W9-BMY-125

PSYCHOLOGY

PSYCHOLOGY

THIRD EDITION

MARGARET W. MATLIN

SUNY Geneseo

HARCOURT BRACE COLLEGE PUBLISHERS

Fort Worth Philadelphia San Diego New York Orlando Austin San Antonio
Toronto Montreal London Sydney Tokyo

Dedication

To Beth and Sally Matlin
and all college students who care about people
and want to learn more about them.

Publisher	EARL MCPEEK
Acquisitions Editor	CAROL WADA
Market Strategist	KATHLEEN SHARP
Product Manager	JO-ANNE WEAVER
Developmental Editor	TRACY NAPPER
Project Editors	TAMARA NEFF VARDY / ANGELA WILLIAMS URQUHART
Production Manager	ANDREA A. JOHNSON
Art Director	BURL SLOAN

Cover image © Ron Watts/Westlight.

ISBN: 0-15-505495-3
Library of Congress Catalog Card Number: 97-71493

Copyright © 1999, 1995, 1992 by Holt, Rinehart and Winston

All rights reserved. No part of this publication may be reproduced or transmitted in any form or by any means, electronic or mechanical, including photocopy, recording, or any information storage and retrieval system, without permission in writing from the publisher.

Requests for permission to make copies of any part of the work should be mailed to: Permissions Department, Harcourt Brace & Company, 6277 Sea Harbor Drive, Orlando, Florida 32887-6777.

Special acknowledgments of copyright ownership and of permission to reproduce works (or excerpts thereof) included in this edition begin on page 699 and constitute an extension of this page.

Address orders to:
Harcourt Brace & Company
6277 Sea Harbor Drive
Orlando, FL 32887-6777
1-800-782-4479

Address editorial correspondence to:
Harcourt Brace College Publishers
301 Commerce Street, Suite 3700
Fort Worth, TX 76102

Web site address:
http://www.hbcollege.com

Harcourt Brace College Publishers will provide complimentary supplements or supplement packages to those adopters qualified under our adoption policy. Please contact your sales representative to learn how you qualify. If as an adopter or potential user you receive supplements you do not need, please return them to your sales representative or send them to: ATTN: Returns Department, Troy Warehouse, 465 South Lincoln Drive, Troy, MO 63379.

Printed in the United States of America

8 9 0 1 2 3 4 5 6 7 032 10 9 8 7 6 5 4 3 2 1

Harcourt Brace College Publishers

ABOUT THE AUTHOR

Margaret W. Matlin received her BA in psychology from Stanford University and her MA and PhD in experimental psychology from the University of Michigan. She holds the title of Distinguished Teaching Professor at State University of New York at Geneseo, where she has taught courses since 1971 in introductory psychol-ogy, experimental psychology, statistics, sensation and perception, cognitive psychology, human memory, human development, conflict resolution, is-sues in feminism, and the psychology of women. In 1977, she received the State Uni-versity of New York Chancellor's Award for Excellence in Teaching, and in 1985 she was awarded the American Psychological Association Teaching of Psychology Award in the four-year college and university division. Most recently, in 1995, she received the American Psychological Foundation's Distinguished Teaching in Psychology Award. Margaret Matlin's other books include The Pollyanna Principle: Selectivity in Language, Memory, and Thought; Human Experimental Psychology; Sensation and Perception *(with coauthor Hugh Foley, 4th edition)*; Cognition *(4th edition); and* The Psychology of Women *(4th edition, in preparation).*

Margaret Matlin's husband, Arnie, is a pediatrician in Geneseo, New York. Their daughter Beth teaches elementary school in the Boston public schools. Their daughter Sally works with Latin American clients in an immigration law office in San Francisco.

PREFACE

In August of 1996, I began writing the third edition of *Psychology*. At the same time, I was preparing to teach Introductory Psychology for the 20th time at SUNY Geneseo. A new edition—like a new teaching semester—provides an ideal opportunity to step back, evaluate previous experiences, and decide upon important goals. Our discipline of psychology continues to span topics as different as a single cortical neuron and international conflict resolution. How can a single book—or a single introductory psychology course—capture all of this rich diversity of information? To achieve this ambitious objective, I devised a set of goals and pedagogical tools, and made some key revisions to this edition. These guidelines, along with a set of carefully prepared supplementary materials, makes this edition particularly strong.

GOALS

Six major goals have guided me in writing this third edition:

1. To synthesize the broad range of knowledge about psychology, emphasizing the most recent research. Since completing the previous edition of *Psychology*, I have written the third edition of *The Psychology of Women,* the fourth edition of *Cognition,* and the fourth edition of *Sensation and Perception* with my coauthor Hugh Foley. My background in such diverse areas provides the perfect preparation for writing an up-to-date introductory textbook. From my work on the latest edition of *The Psychology of Women,* I know the most recent information about gender stereotypes, gender comparisons in social and intellectual domains, gender issues in clinical psychology, and the complex interplay between gender and ethnicity. My revision of *Cognition* has provided me with current perspectives on memory, language, and higher mental processes. The newest research in *Sensation and Perception* helps me write knowledgeably about the more biological components of psychology.

This broad perspective also enables me to point out relationships among topics that might initially seem unrelated. For example, in the social psychology of stereotypes, I'll emphasize that people are guided by heuristics similar to those used in cognitive tasks. I've also constructed three important themes throughout the textbook, which are described more under "Features" on page ix, to provide even further cohesiveness.

2. To present complex topics in an interesting, clear, and well-organized fashion. My academic background in cognitive psychology inspires me to apply the principles of that discipline in developing this introductory textbook. For instance, the research in human memory demonstrates that students recall high-imagery material quite accurately. I apply this principle by including numerous concrete examples that describe my students' experiences as well as my own. Over the years, I've received letters and comments from hundreds of students and professors, praising the clarity and interest level of my textbooks. Using that feedback, I have tried to write this third edition so that the features readers most appreciate are even stronger than in the two previous editions.

Research in cognitive psychology also emphasizes the importance of organization. Therefore, each chapter in this textbook is organized into two to five sections, each followed by a section summary that encourages students to integrate their current knowledge before they begin the next section. Within each of the sections, I often review what we have discussed and preview what we will cover next.

The textbook also features numerous pedagogical aids (see pages 25 to 26). Some authors assume that student-oriented features are useful only for lower-level students. I strongly argue that students with all levels of ability can profit when these features are carefully conceived. The clear majority of students in my own introductory psychology classes at SUNY Geneseo ranked in the top 10% of their high school classes. Even the best of these students tell me that they appreciate such features as section summaries, mnemonic tips, and pronunciation guides.

Finally, research on the self-reference effect in memory has shown that people retain material better if they relate it to their own experience. An important objective in writing *Psychology* was to encourage students to think about their own psychological processes. This principle is equally important, whether students are learning about saccadic eye movements in the chapter on sensation and perception, or whether they are thinking about the fundamental attribution error in the chapter on social cognition.

3. To emphasize research methodology. When I was a beginning college student, the excitement of psychological research lured me away from a biology major. Later, I received my PhD in experimental psychology, and the first textbook I wrote was *Human Experimental Psychology*. As we approach the 21st century, I'm even more convinced that a separate chapter on research methods is essential in an introductory psychology textbook. Therefore, Chapter 2 discusses the major research methods in detail. This chapter also considers important issues such as gender, ethnic, and cultural biases in research—in addition to more standard topics such as research ethics, sampling, and statistical analyses.

Research methodology is also emphasized throughout the rest of the textbook. For example, the In Depth Sections in Chapters 2 through 18 encourage students to review methodological issues and see how they are applied in the diverse disciplines within psychology.

4. To develop students' critical thinking skills. Both my classroom teaching and my textbooks have consistently focused on critical thinking. I have always emphasized to students that the specific "facts" of psychology may be substantially different 20 years from now. Nevertheless, students who have developed the ability to analyze a study critically will still be able to evaluate new research and to question studies that were not appropriately conducted. An important change in this edition of *Psychology* is a strengthened emphasis on critical thinking. Chapter 1 introduces the basic principles of critical thinking, together with some cautions about common errors in thinking about psychological principles. Throughout each remaining chapter in the book, I have included several critical-thinking exercises. These exercises encourage students to reflect about the research on a specific topic. Students are instructed to describe why the authors of the research used a specific precaution, to discuss a potential problem with the design of a study, or to design a component of a hypothetical study.

This textbook also encourages students to apply the principles of critical thinking to their own experiences. Students need to learn that their analytic skills need not be confined to formal research. Another feature of this textbook that encourages critical thinking is the review questions at the end of each chapter. This pedagogical feature encourages students to interrelate concepts that might initially seem unrelated, to apply their knowledge to real-life situations, and to provide evidence for a particular viewpoint.

5. To emphasize active learning. Inspired by a number of workshops and conferences I've attended, my classroom teaching increasingly emphasizes active learning. Unfortunately, many students approach their college courses with the basic request to their professors, "Just tell me what I need to know" (Mathie, 1993). However, those of us who teach psychology are now more likely to emphasize the *process* of thinking about psychology, not simply the collection of facts to be conveyed in a lecture or a textbook.

Furthermore, the research in cognitive psychology shows that students are often overconfident when they read psychology textbooks; they may believe that they understand a passage, but a test on that material reveals that they do not (e.g., Maki & Berry, 1984). Students need to become actively engaged with the material to understand whether they have mastered it.

When I teach introductory psychology, I often pause during class and ask a significant question; all students are instructed to write down their own answers. Then I ask for volunteers to share their responses. In the traditional question-and-answer format, we typically find that the same small group of eager students will raise their hands, leaving the remainder silent and uninvolved. With these brief active-learning exercises, virtually all the students begin writing in their notebooks, and a greater variety of students raise their hands to contribute an answer. I'm also extremely enthusiastic about the improved quality of the responses with this system; the students' answers are more complete, more thoughtful, and more analytical (Nodine, 1994).

Inspired by these classroom results, I've incorporated active learning into this textbook in several ways. The critical-thinking exercises, described above, allow students to test their analytical skills. I encourage students to write out their answers to these exercises, because my own experience has convinced me that their analyses of the issues will be more complete. Otherwise, students may be tempted to look at a critical thinking question and simply muse to themselves, "Yes, I know the answer." Sometimes, as they begin to write a response, they may realize that they really cannot provide the details they thought they knew; this discrepancy should encourage them to review the section. I also made the decision to include the answers to the critical-thinking exercises so that students can discover whether their own responses were appropriate. However, these answers appear at the end of each chapter; learning can be temptingly passive if the answer appears immediately below each question.

A second active-learning exercise in this textbook is the demonstrations, which invite students to participate in an active fashion. Sometimes these demonstrations replicate a classic study, and sometimes they illustrate an important psychological principle. In each case, however, the rationale for the demonstration is fully explained. Students may enthusiastically try an interesting demonstration, but the pedagogical value of that exercise is lost if a textbook does not explain how that demonstration is relevant to the topic!

A third active-learning exercise is the review questions at the end of each chapter. These conceptual questions encourage students to apply their knowledge and to integrate information on a given topic. These review questions also encourage students to test their knowledge and emphasize the importance of reviewing the chapter if their information is incomplete.

6. To convey the variety and diversity of human experience. As psychologists, we must consider how people's lives may be influenced by such factors as gender, ethnicity, age, sexual orientation, and social class. My own expertise in the psychology of women has sensitized me to the issue of gender in psychology textbooks. In this textbook, you'll find that the biological drawings depict gender-neutral skulls, rather than the masculine heads that often seem to be standard in biopsychology chapters. You'll also find that issues of gender are integrated throughout the book, wherever I believe that the topic is appropriate. Gender is discussed, for example, in the chapters on research methods, biopsychology, thinking, and language. However, gender is an especially important part of the chapters on child and adult development, psychotherapy, social psychology, and health psychology.

My background in gender research has also sensitized me to the invisibility of many other social groups in psychology textbooks. This textbook frequently explores the experiences of people of color and people from cultures outside the United States and Canada. This information is examined in virtually every chapter—rather than in just a single portion of the textbook.

Many other introductory textbooks assume that human development is a topic limited to infants, children, and adolescents; in contrast, my textbook also emphasizes the experiences of the elderly. This textbook also discusses gay and lesbian issues within the framework of adult love relationships, rather than in the discussion of sexuality or—worse still—sexually transmitted diseases. Yet another source of diversity is social class, a topic often ignored by psychologists. I've tried to address social class issues whenever possible, especially in the In Depth section of Chapter 18. In addition, I've incorporated some information about deaf individuals, especially in Chapters 4, 11, and 15.

As we draw close to the end of the 20th century, psychologists are increasingly aware that the generalizations we have assumed to be typical of all humans simply do not apply to the wide range of humanity on our planet. As we prepare to enter the 21st century, an introductory psychology textbook especially benefits from a multicultural perspective that admires and respects diversity.

FEATURES

Consistent with these six goals, I have developed some important features that both students and professors have appreciated.

1. *Three important themes* are emphasized throughout the book:

    • Humans are extremely competent; their performance is generally rapid and accurate, and most errors can be traced to strategies that are typically adaptive.
    • Humans differ widely from one another; as a result, people often respond differently to the same stimulus situation.
    • Psychological processes are complex; most psychological phenomena are caused by multiple factors.

2. *Section summaries* appear at frequent intervals throughout the chapter so that students can integrate the previous material before proceeding to a new topic.

3. Chapter 1 explores critical thinking, and several *critical-thinking exercises* are integrated into each subsequent chapter, encouraging students to carefully analyze research techniques and conclusions.

4. *Demonstrations* or informal experiments encourage students to illustrate a well-known study or an important principle, making the material more memorable.

5. *New terms* are shown in boldface type, with a definition included in the same sentence. These terms are listed at the end of each chapter so that students can test themselves, and they also appear with definitions in the glossary at the end of the book.

6. Chapters 2 through 18 each include an *In Depth section* that examines recent research on a selected topic. This feature is an important mechanism for achieving depth as well as breadth in an introductory psychology textbook. In addition, these sections provide an opportunity to emphasize research methodology.

7. *A list of recommended readings,* appropriate for introductory psychology students, provides resources for students who want additional information on concepts related to the chapter topics.

WHAT'S NEW IN THE THIRD EDITION?

The first two editions of *Psychology* received strong praise for their writing style, chapter organization, and pedagogical features. I retained these strengths in the third edition. In addition, I added more than 80 critical-thinking exercises, as described earlier. Another new feature is a vignette designed to open each chapter. Each vignette tells a story and provides a preview of important issues that will be explored in the chapter. In addition, the text now includes 18 chapters—instead of 19—to facilitate chapter assignments within a one-term format.

The third edition is dramatically different from the second edition because it includes more than 1,600 new references. Furthermore, 2,040 of the 2,815 references in the book were published in the 1990s. Our discipline of psychology has made impressive advances in just a few years, and our introductory psychology students should be informed about this cutting-edge research. Although every page of this textbook has been rewritten and updated, some of the more noteworthy changes are the following:

- Chapter 1 has added an extended discussion of critical-thinking principles, to provide a background for students' critical analyses of material throughout the textbook.
- Chapter 2 includes new examples for the research methods, as well as a discussion on evaluating psychological tests.
- Chapter 3 has a new section on evolutionary psychology; it also discusses recent research on the cerebral cortex and a new brain-imaging technique.
- Chapter 4 is supplemented by a new In Depth section on the long-term effects of noise, as well as recent research on vision.
- Chapter 5 features a new In Depth section on the consequences of alcohol use and the incidence of alcohol-related problems on college campuses.
- Chapter 6 has new information about the classical conditioning of the immune system, as well as updated coverage of observational learning.
- Chapter 7 now features an In Depth section on working memory, as well as a reorganized and updated section on long-term memory.
- Chapter 8 now incorporates the section on intelligence testing from the second edition's Chapter 14; a new In Depth section on the framing effect has been added to the section on decision making.
- Chapter 9 emphasizes new research on neurolinguistics, as well as updated information on bilingualism.
- Chapter 10 features new research on infant perception, children's cognitive development, gender-role development, and cross-cultural psychology.
- Chapter 11 includes updated information on gender, sexual orientation, ethnicity, and cross-cultural psychology.
- Chapter 12 examines new research on obesity, sexual aggression, and emotion, as well as a new In Depth section about cross-cultural research on facial expressions.
- Chapter 13 now features an In Depth section on cross-cultural views of the self, in addition to updated information about the social-cognitive approach and the biological basis of personality.
- Chapter 14 contains a new In Depth section on gender and depression, and updated coverage on anxiety disorders, mood disorders, and schizophrenia.

- Chapter 15 includes current developments in the psychodynamic approach, as well as current information about therapy and gender, therapy and ethnicity, and therapy and the deaf.
- Chapter 16 emphasizes the new research on impression formation, racism, sexism, stereotype threat, in addition to a critical analysis of the evolutionary psychology approach.
- Chapter 17 is supplemented with recent research on group processes, conformity, aggression, and altruism.
- Chapter 18 features a new In Depth section on socioeconomic status and health, as well as new material on cognitive appraisal, gender, ethnicity, AIDS, and smoking.
- The appendix now includes information about how distorted graphs and figures can encourage incorrect conclusions.

SUPPLEMENTARY MATERIALS

My editors and I agreed that ancillary material developed for many introductory psychology textbooks often appears to have been hastily written, with little or no attempt to coordinate the separate books. In contrast, the ancillary authors for this textbook have exchanged material with one another to increase the compatibility of these resources. In addition, I have thoroughly reviewed every page of these ancillaries to insure their accuracy and stylistic consistency. I truly admire the teaching and writing skills of the three ancillary authors who worked on these projects!

Study Guide
(by Drew C. Appleby and Margaret W. Matlin)

Drew Appleby is an award-winning professor at Marian College in Indiana and is well-known for numerous projects focusing on the teaching of psychology. Dr. Appleby's sensitivity to students and his mastery of the subject matter are clear in all parts of the Study Guide. We decided to organize the exercises in the Study Guide so that the first task in each section is the easiest (matching). Students next attempt a related task (fill-in-the-blank), and then they try the task most similar to the one on typical in-class examinations (multiple choice). Each section ends with thought projects that encourage students to contemplate and answer more comprehensive questions. The Study Guide emphasizes an organization by sections so that students can read a section in the textbook and then immediately work on that same material in the Study Guide.

Test Bank
(by Lucinda DeWitt and Margaret W. Matlin)

Lucinda DeWitt, a new addition to our team, has academic interests that closely mirror my own. She has been on the faculty at DePauw University and at Concordia College and currently teaches courses in introductory psychology, cognitive psychology, and the psychology of women at Moorhead State University. Dr. DeWitt created hundreds of creative new questions for this third edition, and she also carefully updated the old ones to reflect the current coverage. The new Test Bank includes approximately 200 items for each chapter; it emphasizes conceptual questions and applied questions that require synthesis and application. It also includes factual questions that test the acquisition of basic information.

Instructor's Manual
(by Lori R. Van Wallendael and Margaret W. Matlin)

Lori Van Wallendael is an enthusiastic and well-read faculty member at the University of North Carolina at Charlotte. Dr. Van Wallendael drew from her expertise in teaching both classic and highly current topics in introductory psychology to produce an exceptional set of lecture ideas. She also developed many wonderful classroom demonstrations (many new to this edition) that she had found helpful in her own introductory psychology classes. In addition, Dr. Van Wallendael and I each previewed dozens of psychology videos because we are convinced that instructors will find our "media reviews" to be more helpful than the capsule summaries supplied by film distributors.

Other Teaching Aids

- Computerized versions of the testbank are available in DOS 3.5", Windows, and Macintosh versions. The testbank software *EXAMaster+*™ offers three unique features to the instructor. *EasyTest* creates a test from a single screen in just a few easy steps. Instructors choose parameters, then either select questions from the database or let *EasyTest* randomly select them. *FullTest* offers a range of options that includes selecting, editing, adding, or linking questions or graphics; random selection of questions from a wide range of criteria; creating criteria; blocking questions; and printing up to 99 different versions of the same test and answer sheet. *EXAMRecord*™ records, curves, graphs, and prints out grades according to criteria the instructor selects, and can display the grade distribution as a bar graph or a plotted graph.

For the instructor without access to a computer, Harcourt Brace College Publishers offers *RequesTest.* By calling 1-800-447-9457, a software specialist will compile questions according to the instructor's criteria and mail or fax the test master within 48 hours.

- Available for your use is a set of 50 **overhead transparencies** that correspond specifically to this textbook, or you can choose the Harcourt Brace Introductory Psychology Transparency package, which has more than 200 full-color acetates and an accompanying guide.

Multimedia and Interactive Software

- **The Explorer,** the accompanying CD-ROM prepared by John Mitterer of Brock University, is an innovative learning tool that allows students to explore and understand the realm of psychology in an interactive, multimedia environment. *The Explorer* allows students to interactively explore the dynamic processes illustrated graphically in the text, with a wave of the mouse. In addition to further explorations of graphic material from *Psychology,* Third Edition, *The Explorer* allows students to repeat experiments on classic psychological phenomena, such as the Stroop effect and the Müller-Lyer illusion. Links to Web pages from *The Explorer* give students the power and recency of the World Wide Web. In addition, this CD-ROM allows students to test their mastery of the material in a series of test questions, based on the material in *Psychology,* Third Edition.
- **The Instructor's Explorer,** included on *The Explorer* CD-ROM, allows you to integrate multimedia into your lectures. Projection quality simulations, demonstrations, and experiments from *The Explorer* enhance the teaching of key concepts in psychology.
- **Dynamic Concepts in Psychology II,** a highly successful videodisk developed by John Mitterer of Brock University, covers every major concept of introductory psychology. Media include animated sequences, video footage, still images, and demonstrations of well-known experiments. A modular format allows instructors to tailor the program to their course. Lecture-Active presentation software (Windows, Macintosh) accompanies *Dynamic Concepts in Psychology II.* This software gives instructors the ability to

preprogram classroom presentations as well as to import material from other multimedia sources, such as other videodisks, CD-ROMs, or computer hard drives.

- **Psychology MediaActive™** is a CD-ROM-based psychology image bank to be used with commercially available presentation packages like Power-Point™ and Astound™, as well as Harcourt Brace's LectureActive™ for IBM and Macintosh.

- **The Whole Psychology Catalog: Instructional Resources to Enhance Student Learning, 1997,** by Michael B. Reiner of Kennesaw State College, allows instructors to easily supplement course work and assignments. It has perforated pages containing experiential exercises, questionnaires, and visual aids. Each activity is classified by one of eight learning goals central to the teaching of psychology. Also included in the new version is an informative section on using the Internet and the World Wide Web.

- **The Harcourt Brace Multimedia Library** provides additional media for instructors to use in the classroom. The library includes videos from Films for the Humanities and Sciences and Pyramid Films, as well as series, such as *The Brain* teaching modules, *The Mind* video modules, the *Discovering Psychology* telecourse, *Childhood, Seasons of Life,* and *Time to Grow.* Contact your local Harcourt Brace representative for qualifying details and further information.

- **World Wide Web**—For up-to-date instructor's resources, student's resources, and links to dynamic Web sites that will enhance your teaching and learning about psychology, visit us on the World Wide Web at htt://www.hbcollege.com.

- **Software Technical Support**—Technical support for all of our software is available by calling 1-800-447-9457. This service is available Monday through Friday, 7 a.m. to 6 p.m., central time.

ACKNOWLEDGMENTS

When we teach our classes, we rarely have the opportunity to thank publically the individuals who have helped and inspired us. Fortunately, a textbook is different: Now I can acknowledge in writing the gratitude I feel for the dozens of people who have guided the creation and development of this book. Harcourt Brace publishes three of my textbooks, and I continue to be impressed with the many highly competent people associated with this company.

As we contemplated the third edition of *Psychology,* Publisher Earl McPeek encouraged me to clarify the goals for this book. For example, he helped me develop an innovative approach to teaching critical thinking. Critical thinking has always been implicit in my textbooks. However, Earl helped me plan how to make this approach more explicit in this third edition; our discussions clarified the treatment of critical thinking in Chapter 1, as well as the exercises throughout the book. Carol Wada, Executive Editor, supervised the later editorial phases of the book. I admire Carol's expertise, constructive comments, and good judgment.

My developmental editors, Van Strength and Tracy Napper, located superb reviewers, handled the mountains of necessary paperwork, coordinated the ancillary materials, arranged for my visits to Fort Worth, and kept me informed about numerous aspects of the project. Amy Hester, Cindy Hoag, and John Matthews also helped during crucial phases of the book's development.

Tamara Vardy, project editor extraordinaire, has now worked with me on all three of my Harcourt textbooks. I especially appreciate her intelligence, organizational abilities, cheerfulness, and encouragement throughout this project. I hope our partnership can continue for many future editions. Thanks, also, to Angela Urquhart, who filled in during Tamara's absence toward the end of the project and worked heroically to keep the book on schedule. Burl Sloan, the art director for this edition, created a wonderful design for both the cover and the interior pages. Marcy Lunetta was especially conscientious in tracking down the literary permissions. Linda Webster, my longtime associate, again performed a superbly professional and efficient job on the glossary and the indexes. Finally, Andrea Johnson—the production manager—deserves my gratitude for her careful attention to important details and time constraints.

Sandra Lord is an ideal photo researcher. She has an uncanny ability to translate my prose descriptions into interesting and unique photo choices. She also heroically tracked down unusual photo requests for pictures of Chicana vocalists, interesting elders, people in unusual professions, and even a sample of kombucha for Chapter 1. I truly enjoyed working with Sandra.

Michele Gitlin, my wonderful copy editor on this edition, has an exceptional ear for the English language. I especially admired the way she can modify a few words in a paragraph, conveying the precise meaning that I had originally intended. Her intelligent questions also forced me to redefine some crucial terms, clarify some principles in more detail, and provide appropriate examples for complex concepts. Her meticulous attention to general concepts—as well as specific details—transformed the phase of the production process into an enjoyable experience. Thanks also to my proofreader, Roberta Kirchhoff, for her careful work throughout the page proof stage.

Numerous psychologists deserve praise for their suggestions, comments on content and style, and lists of additional references. These reviewers and consultants helped me write a much more accurate and lucid textbook than I could have managed on my own.

I would like to thank the individuals who reviewed both the first and second editions of *Psychology*. In addition, I want to acknowledge the knowledgeable, informed comments from the following reviewers for this third edition:

Tom Brothen, *University of Minnesota*
David Clement, *University of South Carolina*
Lucinda DeWitt, *Concordia College*
Lee Fargo, *University of California at San Diego*
Lawrence Fehr, *Widener University*
Kathleen Flannery, *St. Anselm College*
Mindi Foster, *University of North Dakota*
Tresmaine Grimes, *South Carolina State University*
Doxey Hatch, *University of Montana*
Lisa Isenberg, *University of Wisconsin–River Falls*
Kevin Keating, *Broward Community College*

Norman Kinney, *Southwest Missouri State University*
Charles Levin, *Baldwin-Wallace College*
Brady Phelps, *South Dakota State University*
Michael Renner, *West Chester University*
Joan Piroch, *Coastal Carolina University*
David Pittenger, *Marietta College*
Vicki Ritts, *St. Louis Community College–Meramec*
Nancy Simpson, *Trident Technical College*
Irene Staik, *University of Montevallo*
Donna Thompson, *Midland College*
Phyllis Walrad, *Macomb Community College*

My thanks also go to my superb student reviewers, who conscientiously read either the manuscript for the first edition or made suggestions for the other editions. I was truly impressed with their expertise, diligence, and honesty. My appreciation goes to Rachel Andrews, Amy Bolger, Jonathan Blumenthal, Sheryl Mileo, Claudia Militello, Matthew Prichard, Heather Wallach, Joseph Wesley, and Martin Williams.

In addition, many colleagues, students, and friends supplied examples, ideas, information, and references. I thank James Allen, Susan Arellano, Anni Ashford, Joan Ballard, Charles Brewer, Ganie DeHart, Karen Duffy, Lisa Elliot, Frederick Fidura, Hugh Foley, Jennifer Gullo, Diane Halpern, Tina Howard, Patricia Keith-Spiegel, Maria Kountz, Mary Kroll, Warren Lord, James McNally, Jeffrey Mounts, Peter Muzzonigro, Barbara Nodine, Lynn Offerman, Paul Olczak, Robert Owens, Catherine Perna, Paul Pizzano, Cathleen Quinn, Darmendra Ramcharran, George Rebok, Ramon Rocha, Lanna Ruddy, Donna Shapiro, M. Shelton Smith, John Sparrow, Maura Thompson, Leonore Tiefer, Gail Walker, Helen S. White, Susan K. Whitbourne, Edward Whitson, and Melvyn Yessenow.

My dear friend Mary Roth Walsh died tragically just shortly after I finished this third edition of the textbook. Mary was one of my strongest supporters. She also provided suggestions, references, and interesting points of view on numerous issues throughout this book. I will think of her often and greatly miss her wonderful enthusiasm.

Thanks also to Drew Appleby, Lucinda DeWitt, and Lori Van Wallendael for their exemplary work on the ancillaries for this textbook. Not only did they write exceptionally strong books themselves, but they also provided useful feedback that helped shape my own textbook.

I would also like to thank many of my undergraduate students at SUNY Geneseo who located errors or unclear sections in the earlier editions of *Psychology*. Their careful suggestions were helpful in revising the textbook. Thanks are due to Rachel Andrews, Shannon Basher, Mary Rose Bayer, Cynthia Behrent, Christopher Brown, Jennifer Clarke, Kevin Donsbach, Lisa Dunham, Jenny Eng, Katherine Eng, Amelie Feroce, Margaret Gee, Jennifer Halleran, Helen Hanwit, Kimberley Kittle, Erika Mack, Kelly Meyer, Kathleen Quinn, Jeanette Rosenbaum, Amy Samartino, Patricia Seith, Gretchen Teal, Noel J. Thomas, Rosanne Vallone, Thomas A. P. van Geel, Joseph Wesley, and Lotus Yung.

However, no acknowledgment section would be complete without emphasizing contributions from my professors. They inspired me to pursue psychology and encouraged me to view our field as an evolving discipline in which every answer provokes a still greater number of questions. I would like to thank Leonard Horowitz—my undergraduate mentor, Gordon Bower, Albert Hastorf, Douglas Lawrence, Eleanor Maccoby, Walter Mischel, and Karl Pribram of Stanford University. Thanks, also, to Bob Zajonc—my dissertation advisor, John Atkinson, David Birch, Robyn Dawes, Edwin Martin, Arthur Melton, Richard Pew, Irving Pollack, W. P. Tanner, and Daniel Weintraub at the University of Michigan.

Many other people have helped in various phases of the preparation of this book. Carolyn Emmert, Shirley Thompson, and Constance Ellis provided countless services that allowed me to devote more time to writing. Several students—Melissa Katter, Elissa Burke, Colleen O'Loughlin, Benjamin Griffin and Vincent Carroll—were exemplary in tracking down references, photocopying material, sending for reprints, and checking the accuracy of my bibliography. In addition, several members of the Milne Library staff at SUNY Geneseo provided superb expertise and assistance: Judith Bushnell, Paula Henry, Diane Johnson, Mina Orman, Harriet Sleggs, and Paul MacLean. Drew Appleby, Ron Pretzer, and Louise Wadsworth all deserve high praise for their wonderful photos of students, children, and an assortment of unlikely objects.

My last, most enthusiastic acknowledgment goes to the members of my family. Thanks to my daughters, Beth and Sally, for providing helpful examples, posing for photographs, helping to develop some of the demonstrations . . . and also for being wonderful human beings who inspire me to write for people like themselves. To my husband, Arnie, I give my deepest thanks for this technical expertise and suggestions, and also for helpfully reading through his medical journals to locate relevant articles for me. More importantly, I appreciate his love, his committed encouragement, and his spectacular sense of humor. My parents deserve the final note of appreciation: Thanks to Helen White for encouraging my enthusiasm for learning and my love of language, and to Donald White for encouraging my enjoyment of science and for providing a model of a professional who is truly excited about his work.

Margaret W. Matlin

CONTENTS IN BRIEF

CONTENTS

INTRODUCTION

PSYCHOLOGY'S PAST

Wilhelm Wundt

William James

American Psychology in the Early Twentieth Century

European Psychology in the Early Twentieth Century

PSYCHOLOGY TODAY

Six Contemporary Approaches in Psychology

Professions in Psychology

THREE IMPORTANT THEMES IN PSYCHOLOGY

Theme 1: Humans Are Extremely Competent

Theme 2: Humans Differ Widely From One Another

Theme 3: Psychological Processes Are Complex

CRITICAL THINKING

Guidelines for Critical Thinking

Why Critical Thinking Is Important in Psychology

What Factors Hinder Critical Thinking?

HOW TO USE THIS BOOK

CHAPTER 1

Billings, Montana, is a typical North American town of 84,000 people—a town where people usually greet each other on the street, go to church on Sunday, and enjoy the rodeo. But several years ago, a wave of hate crimes struck Billings. A Black man received a death threat. Gays and lesbians were harassed. A Native American woman named Dawn Fast Horse was at home with her four children, when a group of white supremacists painted hate messages on the side of her house—messages such as "Kill" and "Indians Suck." In early December 1993, someone threw a cement block through a child's bedroom window in the home of Brian and Tammie Schnitzer, a Jewish family who had displayed a menorah. Luckily, young Isaac Schnitzer was not in bed, or he could have been killed. The Billings story shows us that under some circumstances, people treat others with hatred and violence.

Fortunately, the residents of Billings reacted with compassion and outrage. Thirty members of the Painters Union Local arrived to paint over the hate-filled messages on Dawn Fast Horse's home, and dozens of community members showed up to offer their support. More than 6,000 people signed a petition condemning hate crimes. Religious and community groups also held meetings and town gatherings to demonstrate their support for diversity (see the photo above). Gary Svee, an editor of the *Billings Gazette,* responded creatively to the violence at the Schnitzer home. He recalled how the king of Denmark had reacted during World War II to the Nazi demand that Danish Jews must wear yellow stars; the king also began to wear a yellow star. Similarly, the *Gazette* printed a full-page picture of a menorah, and close to 10,000 homes in this largely Protestant town displayed the menorahs in their windows. This part of the Billings story shows us that under some circumstances, people treat others with compassion and love (O'Neill et al., 1995).

In this textbook, we will explore **psychology,** or the scientific study of behavior and mental processes. The behaviors include physical actions that can be seen or heard, such as volunteering to repaint a neighbor's home. The mental processes, which cannot be seen or heard, include thoughts about prejudice and emotions such as anger. As we will see throughout this book, psychologists study these issues scientifically, by conducting controlled experiments and by carefully observing behavior.

Research-oriented psychologists emphasize the following goals:

1. *Describing* behaviors and mental processes, using careful, systematic observation;

2. *Explaining* why these behaviors and mental processes occurred; and

3. *Predicting* what an individual will do in the future, based on past events.

In contrast, **applied psychologists** are typically more concerned with a fourth goal, *changing* behaviors and mental processes.

Let's clarify these different goals, using examples of how psychologists might study children's aggression. Some psychologists *describe* children's aggressive behavior in a classroom. Others *explain* why children are more aggressive after watching a violent movie. Still others might *predict* children's aggressiveness in first grade, based on their aggressiveness during kindergarten. Finally, applied psychologists might try to *change* the children's behavior, to make them less aggressive.

We've noted that psychologists pursue different goals. We also see this diversity of perspectives when we look at the past history of psychology, when we consider the current theoretical approaches to psychology, and when we explore some of the most common careers in psychology. This chapter examines these three issues, outlines three important themes that recur throughout this textbook, and introduces the important topic of critical thinking in psychology. Our final section in this chapter suggests how you can use the textbook most effectively.

PSYCHOLOGY'S PAST

Greek philosophers such as Plato and Aristotle speculated about human nature more than 2,000 years ago. For many centuries, philosophers continued to use an "armchair approach," reasoning and speculating about psychology, but not studying the issues scientifically. Casual speculation sometimes leads us to correct answers, but it also produces the wrong conclusions. For instance, try Demonstration 1.1, which asks you to evaluate some popular sayings based on the armchair approach and casual observation.

In contrast to the armchair approach, psychologists in recent years have relied upon **empirical evidence,** or scientific evidence obtained by careful observation and experimentation. If you check the answers to Demonstration 1.1, you'll see that

DEMONSTRATION 1.1 Evaluating Popular Sayings

Here are 10 popular sayings that psychologists have examined. Read each one and decide whether you think that the psychological evidence supports it; write *true* or *false* in front of each saying. Turn to the end of the chapter to find what current researchers have concluded.

_____ 1. Misery loves company.
_____ 2. Spare the rod and spoil the child.
_____ 3. The squeaky wheel gets the grease.
_____ 4. Actions speak louder than words.
_____ 5. Beauty is only skin deep.
_____ 6. Cry and you cry alone.
_____ 7. Marry in haste, repent at leisure.
_____ 8. Familiarity breeds contempt.
_____ 9. He who lives by the sword dies by the sword.
_____ 10. Opposites attract.

empirical evidence often contradicts our intuitions. This textbook emphasizes the empirical approach.

Any attempt to specify a date for the beginning of empirical psychology is somewhat arbitrary (Danziger, 1990). However, most psychologists consider the birthdate to be 1879, the year in which Wilhelm Wundt (pronounced "*Vill*-helm Voont," 1832–1920) founded his laboratory. Let's begin our history with this German pioneer and with an American pioneer named William James. Then we will move into the twentieth century in both the United States and Europe.

Do opposites attract? People who favor the armchair approach might speculate about whether people in romantic relationships are similar or different. However, psychologists who use the empirical approach conduct research to determine whether people do prefer those who differ in characteristics such as appearance, personality, and leisure activity.

Wilhelm Wundt (1832–1920). Founder of academic psychology.

Wilhelm Wundt

In 1879, Wundt created the first institute for research in experimental psychology at the University of Leipzig, Germany. For the first time in history, students in this new discipline could conduct psychological research. We are now so accustomed to psychology as an academic subject that we need to remind ourselves that psychology courses were not available prior to Wundt's era.

Wundt argued that psychology should abandon casual armchair speculation and develop more formal, careful methodology. For example, some of his research featured **introspection,** or carefully observing one's own conscious psychological reactions. Wundt insisted that introspection should be rigorously conducted, after training in standardized techniques for introspection. Wundt's approach, which was developed more fully by his students, was called structuralism. **Structuralism** examines the structure of the mind and the organization of the basic elements of sensations, feelings, and images. Structuralists argue that every experience can be broken down into its primitive components.

One reason Wundt is so important in the history of psychology is that he was impressively productive as a researcher. In roughly 50 years of work, he published about 500 research papers and books, writing about 60,000 printed pages (Gardner, 1985; Schlesinger, 1985). His interests ranged widely and included memory, language, emotion, abnormal psychology, religion, history, and art (Blumenthal, 1975).

Consider a typical Wundt study, one on memory. For a fraction of a second, Wundt presented to trained observers a set of letters such as this:

r   v   n   e
w   o   z   g
m   b   t   u

Wundt found that most observers could report no more than six letters, yet they claimed they *saw* more (Wundt, 1912/1973). The additional letters seemed to slip away from memory in the process of recalling them. As you will see in Chapter 7, this fragile, fleeting characteristic of memory was explored again half a century later in an important study. This topic is now called sensory memory (Sperling, 1960). Impressively, the basic phenomenon was initially described by psychology's first systematic researcher.

Wundt deserves credit not only for his findings, but also for his methods. For example, he emphasized the importance of **replications,** or studies in which a phenomenon is tested several times, often under different conditions. For instance, the study with the letters could be repeated several times, each time with a different group of participants and a different arrangement of letters. When a study has been replicated, we can be more confident that its conclusions are accurate.

William James (1842–1910). First major American psychologist.

William James

American psychologists at the end of the nineteenth century were more influenced by William James (1842–1910) than by Wilhelm Wundt. James's less formal approach emphasized the kinds of questions we encounter in daily life. He wrote extensively about consciousness, which we now define as our awareness of the outside world and of our perceptions, images, and feelings (Chapter 5). James also developed a theory that our emotional reactions arise from the way we perceive our physiological responses (Chapter 12). For example, you feel afraid when you perceive that your heart is pounding. His view on numerous other topics—perception, reasoning, and racial injustice, and peace psychology—are still considered relevant (Dember, 1990; Nickerson, 1990; Plous, 1994; Simon, 1998).

James was particularly interested in how consciousness and other psychological processes help human beings. This emphasis on the functions of psychological activities inspired the name for James's approach to psychology, called functionalism.

Functionalism argues that psychological processes are adaptive; they allow humans to survive and to adapt successfully to their surroundings.

Wilhelm Wundt was known for his laboratory, but James was known for his textbooks. For several decades, American psychology students read either the two-volume *Principles of Psychology* (1890) or the shorter version, *Psychology, Briefer Course* (1892). Professors referred to the longer version as "James," and they nick-named the shorter version "Jimmy" (Hilgard, 1987). A century later, the two-volume work has been called "probably the most significant psychological treatise ever written in America" (Evans, 1990, p. 11).

Many of James's ideas seem remarkably modern. For example, he emphasized that the human mind is active and inquiring, a view still current today (Matlin, 1998). James also suggested that humans have two different kinds of memory. As we'll see in Chapter 7, this proposal was reemphasized nearly 80 years later (Atkinson & Shiffrin, 1968).

American Psychology in the Early Twentieth Century

William James remained a dominant force in the United States at the beginning of the twentieth century. In addition, many of Wilhelm Wundt's students came to the United States from Germany (Benjamin et al., 1992). Some of them, such as Edward Titchener, continued in Wundt's tradition. Titchener founded a psychology laboratory at Cornell University and expanded the introspection technique to areas such as thinking and complex feelings (Danziger, 1990). However, other students developed different agendas. For example, G. Stanley Hall, at Johns Hopkins University, founded the American Psychological Association and promoted research on child development (Sokal, 1992). Figure 1.1 describes eight men and women who made important early contributions to psychology in the United States.

One of these early psychologists, John B. Watson (1878–1958), proposed a new approach to psychology known as behaviorism. **Behaviorism** emphasizes the study of observable behavior, as opposed to hidden mental processes. Watson had originally conducted research with animals, because he thought he could conduct objective research on their observable behaviors. In contrast, he opposed studying consciousness or other components of the human mind. He also opposed using the introspective techniques proposed by Wundt, which he believed to be too subjective (Buckley, 1989; Popplestone & McPherson, 1994; Watson, 1913).

American psychologists found behaviorism appealing because it offered some practical applications (O'Donnell, 1985; Schnaitter, 1987). Wundt's introspection technique and James's ideas about the nature of consciousness and emotions both provided interesting theories about psychology, but neither approach could be applied in everyday life.

Because these early behaviorists emphasized observable behavior, they rejected any term referring to mental events, such as *idea, thought,* or *mental image.* In fact, many early behaviorists classified thinking as simply a form of speech. They proposed that researchers should be able to detect tiny movements of the tongue (an observable behavior), which would reveal thought—if only they could develop the appropriate equipment. Watson argued that vague, invisible constructs such as *thought* were simply unnecessary.

Although many behaviorists were less extreme than Watson, behaviorism had a strong influence on North American psychology from the 1920s through the 1950s (Innis, 1992; Thompson, 1994; Todd & Morris, 1995). As one author wrote: "If you were to knock on the door of an academic psychologist's office in the 1930s, the chances were better than nine out of ten that you would be answered by a behaviorist" (Schlesinger, 1985, p. 13). Thus, most American research psychologists in the early twentieth century rejected unobservable mental processes, consciousness, and introspection. Instead, they embraced the behaviorist approach, which emphasized observable behavior.

G. Stanley Hall (1844–1924). Student of Wilhelm Wundt; founder of the American Psychological Association.

Christine Ladd-Franklin (1847–1930). Taught at Johns Hopkins and Columbia universities; formulated a theory of color vision.

Mary Whiton Calkins (1863–1930). Student of William James; pioneer in memory research; first woman president of the American Psychological Association.

Edward Bradford Titchener (1867–1927). Student of Wilhem Wundt; developed introspection techniques in the United States; taught at Cornell.

Margaret Floy Washburn (1871–1939). First woman to receive a PhD in psychology; wrote a book on animal behavior that foreshadowed behaviorism.

Edward Lee Thorndike (1874–1949). Student of William James; investigated trial-and-error animal learning.

John B. Watson (1878–1958). Founder of behaviorism, which influenced U.S. psychology for over 50 years.

Leta Stetter Hollingworth (1886–1939). Pioneer in the psychology of women; she discredited the view that menstruation was debilitating to women.

FIGURE 1.1

Some early U.S. psychologists.

FIGURE 1.2

According to Gestalt psychologists, this square forms a well-organized, complete figure.

European Psychology in the Early Twentieth Century

Behaviorism may have captivated North Americans, but it did not have a loyal following in Europe. Instead, European psychology in the early part of the twentieth century was influenced by three new approaches: Gestalt psychology, the psychoanalytic approach of Sigmund Freud, and the early cognitive psychology approach.

The Gestalt (pronounced "Geh-*shtahlt*") approach originated in Germany at the beginning of the twentieth century. According to the **Gestalt approach,** we perceive objects as well-organized, whole structures, instead of separated, isolated parts (Sherrill, 1991). Gestalt psychologists emphasize that we see shapes and patterns because of subtle relationships among the parts. For instance, consider the square shown in Figure 1.2. Followers of Wilhelm Wundt might suggest that this square could be broken down into its four component lines (Rachlin, 1994). In contrast, Gestalt psychologists would argue that the object looks well organized; we perceive it as a complete figure—a cohesive square—rather than four isolated lines. The Gestalt psychologists influenced research in visual perception (Chapter 4), problem solving (Chapter 8), and group processes (Chapter 17).

Europe's most important contribution to psychology came from Sigmund Freud (1856–1939), an Austrian physician. Freud was specifically interested in neurology and psychological problems. He argued that people are driven by sexual urges, a view that was not warmly greeted when it was introduced to straitlaced Victorians! In addition, Freud emphasized that human behavior is motivated by the unconscious—by thoughts and desires far below the level of conscious awareness. Psychologists trained in Wundt's laboratory did not welcome this focus on unconscious experiences.

Freud's emphasis on sexuality and unconscious processes meant that he entered the game with two strikes against him. Still, Freud's theories eventually became popular among therapists in both North America and Europe. However, his psychoanalytic theory had little influence on *research* psychology. Instead, early researchers in North America supported behaviorism. Researchers in Europe were likely to favor Wundt's approach, the Gestalt approach, or else a new orientation called the cognitive psychology approach.

The cognitive psychology approach emphasizes mental processes, and its best known European advocate during the early twentieth century was Jean Piaget (pronounced "Zhohn Pea-ah-*zhay*"). Piaget (1896–1980) was a Swiss theorist whose ideas helped shape our knowledge about children's thinking. Piaget proposed that even young babies think, although their thoughts are connected with their senses and their body movements. He argued that their thinking changes during childhood, becoming more abstract and complex. Chapter 10 explores Piaget's theories about children's cognitive development in some detail. We'll also see that the cognitive approach is one of the most important theories throughout contemporary psychology.

Following psychology's early beginnings in Wundt's laboratory in Germany, the discipline developed and diversified. By the 1930s, the field included behaviorists in North America, many Europeans continuing in Wundt's tradition, therapists practicing Freudian psychoanalysis, Gestalt psychologists investigating organizational principles, and cognitive psychologists exploring human thinking.

Jean Piaget (1896–1980). Formulated theory of children's thinking that helped shape current ideas about developmental psychology.

SECTION SUMMARY: *PSYCHOLOGY'S PAST*

1. Psychology, the scientific study of behavior and mental processes, was first studied systematically by Wilhelm Wundt, who emphasized careful research techniques.

2. William James examined human consciousness and other psychological issues relevant to everyday life; he also wrote influential psychology textbooks.

3. Important European trends in the early twentieth century included the Gestalt approach, Sigmund Freud's psychoanalytic approach, and the cognitive approach.

PSYCHOLOGY TODAY

As we move into the twenty-first century, some of the earlier psychological approaches have lost their strong support. However, they have influenced contemporary approaches. For instance, Wundt's emphasis on careful research and replications is still current. Modern cognitive psychology is clearly inspired by ideas about mental processes proposed by Wundt, James, and Gestalt psychologists (Simon, 1992). Let us now shift our attention from psychology's past to contemporary psychology.

Six Contemporary Approaches in Psychology

The scope of psychology is impressive—from microscopic neurons to large crowds of people. In fact, psychology spans the enormous distance between **biology,** which examines the structure and function of living things, and **sociology,** which studies how groups and institutions function in society. It would be impossible for a single approach to be endorsed by researchers as diverse as a psychologist investigating the neurons in the visual system and a social psychologist interested in stereotypes about gender.

Six general approaches dominate contemporary psychology. Let's summarize them in the same order as they will be addressed in later chapters of this textbook.

The Biological Approach   In recent decades, an increasing number of psychologists have favored the biological approach to behavior and mental processes (Boneau, 1992; Thompson, 1994). This **biological approach** or **neuroscience approach** proposes that every behavior, emotion, or thought is caused by a physical event in the brain or other part of the nervous system. People who favor this approach are likely to examine how various regions of the brain and various brain chemicals are related to psychological processes.

The psychologists we discussed in the previous section could not use the biological approach because early techniques were not sophisticated enough to reveal useful information about the brain. Chapter 3 will introduce you to some research techniques that are currently used by psychologists and neuroscientists. For example, researchers can record how brain activity changes when people look at a specific written word (Posner & Raichle, 1994). Researchers can also examine individuals who have unusual disorders. For instance, neuroscientists interested in memory examined a young man who was accidentally stabbed through his nostril—into his brain (Squire, 1987). He now has a very specific problem; he cannot learn any new material. Researchers also use the biological approach to study topics such as drug abuse and psychological disorders.

The Behaviorist Approach   In the preceding section, we introduced the behaviorist approach, with its emphasis on observable behavior. Chapter 6 will examine how this approach was further developed by B. F. Skinner (1904–1990). Skinner was an influential behaviorist who had an especially strong impact on the psychology of learning and the applications of learning principles to human behavior (Bjork, 1993; Lattal, 1992). Chapter 15 will also describe how behavioral approaches are used in treating many psychological disorders.

The Cognitive Approach   Earlier, we noted that Wilhelm Wundt, William James, and Jean Piaget all provided important contributions to the cognitive approach. However, the behaviorist influence on psychology was so strong from about 1920 to 1960 that researchers in North America paid little attention to hidden mental processes.

B. F. Skinner (1904–1990). Promoted the behaviorist approach during the 60-year span of his career.

In contrast to the behaviorist approach, however, the **cognitive approach** focuses on unobservable mental processes such as perceiving, remembering, thinking, and understanding. For instance, as your eyes are now racing across this page, you perceive meaningful letters, and you remember the meaning of words. You might even be thinking about whether you understand the definition of *cognitive approach*. And you can understand complex ideas (for instance, why behaviorism and the cognitive approach might diverge on certain points). Researchers in cognitive psychology try to create precise definitions for invisible mental processes, and they devise methods for measuring these processes objectively.

Cognitive psychologists and behaviorists view humans differently. The early behaviorists held that humans are relatively passive organisms, who wait for an appropriate stimulus from the environment before they respond. In contrast, the cognitive approach argues that people eagerly and actively acquire information. People combine information from several sources, and their cognitive processes often transform this information. For example, think about an occasion when two friends each told you a different story about the same event. Think how your cognitive processes worked overtime as you tried to reconcile the discrepancies, and how you also reinterpreted some portions of each story.

Beginning in the 1960s, many North American psychologists shifted their loyalty away from behaviorism (Hilgard et al., 1991; Sperry, 1993). Psychologists had discovered that most complex mental processes could not be explained using only the terms from behavioral learning theory. For example, behaviorist approaches cannot account for the complexity of the sentences we produce or the way our memory synthesizes information. In addition, Jean Piaget's theories of human development had won the admiration of child psychologists and educators.

By about 1975, most researchers interested in memory, thinking, and language began calling themselves *cognitive psychologists*. The cognitive approach was soon applied to other areas, such as motivation, personality, and psychotherapy. In each case, researchers and theorists emphasized the importance of people's thoughts and how the human mind can manipulate, transform, and even distort these thoughts. The cognitive approach influences most topics discussed in this textbook. In future chapters, we will also examine new theoretical developments in cognitive psychology.

The Sociocultural Approach   According to the **sociocultural approach,** our social context strongly influences our behavior and mental processes. This social context includes factors such as culture, ethnic group, gender, and social class. Many current psychologists emphasize that these sociocultural factors affect our behaviors and thoughts. Some of the relevant topics we will consider later in the book include these questions: (1) How do bilinguals differ from people who know only one language? (2) How does a person's ethnic group influence his or her parenting style? (3) Why are women more likely than men to suffer from depression? (4) How does social class influence a person's health?

The Psychodynamic Approach   The cognitive approach and the sociocultural approach are both extremely popular among psychologists. However, most students in an introductory psychology course are more likely to recognize the name of Sigmund Freud (1856–1939). The **psychodynamic approach** emphasizes two central points: (1) childhood experiences determine adult personality, and (2) unconscious mental processes and conflict influence most human behavior. A narrower term, the **psychoanalytic approach,** refers specifically to Freud's original theory. Compared with Freud, recent psychodynamic theorists place more emphasis on social factors and less emphasis on sexual forces.

The psychodynamic approach provides an extremely influential theory of personality disorders. Even therapists who prefer other approaches have studied psychodynamic theory extensively. Think about it: You've often seen terms such as *unconscious, ego,* and *repression;* in fact, you've probably used these psychodynamic terms yourself. In comparison, does your Sunday newspaper use terms from cognitive psychology such as *schema, heuristic,* and *working memory?*

We discussed earlier how Sigmund Freud developed his theory at the beginning of the twentieth century. In Chapter 13, you'll read how the psychodynamic approach is applied to personality development. In Chapter 15, you'll see how this approach is used to treat psychological disorders. Also, Chapters 10 and 11 explore a theory of identity development proposed by Erik Erikson, one of the most prominent psychodynamic theorists.

The Humanistic Approach   You've learned that theorists developed behaviorism when they were dissatisfied with Wundt's and James's approaches, and other theorists developed the cognitive approach when they were dissatisfied with the behaviorist approach. Similarly, another group of psychologists became dissatisfied with the two major theories that dominated the first half of the twentieth century—that is, the psychoanalytic and the behaviorist approaches. Specifically,

Sigmund Freud (1856–1939). Founder of the psychoanalytic theory.

Carl Rogers (1902–1987). Major humanistic theorist.

American psychologists—such as Carl Rogers (1902–1987) and Abraham Maslow (1908–1970)—argued that the psychoanalytic approach focuses on the "sick" side of our lives. They also pointed out that behaviorism only examines simple behaviors. They preferred a theory that would emphasize the more positive human qualities and our more complex and noble human goals.

This **humanistic approach** emphasizes that we humans have enormous potential for personal growth. We can care deeply for other people, and we try to establish meaningful and productive lives for ourselves. This optimistic theoretical approach accounts quite well for the heroism of the housepainters and the newspaper editor in Billings, Montana—though it might flounder in trying to explain the racism, hatred, and intolerance of some of the other residents. Chapter 13 examines Carl Rogers's person-centered approach to personality and psychotherapy, as well as Abraham Maslow's theory that people try to fulfill their true potential.

Now inspect Table 1.1. As you can see, the biological approach is introduced in the biopsychology chapter, behaviorism influences the learning chapter, and the cognitive approach is first examined in the memory chapter. The sociocultural approach begins to play a role in the chapter on thinking. In contrast, the psychodynamic and humanistic approaches are emphasized in the last half of the book.

Psychology in the 1990s We've been tracing the origins of psychology. The chapter began with Wundt's efforts to transform the discipline into an empirical science and James's ideas about human consciousness. We continued through the founding of behaviorism in the United States and the development of Gestalt, psychoanalytic, and cognitive approaches in Europe. Then we examined six modern perspectives: the biological, behaviorist, cognitive, sociocultural, psychodynamic, and humanistic approaches. We've seen in this overview that psychologists have not been inspired throughout their history by one all-encompassing theory, one single truth.

When Wilhelm Wundt decided to conduct research on people's mental processes, no one handed him a proclamation about the best way to proceed. Instead, he began at a logical starting point, by asking people to report on their own psychological processes and by conducting some basic experiments. Behaviorists advanced psychology by emphasizing that concepts should be precisely defined and that responses must be objectively measured. Cognitive psychologists then adopted this emphasis on precision and objectivity, and they applied these techniques in studying mental processes.

Viewpoints in research psychology continue to change. Each new approach attempts to improve upon the earlier approaches or else to address other issues. The history of psychology is not smoothly continuous. Instead, it is fragmented, and different approaches emphasize different aspects of behavior and mental processes (Hilgard et al., 1991; R. Smith, 1988).

The viewpoints on treating psychological disorders have also continued to change. We can safely say that few current therapists uphold every word that Sigmund Freud ever wrote (Slipp, 1993). Also, most therapists acknowledge that some psychological disorders can be partly linked to a biological problem, so that drug treatment may be helpful. Most therapists also use some behaviorist techniques based on learning theory and some cognitive techniques designed to change inappropriate thought patterns. Therapists may also practice humanistic methods for listening to their clients, and they may try to understand how sociocultural factors influence their clients' lives. In other words, a therapist may strongly prefer one of the six theoretical approaches, but may still borrow techniques from the other five. The complexity of human psychology requires a complex approach in treating disorders, rather than strict loyalty to just one approach.

TABLE 1.1 Chapters in the Textbook Emphasizing the Six Major Current Approaches in Psychology

	THE CURRENT APPROACHES					
	Biological	Behaviorist	Cognitive	Sociocultural	Psychodynamic	Humanistic
Ch. 3: Biopsychology	●					
Ch. 4: Sensation and Perception	●					
Ch. 5: States of Consciousness	●					
Ch. 6: Learning	●	●				
Ch. 7: Memory	●		●			
Ch. 8: Thinking and Intelligence			●	●		
Ch. 9: Language and Conversation	●		●	●		
Ch. 10: Development in Infancy and Childhood			●	●		
Ch. 11: Development From Adolescence Through Old Age			●	●	●	
Ch. 12: Motivation and Emotion	●		●	●		
Ch. 13: Personality	●	●	●	●	●	●
Ch. 14: Psychological Disorders	●	●	●	●	●	
Ch. 15: Treating Psychological Disorders	●	●	●	●	●	●
Ch. 16: Social Cognition			●	●		
Ch. 17: Social Influence				●		
Ch. 18: Health Psychology	●	●	●	●		

Professions in Psychology

We have emphasized the diversity in psychology's goals, as well as in the historical and modern approaches to psychology. This diversity also applies to the occupational specialties within psychology. Let's first discuss four representative specialties that emphasize basic research and then consider three applied specialties that illustrate practical applications of psychological knowledge.

Cognitive psychologists conduct research on topics such as memory, thinking, and language. As you might imagine, their theoretical orientation is the cognitive approach.

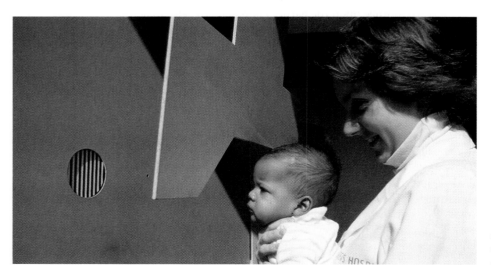

Developmental psychologists examine infants to study perception and cognitive processes.

Social psychologists study how our psychological processes are influenced by other people. For example, will this woman be less likely to litter if she has seen this man pick up someone else's trash?

Dr. Maria Kountz. Clinical psychologist who teaches at Beaver College in Glenside, Pennsylvania, and counsels clients who have personal problems.

FIGURE 1.3

J. Henry Alston. First Black psychologist to publish a paper in a major psychology journal.

Developmental psychologists examine how humans mature and change throughout their lives. Most developmental psychologists specialize in one part of the life span, such as childhood or old age.

Personality psychologists discover how people are influenced by relatively stable inner factors. A typical research question would be whether risk-taking is a characteristic that is likely to be inherited.

Social psychologists examine how our thoughts, feelings, and behaviors are influenced by other people. For example, a typical social psychology researcher might investigate the social conditions that encourage us to perform more energetically, as well as the conditions that promote social loafing (Sanna, 1992).

Throughout this textbook, you'll learn about other kinds of research psychologists. About half of research psychologists work in universities and colleges; others work for the government or private organizations (Azar, 1996).

Applied psychologists often work with people who have psychological problems. For example, **clinical psychologists** assess and treat people with psychological disorders. By using interviews and psychological tests, they suggest a diagnosis of the problem. Then they provide either individual or group psychotherapy. Like clinical psychologists, **counseling psychologists** assess and treat people, but their clients usually have less severe problems. Some counseling psychologists provide marriage or career counseling; others work in college mental health clinics.

Incidentally, many people confuse clinical and counseling psychologists with a group of medical professionals known as psychiatrists. **Psychiatrists** receive training in medicine, rather than psychology; their medical orientation emphasizes treating certain disorders with medication. Thus, psychiatrists are *not* psychologists.

One other major profession in applied psychology—besides clinical and counseling psychology—is industrial/organizational psychology. **Industrial/organizational psychologists** study how humans behave in business and industry. Some may help organizations hire and train employees. Others study the work setting, with the goal of improving people's productivity, morale, and job satisfaction. Still others measure people's attitudes toward a company's products.

Now that we have looked at several research and applied specializations within psychology, you may be curious about some of the characteristics of psychology students and psychologists. For example, in 1993 almost 67,000 U.S.

students received bachelor's degrees in psychology, with women receiving 73% of these degrees (McGovern & Reich, 1996). Also, 72% of master's degrees in psychology are awarded to women, in both the United States and Canada (McGovern & Reich, 1996; Pyke, 1995). Women now receive the majority of PhD degrees in psychology, too—62% in the United States and 68% in Canada (McGovern & Reich, 1996; Pion et al., 1996; Pyke & Greenglass, 1997). As you might imagine, women's status in psychology has changed considerably during the past century (Scarborough, 1994). During psychology's early history, Harvard University refused to grant a PhD to Mary Whiton Calkins—whose photo you saw in Figure 1.1—even though William James had described her as his very brightest student (Russo, 1983; Scarborough & Furumoto, 1987).

Table 1.2 lists the number of people who received bachelor's and PhD degrees in psychology in the United States, according to ethnic group. The early history of Black and Hispanic psychologists has been traced by Guthrie (1998). A prominent pioneer was Gilbert Haven Jones, the first Black psychologist with a PhD to teach in the United States. J. Henry Alston, shown in Figure 1.3, was the first African American to publish research in a major psychology journal. His 1920 article examined how people perceive heat and cold, a topic we'll mention in Chapter 4. Many Black and Hispanic psychologists have studied how children from different ethnic groups score on intelligence tests, a topic we'll consider in Chapter 8. For instance, Figure 1.4 shows George Sanchez, one of the first psychologists to discuss how these tests produced biased scores for Mexican American children (Guthrie, 1998). Sanchez is sometimes called the father of Chicano psychology (Padilla, 1988). Stanley Sue's (1992) report on Asian Americans in psychology describes how Asian students in previous decades were not encouraged to enter the field. In 1971, for example, Dr. Sue was the only full-fledged clinical psychologist from a Chinese background in a U.S. university. (See Figure 1.5.)

In recent years, several programs have been developed to encourage people of color to pursue graduate degrees. For example, the Minority Fellowship Program, sponsored by the American Psychological Association, offers financial assistance for graduate students in research, the neurosciences, and clinical psychology.

In this section, we've seen how the variety of theoretical approaches and professions illustrate the diversity of psychology. However, psychologists share a unified concern that underlies this diversity. All psychologists—no matter what specialty they pursue—are concerned with the scientific study of behavior and mental processes. In the next section, we'll see that three themes can be traced throughout many diverse areas within psychology.

FIGURE 1.4

George Sanchez. Early critic of intelligence tests that were biased against Hispanics and other people of color.

FIGURE 1.5

Stanley Sue (1944–   ). Clinical researcher who has conducted research on sociocultural factors that influence psychological disorders and their treatment.

TABLE 1.2 Ethnic Group Representation Among U.S. Recipients of Bachelor's and PhD Degrees in Psychology for 1992–1993

Ethnic Group	Number of Bachelor's Degrees in Psychology	Number of PhD Degrees in Psychology
White (non-Hispanic)	55,057	3,027
Black (non-Hispanic)	4,727	126
Hispanic	3,175	140
Asian	2,596	93
Native American	344	11

Source: Snyder et al., 1996.

SECTION SUMMARY: *PSYCHOLOGY TODAY*

1. The biological approach to psychology proposes that every behavior and mental process can be linked with a physical event in the brain or other part of the nervous system.

2. The behaviorist approach emphasizes behavior; it contributes to learning theory and psychotherapy.

3. The cognitive approach focuses on unobservable mental processes; it emphasizes how people actively acquire, combine, and transform information.

4. The sociocultural approach argues that psychological processes are influenced by factors such as culture, ethnic group, gender, and social class.

5. The psychodynamic approach points out the importance of childhood experiences, unconscious mental processes, and conflict.

6. The humanistic approach emphasizes humans' enormous potential for personal growth.

7. Viewpoints in both research psychology and psychotherapy have continued to change in the current era.

8. Some occupations in psychology emphasize research (e.g., cognitive, developmental, personality, and social psychologists); other occupations emphasize applications (e.g., clinical, counseling, and industrial/organizational psychologists).

9. In North America, the majority of bachelor's, master's, and PhD degrees in psychology are currently awarded to women; people of color still receive a relatively small fraction of psychology degrees.

THREE IMPORTANT THEMES IN PSYCHOLOGY

I asked myself the following question while writing this textbook: Suppose that 10 years from now, students who had read this book were asked to list several main points they recalled from their reading. What points would I most want them to remember? To me, three themes that recur throughout psychology seem most important. These themes are neither obscure nor surprising—instead, they are straightforward. Keep the themes in mind as you read the textbook. I'll frequently point out the themes in future chapters. However, you can aid your learning by trying to identify additional examples, even when they are not specifically noted.

Theme 1: Humans Are Extremely Competent

You've had many years of experience as a human being. Still, you probably do not fully appreciate the talents that you and other humans share. For instance, suppose you answer your telephone, and you hear the speaker say, "Is this Maxine's Pizza Parlor?" You manage to decode that stream of sounds effortlessly, understand the speaker's question, and answer—equally effortlessly—"No, I'm sorry, but you have the wrong number." Your actions may not sound particularly dazzling unless you realize that no computer can analyze language and respond with even a fraction of your own degree of competence.

The theme that humans are competent is especially prominent in the first half of the textbook. The theme is first introduced in Chapter 3 when we discuss the biological basis of behavior and mental processes. Here we will see that the human nervous system permits information to travel quickly. The brain also has numerous specialized regions that performs specific functions. Our impressive psychological skills can be traced to our impressive nervous system.

You'll also find the competence theme frequently in Chapter 4 (Sensation and Perception), particularly in the discussion of vision and hearing. However, the theme is most prominent in the chapters on human cognition—Chapter 7 (Memory), Chapter 8 (Thinking and Intelligence), and Chapter 9 (Language and Conversation). Our cognitive processes are fast, accurate, and flexible. Naturally, all of us make occasional errors. However, in many cases, these errors can be traced to a general strategy that usually produces correct responses. So, even our errors tend to be "smart mistakes." By the time you have completed this textbook, you should be very impressed with your own mental abilities.

Theme 2: Humans Differ Widely From One Another

We noted earlier that one goal of psychologists is to predict behavior. However, humans differ so impressively from one another that prediction is often difficult. Consider, in contrast, how easily we can make predictions in some other disciplines. For example, if I take a tablespoon of vinegar and add it to a tablespoon of baking soda, I can predict that the mixture will foam and produce a fizzing noise. In fact, I tried that three times, each with a different kind of vinegar, and the results were boringly predictable. Each time, the mixture foamed and fizzed. In psychology, however, we cannot make predictions with the same accuracy. I can take one student, add a lecture on visual perception, and that student will foam and fizz with excitement. Another student, similar from all outward appearances, may soon fall asleep. The individual differences among students—or any other humans—mean that they often respond in different ways to the same identical stimulus.

Individual differences are not especially prominent when we consider the processes that are largely biological, as in Chapter 3 (Biopsychology) and Chapter 4 (Sensation and Perception). However, beginning with Chapter 5 (States of Consciousness), we will often focus on this human variability.

Because of these individual differences, psychology researchers may have trouble obtaining consistent results. For instance, suppose that a group of researchers wants to see whether a new experimental program makes college students more interested in learning about other ethnic groups. Students first take a test that measures their interest in ethnic diversity. Next, they participate in the experimental program, and then they take a second test about interest in diversity. Compared to the first task, some students' scores improve, some decline, and some remain the same—demonstrating large individual differences. The researchers must then determine whether the first set of scores differs significantly from the second set of scores, taking into account the individual differences.

Researchers in some areas of psychology consider individual differences to be a nuisance, a factor that decreases their chances of finding significant experimental results. However, researchers in other areas—particularly in the psychology of personality—concentrate specifically on investigating these individual differences. In fact, personality researchers examine the factors that produce these individual differences. So, one psychologist's garbage is another psychologist's favorite dish.

Throughout this textbook, we will often compare various groups of humans when we focus on people who differ in characteristics such as gender, ethnic group, and sexual orientation. In general, we will conclude that differences *within* groups are larger than differences *between* groups. For example, in Chapter 8, we'll note that

Students in a classroom, like any group of humans, display individual differences.

males occasionally score higher than females on some mathematics tests. However, the difference between males and females is small compared to the differences within males or the differences within females. Just consider the variation within males, for example. You probably know males who are extremely skilled in math, yet you also know males who find the subject overwhelming. The variation within any human group is an important example of the general theme that humans differ widely from one another.

Theme 3: Psychological Processes Are Complex

When we examine the factors that influence human behavior, we seldom identify just one important factor. For example, suppose that researchers want to determine why 10-year-olds receive higher scores on a memory test than 6-year-olds. They will probably find that the explanation is complex and involves many contributing factors. One factor may be that the older children are more familiar with the words on the memory test. Another factor may be that the older children are more likely to figure out relationships between the words on the list and remember the words in clusters. Still another factor may be that the older children realize that they need to use a memory strategy, whereas the younger children don't believe they need to make a special effort to coax the words into memory. In short, most psychological processes are caused by multiple factors.

This complexity theme also operates when we try to figure out why two kinds of behavior are related to each other. For instance, in Chapter 6, we will see that the amount of violent television a child watches is related to that child's aggressive behavior. Three different factors probably contribute to this relationship:

1. Watching violent television encourages children to act aggressively;

2. Aggressive children like to watch violent television programs; and

3. The kind of family that allows children to watch violent television also tends to allow children to act aggressively.

In most relationships between psychological variables, a single explanation is not sufficient.

You'll see the complexity theme throughout this textbook. For example, in Chapter 4, you'll learn that our ability to hear depends upon an elaborate arrangement of auditory receptors, neurons, and tiny bones. Near the end of the book, in Chapter 17, you'll see that your tendency to be altruistic and helpful depends upon a complex set of factors, such as whether you can empathize with another person and whether you are in a hurry.

The complexity theme should encourage you to be suspicious of simple, one-factor explanations. For example, suppose you read in the newspaper that fathers who are emotionally cold and unresponsive are likely to have daughters who develop eating disorders. Remember that many factors—other than the father's emotions—contribute to eating disorders. Furthermore, the individual differences theme should lead you to realize that emotional unresponsiveness may promote an eating disorder in some young women, but it may have no effect on some other young women.

If humans were less competent, if individual differences were smaller, and if psychological explanations could be simple, this textbook would be very short. We would have all the answers, researchers would be unemployed, and we would not need therapists or other applied psychologists. However, the reality is that humans are amazingly competent, so we need to explain all their different talents. Humans also differ enormously, so we need to realize that people may respond differently to the same stimulus, and we need to explain these individual differences. Finally, psychological processes are complex, and the explanations for behavior are difficult to unravel. Psychologists have probably discovered more about behavior and mental processes in the last 30 years than in the previous 3,000. Still, we do not have all the answers. In fact, we have not even asked all the interesting questions.

Your ability to hear the tones produced by this violinist depends upon a complicated arrangement of structures in your auditory system. This is an example of Theme 3.

SECTION SUMMARY: *THREE IMPORTANT THEMES IN PSYCHOLOGY*

1. Theme 1 states that humans are extremely competent, especially in their perceptual and cognitive abilities.

2. Theme 2 states that humans differ widely from one another; these individual differences often make it difficult to obtain consistent results.

3. Theme 3 states that psychological processes are complex; for example, when two kinds of behavior are related to each other, we'll typically find that several factors contribute to the relationship.

CRITICAL THINKING

According to Betsy Pryor, this butterscotch-colored fungus can cure tired blood, heighten sex drives, and improve energy levels. Critical thinkers would ask for more compelling empirical evidence.

A course in introductory psychology should increase your knowledge about behavior and mental processes. In addition, this course should help you develop an extremely useful skill, called critical thinking. **Critical thinking** requires you to do the following:

1. Ask good questions about what you see or hear;

2. Determine whether conclusions are supported by the evidence that has been presented; and

3. Suggest alternative interpretations of the evidence.

We'll soon consider some guidelines for critical thinking. Before we begin, though, let's consider a typical situation in which critical thinking might be useful. A few years ago, *People* magazine featured an article about a kind of medicinal fungus called kombucha ("Yeast Meets West," 1995). According to the people who are trying to market this miracle cure, kombucha has been used as a folk medicine for at least 2,000 years in Manchuria—or maybe it was Egypt. At any rate, kombucha is supposed to cure tired blood, heighten your sex drive, improve your energy level, and even eliminate pimples! All you have to do is buy a starter kit (for $50), brew your own beverage, and drink three small glasses of this delightful fungus drink each day. One of the marketers, Betsy Pryor, had been encouraged by her guru in West Hollywood to try this miracle cure. Pryor then proclaimed, "Within a few days, my energy started to lift, and my skin started to clear up" (p. 192). If you approach the kombucha story using critical thinking skills, you should be asking questions such as the following:

1. What kind of specific behaviors or mental processes are supposed to improve after consuming this beverage? We'll leave the pimples to the dermatologists, but is "tired blood" a psychological characteristic? Is it the same as energy level? Is sex drive somewhat different?

2. How can these psychological processes be objectively measured? For example, I'd suspect that the kombucha marketers relied simply on their own subjective impressions, rather than on any careful, empirical measure of energy level.

3. A proper study would need to compare the results obtained when people had consumed kombucha with results when people had *not* consumed kombucha. Did the marketers include any comparison group?

4. What other kinds of explanations could account for the post-kombucha improvement? For example, perhaps Pryor began to feel more energized because she *expected* her energy to lift.

After asking questions like these, critical thinkers should realize that their $50 would be better spent on their favorite charity than on a Manchurian-Egyptian fungus drink.

Let's now consider critical thinking in more detail. What guidelines can critical thinkers employ? Why is critical thinking vitally important in psychology? What factors can hinder critical thinking?

Guidelines for Critical Thinking

Throughout this textbook, we'll be exploring many specific components of critical thinking. However, six general guidelines can help you navigate through a wide variety of problems:

1. *Examine how the terms are defined.* For example, suppose that a newspaper headline proclaims "Laughter Found to Improve Health." As you read the article, you find that the study compared people who were shown television sitcoms for one hour each day with people who were shown detective programs for the same amount of time. Those who has seen the sitcoms later rated their physical health as 5.9 on a scale with a maximum score of 7.0, whereas those watching the detective programs rated their health as only 4.7. Notice that the study relies on self-report, rather than on some more objective measures of health—such as visits to a health provider, number of days of work missed due to illness, or blood pressure. Throughout this book, we'll often see that researchers' conclusions may change when they use different definitions for their terms.

2. *Inspect the evidence.* Suppose an article reports on the caring concern that a group of young women expressed about their closest female friends. Then suppose the article concludes that gender differences in this area are very large. However, on closer inspection, you might discover that no one actually gathered data on a similar group of young men.

You should also inspect any data that the report does include. As you might suspect, researchers must conduct statistical analyses to determine whether their results are significant. Still, you can informally assess whether any differences seem to be large or small. For example, I recently saw an article titled "More Students Quitting College Before Sophomore Year, Data Show" (Geraghty, 1996). However, an inspection of the evidence showed only a small increase. The proportion of students at private four-year colleges who do not return for their sophomore year had increased from 23% in 1983 to 26% in 1996—only a minimal increase. The similar figures for public colleges were 29% and 29%—no increase at all. You need to determine whether the evidence genuinely supports the reported conclusions.

3. *Look for potential biases.* For instance, if you are reading an advertisement, be suspicious of any "research" that the company itself has conducted. Would you really trust them to report that their product was useless? Should you believe tobacco companies when they argue that cigarettes do not cause cancer?

You should also look for your *own* biases. Many students find that an introductory psychology course forces them to reexamine some beliefs that they have not previously questioned. For example, some of the students in my introductory psychology classes believe at the beginning of the semester that children raised by gay or lesbian parents must have more psychological problems than children raised by heterosexual parents. These are the messages they have received from their family and community for the past 18 years or more. However, reviews of the psychology research contradict their assumptions. As C. J. Patterson (1996) concludes, these studies "provide no evidence that psychological adjustment among lesbian mothers, gay fathers, or their children is impaired in any significant respect relative to heterosexual parents or their children" (p. 291). Although many of the conclusions in psychology will match your own views, you should also be prepared to change your mind when the evidence is compelling.

According to numerous studies and reviews of literature, children raised by gay and lesbian parents are similar in their psychological adjustment to children raised by heterosexual parents. However, many people may have trouble accepting the empirical evidence on this issue because of their prior biases.

4. *Ask whether the conclusions have been oversimplified.* As you know, one of the themes of this textbook is that psychological processes are complex. Therefore, you should be very suspicious whenever a report seems to oversimplify a relationship, trying to argue that a complicated psychological relationship can be distilled into a single important explanation. For example, we'll see in Chapter 6 that children who watch violent television programs tend to be more aggressive. However, critical thinkers acknowledge that no psychological relationship can be entirely straightforward. Yes, television violence is probably one important cause of aggressive behavior. But aggressive behavior is also promoted by seeing violent behavior in the family or community and by misinterpreting the behavior of other people (Chapter 17). You should always be suspicious of single-factor explanations.

5. *Ask whether the conclusions have been overgeneralized.* An article in the *Los Angeles Daily News* proclaimed, "Women have a gender-specific, natural pain-relief system that depends on estrogen, say researchers at UCLA" ("Gender-Specific Pain Relief," 1993, p. C1). However, the UCLA researchers were actually reporting on responses to pain in male and female *mice* (Mogil et al., 1993). You should mistrust any research whose conclusions leap across to a different species from the one that was tested. You should also mistrust any research that generalizes to different human populations from the one that was examined. For example, a study on eating disorders on upper-middle-class European American suburban teenagers in the northeastern United States may not be relevant for low-income African American rural 30-year-olds in the Southeast. Responsible researchers acknowledge that their conclusions must be limited to the population they have examined.

6. *Consider other possible interpretations.* Healthy skepticism is one of the trademarks of critical thinking, and critical thinkers enjoy pursuing alternative explanations for a study's findings. Suppose that a developmental psychologist discovers that 3-month-old infants spend the same amount of time looking at a triangle and a square. She therefore concludes that infants cannot visually distinguish between the two shapes. However, another possible explanation for these results is that the babies can indeed see the difference between the two stimuli—still, they like them equally well, so they spend equal time looking at them. Conscientious researchers conduct additional studies to rule out these alternative explanations.

In other cases, a variable may initially seem to influence behavior, but closer inspection shows that a different variable is really responsible. For example, early studies on bilingualism reported that bilingual children scored lower on intelligence tests than did children who spoke only one language. However, critics noticed that the researchers had been comparing bilingual children from lower socioeconomic backgrounds with middle-class monolingual children (e.g., Reynolds, 1991). Social class—rather than bilingualism—was probably responsible for the differences in intelligence. In fact, when later research equated the two groups for social class, bilinguals performed slightly better on tests measuring language and academic ability (Peal & Lambert, 1962). Like a detective, you need to search for clues about alternative explanations.

You can apply these critical-thinking principles in your daily life, as well as in psychology research. In my introductory psychology class, for example, I give students the assignment of critically examining some conclusion they have drawn about psychological processes. Students typically realize that they had originally failed to consider alternative explanations for their experiences. For instance, one semester, a student named Amelie Feroce described how she had concluded that her grades were higher than her roommate's because she had attended a private high school. (Her roommate had attended a public high school.) On closer inspection, however, Amelie realized that she had selected relatively easy courses, whereas her roommate was a biochemistry major—one of the most difficult majors on campus. Also, Amelie's older brother was a college junior who had given her extensive advice about study skills; her roommate had no similar guidance. In fact, Amelie identified four other factors—in addition to high school experience—that could have explained the difference in grades (Feroce, 1992). As we noted, critical thinking encourages us to ask good questions, determine whether the evidence supports the conclusions, and suggest alternative interpretations of the evidence.

Why Critical Thinking Is Important in Psychology

Critical thinking is a valuable skill for all students to acquire—not just psychology students. One reason is that you'll learn material more thoroughly if you carefully think about the material you are reading and analyze its implications (King, 1992; Paul, 1992). Also, if you can analyze an argument and find flaws in its conclusions, you'll find that this skill can help you think more clearly about both your professional life and your personal life. But critical thinking is especially important in psychology. Let's consider some reasons.

1.   During your years of experience as a human being, you have established some firm beliefs about how people think and act. We humans often cling to our strongly held beliefs, even when we have little evidence (Nissani, 1994). In fact, most people think of themselves as "amateur psychologists" who give useful advice and understand human nature. (Interestingly, the people I know never think of themselves as "amateur dentists" or "amateur chemists"!) You'll therefore be reluctant to throw your fondest beliefs overboard and calmly analyze why your previous reasoning may have been flawed (Stanovich, 1998).

2.   A vivid example of a single individual can often be more seductive than several pages of rational data (Nisbett & Ross, 1980; Stanovich, 1998). Politicians

know that one compelling story about a welfare mother who acquired funds illegally is often all they need to persuade voters to support cutbacks in welfare spending. In fact, that one story may be much more persuasive than an academically sound article about the genuine needs of welfare recipients and the difficulty of finding employment in their community.

3. Many of the most deceptive advertisements offer products that claim to have psychological effects. In North America, we are surrounded by advertising. In fact, the average person encounters 30,000 advertisements each year (Postman & Powers, 1992). Start noticing how many of these ads promise psychological benefits, even when the product focuses on an entirely different problem. For example, if you rid your scalp of dandruff, you'll achieve instant popularity! In Chapter 2, we'll also examine "subliminal tapes." The ads claim that such tapes will help you conquer your personal weaknesses—but we'll see that the tapes do not live up to the advertisements (Druckman & Bjork, 1991).

As I was writing this section on critical thinking, I received a catalog that offered—for a mere $19.95—a "Crystal Spellbox." Here is the text of the advertisement:

> Do you dream about sharing your life with someone special? Open your heart and mind to the limitless possibilities of love with the secrets of this true love spell. The spellbox contains everything you'll need to cast the spell to help you find your soul mate. It includes candle, incense, instructions, and more! You supply imagination and desire!

Throughout this textbook, I'll include a number of exercises to help you develop your critical thinking skills. In each case write out your response to the questions; the writing process forces you to clarify your answers. Here's our first example; you can find the answer at the end of this chapter (on Page 29).

Critical Thinking Exercise 1.1

Write down your answers to the following questions about the "crystal spellbox" and critical thinking:

a. In the advertisement for the crystal spellbox, what end result does the ad *imply?* When you look more closely, what terms are used to describe what you can actual *do* with the spellbox?

b. What evidence is offered that the spellbox has been demonstrated to be successful?

c. What potential biases might encourage the advertisers to be less than fully honest in the ad?

d. If you actually purchased this spellbox and you really did locate your soul mate, what other explanation might account for your success?

What Factors Hinder Critical Thinking?

Earlier in this section, we examined six guidelines to help you pursue critical thinking. Now let's consider several factors that can derail critical thinking and encourage inappropriate conclusions. If you spot any of these four factors in an article or an advertisement, be suspicious that someone is trying to keep you from thinking critically.

1. *Appeals to the popularity of a program or an idea* (Gibbs et al., 1995; Halpern, 1996a). At the time I was writing this section, the book *Men Are From*

What would be your emotional reaction to this soldier if he were described as a freedom fighter? How would your reaction change if he were described as a terrorist? Biased language is one of the factors that hinders critical thinking.

Mars, Women Are From Venus (Gray, 1992) had been on the best-seller list for three years and had been translated into 86 languages. From the book's popularity, you might be tempted to believe that gender differences in interpersonal relationships are clear-cut, straightforward, and universal (Bader, 1996). However, more careful reviews of the research show that gender similarities are typically more common (e.g., Hyde, 1996a; Matlin, 1996a; Unger & Crawford, 1996). Popularity is no substitute for empirical evidence!

2. *Incomplete comparisons* (Halpern, 1996a). Suppose you read in a magazine that a certain drug "provided more relief from depression." Your first response should be, "Compared to what?" We cannot know whether the drug was successful unless we have been told whether the drug condition was compared with a therapy condition, with a condition that received a different drug, or with a condition that received no treatment. You'll see in this textbook that many psychological studies emphasize comparisons between different conditions.

3. *Using biased language.* You should be alert for biased language in news reports. For example, a group of individuals in another country may be called "freedom fighters" if our government supports them, but "terrorists" if the group has different goals (Paul, 1992). Similarly, look for biased wording in reports of psychological research. For example, you might read, "Only 59% of children from day care programs showed close attachment to their mothers, in contrast to fully 62% of children whose mothers did not work outside the home." The contrast between the terms "only" and "fully" masks the fact that a mere 3% separated the two groups. You should continually watch for phrases that imply more than the data reveal.

4. *Stating claims with certainty.* We humans prefer the reassurance of certainty to the dissatisfaction of uncertainty (Carlson, 1995). Students in my introductory psychology class often want me to make a definite statement, such as "Yes, people definitely recall more material if they try to remember the material in the same setting in which they originally learned it—rather than in a different setting." However, I encourage them to tolerate uncertainty, especially in an area as complex as psychology. I know they are disappointed when I hedge with a conclusion, such as "Sometimes people recall more when they are in the same setting, but sometimes the setting does not influence recall." Throughout this book you'll find numerous examples of uncertainty, rather than clear-cut conclusions. That's simply the nature of our discipline! Because reality is uncertain, you should be suspicious of any argument suggesting that certain results are clear-cut.

As you'll discover, critical thinking is not limited to a simple list of guidelines and cautions that can be mastered in one short section. We'll return to this topic in Chapter 2, when our examination of research methods provides some more tools for evaluating conclusions in psychology.

SECTION SUMMARY: *CRITICAL THINKING*

1. Critical thinking requires asking good questions, determining whether the evidence supports the conclusions, and suggesting alternative interpretations.

2. Several important guidelines for critical thinking include the following: examine how the terms are defined; inspect the evidence; look for potential bi-

ases; ask whether the conclusions have been oversimplified; ask whether the conclusions have been overgeneralized; and consider other possible interpretations.

3. Critical thinking is a useful intellectual skill for all students; however, it is especially useful for psychology students—because they are likely to have

formed some strong beliefs; because vivid examples may compellingly contradict empirical data; and because many advertisements address psychological issues.

4. Important factors that hinder critical thinking include the following: appeals to an idea's popularity; incomplete comparisons; biased language; and people's preference for certainty.

HOW TO USE THIS BOOK

Psychology includes several features to help you think about, understand, and remember the material. Here's how you can use these features most effectively.

Notice that each chapter begins with an outline. Before reading a new chapter, inspect the outline and try to understand the structure of the topic. For instance, on Page 30, notice that Chapter 2 is divided into four sections: "The Major Research Methods," "Research Issues," "Constructing and Evaluating Psychological Tests," and "Analyzing the Data."

Another important feature of this textbook is a "section summary" at the end of each major section of a chapter. These summaries encourage you to review the material often and to master relatively short topics before moving on to a new area. When you reach the end of a section, test yourself to see whether you can remember the important points. Then read the section summary and mark the items you forgot or remembered incorrectly. Finally, test yourself again and recheck your accuracy. Some of my introductory psychology students have told me that they like to read one section at a time, check themselves on the section summary, and then take a break. Then when they return to the textbook, they find it helpful to review previous section summaries before beginning the new material.

I have applied many psychological principles in writing this textbook. Research on memory has demonstrated that people remember material better when it is illustrated with examples. Therefore, I've included many examples from my experience, as well as examples my students have provided. You will also remember more effectively if you think about examples from your own experience. For instance, the section on working memory in Chapter 7 points out that memory is often fragile; an item you just heard can disappear from memory if your attention is distracted. When you read a statement like the one about memory, try to determine whether it matches your own experiences. Pause, try to recall some specific examples, and write them in the margins. Psychologists have found that one of the most effective methods of enhancing recall is to ask people to relate the material to themselves (e.g., Rogers et al., 1977). You have lived with yourself for many years now, so take advantage of your experience!

This textbook also includes informal experiments labeled "demonstrations." You've already tried a demonstration about popular sayings, on Page 5. Each demonstration can be done quickly and usually requires no special equipment. In most cases, you can perform the demonstrations by yourself, but some require you to work with a partner. These demonstrations should also help make the material more concrete and easy to remember. More tips on improving memory are discussed throughout Chapter 7.

The "critical thinking" exercises will help you develop your analytic skills. For example, the first of these exercises, on Page 23, helped you think more critically about an advertisement. As you learn more about research methods in Chapter 2, many of these exercises will focus on the strengths and weaknesses of research design. Whenever possible, write down your answers to these exercises. Writing encourages you to reflect carefully about a complex question, rather than simply supplying a rapid response (Wade, 1995).

Notice, also, that new terms appear in boldface type (for example, **psychology**). I've included the definition in the same sentence as the term, so that you don't need to search an entire paragraph to discover its meaning. Each term also appears in the glossary at the end of the book and in the index. If your professor uses a psychological term during a lecture, and you cannot recall its meaning, check the glossary for a brief definition, or look in the index to find where the topic is discussed in more detail. A phonetic guide is provided where a term or a person's name (like Wilhelm Wundt) does not have an obvious pronunciation. (The accented syllable will appear in italics.) My students have told me that they appreciate knowing how to pronounce a word when they first see it defined, rather than having to make a wrong guess or check the glossary at the end of the book.

Chapters 2 through 18 each contain an "In Depth" feature, which discusses recent research on a selected topic relevant to the chapter. These discussions look closely at the research methods and the results of studies on a topic that currently intrigues psychologists.

You will find a set of review questions at the end of each chapter. Many review questions ask you to apply your knowledge to a practical problem. Other questions encourage you to integrate information from several parts of a chapter. Prior to an exam, you may find it helpful to review all the section summaries in a chapter, and then try to answer the review questions.

You can also find a list of new terms at the end of each chapter. These are the words and phrases that appeared in bold type in the chapter text. The best way to study these new terms is by trying to supply a definition and—where relevant—an example for each. You can monitor your accuracy by checking either the glossary or the pages of the textbook.

The final feature of each chapter is a list of "recommended readings." This list supplies you with resources if you want to write a paper on a particular topic or if an area interests you. In general, I've included books, chapters, and articles that provide more than a general overview of a topic but are not overly technical.

In summary, psychological principles can be used to help you master psychology. When you actively think about the material and review it systematically, you'll find that you can remember more of the important concepts in psychology.

SECTION SUMMARY: *HOW TO USE THIS BOOK*

1. This section provides many tips to help you learn the materials more effectively.

2. You'll recall more if you review the material frequently, thinking of examples of psychological principles from your own life, and testing your knowledge.

REVIEW QUESTIONS

1. Wilhelm Wundt is often considered the founder of contemporary psychology. What did he study, and how rigorous were his methods? Describe a theoretical question in which he and Gestalt psychologists would be likely to *disagree*.

2. Three important facets of American research psychology have been the psychology of William James, the behaviorist movement, and the cognitive psychology framework. Describe each of these approaches, and contrast them with respect to factors you consider to be important.

3. Before you began this chapter, what had you heard about Sigmund Freud's theory? Does that information match what you read here? Why or why not?

4. What does the cognitive psychology approach emphasize? What are its origins in European psychology, and what does it borrow from American psychology? Why did its popularity increase later in the twentieth century? What is the humanistic approach, who are its major theorists, and how did it come about?

5. Describe the six current approaches to psychology: biological, behaviorist, cognitive, sociocultural, psychodynamic, and humanistic. If you were to pursue a career in psychology or in some related area, which approach would be most personally useful? Which approach(es) would be most relevant for a physician? A classroom teacher? A businessperson? A social worker?

6. Contrast the view of human nature provided by those who favor the behaviorist, cognitive, psychodynamic, and humanistic approaches. Which approach(es) do you find most consistent with your own view of humans?

7. Imagine that psychologists from a variety of specialty areas in psychology have gathered for a conference on aggression. Each of the following will present a paper on his or her work related to aggression: a cognitive psychologist, a developmental psychologist, a social psychologist, a clinical psychologist, a counseling psychologist, and an industrial/organizational psychologist. Suggest a sample paper topic for each of these six psychologists.

8. What are the three themes of this book, presented just before the section on critical thinking? Explain each theme, and provide your own example for each one, based on something you have observed in the last few days.

9. Try to recall the six general guidelines for critical thinking. Then think of an important decision you have made in the last year, and apply those rules to evaluate how you chose between two or more options. For example, if you decided "College X is better than College Y," examine how you defined the term "better," and then continue through the other five guidelines.

10. What factors hinder critical thinking? How could those factors have hindered your critical thinking for the decision you described in Question 9. How are these factors related to the armchair approach, which we examined at the beginning of the chapter?

NEW TERMS

psychology (p. 4)
applied psychologists (p. 4)
empirical evidence (p. 4)
introspection (p. 6)
structuralism (p. 6)
replications (p. 6)
functionalism (p. 7)
behaviorism (p. 7)
Gestalt approach (p. 8)
biology (p. 9)
sociology (p. 9)
biological approach (p. 10)
neuroscience approach (p. 10)
cognitive approach (p. 10)

sociocultural approach (p. 11)
psychodynamic approach (p. 11)
psychoanalytic approach (p. 11)
humanistic approach (p. 12)
cognitive psychologists (p. 13)
developmental psychologists (p. 14)
personality psychologists (p. 14)
social psychologists (p. 14)
clinical psychologists (p. 14)
counseling psychologists (p. 14)
psychiatrists (p. 14)
industrial/organizational psychologists
  (p. 14)
critical thinking (p. 19)

RECOMMENDED READINGS

Guthrie, R. V. (1998). *Even the rat was white: A historical view of psychology* (2nd ed.) Boston: Allyn & Bacon. The title of the book refers to psychology's early neglect of racial and ethnic minorities;

this up-to-date book helps to correct this neglect, especially by presenting biographies of pioneering Black and Hispanic psychologists.

Halpern, D. F. (1996). *Thought and knowledge: An introduction to critical thinking* (3rd ed.). Mahwah, NJ: Erlbaum. Diane Halpern is one of the foremost experts on the teaching of critical thinking; her textbook relates critical thinking to the discipline of cognitive psychology in a clear and interesting fashion.

Popplestone, J. A., & McPherson, M. W. (1994). *An illustrated history of American psychology.* Madison, WI: Brown & Benchmark. I'm especially enthusiastic about this book on psychology's history because of its wonderful photos of the early psychologists, their laboratories, and their research equipment.

Scarborough, E., & Furumoto, L. (1987). *Untold lives: The first generation of American women psychologists.* New York: Columbia University Press. This fascinating book features chapter-long biographies of several early female psychologists, including Calkins, Washburn, and Ladd-Franklin, as well as shorter portraits of other pioneering women; an especially useful section analyzes the forces that limited women's academic achievements at the beginning of the twentieth century.

Schultz, D. P., & Schultz, S. E. (1996). *A history of modern psychology* (6th ed.). Fort Worth, TX: Harcourt Brace. This textbook provides a readable, mid-level overview of psychology's history. It emphasizes behaviorism and the psychodynamic perspective; the final chapter on gender and ethnicity includes some interesting information.

Stanovich, K. E. (1998). *How to think straight about psychology* (5th ed.). New York: HarperCollins. Here's a wonderfully clear and concise guide to critical thinking in psychology, focusing on some of the most prominent errors that people commit.

Answers to Demonstrations

Demonstration 1.1

1. True—Depressed people are more likely to seek emotional support from others than are people who are not depressed.

2. False—Children who are severely punished when young are more likely to develop psychological problems in adulthood than are those whose parents "spared the rod."

3. True—When management students were asked to decide the salary levels of various job candidates, they awarded higher salaries to the applicants who had requested higher salaries.

4. True—When students watched videotapes of people whose self-descriptions conflicted with their actual behavior on characteristics such as "shy" and "friendly," their judgments were influenced much more strongly by what the people did than what they said.

5. False—Attractive people turn out to have higher self-esteem and to be better treated than less attractive people. (We discuss the issue of physical attractiveness in detail in Chapter 2.)

6. True—Students who had talked on the phone to depressed people were not interested in spending time with these people, compared to students who had talked to nondepressed people.

7. True—People who marry young or after just a short courtship are more likely to seek a divorce later on, in comparison to those who marry after age 20 or after a long courtship.

8. False—In a variety of studies, people have indicated their preference for items (such as words, symbols, and photos) that they have seen frequently.

9. True—If we transform the ancient sword into the modern handgun, the saying has clear support; gunshot deaths are three times more likely to occur in homes where a gun is kept, (compared to homes with no guns). Also, guns are more likely to kill a resident than an intruder, by a ratio of about 350 to 1.

10. False—Numerous studies on both friendships and romantic relationships show that people tend to be attracted to individuals who are similar to themselves, not different.

Sources: Jordan, 1989; Kellermann et al., 1993; Kohn, 1988.

ANSWERS TO CRITICAL THINKING EXERCISES

Exercises 1.1

a. The ad implies that you will find true love. However, when you look more closely, it *says* that you will open your heart and mind to the possibilities of love and that you will have the ingredients to cast a spell (not that it will necessarily work).

b. No evidence of success is presented.

c. Clearly, the advertisers want your money, so they would not be likely to tell you that the spellbox's success has not been demonstrated.

d. The spellbox may have made you more self-confident, or more eager to seek out places where you could meet your soul mate, or more likely to believe that someone you meet is indeed your soul mate. Also, you may have met this individual—even if you hadn't purchased the spellbox.

RESEARCH METHODS IN PSYCHOLOGY

THE MAJOR RESEARCH METHODS

The Experimental Method

The Quasi-Experiment

The Correlational Method

The Survey Method

In-Depth Interviews and Case Studies

Naturalistic Observation

Comparing the Methods

RESEARCH ISSUES

Sampling

Measuring Responses

Avoiding Gender, Ethnic, and Cultural Biases

Social Aspects of Research

Ethical Aspects of Research

In Depth: Research on Physical Attractiveness

CONSTRUCTING AND EVALUATING PSYCHOLOGICAL TESTS

Standardization

Norms

Reliability

Validity

ANALYZING THE DATA

Descriptive Statistics: Summarizing the Data

Inferential Statistics: Drawing Conclusions About the Data

CHAPTER 2

Imagine that you are a resident of New Haven, Connecticut. You have responded to a newspaper ad, and you are scheduled to report to a laboratory at Yale University. You've been told that the study explores memory and learning. You meet the researcher, as well as another participant who has arrived at the same time, a pleasant middle-aged man. The two of you draw slips of paper from a hat, and you are assigned the role of the "teacher"; the other participant will be the "learner." As the teacher, you must press a switch on the equipment shown above and administer an electric shock to the learner whenever he makes a mistake on the learning task. You are also instructed to raise the shock level by 15 points after each subsequent mistake. Your first assignment is to help strap the learner into a chair, so that the electrodes attached to a shock generator will not fall off if he moves excessively. You are reluctant to harm another person, especially when he begins to scream out in pain. However, when you hesitate before delivering a shock, the experimenter urges you: "The experiment requires that you go on." What would you do in this situation?

This scenario describes the research of Dr. Stanley Milgram (1963, 1974)—shown above—one of the best-known experiments in the history of psychology (A. G. Miller et al., 1995a). Milgram described a typical "teacher"—in this case, a middle-aged businessman:

I observed a mature and initially poised businessman enter the laboratory smiling and confident. Within 20 minutes he was reduced to a twitching, stuttering wreck, who was rapidly approaching a point of nervous collapse. He constantly pulled on his earlobe, and twisted his hands. At one point he pushed his fist into his forehead and muttered: "Oh, God, let's stop it." And yet he continued to respond to every word of the experimenter, and obeyed to the end. (Milgram, 1963, p. 377)

Incidentally, at this point, we need to emphasize that the "learners" in Milgram's studies were really research assistants. They received no actual shock.

Under the conditions we have discussed, 65% obeyed completely, delivering what they believed to be the full 450 volts of shock (Milgram, 1974). In the most tormenting condition, the teacher was instructed to press the hand of the screaming victim down onto the shock plate—so that the electric shock could be delivered appropriately. Even here, 30% of the participants obeyed completely (Milgram, 1974). More than 1,000 individuals participated in this research, the majority delivering the full amount of electric shock to another human being (Elms, 1995).

The Milgram research has been widely debated in the decades after it was conducted (A. G. Miller et al., 1995b). In particular, psychologists have discussed whether this research was ethically appropriate and whether the results can be applied to the everyday evil that people commit in their normal lives. Indeed, Milgram had designed the experiment to examine obedience to destructive authority, an important social issue during the 1960s (Elms, 1995). The Holocaust had ended less than two decades before. Also, Adolf Eichmann had recently received the death sentence for his role in the Holocaust, although he argued that he had simply been "following orders." Milgram's research was important because it demonstrated that obedient Nazis are not the only ones who follow orders. Ordinary American citizens, living in New Haven, Connecticut, will follow the commands of a psychology researcher, even though they realize they may be endangering the safety of another individual.

Philosophers and historians may theorize about the nature of evil and the conditions that are likely to encourage aggression and violence. Psychologists adopt a different approach, conducting research to determine how people will actually behave in certain situations. This chapter explores the methods psychologists use to explore human behavior and thought.

In the preceding chapter, you learned some general guidelines about improving your critical thinking. The current chapter on research methods will provide more specific background information to help you analyze psychology research more critically. Once you understand some of the important features of research, you'll be able to think more analytically about the studies described throughout this textbook. Even more important, you'll develop a healthy skepticism about the research you encounter in the media. Several years from now, you may not recall much of the specific information in this book. However, if you have improved your understanding of psychology research and critical thinking, you'll still be able to use the basic principles of research methods to evaluate claims in psychology and related areas (Stanovich, 1998).

Let's consider an example. Suppose a newspaper article summarizes a study in which 92% of adolescent women with eating disorders described their relationships with their fathers as "distant." After reading this chapter, I hope you'll ask critical questions about such reports. For instance, what percentage of adolescent women *without* eating disorders also describe distant relationships with their fathers? Is it possible that the relationships are not really "distant" at all, but are just being perceived inaccurately by the young women? Further, the article implies that distant fathers cause their daughters to develop eating disorders; instead, could the daughters' unusual behavior cause alienation in the fathers? Asking critical questions about research methods and reported findings can help you put research results in proper perspective.

Another advantage to understanding research is more personal: You can think more clearly about your own behavior and make more rational decisions. For example, suppose you study conscientiously for a biology exam, you sleep eight hours the night before, and you receive a C+. For the next exam, you study less and sleep less, and receive a B. Can you conclude that you will receive an even higher score on the third exam by studying and sleeping even less? After reading this chapter, you should be on the lookout for alternative explanations of relationships. (For instance, the second exam might have been easier, or you may have become more accustomed to the instructor's test format.)

We'll begin this chapter by exploring several major research methods. Then we'll discuss some important research issues, such as the problem of measuring behavioral responses and the issue of avoiding biases in psychological studies. The third section in this chapter examines how psychological tests are constructed and evaluated. Our final section briefly considers the analysis of psychological data.

THE MAJOR RESEARCH METHODS

Psychological research uses the scientific method. The **scientific method** includes these four basic steps:

1. Identify the research problem, aided by the previous research.
2. Design and conduct a study, gathering appropriate data.
3. Examine the data.
4. Communicate the results.

Psychologists use six major research methods to explore behavior. Each method approaches the steps of the scientific method from a different perspective. As you might expect, each of the six methods has strengths and weaknesses. By combining several approaches, researchers can acquire a much more complete picture of psychological processes. For instance, the experimental method is most useful for determining the *cause* of a particular behavior. In contrast, naturalistic observation tells us little about causes for behavior, but it helps us understand how people and animals *behave* in their normal lives.

The six methods also differ in the amount of control the researchers can exercise when they conduct their studies. In experimental studies, researchers can control what the participants see, hear, and do. In naturalistic observation, the participants control their own behavior; the researchers observe but do nothing to control or change the participants' behavior.

The Experimental Method

The experimental method is the most effective way to identify a cause-and-effect relationship. In an **experiment,** researchers systematically manipulate a variable under controlled conditions and observe how the participants respond. For example, suppose you want to see whether students write more effective essays if they first construct an outline. In an experiment, you could systematically manipulate the instructions given to the students: Perhaps half of the students are told to begin by outlining the major topics they plan to cover; the other half are told to begin writing immediately.

In an experiment, researchers manipulate one variable, such as presence or absence of instructions about an outline. Then the researchers observe how the participants respond—for example, in terms of the writing quality of their essay. (This quality could be assessed by well-qualified judges, who are unaware whether the students had prepared an outline.) The researchers try to hold constant the other variables that are not being tested (e.g., the topic of the essay and the lighting in the room). If the results change when only that one manipulated variable is changed, then the researchers can conclude that they have discovered a cause-and-effect relationship. For example, they may conclude that preparing an outline causes students to write a more effective paper. By the way, you should know that students who have prepared outlines really *do* write more effective papers than do students who have not prepared outlines (Kellogg, 1988, 1994).

Independent and Dependent Variables   When you design an experiment, the first step is to state a hypothesis. A **hypothesis** is a tentative set of beliefs about the nature of the world (Halpern, 1996a). It's a statement about what you expect to happen if certain conditions are true. A hypothesis can be stated in an "if . . . then" format: *If* certain conditions are true, *then* certain things will happen. For example:

If (students prepare an outline)   **then**   (they will write more effective papers.)

A hypothesis tells what relationship a researcher expects to find between an independent variable and a dependent variable. The **independent variable** is the variable that the experimenters manipulate. They decide how much of that variable to present to the participant. The independent variable is described in the *if* part of the "if . . . then" statement of the hypothesis. In the preceding example, the independent variable is whether or not the students prepare an outline.

The **dependent variable** concerns the responses that the participants make; it is a measure of their behavior. The dependent variable is described in the *then* part of the "if . . . then" statement of the hypothesis. In our example, the dependent variable is the effectiveness of the papers, as rated by well-qualified judges.

You can remember the two kinds of variables by noting that the dependent variable *depends* upon the value of the independent variable. For example, the writing quality (dependent variable) *depends* upon the presence or absence of an outline (the independent variable). Students often have difficulty identifying the independent and dependent variable in an example, even when they can define these terms perfectly (McKelvie, 1992). Demonstration 2.1 helps you apply your knowledge of these important terms.

Experimental and Control Conditions   In an experiment, the researcher must arrange to test at least two conditions that are specified by the independent variable. In the simple example of the writing experiment, we could test one group of students in a "no-outline" condition and a second group in an "outline" condition. In other words, one group, the **control condition,** is left unchanged; the students receive no special treatment. The second group, the **experimental condition,** is changed in some way. A particular variable is present in the experimental condition that is absent in the control condition. (In this study, the outlining is either present or absent.)

Most of the experiments described in this book include more than just two conditions. The writing study could compare three conditions: a no-outline control

DEMONSTRATION 2.1   Identifying the Independent and the Dependent Variables

To help you understand independent and dependent variables, read the first two examples. Then, for the next three examples, list what you believe to be the independent and the dependent variables. You can check the answers at the end of this chapter.

HYPOTHESIS	INDEPENDENT VARIABLE	DEPENDENT VARIABLE
1. If prison guards treat inmates courteously, then inmates will comply better with prison rules.	Nature of guards' interactions (courteous vs. rude)	Extent of compliance with rules (e.g., proper mealtime conduct)
2. If residents in a nursing home can control aspects of their lives, then they will be healthier.	Personal control (e.g., allowed to decide about bedroom decorations vs. no input in decision)	Health measures (e.g., number of days with medical complaints)
3. If people consume caffeine prior to bedtime, then they will take longer to fall asleep.	?	?
4. If another person is present in the room, then an individual will take longer to respond to an emergency.	?	?
5. If people are praised for helping another person, then they are more likely to help others in the future.	?	?

Note: Hypotheses are often stated in formats that do not use the specific words *if* and *then*. For example, Hypothesis 1 might appear as *Inmates comply better with prison rules when prison guards treat them courteously.* To identify the independent and dependent variables, simply reword the hypothesis in an "if . . . then" format.

and two experimental conditions (brief outline and detailed outline). However, all experiments require some kind of comparison between conditions. If you have only one condition, you do not have an experiment, and you cannot draw conclusions about cause and effect.

Let's consider why we cannot draw causal conclusions from just a single condition. You have probably read advertisements for so-called "subliminal" tapes. Each tape recording presumably contains positive messages, spoken so quietly that they cannot be consciously heard. Instead, the listener hears only soothing music or natural sounds, such as gentle winds or ocean waves. The ads claim, however, that the subconscious mind responds to the hidden messages and that these messages will transform your life. Each ad features testimonials from people about their weight loss, improved self-image, increased memory, better sex life, and other life transformations. One testimonial on weight loss stated the following:

> I have lost 15 pounds without too much effort using your [weight control] tape. To say I'm extremely pleased is putting it mildly. Thank you so much for making this help available.

Intrigued by these ads, I wrote to seven companies that offered subliminal tapes. In each case, I requested information on experimental studies that contrasted the performance of experimental and control groups. So far, no company has replied. The companies probably never tested the tapes experimentally. As a result, we hear testimonials, and their enthusiasm might convince an uncritical thinker that the tapes work miracles.

However, suppose that one company decides to test the weight-loss tape using a single condition. In this single condition, everyone listens to the tape, complete with the subliminal message. Suppose, as well, that 80% of the people report at least some weight loss. The problem is that we do not know what percentage of people in a control condition—who never listened to subliminal tapes—would also have reported at least some weight loss. Without a comparison condition, we cannot draw conclusions.

This student is listening to a subliminal tape while he studies. However, we do not have research evidence that these tapes are effective.

Let us sketch the basic design for an experiment to test the effects of the tape. People could be assigned to either the control condition (tape with no subliminal message) or the experimental condition (tape with "subliminal" message). The participants would be weighed, given the necessary instructions, and then weighed again several weeks later. If the people in the experimental group lost substantially more weight than those in the control group, we could conclude that the tapes might have caused the effect. Proper controls allow researchers to draw cause-and-effect conclusions that they cannot draw when the control group is missing.

The companies that market the tapes may not have tested them scientifically, but several psychologists have. Moore (1991, 1992a, 1992b), Druckman and Bjork (1991), and Greenwald and his colleagues (1991) have all tested tapes. If you believe the companies' advertisements, these tapes will help you lose weight, stop smoking, read faster, improve your memory, relieve pain, prepare for a divorce, and enhance your self-esteem. *None* of these studies demonstrated that the tapes objectively fulfilled their claims.

Confounding Variable   A **confounding variable** is any variable (other than the independent variable) that is not equivalent in all conditions and could possibly influence the dependent variable. Confounding variables are sometimes called **confounding factors.**

Confounding variables can lead researchers to draw incorrect conclusions. Suppose that at the beginning of the weight loss study, the people in the "subliminal" condition were all college students, whereas the people in the control condition were all people of the same age who were working in a nearby community. Type of participants would then be a confounding variable. If people in the "subliminal" condition lost more weight, this advantage might really be traceable to differences between the two populations, such as the kind of food that is available to them. The subliminal message might really have had no effect on weight loss.

How can researchers guard against confounding variables? Many researchers use random assignment. As the name implies, **random assignment** means that people are assigned to experimental and control groups using a random system, such as a coin toss. For example, a coin could be tossed for every name on the sign-up sheet. "Heads" might indicate the experimental group and "tails" the control group. This kind of random assignment ensures that everyone has an equal chance of being assigned to any condition (Levine & Parkinson, 1994). If the number of participants in the study is sufficiently large, then random assignment usually guarantees that the various groups will be reasonably similar with respect to important characteristics.

When researchers use precautions such as random assignment to reduce confounding variables, then they have a **well-controlled study.** With a well-controlled study, we can feel more confident about drawing cause-and-effect conclusions in an experiment.

Critical Thinking Exercise 2.1

Write down your answers to the following questions about confounding variables:

a. Suppose a group of researchers wants to investigate whether the presence of another individual influences people's conscientiousness. Students are told that they can sign up for the experiment in the psychology department office. The first 20 who sign up are placed in the other-person-present condition; the last 20 are placed in the other-person-absent condition. What is the independent variable in this study, and what is the dependent variable? Can you describe a potential confounding variable?

b. Suppose the results of this study show that people are more conscientious when another person is present. Why would it be difficult to claim that the presence of the other person *caused* the increase in conscientiousness?

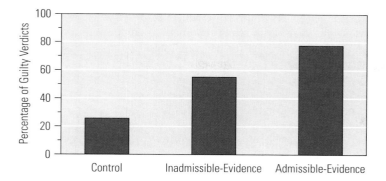

FIGURE 2.1

Conviction Rates for the Control, Inadmissible-Evidence Condition, and Admissible-Evidence Condition
Effect of condition on judgments about guilt.
Source: Based on Kassin and Sommers, 1997.

An Example of an Experiment   Let's consider an example of an experiment, a study by Saul Kassin and Samuel Sommers (1997). These researchers wanted to determine whether jurors are influenced by inadmissible testimony. You've probably seen a court-room drama on TV or in a movie in which a lawyer discloses some information in the court, the opposing lawyer objects, and the judge agrees that the evidence was "inadmissible." In this case, the judge typically tells jury members to disregard that information. You may have wondered, however, whether people can truly ignore this information. At some point, couldn't this inadmissible evidence influence the jurors' judgment?

Kassin and Sommers asked undergraduate students to play the role of mock jurors. Participants were randomly assigned to conditions; we'll discuss three of these conditions. In the control condition, the prosecutor presented weak evidence that a man had murdered his estranged wife and male neighbor. In a second condition (the inadmissible-evidence condition), a police officer revealed that a wiretap from an unrelated case had recorded a conversation in which this defendant had confessed the murder to a friend. The defense lawyer objected to this disclosure because it had been obtained without an appropriate warrant. The judge sustained the objection and told the jury to disregard this evidence. A third condition was identical until the final part, when the judge overruled the objection and told the jury that the taped information was appropriate evidence (the admissible-evidence condition).

We've seen that the independent variable in this study was the information provided to the jurors. The dependent variable was the percentage of guilty verdicts. As you can see from Figure 2.1, few jurors in the control condition concluded that the defendant had been guilty. In contrast, most people in the admissible-evidence condition concluded he had been guilty. The most interesting results are that the people in the inadmissible-evidence condition continued to be influenced by that evidence. They did *not* successfully ignore the taped information when they were deciding whether the defendant was guilty. Notice that the individuals in this condition were about twice as likely as control-group individuals to issue a guilty verdict.

Because Kassin and Sommers (1997) had carefully designed their study to eliminate confounding variables, they could draw cause-and-effect conclusions. Specifically, inadmissible evidence *does* influence jurors, even though they have been instructed to ignore it. We will discuss related aspects of eyewitness testimony in Chapter 7.

Conclusions About Experiments   The experimental method has one clear advantage over the other approaches. It is the only method that allows us to draw firm cause-and-effect relationships. With some other methods that are less well controlled, alternative explanations prevent the researchers from concluding that the independent variable actually *caused* a change in the dependent variable. In still other methods, the researchers' goal is to observe, rather than to interpret the cause of behavior.

The strength of the experimental method—its control over the important variables—is also its weakness. That is, any situation in which all the variables are carefully controlled is artificial. Studies using the experimental method may lack **ecological validity** if the conditions in which the research is conducted are very

In this social psychology study, two people are forming first impressions of one another in the psychology laboratory. However, this study may lack ecological validity: The results may be difficult to generalize to the social situations in which two people meet in "real life".

different from the natural setting to which the results are to be applied (Whitley, 1996). For example, consider a study in which students memorize nonsense words presented on a computer screen in a psychology laboratory. This study may lack ecological validity if we want to apply the results to students who are learning about introductory psychology in a college classroom.

Let's now explore the five other kinds of research methods—those in which the experimenter has less control. We often need to use one of these other methods when it is impossible to assign people randomly to groups or to manipulate the independent variable. These methods are also particularly useful for informing us about how people and animals behave in their normal lives.

The Quasi-Experiment

The prefix *quasi-* means "resembling" or "sort of," as in the word *quasi-official*. Similarly, a **quasi-experiment** resembles an experiment, but it does not meet all the criteria of a full-fledged experiment. The most important criterion missing from a quasi-experiment is random assignment to groups. In an experiment, the researcher uses a coin toss or some other random system to decide which person belongs in which group (for instance, which students are assigned to the experimental group and which to the control group).

However, random assignment is often impossible for ethical or practical reasons. Consider a study about whether sibling jealousy was influenced by an older child's presence at the birth of a younger sibling (DelGiudice, 1986). The researchers certainly could not randomly assign these families to the present-at-birth or the absent-at-birth condition. Instead, the family and the older sibling needed to make that decision. In other words, the participants assigned themselves to one of the two conditions. This study therefore qualifies as a quasi-experiment. (Incidentally, the results showed no difference between the two conditions in sibling jealousy.)

An excellent example of a quasi-experiment is one by Jerald Greenberg (1990), who examined theft rate among employees of three manufacturing plants owned by the same parent company. The plant executives decided to temporarily reduce the salaries of the employees in two of the plants because the company had lost some manufacturing contracts. (The executives had chosen to implement an across-the-board 15% pay cut for six weeks, rather than firing some employees.) Greenberg was invited to study the situation, and he hypothesized that the theft rate would be lowest for the plant where salaries were not cut. He also hypothesized that the theft rate would be intermediate for the plant where employees received a thorough, sensitive

Would this employee be more likely to steal some of his tools if his pay had been cut and he had not been given an appropriate explanation for the reduction?

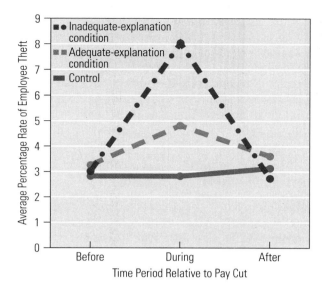

FIGURE 2.2

Average Percentage Rate of Employee Theft (as a function of condition and time period)
Source: Adapted from Greenberg, 1990.

explanation for the pay cuts. Finally, the theft rate should be highest for the plant where the explanation was very brief.

Now let's look at the study in more detail. As you can imagine, the employees could not be randomly assigned to the plants, so Greenberg was concerned that the employees in the three plants might differ initially on some important characteristic. However, he assessed that the three groups were similar with respect to their age, gender, length of time with the company, level of education, and unemployment rate in the community.

The independent variable in this study was the amount of explanation given for the pay cuts. Employees in the control condition experienced no change in salary. Employees in the adequate-explanation condition were invited to a 90-minute meeting in which the company president explained the situation in detail and with compassion, pointing out that he would also take a pay cut. Employees in the inadequate-explanation condition were invited to a 15-minute meeting in which a company vice president provided basic information without apology or regret. He did not describe the executive pay cuts, and he did not mention that the company thought the temporary pay cuts would be preferable to layoffs. He also explained that he did not have time to answer more than one or two questions.

The dependent variable in this study was the theft rate for tools and supplies, which a company representative determined by inspecting the workplace at night once a week. As you can see from Figure 2.2, employees in the control condition showed no change in their theft rate before, during, and after the pay cut. The theft rate among employees in the adequate-explanation condition showed some increase during the pay cut. In contrast, the employees in the inadequate-explanation condition more than doubled their theft rate during the pay cut.

Critical Thinking Exercise 2.2

Based on your knowledge of Greenberg's (1990) study, write your response to each of the following questions:

a. Why was it important for Greenberg to measure the theft rate before and after the pay cut, and not just during the cut?

b. Greenberg determined that the employees in the three plants were similar on several important variables. Can you think of any variable that might possibly be different for the three groups that could account for the differences in theft rates during the pay cut period?

We have seen that quasi-experiments can be used to study the behavior of employees in an industrial setting. Quasi-experiments are also practical when researchers want to determine whether a new program works in a school, for instance, or in a community. In these real-life situations (unlike the psychology laboratory), we typically cannot randomly assign people to conditions; they already belong to an established group. However, by obtaining the appropriate measures before the study begins, we can determine whether the groups are somewhat similar. Then we can manipulate the independent variable and draw tentative conclusions. Clearly, however, when researchers report the findings of a quasi-experiment, they need to discuss potential confounding variables.

The Correlational Method

In **correlational research,** psychologists try to determine whether two variables or measures are related. They obtain two measures on each person (or situation) and try to establish whether the data reveal a systematic pattern. Correlational research involves neither random assignment to groups nor the manipulation of variables. Researchers do not intentionally *change* anything, though they may administer a test or a questionnaire to gather necessary data.

After obtaining measures on the group that is being studied, the researchers calculate a statistic called the correlation coefficient. A **correlation coefficient** is a number that indicates the direction and the strength of a relationship between two variables; it can range between -1.00 and $+1.00$. The correlation coefficient is often symbolized as r (e.g., $r = +.28$).

Correlations allow researchers to make predictions about future behavior, based on previous behavior. (You may recall that one goal of psychology, mentioned in Chapter 1, is to predict behavior.) When two variables concerned with behavior are strongly correlated, we can predict future behavior quite accurately on the basis of past behavior. In contrast, when the correlation is weak, predictions are not accurate. For example, we know that there is a moderately strong correlation between grades in high school (Variable 1) and grades in college (Variable 2). Therefore, if administrators know a student's high school grades, they can predict this student's college grades with a moderate degree of accuracy.

Kinds of Correlations Correlational research can produce a positive correlation, a zero correlation, or a negative correlation. In a **positive correlation,** people who receive a *high* score on Variable 1 are likely to receive a *high* score on Variable 2. Likewise, people who receive a *low* score on Variable 1 are likely to receive a *low* score on Variable 2.

Consider this example of a positive correlation. Shaver and Brennan (1992) wanted to determine whether various personality characteristics were correlated with the way people feel about their romantic partners. One correlation they calculated concerned the relationship between warmth and a secure style in romantic relationships. Shaver and Brennan reported a positive correlation between these two measures. In other words, those who considered themselves to be very warm people tended to report that they could easily get close to others (secure style); those who considered themselves not to be very warm tended to report that they had difficulty achieving close relationships. Figure 2.3 shows data consistent with these results.

Correlations whose values are close to zero (e.g., +.09, .00, and −.09) are called zero correlations. A **zero correlation** indicates no substantial relationship between the two variables. Consider the following example of a zero correlation—one that might surprise you. Some people believe that the full moon brings forth peculiar behavior. For instance, a lawyer friend of mine claims that whenever she receives numerous phone calls about robberies and murders—rather than more ordinary legal cases— her calendar consistently indicates that the moon has been full. (In fact, the word *lunacy* is based on the Latin word for moon, *luna.*) I am sorry to disappoint you, but a comprehensive study by Rotton and Kelly (1985) indicated a zero correlation between phases of the moon and several different measures of "lunacy," such as murders, other

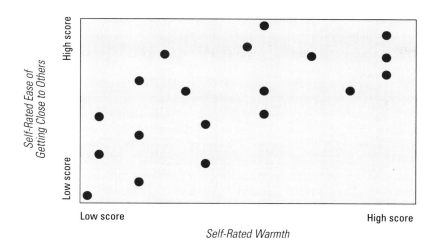

FIGURE 2.3

Positive Correlation

An example of a positive correlation between people's ratings of whether they are a warm person and whether they easily get close to other people in a romantic relationship. Note: Each dot represents the values on the two variables measured for one student. For example, the dot in the lower left corner represents a student who received low scores on both "getting close to others" and "self-rated warmth."
Source: Hypothetical data, consistent with Shaver & Brennan, 1992.

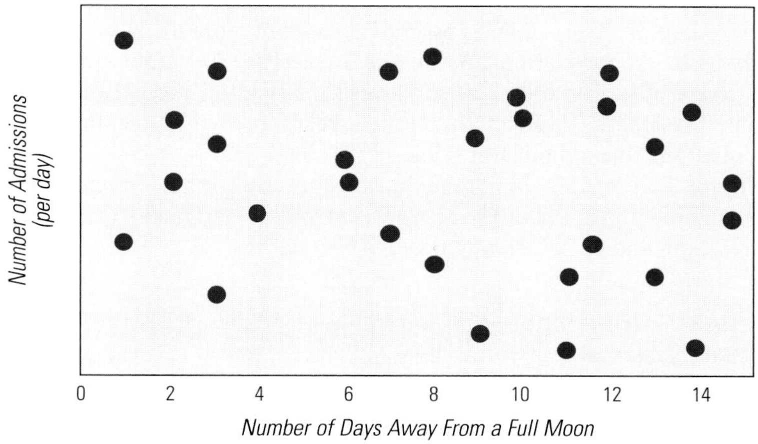

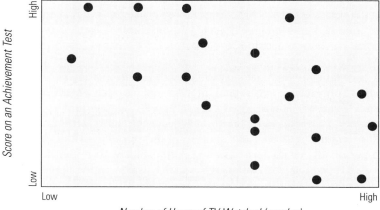

FIGURE 2.4

No Correlation

An example of a zero correlation; phase of the moon is not correlated with the number of admissions to psychiatric hospitals.
Source: Hypothetical data, consistent with findings of Rotton & Kelly, 1985.

FIGURE 2.5

Negative Correlation

An example of a negative correlation between the number of hours of television a student watches each day and his or her score on an achievement test. Note: Each dot represents the values on the two variables measured for one student.
Source: Hypothetical data, consistent with Keith et al., 1986.

criminal offenses, and admissions to mental hospitals. Figure 2.4 shows a typical example of no relationship between two variables.

A **negative correlation** means that people who receive a *high* score on Variable 1 usually receive a *low* score on Variable 2. Similarly, people with a *low* score on Variable 1 usually receive a *high* score on Variable 2. Consider the example of a negative correlation shown in Figure 2.5. According to research by Keith and his colleagues

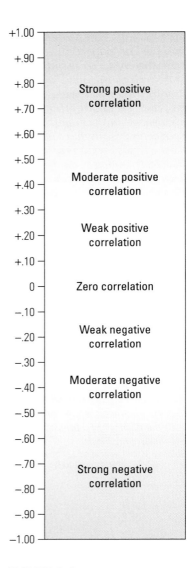

FIGURE 2.6

Interpreting the Strength of Various Correlation Coefficients.

(1986), high school seniors who spend a large number of hours watching television each day (i.e., high scores on that variable) tend to receive low scores on an academic achievement test. Furthermore, students who seldom watch television are likely to receive high scores on an achievement test.

So far, we have emphasized the *direction* of the correlation—that is, whether the correlation is positive or negative. We also need to discuss the *strength* of the correlation. A correlation is strong if the absolute value of the correlation coefficient is close to 1.00. Thus, when $r = +.93$, we have a strong positive correlation. Similarly, when $r = -.93$, we have a strong negative correlation. In fact, those correlations are equally strong, because $-.93$ is just as close to -1.00 as $+.93$ is to $+1.00$. Students often mistakenly believe that strength depends upon direction, so that any positive correlation would be stronger than any negative correlation. However, strength is independent of direction. To assess strength, just ignore the + or – sign in front of the number. Incidentally, in this textbook and elsewhere, you will often see examples of correlations unadorned by + and – signs; these are all positive correlations. In other words, assume that .47 is positive *unless* it is preceded by a – sign.

A correlation is weak if the absolute value of the correlation coefficient is close to zero (e.g., $+.21$ or $-.23$). In psychology, we are more likely to find weak correlations than strong correlations. As Theme 3 (see Page 18) emphasizes, behavior is complex; many other variables can contaminate a relationship between our two target variables, reducing the strength of the correlation. We will see many examples of weak correlations throughout this book.

Figure 2.6 provides some guidelines for interpreting correlation coefficients. Notice that a relationship can range from a strong negative correlation, through a zero correlation, and on to a strong positive correlation.

Interpreting Correlations Correlational research is useful when psychologists want to determine whether two variables are related to each other but when random assignment and manipulation of variables are not possible. For example, a study by Taylor and Brown (1988) examined the relationship between psychological adjustment and awareness of one's faults. They could not possibly assign people at random to the well-adjusted and maladjusted groups. ("OK, Sam, you're in the well-adjusted group. Tough luck, Joe, get over here in the maladjusted group.") Nor could they actively manipulate variables. ("OK, Sam, here's what we're going to do to improve your life. And Joe, here's how we'll make you miserable.") Instead, researchers using correlational methods must study the characteristics that people bring with them to the study.

A correlational study tells us whether or not two variables are related. However, when we only have correlational information, we often cannot determine which variable is the cause and which is the effect, or whether another explanation may be possible.

For example, let's consider another finding in Shaver and Brennan's (1992) study on personality characteristics and relationships with romantic partners. They also reported a positive correlation ($r = +.32$) between depression and an avoidant style in romantic relationships. (An avoidant person reports feeling uncomfortable being close to other people.) Here are two possible explanations for the correlation:

1. A person who is depressed will avoid becoming close to other people, including potential romantic partners.

2. A person who has difficulty developing close relationships with other people, including romantic partners, will become depressed.

In reality, *both* explanations are probably correct. In many situations, the psychological relationships underlying a correlation are complicated—as you might guess from Theme 3 as presented in Chapter 1. Variable 1 partly causes Variable 2, but Variable 2 also partly causes Variable 1. We can indicate these two causal relationships in Figure 2.7 by showing arrows going in both directions.

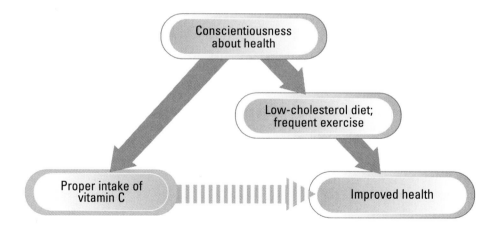

Depression ⟷ **Avoidant style in romantic relationship**

FIGURE 2.7

Interpreting a correlation
Depression and an avoidant style in romantic relationships are correlated; Both of these casual relationships probably contribute to the correlation.

Psychologists often use the phrase "correlation is not necessarily causation" when they are trying to interpret correlations. Just because two variables are correlated, we cannot conclude that the first variable actually *causes* the second variable. Yes, it *may* be that Variable 1 causes Variable 2. However, Variable 2 may really cause Variable 1.

Correlations are also difficult to interpret because of another complication called the third-variable problem: In many cases, a third variable (perhaps not yet identified) causes both Variable 1 and Variable 2. For example, a study reported that people's vitamin C intake is correlated with various measures of health (Cowley & Church, 1992). Specifically, the study found that people who consumed large amounts of vitamin C (either from fruits and vegetables or from vitamin supplements) tended to have a low incidence of heart disease.

Can you see why these results are difficult to interpret? Yes, perhaps vitamin C directly causes improved health. However, another variable may really be responsible: conscientiousness about health. Maybe people who are very conscientious about their health make certain that they consume enough vitamin C. In addition, they also make sure that they eat low-cholesterol diets and that they exercise frequently. Both of these precautions would produce a lower incidence of heart disease. Perhaps most of the correlation between vitamin C intake and health can actually be explained by the fact that each variable is correlated with a third variable, conscientiousness about health. Figure 2.8 illustrates this potential explanation.

Conscientiousness about health
Low-cholesterol diet; frequent exercise
Proper intake of vitamin C
Improved health

FIGURE 2.8

Interpreting a correlation with a third variable
Taking vitamin C may not directly cause improved health. Instead, the kind of people who are conscientious about their health may consume enough vitamin C, and they may also take other precautions (such as diet and exercise) that produce improved health.

Critical Thinking Exercise 2.3

Write down your answers to the following questions about correlation:

a. Some years ago, research on motorcycle accidents revealed that the number of accidents was highly correlated with the number of tattoos the riders had on their bodies (Martin, 1990). Do accidents cause tattoos? Do tattoos cause accidents? Could you suggest, instead, a third variable that might be entirely responsible for the correlation?

b. Look back at Figure 2.5, which shows the relationship between the number of hours of television watched and scores on an achievement test. Explain how Variable 1 may indeed cause Variable 2. Then explain how Variable 2 might instead cause Variable 1. Then explain how a third variable might be at least partly responsible for the correlation.

In summary, then, the correlational method allows us to discover whether variables are related to each other. This method is particularly helpful in real-life settings where an experiment would be impossible. However, a major disadvantage of correlation research is that we cannot draw the firm cause-and-effect conclusions that an experiment permits. In many cases, though, correlational research does generate cause-and-effect *hypotheses* that can be tested later, using the experimental method. For example, the study on vitamin C suggests that an experiment should be conducted in which people are randomly assigned either to an experimental condition where they receive vitamin C or to a control condition.

The Survey Method

In the **survey method,** researchers select a large group of people and ask them questions about their behaviors, thoughts, and attitudes. Typically, the researchers also collect **demographic information** about the characteristics often used to classify people, such as gender, age, marital status, race, education, income, and so forth. As anyone can testify who reads newspapers during an election year in either the United States or Canada, people thrive on surveys!

When researchers have collected survey results for many years, they can determine whether the responses have changed systematically across time. For instance, Figure 2.9 shows the trend since 1976 in the percentage of college students who said that an important reason for attending college is "to gain a general education" and "to make more money" (McNally, 1998; Sax et al., 1997).

Think about some of the ways in which surveys may *not* accurately represent people's behaviors, thoughts, and attitudes:

1. The sample studied in a survey may not be typical of the entire population, a point we'll cover more thoroughly later in this chapter when we discuss sampling.

2. People may distort their answers to make themselves appear more positive (Crossen, 1994; Foddy, 1993).

3. People may not recall information accurately (Foddy, 1993; Sudman et al., 1996). For example, in one study, students systematically underestimated the number of times they had consumed alcohol during a five-week period (Mingay et al., 1994).

In summary, the survey produces valuable descriptive information. Survey results may also be useful in other research. For instance, researchers could determine whether the relationship between a student's family income and the

FIGURE 2.9

Why Students Attend College
Reasons noted as very important in deciding to go to college.
Source: McNally, 1998; Sax et al., 1997

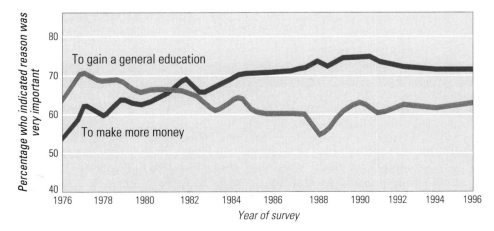

Critical Thinking Exercise 2.4

Write down your answers to the following questions about surveys:

a. A catalog displaying moderately expensive clothing invited U.S. customers to participate in a poll just prior to the 1996 presidential election. By purchasing a necktie decorated with either donkeys or elephants (for $32), you could indicate your preference. What problems might reduce the accuracy of this "survey"?

b. Suppose a psychologist surveys the students on your campus by handing out surveys that ask them about the number of times they have cheated since coming to college. The psychologist asks students not to write their names on the survey, but to return them to a box in the library. How could all three of the biasing factors listed in the discussion of the survey method reduce the accuracy of this survey?

selection of the goal "to make more money" (Refer again to Figure 2.9.) involves a positive, zero, or negative correlation. (What would you guess?) Keep in mind, however, that many potential biases can distort survey results. Furthermore, the survey method typically cannot be used to determine the causes of human behavior.

In-Depth Interviews and Case Studies

So far, we have discussed research methods in which the ideal psychologist remains distant, uninvolved, and neutral. Researchers meet the participants briefly (if at all) and interact with them minimally in order to gather quantitative data. Some theorists argue, however, that these methods have their limitations. They point out that qualitative methods—such as interviews and case studies—provide essential information about human behavior, thought, and emotion (Hamel, 1993; Weiss, 1994).

An **in-depth interview** requires the interviewers to gather answers to open-ended questions—ones that do not have simple answers like "yes" or "no"—often over a period of many hours or days. These interviews often require the interviewer to achieve warmth and rapport with participants (Benmayor, 1987). For instance, Alvarez (1987) conducted an in-depth interview with a Black Puerto Rican woman. Alvarez would have learned relatively little if she had not been fluent in Spanish and if she had not grown close to the woman during previous meetings. In this excerpt from the interview, the woman shared her thoughts about child rearing:

> I brought my children up in the twentieth century. I wasn't too free with them but neither was I too strict. . . . I raised them without having to fight, without having to hit them . . . and with my daughters little by little I went on explaining to them about sex because, you know, it's not good to live in ignorance. (p. 60, translated from Spanish)

A **case study** is an in-depth examination of a single person or group, usually conducted over a long period of time (Whitley, 1996). A case study of an individual typically includes an interview, observation, and test scores. The individual selected for a case study usually has unique characteristics.

Consider the case study that Oliver Sacks (1995a) reported on Stephen Wiltshire, a young West Indian man living in London. Stephen had been diagnosed with **autism**, a disorder in which social interactions and language skills are extremely limited (American Psychiatric Association, 1994a). Sacks quotes Lorraine Cole, the headmistress at Stephen's special school for children with developmental disabilities:

FIGURE 2.10

A sketch of St. Mark's Cathedral in Venice, drawn at the age of 15 by Stephen Wiltshire, a young man who is autistic.
Source: From Sacks, 1995a.

He had virtually no understanding of or interest in the use of language. Other people held no apparent meaning for him except to fulfill some immediate, unspoken need; he used them as objects. He could not tolerate frustration, nor changes in routine or environment and he responded to any of these with desperate, angry roaring. He had no idea of play, no normal sense of danger and little motivation to undertake any activity except scribbling. (p. 47)

Stephen was given an intelligence test, and his IQ was estimated to be only 52, indicating moderate mental retardation. However, Sacks (1995a) notes that about 10% of individuals with autism display unusual talents. Stephen Wiltshire's special talent—suggested by Ms. Cole's remarks—is a remarkable artistic ability for capturing elaborate architectural structures. After a brief glance, he can hold the details of a building in memory, later sketching it with astonishing accuracy and vibrant energy. For example, Figure 2.10 shows Stephen's sketch of St. Mark's Cathedral in Venice.

Both the in-depth interview and the case study provide a much fuller appreciation of an individual than any other methods. A skillfully conducted study helps us understand what it's like to live inside someone else's skin. Also, interviews and case studies are useful for providing ideas that can be explored further using other research methods. Of course, the researchers cannot claim that their findings hold true for all people—or even many people. Nor do they claim that we can draw cause-and-effect conclusions from the observations.

Naturalistic Observation

One of the goals of psychology discussed in Chapter 1 is to describe behavior. Naturalistic observation is especially appropriate for this goal. As the name implies, **naturalistic observation** examines individuals "in their natural environments, performing their natural behaviors in response to natural stimuli" (Whitley, 1996, p. 358).

An important function of naturalistic observation is to gather descriptive information about the typical behavior of people or animals. For example, Hedwige Boesch-Achermann and her coauthor Christopher Boesch (1993) studied how wild

Suppose that you wanted to conduct naturalistic observation in this college classroom. Some behaviors you might choose to explore include where students sit in relation to the front of the classroom, whether people tend to sit near others of their own ethnic group, what the demographic characteristics are of students who ask questions, and how long before the end of the lecture students begin to pack up their books. Can you think of other possible topics?

chimpanzees construct and use tools in the tropical rain forests of West Africa. Adult chimps gather stones to use as hammers for cracking wild nuts. They also prepare small sticks to extract the nuts from the shells. These researchers also discovered that mother chimps instructed their young offspring in the art of nut cracking, for example, by correcting their grip on the hammer.

A second function of naturalistic observation is to identify variables that would be worthwhile to study with one of the other research techniques. A third function is to provide data for use with one of these other techniques, such as the experimental method, the quasi-experiment, or the correlational method. For example, Levine (1990) gathered a variety of measures on the "pace of life" in several U.S. cities. These measures, obtained by naturalistic observation, included the percentage of people wearing wristwatches and the walking speed of pedestrians. Impressively, Levine found a +.50 correlation between a city's "pace of life" measure and that city's death rate from heart attacks! (Incidentally, would you want to conclude that you'd be less likely to die of a heart attack if you remove your watch?)

We have noted that naturalistic observation is useful for gathering descriptive information, generating research ideas, and providing data for other studies. Unfortunately, though, researchers cannot draw cause-and-effect conclusions, because behavior is simply observed and not manipulated. Furthermore, researchers have little control over the research situation, making it difficult to conduct observations for behavior that occurs infrequently.

Comparing the Methods

Table 2.1 lists the six research methods we have discussed, together with each method's advantages and disadvantages. Clearly, some questions can be more readily answered with one method than with others. However, psychologists are increasingly likely to favor a multimethod approach, with studies using several different research techniques.

TABLE 2.1 Comparing Psychological Research Methods

METHOD	ADVANTAGES	DISADVANTAGES
Experiment	1. Can control potentially confounding variables. 2. Can draw cause-and-effect conclusions.	1. May be difficult to generalize to real-world settings. 2. Cannot manipulate many variables.
Quasi-experiment	1. Can study behavior in real-world settings. 2. Can draw tentative cause-and-effect conclusions.	1. Cannot control confounding variables as well as in an experiment. 2. Cause-and-effect conclusions are not as firm as with experimental method.
Correlation	1. Can study behavior in real-world settings. 2. Can determine whether two variables are related.	1. Cannot draw cause-and effect conclusions
Survey	1. Can obtain descriptive information about large groups of people. 2. Provides data for use in studies using other methods.	1. May produce biased results because of atypical sample, overly positive answers, and/or inaccurate recall. 2. Cannot draw cause-and-effect conclusions.
Case study and in-depth interview	1. Provides in-depth information on individuals. 2. Provides ideas for further research.	1. Cannot generalize the results to other individuals. 2. Cannot draw cause-and-effect conclusions.
Naturalistic observation	1. Provides information about people and animals in real-world settings. 2. Provides ideas for further research and data for use in studies using other methods.	1. Cannot draw cause-and-effect conclusions. 2. May be difficult to conduct research on infrequent behavior.

SECTION SUMMARY: *THE MAJOR RESEARCH METHODS*

1. Critical thinking can be enhanced by knowledge about research methods; the scientific method requires identifying the research problem, conducting a study, examining the data, and communicating the results.

2. In the experimental method, researchers manipulate variables and observe how the participants respond; conditions are carefully controlled, and participants are randomly assigned to conditions.

3. Quasi-experiments are used when random assignment is impossible; however, variables can still be manipulated with this method.

4. Correlational research establishes whether two variables are related; this method uses neither random assignment nor manipulation of variables. With correlational research, researchers typically cannot identify which variable is the cause and which is the effect, or whether a third unidentified variable is responsible for the relationship.

5. The survey method is used to collect information about the behaviors, thoughts, and attitudes of a relatively large group of people.

6. In-depth interviews require extensive questioning of participants; case studies typically include an interview, observation, and psychological testing.

7. In naturalistic observation, the researcher observes people or animals in their natural setting.

8. Each research method has its strengths and weaknesses; many psychological questions can be most effectively answered by combining several research methods.

RESEARCH ISSUES

In the preceding section, we examined six research methods commonly used in psychology, and we noted some problems associated with each one. However, other potential problems are more general; they are not limited to just one of the six methods. In this section, we'll consider these more general research issues, which focus on sampling, measuring responses, and avoiding biases. We'll also discuss social and ethical issues in psychological research. This section concludes with an "In Depth" feature discussing some research on physical attractiveness. In this feature, we'll consider how several different research methods have approached the important topic of personal appearance.

Sampling

When researchers want to test a hypothesis, they must select participants for the study. We seldom have the resources to study an entire population—for instance, all humans living in North America. Instead, we gather a **sample** by selecting a small group of individuals from a larger population of individuals. Our goal is to discover something about the general population from which this particular sample was chosen. For instance, the American Council on Education's study on college students' reasons for attending college, shown earlier in Figure 2.9, examined a sample of several hundred thousand students, rather than all U.S. college students.

An important factor relevant to sampling is that the participants should be carefully chosen. Researchers aim for a **representative sample,** in which the characteristics of the sample are similar to the characteristics of the population. A sample is more likely to be representative if it is a **random sample,** where every member of the population has an equal chance of being selected. In contrast, in a **biased sample,** the sample is not representative. That is, some members of the population are more likely than others to be chosen.

The sample must be similar to the population because eventually we want to generalize our findings to the population from which the sample was selected. For example, from the data gathered by the American Council on Education, we want to say something more general about all U.S. college students. Fortunately, the sample in this survey is representative of all U.S. college students, so we can generalize the results.

You already had a chance to think about biased samples in Critical Thinking Exercise 2.4, on the "Necktie" election poll. Consider one of the most famous cases of a biased sample, which occurred during the presidential campaign of 1936 (Crossen, 1994; Snodgrass et al., 1985). A magazine named *Literary Digest* conducted a poll based on more than 2 million responses, and it predicted that the Republican candidate Alf Landon would win the election. You don't remember President Landon? Actually, Franklin D. Roosevelt won that election, receiving close to two-thirds of the popular vote.

The problem was that the *Digest* used a biased sample, because the sample was selected from telephone directories and lists of *Digest* subscribers. The sample had overrepresented wealthy people, who could afford telephones and magazine subscriptions during the Depression era—and who tended to vote Republican. The sample was not representative of the population of Americans who actually cast votes in that election.

A second important factor relevant to sampling is the study's sample size. You can typically trust an experiment or a survey conducted on 1,000 people more than one conducted on only 100 people. For example, you can trust the results derived from the survey on reasons for college attendance, illustrated in Figure 2.9, more than if the sample had been smaller. Large samples are more trustworthy because they are more likely to be representative of the population from which they are drawn.

Large, unbiased samples are important in surveys when we want to assess the views of a large population. However, sampling is also important in other research methods when we want to make general statements about the results. We can only generalize the results to people similar to our sample. For example, Greenberg's

(1990) quasi-experiment on employee theft was conducted with employees of three medium-sized manufacturing plants in the midwest. Perhaps employees in other regions or in other kinds of jobs would not have been influenced by the kind of explanation offered for salary cuts.

Measuring Responses

In order to measure the responses of research participants, psychologists must carefully construct operational definitions. An **operational definition** is a precise definition that specifies exactly what operations will be performed in order to measure the concept. For example, the introduction to this chapter described Milgram's (1963, 1974) study on obedience. His operational definition for "obedience" was whether an individual delivered the full 450 volts of electric shock.

One advantage of operational definitions is that they allow other researchers and observers to understand exactly how a variable was measured. Research can therefore be more objective than if the criteria are ambiguous. For example, Nobel Prize winner Linus Pauling was a longtime advocate of vitamin C as a cold preventer. He was once asked whether it was true that he and his wife (both of whom consume large amounts of vitamin C) no longer suffer from colds. He apparently responded that it was true; they do not get colds at all, just sniffles (Gilovich, 1991). Wouldn't you feel more reassured if you were convinced that Pauling's operational definition for "sniffles" was substantially different from the operational definition for "a cold"?

A second advantage of operational definitions is that they permit other researchers to replicate a study using the same system of measurement. Similarly, if two researchers are examining the same topic and their results differ, the discrepancy can often be traced to a difference in their operational definitions.

Let us consider three representative approaches to measuring responses—in other words, three different classes of operational definitions. These include self-report, behavioral measures, and physiological measures. As you will see, the conclusions that researchers draw from their study often depend on the operational definitions they choose. Let's illustrate this point using examples from research on gender comparisons in empathy. (You show empathy when you feel the same emotion that another person experiences. So a person who is empathic can hear a friend describe the death of a favorite relative and share the same feelings of sadness, loneliness, and loss.)

Suppose that a cafeteria on your campus wanted to assess the popularity of this new vegetarian main course, which is nutritious and low fat. What kinds of operational definitions could they use to assess students' reactions?

DEMONSTRATION 2.2 Gender Comparisons

Assemble 10 index cards and one blank envelope, and go to a location with a large number of males and females. (If you live in a coed dorm, you are all set.) Approach five females and five males individually and ask if they have a spare moment. Explain that you are conducting an informal survey. Hand everybody an index card, and ask them to rate themselves on a scale where 1 = "not at all" and 7 = "very much." Then explain that the item you would like them to rate themselves on is "I tend to get emo-

tionally involved in a friend's problems." Everyone should simply supply a number from 1 to 7, and then indicate F for female and M for male. Emphasize that they should not write their name on the card but should place it face down in the envelope. When you have collected all 10 responses, figure out an average score for females by adding up the scores for the five female respondents and dividing by 5. Repeat the process for the male respondents. Are the two averages substantially different from each other?

Self-Report   When researchers assess psychological processes by **self-report,** they ask participants to report their own thoughts, emotions, behaviors, or intentions. Self-reports are usually measured with a rating scale, such as the one shown in Demonstration 2.2. The rating scale allows us to capture an internal experience—such as empathy or anger or happiness—and represent it with a concrete number. The numbers can then be analyzed statistically, as the last section of this chapter illustrates. In many cases, self-report is the most useful measure of people's subjective experience.

An important drawback to self-reports is that people are likely to give biased answers, reporting that they are much more noble, normal, and nice than they truly are. Psychologists would like the response measure to reflect reality. However, when we try to measure reality, the measurement process often intrudes on people's normal responses, giving us a distorted, rose-colored view of reality.

One kind of bias in self-reports is that people often tend to respond the way they believe they are *supposed* to respond. According to a common stereotype, women are supposed to show empathy, whereas men are supposed to remain cool and objective. The research on empathy indeed shows a substantial gender difference in self-reported empathy. In a review of the research, Eisenberg and Lennon (1983) found that women consistently rated themselves higher than did men on self-report statements such as the one in Demonstration 2.2: "I tend to get emotionally involved in a friend's problems." One semester, I asked students in my introductory psychology class to rate themselves on this term on a slip of paper, indicating their gender but omitting their name. The average man rated himself 4.0, whereas the average woman rated herself 5.0. (The maximum score was 7.0.)

Do these self-reports reflect reality, or are they biased, drifting in the direction of the popular stereotypes about "appropriate" behavior for women and men? Unfortunately, we cannot peel away a person's scalp, look at a little dial on the brain, and discover that the *true* empathy rating (unbiased by stereotypes) is really a 3.2. However, two other methods for measuring responses may seem more appealing: behavioral and physiological measures.

Behavioral Measures   We use **behavioral measures** to objectively record people's observable behavior. For example, psychologists who want to measure a person's aggressive tendencies might use naturalistic observation, recording the number of physically aggressive acts performed in a specified time. They might argue that these measures would be more objective and less biased than the person's self-report about aggressive tendencies.

One kind of behavioral measure assesses nonverbal behavior, such as facial expressions. In a study of children's empathy, boys and girls listened to a tape recording of an infant crying. Measuring facial expression, the researchers found no gender differences in empathy (Eisenberg & Lennon, 1983).

Of course, if individuals know they are being observed, their behavior could be just as biased a reflection of reality as any self-report. Also, behavioral measures cannot be used to examine most mental processes. How would you obtain behavioral measures on something entirely invisible and private, such as the content of people's daydreams?

One physiological measure of psychological processes is called the electrodermal response. When you perspire more, your skin changes its electrical conductivity, as registered by this machine.

Physiological Measures A third option in measuring psychological processes is to obtain **physiological measures,** which are objective recordings of physiological states such as heart rate, breathing rate, perspiration, and brain activity. We will examine some of these physiological measures in Chapter 3 (on the biological basis of behavior), in Chapter 5 (on sleep patterns), and in Chapter 12 (on emotions).

Physiological measures provide objective numbers that are unlikely to be distorted by the desire to "look good." The problem, however, is that the body has only a limited number of ways of responding, and many different emotions can produce the same response. Suppose, for instance, that a man's palms start to sweat (as measured by an index called the electrodermal response). That physiological response could reflect increased excitement, anxiety, or sexual arousal. Which one should we choose? A physiological measure simply tells us we have more sweat—the sweat droplets do not appear with little labels identifying which emotion generated them.

Let us return to the question of gender comparisons in empathy. According to Eisenberg and Lennon (1983), researchers have obtained a variety of physiological measures on people watching an adult being shocked or an infant crying. Physiological measures such as heart rate, pulse, and blood pressure show no gender differences in empathy.

Conclusions About Response Measurement Approaches You have learned that self-reports may be biased, that behavioral measures cannot be gathered for some psychological processes, and that we often cannot interpret the origin of physiological measures. Should psychology researchers just pack up and go home? Obviously not. It's true that no flawless response measure exists, just as no flawless research method exists. However, psychologists can obtain a more accurate picture of reality when they conduct research on a particular topic by using a variety of response measures. In the case of empathy, for instance, you should be suspicious that gender differences appear in self-report, but they evaporate when measured behaviorly or physiologically. Men and women are probably similar in their empathic reactions, and their self-reports are probably distorted to match the common stereotype that women *should* be empathic and men *should* be emotionally distant. As you can see, the complicated relationship between gender and empathy is a clear example of Theme 3: Psychological processes are complex.

Critical Thinking Exercise 2.5

Write down your answers to the following questions about sampling techniques and response measurement:

In 1993, Robert Levine published a study in which he rated 36 cities on their friendliness, in terms of pedestrians' helpfulness to strangers.

a. Can you suggest three or four operational definitions for this kind of friendliness? Would you use self-report, behavioral measures, or physiological measures?

b. If you actually gathered these measures the way you described, would you be able to obtain a representative sample of each city's residents? If not, how might the sample be biased?

Avoiding Gender, Ethnic, and Cultural Biases

Many parts of this chapter discuss biases that can creep into psychological research and distort the results. For example, a biased sample will not provide an accurate picture of the population, and a biased self-report will not provide an accurate picture of an individual's true reactions. One of psychology's goals is to discover how psychological processes operate, and biases like these can lead us to incorrect conclusions.

Biases can be especially harmful when the results are used to discriminate against certain groups of people. These biases may operate at any stage of the research process: in formulating the hypothesis, designing and performing the study, interpreting the data, or communicating the findings (Halpern, 1992; Matlin, 1996a). For instance, researchers should avoid studying single-sex samples, unless they have a plausible reason for doing so—such as undertaking a study about emotional reactions to one's own pregnancy (Cotton, 1990; Gannon et al., 1992). Also, participants should be carefully selected to avoid confounding variables. Imagine, for example, that we are studying gender, and we want to examine the mental health of men and women. We should make certain that the two groups are similar with respect to employment status, because nonemployed people are more likely than employed people to have psychological problems (McHugh et al., 1986; Warr & Parry, 1982). Thus, if we were to compare employed men with nonemployed women, employment status would be an important confounding variable. Any gender difference in this study might be traceable to the confounding variable of employment.

Researchers should also avoid ethnic biases. For example, a study on ethnic differences in child rearing should control for social class, an important potential confounding variable (Betancourt & López, 1993). Research that examines some ethnic groups must address additional problems, such as translating the instructions appropriately, as Marín and Marín (1991) point out in their book, *Research With Hispanic Populations*.

Biases can also enter when the researchers interpret their data and write summaries of their results. One common mistake, for example, is that researchers are likely to report any gender differences demonstrated in their study. In contrast, if they find no gender differences, they yawn and fail to report this finding; gender similarities may seem boring. You can anticipate the problem that arises: Psychology journals will include many published articles reporting gender differences. Meanwhile, gender similarities will be underrepresented (Denmark et al., 1988; Matlin, 1996a).

A second mistake researchers make when they write their research summaries is to overgeneralize the results, a problem we introduced in the section on critical thinking in Chapter 1. For example, Triandis (1996) points out that almost all of the research and theory in psychology is based on North Americans, Europeans, and others from Western populations. Psychology articles based on these individuals typically imply that the findings hold true for everyone. However, about 70% of all the world's people live in non-Western cultures. We do not know whether research can be applied to these other populations.

The previous examples on bias have focused on gender, ethnicity, and cultural groups. However, researchers should also guard against all kinds of biases and assumptions about social class, disability, age, and sexual orientation. Whenever biases favor one group, they may harm another group, limiting their potential for achievement and life satisfaction.

Social Aspects of Research

Whenever people interact, they have the potential to influence one another. Chapters 16 and 17 examine these social interactions in some detail. However, we need to remember here that researchers and participants interact socially in most psychological studies. During these interactions, researchers may convey certain expectations, and participants may develop other expectations. Both sets of expectations can influence the outcome of a study, leading the researchers astray in their search for accurate information about psychological processes.

Demand characteristics are the clues that the research participants discover about the nature of the study. In this study, one important source of demand characteristics would be the equipment being pointed out by the researcher.

Experimenter Expectations   The term **experimenter expectancy effects** means that researchers' biases and expectations can unwittingly influence the outcome of an experiment (Martin, 1994). More than 300 studies have been conducted in areas as diverse as laboratory rats learning mazes and children answering questions on classroom tests (Darley & Oleson, 1993; Rosenthal, 1993, 1994). For example, elementary school teachers who expected certain students to be bright actually obtained better performance from these students, relative to other students with similar ability (Rosenthal, 1968, 1973). Obviously, experimenter expectations do not always influence people's responses. Still, they operate often enough that we should consider the possibility of this additional source of bias (Darley & Oleson, 1993).

Participants' Expectations   The participants—as well as the experimenters—develop expectations about what is supposed to happen in a research study. We humans are curious creatures who constantly think about our surroundings, trying to figure out what we are supposed to do (Kihlstrom 1995).

The clues that the participants discover about a research study are called the **demand characteristics** (Orne, 1962). Demand characteristics include the description supplied when they signed up to participate in the study, the activities and remarks of the researchers, and the laboratory setting itself. All of these clues are called demand characteristics because the research participants believe that these clues *demand* certain responses. For instance, suppose you have heard rumors about the study in which you're participating. Specifically, you've heard that the researchers want to see whether people will conform to the opinion of the majority. These clues *demand* that you conform. As a result, people may behave the way they *think* they should behave, instead of responding normally.

In summary, bias can intrude, based on the expectations of either the researcher or the participants. These biases can compromise the results of a study.

Ethical Aspects of Research

Psychologists study living creatures. We need to make certain that we do not harm these creatures in the process of learning more about them. The American Psychological Association, the Canadian Psychological Association, and a variety of government agencies have therefore developed ethical principles and regulations. These documents specify how people and animals should be treated in psychological research (American Psychological Association, 1990, 1992; Canadian Psychological Association, 1991; Office for Protection From Research Risks, 1986). Table 2.2 lists some of the ethical principles that concern human participants. In colleges and universities where psychological research is conducted, ethics committees must approve research involving humans and animals (Canter et al., 1994).

As you can see, even the first contact with the participants requires ethical treatment. For example, the researchers must describe the study carefully, pointing out any potential dangers (see Item 1 in the table). Participants also have the right to leave at any point during the study (see Item 2). Let's examine the other three items in more detail and then consider the ethical treatment of animals in psychological research.

Avoiding Potential Harm   Researchers must avoid any research study that is likely to cause permanent harm. When researchers need to study physical pain in an experiment, they should participate in the study themselves before testing any participants.

Researchers must avoid mental harm, as well as physical harm. They must keep in mind the important principle of respecting the dignity of other people (Canadian Psychological Association, 1991). Thus, a study that lowers the participants' self-esteem

TABLE 2.2 Some of the APA Ethical Principles for Research With Human Participants

1. The researcher must inform participants about all aspects of the research that are likely to influence their decision to participate in the study, including factors such as risks and discomfort.
2. Participants must have the freedom to say that they do not wish to participate in a research project; they may also withdraw from the research at any time.
3. The researcher must protect the participant from physical and mental discomfort, harm, and danger.
4. If deception is necessary, researchers must determine whether its use is justifiable; participants must be told about any deception after they have completed the study.
5. Information supplied by participants must be kept confidential, and researchers must be sensitive about invading the participants' privacy.

Source: American Psychological Association, 1990, 1992.

would be ethically questionable. Fortunately, you are not likely to participate in a study requiring either physical or mental harm, because of psychologists' current awareness of ethical principles, as well as governmental regulations.

Avoiding Unnecessary Deception   The relationship between the researcher and the participants should be based on openness and honesty (Fisher & Fyrberg, 1994). In some studies, however, modest deception may be necessary. If researchers describe precisely what will happen during some studies, demand characteristics can distort the results and make them meaningless. For example, in some studies on perceptual attention, participants are told to pay attention to the sentences presented via earphone to their right ear. Later, they are tested on these sentences, as well as on other sentences presented to their left (unattended) ear. Imagine what would happen if they had been told initially that they would be tested on these other sentences. Their attention certainly would have shifted, and the results would be useless. Some research uses more extensive deception, but such research must be judged appropriate by an ethics review board. Fortunately, research participants rarely complain about deception in psychological research (Sharpe et al., 1992).

A crucial part of any psychological research is debriefing. Proper **debriefing** requires telling the participants—as soon as possible—about the purpose of the study, the nature of the anticipated results, and any deceptions used (Canter et al., 1994). Debriefing also has educational value. If people donate their time to a project, they deserve to learn something from the experience. If deception was used, the debriefing also explains any false information. Researchers must be certain that participants' questions have been answered and that all of their concerns have been addressed.

Ensuring Privacy   Privacy means that people can decide for themselves whether they want to share their feelings, thoughts, and personal information with others. For example, participants must feel free to say that they do not choose to answer personal questions on a survey. In addition, any personal information should be kept confidential, rather than being shared with other people. In general, data must also be gathered anonymously, so that the researchers cannot identify which person supplied which data.

We have seen that human subjects must be treated humanely in psychological research, avoiding physical harm, mental harm, unnecessary deception, and invasion of privacy. Try Demonstration 2.3 to discover your own ideas about ethical issues in psychology. Then we'll turn our attention from human participants to animals.

DEMONSTRATION 2.3 Ethical Issues in Psychological Research

Each of the following paragraphs describes a research study that was actually conducted. After reading them, rank all in terms of their compliance with ethical standards discussed here. Give a ranking of 1 to the most ethical study and a ranking of 6 to the one you consider least ethical. It should be stressed that the clear majority of psychological research complies with all ethical principles; most cases cited here are unusual ones presented to ethics review committees.

_____ A. A researcher wanted to create a realistic experiment, so he told participants that they were being hired for a semipermanent job. At the end of the day, they were told it was only an experiment. One person had turned down other job offers because of this job.

_____ B. A professor asked her students to do her a favor by staying after class to fill out a brief questionnaire. She added that the task was voluntary, but when one of the students began to leave, she said, "Well, I'm certainly glad the _rest_ of you are willing to help me out."

_____ C. Students are given a list of paired words to memorize. Afterward, their recall is tested. The researcher then announces, "Now we'll go on to something else," and instructs them to solve simple jigsaw puzzles. Fifteen minutes later, the students are again asked to recall the pairs, even though they

had been led to believe they would not be tested further on this material.

_____ D. As part of a study, students completed a "life-goals inventory" and a "graduate school potential test." The researcher then informs some of them that the test results indicated that they are not graduate school material. One student decides to give up her goal of graduate work in English. The researcher later informs them that the purpose of the research was to see whether life goals would be clarified by discouraging or encouraging evaluations.

_____ E. An experimenter gave research participants an insoluble task to perform. He assured them that the task could be solved, intending to make them angry.

_____ F. Students participating in a survey about cheating are told that they should not write their names on the survey so that the results could be kept confidential. However, the questionnaire includes many demographic questions, asking students to supply their gender, major, year, and so forth. After turning in the questionnaire, several students worry that the information may allow them to be identified.

Turn to Page 71 to see how this demonstration was answered by a psychologist who specializes in ethical issues.

Sources: American Psychological Association, 1973; Faden et al., 1986; Keith-Spiegel & Koocher, 1985.

Ensuring the Ethical Treatment of Animals Ethical standards have been set by the American Psychological Association (1992), the Canadian Psychological Association (1991), and the Committee on the Use of Animals in Research (1991). All of these documents contain information about the high standards of care required for treating animals humanely. Federal regulations also specify strict guidelines when research involves surgery, pain, or potential harm.

The United States and Canada now have more than 200 animal rights groups (Plous, 1991). Often these activists and people who do research with animals seem to be talking across an abyss, with little genuine communication (Blum, 1994; Sperling, 1988). Animal rights activists have broken into research laboratories, releasing animals and creating damage that exceeds $1 billion (N. E. Miller, 1991). Meanwhile, the researchers argue that the activists' claims about harm to animals have been greatly exaggerated (Coile & Miller, 1984; Greenough, 1992).

Research with animals has helped biologists and medical researchers to develop treatment for high blood pressure, diabetes, blood diseases, arthritis, Parkinson's disease, Alzheimer's disease, and AIDS (Szymczyk, 1995). Animal research has also helped veterinarians learn more about diseases in animals. Psychologists have studied animals to establish the basic principles of learning (Chapter 6). They have also used animals in such research areas as the biological basis of behavior, developmental psychology, eating disorders, and pain relief (Committee on the Use of Animals in Research, 1991; Domjan & Purdy, 1995; Greenough, 1991; Miller, 1985). Researchers also test animals when they develop drugs used to treat mental illness.

Obviously, research animals should be well treated, and all unnecessary pain must be avoided (Canter et al., 1994). Ultimately, you need to decide for yourself whether you support animal research. You may truly believe that human lives

The ethical standards for research on animals specify that all animals should be well treated, avoiding unnecessary pain.

should not have priority over animal lives, and you may conscientiously avoid eating meat or wearing leather products. Or you may agree with most psychologists, who maintain that no animals should suffer needlessly, but that animal research is usually justified in producing results that may ultimately promote human welfare.

IN DEPTH

Research on Physical Attractiveness

Be honest. Can you truthfully say that you pay no attention to physical attractiveness when you meet a person for the first time? If your self-report is honest, you'll probably admit that personal appearances do affect your judgment. You've often heard about bias that is based on ethnicity or gender. This "In Depth" feature examines another form of discrimination: specifically, bias on the basis of personal appearance.

According to many studies, attractive people are judged to have more socially desirable personalities than less attractive people (Dion, 1986; Feingold, 1992a). This effect extends to different ethnic groups and to different age groups. For instance, Black, European American, and Mexican American students think that cute babies from all three ethnic groups are more likely than less attractive babies to be happy, well behaved, and smart (Stephan & Langlois, 1984).

In this "In Depth" discussion, we'll consider several studies that illustrate how different research methods approach a specific psychological question. We will first discuss the experimental method, then a study that combines naturalistic observation and correlational research, and finally an in-depth interview.

Experimental Method

Most people believe that they have acquired their standards of attractiveness through many years of exposure to the media (Langlois & Musselman, 1995). From watching television and looking at advertisements, they gradually learned which faces are considered most attractive. However, research by Judith Langlois and her colleagues (1991) demonstrates that even young infants prefer to look at attractive faces, rather than unattractive faces.

If you respond like the student in Stephan and Langlois's (1984) study, you would judge that this baby is happier, better behaved, and smarter than babies who are less attractive.

(IN DEPTH continued)

Before testing the infants, Langlois and her coauthors asked male and female students to rate the attractiveness of 440 slides of European American adult faces. From these ratings, the researchers assembled 16 pairs of slides. In each pair, one slide had been rated very attractive and one slide had been rated very unattractive. Eight of the pairs were of women, and eight were of men, and in each pair the faces were matched for facial expression, hair length, and hair color. Thus, the researchers held constant a number of potentially confounding variables.

The participants in this study were 60 infants who were 6 months old and predominantly European American or Hispanic. Because each baby would be seeing both attractive and unattractive faces, the babies did not need to be randomly assigned to conditions. However, because the babies would be seeing both faces (one attractive, one unattractive) at the same time, the researchers needed to control for another potentially confounding variable: position of the slide. Half of the time, the attractive photo appeared on the right; half of the time it appeared on the left. Suppose—instead—that the attractive photo always appeared on the right, and babies have a systematic preference for looking to the right. Then we could not draw conclusions about the reasons for their preferences.

Each pair of slides was exposed for 10 seconds, and an experimenter recorded the number of seconds the infant looked at each slide. The equipment was arranged so that the experimenter could only see the infant's eye movements, not the slides that were being projected. (Otherwise, experimenter expectancy might operate.)

The results showed that the infants looked substantially longer at the more attractive faces. This preference for attractive faces was true for both male and female faces. Furthermore, Langlois and her coauthors (1991) later tested infants using Black adult female faces and European American infant faces. For both these categories, infants again looked longer at the attractive faces. In short, infants prefer to look at attractive faces, even before they have been extensively exposed to media images.

Combining Naturalistic Observation and Correlational Research

The research by Langlois and her colleagues demonstrated the importance of attractiveness, using an experiment in the laboratory. But what happens in real life? Are people really treated differently if they are attractive?

Research by Gregory Smith (1985) combines naturalistic observation with correlational methods to provide some interesting answers with young children. Smith studied middle-class European American preschoolers between the ages of 2 years, 9 months, and 5 years, 7 months. Using naturalistic observation, he recorded the behavior of each child in the preschool classroom for a five-minute session on five separate days. In particular, he recorded how other children treated this child. Were the other children prosocial—helping, patting, and praising the target child? Were these other children physically aggressive—hitting, pushing, or kicking this child?

The next step was to establish whether these naturalistic observations about behavior toward a child were correlated with that child's attractiveness. As an operational definition of attractiveness, Smith asked college students to rate each child, based on a photograph of the child's face.

Interestingly, attractiveness was correlated with the way little girls were treated, but not little boys. Specifically, the more attractive little girls tended to receive more prosocial treatment; the correlation was +.73. Furthermore, the more attractive little girls also tended to receive less physical aggression; the correlation was −.41. In other words, cute little girls get helped more, and they are hit less. How about the little boys? For them, physical attractiveness was not related to either prosocial behavior ($r = +.05$) or physical aggression ($r = +.03$). Smith's study is especially interesting because it illustrates one positive correlation, one negative correlation, and two zero

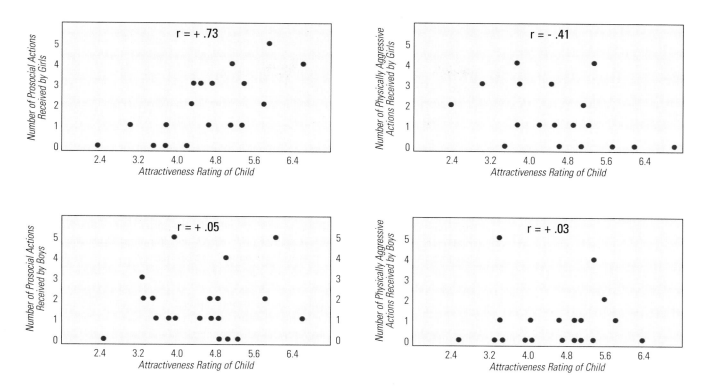

correlations. Figure 2.11 shows Smith's actual data for these four correlations. Notice that attractiveness matters more for little girls than for little boys, consistent with the greater emphasis on attractiveness for females of all ages (Freedman, 1986; Leinbach & Fagot, 1991; Wolf, 1991).

In the discussion of the correlational method earlier in the chapter, we emphasized that we cannot typically identify the cause and the effect in a correlation. In the case of attractiveness and prosocial behavior toward little girls, for instance, the major part of the correlation can probably be traced to the fact that a pretty face elicits pleasant behavior from other people (A → B). However, another factor may also contribute to the correlation; pleasant behavior produces smiles and self-confidence in a little girl, and so she looks especially attractive in a photograph (A ← B).

In-Depth Interviews

So far, beauty seems to bring benefits, at least to females. However, the interview approach suggests that the relationship is more complex. For instance, Hatfield and Sprecher (1986) interviewed several people who pointed out that good looks can create disadvantages. In this case, then, the in-depth interview provided a different perspective on the effects of attractiveness. Here is a short excerpt from one professional woman they interviewed:

Here's something that happened to me recently: I was elected to be on an important state committee—a 30-member committee, all men. But I was nominated in a devastating way. An important committee member stood up and announced in front of everyone, "We have to have Audry on the committee—she's the prettiest thing here." I was stunned! Shocked! I couldn't say anything. I wasn't prepared for such a statement. . . . We were all there because we had professional credentials. After getting over my initial astonishment, my reaction was to get very, very angry. (pp. 66–67)

Conclusions About Attractiveness

From the experiment by Langlois and her colleagues (1991), we learned how even young infants prefer attractive faces. Smith's (1985) study, which combined naturalistic

FIGURE 2.11

Results of Smith's Attractiveness Study

(upper left) For girls, attractiveness is positively correlated with prosocial treatment.

(upper right) For girls, attractiveness is negatively correlated with physically aggressive treatment.

(lower left) For boys, attractiveness is not correlated with prosocial treatment.

(lower right) For boys, attractiveness is not correlated with physically aggressive treatment.

Source: Smith, 1985.

(IN DEPTH continued)
observation with correlational research, showed how attractiveness is related to the way children are treated in a real-life situation. Finally, in-depth interviews help complete the picture, illustrating that good looks may sometimes distract other people from an individual's professional competence.

Other researchers have identified additional characteristics associated with attractiveness. For instance, attractive children are judged more favorably by their teachers than are less attractive children (Ritts et al., 1992). Physically attractive adults are also more likely than less attractive adults to have higher status jobs and to be very satisfied with their lives (Collins & Zebrowitz, 1995; Diener et al., 1995).

Two reviews of the literature show that attractive individuals are also perceived differently by others. In general, people say that physically attractive individuals are more sociable, popular, socially skilled, and sexually warm than are less attractive individuals (Eagly et al., 1991; Feingold, 1992a). The effect is weaker when people make judgments about adjustment and intelligence, and the effect is weaker still for judgments about personal integrity and concern for others. Physical attractiveness also has a dark side: People believe that attractive people are more likely to be vain (Eagly et al., 1991).

In summary, the complicated nature of the relationship between physical attractiveness and perceived personal characteristics depends upon our operational definition of those personal characteristics—consistent with the complexity theme of psychology presented on Page 18.

SECTION SUMMARY: *RESEARCH ISSUES*

1. A sample should be unbiased and also sufficiently large.

2. An operational definition specifies exactly how a psychological concept is to be measured; the operational definition of participants' responses can be assessed by self-report, behavioral measures, and physiological measures.

3. Researchers must guard against gender, ethnic, and cultural biases at every step in the research process.

4. Two social factors—experimenter expectations and participants' expectations—can distort research results.

5. Important ethical considerations include recruiting participants honestly, avoiding potential harm and unnecessary deception, ensuring privacy, and treating animals properly.

6. Psychologists can learn most about a research issue such as physical attractiveness when they combine several different research approaches.

CONSTRUCTING AND EVALUATING PSYCHOLOGICAL TESTS

In the last part of this chapter, we'll consider two important topics connected with research data. First, we'll see how tests should be constructed to measure psychological processes appropriately. In the next section, on data analysis, we'll see how psychologists draw conclusions from the data they have gathered.

A **psychological test** is an objective, standardized measure of a sample of behavior. For instance, psychologists might test a child's arithmetic skills, an employee's honesty, or students' attitudes toward people with disabilities. Psychological tests allow us to measure those individual differences that are the focus of Theme 2: Humans differ widely from one another.

A proper psychological test features four important properties: standardization, norms, reliability, and validity. This discussion should convince you that a high-quality test cannot be constructed casually. Incidentally, we'll explore applications of intelligence tests in Chapter 8 and examples of personality tests in Chapter 13.

Standardization

An important early step in test construction is to administer it to a large group of people, who all take the test in situations as uniform as possible—a process called **standardization.** The scores would be meaningless, for instance, if one group had only 45 minutes to complete the test, with no opportunity to ask questions, and another group had no time limits, with the opportunity for questions. Thus, an initial step in standardizing a test requires the systematic administration of the test under uniform conditions.

When a test is standardized, it must be administered under uniform conditions.

Norms

Suppose that you take a test of writing ability during the orientation for new students at your college, and you receive a score of 29. By itself, this score is meaningless— you cannot tell whether it is high, average, or low. To make this score meaningful, you must compare it with a norm or standard.

A second important step in creating a psychological test is to calculate **norms,** or established standards of test performance. An individual's score on the test is meaningful only by comparing that score with those norms. For instance, suppose that the average student received a 20 on the writing ability test for which you received a score of 29. This information is useful, because you now know that your score was better than average. However, you also need some normative information about variability. Suppose that most people receive a score within 3 points of 20, so that the variability on the test is small. Then your score of 29 would be spectacular. However, if most people received a score within 10 points of 20—so that the variability is large—your score of 29 is still good, but not truly outstanding. The norms include information about both the average score and the variability of the scores—or, using the statistical terms discussed at the end of this chapter and in the Appendix, the *mean* and the *standard deviation.*

We also need to emphasize another point about testing procedures: The population you are testing must be comparable to the population on which the test norms are based. For example, a test that is carefully normed on school-age children living in a small midwestern town may not be useful for students living in Los Angeles, where the ethnic background, mastery of English, and school curriculum may be very different (Cohen et al., 1992; Kline, 1993).

Reliability

Reliability refers to the consistency of a person's scores. This consistency is established by reexamining the test takers or by examining the consistency within a test (Kline, 1993).

Every test produces some measurement error. Even objective measurements show variation. If you weigh yourself now and one hour from now, your two weights probably will not be identical. However—if your scale is reliable—your weight will be reasonably consistent.

Unfortunately, psychological tests are not as reliable as bathroom scales, because psychological characteristics are more difficult to assess than physical characteristics. Still, reliability is one of the most important requirements of a high-quality psychological test.

The reliability of a test can be measured in several different ways. One of the most widely used methods is called test-retest reliability. In **test-retest reliability,** the same identical test is administered on two occasions, usually one day to several weeks apart. The test-retest reliability is high if each person's score is similar on the two tests.

When measuring reliability, the researcher calculates a correlation coefficient, or r. As we noted earlier in this chapter, a correlation coefficient tells us whether a person's score on one measure is related to his or her score on another measure. A test is reliable if a person who receives a high score on the first test also receives a high score on the second test; medium- and low-scorers must also show this same consistency.

An r of 1.00 indicates a perfect correlation, or absolute consistency in the two scores. Psychological tests do not achieve r's of 1.00, because the tests are not perfect, and because human behavior is too complex to be absolutely consistent. However, the reliability of psychological tests is reasonably high. For example, one study examined reliability measures on psychological tests described in previous issues of the *Journal of Counseling Psychology*. About 70% of those reliability measures were between .80 and .90 (Meier & Davis, 1990).

Validity

Validity refers to a test's accuracy in measuring what it is supposed to measure (Meier, 1994). For instance, if a test is a valid measure of intelligence, people's scores on that test should be strongly correlated with their grades in school.

Consider this real-life example of a potentially invalid test. On June 20, 1989, the answer key to the year-end New York State Regents Examination in chemistry was stolen, and the answers were published in a newspaper, the *New York Post*. The criminal and ethical aspects of this theft were extremely important. However, high schools throughout the state also faced a major practical problem: Should they actually give students the Regents Exam? Most high schools near New York City decided not to administer the test. If they had given the test, it would have been invalid. The test would have measured students' ability to locate and buy the *New York Post*, rather than their knowledge of chemistry. In other words, the test would not have measured what it is supposed to measure.

For an ideal test, researchers use a variety of methods to establish validity. We'll consider two approaches: content validity and criterion validity.

Several years ago, I spoke with an irate student who complained that her final examination in a psychology course had contained an essay question on material that had not been conveyed in either the class lectures or the textbook. She had spoken to her professor, who confirmed that this topic had indeed not been covered; however, he thought that the topic was something that every psychology undergraduate ought to know.

This particular test had been low in content validity. **Content validity** is the degree to which the test covers the complete range of material that it is supposed to cover. (I assume you agree with me that a test should not cover material never mentioned in a course!) A test should not cover too much, and it also should not cover too little. Suppose your psychology professor announces that your final examination in this course will be comprehensive. However, when you take the exam, you discover that it includes no questions on learning, memory, or thinking. This exam would lack content validity.

A second kind of validity measure is **criterion validity,** or a test's ability to predict a person's performance on a second measure—that is, an independent criterion. For example, suppose that researchers want to assess criterion validity for a test of intelligence. They could measure whether scores on that test are correlated with the number of years of education that each person achieves (Anastasi, 1988).

What other criteria would you consider important if you were developing a new intelligence test? One potential criterion is grades in school. We know that current intelligence tests predict students' grades in school quite accurately (Richardson, 1991). But perhaps you want to predict something more ambitious, such as

Criterion validity is useful only if the criterion is compelling. For example, a test designed to assess racism in European Americans might include a criterion that assesses whether they help a stranger who is African American.

professional success. Psychologists would disagree upon the operational definition for "professional success." Should it be income, prestige of the profession, or . . .? (You fill in the blank.) At present, theorists disagree about whether current intelligence tests are correlated with any important measures of success in life (e.g., Barrett & Depinet, 1991; Ree & Earles, 1992; Sternberg, 1990a). As you can imagine, criterion validity is useful only if the test makers select a compelling criterion.

Critical Thinking Exercise 2.6

Write down your answers to the following questions about constructing a psychological test:

a. Suppose that you decide to construct a psychological test to measure attitudes towards women. For simplicity's sake, assume that you will only be interested in assessing these attitudes on your college campus. How could you use the test-retest method for measuring the reliability of the test?

b. Why would it be important to think about the content validity of this test? How could you assess criterion validity for this test?

SECTION SUMMARY: *CONSTRUCTING AND EVALUATING PSYCHOLOGICAL TESTS*

1. A psychological test is an objective, standardized measure of a sample of behavior.

2. To achieve standardization, people must be tested under uniform conditions.

3. Norms must be established by calculating the average score for a test, as well as a measure of the scores' variability.

4. Reliability—or consistency—can be measured in terms of test-retest reliability.

5. Validity—or a test's ability to measure what it is supposed to measure—can be assessed in terms of content validity and criterion-related validity.

ANALYZING THE DATA

Many portions of this chapter have focused on gathering data by using various research methods and by avoiding biases that could distort the data. After the data are gathered, researchers must summarize and interpret them. For example, suppose you tried Demonstration 2.2, asking five women and five men to rate themselves using numbers between 1 and 7 on the statement: "I tend to get emotionally involved in a friend's problems." Let's say that you gathered the data shown in Table 2.3. Researchers who want to convey their findings to other psychologists would find it awkward to write: "The five women gave ratings of 4, 5, 5, 5, and 6, whereas the five men gave ratings of 2, 4, 4, 4, and 6." And the situation becomes preposterous when you test hundreds of people, rather than just 10.

To avoid listing every individual person's score, researchers have developed standardized, efficient methods for describing their data. They have also developed standardized methods for drawing conclusions about their data. These methods allow them to determine whether the differences between groups are significant, and also whether the correlations between two variables are significant. Let us first discuss how researchers describe data and then consider how they draw conclusions. (The Appendix provides more detailed information about statistics, with an emphasis on statistical formulas and calculations.)

TABLE 2.3 Calculating the Mean, Median, and Mode

Imagine that you tried Demonstration 2.2 and gathered the following data on men's and women's empathy:

Women: 4   5   5   5   6
Men: 2   4   4   4   6

1. Calculate the **mean** for each group:

For the women $= \dfrac{4+5+5+5+6}{5} = \dfrac{25}{5} = 5.0$

For the men $= \dfrac{2+4+4+4+6}{5} = \dfrac{20}{5} = 4.0$

2. Calculate the **median** for each group:

For the women = 4   5   ⑤   5   6   5 is the score in the middle
For the men   = 2   4   ④   4   6   4 is the score in the middle

3. Calculate the **mode** for each group:

For the women = 4 ⟨5   5   5⟩ 6   5 is the most frequent score
For the men   = 2 ⟨4   4   4⟩ 6   4 is the most frequent score

Descriptive Statistics: Summarizing the Data

In any group of data, two of the most important features you would like to know are some measure of central tendency ("What is the typical score?") and a measure of variability ("Are the other scores clustered closely around the typical score, or are they more spread out?"). These **descriptive statistics** allow us to summarize data in a brief, useful form that other researchers can easily interpret.

Central Tendency   When we summarize the data, we need some measure of **central tendency,** or a measure of the most typical, characteristic score. For instance, with the men's scores in Table 2.3, what is the number that best captures their ratings? (The name *central tendency* makes sense if you realize that all the numbers have a *tendency* to cluster toward some *central* number.) We have three ways of measuring a central tendency.

1.   The **mean** is the simple average of all scores, obtained by adding all the scores together and dividing by the number of scores. For the women, we perform this calculation:

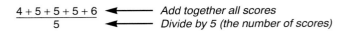

$$\frac{4+5+5+5+6}{5}$$ ←———— *Add together all scores*
   ←———— *Divide by 5 (the number of scores)*

The mean for women is 5.0, whereas a similar calculation for the men yields a mean of 4.0. The mean is usually the most valuable measure of central tendency, because it is used when we want to draw conclusions about the data (as shown in the discussion of inferential statistics and in the Appendix).

2.   The **median** is the score that falls precisely in the middle of a distribution of scores. (In fact, the word *median* sounds like *middle.*) One common way to calculate a median is to arrange the scores in order, from lowest to highest. Then identify the score exactly in the middle, with half of the scores below and half the scores above. For the data in Table 2.3, the median for the women is 5, and the median for the men is 4.

TABLE 2.4   The Median Is Sometimes a More Representative Measure of Central Tendency Than Is the Mean

Annual income of seven graduates of a hypothetical psychology bachelor's program:

$18,000 $19,000 $22,000 $24,000 $25,000 $27,000 $120,000

Mean income for the graduates = $36,429. Note that the mean is greatly increased by the one extremely high income.

Median income for the graduates = $24,000. Note that the median is not greatly increased by the one extremely high income; the median is therefore more effective than the mean as a measure of central tendency for this distribution.

The median is an especially useful measure of central tendency when a small number of scores lie extremely far from the mean. For example, suppose that a psychology department collects data on the first-year salaries of students who have graduated from their bachelor's program, as shown in Table 2.4. Notice that the median income, $24,000, is close to the majority of scores. In contrast, the mean income is $36,429. The single high score, $120,000, produces an enormous distortion in the mean, but not in the median.

3. The **mode** is the score that occurs most often in a group of scores. The mode can be established by simply inspecting the data and noting which number appears most frequently. For the data in Table 2.3, the mode is 5 for the women and 4 for the men. (Incidentally, in Table 2.3, the mean, median, and mode are all the same within each distribution—an unusual occurrence in most studies. In Table 2.4, you can see that the mean and median are different.)

Variability   Once we know a measure of central tendency such as the mean, we have some feeling for the general nature of the data. However, these central-tendency measures can only tell us where the center of the data lies—not the degree to which the scores are spread out. Measures of **variability** give us a feeling for the extent to which the scores differ from one another. If Theme 2 were not true—that is, if individual differences were small—variability would be minuscule.

An example can illustrate why we need information about variability—as well as central tendency—to convey an adequate statistical picture of the data. Suppose that Dr. Ted Schwartz teaches introductory psychology at two different colleges. Class A and Class B each have 40 students. He grades the first examination and calculates that the mean number of items correct is 35 (out of 50) for each of the two classes. In addition, he calculates that the median for each class is also 35, and the mode is 35 as well. For each class he constructs a **histogram,** a bar graph in which the data are arranged so that they show the frequency of each score (Figure 2.12).

The three measures of central tendency are identical for the two classes. However, you can see from the histograms that Class A shows great variability, with the scores widely scattered. In contrast, the scores in Class B are clustered close to the mean. Dr. Schwartz could make good use of this information about the variability of test scores. With Class A, he may need to give extra help to people with low scores, and he might contemplate special enrichment material for the outstanding students. In contrast, with Class B, he knows that if he aims the lectures at the average students, the level will be appropriate for everyone, because of the low variability.

Let us consider two ways of measuring variability.

1. The **range** is the difference between the highest and the lowest scores. Class A's scores are spread between 23 and 47, so the range is 24 (that is, 47 minus

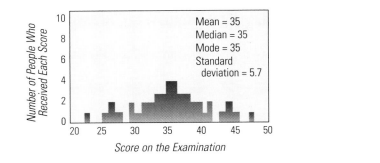
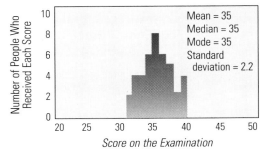

FIGURE 2.12

Examples of variability.

(left) The histogram for Class A (hypothetical data).

(right) The histogram for Class B (hypothetical data).

23). Class B's scores, in contrast, have a range of only 8 (39 minus 31). The range gives us a very quick estimate of variability in the scores.

2. The **standard deviation** is the more commonly used measure, and it is based on how far each score deviates from the mean. Psychologists use the standard deviation when they want to draw conclusions about their data—for instance, to see whether they have an important difference between two groups. It takes much longer to calculate the standard deviation than to calculate the range. (The formula is shown in the Appendix.) However, the standard deviation gives a much more complete picture of the variability than does the range, because the standard deviation takes into account the specific value of *every* number in the distribution, not just the highest and the lowest. A calculation for the two distributions in Figure 2.12 lists the standard deviation as 5.7 for Class A, but only 2.2 for Class B. As you might imagine, larger standard deviations indicate greater variability.

Inferential Statistics: Drawing Conclusions About the Data

So far, we have only discussed descriptive statistics, which describe a distribution's central tendency and variability. However, when psychologists conduct experiments, quasi-experiments, and correlational research, they want to draw conclusions. They use **inferential statistics** to draw these conclusions about their data.

In everyday language, an inference is a conclusion based on evidence. For instance, from a friend's scowling face, you draw an inference about angry emotions. Our everyday inferences are very casual. In contrast, inferential statistics provide a formal procedure for using data to test for **statistical significance** (that is, whether the findings are likely to be due to chance alone) or whether the differences are major (that is, greater than expected by chance). Three important issues in inferential statistics include how inferential statistics can help us draw conclusions about two groups, statistical versus practical significance, and meta-analysis.

Using Inferential Statistics to Draw Conclusions About Two Groups Let us return to the example of men's and women's self-ratings on the statement "I tend to get emotionally involved in a friend's problems." One semester, I asked students in my class to rate themselves on that statement, using a 7-point scale. The 41 men in the class supplied a mean rating of 4.0, whereas the 100 women supplied a mean rating of 5.0. Inferential statistics allowed me to decide if the difference between those two means—roughly 1 point on the rating scale—was statistically significant.

A single point on a rating scale might not seem to merit a statistical analysis. However, when comparing two groups statistically, we need to consider three factors:

1. The size of the difference between the two means (a large difference is more likely to produce a statistically significant difference);

2. The size of the standard deviations (small standard deviations are more likely to produce a statistically significant difference); and

3. The number of people tested (large numbers are more likely to produce a statistically significant difference).

In the case of this comparison, the standard deviations were fairly small and the number of people tested was fairly large, so that a 1-point difference might indeed be important.

An analysis that uses inferential statistics tells us how likely it is that the results we obtained could have occurred by chance alone. Suppose, for instance, that the analysis told us that a difference of 1 point or larger would be likely to occur by chance about 50% of the time—that is, with a probability *(p)* of .50. We would respond with a yawn—that difference is certainly not worth any excitement. However, if a difference of that size occurred by chance only 10% of the time ($p = .10$), we might become somewhat more excited—but would we have reason to become *very* excited? By tradition, psychologists have agreed that they are willing to say a finding is statistically significant if it is likely to occur by chance alone less than 5% of the time (Cohen, 1994). We symbolize this significance with the notation, $p < .05$. In other words, this is the formal boundary between what psychologists consider to be ho-hum results and a major difference that we would be likely to duplicate if we repeated the study.

Let's return to the men's and women's responses to the question about emotional involvement. A statistical analysis of the data collected from my class showed that a 1-point difference between the groups (with 141 participants and the specified standard deviations) would be likely to occur less than 1 time in 10,000 ($p < .0001$). This probability is far less than .05, so we can conclude that the difference is statistically significant.

Statistical analyses allow us to compare two or more groups, to see if they are different. We can also conduct statistical analyses with correlational data, to determine whether the relationship between two variables is statistically significant.

Statistical Versus Practical Significance   Statistical significance means that the data were tested with a standard statistical test, and they met the established criterion for significance. In contrast, **practical significance** means that the results have some important, practical implications for the real world. A study may

On the standardized mathematics test these students are taking, the males may receive an average score that is less than a point higher than the average score for females, indicating statistical significance. However, these results would have no practical significance for the way the teacher instructs males and females in the classroom.

therefore demonstrate statistical significance but not practical significance. For instance, one study examined gender comparisons in mathematics performance, testing 440,000 high school students. The results demonstrated a statistically significant gender difference, with male students performing better (Fox et al., 1979). Bear in mind, however, that nearly half a million people were tested. With such a large sample size, even a small difference can produce statistical significance. An inspection of the means for the test scores indicated that the males' scores were six-tenths of a point higher than the females' scores. It is hard to imagine how roughly half a point difference could have practical significance—that is, any important implications for the way people should treat male and female students in the real world.

Meta-Analysis Let us consider one final issue in inferential statistics. Suppose that several clinical psychologists are interested in the treatment of **phobias,** which are intense, irrational fears of particular objects (for example, snakes). They have systematically examined all the studies published in psychology journals to determine whether Therapy A or Therapy B is most effective in treating phobias. In all, 20 studies favor Therapy A, 8 favor Therapy B, and 3 show no difference. What should the psychologists conclude? If they simply tally the outcomes, Therapy A seems preferable, but not consistently so.

A technique called meta-analysis helps psychologists draw conclusions when the previously published psychology articles show conflicting results. **Meta-analysis** is a systematic statistical analysis of the results from many individual studies, designed to integrate the findings (Cooper & Hedges, 1994; Hyde, 1986a). This method statistically combines the results from all these studies, producing a single number that tells us whether a particular variable has an overall effect on behavior.

Consider a study by Wolraich and his colleagues (1995), who were curious about a hypothesis you may have contemplated: Does sugar affect children's behavior and thought processes? Generations of parents and teachers have sworn that large quantities of sugar will cause children to behave wildly. But what is the empirical evidence?

Wolraich and his coauthors located 23 well-controlled studies on this issue. Most of these studies included several dependent variables, each focusing on the child's behavior. These dependent variables could be grouped into 14 clusters (for example, aggression, mood, and direct observation). The researchers conducted 14 meta-analyses. Not one of the meta-analyses yielded a significant difference between performance with sugar and without sugar. For example, the meta-analysis for the dependent variable of direct observation of physical activity was based on one study showing greater observed activity after consuming sugar—and 12 studies showing no difference. As you might imagine, this meta-analysis of the 13 studies demonstrated no overall difference. Of course, sugar may possibly influence a small number of children adversely, but it has no overall effects.

The meta-analysis technique is now widely used in psychology. It will therefore be mentioned many times throughout this book, for example in the discussion of intellectual abilities, psychological therapy, and social psychology.

Data analysis is important in all sciences. It is particularly critical in psychology because most psychological research yields numbers. As emphasized by two of the themes presented in Chapter 1, humans vary greatly from one another, and behavior is extremely complex. Therefore, a casual inspection of these data seldom allows us to draw a clear-cut conclusion. Instead, psychologists must calculate descriptive statistics, which portray the data's central tendency and variability, and inferential statistics, which provide a systematic method for drawing conclusions about statistical significance.

According to the meta-analysis by Wolraich and his colleagues (1995), sugar should not have a noticeable effect on the child's behavior or thought processes.

SECTION SUMMARY: *ANALYZING THE DATA*

1. The central tendency can be measured in terms of the mean, median, and mode.

2. The variability can be measured in terms of the range and the standard deviation.

3. Inferential statistics describe the formal procedures that researchers use to test statistical signifi-

cance, in order to draw conclusions from the data.

4. A study may show statistical significance without having substantial practical significance; meta-analysis is a technique that allows us to draw conclusions that are based on a large number of individual studies.

REVIEW QUESTIONS

1. Name and briefly describe each of the six major research methods, listing their advantages and disadvantages. Then, concentrating on the topic of eating and body weight, describe an example of a study that could be conducted using each of the six methods.

2. Suppose that you are interested in the factors that influence college students' performance on examinations. With your classmates' consent, you would like to collect data on their performance on their first examination in introductory psychology. These scores therefore provide one variable for your study. Describe how you could conduct three different studies on this topic, using the experimental, the quasi-experimental, and the correlational methods.

3. Suppose that you are interested in the topic of attitudes toward people from different ethnic groups. Describe how you could conduct four different studies on this topic, using the correlational, survey, case study, and naturalistic observation methods.

4. What does the phrase "correlation is not necessarily causation" mean? Suppose that you gather data on sixth graders in gym class. You discover that there is a positive correlation between the number of positive remarks the gym teacher makes to each child and the athletic performance of the child. What three explanations could you provide for this correlation? Suppose that you want to establish more firmly that one of these explanations is correct—that praise enhances athletic performance. How would you conduct this study?

5. Dr. Mayra López is a clinical psychologist who would like to assess a new method of helping clients overcome snake phobia. Suppose that she would like to use each of the three methods of measuring responses discussed in the second section of this chapter (self-report, behavioral measures, and physiological measures). How might she assess the dependent variable—that is, people's responses to snakes both before and after therapy—using each method?

6. Imagine that a new magazine is being published, aimed exclusively at college students and costing $6 an issue. The first issue includes a survey, inviting readers to respond. The survey concerns college students' attitudes toward part-time work, favorite kinds of leisure activities, and scholarships. How might the sample of students who respond be biased, and what biases might influence their responses? Why should any summary of the study be cautious about its generalizations?

7. Suppose that you want to design a new test to assess high school students' academic motivation. Imagine that you do not need to be concerned about financial considerations. Describe how you could address the issues of standardization, reliability, and validity for this new test.

8. Analyze the Milgram (1963, 1964) research on obedience—described at the beginning of this chapter—from the standpoint of the social aspects of the experiment, specifically experimenter expectancy effects and demand characteristics. You may find it useful to imagine yourself participating in this study.

9. Return to Demonstration 2.3, on the ethics of psychological research. Point out which ethical principles may be violated by each of the studies described in that demonstration. Do the same for the studies by Milgram (1963, 1974), discussed at the beginning of the chapter.

10. Psychologists try to discover accurate factual information about psychological processes. Name as many factors and biases as you can recall from this chapter that would interfere with the discovery of accurate results.

NEW TERMS

scientific method (p. 33)
experiment (p. 33)
hypothesis (p. 34)
independent variable (p. 34)
dependent variable (p. 34)
control condition (p. 34)
experimental condition (p. 34)
confounding variable (p. 36)
confounding factors (p. 36)
random assignment (p. 36)
well-controlled study (p. 36)
ecological validity (p. 37)
quasi-experiment (p. 38)
correlational research (p. 40)
correlation coefficient (p. 40)
positive correlation (p. 40)
zero correlation (p. 40)
negative correlation (p. 41)
survey method (p. 44)
demographic information (p. 44)
in-depth interview (p. 45)
case study (p. 45)
autism (p. 45)
naturalistic observation (p. 46)
sample (p. 49)
representative sample (p. 49)
random sample (p. 49)
biased sample (p. 49)
operational definition (p. 50)

self-report (p. 51)
behavioral measures (p. 51)
physiological measures (p. 52)
experimenter expectancy effects (p. 54)
demand characteristics (p. 54)
debriefing (p. 55)
psychological test (p. 60)
standardization (p. 61)
norms (p. 61)
reliability (p. 61)
test-retest reliability (p. 61)
validity (p. 62)
content validity (p. 62)
criterion validity (p. 62)
descriptive statistics (p. 64)
central tendency (p. 64)
mean (p. 64)
median (p. 64)
mode (p. 65)
variability (p. 65)
histogram (p. 65)
range (p. 65)
standard deviation (p. 66)
inferential statistics (p. 66)
statistical significance (p. 66)
practical significance (p. 67)
phobias (p. 68)
meta-analysis (p. 68)

RECOMMENDED READINGS

Blum, D. (1994). *The monkey wars.* New York: Oxford University Press. This well-written book examines the ethics of animal research in a thoughtful fashion, providing perspectives on both sides of the controversy and focusing specifically on nonhuman primates.

Blanck, P. D. (Ed.). (1993). *Interpersonal expectations: Theory, research, and applications.* New York: Cambridge University Press. If you are intrigued by the way researchers' expectations can influence participants' responses, this book is ideal for you. It includes a review of the field by Robert Rosenthal, as well as other theoretical and applied chapters on the topic.

Foddy, W. (1993). *Constructing questions for interviews and questionnaires: Theory and practice in social research.* New York: Cambridge University Press. Here's a book that is ideal for students who want to learn more about surveys, questionnaire construction, and in-depth interview techniques.

Kline, P. (1993). *The handbook of psychological testing.* New York: Routledge. If you would like to learn more about constructing psychological tests, this book provides a clear yet detailed overview.

Whitley, B. E., Jr. (1996). *Principles of research in behavioral science.* Mountain View, CA: Mayfield. This well-written mid-level textbook provides an excellent introduction to a variety of research methods, and it also discusses research ethics and writing research papers.

Answers to Demonstrations

Demonstration 2.1

3. The independent variable is caffeine consumption (caffeine present versus caffeine absent), and the dependent variable is the amount of time taken to fall asleep.

4. The independent variable is the presence or absence of another person in the room, and the dependent variable is the amount of time taken to respond to an emergency.

5. The independent variable is the presence or absence of praise; the dependent variable is whether or not the person provides help in a specified situation.

Demonstration 2.3

Dr. Patricia Keith-Spiegel, an expert in psychological ethics, was invited to provide her assessment of the ethics of these six episodes. She responded:

Although I would want more information about each of these studies before making definitive ratings, I have ranked the studies on the basis of their potential for harms and wrongs as a consequence of participation. Studies C (rated first, or least objectionable) and E (rated third) may create momentary upsets among some participants, assuming that they will be "debriefed" *promptly* after the experimental trial. Study E is the more unsettling of the two because the attempt to elicit an *uncomfortable* emotion was purposeful and willful. Neither study appears, on the basis of the information given, to be a particularly significant piece of work, nor do we know if any attempt was made to study the phenomenon of interest in a way that did not involve deception. Two of the conditions that should pertain in order to justify the use of deception techniques are (1) the research should hold out the prospect for important findings, and (2) all other alternatives to deception should be carefully considered and ruled out as unfeasible.

Study F (rated second) is judged as only somewhat objectionable as opposed to a serious violation of the participants' rights to confidentiality. (I am assuming that the researchers were simply insensitive to the possibility that participants might fret because of the delicate subject of the survey and that the researchers have no intention of identifying anyone.)

Study B (rated fourth) illustrates the ethical infraction of coercion; that is, a professor places students over which she holds some power (i.e., the assignment of a grade) in a position where full voluntary consent is not possible. This concern is proven out when she ridicules a student for exercising the right to refuse participation.

Studies A (rated fifth) and D (rated sixth) are of greatest concern because the potential for wrong and harm to participants is high. Study A illustrates a harm that actually materialized. The more typical participant in Study A probably lost a day of life that might have been spent in more meaningful and productive ways otherwise and endured some degree of disappointment. Study D is rated as the most reprehensible because trusting students, most of whom are struggling with their decisions about their futures and feeling vulnerable about them, are given bogus feedback that could deflate their self-confidence. Had the researchers "debriefed" within an hour after inflicting the deception, little harm would probably have been done (although one always wonders what happens to the trust of deceived participants toward psychologists!). The most unsettling element of Study D is that considerable time was purposely allowed to pass before the researchers "came clean" with the students. The students had the time to fret, to possibly begin to doubt themselves, to become confused. Here is also an instance where debriefing the participants does not necessarily "disabuse" them. That is, even when the students learn that it was all "just research," that does not necessarily restore them to their former senses of self. (Keith-Spiegel, 1990)

In summary, Dr. Keith-Spiegel's rankings (where 1 = most ethical) are as follows: A. 5; B. 4; C. 1; D. 6; E. 3; and F. 2.

Answers to Critical Thinking Exercises

Exercise 2.1

a. The independent variable is presence or absence of another person; the dependent variable is conscientiousness. The confounding variable is the order of signing up for the study, which is not equivalent for the other-person-present and the other-person-absent conditions. This variable could indeed influence the dependent variable; those who sign up early might indeed be more conscientious than those who sign up late.

b. The difference in conscientiousness might be entirely traceable to the confounding variable; the presence or absence of the other person may be irrelevant. In a better-controlled study, you could toss a coin for each participant; when the coin lands "heads," the participant is in one condition, and "tails" indicates the other condition.

Exercise 2.2

a. It was important to know that the three groups were similar on the crucial dependent variable before the independent variable was manipulated; it was also reassuring that the three groups were also similar after the normal salaries were restored.

b. The three plants were located in three different cities. Because the employees were not randomly assigned to condition, they may have differed in personality characteristics, such as the ability to resist theft when theft seems like an excusable behavior. Also, the president of the company in the adequate-explanation condition might be more believable than the vice president of the company in the inadequate-explanation condition (Greenberg, 1990).

Exercise 2.3

a. A third variable such as risk-taking may be entirely responsible for the correlation. People who are risk-takers are more likely to have motorcycle accidents, and they are also more likely to get tattoos.

b. The variable of TV watching may cause the variable of achievement test scores; in other words, if you watch TV often, you'll study less, and your achievement test scores will drop. However, the variable of achievement test scores may also cause TV watching; students who don't do well academically may be likely to watch television often, because studying isn't interesting or enjoyable. A possible third variable is the conscientiousness of the parents; conscientious parents don't let their children watch much TV, and they encourage children to study.

Exercise 2.4

a. Supporters of the two political parties may differ in numerous characteristics, such as (1) the likelihood of receiving the catalog, (2) their interest in neckties, (3) the fact that women aren't likely to "vote" in this survey, and (4) their income level. The survey is therefore not accurate.

b. Those who return the survey may be more conscientious and less likely to cheat than the typical student. They may also underreport their cheating. Finally, they may not recall every instance of their cheating.

Exercise 2.5

a. You undoubtedly selected different operational definitions. However, Levine (1993) included the following: (1) "accidentally" dropping a pen and noting whether a pedestrian picked up the pen and returned it; (2) walking with a large, visible leg brace and then "accidentally" dropping a pile of magazines, noting whether a pedestrian helped; and (3) politely requesting change for a quarter. These three of Levine's operational definitions were all behavioral measures, and yours may have been, too. However, you may also have included self-reports. Probably none were physiological measures!

b. The sample was probably not representative, because it would usually be gathered from a public place or street. It would underrepresent people who live a distance from that location, those who are at work or at home with small children, and individuals with health problems.

Exercise 2.6

a. You could assess test-retest reliability by giving the same test on two occasions, perhaps two weeks apart. Then you would calculate the correlation between the two sets of scores.

b. Because you would be concerned about content validity, you would want to make certain that your test assessed a wide variety of attitude areas. For example, a test that assessed only attitudes toward women in the workplace would lack content validity. To assess criterion validity, you would need to identify a plausible criterion that should be correlated with attitudes towards women. Several possibilities include number of women's studies courses taken, willingness to sign a petition on a women's issue, or correlation with one of several existing standardized tests, which are designed to measure attitudes towards women.

BIOPSYCHOLOGY

INTRODUCTION TO THE NERVOUS SYSTEM

The Neuron

Chemical Message Systems

Neuroscience Research Methods

Divisions of the Nervous System

THE BRAIN

Regions of the Human Brain

The Two Cerebral Hemispheres

Brain Disorders

In Depth: Neuroscience Research on Visual Object Recognition

BEHAVIORAL GENETICS AND EVOLUTIONARY PSYCHOLOGY

Genes and Chromosomes

Methods for Studying Behavioral Genetics

The Nature-Nurture Question

Evolutionary Psychology

CHAPTER 3

Consider the case of H.M., a man who suffers from such severe amnesia that he cannot recall what he ate for lunch several hours earlier. H.M. had a normal childhood, but he began having serious epileptic seizures as a teenager. These seizures became so disabling that neurosurgeons removed portions of his temporal lobes and his hippocampus, structures we'll discuss later in this chapter (Bradshaw & Mattingley, 1995; Corkin, 1984; Milner, 1966). This surgery successfully reduced H.M.'s epilepsy, but it left him with severe memory deficits.

H.M. can draw an accurate floor plan of the house where he lived in earlier years. In fact, he believes he still lives there. He actually lives in a nursing home, where he has walked thousands of times from the ground floor to his room one flight up. When he is asked to guess the current year, his estimate may be off by more than 40 years. He also has to be reminded to brush his teeth, comb his hair, and shave. He has great difficulty learning and retaining new information. For example, anyone he met on a Monday would not look familiar on a Tuesday! H.M. might meet with this physician today (see above) and report that he looks like a perfect stranger tomorrow.

Despite these gaps, H.M. receives average scores on intelligence tests, and he can carry on a normal conversation. Surprisingly, he can learn new motor skills. For instance, he deals comfortably with both computerized tests and portable radios.

H.M.'s combination of abilities and disabilities is typical of the kinds of paradoxes we'll encounter in this chapter. As we'll see in this exploration of biopsychology, a person whose brain is not intact may seem perfectly normal on some tasks and completely helpless on other tasks.

The scientific study of the biology of behavior and mental processes is called **biopsychology.** In this chapter, we will examine the human brain and the rest of the nervous system, providing extensive evidence for the remarkable capabilities of these structures. We will also see how genetics and evolutionary processes are relevant to psychology. This chapter will illustrate three important principles that are related to human competence (Theme 1) and human complexity (Theme 3):

1. The structure of the brain is impressively complex, as we would expect of any organ that must accomplish so many tasks. We'll also emphasize the complexity of genetics and heredity, which account for the inheritance of psychological characteristics.

2. Many different regions of the brain must cooperate in order to produce most psychologically interesting activities. For example, as you read this sentence, your eyes jump forward several letters. This movement seems effortless, yet it requires the close collaboration of a variety of brain structures.

3. Different regions of the nervous system have different, specialized functions (Broca, 1861; Churchland & Sejnowski, 1992). For example, cells in a region toward the back of your brain respond only to simple lines, whereas cells located on the top of your brain direct the movement of your left thumb.

We'll begin this chapter by examining the general organization of the nervous system, as well as the techniques that researchers use to investigate the nervous system. The second section looks more carefully at the human brain, discussing both the normal brain and brain disorders. The chapter concludes with an overview of genetics and evolution; we will see that 23 microscopic chromosome pairs carry the complete genetic formula for producing a new human being.

INTRODUCTION TO THE NERVOUS SYSTEM

The Neuron

The **neuron** is a specialized cell that processes, stores, and transmits information throughout your body. No one really knows how many neurons the central nervous system contains. However, one well-educated guess is about 1 trillion—that is, 1,000,000,000,000—neurons (Ferster & Spruston, 1995). We should emphasize that even this basic unit in the nervous system is impressively complex, so this chapter can provide only a brief overview of the topic.

Neuron Structures   Neurons come in an impressive variety of sizes and shapes, depending on their function in the nervous system (Prince, 1995). Figure 3.1 illustrates one representative neuron, drawn schematically to show the important parts: the dendrites, cell body, and axon. Figure 3.2 is a photograph of an actual neuron, greatly magnified so you can appreciate its structure. Let us discuss some of the features of a typical neuron.

The **dendrites** of neurons are slender, branched fibers that receive information from other neurons, and transmit that information to the cell body in a neuron. The name *dendrite* comes from the Greek word for "tree." If you use your imagination, you

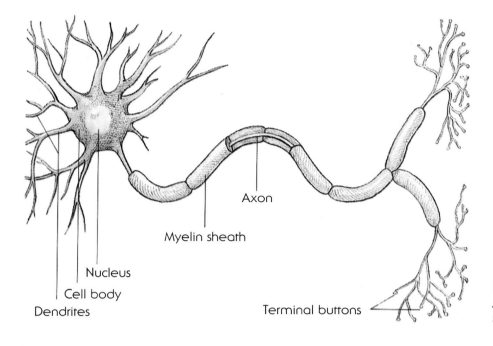

FIGURE 3.1

A schematic drawing of a representative neuron.

can indeed see a tree-like structure in the dendrites. Dendrites basically expand the neuron's receptive surfaces. The greater the area of the dendrites, the more information they can receive from other neurons (Kalat, 1995; Thompson, 1993). Dendrites have typically been portrayed as solid citizens whose work isn't very interesting. However, current research suggests that they do not merely send information from other neurons to the cell body; they also relay information from the cell body back down to the ends of the dendrites. This information seems to modify the dendrites' responses to further signals (Barinaga, 1995a).

The prominent central structure in Figure 3.1 is the **cell body,** the area of the neuron that contains the cell nucleus, as well as other structures that help the cell function properly. However, keep in mind that Figures 3.1 and 3.2 show greatly enlarged neurons. Even though the cell body is thicker than other parts of the neuron, the cell bodies found in humans are usually less then 0.1 mm in diameter, barely visible to the human eye (Kalat, 1995).

The final major structure in the neuron is the **axon,** the long fiber in the middle of Figure 3.1. The axon carries information away from the cell body, toward other neurons. The information is in the form of electrical impulses that move along the axon at a speed as high as 180 miles per hour (Nicholls et al., 1992). (You can remember that neural impulses travel through the structures in the neuron in reverse alphabetical order: dendrite, cell body, axon.)

Neuron Function   The neuron is not a simple biological device that passively relays signals (Trehub, 1991). Instead, it is part of an electrochemical system in which chemical substances and electrical signals interact in a complex fashion. Specifically, an inactive neuron has many negatively charged atoms and molecules inside its cell membrane. When the dendrite is stimulated, the cell membrane opens up its miniature passageways. The positively charged atoms and molecules rush inward. As a result, the neuron's charge becomes less negative (depolarized) for an instant. That depolarization spreads down the dendrite and into the cell body.

The neuron is somewhat finicky, however. If a neuron receives an electrical signal that is too weak, it will not pass on the message to a nearby neuron. A structure within the cell body combines all these weak signals. If the cumulative excitatory signal is strong enough to reach a certain threshold, then the axon membrane depolarizes. This rapid change in an axon's electrical charge is called an **action potential** (Strange, 1992). This electrical signal then travels rapidly down to the far end of the axon.

FIGURE 3.2

A photograph of a neuron from a cat's cerebral cortex (greatly magnified).

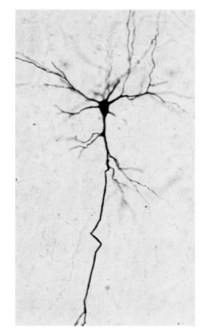

Action potentials obey an all-or-none law. If the total input from all signals reaches the specified threshold, an action potential occurs, and the impulse is transmitted. If the total input falls short of the threshold, no action potential occurs. In other words, the nervous system does not allow any partial action potentials. Impressively, under ideal conditions, a neuron can produce as many as 1,000 action potentials per second.

A feature that aids the transmission of neural messages is that the larger axons in the nervous system are coated with an insulating material called the **myelin sheath,** which is part fat and part protein. The myelin sheath operates like the insulation covering an electric wire. It helps the action potential travel faster along the axon. It also helps insulate the axon from other nearby axons. Without the myelin sheath, the messages in neighboring axons might become scrambled. Obviously, a sophisticated message system must avoid scrambled communications. As you may know, **multiple sclerosis (MS)** is a disease that destroys the myelin sheath. People with MS have varying symptoms, depending on which part of the nervous system is affected. Common symptoms include numbness or tingling in the arms and legs, blurred vision, and cognitive problems (Beatty, 1996).

All of the fine qualities of the neuron would be wasted if there was no way for neurons to communicate with one another. Clearly, neurons must deliver their messages to other neurons. The small gap between the axon of one neuron and the dendrite of a neighboring neuron is called the **synapse.** Your brain is so densely packed with synapses that one microliter (that is, 0.000001 liter) of brain tissue contains roughly 1 billion synapses (Stevens, 1995). Now turn back to Figure 3.1 and notice the knobs located at the far end of the axon; these knobs are called **terminal buttons.** (Figure 3.3 shows a highly magnified view of several of these terminal buttons.)

Incidentally, early researchers thought that the terminal buttons from one axon rested directly on the dendrite of the adjoining axon. However, with more refined microscopic investigation of the synapse, researchers discovered that a narrow space separates the two adjacent neurons. The two neurons do not actually touch.

How does the electrical message from one neuron leap across the synapse to reach the neighboring neuron (the postsynaptic neuron)? Figure 3.4 shows a schematic diagram of one of the approximately 10 trillion synapses in the brain. As you can see, the electrical signal is conducted down the axon to the terminal button. The arrival of this electrical signal triggers the release of **neurotransmitters,** which are chemical substances stored in the terminal buttons. The neurotransmitters are released from tiny vesicles (containers) in the terminal buttons; each vesicle contains a fairly standard number of molecules of the neurotransmitter (Greengard et al., 1993). As each vesicle dumps its entire contents into the synapse, these chemicals spread across the channel to the postsynaptic neurons (Agnati et al., 1992). Let us examine these neurotransmitters and other chemical messengers in more detail.

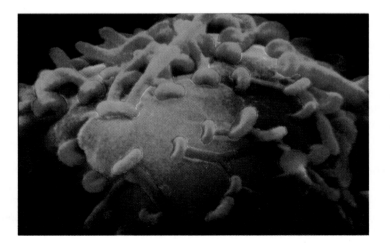

FIGURE 3.3

An electromicrograph of the terminal buttons (magnified about 10,000 times their normal size).

Chemical Message Systems

We have seen that the neuron can transmit information from its cell body down its axon both quickly and efficiently. This information causes the release of neurotransmitters from the axon's ending. Your body releases not only neurotransmitters, but also two other kinds of chemical messengers, called neuromodulators and hormones.

Neurotransmitters   As we discussed, the synaptic vesicles release neurotransmitters. Depending on both the nature of the neurotransmitter and the kind of receptor, the postsynaptic neuron can be either excited or inhibited. In an **excitatory potential,** the vesicles release a neurotransmitter that excites the postsynaptic neuron. As a consequence, that postsynaptic neuron is more likely to produce an action potential. In contrast, in an **inhibitory potential,** the vesicles release a neurotransmitter that inhibits the postsynaptic neuron. As a result, this second neuron is less likely to produce an action potential.

Any given neuron can have many excitatory and inhibitory synapses on it. The rate at which this neuron produces action potentials will depend largely on the combination of excitatory and inhibitory inputs at any point in time.

Table 3.1 lists four major neurotransmitters that you will encounter again in other parts of this book. One important neurotransmitter is **acetylcholine,** abbreviated **ACh.** ACh is found in synapses in the brain, where it is important in such functions as arousal, attention, memory, aggression, sexuality, thirst, and sleep (Carlson, 1994; Panksepp, 1986). For example, research on memory suggests that ACh helps change the connection strengths among neurons. As a result, ACh helps form new patterns of associations (Kosslyn & Koenig, 1992).

A second neurotransmitter, **dopamine,** can act as an inhibitory neurotransmitter in the brain. You may know someone with **Parkinson's disease,** which involves symptoms such as weakness and tremors in the hands, altered posture, and difficulty walking (Soukop & Adams, 1996). Parkinson's disease has been traced to a dopamine deficit. In Chapter 14, we'll also see that dopamine deficits are associated with some psychological disorders (e.g., Lieberman et al., 1994).

Researchers have now identified at least 50 human neurotransmitters (Changeux, 1993). How do these neurotransmitters influence the postsynaptic neuron? It takes about 50 microseconds (0.00005 second) for a neurotransmitter to reach the dendrite of the postsynaptic neuron. Once the neurotransmitter reaches the other side, it interacts with specialized membranes. These membranes contain gates that are "guarded" by protein molecules. In much the same fashion as a key opens a lock, the neurotransmitter enters the membrane by moving the protein molecules aside and fitting neatly into the "keyhole."

The neurotransmitter then attaches itself in position onto the dendrite on the other side of the synaptic cleft, which upsets the electrical balance in the dendrite. In an excitatory potential, the nature of this imbalance makes an action potential more likely to occur in the axon of this second neuron. Figure 3.5 summarizes the stages

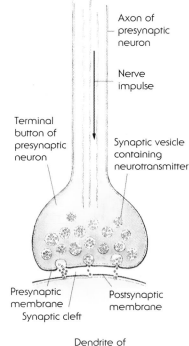

FIGURE 3.4

A schematic diagram of a synapse.

TABLE 3.1   Some Important Neurotransmitters and Their Functions

NEUROTRANSMITTER	FUNCTION
Acetylcholine (ACh)	Important in arousal, attention, memory, aggression, sexuality, thirst, and sleep.
Dopamine	Important in regulating muscle action, learning, and memory; dopamine deficits associated with Parkinson's disease and some psychological disorders.
Norepinephrine (also called noradrenaline)	Involved in arousal, memory, sleep, and mood.
Serotonin	Involved in sleep, pain perception, and emotion.

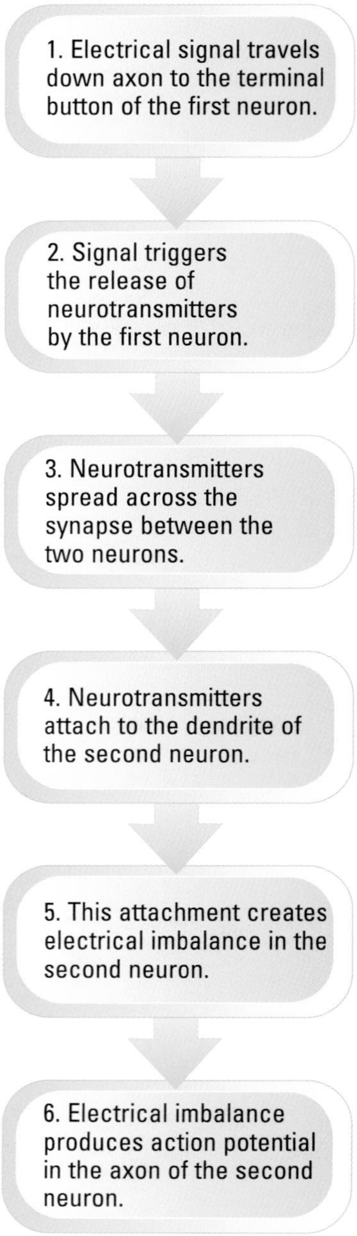

1. Electrical signal travels down axon to the terminal button of the first neuron.

2. Signal triggers the release of neurotransmitters by the first neuron.

3. Neurotransmitters spread across the synapse between the two neurons.

4. Neurotransmitters attach to the dendrite of the second neuron.

5. This attachment creates electrical imbalance in the second neuron.

6. Electrical imbalance produces action potential in the axon of the second neuron.

FIGURE 3.5

The stages in excitatory synaptic transmission.

in excitatory synaptic transmission. In an inhibitory potential, the action potential is *less* likely to occur in the postsynaptic neuron.

Neuromodulators   Besides releasing neurotransmitters, neurons release additional chemical substances called neuromodulators, which also act at the synapse. As the name suggests, **neuromodulators** modify the effects of neurotransmitters. As a consequence, neuronal activity is either increased or decreased. Neuromodulators are released in relatively large quantities, and they are likely to spread beyond the synapse and influence larger regions of the brain (Carlson, 1994).

One important category of neuromodulators is the endorphins, substances that were discovered in the early 1970s (e.g., Goldstein, 1976; Pert & Snyder, 1973). **Endorphins** are chemicals that occur naturally in the brain; when they are released, endorphins make people less sensitive to pain.

Many of the drugs that are used to treat psychological disorders act like neuromodulators. In fact, most drugs used in psychiatry act by increasing or decreasing neuronal activity at the synapse. We'll discuss neuromodulators again when we examine pain perception (Chapter 4) and medications used in treating psychological disorders (Chapter 15).

The Endocrine System   The nervous system and neurotransmitters provide extremely rapid service for messages; neuromodulators operate in a somewhat more leisurely fashion. The endocrine system is the slowest of the three systems in transmitting messages.

The **endocrine system** is a collection of glands that release their chemicals into the bloodstream. (See Figure 3.6.) We saw that the nervous system has its own independent communication network provided by the neurons. In contrast, the endocrine system is cleverly and economically designed to spread its messages through the bloodstream. The chemicals released by the endocrine system are called **hormones.** These hormones therefore travel by the bloodstream to other organs, whose activity is influenced by the hormones.

The most important gland in the endocrine system is the pituitary gland. Part of the **pituitary gland** contains neurons, which receive neural messages via axons from the brain. A different part of the pituitary receives hormonal messages through the bloodstream. The pituitary receives these neural and hormonal messages and responds by releasing its own hormones. One substance it releases is growth hormone. If it releases too little growth hormone during childhood, the child will become a midget (Rieser & Underwood, 1990). If it releases too much, the child will become a giant.

Pituitary hormones also influence the hormone production of other endocrine glands. For example, one pituitary hormone influences the **thyroid gland,** a gland producing its own hormone that is important in regulating the body's metabolism.

A second pituitary hormone stimulates the **adrenal glands,** which are two lumpy structures perched on top of the kidneys. The adrenal glands produce several dozen hormones, which perform such critical tasks as regulating the concentration of minerals in the body. The adrenal glands also produce sex hormones, such as the androgens and the estrogens. **Androgen hormones** produce changes in males during early prenatal development, guiding the development of the male reproductive system; the androgens also influence male physical changes at puberty (e.g., deepened voice and pubic hair). **Estrogen hormones** are not very active during early prenatal development; however, estrogens influence female physical changes at puberty (e.g., breast development and the beginning of menstruation). However, consistent with Theme 3 presented in Chapter 1, the endocrine system is complex: Females manufacture some androgen hormones, and males manufacture some estrogen hormones (Collaer & Hines, 1995). In addition to the sex hormones, the adrenal glands manufacture **epinephrine** (also known as *adrenaline*). Epinephrine makes your heart pound vigorously if you are frightened.

A third pituitary hormone stimulates the **gonads,** or sex glands. As Figure 3.6 shows, the gonads include the testes in males and the ovaries in females. Like the adrenal glands, the gonads produce a variety of hormones that are crucial in sexual development and reproduction.

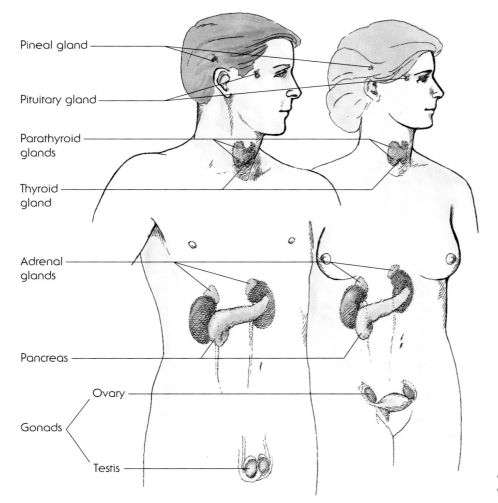

Pineal gland

Pituitary gland

Parathyroid glands

Thyroid gland

Adrenal glands

Pancreas

Ovary

Gonads

Testis

FIGURE 3.6

Some of the more important endocrine glands in the human body.

In summary, then, the endocrine system contains several glands that manufacture important hormones, which are transported via the bloodstream. The efficiency of using the circulatory system for both blood and hormones is another example of Theme 1: Humans are extremely competent. In fact, imagine the alternatives if hormones could not be conveyed through bloodstream. Our bodies would need to be equipped with a separate, special-function system, or else hormones would be circulated in a haphazard fashion—with dire consequences for our growth and metabolism.

So far, we have considered the body's elaborate communication systems. The neurons allow messages to be transmitted in a fraction of a second, using neurotransmitters as the chemical messengers. Two other chemical messengers—neuromodulators and hormones—allow more leisurely communication and regulation.

Critical Thinking Exercise 3.1

Write down the answers to each of the following questions about chemical message systems:

a. Why do neurotransmitters need a special communication system? Why can't the neural messages simply travel through the bloodstream?

b. Why don't hormones need a special communication system? Why does it work well for them to travel through the bloodstream?

Neuroscience Research Methods

Researchers in the interdisciplinary field of neuroscience have developed techniques as diverse as observing the behavior of an individual with brain damage and recording messages from a single neuron. As we will see later in the "In Depth" feature, researchers often obtain a more complete picture of brain functioning when several methods are used to attack the same problem. You may recall that we reached the same conclusion about psychology research methods in Chapter 2.

Case Study   As Chapter 2 explained, a **case study** is a careful in-depth examination of one individual. Researchers have advocated using the case study method with brain-damaged people, to help them understand the functioning of people with normal brains. You'll recall the case study of H.M., discussed at the beginning of the chapter.

Consider the case of a man known by his initials, N.A., who had joined the Air Force after a year at a community college. His roommate was playing with a miniature fencing sword when N.A. turned suddenly toward him and was stabbed through the right nostril, a thrust that was deep enough to penetrate the brain. (Later research showed that the sword had damaged a portion of the thalamus—shown in Figure 3.13 later in the chapter—that is associated with memory.) N.A. lost consciousness temporarily, and he also showed some temporary paralysis. Twenty years later, Squire (1987) reported that N.A. had a high intelligence quotient (IQ), and he carried on normal conversations. However, N.A. has a very specific deficit: He forgets some kinds of new material. For example, he loses track of his belongings, and he forgets what he has done. His mother, who lives nearby, prepares meals for him. However, he often forgets that the meals are in the refrigerator, and he goes out to a restaurant instead. He forgets to take his medication, and he forgets to refill his prescriptions. The destruction of a small portion of N.A.'s brain has affected his entire life!

Lesion Production   A **lesion** is a wound or disruption of the brain. Lesions can be produced in laboratory animals to confirm some suspicions about the functions of brain structures. (In contrast, case studies—the method just described—focus on brain lesions that occur by accident in humans.)

The reasoning behind the lesion production technique is that researchers can figure out which kind of behavior is changed in an animal once an area of his brain has been destroyed. That part of the brain may be responsible for the altered behavior. For example, if an animal can no longer see—after a region of the brain has been destroyed—we can conclude that this region plays some role in vision. Thus, the lesion technique provides a reasonably controlled method for examining the brain (Terry, 1995).

FIGURE 3.7

An example of the EEG technique, which records on this paper an electrical message from the neurons located beneath electrodes on a person's scalp.

Brain Recording   At the beginning of the chapter, we saw that neurons produce electrical signals in the brain. Neuroscientists use several methods to record these brain signals. For example, in an **electroencephalography** or **EEG** method, they place electrodes on the scalp. The electrical messages from the thousands of neurons beneath the electrodes are then recorded on graph paper, as Figure 3.7 shows. The EEG technique has been used since the 1930s, and it is still helpful in diagnosing brain disease (Alper, 1993; Churchland & Sejnowski, 1992). It has also provided useful information about brain activity when people are sleeping, as we will see in Chapter 5. Unfortunately, however, the EEG cannot provide precise information about brain activity. After all, an EEG "listens" to thousands of neurons at once.

A second brain-recording technique obtains more precise information. This method is used with animals, rather than humans, because it can cause neurological damage. In the **single-cell recording technique,** the researcher inserts a tiny electrode next to (or even into) a single neuron. This technique has been used, for example, to help us understand how individual neurons function. We will consider the technique again in Chapter 4. As we'll discuss, researchers can insert an electrode into a neuron of an animal's visual cortex. By presenting a variety of stimuli,

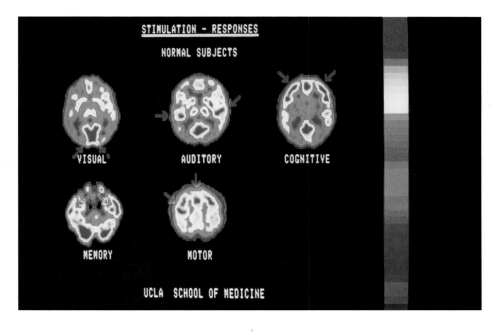

FIGURE 3.8

PET Scans of Normal People Performing Five Different Tasks
The front of the brain is at the top of each PET scan. Red indicates the highest level of cell activity; purple indicates the lowest level. The figure illustrates the following five tasks:

Visual—participants open their eyes and look at a visual screen. This activates the visual cortex (arrows).

Auditory—participants listen to music and language, which activates the right and left auditory cortex (arrows).

Cognitive—participants count backward from 100 by 7's. This activates the frontal cortex (arrows).

Memory—participants are asked to recall previously learned facts. This activates small structures called the hippocampus (arrows).

Motor—participants touch their fingers to the thumb of the right hand. This activates the left motor cortex (slanted arrow) and supplementary motor cortex (vertical arrow).

the researchers can determine the kind of visual pattern that produces the most vigorous electrical activity from the neuron.

Imaging Techniques Several newer techniques provide a picture of the living human brain, typically using computers to combine a series of brain images. These techniques are invaluable in diagnosing the part of the brain that might be affected by head injury, a stroke, or a tumor. They also provide useful information for researchers who want to identify the biological basis of psychological processes. The three most common imaging techniques are known by their initials: CT scan, PET scan, and MRI.

A **computed tomography,** or **CT scan,** passes x-ray beams through the head from a variety of angles; the computer then reconstructs a two-dimensional picture that resembles a horizontal "slice" through the brain (Posner & Raichle, 1994). Then the person's head is moved either up or down, and a second picture is reconstructed, based on this new position. Finally, an entire series of computer-generated pictures is assembled.

A **positron emission tomography,** or **PET scan,** traces the chemical activity of various parts of the living brain. A tiny amount of radioactively labeled water is injected into a blood vessel that carries the chemical to the brain. Within one minute, the brain cells that are currently active temporarily accumulate this chemical. A machine then passes x-ray beams through the head (Hartshorne, 1995; Posner & Raichle, 1994; Resnick, 1992).

Figure 3.8 shows a series of PET scans of normal people who were asked to perform various tasks while the PET scans were taken. Each picture represents a slice of the brain, with the front of the brain at the top of the page and the back of the brain at the bottom of the page.

A third imaging technique is **magnetic resonance imaging,** or **MRI,** which passes a strong (but harmless) magnetic field through a person's head. The MRI scanner picks up signals from the hydrogen molecules that are present in different concentrations in different tissues (Raichle, 1994). This technique provides a picture of a "slice" of the human brain. Figure 3.9 shows an MRI of a normal human brain. An MRI provides a much sharper image than a CT scan does. As Pool (1994) describes the comparison, moving from a CT scan to an MRI image is something like the experience of an extremely nearsighted person putting on glasses! This technique is especially useful for detecting lesions and neurological diseases such as multiple sclerosis.

During the 1990s, neuroscientists developed an important modification of the MRI technique. **Functional magnetic resonance imaging (fMRI)** produces images of

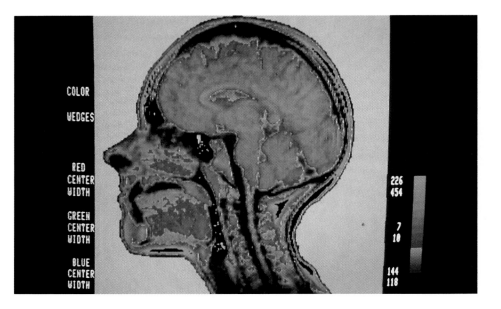

FIGURE 3.9

An Example of Magnetic Resonance Imaging (MRI)
This is an image of a normal human brain, which can be compared with the schematic drawing in Figure 3.12.

the increase in blood flow to the brain (Raichle, 1994). The fMRI technique makes these images quickly, and it provides a much sharper image than a PET scan does.

In summary, then, two of these techniques produce images of the brain's structure; however, the MRI makes clearer images than does the CT scan. The other two techniques produce images of how the brain functions; however, the fMRI makes clearer images than does the PET scan.

As this section has demonstrated, neuroscientists have observed the nervous system at all levels, from the isolated neuron to the normal human brain. As we will see in later chapters, their research has clarified topics as diverse as a rabbit blinking when a tone is presented (Chapter 6), a person trying to recall an acquaintance's name (Chapter 7), and someone trying to cope with severe depression (Chapter 14).

Critical Thinking Exercise 3.2

Write down the answers to each of the following questions about the methods used in neuroscience research:

a. Based on your knowledge of the case study method—as discussed in Chapter 2 as well as here—list some *disadvantages* of this technique for biopsychology.

b. A group of biopsychologists wants to examine schizophrenia, a serious disorder involving disorganized thoughts. Suppose that they want to determine which part of the brain is active when a person with schizophrenia reports hearing voices. Which neuroscience methods could be used, and which one is preferable?

Divisions of the Nervous System

You've learned about the structure of the neuron, three kinds of chemical messengers, and the techniques used to probe the nervous system. Let's place the nervous system in context in the human body. Figure 3.10 shows the major divisions of the nervous system. As you can see, the most important distinction is between the central and the peripheral nervous systems. Most of this chapter examines the central nervous system, specifically the brain. However, we'll begin with the peripheral nervous system. Without this vitally important system, you could not stay alive long enough to finish reading this sentence!

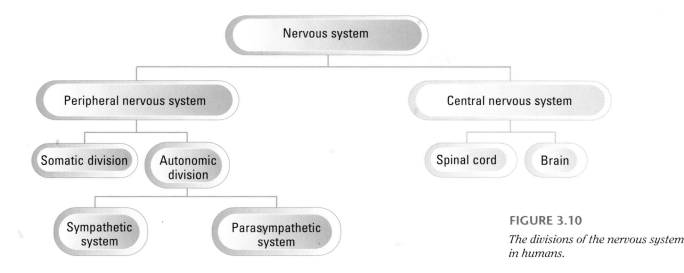

FIGURE 3.10

The divisions of the nervous system in humans.

Peripheral Nervous System   The word *peripheral* means "not central." Thus, the **peripheral nervous system** consists of everything in the nervous system except the spinal cord and the brain. The peripheral nervous system transmits messages from the sensory receptors to the **central nervous system** (that is, the spinal cord and the brain), and it also transmits messages back out from the central nervous system to the muscles and glands. This communication between the two nervous systems typically takes place via **nerves,** which are bundles of axons from neurons in the peripheral nervous system.

The peripheral nervous system is further divided into two parts: the somatic division and the autonomic division. The **somatic division** permits communication between the central nervous system and the skin and muscles. You use this somatic division when you scratch your nose, chew gum, or perform any other voluntary action. In contrast, the **autonomic division** helps control the glands, the intestines, the heart, blood vessels, and other internal organs. The autonomic nervous system usually works automatically. Unlike the voluntary actions in the somatic division, you do not need to decide whether to make your heart beat for the next 60 seconds. The autonomic division is further divided into two parts: the sympathetic nervous system and the parasympathetic nervous system.

The **sympathetic nervous system** prepares the body for action. The neurons in the sympathetic system secrete epinephrine—a substance we discussed on Page 80—which increases your heart rate and dilates the pupils of your eyes. The sympathetic system makes you sweat, and it makes you blush. The next time you find yourself in a frightening situation, notice how your heart beats faster, your pupils grow wider, and you sweat and blush.

The **parasympathetic nervous system** generally works in the opposite direction, though researchers are discovering exceptions (e.g., Berntson et al., 1994). This system tends to slow down your body functions, and it conserves energy. For example, the parasympathetic system slows your heartbeat and constricts your pupils. This is accomplished by the secretion of the neurotransmitter ACh. (Incidentally, you can remember that the sympathetic system spends energy; the parasympathetic system preserves it.) Working together, these two systems help your body maintain its balance. During a frightening experience, the sympathetic system is dominant. Soon after, however, the body's alarm system alerts the parasympathetic system to relax the functions and bring the body back to normal.

The sympathetic and the parasympathetic systems often work in an opposing fashion, with one increasing and the other decreasing an organ's activity. This pattern is true for the heart, the pupils, the intestines, and the lungs. The two systems work together, balancing each other to achieve **homeostasis,** or a constant, ideal internal environment. However, the two systems sometimes work in parallel (simultaneously but separately). For example, during sexual activity, the parasympathetic system causes the sexual organs to swell, and the sympathetic system is responsible for orgasm. The impressive coordination of the two systems is an important example of Theme 1, that humans are well designed to function in their environments.

Central Nervous System   The other major division of the nervous system is the central nervous system. As Figure 3.10 shows, the two components of the central nervous system are the spinal cord and the brain.

The **spinal cord** is a column of neurons that runs from the base of the brain, down the center of the back. A series of bones protects the spinal cord, just as the skull protects the brain. For more primitive vertebrate animals, the spinal cord forms the major part of the central nervous system. For humans, it performs more basic functions, providing a gateway for signals to and from the peripheral nervous system.

You could not function without the various parts of the peripheral nervous system, and damage to the spinal cord—in the central nervous system—causes major disabilities. However, psychologists are much more interested in the one remaining structure in the nervous system—the brain. We will consider the brain in the next section of this chapter.

SECTION SUMMARY: *INTRODUCTION TO THE NERVOUS SYSTEM*

1. Three general principles of biopsychology are that the brain's structure is complex, that most activities require the cooperation of many brain regions, and that the brain regions have specialized functions.

2. The neuron consists of dendrites, a cell body, and an axon; it transmits messages to nearby neurons via neurotransmitters.

3. Neurotransmitters can be excitatory or inhibitory; each neurotransmitter is responsible for different psychological functions, including memory, motor movement, and psychological well-being.

4. Neuromodulators modify neurotransmitter activity; endorphins (one category of neuromodulators) modify pain perception.

5. The endocrine system releases hormones; the most important gland in the endocrine system is the pituitary, which stimulates other glands such as the thyroid gland, the adrenal gland, and the gonads.

6. Some methods used in neuroscience research include the case study, lesion production, brain recording (EEG and the single-cell recording technique), and imaging techniques (CT scans, PET scans, MRIs, and fMRIs).

7. The nervous system has two major components—the peripheral nervous system and the central nervous system—each of which is further subdivided.

THE BRAIN

The human brain doesn't look very impressive. In fact, it resembles a 3-pound lump of leftover lukewarm oatmeal. However, consistent with Theme 3, the human brain is the most complicated object known. The brain never rests, even when we are asleep. The various electrical signals and chemical secretions are changing constantly, directing our extremely complex psychological processes.

In this section, we will first explore the regions of the human brain and then consider the two cerebral hemispheres and brain disorders. We'll conclude with an "In Depth" feature about neuroscience research on visual object recognition.

Regions of the Human Brain

Let's now focus on the final component of Figure 3.10, the human brain. We'll verbally dissect this astonishing brain to help you appreciate its structures. Figure 3.11

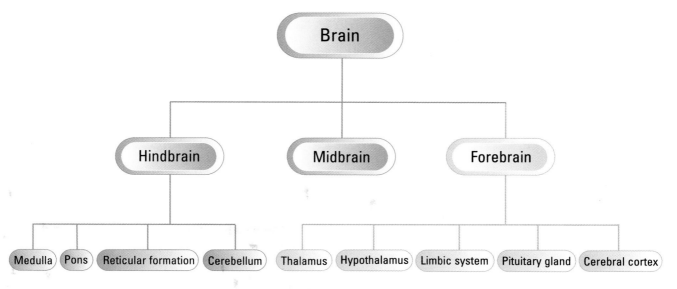

FIGURE 3.11

The major parts of the brain.

provides an overview of the brain's organization to help you appreciate how the components fit into the overall system. Figure 3.12 shows a schematic diagram of important structures in the brain.

The Hindbrain The **hindbrain** is located in the bottom portion of the brain, and it includes several important structures. One of these structures, the medulla, can be found just above the spinal cord. In fact, it can be considered a thicker, more complex extension

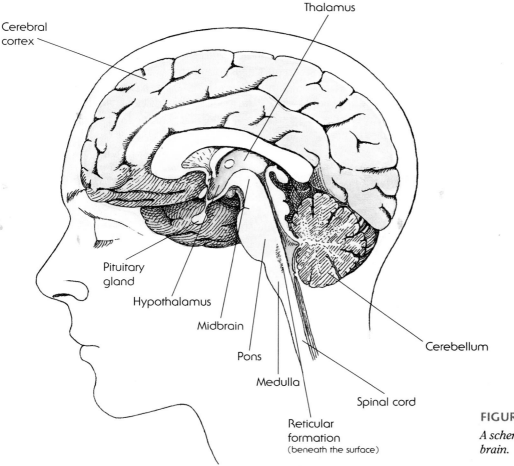

FIGURE 3.12

A schematic view of the human brain.

DEMONSTRATION 3.1   The Finger-Nose Test

With your eyes open, stretch your dominant hand out in front of your face. (Use your right hand if you are right-handed, and your left hand if you are left-handed.) Point your index finger and then bring it in quickly to touch your nose; repeat this several times. Now close your eyes and once again bring your pointed finger in to touch your nose.

People with a lesion in the cerebellum can pass the basic finger-nose test, because they use their vision to guide the finger. With eyes closed, however, this motor skill is impaired.

Source: Adapted from Glees, 1988.

The cerebellum is important in the control of this dancer's motor movements.

of the spinal cord. The **medulla** has several important functions, such as controlling heart rate and breathing. The *medulla* sounds rather *dull,* but you could not survive without it.

Notice that the pons is a bulging structure located above the medulla. The word *pons* means "bridge," and this structure forms a bridge between the lower brain regions and the higher brain regions. The **pons** is important in muscle control; for example, it plays a role in facial expression (Thompson, 1993). The pons is also important in regulating sleep and attention.

Another structure, buried inside the top portion of the spinal cord, is called the reticular formation. This structure runs up from the hindbrain to the midbrain. The **reticular formation** is important in attention and in sleep (two topics covered in Chapter 5), and it also helps maintain your muscle tone, breathing, and circulation (Kinomura et al., 1996; Pinel, 1997).

Finally, notice the **cerebellum,** a structure that controls motor movement, maintains posture, and plays an important role in basic learning (Raymond et al., 1996; Welsh & Harvey, 1992). Demonstration 3.1 illustrates the finger-nose test. People with a lesion in the cerebellum have trouble passing the test with their eyes closed, because the cerebellum directs this kind of motor coordination (Glees, 1988).

For many years, researchers viewed the cerebellum as a competent athlete, but they did not appreciate its role in higher mental processes. Within the last decade, however, neuroscientists have discovered that neurons from the cerebellum extend into the cerebral cortex (Middleton & Strick, 1994). By using functional magnetic resonance imaging, researchers have found that the cerebellum is active when people judge the roughness of sandpaper, estimate the passage of time, and solve problems that require spatial skills (Barinaga, 1996a; Gao et al., 1996). Thus, the cerebellum seems to play a role in perceptual and cognitive processes—the kinds of processes that are uniquely human (see Chapters 4 and 8).

The Midbrain   As Figure 3.12 shows, the **midbrain** is the top portion of the spinal cord; all signals between the spinal cord and the forebrain must pass through this structure. Furthermore, visual information passes through the midbrain on its route from the eyes to the forebrain. In the midbrain, visual information is also coordinated with motor movements, as Demonstration 3.2 illustrates. The midbrain also helps control other motor movements, regulates shifts in attention, and plays a role in sleep (Posner, 1996).

Before we approach the more complex forebrain region, let's review where we have been. The hindbrain controls some basic functions such as breathing and

DEMONSTRATION 3.2   The Midbrain: Coordinating Vision and Motor Movements

Stand in front of a mirror and look at yourself. Turn your head to the left, while continuing to look at your face in the mirror. Notice that your eyes move in a direction that is the opposite of your head movements. This coordination is one of the tasks performed by the midbrain.

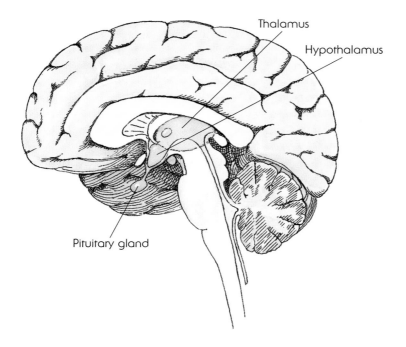

Thalamus

Hypothalamus

Pituitary gland

FIGURE 3.13

The thalamus, the hypothalamus, and the pituitary gland.

heart rate (the medulla), and it connects the lower and higher brain regions (the pons). It is important in attention, sleep, and learning (the reticular formation), and it controls movement while having some influence on selected higher mental processes (the cerebellum). The midbrain plays a role in vision, motor movements, attention, and sleep. You could not survive without your hindbrain or your midbrain. However, the forebrain is most important in perception, memory, thinking, and social behavior—those aspects of human life most relevant to psychology.

The Forebrain   In humans, the **forebrain** is the largest part of the brain. It includes the cerebral cortex, the structure that interests us most. However, several other parts of the forebrain are also critical in human behavior. Many structures discussed here come in pairs, although biopsychologists usually speak of them in the singular. For example, your cortex has both a right temporal lobe and a left temporal lobe. Later in this chapter, we'll discuss some consequences of this cortical arrangement. For now, let's take an overview of the forebrain's structures.

   1.   The **thalamus** can be compared with a central switchboard (Taubes, 1994); it receives information about emotion from the limbic system—which we'll discuss shortly—and information from the senses. (Figure 3.13 highlights the thalamus.) The thalamus does not simply send messages along in a passive fashion. Instead, it filters and organizes this information. Critical Thinking Exercise 3.2 mentioned schizophrenia, a psychological disorder involving disorganized thoughts. Andreasen and her colleagues (1994) used a modified MRI technique to analyze images of the thalamus. They reported that the thalamus is significantly smaller in individuals with schizophrenia than in control-group individuals. This finding makes sense, because people with a defective thalamus may be overwhelmed with stimuli. Disorganized thinking would be a natural consequence.

   2.   The **hypothalamus** controls the autonomic nervous system and regulates different kinds of motivated behavior. As Figure 3.13 shows, it lies just below the thalamus (the prefix *hypo-* means "under"). This relatively small structure is therefore responsible for directing the activity of the glands, blood vessels, and

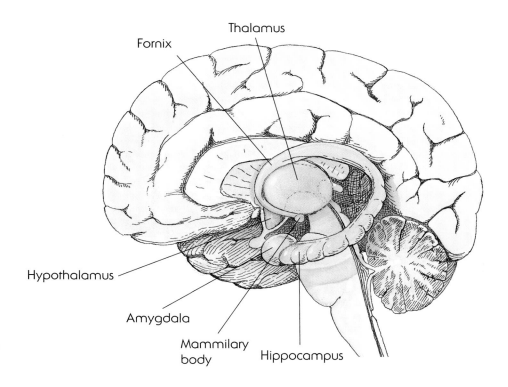

FIGURE 3.14

The components of the limbic system. Note: This diagram shows only the left member of each pair.

internal organs. With respect to motivated behavior, the hypothalamus features several distinct clusters of neurons that control eating, drinking, sexual behavior, aggression, and activity level. This structure is no larger than a kidney bean, and yet each of its regions is critically important to normal functioning. For example, when one region of the hypothalamus is stimulated, an animal will gorge itself—even after a full meal. When a nearby region is stimulated, the animal will stop eating entirely.

3. The pituitary gland is the hormone-producing gland that we discussed in connection with the endocrine system (Page 80). The pituitary gland is not technically part of the brain, but it is regulated in the forebrain by the nearby hypothalamus.

4. The **limbic system** comprises a part of the forebrain that helps regulate the emotions, and it also plays a critical role in motivation, learning, and memory (Aggleton, 1992; Squire, 1992a). As Figure 3.14 shows, the limbic system consists of several related parts, such as the hippocampus and the amygdala. (It is classified as a system because the components are connected with one another, and they work together in an integrated fashion.)

This complex system also helps regulate pleasant and unpleasant emotional reactions. For example, a woman whose limbic system showed electrical abnormalities frequently attacked another person with a knife or a pair of scissors (Restak, 1994). In later chapters, we'll emphasize the role of the limbic system in memory. We know, for example, that people with lesions in the hippocampus may have accurate memory for events that happened long ago. However, they cannot recall an event that occurred 5 minutes ago (McClelland et al., 1995; Swanson, 1992). Memory deficits are especially noticeable on difficult cognitive tasks (Isaacson, 1993). In fact, the chapter began with the case of H.M., who had a lesion in his hippocampus.

5. The **cerebral cortex** is the outer surface of the two cerebral hemispheres of the brain; it processes all perceptions and complex thoughts. The cortex is thinner

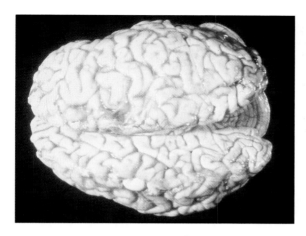

FIGURE 3.15

The cerebral cortex (as seen from overhead).

than the cover of this textbook, but it is essential in perception, memory, and higher mental processes.

Figure 3.15 shows another view of the brain, looking down from above. As you can see, the brain has a walnut-like shape and a wrinkled appearance. If you could somehow smooth out the cerebral cortex, it would occupy a space as large as four of these textbook pages. In contrast, a rat's brain would fit on a postage stamp (Calvin, 1994).

Figure 3.15 also highlights the fact that the brain has two cerebral hemispheres. Although these two half-brains look nearly identical, we will see that they perform somewhat different functions. Figure 3.16 is a schematic drawing of the left side of the brain. As you can see, the brain is divided into four lobes or regions, based on their structure and function. We'll now look at these regions more closely.

Let's start our examination of the cerebral cortex with the **occipital lobe** (pronounced "ox-*sip*-ih-tul"), which processes basic visual information. The occipital lobe

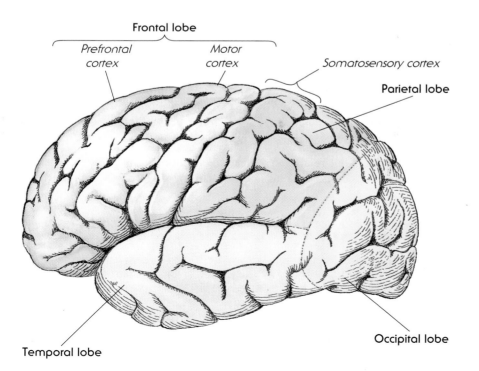

FIGURE 3.16

A schematic drawing of the cerebral cortex, as seen from the side.

DEMONSTRATION 3.3 The Spatial Arrangement in the Visual Cortex

Stand in front of a full-length mirror. An image of yourself is now being registered on the retina, at the back of each eye. We could make a map illustrating how each point on the retina is represented on the visual cortex. When you look at a road map, you see that Illinois is closer to Michigan than it is to California. This road map therefore corresponds to geographic reality. Similarly, when you look at yourself in this mirror, the map on your visual cortex represents your left eyebrow as being closer to your left eye than it is to your feet. This visual-cortex map is therefore similar to the pattern of stimulation on your retina.

However, do not take this retinotopic arrangement too literally because many factors make this representation less than perfect. For example, about half of the neurons in the visual cortex receive information from the very small portion in the central part of your retina. This is the part of the retina in which vision is crisp and clear. If you look in the mirror at your chin, for instance, you will see your chin very clearly. At this moment, your chin is taking up far more than its fair share of your visual cortex. If you maintain your gaze on your chin, note that the part of your body below your waist becomes increasingly blurry. Your knees and toes occupy only a small part of the visual cortex.

is located at the back of the head, just above your neck. As Chapter 4 explains, information travels from the receptors in the eyes, through the thalamus, to the visual cortex of the occipital lobe. One feature of the visual cortex is its spatial arrangement. Specifically, the pattern of information received by the eyes' sensory receptors corresponds fairly closely to the pattern of information on the visual cortex; this correspondence is called a **retinotopic arrangement.** Try Demonstration 3.3 to appreciate this retinotopic arrangement.

Moving upward and forward from the occipital lobe, we reach the parietal lobe (pronounced "puh-*rye*-ih-tull"). The **parietal lobe** processes information about body movement, the location of body parts, and touch. At the front of the parietal lobe is the **somatosensory cortex,** the part of the brain that handles the skin senses. Take a moment to appreciate these senses, though we will discuss them more completely in the next chapter. Right now, your right hand may be touching a page of this textbook, you may feel a slight pressure from the watch on your wrist, and the room temperature may seem slightly cold. Each of these skin senses will be registered on your somatosensory cortex.

You've probably noticed that some parts of your skin are more sensitive to touch than other parts. Demonstration 3.4 illustrates this point. In general, body parts that are represented by large regions of the somatosensory cortex are relatively sensitive in discriminating between one index card and two index cards on this task (Matlin & Foley, 1997).

Now let's consider the temporal lobes, which are located on each side of your head. (You can remember that the *temporal* lobes are near your *temples*.) The **temporal lobes** contain the auditory cortex, which processes information about sounds, speech, and music. A person with a lesion in the left temporal lobe may have difficulty understanding or producing language. However, the specific pattern of deficits is not related in a clear-cut fashion to the part of the temporal lobe that is damaged (Zurif, 1992). Interestingly, researchers have used brain

DEMONSTRATION 3.4 Sensitivity to Touch

Fold an index card in half so that the two edges are just barely separated. Touch their corners to your lips, and you can easily feel the two distinct surfaces. Now hold the cards in the same position to touch your arm; does it feel like just one thick surface? How far apart do you need to hold the two cards to sense two distinct surfaces? Try experimenting with other parts of your body. One of the least sensitive parts should be the heel of your foot—a body part that is represented by a relatively small space on the somatosensory cortex. Interestingly, when blind adults learn to use a forefinger to read braille, the region of the somatosensory cortex representing that forefinger expands into regions that had previously been dedicated to the other fingers.

Source: Adapted from Barinaga, 1994a.

imaging techniques to examine people with schizophrenia when they are experiencing auditory hallucinations—or hearing voices that do not really exist. According to this research, the blood flow increases to the auditory cortex during these hallucinations (McGuire et al., 1993). In other words, the cortex is active during *imagined* auditory messages, as well as real ones.

Part of the temporal lobe also accomplishes complex visual tasks, such as identifying whether the next person you see is male or female (Ungerleider, 1995). In fact, a person with a lesion in part of the temporal lobe might have difficulty recognizing that a particular arrangement of features is actually a face! Later in the chapter, our "In Depth" feature will focus on people who have trouble recognizing complex visual objects, due to lesions in their temporal lobe.

Finally, let's consider the **frontal lobe,** the region of the brain that contains the motor cortex, as well as regions of the brain responsible for memory, thinking, and other complex human activities. The motor cortex does not contain an orderly map of body parts that move in response to its commands (Barinaga, 1995b). Instead of a systematic one-to-one correspondence between the motor cortex and body parts, the fMRI technique has revealed that individual muscles receive input from a variety of locations on the motor cortex (Sanes et al., 1995). Like many other parts of the brain, the motor cortex illustrates the complexity of human psychological processes (Theme 3).

In general, however, the parts of the body that humans use the most tend to correspond to the largest parts of the motor cortex. We use our fingers often, and we make very precise movements with them. (Notice the precise movements you make with your pen to differentiate the handwritten letter *a* from the letter *o*.) Your fingers correspond to a relatively large space on your motor cortex. Without special training, you could never do this with your toes (which correspond to a relatively small part of the motor cortex).

Large parts of the motor cortex are also devoted to the lips and tongue, which humans use to make very precise discriminations when they talk (Passingham, 1993). Notice how your tongue makes only a slight adjustment inside your mouth to turn *save* into *shave* or *tip* into *chip.* Fortunately, you are blessed with an agile tongue to make these important motor movements. Your speech would be slurred if your mouth contained a body part associated with less precise movements, such as your knee or your elbow.

The **prefrontal cortex** is responsible for our most complex intellectual tasks (Benson, 1994). Many neuroscientists claim that the prefrontal cortex is the least understood and most complex region of the brain (Benson, 1994; Goldman-Rakic, 1988). The prefrontal cortex handles working memory, our memory for the material we are currently processing. Demonstration 3.5 illustrates a task that requires working memory. J. D. Cohen and his colleagues (1994) used the fMRI technique to measure activity in the prefrontal cortex while people completed this working memory task. The results showed increased activity in the prefrontal cortex, compared to the results for people who worked on a simple detection task, responding whenever they saw the letter X in the same list.

DEMONSTRATION 3.5   A Working Memory Task That Involves the Frontal Cortex

Cut a narrow window in a sheet of paper; the window should be just wide enough to expose one letter at a time in a sequence of letters. Your task is to examine one letter at a time in the letter series below and to say "yes" when you see any letter repeated with exactly one different letter in between. Thus, you would say "yes" if you see the sequence "A R A," but not "A A" or "A C R A." Here is the letter series:

X V A R V B Q B S N I N O K K L N E N T T W T V X V

The frontal lobe of this tennis player is extremely active as she uses her arm to hit the ball, considers her strategy for winning the game, and shows the appropriate emotional reaction when she has played well.

The prefrontal cortex is also responsible for complex cognitive tasks, such as making plans, forming concepts, and inhibiting actions that are inappropriate (Benson, 1994; Grafman, 1989). For example, I know a man with a lesion in the prefrontal cortex who is very intelligent and well informed. However, he often asks inappropriate questions at the wrong time during a group discussion. We'll be talking about the unemployment rate in Nicaragua, and he'll interrupt to tell us all to write letters to our senators about the U.S.-run sweatshops in Northern Mexico.

The prefrontal cortex also helps regulate your mood. People with a lesion in this region are often depressed (Stuss et al., 1992). They may laugh or cry at inappropriate moments (Benson, 1994; Haaland, 1992). Furthermore, they seem to be unaware of their deficits (Stuss, 1991). In summary, the prefrontal cortex is a critically important region of the brain in humans. It manages our emotions and takes responsibility for the kinds of higher mental functions that make us into socially sensitive beings who have long-range goals.

We have identified several important structures in the four lobes of the cerebral cortex. In many cases, a specific location on the cerebral cortex is associated with a specific function, as in the case of part of the visual cortex in the occipital lobe. However, many mysteries remain. For example, brain damage in some areas of the frontal lobe often produces no major deficits in behavior (Stuss & Benson, 1984). Students in introductory psychology courses sometimes assume that psychologists have already answered all the interesting questions. Although neuroscientists have made tremendous progress in recent years, many areas of the brain remain uncharted.

Furthermore, different parts of a structure may perform more than one function. For example, we discussed how the reticular formation handles processes as different from each other as sleep and learning.

In addition, most psychological processes require the participation of more than one portion of the brain. For example, Chapter 4 considers saccadic eye movements, which are used when you read or drive. They do not seem particularly complicated. However, researchers have determined that saccadic eye movements require the cooperation of many structures in the brain, including part of the midbrain, a region of the cerebral cortex, and probably additional structures that have not yet been identified (Goldberg & Bruce, 1986).

This discussion should remind you that most psychological processes have more than one explanation—more than one cause (Theme 3). Naturally, this complexity challenges introductory psychology students, who must try to make sense out of the information. Clearly, the human nervous system did not evolve into a neat, orderly set of organs, each with only a single, well-defined function. Evolution did not have the goal of developing a brain whose structures would be easy to memorize. Instead, evolution has produced a brain that is amazingly skillful in performing a wide variety of tasks both quickly and accurately. The speed and accuracy of human behavior, as you will recall, is itself another theme of this textbook.

Critical Thinking Exercise 3.3

Write down your answers to each of the following questions about research on the cerebral cortex:

a. Suppose that people with a particular psychological disorder have MRIs or fMRIs that differ from the comparable brain images obtained from people who do not have this disorder. Why should researchers be cautious when they interpret these results?

b. The study by J. D. Cohen and his colleagues (1994) found that people who searched for a particular kind of sequence of letters had more activity in the prefrontal cortex than did people in a control group who simply searched for the letter X. Why was a control group necessary in this study?

Let's now consider three additional issues related to the human brain. Do the two hemispheres of the brain function differently? What happens when part of the brain is destroyed, through a stroke or Alzheimer's disease? What have neuroscientists determined about the part of the cortex responsible for recognizing complex objects?

The Two Cerebral Hemispheres

Turn back to Figure 3.15 to remind yourself that the cortex is divided into two distinct hemispheres. One important characteristic of the brain is that for the sensory and motor areas of the cortex, the right side of the cortex is more strongly connected with the left side of the body. Furthermore, the left side of the cortex is more strongly connected with the right side of the body. This crossover pattern is known as a **contralateral arrangement.** Because of this crossover arrangement, you may know someone who has great difficulties with the *right* side of the body, traceable to a stroke in the *left* cerebral cortex. For example, I know a man who cannot use his right hand skillfully (due to left motor cortex damage), and this hand is also numb (due to left somatosensory cortex damage).

A second important characteristic of the brain is called lateralization. **Lateralization** means that the two hemispheres have somewhat different functions, though we should not exaggerate these differences. We can learn about lateralization from a small number of people who have had a special operation called the split-brain procedure and also from more subtle observations on normal humans with intact brains.

Lateralization and the Split-Brain Procedure   In the normal brain, a bridge between the two hemispheres is called the **corpus callosum,** which is a thick bundle of about 200 million nerve fibers (Giedd et al., 1994). The corpus callosum permits information to be transferred between the two hemispheres, so that a message received in one hemisphere can be quickly transmitted to the other hemisphere (Hellige, 1993a). Figure 3.17 shows where the corpus callosum is located.

During the 1960s, a group of researchers—which included psychologists Roger Sperry and Michael Gazzaniga—began to explore what happens when the corpus callosum is cut. This operation literally produces a split brain. Researchers examined people who had such disabling epilepsy that a seizure beginning in one hemisphere would spread across the corpus callosum to the other hemisphere. Encouraged by earlier research with cats and monkeys, these researchers hoped they could reduce the intensity of seizures by cutting the corpus callosum that linked the two hemispheres. (As you might imagine, this kind of operation is only used as a last resort.)

Operations on a small number of people with severe epilepsy have typically been successful. After the operation, individuals usually experience fewer, less severe epileptic seizures. Furthermore, they seem to behave normally in their daily lives. However, research in the laboratory reveals subtle deficits—which we will consider shortly. These deficits allowed researchers to examine how each hemisphere functions when it is separated from the other hemisphere.

To understand this research, you need to keep in mind the contralateral arrangement of the brain. For example, everything that appears in your left visual field would be registered in the *right* side of your visual cortex. In contrast, everything that appears in your right visual field would be registered in the *left* side of your visual cortex. Notice that this contralateral arrangement is shown in Figure 3.18.

In the normal brain, information about an object in the left visual field (and therefore the right hemisphere) can be shared with the left hemisphere; the signal travels across the corpus callosum. Imagine what would happen if this structure were

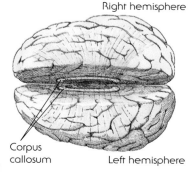

Right hemisphere

Corpus callosum   Left hemisphere

FIGURE 3.17

An overview of the corpus callosum, dissected to indicate how it joins the two hemispheres together.

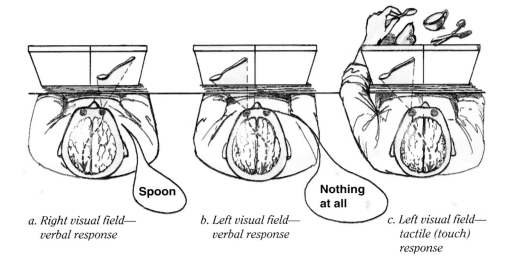

FIGURE 3.18

Testing a split-brain patient in three different conditions.

a. *Right visual field— verbal response*

b. *Left visual field— verbal response*

c. *Left visual field— tactile (touch) response*

Spoon

Nothing at all

cut, as in Figure 3.17. Information in the left visual field would still reach the right hemisphere. However, it could not travel across to the left hemisphere. (Of course, a person with a split brain could register this object in the left hemisphere by turning his or her head until the object was included in the right visual field—something that can be easily done in daily life.)

In the laboratory, researchers asked the split-brain patients to sit at a table and gaze straight ahead (Gazzaniga & LeDoux, 1978; Hellige, 1993b; Sperry, 1982). Then the researchers presented a photo of an object, perhaps a spoon, to the right visual field (i.e., the left hemisphere). The patients had no difficulty saying the name of the objects (see Figure 3.18a). These results confirmed researchers' strong suspicions that the left hemisphere is actively involved in processing language.

Now let us consider what happens when the same photo of the spoon was presented to the left visual field (i.e., the right hemisphere). When asked what they had seen, patients typically replied "Nothing" (Figure 3.18b). In this condition, the information about the spoon is sent to the right hemisphere, where it is trapped. In a person with a normal brain, that information could travel across the corpus callosum to the "verbal" left hemisphere, and the person could easily reply "Spoon." However, in a person with a split brain, the isolated right hemisphere apparently lacks the verbal skills to report that the object is a spoon.

The right hemisphere may be mute, but it is not helpless. Figure 3.18c shows a second left-visual-field condition. Here, patients were asked to reach behind the screen with their left hand and use the sense of touch to identify the object that had been presented on the screen. As you can see, the patient correctly grasps the spoon. These results confirmed researchers' strong suspicions that the right hemisphere is skilled in identifying spatial information, such as the shapes of objects. With the help of the left hand (also controlled by the right hemisphere), the patient could easily identify the spoon-shaped object. The split-brain research has therefore illustrated a clear-cut difference between the two hemispheres (Gazzaniga, 1983; Iaccino, 1993).

Lateralization in People With Intact Brains   Only about 100 people with split brains have been studied for lateralization effects. Unless you are one of those rare individuals, you may wonder if lateralization is relevant to your brain. As it turns out, research on people with normal communication between the hemispheres reveals some important differences between the left and the right hemispheres. However, individual differences are large, and we must be careful not to exaggerate the hemispheric differences (Hellige, 1993a; Hellige et al., 1994).

TABLE 3.2   Some Tasks on Which One of the Hemispheres Shows Superiority

TASK	LEFT HEMISPHERE	RIGHT HEMISPHERE
Vision	Translating letters into sounds.	Recognizing faces.
	Encoding small patterns (better than large patterns).	Encoding large patterns (better than small patterns).
Hearing	Interpreting language sounds.	Interpreting nonlanguage sounds, music.
	Distinguishing high-pitched tones.	Distinguishing low-pitched tones.
Memory	Using verbal memory.	Using visual memory.
	Drawing inferences in memory.	Storing more exact memory traces.
Language	Interpreting grammar, relations among word concepts.	Interpreting humor, emotional content; integrating information from several sentences.
Mathematics	Doing arithmetic.	Doing geometry.
Complex tasks	Performing tasks that must be completed one part at a time.	Performing tasks for which all parts must be completed simultaneously.

Sources: Hellige, 1993a; Ivry & Lebby, 1993; Joanette & Brownell, 1990; Kosslyn et al., 1994; Metcalfe et al., 1995; Witelson, 1995.

Research on people with intact brains shows increased brain wave activity, metabolism, and blood flow in the left hemisphere when a person is speaking. In contrast, these same measures show that the right hemisphere is more active when a person performs tasks involving spatial perception, as in Figure 3.19 (Iaccino, 1993; Springer & Deutsch, 1989). However, the differences are not overwhelming. In most cases, the less active hemisphere is simply responding at a lower level.

One method for studying lateralization requires dichotic (pronounced "dye-*kot*-ick") listening. In the **dichotic listening technique,** people wear earphones that present two different simultaneous messages, one to each ear. In a representative dichotic listening study, right-handed people listened to two syllables presented at the same time, one to each ear (Hellige et al., 1994). For example, on one trial, the participant might hear "ga" in the right ear and "pa" in the left ear. The participants correctly recognized 74% of the syllables presented to the right ear (left hemisphere), in contrast to 66% of the syllables presented to the left ear (right hemisphere). Notice, then, that the right-ear advantage is not large; however, this difference is statistically significant.

We have been singing the praises of the left hemisphere. What can the right hemisphere do? As mentioned earlier, the right hemisphere specializes in spatial tasks and tasks requiring complex visual perception. Hellige and his colleagues (1994) showed that the right hemisphere was dominant when participants made judgments about people's facial expressions. Also, children with damaged right hemispheres typically have trouble in geometry and map drawing (Iaccino, 1993).

Table 3.2 shows some of the tasks for which the left and right hemisphere are at least somewhat specialized. Remember, however, that the two hemispheres do *not* function like two independent brains. Instead, they work cooperatively (Hellige, 1993a; Hoptman & Davidson, 1994). For example, when you read a story, your left hemisphere is more active in translating the written words into their appropriate sounds, figuring out grammatical relationships in the sentence, and noting the relations among word concepts. Your right hemisphere is more active in decoding the visual information, understanding metaphors, figuring out the story's structure, and appreciating the story's humorous and emotional aspects. In addition, both hemispheres are important in tasks requiring creativity or logic. Interestingly, when a task is difficult, performance is better when both hemispheres are active (Hellige, 1991, 1993b; Hoptman & Davidson, 1994; Joanette & Brownell, 1990).

FIGURE 3.19

When people are asked to construct this block design out of these blocks, the task primarily requires right-hemisphere activity.

We must conclude that both hemispheres can perform most tasks, but one hemisphere is usually faster and more accurate. As Hellige (1993b) writes:

> During the past 30 years or so, emphasis on the functional differences between the left and right hemispheres has resulted in the brain being taken apart, with a tendency for the pieces to be analyzed separately. It is time to put the brain back together again. (p. 25)

In summary, we have one complete brain, not two independent hemispheres.

Critical Thinking Exercise 3.4

Write down your answers to the following questions about hemispheric lateralization:

a. Why should researchers be cautious in drawing conclusions based on research involving split-brain patients?

b. You have probably seen popular psychology articles that describe "left-brain people" and "right-brain people." Why should you be skeptical when you read these articles?

Brain Disorders

Brain Injury Every year, between 150,000 and 500,000 U.S. residents experience significant brain damage from accidents, sports injuries, gunshot wounds, and other traumatic events (Beers, 1992; Ruff, 1993). Many will be left with cognitive, motor, and personality problems. In addition, many seem unaware that they have a problem (Prigatano, 1992; Williamson et al., 1996). You probably know someone who has had a **concussion,** which is a disruption of neurological function produced by trauma such as a direct blow to the head, often accompanied by loss of consciousness (Beers, 1992). Even mild head injury can have long-term consequences. Beers and her colleagues (1994) found that college students who had reported mild head injury as adolescents scored lower than students in a control group on tests of attention, memory, spatial skills, and problem solving.

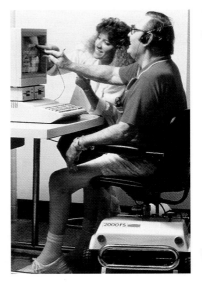

A hospital therapist working with a stroke victim.

Another common cause of brain damage is a **stroke,** a disorder in which a blood clot or some other obstruction reduces the blood flow to a region of the brain (Zivin & Choi, 1991). According to medical reports, 1% of all people in their sixties experience a stroke in any given year (Kalat, 1988). A stroke is a life-threatening event, because 30% to 40% of stroke victims die within one year, and 20% to 30% are left with a severe, permanent disability (Anderson, 1992; Zivin & Choi, 1991). These disabilities include paralysis, loss of vision, and aphasia (Anderson, 1992). **Aphasia** is difficulty in speaking, understanding, or writing, caused by damage to the speech areas of the brain (Thompson, 1993).

In the near future, stroke victims may be treated with a new compound called tissue plasminogen activator, a substance that rapidly removes blood clots and limits the extent of the brain damage (Zivin & Choi, 1991). At present, the brain imaging techniques we discussed earlier allow physicians to locate the exact site of the damage (Brown & Bornstein, 1991). Therapists also work with stroke victims—for example, in helping people with aphasia to recover their communication abilities (Sarno, 1991).

Occasionally, the brain demonstrates plasticity or flexibility. That is, when one part of the brain is injured, another part may take over some of those functions. Plasticity is relatively common during childhood. Unfortunately, however, plasticity is rare during adulthood. Usually, adults recover from a stroke very slowly, and they may never regain their original level of functioning (Barinaga, 1994b).

Alzheimer's Disease   This year, several hundred thousand North Americans will begin to lose their ability to remember simple things. They will not recall whether they turned off the oven or whether they let the cat out. They will not remember the names of common objects, and they will no longer be able to balance a checkbook. They have a specific disorder called **Alzheimer's disease,** a condition that involves a severe decline in memory, language, and thinking skills, which gradually grows worse over time (Brinkman, 1995; Nebes, 1992). According to current estimates, between 5% and 15% of people over the age of 65 have probable Alzheimer's disease (Albert, 1992; Rebok & Folstein, 1993; Scinto et al., 1994).

Individual differences in the symptoms of Alzheimer's disease are large. One person may look visibly confused and depressed. Another person may be able to carry on a brief conversation without any obvious problems.

Unfortunately, no standardized biochemical test can reliably identify Alzheimer's disease (Rebok & Folstein, 1994). Instead, physicians make a diagnosis on the basis of medical history, physical examination, appropriate psychological tests, and brain imaging techniques such as the MRI (Bair, 1993; Rebok & Folstein, 1993, 1994). The diagnosis can be positively confirmed only after death, through brain autopsy.

Consistent with Theme 2, individuals differ widely in the nature and the severity of Alzheimer's symptoms (Edwards, 1993). However, here are some of the more common problems:

1. Decreased memory, especially memory for events (Nixon, 1996; Zec, 1993);

2. Deterioration of language skills, such as finding the appropriate name for a common object (Johnson & Hermann, 1995; Nebes, 1992; Rebok et al., 1990) or writing a sentence (see Figure 3.20);

3. Decreased spatial ability, including poor performance on spatial tasks such as the one in Figure 3.19 or getting lost in familiar environments (Rebok et al., 1990; Zec, 1993);

4. Slower responses on problem solving and other thinking tasks (Nebes & Brady, 1992; Zec, 1993); and

5. Mood problems, including depression and irritability (Teri & Wagner, 1992) and other symptoms of psychological disorders, such as hallucinations (Gilley, 1993).

As you can see, these are cognitive abilities we take for granted; *of course* we can remember, speak, know where we are, and think quickly! However, people with Alzheimer's disease can survive more than 25 years after the symptoms first develop. Their midbrain and hindbrain regions are fairly normal, and these structures keep them alive. During that extended period, people with Alzheimer's disease will often interact normally with a visitor. Sadly, however, a few minutes later they may not recognize the visitor or know what year it is.

FIGURE 3.20

A woman with Alzheimer's wrote this sentence. She reported that she was trying to write, "I like the country."

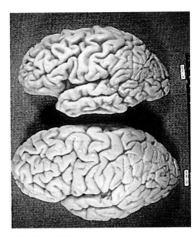

FIGURE 3.21

Examples of the brain of a person who had Alzheimer's disease (upper) and of a normal brain (lower).

Alzheimer's disease causes profound changes in the human brain. One major change is a dramatic loss of neurons in the cortex and the limbic system. Sometimes, as many as 50% to 70% of brain cells may be affected (Edwards, 1993). Figure 3.21 compares the brain of a person who had Alzheimer's disease with the brain of a person without the disease. As you can see, the cortex is much smaller. Even the neurons that remain may show degeneration. Another common brain abnormality is numerous amyloid plaques, which are clumps of protein that form around the degenerated nerve cells (Hardy & Higgins, 1992; "Update on Alzheimer's Disease," 1995). Individuals with Alzheimer's also have less of a substance that produces the neurotransmitter acetylcholine (Price & Sisodia, 1992). As Table 3.1 noted, acetylcholine is important in cognitive functions such as attention and memory.

In recent years, neuroscientists have developed several drugs designed to treat Alzheimer's disease. However, many that once looked promising have been disappointing (Price & Sisodia, 1992). A drug called tacrine currently shows some promise, though it does have potentially dangerous side effects ("Update on Alzheimer's Disease," 1995). Unless a more effective drug is developed, Alzheimer's disease will remain one of the most serious threats to the health and well-being of people throughout North America.

Critical Thinking Exercise 3.5

Write down the answers to the following questions about brain damage and Alzheimer's disease:

a. The discussion on brain injury examined research by Beers and her colleagues (1994) on the cognitive abilities of college students who had reported head injuries. Why would these researchers need to be extremely careful in selecting a comparable control group? Can you suggest a suitable control group for these students?

b. The rate of Alzheimer's disease is expected to triple in the next 50 years (Zec, 1993). Some might argue that this increase could be traced to chemicals in the environment, lifestyle changes, or some other behavioral difference. Can you think of an alternative explanation?

IN DEPTH

Neuroscience Research on Visual Object Recognition

Imagine your frustration if you awoke tomorrow morning and could not name the objects around you—even common objects such as a book, a chair, and a cup of coffee. This disorder is called associative visual agnosia (pronounced "ag-*know*-zhia"). In **associative visual agnosia,** a person has normal basic visual abilities and no evidence of a general disorder such as Alzheimer's disease; however, he or she cannot recognize objects by sight (Farah, 1990, 1994).

Associative visual agnosia is a relatively rare disorder that has been studied extensively by Martha Farah. Because of her research on vision, Farah received the prestigious National Academy of Sciences Troland Award in 1992. As Farah (1990) points out, people with associative visual agnosia have vision that appears to be normal on many tasks. For example, when a man with this disorder was asked to copy a drawing of a horse, he produced the sketch in Figure 3.22 (Farah et al., 1991). As you can see, his drawing is adequate. People with associative visual agnosia can see angles, lines, and curves. However—amazingly—this man could not name the object he had just drawn.

Let us examine visual object recognition in some detail, because this topic illustrates how neuroscience research can help us understand a normal human skill that we typically take for granted. The study of visual object recognition has primarily been advanced through three techniques we discussed at the beginning of this chapter: the case study method, lesion production, and the single-cell recording technique. We'll see that this research has identified the temporal lobe of the cortex as the site for visual object recognition.

FIGURE 3.22

Figure produced by L. H., a 36-year old man whose case is discussed on this page.

Case Study Method

A classic case study provides a vivid example of prosopagnosia (pronounced "pro-soap-ag-*know*-zhia"). **Prosopagnosia** is a very specific kind of associative visual agnosia, where a person has difficulty recognizing human faces following brain damage (Farah, 1994, 1996). In this early case study, Pallis (1955) described a brain-injured man who was worried because he saw a stranger staring at him in a restaurant. He then asked a nearby person to identify this stranger. As it turned out, he had been looking at himself in a mirror!

Let's consider in more detail the case of L.H., a middle-aged man who had been in an automobile accident as a young man (Farah, 1996; Farah et al., 1991). The brain injury affected the occipital lobe, the right temporal lobe, and the right side of the frontal lobe. (Check Figure 3.16 to remind yourself where these structures are located.) Nevertheless, he recovered remarkably well from the accident and subsequent surgery, and he even completed college and graduate school. His conversational skills are normal, and he has no difficulty finding words. His basic visual skills are generally normal; his drawing of a horse is shown in Figure 3.22. However, he correctly identified only 52% of all drawings of living things, compared with 84% of nonliving things.

Face recognition is especially difficult for L.H. In fact, he cannot recognize his wife and children by simply looking at their faces. Martha Farah and her coauthors Karen Levinson and Karen Klein (1995) explored this prosopagnosia in more detail. These researchers studied L.H., as well as 10 normal participants without brain damage. Each person first examined a set of photographs of faces and other objects, such as the face and the chair at the top of Figure 3.23. Later, they were shown some entirely new items (such as the face and the chair on the bottom left of the figure) and some different views of the familiar items (such as the face and the chair on the bottom right). In each case, they were to judge which item was old and which was new. The normal people responded correctly for 86% of the faces and 85% of the objects. Thus, they were equally accurate for both kinds of stimuli. In contrast, L.H. responded correctly for only 62% of the faces, in contrast to 92% of the objects. In other words, L.H. has a specific deficit for face recognition.

In our discussion of research techniques earlier in this chapter, we mentioned some problems with the case study method. For example, when people are in an accident—unfortunately for both themselves and for science—the brain damage is not limited to a neat, well-defined region of the cortex. In the case of L.H., for example, any of several regions of the brain might be linked with his associative visual agnosia. Researchers need to supplement the case histories with experimental research techniques, in which they have greater control over the region of the brain they examine.

Lesion-Production Technique

David Plaut and Martha Farah (1990) describe how the lesion-production technique has been used in animal research. For example, in the classic research, neuroscientists removed small portions of the temporal lobe of the cortex in monkeys in order to identify which brain regions were associated with which visual skills.

Naturally, the researchers could not use a verbal naming task with monkeys, so they needed to devise a dependent variable that could reveal the monkeys' visual

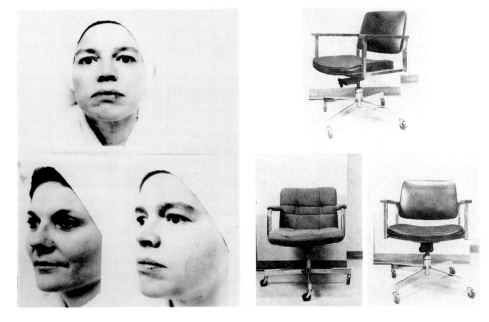

FIGURE 3.23

The stimuli used in research by Farrah, Levinson, and Klein (1995). Participants first saw the face and the chair on top; later they had to specify whether each item on the bottom was new or a different view of an old item.

(IN DEPTH continued)

deficits. They selected a visual discrimination task, in which monkeys saw two visually similar designs. If the monkeys pressed a button next to one design, they received a reward. If they pressed the button next to the unrewarded pattern, they received nothing. Monkeys in a control condition easily learned which design will be rewarded. However, monkeys with lesions in the lower part of the temporal lobe (a section called the inferotemporal cortex) performed very poorly on this task and other similar ones (e.g., Blum et al., 1950; Mishkin, 1966; Pribram, 1954). In other words, visual object recognition was virtually impossible without this part of the cortex.

Single-Cell Recording Technique

Research using the single-cell recording technique confirms that the inferotemporal cortex is involved in recognizing visual objects. As you'll learn in Chapter 4, vision researchers were frustrated in their early attempts to understand which parts of the brain were involved in vision. They inserted a tiny electrode into many regions of an animal's cortex, presented a variety of simple stimuli, and found that the neurons refused to respond.

Later, the researchers discovered that the cells in the inferotemporal cortex did not respond to simple lines and angles, but they did respond to more complex stimuli. For example, Robert Desimone and his colleagues (1984) located neurons in the inferotemporal cortex that showed only random production of action potentials when a stimulus such as a hand or a brush was displayed in the visual field. However, as Figure 3.24 shows, these same neurons responded somewhat more enthusiastically when a picture of a monkey's face—seen at an angle—was displayed. Furthermore, you can see that the neurons were even more responsive when either of the two front-view pictures of monkey faces were presented. Since this study, more than a dozen other research projects have reported similar results (Desimone, 1991).

Naturally, we cannot generalize from the research on monkeys and assume that the research applies equally well to humans (Plaut & Farah, 1990). Furthermore, we cannot generalize the research on faces to explain how we recognize other objects. For example, you do not have a region in your inferotemporal cortex that allows you to recognize your psychology textbook! However, the current research suggests that

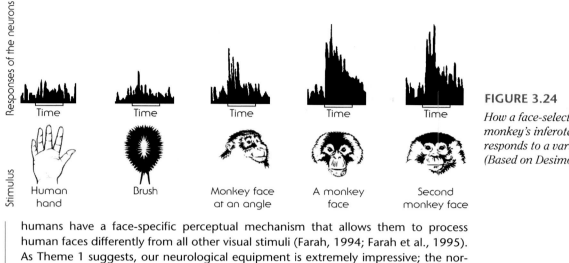

FIGURE 3.24

How a face-selective cell in a monkey's inferotemporal cortex responds to a variety of stimuli. (Based on Desimone et al., 1984).

humans have a face-specific perceptual mechanism that allows them to process human faces differently from all other visual stimuli (Farah, 1994; Farah et al., 1995). As Theme 1 suggests, our neurological equipment is extremely impressive; the normal human brain is designed to recognize human faces even more accurately than other similarly complicated visual stimuli.

SECTION SUMMARY: *THE BRAIN*

1. The hindbrain includes the medulla, the pons, the reticular formation, and the cerebellum; this regions helps regulate basic functions such as breathing, sleep, and body movement.

2. The midbrain is important in such processes as vision, motor movements, attention, and sleep.

3. The forebrain includes the thalamus, the hypothalamus, the pituitary gland, and the limbic system (all structures critical in relaying information, controlling hormone production, and regulating motivation and emotion).

4. The forebrain also includes the cerebral cortex, which is responsible for vision, the skin senses, hearing, motor movement, and all complex thought processes.

5. The two hemispheres of the brain have a contralateral arrangement; also, the hemispheres show some lateralization, but the differences in their functions should not be exaggerated.

6. Brain disorders can result from injuries (e.g., a head injury or a stroke). Alzheimer's disease produces decreased memory, language skills, spatial ability, and problem solving, as well as mood problems; changes can be observed in the brain structure of people with Alzheimer's disease.

7. Research on visual agnosia has employed the case study method, lesion production, and the single-cell recording technique to demonstrate that the inferotemporal cortex plays a role in visual object recognition, and more specifically in face recognition.

BEHAVIORAL GENETICS AND EVOLUTIONARY PSYCHOLOGY

So far, this chapter has emphasized two of the three themes of this textbook. We have seen that the biological basis of psychological processes is complex (Theme 3); even simple behaviors require the cooperation of many neurons and many regions of the brain. We have also seen that the nervous system allows humans to function quickly and efficiently (Theme 1). However, Chapter 3 has only hinted at Theme 2, individual differences. This section examines how genetics influences behavior, so we will discover important implications for the variation among humans.

Furthermore, genetics is central to this chapter because the information in your genes has controlled your development from a single-celled creature into a fully functioning

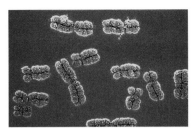

FIGURE 3.25

Human chromosomes (greatly magnified)

adult. Your genes are responsible for the fact that your adrenal glands secrete epinephrine in response to a fearful situation; your cerebellum controls your balance; and part of your temporal lobe recognizes complex patterns.

At several points throughout this textbook, we will discuss how genetics and evolution may influence behavior. For example, Chapter 8 examines how hereditary factors are related to intelligence. Chapter 10 discusses the influence of genetics on prenatal development and on children's personality. Chapter 14 points out that depression and schizophrenia are at least partly inherited. In Chapter 16, we'll consider a controversial proposal that evolutionary factors partly determine mate selection. To provide a basis for these future discussions, we need to discuss several topics: Genes and chromosomes, methods for studying behavioral genetics, the nature-nurture question, and evolutionary psychology.

Genes and Chromosomes

Genes are the basic units of the hereditary transmission of characteristics. In humans, the genes are located on 23 pairs of chromosomes. **Chromosomes** are the rod-shaped genetic structures that are located in the cell nucleus. In fact, virtually every cell in your body contains all 46 chromosomes, which carry the genetic information that played a critical role in making you into yourself. One set of 23 chromosomes was contributed by your father; the other set came from your mother. Figure 3.25 shows several chromosome pairs.

One of those 23 pairs of chromosomes determined whether you would be male or female; this pair is called the **sex chromosomes.** Females have a pair of sex chromosomes called X chromosomes (symbolized XX). Males have one sex chromosome called X and a much smaller one called Y (symbolized XY). Ironically. then, a single chromosome pair determines a characteristic that most humans consider to be vitally important—whether you are male or female. When we discuss gender comparisons and gender stereotypes in later chapters, keep in mind that all this controversy can be traced to a pair of chromosomes so tiny that they must be magnified hundreds of times before they are visible.

The full set of genes for any given organism is known as the **genome.** Biologists and medical researchers launched an ambitious program in 1990 called the Human Genome Project. The goal of the Human Genome Project is to construct a map of the exact sequence of genetic landmarks for the human genome (Cox et al., 1994; Roberts, 1992). For example, two journal articles reported on three years of work conducted by a group of about 50 researchers, who had identified more than 15,000 landmarks distributed throughout all the human chromosomes (Hudson et al., 1995; Marx, 1995). Genetic research like this has been important in mapping the genetic location of diseases such as breast cancer and cystic fibrosis (NIH/CEPH Collaborative Mapping Group, 1992; Nowak, 1994). Let's now turn our attention to the research techniques used to study the genetic basis of psychological characteristics.

Methods for Studying Behavioral Genetics

Researchers interested in genetics have devised several methods for understanding more about the relationship between genetics and psychological characteristics. These techniques include (1) investigating genetic abnormalities, (2) studying twins, and (3) studying children who have been adopted. These three methods are most likely to be used in studying cognitive abilities, personality, and psychological disorders (Plomin & Neiderhiser, 1992).

Investigating Genetic Abnormalities   Researchers have discovered many genetic abnormalities that are related to psychological characteristics. One of the most prominent, Down syndrome, usually results from having a third 21st chromosome, rather than the normal two chromosomes. Individuals with **Down syndrome** typically have mental retardation and have smaller brain size. When interacting with other people, they are often friendly and cheerful. More than 300 abnormal characteristics have been identified for Down syndrome (Plomin et al., 1990). As Figure 3.26 shows, people with Down syndrome often have distinctive round faces, with small folds of skin across the inner edge of the eyes.

Furthermore, some psychological disorders now seem to have a genetic origin. For example, a gene on chromosome 6 is responsible for some cases of reading disability (Cardon et al., 1994). Also, recent research suggests that Alzheimer's disease is linked with chromosomes 1, 14, and 21 (Barinaga, 1995c; Dewji & Singer, 1996; Schellenberg et al., 1992).

Twin Studies Jerry Levey and Mark Newman are identical twins who were separated at birth. When they were finally reunited, the two middle-aged bachelors discovered that they shared an uncanny number of peculiar characteristics. Both were compulsive flirts, and both were raucously good-humored. They both liked beer and preferred the same brand. Both drank from the bottle, with the little finger extended underneath the bottom of the bottle. Both were volunteer firefighters (Horgan, 1993; Rosen, 1987).

Anecdotes like this are certainly impressive. However, we need to recall the principles of critical thinking and remain skeptical. For example, where is the control condition? Any pair of unrelated individuals who were born on the same day in the same country would probably be able to identify a number of amazing coincidences (Horgan, 1993; Plomin et al., 1990).

Researchers are more likely to compare identical twins with fraternal twins. **Identical twins** come from a single fertilized egg that divided within two weeks after conception; identical twins are therefore genetically identical (Segal, 1993). **Fraternal twins** come from two separate eggs, each fertilized by a different sperm cell; fraternal twins are no more genetically similar than two siblings from the same parents. These comparisons of identical and fraternal twins are called **twin studies.** In most research, identical twins are more similar to each other than are fraternal twins (e.g., Plomin et al., 1990; Scarr, 1996).

FIGURE 3.26

This young woman has Down Syndrome, yet she can interact helpfully with children in a day care setting.

The identical twins on the right probably behave somewhat similarly. In contrast, the fraternal twins on the left probably display greater differences.

Adoption Studies A third approach in behavioral genetics is to study individuals who have been adopted. **Adoption studies** compare the resemblance between biological relatives—who have lived apart—with the resemblance between unrelated individuals who share the same home (Segal, 1993). For example, researchers might examine a specific characteristic such as optimism-pessimism. In some adoption studies with parents and children, the adopted children are more likely to resemble their biological parents than their adoptive parents. For example, studies have been conducted on schizophrenia, which involves disordered thought—as we discussed earlier in the chapter. The adoption research shows that an adopted person who develops schizophrenia is more likely to have a biological parent with schizophrenia than to have an adopted parent with schizophrenia (Plomin et al., 1990). In this case, genetic factors are more important than home environment.

Both twin studies and adoption studies assess the relative contribution of genes and environment to human behavior. These studies provide important information for a long-standing controversy in psychology known as the nature-nurture question.

The Nature-Nurture Question

Stop reading for a moment and try to think of a particular characteristic that makes you unique. How would you explain this particular attribute? Is it determined by the genes you inherited from your biological parents—in other words, is it traceable to **nature?** Alternatively, is this characteristic due to the experiences you had as you were being raised—in other words, is it traceable to **nurture?** You probably cannot draw a simple conclusion; the issue is complex, as Theme 3 suggests. For example, suppose you are musically gifted, and you know that one parent is also extremely musical. Perhaps that parent passed on the relevant genes to you. However, another reasonable explanation is that a musical parent is likely to encourage musical talent in a child.

We'll raise the nature-nurture question at several points throughout this book, because it is a major theme in psychological research. As you'll see, psychologists cannot provide a clear-cut "It's all nature" or "It's all nurture" answer. However, psychologists now acknowledge that many characteristics have a substantial genetic (or nature) component. These characteristics include intelligence, school achievement, reading disabilities, psychological disorders, tendency to smoke, criminal behavior, career choice, some personality characteristics, and some attitudes (Goldsmith, 1993; Loehlin, 1992; Plomin et al., 1990; R. J. Rose, 1995; Tesser, 1993).

An important concept in the nature-nurture debate is heritability. **Heritability** estimates how much of the variation in a specific characteristic can be traced to differences in heredity, as opposed to differences in environment (Kalat, 1995). Researchers use an index of heritability that ranges between 0% and 100%. A heritability figure near 0% indicates that little of the variation among people can be traced to heredity. In contrast, a heritability figure near 100% indicates that almost all of the variation can be traced to heredity. For example, research suggests that the heritability for intelligence is between 50% and 70% (DeFries et al., 1987; Loehlin et al., 1988; Plomin, 1990). We cannot state a specific heritability figure for any given psychological characteristic. Instead, the heritability figure varies substantially, depending on the populations that are studied, the environment in which the individuals were reared, and the way they were tested.

Evolutionary Psychology

Charles Darwin (1809–1882) proposed the theory of evolution to explain why certain species have certain characteristics (Darwin, 1859). More specifically, **evolutionary theory** proposes that various species gradually change over the course of many generations in order to adapt better to their environment (Hayes, 1994). A central concept in evolutionary theory is **natural selection,** a process in which the better adapted members of a species are more likely to stay alive until they produce offspring (D. E. Brown, 1991). As a result, the well-adapted individuals are more likely to pass on their genetic material, and their genes will become more common in the population. In contrast, the poorly adapted individuals are likely to die before passing on their genetic material, so their genes will become less common.

Most evolutionary changes occur very slowly, over thousands of years. Occasionally, however, biologists discover more rapid changes. One of the best-known rapid evolutionary changes has occurred with a particular species of moth that can range in color from dark gray to light gray. In nineteenth century England, the surfaces of trees had become darkened by pollution from coal-burning factories. Under these conditions, the dark gray moths were well adapted; in contrast, predators could easily spot the light gray moths and eat them. As a result, the dark moths became much more common than the light ones. However, by the middle of the twentieth century, English factories had installed devices to control the pollution, so the surfaces of trees became lighter. Since then, the light gray moths have become much more common, because the dark gray moths are eaten by predators. (See Figure 3.27.)

Evolutionary theory has become so standard in biology that the basic principles are no longer debated (Buss, 1995a; Premack, 1996). However, the widespread application of evolutionary principles to psychology is much more recent, becoming popular only since 1990 (e.g., Barkow et al., 1992; Buss, 1995a). **Evolutionary psychology** proposes that psychological mechanisms have evolved in humans to solve specific adaptive problems—problems that confronted our distant ancestors many years ago (Buss, 1995a).

Those who favor evolutionary psychology also support two interrelated concepts:

1. They endorse the "nature" side of the nature-nurture controversy, arguing that genetic forces are more crucial for a person's development than the way the individual was reared. For example, they would argue that genetic explanations are more effective than parents' treatment in explaining a child's temperament (Gazzaniga, 1992).

2. They argue that many human characteristics are universal—shared by all humans in all cultures—because of similar evolutionary forces (D. E. Brown, 1991). For example, we'll see evidence in Chapter 12 that basic facial expressions are shared by people in diverse cultures.

Evolutionary psychologists have proposed many different human characteristics that they believe can be explained by evolutionary forces. For example, people prefer food that is rich in fats and sugar, a preference that increases our intake of calories (Buss, 1995a). Also, infants seem to have an inborn knowledge about how objects move, a skill that should be adaptive when infants interact with objects in their environment (Spelke et al., 1994). Furthermore, people are more likely to have an inborn fear of snakes than a fear of less dangerous animals, a strategy that protects them from the snake's venom (Buss, 1995a). In Chapter 16, we'll consider whether males and females emphasize different characteristics when they choose a mate, a controversial topic that could be consistent with evolutionary principles.

Evolutionary psychology seems to be gaining popularity. However, this approach does have some problems. One problem is that many characteristics are difficult to test empirically. For example, some theorists have suggested that women's morning sickness during pregnancy developed via evolution in order to protect them from eating food that

FIGURE 3.27

When the surface of English trees was dark gray, the dark variety of a moth was more common (left). When the surface became light gray, the light variety of the moth was more common (right).

might harm the developing fetus (Buss, 1995a). How can this be tested using standard psychology research techniques?

Another problem is that researchers construct elaborate evolutionary theories to explain effects that are too weak to require complex explanations. For instance, Buss (1995a) argues that males are superior to females in their spatial abilities because in prehistoric eras, men were the hunters, and hunters required these skills. However, we'll see that the gender differences in spatial skills are small and inconsistent (Favreau, 1993). Furthermore, these gender differences can be easily erased when people are given the right kind of training (Vasta et al., 1996).

Still, evolutionary psychology is an intriguing approach that provides a comprehensive, well-organized view of human characteristics. We will discuss this theory in several chapters later in this book (e.g., Chapters 4, 10, 12, and 16).

Critical Thinking Exercise 3.6

Write down your answers to the following questions about genetics and evolution:

a. Suppose that you conduct a study on identical twins who are one day old, and you discover that they differ somewhat in their size and in their temperament. Can you conclude that these differences are traceable to one day's experience in the world, or can you think of another explanation?

b. Suppose that you read a newspaper article claiming that males show more sexual jealousy than females do; the article argues that the gender differences can be explained by evolutionary psychology. What kinds of questions would you ask before trusting the results?

SECTION SUMMARY: *BEHAVIORAL GENETICS AND EVOLUTIONARY PSYCHOLOGY*

1. Humans have 23 chromosome pairs, each pair containing a number of paired genes.

2. Techniques for studying behavioral genetics include the study of genetic abnormalities (e.g., Down syndrome), twin studies, and adoption studies.

3. The nature-nurture question considers what portion of the variability in psychological characteristics can be traced to nature (genetics) and what portion can be traced to nurture (rearing); heritability is a measure of the relative contribution provided by genetics.

4. Evolutionary psychology, based on Darwin's evolutionary theory, argues that psychological mechanisms have evolved in humans to solve specific adaptive problems (e.g., nutritional needs).

REVIEW QUESTIONS

1. Draw a schematic neuron, labeling the dendrites, cell body, axon, myelin, synapse, and terminal buttons. Then describe the functions of each structure.

2. Name the three kinds of chemical messengers discussed in this chapter. What function does each kind of messenger perform, and how do the three kinds differ from one another?

3. Figure 3.10 outlined the divisions of the nervous system. Try to reproduce this figure without referring to the text, beginning with "the nervous system" at the top of your diagram. Include the following titles in the appropriate location of your diagram: autonomic division, central nervous system, sympathetic system, brain, peripheral nervous system, spinal cord, somatic division, and parasympathetic

system. Then recall some recent activity that used each portion of the nervous system. Check your accuracy by consulting Figure 3.10 on Page 85.

4. Suppose that neuroscientists wanted to know more about the way that auditory stimuli (sounds) are processed by the brain. List each neuroscience research method described in this chapter, and suggest how each could be used to provide information about hearing.

5. You probably know someone who required one of the imaging techniques described in this chapter, because of a head injury, a stroke, or a serious disease. Describe in as much detail as possible the way these medical procedures are performed.

6. Figure 3.11 outlined the organization of the brain. Without referring to the text, draw a diagram that lists as many of the structures as you can recall, listing them under the headings of hindbrain, midbrain, and forebrain. Then consult Figure 3.11 (Page 87) to add any structures you may have missed. Now switch to a pen of a different color and jot down notes about the functions performed by each structure. Try to identify overall differences among the functions of the three major regions of the brain.

7. Define the term *contralateral arrangement* and explain how this term is relevant for a person who has had a stroke affecting one hemisphere. Then define the term *lateralization,* and explain how research on the split-brain procedure and on dichotic listening provides information about lateralization.

8. Imagine that a friend has just discovered that an elderly relative has been diagnosed as having Alzheimer's disease. What information could you supply about the general nature of the disease, its symptoms, and its neurological changes? Also, briefly summarize what this chapter described about several other problems: Parkinson's disease, multiple sclerosis, head injuries, strokes, and Down syndrome.

9. Suppose that you are interested in conducting genetic research on sensitivity to sweet tastes. How could you conduct twin studies and adoption studies to examine this characteristic? If you and your sibling (who were both raised in the same household) have the same kind of sensitivity, why would it be difficult to resolve the nature-nurture controversy? Finally, how would an evolutionary psychologist explain why humans may be sensitive to sweetness in foods?

10. In preparation for Chapter 4, summarize what you know about the way the brain processes sight, sound, and touch. Your information should be most complete for sight, because we discussed how the brain processes both simple visual stimuli and complex visual stimuli.

New Terms

biopsychology (p. 76)
neuron (p. 76)
dendrites (p. 76)
cell body (p. 77)
axon (p. 77)
action potential (p. 77)
myelin sheath (p. 78)
multiple sclerosis (MS) (p. 78)
synapse (p. 78)
terminal buttons (p. 78)
neurotransmitters (p. 78)
excitatory potential (p. 79)
inhibitory potential (p. 79)
acetylcholine (ACh) (p. 79)

dopamine (p. 79)
Parkinson's disease (p. 79)
neuromodulators (p. 80)
endorphins (p. 80)
endocrine system (p. 80)
hormones (p. 80)
pituitary gland (p. 80)
thyroid gland (p. 80)
adrenal glands (p. 80)
androgen hormones (p. 80)
estrogen hormones (p. 80)
epinephrine (p. 80)
gonads (p. 80)
case study (p. 82)

lesion (p. 82)
electroencephalography (EEG)
    (p. 82)
single-cell recording technique
    (p. 82)
computed tomography (CT scan)
    (p. 83)
positron emission tomograpy
    (PET scan) (p. 83)
magnetic resonance imaging (MRI)
    (p. 83)
functional magnetic resonance
    imaging (fMRI) (p. 83)
peripheral nervous system (p. 85)
central nervous system (p. 85)
nerves (p. 85)
somatic division (p. 85)
autonomic division (p. 85)
sympathetic nervous system (p. 85)
parasympathetic nervous system
    (p. 85)
homeostasis (p. 85)
spinal cord (p. 86)
hindbrain (p. 87)
medulla (p. 88)
pons (p. 88)
reticular formation (p. 88)
cerebellum (p. 88)
midbrain (p. 88)
forebrain (p. 89)
thalamus (p. 89)
hypothalamus (p. 89)
limbic system (p. 90)

cerebral cortex (p. 90)
occipital lobe (p. 91)
retinotopic arrangement (p. 92)
parietal lobe (p. 92)
somatosensory cortex (p. 92)
temporal lobes (p. 92)
frontal lobe (p. 93)
prefrontal cortex (p. 93)
contralateral arrangement (p. 95)
lateralization (p. 95)
corpus callosum (p. 95)
dichotic listening technique (p. 97)
concussion (p. 98)
stroke (p. 98)
aphasia (p. 98)
Alzheimer's disease (p. 99)
associative visual agnosia (p. 100)
prosopagnosia (p. 101)
genes (p. 104)
chromosomes (p. 104)
sex chromosomes (p. 104)
genome (p. 104)
Down syndrome (p. 105)
identical twins (p. 105)
fraternal twins (p. 105)
twin studies (p. 105)
adoption studies (p. 106)
nature (p. 106)
nurture (p. 106)
heritability (p. 106)
evolutionary theory (p. 106)
natural selection (p. 106)
evolutionary psychology (p. 107)

RECOMMENDED READINGS

Adams, R. L., Parsons, O. A., Culbertson, J. L., & Nixon, S. J. (Eds.). (1996). *Neuropsychology for clinical practice: Etiology, assessment, and treatment of common neurological disorders.* Washington, DC: American Psychological Association. This excellent resource includes chapters on such topics as traumatic brain injury, Alzheimer's disease, multiple sclerosis, and learning disabilities.

Buss, D. M. (1995). Evolutionary psychology: A new paradigm for psychological science. *Psychological Inquiry, 6,* 1–30. David Buss is one of the foremost theorists in the evolutionary psychology approach; this article provides a readable overview of the topic.

Hellige, J. B. (1993). *Hemispheric asymmetry: What's right and what's left.* Cambridge, MA: Harvard University Press. Hellige is one of the major researchers on lateralization, and his book is a good blend of research and interesting examples.

Kalat, J. W. (1995). *Biological psychology* (5th ed.). Pacific Grove, CA: Brooks/Cole. Students who used Kalat's textbook in a course in biopsychology at my college were especially enthusiastic about this straightforward, interesting book; it also includes numerous color photos and diagrams.

Nicholls, J. G., Martin, A. R., & Wallace, B. G. (1992). *From neuron to brain: A cellular and molecular approach to the function of the nervous system* (3rd ed.). Sunderland, MA: Sinauer. For students who already have a fairly strong background in biology, this book provides a clear description of neurons, neural communication, the development of the nervous system, and neurons in the visual system.

Answers to Critical Thinking Exercises

Exercise 3.1

a. The neurotransmitters require a very precise communication system that will deliver messages quickly, to an exact location in the nervous system. The bloodstream cannot convey neural messages because it is far too slow, and it cannot deliver its contents to a precise location.

b. Hormones do not need a special communication system because split-second speed is not an issue for hormones that must be slowly released over a period of days (or years). The bloodstream can convey hormones to the relevant organs as quickly as necessary.

Exercise 3.2

a. One disadvantage is that we may not be able to generalize from that one individual to other humans. Another disadvantage is that brain damage in an accident is not limited to one small region; several areas—each with different functions—may be affected. As a result, we cannot link a specific brain structure with a specific psychological function.

b. In this case, researchers want to examine brain functioning, so they could use a PET scan, but the fMRI technique would offer more precise information.

Exercise 3.3

a. Basically, these data are correlational: Brain structure X tends to be associated with psychological disorder Y. It might be tempting to conclude that some deficit in a brain structure *causes* a psychological disorder (X → Y). However, we cannot rule out the possibility that the disorder causes a change in the brain structure (Y → X) or that some third variable produces a change in both the brain structure and in psychological functioning.

b. J. D. Cohen and his colleagues (1994) wanted to see whether the prefrontal cortex is active during a working memory task. However, if they recorded prefrontal cortex activity during this particular task, this brain activity might be due to searching for letters or identifying letters. Thus, they needed to compare prefrontal cortex activity during a working memory task with activity during a similar task that involved only searching and letter identification.

Exercise 3.4

a. People who have had a split-brain operation have all suffered from severe epilepsy, so they are likely to have neurological abnormalities. These abnormalities may have produced some patterns of hemispheric lateralization, even before they had the split-brain surgery (Hellige, 1993a).

b. As you have seen in the preceding discussion, both hemispheres are active in most of the complex tasks we accomplish. Therefore, people do not simply use just their right brain or just their left brain.

Exercise 3.5

a. People who have experienced head injuries may be greater risk-takers than the general college population, and their cognitive skills may have been different *before* the accident. Cleverly, Beers and her colleagues (1994) matched each head-injured student with a friend of that student, based on the reasonable assumption that friends are typically similar on these relevant characteristics.

b. The increase in Alzheimer's disease can be entirely traced to the fact that people are living longer, and Alzheimer's is much more common among very elderly people. Interestingly, the rate of this disease has remained the same since the 1940s, if you consider any given age group ("Update on Alzheimers's Disease," 1995).

Exercise 3.6

a. One possibility is that the twins differed in their *prenatal* environment—that is, their environment in the uterus prior to birth. Some research suggests that identical twins differ in the amount of nutrition they receive in the uterus, as well as in their hormone levels (Aldhous, 1992).

b. Some of the questions you might ask include the following: How is sexual jealousy measured? Are the gender differences really large? (That is, do they have both practical significance and statistical significance?) How did the researchers establish that any gender difference was due to evolutionary forces? Simply discovering gender differences does *not* establish that these differences were caused by evolutionary factors; many other explanations are more plausible.

SENSATION AND PERCEPTION

CHAPTER 4

Try to imagine what it would be like to have lived for the last 45 years without any functional vision and then—suddenly—to have your vision restored. This was the situation of Virgil, who had experienced visual problems since birth. As a young boy, he developed cataracts; the lens within each eye grew cloudy, and he was considered blind. Virgil learned braille, and he found a job at the YMCA as a message therapist, a job he seemed to enjoy (Sacks, 1995b).

At the age of 50, he became engaged to an energetic woman who urged him to have his cataracts surgically removed. You'd probably expect Virgil to cry out—as soon as the bandages were removed—"I can see!" To everyone's dismay, Virgil reported only a meaningless blur of color and movement. Surprisingly, he could read the letters on an eye chart, but he could not combine the letters into words. Also, complex visual scenes were overwhelming—a trip to a supermarket such as the one in the photo above revealed a confusing jungle of colors, shapes, and sizes. He far preferred an uncluttered view of green hills and grass. Virgil could pick up visual details such as an angle, a color, or movement, but he could not combine them into a complete object. Instead of an entire cat, he might report a nose, an ear, and a twitching tail.

The case history of Virgil reminds us that vision and other perceptual experiences are complicated (Theme 3). Even when the eyes can properly gather information, we still may not "see." Most of us take vision for granted; we fail to appreciate why seeing should be such a complex procedure.

In this chapter, we'll consider **sensation,** the immediate, basic experience generated by a simple stimulus. Sensations include the experience of cold when rain strikes your cheek or the experience of red from a blotch of color on a painter's canvas. In contrast, **perception** requires you to *interpret* those basic sensations, giving them organization and meaning. Suppose that a friend plays a note on the piano. The loudness and pitch of that note are *sensations*. However, if you hear the first five notes and realize that they form a melody—rather than random sounds—you experience a *perception*.

In reality, the distinction between sensation and perception is not clear-cut. How complex can a stimulus become before it crosses the boundary into perception? How much interpretation is required before sensation wanders into the territory of perception? Psychologists concede that the boundary between these two terms is blurred.

People usually take sensation and perception for granted. After all, you manage without effort to see, hear, touch, smell, and taste. These processes seem so commonplace, yet they have intrigued psychologists and philosophers for centuries. Here is the basic question: How are the qualities of objects—such as the frog in Figure 4.1—re-created inside your head? This picture lies an arm's length in front of you. Still, the frog's color, shape, and features are conveyed to your cortex so that you experience a reasonably accurate, well-organized representation of the frog.

This chapter explores how we achieve accurate, well-organized perceptions of sights, sounds, skin senses, smells, and tastes. We'll begin by exploring psychophysics, which focuses on measuring sensations.

PSYCHOPHYSICS

How can we measure how the world appears? Sensation is a private activity. If you decide to watch a friend's sensory processes at work, you'll soon grow bored because so little activity is visible. **Psychophysics** is an area of psychology that examines how physical stimuli (such as sights or sounds) are related to people's psychological reactions to those stimuli. Consider the following situation. A conductor of a college marching band is listening to two trombone players play a C on their instruments, and Jo's C is slightly higher than Carlos's C. In other words, the two *physical* stimuli differ slightly. Will their conductor be able to discriminate between these two tones, indicating that they are *psychologically* different?

A typical study in psychophysics might assess people's psychological reactions to a faint tone. Psychologists can easily measure the intensity of the physical stimulus—that faint tone—in precise units designed by physicists. Measuring people's psychological reactions is much more challenging. For more than a century, researchers have been devising psychophysical methods for converting these private psychological reactions into objective numbers. These numbers inform us about human sensory ability, and they also provide objective measures for research in perception.

Psychophysicists ask two basic questions: (1) Can people detect this low-intensity stimulus? (2) Can people discriminate between these two similar stimuli? Let's consider both detection and discrimination research.

FIGURE 4.1

Perception requires you to interpret basic sensations, such as the green color of this frog.

TABLE 4.1 **Several Approximate Detection Threshold Values**

SENSORY PROCESS	APPROXIMATE DETECTION THRESHOLD
Vision	A candle flame seen at 30 miles on a dark clear night.
Hearing	The tick of a watch at 20 feet under quiet conditions.
Touch	The wing of a bee falling on your cheek from a distance of ½ inch.
Smell	One drop of perfume diffused into the entire volume of a three-room apartment.
Taste	One teaspoon of sugar in 2 gallons of water.

Source: Adapted from Galanter, 1962. Used with permission.

Detection

Suppose you are tasting a fruit punch at a party. Is that subtle flavor some kind of alcohol? Or suppose your neighbors have asked you to keep an eye on their house while they were away on vacation. Is that a faint light in their living room? These two situations require detection. In **detection** research, psychologists present low-intensity stimuli and record whether people report them. Psychologists can study detection using either of two major approaches to detection: the classical psychophysics approach or the signal detection theory approach.

Classical Psychophysics Approach   The goal of the classical psychophysics approach to detection is to establish a threshold. A **detection threshold** is defined as the smallest amount of energy required in order for a person to report the stimulus on half (50%) of the trials. For example, if researchers want to measure the detection threshold for a particular light, they must figure out how intense the light must be for the observer to say "I see it" half the time and "I don't see it" half the time.

Just how sensitive are the senses? Table 4.1 shows examples of some very impressive detection thresholds. However, do not conclude that psychophysicists sit in their laboratories dropping bee wings on people's cheeks. They are more likely to use carefully calibrated hairlike fibers to detect thresholds for touch. Furthermore, you may notice a problem with these thresholds. Would you always be able to hear a watch ticking 20 feet away? Wouldn't your threshold be different if a noisy jet plane had just flown overhead before you listened for the stimulus? Wouldn't you be more likely to say "Yes, I hear it" if the researcher had promised you a dollar for every stimulus you correctly detected?

Signal Detection Approach   The more current approach to detection rejects the concept of an absolute threshold, in which a stimulus is consistently perceived if it is above the threshold and not perceived if it is below the threshold (Luce & Krumhansl, 1988; Swets, 1996). Psychophysicists acknowledge that a variety of factors (such as prior noise) have an important impact on thresholds. More important, the current approach emphasizes that your likelihood of hearing a faint noise depends on your expectations and your motivation, as well as your sensitivity.

A student, Bruce Edington, provided a good example of how both expectations and motivation influence our responses. Bruce had applied for a job, and the manager had emphasized that Bruce should expect a phone call between 3:30 and 4:00 on a particular afternoon. During that 30-minute period, Bruce was convinced that he heard the phone start to ring two or three times. His "I hear it" responses were more frequent than in other circumstances because of two factors: (1) His expectations were high because of the high probability that the phone should actually ring during that period; (2) his motivation was high because of the important benefits of answering the phone if it did actually ring—in contrast to the major drawbacks of not answering the

Signal detection theory predicts that the expectations and motivations of this air traffic controller will influence the likelihood of his detecting an incoming plane on the horizon.

phone. In fact, Bruce's expectations and motivation were so strong that he probably would have run to the phone if the *doorbell* had rung!

The classic psychophysics approach ignores factors such as a person's motivations for saying "Yes, I detect the stimulus." Instead, that approach simply records the number of "Yes" and "No" responses. In contrast, **signal detection theory** assesses both the observer's sensitivity and his or her criterion. **Sensitivity** is the ability to detect a weak stimulus. Thus, Bruce Edington's responses in the phone call situation depended on the sensitivity of his hearing. The observer's **criterion** is his or her willingness to say "I detect the stimulus," when it is not clear whether the stimulus has been presented. Notice that Bruce's expectation and motivation regarding the phone call encouraged him to adopt a lenient criterion when he was waiting for the call. He was willing to believe that the phone had rung, even if there was only the *slightest* chance that it rang.

In signal detection studies, researchers present hundreds of stimuli (Kadlec & Thompson, 1992), and observers report whether or not they detect the stimulus. On many trials, however, no stimulus is presented. Signal detection researchers find that two common determinants of a person's criterion are (1) the probability that the stimulus will occur and (2) the benefits and drawbacks associated with making the particular response. When both the probability and the benefits are high—as they were in Bruce Edington's case—people often answer "I heard it," even when no stimulus had occurred.

The important contribution of signal detection theory to psychophysics is that it reminds us of the variability within each human. We are not rigid "detection machines" who consistently report "I perceive it" whenever a stimulus reaches a specific intensity. Instead, our knowledge of the situation determines how we respond to a particular stimulus.

Discrimination

In detection studies, people try to detect a weak stimulus. In **discrimination** studies, people try to determine whether two stimuli are distinguishably different. We perform discrimination tasks every day. For example, when you sing the national anthem before a ballgame, does your note match the one sung on the loudspeaker, or is it slightly lower? Does this chicken recipe have the same amount of lime as the one in the Afrilanka Restaurant, or is it more sour?

The classical research on discrimination produced an important concept, the just-noticeable difference. As the name implies, the experimenter changes the physical stimulus slowly until a **just-noticeable difference (jnd)** is produced. For instance, researchers have found that humans can just barely notice the difference between 60 candles burning in one room and 61 candles in the same room.

An early researcher, Ernst Weber (pronounced "*Vay*-bur"), noticed that two stimuli must differ by a constant proportion in order to create a just-noticeable difference. According to **Weber's law,** a weak or small stimulus does not require much change before we notice that it has changed; a strong or large stimulus requires a proportionately greater change before we notice that it has changed. So, for example, Uma may just barely notice the difference between 60 candles and 61 candles. However, if we begin with 120 candles (a stimulus that's twice as intense), then we'll need to increase the number of candles to 122 for her to notice the change.

Research on Weber's law shows that the exact value of the constant proportion will vary from task to task. For instance, we are very sensitive to changes in the pitch of a tone. If two tones differ by less than 1% (0.33%, to be exact), we can detect the difference between them. On the other hand, we are not very sensitive to changes in the intensity of tastes. Two tastes must differ by about 25% for us to detect the difference between them. For example, you should be able to tell the difference between 4 and 5 teaspoons of sugar added to a quart of iced tea.

Is Weber's law accurate? Researchers know that judgments are influenced by the context in which the stimuli appear (Poulton, 1989). Still, a wide variety of studies on vision, hearing, and the other senses demonstrate that Weber's law is reasonably accurate in predicting sensory discrimination (Laming, 1985).

Just-noticeable difference: Suppose that you can just barely discriminate between the length of Rods A and B, which are 1.0 and 1.1 centimeters long. Then, if you were presented with Rod C, which is 2.0 centimeters long, a fourth rod, D, would need to be 2.2 centimeters long to be barely discriminable.

A

B

C

D

Think about some applications of Weber's law. For example, you may notice a 5-pound weight loss on a slender friend, but a heavier friend may need to lose 10 pounds to produce a just-noticeable difference. Similarly, people complain about a 4-cent raise in the price of a postage stamp, but they may not notice a 4-cent increase in the cost of a gallon of gasoline.

Psychophysics is a useful tool for assessing people's private sensory responses and for converting those private responses into numbers. These numbers can be useful in research on sensation and perception. Also, the detection thresholds and some of the discrimination thresholds illustrate the theme that humans are endowed with extremely impressive sensory equipment (Theme 1). This equipment allows them to perform both accurately and efficiently.

Critical Thinking Exercise 4.1

Write down your answers to the following questions about psychophysics:

a. Suppose that Jim reports seeing a faint light in a psychophysics study, but Pat does not. Can you conclude that Jim has more sensitive hearing than Pat? What potential confounding variable might explain the difference?

b. How might an evolutionary psychologist explain why our detection thresholds (e.g., for taste) are generally more impressive than our discrimination thresholds?

SECTION SUMMARY: *PSYCHOPHYSICS*

1. Sensation refers to the immediate experiences generated by simple stimuli; perception requires interpretation, organization, and meaning. In reality, the distinction between the two processes is blurred.

2. Psychophysics investigates the relationship between physical stimuli and psychological reactions to those stimuli.

3. To study detection, psychologists use either the classical psychophysical approach (which measures detection thresholds) or signal detection theory (which points out that expectations and motivations influence an observer's criterion).

4. In research on discrimination, Weber's law says that small changes can be readily noticed when the stimulus is weak or small; strong or large stimuli require proportionately greater changes before people notice those changes.

VISION

Take a minute to notice your perceptual experiences at this very moment. You may be aware of sound, touch, smell, and taste. However, your visual experiences are probably most prominent. This extraordinarily rich visual sense supplies you with knowledge, for example, when you read about Weber's law, as well as social cues (a friend's scowling face). Vision also provides us with survival information and entertainment. Vision typically dominates our perceptual experiences, and it also dominates the research in sensation and perception. As a result, our knowledge about the visual system, sensory processing, and complex visual phenomena is much more complete than the knowledge about the other senses. Let's begin by considering the structure of the eye and the rest of the visual system.

The Visual System

The human eye is about the size of a large olive, yet it performs an impressive variety of tasks with remarkable accuracy and efficiency. The eye gathers information about color, shape, motion, and distance—even though it is less than 2 inches wide.

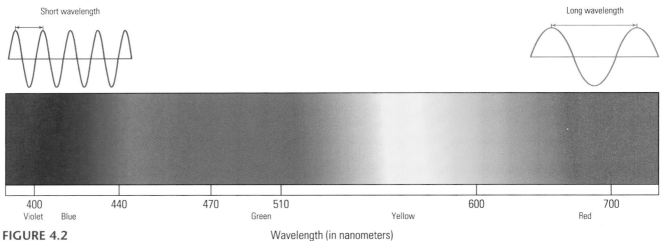

Short wavelength

Long wavelength

400
Violet   Blue
440
470
510
Green
600
Yellow
700
Red

FIGURE 4.2
The Visible Spectrum

Wavelength (in nanometers)

The visual stimulus that initiates this impressive variety of tasks is light, which is one form of electromagnetic radiation. Figure 4.2 shows you the visible spectrum, the portion of the electromagnetic spectrum that humans can see.

Light travels in waves, and **wavelength** is the distance between two peaks in these waves. This distance is measured in nanometers (abbreviated nm); one nanometer equals one-billionth of a meter (0.000000001 m). We can see light in the wavelength range between about 400 nm (violet) and 700 nm (red).

Wavelength is a characteristic of light that helps to determine the **hue** or color of a visual stimulus. The height of the light wave, or **amplitude,** is the characteristic that determines the **brightness** of a visual stimulus. Thus, the wavelengths in a bright sky-blue color are relatively close together and tall, whereas the wavelengths in a dark shade of red are relatively far apart and short.

Anatomy of the Eye Figure 4.3 shows the major structures of the eye. The **cornea** is a clear membrane with a curved surface, which helps to bend light rays when they enter the eye. Just behind the cornea is the **iris,** a ring of muscles that contracts and dilates to change the amount of light that enters the eye. The color of the iris can range from pale blue to dark brown. The **pupil** is the opening in the center of that colored iris.

Directly behind the iris and the pupil is the **lens,** a structure that changes its shape to focus on objects that are nearby or far away. The lens completes the process—begun by the cornea—of bending the light rays so that they gather in focus at the back of the eye, at a point on or near the retina.

The **retina** absorbs light rays and converts them into patterns of action potentials that can be transmitted to the brain by the neurons. The retina is a critically important part of the eye, even though it is only as thick as a page of this book. Notice the tiny region in the center of the retina called the fovea (pronounced "*foe*-vee-uh"). The **fovea** is the area of the retina in which vision is the most precise.

Cells in the Retina Several different kinds of retinal cells play a critical role in converting light into sight. The two kinds of cells that respond to light are called **receptor cells,** or cones and rods. (See Figure 4.4.) **Cones** are responsible for color vision, and they operate best when the lighting is good. **Rods** do not code color; they code all stimulus wavelengths as blacks, grays, and whites. When the lighting is poor, rods function better than cones. When you go outside at night, you cannot see an object's customary color. However, the rods do allow you to see various shades of gray.

These two kinds of receptors also differ in their distribution throughout the retina. Cones are concentrated primarily in the fovea; rods are located mostly outside

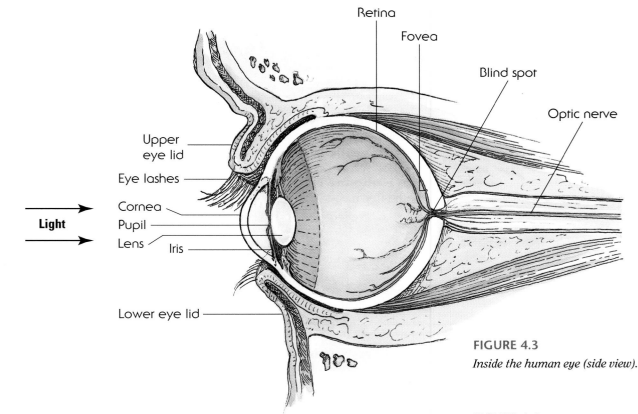

Retina

Fovea

Blind spot

Optic nerve

Upper
eye lid

Eye lashes

Cornea

Light

Pupil

Lens   Iris

Lower eye lid

FIGURE 4.3

Inside the human eye (side view).

FIGURE 4.4

A photograph of rods and cones on the retina, as shown by an electron microscope (magnified roughly 1,000 times normal size). The two tapered structures at the front are cones, and the rod-shaped structures are rods. These receptors are shown in the same orientation they would have on the retina, with their tips pointing toward the back of the retina. (See Figure 4.3.)

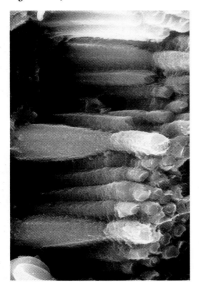

the fovea. Each retina contains only about 6 million cones, in contrast to about 125 million rods (Pugh, 1988).

A poorly designed visual system might feature only one kind of light receptor, which would need to perform a variety of tasks in a variety of different conditions. Instead, humans have two specialized kinds of receptors, each excelling in its own area. This dual receptor system is another illustration of the theme that humans are remarkably well equipped to function in our environment. Your cones excel in transmitting color information in a well-lit situation, as when you inspected the photograph of the frog in Figure 4.1. In contrast, rods are active when you walk outside at night. Rods are highly sensitive in detecting faint spots of light when the illumination is poor (Schnapf & Baylor, 1987). Because we have two specialized receptor systems, we can see under a much broader range of lighting conditions than if we had only cones or only rods.

The cones and rods use transduction to convert light into electrical activity at the cell membrane. This electrical message is received by the *bipolar cells* and then passed on to the ganglion cells. The **ganglion cells** collect messages from the bipolar cells and then send this information (in the form of action potentials) out of the eye, in the direction of the brain.

Each retina contains more than 130 million cones and rods, but only about 1 million ganglion cells. As a result, many receptor cells must share synaptic connections with each ganglion cell. On the retina—as in life itself—the sharing is far from equal. Specifically, the cones receive far more than their equal share. In the foveal region of the retina, which is rich with cones, a ganglion cell might receive information from just one or two cones (Masland, 1996). When you are examining a detailed picture, that cone-rich area of the retina will pass on most of the tiny details to the ganglion cells. In contrast, in the rod-rich edges of the retina, a ganglion cell might receive information from 200 rods. Suppose that this region of the retina was exposed to a pattern of very narrow black-and-white stripes. The rods might accurately pick up that detailed information about the stripes. However, all this information is fed into just one ganglion, which does not have the ability to transmit all that detail. Instead of precise stripes, the ganglion cell would simply code a blurry gray. An important implication of this unequal sharing of ganglion cells is that vision is sharper in the cone-rich fovea than in the rod-rich edges.

The axons of the ganglion cells gather together to form the optic nerve. The **optic nerve,** which is slightly narrower than your little finger, travels out of the eye and onward to higher levels of visual processing. Turn back to Figure 4.3 and notice that the location where the optic nerve leaves the retina is called the **blind spot.** Neither rods nor cones inhabit this blind spot. As a result, if a small, isolated stimulus reaches this part of the retina, you will not see it. Try Demonstration 4.1 to experience your own blind spot.

From the Eye to the Brain Figure 4.5 illustrates how information travels in its route to the visual cortex. As you can see, the two optic nerves come together at a point called the optic chiasm (pronounced "*kye*-as-em"). At this point, the axons from the ganglion cells regroup. Trace the pathways in the figure to show that everything that was originally registered on the left half of each retina ends up on the left side of the brain; everything from the right half of each retina travels toward the right side. As you might guess, this complex partial crossover arrangement accomplishes something important for the human visual system: We have **binocular vision;** our two eyes work together, and we have partially overlapping fields of view. An object toward your left is registered on both retinas. However, information from that object will eventually end up on the left side of your brain, where the information from both eyes can be compared. The images from the two eyes are slightly different; later in the chapter, we'll see how this binocular disparity helps us with distance perception.

Those ganglion cells that originated in the retina and passed through the optic chiasm transfer their messages to new sets of neurons in the midbrain and in the thalamus. (As Pages 88–89 noted, these structures play important roles in perception.) These new neurons then send messages to the visual cortex. As Chapter 3 pointed out, the **visual cortex** is the part of the brain that is concerned with vision. It is located at the back of your brain, just above your neck, and it is about the size of a credit card (Livingstone, 1987).

Cortical Neurons How do the cells in the visual cortex operate? Neuroscience researchers have discovered important information about the structure and the function of the visual cortex. Much of this research has used the single-cell recording technique. As Chapter 3 described, the **single-cell recording technique** requires inserting a microelectrode into an animal's cortex in order to record action potentials from individual cells.

Two prominent researchers, David Hubel and Torsten Wiesel, examined the primary visual cortex—the region of the visual cortex where the information from

---

DEMONSTRATION 4.1 The Blind Spot

Close your right eye, and with your left eye look at the X in the box below. Gradually move this page toward your eye and then away. Keep the distance in the range of 8–24 inches, and do not let your focus drift away from the X. At some point, the tree will fall on your blind spot, and it will seem to disappear.

In daily life, you are usually not aware of your blind spot for two reasons. First, each eye usually picks up an object that the other eye misses. Secondly, the human visual system spontaneously completes an object in which a part is missing (Ramachandran, 1992a, 1993; Ramachandran & Gregory, 1991). A later part in this chapter examines illusory contours, a similar tendency in which the visual system actively fills in the missing information.

X

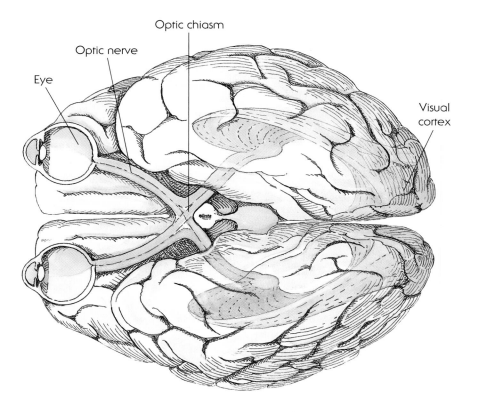

Optic chiasm

Optic nerve

Eye

Visual cortex

FIGURE 4.5

The visual pathway from the eye to the cortex.

the retina first arrives (Hubel, 1982; Hubel & Wiesel, 1965, 1979). First, they inserted the microelectrode into a specific cortical neuron of a cat. Then they systematically presented a series of visual stimuli to the specific region of the retina that was thought to be monitored by that cortical neuron. For each stimulus, Hubel and Wiesel recorded the response rate. Then they moved on to another cell to test its sensitivity to the visual stimuli.

Studies by Hubel and Wiesel and later researchers have demonstrated that neurons in the primary visual cortex—called simple cells—respond most vigorously to a stimulus with a specific orientation presented in a specific location (Heeger, 1994; Maunsell, 1995). For example, one particular neuron located in your primary visual cortex will produce a sudden burst of activity only when a line tilted 15 degrees is presented exactly in front of your retina. We'll see some important consequences of this orientation sensitivity later in the chapter. Other cells in the primary visual cortex—called complex cells—respond best to moving stimuli (Bruce & Green, 1990; Lennie, 1980).

Beyond the primary visual cortex, researchers have now identified more than 30 areas in the primate brain that are concerned with vision (Kosslyn & Koenig, 1992; Schiller, 1994; Sereno et al., 1995; Van Essen et al., 1992). Research in these other visual areas is especially challenging, though studies are now using a variety of imaging techniques to explore these more mysterious areas (Cowey, 1994; Sereno et al., 1995). In one set of studies, Zeki (1992) used the PET scan technique to study the human visual system. As Chapter 3 discussed, the **PET scan (positron emission tomography)** traces the chemical activity within the brain when people perform specific tasks. Zeki found that a boldly colored abstract painting produced the greatest activity in an area close to the center of the visual cortex. In contrast, a pattern of moving black-and-white squares produced the greatest activity in a different area, closer to the ear.

Neurons in several other areas of the cortex respond only to complex visual patterns. Thompson (1993) describes how Charles Gross and his colleagues at Harvard University stumbled upon the ideal stimulus for one region of the cortex. Some years ago,

Gross and his colleagues were using the single-cell recording technique in a monkey. They had presented the customary variety of visual stimuli, such as simple lines and bars of light. The neuron being monitored by the electrode failed to respond to any of these stimuli, and so the researchers decided to move on to another cell. One experimenter gave that cell a symbolic farewell by waving his hand in front of the monkey's eye. To the researchers' surprise, the cell immediately began to fire rapidly to the moving hand! The excited researchers then cut out a variety of hand-shaped stimuli and waved them in front of the monkey's eye. They found that this cell responded most strongly to a hand that was shaped like a monkey's paw. You'll recall from the "In Depth" feature in Chapter 3 that the inferotemporal cortex is one region of the brain that has been explored in some detail. Specifically, neuroscientists now know that this region is crucial in recognizing complex stimuli in both monkeys and humans (Farah & Ratcliff, 1994).

In our tour of the visual system, we have seen that the cells in the first step of visual processing—the rods and the cones—only require light in order to respond. Within the visual cortex, however, the cells become increasingly "picky," until they respond only to selected stimuli containing certain contours and movement patterns. Later in this chapter, we will examine the distinctive-features approach to shape perception. This approach argues that the cortical cells' specific sensitivity to lines, angles, and contours helps us recognize shapes such as letters of the alphabet.

Basic Visual Functions

We have seen that the visual system can extract information about the lines and angles in an object's shape. In addition, the visual system can appreciate fine details, and it can also adapt to a wide variety of lighting conditions. To perform other tasks, the eyes can also move in ways you may not have previously appreciated. However, the visual system is somewhat fragile, and so several kinds of visual disorders are worth exploring.

Acuity Suppose you are walking and you spot a shape in the distance—is it a person or a tall bush? Does the dot on the horizon represent one tree or two trees close together? Is that someone's glove next to the classroom entrance? These all represent acuity tasks. **Visual acuity** is the ability to see precise details in a scene.

What does it mean to have 20/40 vision on an acuity test? Usually this kind of score is obtained when an observer reads an eye chart that has rows of letters ranging from large to small, while standing 20 feet away from the chart. If you can read the letters that a person with normal vision can read at 20 feet, then you have 20/20 vision. Suppose you can read letters at 20 feet that a person with normal vision can read at 40 feet. Your acuity would then be called 20/40 vision. A person whose vision with corrective lenses is poorer than 20/200 is considered legally blind (Tielsch et al., 1995).

Dark Adaptation You have probably had an experience like this: In the middle of a sunny afternoon, you enter a movie theater. The movie has already started, and you grope your way through the theater, reaching for what you hope is the back of an empty seat, rather than someone's shoulder. (My grandfather was once asked whether he had known the woman who sat on him in a dark theater. Thinking fast, he replied that he did not know her name, but he could identify her nationality: She was a Laplander.) After several minutes in the dark, however, you can easily see which seats are empty.

The darkened theater experience is one example of **dark adaptation;** your eyes adjust and become more sensitive as you remain in the dark. As you have discovered, your sensitivity increases tremendously after just 10 minutes. Dark adaptation allows us to extend the range of light levels in which the visual system can function. The illumination from the bright noon sun is about 100 million times as intense as the illumination from the moon (Hood & Finkelstein, 1986). Nonetheless, the visual system is so superbly designed that we can function in both kinds of illumination, as well as in the vast intermediate region.

How can we explain dark adaptation? Consistent with the theme that humans are complicated, most psychological processes have more than one explanation. Three mechanisms help account for dark adaptation: (1) The pupils dilate to let more light pass through. (2) In comparison to rods exposed to light, our dark-adapted rods contain a greater amount of the special chemical that determines sensitivity (Pugh, 1988). (3) Neurons at higher levels in the cortex must also play an important role, although the details of this process are not clear (Frumkes, 1990; Green & Powers, 1982).

Your eyes use smooth pursuit movements to follow the flight of a bird.

Eye Movements   Another function of the visual system is so obvious that we seldom appreciate what it accomplishes for us: Our eyes move, rather than remaining in a fixed position. One kind of eye movement is called **pursuit movement,** which is the eye movement we use to track a moving object.

Demonstration 4.2 illustrates a second important kind of eye movement, known as saccadic movement (pronounced "suh-*kaad*-dick"). **Saccadic movement** is the rapid, jerky movement that we use to read or scan a visual scene (Abrams, 1994). Turn back to Figure 4.3 and notice the fovea, the tiny region of the retina with the best acuity. You need saccadic movements in order to bring the fovea into position with the object you want to look at next (Rayner, 1993).

When you read, the size of the average saccadic movement is about 8 or 9 letters (Rayner, 1993). Researchers have devised equipment that monitors eye movement and pauses, so psychologists now know many details about these saccadic movements (Ferreira, 1994). For example, psychologists have found that the eye fixates longer on the most information-rich parts of a sentence and on scenes that are surprising rather than expected (Balota et al., 1985; De Graef, 1992; Rayner & Pollatsek, 1987).

When you examine perceptual processes, you often realize that a skill you take for granted is really quite mysterious. A major mystery concerned with saccadic eye movements is this: We make about three saccades every second, so that objects in our world occupy different positions on the retina from one moment to the next. Nevertheless, your visual world seems coherent and stable, rather than a turmoil of disjointed photographs (Ferreira, 1994; Irwin, 1996). The explanation for this stability is still elusive, but it may depend on the fact that our eyes pause during a fixation for a period of time that is about 10 times as long as the saccadic movement. Thus, the stable images are relatively long-lasting (Irwin, 1992, 1996).

The information about saccadic movements provides clear evidence for Theme 1, that humans are well equipped to function in their environment. The eye is designed so that a small region of the retina has excellent visual acuity. Furthermore, the visual system allows our eyes to jump across the page, exposing new words and new scenes to the fovea. Finally our eye movements take in the most useful and unusual region of a stimulus, and the visual system conveys a sense of stable images, rather than chaos.

Visual Disorders   Table 4.2 lists some of the more common visual disorders, beginning with three major focusing disorders that reduce our ability to see fine details. Notice also that people can experience difficulty with depth perception if the two eyes do not work together. Furthermore, visual impairment can be caused when the lens, retina, cornea, or ganglion cells are somehow damaged. This table points out the importance of eye checkups in order to prevent significant visual problems.

DEMONSTRATION 4.2 Saccadic Eye Movements

Glance over at the opposite page and select a word in the middle of the page. Focus on that specific word, and notice how the letters are increasingly fuzzy in the words that are farther from your target word. (If you cannot explain why, check the discussion of rods and cones in the retina.)

Now start to read the entire sentence. Are you aware that your eye is advancing across the page in small, jerky leaps? Try to read the next sentences by letting your eyes roll smoothly across the page. You will probably find that your eyes can indeed move smoothly, but you do not seem to be perceiving the words.

TABLE 4.2 Some Common Visual Disorders

FOCUSING DISORDERS

- *Nearsightedness.* If the eyeball is too long or the lens of the eye is too thick, the images of objects are focused in front of the retina. Nearsighted people can see only *nearby* objects clearly.
- *Farsightedness.* If the eyeball is too short or the lens of the eye is too thin, the images of objects are focused at a point behind the retina. Farsighted people can see only *distant* objects clearly.
- *Astigmatism.* People with astigmatism have a cornea that is irregularly curved, with some areas having more curvature than others. As a result, some regions will appear blurry.

DISORDERS INVOLVING EYE COORDINATION

- *Strabismus.* This disorder occurs when the muscles of the two eyes do not work together. Thus, an object that is registered on the fovea of one eye will not be registered on the other fovea. This disorder should be corrected in early childhood to allow the development of proper binocular vision. The disorder occurs in about 2% of all children (Vaughan et al., 1995).
- *Stereoblindness.* If strabismus is not corrected, stereoblindness develops. People with this disorder cannot use the depth information from binocular vision to aid distance perception (discussed on Pages 130–131).

DISORDERS OF THE LENS AND RETINA

- *Cataracts.* Cataracts occur when the lens loses its transparency and becomes too cloudy; light cannot pass through to the retina. Some loss of lens transparency is normal in people over the age of 70 (Vaughan et al., 1989). If vision is seriously impaired, the lens of the eye can be surgically removed and a substitute lens implanted, or special corrective lenses can be worn.
- *Diabetic retinopathy.* This disorder occurs when people have had severe diabetes for many years, causing fluid to leak out from the thickened blood vessels that supply the retina. Diabetic retinopathy is the leading cause of blindness among people between the ages of 25 and 74 (D'Amico, 1994).

OTHER VISUAL DISORDERS

- *Corneal damage.* An object can scratch the cornea or become lodged in the cornea. The outer layer of the cornea protects the eye from disease germs. Consequently, anyone with corneal damage should immediately receive medical care.
- *Glaucoma.* Normally, the fluids inside the eyeball maintain the eye's characteristic shape. However, in glaucoma, extra fluid within the eye causes too much pressure and can lead to deterioration of the ganglion cells in the retina and optic nerve. In the United States, 1.5% of people over the age of 40 have glaucoma. People over 40 should be regularly tested for glaucoma in order to prevent blindness.

Critical Thinking Exercise 4.2

Write down your answers to the following questions about basic visual functions:

a. Acuity is often measured with an eye chart containing rows of letters. What is a potential problem with this measure of acuity?

b. Recent research has shown that residents of nursing homes are more likely to be blind than people of the same age who live in the community (Klein & Klein, 1995; Tielsch et al., 1995). Something about living in a nursing home could encourage blindness, but can you think of a more likely explanation?

Color Vision

I know an artist who had just finished preparing the family meal when she noticed that everything she was about to serve was yellow. To add visual interest to the dinner, she stirred several drops of blue food coloring into the creamed corn. Her father refused to eat the lime-green corn; his expectations about customary food color had been entirely disrupted. Color is such a critical part of an object's identity that we may protest when that color is altered.

Most of the early research on color vision was inspired by a debate about two different color vision theories, called trichromatic theory and opponent-process theory (Kaiser & Boynton, 1996). Some creative theorizing and more recent research on the physiology of color vision have resolved the conflict peacefully. We now know that both color vision theories are correct. However, they apply to different stages of the visual processing system. Let's see how the two theories have been integrated.

Trichromatic Theory   According to the **trichromatic theory** of color vision, the retina contains three kinds of cones, each sensitive to light from a different portion of the spectrum (Kaiser & Boynton, 1996). This theory was originally proposed in the 1800s, and researchers began to uncover physiological evidence for three kinds of cones about a century later (Dartnall et al., 1983; Rushton, 1958). Perception researchers refer to these cones in terms of the wavelength to which they are most sensitive: short (in the 430 nm range), medium (in the 530 nm range), and long (in the 560 nm range). By combining different stimulation levels from each of these three kinds of cones, the visual system can code the wide variety of colors we see in our daily lives.

Trichromatic theory explains how we can discriminate among the various colors of the spectrum, but it leaves some questions unanswered. For example, why can we perceive a greenish blue, but why is a yellowish blue impossible? And how can we explain chromatic adaptation—a phenomenon illustrated in Demonstration 4.3—in which prolonged exposure to yellow produces blue, and prolonged exposure to green produces red?

Opponent-Process Theory   The opponent-process theory was developed in the late 1800s to account for color phenomena such as impossible color combinations and chromatic adaptation. According to the current interpretation of color vision, trichromatic theory explains how the cones gather color information. This information is then passed on to the ganglion cells and other cells, which operate in an opponent-process fashion (Kaiser & Boynton, 1996).

The current version of **opponent-process theory** states that ganglion cells and other cells closer to the visual cortex operate in an opponent fashion. Specifically, the cells respond by increasing their activity when one color is present and decreasing their activity when another color is present. For example, one ganglion cell might increase its activity when yellow is present and decrease it when blue is present. A different ganglion cell will increase activity when blue is present and decrease it when yellow is present.

DEMONSTRATION 4.3   Chromatic Adaptation

Set a sheet of plain white paper to the side of the picture below. Stare at the picture for 30 to 40 seconds, focusing on the star in the lower right corner and being certain not to move your eyes. Quickly transfer your gaze to the white paper and notice the afterimage. You can blink several times to preserve the afterimage.

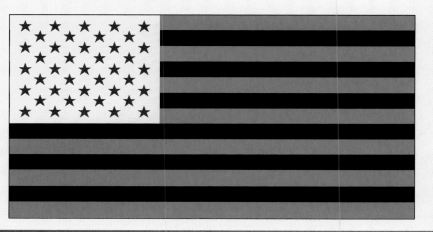

Therefore, this set of cells works in an opposing, mirror-image fashion. A second opponent works the same way for red and green. A third opponent system responds to light and dark. These three opponent processes occur at the ganglion level and also in the thalamus, a location on the route to the visual cortex.

How does opponent-process theory explain the two color phenomena discussed earlier? You cannot see a yellowish blue because any cell that increases its activity to yellow will decrease its activity to blue and vice versa. (You also cannot see a greenish red.) Furthermore, you saw a blue background for the stars in Demonstration 4.3 when you shifted your eyes to the white paper, because prolonged viewing of yellow weakens the cells' response to yellow stimuli. As a result, the opponent color—blue—remained relatively strong and activated. Similarly, prolonged staring at the green stripes leaves the opponent color—red—relatively strong; staring at the black stripes and black stars leaves the opponent process—white—relatively strong.

Color Deficiencies Some of you reading this section may not experience the color vision effects we've been discussing. You may have a **color deficiency,** or difficulty in discriminating among different colors. For example, about 8% of males and less than 1% of females have some form of red-green color vision deficiency (Birch, 1993). Try Demonstration 4.4, which shows two typical items in a much more extensive test for color deficiencies.

Notice that the appropriate term is color deficiency. The term *color blindness* is inaccurate because almost all of the people affected do see some colors. Only a very small number of people with only one type of cone receptor—or with none at all—are truly color blind (Kaiser & Boynton, 1996).

Shape Perception

We have examined how the visual system can see fine details in a scene (acuity). We can function in both bright sunlight and pale moonlight (light adaptation and dark adaptation). Our eyes can also execute several specialized movements, such as pursuit movement and saccadic movement. The visual system also registers information about color. However, this list is only a small sample of the visual system's talents. Now let's move away from sensation to consider the topics more commonly associated with visual perception. These topics include the perception of shape, motion, distance, constancy, and illusion.

DEMONSTRATION 4.4 Examples of Items From a Color-Deficiency Test

Find a location in which the lighting is a little less bright than you normally would use for reading. Examine the two test items below. What numbers do you see? The answers appear at the end of the chapter. These items test for sensitivity to reds and greens. A complete test of color deficiencies would include a large number of items in each of many colors.

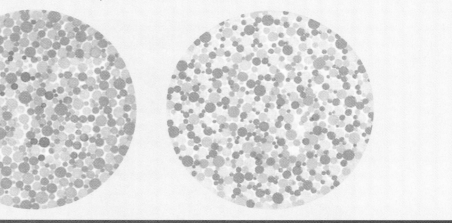

Without shape perception, our visual world would consist of random patches of light and dark, a disorderly mass of colored and uncolored fragments. However, our perception is quite orderly. For example, look up from your book right now and notice that your visual world contains objects with distinct borders and clear-cut shapes. Even the messiest room reveals pattern and organization, so that you can recognize objects—a lamp, a psychology professor, and a letter of the alphabet. Despite all the visual clutter, our shape perception is usually a highly accurate mirror of reality—consistent with our theme of human competence. Several important aspects of shape perception include the figure-ground relationship, the laws of grouping, and pattern recognition.

Figure-Ground Relationship   If you look out a nearby window, you'll appreciate how well your vision world is organized. An automobile forms a distinct shape against the parking lot in the background, and the lamppost does not blend into the grass beneath it. An important component of this organization is called the **figure-ground relationship:** When two areas share a common boundary, the figure is the distinct shape with clearly defined edges, and the ground is the part that is left over, forming the background in the scene. For example, in Figure 4.6, the pitcher is the figure and the wall is the ground.

The history section in Chapter 1 introduced the Gestalt approach. According to the **Gestalt approach,** we perceive objects as well-organized, whole structures, instead of separate, isolated parts. Gestalt psychologists emphasized that factors such as the figure-ground relationship help us achieve this organization. These early researchers described several characteristics of the figure-ground relationship. For example, the figure has a distinct shape, whereas the ground seems shapeless. Also, the ground seems to continue behind the figure. Finally, the figure seems closer to the viewer, in comparison to the ground (Rubin, 1915/1958). Notice how the figure and the ground in Figure 4.6 follow all three principles.

In our daily lives, the figure-ground relationship is almost always clear-cut. But sometimes you'll perceive an ambiguous relationship, perhaps because an artist has created one. Notice how you must work to force the faces in the background of Figure 4.7 to become figures. In fact, many people have difficulty spontaneously reversing ambiguous figures (Rock & Mitchener, 1992).

Laws of Grouping   We've discussed how Gestalt psychologists emphasize figure-ground relationships. Gestalt psychology's second important contribution to shape

FIGURE 4.6

An Illustration of the Figure-Ground Relationship
This pitcher and its background illustrate the figure-ground relationship.

FIGURE 4.7

Ambiguous Figure-Ground Relationship
"The Forest Has Eyes" by Bev Doolittle, 1984. © The Greenwich Workshop, Inc.

perception is the laws of grouping, which describe why certain objects seem to go together, instead of remaining isolated and disorganized (Palmer, 1992). Here are the four most common Gestalt laws of grouping:

1. The **law of proximity** states that objects near each other tend to be perceived as a unit.

2. The **law of similarity** states that objects similar to each other tend to be seen as a unit.

3. The **law of good continuation** states that we tend to perceive smooth, continuous lines, rather than discontinuous fragments.

4. The **law of closure** states that a figure with a gap will be perceived as a closed, intact figure.

Each of these Gestalt laws is illustrated in Figure 4.8.

The Gestalt psychologists first proposed these laws of grouping at the beginning of the twentieth century, but they continue to inspire current research. Psychologists are still discovering new laws of grouping (Palmer & Rock, 1994) as well as new psychological processes operating for some of the familiar laws (Foley et al., 1997). Some of the recent research also examines an unresolved controversy about how the laws work. The early Gestalt psychologists proposed that the laws of grouping operate as soon as we see a stimulus, before we analyze it. However, current psychologists are suggesting that we must recognize an object before the laws of grouping can operate (Palmer et al., 1996; M. A. Peterson, 1994; Peterson & Gibson, 1994). Let's now consider this related topic of pattern recognition.

Pattern Recognition How do we recognize a visual pattern? The process seems so simple. When you read, you recognize the letters in a word. A tall, slender person

FIGURE 4.8

The Gestalt Laws of Grouping

(upper left) The law of proximity. You perceive the four stamps in the lower left as a unit, because you group items together that are near each other.

(upper right) The law of similarity. You group this arrangement in terms of horizontal rows, grouping together the cats on this wrapping paper because they are facing the same direction.

(lower left) The law of good continuation. You see each pencil as forming a straight, continuous unit, rather than a series of right-angle zigzags.

(lower right) The law of closure. You see the left-hand border of this greeting card as a closed, intact edge, even though it is interrupted by the leaf that the dove is carrying.

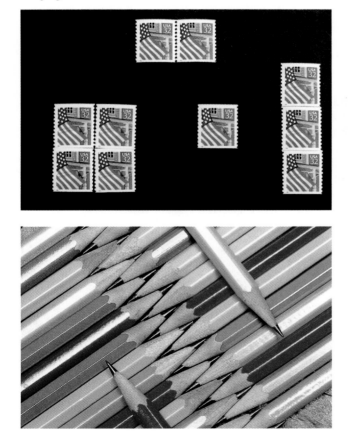

approaches—with a moustache, flannel shirt, and jeans—and you recognize Henry from your political science class. Let's consider how we might recognize simple patterns such as letters and more complex, three-dimensional objects.

Eleanor Gibson (1969) proposed that we differentiate between letters of the alphabet on the basis of **distinctive features,** or characteristics such as straight versus curved lines. Thus, the letter E has four straight lines, whereas the letter O has none. We recognize the letter C because it is the only curved letter with an opening at the side that is also symmetrical. The distinctive-features approach to pattern perception is supported by neuroscience research discussed on Page 121, showing that neurons in the visual cortex are sensitive to lines, angles, and contours.

A more recent theory proposed by Irving Biederman (1987, 1990) explains that we recognize more complex, three-dimensional patterns in terms of their parts or components. The basic assumption of **recognition-by-components theory** is that an object can be represented as an arrangement of simple three-dimensional shapes. Gibson showed that lines and curves can be combined to create an alphabetical letter. Similarly, Biederman argues that basic 3-D shapes, called *geons,* can be combined to create meaningful objects. Figure 4.9 shows five of the proposed geons, together with several objects that can be constructed from the geons. The recognition-by-components model has not yet been extensively tested. However, the early reports—based on people with specific visual deficits, as well as on normal people—are compatible with the model (Banks & Krajicek, 1991; Biederman et al., 1991).

Both the distinctive-features approach and the recognition-by-components theory focus on bottom-up processing. **Bottom-up processing** emphasizes the role of the sensory receptors in processing the basic stimuli. Processing begins, for example, when a slanted line in the letter N is registered on the retina. The rods, cones, and other neurons at the bottom (or most basic) level of perception will produce bursts of electrical activity, which ultimately reach the visual cortex and even higher levels of visual processing (Dodwell, 1993).

However, shape perception also requires top-down processing. **Top-down processing** emphasizes the importance of the observers' concepts, expectations, and prior knowledge—the kind of information stored at the top (or highest) level of perception. Part of the reason you recognize your classmate Henry, when you see him, is that you expect to see him in the hallway near your classroom. Out of context—in your hometown hardware store—he would be more difficult to recognize. We've already mentioned the importance of these cognitive factors in the discussion of signal detection theory earlier in this chapter. We saw that expectations and prior knowledge influence the probability of saying "Yes, I perceive the stimulus." Perception therefore depends on both bottom-up and top-down processing.

Some of the most convincing evidence for top-down processing comes from research on letter recognition. According to the **word-superiority effect,** we perceive letters more accurately when they appear in words than in strings of unrelated letters or by themselves (Jordan & Bevan, 1994; Krueger, 1992). For example, suppose you are looking at a sequence of blurry letters. You can recognize the letter A more easily when you see it in the word HATS than when you see it in the meaningless nonword TASH or by itself, as the isolated letter A (Jordon & Bevan, 1994; Reicher, 1969). The surrounding letters in the word HATS provides a context that helps you recognize each letter. If the word-superiority effect (and, more generally, top-down processing) did not operate, you could not read so quickly and so accurately. In fact, you would probably still be reading through the first chapter of this book!

Motion Perception

So far, we've discussed shapes that are static—a letter frozen on a textbook page or a horse immobilized in a painting. But you glance up from your textbook to a world rich with motion. Consider the complexities of your motion perception as you leave your psychology classroom. You see a swirl of moving bodies and stationary objects, and your own perspective changes as you move through this visual chaos (Cutting et al., 1995).

FIGURE 4.9

Examples of geons(above) and representative objects that can be constructed from the geons (below).
Source: From Biederman, 1990.

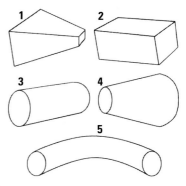

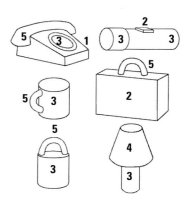

FIGURE 4.10

To illustrate biological motion, a man wears flashlight bulbs at his joints, and a film is made of his movements. In this photo, the camera shutter was kept open for several seconds and the lights trace paths in the picture. The man was initially sitting in a chair at the right of the photo with one leg swung over the other. Then he stood up and walked across the floor to the left.

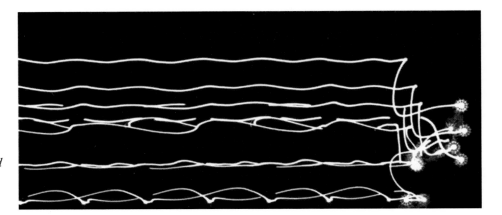

Motion perception is such a basic skill that even primitive insects like the fly are superbly talented in this domain (Johansson, 1985; Ullman, 1983). Some of the most interesting discoveries about motion perception concern **biological motion,** which is the pattern of movement made by people and other living things. Gunnar Johansson, a Swedish psychologist, attached small flashlight bulbs to the major joints of a male colleague, as shown in Figure 4.10. Johansson made a movie of this man, who moved around the darkened room. Then Johansson showed the movie to groups of observers who were asked to interpret the pattern of lights. Even though the movie showed only 12 tiny lights, the observers could readily tell the difference between walking and jogging. When the man pretended to limp, the observers easily identified the change in body movement (Johansson, 1975, 1994; Johannson et al., 1980).

Other researchers have discovered that observers watching a pattern of lights can distinguish a female walker from a male walker (Cutting, 1983). They can also appreciate biological motion when as many as 66 irrelevant moving dots are superimposed on the walking figure (Bertenthal & Pinto, 1994).

Biological motion is complicated to describe mathematically, yet it is easy for our visual system to process. Because we are so quick and so accurate in identifying human movement, researchers have proposed that some neurons may be specially organized to decode and interpret this kind of motion (Johansson, 1985, 1994). Notice that this suggestion is highly consistent with the evolutionary psychology approach.

FIGURE 4.11

Distance is obvious in this photo because it provides information about relative size, overlap, texture gradient, and linear perspective.

Distance Perception

Except when we read, our visual activity usually involves objects that are solid, rather than flat, or else figures on television screens that convey depth and distance. So let's move into the third dimension as we consider distance perception.

A major challenge for psychologists interested in perception is to explain how we can appreciate that objects have depth, as well as height and width, and how we realize that an eraser is closer to us than the chalkboard. After all, your retina only registers height and width; the chalkboard is not represented as being *deeper* into the surface of the retina, in comparison with the eraser.

As it happens, our visual world is rich with information about depth and distance (Epstein, 1995). In fact, most perception textbooks list at least a dozen (e.g., Coren et al., 1994; Goldstein, 1996; Matlin & Foley, 1997). As you can probably guess, any process that occurs so automatically and so accurately is likely to be aided by a variety of factors.

Some of these sources of distance information are **monocular**—they can be seen with just one eye and can also be represented in a painting or a photograph (Cutting & Vishton, 1995). These monocular factors include the following:

1. *Relative size:* If two similar objects appear together, the one that occupies more space on the retina seems closer to us (S. Rogers, 1995). For example, notice the relative size of the arches in Figure 4.11.

FIGURE 4.12

In this photo, distance is conveyed by monocular factors such as relative size (the hills) and texture gradient (the wheat).

2. *Overlap:* One of the most persuasive distance cues is overlap; when one object partly covers another, the completely visible object seems closer than the partly covered object (Cutting & Vishton, 1995).

3. *Texture gradient:* The texture of surfaces is denser for more distant objects. Texture gradient is an important factor in distance perception, but its value has only recently been acknowledged (Gibson, 1979; Hagen, 1985; R. Schwartz, 1994). Notice, for example, how the texture of the wheat in Figure 4.12 is much more tightly packed and dense toward the horizon. To appreciate texture gradient, turn the picture upside down. Doesn't the texture look bizarre?

4. *Linear perspective:* Parallel lines seem to meet in the distance, as you probably learned in art class. We now take perspective for granted when we look at art, but paintings prior to the fifteenth century look flat because artists did not show linear perspective cues (Wade & Swanston, 1991).

5. *Atmospheric perspective:* Distant objects often look blurry and bluish gray (O'Shea et al., 1994). The series of mountains in Figure 4.13 is a good example of atmospheric perspective.

Other depth information is **binocular,** requiring two eyes. The most important binocular factor can be traced to the fact that your eyes are about 3 inches apart. This distance guarantees that any object closer than about 30 feet will present a slightly different view to each eye (Cutting & Vishton, 1995). On Page 120, we noted this difference between the two retinal images of an object, a difference known as **binocular disparity.** Your visual system is so sensitive to binocular disparity that it can detect different views that correspond to one-thousandth of a millimeter (0.001 mm) when registered on the retina (Yellot, 1981). To give you a feeling for this degree of precision, the wire on a paperclip is about 1 millimeter thick; imagine splitting this slender wire into 1,000 parts to create a detectable difference. The visual cortex contains cells that are sensitive to these tiny discrepancies. These cells fire rapidly when they detect binocular disparity (Nakayama & Shimojo, 1992; Ohzawa et al., 1990; Poggio, 1995).

Binocular information is extremely helpful in depth perception, and people are much more accurate when they receive information from both eyes, rather than just one eye (Foley, 1980, 1985). Take a moment to review the visual disorders involving eye coordination (Page 124), so you can see why these disorders should not be treated casually.

FIGURE 4.13

Notice the atmospheric perspective in this photo of mountains in the Adirondacks.

FIGURE 4.14

Size and Shape Constancy
You perceive this book as maintaining its normal size, even when it is moved farther away from you (size constancy). You also perceive the book as maintaining its rectangular shape, even though it projects a trapezoidal image when viewed from a different angle (shape constancy).

Constancy

When you move around in the world, you approach objects and then move away. However, the telephone does not seem to grow in size as you run to answer it. As Figure 4.14 shows, a book assumes a different shape on your retina when you view it from a different angle—it becomes a trapezoid shape, rather than a rectangle. Still, you know that it did not *really* change its shape. These examples illustrate constancy. **Constancy** means that we perceive objects as having constant characteristics (such as size and shape), even when there are changes in the information that reaches our eyes (Wade & Swanston, 1991). Perception therefore allows us to move beyond the information that our retinas register.

Size constancy means that an object's perceived size stays the same, even when the distance changes between the viewer and the object. Demonstration 4.5 illustrates size constancy. One factor that contributes to size constancy is that we are familiar with many objects' customary size, such as the size of your hand. Another explanation for size constancy is that we unconsciously and automatically take distance into account when we see an object (Rock, 1983). Without being consciously aware of the process, we can figure out an object's true size with impressive accuracy

---

DEMONSTRATION 4.5 Size Constancy

Hold up your right hand, with your palm facing you, about 10 inches in front of your face. At the same time, hold up your left hand—also with your palm facing you—but stretch out your left arm as far as possible. Your hands create images of two different sizes on your retina. However—unless you are truly unusual—you'll report size constancy.

Source: Based on Wade & Swanston, 1991.

(McKee & Welch, 1992). The process cannot involve complicated mathematical calculations, however, because even animals use size constancy (Gogel, 1977).

An important American theorist, James J. Gibson (1959), argued that perception is much more direct. We do not need to perform any calculations—conscious or unconscious—because the environment is rich with information. For example, you know the size of an object by comparing it with the texture of the surrounding area. If you place this textbook on a tile floor, it would cover one linoleum tile, whether you viewed it from a distance of 3 feet or 30 feet. Tile, grass, strands of yarn in a carpet, and other kinds of background textures all provide a kind of yardstick for preserving size constancy.

We also have shape constancy, as shown in Figure 4.14. **Shape constancy** means that an object's perceived shape stays the same, even though an object changes its orientation toward the viewer. A compact disc does not distort itself into an oval when you view it from an angle; you know it remains round. Psychologists who favor the evolutionary perspective would argue that our ancestors needed information about the size and shape of dangerous animals in order to survive (McKee & Welch, 1992).

One other important constancy is **color constancy;** in general, an object's perceived hue tends to stay the same, despite changes in illumination (Brainard et al., 1993; Craven & Foster, 1992). Although our color constancy may be less accurate than the other constancies, a blue shirt seems to stay about the same color, whether we view it in the bright sunlight, in artificial light, or even under a yellow lightbulb. You may have noticed that your color constancy is less than perfect. For example, some colors in a painting may appear slightly different if you look at them by daylight and then under incandescent illumination at night (Jameson & Hurvich, 1989; Thompson et al., 1992).

Notice how the constancies simplify our perceptual world. We can rely on objects to stay the same, even when we change the way we view those objects. Otherwise, imagine the nightmare we would face! Objects would expand and shrink, stretch into uncharacteristic shapes, and take on unexpected colors. Perhaps a movie producer will adopt this nightmarish idea: Coming soon, to a theater near you . . . the new motion picture, *A World Without Constancies!*

Illusions

Before you read further, try Demonstration 4.6, which shows the Poggendorff illusion. An **illusion** is a discrepancy between perception and reality, which occurs as a result of normal sensory processes (Wenderoth, 1992). Illusions lead us to make errors in the orientations of lines (as in Demonstration 4.6), in the length of lines, and in the perception of contours.

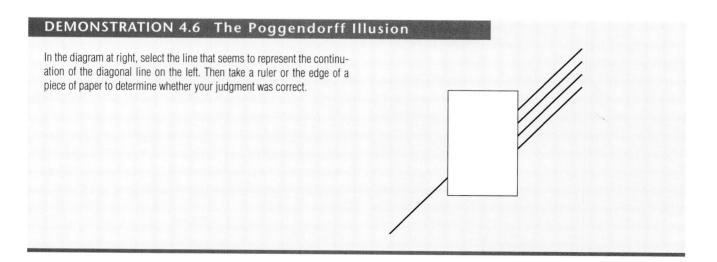

DEMONSTRATION 4.6 The Poggendorff Illusion

In the diagram at right, select the line that seems to represent the continuation of the diagonal line on the left. Then take a ruler or the edge of a piece of paper to determine whether your judgment was correct.

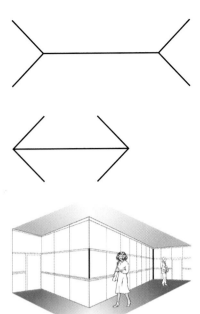

FIGURE 4.15

Two Versions of the Müller-Lyer Illusion

(top) The classic Müller-Lyer illusion.

(bottom) In this variant of the classic Müller-Lyer illusion, which of the two dark vertical lines looks longer? The additional distance cues typically make the illusion even stronger.

FIGURE 4.16

The Ponzo Illusion

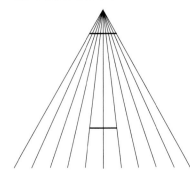

Why do psychologists study visual illusions? One reason is that they are intriguing; our perception is usually so accurate that a mistake is interesting. A second reason is that illusions help us understand our underlying perceptual processes. If the visual system makes consistent mistakes, we can draw conclusions about how visual information is altered when it passes from the retina to the cortex. We'll also see in the chapters on memory and cognition that psychologists study our occasional errors in these areas to help identify some general principles about how people remember and think.

A final reason for studying illusions is that they can have practical applications. For example, in 1965, the Poggendorff illusion was responsible for a tragic plane crash (Coren & Girgus, 1978). Two airplanes were about to land in the New York City area. A cloud formation separated them, and the Poggendorff illusion created the perception that they were heading directly toward each other—similar to the line on the left and the bottom right line in Demonstration 4.6. Quickly, the two pilots changed their paths to correct what seemed to be an error. The planes collided. Four people died and 49 others were injured—and only an illusion was to blame.

Let's look more closely at two common categories of illusions, those involving line length and those that include an illusory contour.

Line-Length Illusions Figure 4.15 shows two versions of the most famous visual illusion, the Müller-Lyer illusion. In each case, the two lines are actually the same length. However, the "wings outward" version of the classic illusion looks about 25% longer than the "wings inward" version. One of several factors that creates this illusion is that people move their eyes a longer distance to perceive the entire figure in the "wings outward" version. When our eyes move a longer distance, we tend to perceive the figure to be longer (Coren, 1981).

Figure 4.16 shows the Ponzo illusion, a second line-length illusion. The bar on top looks longer in this illusion. Can you figure out why? According to one popular explanation, we interpret the converging set of 11 lines as conveying linear perspective. The top of the figure definitely seems farther away. Therefore, the horizontal bar that appears in the "distant" part of the figure must also be farther away. The rules of constancy tell us that we must consider distance when we judge the size of an object, so we judge that "distant" bar to be bigger. This explanation for the Ponzo illusion and others that contain strong depth cues is called the **theory of misapplied constancy** (Gillam, 1980).

Our susceptibility to illusions such as the Ponzo illusion seems to contradict the theme that humans are extremely competent and accurate. However, this theme also noted that many of our errors can be traced to strategies that usually produce correct responses. In most cases, cues suggesting linear perspective *do* mean that the point of convergence is more distant. We therefore make a "smart mistake" when we see depth in Figure 4.16.

Illusory Contours Figure 4.17 is an example of an **illusory contour,** a figure in which we see edges even though they are not physically present. For example, this figure seems to show a white triangle against a background of three circles and an outlined triangle.

Illusory figures have two important characteristics (Meyer & Petry, 1987). First, a distinct surface—such as a solid white triangle—seems to be present. This surface often seems to be brighter than the background, even though the intensity registered on the retina is actually identical (Kanizsa, 1976). Second, a distinct edge or contour appears to surround the illusory figure. The edge even continues in the regions that lack a true contour (such as the white regions between the black circles and the outlined triangle in Figure 4.17).

Why do we see illusory contours? Coren and Porac (1983) argue that we create illusory contours because we prefer to see simple, familiar figures—rather than meaningless, disorganized parts. As the Gestalt approach argues, our perceptions tend to be well organized. In Figure 4.17, for example, we could see circles with wedges sliced out, alternating with three V-shaped lines. However, instead of this unnecessarily complicated interpretation, our visual system prefers to use distance cues—such as overlap—to sort out the picture. Therefore, we see a white triangle placed in front of the background.

As some researchers argue, illusory contours arise because the visual system essentially tries to solve a mystery when it attempts to sort out figure and ground (Parks, 1986; Rock, 1987). Notice that this distance-cue explanation requires top-down processing. Our expectations and prior knowledge—about the way one object blocks the objects behind it—make sense of an otherwise puzzling and disorderly jumble.

So far, our discussion of illusory contours has emphasized top-down processing. However, some researchers are beginning to examine bottom-up explanations for the phenomenon (Gordon & Earle, 1992). For example, some cells in the visual cortex seem to respond to illusory contours (e.g., Ramachandran, 1987; Sheth et al., 1996; Winckelgren, 1992). Researchers continue to create illusory contours, such as the ones in Figure 4.18, and they continue to explore their characteristics. However, the complete explanation for illusory contours has not yet been developed. As Diane Halpern and her coauthors (1983) remarked, "The search for the best theory to explain the perception of contours that do not physically exist has proven as illusory as the nature of the contours themselves" (p. 293).

FIGURE 4.17

An Example of Illusory Contour
Note that the white upright triangle appears to be bordered by a clear-cut contour, even in the regions where no physical contour actually appears.
Source: From Kanizsa, 1976.

Critical Thinking Exercise 4.3

Write down your answers to the following questions about illusions:

a. What would an evolutionary psychologist be likely to say about the frequency of illusions in our daily lives?

b. Suppose a psychologist was examining the Müller-Lyer illusion, and he presented the two versions of the line exactly as you saw them in Figure 4.15. Observers were instructed to adjust the length of the line in the "wings inward" version until it equaled the length of the line in the "wings outward" version (which always appeared on top). The researcher found that the observers created a "wings inward" line that was 28% longer than the "wings outward" line. How would you criticize the methodology of this study?

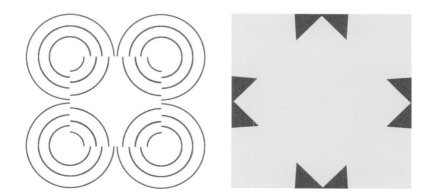

FIGURE 4.18

Two Examples of Illusory Contour
Note that illusory contours can be obtained with colored figures, as well as black-and-white ones.

SECTION SUMMARY: *VISION*

1. The cones and the rods in the retina absorb light rays. The light is converted to action potentials, which are passed on to other neurons and eventually reach the visual cortex.

2. Several dozen regions in the cortex—beyond the primary visual cortex—are responsible for more complex visual processing.

3. Two important visual skills are visual acuity and dark adaptation. In addition, the eye can make pursuit movements and saccadic movements.

4. Two processes are important in color perception: (a) The three kinds of cones are sensitive to different parts of the spectrum, as trichromatic theory points out; and (b) pairs of cells at the ganglion level and beyond function in an opponent-processing fashion.

5. Shape perception is aided by the figure-ground relationship and by the Gestalt laws of grouping.

6. Eleanor Gibson proposed a distinctive-features approach to explain how we perceive simple shapes such as letters; Irving Biederman's recognition-by-components theory is designed to explain our perception of complex three-dimensional figures. Top-down processing also facilitates pattern recognition.

7. Humans can readily recognize biological motion and can accurately identify subtle differences in human motion.

8. We perceive distance and depth because of a variety of monocular factors—such as overlap and texture gradient—and also because of binocular disparity.

9. The visual system demonstrates constancy. Size constancy, shape constancy, and color constancy ensure that an object's qualities are perceived as staying the same, even when we view that object from different distances and angles and in different lighting conditions.

10. An illusion is a discrepancy between perception and reality; illusions help psychologists to identify important consistencies in visual processes. For example, the Ponzo illusion shows that we may rely too strongly on constancy, and illusory contours demonstrate the importance of top-down processing.

HEARING

Vision is certainly our most prominent perceptual ability. However, people who are both deaf and blind often miss their hearing more than their vision. For example, Helen Keller once wrote the following in a letter:

> I am just as deaf as I am blind. The problems of deafness are deeper and more complex, if not more important, than those of blindness. Deafness is a much worse misfortune. For it means the loss of the most vital stimulus—the sound of the voice that brings language, sets thoughts astir and keeps us in the intellectual company of [other people]. . . . If I could live again I should do much more than I have for the deaf. I have found deafness to be a much greater handicap than blindness. (Cited in Ackerman, 1990, pp. 191–192)

To examine hearing, let's first consider the characteristics of sound and the auditory system. Then we'll examine how the auditory system registers pitch, as well as several sensory characteristics of sound. We'll also discuss hearing impairments and the psychological consequences of noise. Later in this book, Chapter 9 explores the important topic of speech perception. Also, Chapter 10 considers the recent research on infants' astonishing speech-perception skills.

Physical Characteristics of Sound

Concentrate for a moment on the variety of sounds that surround you right now. Even if you are reading this paragraph in a relatively quiet location, you can probably hear raindrops, a distant radio, some muffled voices, or your own breathing. In fact, close your eyes at the end of this sentence and concentrate on this rich variation of auditory experiences.

Each of these widely different sounds in your environment is caused by tiny disturbances in air pressure called **sound waves.** The air pressure rapidly compresses and expands as the sound waves travel to your eardrum, causing it to move slightly. The successive pressure changes that move your eardrum are called **sound.** Amazingly, the movement of invisible air molecules is strong enough to produce hearing.

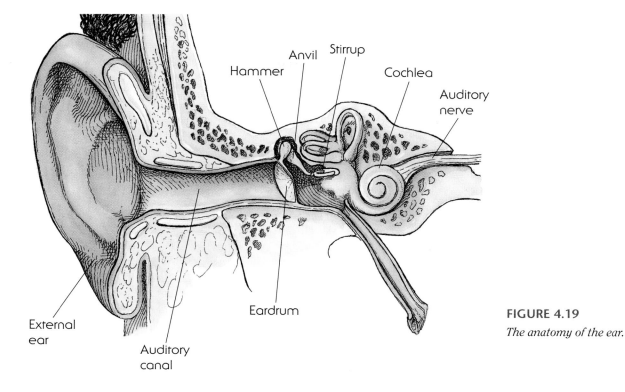

FIGURE 4.19
The anatomy of the ear.

One important physical characteristic of sound is **frequency,** which is the number of cycles a sound wave completes in 1 second. If you strike middle C on the piano, you produce a sound wave that vibrates up and down 262 times each second. Another important physical characteristic of sound is **amplitude,** or the size of the change in pressure created by a sound wave. As we'll discuss in more detail later, the physical quality of frequency is roughly equivalent to the psychological experience of *pitch,* whereas the physical quality of amplitude is roughly equivalent to the psychological experience of *loudness.*

The Auditory System

The sound waves that bounce against your eardrum need to be transformed into neural messages, and the auditory system is neatly designed to accomplish this. As Ackerman (1990) writes, the auditory system looks like a contraption that an ingenious plumber has put together with spare parts! Still, each structure in the auditory system accomplishes some function. Figure 4.19 shows how sound enters the auditory canal, the tube running inward from the outer ear. The sound waves bounce against the **eardrum,** which is a thin membrane that vibrates in sequence with the sound waves.

Resting on the other side of the eardrum are three small bones in the middle ear, which an imaginative early anatomist named the hammer, the anvil, and the stirrup. These bones are the smallest ones in the human body, but they have a very important function. Specifically, these bones are superbly constructed so that they intensify the pressure on the cochlea.

The most important structure in the inner ear is the cochlea (pronounced "*coke*-lee-uh"). The **cochlea** is a bony, fluid-filled coil that contains the auditory receptors, which are called **hair cells.** The hair cells are therefore equivalent to the receptors in vision—that is, the cones and rods. These hair cells are embedded in the **basilar membrane,** a specialized membrane located inside the cochlea. The hair cells are illustrated in greatly magnified form in Figure 4.20.

When pressure is transmitted from the stirrup to the cochlea, this pressure causes waves in the fluid within the cochlea. These waves, in turn, produce a vibration

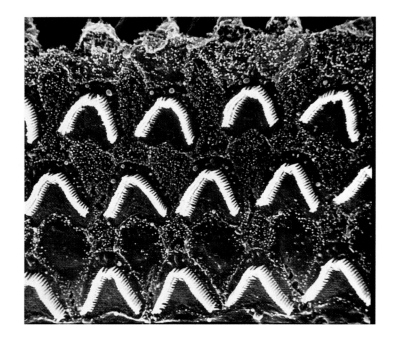

FIGURE 4.20

Overhead view of hair cells embedded in the basilar membrane of the cochlea. Each little fiber in the V-shaped patterns represents one hair cell. This photograph is greatly magnified. Each hair cell is about 35µ in length, which is about ¹/₂₀ of the thickness of one textbook page.

Frequency theory accounts for how you hear the low notes produced by this bass player; your basilar membrane vibrates at the same number of cycles as the very low note he plays.

in the membrane on which the hair cells are sitting. When those hair cells move as little as one-*billionth* of a meter, they trigger action potentials (Hudspeth, 1989). The auditory nerve then picks up those impulses. In other words, the vibration of air molecules, the pounding of a miniature hammer, the sloshing of the fluid in the cochlea, and the stimulation of microscopic hairs are all necessary in order to convert sound into a form that the auditory nerve can receive.

The **auditory nerve** is a bundle of axons that carries information from the cochlea toward higher levels of processing. Along the way, this auditory information passes through several structures, including a part of the thalamus near the location where visual information also passes.

The auditory information eventually travels to the **auditory cortex,** which is primarily located in a deep groove in the temporal lobe of each side of the brain. Recent research using PET scans and other imaging techniques has identified regions of the auditory cortex that respond to simple tones. Other regions respond to tone sequences that move from low to high frequency, and others respond only to clicking sounds. Still others respond only to words—but not to simple tones and not to isolated vowels (Evans, 1982a; Posner & Raichle, 1994). The auditory cortex is relatively large in humans, probably because language is more developed in humans than in other animals (Kiang & Peake, 1988).

Basic Auditory Functions

When you hear a sound, you can distinguish four basic characteristics: pitch, loudness, timbre, and localization. Let's consider these features.

Pitch We define **pitch** as the psychological reaction that corresponds to the physical characteristic of frequency (or cycles per second). We noted earlier that frequency is the number of cycles a sound wave completes in 1 second. For example, when you play a middle C on a piano, the frequency of that tone is 262 cycles per second, or 262 Hz (pronounced "hurts"). The lowest pitch we can hear is about 20 Hz, and the highest is about 20,000 Hz. The notes on a piano range between 28 Hz and 4,186 Hz. Notice, then, that the piano includes only a limited portion of our sensory capacities (Butler, 1992; Matlin & Foley, 1997).

How does the complex auditory system manage to record these different frequencies? When we discussed color vision earlier, we examined two theories that were

TABLE 4.3 Some Representative Amplitudes of Everyday Noises, as Measured by the Decibel Scale of Loudness

LEVEL	LOUDNESS (DECIBELS)	EXAMPLE
Substantial hearing loss	180	Rocket launching pad
	160	Loudest rock band
Intolerable	140	Jet airplane taking off
	120	Very loud thunder
Very noisy	100	Heavy automobile traffic
Loud	80	Loud music from radio
Moderate	60	Normal conversation
Faint	40	Quiet neighborhood
	20	Soft whisper
Very faint	0	Softest sound detectable by human ear

once considered incompatible. We now know that both theories are correct. Similarly, the history of auditory research once featured a battle between two theories about the way the auditory system registers frequency. Researchers now conclude that both theories are correct. As you'll see, frequency theory explains how we process very low tones, and place theory explains how we process both middle and high tones.

Frequency theory states that the entire basilar membrane vibrates at the same frequency as the tone that is sounded. (Remember that the basilar membrane contains the hair cells, which are the receptors in the auditory system.) So, if you are listening to jazz, and the bass player strikes the lowest F on the musical scale (44 Hz), your basilar membrane responds by vibrating at a rate of 44 cycles per second. Researchers have concluded that frequency theory applies only to auditory stimuli in the low-frequency range.

Place theory, in contrast, proposes that each tone frequency produces a vibration in a particular *place* on the basilar membrane. The lowest tone a violin can play creates the greatest vibration in the part of the basilar membrane that is farthest away from the stirrup. The violin's highest tone creates the greatest vibration closer to the stirrup. Researchers believe, then, that place theory accounts for our perception of auditory stimuli in the middle and high range.

Loudness   When we refer to **loudness** we mean the psychological reaction that corresponds to the physical characteristic of amplitude. Loudness is measured in decibels, abbreviated dB. Table 4.3 shows some representative sounds of different amplitudes. As you might imagine, lengthy exposure to extremely loud noises can be hazardous. For example, one study found that the sound level at two bars near a college averaged about 125 dB. One-third of the college students who regularly visited these places showed substantial hearing loss (Hartman, 1982).

Timbre   The term **timbre** (pronounced "*tam*-burr") refers to sound quality; timbre is the characteristic that distinguishes among different sounds when the pitch and loudness are the same. In other words, timbre is a "wastebasket" category, accounting for those leftover qualities that remain when we have accounted for the two straightforward characteristics (Butler, 1992). The squeaky brakes on your friend's car may produce a sound that exactly matches the pitch and loudness of a tone produced by the finest soprano in the Metropolitan Opera Company. However, these two sounds differ in timbre. Also, you can immediately recognize voices on the telephone that are identical in pitch and loudness—again, because they differ in timbre.

If pitch is related to frequency, and loudness is related to amplitude, what physical feature of sound corresponds to timbre? The answer is tone complexity.

Place theory accounts for how you hear the middle and high notes on a piano; the basilar membrane vibrates at a particular place in response to these specific notes.

These two Latina singers may be singing the same middle C note, and their voices may be equally loud, but you can still tell the differences between their voices because of their timbres.

DEMONSTRATION 4.7 Sound Localization

Locate an object that makes a distinctive above-threshold noise (e.g., a dripping faucet, a ticking clock, or a faintly humming appliance). This object should be located in a room that is uniformly lit. One you have selected the object, stand several feet away, plug your ears with your fingers, close your eyes, and turn around several times until you are not certain which direction you are facing. Then stop and keep your eyes closed, but unplug your ears. Point to the source of the sound as quickly as possible. How accurate were you? Repeat this demonstration but keep one ear plugged. Compare your accuracy with the two-ear condition.

Your auditory system provides localization information, as well as pitch, loudness, and timbre. The members of this audience listening to the musical, "Rent," for example, can report that this female singer is on the right of this male singer.

Some sounds are composed of a small number of sound waves; the timbre of these sounds is pure and clean. For example, think about the timbre of a tone played by an accomplished flutist. Other sounds combine many different sound waves; the timbre of these sounds is richer and less crisp-sounding. For example, consider the timbre of a guitar. When people describe timbre, they mention qualities such as richness, mellowness, and brightness (Evans, 1982b; Handel, 1995).

Localization   The concept of **localization** refers to our ability to determine the direction from which a sound is coming. When you hear water dripping, you can locate the appropriate faucet. When your alarm rings in the early morning hours, your arm reaches out in (approximately) the correct direction. How do we manage to localize sound? The hair cells in your ear can register the physical characteristics of sound such as frequency, amplitude, and complexity. However, hair cells cannot code the information that your alarm is ringing near your left arm, rather than near your right knee (Oldfield & Parker, 1986). An additional problem is that your auditory system must sort through a complex input of sounds. At any one moment, you might hear a chair squeaking to your left, a car with a defective muffler in front of you, and someone turning a page directly behind you (Yost, 1992).

In the section on vision earlier in this chapter, we saw the usefulness of binocular vision. We can figure out where objects are located because we have two eyes. Similarly, we can figure out where a sound comes from because we have two ears. To some extent, we can localize sounds by using just one ear (Middlebrooks & Green, 1991). However, the major factors that explain sound localization can be traced to the fact that your two ears are about 6 inches apart. As a consequence, they receive somewhat different stimuli. For example, when the alarm clock rings near your left arm, the noise reaches your left ear slightly before it reaches your right ear. In addition, your head creates a barrier, so the amplitude of the sound is somewhat fainter when it reaches your right ear. These two factors and other sources of information about a sound's location enable us to localize a sound within 1 degree of its true source (Grantham, 1995; Matlin & Foley, 1997; Phillips & Brugge, 1985). Now try Demonstration 4.7 to illustrate your own accuracy in localizing sounds.

Critical Thinking Exercise 4.4

Write down your answers to the following questions about the characteristics of sound:

a. The discussion of pitch mentioned that the lowest pitch we can hear is about 20 Hz. Suppose that a company is hiring individuals for a position that requires people to detect very low tones, and that applicants' hearing is first tested to determine their suitability for this task. What precautions should the company take in administering the hearing test?

b. In Demonstration 4.7, why did the instructions state that the room had to be uniformly lit?

Hearing Disabilities

More than 28 million Americans have hearing disabilities (Soli, 1994). One kind of impairment, called conduction deafness, involves problems in either the outer or the middle ear. In Figure 4.19, this region applies to everything to the left of the cochlea. **Conduction deafness** involves a defect in the mechanical aspects of the auditory system, so that the sound cannot be conducted appropriately from the eardrum to the receptors (Gulick et al., 1989). A hearing aid is typically useful for a person with conduction deafness.

The other kind of hearing impairment, called **nerve deafness,** involves problems in the inner ear, specifically in the cochlea or the auditory nerve. For example, the hair cells shown in Figure 4.20 can be destroyed by repeated exposure to very loud noises (Gulick et al., 1989). In unusual situations, a single extremely loud noise can even cause permanent nerve deafness. People who work with very noisy equipment or listen to loud music for an extended period of time—without protection—may experience nerve deafness. A person with complete nerve deafness cannot be helped by a simple hearing aid. The hearing aid can *conduct* the sound waves, but the receptors or the auditory nerve are too damaged to receive or transmit the message.

Current hearing aids, such as this one, are created to fit the shape of a person's ear. A hearing aid can help an individual with conduction deafness but not nerve deafness.

Consequences of Long-Term Exposure to Noise

In New York City, 250,000 residents listen each day to the roar of the subway's elevated trains, with a measured sound level of 70 dB. Also, 60% of residents living within a mile of New York's JFK airport report sleep disturbances. Still other New York City residents are bombarded with music designed to entertain other people. One man asked the promoter of a rock concert in Central Park how loud he felt the music at the concert should be. The promoter responded: "Your ears should be bleeding." Other city dwellers are subjected to the noise of urban violence. And one man living at an elegant address on the Upper East Side complained about the people who make noise near his apartment:

> It's impossible to get any sleep at all. And these aren't poor kids; they're kids in coats and ties throwing garbage cans into the street, breaking windshields, busting down doors, ringing buzzers in all the buildings. . . . Last week a kid tossed a barbecue grill onto a parked car. (Cooke, 1992, p. 31)

So far in the section on hearing, we've seen that loud sounds can produce hearing impairment. Now, we'll look at some of the other consequences of environmental noise. But first, how do we define noise? According to most sources, **noise** is sound that is unwanted (Bell et al., 1996; Kryter, 1994; Smith & Jones, 1992). Notice, then, that we cannot simply measure a sound and declare that everything above, say, 80 dB should be classified as noise. Instead, we must consider people's *subjective* reactions to the sound—their interpretations of these auditory sensations (Staples, 1996). In other words, we must cross the border from sensation into perception in order to examine noise. The people who attended that (literally) ear-splitting concert in Central Park wouldn't consider the music to be noise; for many of the people living nearby, however, that sound was clearly unwanted.

The topic of noise perception is interesting to psychologists who study perception and also to those who study environmental psychology. **Environmental psychology** studies interactions between people and the environment—both the natural environment and the environment created by humans (Bell et al., 1996). Let's consider a comprehensive study that illustrates a large variety of psychological

If the sounds produced by this drummer are unwanted, they qualify as "noise"; because we must consider the interpretation of basic sensations, this area of research is called "noise perception."

According to the research by Evans and his colleagues, children who live in a quiet neighborhood would be more likely than children who live in a noisy neighborhood to persist on a challenging puzzle.

(IN DEPTH continued)

consequences of environmental noise. This study was conducted by an international team of researchers: Gary Evans of the United States, Staffan Hygge of Sweden, and Monika Bullinger of Germany.

Evans and his coauthors (1995) studied 135 third graders and fourth graders living in Munich, Germany. Roughly half of the children lived in a relatively quiet urban neighborhood (average level of sound = 59 dB) and roughly half lived in a neighborhood surrounding the Munich International Airport (average level of sound = 68 dB). A 9 dB difference may not sound substantial, but decibels are based on a logarithmic scale. As a result, the noisy neighborhood sounded about twice as loud.

These researchers gathered from the children a variety of physiological measures that are considered indicators of stress. For example, the children in the noisy neighborhood had elevated levels of epinephrine and norepinephrine in their urine. These children also showed a blood-pressure pattern that is characteristically related to stress.

The children were also tested on a variety of cognitive tasks. All the testing occurred in a relatively soundproof trailer near the children's schools. In one memory test, children read a story and tried to recall it the next day; the children from the quiet neighborhood scored significantly higher than those from the noisy neighborhood. However, the two groups were similar in the number of alphabet letters they recalled several seconds after presentation. Children from the quiet neighborhood also scored significantly higher on a standardized reading test.

Evans and his coauthors also examined measures of the children's adjustment. A measure of motivation, for example, assessed the children's persistence on a difficult puzzle. The children from the quiet neighborhood tried the task an average of 6.8 times. The children from the noisy neighborhood gave up earlier, after trying an average of only 5.5 times. Other measures demonstrated that the children from the noisy neighborhood were significantly more annoyed by the level of noise in their community, and they also gave lower ratings on a scale assessing psychological aspects of their satisfaction with life.

Evans, Hygge, and Bullinger point out that their study does not qualify as a true experiment. However, their results do suggest that living in a noisy community is a stressful experience that is associated with both cognitive and emotional consequences. They also note that more than 10 million American schoolchildren live near equally noisy airports in the United States. Furthermore, many other studies report similar consequences for both children and adults living in noisy environments (Bell et al., 1996; Smith & Jones, 1992; Staples, 1996). Despite the impressive research on the consequences of noise, however, public policy has not changed. In fact, the Office of Noise Control was actually eliminated from the Environmental Protection Agency during the early 1980s (Staples, 1996). In the future, we can hope that environmental psychologists will work together with citizens' groups to address the significant problems of living in noisy communities.

Critical Thinking Exercise 4.5

Write down your answers to the following questions about the study, conducted by Evans and his colleagues (1995), on long-term exposure to noise:

a. The researchers established, at the beginning of the study, that the two groups of children were similar in socioeconomic status and that all children had normal hearing. Why are these precautions important?

b. Why isn't this study a true experiment? What precautions would be necessary to convert the study into an experiment, and what problems would arise if this proposed experiment could be conducted?

SECTION SUMMARY: *HEARING*

1. In hearing, the auditory system converts sound waves into neural messages in the form of action potentials. The auditory nerve transmits information from the cochlea to regions in the auditory cortex.

2. Humans can appreciate four sensory characteristics of sound: pitch (which is explained by both frequency theory and place theory), loudness, timbre, and localization.

3. Two different hearing disabilities are conduction deafness and nerve deafness.

4. Long-term exposure to noise can be associated with decreased scores on cognitive tasks, motivation tests, and satisfaction with life.

OTHER PERCEPTUAL SYSTEMS

Vision and hearing dominate your perceptual experiences. But imagine your life without your other perceptual systems. Without touch and your other skin senses, you'd be cut by sharp objects and burned by hot ones. Without your sense of smell, you'd exposure yourself to dangerous smoke and gases. Without taste, you might not eat. Let's examine these three so-called "minor senses."

Touch and the Other Skin Senses

Your skin is the largest sensory system you own. It features more than 2 square yards of skin receptors located across your entire body, dwarfing the relatively small receptive surfaces of your retina and your basilar membrane. The skin senses provide information about touch, pain, and temperature. Let's consider these first two topics in more detail.

Touch Think about the variety of ways in which you can experience touch. In **passive touch,** an object is placed on your skin. For example, researchers may measure detection thresholds for different parts of the body. You are more sensitive to a light touch on your lip than on the bottom of your toe (Weinstein, 1968). Two important topics related to passive touch are adaptation and the importance of touch in early development.

In **adaptation,** the perceived intensity of a repeated stimulus decreases over time. All your skin surfaces—whether on your lip or on your toe—show adaptation. For example, are you aware right now of the pressure of your watch against your wrist? The wristband is pressing your skin's surface just as much right now as when you slipped the watch on this morning. However, touch adaptation guarantees that you will stop noticing touch after just a few minutes of mild constant pressure. Our nervous system is designed to notice *change,* rather than continuous stimulation; adaptation is an excellent example of this tendency (Partridge & Partridge, 1993).

Touch is more important than many people realize. For example, Tiffany Field (1993, 1995) demonstrated that touch is vitally important to young infants. Her research showed that premature babies thrive when they receive 45 minutes of massage each day for 10 days. Compared to premature infants with no special treatment, the massaged infants gained more weight, showed fewer signs of tension such as fist clenching, and stayed awake longer.

In passive touch, people are prodded, poked, and touched by other people or by objects. In contrast, we use **active touch** when we actively explore objects. In everyday life, we use active touch much more frequently than passive touch (Heller, 1991). At this moment, for example, you may be running your finger along the right-hand margin of this textbook, preparing to turn the page. Unaided by vision, you use active touch to fasten a zipper, determine whether fruit is ripe, or thread a nut onto a

This person is using active touch to read braille.

hidden part of your automobile (Heller & Schiff, 1991). By picking up a pencil or a fork, you can determine—without even looking—how long it is and how it is oriented in relation to your body (Turvey, 1996).

You can even recognize your friends fairly accurately, simply by using active touch. Kaitz (1992) found that adults were accurate 58% of the time in identifying their romantic partner's face—by touch alone—in a situation where chance accuracy was 33%. Incidentally, students sometimes wonder about gender comparisons in perceptual sensitivity. On this particular task, males and females were similarly accurate. On passive-touch tests, females are sometimes more sensitive, but the results are inconsistent (Fucci et al., 1990; Petrosino et al., 1988; Weinstein, 1968). On tasks measuring other perceptual abilities, the gender similarities are more impressive than the differences.

Pain   It's easy to understand why we need vision, hearing, and touch. But why do we need pain? Some people cannot feel pain, and you might envy them at first. However, children who are born without pain sensitivity have bitten off their tongue and fingers by mistake. Adults may not detect a ruptured appendix or cancer in time to seek adequate treatment (Sternbach, 1968, 1978).

Pain is a complex perceptual experience, involving sensory, emotional, and evaluative components (Fernandez & Turk, 1992; Turk, 1994). Pain can produce stress, depression, and lowered immunity (Cannon, 1996; Turk & Rudy, 1992). The emotional components can be so intense that the pain may drive a person to suicide (Melzack, 1990). Pain is also mystifying. Consider these observations:

1. About 70% of people who have had an arm or a leg amputated continue to report pain in the missing limb—even though there are no pain receptors; this phenomenon is called **phantom limb pain** (Melzack, 1992).

2. A soldier in World War II reported intense pain when a bullet nicked his forehead. However, he felt nothing some time later when his leg was completely torn off (Wallis, 1984).

3. A patient believed that her leg pain was caused by a minor problem, and she controlled the pain with small doses of codeine. When she discovered the pain was due to cancer, she needed much greater amounts of medication (Cassel, 1990).

Endorphin seem to play a major role in the gate-control explanation of pain perception. For this basketball player, stress-induced analgesia may reduce the pain of the injury.

These examples illustrate that pain requires not only a biological explanation, but also a psychological explanation (Melzack, 1986). The most widely accepted explanation of pain is Ronald Melzack and Patrick Wall's **gate-control theory,** which proposes that you experience pain only if the pain messages can pass through a gate in the spinal cord on their route to the brain. When the gate is open, we feel pain. Conditions that open this gate are anxiety, depression, and focusing on the pain. However, the brain can send messages to the spinal cord, indicating that the gate should be closed. If the gate is closed, pain messages are blocked from reaching the brain. Factors such as relaxation, optimism, and distraction close the gate. In other words, pain involves far more than the sensations delivered by the pain receptors. Instead, pain is a complex perception in which mechanisms in both the brain and the spinal cord contribute to the experience (Druckman & Bjork, 1991; Melzack & Wall, 1965; Novy et al., 1995; Turk & Melzack, 1992).

In short, gate-control theory shows how top-down processing (discussed in connection with visual pattern perception) can also influence pain perception. For example, the brain's message probably helped to block pain perception for the soldier who lost his leg, and they probably helped to increase the pain perception for the woman suffering from cancer.

Chapter 3 discussed **endorphins,** which are neuromodulators that occur naturally in the brain and decrease a person's sensitivity to pain. Endorphins probably play an important role in the gate-control mechanisms, though the specific details about endorphins and cortical processing of pain are not well understood (Talbot et al., 1991). However, researchers have discovered a phenomenon called **stress-induced analgesia;** psychological stress triggers the release of endorphins, making painful stimuli seem less intense (Coren et al., 1994; Lewis et al., 1984; Wiertelak et al., 1992).

We also know that cognitive processes can alter pain perception—for example, during prepared childbirth. **Prepared childbirth** uses techniques such as relaxation and distracting attention away from the pain. Cognitive distraction has a clear impact on pain perception (Irving, 1997; Livingston, 1993). In fact, a review of 150 studies showed that people reported less pain when they used strategies such as thinking about pleasant images (Fernandez & Turk, 1989). Once again, top-down processes influence perception.

This discussion of the skin senses shows that our perceptual processes provide us with the ability to *stop* noticing a stimulus. They also permit us to recognize objects and people when we use active touch. These perceptual processes allow us to feel pain in some circumstances, but to stop feeling pain in other situations. Once more, we see that humans are well equipped to interact in their environment.

Critical Thinking Exercise 4.6

Write down your answers to the following questions about active touch and pain perception:

a. Consider Kaitz's (1992) study in which people tried to identify their romantic partners by using active touch. What kind of precautions should be taken in a study like this one to make certain that the participants are not relying on perceptual cues other than touch?

b. Suppose you take a painkiller to help relieve a headache, and you do feel better 45 minutes later. Why should you be cautious in attributing your improvement to the painkiller? What other mechanism could account for the improvement? How could a properly controlled study be conducted to test this medication?

Smell

Smell is mysterious. Of all the research in perception, only 2% of journal articles examine smell (Almagor, 1990; Teghtsoonian, 1983). One reason for this neglect is that smell is simply less important to humans than the other senses. Another reason is the difficulty of classifying odorous stimuli. We can easily describe visual and auditory stimuli in terms of wave frequency and amplitude. But how can we transform the stench of an ancient tuna sandwich or the fragrance of chocolate chip cookies into wavelengths? With odorous stimuli, we typically settle for qualitative descriptions such as "spicy," "minty," and "citruslike."

Several researchers have explored the nature of odor receptors. They have discovered a large family of genes that seem to be associated with proteins located in the nasal passages. These receptor proteins resemble the proteins that bind neurotransmitters, so a lock-and-key mechanism may explain how each smell is coded in the nasal passages (Barinaga, 1991a; Buck & Axel, 1991). It's also possible that the receptor proteins can be categorized into subfamilies that handle odors with similar fragrances. If this idea is confirmed, then we may be able to develop a more objective method for classifying odors (Bartoshuk & Beauchamp, 1994).

In the previous discussion, you learned about adaptation to touch. We also adapt to odors. Have you ever walked into a locker room, pungent with odor of dozens of sweaty bodies? You may have noticed that the odor was initially strong, but

After smelling some chocolate chip cookies for about one minute, the intensity of the fragrance will be only about one-third of its original strength.

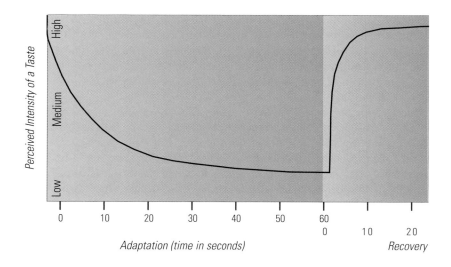

FIGURE 4.21

Adaptation to a specific taste, and subsequent recovery.

a few minutes later, you didn't notice it. In fact, the perceived intensity of an odor decreases substantially during adaptation (Berglund & Engen, 1993; Cain, 1988; Engen, 1991). Within one minute the perceived intensity may drop to about 30% of its original level.

We humans are reasonably competent at detecting odors, but we are not especially accurate in identifying a specific odor (de Wijk et al., 1995; Engen, 1991; Richardson & Zucco, 1989). In my classes, I sometimes ask students to sniff and identify the contents of several opaque jars. The students' faces grow puzzled as they try to identify mysteriously familiar substances such as crayons and pencil shavings. This ability to recognize that an odor is familiar—combined with the inability to identify its name—is called the **tip-of-the-nose-phenomenon** (Engen, 1987; Lawless & Engen, 1977). This experience is similar to the more common tip-of-the-tongue phenomenon (Chapter 7), in which a word for which you are searching refuses to leap forth from memory.

Some odors can be recognized easily; coffee, paint, and chocolate pose no challenge. In contrast, fewer than 20% of participants in one study could correctly identify odors such as ham, sawdust, cat feces, and cigars (Desor & Beauchamp, 1974).

Let's now consider the last of the perceptual systems—taste. As we'll see, smell and taste help create the experience of flavor.

Taste

Taste refers to the perceptions created when a substance makes contact with the specialized receptors in the mouth (Bartoshuk, 1991a). When psychologists use the word *taste* correctly, they mean perceptions such as sweetness. So taste refers to only a narrow range of sensory experiences—sweet, sour, bitter, and salty.

Flavor, a much broader term, includes smell, touch, temperature, and pain—in addition to taste (Bartoshuk, 1991b). For example, the flavor of spicy chili includes impressions such as the pungent smell of cumin and sauteed onion, the creamy smooth texture of an exploded bean on your tongue, the piping-hot temperature, and the distinct pain from the chili pepper.

One of the most important taste phenomena is taste adaptation. A first sip of lemonade is so sour that your lips instantly pucker. After a few sips, though, the drink is more tolerable and less sour. As you might imagine, taste adaptation resembles the touch adaptation and odor adaptation we've already discussed. Figure 4.21 shows how the perceived intensity of a taste decreases. After about half a minute of sipping, the lemonade does not taste nearly as sour as the first mouthful. However, we recover rapidly from adaptation. If you stop drinking the lemonade for a few seconds and then take another sip, your lips will pucker once again.

The most important application of taste is in the area of food technology. Before it reaches the customers, a new breakfast cereal will be judged on qualities such as sweetness, crispiness, and aroma. Flavor enhancement is a new branch of food technology that contributes to medical therapy. For example, a man who was recovering from surgery had a craving for mashed potatoes that clearly could not be satisfied by the intravenous feeding required during the postoperative period. Dr. Susan Schiffman, a prominent researcher in the area of flavor and taste, was able to supply him with a powder that smelled and tasted exactly like mashed potatoes, yet it dissolved completely on the tongue (Blackburn, 1988). Schiffman also helped to develop powders and sprays with flavors such as peanut butter and jelly, pizza, and—one surgical patient's request—southern boiled fatback and green beans.

These flavor enhancers can also help treat obesity and encourage elderly people to eat. Some elderly people have decreased taste sensitivity. They eat less, because the food seems so boringly bland. In contrast, Schiffman found that elderly individuals at a retirement home ate more beef when its flavor had been boosted by a beef flavor enhancer. If fashion magazines are filled with scent strips from luxury perfumes, what can we expect in the future from the gourmet food magazines? Will *Bon Appétit* include flavor strips for well-aged Camembert cheese? Will *Gourmet* reek with Peking duck flavor enhancer? Clearly, the research on sensation and perception can produce practical applications as well as theoretical advances.

Food technology is vital to the economy of many cultures outside North America. This photo shows A. K. Das, a professional tea taster in Assam, India. However, he does not simply judge the taste of a tea. He also assesses the color and texture of the dry tea leaves, as well as the color and fragrance of the tea liquid.

SECTION SUMMARY: *OTHER PERCEPTUAL SYSTEMS*

1. Research on touch shows that different parts of the body have varying thresholds for touch, that we adapt to touch after continued stimulation, and that touch can help premature infants to thrive. People are fairly accurate in using active touch to identify the faces of romantic partners.

2. Pain requires a psychological explanation in addition to a biological explanation, because higher level, top-down factors influence pain perception.

3. Gate-control theory points out that brain and spinal cord mechanisms influence pain perception; pain perception is also influenced by endorphins, stress-induced analgesia, and cognitive processes.

4. Receptor proteins in the nasal passages may code odorous stimuli. People adapt to odors, but they may have trouble identifying some familiar odors.

5. Taste is a more limited term than flavor. People adapt to tastes, as well as touch and odor. Flavor enhancers are helpful in medical therapy.

REVIEW QUESTIONS

1. Describe a recent experience that required you to detect a stimulus. How could you measure a detection threshold in that situation, using the classical psychological approach? If the signal detection approach were used instead, what factors would have determined your criterion? Now describe a recent situation requiring discrimination. Discuss how the concept of just-noticeable differences could be applied here.

2. Imagine that you are witnessing a car crash. Simultaneously, you register both the visual and the auditory stimuli. Trace how these two kinds of stimuli would be processed, beginning with the receptors and ending at the cortex.

3. Vision and hearing share several similarities. For example, color perception and pitch perception each have two theoretical explanations. Describe as many other similarities as you can recall.

4. What factors provide visual information about an object's location? What factors provide information about the location of an auditory stimulus?

5. The discussion of shape perception described how the figure-ground relationship and the Gestalt laws of grouping help organize visual stimuli. Discuss these two topics, listing the characteristics of the figure versus the ground and also listing the Gestalt laws. Now apply each of these items to auditory stimuli: How is our hearing organized?

6. The discussion of shape perception explained how perception involves both bottom-up and top-down processes. Describe these two kinds of processes, and then discuss how they could be applied to signal detection theory, shape perception, and illusory contour.

7. What consequences do loud noises have for hearing disabilities, for cognitive abilities, and for emotional well-being?

8. The concept of adaptation was discussed in connection with vision, touch, smell, and taste. Describe these four topics, providing an example of each one, based on your recent experience.

9. Pain seems to be more than the mere registration of painful stimuli from the receptors. Explain this statement, discussing gate-control theory and other factors that influence pain perception.

10. This chapter emphasized vision and hearing more than the other senses. However, some of the same principles apply to touch, smell, and taste. Describe how you would apply each of the following concepts to one of these other sensory processes: (a) signal detection theory applied to odor detection; (b) figure-ground perception applied to taste; (c) constancy applied to the intensity of a smell when you take a deep breath of an odor, rather than a small breath; (d) the law of nearness applied to touch.

NEW TERMS

sensation (p. 114)
perception (p. 114)
psychophysics (p. 114)
detection (p. 115)
detection threshold (p. 115)
signal detection theory (p. 116)
sensitivity (p. 116)
criterion (p. 116)
discrimination (p. 116)
just-noticeable difference (jnd) (p. 116)
Weber's law (p. 116)
wavelength 118
hue (p. 118)
amplitude (vision) (p. 118)
brightness (p. 118)
cornea (p. 118)
iris (p. 118)
pupil (p. 118)

lens (p. 118)
retina (p. 118)
fovea (p. 118)
receptor cells (p. 118)
cones (p. 118)
rods (p. 118)
ganglion cells (p. 119)
optic nerve (p. 120)
blind spot (p. 120)
binocular vision (p. 120)
visual cortex (p. 120)
single-cell recording technique (p. 120)
PET scan (positron emission tomography) (p. 121)
visual acuity (p. 122)
dark adaptation (p. 122)
pursuit movement (p. 123)
saccadic movement (p. 123)
trichromatic theory (p. 125)

opponent-process theory (p. 125)
color deficiency (p. 126)
figure-ground relationship (p. 127)
Gestalt approach (p. 127)
law of proximity (p. 128)
law of similarity (p. 128)
law of good continuation (p. 128)
law of closure (p. 128)
distinctive features (p. 129)
recognition-by-components theory (p. 129)
bottom-up processing (p. 129)
top-down processing (p. 129)
word-superiority effect (p. 129)
biological motion (p. 130)
monocular (p. 130)
binocular (p. 131)
binocular disparity (p. 131)
constancy (p. 132)
size constancy (p. 132)
shape constancy (p. 133)
color constancy (p. 133)
illusion (p. 133)
theory of misapplied constancy (p. 134)
illusory contour (p. 134)
sound waves (p. 136)
sound (p. 136)
frequency (p. 137)

amplitude (hearing) (p. 137)
eardrum (p. 137)
cochlea (p. 137)
hair cells (p. 137)
basilar membrane (p. 137)
auditory nerve (p. 138)
auditory cortex (p. 138)
pitch (p. 138)
frequency theory (p. 139)
place theory (p. 139)
loudness (p. 139)
timbre (p. 139)
localization (p. 140)
conduction deafness (p. 141)
nerve deafness (p. 141)
noise (p. 141)
environmental psychology (p. 141)
passive touch (p. 143)
adaptation (p. 143)
active touch (p. 143)
pain (p. 144)
phantom limb pain (p. 144)
gate-control theory (p. 144)
endorphins (p. 144)
stress-induced analgesia (p. 145)
prepared childbirth (p. 145)
tip-of-the-nose phenomenon (p. 146)
taste (p. 146)
flavor (p. 146)

RECOMMENDED READINGS

Bell, P. A., Greene, T. C., Fisher, J. D., & Baum, A. (1996). *Environmental psychology* (4th ed.). Fort Worth, TX: Harcourt Brace. Here's an interesting book that provides more details on the consequences of noise; other environmental psychology topics include the effects of weather, natural disasters, and crowding.

Coren, S., Ward, L. M., & Enns, J. T. (1994). *Sensation and perception* (4th ed.). Fort Worth, TX. Harcourt Brace. This upper-level book provides a complete overview of sensation and perception, including chapters on individual differences in perception, as well as the role of experience in perception.

Engen, T. (1991). *Odor sensation and memory.* Westport, CT: Praeger. This book is written by a very prominent researcher in the discipline of smell. It includes readable discussions of topics such as odor memory, odor pollution, and loss of odor sensitivity.

Kaiser, P. K., & Boynton, R. M. (1996). *Human color vision* (2nd ed.). Washington, DC: Optical Society of America. Robert Boynton is one of the most active researchers in the area of color vision; he and his colleague Peter Kaiser have written a book that examines such topics as the history of color vision research, subjective color phenomena, color discrimination, and color naming.

Matlin, M. W., & Foley, H. J. (1997). *Sensation and perception* (4th ed.). Boston; Allyn & Bacon. This mid-level book emphasizes top-down processes in perception; it contains many applications for the professions and for everyday experiences.

Rayner, K. (Ed.). (1992). *Eye movements and visual cognition: Scene perception and reading.* New York: Springer-Verlag. The topics in this book include how we program saccadic eye movements and how we use them to search, perceive scenes, and read text. One interesting chapter examines eye movements when we look at a cartoon.

ANSWERS TO DEMONSTRATIONS

Demonstration 4.4
   57, 15

ANSWERS TO CRITICAL THINKING EXERCISES

Exercise 4.1

   a. No, Jim does not necessarily have more sensitive hearing. Instead, Jim may have a more lenient criterion for saying "Yes, I hear it." Because of this potential confounding variable, we cannot draw a firm conclusion that Jim has more sensitive hearing.

   b. An evolutionary psychologist (see Pages 106–108 in Chapter 3) may argue that it's adaptive to be able to detect something (e.g., a spoiled taste in food), but it isn't necessary to be precise in discriminating between two stimuli (e.g., two spoiled samples of food).

Exercise 4.2

   a. A problem is that the eye chart may not be a valid measure of acuity; it may measure a person's ability to memorize an eye chart, rather than his or her ability to see fine details.

   b. People who are having visual difficulties may possibly be admitted into nursing homes more often than people with normal vision, because they or their relatives may be concerned about their safety when they cannot see well.

Exercise 4.3

   a. If our sensory processes were frequently deceived, the human species would have become extinct long ago (Cutting & Vishton, 1995). We would have bumped into trees, fallen into pits, and misjudged the nearness of dangerous animals. Thus, illusions are the exception, rather than the norm.

   b. An important confounding variable in this study is that the "wings outward" version always appears on top; it's possible that we perceive a line on top to be consistently larger (or else consistently smaller). To design the study properly, the "wings outward" version should appear on top half the time and on the bottom half the time. Also, in this hypothetical study the observers only adjust the length of the "wings inward version"; to understand the illusion more completely, the observers should adjust the length of the "wings outward" version on half of the trials.

Exercise 4.4

   a. Because a prospective employee's motivation is probably extremely high, this person may say "I hear it" whenever there is the slightest chance that a tone has been presented. Therefore, the company should include some trials on which no tone is presented, to see whether the individual still says "I hear it." This kind of precaution is actually part of the signal detection approach.

   b. If the room featured light streaming in from one window, you would perceive this region of brightness, even with your eyes closed; you could therefore locate the noisy object in relation to that window—rather than simply on the basis of auditory cues.

Exercise 4.5

   a. In general, wealthier families are more likely to live in quieter neighborhoods. This confounding variable of family income is important because children from wealthier families may perform better on cognitive tasks. Without this precaution, we wouldn't know whether noise or factors related to family income were responsible for the differences in test scores (Kryter, 1994). Also, the authors wanted to make sure that all the children had normal hearing because if the children in the noisy neighborhood had hearing impairments, they could have trouble with language skills (e.g., scores on reading tests).

b. This study is not a true experiment because the children were not randomly assigned to quiet and noisy neighborhoods, as Evans and his coworkers (1995) acknowledge in their article. Although they made sure that the children were similar in social class and in hearing ability, the kinds of families who choose to live in noisy neighborhoods may differ in some other important ways from those who choose to live in quiet neighborhoods (e.g., interest in academics). Theoretically, researchers could conduct an experiment in which children were randomly assigned to groups and one group heard loud noise for many years. However, this study would be ethically inappropriate, as well as difficult and expensive to conduct.

Exercise 4.6

a. In Kaitz's study, the people who tried to identify their partner were blindfolded, and four layers of cloth were also placed over the nose; both visual and odor cues were therefore diminished. In addition, Kaitz played a fairly loud recording of a masking sound, so that they could not identify any unusual identifying noises (e.g., breathing sounds) that their partners might make.

b. It's possible that the headache would have disappeared on its own, without any medication. It's also possible that your *expectation* about decreased pain could have played a role; as you know, gate-control theory points out that cognitive factors can play a role. To conduct a proper study, a large number of people would need to be randomly assigned to groups. People in one group take the painkiller and people in the other group take a similar-looking pill (a placebo) that does not have any biological effect on pain. Later, you compare the pain reports of the two groups. Research suggests that these "placebo control groups" typically report substantial pain reduction (Turner et al., 1994).

STATES OF CONSCIOUSNESS

WAKING CONSCIOUSNESS AND ATTENTION

Consciousness About Thought Processes

Mental Control

Attention

SLEEPING AND DREAMING

Circadian Rhythms

Stages of Sleep

Effects of Sleep Deprivation

Why Do We Sleep?

Sleep Disorders

Dreaming

DRUGS THAT INFLUENCE CONSCIOUSNESS

Basic Terms

In Depth: Alcohol

Opiates

Stimulants

Hallucinogens

Psychoactive Drug Use

HYPNOSIS

Hypnotic Phenomena

Theories of Hypnosis

CHAPTER 5

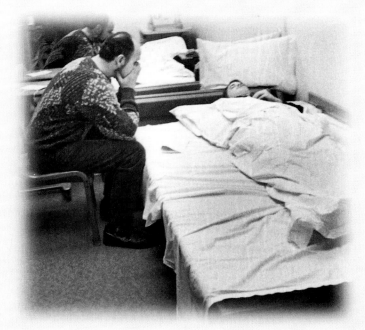

On a Wednesday afternoon, the body of a 14-year-old boy is wheeled into the emergency room at the University of Michigan Hospital in Ann Arbor. He is pronounced dead on arrival, and a doctor reports blood tests establishing that more than half of his blood volume is alcohol. Apparently, he had attended an unsupervised party at a friend's house. Someone had found him unconscious and called an ambulance. Alcohol poisoning had caused cardiorespiratory arrest (Finn, 1996).

A man believed to be the teenager's father soon arrived. The hospital's chaplain greets him with chilling words: "We're pretty sure we have your son, but he has no ID on him so we need you to identify the body" (Finn, 1996, p. 14). The man enters the morgue, sees the face of his son, and confirms that it is his oldest child inside the body bag. The chaplain offers a prayer and asks the father about the possibility of tissue donation and an autopsy. The father gazes on the white shroud in front of him and his son's familiar face, now eerily still.

And then his son sits up, wriggles out of the body bag, and hugs his father. As it happens, this father and son were participating in an educational program at the University of Michigan, designed to expose adolescents and their families to the consequences of alcohol and drug use. In addition to guest speakers and role-play exercises, the students also tour the intensive care unit and the morgue, where they are shown real brains, livers, hearts, and lungs—all visibly damaged by alcohol and other drugs. As the director of this program explains, "The goal is to bring kids through the front door of the hospital now instead of through the emergency room later" (p. 15).

The program certainly has an immediate emotional impact on the participants. As the father in this scenario commented afterwards, "I wasn't ready for the emotional impact it had on me. . . . I knew it was a simulation, but it was just too real; I couldn't control myself. I realized at that moment that this really could happen, and that I didn't feel I was doing enough to make sure it didn't." For his son, the experience was equally realistic: "I knew that alcohol and drugs weren't good, but here, it just really hit home. Much more than 'Just Say No'" (p. 15).

Our topic for this chapter is **consciousness**—our awareness of the outside world and our perceptions, thoughts, and feelings (Hirst, 1995; Posner, 1994). We'll also explore some altered states of consciousness, like those induced by alcohol and other drugs.

The topic of consciousness has varied tremendously in its popularity throughout the history of psychology. Scientific psychology actually began with the study of consciousness; we discussed Wilhelm Wundt's introspection technique in Chapter 1. William James included a chapter on consciousness in his groundbreaking textbook (James, 1890). But several decades later, the behaviorists rejected consciousness. They considered the topic inappropriate for scientific study: How could researchers observe consciousness or measure it with a clear-cut operational definition? By the middle of the twentieth century, then, consciousness had vanished from the psychological scene (Cabanac, 1996; Chalmers, 1995). However, when cognitive psychology gained popularity during the 1960s, consciousness was "rehabilitated." Currently, the topic of consciousness is popular among both researchers and theorists (Chalmers, 1995; Farthing, 1992).

We'll begin our exploration of consciousness by looking at waking consciousness and attention, which occupy the major part of our lives. Then we'll examine two altered states of consciousness—sleeping and drug-induced states. Our final topic, hypnosis, is more controversial; psychologists disagree about whether hypnosis can induce a truly altered state of consciousness.

WAKING CONSCIOUSNESS AND ATTENTION

Most of this textbook focuses on our normal waking state. When you remember, think, and speak, you are aware and conscious. Your social interactions also emphasize normal waking consciousness. Psychologists have been intrigued by two questions about this normal waking consciousness: (1) Are we really aware of our thought processes? and (2) What happens when we try to eliminate a thought from consciousness? Another important issue that is often intertwined with consciousness—attention—is our final topic in this section.

Consciousness About Thought Processes

What is the name of your psychology professor? Now consider this second question: How did you arrive at the answer to the first question? As psychologists have pointed out, we often cannot fully explain our thought processes (Miller, 1962; Nisbett & Wilson, 1977). We can remember information and solve problems, but we usually are not conscious of the process that created these answers (Lyons, 1986).

However, we can be conscious of other, more leisurely thought processes (Nelson, 1992). If you're trying to remember where you left your keys, you can trace back over your recent activities in a linear, logical fashion until you remember placing them on the cafeteria counter. In summary, some mental processes are available to consciousness, whereas others remain hidden and relatively mysterious (Farthing, 1992; Nelson, 1996).

Critical Thinking Exercise 5.1

Write down your answers to these questions about the introduction to this chapter and about the accuracy of human's reports about their thought processes.

a. The introductory example of the alcohol awareness program at the University of Michigan suggested that the project would be helpful. What research method was used in this example? If you wanted to test the program, how would you design the study using the experimental method? What dependent measures would you use? List at least three of them.

b. Suppose some researchers did conduct an experiment. The dependent variables they studied were responses to questionnaire items such as "I do not intend to drink alcoholic beverages" and "I can say no to alcohol and other drugs." Taking into account the information presented here on consciousness about thought processes (and any other factors), how would you critique this study?

Mental Control

Take a moment to think of your very favorite food, and then try to remove every trace of this thought from your consciousness. This exercise requires **mental control,** which is defined as the influence we exercise over our consciousness (Wegner & Wenzlaff, 1996). You use mental control whenever you change your thoughts and emotions according to priorities you have set. When you use mental control, you try to change the contents of consciousness.

If we were completely successful at mental control, people on a diet would never think about forbidden foods. Smokers trying to abandon their cigarettes wouldn't long for just one puff. Depressed people could transform their moods into eternal optimism. And no one would ever mourn for a lost love.

Unfortunately, we humans are not always successful in our mental control. Specifically, we may have difficulty with **thought suppression,** which is the intentional, conscious removal of a thought from consciousness (Wegner, 1992). Consider, for example, a study by Wegner and Gold (1995), which examined people's thoughts about an "old flame." In this study, undergraduates were asked to think out loud about a previous romantic partner. Next, they were asked to try to suppress any thoughts of this individual from their consciousness. Finally, they were told that they could think about anything at all.

The results were different for those who no longer yearned for the lost love and for those who still had strong feelings. Relative to a control group, those who no longer yearned for this lost love expressed significantly more thoughts about this individual during that final period. They showed a rebound effect. That is, when they tried to eliminate memories from their consciousness, those memories came back even stronger at a later time. These results are consistent with numerous other studies (e.g., Wegner & Pennebaker, 1993; Wegner et al., 1987).

In contrast, however, people who *did* still yearn for their lost love showed no such rebound. Wegner and Gold (1995) speculate that these people may be accustomed to suppressing their romantic thoughts. When the researcher tells them that they can now think about this person, their natural suppression tendencies swing into action.

If you are successful at controlling the contents of your consciousness, you can easily suppress any thoughts about favorite desserts or other pleasures you are trying to avoid. According to the research of Daniel Wegner and his colleagues, mental control is often extremely difficult.

You can see Theme 3 in action here. Psychological processes are indeed complex: Thought suppression is not successful in some cases, but it's effective in other cases.

Notice an interesting contrast between the two topics we've been discussing in connection with consciousness. We first saw that people may have difficulty bringing into consciousness their thoughts about their memory and cognitive processes. Then we saw in this section on mental control that people may have difficulty eliminating some thoughts from their consciousness. Consciousness is not a perfectly accurate mirror of our thinking, and it is not a process that can be easily controlled.

Attention

Consciousness and attention are closely related. Consciousness is your awareness of stimuli; **attention** means a concentration of mental activity. Right now, you may be conscious of many stimuli around you. However, your attention may be focused on the material you are reading. Let's look at three components of attention: divided attention, selective attention, and search.

Divided Attention   Think about the last time you tried to listen simultaneously to a professor and to a nearby conversation. This is an example of **divided attention,** which occurs when we try to distribute our attention between two or more competing tasks. As you've undoubtedly discovered, your attention has a limited capacity, and your performance becomes less accurate when you try to do too many things at once (Koelega, 1996). For example, Reinitz and his colleagues (1994) asked some people to study a series of faces (control group); others counted a sequence of dots that appeared on the faces while they studied the faces (divided-attention group). Later, those in the divided-attention group correctly recognized only 60% as many faces as those in the control group.

Divided attention is difficult when we first begin learning a task. However, practice clearly improves our performance. For example, in one study, college students successfully learned to read stories to themselves while simultaneously categorizing words that were read to them, such as writing down "animal" when hearing the word "dog" (Spelke et al., 1976). Similarly, when you first began to drive, you probably found that you couldn't pull out of a driveway and listen to a radio simultaneously. Now, you may have trouble remembering that the task was ever challenging!

Selective Attention   In **selective attention,** two or more messages are presented simultaneously; people must focus attention on one message and ignore everything else. Notice that divided attention and selective attention both involve two or more simultaneous tasks. However, in divided attention, you must pay attention to two or more tasks. In contrast, selective attention requires you to focus on only one task.

Think about a selective-attention task you recently faced. Maybe you tried to listen to the news while a conversation elsewhere in the room threatened to distract you. You have probably discovered that if you conscientiously attend to one message, you notice little about other messages presented at the same time.

In the laboratory, auditory selective attention is often studied in a dichotic listening task. As Chapter 3 discussed, in a **dichotic listening task,** people are instructed to repeat a message presented to one ear, while ignoring a different message presented to the other ear. The research generally shows that people seldom notice important features of the unattended message. For example, if you are supposed to follow an attended message that is spoken quickly, you may not even notice whether the message in the unattended ear is in English or in German (Cherry, 1953). You'll be somewhat more likely to recognize your own name in an unattended message. For example, in a well-controlled study, Wood and Cowan (1995) found that 35% of the participants reported hearing their name in a message that they were supposed to ignore.

Try Demonstration 5.1, which illustrates the difficulty of *visual* selective attention in a Stroop-effect task. In tasks that measure the **Stroop effect,** people take much

Because of selective attention, these students can focus their attention on the conversation in their own group and ignore the other conversation.

DEMONSTRATION 5.1 The Stroop Effect

For this demonstration, you will need a watch with a second hand. First, measure how long it takes to name the colors listed immediately below. Your task is to say out loud the names of the ink colors, ignoring the meaning of the words. Measure the amount of time it takes to go through this list *five* times, (Keep a tally of the number of repetitions.) Record that time.

RED   **BLUE**   **GREEN**   **YELLOW**   GREEN   **RED**   BLUE   **YELLOW**   **BLUE**   RED

YELLOW   GREEN   **YELLOW**   **GREEN**   BLUE   RED   **RED**   GREEN   **YELLOW**   BLUE

Now try a second color-naming task. Measure how long it takes to name the colors listed below. Your task is to say out loud the names of these ink colors. Measure the amount of time it takes to go through this list five times. (Again, keep a tally of the number of repetitions.) Record that time.

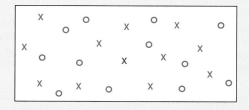

longer to say the color of a stimulus when it is used in printing an inappropriate color name, rather than when it appears as a simple solid color. For example, in Demonstration 5.1 you probably took much longer to say the color "yellow" when that color was used to print the inappropriate color name *red* than when it appeared as a solid yellow rectangle. The Stroop effect illustrates selective attention because you take longer to name a color when you are distracted by another very prominent feature of the stimulus presented at the same time. In a Stroop task, the message you are supposed to ignore is the meaning of the word itself. However, as an adult reader, you attend primarily to word meaning and find it difficult to attend to a less salient feature—in this case, the color of the stimulus.

The effect was first demonstrated by J. R. Stroop (1935), who found that people took roughly twice as long on the selective-attention task as on the task of naming the colors of solid rectangles. Since the original experiment, more than 400 additional studies have examined variations of the Stroop effect (e.g., MacLeod, 1991; Richards et al., 1992; Sugg & McDonald, 1994).

Try noticing your own attention patterns. Which selective-attention tasks seem most challenging? When do you notice the characteristics of the message that you are supposed to be ignoring? Does a selective-attention task suddenly become a divided-attention task when you try to monitor *two* interesting conversations?

Search   Searching requires you to focus your attention on locating specific targets. Try Demonstration 5.2 and note which search task is faster. From the research of Anne Treisman and her colleagues, we know that search uses either of

DEMONSTRATION 5.2 Preattentive Processing Versus Focused Attention

Cover the two designs below before you read further.

A. In this part of the demonstration, see how long it takes you to locate the blue figure. Remove the cover from the left-hand design and find the blue figure.

B. Now see how long it takes you to locate the blue X in the other design. Remove the cover and find the blue X.

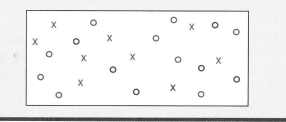

two kinds of attention (Treisman, 1986, 1991, 1993; Treisman & Gelade, 1980). In one kind of search, called **preattentive processing,** you automatically register the features in a display of objects. For example, in Part A of Demonstration 5.2, you used preattentive processing because the blue figure seemed to "pop out" effortlessly. In this low-level kind of attention, you attend only to isolated features, such as "blue."

The second, more complicated kind of search is called focused attention. **Focused attention** requires you to process objects one at a time. In Part B, you used focused attention to examine each object in the box. The blue X did not simply "pop out" from the display as it did in Part A. As you can imagine, focused attention is more time-consuming than preattentive processing. Notice how you use focused attention when searching a telephone directory for a friend's name, because you must skim through every name in a section of the list. In contrast, you use preattentive processing to locate the one blue shirt when all the other shirts on the rack are white.

SECTION SUMMARY: *WAKING CONSCIOUSNESS AND ATTENTION*

1. The topic of consciousness has fluctuated dramatically in its popularity throughout the history of psychology.

2. We seem to have only limited access to some memory and thinking processes, yet we are apparently conscious of other more leisurely mental activities.

3. We use mental control when we try to change the contents of consciousness; however, thought suppression is sometimes difficult.

4. In divided attention, people have difficulty performing two tasks simultaneously; however, practice improves their accuracy.

5. In selective attention, people pay complete attention to one task and typically notice little about the unattended message; the Stroop effect is illustrated by a visual selective-attention task in which a word's meaning interferes with naming the color of the ink.

6. Two kinds of search are the relatively automatic preattentive processing and the more time-consuming focused attention.

SLEEPING AND DREAMING

If you are like most people, you'll spend close to 25 years asleep during your lifetime. During **sleep,** your body is less active and you are less responsive to the environment (Oswald, 1987a). When you are asleep, you may be relatively unresponsive, but your brain is still very active. In fact, your overall level of neuron activity is not much lower than if you were sitting in a chair, reading a novel (Webb, 1992).

Let's begin by looking at the sleeping-and-waking cycle. Then we'll consider the stages of sleep, sleep deprivation, the reasons why we sleep, and sleep disorders. The final part of this section examines dreams; we'll see that your brain is especially active during dreaming.

Circadian Rhythms

Every day of your life, you complete a cycle that includes both a sleeping and waking period. A **circadian rhythm** (pronounced "sur-*kay*-dee-un") has a cycle lasting about 24 hours. If you lived in an environment with no clues about the time of day, you would probably maintain a cycle that is closer to 25 hours, rather than 24 hours. Part of the reason you maintain a 24-hour cycle is that your world is filled with zeitgebers (pronounced "*tsite*-gay-burs"). **Zeitgebers** are clues—such as clocks and the brightness of the sky—that encourage you to adopt a 24-hour cycle.

What happens when we are deprived of zeitgebers? To answer this question, researchers have asked volunteers to live for several weeks in places where sunlight cannot penetrate, such as underground caves or in specially constructed laboratories. The volunteers also give up their watches, radios, and television.

If people had sleeping-and-waking cycles that lasted exactly 24 hours, they could maintain their 24-hour-cycles, even without zeitgebers. However, most people soon adopt a 25-hour cycle. This natural tendency to adopt a 25-hour cycle is known as **free running** (Coren, 1996; Kronauer, 1994). Because of this free-running tendency, people deprived of zeitgebers for about two weeks begin requesting their breakfast at 8:00 in the *evening*.

It is daytime in this airport, but these jet passengers are still operating according to biological clocks established in their own countries.

Disrupted Circadian Rhythms In modern-day North America, people are likely to experience disrupted circadian rhythms for two reasons: shift schedules and jet lag. In both cases, sleep patterns become irregular, and people make more errors when they are awake (Coren, 1996).

About 20% of workers in the United States are on **shift schedules** in which they must work during the normal sleeping hours (Moorcroft, 1993). As a result, they sleep fewer hours, and they wake up more often during sleep. The research conducted on shift work has shown that about 60% of shift workers complain about sleep disturbances, in contrast to about 20% of day workers (Coleman, 1986; Moorcroft, 1993). You can understand why shift workers have trouble sleeping during the day, because sunlight streams in and the rest of the world makes daytime noises. Furthermore, shift workers often fall asleep on the job (Coleman, 1986; Coren, 1996). The brief naps may be harmless in some cases, but they can be very serious for airplane pilots, truckers, and others whose sleepiness can kill dozens of people. In one case, an unannounced late-night inspection of a nuclear power plant found 5 of the 13 employees asleep—a report that did not amuse nearby residents.

Jet travel also disrupts circadian rhythms. **Jet lag** is the term for the disturbances in body rhythm caused by lengthy journeys requiring time-zone changes. In contrast, travelers do not experience jet lag when they fly in a north-south direction, without changing any time zones.

Variations in Amount of Sleep Our theme of individual differences is prominent when we look at the variations in the number of hours that people spend sleeping. Figure 5.1 shows how normal undergraduates vary in their sleep duration (Hicks et al., 1990). As you can see, some students require three times as much sleep as others.

Age has a significant influence on sleep. Newborns sleep about 17 hours a day (Mindell, 1993). Elderly people sleep about 6 hours a day and are more likely to report difficulty falling asleep and staying asleep (Friedman at al., 1991; Monk et al., 1991).

Critical Thinking Exercise 5.2

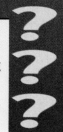

Write down your answers to the following questions about circadian rhythms.

a. What special kinds of precautions should researchers take when they interact with participants in a free-running study, so that they do not reveal the true time of day?

b. Why might the people who have shift-work jobs be unrepresentative of the general population? What about the people on whom jet-lag data are gathered—are they representative of the general population?

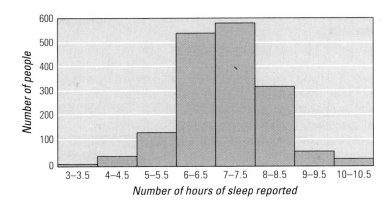

FIGURE 5.1

Self-Reported Sleep Durations for College Students
Source: Based on data from Hicks et al., 1990.

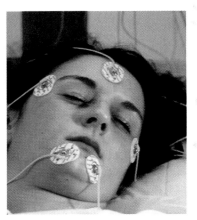

FIGURE 5.2

A person prepared for a night's sleep in a sleep laboratory.

Stages of Sleep

We've been examining our 24-hour cyclic pattern of sleeping and waking. We also have shorter cyclic patterns during sleep, consisting of five different stages of sleep.

Conducting Sleep Research To study sleep, researchers cannot casually stroll into a volunteer's house, perch on a chair near the bed, and watch this somewhat self-conscious individual begin to snooze. Instead, research must be conducted in a sleep laboratory, which includes an observation room next to several bedrooms.

Imagine that you have volunteered to participate in a sleep study, and you have just arrived at the lab. You introduce yourself to the researchers; because you have just finished reading about circadian rhythms, you realize that they qualify as shift workers. After you get ready for bed, the researchers tape the electrodes of an electroencephalogram onto your scalp. (You also remember reading in Chapter 3 that the EEG painlessly measures electrical activity in the brain.) In addition, the researchers attach additional electrodes to measure your eye movements and your muscle tension. (See Figure 5.2.) They may also measure your breathing rate, your heart rate, and your level of genital arousal (Anch et al., 1988; Coren, 1996).

As you might imagine, researchers generally ignore data collected on the first night, because sleep patterns are usually distorted by the unfamiliar situation (Moorcroft, 1993). The following night, though, the sleep project begins in earnest, and the researchers start to collect various measures. When you close your eyes and relax, your EEG shows a pattern of alpha waves, which you can see at the top of Figure 5.3. Soon afterwards, you begin to drift from a pleasant drowsiness into the stages of sleep.

The Five Stages Throughout the night, you will drift back and forth among five sleep stages.

In Stage 1 sleep, the EEG records small, irregular brain waves. You are drifting into a light sleep. You can be readily awakened from Stage 1 sleep.

In Stage 2 sleep, the EEG shows very rapid bursts of activity known as sleep spindles. If a sleep researcher sneezed next door, you probably would not hear it.

In Stage 3 sleep, your EEG begins to show a few delta waves, at the very slow frequency of about 2 per second. Sleep researchers determine whether you are in Stage 1, 2, 3, or 4 in terms of the ratio between the number of sleep spindles and the number of delta waves (Munglani & Jones, 1992). During Stage 3 sleep, your breathing slows substantially, and your muscles are completely relaxed.

In Stage 4 sleep, the EEG now shows almost exclusively delta waves. You are now in deep sleep. A sleep researcher could probably wander into your room without waking you.

These four stages of sleep do not tell the complete story, however. You do not slowly drift downward into deep sleep during the first half of the night and then drift upward into light sleep as morning approaches. Instead, you spend the first 30 to 45

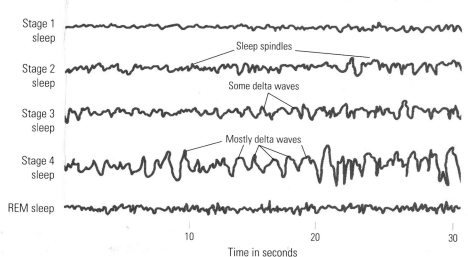

Alpha waves

Stage 1 sleep

Sleep spindles

Stage 2 sleep

Some delta waves

Stage 3 sleep

Mostly delta waves

Stage 4 sleep

REM sleep

10   20   30
Time in seconds

FIGURE 5.3

EEG Patterns (measured by changes in voltage)
Patterns shown represent (from top) the stage prior to sleep, the four non-REM stages, and REM sleep.

minutes progressing from Stage 1 to Stage 4, and the next 30 to 45 minutes reversing the direction, back up to Stage 1.

Then from Stage 1, you enter a very different stage called REM sleep. During **REM sleep** (rapid eye movement sleep), your eyes move rapidly beneath your closed eyelids. Notice that the delta waves disappear in REM sleep. REM sleep is quite different from non-REM sleep. For instance, brain-imaging studies show that the neurons in the cerebral cortex become much more active (Munglani & Jones, 1992). Your heart beats more rapidly, and you breathe quickly and irregularly. Your genitals are likely to show arousal—with moisture and swelling in the vaginal area for women and erections for men.

REM sleep is also more likely to be associated with dreaming. When people are awakened during REM sleep, about 80% report that they just had a vivid dream—even if they had claimed beforehand that they never dream (Squier & Domhoff, 1998). We will discuss dreams in more detail later in this section.

A healthy adult usually has between four and six sleep cycles every night, with each cycle lasting about 90 minutes (Anch et al., 1988; Moorcroft, 1993). Figure 5.4 shows how a person might sleep in a typical night.

The brain's activity, as revealed by the EEG, is related to the stages of sleep. Researchers have determined that several brain structures are responsible for sleep. As Chapter 3 mentioned, the reticular formation in the hindbrain seems to play an important role. For example, it helps regulate REM sleep. Furthermore, when the reticular formation receives electrical stimulation, a sleeping person wakes up (Kalat, 1995). The hypothalamus and other structures in the limbic system are crucial in producing sleep (Adler, 1993; Kalat, 1995; Sherin et al., 1996). However, the details of this process—and the brain chemicals related to sleep—are still quite mysterious (Cravatt et al., 1995). Consistent with the complexity theme (Theme 3) of this book, several different structures must work cooperatively to regulate our patterns of sleep.

Effects of Sleep Deprivation

Think about a day when you had little or no sleep on the previous night. Did you find that you performed normally on some tasks, but your accuracy suffered on other tasks? Babkoff and his colleagues (1991) argue that the effects of sleep deprivation are complicated, a conclusion that certainly supports Theme 3 of this textbook. In other words, we cannot simply say "Yes, sleep deprivation affects behavior" or "No, sleep deprivation has no effect on behavior."

FIGURE 5.4

A Typical Pattern of Normal Sleep

Note that we have four stages of sleep; the black bars represent REM sleep.

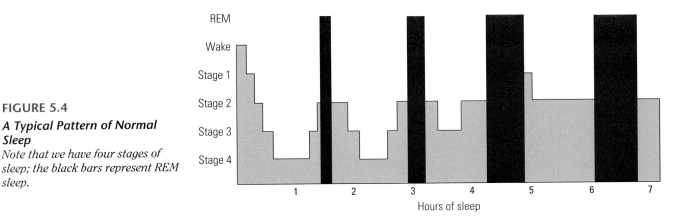

For example, performance on a boring task often shows a decline after just a few hours of sleep deprivation (Babkoff et al., 1991). If the task is interesting, sleep deprivation has little effect. A second important factor, as you might imagine, is task difficulty. If the task is difficult, performance declines after moderate sleep deprivation. If the task is easy, sleep deprivation has little effect (Babkoff et al., 1991). Motivation is also important (Dinges & Kribbs, 1991). If you're not highly motivated, sleep deprivation affects performance. On the other hand, if you can persuade yourself to try hard, sleep deprivation has little effect.

A fourth factor—time of day—is more subtle. If you try a task at a time of day when you typically perform poorly, your performance will decline after only moderate sleep deprivation. If you try the task when you're at your best, sleep deprivation has little effect (Babkoff et al., 1991). Figure 5.5 shows a typical task in sleep-deprivation research. On this boring, difficult task, sleep-deprived people perform disastrously at the "wrong" time of day.

This research should encourage you to think about whether you really should stay up all night studying for an important exam. If you expect the test to be both interesting and easy, if you're highly motivated to do well, and if the test is scheduled for an ideal time of day, sleep deprivation may not hurt you. In other cases, you may want to read the last part of Chapter 7 in this text (on effective study techniques), follow those hints, and go to bed at the normal time!

Critical Thinking Exercise 5.3

Write down your answers to the following questions about sleep deprivation.

a. Suppose that researchers at University A assess the effects of sleep deprivation on memory. They find that people remember much more material if they are well rested than if they have been sleep deprived. Researchers at University B try to replicate the study, using the same instructions and the same stimuli. They find that sleep deprivation does not influence recall. How might you explain the discrepancy?

b. Suppose you read in a newspaper that a man has gone without sleep for one full week. According to the report, "He's never felt better!" What questions would you ask before trusting the article?

Why Do We Sleep?

As you know, a particular behavior probably has more than one explanation. Because we sleep for about one-third of our life, we probably have more than one reason for sleeping.

FIGURE 5.5

This is a typical task studied in sleep-deprivation research. People are instructed to trace the star, using their nondominant hand, watching their hand in a mirror. Because the task is boring and difficult, sleep-deprived people make many errors if their motivation is low and they are tested at the "low" point in their circadian cycle.

The answer to the puzzling question of why we sleep is far from clear (Coren, 1996). However, two likely reasons are that sleep is restorative and that sleep is adaptive.

- *The restorative function:* Researchers have found that the body manufactures useful substances while we are sleeping. Specifically, the body produces growth hormones and brain protein during sleep, and more energy is stored in the cells during this period (Anch et al., 1988; Moorcroft, 1993). Also, if you've been sleep-deprived for a long period, you'll sleep longer once you have the opportunity (Moorcroft, 1993), though you won't make up entirely for the lost sleep. This partial compensation supports the restorative function of sleep.

- *The adaptive function:* Another possibility emphasizes the evolutionary approach. Consistent with our discussion of this approach in Chapter 3, the specific pattern of sleep developed by each species may have increased the likelihood of that species' survival. The humans who spent their dark hours sleeping in caves may have been more likely to pass on their genes to future generations. In contrast, humans who spent their nights wandering around in the dark probably encountered wild beasts and other perils. The mechanisms for sleep may persist in modern humans, even though we no longer need sleep for the same reasons as our distant ancestors (Moorcroft, 1993; Webb, 1992).

The problem, of course, is that we cannot directly test either of these explanations. For instance, our bodies may restore the levels of certain substances during sleep, but this observation does not demonstrate that we need sleep for this reason. And no one will be able to demonstrate experimentally that sleep-needy prehistoric humans were more likely to survive (Coren, 1996). At present, then, we have two plausible guesses for why we humans need to sleep, but we still need more persuasive evidence in order to accept either explanation.

Sleep Disorders

So far, we have emphasized normal sleep patterns. However, millions of North Americans do not enjoy a normal night's sleep. For instance, the American Sleep Disorders Association listed 368 accredited sleep centers in the United States in 1998, and Sleep/Wake Disorders Canada lists 75 in that country. We'll consider two sleep disorders, insomnia and sleep apnea.

Insomnia   The term **insomnia** refers to difficulty in falling asleep or remaining asleep (American Psychiatric Association, 1994a). Insomnia is a persistent problem for 10% to 17% of adults, and countless others struggle with insomnia from time to time (Morin et al., 1994; Stepanski, 1993). In general, older people have more problems than younger people, and women have more problems than men (Morin, 1993; Stepanski, 1993).

TABLE 5.1 Treating Insomnia

Here are some general recommendations proposed by some resources on insomnia.

1. Do not read or do work in bed; the bed should be a powerful stimulus to sleep.
2. Go to bed only when you are sleepy, and don't sleep late to compensate for lost sleep.
3. Do not lie in bed thinking or worrying. Get up and do something boring until you feel sleepy. Some people find it helpful to describe their worries briefly on a sheet of paper.
4. If you keep glancing at a clock, remove it.
5. Once you are in bed, relax your muscles and imagine yourself in a soothing setting.
6. Avoid caffeine and alcohol after about 4:00 p.m.
7. Avoid long-term use of sleeping pills. Some pills are useless; others produce dependency, and some have dangerous side effects.
8. Improve your sleeping environment; make sure that the room is quiet, dark, and the correct temperature.
9. If all else fails, contact one of the hundreds of sleep centers throughout North America. U.S. residents should write to the American Sleep Disorders Association, 1610 Fourteenth Street, NW, Suite 300, Rochester, MN 55901. Canadian residents should write to Sleep/ Wake Disorders Canada, 3080 Yonge Street, Suite 5055, Toronto, Canada M4N 3N1, or call 1-800-387-9253. (This number can be accessed only from a phone in Canada.)

Sources: From Coleman, 1986; Cowley, 1991; Moorcroft, 1993; Morin, 1993; Morin et al., 1994; "Sleep Disorders," 1994; Stepanski, 1993.

Researchers have identified several kinds of insomnia. For example, most people have experienced transient insomnia at some time in their lives, perhaps just before a major exam or after a fight with the boss. Transient insomnia does not need any special attention. In the case of learned insomnia, people are extremely anxious about whether they will sleep well. People with learned insomnia can usually be treated with about five hours of therapy. This therapy includes relaxation training, as well as information about helpful sleep habits (Morin et al., 1994). Other insomnias arise from psychiatric problems such as depression (Buysse & Nofzinger, 1994; "Sleep Disorders," 1994). Finally, subjective insomnia occurs when a person complains of insomnia, even when he or she has normal sleep patterns. In fact, most insomniacs underestimate their total nightly sleep (Bonnet & Arand, 1994). Table 5.1 lists some suggestions for correcting insomnia.

Sleep Apnea   When a person has **sleep apnea,** that person's breathing actually stops for at least 10 seconds during each episode (Westbrook, 1993). Someone with sleep apnea may experience interrupted breathing more than 300 times each night (Mead, 1996). Each time, the individual wakes up briefly with a loud snort and then begins to breathe normally again. Apnea can usually be traced to physical explanations, such as a narrow respiratory passage (Mead, 1996; Westbrook, 1993). As you might imagine, people who awake dozens of times each night will be sleepy during the day, and they are at risk for accidents (Westbrook, 1993). People with apnea should visit a sleep clinic, because this disorder can be dangerous as well as unpleasant.

Dreaming

In our dreams, we can overcome the constraints of our conscious daytime thoughts. Some dreams are so different from ordinary awareness that they were once thought to be caused by the visits of alien beings (Oswald, 1987b). Figures 5.6 and 5.7 show two representations of these night visitors. Before you read further, try Demonstration 5.3.

We mentioned earlier that dreaming is more likely with REM sleep than with non-REM sleep. For example, when researchers wake sleepers during REM sleep, about 80% of participants report dreaming. When sleepers are awakened during non-REM sleep, about 30% to 50% of participants report dreaming (Schatzman &

FIGURE 5.6
"A Maiden's Dream" by Lorenzo Lotto.

FIGURE 5.7
"Nightmare" by Henry Fuseli.

Fenwick, 1994; Squier & Domhoff, 1998; Strauch & Meier, 1996). People who had been in one of the non-REM stages of sleep often report that they were thinking, a more orderly, unemotional activity. Let's examine the information about the content of dreams, and then we'll discuss several explanations for why we dream.

The Content of Dreams   College students often report dreams in which they are being chased by a threatening figure; even people who live in crime-free neighborhoods report these dreams. College students also report dreams about falling, flying Superman-style, and wearing inappropriate clothes . . . or no clothes at all. To some extent, though, these reports may simply reflect stereotypes about what we are supposed to dream about (Squier & Domhoff, 1998). Examination-anxiety dreams are also common: You can't find the place where you are supposed to take an exam, or your pen won't write, or you're running out of time (Van de Castle, 1993). The dreams that people report often include bizarre events or discontinuities in the narrative, for example

---

DEMONSTRATION 5.3   Beliefs About Dreams

Answer each of the following questions; write either *true* or *false* in front of the item. The answers can be found at the end of the chapter, on Page 183.

_____   1.   When some people dream, they are aware that they are dreaming.
_____   2.   Most dreams are in black and white.
_____   3.   Eating weird food (like sauerkraut or pickled tomatoes) causes you to dream more.
_____   4.   Dreams can incorporate sounds that occur in the environment surrounding a sleeper.
_____   5.   Although dreams seem like they go on for a long time, they really occur in a flash.
_____   6.   Blind people do not dream.
_____   7.   At present, we have no evidence that people can manage to control the outcome of their dreams.

with dancers suddenly appearing out of nowhere (Kahn & Hobson, 1994). The content of your dreams is sometimes related to the thoughts you had just before falling asleep (Botman & Crovitz, 1989–1990; Rados & Cartwright, 1982).

Some dreams are nightmares. A **nightmare** is an intense dream that occurs during REM sleep and causes anxiety or fear (Moorcroft, 1993; Oswald, 1987b). Typically, a nightmare occurs during the second half of the sleep period, during a long REM period of at least 15 minutes. This REM period may show somewhat more eye movement than other REM segments (Hartmann, 1993). In a nightmare, you often respond to a threat by moving—both in the dream and in reality. This movement is typically followed by awakening (Moorcroft, 1993).

Why Do We Dream?   Earlier, we noted that researchers have not clearly identified the reasons why we sleep. Their explanations for why we dream are similarly unsuccessful. Nevertheless, we will explore some of these theories here.

Sigmund Freud provided the first major theory of dreams; we'll examine his influential work more thoroughly in later chapters. In his book, *The Interpretation of Dreams,* Freud (1900/1953) argued that dreams are connected with our waking life. Specifically, a dream represents the fulfillment of wishes we hold in our unconscious when we are awake (Schatzman & Fenwick, 1994; Trosman, 1993). According to this approach, our dreams express—in disguised form—the sexual and aggressive impulses that inhabit our unconscious minds. This theoretical framework supposedly facilitates dream interpretation, and analysts work to uncover the true meaning of dreams. For example, a dream about a tunnel might represent a vagina, whereas a dream about shaving might represent masturbation. An analyst could presumably uncover these hidden messages and provide awareness to the dreamer.

Freud argued that we can satisfy some of our sexual wishes and other forbidden desires through our dreams. Therefore, our dreams provide "safety valves." Without them, energy from these desires would reach unacceptable levels and threaten our psychological well-being. Current theorists propose that Freud should be praised for pointing out how dreams express emotional concerns. However, his specific theories of dream formation have not been supported (Squier & Domhoff, 1998).

A very different view of the function of dreams, based on current neurophysiology and cognitive psychology, is called the **neurocognitive model.** This approach has been developed primarily by J. Allan Hobson and John Antrobus. An essential part of this model is the **activation-synthesis hypothesis,** which proposes that the hindbrain transmits a chaotic pattern of signals to the cerebral cortex *(activation)*, and then higher-level cognitive processes in the cerebral cortex try to integrate the signals into a dream plot *(synthesis)* (Hobson, 1988, 1990; Hobson & Stickgold, 1995). However, even the most competent cortex can't completely weave together the plot elements from these chaotic signals. As a result, our dreams are filled with discontinuities, such as dancers appearing out of nowhere.

John Antrobus developed this activation-synthesis model further (Antrobus, 1990, 1991; Antrobus & Bertini, 1992). He describes it in terms of the connectionist approach, a new facet of cognitive psychology that we will discuss in more detail in Chapter 7. According to the **connectionist approach,** a stimulus cue activates a concept, which leads to the activation of other, related concepts. When you are awake, and you see your friend Chris, the visual stimulus of Chris activates in your cerebral cortex some other concepts that you have associated with Chris (perhaps the name of Chris's hometown, her major, when you first met her, and so forth). When you are asleep, the outside world does not provide any signals to your cerebral cortex. However, the hindbrain provides signals, and your cortex treats those signals as if they came from the outside world. Specifically, each signal still leads to the activation of other, related concepts.

Sometimes the signals from the hindbrain reach the portions of the central cortex that are concerned with vision. Activation of this part of the cortex will produce a visual image that is bright, clearly focused, and colorful. This activation will spread to other, connected concepts. Meanwhile, another signal from the hindbrain

Researchers disagree about the function of dreams: Are they symbolic, as the Freudian approach argues, or do they represent the brain's attempt to interpret random signals, as the activation-synthesis model proposes?

may reach a different part of the visual cortex, producing a visual image that is unrelated to the first image. This activation also spreads to other connected concepts. Other signals activate still other parts of the cortex (including nonvisual areas). The arrival of these hindbrain signals in the cortex points out that bottom-up processes are important in dreaming, just as they are when we perceive stimuli in the external world (Hobson & Stickgold, 1995). We discussed these bottom-up processes in Chapter 4, in connection with pattern recognition.

Furthermore, our cognitive processes are as active when we dream as when we perceive and think during our waking hours. These cognitive processes work to make sense of this complex pattern of stimuli in the cortex. Basically, they try to "dream up" a story line that weaves together these unrelated items. To some extent, the top-down processes (also described in Chapter 4) will use our concepts and expectations to make sense out of this chaos. Also, our motivations (e.g., for food, sex, or achievement) may guide these efforts to construct a sensible solution. However, Antrobus (1991) argues that the primary flow of information during sleep is bottom-up—from the hindbrain to the cortex. You've probably also noticed that our dreams do *not* make as much sense as the events in our lives, though most are reasonably well organized (Weinstein et al., 1991).

To help you understand the neurocognitive approach to dreams, try Demonstration 5.4.

DEMONSTRATION 5.4 Relating the Neurocognitive Model to Your Own Dream

To try this demonstration, you need to remember the major themes of one dream. You may find it easier to recall a dream if you arrange to lie in bed for a few minutes after awakening one morning; try to lie quietly, letting your mind flow freely. Write down a few key words, and fill in any gaps when you review the dream a few minutes later.

Try to identify those elements of your dream that seem vividly visual; Hobson and Antrobus would suggest that these fragments were produced by stimulation from the hindbrain to the visual cortex. Can you identify any fragments that would suggest stimulation of other senses (e.g., motor or auditory)? Now figure out how the connectionist approach would explain how each basic clue (e.g., a visual image) was enriched by related concepts. How did the story line of your dream manage to connect the elements of your dream? Did any elements remain unconnected?

Keep in mind, however, the earlier point that we often lack insight about the way our higher mental processes operate. Our after-the-fact speculations may not match what really happened!

SECTION SUMMARY: *SLEEPING AND DREAMING*

1. We maintain circadian rhythms partly because of zeitgebers and partly because of our internal clocks; without zeitgebers, we would run on a slightly longer internal clock of about 25 hours.

2. Shift schedules and jet lag disrupt the normal circadian rhythms, producing irregular sleep and poorer work performance.

3. People vary widely in the amount of sleep they obtain; sleep decreases markedly across the life span.

4. When people fall asleep, they drift from light sleep (Stage 1) through deep sleep (Stage 4) and then back again to light sleep; at this point, they enter REM sleep, when most dreaming occurs; this cycle is repeated four to six times each night.

5. Structures in the brain that regulate sleep include the reticular formation, the hypothalamus, and the limbic system.

6. Sleep deprivation has little influence on later performance if the task is interesting and easy, if your motivation is high, and if you are tested at an ideal time of day; in other situations, sleep deprivation can harm your performance.

7. According to one theory, we need sleep because it is restorative. According to the evolutionary approach, it is adaptive.

8. Insomnia is a common sleep disorder that has many causes; in sleep apnea, breathing may stop hundreds of times each night, producing sleep disruption.

9. Common dream themes include being chased, falling, flying, wearing inappropriate clothes, and experiencing test anxiety; dream content is often related to thoughts that precede sleep.

10. One theory of dreams is the Freudian theory that dreams are symbolic. Another theory is the neurocognitive model, which proposes that the hindbrain sends random signals, and the cerebral cortex makes sense of these signals by relying on connections with related concepts (connectionism), with some assistance from concepts and expectations (top-down processing) and from motivational factors.

DRUGS THAT INFLUENCE CONSCIOUSNESS

We began this chapter by examining normal waking consciousness. Then we explored sleep, an altered state of consciousness associated with different electrical activity in the brain, as well as less coherent thoughts. Both of these states of consciousness occur quite naturally as part of everyday life. However, consciousness can also be altered when people use drugs. In this section, we'll begin by defining some basic terms, then consider four categories of drugs, and finally examine patterns of drug use. In Chapter 10, we'll discuss how drug use during pregnancy can harm the developing embryo and fetus, and Chapter 18 explores the deadly effects of cigarette smoking.

Basic Terms

Psychoactive drugs are chemical substances that influence the brain, alter consciousness, and affect people's behavior, emotions, and thinking (Landry, 1994). Psychoactive drugs usually work via neurotransmitters. As we noted in Chapter 3, **neurotransmitters** are chemical substances stored in the neurons that alter the electrical activity of the postsynaptic neuron. Psychoactive drugs typically increase or decrease the availability of neurotransmitters, or they may even compete with these neurotransmitters.

Frequent use of a psychoactive drug can produce addiction. **Addiction** is defined as a pattern of behavior in which people repetitively and compulsively take a psychoactive drug (Heishman et al., 1997). Frequent use of a psychoactive drug can also produce **tolerance,** a condition in which the same amount of a drug comes to have a reduced effect. As a result, the drug user needs larger amounts of the drug to produce the same sensation (Heishman et al., 1997; Landry, 1994).

Sometimes people who have been frequently using a psychoactive drug will stop taking it. After several hours without the drug, they may experience **withdrawal symptoms,** which are the undesirable effects of discontinued drug use. These symptoms vary, depending upon the nature of the drug. However, they may include intense depression, agitation, nausea, abdominal cramps, and muscle spasms (Goldstein,

TABLE 5.2 Some Important Psychoactive Drugs

1. Depressants
   a. Alcohol
   b. Tranquilizers
2. Opiates
   a. Morphine
   b. Heroin
3. Stimulants
   a. Caffeine
   b. Nicotine
   c. Amphetamines (e.g., Dexedrine)
   d. Cocaine and crack
4. Hallucinogens
   a. Marijuana
   b. Lysergic acid diethylamide (LSD)

1994; Heishman et al., 1997; Landry, 1994). It may take weeks for the individual to feel normal in the absence of the drug.

Psychoactive drugs include illegal drugs such as cocaine and LSD. Psychoactive drugs also include the alcohol in the holiday eggnog, the caffeine in a cup of coffee, and the nicotine in a package of cigarettes. Although these three drugs are legal, they alter consciousness and can cause as much harm as illegal drugs. Psychoactive drugs also include the prescribed medications that are used in treating psychological disorders; we'll postpone our discussion of these drugs until Chapter 15. In this section, we'll consider four categories of psychoactive drugs: alcohol, opiates, stimulants, and hallucinogens. Table 5.2 lists some of these drugs.

Alcohol

Alcohol is a **depressant**—that is, a drug that depresses central nervous system functioning. Other depressants include tranquilizers such as Valium and barbiturates such as Seconal. These depressants are prescription drugs used to treat psychological disorders; we'll discuss them in Chapter 15. In this chapter, we'll focus on the most commonly used depressant, alcohol.

Before you read further, try Demonstration 5.5, on Page 170, which is based on a survey we'll discuss shortly. In this "In Depth" feature, we'll examine the extent of the alcohol problem, as well as the influence of alcohol on psychological processes.

The Scope of the Alcohol Problem

When we examine the nature of the alcohol problem, we can explore a variety of dependent variables. We can look at the physical effects of long-term drinking and discover that the liver, pancreas, heart, and central nervous system are all affected (Rivers, 1994). For instance, PET scans of alcoholic individuals show that their brain metabolism is much lower than the metabolism of nonalcoholic individuals (Parsons, 1996a).

We can look at the national statistics and learn that between 18,000 and 19,000 U.S. automobile fatalities each year can be traced to alcohol (Brake, 1994; Brewer et al., 1994). A disproportionate number of deaths from drowning, fires, violent crimes, and suicides are also alcohol related (Brake, 1994; Rivers, 1994). In fact, alcohol kills more than five times as many people every year as all illegal drugs combined (Royce & Scratchley, 1996). We can even measure the effects of alcohol in financial terms. The total loss in the United States from alcoholism and other alcohol problems is estimated to be $148 billion (Royce & Scratchley, 1996).

When we look at the percentage of U.S. residents with alcohol-related problems, we find that the rate has decreased during the last decade (Midanik & Clark, 1995; Royce & Scratchley, 1996). However, alcohol problems have actually *increased* in recent years on college campuses (Parsons, 1996a; Wechsler et al., 1994; Wechsler et al., 1995).

Drunk-driving accidents kill between 18,000 and 19,000 U.S. residents every year.

DEMONSTRATION 5.5 Questionnaire About Alcohol Consumption and Its Behavioral Consequences

Answer each of the following questions as accurately as possible.

1. Think about your behavior during the last two weeks. How many times have you had four or more drinks in a row if you are female, *or* five or more drinks in a row if you are male? (The operational definition of a "drink" is 12 ounces of beer or a wine cooler, 4 ounces of wine, or 1.25 ounces of liquor.) _____

2. Since the beginning of this school year, how many times have you personally experienced each of the following problems as a consequence of drinking alcohol?

_____ a. Had a hangover
_____ b. Missed a class
_____ c. Fallen behind in schoolwork
_____ d. Done something you later regretted
_____ e. Forgotten what you did
_____ f. Argued with friends

_____ g. Had unplanned sexual activity
_____ h. Failed to use protection when you had sex
_____ i. Damaged property
_____ j. Got into trouble with campus or local police
_____ k. Got injured or hurt
_____ l. Required medical treatment for an alcohol overdose

Source: Based on Wechsler et al., 1994.

(IN DEPTH continued)

Let's look at a carefully conducted study of drinking behavior among U.S. college students. Henry Wechsler and his coauthors (1994) mailed questionnaires to students at 140 colleges that were selected to be representative of all U.S. colleges. A total of 17,592 students returned the 20-page questionnaire. The response rate, about 70%, was impressively high for such a long questionnaire.

One of the most striking findings was the large percentage of students who engaged in **binge drinking**—defined as four or more drinks in a row for females and five or more drinks in a row for males—during the preceding two weeks. (The researchers specified lower alcohol consumption for females because their body weight is generally lower.) Specifically, 50% of the males and 39% of the females could be categorized as binge drinkers. Binge drinking was more common among college students in the Northeast or North Central regions of the United States (in comparison to the West or the South). Students at women's colleges and at historically Black institutions were *less* likely to binge than students at other institutions.

The questionnaire also included items that assessed the behavioral consequences of drinking. The 12 items in Question 2 from Demonstration 5.5 are based on similar items from the questionnaire designed by Wechsler and his colleagues (1994). The majority of binge drinkers had experienced a hangover, and about half reported missing a class or doing something they later regretted. Those who had binged at least three times during the previous two weeks also frequently reported forgetting what they had done, getting behind in schoolwork, arguing with friends, and engaging in unplanned sexual activity. Surprisingly, however, less than 1% of these frequent binge drinkers classified themselves as "problem drinkers."

The incidence of binge drinking is worrisome, but we need to keep in mind that many U.S. college students do not have an alcohol problem. Specifically, 15% of the men and 16% of the women reported that they did not drink alcohol; 35% of the men and 45% of the women also reported that they drank occasionally, but had not had a binge-drinking episode in the previous two weeks. However, these students are still likely to suffer—from the problems created by other students who are binge drinkers. For example, the majority of respondents to this survey said that their sleep or studying had been interrupted by a drunken student or that they had taken care of a student who was drunk.

So far, we've looked at the dimensions of the alcohol problem, especially on college campuses. Now let's consider how alcohol influences psychological processes.

The Effects of Alcohol on Psychological Processes Let's examine in some detail how alcohol impairs thought and raises levels of violence. We'll also see that people who *believe* they have consumed alcohol may change their behavior—even when their drink actually contained no alcohol.

We know that alcohol can influence thinking. For example, alcohol affects performance on **vigilance tasks**—that is, tasks that require detecting and responding to a stimulus (Koelega, 1995). We also know that alcohol affects people's memory (e.g., Goldman et al., 1991; Read et al., 1992).

In fact, as Steele and Josephs (1990) argue, alcohol intoxication impairs almost every aspect of thinking. For instance, a person who is drunk will have trouble processing several cues at the same time. A person who is drunk will also have difficulty encoding meaning from incoming information, as well as difficulty forming abstract concepts. As a result, a drunk person may pick up some important cues that encourage action, but this same person may miss other cues that suggest he or she should definitely *not* act.

Steele and Josephs propose that the impaired thinking has an important consequence for a person who is drunk: He or she will not respond normally to important cues. Imagine this situation. You are living off campus and have just had a fierce argument with your landlord. You're now at a party at the house next door, and you turn your head to face this despised landlord. If you are sober, you will experience response conflict. On the one hand, you want to scream at him, but you also realize an instant later that a terrible scene would be embarrassing—and you might even be evicted. So you grit your teeth and suppress your rage. However, suppose that you encounter your landlord after several drinks. His face is a cue that provokes anger, but alcohol has suppressed your awareness of the unfortunate consequences of telling him off. So your anger erupts . . . and the next morning, you're searching for a new apartment.

The term *alcohol myopia* (pronounced "my-*owe*-pea-uh") is used to describe this important effect of alcohol (Josephs & Steele, 1990). **Alcohol myopia** means that a person under the influence of alcohol becomes "shortsighted," processing fewer cues and also processing those cues less accurately. Research generally supports the concept of alcohol myopia (Ito et al., 1996; Josephs & Steele, 1990; MacDonald et al., 1995).

We can see how this shortsightedness—and failure to consider negative consequences—can lead to violence in social situations. For example, alcohol is involved in about 65% of murders, 88% of knifings, 65% of spouse batterings, and 55% of physical child abuse cases (Kent, 1990; Rivers, 1994; Steele & Josephs, 1990). Moreover, as Pernanen's (1991) survey of a Canadian community illustrated, many incidents of alcohol-related violence are not reported to the police. Reviews of the research confirm that alcohol often increases aggression (Bushman & Cooper, 1990; Ito et al., 1996).

As you have been reading about the effects of alcohol, perhaps you've thought about a potential problem with this research. In Chapter 2 you learned that people's expectations can influence the dependent variable. Perhaps people who have had too much to drink have confused thoughts and act violently because they *expect* alcohol to make them this way. Psychologists have become increasingly interested in the importance of people's expectations (Goldman et al., 1991; Leigh, 1989; McKim, 1991). To what extent does a drinker's expectations about the effects of alcohol actually influence his or her behavior?

A special research design can be used to sort out the effects of the drug itself, as opposed to the effects of people's expectations about how they *should* behave. This design, called the **balanced-placebo design,** consists of four groups of participants, half of whom expect that they will be drinking alcohol and half of whom do not. Furthermore, half of the participants actually do receive alcohol and half do not. (See Table 5.3.) This kind of design allows researchers to discover the situations in which behavior is influenced either by alcohol or by expectations about alcohol. For example, it is possible that alcohol makes people uncoordinated only when they think that they are drinking alcohol (Condition 1), but it has no effect when they think their beverage contains no alcohol (Condition 2).

TABLE 5.3 The Balanced-Placebo Design to Test the Effects of Alcohol

		Expected Beverage Content	
		Alcohol	No Alcohol
True Beverage Content	Alcohol	Condition 1	Condition 2
	No Alcohol	Condition 3	Condition 4

(IN DEPTH continued)

Jay Hull and Charles Bond (1986) located a total of 36 experiments that used the balanced-placebo design. They then conducted a meta-analysis. These researchers concluded that alcohol *consumption* had a significant effect on behavior that is not social. Specifically, it impaired memory and motor behavior, and it improved mood. These three effects occurred whether or not people thought they were drinking alcohol. (In other words, Condition 1 and Condition 2 in Table 5.3 were similar.) Surprisingly, however, alcohol consumption did not make people feel more sexually aroused. In contrast, the current conclusion is that alcohol consumption does significantly increase aggression (Bushman & Cooper, 1990; Hull & Bond, 1986; Ito et al., 1996).

How did alcohol *expectation* affect behavior? That is, do people who think that the orange juice contains vodka actually behave differently from those who think they are drinking straight orange juice? People who thought they were drinking alcohol were no more likely to experience impaired memory or motor behavior or improved mood; expectations also have no effect on aggression. However, those who thought they were drinking alcohol were more likely to report increased sexual arousal.

Let's apply these conclusions. Suppose that a young man has opened a bottle of vodka and consumed several ounces of it. The physiological effects of the alcohol cause him to forget, to be uncoordinated, to feel happy, and to become more aggressive. (As Table 5.4 shows, all four of these items list a significant effect.) Because this man knows he has consumed alcohol, he also reports feeling more sexually aroused; expectancy—rather than the alcohol itself—causes this increase in sexual arousal. Now imagine that this young man is at a party where he meets an attractive woman. Josephs and Steele's (1990) concept of alcohol myopia helps to explain why acquaintance rape is relatively common after binge drinking. This man may see a faint smile on the woman's face, but fail to pick up the fear in her eyes as he begins to remove her clothes. Aggression, sexual arousal, and poor judgment could have serious social consequences for both of these individuals.

Critical Thinking Exercise 5.4

Write down your answers to the following questions about alcohol consumption and behavior.

a. The large-scale study by Wechsler and his coauthors obtained an impressive 70% return rate from college students. As a college student yourself, how do you think they motivated so many students to return their questionnaires? Do you believe that the respondents would be representative of all college students, with respect to alcohol consumption?

b. In the balanced-placebo design, some people have been told that they are drinking a beverage containing alcohol; however, the drink actually has no alcohol. Why might some participants not be convinced that their drink contains alcohol, and how might you address this problem?

TABLE 5.4   The Effects of Alcohol Consumption and Alcohol Expectation on Behavior

	Alcohol Consumption	Alcohol Expectation (without consumption)
Memory	Significant effect	No effect
Motor Behavior	Significant effect	No effect
Mood	Significant effect	No effect
Aggression	Significant effect	No effect
Sexual Arousal	No effect	Significant effect

Sources: Based on Bushman & Cooper, 1990; Goldman et al., 1991; Hull & Bond, 1986; Ito et al., 1996; Read et al., 1992.

Opiates

Opiates are a class of drugs that have three effects: They depress the functioning of the central nervous system; they relieve pain; and they also encourage sleep (Jaffe, 1991; Julien, 1995). Opiates—which include both morphine and heroin—imitate the action of endorphins. As discussed in Chapters 3 and 4, **endorphins** occur naturally in the brain; when released, they decrease a person's sensitivity to pain. Addicts who inject opiates report a blissful feeling and decreased anxiety. When they stop taking an opiate, they often experience severe withdrawal symptoms.

Non-addict patients who receive opiates for pain relief often report only a sense of tranquillity, rather than a major alteration in mood (Jaffe, 1991). However, people who are "recreational" users of heroin receive a positive reaction that encourages addiction. A long-term study of heroin addicts showed that substance use and criminal activity were still common—among the survivors—24 years later (Hser et al., 1993). Addiction to heroin and other opiates is a serious problem that is difficult to treat ("Treatment of Drug Abuse," 1995).

Stimulants

Stimulants, as the name implies, are chemicals that increase central nervous system functioning. In general, they operate by increasing the release of neurotransmitters, such as dopamine in the cortex and the reticular activating system (Dusek & Girdano, 1987). Stimulants include caffeine, nicotine, the amphetamines, cocaine, and crack.

Caffeine is the stimulant found in coffee, tea, and some soft drinks. Caffeine increases your metabolism, creating a highly awake state. After drinking coffee, your heart may pound faster, and your blood pressure may increase. A study using PET scans showed that blood flow in the cerebral cortex increased by 30% after people consumed a dose of caffeine comparable to two cups of coffee ("Brain Imaging and Psychiatry," 1997). Caffeine may seem innocent, yet the caffeine in 20 cups of coffee could be deadly if consumed all at once (Dusek & Girdano, 1987).

Next to caffeine, nicotine is the stimulant that is most widely used in the United States. As you know, nicotine is found in cigarettes and other tobacco products. Nicotine clearly causes drug dependence, and in fact it operates throughout the nervous system in a manner similar to the illegal drug, cocaine (Pich et al., 1997). Cigarette smoking is the largest single preventable cause of early death and disability in North America. Smoking has such harmful health consequences that we'll discuss it in detail in the health psychology chapter (Chapter 18).

Amphetamines, such as Dexedrine, stimulate both the central nervous system and the sympathetic regions of the autonomic nervous system. These highly

The caffeine in coffee has been shown to increase cerebral blood flow. However, large quantities of caffeine can be deadly.

addictive drugs increase the concentration of dopamine and norepinephrine at the synapses. Specifically, amphetamines enhance the release of neurotransmitters, and they also block the reuptake (Fischman & Foltin, 1991). As a consequence, neurotransmitters continue to bombard the receptors. Amphetamines can produce irritability and anxiety, and they also interfere with sleep. Some students disregard the harmful effects of amphetamines and take them prior to an all-night study session before an examination. However, when exam-time comes, they are likely to have problems paying attention, solving problems, and responding accurately (Dusek & Girdano, 1987).

Cocaine is an even more potent and dangerous stimulant. Cocaine blocks the reuptake of dopamine and norepinephrine, producing feelings of excitement and pleasure in the drug user (Holloway, 1991). Large doses and repeated use can produce anxiety, hallucinations, insomnia, and aggressive behavior. In some cases—especially among cigarette smokers—even a relatively small dose can lead to a stroke, a heart attack, or death (Gold, 1993; Moliterno et al., 1994; Pagliaro, 1996).

In the mid-1970s, a powerful, extremely addictive form of cocaine appeared on the market; it is known as crack. When crack is smoked, the active ingredients travel to the brain within 10 seconds, providing an even more potent "rush" than cocaine (Gold, 1993; Wallace, 1991). Crack may also produce more medical complications and more psychological disorders than cocaine (Gold, 1993; Honer et al., 1987).

Hallucinogens

Hallucinogens are chemical substances that alter people's perceptions of reality and may cause vivid hallucinations. A **hallucination** is a strong mental image that seems as if it truly occurred, even though no physical stimulus has been registered by a sensory organ (Landry, 1994). Hallucinogens include several substances extracted from plants, such as marijuana and peyote, as well as several synthetic drugs, such as LSD.

Marijuana is a hallucinogen that is derived from the flowers and leaves of a weed called *Cannabis sativa*. Like other hallucinogens, marijuana alters the perception of sights, sounds, and touch. Marijuana is frequently in the news—for example, when voters in some states decide to legalize marijuana for medical purposes. Criminal arrests for possessing or selling marijuana also sometimes make the news. In fact, about 225,000 U.S. residents are arrested each year for possessing marijuana, making this the fourth most common cause of arrest in the United States (Grinspoon & Bakalar, 1994).

With all the publicity about marijuana, you might expect that researchers have clearly documented the effects of this drug. We do have some evidence that it affects thought processes. It seems to influence the hippocampus region of the limbic system (see Figure 3.14), which may explain why marijuana affects concentration and attention (Johnson, 1991). It also impairs cognitive activities such as reading comprehension, memory, arithmetic, and problem solving (American Academy of Pediatrics, 1991; Dusek & Girdano, 1987; Stephens & Roffman, 1993). However, the research is not extensive. Also, the physiological explanations for the hallucinations are not clear (D. Brown, 1996; Stephens & Roffman, 1993).

People who regularly use marijuana tend to have poor academic performance, and they are more likely to commit theft and vandalism. Heavy marijuana users may have problems in social interactions, and they may be less likely to be concerned about goal-directed behavior (American Academy of Pediatrics, 1991; Dusek & Girdano, 1987; Stephens & Roffman, 1993). In short, recent information suggests that marijuana is not an innocent substance, because it is associated with cognitive, social, and motivational problems.

The Huicholes, an indigenous community in Mexico, often use the hallucinogen peyote. The vivid, unusual figures in this yarn painting are characteristic of the hallucinations produced by peyote.

LSD, or lysergic acid diethylamide, is an extremely powerful hallucinogen. A tiny speck can alter consciousness within 15 minutes and last up to 12 hours (Strange & Shapiro, 1991). Shortly after taking LSD, a person typically becomes extremely emotional, with intense laughing or crying. The shapes and colors of objects in the room soon look altered. For example, a person under the influence of LSD may look at a friend's face and perceive that it is made of wax and dripping as if it were melting in the hot sun (Schwartz, 1995). Some users experience hallucinations, reporting that they see religious figures or enchanted places. LSD clearly impairs cognitive processes, because a person under the influence of LSD has difficulty concentrating, perceiving, and performing simple intellectual tasks (Schwartz, 1995). Other LSD users may experience intense panic, or they may attempt suicide. With respect to LSD, the dangers do seem clear-cut (Schwartz, 1995).

Psychoactive Drug Use

During a typical month in the United States, at least 14 million people consume some type of illicit drug (Lipsitt & VandenBos, 1992). According to estimates, the United States has about 1 million heroin addicts and about 2.4 million crack and cocaine addicts (Holloway, 1991).

Some demographic factors seem to be related to drug use, though methodological problems make it difficult to find accurate estimates. Gender is typically related to drug use. Probably the only psychoactive, nonprescription drug that males and females use equally is nicotine (Johnston et al., 1991). We saw in the "In Depth" feature on alcohol that college males are more likely than college females to be binge drinkers (Wechsler et al., 1994). Males in college and in the general population are also more likely to use illegal drugs, if we consider all age groups (Alexander & LaRosa, 1994; Johnson et al., 1991; Johnston et al., 1991; National Institute on Drug Abuse, 1989). However, some research suggests that the gender ratio may be changing, and women may soon be using illegal drugs as often as men do (Van Den Bergh, 1991; Walker et al., 1991).

Some researchers have reported ethnic differences in drug use, though we should be cautious about interpreting these findings. For example, alcohol problems and alcohol-related deaths are especially high among Native Americans (Center for Substance Abuse Treatment, 1994; Gibbons, 1992). African Americans are more likely than European Americans to be nondrinkers. However, a greater percentage of African Americans also report drinking problems (Rivers, 1994).

Sometimes the race differences are complicated by gender effects. For example, alcohol problems are more common for Mexican American and Puerto Rican men than for European American men. However, alcohol problems are *less* common for Mexican American and Puerto Rican women than for European American women (Gilbert, 1989). Also, African American and Latino men may be more likely than European American men to use illegal drugs, but the drug-use rates are reasonably close for African American, Latina, and European American women (Center for Substance Abuse Treatment, 1994). That is, cultural norms often depend upon a person's gender. Researchers continue to examine the cultural norms that produce these complex patterns of group differences.

Still, almost every group in North America experiences some drug problems. For instance, when you think of an alcoholic, don't you think of a middle-aged person? Unfortunately, about 1 million alcoholics in the United States are elderly (Finn, 1991). Also, despite the publicity about young people who abuse illegal drugs, many reports suggest that the typical drug user is older than 30 (Males, 1996).

Let's look at the drug use of college students. Figure 5.8 shows the percentage of full-time college students in the United States who report ever using the specified

FIGURE 5.8

Drug Use Among U.S. College Students

Drug use among full-time college students in the United States, illustrating the percentage who report using the drug at least once in their lifetime.

Source: Based on Johnston et al., 1991.

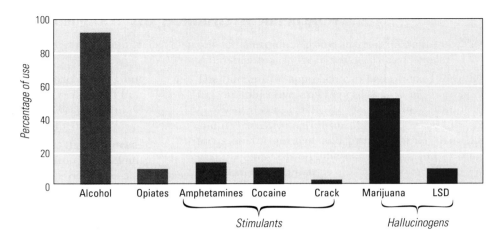

drug. Figure 5.9 is based on both college and noncollege Canadians, and you'll notice that the drugs are categorized somewhat differently from those in the U.S. survey. Still, both surveys show that nearly everyone tries alcohol, but a much smaller proportion try marijuana and other drugs.

Other researchers are trying to develop theories to explain why some individuals use drugs and some do not. For example, Petraitis and his colleagues (1995) point out the complexity of the issues, consistent with our Theme 3. Specifically, an adolescent's decisions to use illegal drugs may be influenced by role models, the behavior of peers, personality traits, attitudes, and decision-making factors. Given the complicated nature of these factors, a simple "Just Say No" approach cannot be effective in preventing young people from using drugs.

Critical Thinking Exercise 5.5

Write down your answers to these questions about psychoactive drug use.

a. What factor may help to account for the fact that researchers report that men are more likely than women to abuse alcohol?.

b. What factors may help to account for the fact that researchers report ethnic differences in drug use?

FIGURE 5.9

Drug Use Among Canadians (ages 15–24, college and noncollege)

Source: Based on Eliany et al., 1992.

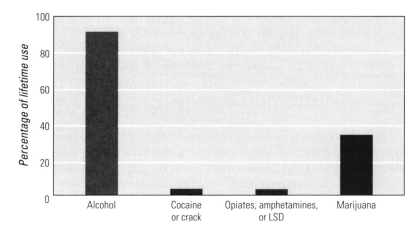

SECTION SUMMARY: *DRUGS THAT INFLUENCE CONSCIOUSNESS*

1. *Addiction* means that a psychoactive drug is used frequently and compulsively. The same amount of a drug now has a reduced effect (tolerance). Withdrawal symptoms are the undesirable effects of discontinued drug use.

2. Alcohol has harmful effects on body systems and brain metabolism, and it is responsible for many more deaths than all illegal drugs combined.

3. Although alcohol-related problems have decreased among U.S. residents overall, these problems have increased among college students, where 50% of males and 39% of females reported binge drinking.

4. Alcohol impairs thinking, encourages people to process fewer cues (alcohol myopia), and encourages violence. Research using the balanced-placebo design show that alcohol consumption significantly affects memory, motor behavior, mood, and aggression; alcohol expectation does not influence these processes. Alcohol expectation influences sexual arousal, but alcohol consumption has no effect.

5. Opiates depress the central nervous system, relieve pain, and encourage sleep; addicts who stop using opiates experience severe withdrawal symptoms.

6. Stimulants—which increase functioning of the central nervous system—include caffeine, nicotine, the amphetamines, cocaine, and crack.

7. Hallucinogens, such as marijuana and LSD, alter people's perception, memory, and other cognitive abilities; LSD is especially likely to have harmful consequences.

HYPNOSIS

In the first section of this chapter, we examined normal, waking consciousness. The sections on sleep and drug-induced states explored two conditions that psychologists agree are different from the normal waking state. Two other topics are more controversial. **Meditation,** which is a focusing of attention designed to avoid worried thoughts (Druckman & Bjork, 1991; Shapiro, 1984), was once proposed as an altered state of consciousness. However, properly controlled research shows that meditation is similar to waking experiences. Also, meditation does not significantly reduce hypertension or other health problems (Druckman & Bjork, 1991; Holmes, 1984a, 1987).

Hypnosis is a second controversial topic. For more than a century, psychologists maintained that hypnosis was a different state of consciousness. As we'll see, most psychologists have now abandoned this "special status" position.

Hypnosis is defined as a procedure in which a person designated as a hypnotist suggests to another person that he or she will experience changes in perception, thoughts, feelings, or behavior (Kirsch & Lynn, 1995; Kirsch et al., 1993). We should emphasize that hypnosis is *not* sleep. In fact, EEG records and other brain measures have not demonstrated significant differences between the hypnotic state and normal waking consciousness (P. Brown, 1991; "Hypnosis," 1991; Kirsch & Lynn, 1995).

The hypnotist has encouraged this woman to relax. A susceptible person may be hypnotized within 15 minutes.

To induce a hypnotic trance, hypnotists encourage participants to relax. They may repeat suggestions—such as "Your eyelids are getting heavy"—in a rhythmic, monotonous voice, or they may suggest that the participants visualize themselves in a peaceful relaxing setting (Kirsch et al., 1993). Some hypnotists may ask participants to watch a swinging pocket watch. Susceptible people can be hypnotized by a trained hypnotist within 15 minutes, although many people report no changes in their experiences (Hilgard, 1991; "Hypnosis," 1991).

We should note that "stage hypnotists" count on their participants to cooperate and fake some of the suggestions. Thus, the volunteer who apparently believes that he is Frank Sinatra crooning "Strangers in the Night" is probably an extravert who does not want to disappoint the audience (Barber, 1986). The majority of people who have participated in stage hypnosis can recall what they did, and they report that the hypnotist did not have control over their behavior (Crawford et al., 1992).

DEMONSTRATION 5.6 Beliefs About Hypnosis

Based on the information you've read and heard about hypnosis, answer each of the following questions; write either *true* or *false* in front of the item. The answers can be found at the end of the chapter, on Page 183, and these answers are also provided throughout this section.

_____ 1. People who have been hypnotized may simply be acting the way they think they are supposed to act.
_____ 2. During hypnosis, you can literally reexperience your childhood.
_____ 3. When the hypnotist instructs people that they will be unable to see a visual stimulus, that stimulus becomes truly invisible.
_____ 4. If a woman is hypnotized during childbirth, her labor pains can be reduced.
_____ 5. Hypnosis increases the accuracy of a person's memory about forgotten events.
_____ 6. Under hypnosis, people are more likely to "recall" events that never really occurred.
_____ 7. Under hypnosis, people can be "regressed" so that they reexperience previous lives.

Let's continue by looking at several hypnotic phenomena. Then we'll consider some theoretical approaches to hypnosis. Before reading further, however, try Demonstration 5.6.

Hypnotic Phenomena

Part of the reason that hypnosis is so intriguing is that hypnotized people seem to behave quite differently from people in the normal waking state. Let's examine four kinds of reported hypnotic phenomena.

Memory You've surely seen some movies in which a person who has witnessed a crime suddenly remembers all the details, under the spell of hypnosis. Unfortunately, the research on hypnosis typically shows that hypnosis is no more effective than control-group instructions in retrieving inaccessible memories (Geiselman, 1992; Register & Kihlstrom, 1987; Sheehan, 1988).

A major problem with "hypnotically refreshed" memory is **confabulation;** hypnotized participants may simply make up an item to replace one that they cannot retrieve. In one study, for instance, Dwyan and Bowers (1983) presented 60 pictures of common objects. Then the participants in the study were encouraged to remember as many pictures as they could, over a period of one week. By this time, the typical individual had recalled 38 of the 60 items. Then came the critical test: Would hypnosis bring forth more memories than standard instructions? Half of the participants were then hypnotized and told to relax, focusing all their attention on the pictures they had seen a week ago. The other half were not hypnotized; they were simply told to relax and focus their mental attention on the pictures.

As Figure 5.10 shows, the hypnotized people recalled just slightly more correct items than did people in the control group. However, the hypnotized people also recalled many more incorrect items, ones that were not on the original list. Hypnotized people may simply be less cautious about reporting items as true memories. Sometimes they will report something they actually saw, but they are likely to simply manufacture a memory.

The research on hypnosis and confabulation has had an important impact on the use of hypnosis in the courtroom. Specifically, the American Medical Association recommends that witnesses who have been previously hypnotized should not give courtroom testimony (Orne, 1986). In short, hypnosis is not a magical key that unlocks the unconscious and reveals buried memories.

Age Regression In **age regression,** a hypnotized person is given suggestions to reexperience an event that occurred at an earlier age and to act like and feel like a child of that particular age. The concept of age regression seems very dramatic.

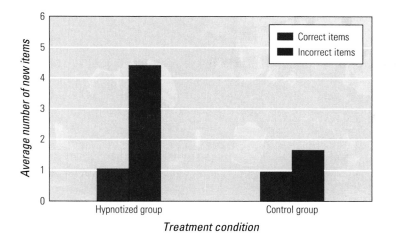

FIGURE 5.10

"Remembering" and Hypnosis
*Number of correct and incorrect
items recalled by hypnotized and
control groups.*
Source: Based on Dwyan & Bowers, 1983.

Suddenly a 40-year-old begins to print like a kindergartner! However, these actions are not really childlike when you look more closely. For example, one person who was regressed to age 6 wrote with childlike printing—but perfect spelling—"I am conducting a psychological experiment which will assess my psychological capacity" (Orne, 1951). Reviewing the research on age regression, researchers have concluded that age regression does not produce genuinely childlike behavior (Kirsch et al., 1993; Nash, 1987).

You've probably also heard of **past-life regression,** in which a hypnotized person is supposedly age-regressed beyond birth until a "past-life personality" is reinstated. As you might guess, psychologists are not likely to trust someone who reports, under hypnosis, that he used to be Elvis Presley. One of the foremost researchers in hypnosis, Nicholas Spanos, worked together with his colleagues to try to regress undergraduate students to a previous life (Spanos et al., 1991). In all, 32% reported a past-life identity. However, none of the participants provided a historically accurate portrait of the time period. Thus, the simplest explanation is that the hypnotized participants merely (and perhaps unknowingly) constructed some interesting fantasies.

FIGURE 5.11

*The Ponzo illusion (top) and same
horizontal lines without the slanted
framing lines (bottom).*

Hallucinations   Hypnotists can encourage people to perceive objects that are not present (**positive hallucinations**). For example, a hypnotized woman may be encouraged to "see" a mosquito buzzing around her head. People can also be encouraged *not* to see objects that are present (**negative hallucinations**). A hypnotized person may report that a nearby chair is not visible (Kihlstrom et al., 1992).

Several studies on negative hallucinations suggest, however, that the brain still processes the sensory information. For example, one group of researchers studied the Ponzo illusion (Figure 5.11a) and suggested to hypnotized participants that the slanted lines on each side would disappear. Participants were then instructed to judge the relative length of the two horizontal lines. If the two slanted lines were truly invisible, people should report that the horizontal lines are equally long. After all, they should see just the two lines shown in Figure 5.11b. In fact, people reported that the top line was longer, indicating that their visual systems were still processing the slanted lines (Miller et al., 1973). Thus, those slanted lines were registered in the participants' visual systems, even though people reported not seeing them.

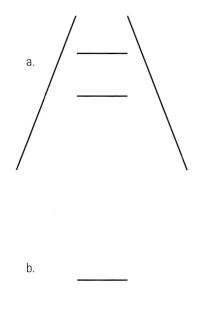

Pain Perception   So far, we have found that the evidence undermines the popular perception that hypnosis can improve memory, encourage age regression, and produce genuine hallucinations. In this last part of the discussion, we'll see that the results for pain perception are more encouraging. In general, people who have been hypnotized respond to a painful stimulus differently from the way un-hypnotized people do (Spiegel et al., 1989). In childbirth, for instance, women who have been hypnotized report less pain during labor, and the actual duration of labor is shorter.

Hypnosis has also been used effectively for people suffering from severe burns. When the hypnotist suggests that the patient feels cool and comfortable, people report less pain. They also request less narcotic medication (Chaves, 1993; Kihlstrom, 1985; Venn, 1986). A well-controlled experiment has confirmed that hypnotized burn patients are more likely than control-group patients to report a reduction in pain (Patterson et al., 1992). Other research has shown that hypnotized people give lower pain ratings than control-group people when a sharp weight was applied to their finger (Hargadon et al., 1995).

In Chapter 4, we noted that pain is influenced by psychological factors as well as biological factors. The research on hypnosis provides additional evidence that thoughts and suggestions influence our pain perception. However, the explanations for the effectiveness of hypnosis are not yet clear (Hargadon et al., 1995).

Theories of Hypnosis

We have reviewed some of the research about the influence of hypnosis on a variety of dependent variables. How can we explain these results? As Kirsch and Lynn (1995) explain, the theories of hypnosis can be arranged along a continuum. At one extreme of this continuum are some psychodynamic theorists such as Milton Erickson (1941/1980). These theorists argue that hypnosis is indeed a state of consciousness that is distinctly different from our normal waking mode. Therapists in this tradition argue that they have easier access to the unconscious when a person has been hypnotized (Kirsch & Lynn, 1995).

In the middle of the continuum are theorists who propose that hypnosis is *somewhat* different from the normal waking mode. For example, a person who has been hypnotized may be in a state that resembles daydreaming, a kind of trance (Kirsch & Lynn, 1995).

However, most current researchers currently argue that hypnosis is really identical to the normal waking state. They point to the research, which shows that people are not substantially more receptive to suggestions when they are hypnotized than when they are in a control group (Kirsch & Lynn, 1995; Lynn et al., 1996). The sociocognitive perspective is a theory typical of those who argue that hypnosis is nothing special. According to the **sociocognitive perspective,** the behavior of people who have been hypnotized can be traced to their attempts to understand the social situation of a hypnosis study and to figure out what they are supposed to do (Barber, 1979; Spanos, 1991). The sociocognitive approach argues that people bring certain expectations with them to a hypnosis experiment. This approach is consistent with our discussion of demand characteristics in Chapter 2.

The sociocognitive theorists argue that—when a hypnotist tells hypnotized individuals they cannot see the numeral "8" on the paper in front of them—they consider the role demands of the situation. They reason that they are supposed to say they see nothing, so that's what they report (Spanos, 1991). Similarly, they may print like 6-year-old children, and they may report that a sharp weight is not painful. As we will see later in the book, people's expectations about how they are supposed to act have an important influence on their behavior. At present, most research psychologists argue that these same expectations are responsible for the way people behave when they are in a hypnosis situation.

Critical Thinking Exercise 5.6

Write down your answers to the following questions about hypnosis.

a. You read in a newspaper about a person who witnessed a robbery, but she remembered none of the details that might help locate the criminals. However, under hypnosis, she recalled some useful details, including the license plate number of the criminals. How would you respond to this supposed demonstration of the value of hypnosis?

b. If hypnosis is nothing more than playing the expected role in a social situation, how could you design a study to support this theory? Use a negative hallucination study, in which the numeral "8" is presented to people on a sheet of paper in front of them, and 15 out of 45 hypnotized individuals have just reported that this paper is blank. What second phase would you include in this study to demonstrate that the hypnotized participants really did see the numeral "8"?

SECTION SUMMARY: *HYPNOSIS*

1. In hypnosis, a person designated as a hypnotist suggests to a participant that he or she will experience altered perception, thoughts, feelings, or behavior.

2. People who have been hypnotized recall no more than control-group individuals. They apparently do not experience genuine age regression or past-life regression, and they do not really have positive or negative hallucinations. However, they may show altered pain perception.

3. Theories of hypnosis can be arranged along a continuum, with some who argue that hypnosis is a genuine altered state. At the other end of the continuum are those who say hypnotized people are merely responding according to the demands of the social situation (the sociocognitive perspective).

REVIEW QUESTIONS

1. What is consciousness? Briefly describe the major topics in this chapter, noting those that seem to involve major changes from the active mode of consciousness and those that may not differ substantially from normal waking consciousness.

2. The section on waking attention emphasized three related phenomena. Specifically, we often have difficulty (1) removing an idea from consciousness; (2) dividing attention between two tasks; and (3) noticing the characteristics of one task when we are paying attention to another task. Discuss the research in these three areas and think of an example of each area that you have recently encountered.

3. How do zeitgebers help us maintain circadian rhythms? How are the concepts of free-running, shift schedules, and jet lag all relevant to circadian rhythms? Think of examples of each concept.

4. Imagine that you have had no sleep for the last two nights. Select six tasks that you must perform at some point today. Predict—on the basis of the research on sleep deprivation—how well you would perform each task, compared to your performance when well rested.

5. Imagine that a high school student you know is intrigued with the topic of sleep and asks you, "Why do we sleep?" Summarize the major reasons as clearly as possible. Then suppose the student asks, "Why do we dream?" Again, explain the major theoretical approaches.

6. Based on the information in the section on drugs that influence consciousness, describe the factors that are associated with drug use, both on college campuses and in the general population.

7. Explain Josephs and Steele's (1990) proposal that alcohol alters attention to cues, creating your own example to clarify their proposal. How is their approach related to the material at the beginning of the chapter on divided and selective attention?

8. What are the four major categories of psychoactive drugs described in this chapter? For each category, make a list of some general physical and psychological effects. We discussed expectancy effects in connection with alcohol. How could expectancy effects be relevant for some of the other drugs?

9. From what you read and heard prior to reading this chapter, would you have concluded that hypnosis is substantially different from the normal waking state? What would you conclude now, based on the research discussed in this chapter?

10. Top-down processing was mentioned or implied in several parts of this chapter. Explain how it is relevant for the neurocognitive model of dreaming, expectations about the effects of alcohol, and the sociocognitive theory of hypnosis.

New terms

consciousness (p. 154)
mental control (p. 155)
thought suppression (p. 155)
attention (p. 156)
divided attention (p. 156)
selective attention (p. 156)
dichotic listening task (p. 156)
Stroop effect (p. 156)
preattentive processing (p. 158)
focused attention (p. 158)
sleep (p. 158)
circadian rhythm (p. 158)
zeitgebers (p. 158)
free running (p. 159)
shift schedules (p. 159)
jet lag (p. 159)
REM sleep (p. 161)
insomnia (p. 163)
sleep apnea (p. 164)
nightmare (p. 166)
neurocognitive model (p. 166)
activation-synthesis hypothesis (p. 166)
connectionist approach (p. 166)

psychoactive drugs (p. 168)
neurotransmitters (p. 168)
addiction (p. 168)
tolerance (p. 168)
withdrawal symptoms (p. 168)
depressant (p. 169)
binge drinking (p. 170)
vigilance tasks (p. 171)
alcohol myopia (p. 171)
balanced-placebo design (p. 171)
opiates (p. 173)
endorphins (p. 173)
stimulants (p. 173)
hallucinogens (p. 174)
hallucination (p. 174)
meditation (p. 177)
hypnosis (p. 177)
confabulation (p. 178)
age regression (p. 178)
past-life regression (p. 179)
positive hallucinations (p. 179)
negative hallucinations (p. 179)
sociocognitive perspective (p. 180)

Recommended readings

Coren, S. (1996). *Sleep thieves: An eye-opening exploration into the science and mysteries of sleep.* New York: Free Press. Here's an interesting book on sleep deprivation, shift work, and other factors that encourage sleepiness—as well as its consequences.

Farthing, G. W. (1992). *The psychology of consciousness.* Englewood Cliffs, NJ: Prentice Hall. Farthing's textbook offers a mid-level overview of every topic in this chapter, as well as discussion of related topics such as introspection and daydreaming.

Goldstein, A. (1994). *Addiction: From biology to drug policy.* New York: Freeman. This book examines neurotransmitters, endorphins, alcohol, and the other drugs discussed in this chapter at a level appropriate for undergraduates.

Kirsch, I., & Lynn, S. J. (1955). The altered state of hypnosis: Changes in the theoretical landscape. *American Psychologist, 50,* 846–858. I would recommend this article for a brief overview of the theories and research on hypnosis.

Moorcroft, W. H. (1993). *Sleep, dreaming, and sleep disorders: An introduction* (2nd ed.). Lantham, MD: University Press. This is a clearly written overview of sleep, dreams, and sleep disorders.

Royce, J. E., & Scratchley, D. (1996). *Alcoholism and other drug problems.* New York: Free Press. Here's a helpful introduction to alcohol and other drugs, with additional information about prevention and treatment.

Answers to demonstrations

Demonstration 5.3

1. True—some people experience lucid dreaming, in which a dream seems vivid, yet they are aware they are dreaming.

2. False—most dreams are in color.

3. False—it's possible we don't sleep as soundly if we have indigestion, but we do not dream more.

4. True—we can incorporate the stimulus into the dream, and we fail to perceive that it comes from the external world. However, these episodes are relatively rare.

5. False—dreams take about as much time as the comparable real-world experience takes.

6. False—blind people dream, though their dreams may emphasize auditory experiences, rather than visual ones.

7. True—at present researchers have not discovered methods that can be used for dream control.

Sources: LaBerge, 1990; Moorcroft, 1993; Squier & Domhoff, 1998.

Demonstration 5.6

1. True 2. False 3. False 4. True 5. False 6. True 7. False

Answers to critical thinking exercises

Exercise 5.1

a. This example was basically a case study about a program. To test the effectiveness of this program more rigorously, a true experiment should be conducted, in which students are randomly assigned to two groups. One group receives the standard informational lectures, and the other group receives the more active-learning approach. The dependent variable could include self-report measures (either about their intentions with respect to alcohol or self-reported drinking). It also could include behavioral measures, gathered over several years, on drunk-driving arrests and other alcohol-related problems.

b. A problem with these self-report items is that, as the text points out, people do not always have access to their true thoughts, so the reports may not be accurate. Another problem is that people are not very good at predicting how they will act in a particular situation, based on their attitudes (as we'll see in Chapter 17).

Exercise 5.2

a. The researchers should be careful not to wear watches. They must also avoid time-related greetings such as "Good morning" or "Are you ready for breakfast?"

b. Certain jobs are not likely to be represented in the samples of people who do shift work (e.g., sanitation workers, schoolteachers, college professors, lawyers). Perhaps even more important, people who cannot get accustomed to working at night will leave shift-work occupations. As a result, studies of shift work are conducted on "survival samples"—only those people who are most successful at adapting to night work. Jet-lag data are gathered only on those who have occupations or income levels that allow jet travel. These individuals are more likely to be well educated and financially well off—but it's not clear whether these people would be more or less adaptable than the general population.

Exercise 5.3

a. The students at University B might be more academically gifted than those at University A, so that they find the memory task interesting and/or easy; they may also be more motivated. It's also possible that the researchers tested them at an optimal time of day. Each of these four factors would decrease the likelihood that sleep deprivation would influence their performance.

b. Don't trust this report unless you know that this man had been monitored in a sleep lab to verify that his EEG showed no signs of sleep. Also, you'd want to know what dependent variables were used; did the researchers test this man's accuracy and speed on some boring, difficult tasks? Furthermore, you'd want to compare his performance after sleep deprivation with his performance without sleep deprivation.

Exercise 5.4

a. To obtain such a high return rate, the authors offered students money (surprise!). Specifically, they promised that they would award $1,000 to a student whose name was drawn from the students responding within one week; one $500 award and ten $100 awards would also be selected from all those who responded (Wechsler et al., 1994). Still, the sample probably was not representative of the college population, with respect to drinking habits. We would suspect that those with the most serious alcohol problems would be less likely to complete and return the questionnaire. The authors report that 49% of the respondents had a grade-point average between an A and a B+; conscientious students—who tend to be nonbingers—might therefore be overrepresented. The true, unbiased binge-drinking rates actually may be higher.

b. The problem is that students who are familiar with the smell and taste of alcohol would not believe that they are drinking alcohol if you hand them a glass of plain water. In a typical study using a placebo, Read and his colleagues (1992) used a basic beverage of fruit juice and a carbonated soft drink. A strong dose of alcohol was added to the drink for those in the "alcohol" condition. For those in the "no-alcohol" condition, a thin layer of vodka (not enough to change the blood alcohol) was floated on top of the basic beverage, and the deception was apparently convincing.

Exercise 5.5

a. Research shows that people judge an intoxicated woman much more harshly than an intoxicated man (Forth-Finnegan, 1991). Women may also be less likely to brag about heavy drinking. As a result, women may be less likely than men to self-report heavy drinking. Women with alcohol problems may remain relatively invisible (Matlin, 1996a).

b. The estimates may be biased by a number of factors. For example, a Black teenager is much more likely than a White adult to be arrested for drugs. As a result, reports based on arrest records could be biased (Males, 1996). Also, upper-class European Americans may be able to arrange for treatment for drug and alcohol abuse in private facilities, so their abuse problems may be less visible. Cultural norms about the acceptability of drug use may also depend on ethnicity.

Exercise 5.6

a. You should be suspicious because, with only one individual, they could not include a control condition. Suppose that after the same amount of time had elapsed since the crime, the same witness had been seated in a comfortable chair, encouraged to relax, and invited to try to visualize the scene of the crime. The research suggests that she would be just as likely to remember these details as if she had been hypnotized.

b. Spanos and his colleagues (1989) began with just this setup. After these 15 people reported that they could see nothing, a different individual came into the room. She told each participant that people who are deeply hypnotized report that they had initially seen a number on the sheet, but it gradually faded. In contrast, she told them, fakers insist that they never saw anything. Under these instructions, 14 of the 15 participants drew the numeral "8" on a sheet of paper (Spanos et al., 1989). According to the sociocognitive perspective, people figure out that they don't want to be perceived as fakers, so they now "remember" seeing the numeral "8."

LEARNING

CLASSICAL CONDITIONING

    Influential Research in Classical Conditioning

    Components of Classical Conditioning

    Recent Developments in Classical Conditioning

    Biological Aspects of Classical Conditioning

    Applications of Classical Conditioning

OPERANT CONDITIONING

    Influential Research in Operant Conditioning

    Components of Operant Conditioning

    Recent Developments in Operant Conditioning

    Biological Aspects of Operant Conditioning

    Applications of Operant Conditioning

OBSERVATIONAL LEARNING

    Influential Research in Observational Learning

    Components of Observational Learning

    In Depth: Media Violence and Observational Learning

    Applications of Observational Learning

CHAPTER 6

When A.S. was 7 years old, his father would play a bizarre bedtime game in which he became the "wild pig man." He would snort loudly and race down the hall, searching for his sons to eat as an evening meal. A.S. customarily sought refuge in a closet that had a sliding door. One time, however, a stick fell into the tracks of the sliding door, and he couldn't get out. A.S. was trapped in the dark in a small enclosure, with no means of escape—and the "wild pig man" was coming closer and closer. When A.S.'s brothers learned that he was afraid of dark, enclosed places, they began locking him in unlit storage rooms. Not surprisingly, A.S. developed a fear of enclosed places in which the lights *might* go out. In fact, as an adult, he quit a good job as a telephone repairman because he was asked to repair the phones in elevators—even in well-lit elevators like the one above.

To overcome his intense fear, A.S. enrolled in a course on self-change (Watson & Tharp, 1993). He started by addressing his specific fear of elevators. At the beginning, he would simply walk into an unoccupied elevator—keeping one hand on the door—then press a button, and then walk out. During each session, he was careful to practice relaxation exercises. Gradually, he worked up to letting the doors close before exiting, rewarding himself for each successful session. Eventually, he "graduated" to riding in the elevator for longer and longer distances. As he reported, "At the end of my project I was riding all the elevators I came into contact with. I'm still not totally comfortable being in one, but I'm not avoiding them, either" (Watson & Tharp, 1993, p. 12). In this example of classical conditioning, A.S. had learned to be afraid of elevators, and then he learned how to reduce this fear.

In Chapter 4, we examined how your sensory systems allow you to perceive sights, sounds, tactile and painful stimuli, smells, and tastes. Chapter 5 discussed how you sometimes pay attention to these perceptions and sometimes ignore them. However, those perceptions do not simply lie trapped and useless in your cerebral cortex. As the next four chapters emphasize, you use this perceptual information when you learn, remember, think, and use language.

Our current chapter focuses on three kinds of learning, beginning with the *classical conditioning* that A.S. experienced. We'll also consider operant conditioning and observational learning.

One of my students described this example of *operant conditioning* (Basher, 1991). A 4-year-old child named Rick talked constantly and disrupted activities at his day care center. His parents decided to award him a star sticker every time his day care teacher gave them a positive report. The stickers could later be exchanged for enjoyable activities, such as going to the movies or inviting a friend over to play. After several months of this program, Rick's behavior was much less disruptive.

I observed the following example of *observational learning* in a kindergarten classroom. Throughout the year, the teacher had encouraged the children by praising their attempts to print letters and complimenting them on their artwork. On the particular day I was observing, their assignment was to write the letter O and to draw some object beginning with this letter. One little girl wandered over to observe the work of a classmate. "Oh, Anteus," she said excitedly, "your O is so nice and round, and your octopus is really good!" Through observational learning, with her teacher as the model, this little girl had mastered the art of praising others.

What characteristics are shared by the man who overcame his fear of elevators, the boy whose behavior became less disruptive, and the girl who imitated her teacher's instructional techniques? They all illustrate different kinds of **learning,** which is defined as a relatively permanent change in behavior or knowledge, due to experience. Notice that the change can involve knowledge, as well as behavior. For example, you may know how to bandage a sprained ankle after watching a first-aid video, even if you have never actually performed this activity. We also need the phrase "due to experience" because learning does not involve behavior that changes as a result of drugs, fatigue, genetics, and maturation (Lutz, 1994).

We'll begin this chapter on learning with classical conditioning, a topic that is more complex than it initially appears. In the section on operant conditioning, we'll consider how rewards and punishments influence behavior. Finally, we'll discuss how people learn by watching others, in the section on observational learning.

CLASSICAL CONDITIONING

In **classical conditioning,** a previously neutral stimulus acquires the ability to produce a response, because it has been associated with a stimulus that already produces a similar response. Consider this example provided by one of my students. This student had recently been walking through a field of goldenrod on a September day when the goldenrod was especially laden with pollen. Soon, he began sneezing energetically; in an allergic person, pollen irritation typically produces a sneezing

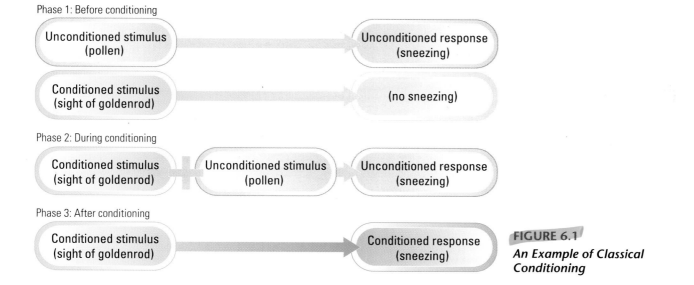

Phase 1: Before conditioning

Unconditioned stimulus
(pollen) → Unconditioned response
(sneezing)

Conditioned stimulus
(sight of goldenrod) → (no sneezing)

Phase 2: During conditioning

Conditioned stimulus
(sight of goldenrod) + Unconditioned stimulus
(pollen) → Unconditioned response
(sneezing)

Phase 3: After conditioning

Conditioned stimulus
(sight of goldenrod) → Conditioned response
(sneezing)

FIGURE 6.1

An Example of Classical Conditioning

response. The next day, this student was watching a program on Colorado, and a field of goldenrod suddenly occupied the whole television screen. Almost instantly, he began to sneeze.

In classical conditioning, prior to any learning, an unconditioned stimulus reliably elicits an unconditioned response. The **unconditioned stimulus** is defined as the stimulus in classical conditioning that elicits an unlearned response. The **unconditioned response** is defined as an unlearned response to a stimulus—a response that occurs naturally.

In the goldenrod example, the pollen can be labeled as an unconditioned stimulus, and the sneeze can be labeled as an unconditioned response (Figure 6.1, Phase 1). The visual appearance of goldenrod was initially a neutral stimulus that produced no reaction. However, by association with the pollen, the sight of goldenrod can eventually produce sneezing, even when no pollen is present (Phase 3).

During conditioning, an individual learns that the conditioned stimulus (for instance, the sight of goldenrod) is associated with the unconditioned stimulus (for instance, the pollen). When classical conditioning has occurred, the conditioned stimulus now elicits a conditioned response. The **conditioned stimulus** is defined as the previously neutral stimulus that is associated with the unconditioned stimulus. The **conditioned response** is defined as the response that is elicited by the conditioned stimulus.

Take a few minutes to review these four terms and learn them, because they are used throughout this section. Keep in mind that *unconditioned* refers to stimuli and responses that do not require learning. In fact, this reaction occurs spontaneously, and it typically involves a reflex. The other two terms—*conditioned* stimuli and *conditioned* responses—require conditioning; learning produces this conditioning.

Try applying these terms to a different example, the tickle response (Newman et al., 1993). Suppose that a young girl named Marta is extremely ticklish. Every time someone lightly strokes the bottom of her foot, she squirms and giggles. Her older sister has recently begun wiggling her fingers and saying "tickle, tickle" before she begins to tickle Marta. Now, Marta only needs to see those fingers and hear "tickle, tickle" in order to begin squirming and giggling. Take a minute to identify the unconditioned stimulus, the unconditioned response, the conditioned stimulus, and the conditioned response. Then try an example of classical conditioning in Demonstration 6.1, which also contains the answer to the question about tickling.

Classical conditioning can produce extremely powerful and sometimes unexpected reactions. For example, a Latin American refugee who had fled to Canada

For an extremely allergic person, the mere sight of goldenrod (a conditioned stimulus) can provoke a conditioned response of sneezing.

DEMONSTRATION 6.1 An Example of Classical Conditioning

Take a balloon and blow it up until it is as inflated as possible. Ask a friend to participate in a brief demonstration, and stand with the balloon about 2 feet from your friend. Take a sharp pair of scissors and move the point toward the inflated balloon, watching your friend's facial expression and body movements. People usually shut their eyes and contract the muscles in the upper part of their bodies during this demonstration. In this case, the loud noise of a balloon popping is the unconditioned stimulus, and the changes in facial expression and body movements represent the unconditioned response. The sight of a balloon about to be popped is the conditioned stimulus (often predictive of a popping noise), which through classical conditioning comes to produce the change in facial expression and body movements, or the conditioned response.

Incidentally, in the example of the ticklish girl presented earlier, the light stroke on the foot is an unconditioned stimulus; the squirming and giggling are unconditioned responses; the wiggling fingers and the phrase "tickle, tickle" are the conditioned stimulus; and the squirming and giggling in response to the sister's actions are the conditioned response.

froze in terror when a well-wisher presented him with a gift basket. The basket contained two pineapples, a welcome gift for most people. However, before fleeing his native country, this refugee had been forced to watch while a military guard hacked several prisoners to death with a machete. Then—without wiping the blade—the guard had calmly carved up a ripe pineapple and eaten the bloodstained slices.

Classical conditioning was traditionally considered to be a low-level, automatic kind of learning. In fact, critics typically claimed that classical conditioning was "all spit and twitches" because researchers usually examined salivary responses and reflexes using muscle movements. In recent decades, that view has changed. Classical conditioning is certainly simpler than the kinds of learning we'll investigate in Chapters 7 and 8. However, classical conditioning can require remembering stimuli for hours or even days. Furthermore, conditioning is more than the simple pairing of the conditioned stimulus with the unconditioned stimulus. As this chapter will demonstrate, even classical conditioning provides examples of our theme about the complexity of behavior.

To understand classical conditioning more fully, let's first discuss two well-known early studies and then examine important components of classical conditioning, such as acquisition and stimulus generalization. Then we'll explore some important new theoretical developments that have changed the way psychologists view classical conditioning. Our final two topics are the biological basis of classical conditioning and several practical applications of this kind of learning.

Influential Research in Classical Conditioning

Pavlov's Conditioned Salivation Experiment   The history of many disciplines might have been completely different if a particular early researcher had been somewhat less curious or less persistent. For example, the Russian physiologist Ivan Pavlov was studying the digestive system of dogs when he discovered something unusual. Not surprisingly, a dog's saliva production increases when meat powder is placed in the dog's mouth. However, Pavlov observed that the mere *sight* of food caused an increase in saliva production. Even the sound of the experimenter's footsteps elicited salivation.

Pavlov prided himself on being an objective scientist. In fact, the workers in his laboratory were fined if they used any subjective, nonphysiological language (Hergenhahn, 1988). His decision to abandon the physiological emphasis and to explore the psychological determinants of salivation was therefore a difficult one.

Figure 6.2 shows the experimental equipment Pavlov used in his early research on classical conditioning. Notice that the tube running from the dog's cheek allowed the saliva to be collected and measured. Later, Pavlov and his associates developed more refined equipment that permitted more precise recordings of saliva production (Goodwin, 1991).

FIGURE 6.2

Sketch of Pavlov's early apparatus.
Source: Based on Yerkes and Morgulis, 1909.

The three critical phases of Pavlov's research design are shown in Figure 6.3. Before conditioning had begun, the unconditioned stimulus (meat powder) produced an unconditioned response (salivation). Pavlov had selected the sound of a bell to serve as the conditioned stimulus. Before conditioning, the bell produced no salivation. Instead, the dog simply looked in the direction of the sound.

During conditioning, the conditioned stimulus (the bell) was followed by the unconditioned stimulus (the meat powder), which continued to produce the unconditioned response (salivation). The conditioned stimulus and the unconditioned stimulus were paired together in this fashion for several trials.

After a number of conditioning trials, Pavlov discovered that the sound of the bell was sufficient to produce salivation. The meat powder did not need to be presented at all. Similarly, an allergic person may sneeze at a picture of goldenrod—the pollen does not need to be present. Also, your friends may tense their muscles when a pair of scissors approaches a balloon, even though it has not yet popped.

Watson and Rayner's Conditioned Fear Study Another well-known study was conducted in the United States by John Watson and Rosalie Rayner (1920). Chapter 1 discussed Watson's contributions to the behaviorist approach. In this highly publicized study, he and Rayner argued that a simple conditioning principle could be combined

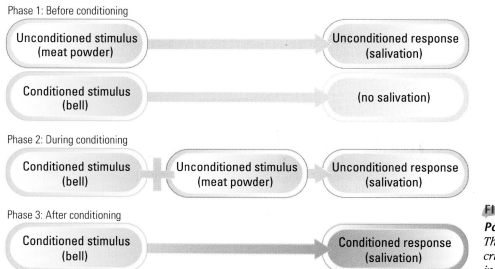

FIGURE 6.3

Pavlov's Research Design
This diagram illustrates three critical phases of Pavlov's research in classical conditioning.

with fundamental emotions such as fear, to weave a complex web of emotions (Coon, 1994). These researchers tested an 11-month-old baby named Albert, who showed no fear of animals prior to testing. However, he showed a clear-cut fear reaction whenever a researcher made a loud noise by striking a hammer against a large steel bar located immediately behind Albert's back. (The noise therefore served as the unconditioned stimulus, and the fear reaction was the unconditioned response.)

Watson and Rayner used a white rat as the conditioned stimulus. Whenever Albert reached out to touch the rat, the hammer clanged loudly against the steel bar. After seven pairings of the rat and the noise, Albert cried and avoided the rat, even when the loud noise was no longer delivered. Watson and Rayner concluded that fear could be learned through conditioning.

Although this study is one of the most famous in all psychology, it was not one of the best (Harris, 1979; Todd, 1994; Turkkan, 1989b). For example, the research design does not technically qualify as an example of classical conditioning. Specifically, the researchers waited until Albert reached for the rat, before striking the steel bar. (As you will learn shortly, this setup is closer to operant conditioning, in which a response may be followed by a punishing stimulus.)

Critical Thinking Exercise 6.1

Write down your answers to the following questions about the two well-known studies in classical conditioning that were presented here.

a. A recent article in a travel magazine contained one paragraph on each of the 50 U.S. states. According to their description of Ohio, "It's practically Pavlovian: Mention Ohio, and even broad-minded types think of soybeans and buckeyes." The article therefore implies that this is an example of Pavlovian conditioning, because people often hear the words *Ohio, soybeans,* and *buckeyes* mentioned together. Do you think this qualifies as Pavlovian conditioning?

b. Watson knew a month in advance that Albert's mother planned to remove him from the research project. Still, Watson apparently did not decondition the child to make certain that he had no remaining fear of rats. At the time, psychologists were not especially concerned about the ethics of this study (Todd, 1994). However, what ethical concerns would you raise, based on your knowledge of ethical principles?

Components of Classical Conditioning

Now that we have discussed several examples, let's examine some components of classical conditioning more closely. Once conditioning has been acquired, you'll see that it can be applied in some new circumstances (stimulus generalization)—but not all (stimulus discrimination). Also, a conditioned response can be eliminated (extinction), though it may return again (spontaneous recovery). In this discussion, then, we'll explore some of the complexities of classical conditioning. This form of learning involves more than the acquisition of a single conditioned response that remains unchanged throughout a lifetime.

Acquisition We use the term **acquisition** to describe the process of learning a new response. In classical conditioning, acquisition involves producing a conditioned response to a conditioned stimulus. Figure 6.4 shows a typical acquisition curve. As you can see, at the beginning of testing, the conditioned stimulus does not elicit the conditioned response. For example, Pavlov's dogs did not initially salivate when the bell rang. During the first few trials, however, the strength of the conditioned response grows rapidly. Later in the testing session, the increase in the strength of the conditioned response is more gradual.

Figure 6.4 shows a fairly leisurely acquisition rate, in which many trials are necessary for the conditioned response to reach its maximum strength. You can

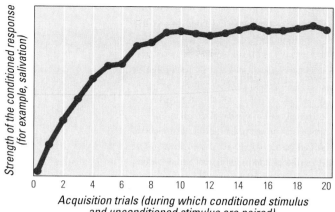

Strength of the conditioned response
(for example, salivation)

Acquisition trials (during which conditioned stimulus
and unconditioned stimulus are paired)

FIGURE 6.4

Typical Acquisition Curve
Data illustrate the acquisition of a conditioned response.

probably think of many exceptions to this pattern—cases that require only a single pairing of the conditioned stimulus and the unconditioned stimulus. The Latin American exile mentioned earlier in the chapter acquired his fear of pineapples from a single barbaric act. Another example of one-trial learning occurred several years ago, when my family and I were driving together and had stopped at an intersection, with our flasher indicating a left-hand turn. An inattentive driver rear-ended us, causing some injuries and demolishing our car. For weeks afterward, we all experienced anxiety whenever we were stopped at an intersection and a car approached quickly from the rear. No repeated pairings were necessary; we had learned this anxiety in a single trial. In classical conditioning, acquisition can be rapid—even immediate—when the unconditioned stimulus is intense.

Stimulus Generalization   Both people and animals show **stimulus generalization,** which means that if they learn a response to one particular stimulus, similar stimuli will also tend to elicit that response (Houston, 1991). For example, the car that rear-ended my family's car was large, old, and beige. Nevertheless, our fear of cars approaching from the rear was not limited to just this kind of car. I suspect that a large, old *blue* car would have produced a substantial anxiety response during the month after the accident. We probably would have experienced some anxiety, even if a brand-new red sports car had approached too quickly.

As you might expect, new stimuli that are highly similar to the conditioned stimulus are more likely than dissimilar stimuli to produce the conditioned response. For example, Figure 6.5 shows data from rabbits that had been conditioned to blink their eyes to a particular tone with a frequency of 1200 Hz (that is, a pitch slightly more than two octaves above middle C). Conditioning was produced by presenting a brief puff of air to the eye, immediately after the tone had been sounded. When the rabbits were tested later, the largest number of conditioned responses was produced by the original tone, 1200 Hz. However, other tones produced some conditioned responses as well. For instance, a tone of 800 Hz (3 notes lower on the piano) produced a substantial response rate, and even a tone of 400 Hz (11 notes lower on the piano) produced some conditioned responses.

Stimulus generalization is useful, both for animals and for humans. Our learning would be limited indeed if we never generalized beyond the exact same conditioned stimulus that was originally presented. Instead, generalization allows us to predict what is likely to happen in new situations. Stimulus generalization is an example of the theme that organisms are well equipped to function in their environments.

Stimulus Discrimination   Of course, stimulus generalization could be carried too far. If we generalized to every new stimulus that vaguely resembled the conditioned

The blinking red light on top of an ambulance is a conditioned stimulus for most people, because the unconditioned stimulus (the siren) with which it is associated produces an unconditioned response (your heart beats faster).

Most people show some stimulus generalization from the ambulance's red light to the blinking yellow light on the top of a tow truck.

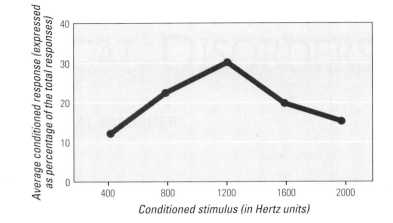

FIGURE 6.5

Stimulus Generalization
Data are for rabbits originally
conditioned to respond to a tone of
1200 Hz frequency.
Source: Based on Liu, 1971.

People who have allergic reactions
to shellfish can usually eat "finny"
fish safely—and vice versa.
Stimulus discrimination allows
people to learn that it's fine to eat
one category of fish, but not the
other, even though both are called
fish and live in similar habitats.

stimulus, we would often act inappropriately. Therefore, we need to differentiate between similar stimuli, through a process called **stimulus discrimination.** For example, a child who has been burned by a gas stove will not show a fearful emotional response to a photograph of a fire. Thus, stimulus generalization and stimulus discrimination work together. Stimulus generalization ensures that we expand our learning beyond the immediate conditioned stimulus. However, stimulus discrimination operates to guarantee that we do not generalize too broadly or inappropriately.

Extinction Suppose that a dog has learned to salivate to a bell, and the bell is presented many times *without* the meat powder. Would the dog continue to drool? Pavlov reported that, after only five or six trials without meat powder, the dogs no longer produced saliva when the bell was sounded. This is an example of **extinction,** which occurs when a conditioned stimulus loses its ability to elicit a conditioned response when it is later presented without the unconditioned stimulus (Bouton, 1994a, 1994b). Several months after our car accident, for example, my heart no longer pounded when another car approached from behind.

In general, extinction allows us to stop responding when a conditioned stimulus is no longer associated with the unconditioned stimulus. For example, during the years since the car accident, *car approaching from behind* has not been associated with *car crash.* I hope to live the rest of my life with no other car approaching from behind, producing a car crash. People and animals need extinction so that they can keep adapting to an environment that changes (Bouton, 1994b). Notice that this information on extinction is consistent with the views of the evolutionary approach, discussed in Chapter 3.

Spontaneous Recovery However, classical conditioning can easily recover following extinction, because extinction can be forgotten (Bouton, 1994a, 1994b). This phenomenon is called **spontaneous recovery;** when time has passed after extinction —and the conditioned stimulus is presented once more—the conditioned response may reappear. For example, Figure 6.6 shows data gathered by Pavlov (1927). When the unconditioned stimulus (meat powder) was no longer presented, salivation gradually dropped to zero. Then Pavlov waited about two hours and presented the conditioned stimulus (the bell) once again. Notice that the conditioned stimulus now elicited a noticeable amount of saliva during spontaneous recovery. However, with further presentations of the conditioned stimulus—and no unconditioned stimulus —the response would quickly extinguish once more.

Recent Developments in Classical Conditioning

Several decades ago, the research on classical conditioning seemed to be dying out (Turkkan, 1989a). Psychologists thought that they completely understood this form

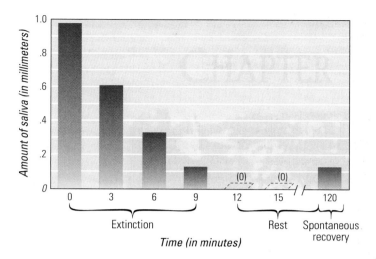

FIGURE 6.6

Extinction and Spontaneous Recovery of a Conditioned Response
Source: Based on Pavlov, 1927.

of learning. After all, what could possibly be left to learn about drooling dogs and blinking rabbits? However, researchers uncovered some unexpected findings. For example, they found that the conditioned stimulus and the unconditioned stimulus could be separated by a delay of several hours; classical conditioning does not always require split-second timing (e.g., Revusky, 1971). Researchers have found that people can develop a distaste for a nausea-producing food, even when the nausea occurs four hours after they ate that particular food. Two other topics that researchers have actively explored are biological preparedness and the cause of classical conditioning.

Biological Preparedness   Psychologists originally believed that any perceivable stimulus could serve as a conditioned stimulus. However, research by John Garcia and his colleagues showed that some associations are much more readily learned than others (Garcia, 1984; Garcia & Koelling, 1966; Garcia et al., 1972). These studies examined the effects of radiation on the eating behavior of laboratory rats. Radiation (an unconditioned stimulus) produces nausea (an unconditioned response). The research examined **taste aversion,** the development of intense dislike for a food through conditioning.

Garcia and his colleagues found that *taste* could easily serve as a conditioned stimulus. After a single trial in which sweet-tasting water was paired with radiation, rats learned to avoid the sweet-tasting water. However, these researchers discovered that *sight* and *sound* could not serve as conditioned stimuli. In a second condition, bright, noisy water (that is, water accompanied by flashing lights and loud noises) was paired with radiation. No conditioning occurred; the rats did not learn to avoid the water.

Apparently, the nervous system of mammals has developed through evolution so that they learn certain associations more easily than others. In the case of rats, the nervous system is "biased" to remember the taste of foods that are associated with nausea. However, sight and sound are not typically related to nausea. As a result, they cannot serve as conditioned stimuli for nausea.

Biological preparedness is the name for this built-in bias, which ensures that humans and other animals will learn some relationships between stimuli and responses (e.g., taste and nausea) more easily than other relationships (e.g., sight and nausea) (Barker, 1994). As you might imagine, biological preparedness is an important part of the evolutionary approach to psychology. The concept of biological preparedness altered the traditional view of classical conditioning by demonstrating that all stimuli are *not* created equal. Depending upon the conditioning situation, some stimuli are easier to learn than others.

The Cause of Classical Conditioning   For many years, psychologists had argued that classical conditioning could be explained by *contiguity;* the closer the conditioned stimulus and the unconditioned stimulus occurred in time, the quicker the learning.

Biological preparedness explains why coyotes can easily acquire taste aversion. In one program, ranchers placed a nausea-producing substance on lamb carcasses. Coyotes that ate this meat often avoided killing lambs in the future.

However, taste aversion research showed that learning could occur rapidly when the two stimuli were separated by several hours. Also, learning is faster when the conditioned stimulus slightly precedes the unconditioned stimulus. In contrast, learning is actually much slower when the two stimuli are presented at the same time—with maximum contiguity (Barker, 1994; Lutz, 1994).

Robert Rescorla and his colleagues have argued that contiguity is *not* sufficient; the relationship also must be predictive (Rescorla, 1968, 1988; Rescorla & Wagner, 1972). In a predictive relationship, whenever the conditioned stimulus occurs, the unconditioned stimulus will follow. In other words, the conditioned stimulus provides information about what will happen (Lutz, 1994). These researchers found that animals learned better when the relationship between the two stimuli was predictive. This view of classical conditioning has become the dominant explanation over the last 20 years. Although other components of the model have been criticized, Rescorla's model remains the dominant explanation of classical conditioning (R. R. Miller et al., 1995; D. A. Williams et al., 1992).

In short, the newer research on classical conditioning has pointed out that the conditioned stimulus and the unconditioned stimulus can be separated by several hours. In addition, some stimuli produce better conditioning than others. Finally, predictability is the essential feature of classical conditioning, rather than simple pairing. The recent research illustrates that even this relatively simple learning is more complex than psychologists had originally suspected (Theme 3).

Biological Aspects of Classical Conditioning

Research on the biological basis of classical conditioning offers additional support for our theme of complexity. Specifically, different neural structures seem to be activated for different kinds of learning (Ivry, 1992). For example, when a lesion is made in a rabbit's cerebellum, the rabbit will not be able to learn a specific kind of eye-blink response. However, the lesion will have no effect on heart-rate conditioning (Daum & Schugens, 1996; Lavond et al., 1984).

Let's examine this eye-blink response in more detail, because the biological explanation for this response has been extensively studied in recent decades. As it happens, rabbits have an unusual inner eyelid called the nictitating membrane, which slides over a rabbit's eye to protect it when a puff of air is presented; this response is called the **nictitating-membrane reflex.** A rabbit can be conditioned by presenting a tone (the conditioned stimulus) just before the puff of air. At first, the rabbit does not respond to the tone. However, with repeated trials, the nictitating membrane slides over the eye in response to the tone, even when the puff of air is not presented. Classical conditioning has occurred.

One brain structure that is involved in nictitating-membrane conditioning is the cerebellum. (See Figure 3.12 for the location of the cerebellum in humans.) For example, when a lesion has been made in the rabbit's cerebellum, the animal no longer shows evidence of conditioning; when the tone is presented, the nictitating membrane no longer moves. However, the unlearned reflex is not harmed; when the puff of air is presented, the normal nictitating-membrane reflex occurs (Daum & Schugens, 1996; McCormick et al., 1982). Incidentally, case studies in humans who have cerebellum damage also show that they cannot be classically conditioned to blink in response to a tone that has been paired with a puff of air (Daum & Schugens, 1996).

Another brain structure responsible for some conditioning tasks is the hippocampus. (Figure 3.14 shows the location of the hippocampus in humans.) The hippocampus is *not* involved when the conditioning task is simple and the tone stays on while the puff of air is presented. However, the hippocampus *is* involved when the tone is turned off half a second before the puff of air is presented. A rabbit with a lesion in the hippocampus cannot acquire this more complicated conditioning (Solomon et al., 1983). Current researchers are trying to establish how the hippocampus is involved in

Researchers interested in the biological basis of classical conditioning have often studied the nictitating-membrane reflex in rabbits.

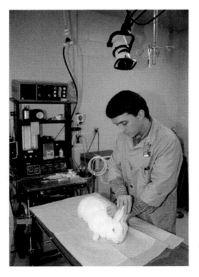

remembering the tone for a short period of time before the puff of air is presented and how the hippocampus may account for processing complex conditioned stimuli. They are also studying how the hippocampus and the cerebellum interact (Schmajuk & Blair, 1993; Schmajuk & DiCarlo, 1991, 1992).

Other researchers have used neuroscience techniques to explore classical conditioning in humans. For example, one patient had brain damage in the amygdala (Figure 3.14), but his brain was otherwise intact (Bechara et al., 1995). The researchers tried a classical-conditioning study with this patient in which a blue stimulus was paired with a startling sound. Normal people soon react with a startle response to the blue stimulus, but this particular individual never acquired the conditioned response. However, he was able to describe verbally how the blue stimulus was always followed by the sound. Without a functioning amygdala, he could still notice and remember information, but he could not learn a simple conditioned response.

Finally, other researchers have used brain-imaging techniques to explore how the cerebral cortex is involved in human classical conditioning. Hugdahl and his colleagues (1995) obtained PET scans on people who were participating in a classical conditioning experiment. The PET scans showed increased activation mostly in the right hemisphere, especially in the frontal lobe.

In summary, even the simplest form of learning is really not so simple. Classical conditioning can involve the cerebellum and the hippocampus; in humans, it can involve the amygdala and the cerebral cortex, as well.

Applications of Classical Conditioning

Psychologists have discovered a number of important applications of classical conditioning. One important field is the application of classical conditioning to psychotherapy, a topic we'll consider in Chapter 15. Here, we'll look at two other important applications: Classical conditioning can be applied to two issues in medicine, taste aversion in cancer patients and conditioning in the immune system.

Taste Aversion In the earlier discussion of biological preparedness, we saw that rats could develop taste aversion to sweet-tasting water that had previously been paired with nausea-producing radiation. Conditioned taste aversion may be one of the best-documented learned responses. In fact, more than 1,300 articles on the subject were published prior to 1989 (Bernstein & Meachum, 1990: Locurto, 1989). Humans —as well as animals—can easily acquire taste aversions (Schafe & Bernstein, 1996).

For a number of years, Ilene Bernstein and her colleagues have been examining how taste aversion develops in young cancer patients. Children who receive chemotherapy often acquire an intense dislike for the particular food they ate prior to chemotherapy. In an important early study, Bernstein (1978) tested whether children would develop conditioned taste aversion to a new flavor of ice cream, which she labeled "Mapletoff." Half of the children, who were between the ages of 2 and 16, were given a serving of Mapletoff ice cream prior to chemotherapy with a drug that causes nausea and vomiting. The other half of the children served as a control group. The control group received similar drug treatment, but no Mapletoff beforehand.

Two to four weeks later, the children in both groups were given a choice: They could either eat Mapletoff ice cream or play with a game. Only 21% of the children who had eaten Mapletoff prior to chemotherapy chose to eat the ice cream, in contrast to 67% of the children who had no previous experience with the Mapletoff (Bernstein, 1978). Clearly, most children in the experimental group had been conditioned to dislike the Mapletoff flavor.

Conditioned taste aversion creates nutritional problems, especially because taste aversion is typically strongest for meat and other sources of protein (Midkiff & Bernstein, 1985). Cancer patients need to eat, and they also need their chemotherapy. How can the dilemma be solved? We saw in an earlier section that the problem cannot be solved by waiting until several hours after eating before giving the drug.

If cancer patients who are about to receive chemotherapy eat unusually flavored candy after a normal meal, conditioned taste aversion may develop for the unusual candy, rather than the nutritious food.

TABLE 6.1 Setup for Broberg and Bernstein's Study on Conditioned Taste Aversion

	SEQUENCE OF EVENTS		
	1	**2**	**3**
EXPERIMENTAL GROUP	Meal	Life Savers	Chemotherapy
CONTROL GROUP	Meal	(nothing)	Chemotherapy

Source: Broberg & Bernstein, 1987.

Broberg and Bernstein (1987) devised a clever answer. Conditioned taste aversion is especially likely to develop for unfamiliar tastes. (After all, a familiar food such as a pancake is likely to have a long history of positive associations.) Therefore, these researchers gave children in the experimental condition an unusual flavor of Life Savers candy to eat immediately after the meal. The researchers selected two uncommon flavors, root beer and coconut, so that an intense dislike for these flavors would not have an effect on later nutrition. Children in the control group received no Life Savers. All were then given chemotherapy (see Table 6.1).

Later testing showed that the children who had received the Life Savers were more positive about eating the kinds of food that had been included in the earlier meal. In contrast, the control-group children were more likely to have developed taste aversions to the food in the meal. It seems that the Life Savers had served as a scapegoat for the first group, protecting the more nutritious food from acquiring taste aversions.

More recent research has demonstrated that aversions are more likely to be associated with the *smell* of the food, rather than its taste (Bartoshuk, 1991a). Perhaps further research will focus more on modifying the classical conditioning of odors.

Conditioning in the Immune System The **immune system** protects our bodies from damage by invading bacteria, viruses, and parasites. **Psychoneuroimmunology** is an interdisciplinary area that examines the relationship between the central nervous system and the immune system (Cohen & Herbert, 1996). In Chapter 18, we'll explore many ways in which psychological factors can influence our health via the immune system. Here, we will look at one component of psychoneuroimmunology: How classical conditioning can operate in the immune system.

After researching taste aversion in rats, Ader and Cohen (1985) extended these conditioning techniques to the immune system. Specifically, they paired two stimuli: (1) water sweetened with saccharin (the conditioned stimulus) and (2) injections of a drug that suppresses the immune system (the unconditioned stimulus). After the sweetened water had been repeatedly paired with the drug, Ader and Cohen found that the water alone could produce a suppression in the immune system. That is, the suppression occurred even when the drug was no longer presented. With a suppressed immune system, an organism is more susceptible to disease, so this discovery is potentially important.

Additional research has shown that classical conditioning has a small but reasonably reliable effect on the immune system (Ader & Cohen, 1993). Furthermore, the immune system can be either suppressed or enhanced by conditioning (Barker, 1994). However, researchers have not yet discovered the neural, endocrine, and immune system pathways that are involved during the conditioning process (Ader & Cohen, 1993).

The research on classical conditioning in the immune system has not yet been systematically applied in treating disease in humans. However, classical conditioning may help account for the placebo effect. In the **placebo effect,** a person is

By classical conditioning, this nurse and this container for the medicine may be associated with the actual drug. Later, the nurse and the container may produce a conditioned response, consisting of relief from symptoms. According to Ader (1995), this classical conditioning may partially account for the placebo effect.

given a substance that contains no active ingredients, and yet he or she experiences some relief from specific symptoms (Ader, 1995; Dodes, 1997). Psychologists and medical researchers have typically proposed that the placebo effect can be traced to people's expectations about the substance's effects. However, at least in some cases, classical conditioning may be partly responsible. For example, an individual may have taken a medicine that the nurse consistently administered from a round, brown bottle. By association with the actual drug (the unconditioned stimulus), the nurse and the bottle (the conditioned stimuli) may be able to elicit a conditioned response. This conditioned response may resemble the unconditioned response (relief from symptoms) associated with the original drug (Ader, 1995).

Critical Thinking Exercise 6.2

Write down your answers to the following questions about classical conditioning and taste aversion.

a. In the study in which Life Savers candy acted as a scapegoat, why would Broberg and Bernstein (1987) need to pretest the root beer and coconut Life Savers to see whether children liked them or disliked them?

b. In that same study, why did the researchers need to include a control group?

SECTION SUMMARY: *CLASSICAL CONDITIONING*

1. Learning is a relatively permanent change in behavior or knowledge.

2. In classical conditioning, a previously neutral stimulus acquires the ability to produce a response, because it has been associated with a stimulus that already produces a similar response.

3. In his influential study with dogs, Pavlov paired a bell (conditioned stimulus) with meat powder (unconditioned stimulus). Later, the sound of the bell produced salivation (conditioned response), even when the meat powder was no longer presented.

4. In another influential study, Watson and Rayner conditioned a baby to be afraid of a rat by pairing the rat with a loud noise.

5. Five important components of classical conditioning are acquisition, stimulus generalization, stimulus discrimination, extinction, and spontaneous recovery.

6. According to current theory about classical conditioning, (a) the conditioned and unconditioned stimulus don't have to be presented together; (b) biological preparedness ensures that some relationships between stimuli and responses will be learned more readily than others, and (c) classical conditioning requires a predictive relationship, so that the conditioned stimulus is always followed by the unconditioned stimulus.

7. Different kinds of classical conditioning involve different brain structures. The nictitating-membrane reflex in rabbits involves the cerebellum and—in more complex learning situations—the hippocampus. At least in humans, the amygdala and portions of the cerebral cortex may also be involved.

8. Some applications of classical conditioning include taste aversion and conditioning in the immune system.

OPERANT CONDITIONING

We have seen that classical conditioning can explain how people learn to dislike certain foods and why your heart pounds harder when you see a flashing signal on a tow truck. Classical conditioning can also account for some emotional reactions, both positive and negative. However, it cannot explain how a child learns to put away her toys or why you are reading this textbook right now—rather than watching television or going out with your friends. We need to turn to a second kind of conditioning to explain these behaviors.

FIGURE 6.7

Experimental setup for Thorndike's research on operant conditioning.

In **operant conditioning,** or **instrumental conditioning,** we learn to make a response because it leads to a reinforcing effect; we also learn *not* to make a response because it leads to a punishing effect. For example, a child learns to put away her toys because it leads to a reinforcing effect such as praise from a parent. You also learn *not* to repeat a joke on Wednesday that produced only an embarrassed silence from your friends on Tuesday.

Before describing operant conditioning in more detail, we should clarify the distinction between classical conditioning and operant conditioning. In classical conditioning, we respond to conditioned and unconditioned stimuli that we cannot control. In contrast, we respond *voluntarily* to the stimuli in an operant-conditioning situation (Kimble, 1996). Children can decide whether or not to pick up their toys, and you can choose whether to read a textbook.

Let's begin by examining two well-known studies that demonstrate operant conditioning. Then we will consider the important components of operant conditioning, new developments in this area, and biological explanations for operant conditioning. Our final discussion explores some applications for this important kind of learning.

Influential Research in Operant Conditioning

Thorndike's Puzzle Box Even before Pavlov investigated dogs who drool, the American psychologist Edward L. Thorndike (1898) examined cats who solved puzzles. As Figure 6.7 shows, a hungry cat was placed inside a cage. When the cat stepped on a special level, the door would open. The cat could then escape from the box and receive a food reward.

The cats did not show any systematic strategies in trying to escape from the puzzle box. Instead, they would scramble around the cage until they accidentally stepped on the lever. A typical cat might require 40 trials before it mastered the art of pressing on the lever, then quickly escaping through the door. Thorndike proposed the law of effect to explain the cats' behavior. The **law of effect** says that organisms learn responses that result in rewarding consequences; in contrast, responses with punishing consequences are weakened and not learned (Schunk, 1991; Thorndike, 1913). In Thorndike's research, the cats learned the behavior of pressing the lever because of its rewarding consequences.

Skinner's Conditioning Research B. F. Skinner was a prolific researcher whose work was central to modern behaviorism. He decided to design a simple environment in which the principles of animal learning could be discovered—an environment in

TABLE 6.2 Two Kinds of Reinforcement and Two Kinds of Punishment

	TWO KINDS OF STIMULI	
	Positive	**Negative**
ADD SOMETHING	Positive reinforcement	Punishment
TAKE AWAY SOMETHING	Punishment	Negative reinforcement

Note: A stimulus can be positive or negative, and it can be added or taken away.

which irrelevant factors could be eliminated (Rachlin, 1994). His learning chamber contained either a lever that a rat could press or a disk that a pigeon could peck to receive a food reward.

Figure 6.8 shows a pigeon pecking a disk, which allows a food pellet to drop into the tray below. The apparatus also records the number of times the pigeon pecks the disk. This recording provides a clear picture of the rate of learning, and it allows researchers to examine how a particular independent variable affects behavior. For example, they could examine how the pecking rate is influenced by the frequency of the food reward (for example, food on every trial versus food on every 10th trial).

Components of Operant Conditioning

Let's explore some important components of operant conditioning. We will begin with an overview of reinforcement and punishment, and then consider other features such as shaping, the discriminative stimulus, and extinction.

Reinforcement and Punishment In an effort to make academic advising more effective, West Chester University has faculty advisers write letters to students to congratulate them on their academic achievements. However, if a student misses a scheduled appointment with an adviser, the adviser posts a "wanted" poster—complete with the student's picture—near the dormitory cafeterias (Dodge, 1992). The advisers hope that the reinforcement will encourage further achievements, and that the punishment will discourage missed appointments.

We have two ways of offering reinforcement and two ways of providing punishment, as illustrated in Table 6.2. As you can see, **positive reinforcement** involves adding something positive to the situation after the correct response has been made. For example, one of my students baby-sat for a 7-year-old named Melissa while her parents went on a two-week business trip. The student praised Melissa warmly for her high math scores, and Melissa ended the semester with her first A in math (Ianazzi, 1992).

In **negative reinforcement,** something negative is taken away or avoided. For example, when you sit down to drive a car and you fasten your seat belt, the unpleasant sound of the seat-belt buzzer is removed. (Think how stunningly ineffective that signal would be if it played a selection by your favorite musician, rather than making that obnoxious noise!) Unfortunately, the term *negative reinforcement* confuses more students than virtually any other phrase in psychology (Kimble, 1992). One problem is that "negative" usually implies something bad or punishing, yet negative reinforcement actually ends up being pleasant. It may be helpful to emphasize the upbeat word *reinforcement* in this phrase.

Positive and negative reinforcement have similar consequences; they both strengthen or reinforce the behavior they follow and increase the chances that the behavior will be repeated. Thus, positive reinforcement from a baby-sitter should increase the probability of good math performance, and negative reinforcement from the cessation of the seat-belt buzzer should increase the probability of fastening the seat belt.

FIGURE 6.8

The experimental setup for Skinner's research on operant conditioning.

DEMONSTRATION 6.2 Understanding Reinforcement and Punishment

The following quiz tests your mastery of the concepts of reinforcement and punishment. The answers are at the end of the chapter on Page 222.

1. Is negative reinforcement used to increase or decrease behavior?

2. Can people look forward to negative reinforcement?

3. Do you think teachers should completely avoid using negative reinforcement?

4. Which of the following is an example of negative reinforcement? (You can select more than one.) Also, categorize each of the other examples.

   a. "Because you talked back, you have to stay after school."

   b. "You will have to stay after school until you clean your desk."

   c. "If you do all of your reading assignments without bothering other students, I will not have to call your parents."

   d. "Because you scored lower than 80% on this test, you will be required to submit a final paper."

   e. "If you submit all of your remaining weekly assignments on time, you may toss out your lowest quiz grade."

5. In terms of its effects on students' behavior, is negative reinforcement more similar to punishment or positive reinforcement?

Source: Based on Tauber, 1988.

An example of negative reinforcement would be if this child were told by a parent, "If you eat all your salad, you won't have to eat your lima beans"—thereby taking away something unpleasant.

Let's also consider the two kinds of punishment. **Punishment** can involve adding something negative; punishment can also involve taking away or preventing something positive (Skinner, 1953). One student recalled a high school coach who routinely used the "adding something negative" kind of punishment. Any baseball player who made an error during practice would be required to stay late and run an extra lap (Bilyk, 1992). Another student vividly remembered how her parents encouraged their children with the "preventing something positive" form of punishment: "If you kids aren't ready for bed by 7:30, you can't watch *The Muppet Show!*" (Seith, 1992).

Punishment tends to decrease the probability of the response that it follows, making that response less likely in the future. For example, the baseball team members may make fewer errors, and young children may procrastinate less. Now try Demonstration 6.2 to make certain that you understand the concepts of reinforcement and punishment.

The Punishment Dilemma Punishment is a controversial topic, although it is often used in one form or another. For example, naturalistic observation of elementary and junior high teachers shows that they yell at students at the rate of one scolding every two minutes (Schwartz, 1989; Van Houten & Doleys, 1983). Here are some of the problems with punishment:

1. Punishment may decrease the frequency of an inappropriate behavior, but it does not automatically increase the frequency of the behavior we want. A father may swat his daughter for saying something rude to the neighbor, and she may utter fewer rude remarks in the future. However, she does not learn what remarks *are* appropriate.

2. Through classical conditioning, fear and anxiety may become associated with the punisher or the environment in which punishment is given. For example, if a teacher yells loudly at a young boy for poor performance, then the teacher, the classroom, and even studying may arouse anxiety (Lieberman, 1990).

3. In order to deliver punishment, the punisher must pay attention to the offender. This attention may in fact be reinforcing—precisely the opposite of the desired effect (Mace et al., 1993). A teacher who spends a full two minutes lecturing Spike, the class bully, may find that attention reinforces him for his previous aggressive behavior. In the future, Spike may be even more likely to brutalize his classmates (Serbin & O'Leary, 1975).

4. Punishment provides a model of aggressive behavior, via observational learning (to be discussed in the next section). The person who is being punished learns that aggression is a way to solve problems. The research on child abuse provides a tragic example of how people learn to imitate an aggressive model.

This research has noted that many people who were abused as children—though certainly not all—will grow up to be abusing parents ("How Often," 1991; Straus & Gelles, 1980; Widom, 1989).

Realistically, however, we are not likely to eliminate punishment. Every parent, teacher, or pet owner occasionally feels that some kind of punishment is necessary. Nonetheless, several guidelines can help you use punishment more effectively. Specifically, punish the misbehavior consistently; a teacher will not be effective if she punishes cheating today but allows children to cheat without punishment tomorrow. Also, the delay between the response and the punishment should be as short as possible. Children will not learn from a threat such as "You just wait until your father gets home!" (Lutz, 1994; Pierce & Epling, 1995).

A better alternative to punishment is to reinforce a response that is incompatible with the unwanted response. If you want children to be less aggressive, praise them when they are interacting in a friendly fashion. This technique requires more thought than punishment does, but it is more likely to produce long-term behavior change (Iwata et al., 1993; Skinner, 1971, 1988a).

I recall learning as an undergraduate student about the virtues of reinforcing incompatible responses, but I was never fully convinced until about 10 years later. We had invited a family from a nearby city to join us for brunch. We had not met the two sons, Roy and Reginald, but we expected a pleasant morning because they were about the same age as our preschool daughters. The doorbell rang, we opened the door, and the older boy greeted us, saying "I am a lion and I'm going to tear your house apart." Apparently he was speaking for his younger brother as well, because the two proceeded to rip apart books, scatter toys everywhere, and intimidate our daughters. Every few minutes, a parent would mutter, "Stop that, Roy" or "Don't do that, Reginald." The parents may have intended these remarks as punishment, but they were ineffective.

At one point, though, we looked over to see that Roy, Reginald, and our daughters were quietly talking and playing tea party. My husband commented, "My goodness, you are all playing so nicely together now! That's wonderful!" Roy and Reginald looked up and their jaws dropped with astonishment. Their mother remarked, "They're not used to praise." Now I am not going to claim that their behavior during the rest of the morning qualified them for the Children-of-the-Month Award, but they were noticeably nicer for the rest of the visit. They had been reinforced for pleasant social interactions, and these responses are incompatible with antisocial behavior.

Shaping   Imagine a 6-year-old boy learning to swim. His teacher has asked him to try the basic crawl for the first time. The boy's legs are bent, his arms are awkward, and his head protrudes too far out of the water. Still, the teacher shouts an encouraging, "Good, keep it up." By the end of the lesson, the teacher would require a more refined technique before praising the swimmer. If the boy later trains for the swim team, he would have to be much better before earning reinforcement. Teachers, parents, and other people who want to encourage a particular behavior are likely to use shaping. **Shaping** is the systematic reinforcement of gradual improvements toward the desired behavior.

Shaping works because both humans and animals show great variability in their behavior (Epstein, 1991). During shaping, the teacher or the researcher reinforces only the responses that are closer and closer to the desired goal.

Shaping is a valuable tool because it encourages the learner to acquire a new behavior relatively quickly. To encourage a rat to press a lever, for instance, the researcher first delivers a food reinforcement when the rat is in the general vicinity of the lever (see Figure 6.9). The criterion is then made increasingly stricter. To earn the food, the rat must lift its paw in the vicinity of the lever. Ultimately, the researcher reinforces only those responses in which the rat completely depresses the lever. Thus, both the swimmer and the lever-pressing rat are reinforced for gradual improvements in performance.

FIGURE 6.9

At the end of shaping, the rat would need to completely depress the lever with its paw in order to receive the pellet of food.

TABLE 6.3 Four Common Partial Reinforcement Schedules

		REINFORCEMENT DEPENDS UPON	
		Number of Responses	**Passage of Time**
REINFORCEMENT IS	**Regular**	Fixed ratio	Fixed interval
	Irregular	Variable ratio	Variable interval

Schedules of Reinforcement   Think about how operant learning applies to your own life. How often do you receive reinforcement for good behavior or correct responses? Unless you are a very fortunate person, you'll answer "Not very often." In operant learning, the term **continuous reinforcement schedule** applies to situations in which the individual is reinforced on every correct trial. Candy machines typically reinforce the user according to a continuous reinforcement schedule. Every time you insert the appropriate coins, you should be rewarded by receiving the appropriate candy. In our daily lives, however, other humans rarely provide continuous reinforcement for appropriate behavior.

We are much more likely in our daily lives to receive a **partial reinforcement schedule,** in which reinforcement is provided only part of the time. Let's examine four kinds of partial reinforcement, which are listed in Table 6.3. In each case, the person or the animal needs to make the appropriate response before reinforcement can be delivered.

1. In a **fixed-ratio schedule,** reinforcement is given after a fixed number of responses have been made. For example, my local bagel store issues a card on which they mark their patrons' purchases. After I accumulate 12 tally marks, I will be rewarded with a dozen free bagels.

2. In a **fixed-interval schedule,** reinforcement is given for the first correct response made after the specified period of time (e.g., 30 minutes) has passed. For example, imagine a work setting in which the manager circulates around the office every hour, complimenting clerks who are working industriously. Some clerks are away at a meeting, so she waits until they are back working at their desks before she compliments them (Sulzer-Azaroff & Mayer, 1991). In a fixed-interval schedule, the reinforcement doesn't simply come after the appropriate time period. Instead, it is also contingent upon the correct behavior.

3. In a **variable-ratio schedule,** reinforcement is given after a varying number of responses have been made. For example, a figure skater may receive praise from her coach for an average of four out of every five jumps. Notice that the coach doesn't consistently praise the first four jumps and withhold praise for every fifth jump. Over a period of time, however, an average of four out of five jumps receives applause. Similarly, gamblers who play slot machines operate on a variable-ratio schedule, though they usually are not reinforced at the average rate of four out of five trials!

4. In a **variable-interval schedule,** reinforcement is given for the first response you make after a varying period of time has passed. For example, suppose you have a friend whose telephone is often busy. When you want to reach him, you typically dial the number every few minutes until you are successful. Sometimes you have a 20-minute wait, but other times you are successful after just 2 minutes.

The different schedules of reinforcement produce different response patterns. For instance, your response rate will be higher with the two kinds of ratio schedules, because reinforcement is linked to the number of responses. Furthermore, the two kinds of variable schedules produce a steadier rate of responding. Wouldn't you study more regularly if you did not know which day your professor would give a weekly quiz than if you could expect a quiz every Friday?

Secondary Reinforcers   When researchers reinforce a hungry rat with a pellet of food for pressing a lever, they are delivering a primary reinforcer. A **primary reinforcer** is a reinforcer that can satisfy a basic biological need, most likely food or water. Most human behavior, however, is controlled by **secondary reinforcers,** which are reinforcers that do not satisfy a basic biological need but acquire their rewarding power by association with another established reinforcer (Mazur, 1993).

   For example, many learning chambers are designed so that they make a clicking noise as they release a pellet of food. The animal associates that click with the primary reinforcer, food. Soon, the clicking sound serves as a secondary reinforcer. Try to think of the things that are most reinforcing to you—perhaps money, praise from someone you admire, or a good grade. Can you really argue that a good grade satisfies a basic biological need? Instead, it is a secondary reinforcer.

The Discriminative Stimulus   A **discriminative stimulus** is a stimulus signaling that a response will be reinforced. For example, a pigeon in a learning chamber may learn that only when a red button is lit up (the discriminative stimulus) will its pecking (response) lead to food (reinforcement). If the button is not lit up, the pigeon could peck incessantly without producing a morsel of food. Similarly, a headache serves as a discriminative stimulus for taking an aspirin or other painkiller (Pierce & Epling, 1995). Also, a ringing telephone serves as a discriminative stimulus for answering the phone. Without this discriminative stimulus, your response of picking up the receiver will not be reinforced by a conversation.

Extinction   You know the term *extinction* from classical conditioning. Extinction occurs when the conditioned stimulus is presented repeatedly without the unconditioned

For this child, winning an award serves as a secondary reinforcer.

FIGURE 6.10

Extinction Patterns (partial versus continuous reinforcement)
During extinction, the response rate drops much more rapidly when animals previously had continuous reinforcement than when they previously had partial reinforcement (typical results).

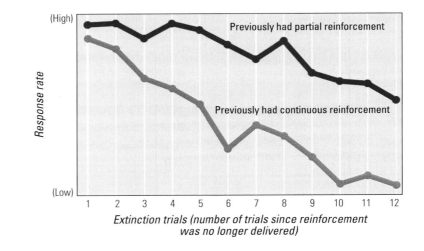

stimulus. In operant conditioning, extinction occurs when an organism repeatedly makes a response, and reinforcement is withheld. You are certainly familiar with extinction if you have ever inserted coins into a vending machine and received no food. After two or three unsuccessful attempts, you *should* show extinction!

An important principle of learning is that both people and animals show rapid extinction if they previously received continuous reinforcement, rather than partial reinforcement. Suppose you have a car that has always started reliably for more than two years. With this continuous reinforcement schedule, you will extinguish very quickly if you turn the key several times one morning and you are not reinforced by the purr of the motor. In contrast, suppose that you have a car that often does not start until the third or fourth attempt. With this partial reinforcement schedule, you may keep trying on one particular morning. In fact, you may wear out the battery before you extinguish.

The principle of slow extinction—following partial reinforcement—helps us understand the extraordinary persistence of some individuals. Maybe an uncle of yours keeps trying out for a role in the local theater productions because once— seven years ago—he was rewarded with a small part. Athletes, musicians, and other artists all keep working, sustained by the hope that the next attempt may bring them reinforcement. Or consider a toddler in her crib whose parents sometimes (but not always) let her out of bed at night when she has cried for a long time. She is likely to keep crying, lured by the hope that the next heart-wrenching sob may win her freedom. Figure 6.10 compares the extinction patterns of animals who have learned under continuous reinforcement or partial reinforcement.

Critical Thinking Exercise 6.3

Write down your answers to the following questions about the components of operant conditioning.

a. Suppose that a fourth-grader is learning to play the clarinet. Give an example of how her music teacher might apply the following components of operant conditioning: negative reinforcement, shaping, variable-interval schedule, and secondary reinforcers.

b. A parent holds out a cookie (a discriminative stimulus) to a child; the child says "cookie" (the response) and receives the cookie (positive reinforcement). A learning theorist says that this behavior can be totally explained by operant conditioning, because this is the same process by which a rat learns to press a lever to receive a food pellet. How would you respond to this claim?

Recent Developments in Operant Conditioning

In the first section of this chapter, we saw that major new developments in classical conditioning focus on the relationship between the conditioned stimulus and the unconditioned stimulus. In operant conditioning, the major new developments concern the role of the discriminative stimulus and the evolutionary psychology approach to operant conditioning.

The Role of the Discriminative Stimulus   Early theories of operant conditioning argued that during learning, an association forms between the discriminative stimulus and the response. Later theories suggested that the critical association is between the stimulus and the reinforcement. However, consistent with our theme of complexity, the current view is that the discriminative stimulus becomes associated with the *relationship* between the response and the reinforcement—rather than with either of them individually (Colwill & Rescorla, 1990; Rescorla, 1991; Roitblat & von Fersen, 1992). According to this newer view, the discriminative stimulus sets the occasion during which the response produces the reinforcement. For example, the ring of a telephone sets the occasion during which answering the phone will be reinforced by a conversation.

The Evolutionary Psychology Approach to Operant Conditioning   Charles Darwin's theory of evolution prompted scientists to study animal learning as a way of tracing the roots of human intelligence. Many researchers have tried to determine the upper limits of animals' intelligence. For example, we'll see in Chapter 9 that psychologists have been moderately successful in teaching chimpanzees to communicate using sign language and other symbolic languages. Some have also reported the impressive abilities of insects, birds, dogs, and other animals to appreciate time, number, language, spatial relationships, and the use of tools (e.g., Candland, 1993; Gallistel, 1990; Griffin, 1991).

Still other researchers have demonstrated that animals can acquire subtle concepts (Herrnstein, 1984; Roitblat, 1987). Consider a study in which pigeons acquired the concept of *tree* by watching a series of slides (Herrnstein et al., 1976). About half of these slides were pictures of trees—sometimes a part of a tree, sometimes one tree, and sometimes a forest. Pictures of trees served as the discriminative stimulus in this study. That is, when a picture of a tree was presented, the pigeon could peck at a key and receive a food pellet. Pecking when the other pictures were present earned no pellet. After a number of training sessions, a new set of pictures was presented as a test. The pigeons were highly accurate in discriminating tree from non-trees (see Figure 6.11). This kind of achievement makes us wonder whether the term "birdbrain" is really more a compliment than an insult!

Other researchers, however, have emphasized the limits of animal learning. That is, animals may seem smart when they learn some tasks that are compatible with their natural abilities, but they seem slow-witted on other tasks that do not match these natural abilities (Gould & Marler, 1987).

Furthermore, the principle of **instinctive drift** argues that when an animal is engaged in operant conditioning, its behavior will drift in the direction of instinctive

FIGURE 6.11

Using photographs like these, the research of R. J. Herrnstein and his colleagues revealed that pigeons can distinguish a variety of tree photos from pictures of irrelevant objects.

FIGURE 6.12

Because raccoons instinctively handle objects, it is difficult to teach them to perform a trick in which they must release the objects; this is an example of instinctive drift.

behaviors related to the task it is learning (Breland & Breland, 1961; Pierce & Epling, 1995). For example, Breland and Breland tried to train a raccoon to pick up a single coin and deposit that coin in a piggy bank. However, they found that the raccoon would typically clutch the coin firmly, refusing to deposit it in the bank. Evolutionary factors have encouraged raccoons to instinctively manipulate objects, as Figure 6.12 shows. Holding objects is adaptive for raccoons, and so they cannot easily learn to give them up (Gray, 1996). We saw earlier in the chapter that biological preparedness limits animals' ability to learn that bright, noisy water predicts nausea in classical conditioning. Similarly, the instinctive drift principle limits animals' ability to learn operant conditioning tasks that are incompatible with their instincts.

Biological Aspects of Operant Conditioning

Researchers who examine the biological components of learning point out that classical conditioning is easier to study than operant conditioning (Thompson & Donegan, 1986). Still, neuroscientists have made some progress in identifying the neural structures that account for operant conditioning. For example, when the operant task requires mastering a spatial map such as a maze, the parietal cortex is involved. (See Figure 3.16 for the location of the parietal lobe in humans.) However, when the operant task emphasizes a sequence of events (e.g., the components must be performed in a certain order), then part of the frontal region of the cortex is involved. These localization findings may remind you of the findings in classical conditioning. Specifically, we noted on Page 196 that the parts of the brain involved in eye-blink conditioning are different from those involved in heart-rate conditioning.

The limbic system is active in both classical conditioning and operant conditioning. We saw that classical conditioning involves the hippocampus, at least on some tasks. Operant conditioning also uses the hippocampus, but it makes more use of the amygdala (Schmajuk & Blair, 1993; White & Milner, 1992). (See Figure 3.14 for the location of the amygdala in humans.) Consider the research by Gaffan and Harrison (1987), in which monkeys had been trained to discriminate between visual stimuli by receiving a tone as secondary reinforcement. (The tone had previously been associated with a food reward.) After lesions were made in the amygdala, the animals could no longer perform accurately.

Epinephrine seems to be the relevant neurotransmitter in the amygdala (McGaugh, 1989). Furthermore, memory for an operant response is enhanced by low to moderate amounts of epinephrine, and it is impaired by larger amounts (McGaugh & Gold, 1988). In summary, then, the region of the cortex that is involved in operant conditioning depends upon the specific nature of the task. Within the limbic system, however, the amygdala is the most important structure, and epinephrine is probably the critical neurotransmitter.

Critical Thinking Exercise 6.4

Write down your answers to the following questions about recent developments and biological research in operant conditioning.

a. Herrnstein and other researchers have argued that pigeons could acquire the concept of *tree*—a concept that included the stimuli in Figure 6.11. What kinds of precautions must researchers take when they select stimuli in order to avoid confounding variables in this kind of study?

b. Two groups of researchers are studying the effects of epinephrine on memory for an operant response in rats; each group tests two dosages—a "smaller" amount and a "larger" amount. Group 1 claims that their rats remembered better with their "smaller" amount of epinephrine; Group 2 claims that their rats remembered better with their "larger" amount. Without knowing anything further, how do you suspect that their data could be reconciled?

Applications of Operant Conditioning

The most popular applications of operant conditioning focus on **behavior modification,** which is the systematic use of techniques from learning theory to change human behavior. Behavior modification can be used in treating problems as diverse as drug addiction, depression, delinquency, sexually transmitted disease, and pain management (Bellack et al., 1990; Kazdin, 1994). Behavior modification has also been used to help individuals who are mentally retarded, especially with language and social skills (Matson, 1990; Whitman et al., 1990).

Behavior modification programs include several important steps (Kazdin, 1994; Martin & Pear, 1992; Pierce & Epling, 1995; Watson & Tharp, 1993):

1. Define the problem in behavioral terms that are concrete and observable. For example, a teacher who wants to decrease a child's aggressiveness may select three target behaviors: hitting, kicking, and biting. The definition of the problem emphasizes actions, rather than thoughts or wishes. You may decide to decrease a certain behavior, or you may decide to increase another behavior.

2. Decide on an operational definition for the target behavior, and determine how you will measure it in a consistent manner. For example, if you have decided that you want to increase the amount of time you spend studying, you might measure that behavior in terms of hours per day.

3. Take a **baseline measure,** which is the frequency of the response or the time spent responding *before* you begin the behavior modification program.

4. Figure out reinforcers or punishers for the target behavior. Continue to measure the response rate while you carry out the program.

5. If the program is going well, continue. If it is not, try changing the reinforcer or punisher. You may find, for example, that you initially chose an inappropriate reinforcer. For instance, in one behavior modification program, staff members had originally selected candy as a reinforcement for a young girl. Candy was not effective, but she later responded well when they switched to a reinforcer of allowing her to play briefly with a toy purse.

This teacher is handing the student a token, which can be exchanged later for an appealing reward.

DEMONSTRATION 6.3 Applying the Principles of Behavior Modification

Identify one specific behavior of yours that you would like to change. Perhaps you would like to spend more time studying or participate more in class. Or you may want to reduce a certain behavior, such as snacking less between meals or making fewer sarcastic comments. Select a target behavior and follow these suggestions.

1. Define the problem in terms of concrete behavioral terms that are specific, rather than general.

2. Determine how you will measure this behavior consistently and how you will record it systematically. Construct a tally sheet that you can carry with you to record the number of responses you make each day.

3. For one week, take a baseline measure before you begin with rewards. This process may also help you identify the circumstances in which

you are likely to perform an unwanted behavior or to avoid performing a desirable behavior.

4. Identify an attractive reward. (For the purposes of this demonstration, avoid punishment and negative reinforcement.) The reward might be something small or else something large for which you can accumulate tokens (e.g., check marks) over a period of time. Begin the program and record your behavior for two weeks.

5. If the program is going well, continue. You may want to alter the reinforcement schedule, however. If it is not going well, reassess and try to find a more attractive reward.

Note: Watson and Tharp (1993) include many details on applying behavior modification to your own life.

Sources: Based on Michael, 1985; Watson & Tharp, 1993.

In behavior-modification programs in an industrial setting, praise can act as a reinforcer.

An important concept in behavior modification is the token economy. In a **token economy,** good behavior is immediately reinforced by a token object, such as a ticket or a star; these tokens can be accumulated and exchanged later for a reinforcer (Kazdin, 1994). For example, a sixth grade teacher applied a token economy by handing out a token every time a student finished an assignment. Students wrote their names on the tokens, which served as lottery tickets for prizes such as a small pocket radio. Her students showed a dramatic improvement in the number of assignments they completed (Skinner, 1988b).

Behavior modification has been used in business as well as in education. Programs have been implemented to improve productivity, worker safety, and management-employee relations, as well as to reduce shoplifting, tardiness, and absenteeism (Martin & Pear, 1992). Chapter 15 also examines how behavior therapy can be used for treating psychological disorders.

Now that you have been introduced to the basic principles of operant conditioning and behavior modification, try Demonstration 6.3.

SECTION SUMMARY: *OPERANT CONDITIONING*

1. In operant conditioning, an organism learns to make a response because it produces a rewarding effect; the organism may also learn *not* to make a response because it produces a punishing effect.

2. Two important early demonstrations of operant conditioning showed cats learning how to escape from a puzzle box (Thorndike) and animals pressing a lever or a disk to receive a food reward (Skinner).

3. Psychologists distinguish among positive reinforcement, negative reinforcement, and two kinds of punishment; in general, reinforcing a response that is incompatible with an undesired response is more effective than administering punishment.

4. Other important components of operant conditioning include shaping, schedules of reinforcement, the discriminative stimulus, secondary reinforcers, and extinction.

5. New developments in operant conditioning include (a) the view that the discriminative stimulus is associated with the relationship between the response and the reinforcement, and (b) the finding that animals have impressive learning capacities—although the evolutionary psychology approach emphasizes that these capacities may be limited by instinctive drift.

6. The brain structures involved in operant conditioning include regions of the cortex and the limbic

system; epinephrine is apparently the crucial neuro-transmitter.

7. Operant conditioning has been applied in a wide variety of behavior modification programs, such as improved students' completion of assignments and improving workers' productivity.

OBSERVATIONAL LEARNING

So far, we have seen that classical conditioning can explain how we acquire fears, salivary responses, eye blinks, and motor performances. We have also noted that operant conditioning can account for a much wider range of learned behaviors. However, many of your daily actions cannot be explained by even the broadest interpretation of conditioning approaches. Classical and operant conditioning are especially limited in accounting for the rapid acquisition of *new* behaviors (Schunk, 1991).

Consider, for example, your very first attempt to drive a car. You knew exactly where to insert the key and exactly where to place your hands on the steering wheel. Of course, operant conditioning helps explain how you perfect your skills and how you maintain them. However, neither classical conditioning nor operant conditioning can account for the speed and accuracy with which you acquire a behavior that you have never previously attempted.

To account for numerous accomplishments—especially those you perform for the first time—we need to consider the third major kind of learning: observational learning. In **observational learning,** we acquire behaviors by watching and imitating the behavior of others. Observational learning is also called **modeling,** because the learner imitates a model. It is also called **social learning,** because learning occurs in a social situation by watching other people. Incidentally, we should note that researchers have reported imitation in monkeys, rats, birds, and octopuses (Fiorito,

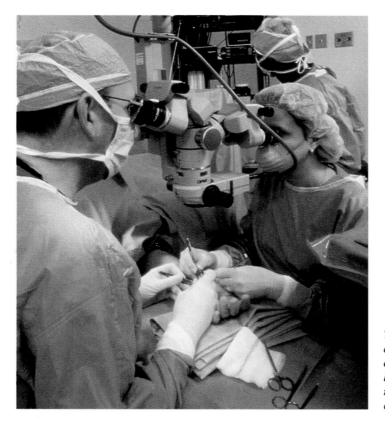

This physician's skill in performing a surgical operation can be explained better by observational learning than by the trial-and-error mechanisms of operant conditioning.

1993; Fiorito & Scotto, 1992; Heyes & Galef, 1996). As you might imagine, this topic is especially interesting to evolutionary psychologists. However, we'll concentrate on observational learning in humans.

Let's begin our discussion of observational learning by considering some important early research, as well as the components of observational learning. Next, the "In Depth" feature discusses the relationship between media violence and aggression. We'll end with a brief overview of applications of observational learning.

Influential Research in Observational Learning

In the most widely cited research in observational learning, children watched adults as they behaved aggressively with a large inflated toy doll. Throughout a series of studies, Albert Bandura and his colleagues (1961, 1963) examined whether these children would imitate the adult models. In a typical session in the Bandura studies, a nursery school child works busily on a picture. Than an adult in a different part of the room approaches a Bobo doll, an inflatable clownlike toy that is weighted on the bottom so that it pops back up whenever it is knocked down. For about 10 minutes, this adult brutalizes Bobo, hitting it with a hammer, knocking it down, and sitting on it. The adult accompanies these aggressive actions with remarks such as "Kick him" and "Sock him in the nose."

The child is then led into a second room, filled with many enticing toys. However, the child is told that the toys are being saved for other children, a comment guaranteed to arouse frustration. Finally, the child is brought to a third room, containing several toys and—you guessed it—a Bobo doll. Bandura and his colleagues watched through hidden windows and noted the children's behavior.

The children who had been exposed to the violent model were likely to hit Bobo, even repeating the same phrases and mimicking the identical aggressive actions. Children showed this observational learning, whether they directly observed the aggressive adult or viewed the aggression in a film. In contrast, other children who had not observed a violent adult model were much less likely to treat Bobo aggressively. Later research showed that children were even more likely to imitate aggression when the adult model had been praised for acting aggressively (Rosekrans & Hartup, 1967).

Components of Observational Learning

In observational learning, people learn how to perform an action, even when they receive no reinforcement themselves. However, we have just seen that learning can be enhanced when a model receives praise. An important concept in observational learning is called **vicarious reinforcement,** which occurs when the model receives reinforcement. Similarly, **vicarious punishment** occurs when the model receives punishment (Bandura, 1986). Suppose, for example, that you are enrolled in a course in which students make class presentations. Your professor has just praised a presenter's effective use of vivid examples but criticized this presenter's tendency to say "um" and "er" between phrases. You experience both vicarious reinforcement (for the examples) and vicarious punishment (for the extraneous noises). Your own presentation may be influenced by these vicarious experiences.

Bandura also emphasizes that people can experience **intrinsic reinforcement,** an internalized sense of satisfaction when they perform well. For example, you may experience intrinsic reinforcement when you are pleased with a painting you've just completed, even though no one else is present. Alternatively, **intrinsic punishment** occurs when you scold yourself for poor performance. If you receive a low score on a section of the Study Guide for this chapter, you may experience intrinsic punishment, even though no one else will see your score.

Bandura's more recent additions to observational learning theory reflect the current emphasis on cognitive psychology (Bandura, 1986, 1992a). In particular, he emphasizes that a learner observing a model does *not* acquire a perfectly accurate, exact replica of the model's behavior. Instead, the learner acquires a **schema** (pronounced "*skee*-muh")—a generalized idea that captures the important components, but not every exact detail. The learner actively transforms the information about modeled behavior into a set of rules for generating new behavior. Thus, a child who has watched an adult attacking a Bobo doll may later show many important components of the adult's behavior, but this child will not exactly duplicate every gesture and comment. In the next chapter, we'll discuss how schemas can influence your memory.

Psychologists believe that observational learning theory is particularly effective in explaining social behavior. For example, children may learn many gender stereotyped behaviors by imitating models, either people they know or characters from television programs and movies (Matlin, 1996a; Mischel, 1966). For example, a young girl may learn from these models that she is supposed to act helpless in an emergency. I recall watching a Saturday morning cartoon in which the only female character was a mother who fainted during an interplanetary crisis. (Her preteen son came to the rescue and saved the universe.)

Vicarious reinforcement is another concept that explains social behavior. For instance, a young boy may watch as a male teenager receives smiles and cheers for hitting a fellow student who seemed to be taunting him. A girl in junior high may experience intrinsic reinforcement as she practices a demure, stereotypically "feminine" smile in the mirror. Observational learning helps account for the differences in body language shown by the young girl and boy in Figure 6.13. However, one of the most important applications of observational learning focuses on the media.

FIGURE 6.13

Observational learning may have encouraged these young children to acquire their gender-stereotyped nonverbal behavior.

IN DEPTH

Media Violence and Observational Learning

Several years ago, a group of scholars and television professionals met to discuss a significant issue: Do children learn to be aggressive by watching television violence? The moderator of the discussion interviewed Dick Wolf, the producer of violent programs such as *Miami Vice* and *Law & Order*. Part of their conversation is revealing:

> **Wolf:** *I have an 8-year-old and a 5-year-old child. They've never seen any of the shows I've ever produced. They shouldn't be watching them. They're not allowed to watch Saturday-morning cartoons.*
>
> **Moderator:** *Why not?*
>
> **Wolf:** *Why not? Because they're extremely violent. (Eron, 1993, p. 6)*

We saw in the early research on observational learning that children become more aggressive after watching a violent model (Bandura et al., 1961, 1963). In a popular magazine, Bandura (1963) pointed out that parents were unwittingly exposing their children to violent models on television. Bandura (1994) continues to point out that children can learn to be aggressive by observing violence on television. For example, children experience vicarious reinforcement when a television hero is praised for killing another individual.

Media violence remains a major problem as we move into the twenty-first century. According to some estimates, in a typical year the average American child sees between 1,000 and 10,000 murders, rapes, and assaults on television. Children also see nearly 20,000 commercials each year, often featuring toys that encourage further aggression (Comstock & Strasburger, 1993; Strasburger, 1991). Children and adolescents watch between 21 and 40 hours of television each week (Centerwall, 1992; Committee on Communications, 1995; Klein et al., 1993). By the time they graduate from high school, teenagers have usually spent 15,000 to 18,000 hours in front of the TV set, in contrast to 12,000 hours in classroom instruction (Strasburger, 1991). Thus, American children have the opportunity to learn more from television than from the educational system.

For nearly four decades, researchers have examined how television violence influences viewers' behavior. Consistent with Theme 3 of our book, the picture that

Children watch violent programs on television, and they also see ads for toys that encourage even more violence, such as this toy in which the dummies' body parts fly off when the car crashes.

(IN DEPTH continued)

emerges is complex. As this "In Depth" feature illustrates, exposure to media violence does not inevitably cause viewers to become aggressive. However, it does make aggression more likely in certain situations. We'll also see that observational learning is not the only mechanism that encourages a relationship between television violence and aggressive behavior.

An additional benefit of examining the relationship between media violence and aggression is that the topic lets us compare several research methods: the experiment, the quasi-experiment, and the correlational technique. We introduced these research methods in Chapter 2, and now we will review them.

The Experimental Method

In the **experimental method,** the researchers manipulate the independent variable to determine its effects on the dependent variable—that is, the behavior of the participants in the experiment. In research on television violence, the independent variable is typically the kind of television show that people watch. The dependent variable is some measure of their aggressive behavior or aggressive tendencies.

Let's consider a representative study by Wendy Josephson (1987), who examined both the effects of violent television programs and the effects of a cue reminding children about the violence they had viewed. She studied boys in the second and third grades, placing them in groups of six children. Consistent with one criterion of the experimental method, the groups of children were randomly assigned to conditions. Children in the nonviolence control group saw a 14-minute segment of a television program about a boys' bike-racing team. Children in the violence condition saw a 14-minute segment of a television program that began with the brutal killing of a police officer by a group of snipers; it ended with all the snipers being dead or unconscious. (The researchers had established by rating scales and physiological measures that these two segments differed in violence, but not in excitement or interest level.) Children in the third group, the violence-plus-cue condition, saw the same violent program, but they were also shown a reminder cue (a walkie-talkie, similar to one in the violent show) just before the dependent variable was measured.

The dependent variable in Josephson's study was the number of aggressive behaviors each group of six made during a subsequent game of floor hockey. These behaviors included hitting another boy with a hockey stick, pulling his hair, and calling him names.

Figure 6.14 shows the average number of aggressive behaviors for each of the three conditions during the nine minutes of the floor hockey game. As you can see, aggression was relatively low for the boys who had seen the nonviolent TV segment. It was significantly higher for those who had seen the violent TV segment. However, aggression was even higher for those who had seen the violent TV segment plus the reminder cue.

As you may recall from Chapter 2, a **meta-analysis** is a systematic statistical method for synthesizing the results from numerous studies on a given topic. Fortunately, researchers have conducted two recent meta-analyses on studies using the experimental method. The two research groups included somewhat different studies in their meta-analysis. However, both concluded that exposure to media violence does indeed increase aggression in children and adolescents. Wood and her colleagues (1991) found that the strength of the effect was in the small-to-moderate range; Paik and Comstock (1994) reported that the strength of the effect was large.

Let's translate this statistical information into a more meaningful format. As Eron (1995a) reports, the strength of the relationship between television violence and aggression is about the same as the relationship between smoking and lung cancer. As Eron cautions, "Not everyone who smokes gets lung cancer, and not everybody who has lung cancer ever smoked. . . . Similarly, not everyone who watches violent TV becomes aggressive, and not everyone who is aggressive watched violent television" (p. 4). Still, television violence does have a noteworthy causal effect on aggression, when studied in experimental research.

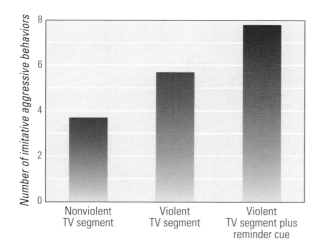

FIGURE 6.14

Effects of TV Violence on Young Boys

Average number of aggressive behaviors made by each group of six boys, as a function of condition. Source: Based on Josephson, 1987.

Critical Thinking Exercise 6.5

Write down your answers to the following questions about the experimental method and research on media violence.

a. What are some of the *advantages* of the experimental method, as represented by Josephson's study, in comparison to the correlational method?

b. What is an important *disadvantage* of the experimental method, in comparison to other research methods?

The Quasi-Experimental Method

As Critical Thinking Exercise 6.5 pointed out, we may have trouble generalizing the results of an experiment to real-life settings. For this reason, researchers also need to conduct quasi-experiments and correlational research in order to answer complex questions.

In a **quasi-experiment**, the researchers cannot randomly assign participants to different groups. Instead, they locate a situation in which groups already exist that differ substantially from one another. For example, Joy, Kimball, and Zabrack (1986) located a town in a remote part of Canada that had no television prior to 1974, when one station was made available. This town therefore experienced a *change* in television viewing patterns. In contrast, a second town had one station available both before and after 1974. A third town had four stations available both before and after 1974. Notice that the second and third towns did not experience a change in television viewing patterns.

Figure 6.15 shows the increase in the number of physically aggressive responses, between 1973 and 1974, made by children in the three towns. When television was introduced to children in the first town, their aggression increased substantially. In contrast, children in the other two towns—where television availability did not change between 1973 and 1974—did not dramatically change their aggressive behavior.

This quasi-experiment shows us that introducing television to a community might have a real-life impact on the children's aggressive tendencies. However, keep in mind that the experimenters did not randomly assign the children to the three community groups. Therefore the three groups may have differed substantially, even before the study began. The researchers established from census figures that the three towns were identical in population size and income level, but they might have differed in some characteristics not measurable in a census. We must therefore be cautious about concluding that the introduction of television *caused* the increase in aggression.

FIGURE 6.15

Increases in Violence Among Children in Three Canadian Towns

The increase in the number of aggressive responses, as a function of change in television availability. *Source:* Based on Joy et al., 1986.

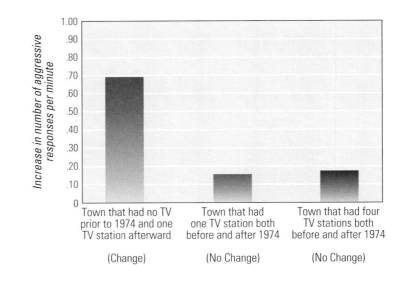

(IN DEPTH continued)

Correlational Research

A variety of studies on media violence have used the correlational approach. **Correlational research** attempts to determine whether two variables are related. As in a quasi-experiment, researchers gather data in real-life settings. In correlational studies, the researchers do not actively manipulate any variable. Many studies have shown that television viewing patterns and aggressive behavior are significantly correlated (e.g., Greenberg, 1975; Huesmann, 1986; Singer & Singer, 1981). In general, these correlations are moderate, rather than strong (Condry, 1989; Dubow & Miller, 1996; Eron & Huesmann, 1987; Paik & Comstock, 1994). We would not expect the correlations to be strong, because so many factors other than media viewing could influence aggressive behavior (Wood et al., 1991).

Correlational research presents several major problems. One problem is that the researchers cannot control the independent variable. In the case of research on media violence, researchers cannot control which programs the viewers watch and the conditions under which they watch these programs.

We discussed a second problem in Chapter 2: Some "third variable" may be responsible for the apparent relationship between two variables. As we have noted, the amount of violent television a child watches is correlated with his or her aggressive behavior. However, that relationship may really be traceable to a third variable, the characteristics of the child's parents. Specifically, the kind of parents who prohibit their children from watching violent TV shows are also likely to discourage aggressive behavior in their children. Fortunately, researchers can use statistical techniques to determine whether television viewing patterns and aggressive behavior are still correlated, after we have taken some of these possible "third variables" into account. In general, the studies show that the correlation does remain significant (e.g., Dubow & Miller, 1996; Hughes & Hasbrouck, 1996; Liebert & Sprafkin, 1988; Paik & Comstock, 1994; Singer et al., 1984).

A third major problem with correlational studies is known as the "directionality problem." As Chapter 2 discussed, a correlational study cannot tell us whether Variable A caused Variable B or whether Variable B caused Variable A. In fact, *both* explanations could apply to the media violence issue:

1. Television violence causes aggressive behavior.

2. Aggressive behavior causes viewing of television violence. (For example, children who are already aggressive may like to watch violent programs, but less aggressive children may prefer nonviolent programs.)

Extensive research on television violence and aggression in five different countries suggests that both of these explanations of the correlation are correct. Once again, psychological processes require complex explanations. L. Rowell Huesmann and Leonard Eron (1986) arranged for children between the ages of 6 and 11 to be studied over a two-year period in Australia, Finland, Poland, Israel, and the United States. Their analysis of the results led them to conclude that children who frequently watch violent TV programs are indeed more likely to learn how to behave aggressively. Furthermore, children who have learned how to behave aggressively are more likely to enjoy watching even more of these violent TV programs. A vicious circle begins, encouraging even more aggressive behavior.

Conclusions About Media Violence

The research we have examined is representative of hundreds of studies on media violence that have been summarized in other resources (e.g., Geen, 1994; Huesmann et al., 1992; Paik & Comstock, 1994; Wood et al., 1991). Almost all of these reviews conclude that exposure to media violence does increase viewers' aggression, although a few researchers disagree (Freedman, 1986, 1992; Potts et al., 1986; Sprafkin et al., 1987).

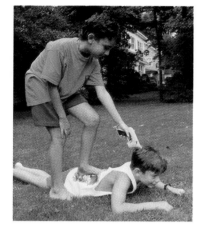

This child may have learned his aggressive behavior from watching violent television, but he also may have been more likely to watch violent television because he was more aggressive than other children.

Furthermore, some children are clearly more affected by media violence than others. For instance, Heath and her colleagues (1986) concluded that television violence is particularly dangerous for children who have been abused. These children see aggression modeled in their daily lives, as well as on the television set. In contrast, children with little real contact with violence may not be as likely to learn aggressive behavior from the media (Dubow & Miller, 1996). These conclusions are clearly consistent with our theme of individual differences. Future research on this topic should examine other individual-difference factors that may influence whether television violence has a strong impact on children's aggression.

Psychologists also acknowledge that several different mechanisms account for the relationship between television violence and aggressive behavior. Here, we have focused on observational learning. Consistent with our theme of complexity, we need to consider additional influential factors. For example, the violence in a cartoon program may arouse children and make them more excited; excited children are likely to be more aggressive. Furthermore, children who watch violent programs over the course of several months or years may become desensitized. They may require increased levels of violence to feel satisfied, and they may not be concerned about real violence that occurs in their everyday lives (Gunter, 1994).

In summary, we have seen that television violence does have a significant effect on children's aggression. Naturally, though, television violence is just one cause of aggressive behavior (Eron, 1995b); we'll examine other causes in Chapter 17. Furthermore, observational learning is not the only mechanism that explains how television violence influences the aggression level of children.

Many of you who are concerned about media violence may wish to have additional information. Here are three excellent organizations:

Critical Thinking Exercise 6.6

Write down your answers to the following questions about quasi-experimental and correlational research on the relationship between TV violence and children's aggression.

a. The discussion of the quasi-experiment by Joy, Kimball, and Zabrack (1986) noted that the three community groups may have differed in some characteristics other than their town's population and income level. Can you think of a potential confounding variable that could account for the differences in aggression shown in Figure 6.15?

b. Research shows that the number of television sets in North America has systematically increased since 1950. During the same period of time, the homicide rate has also systematically increased. Suppose that someone is trying to argue that these data demonstrate that television violence therefore causes aggressive behavior. What would you reply?

(IN DEPTH continued)
- Action for Children's Television, 975 Memorial Drive, Cambridge, MA 01020
- American Academy of Pediatrics, Committee on Communications, 141 Northwest Point Blvd., P.O. Box 927, Elk Grove Village, IL 60007-1098
- Stop War Toys Campaign, c/o WRL, 339 Lafayette Street, New York, NY 10012

Applications of Observational Learning

In Chapter 13, we will discuss how Albert Bandura applied observational learning to personality development. Two other areas in which observational learning has been applied include educational psychology and clinical psychology.

Educational Psychology   In the section on operant conditioning, we discussed how behavior modification has been used in education. Clearly, observational learning also has numerous applications in teaching. For example, students learn how to pronounce French vocabulary and how to play football, mostly by observational learning. Also, observational learning plays an important role when student teachers learn how to teach.

Cognitive psychologists have developed additional techniques based on observational learning. For example, in **cognitive modeling,** a teacher performs actions while explaining the reasons for those actions (Schunk, 1991). For instance, suppose that a teacher wants to use cognitive modeling to show students how to solve an arithmetic problem: 245 divided by 5. The teacher could solve the problem on the board, while commenting as follows:

> First I need to decide what number to divide the 5 into. I start on the left and move to the right until I find a number that is large enough. Is 2 large enough to be divided by 5? No, but 24 is. OK, so my first division will be 5 into 24. Now I want a number that I can multiply by 5 that will give me an answer that's the same as or slightly smaller than 24. How about 5? Well, 5 times 5 is 25, so that's too large. But 4 times 5 is 20, so that will work. . . .

Notice that the teacher models how to cope with mistakes, as well as how to solve the problem correctly. Research on cognitive modeling shows that children learn division more effectively using this technique than with more traditional teaching methods (Schunk, 1991). Modeling has also been used in education to teach job interviewing skills, improve students' athletic skills, and correct language deficits (Sulzer-Azaroff & Mayer, 1991).

Clinical Psychology   Observational learning is also important in the origins and treatment of phobias. A **phobia** is an intense and persistent fear of a specific object or situation (American Psychiatric Association, 1994a). At one point, many theorists believed that phobias were caused by classical conditioning. For example, they suggested that a person might develop a snake phobia following a snake bite, producing an extreme fear of the sight of snakes. A.S., who was described at the beginning of the chapter, probably acquired his fear of enclosed spaces via classical conditioning. However, most people with phobias cannot recall a traumatic conditioning experience to account for their fears (Barlow, 1988).

Instead, observational learning seems to be the major reason that people acquire phobias. In a series of studies, laboratory-reared monkeys learned to fear snakes. At the beginning of the research, these young monkeys showed no fear of snakes. Then they were introduced to their parents, who had been reared in the wild. The young monkeys watched as their parents reacted fearfully to snakes. After brief observation periods, the offspring avoided snakes and appeared afraid of them, showing behaviors similar to their parents (Cook et al., 1985; Mineka et al., 1984).

A therapist may suggest that a mother help her daughter overcome her fear of cats by modeling how to handle the cat in a relaxed manner.

In short, phobias seem to arise when we watch someone being afraid, rather than when we experience pain directly. Many therapists now help people overcome their phobias by asking them to watch a person dealing with the feared animal and showing no apparent signs of anxiety. In other cases, people may watch videos showing a person interacting in a relaxed manner with the feared animal or object (Kazdin, 1994). Thus, observational learning can help people overcome their phobias.

In this chapter, we have examined three kinds of learning: classical conditioning, operant conditioning, and observational learning. Each approach provides an important mechanism for acquiring new skills and changing behavior. However, since you began reading this chapter, you have learned many concepts and changed many behaviors. Only a fraction of these changes can be traced to these three kinds of learning. As a human, you also have the capacity to learn and change because of your ability to remember, think, and use language. The next three chapters examine these topics.

SECTION SUMMARY: *OBSERVATIONAL LEARNING*

1. In observational learning, we acquire behaviors by watching and imitating the behavior of others.

2. Bandura's research showed that children can learn to imitate an adult's aggressive behavior toward a Bobo doll.

3. Important components of observational learning include vicarious reinforcement and punishment, intrinsic reinforcement and punishment, and the acquisition of schemas.

4. Research on the relationship between television violence and children's aggression has used the experimental, quasi-experimental, and correlational methods. Most research shows that TV violence is moderately related to aggression. However, the

relationship is complex. Also, many mechanisms other than observational learning are responsible for the relationship between media violence and children's aggression.

5. Observational learning has applications in classroom teaching and in explaining and treating phobias.

REVIEW QUESTIONS

1. Suppose that you are driving along the road, and you spot a pothole immediately in front of you. As soon as you see it, your body automatically tightens and you flinch, in preparation for the jolt. Explain how classical conditioning accounts for your reaction. Be sure to use the appropriate terms. When you are done, compare your explanation with the diagram in Figure 6.1.

2. Imagine that you have eaten potato salad at a picnic that turned out to be spoiled, causing severe stomach cramps. If the micro-organisms in the salad are the unconditioned stimulus, what are the unconditioned response, the conditioned stimulus, and the conditioned response? Also, describe how the terms *stimulus generalization, stimulus discrimination, extinction,* and *spontaneous recovery* could apply to this situation.

3. As the discussion of classical conditioning emphasized, this kind of learning involves more than simple pairing of the conditioned stimulus and the unconditioned stimulus. Explain three characteristics of the newer views of classical conditioning.

4. How do classical and operant conditioning differ? Describe how Skinner's influential research differs from the research by Ader and Cohen (1985) on conditioning of the immune system. Be sure to point out the voluntary-involuntary distinction, and also describe the timing of the elements in each kind of learning. Finally, point out why Watson and Rayner's study actually involves some operant conditioning principles.

5. Imagine that you are baby-sitting for a child who makes Bart Simpson look angelic. Describe how you could use positive reinforcement, negative reinforcement, and both kinds of punishment to improve the child's behavior. Mention some of the cautions you should consider in connection with punishment.

6. Think of examples you have encountered in college of each of the four schedules of reinforcement you learned about in this chapter. Also, explain how you learned a particular skill through the use of shaping. Finally, think of examples of discriminative stimuli and secondary reinforcers in your college education.

7. Turn to Figures 3.12, 3.14, and 3.16 in Chapter 3, and identify the brain structures in those figures that are comparable to the animal brain structures that researchers have identified in connection with classical and operant conditioning.

8. Describe how observational learning helped you master a particular skill at which you excel. Apply the following terms to this situation: vicarious reinforcement, vicarious punishment, and schema.

9. Describe the three research methods that were discussed in the "In Depth" feature on media violence and aggression. Point out the advantages and disadvantages of each technique. Did the information presented here match or disagree with your previous thoughts on the issue of media violence?

10. Imagine that you are teaching elementary school mathematics. You have decided to begin a behavior modification program to encourage more accurate performance

on students' in-class arithmetic assignments. Describe how you would design this program. In your description, mention each of the following terms: reinforcement, schedule of reinforcement, shaping, and token economy. Then select some arithmetic concept (other than division), and explain how you would teach that concept using cognitive modeling, as described in the section on observational learning.

New terms

learning (p. 188)
classical conditioning (p. 188)
unconditioned stimulus (p. 189)
unconditioned response (p. 189)
conditioned stimulus (p. 189)
conditioned response (p. 189)
acquisition (p. 192)
stimulus generalization (p. 193)
stimulus discrimination (p. 194)
extinction (p. 194)
spontaneous recovery (p. 194)
taste aversion (p. 195)
biological preparedness (p. 195)
nictitating-membrane reflex (p. 196)
immune system (p. 198)
psychoneuroimmunology (p. 198)
placebo effect (p. 198)
operant conditioning (p. 200)
instrumental conditioning (p. 200)
law of effect (p. 200)
positive reinforcement (p. 201)
negative reinforcement (p. 201)
punishment (p. 202)
shaping (p. 203)
continuous reinforcement schedule (p. 204)

partial reinforcement schedule (p. 204)
fixed-ratio schedule (p. 204)
fixed-interval schedule (p. 204)
variable-ratio schedule (p. 204)
variable-interval schedule (p. 204)
primary reinforcer (p. 205)
secondary reinforcers (p. 205)
discriminative stimulus (p. 205)
instinctive drift (p. 207)
behavior modification (p. 209)
baseline measure (p. 209)
token economy (p. 210)
observational learning (p. 211)
modeling (p. 211)
social learning (p. 211)
vicarious reinforcement (p. 212)
vicarious punishment (p. 212)
intrinsic reinforcement (p. 212)
intrinsic punishment (p. 212)
schema (p. 212)
experimental method (p. 214)
meta-analysis (p. 214)
quasi-experiment (p. 215)
correlational research (p. 216)
cognitive modeling (p. 218)
phobia (p. 218)

Recommended readings

Bryant, J., & Zillman, D. (Eds.). (1994). *Media effects: Advances in theory and research.* Hillsdale, NJ: Erlbaum. This book contains 16 chapters that examine the effects of the media on psychological processes. The chapters by Bandura and Gunter are most relevant to our discussion of aggression, but other chapters explore how the media affect attitude change, sexual behavior, and public health.

Lutz, J. (1994). *Introduction to learning and memory.* Pacific Grove, CA: Brooks/Cole. The first nine chapters in this mid-level textbook provide a clear overview of classical and operant conditioning.

MacBeth, T. M. (Ed.). (1996). *Tuning in to young viewers: Social science perspectives on television.* Thousand Oaks, CA: Sage. This book provides a good complement to Bryant and Zillman's book; it focuses on developmental issues, such as how television socializes young children, how it influences school performance, and how it represents diversity.

Pierce, W. D., & Epling, W. F. (1995). *Behavior analysis and learning.* Englewood Cliffs, NJ: Prentice Hall. Here's a textbook for upper-level undergraduates. It focuses on classical and operant conditioning, including how these principles can be applied to verbal behavior, behavior modification, and evolutionary psychology.

Watson, D. L., & Tharp, R. G. (1993). *Self-directed behavior: Self-modification for personal adjustment* (6th ed.). Pacific Grove, CA: Brooks/Cole. If this chapter has made you curious about how you can apply behavior modification to your own life, I'd recommend that you read this book.

Answers to Demonstrations

Demonstration 6.2

1. Increase   2. Yes   3. No   4. b, c, and e; furthermore, a and d are punishment   5. Positive reinforcement

Answers to Critical Thinking Exercises

Exercise 6.1

a. Pavlovian conditioning should begin with a reflexlike reaction. Pavlov's study began with meat powder producing drooling, and then the bell was paired with the meat powder. The words *Ohio, soybeans,* and *buckeyes,* in contrast, do not spontaneously produce any reflexlike reaction, and no such action could therefore be transferred to other words in this group. Some people may associate these words together in memory, however, by a very different process that we'll discuss in Chapter 9.

b. The study is ethically questionable because Albert certainly experienced discomfort from the loud noise. Also, he may have experienced harm if he continued to fear white objects resembling rats after the experiment had ended.

Exercise 6.2

a. Broberg and Bernstein (1987) needed to establish that the children did not initially have a negative reaction to these two flavors of candy. In classical conditioning, the conditioned stimulus should initially be neutral. Also, if these flavors were initially unpleasant, children might not be willing to eat them.

b. They needed a control group because they required a comparison group in which children would presumably develop taste aversion to the food in the meal. In the experimental group, where children would presumably develop taste aversion to the Life Savers, the researchers speculated that the children would be fairly positive about the food. Suppose that the children in Broberg and Bernstein's (1987) control group did in fact like the food in the meal—just as much as the children in the experimental group did. These results would suggest that, for some reason, neither group experienced taste aversion, so there was no need for the Life Savers to serve as a "scapegoat."

Exercise 6.3

a. To give negative reinforcement, the teacher might say, "If you do a good job on playing your scales the first time, you won't have to repeat them today." (This assumes that the child does not like practicing scales.) To use shaping, the teacher might praise a student initially for making any sound on the clarinet; later, reinforcement would be given only for increasingly skilled notes. A teacher might use a variable-interval schedule by praising the child every five minutes—on the average—sometimes after three or four minutes, sometimes after six or seven, but averaging every five minutes. Secondary reinforcers can come from praise or awards; however, the most important secondary reinforcement comes from the student listening and hearing appropriate notes from the clarinet.

b. We must be careful not to overgeneralize from one species to another. We cannot conclude that operant conditioning is responsible for this behavior. For one reason, we don't know whether the child would have said "cookie" if the discriminative stimulus had not been present and if reinforcement had not been offered. For a second reason, some explanation involving children's inborn understanding of language may contribute to this response, as we will see in Chapter 10.

Exercise 6.4

a. Researchers would need to be certain that they had avoided confounding variables such as the color of the stimulus. Perhaps pigeons learn to respond to slides that are mostly green, and they learn *not* to respond to slides that are other colors. They also need to be sure that the tree slides are not all presented at the beginning of training, with non-tree slides at the end. Their goal must be to make certain that the three slides and the nontree slides differ only with respect to the central object in the slide, not some confounding variable.

b. The very first thing to check would be the exact amount of epinephrine used by the two groups. It's possible that Group 2 used a very small amount and a moderate amount, and Group 1 used a moderate amount and a large amount. The research suggests that as the amount increases, memory at first improves and then grows worse.

Exercise 6.5

a. Josephson could assign the children to the three groups on a random basis, which makes it more likely that the groups were initially similar and that confounding variables would be eliminated. She could also control the nature of the TV program, something that would be impossible in a correlational study with data collected from the "real world." Finally, the children's aggression could be operationally defined and measured in a well-controlled setting, free from the kinds of distractions and complications that abound in a more naturalistic setting.

b. An important disadvantage of the experimental method is that we do not know whether we can generalize from the clean results obtained in a well-controlled setting to the messiness of real-life settings. Also, the experimental method, used in research like Josephson's, presents only brief TV segments. In fact, the meta-analyses may underestimate the effects of television viewing, because the research using the experimental method cannot examine the accumulated effects of years of TV exposure (Hughes & Hasbrouck, 1996).

Exercise 6.6

a. One possibility might be that children in the remote community may have been more likely to have a "frontier attitude." After all, their parents chose to live in this less modern community. They may have welcomed adventures and aggressive confrontations. It is possible (although we cannot know for sure) that they were more responsive to aggression than children in the less rural communities. We don't know whether children in more typical communities would have responded to the increased availability of television by becoming more aggressive.

b. First of all, we should point out that these data are indeed accurate; both the number of television sets and the homicide rates have dramatically increased since 1950 (Hughes & Hasbrouck, 1996). However, correlation does not necessarily imply causation. In fact, the availability of television violence may be partly responsible for the increased homicide rate. However, here are some possible "third variables" that might also be partly responsible for the relationship: The population has increased during the same time period (more people to watch TV, and also more people to commit murders); the use of drugs has increased since 1950 (thereby increasing the number of drug-related murders); the gap between the rich and the poor has also increased since 1950 (thereby increasing the number of financially motivated murders). Other relevant variables may be an increase in citizens' frustration level, an increase in the availability of murder weapons, and a potential change in ethical values.

MEMORY

CHAPTER 7

In 1984, a Mexican American man named Frederico Martinez Macias was accused of murdering an elderly couple and committing armed robbery. Another man had been found with stolen property that had belonged to the couple, and he accused Macias of the actual murder. Two witnesses testified that Macias had been elsewhere on the night of the murder. A third witness claimed that Macias was indeed the murderer, but this witness was not very believable. So the police began to search for another person who had seen Macias at the scene of the crime. One investigator happened to have a conversation with a 9-year-old girl named Jennifer F., who mentioned that she had seen Macias with blood splattered on his shirt and hands, on about the date of the murder. The trial did not emphasize that Jennifer's mother had frequently told her that Macias was a bad man, or that Macias worked in a salsa factory.

Four years later, Macias was scheduled to be executed by lethal injection. Two weeks before the date of execution, Jennifer F. made a statement. In retrospect, she hadn't been certain whether the red stain was blood or salsa. (Think about it: Is the man in the photo above splattered with blood or salsa?) Jennifer also said that many people had asked her questions, and they had encouraged her to say she was more certain than she actually felt. Basically, she had supplied answers because she had wanted to help the adults. Fortunately, however, the court issued a stay of execution, and Macias was eventually set free (Ceci & Bruck, 1995; Leichtman & Ceci, 1995).

In this chapter, we will see that human memory is typically impressive, consistent with Theme 1. However, we'll see that several factors can influence our memory. Like Jennifer F., we may claim we saw something that never really happened.

In **memory,** we store information over time. This information can be stored for less than a second or as long as your lifetime. For example, you use memory when you store the beginning of a word (perhaps *mem-*) for a fraction of a second until you hear the end of the word (*-ory*). You also use memory when you recall an event that occurred when you were just a toddler—perhaps two decades ago.

Memory requires three stages: encoding, storage, and retrieval. During **encoding,** the first stage, we transform sensory stimuli into a form that can be placed in memory. During **storage,** the second stage, we hold the information in memory for later use—perhaps less than a second or perhaps 50 years. During **retrieval,** the third stage, we locate the item and use it.

Throughout this chapter, we will emphasize three general characteristics of human memory:

1. Human memory is active, rather than passive. Your memory does not record an event as accurately as a video recorder. Instead, memory actively blends that event with other relevant information. For example, a memory of an event that occurred when you were a toddler may be influenced by stories you have heard from other family members. Similarly, Jennifer F.'s memory was probably influenced by prejudicial comments her mother had made.

2. Memory accuracy depends upon how we encode material. For example, you will remember the definition for *encoding* if you think about its meaning, but you will forget that definition if you simply glance at it. Similarly, Jennifer F. probably was not paying very close attention to Frederico Macias at the time she saw him; she never would have guessed that a man's life would quite literally have depended upon the accuracy of her observations.

3. Memory accuracy depends upon how we measure retrieval. You may have noticed that you score higher on a multiple-choice test than a fill-in-the-blank exam. Similarly, Jennifer's accuracy was certainly lower because she was being pressured to provide evidence that Frederico Macias had been the murderer. She would have been more accurate if she had been urged, "If you're not really sure, please just say so!"

This chapter is organized in terms of an extremely influential model of memory that was proposed by Atkinson and Shiffrin in 1968. Figure 7.1 presents a modified version of this model. As you can see, this model features three components. Information first enters **sensory memory,** which is a storage system that records information from the senses with reasonable accuracy. Sensory memory can hold a large number of items, but each item fades extremely quickly—in less than two seconds. Some of the material from sensory memory then passes on to working memory. **Working memory**—which is also known as **short-term memory**—contains only the small amount of material we are currently using. Memories in working memory are reasonably fragile, and they can be lost from memory within about 30 seconds

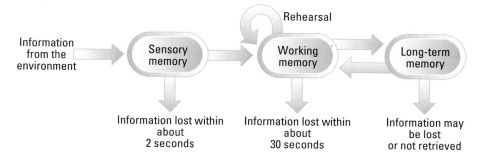

FIGURE 7.1

A simplified version of Atkinson and Shiffrin's model of memory.

unless they are somehow repeated or rehearsed. Our chapter considers sensory memory and working memory in the first section.

As you can see, Figure 7.1 shows that some information passes from working memory to long-term memory. **Long-term memory** has an unlimited capacity. It stores memories that arrived a few minutes ago, and some memories that are decades old. Although some information is eventually lost from long-term memory, these memories are usually more permanent than those in sensory memory or working memory. We'll consider long-term memory in the second section of this chapter. Furthermore, the last section focuses on memory-improvement techniques that are typically used to aid long-term memory.

Many psychologists now believe that the distinction between working memory and long-term memory is more blurry than Atkinson and Shiffrin had originally envisioned. However, current memory theorists typically argue that the model is an effective way to organize the research on human memory (Estes, 1991; Healy & McNamara, 1996; Schacter, 1996). Let's therefore begin with those relatively fragile memories that last for moments, rather than years.

SENSORY MEMORY AND WORKING MEMORY

Your professor announces, "Today we're going to talk about memory." You need to store those words very briefly, long enough to understand the message and jot down a few words. Let's examine sensory memory, as well as several different aspects of working memory.

Sensory Memory

Sensory memory holds information for a brief period after the physical stimulus is no longer available. It holds information in a relatively unprocessed form, instead of making it more meaningful (Hamid et al., 1996). Demonstration 7.1 illustrates several examples of sensory memory.

Sensory memory helps us keep an accurate record of the physical stimulus for a brief period while we select the most important portion for further processing. In

When you drive on a busy street, an enormous number of stimuli enter your sensory memory.

DEMONSTRATION 7.1 Examples of Sensory Memory

Iconic (visual) memory: Take a flashlight into a dark room and turn it on. Swing your wrist around in a circular motion, shining the flashlight onto a distant wall. If your motion is quick enough, you will see a complete circle. Your visual sensory memory stores the beginning of the circle while you examine the end.

Echoic (auditory) memory: With your hand, beat a quick rhythm on the desk. Can you still hear the echo after the beating is finished?

Sensory memory for touch: Rub the palm of your hand quickly along the horizontal edge of your desk. Can you still feel the sharp edge, even after your hand is off the desk?

Iconic memory allows you to see a trace of a visual stimulus for a brief moment after it has disappeared. If someone quickly swings a sparkler, you may briefly see a complete circle.

S	Q	H	M
B	R	L	C
Y	D	V	N

FIGURE 7.2

If you glance quickly at these letters, they will fade from your iconic memory before you can report them all.

Echoic memory guarantees that students will be able to hear this professor's words echoing in their heads, so that they can take notes after the auditory stimulus has disappeared.

Chapter 5 ("States of Consciousness"), you learned that humans cannot pay attention to all stimuli at the same time. Imagine driving down a busy city street, at the peak of rush hour. Your sensory memory briefly records this rich visual stimulation. It might simultaneously record the sound of horns honking, the scratchiness of your sweater, and the stale flavor of cinnamon gum. Sensory memory stores all of these stimuli just long enough for you to pay attention to the stimuli that deserve further processing.

Atkinson and Shiffrin (1968) suggested that we could have sensory memory for all the senses discussed in Chapter 4—vision, hearing, smell, taste, and the skin senses. However, researchers have concentrated almost exclusively on vision (iconic memory) and hearing (echoic memory).

Iconic Memory   Visual sensory memory is called **iconic memory** (pronounced "eye-*conn*-ick"). Iconic memory is so fragile that it is difficult to measure accurately. For example, glance quickly at the letters in Figure 7.2. Then look away and try to recall these letters. Don't you have the feeling that some of these letters are fading during the time it takes to report them? However, Sperling (1960) figured out a clever method to estimate the capacity of iconic memory by asking participants to report the items on only one line of letters. Using this technique, Sperling estimated that iconic memory could hold between 9 and 10 items. Furthermore, this fragile memory lasts less than half a second after the stimulus has disappeared (Crowder, 1992; DiLollo & Bischof, 1995).

Echoic Memory   Auditory sensory memory is called **echoic memory.** The name *echoic memory* is particularly appropriate, because at times a sound may seem to echo briefly inside your head. You've probably noticed that your professor's words seem to reverberate inside your head for a second or two after they have been spoken. Fortunately, this internal echoing allows you to hold the sounds in sensory memory, process them, and write them down a second or two later.

Researchers have estimated that echoic memory holds about 5 items, which is considerably fewer than the 9 or 10 items in iconic memory (Darwin et al., 1972). However, echoic memory lasts about two seconds (Crowder, 1982; Lu et al., 1992)—about four times as long as iconic memory. This information matches our daily experience. We have trouble finding everyday examples of iconic memory because it fades before we are aware it is operating. In contrast, we can easily think of examples of echoic memory. After the clock in a bell tower has struck, does it still seem to reverberate in your head? When a friend has spoken—and you weren't really paying attention—can you reconstruct his words if you immediately "listen" to the echo inside your head?

Working Memory

You've probably had an experience like this. You are standing at a pay telephone, looking up a phone number. You find the number, repeat it to yourself, and close the phone book. You take out the coins, insert them, and raise your finger to dial. Amazingly, you cannot remember it. The first digits were 243, and there was a 5 somewhere, but you have no idea what the other numbers were! They deserted your working memory in about half a minute.

Only a fraction of items from sensory memory make their way into working memory. While you were locating the coins in the phone booth, inserting them, and beginning to dial, your attention was directed away from the phone number. As Chapter 5 explains, we remember very little when we do not pay attention to an item. Less than a minute later, those unattended numbers have departed from your consciousness. In general, items in working memory are lost within about 30 seconds unless they are somehow repeated. Working memory retains information long enough for us to deal with it. However, working memory also allows us to forget trivial material that is no longer useful.

Let's now examine this working memory in some detail. We'll begin with an overview of working memory's structure, and then we'll consider each of its components.

An Overview of Working Memory

For many years, theorists inspired by the classic Atkinson and Shiffrin (1968) model had assumed that working memory consisted of just one component. This single component had a strictly limited capacity. In fact, research suggested that working memory could hold about seven items, perhaps as many as nine or as few as five (Miller, 1956).

Alan Baddeley and his colleagues proposed an alternate view of this brief kind of memory (e.g., Baddeley, 1986; Baddeley & Hitch, 1974). They also proposed a new name: *working memory*. Notice how this name emphasizes active processing of material, rather than the passive storage of material suggested by the name *short-term memory* (Healy & McNamara, 1996). Consistent with Theme 1, our working memory is extremely flexible, and several different systems have evolved that are specialized for different tasks (Gathercole, 1992; Schneider, 1993).

According to Baddely and his coworkers, working memory is a three-part system that temporarily holds and manipulates information as we perform cognitive tasks (Baddeley, 1986, 1992; Gathercole & Baddeley, 1993). Working memory is not a passive storehouse, with a number of shelves to hold partially processed information until it moves on to another location, presumably long-term memory (Smyth et al., 1994). Instead, working memory is more like a workbench where the material is constantly being handled, combined, and transformed.

Before we examine the three components of working memory, let's see why Baddeley rejected the idea of a single-component memory. In an important study, Baddeley and Hitch (1974) found that people were able to **rehearse** (or repeat silently to themselves) a series of random numbers while accurately performing a spatial reasoning task. (See Figure 7.3.) Thus, working memory is not just a single storage bin. Instead, working memory seems to have several components, which can operate partially independently of one another.

One component of Baddeley's model is called the **phonological loop;** this proposed component stores a limited number of sounds. A second component in this model is **visuo-spatial working memory,** which stores visual and spatial information, as well as verbal information that has been encoded into visual imagery (Gathercole & Baddeley, 1993; Logie, 1995). The capacity of each of these components is limited, but the limits of these two components are independent. If several items are cycling through your phonological loop, you can still handle many items in your visuo-spatial working memory.

According to the working-memory model, the **central executive** integrates information from the phonological loop and visuo-spatial working memory, as well as from long-term memory. As the name suggests, the central executive plans, coordinates, and regulates all the operations of working memory. For example, if you are now trying to decide whether to take a break or to read the details about the three components of working memory, your central executive is playing a major role in that decision!

The Phonological Loop

Before you read further, try Demonstration 7.2, which focuses on pronunciation time and memory. This demonstration is based on research by Baddeley and his

The limits of working memory may be frustrating when you forget a phone number moments after you've located it. However, working memory also allows us to forget trivial information we no longer need.

FIGURE 7.3

On this spatial reasoning task, the student must judge whether each statement is correct or incorrect. She can perform this task at the same time she uses her phonological loop to say a series of random numbers. This study led Baddeley and Hitch (1974) to propose that the limits of visuo-spatial working memory and the phonological loop are independent of one another.

DEMONSTRATION 7.2 Pronunciation Time and Memory Span

Read the following list of country names. When you have finished, look away from the page and try to recall them.

Greece, England, Chad, Burma, Nenin, Iceland, Malta

Now try the task again with a different list of country names. When you have finished, look away from the page and try to recall them.

Nicaragua, Switzerland, Namibia, Madagascar,
Venezuela, Mauritania, Sierra Leone

(IN DEPTH continued)

colleagues (1975). These researchers found that people could accurately recall an average of 4.2 words from the list of countries with short names, but only 2.8 words from the list of countries with long names. In other words, the phonological loop seems to have a limited capacity. The second set of country names in Demonstration 7.2 has a greater number of syllables in each name. As a result, your phonological loop is filled to capacity after just two or three words. In contrast, you can probably remember at least four of the shorter country names in Demonstration 7.2.

With impressive consistency, people tend to recall the number of items that they can pronounce in about two seconds (Cowan, 1994; Schweickert & Boruff, 1986). Baddeley (1986) argues that we store a sound-coded representation of each item on a list, but these sounds fade within about two seconds unless we pronounce them silently. The faster we can pronounce these items, the more we can remember. As a result, we can recall a greater number of consonants ("b, x, t, z, m") than shapes ("circle, rectangle, triangle").

Critical Thinking Exercise 7.1

Write down your answers to the following questions about the phonological loop.

a. Suppose that Baddeley and his colleagues (1975) had included only familiar countries (e.g., Norway, France, Spain) in the first list in Demonstration 7.2 and only unfamiliar names (e.g., Myanmar, Namibia, Sierra Leone) on the second list. Why would the results be difficult to interpret?

b. Suppose that researchers have tested people's memory for consonants at the beginning of the experiment, and their memory for shapes at the end of the experiment. Why would the results be difficult to interpret?

Visuo-Spatial Working Memory

The capacity of visuo-spatial working memory is limited, just like the capacity of the phonological loop (Frick, 1988, 1990). You cannot represent a complex geometry problem using just a small scrap of paper. Similarly, when too many items enter into visuo-spatial working memory, you cannot represent all of them accurately. Keep in mind, however, that the limits of visuo-spatial working memory and the phonological loop are independent.

At some point in the near future, ask a friend to help you try Demonstration 7.3. See whether you find it difficult to place these numbers in your visuo-spatial working

DEMONSTRATION 7.3 Interference With Visuo-Spatial Working Memory

Go to a location where you can watch a television screen with the sound off, or where you can look out a window at a busy scene where people are moving about. Then find a friend who can help you by reading the list of in-

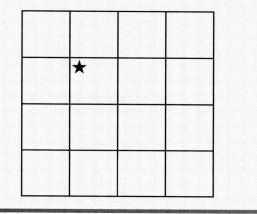

structions at the end of this demonstration. Look at the grid of 16 squares, and notice the location of the black star. Now watch the TV or the busy scene while your friend reads the list of instructions. You should try to visualize (in your visuo-spatial working memory) how the numbers are arranged. When your friend is finished reading the list, cover it up and fill in the numbers on the grid. See the answers on Page 254 to check yourself.

Instructions:
In the square with the black star, put a 1.
In the next square to the right, put a 2.
In the next square to the right, put a 3.
In the next square down, put a 4.
In the next square to the left, put a 5.
In the next square down, put a 6.
In the next square to the left, put a 7.
In the next square up, put an 8.
In the next square to the left, put a 9.
In the next square down, put a 10.

memory when that component of working memory is already quite filled with other visual information.

Demonstration 7.3 is based on a study by Margaret Toms and her colleagues (1994). They asked the participants in their study to perform a spatial task like this one. Let's consider two of the conditions in the Toms experiment. In one condition, participants closed their eyes while listening to the instructions about the numbers; these people experienced no visual interference. In another condition, participants looked at a continuously shifting blue-and-white pattern on a screen. These people experienced great visual interference, just as you do when you try Demonstration 7.3. As you can see from Figure 7.4 on the next page, people performed much better when no visual input could interfere with their visuo-spatial working memory.

Toms and her colleagues also asked their participants to perform a verbal task that required remembering sentences containing no spatial information. They listened to these sentences under the same conditions used on the spatial task. However, because the spatial words were missing, their visuo-spatial working memory was presumably inactive. As you can see in Figure 7.4, the participants recalled about the same amount in the two viewing conditions. This verbal task presumably involves the phonological loop, so that visual input does not provide interference. As the working-memory approach emphasizes, visuo-spatial working memory and the phonological loop operate independently. Furthermore, visual input (from the moving pattern) interferes with visuo-spatial working memory, but it doesn't harm the phonological loop.

The Central Executive

The central executive has been the least researched of the three components of working memory (Logie, 1993). However, the central executive plays a critical role in working memory, because it coordinates information from the other two components. The central executive also decides which issues deserve attention and what should be done first. It also figures out how to tackle a problem, and it selects strategies. The central executive is active when you solve problems, make

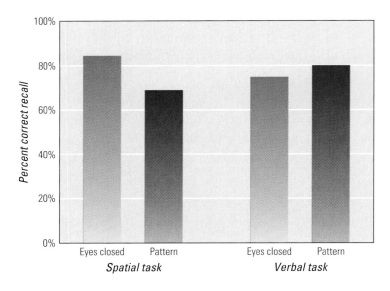

FIGURE 7.4

Percentage correct recall, as a function of task and viewing condition.
Source: Based on Toms et al., 1994.

(IN DEPTH continued)
decisions, perform calculations, and try to understand a sentence (Logie, 1993). In other words, the central executive is the major player in the cognitive processes we discuss in Chapter 8 ("Thinking and Intelligence") and Chapter 9 ("Language and Conversation").

One promising area of research on the central executive uses neuroscience research methods. This research has identified the prefrontal cortex (see Figure 3.16) as the location of the greatest brain activity when people are performing complex tasks that require complex thinking. In fact, turn back to Demonstration 3.5 on Page 93. J. D. Cohen and his colleagues (1994) used the fMRI technique to demonstrate that the prefrontal cortex was extremely active when people performed this complex search task. In contrast, the prefrontal cortex was not active when people simply searched for the isolated letter <u>X</u>.

SECTION SUMMARY: *SENSORY MEMORY AND WORKING MEMORY*

1. Memory is active, rather than passive; memory accuracy depends upon the method of encoding and on the measure of retrieval.

2. Atkinson and Shiffrin's (1968) model of memory includes sensory memory, working memory (short-term memory), and long-term memory.

3. Sensory memory includes iconic memory, which holds about 9 to 10 visual items for approximately half a second, and echoic memory, which holds about 5 items for approximately two seconds.

4. The classic Atkinson and Shiffrin (1968) model viewed short-term memory (working memory) as a single-capacity storehouse; in contrast, Baddeley and his colleagues propose that working memory consists of three components, each with an independent capacity and each actively involved in handling and transforming information.

5. One component of working memory is the phonological loop, which can store approximately the number of items we can pronounce silently in two seconds.

6. Another component of working memory is visuospatial working memory, which stores visual and spatial information; research by Toms and her colleagues (1994) shows that visual input from a moving pattern will interfere with information to be stored in visuo-spatial working memory.

DEMONSTRATION 7.4 Acquisition and Memory

Which of the U.S. coins below is the real one? The correct answer is supplied later in the text.

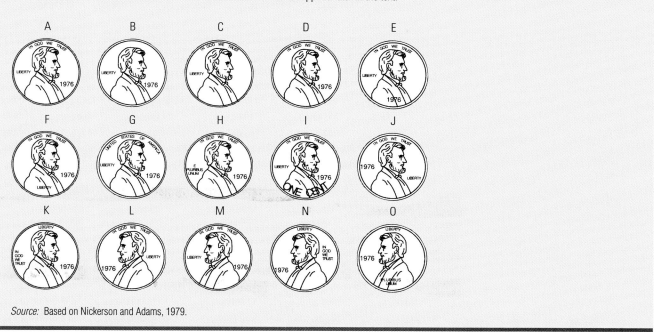

Source: Based on Nickerson and Adams, 1979.

7. The final component of working memory is the central executive, which coordinates the information from the phonological loop and visuo-spatial working memory; it is active in solving problems, making decisions, performing calculations, and trying to understand a sentence.

LONG-TERM MEMORY

What details can you remember about the first day you spent on your college campus? Can you remember what you wore, whom you spoke to, and what you did? Chances are good that you can recall many relatively trivial details about this day, which you have stored in your long-term memory. However, your long-term memory is sometimes disappointing. For example, see how well you do on Demonstration 7.4.

In this section, we'll see how long-term memories are encoded, stored, and retrieved. We'll also discuss a new theoretical approach to memory and several theories of forgetting, as well as the biological basis of memory. Throughout this section, we'll emphasize that our long-term memory usually serves us well. Typically, we remember general, important ideas very accurately. However, factors such as the active nature of memory lead us to forget some details. In addition, our accuracy is influenced by the way we encode material and the way retrieval is measured.

Encoding in Long-Term Memory

During the next 24 hours, you will see and hear thousands of facts, images, and miscellaneous bits of information. How accurately will you recall these items at a later time? Your accuracy will be influenced by three factors associated with encoding: attention, depth of processing, and encoding specificity.

Attention In Demonstration 7.4, did you select the correct coin? In a study by Nickerson and Adams (1979), fewer than half of the participants correctly chose coin A. People also perform poorly when they are asked to draw from memory the "heads" and "tails" of coins. For example, only a third of people correctly draw Lincoln facing to the right on a U.S. penny (Rubin & Kontis, 1983).

Why do we fail to encode this kind of information in long-term memory? We handle pennies every day. However, if you want to use a penny, you only need to notice its general size and color. Once you've extracted that simple information, you immediately stop encoding other characteristics (Schacter, 1996). Consider why this strategy is adaptive. Why should we cram our cerebral cortex with details about a penny when we could be busy encoding and storing more interesting, important information?

Depth of Processing The method people use to mentally process stimuli is called **depth of processing.** In most cases, people remember more when they use a deeper, more complex kind of processing—for example, thinking about a word's meaning (Craik, 1977; Craik & Lockhart, 1972). You'll recall less if you use shallower kinds of processing, for example by simply making judgments about a word's sound (Schacter, 1996).

The deepest, most effective way of processing stimuli is in terms of your own experience—a phenomenon called the **self-reference effect.** Suppose that you are asked to look at a list of adjectives and decide whether each word could be applied to yourself. When people study words using these self-reference instructions, they recall about twice as many items as when they process words in terms of meaning (Klein & Kihlstrom, 1986; Rogers et al., 1977). This self-reference effect operates not only for college students but also for young children and elderly adults (Halpin et al., 1984; Rogers, 1983).

Think about how you can apply this research on depth of processing. When you read a textbook or review your class notes, try to process the material as deeply as possible. Think about what you are reading, and try to give it meaning by rephrasing a section in your own words. Also, take advantage of the self-reference effect. For instance, when you read about encoding specificity in the discussion that follows, try to think of relevant examples of the way your memory is enhanced by contextual cues. At the end of this chapter, we'll discuss memory improvement techniques. As you will see, many of these are effective because they promote deeper and more elaborate processing. In contrast, consider the kind of shallow processing in which your eyes drift across the words, with no real awareness of what you have read. This superficial processing is nearly useless.

Encoding Specificity: The Effects of Context Does this scenario sound familiar? You are in the bedroom and realize that you need something from the kitchen. Once you are in the kitchen, however, you have no idea why you went there. Without the context in which you encoded the item you wanted, you cannot retrieve this memory. Once you return to the bedroom, filled with context cues, you immediately remember what you wanted.

This example illustrates the **encoding specificity principle,** which states that your recall will be better if the retrieval context resembles the encoding context (Schacter, 1996; Tulving, 1983). In contrast, you'll be more likely to forget when the two contexts do not match (for example, the bedroom and the kitchen).

In one test of the encoding specificity principle, participants learned material in two very different settings (Smith et al., 1978). On one day, they learned words in a windowless room, with an experimenter formally dressed in a coat and tie. On another day, these same participants learned a different set of words in a smaller room with two windows, located in a different section of the campus; the experimenter now wore a flannel shirt and jeans. On the third day, people were tested on both word lists. Half of the participants took the test in the windowless room with the formal experimenter, and half took it in the room with windows and the informal experimenter.

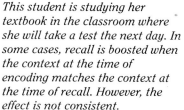

This student is studying her textbook in the classroom where she will take a test the next day. In some cases, recall is boosted when the context at the time of encoding matches the context at the time of recall. However, the effect is not consistent.

The results showed that performance was much better for material that had originally been learned in the same setting. People tested in the same context recalled an average of 14 words, whereas people tested in a different context recalled an average of only 9 words. Thus, if they had learned the word *swan* in the windowless room, students recalled it better if they took the test in that room than in the room with windows.

However, we should not overemphasize the influence of context. The clear majority of research shows at least some modest context effects. However, other carefully conducted studies show no influence (Bjork & Richardson-Klavehn, 1987; Eich, 1995). Theme 3 states that psychological processes are complex, and these contradictory results clearly illustrate this complexity.

Encoding specificity operates often enough that you should try to take advantage of this principle when you are taking a test. Obviously, the effect is not strong enough to compensate for not studying. However, if you cannot recall an answer, try to re-create the context in which you originally learned the material. If the question asks about lecture material, can you visualize your professor discussing the topic?

This discussion has emphasized the importance of encoding; you cannot possibly recall something that you never encoded in the first place! In other words, you will recall material more accurately if you pay attention to it, process it deeply, and match the encoding context with the retrieval context.

Critical Thinking Exercise 7.2

Write down your answers to the following questions about encoding specificity.

a. In the experiment by Smith and his colleagues (1978) on encoding specificity, participants learned lists of words, and their memory for these words was later tested. Can we safely generalize from these results to students hearing a lecture in introductory psychology and then being tested on this material?

b. We noted that some of the research on encoding specificity shows that people do *not* recall better when the retrieval context resembles the encoding context. Another explanation for why encoding specificity sometimes does not help is that people may be able to *imagine* the original encoding situation (S. M. Smith, 1988). How would this factor help explain why encoding specificity may not be helpful in some situations?

FIGURE 7.5

Father Bernard Pagano (top), who was almost convicted of armed robbery, and the real criminal, Ronald Clouser (bottom).

FIGURE 7.6

The effect of type of information and delay on proportion of correct answers.
Source: Loftus et al., 1978.

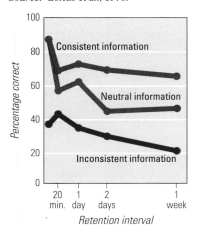

Autobiographical Memory

We have considered several characteristics of the way we encode information into our long-term memory. Let's now examine one of the most important kinds of long-term memory, called autobiographical memory.

Autobiographical memory is defined as memory for information related to yourself (Barclay, 1993). The original research on human memory examined recall for meaningless nonsense syllables (Ebbinghaus, 1885). However, many researchers in the past two decades have changed their focus. Autobiographical memory has become an increasingly popular topic because of the growing emphasis on ecological validity (e.g., Davies & Logie, 1993; Loftus, 1991). **Ecological validity** describes the degree to which the research situation mirrors a situation in everyday life (Whitley, 1996). Research conducted in a laboratory setting sometimes produces findings that are useful for everyday memory. Also, the laboratory certainly provides more control over irrelevant variables than does a real-life setting (Banaji & Crowder, 1989). However, it is easier to generalize research in which people recall real-life events than when they learn lists of meaningless nonsense words.

Here, we'll discuss three topics related to autobiographical memory. Let's begin by examining eyewitness testimony and the current recovered memory/false memory controversy. We'll finish by looking at the phenomenon of flashbulb memory.

Eyewitness Testimony   In 1979, a Catholic priest awaited trial for several armed robberies. Seven witnesses had identified this man as the "gentleman bandit," referring to the polite manners and elegant clothing that the robber had worn. As the trial progressed, one witness after another identified the priest as the one who had committed the robberies. Suddenly, however, the trial was halted: Another man had confessed to the crimes (Rodgers, 1982). Figure 7.5 shows the innocent priest and the real criminal, Ronald Clouser, who certainly do not look like identical twins!

Reports like this one have led psychologists to question the reliability of eyewitness testimony. By some estimates, between 2,000 and 10,000 people are wrongfully convicted each year in the United States on the basis of faulty eyewitness testimony (Cutler & Penrod, 1995; Fruzzetti et al., 1992; Loftus & Ketcham, 1991). Eyewitness testimonies, like other memories, are generally accurate; however, the reports can contain errors (Schacter, 1995). After all, an eyewitness may be asked to remember details about an event that lasted only a few seconds and occurred some time ago. Our memory is generally good, but it cannot be expected to be as accurate as a videotape recorder. The problem is that when eyewitness testimony is not accurate, the wrong person may go to jail or—in the worst cases—be put to death (Loftus & Ketcham, 1991).

Elizabeth Loftus and her colleagues have identified an important source of inaccuracy in eyewitness testimony. After people witness an event, someone may supply misleading information. This misleading post-event information may bias the eyewitness's recall.

In an important experiment, Loftus, Miller, and Burns (1978) showed a series of slides to research participants. In this sequence, a red Datsun stopped at an intersection, and then it turned and hit a pedestrian. Half of the participants saw a slide with a yield sign at the intersection; the other half saw a stop sign. Twenty minutes to one week after the slides had been shown, the participants answered questions about the details of the accident. One critical question was worded differently for each of three separate groups of participants—containing information that was either (a) consistent with a detail from the original slide series, (b) inconsistent with the detail, or (c) did not mention the detail (neutral). For example, some people who had originally seen the yield sign were asked, "Did another car pass the red Datsun while it was stopped at the yield sign?" (consistent). Others were asked the same question with "stop" substituted for "yield" (inconsistent). For still other people, the sign was not mentioned (neutral).

After they had answered the questions, the participants were shown two slides, one with a stop sign and one with a yield sign. They were asked to identify which slide they had originally seen. As you can see in Figure 7.6, participants who had received in-consistent information were substantially less accurate than people in the other two con-ditions. Their original memory of the event was biased by the misleading question.

Several studies have replicated the harmful effects of misleading post-event information (e.g., Cutler & Penrod, 1995; Garry & Loftus, 1994; Schreiber & Sergent, 1996). These results have clear-cut implications for the courtroom: Witnesses who have heard or seen misleading information—following the crucial event—may incor-porate this misinformation into their memory.

The research on eyewitness testimony confirms a point we made at the begin-ning of this chapter. We do not store a memory of an event in a passive fashion, iso-lated from all other information. Instead, post-event information may be incorporated into that memory, changing it substantially (Loftus, 1992). These ob-servations are consistent with the **constructivist approach** to memory, which argues that we continually revise our past in order to reflect our current knowledge. In short, memory does not consist of a list of facts, all neatly stored in intact form. In-stead, memory combines, blends, and replaces the information we have stored about events we have experienced (Kihlstrom & Barnhardt, 1993; Ross & Buehler, 1994).

Critical Thinking Exercise 7.3

Write down your answers to the following questions about eyewitness testimony.

a. Why did Loftus and her coauthors (1978) need to test half of their subjects by including a stop sign in the original slide show, and half with a yield sign? Why didn't they simply show a yield sign to everyone, and then include a yield sign, a stop sign, or no information in the post-event question?

b. Why should we be cautious about applying the results of the study by Loftus and her colleagues to a real accident scene?

The Recovered Memory/False Memory Controversy   If you scan popular magazines such as *Newsweek, People,* and *Ms.,* you won't find articles on echoic memory, the phonological loop, or the encoding specificity principle. However, one topic from cognitive psychology *has* become popular—the issue of adults recalling memories of childhood sexual abuse. Before you read farther, however, be sure that you have tried Demonstration 7.5.

DEMONSTRATION 7.5   Remembering Lists of Words

For this demonstration, you must learn and recall two lists of words. Before beginning, take out a piece of paper. Next, read List 1; then close the book and try to write down as many of the words as possible. Then do the same for List 2. After you have recalled both sets of words, check your accuracy. How many items did you correctly recall?

List 1		List 2	
bed	doze	water	run
rest	slumber	stream	barge
awake	snore	lake	creek
tired	nap	Mississippi	brook
dream	peace	boat	fish
wake	yawn	tide	bridge
snooze	drowsy	swim	winding
blanket		flow	

Source: From Roediger and McDermott, 1995. Used with permission.

Most of the discussion focuses specifically on individuals who, as adults, suddenly remember sexual abuse that they believe they experienced as children. According to the recovered-memory perspective, many people who had experienced sexual abuse during childhood managed to forget that memory for many years. At a later time, often prompted by a specific event or by encouragement from a therapist, the memory came flooding back into consciousness (Alpert, 1996; Briere & Conte, 1993; L. S. Brown, 1996).

A second group of researchers interprets these case studies in a different light. We must emphasize that this second group agrees that child sexual abuse often occurs. However, they deny the accuracy of some individuals' reports that the memory of the abuse was absent for many years and then recovered. Specifically, these researchers argue that many (or all) of these recovered memories are actually false memories, or constructed stories about events that never occurred (Loftus & Ketcham, 1994; Pendergrast, 1995; Wakefield & Underwager, 1994).

Our discussion in this chapter should convince you that memory is less than perfect. For example, we saw that eyewitness testimony can be flawed, especially when misinformation has been provided. Similar problems arise in recalling memories from childhood. For example, some psychotherapists provide suggestions about child abuse that could easily be blended with reality to create a false memory (Forward & Buck, 1988; Lindsay & Read, 1994).

We cannot easily determine whether a memory of childhood abuse is correct. After all, the situation is far from controlled, and researchers can seldom find other independent witnesses who can verify what really happened (Schooler, 1994). Research is much more straightforward when people are simply asked to remember a list of words, and accuracy can be objectively measured. For example, Demonstration 7.5 asked you to memorize and recall two lists of words, and then you checked your accuracy. Take a moment now to check something else. On List 1, did you write down the word *sleep?* Did you write *river* on List 2? If you look again at the demonstration, you'll discover that neither word was listed.

In research with lists of words like those in Demonstration 7.5, Roediger and McDermott (1995) found a false recall rate of 55%. People created false memories of words that did not appear on the lists. Intrusions are common on these lists because each word that *does* appear on a list is commonly associated with at least one other missing word—in Demonstration 7.5, for example, *sleep* and *river.* Similar intrusions could occur with respect to childhood memories. People may falsely recall events related to their actual experiences.

You might correctly argue, though, that we should not generalize results from this word-recall task to the extremely emotional topic of child sexual abuse (L. S. Brown, 1996). However, we obviously cannot perform controlled experimental research on child sexual abuse. Instead, we must rely on a small number of case studies in which an individual was sexually abused as a child, the abuse was documented, the incident was forgotten, and then it was recovered. For example, Schacter (1996) describes a woman named Jane who was sexually abused, at the age of 5, by her father. He admitted this abuse to Jane's mother, but the parents reasoned that Jane would forget it if they did not discuss it with her. Indeed, Jane did not remember the experience until her mother discussed it with her many years later.

As Theme 3 of this textbook has repeatedly argued, psychological processes are complicated. In reality, both the "recovered-memory" and the "false-memory" positions are probably at least partially correct (Schacter, 1996; Schooler, 1994). Indeed, memories of traumatic experiences can vary in their accessibility, sometimes being not available to consciousness and sometimes being painfully present (Schooler, 1994). On the other hand, some individuals have indeed been encouraged to construct events that never really occurred (American Psychological Association, 1996; Loftus, 1993). One clear message from this controversy is that therapists must be meticulously careful not to ask leading questions that might

Because therapists are concerned that their clients may be misled into creating a false memory, they must be extremely careful in asking questions about childhood sexual abuse.

create a misinformation effect (Courtois, 1996). Another clear message is that this controversy should not distract us from the fact that child sexual abuse really does occur in our culture, and this important problem must be acknowledged (American Psychological Association, 1996). Now try Demonstration 7.6.

Flashbulb Memory   Can you remember details about what you were wearing or doing when you heard about an important happy or tragic event? People often have very vivid memories of a situation in which they first learned about a surprising and emotionally arousing event, a phenomenon called **flashbulb memory.**

For example, an Indian friend of mine recalls in detail the circumstances in which Mohandas Gandhi, the nonviolent political leader, spoke to a crowd of people

---

DEMONSTRATION 7.6 Schemas and Memory for Stories

Part 1

Read each sentence below, count to five, answer the question, and go on to the next sentence.

SENTENCE	QUESTION
The girl broke the window on the porch.	Broke what?
The tree in the front yard shaded the man who was smoking his pipe.	Where?
The cat, running from the barking dog, jumped on the table.	From what?
The cat running from the dog jumped on the table.	Where?
The girl who lives next door broke the window on the porch.	Lives where?
The scared cat was running from the barking dog.	What was?
The tree shaded the man who was smoking his pipe.	What did?
The scared cat jumped on the table.	What did?
The girl who lives next door broke the large window.	Broke what?
The man was smoking his pipe.	Who was?
The large window was on the porch.	Where?
The tall tree was in the front yard.	What was?
The cat jumped on the table.	Where?
The tall tree in the front yard shaded the man.	Did what?
The window was large.	What was?

Part 2

Cover the preceding sentences. Now read each of the following sentences and decide whether it is a sentence from the list in Part 1. The answers will be discussed later.

1. The tree was in the front yard. (old ____, new ____)
2. The scared cat, running from the barking dog, jumped on the table. (old ____, new ____)
3. The window was on the porch. (old ____, new ____)
4. The tree in the front yard shaded the man. (old ____, new ____)
5. The tall tree shaded the man who was smoking his pipe. (old ____, new ____)
6. The scared cat was running from the dog. (old ____, new ____)
7. The girl who lives next door broke the large window on the porch. (old ____, new ____)
8. The tall tree shaded the girl who broke the window. (old ____, new ____)
9. The cat was running from the barking dog. (old ____, new ____)
10. The scared cat ran from the barking dog that jumped on the table. (old ____, new ____)
11. The girl broke the large window on the porch. (old ____, new ____)
12. The tall tree in the front yard shaded the man who was smoking his pipe. (old ____, new ____)

Source: Based on Jenkins, 1974.

Do you have a vivid flashbulb memory for your first week at college? These memories may seem extremely clear to you, but memory researchers suspect that they might not be substantially different from more ordinary memories.

in Gauhati, India. My friend was only 5 years old at the time, yet he vividly recalls Gandhi, dressed in white and accompanied by two women. He can recall that his aunt, who was with him, was wearing a white sari with a gold and red border. He can also distinctly remember how the heat of the day had made him very thirsty (Das, 1992).

Research suggests that people are most likely to recall certain characteristics in their flashbulb memory such as where they were, what ongoing event was interrupted by the news, and the person who told them the news (Brown & Kulik, 1977). People typically report that they rehearse these memories frequently, which may make them more vivid.

Are these memories for important events somehow special, significantly more vivid than our more everyday memories? For instance, researchers have found that British students had very vivid and accurate memories for the unexpected resignation of the British prime minister, Margaret Thatcher (Conway, 1995; Conway et al., 1994). However, Conway and his colleagues seem to be in the minority. For example, Neisser and Harsch (1992) found that some people were almost totally incorrect in recalling what they were doing when they learned about the *Challenger* space shuttle disaster. Indeed, people do *claim* that their memories for these events are very vivid and accurate, but in fact the memories are far from perfect (Brewer, 1992; McCloskey, 1992; Weaver, 1993).

Critical Thinking Exercise 7.4

Write down your answers to the following questions about recovered memory/false memory and flashbulb memory.

a. Gail Goodman and her colleagues (1996) conducted research that some psychologists argue has implications for the recovered memory/false memory controversy. She studied young children who had experienced a medical procedure called urethral catheterization, which shares some similarities with sexual assault (i.e., physical pain and genital contact). The children's memories for details of this procedure were very accurate; they showed no evidence of the complete memory loss that some argue is common with sexual assault. Although the ecological validity of this study is relatively strong, why would you be hesitant to generalize these findings to the memory controversy?

b. Your aunt tells you, "I can remember as if it were yesterday when I first heard that President Kennedy was killed in 1963. You're studying psychology. Isn't it true that people have really accurate memories for some important events?" How would you respond?

Schemas and Memory

Take a moment to recall the sequence of events during the last time you went to a fast-food restaurant. You entered the restaurant, stood in line while inspecting the list of options above the counter, told the cashier what you wanted, paid, and received your food. Then you took your tray to a table, ate the food, discarded the waste, and left the restaurant. You have probably visited fast-food restaurants often enough to develop a general idea for the events that will happen and the order in which they will occur. In other words, you have developed a **schema** (pronounced "*skee*-muh"), or a simple, well-structured set of ideas about objects and events associated with a highly familiar activity (Anderson & Conway, 1993; Schank & Abelson, 1995).

Research on schemas shows that we have schemas for a variety of situations, not just fast-food restaurants. We also have schemas for visiting a dentist's office, for the first day of a college course, and even for events that do not have the outcome we expected (Foti & Lord, 1987; Read & Cesa, 1991).

We notice the common features of each of these events through repeated experience with similar kinds of activities (Barclay, 1986). We do not need to remember precise details about much of our daily life. (For example, did the professor hand out the syllabus to the left side of the classroom before the right side?) Instead, we take advantage of schemas. They allow us to process large amounts of material and summarize the many regularities in our lives. Schemas provide structure for memory. In fact, much of our informal and formal education is devoted to discovering which schema other people expect us to follow in which situation (Schank & Abelson, 1995).

Schemas operate at several stages of the memory process. For example, schemas help to determine which items we acquire in memory. Consider a study by Brewer and Treyens (1981), who asked participants to wait, one at a time, in a room that was described as an office. After 35 seconds, the experimenter asked the participant to move to a nearby room and then recall the objects that were in the office.

The results showed that people were likely to recall objects consistent with the "office schema." Nearly everyone remembered the desk and the office chair. However, few recalled objects in the room that were not consistent with the office schema—a wine bottle and a picnic basket. In addition, some people remembered items that were *not* in the room. Many remembered books, though none had been in sight. When we try to reconstruct a memory, schemas encourage us to supply educated guesses that are consistent with these schemas.

Schemas also operate when we hear a story and retain its meaning. Demonstration 7.6 is a simplified version of a study by Bransford and Franks (1971). They asked participants to listen to sentences that belonged to several different stories. The participants later took a recognition test that contained *only new* sentences, many of which were combinations of the earlier sentences. Nonetheless, people were convinced they had seen these exact sentences before. A sentence such as "The tall tree shaded the man who was smoking his pipe" was consistent with the schema they had developed for this particular story. People gather information together from individual sentences to construct a schema. Once the sentences have been fused in memory in the form of a schema, they cannot untangle them into their original components and recall those components word for word.

What is your schema for visiting a dentist's office?

Notice how this information on schemas reveals the active nature of memory. Schemas help shape what we encode into memory—for example, from an office scene. Schemas also mold and integrate isolated sentences into cohesive stories. Schemas even determine what information we'll retain in long-term memory, because concepts incompatible with schemas may be forgotten.

Schemas are closely related to an important principle we will emphasize in the chapter on thinking (Chapter 8). Specifically, many of our thought processes are governed by heuristics. **Heuristics** are general strategies or problem-solving techniques that are usually accurate. The use of schemas is one example of a heuristic; that is, an effective strategy is to organize your memory about a scene or an event. In general, schemas will help you to acquire the important memories, reconstruct the appropriate missing items, and organize isolated sentences into a story. Consistent with Theme 1, our memory usually functions well. However, if we depend too heavily on a heuristic, we can make mistakes. We make mistakes, for example, when we depend too heavily on the office schema and fail to notice the unique features of this particular office. Now let us consider the components of retrieving items from memory.

The Retrieval Process

Take a moment to think about all the information stored in your long-term memory. You store memories of people you have not seen in years, information about songs that left the Top 40 list long ago, ideas about events that occurred when you were in first grade, and a wealth of general information about vocabulary. With this incredibly large storehouse of memories, isn't it amazing that you can manage to retrieve so many specific pieces of information—such as the name of your second grade teacher? Let's consider how long material can be stored prior to retrieval, how we can measure retrieval, and what happens when retrieval fails.

DEMONSTRATION 7.7 Explicit Memory

List the names of the Seven Dwarfs from the fairy tale "Snow White and the Seven Dwarfs." You may list them in any order you wish. Check your answers at the end of the chapter now. The results will be discussed later in this section.

Source: Based on Miserandino, 1991.

Happy, Sleepy, Dopey, Lazy, Grumpy; Sneezy.

Your college courses in academic areas such as psychology almost always use explicit memory tests, such as an essay or fill-in-the-blank test (recall) or a multiple-choice test (recognition).

Explicit and Implicit Measures of Retrieval Before you read farther, try Demonstrations 7.7 and 7.8, which illustrate two ways of measuring retrieval. We'll see in this discussion that memory accuracy depends on how we measure retrieval—an important point made at the beginning of the chapter.

Try to imagine this scene. A young woman is walking aimlessly down the street, and she is eventually picked up by the police. She seems to be suffering from an extreme form of amnesia, because she has lost all memory of who she is. Unfortunately, she is carrying no identification. Then the police have a breakthrough idea; they ask her to begin dialing phone numbers. Amazingly, she dials her mother's number—though she is not aware whose number she is dialing (Adler, 1991a).

This true story illustrates the difference between explicit and implicit measures of memory. **Explicit memory** requires the conscious recollection of your previous experiences (Schacter, 1992). The most common measure of explicit memory is **recall,** in which you must reproduce items that you learned earlier. Demonstration 7.7 measured recall. Another explicit memory measure is **recognition,** in which you must identify which items on a list you had seen earlier. (For example, a recognition test for the Seven Dwarfs would require you to identify which of the following are the correct names: Sleepy, Drippy, Snoozy, Grumpy, Dopey. . .) In other words, explicit memory requires *intentional* retrieval of information.

In contrast, **implicit memory** assesses whether people's actions are influenced by a past experience—without any awareness that they are remembering (Schacter, 1996). A researcher who is testing implicit memory typically avoids using words such as *memory* or *remember.* In the anecdote about the woman with amnesia, dialing a phone number was a test of implicit memory. We typically do not consciously recollect information when we perform skills that require implicit memory. For example, a skilled typist does not need to be conscious of where each letter is located on the keyboard. Similarly, a trained pole-vaulter will not need to pause a moment before jumping, to remember the reason for holding the pole (Nelson, 1993).

DEMONSTRATION 7.8 Implicit Memory

For each of these items, look at the first letters and supply a complete English word. (Incidentally, some may have more than one possible answer; just give the first one that comes to mind.)

GRU_____
DAN_____
SNE_____
COM_____
VIX_____
DOP_____
CUP_____
SLE_____

The answers will be supplied and discussed later in this section.

Source: Based on Miserandino, 1991.

Demonstration 7.8 showed one example of an implicit test, in which you are instructed to form complete words by filling in the blanks. You demonstrate implicit memory on this task by supplying a word from a list of items you saw earlier. For example, some of the items in Demonstration 7.8 could be completed with names of the Seven Dwarfs (Grumpy, Sneezy, Dopey, and Sleepy), which you saw earlier when you checked your answers to Demonstration 7.7, listed at the end of the chapter. In contrast, the control-group items referred to the names of the reindeer in "The Night Before Christmas" (Dancer, Comet, Vixen, and Cupid). Your performance on these control-group items was probably quite poor.

Implicit memory is currently one of the most popular areas in memory research (Greene, 1992; Mitchell, 1991). Psychologists are intrigued by paradoxes, and paradoxes are common when we compare people's performance on explicit and implicit memory tasks. For example, in some studies, patients with amnesia perform disastrously on explicit memory tasks. However, they score just as well on implicit memory tests as do control-group individuals (e.g., Schacter et al., 1994; Warrington & Weiskrantz, 1970).

A skilled pole-vaulter uses implicit memory to accomplish this jump; his actions are influenced by past experiences.

Tip-of-the-Tongue Experience   You have certainly had an experience like this. You are trying to remember the name of a sporting goods store, because you want to call to see how late it is open. You are squirming with frustration because you cannot quite recall it. It is somebody's last name, it's three syllables long, and the first letter is in the middle of the alphabet, maybe a *J*. This is an example of the **tip-of-the-tongue experience,** the sensation you have when you are confident that you know the word for which you are searching, yet you cannot recall it.

A classic study on the tip-of-the-tongue experience was conducted by Brown and McNeill (1966). These researchers challenged people by giving them the definition for an uncommon English word, such as "The green-colored matter found in plants" or "The art of speaking in such a way that the voice seems to come from another place." Sometimes people immediately supplied the appropriate word, and other times they were confident that they did not know it. However, in some cases, the definition produced a tip-of-the-tongue state. Brown and McNeill wrote that this state felt like being on the brink of a sneeze—an accurate description.

People who were in the midst of a tip-of-the-tongue experience were asked to provide words that resembled the target word in terms of sound. When the target word was *sampan,* for example, people provided these similar-sounding words: *Saipan, Siam, Cheyenne, sarong, sanching,* and *symphoon.* In general, research on the tip-of-the-tongue experience shows that people are reasonably accurate in guessing the characteristics of the target word. For example, they guess the first letter of the target word correctly between 50% and 70% of the time. They also guess the appropriate number of syllables between 47% and 83% of the time (A. S. Brown, 1991).

Notice an important characteristic of the tip-of-the-tongue phenomenon. Even when we cannot recall the target word for which we are searching, we do have some knowledge about the way the word sounds. The phenomenon also demonstrates how memory is structured. The word *chlorophyll* is not simply thrown into your memory along with *banana* and *hyphen.* Instead, *chlorophyll* is encoded so that it is closely linked with other similar-sounding words (maybe *chlorine* and *cholesterol*). Similarly, *ventriloquism* is associated with similar-sounding words such as *ventilate.* As you'll see in the following discussion, one of the most prominent current theories of long-term memory emphasizes the interconnections among related items.

So far, our exploration of long-term memory has included the encoding of memories, the nature of autobiographic memories, the influence of schemas, and the retrieval process. Now we'll shift from description to explanation. We'll consider an important new theory called the connectionist approach, several theories about forgetting, and biological factors responsible for long-term memory.

The Connectionist Approach to Long-Term Memory

I am thinking of an object that is orange; it grows below the ground; and it is a vegetable that rabbits like. What is it? Human memory has a remarkable characteristic that we usually take for granted: One thing reminds us of another (Johnson-Laird, 1988). Each of those clues reminded you of several possible candidates, and all the clues converged on *carrot*.

According to an extremely influential model—the **connectionist approach**—the activation of one cue leads to the activation of other, related concepts. As we noted in Chapters 1 and 5, connectionism is a model of the nervous system based on networks that link together individual units. Connectionism is also known as the **parallel distributed processing approach (PDP approach).** Let's examine some of the important characteristics of this complex model.

1. *The processes are parallel, not serial.* When you thought about the answer to the carrot question, you did not conduct a **serial search,** handling the characteristics one at a time. That is, you did not conduct a complete search of all orange objects before beginning a second search of all below-ground objects, and then all rabbit-endorsed vegetables. Instead, you conducted a **parallel search,** handling all the characteristics at the same time. Because the processes are parallel, we can accomplish cognitive tasks very quickly—as Theme 1 emphasizes.

2. *Knowledge is distributed throughout the connections between units, rather than being stored in a specific location in the brain.* James McClelland, one of the major creators of the connectionist model, described how our knowledge about a group of individuals might be stored in terms of connections that link these people together with their personal characteristics. His original example portrayed members of two gangs of small-time criminals (McClelland, 1981). We will use a simpler and presumably more familiar example featuring five college students. Table 7.1 lists these students, together with their college majors, year in school, and political orientation. Figure 7.7 shows how this information could be represented in network form. Naturally, this figure represents only a fraction of the number of people a college student is likely to know, and only a fraction of the characteristics associated with each student.

If the connections are well established, then an appropriate clue allows you to locate the characteristics of a specified individual (McClelland et al., 1986; Rumelhart et al., 1986). For example, if you enter the system with the name *Roberto,* you discover that he is a psychology major, a senior, and politically liberal.

3. *We can draw conclusions, even when we lack appropriate information.* Specifically, the connectionist approach allows us to fill in missing information about an item, based on information about similar items; this process is referred to

TABLE 7.1 Attributes of Representative Individuals Whom a College Student Might Know

NAME	MAJOR	YEAR	POLITICAL ORIENTATION
Joe	Art	Junior	Liberal
Marti	Psychology	Sophomore	Liberal
Sam	Engineering	Senior	Conservative
Liz	Engineering	Sophomore	Conservative
Roberto	Psychology	Senior	Liberal

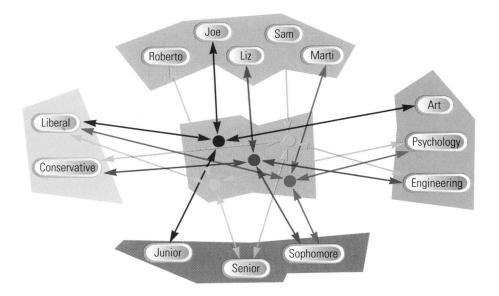

FIGURE 7.7

A figure illustrating the units and connections for the individuals shown in Table 7.1.

as making a **default assignment.** Suppose, for example, that you meet Christina, who is an engineering student. Someone asks you about Christina's political preferences, and you have never discussed politics with her. This question activates information about the political leanings of other engineering students. Based on a default assignment, you reply that she is probably conservative. Notice how the default assignment concept meshes nicely with our discussion on schemas and memory; when we see a photo of an office, we "remember" characteristics of typical offices.

4. *Sometimes we have partial recall for some information, rather than complete, perfect memory.* The brain's ability to provide partial memory is called **graceful degradation.** An example of graceful degradation is the tip-of-the-tongue experience that we discussed earlier. You can often describe exactly what target you are seeking, and you may even know the target's first letter and number of syllables. However, the word itself refuses to leap into memory.

The connectionist approach may represent the most important recent shift in theories about memory and other cognitive processes (Estes, 1991; Rueckl, 1993). Some supporters are especially enthusiastic about this new approach because it seems generally consistent with the neurological design of neurons and the brain (Crick, 1994; Howard, 1995; Lewandowsky & Li, 1995).

The theory works especially well for parallel tasks, in which several processes seem to operate at the same time. The other name for connectionism—parallel distributed processing—emphasizes this parallel-processing characteristic. We seem to use parallel processing when we search memory (the activity we've been discussing here) and also when we recognize patterns (a perceptual activity we discussed in Chapter 4). In summary, connectionism is a prominent new theory that may become the standard approach to explaining memory and some other cognitive activities.

Theories About Forgetting

So far, this section on long-term memory has explained how information is encoded in memory, stored, and retrieved. We have also considered a theoretical approach that emphasizes the interconnections in memory. Now let's consider how

Connectionism is specially useful in explaining pattern recognition and memory search—for example, in recognizing this giraffe and realizing that the word giraffe *is related to words such as* zoo, tall, *and* hippopotamus.

this information may be forgotten. What is the name of the early psychologist who tested cats in puzzle boxes, as described in Chapter 6? Did this name escape your memory, not even approaching the tip of your tongue? How would you explain its disappearance? Let's consider several of the theories that psychologists have proposed for forgetting in long-term memory.

Decay. Psychologists who support the **decay theory** say that each item in memory decays spontaneously as time passes. Several days after you originally saw Thorndike's name, that memory faded. It may have disappeared completely, unless you somehow reviewed it. A basic problem with decay theory, however, is that neuroscientists have not discovered biochemical or structural changes that might account for this decay (Solso, 1995).

Interference. A second approach, **interference theory,** states that forgetting occurs because other items get in the way of the information you want to remember. Figure 7.8 illustrates two kinds of interference. Suppose that you studied Spanish for several years in high school, and then you began to learn French in college. In **proactive interference,** old memories work in a forward direction to interfere with new memories. Specifically, you may have difficulty remembering the new French word *chien,* because the old Spanish word *perro* gets in the way.

In **retroactive interference,** new memories work in a backward direction to interfere with old memories. You may have difficulty recalling the old Spanish word *perro,* because the new French word *chien* gets in the way. (Incidentally, one way to remember these two kinds of interference is to note that *pro*gress means moving forward, whereas *retro*spect means looking backward.)

Try to think of examples of proactive and retroactive interference. For instance, when you are familiar with a particular car, you might experience proactive interference when you drive a different car and try to remember where the light switch is located. As you become accustomed to the new car, however, you'll find that retroactive interference operates. Specifically, you'll forget details about the car you originally drove. Both decay and interference are important sources of forgetting (Mensink & Raaijmakers, 1988; Solso, 1995).

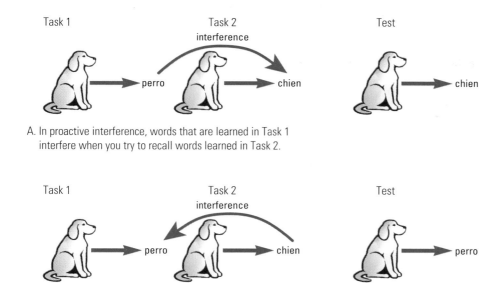

A. In proactive interference, words that are learned in Task 1 interfere when you try to recall words learned in Task 2.

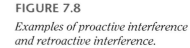

B. In retroactive interference, words that are learned in Task 2 interfere when you try to recall words learned in Task 1.

FIGURE 7.8

Examples of proactive interference and retroactive interference.

Retrieval Failure   I once told a friend that one of the best movies I had ever seen was *The Official Story.* He replied that he had never seen it. "I'm sure you've seen it," I urged. "There's this incredible scene when Norma Aleandro is listening to her friend's description of how she had been tortured." Again, my friend returned a blank look. "OK, it's the film where this schoolteacher slowly realizes that her adopted daughter was probably the child of a woman murdered by the Argentinian military. . . ." The light dawned: "Oh, the film from Argentina! Why didn't you say so?"

You have probably experienced similar frustrations in which an item remains stubbornly buried until the right cue coaxes it forth. This third explanation of forgetting is called **retrieval failure;** it specifies that memory failures occur when the proper retrieval cues are not available. For my friend, the title of the movie, the name of the actress, and a memorable scene could not function as proper retrieval cues, though the name of the country in which it took place immediately prompted recall.

Earlier in the chapter we discussed two topics related to retrieval failure. The encoding specificity principle was covered in our general discussion of encoding. (In

If these children forget the events that occurred during this birthday party, the forgetting may be traced to decay, interference, or retrieval failure.

case you are currently experiencing retrieval failure, it explained how people recalled a greater number of words if they had learned these words in the same room in which they were tested.) Furthermore, the tip-of-the-tongue phenomenon occurs when the retrieval process breaks down.

In summary, then, we forget because of decay, interference, and retrieval failure. Chapter 3 also discussed how head trauma, strokes, and Alzheimer's disease can produce additional forgetting. Consistent with Theme 3 of the book, forgetting is so complex that it requires a variety of different explanations. Now let's consider one final topic in this section, the biological basis of these long-term memories.

The Biological Basis of Long-Term Memory

In the preceding discussion of forgetting, you read the definitions for *proactive interference* and *retroactive interference*. If you processed that information at a deep level, the definitions are now stored in your long-term memory. What brain structures were involved in learning and storing those definitions? What changes took place at the level of the neuron to ensure successful storage? Unfortunately, learning and memory are among the most challenging topics for neuroscientists to explain. Even though researchers have pursued intriguing possibilities for many decades, they do not agree upon a single explanation (Cotman & Lynch, 1990). This difficulty can be traced partly to the impressively vast storage capacity of long-term memory, as well as the variety of kinds of long-term memory. Let's examine the structures in the brain that are most responsible for long-term memory, and then we'll look at some tentative explanations focusing on the neuron and the chemical message system.

Brain Structures That Control Memory.   The regions of the brain that are important in long-term memory include the hippocampus and selected regions of the cerebral cortex. Let's begin with the hippocampus.

The hippocampus appears to be necessary for explicit memories, but not for implicit memories (Squire et al., 1993). Consider the case of a man known by the initials H.M., who had been suffering from life-threatening epilepsy. We briefly considered H.M. in the introduction to Chapter 3. H.M. underwent neurosurgery when he was 27, and the surgeon removed portions of the hippocampus, as well as selected parts of both temporal lobes of the cortex. (Figure 3.14 on Page 90 shows the hippocampus, a structure in the limbic system; Figure 3.16 points out the temporal lobe.)

H.M.'s surgery was successful in controlling his epileptic seizures. However, the operation had an unexpected and tragic side effect that made H.M. the most famous neurology patient of all time. Mysteriously, H.M. could accurately recall events that happened in his childhood, long before his surgery. In contrast, however, he could not remember events that occurred after the surgery (Milner, 1970; Scoville & Milner, 1957).

For example, H.M.'s family moved several months after the surgery. When he was questioned one year after the move, he still had not learned his new address. Forty years after the original surgery, researchers reported that H.M. did not know his age or the current date. He also could not report that his parents had died many years earlier (Cohen & Eichenbaum, 1993).

H.M. suffers from **anterograde amnesia,** an impaired ability for events occurring after the time of brain injury (Bradshaw & Mattingley, 1995). Formal testing reveals many clear-cut deficits. For example, H.M. cannot recognize the names of people who became famous after his operation, and he also cannot recall information about current events (Gabrieli et al., 1988; Ogden & Corkin, 1991). In other words, his explicit memory is defective, and he cannot transfer information from working memory to long-term memory. Surprisingly, however, his implicit memory functions normally (Ogden & Corkin, 1991).

Other persuasive evidence comes from three individuals with clear-cut anterograde amnesia. After they died, an analysis of their brain structures revealed that

This man has anterograde amnesia. In a conversation he appears reasonably normal in many respects. However, he cannot form long-term memories and would be unable to recall your name after several minutes.

each had damage in the hippocampal region, but other brain structures appeared normal (Rempel-Clower et al., 1996).

In short, without a functioning hippocampus, you could not learn about amnesia. Without a functioning hippocampus, you would also have no chance of remembering that we discussed the hippocampus in connection with classical conditioning. (The hippocampus is involved in a conditioned eye-blink response when there is a delay between the conditioned stimulus and the unconditioned stimulus.)

Researchers interested in the biological basis of long-term memory have traditionally focused on the hippocampus. However, portions of the cerebral cortex are also important (Killackey, 1990). For example, the frontal lobe of the cortex (see Figure 3.16) is essential in long-term memory. Individuals with frontal lobe lesions cannot make appropriate judgments about long-term memory. For instance, they are not accurate in predicting how well they know certain information (Kalat, 1995; Squire & Knowlton, 1994).

Changes in the Neuron and Chemical Messengers   For about a century, neuroscientists have assumed that memory must require changes in the synaptic connection between cells (Cotman & Lynch, 1990). More recent research has identified a process that might be responsible for these changes. Specifically, in a series of studies, researchers have presented brief electrical stimulation to neurons in the brains of anesthetized animals (e.g., Bliss & Lømo, 1973; Cotman & Lynch, 1990; Martinez & Derrick, 1996). According to a phenomenon called **long-term potentiation,** this brief electrical stimulation leaves the neuron highly responsive to the same kind of stimulation in the future (Cohen & Eichenbaum, 1993; Kalat, 1995). In other words, that neuron now shows *potentiation*.

Long-term potentiation has a number of characteristics that suggest it may be responsible for forming long-term memories. For instance, long-term potentiation operates in the hippocampus, the cortex, and other regions in the brain that are active during long-term memory. Also, long-term potentiation is limited to the synapses that are active at the time of the electrical stimulation; the inactive synapses are not changed. Finally, like long-term memory, long-term potentiation can last for days or weeks, even though the actual stimulation lasts just a fraction of a second (Abraham et al., 1991; Cohen & Eichenbaum, 1993; Martinez & Derrick, 1996).

Other researchers have argued that the neurotransmitters you read about in Chapter 3 are also vitally important in memory. For example, people with Alzheimer's disease have decreased amounts of the neurotransmitter called acetylcholine (Pool, 1994). Obviously, neurotransmitters play an important role in memory (Kalat, 1995). However, the specific mechanisms need to be more fully clarified.

SECTION SUMMARY: *LONG-TERM MEMORY*

1. In general, we are more likely to encode an item in long-term memory if we have paid attention to it, if we used deep processing, and if the retrieval context matches the encoding context.

2. Eyewitnesses may recall events incorrectly if they heard other, contradictory post-event information; eyewitnesses' confidence is not closely related to their accuracy.

3. Psychologists who favor the recovered-memory perspective argue that many people temporarily forget their painful experiences of childhood sexual abuse, but they can later recover these memories; psychologists who favor the false-memory perspective argue that these recovered memories may actually be false memories—constructed stories about events that never occurred. Both positions are probably at least partially correct.

4. Flashbulb memories seem vivid, but they can be explained by ordinary memory mechanisms.

5. Schemas generally improve our memory for events that happen frequently; however, we make mistakes if we rely on them too heavily.

6. In explicit memory, you consciously remember your previous experiences (e.g., through recall or recognition); in implicit memory, your actions are influenced by a past experience, without being aware that you are remembering (e.g., completing a word fragment to form a word you recently saw).

7. Research on amnesics shows poor performance on explicit memory tests and relatively good performance on implicit memory tests.

8. In the tip-of-the-tongue phenomenon, we have some knowledge of a word for which we are searching, even if we cannot recall the exact target.

9. The connectionist approach is an influential new model based on networks, in which processes are parallel and knowledge is distributed throughout a network; other features include default assignment and graceful degradation.

10. We forget because of decay, interference, and retrieval failure.

11. Research on people with amnesia demonstrates that the hippocampus is important in forming new explicit memories. Portions of the cortex such as the frontal lobe are also essential in long-term memory.

12. Research on the neuronal basis of long-term memory suggests that long-term potentiation may be an important mechanism; neurotransmitters such as acetylcholine may also play a central role.

MEMORY IMPROVEMENT

So far, we have seen that sensory memory is fragile and that working memory has a limited capacity. We have also emphasized the complexity of long-term memory. Now we'll shift from description to application. Your memory has excellent potential; how can you improve it still further?

We've already considered two pointers that can enhance your memory. First, you cannot remember something if it has never entered your memory. If you want to remember something—whether it is the details on a penny or someone's name—pay attention to it. Secondly, be certain that you use a deep level of processing as you learn the material. You've probably had this experience: You suddenly realize that your eyes have moved across several pages of text, yet you have no idea what you have read. This extremely shallow kind of processing will not trap any information in long-term memory. Simple rehearsal—or silent repetition of the material—is also not very effective. Instead, try to think about the meaning of what you have read, and rephrase a passage in your own words. Try to develop rich, elaborate encodings (Pressley & El-Dinary, 1992). When you really need to remember something, try utilizing the self-reference effect. See if you can relate the material to your own experiences.

Let's now consider some other **mnemonics,** which are strategies used to improve your memory. (Mnemonics is pronounced "ni-*mon*-icks," with a silent *m*.) We'll begin by examining some hints related to practice time, and then we'll consider mental imagery and organization—two very useful ways to improve your memory. Our final topic, metamemory, is the most important of all. When you develop your metamemory, you become more aware that you should use memory strategies flexibly and that you need to regulate your study strategies effectively.

Practice

As obvious as it sounds, one way to improve your memory is to increase your practice time. Simply spend longer learning the material, no matter which technique you prefer. Every semester, some of my introductory psychology students come to my office to ask for help after receiving a low grade on an exam. One of my first questions is, "How long did you spend studying?" An amazing number will say something like, "Well, I read every chapter, and I looked over my notes." Most students cannot master the material with only one exposure to the textbook and one review of the lecture notes. Instead, you must read through the material two or three times. Each time, you should also practice retrieving the information (Baddeley, 1993). For example, what are the memory hints we've discussed so far in this section?

The **total time hypothesis** states that the amount you learn depends on the total time you devote to learning (Baddeley, 1990). However, you will not learn effectively if you spend your time allowing your eyes to drift across the pages of your textbook and notebook. You will also waste your time if you simply rehearse the material, repeating it several times, word for word. Instead, spend your study time wisely, using the memory strategies described in this section.

Another important rule about practice is called the **spacing effect;** you will recall more material if you distribute your practice throughout several study sessions. In contrast, you will remember less material if you mass your learning into a single, uninterrupted session. Research consistently supports the spacing effect, and it is one of the most dependable findings in experiments on human memory (Bahrick et al., 1993; Dempster, 1988; Payne & Wenger, 1992). I intentionally divided each chapter of this textbook into two to five sections, so that you can take advantage of the spacing effect. An ideal way to study is to read one section of a chapter, complete the relevant section in the Study Guide, and then take a break. After the break, check the section summary for the part you just read. Then continue with the next section. Also, when you review material before a test, spread your study sessions across several days. Do not try to master it all on one day.

Suppose you are on a job interview, and you meet these three individuals. If you want to remember their names, take advantage of the spacing effect. Practice their names silently, and then let a few minutes pass before rehearsing them again.

Mental Imagery

When we use **mental imagery,** we mentally represent objects or actions that are not physically present. For example, consider a study by Bower and Winzenz (1970). Participants in one condition repeated the pairs silently to themselves, whereas participants in the imagery condition tried to construct a mental image linking the two words in vivid interaction. Each group saw 15 pairs. When they were tested, people in the repetition condition recalled an average of 5.2 items. In contrast, people in the imagery condition recalled 12.7 items—more than twice as many. Visual imagery is clearly a powerful strategy for enhancing your memory (Bellezza, 1996; Paivio, 1995).

The keyword method is one of several mnemonics that relies on imagery. It is particularly useful when you want to link two items together, and one of those items is not an English word. Let's say that you are learning Italian, and you want to remember that *roccia* (pronounced "roach-ee-ah") means *cliff.* From the Italian word *roccia* you could derive a similar-sounding English keyword, *roach.* Then picture a cockroach about to fall off a cliff, as in Figure 7.9. In other words, the **keyword method** uses vivid imagery to link a keyword with another word. When Scruggs and his colleagues (1986) told fourth-graders and fifth-graders how to use this technique, they found that students improved their learning of Italian vocabulary by about 50%. It should be pointed out that some research does not show long-term benefits for the keyword method (e.g., Thomas & Wang, 1996). However, other research shows that the keyword method has improved recall for people's names and for material in spelling, science, and social studies (Hill et al., 1987; Mastropieri & Scruggs, 1991).

This discussion has emphasized that visual imagery is a powerful mnemonic. It is valuable when you simply want to link two English words together. Furthermore, the keyword method can help you learn foreign language vocabulary as well as people's names.

FIGURE 7.9

The keyword representation of the Italian-English word pair, roccia = cliff.

Organization

Your long-term memory resembles a huge library. Unless the information is stored in an organized library, you won't be able to retrieve an item when you need it (Baddeley, 1982). Organization can help in two ways. First, organization relates the newly learned material to your previous knowledge, providing a structured body of information. Second, it arranges the material in your memory, so that when you recall a fragment, you can also access the rest of the material.

One of the most effective ways to organize material is to construct a hierarchy. A **hierarchy** is a system in which items are arranged in a series of classes, from the most general class to the most specific. For instance, earlier in the book, Figure 3.10 on Page 85 showed how the divisions of the nervous system can be arranged in a hierarchy. Hierarchies encourage learners to arrange items into a structured and organized system that can boost recall by more than 200% (Bower et al., 1969; Hirst, 1988).

Metamemory

Perhaps the most important advice about memory improvement is to develop your **metamemory,** or your knowledge and awareness about your own memory (Matlin, 1998). When you try out a mnemonic strategy, ask yourself whether this device seems to be working. As we have emphasized repeatedly, people differ tremendously from one another. A technique like imagery may work for a classmate, but it may fail miserably for you (Belleza, 1996).

You should also monitor your memory. If you think you know a particular list of items, test yourself and see whether your performance matches your expectations. Students are not very accurate in predicting the effectiveness of various memory strategies (Suzuki-Slakter, 1988). Specifically, students may be overconfident if they are using simple repetition, a technique that is not especially helpful. In contrast, they may be underconfident about the effectiveness of more useful memory strategies, such as imagery. When they use imagery, their performance is much better than they expected.

Research on metamemory also tells us that students need to regulate their study strategies more effectively. Specifically, you should spend most of your time on the difficult material that you have not yet mastered, rather than dwelling on the material that is comfortably familiar (Nelson et al., 1994; Nelson & Leonesio, 1988). For example, when you review this chapter for an exam, spend more time mastering the difficult material (perhaps the sections on the connectionist approach and biological aspects of memory), rather than the topics you already know. Plan which strategies you will use for which areas, so that you develop a flexible repertoire of techniques (Herrmann, 1991). Your memory has a tremendous potential to store information. If you focus on metamemory, you can maximize that potential.

SECTION SUMMARY: *MEMORY IMPROVEMENT*

1. This chapter has already discussed several memory hints such as paying attention and deep levels of processing.

2. Memory also improves with increased practice time and when repetitions are spaced.

3. Mental imagery is a useful mnemonic; the keyword method is an example of a mnemonic device that uses imagery.

4. Organization facilitates orderly storage and retrieval; one effective organizational strategy is to create a hierarchy of concepts.

5. Metamemory development is central in memory improvement; some metamemory techniques include checking to see if performance matches expectations and spending more study time on difficult items.

REVIEW QUESTIONS

1. Explain why sensory memory is necessary in both vision and hearing. Provide some examples from your everyday activities. Why is it so difficult to measure?

2. Compare sensory memory, working memory, and long-term memory with respect to their capacity and duration. Describe the kinds of stimuli that are studied for each of these three kinds of memory.

3. Describe the working-memory approach, providing details on each of its three components. What kind of evidence do we have that the capacities of these components are independent of one another?

4. From the discussion of encoding in long-term memory, what kinds of hints can you gather that would increase your chances that you would effectively encode something that you really want to remember?

5. What principle does each of these examples illustrate? (a) A friend who speaks English and Spanish with equal fluency can recall phone numbers better in English than in Spanish; most numbers have one syllable in English and two syllables in Spanish. (b) You were searching a friend's term paper for typographical errors, and you cannot recall much of the paper's content. (c) You cannot remember the words to a song you learned in high school, but they come flooding back when you find your old radio. (d) You cannot recall where the windshield-wiper switch is on your car; however, when you sit in the driver's seat, you reach in the exactly the right direction.

6. Long-term memory is relatively permanent, yet we still forget. What are the three theories of forgetting, and what does the research on flashbulb memories and on eyewitness testimony suggest about the permanence of long-term memory? (Be sure to discuss the recovered memory/false memory controversy.)

7. What evidence does this chapter offer about the active nature of memory? List as many examples as you can, and be sure to mention the constructivist approach.

8. Describe the important characteristics of the connectionist approach to long-term memory. What other memory phenomena from this chapter do these characteristics explain?

9. What do we currently know about the biological basis of memory? Be sure to mention the hippocampus, long-term potentiation, the cerebral cortex, and neurotransmitters; discuss both working memory and long-term memory.

10. Think of as many memory-improvement strategies as you can from the last section of this chapter. Select at least one portion of the chapter to learn using each strategy. Why would you need to consider metamemory as you study for an examination on this chapter?

NEW TERMS

memory (p. 226)
encoding (p. 226)
storage (p. 226)
retrieval (p. 226)
sensory memory (p. 226)
working memory (p. 226)
short-term memory (p. 226)
long-term memory (p. 227)

iconic memory (p. 228)
echoic memory (p. 228)
rehearse (p. 229)
phonological loop (p. 229)
visuo-spatial working memory (p. 229)
central executive (p. 229)
depth of processing (p. 234)
self-reference effect (p. 234)

encoding specificity principle (p. 234)
autobiographical memory (p. 236)
ecological validity (p. 236)
constructivist approach (p. 237)
flashbulb memory (p. 239)
schema (p. 240)
heuristics (p. 241)
explicit memory (p. 242)
recall (p. 242)
recognition (p. 242)
implicit memory (p. 242)
tip-of-the-tongue experience (p. 243)
connectionist approach (p. 244)
parallel distributed processing approach (PDP approach) (p. 244)

serial search (p. 244)
parallel search (p. 244)
default assignment (p. 245)
graceful degradation (p. 245)
decay theory (p. 246)
interference theory (p. 246)
proactive interference (p. 246)
retroactive interference (p. 246)
retrieval failure (p. 247)
anterograde amnesia (p. 248)
long-term potentiation (p. 249)
mnemonics (p. 250)
total time hypothesis (p. 251)
spacing effect (p. 251)
mental imagery (p. 251)
keyword method (p. 251)
hierarchy (p. 252)
metamemory (p. 252)

RECOMMENDED READINGS

Cutler, B. L., & Penrod, S. D. (1995). *Mistaken identification: The eyewitness, psychology, and the law.* New York: Cambridge University Press. If you want to know more about eyewitness testimony, this book is ideal; it emphasizes the factors that influence eyewitness accuracy.

Gathercole, S. E., & Baddeley, A. D. (1993). *Working memory and language.* Hove, Great Britain: Erlbaum. Here is a very clear summary of the working-memory approach, with special applications to reading and language comprehension.

Metcalfe, J., & Shimamura, A. P. (Eds.). (1994). *Metacognition: Knowing about knowing.* Cambridge, MA: MIT Press. This is one of my favorite books in cognitive psychology; it examines memory monitoring, the tip-of-the-tongue phenomenon, and metacognitive aspects of eyewitness testimony.

Pezdek, K., & Banks, W. P. (Eds.). (1996). *The recovered memory/false memory debate.* San Diego, CA: Academic Press. Here's an ideal book if you want to know more about this important controversy, because it features proponents of both positions.

Schacter, D. L. (1996). *Searching for memory: The brain, the mind, and the past.* New York: Basic Books. Daniel Schacter is one of the foremost memory researchers; his book includes fascinating anecdotes and clear summaries about the research on implicit memory, amnesia, the recovered memory debate, and other current topics.

ANSWERS TO DEMONSTRATIONS

Demonstration 7.3

	★ 1	2	3
9	8	5	4
10	7	6	

Demonstration 7.7

The names of the seven dwarfs are Sleepy, Dopey, Grumpy, Sneezy, Happy, Doc, and Bashful.

Answers to Critical Thinking Exercises

Exercise 7.1

a. People may indeed recall more items from the first list because these country names are short. However, we typically recall familiar words more accurately than unfamiliar words. Familiarity is therefore a confounding variable, so we could not draw any conclusions about the cause of the difference between the two lists. To conduct the study properly, the two lists should be equal in familiarity. (My students rated the two lists in Demonstration 7.2 to be equally familiar.)

b. People may indeed recall more consonants than shapes because the consonants have shorter names. However, in this proposed study, people learned the consonants first, when their memory was relatively fresh. They learned the shapes later, when their memory may have been relatively cluttered. The number of previous memory tasks would therefore be a confounding variable. Or you could argue that you'd expect people to perform better on the shapes, because they were now more familiar with the memory task. To control for these "order effects," researchers should test half of the participants on the consonant task first; the other half should be tested on the shape task first.

Exercise 7.2

a. Several factors differ between the two situations. In the standard classroom situation, students take notes on the lecture, and the material is much more complex than a simple list of words. Their motivation for doing well should also be stronger when they will be graded on the material. As the later topic of autobiographical memory emphasizes, list-learning tasks may not be completely applicable to our everyday learning.

b. In a typical experiment on encoding specificity, some people are tested in a situation where the encoding and retrieval cues match; others are tested in a situation where the two cues don't match. However, humans are clever enough to create a mental image of the original encoding situation if they are in the "mismatch" condition. These people may boost their performance up to the level of people in the "match" condition. As a result, the recall for the two groups may be similar.

Exercise 7.3

a. If Loftus and her coauthors had shown everyone a yield sign in the original slide show, then the condition (consistent or inconsistent information) would have been confounded with type of sign (yield or stop). Perhaps stop signs are simply more memorable, so people would readily substitute them for the yield signs. By having half the participants in each condition in the original slide show, we eliminate this potentially confounding variable.

b. Although the ecological validity of this study is relatively high, a situation in which people are shown slides is different from a real-life accident. The slides would be shown at a constant rate under conditions in which you are very likely to pay attention to the accident; the situation is also low in stress. In contrast, in a real-life setting, everything may happen in a split second, and you may have been looking in another direction; your stress level after knowing a human has actually been hit will be substantially higher. Each of these factors may influence memory accuracy.

Exercise 7.4

a. Although Goodman and her coauthors (1996) studied memory for something that was painful and embarrassing, several factors are different from sexual-abuse situations. In sexual abuse, the adult perpetrator may be a relative, and children are likely to realize that the activity is not sanctioned (very different from a procedure in a medical situation). The adult abuser may tell the child never to discuss the incident with anyone, and this adult may never mention the incident again. The medical procedure, in contrast, is not shrouded in secrecy (Goodman et al., 1996). These differences may create a situation that is very different from sexual abuse, with respect to long-term memory consequences.

b. As diplomatically as possible, explain that people do believe their memories for these events are very vivid and accurate. Some researchers have found that these so-called flashbulb memories are highly accurate, but most disagree. The problem is that in real life, we usually do not have any way of verifying what anyone really was doing at the time of a momentous event. So, we can't actually measure memory accuracy.

THINKING AND INTELLIGENCE

CHAPTER 8

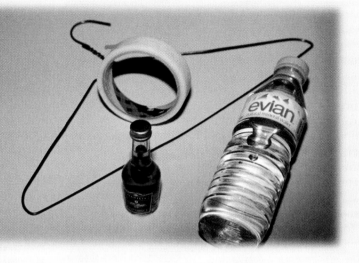

British Airways Flight 32 had taken off from Hong Kong two hours earlier, en route to London. Suddenly, a passenger named Paula Dixon complained of chest pain and difficulty breathing. By good fortune, a physician named Dr. Angus Wallace was also on board. He discovered that she had fallen off a motorbike earlier that day, and he suspected that a broken rib had punctured the membrane surrounding Ms. Dixon's lungs. If so, the air leaking into her chest cavity would form a bubble that would prevent her lungs from inflating. Dr. Wallace judged she would die in less than an hour without surgery, and the plane was now 33,000 feet in the air, with no nearby airport. He would need to operate immediately on the collapsed lung.

In a hospital setting, a surgeon treats a collapsed lung by making an incision in the chest wall, inserting a stiff tube, and bleeding off the air. A jet plane is not exactly a well-stocked hospital, but the emergency kit on Flight 32 did carry a scalpel and a local anesthetic. Fortunately, Dr. Wallace was a top-notch problem solver, and he immediately began to operate, with the assistance of another physician, Dr. Tom Wong.

This impromptu surgical team used the scalpel to cut into Ms. Dixon's chest wall. But what should they use to substitute for surgical clamps? Dr. Wong held the incision open with a knife and fork, which had been sterilized in some brandy. Dr. Wallace had some plastic tubing in his carry-on, but it was too flexible to penetrate into the chest cavity. So Dr. Wallace cut a segment from a metal coat hanger, also sterilized in brandy. He inserted one end of the apparatus into Ms. Dixon's chest cavity, and the other end into a bottle half filled with Evian water. (The photo above illustrates the impromptu "surgical kit.") This precaution allowed air to flow out of Ms. Dixon's chest, without introducing new air into the cavity. When the flight landed in London almost 12 hours later, Ms. Dixon was resting comfortably, as shown in the photo on the right. During those crucial 10 minutes, Dr. Wallace and Dr. Wong solved a life-threatening problem (Adler & Hall, 1995).

In this chapter, we will consider thinking and intelligence. In **thinking,** we manipulate our mental representations to reach a conclusion. **Intelligence** can be defined as the ability to master the information and skills needed to succeed within a particular culture (Locurto, 1991). Both thinking and intelligence are included within the larger category called cognition. **Cognition** involves the acquisition, storage, transformation, and use of knowledge. To solve the collapsed-lung problem, for example, the physicians needed the knowledge that they had acquired from their medical school training and from their subsequent practical experience. This knowledge had been appropriately stored in memory. Then the knowledge was transformed to accommodate the unique limitations of an airplane setting. Finally, the physicians used their knowledge to perform the operation.

The topic of cognition is impressively broad. For example, it includes perception; Chapter 4 emphasized how we use perception to acquire knowledge. Chapter 7 explored how our memory stores and retrieves that knowledge. Cognition also includes language, our topic for Chapter 9. Aspects of cognition are also relevant throughout all the remaining chapters of this book.

The first two sections in this current chapter emphasize how we transform and use our knowledge. For example, in problem solving, we combine isolated facts to help us reach a goal. In decision making, we combine information from different sources to help us make a choice or a judgment. In both cases, we demonstrate our impressive ability to synthesize and use information (Theme 1). The topic of the third section in this chapter, intelligence, emphasizes individual differences in cognitive ability (Theme 2). Here, we will consider human variability with respect to acquiring, storing, transforming, and using knowledge.

Throughout this chapter, we will emphasize top-down processing. As we discussed in Chapter 4 (on sensation and perception), **top-down processing** emphasizes the importance of our concepts, expectations, and prior knowledge. Naturally, thinking also requires **bottom-up processing,** which depends upon the information from our senses. For example, when Dr. Wallace and Dr. Wong solved the collapsed-lung problem, they looked around to perceive and identify a coat hanger, a bottle of brandy, and other visual stimuli (bottom-up processing). However, they also depended upon their prior knowledge and strategies (top-down processing).

When we think, we often use a special kind of top-down processing called heuristics. **Heuristics** are general strategies or problem-solving techniques that are usually accurate. We will see how heuristics typically help us think quickly and accurately when we solve problems and make decisions. This speed and this accuracy are consistent with Theme 1. However, we will see how people occasionally overuse these generally useful strategies; we will see how heuristics can sometimes produce "smart mistakes."

PROBLEM SOLVING AND CREATIVITY

We use **problem solving** when we want to reach a certain goal, but the path toward that goal is not immediately obvious (Squire, 1992b). For example, the two doctors wanted to reach the goal of removing air from Ms. Dixon's chest cavity, but the path toward that goal was far from obvious, outside of a hospital setting.

An auto mechanic must continually use problem solving on the job, because it's often not *obvious why a car isn't working properly.*

Problem Solving and Creativity **259**

DEMONSTRATION 8.1   Representing Problems

Read the information and answer the final question. The answer is at the end of the chapter, on Page 287.

Five people are in a hospital. Each one has only one disease, and each has a different disease. Each one occupies a separate room; the room numbers are 101–105.

1. The person with asthma is in Room 101.
2. Ms. Jones has heart disease.

3. Ms. Green is in Room 105.
4. Ms. Smith has tuberculosis.
5. The woman with mononucleosis is in Room 104.
6. Ms. Thomas is in Room 101.
7. Ms. Smith is in Room 102.
8. One of the patients, other than Ms. Anderson, has gall bladder disease.

What disease does Ms. Anderson have and in what room is she?

In this section, we will discuss problem understanding, problem-solving strategies, expertise, and barriers to problem solving. Our last topic is creativity, a special kind of problem solving. Before you read further, however, try Demonstration 8.1.

Understanding the Problem

When you understand a problem, you construct a mental representation of its important parts (Greeno, 1977, 1991). You pay attention to the important information and ignore the irrelevant clutter that could distract you from the goal. For example, if you pay attention, the following problem proposed by Halpern (1996a) is an easy one:

> Suppose you are a bus driver. On the first stop you pick up 6 men and 2 women. At the second stop 2 men leave and 1 woman boards the bus. At the third stop 2 men leave and 1 woman boards the bus. At the third stop 1 man leaves and 2 women enter the bus. At the fourth stop 3 men get on and 3 women get off. At the fifth stop 2 men get off, 3 men get on, 1 woman gets off, and 2 women get on. What is the bus driver's name? (p. 356)

Many complicated problems become much simpler if you first devise some kind of external representation—for example, some method of representing the problem on paper (Mayer, 1988; Sternberg, 1986). Let us consider several kinds of external representations. (Incidentally, if you still do not understand the bus problem, read the first sentence more carefully.)

Matrices   A **matrix** is a chart that represents all possible combinations, and it is an excellent way to keep track of items, particularly when the problem is complex. Schwartz (1971) asked people to solve "whodunit" problems such as the one in Demonstration 8.1. They were more likely to reach a correct solution if they used a matrix like the one in the answer to the demonstration, at the end of the chapter.

Other Methods   The method of representation that works best depends upon the nature of the problem. A matrix is not always useful. Sometimes a simple list is best. A graph or a diagram can be used to solve a problem that is largely spatial. A visual image is often helpful, as my plumber once discovered when she was trying to fix my humidifier and needed a round metallic part. She represented the problem by trying to visualize this part and then determined where else she had seen an object like this—on an old lamp in her basement.

Problem-Solving Strategies

Once you have represented the problem, you can pursue a variety of heuristics in solving it. Two useful strategies are a means-ends analysis and the analogy approach.

DEMONSTRATION 8.2 The Hobbits-and-Orcs Problem

Try solving this problem: Three Hobbits and three Orcs arrive at a riverbank, and they all wish to cross to the other side. Fortunately, there is a boat. Unfortunately, the boat can only hold two creatures at a time. Another problem is that Orcs are vicious creatures. Whenever more Orcs than Hobbits are on one side of the river, the Orcs will immediately attack the Hobbits and eat them up. Consequently, there can never be more Orcs than Hobbits on any riverbank.

How can you solve this problem? (We should note that the Orcs, though vicious, can be trusted to bring the boat back!) The answer is at the end of this chapter, on Page 287.

Means-Ends Analysis To use **means-ends analysis,** you divide the problem into a number of subproblems, or smaller problems. Then you solve each subproblem by removing the barriers between your present situation and your goal (Mayer, 1991). In other words, you figure out which "ends" you want and then determine what "means" you will use to reach those ends. For example, Dr. Wallace realized that one of the ends he required was some method for sterilizing his improvised equipment; the means he selected was to wash the instruments in brandy with a high alcohol content. He used similar means-ends strategies to solve each of the subproblems in the situation. In fact, means-ends analysis is an especially useful strategy, because it concentrates the problem solver's attention on the difference between the present situation and the goal (Stillings et al., 1995).

Try the Hobbits-and-Orcs problem in Demonstration 8.2. This demonstration illustrates a difficulty with the means-ends approach. Sometimes the correct solution requires you to temporarily increase—rather than reduce—the difference between the original situation and the goal. You'll find it painful to move anybody *backward* across the river to where the creatures originally began (Gilhooly, 1982; Thomas, 1974).

In real life, as in Hobbits-and-Orcs problems, the best way to move forward may be to move backward temporarily. Suppose that you are writing a paper for your sociology course. You think you have successfully solved one subproblem, locating the relevant resources. You are now working on the second subproblem, reading the resources, and you realize that your topic is too narrow. You must now move backward to an earlier stage and locate additional resources before you move forward again.

The Analogy Approach When we use the **analogy approach** in problem solving, we use a solution to an earlier problem to help solve a new one. Analogies are common in human thinking (Halpern et al., 1990; Holyoak & Thagard, 1997). Whenever we try to solve a new problem by referring to a known, familiar problem, we are using the analogy approach.

For example, did you ever consider why the windshield wiper on your car sweeps quickly across the glass and then pauses before taking another sweep? Inventor Bob Kearns was driving in the rain some years ago and realized that he—like many drivers with the old-fashioned wipers—was mesmerized by their leisurely back-and-forth rhythm. He suddenly realized that a windshield wiper should work more like an eyelid. After all, we are rarely distracted when our eyelids sweep rapidly across the surface of our eyes! By creating an analogy between a windshield and the human eye, Kearns invented the intermittent windshield wiper (Seabrook, 1993). Like the means-ends approach, the analogy heuristic usually—but not always—produces a correct solution.

Unfortunately, however, people often fail to apply the analogy heuristic correctly. For instance, people may not successfully transfer from their previous learning when they attempt a new problem (Kolodner, 1997; Mayer, 1988). After solving one algebra problem that involves boats in a river, for example, students may fail to use the same strategies in a comparable problem 15 minutes later. One difficulty is that people tend to focus more on the superficial content of the problem than on the abstract, underlying meaning of the problem (Reeves & Weisberg, 1993, 1994;

The intermittent windshield wiper was invented by someone who created an analogy between the windshield and the human eye.

VanderStoep & Seifert, 1994). In other words, they pay more attention to the prominent **surface features,** which are the specific objects and terms used in the question. Unfortunately, these problem solvers may fail to emphasize the **structural features,** which are the underlying features that must be understood in order to solve the problem correctly. People who have had little practice in solving problems in a discipline are especially likely to form analogies on the basis of surface features, rather than structural features (Cummins, 1992, 1994; Novick, 1988).

In summary, the analogy strategy is often useful. However, problem solvers may fail to notice the correct analogy, and they also make errors in interpreting the analogy.

Critical Thinking Exercise 8.1

Write down your answers to the following questions about understanding the problem and problem-solving strategies.

a. The discussion of understanding the problem noted that people can use devices such as matrices to represent a problem. It also mentioned that Schwartz (1971) found that people were more likely to correctly solve a problem like the hospital-room puzzle in Demonstration 8.1 if they used a matrix. In somewhat more detail, that study allowed people to choose their own methods for representing the problem, and those who decided to use a matrix turned out to be more successful. Suppose some teachers hear about this study. They decide to teach students the matrix method, so that they can improve students' problem-solving skills. How would you critique this proposal?

b. Based on what you have read so far, what kind of dependent variables could psychologists use if they were conducting research on problem solving?

Appropriate Use of Top-Down Processing: How Expertise Facilitates Problem Solving

So far we have discussed how a generic human solves problems; we have not focused on the individual differences emphasized in Theme 2. As you might imagine, however, individual differences in problem solving can be impressive. Cognitive psychologists have examined in some detail the topic of expertise. An individual with **expertise** demonstrates consistently exceptional performance on representative

DEMONSTRATION 8.3 Duncker's Candle Problem

Imagine you are in a room that contains only the materials shown in this picture. You must find a way to attach the candle to the wall of this room so that it burns properly and wax does not drip onto the floor. The solution appears at the end of this chapter, on Page 288.

tasks for a particular area (Ericsson & Lehmann, 1996). Most cognitive psychologists specify that it takes at least 10 years of intense practice to achieve expertise (Anderson, 1993; Ericsson & Charness, 1994).

How do experts differ from **novices,** those individuals who have not acquired expertise in a specific area? Experts are not simply "smarter" than other people in all fields of knowledge. Instead, experts excel primarily in their own domains of expertise (Bédard & Chi, 1992; Glaser & Chi, 1988). After all, you wouldn't expect a racetrack expert to excel at making French pastries! Here are some of the important areas where experts are more skilled than novices:

1. Experts store more information about their discipline in long-term memory, often in the form of schemas (Anderson, 1993; Ericsson & Kintsch, 1995).

2. Experts typically use more sophisticated models to represent abstract problems. They are also more likely to use appropriate mental images or diagrams, which usually facilitate problem solving (Clement, 1991; Larkin & Simon, 1987).

3. Experts are more likely to apply analogies appropriately in their area of expertise. As we noted earlier, experienced problem solvers typically emphasize the problem's structural features, whereas novices are likely to emphasize surface features. Because experts understand the original problem so well, they are more skilled at transferring that knowledge to a new, analogous problem.

4. Experts are faster and more efficient than novices. For example, some people are expert anagram solvers. They seem to consider several alternate solutions at the same time (Novick & Coté, 1992).

5. Experts have superior metacognitive skills related to problem solving in their area. **Metacognition** refers to your knowledge and awareness about your own thought processes. (We investigated one component of metacognition—called metamemory—in Chapter 7.) Experts are more aware when they are making an error, and they are more skilled at distributing their time appropriately when they solve problems (Glaser & Chi, 1988).

In short, experts are more skilled than novices at numerous phases of problem solving. They are even more skilled at assessing their progress as they continue to work on a problem.

Overuse of Top-Down Processing: How Mindlessness Blocks Problem Solving

Before you read this part of the chapter, try Demonstration 8.3, which illustrates one of the barriers to successful problem solving.

Have you ever found yourself solving a problem in the same old familiar way you have handled previous problems—and then discovered that another approach would have been much better? We saw in our discussion of analogies that we often

Judit Polgar, a 15-year-old, plays 20 opponents simultaneously. Compared with a novice chess player, she probably stores more information about chess in her memory, uses more appropriate mental images, makes analogies with previous successful problem solutions, works faster, and shows superior metacognitive skills regarding the solution of chess problems.

solve problems successfully if we use a method that has proved useful in the past. However, we may rely too rigidly on our previous information and overuse our top-down processes, falling victim to mindlessness.

According to Ellen Langer, **mindlessness** is a state that occurs when we use information too rigidly, without becoming aware of the potentially novel characteristics of the current situation (Langer, 1989a, 1989b; Langer & Piper, 1987). In other words, we behave mindlessly when we rely too rigidly on previous categories. We fail to attend to the specific details of the current stimulus; we underuse our bottom-up processes.

One example of mindlessness is **functional fixedness,** which means that the function we assign to an object tends to remain fixed or stable. Successful problem solving often requires overcoming functional fixedness. For example, my sister described a creative solution to a problem she faced on a business trip. She had bought a take-out dinner from a wonderful Indian restaurant. Back in her hotel, she discovered that the bag contained no plastic spoons or forks, and the hotel dining room had closed several hours earlier. What to do? She searched the hotel room, discovered a plastic shoehorn in the "complimentary packet," washed it thoroughly, and enjoyed her chicken biriyani. To overcome functional fixedness, she had to realize that an object designed for one function (putting on shoes) could also serve another function (conveying food to the mouth).

The Duncker candle problem in Demonstration 8.3 is the classic example in which the problem solver must overcome functional fixedness (Duncker, 1945). People typically think of the matchbox as simply a container for matches. Because its function seems fixed, they mindlessly ignore another possible function, as a "candle holder" (Weisberg & Suls, 1973).

Functional fixedness applies to the objects in problem solving. Another kind of mindlessness, *mental set,* applies to people when they solve problems. With a **mental set,** problem solvers keep using the same solution they have used in previous problems, even though there may be easier ways of approaching the problem. For instance, you are familiar with the kind of number puzzles in which you try to figure out the pattern that explains why a sequence of numbers has a particular order. Try figuring out why these numbers are arranged in the following order: 8, 5, 4, 9, 1, 7, 6, 3, 2, 0.

Functional fixedness and mental sets both demonstrate that mistakes in cognitive processing are usually rational. In general, objects in our world have fixed functions. We typically use a shoe horn to help a foot slip into a shoe, and we typically use a spoon to help food slip into our mouths. The strategy of using one tool for one task and another tool for another task is generally wise because each was specifically designed for its own task. Functional fixedness occurs, however, when we apply that strategy too rigidly and fail to realize that a clean shoehorn can make a suitable spoon.

Similarly, you are wise to apply the knowledge you learned in earlier problems when solving the present problem. (After all, that is the basis of the analogy strategy.) However, in the case of mental sets, we mindlessly apply the past-experience strategy too rigidly and fail to notice more effective solutions. For example, you might solve a number-series problem by trying to determine whether two adjacent numbers differ by a constant amount. Instead, you could solve the problem by thinking of other systems for organizing items. (If you haven't yet guessed the answer to the number-sequence problem, check the end of this section on Page 264.)

Creativity

Creativity is the ability to produce unusual, high-quality solutions to a problem (M. W. Eysenck, 1991). According to this definition, a solution can be unusual—even one of a kind—and still not qualify as being creative. For example, a friend of mine who knew I liked both chocolate and garlic brought a plate of chocolate-covered garlic cloves to a dessert potluck. The dish was certainly unusual. However, only two people had the courage to try this dessert, and they did not take second helpings. This project would therefore *not* be considered high-quality.

Characteristics of Creative People If we examine a broad sample of people, we find that intelligence is moderately correlated with creativity (Haensly & Reynolds, 1989; Sternberg & Lubart, 1995). Intelligence seems to be necessary but not sufficient to produce creativity (Hayes, 1989a). Think of the people you know whom you would consider creative. You would probably say that these individuals have above-average intelligence; reasonable intelligence is *necessary* for creativity. However, think of the people you know whom you would consider to be intelligent. You can probably identify several whom you would not consider to be creative; intelligence is not *sufficient* for creativity.

According to Sternberg and Lubart (1995, 1996), creativity must have characteristics beyond intelligence. Specifically, creativity also requires knowledge and motivation. Creativity also requires an encouraging environment, as well as appropriate thinking style and personality. All these six attributes are necessary to produce creativity, according to these theorists. For example, you may qualify in five of the six characteristics, but perhaps you lack motivation. Without this sixth characteristic, Sternberg and Lubart propose that you will not reveal your creativity.

Social Factors Influencing Creativity An important controversial topic within the study of creativity concerns how social factors can influence creativity. For example, Amabile (1983, 1990, 1996) has shown that people are less creative when they know that others will be evaluating their work. In a typical experiment, college students were told to compose a poem. Half were told that the experimenter was simply interested in their handwriting, rather than the content of the poem. These students therefore did not expect to be evaluated on their creativity. The other half of the students were told that the experimenter was interested in the poem's content, and they would receive a copy of the judges' evaluations. In other words, these students knew they would be evaluated.

Each poem was judged by people who were poets. As you can see from Figure 8.1, the creativity scores were much higher for students who had no expectation that their poetry would be judged. In contrast, creativity was reduced when students thought that someone would be judging their poetry. Figure 8.1 shows that creativity was consistently inhibited by concern about evaluation—whether people worked in a group or by themselves.

Other research has examined different social factors. For example, you may be less creative if someone watches you while you are working or when you are offered a reward for creative projects (Amabile, 1990, 1994, 1996). However, in some cases, rewards do not lead to decreased creativity (Eisenberger & Cameron, 1996; Eisenberger & Selbst, 1994). Our theme of individual differences may help to explain why reward decreases creativity in some studies, but not in others. Specifically, some people may become anxious when they know that someone will be judging their performance. Reward may inhibit their creativity. In contrast, other people may not be affected by these social factors. Still others may become even more creative when they know they are being judged or rewarded (Eisenberger & Cameron, 1996). The controversy over creativity and reward is an important example of Theme 3; our psychological processes are so complex that we do not yet have an answer to this question. (Incidentally, if you are still puzzled by the question about the series of numbers on Page 263, notice that the numbers are in alphabetical order (eight, five, four, nine . . .).

FIGURE 8.1

The influence of evaluation expectation and working condition on creativity.
Source: Based on Amabile, 1983.

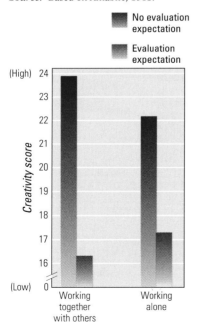

SECTION SUMMARY: *PROBLEM SOLVING AND CREATIVITY*

1. This chapter on thinking and intelligence emphasizes top-down processing.

2. Problem solving requires identifying the real problem and paying attention.

3. A problem is often easier to understand if you construct a representation, for example by using matrices.

4. Heuristics such as a means-ends analysis or the analogy approach are typically useful; however, people

using the means-ends approach may be reluctant to go backward, and people using analogies may not apply this heuristic correctly.

5. Compared to novices, expert problem solvers store more information about their discipline in long-term memory; they use more sophisticated models; they are more likely to apply analogies correctly; they are faster and more efficient; and they have superior metacognitive skills.

6. Problem solving can be blocked by different kinds of mindlessness, such as functional fixedness and men-

tal set; in both of these cases, old ideas inhibit new solutions.

7. Intelligence is a necessary characteristic for creativity, but it is not sufficient; other attributes of creativity are knowledge, motivation, an encouraging environment, and an appropriate thinking style and personality.

8. When people expect to be judged or rewarded, their creativity may be inhibited, but the results are inconsistent in this area.

DECISION MAKING

You make dozens of decisions every day. Which line in the post office will move the fastest? Would the course in child development be more interesting with Dr. Lopez or with Dr. Hastings? Can you finish reading the rest of this chapter before you have to leave for your biology lab?

Decision making requires you to make a choice about the likelihood of uncertain events. You make decisions whenever you make predictions about the future, select from two or more alternatives, and make estimates about frequency in situations with scanty evidence. In decision making, we typically lack clear-cut rules that guide us toward the best decision. Furthermore, we won't know right away whether our decision was correct (Evans et al., 1993). In fact, you may never discover whether Dr. Lopez or Dr. Hastings would have been the better professor for child development.

This woman is trying to decide which shampoo to buy. One has a more familiar name, but the other is less expensive. Heuristics will probably guide her decision.

Decision making, like other thinking tasks, requires us to combine, manipulate, and transform our stored knowledge. When we have no rules or step-by-step procedures to use in decision making, we tend to rely on heuristics. As you know, heuristics are general strategies or problem-solving techniques that are likely to produce a correct solution. Heuristics are typically very useful, especially because they help us simplify the overwhelming amount of information we could potentially consider when we need to make a decision (Hogarth, 1987). Unfortunately, we humans do not always make wise decisions because we fail to appreciate the limitations of these heuristics. In fact, on many occasions, we are "systematically irrational" (Baron, 1991, p. 487). Even good heuristics should be applied with caution.

Throughout this section, we will discuss studies that point out errors in decision making. However, these errors should not lead you to conclude that humans are

---

DEMONSTRATION 8.4 Familiarity and Availability

Read the following list of names:

Louisa May Alcott
Alice Walker
John Dickson Carr
Laura Ingalls Wilder
Thomas Hughes
Jack Lindsay
Edward George Lytton
Margaret Mitchell
Michael Drayton
Henry Vaughan

Edith Wharton
Richard Watson Gilder
Judith Krantz
Agatha Christie
Robert Lovett
Maya Angelou
Virginia Woolf
Judy Blume
George Nathan
Allan Nevins
Henry Crabb Robinson

Jane Austen
Joseph Lincoln
Charlotte Brontë
Arthur Hutchinson
James Hunt
Toni Morrison
Brian Hooker
Harriet Beecher Stowe

Now, before you read further, turn to Page 267 and look at the end of Demonstration 8.5 for further instructions.

unwise and foolish. Instead, we make errors in decision making when we adopt our normally useful heuristics and apply them inappropriately. In other words, we make smart mistakes.

In this section on decision making, we will look at three important heuristics: (1) availability, (2) representativeness, and (3) anchoring and adjustment. Then the "In Depth" feature examines how our decisions are influenced by the way a question is asked or framed. Our two final topics include people's confidence in their decisions and new viewpoints in decision making. But before you read further, try Demonstration 8.4.

The Availability Heuristic

Suppose that someone asks you whether your college has more students from California or from Oregon. Presumably, you have not memorized the geography statistics. Instead, you would probably answer this question in terms of the relative number of people from these two states whose names come to mind. Perhaps you can easily retrieve the names of students from California ("Sara, Lucia, Chi-Ming . . .") because your memory has stored the names of dozens of students from California. However, you may think of only one person's name from Oregon. Because examples of California students were easy to retrieve, you conclude that your college has more of them. In this case, making a decision based on the number of examples that come to mind could be a fairly useful way to answer the question.

We use the **availability heuristic** whenever we estimate frequency or probability in terms of how easy it is to think of examples of something (Tversky & Kahneman, 1973). When deciding whether more students are from California or from Oregon, for instance, it is easier to remember California students than Oregon students. The availability heuristic is accurate whenever the availability (or ease with which examples are remembered) is correlated with true, objective frequency. However, as you will see, other factors can influence memory retrieval that are *not* correlated with objective frequency. These factors distort availability and therefore make our decisions systematically less accurate (MacLeod & Campbell, 1992). As we explore this topic, we will see that recency and familiarity—both factors that influence memory—can potentially influence availability. Figure 8.2 clarifies this relationship.

Recency and Availability As Figure 8.2 shows, one factor that influences availability is recency. In general, we can remember an event better if it happened yesterday, rather than long ago. For example, you can probably recall the details about the latest world crisis more clearly than the details of the 1991 Persian Gulf War.

Research with physicians points out that their diagnoses are also "contaminated" by recency. Specifically, physicians are more likely to select a particular diagnosis if they recently diagnosed a similar case (Weber et al., 1993). When you make a decision, a good precaution would be to ask yourself, "Is my most recent experience with this situation playing too large a role in my decision?"

FIGURE 8.2

The relationship between true frequency and estimated frequency, with recency and familiarity as "contaminating" factors.

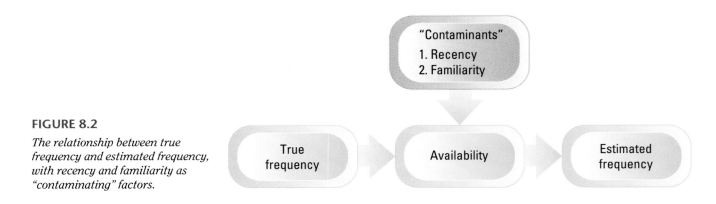

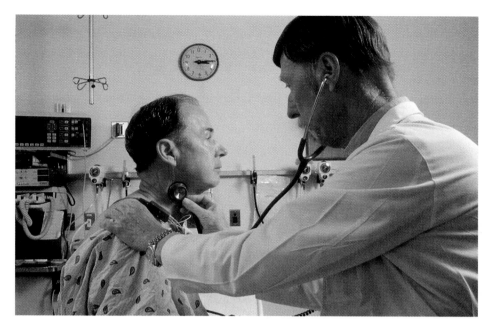

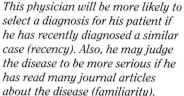

This physician will be more likely to select a diagnosis for his patient if he has recently diagnosed a similar case (recency). Also, he may judge the disease to be more serious if he has read many journal articles about the disease (familiarity).

Familiarity and Availability   Familiarity is a second factor that can contaminate availability. In other words, familiarity distorts estimated frequency in the same way that recency distorts these judgments. Specifically, we are likely to recall items better if they are familiar, rather than unfamiliar. For instance, Demonstration 8.4 listed 14 names of well-known women authors and 15 names of not very familiar men authors. You probably remembered the women's names more easily, and so you estimated that the list contained more women's names than men's names. In other words, availability was more influenced by familiarity than by true, objective frequency. When Tversky and Kahneman (1973) tried this demonstration with 19 names of famous women and 20 names of less famous men, about 80% of the participants mistakenly guessed that the list had contained more women's names.

Familiarity can contaminate medical judgments just as recency does. For example, genetic counselors often overestimate the probability of genetic risks (Shiloh, 1994). This situation is not surprising, because these counselors constantly advise people about birth defects.

Availability also influences the public's opinion of diseases and other causes of death. For example, newspapers do not tend to report deaths due to diabetes or emphysema,

---

DEMONSTRATION 8.5   The Conjunction Error

Read the following paragraph:

Linda is 31 years old, single, and outspoken. She majored in philosophy. As a student, she was deeply concerned with issues of discrimination and social justice, and also participated in antinuclear demonstrations.

Now rank the following options in terms of their likelihood in describing Linda. Give a ranking of 1 to the most likely option and a ranking of 8 to least likely option.

_____ 1. Linda is a teacher in elementary school.

_____ 2. Linda is active in the feminist movement.

_____ 3. Linda works in a bookstore and takes yoga classes.

_____ 4. Linda is a bank teller.

_____ 5. Linda is a psychiatric social worker.

_____ 6. Linda is a member of the League of Women Voters.

_____ 7. Linda is a bank teller and is active in the feminist movement.

_____ 8. Linda is an insurance salesperson.

Further instructions for Demonstration 8.4:

Now you must make a decision about the names you saw in Demonstration 8.4. Were there more men's names or women's names on that list? You cannot answer "about the same."

even though these diseases cause 16 times as many deaths as do accidents (Slovic et al., 1982). We cannot easily think of examples of people dying from these two diseases, so we do not judge them to be very serious. As Yates (1990) points out, the evening news on television is not likely to announce, "Asthma kills 25 in Kansas! Details at 11!"

In summary, we use the availability heuristic when we estimate frequency in terms of how easily we can think of examples. This strategy is generally useful, but it can be distorted by recency and familiarity. Consistent with Theme 1, our decision making is generally quite accurate, but we sometimes make "smart mistakes."

The Representativeness Heuristic

Suppose that you have a normal penny with both a head (H) and a tail (T). You toss it six times. Which seems like the more typical outcome: H H H T T T or T H H T H T? Most people say that T H H T H T looks more typical. After all, you know that coin tossing should produce "heads" and "tails" in random order, and T H H T H T looks perfectly random. It looks like the most typical, representative outcome. Before you read further, try Demonstration 8.5 on the previous page.

When you use the **representativeness heuristic,** you decide whether the sample you are judging looks typical and appropriate. For instance, a sample of coin tosses should have 50% heads and no systematic order in the pattern of heads and tails. As Kahneman and Tversky (1972) found, people follow the representativeness heuristic by judging that random-looking coin tosses like T H H T H T should occur far more often than orderly-looking coin tosses like H H H T T T. Similarly, you've probably had a cashier add up your bill in a store, producing an orderly sum like $22.22. Weren't you tempted to check the arithmetic? After all, this addition process should produce a random-looking sum. A sum such as $21.97 would look much more representative. Representativeness is generally a useful heuristic that produces wise decisions. However, we can make incorrect decisions when we overuse it.

Before we consider more examples, let's make certain that you understand how availability differs from representativeness. When we use the availability heuristic, we are given a general category, and we must supply the specific examples; how easily do those specific examples come to mind? When we use the representativeness heuristic, we are given a specific example, and we ask whether this example looks similar in important characteristics to the general category from which it is drawn.

Representativeness is such a compelling heuristic that we weigh it heavily when making decisions. In fact, we weigh it so heavily that we tend to ignore a very important source of information, called the base rate. We also tend to commit the conjunction fallacy, thereby violating an important statistical principle. Let's consider these two issues.

Base Rate and Representativeness Representativeness is so compelling that people tend to ignore the **base rate,** or how often the item occurs in the population (Hinsz & Tindale, 1992). For example, Kahneman and Tversky (1973) gave people this description:

> Jack is a 45-year-old man. He is married and has four children. He is generally conservative, careful, and ambitious. He shows no interest in political and social issues and spends most of his free time on his many hobbies which include home carpentry, sailing and mathematical puzzles. (p. 241)

People were told that this paragraph described one person selected from a group of 30 engineers and 70 lawyers; what was the probability that he was one of the 30 engineers?

The participants in this study typically ignored the base rate (that is, the fact that 70% of the sample consisted of lawyers). Instead, they focused on the fact that Jack's characteristics were representative of an engineer. As Gilovich (1991) points out, we expect examples to look like the categories of which they are members. That description of Jack looks most like an engineer. We fail to note that—with more than

Would you guess that this man is a poet or a successful businessman? If you focus on representativeness, rather than base rate, you would respond "poet." However, he is the owner of a successful music store in Geneseo, New York.

twice as many lawyers as engineers in the sample—the description probably fits a larger number of lawyers.

The Conjunction Fallacy and Representativeness Be sure that you tried Demonstration 8.5 before you read further. Now look at your answers, specifically Numbers 4 and 7. Which did you think was more likely, "Linda is a bank teller" or "Linda is a bank teller and is active in the feminist movement"?

When Tversky and Kahneman (1983) presented problems like these, students answered that Linda was much more likely to be a bank teller who is active in the feminist movement. Students studying for their PhDs in decision making—who had several advanced courses in probability—were just as likely to make this mistake as undergraduates who had little mathematical background.

Let us see why this decision was incorrect. Which is more likely, that someone is a psychology major or that this person is a psychology major at a college in New York? Whenever we add a restriction such as "at a college in New York," we decrease the probability because we are eliminating some people. There are more bank tellers in this country than there are bank tellers active in the feminist movement—because we have eliminated the group of bank tellers who are *not* active in the feminist movement (see Figure 8.3). Statistically, the probability of any two events occurring together (such as "bank teller and feminist") cannot be greater than the probability of either one of those events occurring alone (such as "bank teller"). However, people often commit the **conjunction fallacy:** They judge the probability of the conjunction (two events occurring together) to be greater than the probability of just one of those events.

The conjunction fallacy can be traced to the representativeness heuristic. The characteristic "feminist" is very representative of someone who is single, outspoken, a philosophy major, concerned about social justice, and an antinuclear activist. A person with these characteristics does not seem likely to become a bank teller, so we give "bank teller" a low ranking in Demonstration 8.5. In contrast, this person seems highly likely to be a feminist. By adding the extra detail of "feminist" to "bank teller," we have actually *decreased* the number of people in the group. However, we have increased the believability of the description. The description is now more representative, so we decide that it is more likely. The Tversky and Kahneman (1983) results have been replicated many times, with generally consistent findings (e.g., Birnbaum et al., 1990; D. Davidson, 1995; Shafir et al., 1990; Wolford et al., 1990).

When used appropriately, the representativeness heuristic can help us make wise decisions. However, we misuse this heuristic so often that we should pause when we are trying to decide which of two options is more likely. One option may sound much more attractive because the description is so very representative—so very typical. However, before you select this option, be sure to pay sufficient attention to the base rate. Also, make certain that you are not committing the conjunction fallacy.

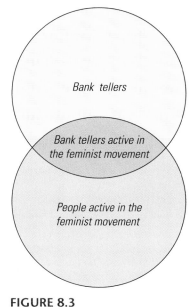

FIGURE 8.3

A diagram showing the relationship between the sets described in Demonstration 8.5. As this diagram shows, the number of bank tellers must be larger than the number of bank tellers who are active in the feminist movement. (See Demonstration 8.5.)

Critical Thinking Exercise 8.2

Write down your answers to the following questions about the availability heuristic and the representativeness heuristic.

a. The availability heuristic would work very well in decision making if every example from a category had an equal chance of being included in the sample. In Chapter 2, you learned that researchers should choose a random sample, but they often choose a biased sample, where some members of the population are more likely to be selected than others. Why does the availability heuristic demonstrate that we often choose biased samples?

b. Chapter 2 also mentioned that researchers aim to collect a representative sample, in which the characteristics of the sample are similar to the characteristics of the population. Why is this concept similar to the representativeness heuristic?

If someone has suggested a very low first approximation (or anchor) for the listing price of this house, this real estate agent might set a much lower listing price than if she had been given a high anchor.

The Anchoring and Adjustment Heuristic

A mail-order catalog contains an advertisement for a pair of boots. The chatty description, written from the perspective of the company president, contained this passage:

> The truth is, I like boots very much. I just don't like most of the boots that I see for sale. I am offended by boots costing $875. I am deeply offended by boots costing $1,200.

The price of this company's boots? A mere $247. I found myself momentarily agreeing that the price seemed reasonable. And then it occurred to me: I had fallen victim to the anchoring and adjustment heuristic. My anchor for a price of boots had been momentarily (and very inappropriately) set as $1,200. Even knocking off a few hundred dollars, $247 seemed justifiable—until I regained a better perspective.

When we use the **anchoring and adjustment heuristic,** we make an estimate by guessing a first approximation (an anchor) and then making adjustments to that number on the basis of additional information. Like the other two heuristics we have examined, this heuristic often leads to a reasonable answer. However, people typically rely too heavily on the anchor, and their adjustments are usually too small (Poulton, 1994; Slovic et al., 1974; Tversky & Kahneman, 1982).

Consider a study in which people were asked to estimate various quantities (Tversky & Kahneman, 1974). A typical question asked participants to estimate the percentage of African countries that belong to the United Nations. Before requesting the reply, the experimenters spun a wheel while the participants watched. At random, the wheel selected a number between 0 and 100. The participants were asked to indicate whether their answer to the question was higher or lower than the selected number, and to supply an estimate.

Even though the selected number had been chosen completely at random, it still acted as an anchor for people's estimates. For example, if the wheel had stopped on 10, people estimated that 25% of the African countries were in the United Nations. If the wheel had stopped on 65, people estimated 45%. In other words, a number that had no real relationship to the question had served as an anchor for the response. People did make adjustments from this number, in the direction of the correct answer. However, these adjustments were typically far too small.

Psychologists have found that the anchoring and adjustment heuristic often influences decisions about financial issues. For example, real estate agents who were given a low anchor for a house, a listing price of about $66,000, suggested that the lowest acceptable offer should be $65,000 (Northcraft & Neale, 1987). Real estate agents who were given a high anchor for this very same house—a listing price of about $84,000—suggested that the lowest acceptable offer should be $73,000. With a high anchor, the offer moved up $8,000. Other research tested business managers with an average of 17 years of work experience (Whyte & Sebenius, 1997). Despite their extensive expertise, these managers were also influenced by the anchoring and adjustment heuristic in setting the price for automobile parts.

Keep the anchoring and adjustment heuristic in mind when you next need to estimate a quantity. Provide an educated guess as a first anchor. Then make adjustments from that anchor, based on other information. However, urge yourself to make appropriately large adjustments, taking into account all relevant additional factors.

IN DEPTH

The Framing Effect

We have seen that decision makers use three heuristics that are generally helpful. They make estimates on the basis of the ease with which they can recall examples (availability). They decide which option is more likely on the basis of whether it looks typical (representativeness). They also estimate quantity by making a first guess and then making overly modest adjustments (anchoring and adjustment). In each case, people may use a heuristic inappropriately, and they underestimate the importance of other relevant information.

In the case of the **framing effect,** people are influenced by two factors that should be ignored: (1) the background context of the decision, and (2) the way in which a question is worded. Before reading further, try Demonstration 8.6.

The Background Context and the Framing Effect

Imagine that you have decided to see a play, and you have paid $10 for the ticket. As you enter the theater, you discover that you have lost the ticket. The office did not record ticket purchases, so you cannot recover the ticket. Would you pay $10 for another ticket for the play? Now change the scenario somewhat. Imagine, instead, that you have decided to see a play, and you plan to pay $10 for the ticket. As you enter the theater, you discover that you have lost a $10 bill. Would you still pay $10 for the ticket for the play?

In both cases, the amount of money involved is $10, yet the decision frame is different for these two problems. We seem to organize our expenses into separate mental accounts. In the first example, buying a second ticket to the play seems to raise the ticket price to $20—perhaps more than we want to spend. When Kahneman and Tversky (1984) asked participants in their study, only 46% said that they would pay $10 for another ticket. In contrast, in the second example, we do not tally the lost $10 in the same account. We view this loss as being generally irrelevant to the ticket. In fact, 88% of the participants in Kahneman and Tversky's study said that they would purchase the ticket in this second condition.

If we consider only mathematics when we make the decision, we would see that the two examples are identical. However, we are distracted by the background information, the context in which each example appears. The framing effect is just as compelling as the famous Müller-Lyer illusion you saw in Figure 4.15. In that illusion, you know that the lines are supposed to be the same length, just as you know that the loss of a $10 ticket equals the loss of a $10 bill. In both cases, however, the frame (either geometric or verbal) influences your interpretation of the situation.

Research on decision frames shows that people are influenced by the way information is worded. Would shoppers be as likely to purchase this ground beef if the label said "20% fat"?

The Wording of a Question and the Framing Effect

We also know that the way a question is worded can have a major effect on the decisions we make. For example, wording can influence consumer behavior. People are much more positive about ground beef that is labeled "80% lean" rather than "20% fat" (Johnson, 1987). The framing effect also holds true for medical decisions (e.g.,

---

DEMONSTRATION 8.6 Examples of the Framing Effect

Problem 1

Version a: You are lying on the beach on a hot day. All you have to drink is ice water. For the last hour you have been thinking about how much you would enjoy a nice cold bottle of your favorite cola drink. A friend offers to bring back a drink from the only nearby place where beverages are sold, a fancy hotel. He says that the cola may be expensive, though. How much would you be willing to pay? _____

Version b: Imagine the same scenario, except that your friend will be going to a small, run-down grocery store. How much would you be willing to pay? _____ (If your answer is different for the two versions of Problem 1, explain why.)

Problem 2

Version a: Imagine that you go to purchase a calculator for $15. The calculator salesman informs you that the calculator you wish to buy is on sale for $10 at the other branch of the store, which is 10 minutes away. Would you drive to the other store? _____

Version b: Imagine that you go to purchase a jacket for $125. The jacket salesman informs you that the jacket you wish to buy is on sale for $120 at the other branch of the store, which is 10 minutes away. Would you drive to the other store? _____ (If your answer is different for the two versions of Problem 2, explain why.)

Source: Based on Frisch, 1993.

TABLE 8.1 Responses to Demonstration 8.6

Problem	Same	Objective Difference	Subjective Difference	No Justification Response Given
Drink on beach	32%	27%	23%	18%
Calculator/jacket	24%	0%	56%	19%

Note: Table shows the percentage of students citing each of the four possible responses to the two problems in Demonstration 8.6.
Source: Based on Frisch, 1993.

(IN DEPTH continued)
Slovic et al., 1982), for using seat belts in automobiles (Slovic et al., 1988), and for paying for public services (Green et al., 1994).

Varying Reasons for the Framing Effect

Deborah Frisch (1993) argues that the framing effect often influences decision making. However, people may have different rationales for different problems. She asked students to try nine problems like the two you tried in Demonstration 8.6. Two independent judges then classified the students' responses into four categories:

1. The student agrees that the two versions are the same.

2. The student believes there is an *objective* difference between the two versions, even though it was not explicitly stated.

3. The student believes there is a *subjective* difference between the two versions, involving psychological factors such as wastefulness.

4. The student gave no justification response.

Table 8.1 shows the percentage of people in each of the four categories for the two problems you tried in Demonstration 8.6. As you can see, students spread their answers fairly evenly across the four categories for the "drink on the beach" problem. Notice, though, that about one-quarter of them (27%) argued for a real, objective difference. Maybe the bottle had been sitting around the wretched grocery store for several years. In contrast, notice that no one argued for an objective difference between the two versions of the "calculator/jacket" problem. Instead, most believed the difference was merely subjective. They responded that it wouldn't seem worthwhile to save $5 on a $125 jacket; in contrast, $5 is a large percentage of the $15 calculator price. (Interestingly, these participants were unwittingly using Weber's law of psychophysics, which you learned about in Chapter 4.)

In other words, framing effects are different in different decision-making situations. In the "drink on the beach" problem, people bring their world knowledge to the problem. They believe that the two situations are objectively different. Given those premises, people *are* acting rationally. But are people making wise, rational decisions in the "calculator/jacket" problem? An economist would probably say no, from a purely dollars-and-cents standpoint. However, most psychologists would probably argue that these subjective, psychological factors may indeed play an important role, and we do not need to classify this behavior as irrational decision making.

Let's review how the framing effect operates. Background information can influence decisions; we do not make choices in a vacuum, devoid of knowledge about the world (Payne et al., 1992). In addition, the wording of the question can influence decisions. Finally, the framing effects are not uniform across situations; people have different justifications for their decisions, depending upon the specific nature of the decision.

This student might travel a distance to save $5 on a $15 calculator, but research on the framing effect suggests she wouldn't travel the same distance to save $5 on a $125 jacket.

Overconfidence About Decisions

In July 1988, the USS *Vincennes* was in the Persian Gulf. Its radar system detected an airplane taking off from an Iranian airport, flying directly toward the ship. Captain Will Rogers was faced with a decision: Was the unknown aircraft attacking his ship, or was it simply a civilian airplane? Captain Rogers decided to launch two missiles at the aircraft. As both Rogers and the rest of the world soon learned, the plane was only a civilian airline, and all 290 passengers aboard the plane died when the plane was shot down. As a panel of decision-making theorists pointed out, Captain Rogers had been overconfident about his original judgment (Bales, 1988). He failed to verify the characteristics of the plane and whether it was ascending or descending.

We saw earlier in this chapter that people often make less than ideal decisions. They use the availability, representativeness, and anchoring and adjustment heuristics too frequently, and they are influenced by the framing of the question. Given these sources of error, people should not be very confident about their decision-making skills. However, instead of being underconfident, people are typically *overconfident*. We are especially likely to be overconfident when the judgment is difficult, and when we are novices in a discipline, rather than experts (Keren, 1987; Plous, 1993; Soll, 1996).

Furthermore, we are more likely to be overconfident that the outcome we *favor* will occur, rather than an undesired result (Griffin & Varey, 1996). Also, students are overly optimistic about how long they will take to complete a project (Buehler et al., 1994). Interestingly, cross-cultural research shows that residents of a variety of Asian countries are much more overconfident than residents of the United States and Great Britain—though the explanation is not clear (Yates et al., 1996).

What are the reasons for people's overconfidence? One factor is that people are often unaware that their knowledge is based on very questionable assumptions (Carlson, 1995; Slovic et al., 1982). Also, we tend to notice evidence that supports our decision, and we ignore evidence that supports the options we have rejected (Baron, 1994; Dawes, 1988). In fact, we may have trouble even recalling those rejected options. If we cannot even recall the other options, we are likely to be overly confident that our decisions are correct (Gettys et al., 1986). The next time you need to make an important decision, ask yourself whether you are inappropriately confident that you are making the right choice!

In 1988, Captain Will Rogers of the USS Vincennes *decided to launch missiles at an airplane taking off from Iran, and 290 passengers were killed. Decision theorists have concluded that this error is an example of overconfidence in decision making.*

New Perspectives on Decision Making

So far, the material on decision making has provided little evidence for human competency as expressed in Theme 1. Especially as compared to our impressive perceptual and memory skills, we humans do not seem to be especially wise decision makers. We rely too heavily on three decision-making heuristics: availability, representativeness, and anchoring and adjustment. We are also plagued by both framing effects and overconfidence. Of course, we should remember that those three heuristics usually serve us well in our daily decision making, and some of the framing effects are either wise or rational.

In recent years, however, a group of more optimistic decision theorists has emerged. These theorists argue that people may not be perfectly rational decision makers, but the research hasn't tested them fairly using naturalistic settings (e.g., Cohen, 1993; Gigerenzer & Hoffrage, 1995; McClelland & Bolger, 1994). Specifically, they argue that people would perform better if psychologists eliminated "trick questions." They point out that many of the classical decision-making questions encourage decision makers to ignore important information like base rates. These optimistic decision theorists may have a point; the classic problems posed by researchers such as Kahneman and Tversky were specifically designed to highlight our weak points. However, the classic research also provides some useful advice. Yes, the heuristics usually serve us well. However, we can become more effective decision makers by realizing the limitations of these general strategies.

Some decision theorists are now moving beyond the straightforward decision problems that have been traditionally studied. Baruch Fischhoff (1996), for example, contrasts the simplicity of problems where the losses and gains are clear-cut, versus the richness of our real-world decisions. A teenager in the real world, for example, may need to decide between two activities for a weekend; she may need to consider her best friend's feelings, her cousin's feelings, her parents' wishes, and her own preferences. Fischhoff (1992) has also analyzed the decisions that women face when they must decide how to respond to sexual assault. Fischhoff's analysis highlights Theme 3's emphasis on complexity. If a woman responds by trying to fight back and attack a rapist, most men will back off. But some men will not, and no clear-cut rules can guide a woman's decision. (We will return to this important topic of sexual assault in Chapter 12.)

Critical Thinking Exercise 8.3

Write down your answers to the following questions about the framing effect and about overconfidence.

a. In Frisch's (1993) study, we noted that two independent judges classified the students' responses to decisions like the "drink on the beach" problem and the "calculator/jacket" problem. What precautions would need to be followed with respect to these judges?

b. The discussion of overconfidence in decision making pointed out that residents of Asian countries are more overconfident than residents of the United States and Great Britain. What kinds of potential confounding variables would you want to rule out before concluding that cross-cultural differences are found with respect to overconfidence in decision making?

So far, this chapter has focused on the way top-down processing and heuristics influence our thinking. When we solve problems and make decisions, we rely on our previous experiences, background knowledge, and some important heuristics. These factors generally help us think quickly and accurately. However, when we overuse previous experience, background knowledge, and heuristics, we make unnecessary errors. In Chapter 16, we'll discuss how these same factors operate in social cognition, when we make decisions about other people and when we try to explain their actions.

SECTION SUMMARY: *DECISION MAKING*

1. Decision making uses heuristics that usually produce correct decisions, but we may overuse them.

2. When we use the availability heuristic, we estimate frequency in terms of how easily examples come to mind. This heuristic is usually accurate, but it can be distorted by recency and familiarity.

3. When we use the representativeness heuristic, we make decisions on the basis of whether the sample we are judging looks appropriate. This heuristic is usually accurate, but people often pay too little attention to the base rate, and they may fall victim to the conjunction fallacy.

4. When we use the anchoring and adjustment heuristic, we typically rely too heavily on the anchor and

make inadequate adjustments when considering additional relevant information.

5. When we make decisions, we are often influenced by the decision frame—that is, by the background context and the question's wording; people provide different justifications for different categories of framing situations.

6. We are likely to be overconfident about the correctness of our decisions.

7. New trends in decision making include (a) the criticism that the classic decision-making problems underestimate people's skills, and (b) the argument that theorists should examine the complexities in people's real-life decisions.

INTELLIGENCE

In this final section of the chapter, we will discuss intelligence. Psychologists have developed numerous definitions for this controversial term. We'll use the general definition mentioned earlier: Intelligence is the ability to master the information and skills needed to succeed within a particular culture (Locurto, 1991). Table 8.2 shows some other characteristics commonly associated with intelligence. You'll notice that the two topics we discussed earlier in this chapter—problem solving and decision making—are therefore more specialized than this final topic of intelligence. Those two topics are typically explored by cognitive psychologists, who search for uniformities in human thought processes. In contrast, the psychologists who examine intelligence tend to focus on the individual differences emphasized in Theme 2. Intelligence includes a wide range of cognitive skills, including perception, learning, memory, knowledge, problem solving, and reasoning (Carroll, 1993; Scarr, 1984).

Let's begin our exploration of intelligence with a brief history of this discipline, as well as background on some current intelligence tests. Then we'll examine the research on mental retardation and giftedness, some theoretical controversies about intelligence, and broader conceptions of intelligence. Our last two topics are the subjects of heated debate: ethnic comparisons and gender comparisons in intelligence.

A Brief History of Intelligence Testing

The first forerunner of modern intelligence tests was constructed early in the twentieth century by the French psychologist Alfred Binet (pronounced "Bin-*nay*"). Binet had been appointed to design a test to identify slower learners in the Paris school system, so that they could receive special instruction. In the test developed by Binet and his colleagues in 1911, older children were given more challenging questions. For example, a 4-year-old might be expected to repeat a three-digit number, whereas an 8-year-old would be tested with a five-digit number (Rogers, 1995).

Testers in the United States welcomed Binet's ideas, and they soon translated and adapted these tests. For example, Lewis Terman, working at Stanford University, constructed the Stanford-Binet Intelligence Scale. When the United States entered

---

TABLE 8.2 Representative Characteristics of an Ideally Intelligent Person, as Judged by Experts in the Field of Intelligence

VERBAL INTELLIGENCE

Displays a good vocabulary
Reads with high comprehension
Displays curiosity

PROBLEM-SOLVING ABILITY

Able to apply knowledge to problems at hand
Makes good decisions
Poses problems in an optimal way

PRACTICAL INTELLIGENCE

Sizes up situations well
Determines how to achieve goals
Displays awareness of world around him or her

Source: Sternberg et al., 1981.

TABLE 8.3 The Wechsler Scales

ABBREVIATION	NAME	INTENDED AGE RANGE
WPPSI-R	Wechsler Preschool and Primary Scale of Intelligence—Revised	4–6
WISC-III	Wechsler Intelligence Scale for Children—Third Edition	6–16
WAIS-R	Wechsler Adult Intelligence Scale—Revised	Adults

World War I in 1917, the military needed a test that could efficiently classify more than 1 million recruits. Accordingly, army psychologists revised some existing tests so that they could be administered in large groups. So began the North American enchantment with intelligence testing; currently, U.S. children take between two and five standardized tests every year (Rogers, 1995).

Current Tests of Intelligence

An **aptitude test** is designed to predict future success on the basis of current performance. Aptitude tests are supposed to draw their material from a broad range of human experience, including information gained outside the classroom. Let's examine two tests of intelligence—the Wechsler scales, which are designed to measure aptitude, and the Scholastic Assessment Test (SAT), which measures both students' aptitude and their achievement in their high school courses.

The Wechsler Scales David Wechsler (pronounced "*Wex*-ler") was a young man during World War I, and he volunteered to help the Army score its intelligence tests (Fancher, 1985). His first task was to design an intelligence test specifically aimed at adults, because the previous tests were modifications of ones designed for children. At present, each of three Wechsler tests is specialized for a particular age range (see Table 8.3).

The **Wechsler scales** include both verbal and nonverbal (or performance) questions. Here are some typical items on the test designed for adults:

1. What does the word *unobtrusive* mean?

2. After you have heard this list of numbers, repeat them in order: 4, 7, 2, 9, 5, 1, 8, 3.

3. Arrange these five pictures in order, so that they tell a story.

4. Assemble these blocks so that they match the design in a booklet.

As with all standardized tests, the reliability and the validity of the Wechsler scales have been examined extensively. As you may recall from Chapter 2, **reliability** refers to the consistency of a person's scores. The reliability is typically very high for these tests. For example, the reliability for the entire WAIS-R is .97, which is very impressive (Kline, 1993).

As Chapter 2 pointed out, **validity** refers to a test's accuracy in measuring what it is supposed to measure (Meier, 1994). Validity studies of the Wechsler scales show satisfactory results, but nothing as impressive as the reliability studies. For example, WISC-III scores are correlated approximately .70 with achievement in elementary school (Rattan & Rattan, 1987).

Intelligence tests like the Wechsler scales yield an **intelligence quotient (IQ),** which is calculated by consulting norms that assign a score of 100 to a person whose score is exactly average for a particular age group. (As you may recall from Chapter 2, **norms** are the standards established for a given test.) Higher and lower IQ scores are

This child is taking the WISC-III.

DEMONSTRATION 8.7 The Scholastic Assessment Test

Answer each of the questions below, which are sample items from the mathematical and verbal portions of the SAT. The answers can be found at the end of the chapter, on Page 288.

1. If the average of four numbers is 37 and the average of two of these numbers is 33, what is the average of the other two numbers?

2. To which of the following is $\frac{a}{b} - \frac{a}{c}$ equal?

   (A) $\frac{a}{b-c}$　　　(B) $\frac{1}{b-c}$

   (C) $\frac{1}{bc}$　　　(D) $\frac{ab-ac}{bc}$

   (E) $\frac{ac-ab}{bc}$

3. Choose the pair that *best* fits the meaning of the sentence as a whole: When Harvard astronomer Cecilia Payne was _____ professor in 1956, it marked an important step in the reduction of _____ practices within the scientific establishment.

   (A) accepted for . . . disciplinary
   (B) promoted to . . . discriminatory
   (C) honored as . . . unbiased
   (D) denounced as . . . critical
   (E) considered for . . . hierarchical

4. Select the lettered pair that *best* expresses a relationship similar to that expressed in the original pair.
   COMPOSER: SYMPHONY::
   (A) playwright: rehearsal
   (B) actor: comedy
   (C) conductor: orchestra
   (D) director: movie
   (E) poet: sonnet

assigned on the basis of where a person's score falls in comparison to the average. Most intelligence tests are designed so that the standard deviation (the measure of variability discussed in Chapter 2) is established as 15 points. Thus, an IQ of 115 tells us that a person scored exactly one standard deviation above the mean (100 + 15).

The Scholastic Assessment Test　Whereas the various Wechsler scales are designed to test several age groups and serve several purposes, the **Scholastic Assessment Test (SAT)** is designed specifically to measure aptitude for college work. Try Demonstration 8.7 to familiarize yourself with this test, in case you did not take it, or to refresh your memory, in case you did. Incidentally, if you took the test before 1994, you knew the SAT as the *Scholastic Aptitude Test*.

The new version of the SAT includes an essay section and a mathematics section in which students must supply the answers (as in Question 1 from Demonstration 8.7). However, an important problem remains on the reading comprehension portion. Students can guess the correct answer with reasonable accuracy, even without reading the appropriate passages. This criticism applies both to the original Scholastic Aptitude Test and to the new Scholastic Assessment Test (Katz & Lautenschlager, 1994; Katz et al., 1990). Unfortunately, then, this portion of the test has a validity problem, because it is measuring something other than the reading ability it is supposed to measure (Katz, 1996).

The Two Extremes of Intelligence

When we examine the concept of intelligence, we need to consider those people whose scores on intelligence tests are either extremely low or extremely high. Let's therefore direct our attention to individuals with mental retardation and to individuals who are gifted.

Mental Retardation　The essential features of **mental retardation** are the following:

1. Intellectual functioning that is significantly below average, with an IQ score of 70–75 or less;

2. Difficulty in two or more skill areas such as communication, self-care, home living, social skills, and health/safety;

3. Onset prior to age 18 (Turkington, 1993).

Notice, then, that individuals who receive low scores on standardized intelligence tests may not be classified as mentally retarded if they can feed and dress themselves and if their communicative and social skills are adequate (Sternberg, 1990b; Turkington, 1993). This relatively new approach eliminates the previous emphasis on categories such as mild, moderate, and severe retardation. It also emphasizes that a valid assessment should consider cultural and linguistic diversity (Turkington, 1993).

According to one estimate, more than 1,000 causes of mental retardation have been identified so far (Azar, 1995a). The causes traditionally have been divided into two general categories: organic and cultural-familial. Between 25% and 50% of retarded individuals have **organic retardation,** traceable to genetic disorders such as Down syndrome (see Chapter 3) or to physical damage to the brain (Zigler & Hodapp, 1991). Some causes of brain damage include infectious disease, medical complications from a premature delivery, and fetal alcohol syndrome. As we'll see in Chapter 10, fetal alcohol syndrome is a result of a mother's heavy drinking during pregnancy.

Between 50% and 75% of people with mental retardation have **cultural-familial retardation;** their disorder has no clear organic cause. They may be retarded because they received fewer genes for high intelligence from their parents, because they grew up in an economically impoverished situation, or a combination of these two factors (Zigler & Hodapp, 1991).

Giftedness   No firm cutoff separates the gifted from other people. However, many school programs specify an IQ above 130, roughly the top 2% of the population (Davis & Rimm, 1989; Gottfried et al., 1994).

We saw that the current definition of retardation specified other skill deficits, in addition to a low IQ. Many argue, similarly, that the definition for **the gifted** should include not only an IQ above 130 but also exceptional creativity, leadership skills, or artistic ability (Webb & Kleine, 1993). Others also specify that people are gifted only if they are highly motivated to complete projects (Khatena, 1992; Renzulli, 1986). As you will remember from our discussion earlier in the chapter, creativity is extremely difficult to measure. Leadership, artistic ability, and motivation are also elusive (Khatena, 1992). Consequently, schools typically assign children to a gifted program on the basis of IQ and teachers' judgments of these other characteristics.

Gifted individuals are particularly exceptional in the kind of planning and organizing required for original projects.

As you might guess, gifted people tend to be exceptional with respect to metacognition (Jackson & Butterfield, 1986). This ability to plan and to monitor progress is especially useful during adulthood. In life outside of a school setting, success often depends on creating and pursuing an original idea, rather than simply doing a task that has been assigned.

Critical Thinking Exercise 8.4

Write down your answers to the following questions about current intelligence tests and the two extremes of intelligence.

a. Suppose that a neighbor is outraged to learn that SAT scores at the local high school have fallen significantly during the last 30 years. Suppose that you know that only 30% of the graduating seniors went to college 30 years ago, but 60% now go to college. How can you reassure your neighbor that the school's intellectual level isn't dropping?

b. Suppose that several researchers are tracking the success of a group of gifted high school students. They send out a questionnaire 10 years after graduation. Virtually all of those who respond have become successful in their chosen careers. Why should the researchers be hesitant about claiming that children classified as gifted continue to be successful individuals?

Theoretical Controversies About Intelligence

We have outlined how intelligence is measured and how mental retardation and giftedness are defined. Let's now explore three theoretical issues that have been important in the research that has been conducted on intelligence. These issues are the nature-nurture question, the stability-change question, and the general-specific question.

The Nature-Nurture Question   We first raised the nature-nurture question in Chapter 3 in connection with genetics. We'll consider it again in Chapter 10, in connection with children's characteristics. Let's now examine the research on the nature-nurture question with respect to intelligence.

A central concept in the nature-nurture controversy is called heritability. This concept focuses on the variability among all IQ scores, which is impressively large. Specifically, **heritability** estimates how much of the variability found in the scores of a group of people is due to heredity (or nature) and how much is due to environment (or nurture). For example, most current research on IQ scores produces heritability indexes between 50% and 70% (Carroll, 1992; Locurto, 1991; Plomin & Rende, 1991; R. J. Rose, 1995). In other words, these studies suggest that between 50% and 70% of all the variability in the scores in these samples can be traced to hereditary factors. These estimates are supported by adoption studies, in which the IQs of adopted children are more strongly correlated with the IQs of their biological parents than with the IQs of their adoptive parents (Turkheimer, 1991).

If the heritability indexes typically range from 50% to 70%, then that means that the percentage of variability due to environment ranges between 30% and 50%. However, psychologists now acknowledge that these environmental factors are subtle. For example, infants differ soon after birth in their personal characteristics. As these infants grow older, adults treat them according to their individual strengths (Locurto, 1991). One child might be encouraged to express artistic talents, whereas another might develop an interest in science. This explanation may account for some of the differences among siblings raised in the same environment.

The Stability-Change Question   Would the smartest students in your fourth-grade class still be intellectually exceptional today? Would the slowest learners still be

To some extent, children's own characteristics determine which interests they pursue in their environment. Some of the variability in IQ scores can be explained because children create different environments for themselves.

Lenny Ng received a perfect 800 on the math SAT exam . . . when he was 10 years old. He received straight A's throughout high school, and he then enrolled at Harvard. The data on stability in intelligence would lead us to predict an extremely high math score if he were to take the math GRE after completing college.

considered slow? In Chapters 10 and 11, we will consider whether personality remains stable through childhood and adulthood. Here, we apply the same question to intelligence.

In general, intelligence test scores remain fairly stable. For instance, intelligence tests administered at age 7 were correlated .74 with test scores at age 13 (Moffitt et al., 1993).

Suppose that you decide to pursue graduate study, and you take the Graduate Record Examination (GRE). A study of about 23,000 students who took both the SAT and the GRE showed that the correlations were .86 for both the verbal and the mathematical sections (Angoff & Johnson, 1988). In other words you can predict your GRE score fairly accurately from your SAT score. In summary, various measures of intelligence seem to show remarkable stability, rather than dramatic change.

The General-Specific Question   One major theoretical argument dominated the early history of intelligence testing, and it still persists today: Does intelligence consist of a single core factor or many separate, unrelated abilities? Think about several intelligent people you know. Are they all intelligent in the same way, or do they have different strengths? Is one person highly verbal, another a whiz at math, and another skilled at fixing mechanical things?

The general-specific question was addressed by Charles Spearman (1904, 1923). He argued that a single general mental ability, which he called the **g factor,** underlies all the varying kinds of intelligence. Spearman did acknowledge that individuals may excel in certain specific areas—such as language, mathematics, or mechanical aptitude. Still, he argued that a person who was exceptional in one area was also likely to be strong in other areas.

As we approach the twenty-first century, an increasing number of contemporary psychologists favor the "specific" side of the general-specific question. They argue that a single factor, *g*, could not adequately capture all the diverse skills that comprise human intelligence (e.g., Ceci, 1994, 1996; Horn, 1989; Perkins, 1995; Sternberg et al., 1995). We'll now explore this perspective in more detail, as we look at alternative theories of intelligence.

Broader Views of Intelligence

So far, our exploration of intelligence has emphasized traditional views of this concept, based primarily on tests that assess verbal and mathematical skills. However, cognitive psychologists have inspired researchers to examine broader definitions of intelligence that consider skills in artistic and interpersonal areas. Let's consider one of these approaches, which has been proposed by Howard Gardner.

Howard Gardner argues that traditional intelligence tests assess only the standard kinds of intelligence. In contrast, **Gardner's theory of multiple intelligences** proposes seven different components of intelligence. This theory includes three standard areas: (1) language ability, (2) logical-mathematical thinking, and (3) spatial thinking. Gardner's theory also includes four other distinct abilities: (4) musical thinking, (5) bodily kinesthetic thinking, (6) intrapersonal thinking, and (7) interpersonal thinking (Gardner, 1983, 1988, 1993).

We are accustomed to individual differences in the first three areas. However, think of people you know who shine in the other four skills—perhaps someone who improvises on the piano (music) or a person who excels in sports (kinesthetic). Someone skilled in *intra*personal thinking has a highly accurate understanding of herself or himself. Someone skilled in *inter*personal thinking has an unusual understanding of other people.

Psychologists have become especially intrigued with emotional intelligence, a skill that is part of interpersonal thinking (e.g., Goleman, 1995; Mayer & Salovey, 1995, 1997). **Emotional intelligence** includes the ability to perceive emotion accurately, to understand it, and to express it. We'll explore this concept in Chapter 12.

Gardner's theory of multiple intelligences specifies several different kinds of intelligence. For example, language ability is necessary to write a paper (left). Interpersonal thinking is critical when comforting a troubled friend (right).

Gardner's ideas about multiple intelligences have aroused interest among both psychologists and educators (e.g., Kantrowitz, 1993). His approach invites us to examine whether intelligence should be defined only in terms of the skills traditionally emphasized in school. Perhaps we should also include other human talents that may be especially valuable in real-life settings.

Ethnic-Group Comparisons in Intelligence

Researchers have discovered that the scores of Mexican, Puerto Rican, and other Hispanic children are an average of 10 to 12 points lower than the scores of European American children on standardized intelligence tests (Dunn, 1987; Neisser et al., 1996). Furthermore, the scores of Black children are typically an average of 10 to 15 points below those of European American children (Brody, 1992; Mackenzie, 1984; Neisser et al., 1996).

As we discuss these ethnic-group comparisons in IQ scores, we need to keep reminding ourselves about an important part of Theme 2: The differences within any group of humans are larger than the differences between groups. For example, that 10- to 15-point difference between groups translates to a difference of 1 standard deviation or less. This number is dwarfed by the fact that the variability *within* any group is about 10 standard deviations (Brody, 1992). Let us first briefly examine the comparison between Hispanics and European Americans. Then we'll discuss in somewhat greater detail the more extensive research on the Black-White comparison.

Comparing the Test Scores of Hispanics and European Americans   You can probably guess some of the reasons that the scores of Hispanic students are somewhat lower than those of European Americans. First of all, the Hispanic students may not be perfectly bilingual—an obvious disadvantage on a test that relies heavily on the English language (Costantino, 1992; Geisinger, 1992; Neisser et al., 1996).

A further problem with the research that reported the 10- to 12-point difference is that it did not control for socioeconomic class (Mercer, 1988; Willig, 1988). Socioeconomic class is correlated about .30 with IQ, so this is an important confounding variable. In most cases, too, the schools that European American students and Hispanic students attend are not comparable. When schools like the one shown in Figure 8.4 are successful in inspiring and teaching Hispanic students, these students are high in achievement motivation and they can receive outstanding intelligence-test scores (Jarboe, 1990).

Comparing the Test Scores of Blacks and Whites   In 1994, psychologist Richard Herrnstein and political scientist Charles Murray published a book called *The Bell Curve: Intelligence and Class Structure in American Life.* Most researchers conduct their studies and then publish their conclusions in scientific

FIGURE 8.4

At El Paso's Cathedral High School, Mexican American students learn that academic subjects should be valued, and successful older students can serve as role models.

journals; other researchers with expertise in the specific discipline must agree that the article is worthwhile before it will be published (Dorfman, 1995). In contrast, Herrnstein and Murray (1994) decided to publish their work in a book intended for general readers. As a result, many North American readers accepted the conclusions of *The Bell Curve,* without understanding why most psychologists disagreed with that viewpoint.

Unfortunately, *The Bell Curve* simply repeated many of the arguments made 25 years earlier by Jensen (1969)—arguments that numerous psychologists had widely disputed (e.g., Brody, 1992; Fancher, 1985). One of the principle suggestions in *The Bell Curve* was that ethnic-group differences in intelligence could be traced to genetic factors.

We cannot summarize all the arguments that have been presented both for and against the genetic interpretation of ethnic differences in intelligence. However, here are some of the major issues that must be considered:

1. Blacks are much more likely than Whites to live in poverty. The environmental disadvantages of poverty are well known. These include poor nutrition, inadequate prenatal care, poorly funded schools, and lack of books and other intellectual resources (Neisser et al., 1996). All these factors widen the gap between White children and Black children.

2. Black individuals are more likely than White individuals to experience racism and other forms of discrimination (Brody, 1992). The cumulative effects of these experiences can have a major impact on people's self-esteem and performance (Brody, 1992; Neisser et al., 1996; Steele, 1997).

3. In general, research has shown that Black children who are adopted and reared in upper-middle-class White homes have IQ scores that are very close to the IQ scores of White children reared in upper-middle-class White homes (Brody, 1992; Nisbett, 1995; Scarr & Weinberg, 1976). These data suggest that environmental factors are more important than biological factors.

In summary, psychologists still have no clear-cut explanation for the ethnic-group differences in IQ scores. However, genetic explanations seem less likely than differences in language, income level, discrimination, and other environmental factors (Brody, 1992). We also need to reemphasize a point made earlier: The differences between ethnic groups are much smaller than the differences within any single ethnic group.

Gender Comparisons in Intelligence

One day I was sitting in the dentist's chair, my mouth open wide and assorted contraptions protruding at various angles. On the other side of a partition, I heard another patient saying to the hygienist, "But it's a well-known fact that girls learn to talk sooner than boys." If I had not been concerned about my dubious credibility in these circumstances, I would have jumped up from the chair and raced in to say, "No, actually, a meta-analysis done in 1988 shows that there is no real gender difference!"

The research on gender comparisons in intelligence is extremely complex, consistent with Theme 3 (Halpern, 1996b). However, consistent with Theme 2, we can conclude that for all these cognitive skills, the differences *within* either gender are much larger than the differences *between* the two genders (Hyde, 1996b).

In many areas, researchers have found no consistent gender differences. For example, females and males do not systematically differ in tests of overall ability, such as IQ (Bishop et al., 1990; McGuinness, 1985; Singleton, 1987; Stumpf, 1995). Gender differences are rarely found in memory performance, problem solving, and reasoning performance (Feingold, 1993; Kimura, 1992; Maccoby & Jacklin, 1974). Keep these many similarities in mind as we explore gender comparisons in verbal, spatial, and mathematical abilities. As you will see, the research in all these areas frequently uses the **meta-analysis** technique, the systematic statistical method for synthesizing the results from numerous studies on a given topic.

Verbal Ability   Research shows occasional gender differences in some kinds of verbal abilities. For example, females score higher on some spelling tasks, and males score higher on some analogies tests (Halpern & Wright, 1996; Stumpf, 1995). However, Hyde and Linn (1988) conducted a meta-analysis of research—involving a total of 1,418,899 people—that showed no overall gender differences in verbal ability. Other research has also shown no gender differences in reading disabilities, when these disabilities are objectively measured (Shaywitz et al., 1990).

Spatial Ability   Try Demonstration 8.8 before reading further. When we examine gender comparisons in spatial ability, the results are more complicated. Part of the problem is that spatial ability really consists of several different components (Halpern & Wright, 1996; Linn & Petersen, 1986).

One kind of ability is spatial visualization, for example, locating a particular object that is hidden in a larger design. Meta-analyses show no gender differences on spatial visualization tasks (Feingold, 1988a; Linn & Petersen, 1986).

Another kind of spatial ability requires mental rotation, as you can see in Demonstration 8.8. Gender differences on mental-rotation are larger than for any other cognitive task (Linn & Petersen, 1986; Voyer et al., 1995). However, in a typical study, the gender differences still account for only 16% of the variability (Sanders et al., 1982). Also, Favreau (1993) points out that significant differences often arise from studies in which most males and females receive similar scores. The statistically significant gender differences can be almost entirely traced to a few females with very slow mental rotation speeds.

Mathematical Ability   Of all the topics discussed in terms of gender differences, mathematics has attracted the most widespread attention. Most of my students are surprised to learn that the only area in which males consistently perform better than females is on the math section of the SAT, where males' scores average about 40 points higher than females' scores (Shea, 1994).

Should we be concerned about gender differences on these SAT scores? A number of researchers say that we should be alarmed. Specifically, the math SAT *underpredicts* how well females will do in their college math courses (Bridgeman & Wendler, 1991; Chipman, 1994; Linn, 1992; Wainer & Steinberg, 1992). For example, if Jane and Bob receive identical grades in college math courses, we can go back to

This boy and girl are probably similar in their ability to solve problems. Here they are trying to design a weight-bearing structure of balsa wood for a school competition.

DEMONSTRATION 8.8   A Test of Mental Rotation (Spatial Ability)

Try these examples from a test of spatial ability. The answers appear at the end of the chapter, on Page 288.

If you mentally rotate the figure on the left, which of the five figures on the right would you obtain?

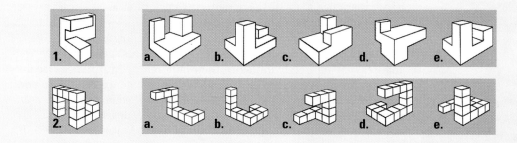

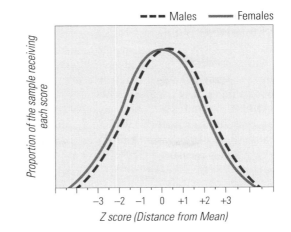

--- Males — Females

Proportion of the sample receiving each score

-3 -2 -1 0 +1 +2 +3
Z score (Distance from Mean)

FIGURE 8.5

Performance of females and males on all mathematics tests except for the SAT.

their records and check their math SATs: Bob's SAT score is likely to have been about 33 points higher than Jane's. To be equitable, then, some educators argue that colleges should add about 33 points to females' math SAT scores (Betz, 1994a).

Ironically, the math SAT is the math test that counts the most in people's lives, and yet it is the only test on which gender differences are prominent. On most standardized math tests, males and females receive similar scores. The most dramatic illustration of this similarity comes from a meta-analysis conducted by Hyde and her coauthors (1990). They analyzed all math tests except the SAT, a sample of more than 2 million people. Figure 8.5 shows that the scores of females and males are nearly identical.

In sum, we have seen that females receive lower scores than males on the math SATs. We have also seen that females and males receive similar scores on other standardized math tests. In contrast, however, females fairly consistently receive higher grades than males in mathematics courses and in statistics courses (Brooks, 1987; Kimball, 1989; Smith & Walker, 1988). Ironically, female's superior performance in terms of grades is not well publicized.

Some of the gender differences in spatial ability can be traced to the fact that males have more experience with video games, which are highly spatial.

Explaining the Results   Numerous theories have been developed to explain gender differences in cognitive abilities. As the years pass and more research accumulates, I'm becoming increasingly convinced that we may not have many gender differences substantial enough to require explaining. Perhaps the only differences in ability involve mental rotation and the kind of math problems that appear on the SAT. However, none of these differences is very large or very consistent. Some researchers have proposed explanations involving biological factors such as lateralization, hormones, or genetics (e.g., Geary, 1995; Halpern, 1992; Voyer, 1996). However, biological explanations may be more powerful than we need in order to account for such minimal differences.

Some social explanations have research support. For example, people who have participated more often in spatial activities, such as video games, score higher on tests of spatial ability. As you might expect, males are more likely than females to have experience with spatial activities (Crawford et al., 1995; Law et al., 1993; Subrahmanyam & Greenfield, 1994). Furthermore, males tend to take more courses in mathematics than females do, which may well contribute to the gender differences (Crawford et al., 1995; Eccles, 1989). Also, parents' gender stereotypes about math abilities may indirectly influence their children's performance (Jacobs, 1991). Complex gender differences in attitudes and self-confidence could also contribute to differences in test scores (Matlin, 1996a; Mura, 1987). The gender differences have been changing significantly within just the last few decades, which argues against a biological explanation (Feingold, 1988a; Murray, 1995; Voyer et al., 1995). It will be interesting to see what the meta-analyses reveal in the twenty-first century!

Critical Thinking Exercise 8.5

Write down your answers to the following questions about ethnic and gender comparisons in intelligence.

a. In Herrnstein and Murray's (1994) book, *The Bell Curve*, the authors suggest that ethnicity actually *causes* social problems. For example, they point out that African Americans are more than twice as likely to have been on welfare, compared to European Americans (in samples that have similar IQs). Although the authors expressed some cautions, the popular press often simplified the argument. Many newspaper articles therefore suggested that being Black, itself, was causally related to being on welfare. How would you criticize this conclusion?

b. Based on the information presented here, what would you conclude about the validity of the SAT, with respect to gender?

SECTION SUMMARY: *INTELLIGENCE*

1. Alfred Binet designed the first forerunner of contemporary intelligence tests, and these tests were adapted for use by the military in World War I.

2. The Wechsler scales are used for testing both verbal and nonverbal intelligence in children and adults; the SAT test is designed to assess aptitude for college work.

3. Two general categories of retardation are organic and cultural-familial retardation. Gifted individuals typically excel at metacognitive skills.

4. Both nature and nurture are important determinants of intelligence; heritability indexes currently range between 50% and 70%; to some extent children's own characteristics determine how adults will encourage their unique intellectual interests.

5. Intelligence tests—such as IQ and the SAT/GRE—show impressive stability over time.

6. Some psychologists, such as Spearman, propose that a single general mental ability *(g)* underlies intelligence; in contrast, most current psychologists favor the "specific" side of the general-specific question.

7. Howard Gardner's theory of multiple intelligences proposes seven specific kinds of intelligence, including skills not measured on traditional tests.

8. Differences between ethnic groups in intelligence are much smaller than differences within any ethnic group; discrepancies between Hispanic and European American IQ scores can probably be traced to differences in English fluency, social class, and the quality of schools.

9. The discrepancy between Black and White IQ scores can probably be traced to environmental factors; the controversial book *The Bell Curve* failed to emphasize these factors, and it overemphasized genetic factors.

10. Gender similarities are found in IQ, memory, problem solving, and reasoning; males and females are also similar in verbal ability, some spatial tasks, and most mathematics tests. Males excel on mental rotation tasks and math SATs, whereas females excel in math grades.

REVIEW QUESTIONS

1. An important theme running through the first two sections of this chapter is that people tend to rely on a small number of general rules. Explain how people use heuristics in problem solving and decision making.

2. At the beginning of the chapter, *cognition* was defined as the acquisition, storage, transformation, and use of knowledge. Explain how each of the three topics in this chapter—problem solving, decision making, and intelligence—fits this definition.

3. The section on problem solving discussed methods of representing a problem. Think of a problem that could be effectively represented by each of the following methods: matrices, graphs, and visual images.

4. How do expertise, functional fixedness, mental set, the analogy approach, and creativity all illustrate the use (or misuse) of top-down processing?

5. Which decision-making heuristic does each of the following examples illustrate? (a) You try to estimate how long it will take to read a chapter in another textbook, based on the fastest rate at which you can read a chapter in this textbook. (b) You see a bearded professor wearing a hand-woven jacket, and you decide that he is a member of the art department (which has 5 members), rather than a member of one of the science departments (which have a total of 40 members). (c) Someone asks you how common amnesia is, and you reply that it is quite common, based on your recall of recent soap opera plots.

6. This chapter contains some practical advice about problem solving and decision making. List 10 to 12 practical tips that you could use to make your thinking processes more effective.

7. Based on the information in this chapter, how would you define intelligence? How has your definition changed since you began reading this chapter?

8. What are the issues in the nature-nurture, stability-change, and general-specific questions? What are the general conclusions on these issues with respect to intelligence?

9. Suppose you are part of a team designing a test for giftedness that will decide which children should be enrolled in gifted programs. Describe how you would measure the test's reliability and validity. (You may want to review Pages 61–63 in Chapter 2 for specific details on measurement techniques.)

10. Probably the two most controversial topics in the field of intelligence concern ethnic-group comparisons and gender comparisons. Summarize the data on both issues, making sure that you acknowledge the complexity of the findings. What kinds of intelligence have typically been examined in this research?

NEW TERMS

thinking (p. 258)
intelligence (p. 258)
cognition (p. 258)
top-down processing (p. 258)
bottom-up processing (p. 258)
heuristics (p. 258)
problem solving (p. 258)
matrix (p. 259)
means-ends analysis (p. 260)
analogy approach (p. 260)
surface features (p. 261)
structural features (p. 261)
expertise (p. 261)
novices (p. 262)
metacognition (p. 262)
mindlessness (p. 263)
functional fixedness (p. 263)
mental set (p. 263)
creativity (p. 263)
decision making (p. 265)
availability heuristic (p. 266)
representativeness heuristic (p. 268)

base rate (p. 268)
conjunction fallacy (p. 269)
anchoring and adjustment heuristic (p. 270)
framing effect (p. 271)
aptitude test (p. 276)
Wechsler scales (p. 276)
reliability (p. 276)
validity (p. 276)
intelligence quotient (IQ) (p. 276)
norms (p. 276)
Scholastic Assessment Test (SAT) (p. 277)
mental retardation (p. 277)
organic retardation (p. 278)
cultural-familial retardation (p. 278)
the gifted (p. 278)
heritability (p. 279)
g factor (p. 280)
Gardner's theory of multiple intelligences (p. 280)
emotional intelligence (p. 280)
meta-analysis (p. 283)

Recommended Readings

Geisinger, K. F. (Ed.). (1992). *Psychological testing of Hispanics.* Washington, DC: American Psychological Association. This book is a good model for the kind of systematic, thoughtful analysis that should be written when examining issues about ethnic groups. Topics include legal issues, biases, test design, testing in industry, and testing for educational purposes.

Matlin, M. W. (1998). *Cognition* (4th ed.). Fort Worth, TX: Harcourt Brace. This mid-level textbook includes chapters on problem solving, creativity, and decision making, as well as related topics such as mental imagery and logical reasoning.

Neisser, U., et al. (1996). Intelligence: Knowns and unknowns. *American Psychologist, 51,* 77–101. This lengthy article is written by 11 experts in the discipline of intelligence; it explores the concept of intelligence, the nature of testing, genetic and environmental factors, and group differences.

Plous, S. (1993). *The psychology of judgment and decision making.* New York: McGraw-Hill. This interesting textbook includes chapters on each of the decision-making heuristics discussed in the present chapter. It also examines other perspectives on decision making.

Answers to Demonstrations

Demonstration 8.1

Ms. Anderson has mononucleosis, and she is in Room 104. To solve this problem you can set up a matrix with the names of the patients and the room numbers listed. Then read through the list of statements. In three cases, we find out which patient is in which room; this information allows us to place the word *yes* (indicated in red on the chart below) in three locations in the matrix, and to eliminate these rooms and these people from the "still uncertain" list. (A blue check on the chart indicates we have taken care of these rooms and people.) We can also note the disease (in green) where appropriate. Because Ms. Jones has heart disease, she cannot be the patient with mononucleosis in Room 104; she must be in Room 103. Therefore, Ms. Anderson must be the patient with mononucleosis in Room 104.

	(asthma)			(mono-nucleosis)	
	101	102	103	104	105
Anderson	✔	✔			✔
(heart disease) Jones	✔	✔			✔
(gall bladder?) Green	✔	✔	✔	✔	yes
(tuberculosis) Smith	✔	yes	✔	✔	✔
(gall bladder?) Thomas	yes	✔	✔	✔	✔

Demonstration 8.2

In the Hobbits-and-Orcs problem, let R represent the right bank and L represent the left bank. Here are the steps in the solution:

1. Move 2 Orcs, R to L.
2. Move 1 Orc, L to R.
3. Move 2 Orcs, R to L.
4. Move 1 Orc, L to R.
5. Move 2 Hobbits, R to L.
6. Move 1 Orc, 1 Hobbit, L to R.
7. Move 2 Hobbits, R to L.
8. Move 1 Orc, L to R.
9. Move 2 Orcs, R to L.
10. Move 1 Orc, L to R.
11. Move 2 Orcs, R to L.

Demonstration 8.3

The solution involves attaching part of the matchbox to the wall, then melting some wax to attach the candle to the platform.

Demonstration 8.7

1. 41;   2. E;   3. B;   4. E

Demonstration 8.8

1. c;   2. d.

ANSWERS TO CRITICAL THINKING EXERCISES

Exercise 8.1

a. The problem is that the data are correlational, because students were not randomly assigned to groups. Those who chose to use a matrix representation were more successful than those who chose other representations. In other words, students self-selected their own conditions. It may be that those who spontaneously used the matrix approach are more talented problem solvers (especially because this is a sophisticated approach). We cannot conclude that teaching students the matrix approach would improve their problem solving. After all, correlation does not imply causation.

b. Some of the dependent variables could be the amount of time required to solve a problem, the number of problems solved in a certain time period, the accuracy of the answers, and the number of false starts before reaching a correct solution. For problems that do not have a single "right" answer, we could have experienced judges rate the quality of the solutions. As you might imagine, the nature of the dependent variable might have an important effect on the conclusions the researcher draws.

Exercise 8.2

a. When we use the availability heuristic and try to think of examples of a general category, we typically collect a biased sample. Specifically, that sample is more likely to include recent examples than examples from long ago. That sample is also more likely to include familiar examples (e.g., examples publicized by the media) rather than unfamiliar examples.

b. In fact, these concepts are very similar. When we use the representativeness heuristic, we should generally think that an example that looks representative of the population from which it is drawn is indeed highly likely to occur. As we know from research methods, we should strive for representative samples. The problem in decision making is that we are *so* impressed by representativeness that we ignore other vitally important information, such as base rate. We are also so impressed by representativeness that we violate statistical rules by committing the conjunction fallacy.

Exercise 8.3

a. These judges should not be informed about the hypotheses that Frisch had devised. The operational definitions for the four categories of responses would also need to be crystal clear. The judges should indeed work independently of one another. Then the researchers would need to check their sets of responses to make certain that the two judges agreed with one another on a high percentage of the students' responses.

b. It's quite possible that the two kinds of populations differed with respect to characteristics such as the following: family income, area of study, general intelligence, and gender. We would also want to make certain that the same problems were used in the two kinds of cultures and that the translations of those problems were equivalent.

Exercise 8.4

a. Thirty years ago, the 30% who might have taken the SATs were probably among the best students at their high schools, so their SAT scores were high. Now that 60% are attending college, this group includes students who are receiving average SAT scores. If you just looked at the SAT scores of this year's top 30%, these scores would probably match those of 30 years ago (Rotberg, 1995).

b. The problem is that many people probably failed to return the questionnaire. We would expect the more successful individuals to be more likely to return the questionnaire. The researchers really cannot generalize from this selected sample to the entire original sample of gifted students (Stanley, 1995).

Exercise 8.5

a. One problem is that several confounding variables were ignored. For example, even when we equate for IQ, African Americans have had fewer opportunities for advanced education, so they may not have the educational background to apply for certain jobs. Another problem is that the argument ignores discrimination based on ethnicity (a topic we'll explore in Chapter 16). Employers may be less likely to hire African Americans, even when they are well qualified. Furthermore, African Americans may be less likely to live in communities where there are many job openings.

b. We said that a test is valid if it measures what it is supposed to measure. If the SAT is supposed to measure how well a student will do in college, it's making low estimates for females' performance. With respect to gender, the SAT has a validity problem.

LANGUAGE AND CONVERSATION

UNDERSTANDING LANGUAGE

Speech Perception

Understanding and Meaning

Reading

PRODUCING LANGUAGE

Speech Planning

Nonverbal Communication

In Depth: Bilingualism

The Chimp-Language Controversy

SOCIAL ASPECTS OF LANGUAGE

Listeners' Background Knowledge

Conversational Interactions

Gender Comparisons in Language and Communication

Gender-Biased Language

CHAPTER 9

For several years during the 1970s, a very unusual student was studying at Columbia University, although he was not taking any formal classes. This student was named Nim Chimpsky, after the famous linguist Noam Chomsky, and in fact he was a chimpanzee. Nim was part of a project, initiated by Herbert Terrace, which was designed to see whether chimpanzees could be taught to communicate using sign language (Terrace, 1979). Some Columbia classrooms were equipped to serve as a nursery school, and a large number of teachers were hired to teach Nim sign language.

On a typical day, Nim would arrive in the classroom, and his teacher would sign to him, "Hang up your coat." Nim would respond appropriately. The teacher would continue to sign throughout the morning activities. When she signed, "Time to eat," Nim would enthusiastically make the *eat* sign with his own hand. (Banana pancakes were a special favorite.) The above photo shows Nim signing *hug*, another favorite activity. Lessons were designed to seem as much like play as possible. For instance, a bag of toys might contain a new surprise. The teacher and Nim would name each object as it emerged from the bag—an orange, a puppet, a mirror, and a shoe. If Nim had trouble producing the sign, his teacher would help by molding his hands appropriately. Nim also had time for play, and his most frequent three-sign combination was "Play me Nim." By the time the project was finished, about four years later, Nim had learned to produce 125 different signs, and he could combine words into short phrases (Michel, 1980; Terrace, 1979). The researchers had recorded more than 20,000 of Nim's short phrases, and they were ready to be analyzed.

Terrace had expected the analysis would demonstrate that chimpanzees could produce language that was remarkably like human language. Disappointingly, his analysis revealed that Nim often simply repeated the signs that his teachers had just produced. Young children, in contrast, are much more likely to produce spontaneous language. Also, Nim often interrupted the signed conversations with his teachers, whereas children are quite skilled at taking turns (Candland, 1993). Nim's "sentences" also remained very short. In contrast, children's sentences quickly lengthen from two words into long streams of conversation. As Terrace concluded, "It would be premature to conclude that a chimpanzee's combinations show the same structure evident in the sentences of a child" (Terrace, 1979, p. 221).

Researchers who study language cannot agree on the definition of this important term (Wallman, 1992). However, most would agree that Nim's communications did not meet the criteria. Yes, he could use symbols to refer to concepts. However, Nim's 125 signs are not in the realm of humans' word mastery. The average college-educated North American has a vocabulary in the range of 75,000 to 100,000 words (Wingfield & Titone, 1998). Also, Nim did not seem to have an abstract set of rules for producing new phrases. In contrast, humans can produce a virtually infinite number of novel sentences they have never heard before (Bickerton, 1995). For example, if we consider only the number of 20-word sentences that you could generate, you would need 10 trillion years to say them all (Miller, 1967; Pinker, 1993).

As you'll see throughout this chapter, language is an astonishing human accomplishment. When we want to understand and produce speech, we must activate our perceptual skills ("Did the speaker say *bear* or *pear?*"). In fact, we need all our cognitive skills, because language depends upon memory, problem solving, decision making, and intelligence—the topics of our last two chapters. However, language is also the most social of our cognitive activities (Clark, 1996). We typically use language with other people, and our knowledge of the social world helps us understand language and select the words we speak. Therefore, this chapter foreshadows the social interactions emphasized in the closing chapters of this book.

This chapter is divided into three sections: understanding language, producing language, and social aspects of language. The important topic of language development is examined separately in Chapter 10.

UNDERSTANDING LANGUAGE

When we understand language, we hear a string of noises or we look at an arrangement of scribbles. Somehow we manage to make sense of them, using our knowledge about sounds, letters, words, schemas, and language rules. An important part of understanding language is speech perception. Other topics in this section include how we understand meaning, how we read written passages, and how neuroscientists are exploring language comprehension.

Speech Perception

You turn on the television, and the soap opera hero says, "But I really love you, Jennifer." His tongue wiggles, his lips contort, and his larynx throbs in order to produce sound vibrations that eventually reach the receptors in your ears (and presumably Jennifer's as well). Your auditory system manages to translate these vibrations into a series of sound that you perceive to be speech.

Speech perception is an extremely complex process (Coren et al., 1994; Matlin & Foley, 1997). The process is especially impressive because an adult speaker produces about 900 sounds each minute (Kuhl, 1994). Fortunately, our top-down processing helps us identify these speech sounds, and it also helps us locate the boundaries between words.

Phoneme Perception   A **phoneme** is a basic sound unit of speech, such as the sounds *th, a,* and *t* in the word *that.* In Chapter 4, we discussed how visual pattern recognition depends on both bottom-up and top-down processing. These processes operate similarly when we perceive speech sounds. **Bottom-up processing** emphasizes the role of the sensory receptors in processing the basic stimuli. In the case of speech perception, the hair cells in the inner ear pick up the vibrations, at the "bottom" level of perception, and they carry the information to higher levels in the auditory system. **Top-down processing** emphasizes the importance of the listener's concepts, expectations, and prior knowledge—in other words, the kind of information stored at the top (or highest) level of perception.

In speech perception, then, the hair-cell receptors gather precise information about pitch and other characteristics of the sound, thanks to bottom-up processing. Top-down processing is also active. If someone says, "The dentist told the girl to brush her tee__," the context of the word and the sentence assure you that the missing phoneme is *th* rather than *b, m,* or *z* (Massaro, 1987).

Humans are so skilled at top-down perception that they sometimes believe they hear a phoneme that is truly missing, an effect known as **phonemic restoration.** In a classic experiment, Warren and Warren (1970) played three sentences for the listeners in their study. These sentences were identical with one exception: A different word was spliced onto the end of each sentence. In each case, as listed below, the same coughing sound was inserted in the location indicated by the asterisk:

1. It was found that the *eel was on the axle.

2. It was found that the *eel was on the shoe.

3. It was found that the *eel was on the orange.

These researchers found that the listeners reported hearing different words, as a function of the context. The "word" *eel* was heard as *wheel* in the first sentence, *heel* in the second, and *peel* in the third.

Phonemic restoration is a kind of illusion. People think that they hear a phoneme, even though the correct sound vibrations never reach their ears (Warren 1984). Additional experiments have confirmed that top-down processing encourages us to "hear" a phoneme or even a word that is not there (Cooper et al., 1985; Huttenlocher & Goodman, 1987; Samuel, 1996, 1997).

We are so tolerant of missing sounds and mispronunciations in sentences that we often fail to notice children's highly inaccurate pronunciations. For instance, one of my students recalled singing a Christmas carol in which the shepherds "washed their socks by night" instead of "watched their flocks by night." Another remembered a carol that began "O come all ye hateful: Joy, Phil, and their trumpet." We typically tolerate children's mispronunciations because our top-down processing encourages us to hear what our expectations predict.

DEMONSTRATION 9.1 Resolving Ambiguous Boundaries Between Words

When we try to determine where the boundaries lie that separate the words in spoken language, we face a task that resembles this one. The string of letters below lacks the white spaces that typically separate the words in written language. Where would you place the boundaries? Two answers appear at the end of the chapter (Page 312), but you may be able to think of others.

THEREDONATEAKETTLEOFTENCHIPS.

Source: Based on Jusczyk, 1986.

Word Boundaries Have you ever overhead a conversation in a language you do not know? The words may seem to run together in a continuous stream, with few boundaries separating them. However, when you hear your native language, you hear distinct words. When you read, you see white spaces clearly identifying the boundaries between words. When you listen, the "white spaces" seem almost as distinct. Before you read further, try Demonstration 9.1.

In most cases, however, the actual spoken language does not have clear-cut pauses to mark the boundaries. In fact, English speakers use a pause or other physical marker for less than 40% of the word boundaries (Flores d'Arcais, 1988; Kuhl, 1994; Miller & Eimas, 1995).

Fortunately, top-down processing usually helps us interpret those unclear boundaries correctly. However, as the previous chapter (on thinking) emphasized, heuristics that *usually* work correctly can *sometimes* produce an error. Consider the grandmother who was listening to a Beatles song. She was more familiar with illness than with hallucinogenic experiences, and so she heard "the girl with colitis goes by," rather than "the girl with kaleidoscope eyes" (Safire, 1979). We can make errors when we rely too heavily on expectations, rather than on the information in the auditory stimulus.

Understanding and Meaning

When we understand language, we do much more than perceive phonemes and identify the boundaries between words. We also decode the meaning of the language we hear. We identify meaning in concepts and in larger units of language.

According to the network model of conceptual meaning, a photo of this rose will activate concepts such as flower, fragrant, thorns, *and perhaps* Valentine's Day.

Conceptual Meaning Psychologists and other language researchers have devised several theories about how humans store conceptual meaning in memory. For example, **network models** propose that concepts are organized in memory in a netlike pattern with many interconnections (e.g., Anderson, 1990; Collins & Loftus, 1975; McClelland et al., 1986). The meaning of a particular concept, such as *apple,* depends upon the concepts to which it is connected, such as *fruit, red,* and *nutritious.* We examined one kind of network model, connectionism, in Chapter 7.

According to network models, when you perceive the name of a concept, that particular location becomes activated. The activation expands or spreads from that location to other concepts with which it is connected, a process called **spreading activation.** So when you perceive the word *apple,* all its important characteristics are activated in your memory.

A second theory of meaning argues that we organize each concept according to a **prototype,** or best example of a concept. Specifically, the **prototype approach** points out that people decide whether an item belongs to a category by comparing that item with a prototype. For example, your prototype for a bird is probably a feathered creature with wings, shaped like a sparrow or a robin. If an unfamiliar creature outside your window resembles this prototype, you categorize it as a bird.

An important assumption of the prototype approach is that all members of a category are *not* created equal. Instead, a category has a **graded structure,** so that the most prototypical members have priority and the category's nonprototypical members have lower status (Neisser, 1987; Rosch, 1973). For example, consider the category *vehicle.* Prototypical vehicles, such as *car* and *truck,* have priority in this category. *Tractor* and *raft* are somewhere further down the line. At the bottom of the pile lie those nonprototypical vehicles, such as *wheelbarrow* and *elevator* (Rosch & Mervis, 1975).

Prototypes have unusual prominence in our language systems. For instance, when people are asked to provide examples of particular categories, they supply prototypes more often than nonprototypes (Mervis et al., 1976). If you ask some friends to name a vegetable, they will probably supply prototypes such as *potatoes* and *carrots,* rather than nonprototypes such as *pumpkin* or *artichokes.* In general, prototypes have a special, privileged status (Smith, 1989).

The network model and the prototype approach both help resolve the question of how we understand conceptual meaning. The network model emphasizes that our thoughts about one concept will automatically activate thoughts about related concepts. The prototype approach explains the organization within categories, so that *vehicle* makes us think of *car,* rather than *wheelbarrow.* Now let us consider larger units of meaning, beyond these individual concepts.

Surface Structure and Deep Structure At the age of 27, the linguist Noam Chomsky described a new approach to language, sometimes referred to as the Chomskyan revolution (G. A. Miller, 1991; Rosenberg, 1993). Chomsky (1957, 1965) proposed that people listening to their native language have the ability to understand the abstract relationships underlying the strings of words they actually hear. His model distinguished between a sentence's surface structure and its deep structure. **Surface structure** is represented by the words that are actually spoken or written. In contrast, **deep structure** is the underlying, more abstract representation of the sentence.

Two sentences may have different surface structures but similar deep structures, as in the following sentences:

The student read the book.

The book was read by the student.

Two ideas can also have identical surface structure but different deep structures, as in this ambiguous newspaper headline:

Two Sisters Reunited After 18 Years in the Checkout Counter

Chomsky devised rules to describe how listeners transform surface structure into deep structure, and how speakers transform the deep structure they wish to express into the specific words they utter. Chomsky's distinction between surface and deep structure completely changed the way psychologists view language, even if some of his more specific predictions may not be widely accepted (Carroll, 1994; Rosenberg, 1993).

Reading

You probably spend several hours a day reading. You read textbooks, notes scribbled on blackboards, notices on bulletin boards, newspapers, and the list of ingredients on cereal boxes. By now, reading is typically automatic, something you can take for granted.

However, reading skills are actually very impressive and complex. Skilled reading requires that numerous component processes work in harmony with one another (Perfetti, 1993). For example, your eyes must move forward in saccadic movements, and you must use shape perception to identify the individual letters. (Both of these processes were examined in Chapter 4.) You must also recognize the words you are

According to the prototype approach to conceptual meaning, a robin is a prototypical bird, whereas a peacock is nonprototypical.

DEMONSTRATION 9.2   Reading a Passage of Text

Read the following passage, and notice whether it seems to flow smoothly and logically.
1. Dick had a week's vacation due
2. and he wanted to go to a place
3. where he could swim and sunbathe.
4. He bought a book on travel.
5. Then he looked at the ads
6. in the travel section of the Sunday newspaper.
7. He went to his local travel agent
8. and asked for a plane ticket to Alaska.
9. He paid for it with his charge card.

Source: Huitema et al., 1993.

---

reading and figure out the meaning of unfamiliar words. Furthermore, you can accomplish all these tasks at the rate of about 300 words per minute (Carver, 1990). Reading is another example of our theme that humans are extremely competent creatures.

Word Recognition   As you read this sentence to yourself, how do you actually recognize the words? This page is decorated with some little squiggles, interrupted by white spaces. How do those squiggles lead you to a word's meaning? According to the most influential model of reading, called the **dual-route hypothesis,** we can reach a word's meaning through either of two routes (Coltheart & Rastle, 1994; Crowder & Wagner, 1992). The dual-route model argues that we can recognize common words directly from the printed symbols. For example, you look at the word *ball,* and that visual pattern leads you directly to information in your memory about that word's meaning.

What happens when you see a difficult or unfamiliar word, such as *pseudoword?* According to the dual-route model, you first translate an unusual word from the ink marks on the page into a sound code. Then you locate the word's meaning. (Think about it. Doesn't it seem that you pronounced *pseudoword* silently as you read it?) This dual-route arrangement helps us read the common words quickly and the uncommon words carefully. Now try Demonstration 9.2 before reading further.

Critical Thinking Exercise 9.1

Write down your answers to the following questions about conceptual meaning and word recognition.

a. The information about prototypes and graded structure was gathered from North American college students. Can we translate the terms—such as *vehicle, car,* and *wheelbarrow*—into other languages and assume that this same graded structure would hold true in another culture?

b. The dual-route model seems to describe the reading process for adults who have some expertise in reading. Educators currently favor two very different ways of teaching reading to young children. From what you have learned about the dual-route model, can you predict what these methods are?

Understanding Discourse   We spend most of our lives understanding language units that are much more complex than words or sentences. In our everyday lives, we continually process **discourse,** or language units that are larger than a sentence (Carroll, 1994). You listen to the news on the radio, you hear a friend telling a story, and you read your psychology textbook. In fact, "Discourse is what makes us human"

(Graesser et al., 1997, p. 164). In contrast, Nim Chimpsky could master words and occasional sentences, but he did not produce connected discourse. Thus, we now turn our attention to this topic. In our discussion we'll consider how we understand *written* discourse when we read—because most of the psychological research focuses on reading. However, keep in mind that you also understand *spoken* discourse whenever you listen to language segments that are longer than one sentence.

We have seen in Chapters 7 and 8 that our background knowledge and top-down processing help us master cognitive tasks. This same background knowledge helps us interpret discourse. According to the widely accepted **constructionist view** of inference, readers usually draw inferences about the causes of events and the relationships between events (Graesser et al., 1997; Graesser & Kreuz, 1993). For example, the first three lines in Demonstration 9.2 lead you to believe that Dick will soon be lounging on a sunny beach. Five lines later, however, you learn that Dick's travel destination is Alaska! Huitema and his coauthors (1993) found that people took significantly longer to read the "Alaska" version of this story than a similar story in which Dick asked for a plane ticket to Florida. Readers found that their schemas were violated, even when the contradictory sentences were separated by several lines.

Metacomprehension   When you were reading about the research on discourse, did you pause for a moment to think about whether you understood this research? If so, you engaged in metacomprehension. **Metacomprehension** refers to our thoughts about reading comprehension, and it is related to the concepts of metamemory (Chapter 7) and metacognition (Chapter 8).

Unfortunately, most college students are not very accurate in their metacomprehension skills. For example, they often believe that they understand a paragraph they have just read. However, when they are given a multiple-choice test on the material, they may choose the wrong answer (Maki & Berry, 1984; Pressley & Ghatala, 1988). College students often think they understand a passage they have read because they are familiar with the general topic. They may not realize that they do not know the specific information well enough to recall it on an examination. One way to improve metacomprehension is to take a pretest, such as those found in a textbook's study guide. The feedback from this pretest can help students assess the accuracy of their metacomprehension (Maki & Serra, 1992; Matlin, 1996b).

Neurolinguistics   So far, we have seen that humans are very competent in understanding language, from the most basic phoneme level to the sophisticated level of discourse. Now let's switch our focus to **neurolinguistics,** which is the discipline that examines the relationship between the brain and language. Research in this area has used the case-study technique to examine individuals with aphasia, as well as imaging techniques such as the PET scan.

As Chapter 3 mentioned, **aphasia** is a condition in which damage to the speech areas of the brain produces difficulty in speaking, understanding, or writing (Thompson, 1993). The research on aphasia underscores Theme 3; language processing is extremely complicated (Alexander, 1997; Kimura, 1993). However, researchers typically discuss two different kinds of aphasia, based on the brain region that is damaged.

A person with **Broca's aphasia** produces speech that is slow, effortful, and grammatically simple (Alexander, 1997; Blumstein, 1995). For example, one person with Broca's aphasia produced this sentence: "Me . . . build-ing . . . chairs, no, no cab-in-nets. One, saw . . . then, cutting wood . . . working . . ." (Jackendoff, 1994, p. 146). In Broca's aphasia, the damage is localized in the front portion of the temporal lobe. (See Figure 3.16.)

The other major aphasia is called Wernicke's aphasia (pronounced "*Ver*-nih-keez"). A person with **Wernicke's aphasia** produces speech that is too abundant, often lacking content; and that person has serious difficulties understanding speech

If these college students are typical, their metacomprehension is not highly accurate. They are likely to believe that they understood a passage in their textbook, yet they will miss the relevant question on their examination.

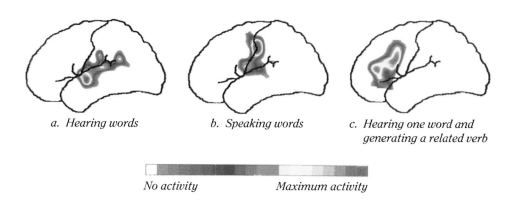

FIGURE 9.1

Brain Activity and Language
*PET scans showing the activity
produced in the brain while a
person is performing three
language tasks; and an index of
activity level (red indicates
maximum activity).*
Source: Photos courtesy of Dr. Marcus
Raichle.

a. Hearing words   *b. Speaking words*   *c. Hearing one word and
generating a related verb*

No activity   *Maximum activity*

(Alexander, 1997; Blumstein, 1995). For example, one man with Wernicke's aphasia was asked, "How are you today?" He replied:

> I feel very well. My hearing, writing been doing well. Things that I couldn't hear from. In other words, I used to be able to work cigarettes I didn't know how . . . (Goodglass, 1993, p. 86)

Other research analyzes brain activity in normal adults using positron emission tomagraphy (Petersen et al., 1989; Posner & Raichle, 1994). As you know from Chapter 3, **positron emission tomography (PET scan)** traces the chemical activity of various parts of the intact brain. For example, Figure 9.1a shows that part of the temporal lobe is especially active when people hear words. When we speak words, a different part of the brain (including the motor cortex) is activated, as shown in Figure 9.1b. When we listen to one word and must generate a related verb (e.g., *hammer* → *pound*), our prefrontal cortex plays a major role, as shown in Figure 9.1c. As you may recall from Chapter 3, the prefrontal cortex is responsible for our most complex intellectual tasks (Benson, 1994). The neurolinguistics research highlights how our human language skills require the talents of a major portion of our cerebral cortex.

SECTION SUMMARY: *UNDERSTANDING LANGUAGE*

1. In contrast to chimps, humans have an enormous speaking vocabulary, from which they can produce a virtually infinite number of sentences.

2. Speech perception requires both bottom-up and top-down processing; the phonemic restoration effect demonstrates the importance of top-down processing.

3. Listeners easily perceive word boundaries, even when no clear-cut pause appears in spoken language.

4. According to network models, concepts are organized in memory in an interconnecting netlike pattern; according to the prototype approach to concepts, people decide whether an item belongs to a category by comparing it with a prototype.

5. According to Chomsky, language can be viewed in terms of both surface structure and deep structure.

6. According to the dual-route model of reading, people access the meaning of a common word directly from the printed page, but an uncommon word must first be translated into sound.

7. People use top-down processes in understanding discourse, and they draw inferences about the causes of events.

8. College students may overestimate how much they understand in a written passage; metacomprehension can be improved with feedback.

9. Broca's aphasia produces slow, simple speech; Wernicke's aphasia produces abundant speech without content, as well as difficulty in understanding speech. Research using PET scans illustrates that different parts of the brain are activated for different linguistic tasks.

PRODUCING LANGUAGE

Every day, we spend hours telling stories, speaking on the telephone, quarreling, and talking to ourselves. In fact, speaking is one of our most complicated cognitive and motor skills (Levelt, 1989, 1994). How do we plan a sentence, how does nonverbal communication operate, and how do bilinguals manage to produce discourse in two or more languages? In this section, we'll also return to the chimp-language controversy to compare human achievements with the more modest accomplishments of other primates.

Speech Planning

To produce a sentence, you must overcome the limits of your memory and attention in order to plan and deliver that sentence (Bock, 1995; Jou & Harris, 1992). You must first work out the gist or the overall meaning of the message. Next you must decide on the general structure of the sentence, and then choose the words. Finally, your tongue, lips, and other vocal apparatus need to move appropriately (Levelt, 1994; Yeni-Komshian, 1998). Two problems that may occur when we construct a sentence are linearization and speech errors.

The Linearization Problem   When you speak, you may have a general thought you want to express. This rather shapeless idea needs to be translated into a linear statement, in which one word follows after another in a line; this challenging situation is called the **linearization problem** (Bock, 1987; Levelt, 1994). Try Demonstration 9.3, which illustrates the linearization problem.

Psychologists have discovered that when people need to list two or more items, they generally place short words before long ones, pleasant items before unpleasant ones, and prototypes before nonprototypes (Kelly et al., 1986; Matlin & Stang, 1978; Pinker & Birdsong, 1979). As you might imagine, this planning process requires longer pauses for longer sentences (Bock, 1995).

Speech Errors   The speech that most people produce is generally very well formed (Bock, 1995), consistent with Theme 1. However, our everyday conversation often deviates from perfect English. As you might imagine, the circumstances of the conversation can influence the number of speech errors. For example, one study examined the speech of people who were calling to make airline reservations. They made errors that they later corrected, at the rate of one error every 10 to 20 utterances (Nakatani & Hirschberg, 1994).

One kind of speech error is a **slip of the tongue,** an error in which sounds are rearranged between two or more separate words. For example, we may exchange phonemes in nearby words, so that *snow flurries* becomes *flow snurries*. We may also exchange words in different parts of a sentence, so that *writing a letter to my mother* becomes *writing a mother to my letter.*

To produce language, this math professor must work out the gist of her message to the class; she must solve the linearization problem; and she must use her vocal apparatus to create a sentence.

DEMONSTRATION 9.3   Struggling With the Linearization Problem

Answer the following question in three or four sentences. As you compose these sentences, say them silently to yourself.

What problems can student cheating cause on a college campus?

Now think about your own thought processes as you constructed these sentences. Did all your ideas immediately fall into a neat, linear order, or did you have to arrange and rearrange them as you thought about the topic?

TABLE 9.1 Some Typical Slips of the Tongue

SPEECH ERROR	WHAT WAS INTENDED
"I was gabberflasted."	"I was flabbergasted."
"I wish there was a refrigerator in this light."	"I wish there was a light in this refrigerator."
"Go lump in a jake."	"Go jump in a lake."
"The shun comes shining through."	"The sun comes shining through."
"My daughter was a real sumbthucker."	"My daughter was a real thumbsucker."

According to one theory of slips of the tongue, which is based on the connectionist theory, a speaker selects many words in a sentence before pronouncing the first word (Dell, 1986, 1990). Once we have selected a word, the sounds within that word becomes activated. We usually speak the sound that is most highly activated. In most cases, that sound is correct. However, sometimes a particular sound has been activated by several different words that you plan to say. For example, consider this familiar tongue-twister: *She sells seashells*. The sound *sh* is highly activated when you are about to pronounce the third word. As a result, you may say *sheshells*. Table 9.1 shows some of the slips of the tongue that my students provided.

Nonverbal Communication

So far, we have only considered verbal language. However, people can also transmit messages by tone of voice, body movement, or facial expression. The term **nonverbal communication** refers to all human communications that do not involve words. Nonverbal communication includes many varied behaviors, such as the following (DePaulo, 1992; Patterson, 1983):

- **Paralanguage,** or vocal cues other than the words themselves, such as voice tone, pitch, pauses, and voice inflection;
- **Gestures,** or movements that accompany speech;
- Body orientation or posture;
- Interpersonal distance;
- Touch;
- Direction of gaze;
- Facial expression.

In Chapter 12, we will discuss how people convey and interpret emotion, especially via facial expression. Right now, however, let's consider how speakers can use two kinds of gestures to convey meaning.

One kind of gesture is called an **emblem.** An emblem is a nonverbal action that is clearly understood by most members of a culture. Each emblem can be translated into a verbal phrase (Deaux & Wrightsman, 1988; McNeill, 1985). A common emblem is a wave of the hand in greeting. We also have emblems for phrases such as "it stinks," "be quiet," and "come here." Middle-class Americans have a smaller number of emblems than people in most other cultural groups, probably fewer than 100 (Ekman, 1976). At this point, try Demonstration 9.4 to see how many emblems you can identify.

One other common kind of gesture is an illustrator. An **illustrator** is a nonverbal action that accompanies speech and quite literally provides an illustration. For example, when you say the sentence, "He was a *very* tall man," you might raise one arm high over your head and bend your fingers forward. Incidentally, when we try to convey spatial information and we are prevented from gesturing, we'll have trouble producing the language (Rauscher et al., 1996).

DEMONSTRATION 9.4 Recognizing Emblems

Make a list of as many emblems as you can recall, eliminating the R-rated and the X-rated ones. Keep working on this list, adding to it whenever you think of a new one, until you have a list of 20 items. Then ask a friend to try to decode your emblems. In each case, do not provide any context or circumstances in which the emblem is likely to be used. Also, do not use any accompanying words. Simply perform one gesture at a time and see whether your friend can guess the appropriate meaning. You may wish to compare your list with others in the class. Working together, can you all identify close to 100 emblems?

Critical Thinking Exercise 9.2

Write down your answers to the following questions about speech planning and nonverbal communication.

a. Some researchers have estimated that only about 5% of published papers in the psychology of language focus on language production; almost all examine how we understand language (Levelt, 1994). Now that you've read some of the research in both areas, why do you suppose that psychologists prefer to conduct experiments on language understanding rather than language production?

b. The discussion of gestures cited a study estimating that middle-class Americans may have fewer than 100 emblems (Ekman, 1976). Why would you be skeptical about *any* estimate about the size of our emblem "vocabulary"?

IN DEPTH

Bilingualism

In this chapter on language, we've considered some impressively challenging cognitive tasks, such as language comprehension, reading, and speaking. To accomplish these tasks, you must simultaneously coordinate many cognitive skills, as well as physical gestures. We can marvel that humans can manage all these tasks in one language—and then we must remind ourselves that many people master at least two languages.

A **bilingual** speaker is a person who uses two languages that differ in speech sounds, vocabulary, and syntax (Taylor & Taylor, 1990). The bilingual's native language is referred to as the **first language,** and the nonnative language is the **second language.**

If we consider the entire world, most people are at least somewhat bilingual (Romaine, 1996; Snow, 1998). Some people live in bilingual regions, such as Belgium, Switzerland, and parts of Canada. Some become bilingual because their first language is not used for school and business. For example, Zulu speakers in South Africa must learn English. People also become bilingual because colonization has imposed another language upon them. Still others become bilingual because they have studied a second language in school. In fact, you may be among the 1.2 million college students in the United States who are currently enrolled in a foreign language course (Cage, 1994).

For many years, North Americans often considered themselves monolinguals. However, 10% of Canadian couples now differ in their first language. For example, one person's original language may be English, whereas the other originally spoke French (Turcotte, 1993). In the United States, about 32 million people speak a language other than English at home (Bialystok & Hakuta, 1994). This number includes about 17 million Spanish speakers, nearly 2 million French speakers, and more than 1 million speakers each for three other languages: German, Italian, and Chinese.

FIGURE 9.2

A notice sent to Boston residents by a telephone company. The languages on the notice are English, Portuguese, Spanish, Vietnamese, French, Chinese, and Cambodian.

What You Should Know About Automatic Dialing Services.

This is an important notice. Please have it translated.
Este é um aviso importante. Queira mandá-lo traduzir.
Este es un aviso importante. Sirvase mandarlo traducir.
ĐÂY LÀ MỘT BẢN THÔNG CÁO QUAN TRỌNG
XIN VUI LÒNG CHO DỊCH LẠI THÔNG CÁO ẤY
Ceci est important. Veuillez faire traduire.
本 通 知 很 重 要 . 请 将 之 译 成 中 文 .
នេះគឺជាដំណឹងល្អ សូមមេត្តាបកប្រែជូនផង

(IN DEPTH continued)

Figure 9.2 shows a message sent to Boston residents, illustrating that many U.S. residents must master new written characters in order to learn English.

In this chapter, we emphasize that language is social as well as cognitive. Naturally, cognitive factors—such as working-memory capacity—influence how easily you can acquire a second language (McLaughlin & Heredia, 1996). However, another important influence is social factors, such as your attitude toward the people who speak the language you want to learn (Leather & James, 1996). In a representative study, researchers tried to predict how well English Canadian high school students would learn French (Gardner & Lambert, 1959; Lambert, 1992). The students' *attitude* toward French Canadians was just as important as their cognitive *aptitude* for learning languages.

Let's consider three topics in this section on bilingualism. We'll first compare bilinguals and monolinguals on a variety of cognitive tasks. Then we'll compare these two groups in more detail on one particular skill, awareness of language. Finally, we'll see how immigrants manage to retain their first language.

General Cognitive Comparisons

According to an early view, bilingualism is harmful. Early theorists believed that if part of your cognitive capacity was occupied by a second language, your other thought processes would suffer (Jespersen, 1922; Lambert, 1990). The early research on bilingualism seemed to support that position. However, this research was seriously flawed by confounding variables. Lower-class bilinguals were compared with middle-class monolinguals. Furthermore, all of the achievement and intelligence testing was conducted in the monolingual child's language, usually English. As you might imagine, scores for verbal IQ are often lower when bilinguals are tested in their second language (Reynolds, 1991; Romaine, 1996).

The first well-controlled study on bilingualism surprised many people. Peal and Lambert (1962) demonstrated that bilinguals were more advanced in school, they scored better on tests of first-language skills, and they showed greater mental flexibility. The original research was conducted in Montreal, and the results have been confirmed by carefully conducted research in Singapore, Switzerland, South Africa, Israel, and New York (Lambert, 1990).

In addition to gaining fluency in a second language, bilinguals seem to have several other advantages over monolinguals:

- Bilinguals actually acquire more expertise in their *first* language after learning a second language. For example, English-speaking Canadian children whose classes are taught in French actually gain greater understanding of English language structure (Diaz, 1985; Lambert et al., 1991).
- Bilingual children are more sensitive to some of the more social aspects of language. For example, English-speaking children whose classes are

For this student who is learning Spanish, her attitude toward Latin Americans is as important as her aptitude in terms of linguistic skills.

taught in French are more aware that you need to supply additional information if the person to whom you are speaking is wearing a blind-fold (Genesee et al., 1975).

- Bilingual children are better at following complicated instructions (Hamers & Blanc, 1989; Powers & López, 1985).
- Bilingual children are more likely to show cognitive flexibility on tests of creativity, such as thinking of a wide variety of different uses for a paper clip (Hamers & Blanc, 1989; Ricciardelli, 1992; Scott, 1973).

The *disadvantages* to being bilingual are minor. For example, bilinguals may subtly change their pronunciation of some speech sounds in both languages (Caramazza et al., 1973). As you can imagine, these disadvantages are easily outweighed by the advantages of being bilingual (Taylor & Taylor, 1990).

Awareness of Language

Now that we have considered how bilinguals perform on a variety of cognitive tasks, let's turn to a more specific question: How do monolinguals and bilinguals compare with respect to metalinguistics? **Metalinguistics** is your knowledge about the form and structure of language, and it is one form of metacognition. We have already considered two other kinds of metacognition, metamemory (knowledge about memory) and metacomprehension (knowledge about comprehension). Metalinguistics does not focus on the meaning of language; instead, it emphasizes people's awareness about the structure or form of language.

Consistent with the themes of complexity and individual differences, bilinguals do not always score higher than monolinguals on tests of metalinguistic awareness (Bialystok, 1991, 1992; Galambos & Goldin-Meadow, 1990; Galambos & Hakuta, 1988). However, we can identify many areas in which bilinguals clearly know more about the way language operates.

Let's focus on a study by Ellen Bialystok (1988), in which she tested linguistic awareness in three groups of Canadian children who were between the ages of 6½ and 7. One group spoke only English. A second group was partially bilingual; they had been raised speaking English, but they were enrolled in a school where they had been taught entirely in French for about two years. A third group was fully bilingual; they had spoken both French and English throughout childhood, and they now attended a French school.

Bialystok gave the children several metalinguistic tasks, which are illustrated in Demonstration 9.5. As you can see, the first task focused on the arbitrariness of language—the fact that the sun is arbitrarily called *sun* in English, but it could just as easily have been called a *glonk* or a *moon*. On the "sun/moon" task, the fully bilingual children received the highest scores.

DEMONSTRATION 9.5 Linguistic Awareness

Try each of the tasks described below. They should not be challenging, because they were designed for children. However, by trying them you can develop your own appreciation of metalinguistics. If you know a child between the ages of 5 and 8, try asking the child these questions.

1. *The Arbitrariness of Language*
   Suppose you were making up names for things, and you decided to call the sun "the moon" and the moon "the sun." What would you call the thing in the sky when you go to bed at night? What would the sky look like when you're going to bed?

2. *Concept of Word*
   What is a word? How can you tell if something is a word?

3. *Correcting Grammatical Errors*
   For each of these two sentences, say the grammatically correct version of the sentence:
   a. There isn't no snow today.
   b. Where they are going?

Source: Based on Bialystok, 1988.

Jim Good, known as Jaime Bueno to his friends in Nicaragua, acquired fluency in Spanish through his many years of humanitarian work in that country. His metalinguistic skills are likely to be more sophisticated than if he had remained monolingual.

(IN DEPTH continued)

The three groups performed similarly on some language tasks. However, the groups differed substantially on Task 2 in Demonstration 9.5. The monolingual children most often answered, "I don't know." The partially bilingual children typically gave a partially correct definition, such as, "A word is something you can say." The fully bilingual children supplied definitions such as, "Words are combinations of letters that mean something"—amazingly sophisticated for first-graders! In correcting grammatical errors, the fully bilingual children were more accurate than the partially bilingual children, who were in turn more accurate than the monolingual children.

Why are bilinguals better on some of these language tasks? Bialystok (1992) argues that bilinguals are simply more sensitive to linguistic input. They are accustomed to hearing things referred to in two different forms. They also know that they must pay attention to the language itself, as well as its meaning. Furthermore, they realize that they sometimes need to address different people in different languages, which draws attention to the alternative forms of language. In short, bilinguals have an enriched perspective because they are more aware of the structure of language.

Maintenance of the First Language Among Immigrants

Many immigrants in the United States and Canada move to communities where their first language is widely spoken. Those individuals who maintain a strong ethnic identity are especially likely to want to maintain fluency in their first language (Hurtado & Gurin, 1995).

Harry Bahrick and his coauthors (1994) tested a total of 801 Spanish-speaking immigrants from Mexico and Cuba, the majority of whom lived either in El Paso, Texas, or Miami, Florida. These researchers tested bilingual immigrants and monolingual English-speakers, who were similar in age and education. In general, the two groups received similar scores on tests of English comprehension and production.

How well did the immigrants remember their Spanish? Bahrick and his colleagues compared the scores of the bilingual group with the scores of Spanish monolinguals, who were similar in age and education and who had recently arrived in the United States. The bilinguals performed slightly *better* on tests of Spanish grammar, Spanish oral comprehension, and Spanish written comprehension. The two groups were equally accurate on a test of Spanish vocabulary recognition. In short, the results suggest an optimistic outcome for these immigrants: They can achieve English language skills without compromising their ability to speak Spanish.

The Chimp-Language Controversy

At the beginning of this chapter, we introduced Nim Chimpsky, one of the most famous figures in the chimp-language controversy. Many other nonhuman primates have played important roles in this drama, both before and after Nim (e.g., Candland, 1993; Wallman, 1992).

Within the last two decades, researchers have focused on a much rarer kind of chimpanzee, known as the bonobo (pronounced "boe-*noe*-boe"). The language skills of one of these bonobos, named Kanzi, surpasses the abilities of all other chimps (e.g., Greenfield & Savage-Rumbaugh, 1991; Rumbaugh, 1993; Savage-Rumbaugh & Lewin, 1994). For example, Kanzi can listen to verbal questions, presented through his earphones, and answer by touching symbols on a board. (See Figure 9.3.)

Kanzi can also respond appropriately to more complicated spoken language. For example, Sue Savage-Rumbaugh once noticed that Kanzi was very interested in some cereal that belonged to another chimp named Austin (Savage-Rumbaugh & Lewin, 1994). So she said, "Kanzi, if you give Austin your monster mask, I'll let you have some of Austin's cereal" (p. 170). Kanzi quickly got the mask and gave it to Austin, and then

FIGURE 9.3

In this picture, a bonobo chimpanzee named Kanzi hears questions through earphones and points to the appropriate answer on a board. The experimenter cannot hear the questions and does not know the answers, so she cannot transmit cues to Kanzi.

pointed to the cereal. He had clearly understood the linguistic bargain. Another important point is that more than 90% of the phrases Kanzi produced were spontaneous, a clear improvement over Nim Chimpsky's tendency to simply imitate his teachers' symbols (Savage-Rumbaum & Lewin, 1994).

What can we conclude about chimp language? Under ideal conditions, chimps can acquire a vocabulary that is dwarfed by a young child's word mastery. Furthermore, chimps primarily communicate about their physical needs, not about signal detection theory, religion, or Jane Austen's novels. Even a bright chimp cannot discuss whether chimps can master language. Chimp language is more sophisticated than we would have guessed 50 years ago. However, chimpanzees cannot match the fluency, flexibility, and complexity of human language.

Critical Thinking Exercise 9.3

Write down your answers to the following questions about bilingualism and the chimp-language controversy.

a. Why is it impossible to conduct a true experiment comparing bilinguals with monolinguals? Why is this a problem?

b. What kind of precautions did the researchers take when formally testing Kanzi's language skills? Why are these precautions necessary?

SECTION SUMMARY: *PRODUCING LANGUAGE*

1. Producing a sentence requires working out the gist of the message, determining its general structure, choosing the words, and producing the words; we often face the linearization problem when formulating a sentence.

2. A connectionist approach has been devised to explain slips of the tongue.

3. Nonverbal behavior enriches verbal communication, as in the case of emblems and illustrators.

4. Bilinguals excel on some general cognitive tasks, such as expertise in their first language, sensitivity to social aspects of language, and metalinguistics.

5. Chimp language is much more primitive than human language.

SOCIAL ASPECTS OF LANGUAGE

You may occasionally talk to yourself or write yourself a reminder note. However, the major reason you talk is to share information with other people. Think about what you have said so far today. You may have requested, informed, persuaded, and complimented. We direct our words to other people, and frequently our goal is to influence the people with whom we are talking (Burgoon, 1990; Dell & Brown, 1991).

Herbert Clark (1991, 1996) proposes that conversation is like a complicated dance, an activity that requires two people to coordinate their efforts. People make numerous assumptions about their conversational partners' knowledge. Dancers make adjustments if they find that their partners do not know a particular step. Similarly, conversational partners make adjustments if their attempts to communicate have not been successful (McCann & Higgins, 1990). Just as two dancers coordinate their actions, conversational partners must also coordinate their turn-taking.

The social aspect of language is known as **pragmatics.** Pragmatics involves how we use language to communicate, how we accomplish our social goals, and how we interpret social messages from other people's language (Green, 1996; Nofsinger, 1991). Let's first consider how speakers attend to their listeners' background knowledge. We'll then consider the nature of conversational interactions. We'll also discuss two ways in which gender is related to language. Specifically, we'll explore gender comparisons in language use. Finally, we'll consider how people interpret gender-biased language. All these topics emphasize that language is the most social of our cognitive activities.

Listeners' Background Knowledge

Speakers are typically concerned about their listeners' familiarity with a topic. You are likely to use simplified language in speaking with children or with people who do not understand your language proficiently. When the listener seems puzzled, you typically replace difficult words with easier ones (Cutler, 1987; Dell & Brown, 1991). In general, we are fairly skilled at judging what our listeners know (Fussell & Krauss, 1992).

Speakers usually assume that listeners have appropriate background knowledge about a conversational topic (Clark, 1996). For example, we noted in Chapter 7 that people develop a **schema,** or a generalized idea about objects, people, and events that are encountered frequently. A typical schema would be the sequence of events that occur when someone attends a concert. So, if you are discussing a concert you attended, you count on your listeners' schemas to "fill in the blanks" about buying the ticket, handing in your ticket at the auditorium door, and so forth.

We also count on our listeners to share background knowledge about people and objects in our culture. For example, if you say, *Jimmy skipped all the way home from school,* you can count on your listener to conclude that Jimmy is a male child. In terms of the network model discussed in connection with word meaning, your listener's network surrounding the name *Jimmy* includes the concept *male.* The networks surrounding *skipping* and *school* both include the concept *child.* Thus, speakers and listeners have an easier time engaging in a conversational dance because they have similar background knowledge and—equally important—because they *know* that they both share this knowledge.

Conversational Interactions

Imagine that Cindy is calling a hair salon to make an appointment with the woman who last cut her hair, though she cannot remember the woman's name. Cindy and the receptionist will perform a short dance as they try to make certain that they are speaking about the same person:

Cindy: *She's short, about five feet two inches.*

Receptionist: *Oh, maybe you mean Marilyn. She has short brown wavy hair.*

Two people participating in a conversation assume that they share similar schemas and background knowledge.

DEMONSTRATION 9.6 Collaborating to Establish Common Ground

For this demonstration, you need to make two photocopies of these figures. Cut the figures apart, keeping each sheet's figures in a separate pile and making certain the dot is at the top of each figure. Then locate two volunteers and a watch that can measure time in seconds. Appoint one person to be the "director"; this person should arrange the figures in random order in two rows of six figures each. This person's task is to describe the first figure in enough detail so that the "matcher" is able to identify that figure and place it in Position 1 in front of him or her. (Neither person should be able to see the other's figures.) The goal is for the matcher to

place all 12 figures in the same order as the director's figures. They may use any kind of verbal descriptions they choose, but no gestures or imitation of body position. Record how long it takes them to reach their goal, and then make sure that the figures do match up. Ask them to try the game two more times, with the same person serving as director. Record the times again, and note whether the time decreases on the second and third trials; are they increasingly efficient in their communication patterns? Do they tend to develop a standard vocabulary (e.g., "the ice skater") to refer to a given figure?

Cindy: *Yes, that's right, and glasses? And she went to Puerto Rico last summer?*

Receptionist: *Yes, that's Marilyn Peters.*

Cindy: *Yes, that name sounds right.*

Notice what happens in this conversational interaction. Both partners put in extra effort together to make certain that they agree they are referring to the same person. Even total strangers collaborate. An important feature of conversational interaction is that participants check, question, and confirm (Clark, 1996; Clark & Brennan, 1991). That part of the conversation is ended only when both are certain that they are talking about the same person and have established common ground.

Researchers have examined how this collaboration process operates when people work together to arrange complex figures. Demonstration 9.6 is a modification of a study by Clark and Wilkes-Gibbs (1986). The participants in this study played this game for six trials. (Each trial consisted of arranging all 12 figures in order.) On the first trial, the "director" required nearly four turns to describe a figure and make certain that the "matcher" understood the reference. However, as Figure 9.4 shows, the director and the matcher soon developed a mutual shorthand. Just as two dancers become more skilled at coordinating their motor movements as they practice together, conversational partners become more skilled in communicating efficiently.

The emotional tone of a conversation is another important component of conversational interactions. For example, people can use humor to increase rapport between conversational partners (Norrick, 1993). Conversational partners also establish a level of politeness. A close friend can say, "May I please borrow your car?" In contrast, suppose you want to ask a professor for a letter of recommendation. Your request will typically be longer, and it may also include an escape option (Brown & Levinson, 1987; Clark, 1992). Thus, after some preliminary small talk, you might ask, "I wonder if you know me well enough to write a letter of recommendation?"

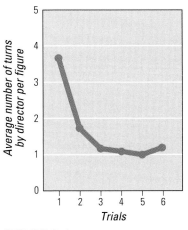

FIGURE 9.4

Average number of turns that "directors" took on each figure, as a function of trial number. See Demonstration 9.6.
Source: Based on Clark and Wilkes-Gibbs, 1986.

Critical Thinking Exercise 9.4

Write down your answers to the following questions about the social aspects of language.

a. Suppose that you wanted to see whether strangers and close friends differ in the way they work on the Clark and Wilkes-Gibbs (1986) setup you tried in Demonstration 9.6. What dependent measure could you use? How would you expect the results to differ for the two groups?

b. Suppose that a group of researchers is studying the topic of politeness. They construct a list of 10 statements, and they ask people to rate these statements, in a laboratory setting, on a 5-point rating scale with the endpoints labeled "Very Impolite" and "Very Polite." Comment on the ecological validity of this study.

Gender Comparisons in Language and Communication

A glance at some best-selling books on gender and communication suggest that women and men cannot understand one another, either in their personal relationships or in work settings. These books suggest that their communication patterns are so different that men and women seem to live on different planets (Gray, 1992; Tannen, 1990, 1994).

In reality, these popularized books oversimplify the situation (Aries, 1996; Crawford, 1995; Matlin, 1996a). They suggest that the gender differences are large and inevitable. These books also ignore individual differences (Theme 2), and they ignore other social variables, such as ethnicity, age, sexual orientation, and social class. Let's consider the research on gender comparisons in both verbal communication and nonverbal communication.

Verbal Communication   The research on language style shows that women may be somewhat more polite in their style, whereas men are more likely to use slang and obscene words (Jay, 1992; Kemper, 1984; Selnow, 1985). Aside from these areas, however, women and men are remarkably similar in their conversational style and in their writing style (Cameron et al., 1993; Rubin & Greene, 1992, 1994). Men do tend to interrupt women more than women interrupt men (Aries, 1996; McMullen, 1992). This difference probably does have social significance, especially because people tend to evaluate a woman negatively when she interrupts a man (LaFrance, 1992).

What do men and women talk about? Are women's conversations limited to gossip, whereas men can only discuss football? Here again, the similarities are more striking than the differences (Aries, 1996). In one study using naturalistic observation, both male and female college students were most likely to talk about jobs, studying, and career plans (Bischoping, 1993).

Research on gender typically shows that gender differences tend to be small when other roles are emphasized (Matlin, 1996a). For example, Wheelan and Verdi (1992) observed professionals in business and government occupations who were attending a conference on group relations. In this kind of setting, work roles would be emphasized more than gender roles. Males and females were found to be similar in their contributions to the discussion groups. For example, these researchers found no gender differences in the number of statements that challenged the leadership or in the number of statements supporting other people's remarks.

In a setting that emphasizes work roles, gender similarities in conversational pattern will be more prominent than gender differences.

Nonverbal Communication   Gender differences in nonverbal communication are typically larger than other kinds of gender differences, including the social behaviors we'll discuss in Chapters 16 and 17 (Hall, 1984; Matlin, 1996a). For example, two women who are talking will sit closer together than two men will (Sussman & Rosenfeld, 1982). Women are also more likely than men to gaze at their conversational partners (e.g., Hall, 1987). Women are also more likely to smile, whereas men are more likely to adopt a neutral or a frowning expression (Mills, 1984; Stoppard & Gruchy, 1993). In addition, two women talking together will touch each other more than two men will—probably no surprise (Hall & Veccia, 1990).

Conclusions About Gender Comparisons in Communication   In all of the areas we have discussed, individual differences are large. As a result, you are likely to know many people whose communication styles are more typical of the other gender. You probably know some women who interrupt more than most men. You probably also know some men who smile more than most women. In many cases, the gender differences disappear when we control for confounding variables. For example, Willson and Lloyd (1990) studied men and women in the arts, and they found no gender differences in smiling.

A recent interpretation of gender, called the **social constructionist viewpoint,** argues that we humans actively organize and construct our view of the world (Beall, 1993; Crawford, 1995). With respect to gender, we construct what it means to be female or male in our society. Our culture provides us with a body of knowledge, which operates like a set of lenses through which we try to make sense of the events that occur in the world (Beall, 1993; Bem, 1993). According to social constructionists, young children are likely to make sense out of their worlds by noticing that men and women are supposed to act differently. Men are supposed to interrupt; women are supposed to smile. However, we don't all receive the exact same set of lenses, and factors such as ethnicity can have an important influence on how we construct our notions about gender.

The social constructionist perspective points out that gender differences are not inevitable. In fact, we can construct an interpretation of the world in which gender roles are not especially relevant in our communication patterns.

Gender-Biased Language

We've just considered how men and women use language. Now let's consider a related question: How does language *represent* men and women? Consider this sentence in a newspaper article quoting a male counselor at a local elementary school: "When a child sees that he has something in common with me, it's like a miracle the way he opens up." Try to visualize the counselor, talking with a troubled child. Is this child a boy or a girl?

The problem illustrated in this example is called the **masculine generic,** the use of masculine pronouns and nouns to refer to all human beings—both males and females—instead of males alone. A teacher may have told you that "he" is supposed to refer to both "he and she," or that "man" is supposed to refer to "men and women." However, the research has shown that these masculine-generic terms are much more likely than gender-neutral terms (such as "he or she" or "they") to produce thoughts about males (Foertsch & Gernsbacher, 1997; Hardin & Banaji, 1993; Matlin, 1996a).

How can researchers examine this question? It's easy to manipulate the independent variable. Some people are given a masculine-generic term, like "he," and others are given a gender-neutral term, like "he or she." The *dependent* variable is more challenging, because we need some way to translate people's thoughts and mental images into measurable responses.

In a representative study, Martyna (1980) constructed sentences such as "When someone prepares for an exam, he must do some studying." Other variations of that sentence used either "they" or "he or she," instead of the masculine generic "he." Students were shown a sentence, accompanied by a picture of someone performing the appropriate activity, such as the photo in Figure 9.5. In each case, the students were asked to decide whether the sentence did or did not apply to the picture. The results showed that the sentence in the "he" format (the masculine generic) was judged not to apply to the photo of the female in 40% of the trials. When people saw "he," they often found it disconcerting to see a picture of a woman. Masculine generic terms like "he" suggest thoughts about men, rather than women. Other research shows that people described mental images of men three times as often with "he" as with "they" (Gastil, 1990).

After examining the research on gender-biased language, the American Psychological Association adopted a policy that specifies nonsexist language. Some of these suggestions are shown in Table 9.2. We will examine some additional gender biases throughout the remaining chapters in this book.

FIGURE 9.5

Many students judge that the sentence "When someone prepares for an exam, he must do some studying" does not apply to this picture.

> **TABLE 9.2 Suggestions for Nonsexist Language**
>
> 1. Use the plural form. "Students can monitor their progress" can replace "A student can monitor his progress."
> 2. Use "his or her" or "her or his," as in the sentence "A student can monitor her or his progress."
> 3. Use "you." The sentence "Suppose that you have difficulty recalling your Social Security number" involves the reader or the listener more than "Suppose that a person has difficulty recalling his Social Security number"—and it is also less sexist.
> 4. Reword the sentence to eliminate the pronoun."The best judge of the value of counseling is usually the client" can replace "The client is usually the best judge of the value of his counseling."
>
> *Source:* Based on guidelines from the American Psychological Association (1994).

Some theorists and researchers have suggested that masculine-generic language is an especially important problem because it encourages a broader gender bias that favors males over females (e.g., Hardin & Banaji, 1993). They often point to the **Whorfian hypothesis,** which states that the structure of language influences the structure of thought (Hudson, 1996; Triandis, 1994; Whorf, 1956). The Whorfian hypothesis was originally applied in cross-cultural research. For example, classical Chinese uses a dozen different characters for varieties of cattle (Hoosain, 1991). The Whorfian hypothesis would argue that people who spoke this language would be able to make more careful distinctions among different types of cattle, in comparison with people who have only a few terms for cattle. The structure of their language would influence the structure of their thought.

Similarly, the Whorfian hypothesis can be extended to masculine-generic language. Suppose you read the sentence "When someone prepares for an exam, he must do some studying." The word *he* restricts your thinking so that you think primarily about males. If the sentence had used the word *they* or *people,* your thinking would show less gender bias. In other words, the structure of language influences the structure of thought. The research we have discussed tends to support this argument.

However, we need to consider the complexity of the gender-bias issue. Yes, our gender-biased language may create additional gender bias. However, that gender-biased language did not emerge out of a vacuum, entirely by accident. Earlier in the chapter, we noted that our culture provides us with a set of lenses. This set of lenses shapes how we use verbal and nonverbal language. These lenses also created a language in which masculine terms have been used to represent both men and women. Still, we can choose to move beyond those limitations. One small way to move ahead is to use language that is equally fair to both women and men.

Critical Thinking Exercise 9.5

Write down your answers to the following questions about gender comparisons and gender bias in language.

a. Suppose you hear that a book has just been written for a general audience; the book is called *Men and Women Are From the Same Planet.* It argues that gender differences are not huge. In fact, when confounding variables are controlled, men and women speak fairly similar languages. Based on the information from previous chapters of this textbook, how well do you think this book will sell?

b. In most studies of gender-biased language, researchers also include phrases and sentences that have nothing to do with gender—in addition to masculine-generic material. Why is this precaution necessary?

SECTION SUMMARY: *SOCIAL ASPECTS OF LANGUAGE*

1. According to the research on conversation, speakers assume that listeners share the same schemas and background knowledge.

2. People in a conversation collaborate to reach common ground; social rules and emotional tone are other important components of a conversation.

3. The research on gender comparisons shows many similarities in conversation and writing style, as well as conversational topic, but men are more likely than women to interrupt. Gender differences are smaller when other roles are emphasized.

4. Women in conversation sit closer to each other than men do; women are also more likely to gaze at their conversational partners and to smile; women are likely to touch each other, but men are not.

5. According to the social constructionist viewpoint, humans construct what it means to be male and female; gender differences are not inevitable.

6. The research on gender-biased language shows that masculine-generic terms are more likely than gender-neutral terms to produce thoughts about males; this research has been interpreted in terms of the Whorfian hypothesis.

REVIEW QUESTIONS

1. How do bottom-up and top-down processes operate when you listen to someone talking? How is speech perception similar to the perception of written words? (You may need to review Pages 128–129 in Chapter 4 to answer this second question.) Why does the phonemic restoration effect demonstrate top-down processing?

2. How do the network approaches and the prototype theory of meaning differ from one another? Combining these two approaches, how would you explain your understanding of the meaning of the word *potato?*

3. A person listening to a sentence can figure out much more information than the physical stimulus registered by the receptors in the cochlea of the ear. Provide support for this statement by discussing the word-boundary issue, the surface structure/deep structure issue, and any other relevant topics.

4. How would the dual-route hypothesis explain how you are able to ascertain the meaning of the words you are reading in this question?

5. Discuss the cognitive and language skills of bilinguals. If the Whorfian hypothesis is correct, speakers of different languages might have different kinds of thoughts. What would be the implications for bilinguals?

6. From your background on the chimp-language controversy, describe the ways in which chimp language resembles human language and the ways in which it differs.

7. In order to carry on a conversation, two people must work together and be finely attuned to each other. Explain how the following factors are important in a conversation: background knowledge, collaboration to establish common ground, and politeness. If men and women really did speak different languages, what would be the implications for each of these factors?

8. Suppose that you know a person who always uses masculine-generic terms such as "he" and "man." What information could you tell him or her about the way people interpret these terms?

9. This chapter discussed two examples of the way we make sense out of the world. Explain the constructionist view of inference and the social constructionist view of the way we create ideas about gender.

10. Many psychologists argue that language is our most impressive cognitive skill. Describe why language requires us to use a wide variety of other cognitive skills, such as perception, attention, memory, problem solving, decision making, and so forth. Also point out why language requires the skillful use of social knowledge.

NEW TERMS

phoneme (p. 293)
bottom-up processing (p. 293)
top-down processing (p. 293)
phonemic restoration (p. 293)
network models (p. 294)
spreading activation (p. 294)
prototype (p. 294)
prototype approach (p. 294)
graded structure (p. 295)
surface structure (p. 295)
deep structure (p. 295)
dual-route hypothesis (p. 296)
discourse (p. 296)
constructionist view (p. 297)
metacomprehension (p. 297)
neurolinguistics (p. 297)
aphasia (p. 297)
Broca's aphasia (p. 297)
Wernicke's aphasia (p. 297)

positron emission tomography
  (PET scan) (p. 298)
linearization problem (p. 299)
slip of the tongue (p. 299)
nonverbal communication (p. 300)
paralanguage (p. 300)
gestures (p. 300)
emblem (p. 300)
illustrator (p. 300)
bilingual (p. 301)
first language (p. 301)
second language (p. 301)
metalinguistics (p. 303)
pragmatics (p. 306)
schema (p. 306)
social constructionist viewpoint
  (p. 309)
masculine generic (p. 309)
Whorfian hypothesis (p. 310)

RECOMMENDED READINGS

Aries, E. (1996). *Men and women in interaction: Reconsidering the differences.* New York: Oxford University Press. Elizabeth Aries has written the ideal book to point out the flaws in the popularized views of gender comparisons in language use. Basing her argument on psychology research and critical thinking, she argues that men and women can display both "masculine" and "feminine" interaction styles, depending on factors such as status and the social situation.

Bialystok, E., & Hakuta, K. (1994). *In other words: The science and psychology of second-language acquisition.* New York: Basic Books. Ellen Bialystok and Kenji Hakuta are well-known researchers in the area of bilingualism; they have written an interesting and accessible summary of the research on this topic.

Carroll, D. W. (1994). *Psychology of language* (2nd ed.). Pacific Grove, CA: Brooks/Cole. I strongly recommend this textbook for any student who wants a clear and comprehensive overview of the psychology of language.

Gernsbacher, M. A. (Ed.). (1994). *Handbook of psycholinguistics.* San Diego: Academic Press. This comprehensive handbook contains 34 chapters on all aspects of the psychology of language, from saccadic eye movements in reading to discourse production and second-language learning.

ANSWERS TO DEMONSTRATIONS

Demonstration 9.1
    Two possibilities are: (1) "There, Don ate a kettle of ten chips" and (2) "The red on a tea kettle often chips."

Answers to Critical Thinking Exercises

Exercise 9.1

a. The graded structure of a concept seems to change in different cultural contexts (Barsalou, 1989, 1993). In many countries of the world, a mango would be a prototypical fruit, and an apple would be nonprototypical. (My daughter recently spent a year in rural Nicaragua, in a town with only six cars; a horse is a more prototypical vehicle than a car.)

b. Some educators favor the whole-word approach, which urges children to connect the written word directly with the word's meaning. In contrast, many favor the phonics approach, in which children must sound out the individual letters of a word to access a word's meaning (Chialant & Caramazza, 1995; Griffith & Olson, 1992).

Exercise 9.2

a. Researchers often ignore language production because they cannot easily control what a person wishes to say; for example, to study speech errors, they must take a sample of speech errors that are naturally produced. In contrast, they can conduct controlled research on what someone hears or reads (e.g., the words can be familiar or unfamiliar, the language can be simple or complex, etc.) (Fromkin & Ratner, 1998). You can also assign people randomly to conditions in research on language comprehension, so the experimental method is easy to apply.

b. Researchers interested in knowledge about emblems probably cannot sample a wide range of communities throughout North America, and emblems may well differ from one region to the next. Also, some emblems become popular for a time, and then they die away. An estimate of emblem vocabulary that was conducted in 1976 may not reflect today's emblem usage.

Exercise 9.3

a. People cannot be randomly assigned to bilingual and monolingual conditions; they arrive at the research setting, already belonging to one of these two groups. This situation creates problems, because the two groups may be different in social class, intelligence, age, education, and other experiences. Researchers therefore must try to match the two groups on relevant characteristics.

b. As Figure 9.3 shows, Kanzi hears the messages through earphones, so that the experimenter cannot hear the questions. The experimenter does not know the answers to the question, and so she or he cannot give hints to the chimp. Kanzi must therefore rely on his own linguistic knowledge.

Exercise 9.4

a. You could use the dependent measure that Clark and Wilkes-Gibbs used, average number of turns by director per figure (Figure 9.4), or you could use the number of minutes taken to complete the matches. With either dependent measure, you would expect communication to be more effective for friends than for strangers, especially for the first and second trials.

b. The problem is that people are being asked about the social nature of language while they are in a research setting that is not very social. This kind of design does not seem very high in ecological validity, because you are not interacting with another social creature. The problem is that, as we noted, it is difficult to study language production in a controlled setting.

Exercise 9.5

a. As Chapter 2 pointed out, people are typically much more excited about gender differences than gender similarities. As a result, this book would be less likely than those proclaiming gender differences to make the best-seller list. Unfortunately, the best-selling books typically overrepresent gender differences.

b. Researchers need to include items that have nothing to do with the variable under investigation if they are worried that participants will discover the purpose of the study. If all the items were concerned with gender, participants might guess that the study examined people's reactions to gender-biased language. They might not respond in a natural, normal way to these sentences.

DEVELOPMENT IN INFANCY AND CHILDHOOD

PHYSICAL AND PERCEPTUAL DEVELOPMENT

Prenatal Development

Hazards During Prenatal Development

Perceptual Development

COGNITIVE DEVELOPMENT

Memory Development

Thinking: Piaget's Approach and Piaget's Critics

Language Development

GENDER-ROLE DEVELOPMENT

In Depth: Children's Concepts About Gender

Theories of Gender-Role Development

PERSONALITY AND SOCIAL DEVELOPMENT

Temperament

Self-Concept

Social Relationships

Prosocial Behavior

The Child Care Controversy

Children and Their Ethnic Backgrounds

The Status of Children in North American Society

CHAPTER 10

Marian Wright Edelman grew up in South Carolina when segregation was an unquestioned reality. This photo shows her at age 6—she is the second from the right. In her book *The Measure of Our Success: A Letter to My Children and Yours*, she recalls the values she learned from her family and neighbors.

> *The adults in our churches and community made children feel valued and important They took time and paid attention to us. They struggled to find ways to keep us busy. And while life was often hard and resources scarce, we always knew who we were and that the measure of our worth was inside our heads and hearts and not outside in our possessions or on our backs. We were told that the world had a lot of problems; that Black people had an extra lot of problems, but that we were able and obligated to struggle and change them; that being poor was no excuse for not achieving; and that extra intellectual and material gifts brought with them the privilege and responsibility of sharing with others less fortunate. . . .*

> *I was fourteen years old the night my Daddy died. He had holes in his shoes but two children out of college, one in college, another in divinity school, and a vision he was able to convey to me as he lay dying in an ambulance that I, a young Black girl, could be and do anything; that race and gender are shadows; and that character, self-discipline, attitude, and service are the substance of life. (Edelman, 1993, pp. 5–7)*

After graduating from Spelman College and Yale Law School, Marian Wright Edelman became the first Black woman admitted to the Mississippi bar. She is currently the president of the Children's Defense Fund,* an organization that promotes the health and well-being of young children. (The photo on the right is a current one.)

---

*You may want to write for a list of the resources available from the Children's Defense Fund. Their address is 25 E Street NW, Washington, DC 20001; phone (202) 628-8787.

The life of Marian Wright Edelman provides a useful framework for our discussion of human development in these next two chapters. As you will see, **development** refers to the changes in physical, cognitive, and social abilities that occur throughout the life span.

Psychologists often raise three important questions in connection with human development. Let's outline them now and raise each one again later in these two chapters:

1. The **nature-nurture question:** Can development be primarily explained by nature, inborn factors, and genetics? Alternatively, is development primarily determined by nurture—that is, by learning and experience? You just read that Marian Wright Edelman grew up to be an individual who cares passionately about helping other people, a characteristic that her parents also shared. Did she become altruistic because of the genetic background she inherited from her parents (nature) or because her parents emphasized altruism in their child-rearing (nurture)?

The nature-nurture question is one of the oldest in psychology (Bronfenbrenner & Ceci, 1994; Kimble, 1994). As you might guess from our complexity theme, the appropriate answer specifies a combination of the two factors. In other words, development is determined by both nature and nurture, just as the area of a rectangle is determined not simply by its width or its length, but by both in combination (Maccoby, 1990a).

2. The **continuity-stages question:** Is development a gradual process, with adults simply having a greater *quantity* of some particular skill? Alternatively, do children and adults differ in the *quality* of their psychological processes? For example, does Marian Wright Edelman practice a qualitatively different kind of altruism as an adult than she did when she was a young child?

A typical example of the continuity-stages debate focuses on the fact that children and adults differ in the amount of material they remember. But do adults simply have *more* memory skills (continuity), or do they have a *different kind* of memory skills (stages)? In this particular area, we find more evidence for stages. As we'll see in the research on memory, older children and adults employ memory strategies that younger children never use. Their approach to memory is qualitatively different, suggesting that memory is primarily characterized by stages, rather than continuity.

3. The **stability-change question:** Do people maintain their personal characteristics as they mature from infants into adults (stability)? Alternatively, do these characteristics shift as a function of a person's current circumstances (change)? Marian Wright Edelman's life shows impressive stability. With her law degree, she could have abandoned her earlier values, but she maintained her commitment to helping needy people. As we'll see in this chapter, a person's temperament remains somewhat stable as infants mature into children. However, the stability is far from complete.

Before we examine the content of developmental psychology, we must briefly consider how researchers in this discipline study age differences. The problem with the age variable is that researchers cannot randomly assign people to different age

In the longitudinal method, a researcher follows a group of people (all the same age) as they grow older. For example, these students could be tested again two and four years later.

categories. For instance, most 30-year-olds would object to being randomly assigned to the 50-year-old age category—and instantly aged by two decades—even if we had the technology to do so. Because researchers cannot use random assignment, they face methodological problems that must be considered from a critical-thinking perspective.

Developmental psychologists typically use one of two methods for assessing age differences. In the **longitudinal method,** researchers select one group of individuals who are the same age and retest them periodically as they grow older. For example, suppose we want to examine children's attitudes toward politics. We might select a sample of 8-year-old children and retest this same group when they are 10 and 12 years old. (In other words, the researchers would need at least four years to complete the study.) If you are especially interested in determining whether personality shows stability or change, the longitudinal method is the logical choice.

In the second approach, the **cross-sectional method,** researchers test individuals of different ages at the same time. For instance, next Tuesday a researcher might select samples of children who are 8, 10, and 12 years old, questioning them about their political attitudes. The cross-sectional method has obvious advantages that appeal to researchers. It requires fewer resources and a study can be completed in a single day, instead of several years.

Each of these two methods has advantages and disadvantages. Neither method uses random assignment. As a result, both can be plagued by confounding variables—although the two methods differ in the kinds of confounding variables that infect them. The problem is that factors other than age can influence the dependent variable. For instance, the longitudinal method can be confounded by time of measurement. Suppose that researchers measure the political attitudes of 8-year-olds in 1998 and return to test the same children in 2000 and 2002. Suppose that the researchers notice that the children are much more negative about politics in 2002. Should the researchers propose that children undergo a major change in their thinking between the ages of 10 and 12? Instead, the researchers would be wise to look for alternative hypotheses, such as the possibility of very negative publicity about politicians in 2002. Another problem with the longitudinal approach is that some of the research participants may drop out or move away before the study has been completed.

The cross-sectional method has a different set of confounding variables. For instance, suppose that researchers would like to determine whether 30-year-olds, 45-year-olds, and 60-year-olds differ in their intellectual functioning. They administer intelligence tests, using three groups of people of the appropriate age. The results indicate a distinct drop in the older groups. Is it all downhill after 30, with intelligence inevitably decreasing? The confounding variable in this case is that each group was born in a different era. The three groups differ in their educational experiences. Many more of the 30-year-olds would have attended college, in comparison to 45- and 60-year-olds. Their higher scores could perhaps be traced to having had greater intellectual stimulation. In fact, cross-sectional research frequently shows a decrease in intellectual performance after age 30. In contrast, longitudinal research, tracing the same group of individuals across time (and therefore controlling for factors such as college attendance) shows little change in intellectual performance up to the age of 60 (Baltes & Kliegl, 1989).

Critical Thinking Exercise 10.1

Write down your answers to the following questions about the nature-nurture question and about research approaches in developmental psychology.

a. Suppose that you know a family in which the parents are both music teachers, and their two children seem to be especially talented musicians. A friend of yours says, "Well, no wonder the children are so musical. After all, they have gone to concerts and had music lessons since they were preschoolers!" How would you respond to this statement?

b. Suppose that you want to test children's knowledge of the rules of grammar, and how this knowledge increases between the ages of 6 and 10. What would be the advantages and disadvantages of using the cross-sectional method to study this question, rather than the longitudinal method?

Now let's consider how infants and children develop in four areas: (1) physical and perceptual changes, (2) cognitive knowledge, (3) gender awareness, and (4) personality and social characteristics. As you can see, the topics in this chapter follow the same order as those in the textbook itself, beginning with the more biological areas and ending with the more social areas.

PHYSICAL AND PERCEPTUAL DEVELOPMENT

In just nine months, a barely visible human egg matures into a baby ready to be born. Newborns have remarkably well-developed perceptual abilities, which continue to develop rapidly after they are born.

At conception, a sperm cell from the father fertilizes an egg cell from the mother.

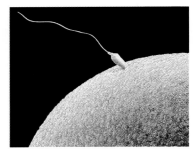

Prenatal Development

During insemination, approximately 200 million sperm cells are released into the female's reproductive tract (Aitken, 1995). **Conception** occurs when a sperm cell from the father fertilizes an egg cell (or ovum) from the mother. The fertilized egg begins to divide rapidly, and it attaches itself to the wall of the uterus.

The **fetal period** begins two months after conception and lasts until the baby is born about nine months after conception. As you can see from Figure 10.1, the four-month fetus has some human features, even though it is only about 6 inches long. The brain, heart, lungs, and other important organs develop further during the remaining months of pregnancy, and the fetus also grows substantially.

Hazards During Prenatal Development

Unfortunately, the developing fetus can be harmed if the mother's nutrition is inadequate. Additional risks come from teratogens (pronounced "*terr*-uh-tuh-jens"). **Teratogens** are substances in the prenatal environment that cause abnormalities during prenatal development. Table 10.1 illustrates a variety of teratogens and diseases.

As you might imagine, researchers find it difficult to estimate how many infants have been exposed to teratogens prenatally. However, Vega and his colleagues (1993) studied a sample of nearly 30,000 pregnant women in California. They estimated that 11.4% of newborns had been exposed to alcohol, tobacco, or an illegal drug within a few days before birth. Let's now consider in more detail the two most common harmful substances—alcohol and tobacco.

Pregnant women who drink alcohol may damage their babies significantly. Heavy drinking can produce fetal alcohol syndrome. As you can see from the photographs in Figure 10.2 (Page 320), the characteristic facial features may include widely spaced eyes and a flattened nose. The diagnosis of **fetal alcohol syndrome (FAS)** is made when a child has abnormalities in the following three categories: (1) the characteristic set of facial features; (2) retarded physical growth; and (3) mild to moderate mental retardation (Jenkins & Culbertson, 1996; Streissguth et al., 1993).

Some studies suggest that even small doses of alcohol can cause lasting effects to the fetus's central nervous system (e.g., Hunt et al., 1995). Therefore, many experts suggest that pregnant women should not consume *any* alcohol (Steinmetz, 1992).

About 30% of pregnant women smoke cigarettes (Brooke et al., 1989; Vasta et al., 1995). Smoking raises the level of carbon monoxide in the blood, which decreases the oxygen available to the fetus. Also, the nicotine in cigarettes indirectly reduces the oxygen supply (Sroufe et al., 1996). Babies of smokers are more likely than the babies of nonsmokers to be born prematurely. If mothers carry their babies to full term, these babies are likely to have a low birth weight and retarded growth (Nieburg et al., 1985; Olds et al., 1994; Sexton & Hebel, 1984). As these babies grow older, they often receive lower scores on tests of attention, reading, arithmetic, and general intelligence (Olds et al., 1994; Vorhees & Mollnow, 1987).

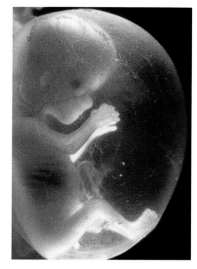

FIGURE 10.1

A fetus four months after conception.

TABLE 10.1 Teratogens and Diseases That Can Affect the Developing Fetus

TERATOGENS	POSSIBLE DANGER
Alcohol	Heavy drinking can produce fetal alcohol syndrome—which includes facial deformities, growth defects, and mental retardation.
Cigarettes	Heavy smoking is associated with premature birth weight, retarded growth, and lower scores on cognitive tasks.
Cocaine	Cocaine use is associated with premature birth, low birth weight, attention problems, irritability, and lower scores on cognitive tasks.
Marijuana	Heavy marijuana use can lead to premature birth, sleep disturbances, and abnormal reactions to stimulation.

DISEASES	POSSIBLE DANGER
Rubella (German measles)	If contracted early in pregnancy, rubella can cause heart defects, deafness, blindness, and mental retardation in babies.
Genital herpes	Genital herpes in pregnant women can cause infant death, blindness, and mental retardation in babies.
Acquired immunodeficiency syndrome (AIDS)	About 25% of HIV-positive mothers transmit the virus to the fetus; about 50% of HIV-positive infants will die by age 3.

Sources: Azuma & Chasnoff, 1993; Dahl et al., 1995; Jenkins & Culbertson, 1996; Mayes et al., 1995; Olds et al., 1994; Sroufe et al., 1996; Streissguth et al., 1993; Vasta et al., 1995; Zuckerman & Frank, 1994.

A 3-year-old girl from Sweden.

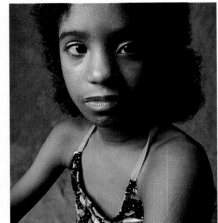

A 10-year-old girl from Chicago.

A 6-year-old boy from Seattle.

FIGURE 10.2

Fetal alcohol syndrome is associated with distinctive facial features in addition to physical and mental retardation.

Sadly, the developing fetus can be harmed even if someone else in the house smokes, providing passive exposure to the harmful substances in cigarettes. A newborn whose *father* had smoked at home faces about two-thirds the risk of reduced birth weight, compared with a newborn whose *mother* had smoked (Rubin et al., 1986; Schwartz-Bickenbach et al., 1987). Advertisements like the one in Figure 10.3 should also mention the hazards that passive smoking can create for the developing fetus.

Perceptual Development

When babies emerge from nine months of gestation, they open their eyes for their first view of the world. What do they see? Is it the disorganized "blooming, buzzing confusion," as claimed by America's first psychologist, William James (1890, p. 488)? And what do these newborns experience in the world of sound, the skin senses, smell, and taste?

Forty years ago, we knew very little about infants' perceptual abilities. After all, infants are too young to talk, so how can they inform researchers about their impressions of their perceptual worlds? Fortunately, researchers have become increasingly skilled at designing techniques for learning about infant perception. This research highlights the extraordinary perceptual competence of young infants (Bertenthal, 1996).

FIGURE 10.3

A stop-smoking ad from the American Cancer Society.

Vision Textbooks used to claim that newborns were blind at birth (Aslin, 1988). The landmark work of Robert Fantz (1961) showed otherwise. He placed infants inside a special chamber and attached pairs of test objects (such as a patch of narrow stripes and a patch of gray) onto the ceiling above them. Researchers recorded the amount of time the infant spent looking at each of the two objects. If little Janie looks significantly longer at the stripes than at the gray patch, then she must be able to tell the difference between the two stimuli. Figure 10.4 shows a patch of narrow stripes that a 1-month-old can just barely differentiate from the gray patch below the stripes. Notice that this method provides a measure of infants' **acuity**—that is, their ability to see precise details.

Babies are also more skilled in recognizing human faces than psychologists once believed. Before they are 1 month old, infants develop the ability to distinguish between a parent and a stranger (Pascalis et al., 1995; Walton et al., 1992). They prefer looking at face-like patterns, rather than other designs, at a very early age—maybe when they are as young as 1 *hour* old (Morton & Johnson, 1991).

Can infants perceive distance? Imagine a 7-month-old girl crawling rapidly from the upstairs bedroom toward the stairway. She pauses on the top step, looking down on the next step. Does that lower step look farther away to her? Figure 10.5

shows an example of a visual cliff, an apparatus in which the infant is exposed to a side that looks shallow and a side that looks deep. Gibson and Walk (1960) found that 6- to 14-month-old babies systematically crawled to the shallow side of the apparatus. In other words, they avoided the side that looked deeper and farther away. Using other measures, researchers have discovered that infants as young as 2 months have acquired some distance perception (Yonas & Owsley, 1987).

Can this early distance perception be traced to nature, or nurture? Unfortunately, we cannot answer this question. A 2-month-old baby may have been born with this skill, or the genetic code may have specified that distance perception should develop during the second month of life. But nurture may also play an important role. By the time they are 2 months old, babies have had experience with objects moving closer and farther, so they have learned some visual cues that are associated with distance. Unfortunately, even the most clever developmental psychologists have not discovered a way for 1-day-olds to "tell" us what they know about distance perception, before they have a chance to interact with objects.

Hearing We have seen that young infants are reasonably precocious in their visual abilities. However, their hearing abilities are even more impressive, especially in the area of speech perception. For instance, infants as young as 1 month old can hear the difference between sounds as similar as *bah* and *pah.* (Try saying these words out loud to appreciate how similar they are.) In fact, by 6 months of age, infants can discriminate between virtually any two **phonemes** (the basic sound units of speech) that are used in language (Aslin & Smith, 1988; Eimas et al., 1971). By 8 months, they are able to identify word boundaries between adjacent words (Saffran et al., 1996).

In fact, 6-month-old infants can even hear distinctions between sounds that older infants and adults can no longer hear. For example, only 10% of English-speaking adults can distinguish between two different kinds of *t* sounds that are important in the Hindi language spoken in India (Werker, 1994). However, 6-month-olds reared in English-speaking households can discriminate between these two sounds (Werker & Tees, 1984). By the ripe old age of 12 months, though, the babies in English-speaking homes could no longer perform accurately on this task.

By the age of 7 months, babies appreciate that a happy voice should come from a happy-looking face. Similarly, an angry voice should come from an angry-looking face (Soken & Pick, 1992; Walker-Andrews, 1986). In summary, then, babies are fairly

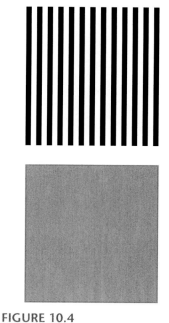

FIGURE 10.4

A 1-month-old infant can just barely discriminate the stripes on the top from the gray patch on the bottom, when both are presented at a distance of 10 inches from the baby's eyes.

FIGURE 10.5

The visual cliff was used by Gibson and Walk (1960) to test distance perception. Notice that the clear glass lies above a surface that appears to be shallow on the right and deep on the left.

By the age of 6 weeks or earlier, the infant can distinguish between the smell of mother and the smell of a stranger.

sophisticated in appreciating the subtle properties of speech sounds. These abilities prepare them to be very receptive to the conversations that surround them. These abilities also prepare them to speak by about the age of 1 year—as we will see when we discuss language development.

Other Perceptual Skills Touch is important in the world of young infants because it provides contact with adults and other people with whom they will form loving relationships. However, researchers have been much slower to appreciate how newborns respond to another skin sense—pain. Twenty years ago, investigators believed that newborns could not respond to painful stimuli that would provoke a response in an older child. Now they acknowledge that the sensory system for pain is well developed in infancy, and newborns should be given appropriate medication prior to surgery (Craig & Grunau, 1993).

Infants also have a fairly well-developed sense of smell. For example, they can smell the difference between their mother and a stranger, perhaps as early as 6 weeks of age (Bornstein, 1992; Cernoch & Porter, 1985).

Taste buds seem to be functional even before birth. For example, 1-day-old babies prefer sweet liquids to unflavored water (Bernstein, 1991; Mennella & Beauchamp, 1996). Unfortunately for our later health, we seem to be born with a sweet tooth—even before we actually have teeth. The preference for sweet tastes can clearly be traced to a nature explanation, because a 1-day-old has not lived long enough for nurture to influence preferences. Sweet tastes are characteristic of carbohydrates—a source of nutrition. Therefore, this inborn preference makes sense from the perspective of evolutionary psychologists.

In summary, the material on perception in young infants provides important support for the theme that humans are remarkably well equipped to function in the world. In fact, developmental psychologists often use the phrase "the amazing newborn," in appreciation of the remarkable capabilities of the young infant.

SECTION SUMMARY: *PHYSICAL AND PERCEPTUAL DEVELOPMENT*

1. Three important issues in human development are the nature-nurture question, the continuity-stages question, and the stability-change question.

2. Developmental psychologists typically use either the longitudinal method or the cross-sectional method to investigate age differences; each method has its advantages and disadvantages.

3. Prenatal development begins with the fertilized egg; the brain and other important organs grow rapidly during the prenatal period.

4. Factors that can harm the fetus during prenatal development include teratogens such as alcohol, cigarettes, cocaine, and marijuana, and diseases such as rubella, genital herpes, and AIDS.

5. Infants have some degree of visual acuity by 1 month of age and depth perception by 2 months.

6. Infants' hearing abilities are even more impressive: They can distinguish phonemes at 1 month; at 6 months they can distinguish phonemes that adults can no longer differentiate; by 7 months they know that facial expression should match a person's tone of voice.

7. Contrary to earlier beliefs, newborns are sensitive to pain, and they have a fairly well-developed sense of smell; they also prefer sweet tastes as soon as they are born.

COGNITIVE DEVELOPMENT

We have seen that young infants possess some remarkable perceptual skills. Their perceptual world is not a "blooming, buzzing confusion." Instead, the world is reasonably orderly. What can they accomplish with these reasonably orderly perceptions? As we will see in this section, infants can remember, think, and use language.

Memory Development

Infancy   We have already seen that infants can remember how their mothers look and smell—before these young babies are 2 months old. However, the most extensive research on infant memory has been conducted by Carolyn Rovee-Collier and her associates, using operant conditioning. As Chapter 6 explained, **operant conditioning** involves learning to make a response because it produces a reinforcing effect. Rovee-Collier applied operant conditioning in her research by connecting the infant's ankle to a mobile with a ribbon, so that when the infant kicked his or her foot, the mobile would move (Figure 10.6). Young infants love this game, and they soon learn the connection between kicking (the response) and movement from the mobile (the reinforcing effect). Then the researchers test memory by waiting several days before presenting the mobile a second time. Will the baby remember to kick?

Rovee-Collier and other researchers demonstrated that a 3-month-old typically remembers how to activate the mobile after a delay as long as 12 days (Rovee-Collier & Boller, 1995; Rovee-Collier & Hayne, 1987). This technique has been used to demonstrate many similarities between infant and adult memory. For example, infants—like adults—recall an event less accurately if they have been exposed to misleading information between the time of the original event and the memory test (Rovee-Collier et al., 1993).

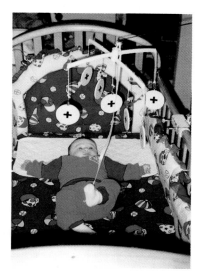

FIGURE 10.6

The operant conditioning technique that Rovee-Collier and her colleagues used to test infant memory.

Childhood   In some respects, children's and adults' memories are similar. For instance, children's recognition memory is reasonably accurate (Kail, 1984; Perry & Wrightsman, 1991). If you show children some magazine ads and later ask them to identify which ads look familiar, they will probably respond accurately.

Children have a strong disadvantage on other kinds of memory tasks, however. Their working memory is clearly limited (Kail, 1992). The average 2-year-old can remember only two items in a row, in contrast to about seven items for 12-year-olds and adults (Dempster, 1981).

The most controversial topic in the development of memory concerns the accuracy of children's eyewitness testimony. As you can imagine, this topic has important implications for the courtroom: Should the eyewitness testimony of a child be trusted? Researchers have discovered some potential problems with children's memories. For example, preschoolers have trouble deciding which memories are real and which are simply imagined (Ratner & Foley, 1994).

Research by Michelle Leichtman and Stephen Ceci (1995) illustrates other potential problems with children's eyewitness testimony. They tested 3- to 6-year-olds in four different conditions. In the *control condition,* a stranger named Sam Stone visited the children's classroom, and the children were provided with no misleading information. In the *stereotype condition,* children had been told beforehand that Sam Stone was clumsy and bumbling. In the *suggestion condition,* children were given misleading post-event suggestions after his visit; they were told that he had accidentally ripped a book and spilled chocolate drink on a teddy bear. In the *stereotype-plus-suggestion* condition, children were supplied with the stereotype information beforehand and the misleading suggestions afterwards.

Ten weeks after Sam Stone's classroom visit, the children were asked what he had done during his visit. As part of the interview, the children were asked whether they had actually seen him tear up the book and spill chocolate drink on the teddy bear. Figure 10.7 shows the percentage of children who said they had witnessed at least one of these events. As you can see, the younger children were much more likely than the older children to report events that had not occurred. It is significant that many of the 3- and 4-year-olds made errors in the stereotype condition. Even more of them made errors in the suggestion condition, and more than 40% of them made errors in the stereotype-plus-suggestion condition. In some cases, though, children's eyewitness reports can be trusted, especially if they are older (Ceci & Bruck, 1993, 1995; Goodman & Bottoms, 1993). However, factors such as stereotypes and suggestions can substantially decrease their accuracy.

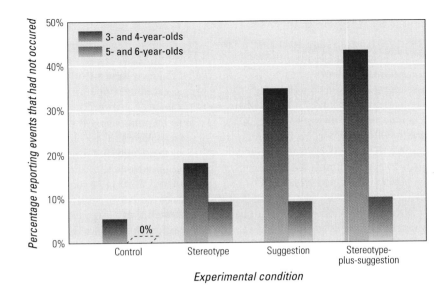

FIGURE 10.7

Children's Eyewitness Testimony
The percentage of children who reported actually seeing one or more events that had not occurred, as a function of experimental condition and age.
Source: Based on Leichtman & Ceci, 1995.

This girl thinks that she can memorize these objects by merely looking at them. Without deep processing, however, she will remember very few items.

Other research has confirmed that young children perform relatively poorly when we measure long-term memory in terms of recall, rather than recognition (Howe et al., 1992a, 1992b; Myers & Perlmutter, 1978). One reason for their poor performance is that they have not yet developed their **metamemory,** or knowledge and awareness about their memory. Specifically, young children do not seem to realize that they need to make a special effort to remember and that they need to use special memory strategies (Kail, 1992; Small, 1990). They think that they will be able to remember a list of items by simply looking at it, without using deep processing. As children grow older, they realize that they need to *work* to improve their memory. They also begin to use strategies such as rehearsal (silent repetition), imagery, and organization in order to enhance their memory performance.

Thinking: Piaget's Approach and Piaget's Critics

Jean Piaget (pronounced "Zhohn Pea-ah-*zhay*") was a Swiss theoretician who lived from 1896 to 1980. Together with Skinner and Freud, Piaget is typically listed as one of the three leading figures in twentieth century psychology (Brainerd, 1996). His theory of cognitive development has had a profound impact on developmental psychology. However, his theory also has some important weaknesses that have been demonstrated by contemporary researchers.

Piaget argued that children are active learners, rather than passive "sponges" that soak up stimuli from the environment. Piaget emphasized that children continually try to create more advanced understandings of how the world works (Siegler & Ellis, 1996).

An important central concept in Piaget's theory can be called meaning-making. **Meaning-making** refers to children's active attempts to make sense of their world, their experiences, and other people (Kuhn, 1992). Children try to construct general principles based on these experiences. For example, children have seen many examples of a glass filled with liquid, and so they construct an idea that the level of liquid in a glass should form a line that is parallel with the bottom of the glass. If you ask children to draw a line showing how the liquid would look in a tilted glass, they would probably draw a line parallel with the bottom of the glass. (See Figure 10.8.) No child has ever *seen* liquid defy the laws of gravity, forming a slanted surface. However, children's drawings do not reflect their visual experiences. Instead, the drawings reflect their meaning-making—that is, their understanding of the relationship between liquids and containers.

Piaget proposed a system of assimilation and accommodation to account for the way people use and modify the stimuli they encounter. This process emphasizes the active nature of children's minds (Flavell, 1996). In **assimilation,** we deal with stimuli in terms of our current thought structures. For example, a girl seeing a little pony for the first time might call it *doggie*, because doggie is a concept that is part of her current thought structure. (You can remember that in *assimilation*, the child treats the stimulus as if it is *similar* to a familiar concept.) Imagine, however, what might happen if children used only assimilation. How could their thought structures grow more complex?

Accommodation, the mirror image of assimilation, occurs when assimilation fails. In **accommodation,** our thought structures change to fit the stimuli we encounter. For example, the previous concept *doggie*—which had been used to refer to medium-sized, hairy, four-legged creatures—might now be divided into two categories, *doggie* and *horsie*.

Piaget described four major periods of human development. With respect to the continuity-stages question discussed at the beginning of this chapter, Piaget clearly voted for "stages." He argued that certain periods in cognitive development appear in a fixed order. Also, each period is necessary for the formation of the period that follows (Piaget, 1983). Furthermore, each period differs qualitatively (in terms of *kind* of thinking) from other periods, rather than simply differing quantitatively (in terms of *amount,* such as number of correct items). An outline of Piaget's four periods is shown in Table 10.2. Let us look at Piaget's description of these periods and then evaluate his theory in light of current research.

Sensorimotor Period   Piaget used the term **sensorimotor period** for the first stage of cognitive development because the infant's major cognitive tasks include sensory activities (such as seeing and hearing) and motor activities (such as kicking, sucking, and reaching). Piaget believed that babies have not yet developed language and symbols, but they can perform some actions. According to Piaget, these actions constitute the first forms of intelligence. In the first weeks of life, basic reflexes like the sucking reflex are most important.

Piagetian theory proposes that young infants do not have a sense of **object permanence,** which is the knowledge that an object exists even if it is temporarily out of sight (see Figure 10.9). Toward the end of the sensorimotor period, however, babies become experts at finding a missing object, even when it is moved several times. As we will discuss, however, recent experimental evidence demonstrates that Piaget underestimated infants' knowledge during the sensorimotor period.

Preoperational Period   A critical characteristic of the **preoperational period** is the development of language. Piaget argued that children can now represent thought by using symbols and words, rather than simple physical actions. Language provides an enormous advantage to children because they can now refer to objects that are not physically present.

Another critical characteristic of the preoperational child is egocentrism. When adults use the word *egocentrism* in everyday speech, we imply selfishness. However, Piaget used **egocentrism** to mean that a child sees the world from only one point of view: his or her own. Little Tanya may annoy her parents by standing directly between them and the television set. *She* can see the program perfectly well; from her point of view, there is no problem. Egocentrism diminishes gradually throughout childhood.

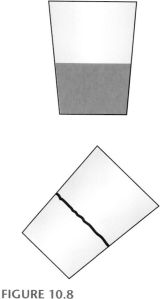

FIGURE 10.8

When children are shown a drawing of liquid in a glass and asked to draw a line indicating the level when the glass is tilted, they draw a line parallel with the bottom of the glass, as in the figure on the bottom.

A young child who sees this pony for the first time can use assimilation and call it a doggie *or use accommodation, creating a new category called* horsie.

TABLE 10.2 An Outline of Piaget's Four Periods of Cognitive Development

PERIOD	APPROXIMATE AGE	DESCRIPTION
Sensorimotor	Birth–2 years	1. The infant interacts with the world through sensory and motor activities. 2. The infant learns that objects exist even when they are not visible.
Preoperational	2–7 years	1. The child represents objects with words and mental images. 2. The child still shows egocentrism.
Concrete operational	7–11 years	1. The child demonstrates conservation. 2. The child shows more logical thinking.
Formal operational	11 years up to adulthood	1. The person can reason abstractly; concrete objects no longer need to be present. 2. The person can form and test hypotheses.

Source: Based on Ginsburg & Opper, 1988.

FIGURE 10.9

Piagetian theory states that the young infant lacks a sense of object permanence; for example, a favorite toy that is hidden beneath the blanket no longer seems to exist. However, recent research suggests that infants do understand object permanence when it is tested with different measures.

Concrete Operational Period During the **concrete operational period,** children acquire important mental operations—that is, methods of manipulating information mentally. One of these operations is called conservation. Children who show **conservation** realize that a given quantity stays the same, no matter how its shape or physical arrangement may change. Figure 10.10 shows a preoperational child, who believes that a tall, thin glass contains more milk. She is so impressed by the height of the liquid in the new container that she fails to realize that the other glass is wider. She also fails to realize that the amounts must be equal because nothing was added or subtracted. Try Demonstration 10.1 to test conservation in children.

Formal Operational Period In the concrete operational period, children can reason logically and maturely on many different problems—as long as the problem is physically present. However, they have trouble with more abstract reasoning. Teenagers and adults who are in the **formal operational period** can think scientifically. They can also construct possible solutions to a problem and then create a systematic plan for selecting a correct solution. They can solve problems without the help of a concrete representation. They can also contemplate complex ideas and think flexibly about a variety of problems.

The Current Status of Piaget's Theory Clearly, Piaget created an extremely comprehensive and complex theory of cognitive development. No other theorist has proposed such a complete picture of children's thinking. In fact, his theories were influential in shifting many psychologists away from behaviorism and toward the cognitive approach (Kessen, 1996).

Piaget identified intriguing concepts—such as object permanence and conservation—that no one else had ever investigated. In addition, his theories have inspired thousands of studies, which is one indication that researchers have judged his work to be extremely valuable (Beilin, 1992; Case, 1987).

Nevertheless, Piaget's theory can be criticized in several respects. For example, he did not pay much attention to individual differences (Case, 1987), a theme emphasized throughout this textbook.

Many studies have also demonstrated that Piaget underestimated the capabilities of young infants (Flavell, 1992). Consider object permanence, for example.

The child believes that two similar glasses contain the same amount of liquid.

She watches the liquid being poured from one container to the other.

She indicates that the taller, thinner glass contains more liquid.

FIGURE 10.10

A preoperational child fails to show conservation.

Piaget assessed object permanence by noting whether the infant manually searched for the missing object. However, infants might perform poorly on this dependent variable because they are limited in their ability to plan their search strategies—not because they have an underdeveloped concept of object permanence (Baillargeon, 1992).

Earlier in this chapter, we saw that psychologists were able to discover remarkable perceptual skills in infants by designing creative research methods. Similarly, Renée Baillargeon and her colleagues used a variety of creative techniques to demonstrate that infants as young as 3 months of age know a great deal about object permanence and other properties of objects (e.g., Baillargeon 1986, 1994; Baillargeon et al., 1985). These studies assess the amount of time an infant looks at an object or an event, rather than Piaget's measure, manual search.

Let's consider a study on object permanence by Baillargeon and DeVos (1991). In this research, 3½-month-old infants watched carrot-like cartoon figures as they traveled along a track, behind a screen. (See Figure 10.11.) The researchers first tested **habituation,** during which a stimulus is presented many times until the individual stops responding to it (in this case, looking at it). They included this condition to make sure that the infants considered the short carrot and the tall carrot to be equally interesting; indeed, the infants looked at both figures for equal amounts of time.

DEMONSTRATION 10.1 The Development of Conservation

In this demonstration, you will be examining conservation of number. First locate one or more children between the ages of 5 and 8. Form two rows of 10 pennies each, with both rows similarly spaced (see *a*). Ask the child whether both rows contain the same number of pennies or whether one contains more. Once the child has determined that the rows contain

the same number, push the pennies in the bottom row closer together (see *b*). Ask again whether the two rows have the same number or whether one row has more. Finally, ask the child to explain his or her answer.

You may also wish to test conservation of liquid, using Figure 10.10 as a guide.

a. Two horizontal rows, each with 10 pennies, lined up so that the two sets of edges are matching.

b. Two horizontal rows, each with 10 pennies, lined up so that the bottom row is denser.

Habituation events

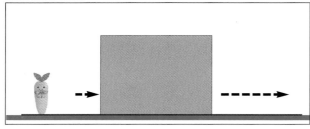

Test events

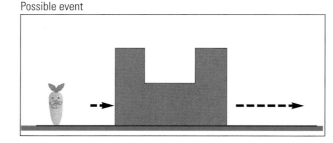

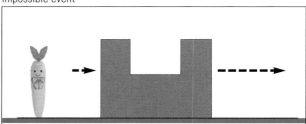

FIGURE 10.11

Studying Infants' Sense of Object Permanence

This is a schematic representation of the research of Baillargeon and DeVos. The habituation phase demonstrated that infants were equally interested in the short and the tall carrot. During the test phase, however, infants looked longer at the impossible event (when the tall carrot was not visible through the opening in the screen) than at the possible event (when the short carrot was not visible).
Source: Based on Baillargeon and DeVos, 1991.

During the test phase, infants sometimes saw a *possible event,* during which the short carrot passed behind a screen without being visible through the opening in the screen. They also saw an *impossible event,* in which the tall carrot passed behind the same screen; it should have been visible in the opening, but it was not. The infants looked significantly longer at the impossible event than at the possible event. This finding suggests that they had expected the tall carrot to maintain its existence, even when it was hidden; they were surprised when it failed to appear in the opening. Infants apparently know that objects should not disappear when they are hidden!

Another feature of Piaget's sensorimotor period that researchers now question is Piaget's claim that infants are not capable of symbolic thought. For example, Mandler argues that infants can form concepts at an early age. Babies as young as 9 months of age can distinguish between the categories of *airplanes* and *birds,* even though both kinds of objects are similar in shape (Mandler, 1992; Mandler & McDonough, 1993).

In general, Piaget was correct about the order in which children master cognitive tasks (Flavell, 1996; Lourenço & Machado, 1996). However, children progress unevenly in their cognitive development, so that a child may be preoperational according to one measure and concrete operational according to a second measure. Also, most current developmental psychologists believe that the "stages" part of Piaget's theory was overstated. They are more likely to see some continuities in cognitive development (Flavell, 1992; Kuhn, 1992). Finally, most developmental psychologists would argue that Piaget's measurment techniques underestimated children's competence (Lourenço & Machado, 1996).

In summary, Piaget proposed a broad, complex theory about the development of thinking. However, even Piaget underestimated the rich, complicated nature of infants' and children's thoughts. The complexity of humans makes it difficult to explain their behavior in any general, sweeping statements. Very clearly, our theme of complexity applies not only to adults, but also to infants and young children.

Critical Thinking Exercise 10.2

Write down your answers to the following questions about memory and cognitive development.

a. Probably one of the major obstacles in studying infant memory and cognitive development is selecting an appropriate dependent variable. What dependent variables have been selected in the research you've read about in these two sections?

b. In the research by Baillargeon and DeVos (1991), why did they need to include a condition in which the infants simply looked at the short and tall carrots (Figure 10.11, top two diagrams)?

Language Development

"Mama!"   (8 months)

"Hi, Mom!"   (1 year, 4 months)

"Don't cry, honey."   (1 year, 5 months)

"My grandma gave me this dolly, Cara. My grandma is my mommy's mommy. I have another grandma, too. She's my daddy's mommy. And Aunt Elli is my daddy's sister."   (2 years, 9 months)

The foregoing selections from the early language of my daughter are typical of the remarkable accomplishment involved in language acquisition. Within a period of 2 to 3 years, all normal children progress from one-word utterances to complex descriptions about relationships. In fact, language acquisition is one of the most impressive intellectual accomplishments we humans perform.

Consider, for instance, that the average 6-year-old has some mastery of about 14,000 words. To acquire a vocabulary this large, children must learn about nine new words each day from the time they start speaking until their sixth birthday (E. V. Clark, 1991). Perhaps even more impressive than the size of children's vocabulary is their skill in combining these words into phrases that are completely original, such as "My dolly dreamed about toys" (2 years, 2 months). Let's see how children's language evolves with respect to early language, grammar, pragmatics, and theoretical explanations for language acquisition.

Early Language   In the discussion of speech perception, we saw that young children have a head start on language. Infants are impressively accomplished at appreciating distinctions among speech sounds.

Children's early vocalizations pass through a series of stages. Infants make cooing sounds around 2 months of age. At 6 to 8 months, babies begin babbling, making sounds such as *dadada* (Locke, 1994; Menyuk et al., 1995). Their speech sounds soon become more similar to adult language. Interestingly, deaf infants who have been exposed to sign language also begin at about this time to "babble" with their hands, producing systematic but meaningless actions that are not found in hearing children (Petitto & Marentette, 1991).

Children say their first words around the time of their first birthday, though individual differences are—as usual—quite striking (Vihman et al., 1994). For example, one study showed that the production vocabulary for 12-month-olds ranged between 0 and 52 words (Fenson et al., 1991). The sudden increase in vocabulary size between 12 and 28 months may be linked to rapid increases in synaptic connections in the cortex (Bates et al., 1992).

Grammar   One important aspect of grammar is **syntax,** or the organizational rules for determining word order, sentence organization, and relationships among words

Jean Mandler's research suggests that infants can form concepts, contrary to Piaget's theory. For example, infants can distinguish between airplanes and birds, even though their shapes are similar.

The telegraphic language of young children omits the nonessential words. For example, this child might describe his pet with the phrase "doggie ball."

(Owens, 1996). Children typically begin producing two-word phrases around the age of 20 months (Bates et al., 1995; Bohannon, 1993). Here are some representative first phrases (Clark & Clark, 1977; de Villiers & de Villiers, 1992):

"Push car"   (action-object)

"Mommy sock"   (possessor-possessed)

"Daddy eat"   (actor-action)

Notice that these early phrases express a wide variety of relationships. Also, the word order in the phrases suggests an early awareness of English word order.

Another characteristic of these sentences is **telegraphic speech,** which includes nouns and verbs but leaves out the extra words that serve only a grammatical function, such as articles (*a, the,* etc.) and prepositions (de Villiers & de Villiers, 1992). Notice that children express only the essential meaning in phrases such as *Push car, Mommy sock,* and *Daddy eat.* As in a telegraph, they omit the extra, less important words.

Pragmatics   As we discussed in Chapter 9, the term **pragmatics** refers to the social aspects of language. Children need to learn what should be said—and what should *not* be said (Ninio & Snow, 1996). One of my students described his family's embarrassment when a younger brother shouted to an elderly gentleman on his way to the bathroom during a party, "Mommy says to make sure to aim straight so you don't get the seat wet!"

We saw that Piaget believed young children have difficulty adopting another person's point of view. However, research on children's language shows that preschoolers can adapt their conversation to their listeners' level of understanding (Siegal, 1996). For example, Shatz and Gelman (1973) found that 4-year-olds described a toy differently when speaking with a 2-year-old than when speaking with a peer or an adult. Specifically, their conversation to 2-year-olds used short, simple utterances, with more repetition. As in some other areas, Piaget apparently underestimated the cognitive skills of young children.

Children learn language so they can accomplish social goals that are important to them (Siegal, 1996). They realize that language is central to the world of adults. To become a genuine person, young children must use language to go beyond their immediate experiences and converse about people's unobservable motivations, the social world beyond their family, and other more complex issues (Shatz, 1994).

Explanations for Language Acquisition   Let us now turn to several explanations that have been proposed for language acquisition. We have emphasized that acquiring a language is an impressive intellectual achievement. The process is facilitated by the fact that children have inborn language skills. They also acquire language by learning. In addition, their cognitive skills allow them to unravel the many mysteries of their native language. Finally, adults help children by providing them with appropriately simple language phrases. Let's consider these four factors.

In speaking to his younger brother, this preschooler would use simpler vocabulary and shorter sentences than when speaking with an adult.

1. *Language is inborn.* According to the inborn view, language skills are genetically programmed. We have seen in this chapter that newborn infants already have impressive speech perception skills. Noam Chomsky (1988), the foremost supporter of the inborn-language view, argues that children acquire language simply by being placed in an appropriate environment, in the same fashion that the child's body grows when provided with appropriate nutrition.

Evidence for this view comes from the observation that language tends to appear at roughly the same age in a wide variety of cultures. Also, the same kinds of meanings are encoded in children's early words and phrases, even though they speak different languages (Rice, 1989; Slobin, 1985). If similar trends occur in such widely different learning environments, then humans must be born with some language-making capacity. However, this language-making capacity must be combined with learning the rules and specific vocabulary of the language in which the child is reared.

2. *Language is acquired by learning.* According to the behaviorist view, language acquisition can be explained by principles of learning such as the ones you read about in Chapter 6. Young children learn to associate certain objects with the sounds of words. They imitate the words and the grammar they hear around them. Adults provide reinforcement for correct language in the form of smiles, hugs, and the food or other objects requested by children (Kymissis & Poulson, 1990; Skinner, 1957). Just as a pigeon in an operant-conditioning task learns to peck a button to receive a pellet of food, a young child learns to say "cookie" to receive a cookie.

Learning theory sounds logical, and learning is clearly an important part of language acquisition. However, it cannot account for all the characteristics of language. For instance, simple imitation cannot explain how children manage to produce grammatical forms and novel sentences they have never heard before. What child has heard his parent say, "I holded two mices"? I assure you my daughter never heard her parents say, "My dolly dreamed about toys."

3. *Language depends upon cognition.* Children who have inborn language ability and numerous opportunities for learning would still make little progress without support from their cognitive abilities. Many theorists therefore emphasize that language depends upon achievements in cognitive development (Rosenberg, 1993; Woodward & Markman, 1998). For example, toddlers begin to say "all gone" about the same time they can solve complicated object-permanence tasks. Once they appreciate what "all gone" means, they begin to talk about it (Rice, 1989).

The cognitive view also emphasizes that children are active language learners (McDonald, 1997; Woodward & Markman, 1998). They continually analyze what they hear, testing hypotheses and trying to fit together the pieces of the language jigsaw puzzle. According to the cognitive view, the child is a junior scientist, actively working to discover the meaning of new words and the rules for combining those words.

4. *Adults provide child-appropriate language.* Another important factor that facilitates children's language acquisition is that adult caretakers tend to use language that is ideally suited for young language-learners. The language spoken to children is called **child-directed speech,** and it uses simple vocabulary, emphasis on important words, well-formed short sentences, long pauses, slow rate of speech, and high voice pitch (Fernald & Mazzie, 1991; Sroufe et al., 1996). (The previous name for this language, *motherese,* is now less common, primarily because of its gender bias.) Cross-cultural research in Europe, Asia, Latin America, and Africa has confirmed a widespread tendency to use this style of language when speaking to infants and young children (Bornstein et al., 1992; Fernald, 1991). Demonstration 10.2 illustrates child-directed speech.

When this Guatemalan girl was about a year old, she began to produce words, like children throughout the world. Children's early words and sentences also capture similar kinds of meanings, which supports the argument that language skills are inborn.

DEMONSTRATION 10.2 Using Child-Directed Speech

Locate a doll that resembles an infant as closely as possible in features and size. Select a friend who has had experience with children, and ask him or her to imagine that the doll is an infant niece or nephew who has just arrived for a first visit. Encourage your friend to interact with the baby as he or she normally would. Observe your friend's language for qualities such as pitch, variation in pitch, vocabulary, sentence length, repetition, and intonation. Also observe nonverbal communication. What qualities are different from the language your friend typically uses with adults?

Source: Based on an idea from Ganie DeHart, 1990.

In summary, children acquire language because they are remarkably well equipped. They supplement their inborn abilities with their learning skills. Furthermore, their cognitive skills encourage them to actively unravel the mysteries of language. Finally, adults help to make language acquisition more manageable by adjusting their communication style to accommodate children's linguistic skills.

SECTION SUMMARY: *COGNITIVE DEVELOPMENT*

1. Research using operant conditioning shows that 3-month-olds can remember an activity up to 12 days later, and that infants—like adults—are less accurate if they have seen misleading post-event information.

2. Children do not differ substantially from adults in their recognition memory. However, children's short-term memory and long-term recall memory are clearly inferior in comparison with adults; for example, young children's eyewitness testimony is highly influenced by stereotypes and suggestions.

3. Children have poorly developed metamemory, and they do not realize that they must use memory strategies in order to improve memory performance.

4. Piaget's theory emphasizes that children actively try to make meaning from the objects and events in their world. He proposed four periods in cognitive development: sensorimotor, preoperational, concrete operational, and formal operational.

5. Piaget's theory has been extremely influential. However, it has been criticized for its lack of attention to individual differences, its underestimation of infants' skills with object permanence and concepts, and its overemphasis on stages.

6. Children's first phrases express a wide variety of relationships, and they are telegraphic; language acquisition also requires mastery of pragmatic rules.

7. An explanation of language acquisition needs to be complex; it must include inborn language abilities, learning skills, the use of active cognitive strategies, and adult language that encourages children's linguistic competence.

GENDER-ROLE DEVELOPMENT

Adults believe that gender is extremely important, even when discussing the gender of an infant. For example, one pair of researchers asked parents of newborns to telephone friends and relatives to announce their baby's birth (Intons-Peterson & Reddel, 1984). In 80% of the cases, the first question the parents were asked was basically, "Is it a boy or a girl?" People eventually asked about the health of the mother or the baby, but only after they had established whether the baby was female or male.

We also know that people make different judgments about baby girls than about baby boys. In a study by Condry and Condry (1976), people watched a series of videotapes featuring an infant. Half of the people had been told the infant was female; half were told the infant was male. At one point, the baby cried when a jack-in-the-box opened suddenly. When people thought they were watching a baby girl, they tended to judge that the baby was afraid. When they thought they were watching a baby boy, they tended to judge that the emotional reaction was more active: The baby was angry. Remember, however, that everyone saw exactly the same videotape. However, the labels "female" and "male" had biased the viewers' judgments. Gender clearly matters to adults.

In the previous sections, we have seen that young children possess impressive perceptual and cognitive talents. As we will see in this section, young children are also very knowledgeable about **gender roles,** which are our expectations about appropriate activities for females and males (Beal, 1994). First, the "In Depth" feature will discuss what children know and think about gender. Then we'll consider some explanations for gender-role development.

IN DEPTH

Children's Concepts About Gender

We have just seen that adults hold different beliefs about male and female infants. At what point do infants make a distinction between males and females? What do young children believe about the characteristics of males and females, and what do they think about members of the other gender?

Distinguishing Between Males and Females

So far in this chapter, we have seen that infants are surprisingly competent. They can make perceptual discriminations, remember objects and events, demonstrate object permanence, and form concepts—even before they are a year old. You may not be surprised, then, to learn that babies can also distinguish between males and females. In one study, Beverly Fagot and Mary Leinbach (1993) used the habituation method you read about on Page 327 in order to test infants between the ages of 5 and 12 months. The infants saw a series of slides of the heads and shoulders of different women. (The slides showed a variety of clothing, hairstyles, facial expressions, and so forth.) After a number of trials, the infants lost interest in the slides of these women; they had habituated. Then the researchers presented a test slide, showing either a male or a female. The infants who were 9 months and older looked significantly longer if the test slide showed a male than if the slide showed a female. In other words, they noticed the difference. The infants showed this same pattern of increased looking-time if they were first habituated to slides of several men and then saw a test slide of a woman. Impressively, then, infants can visually distinguish between males and females before their first birthday.

Beliefs About Personality

Gloria Cowan and Charles Hoffman (1986) studied children's attitudes about gender and personality among boys and girls who were between the ages of 2½ and 4. The children were shown two pictures of infants, one a girl and one a boy. (However, in a pretest, another group of children the same age could not guess the infants' sexes accurately.) For example, the infants in Figure 10.12 might be introduced like this: "This baby is a boy named Tommy (pointing to the baby on the top), and this baby is a girl named Susie (pointing to the baby on the bottom)." Next the experimenters checked to make certain the children recalled which was the girl and which was the boy. Then the children were asked, "One of these babies is big, and one is little; point to the baby which is big." (The experimenters were careful to reverse the photos on half the trials and also to vary the order of the adjectives.) They also asked children to make decisions about seven other adjective pairs, such as mad-scared, strong-weak, and soft-hard.

   The results showed that the children chose a stereotyped response 64% of the time. That is, they tended to say that the boy baby was big, mad, strong, and hard, whereas the girl baby was small, scared, weak, and soft. The results were statistically significant, indicating that even preschoolers have stereotypes about gender.

Concepts About the Other Gender

If you look on any playground, you're likely to notice something striking: Girls play with other girls, and boys play with other boys. This tendency to associate with children of the same gender is called **gender segregation.** In a representative naturalistic observation study, 6½-year-olds played 11 times as often with members of the same gender as with playmates of the other gender. As one girl remarked, sitting next to a boy was like "being in a lower rank or peeing in your pants" (Maccoby & Jacklin, 1987, p. 245).

FIGURE 10.12

Photos of two infants, similar to those used in Cowan and Hoffman's (1986) study.

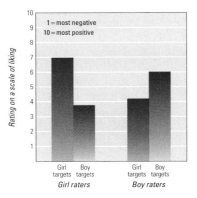

FIGURE 10.13

Ratings supplied by female and male children for the girls and boys in videos. Notice that the data show same-sex favoritism.
Source: Based on Powlishta, 1995a.

(IN DEPTH continued)

As you might expect, children also give more favorable ratings to members of their own gender. For example, Kimberly Powlishta (1995a) showed children a series of brief videotaped interactions between a child and an adult. Three of these segments featured girls, and three featured boys. The children who viewed the film were 9- and 10-year-olds; their ethnic diversity was fairly close to the percentages in the U.S. population. After viewing each video, the children rated the child in the video, using a 10-point scale of liking that ranged from "not at all" to "very, very much."

As you can see in Figure 10.13, girls liked the girl targets in the videos better than the boy targets. In contrast, boys preferred the boy targets to the girl targets. Other research suggests a reason for children's biases in play patterns and preferences. Specifically, children divide the world into two distinct categories, male and female. They tend to prefer the category to which they belong, a phenomenon called **ingroup favoritism** (Powlishta, 1995b, 1995c; Powlishta et al., 1994). Fortunately, however, children grow somewhat more flexible in their ideas and preferences as they grow older (Katz & Ksansnak, 1994; Powlishta et al., 1994).

Theories of Gender-Role Development

As we have seen, children believe that males and females differ significantly. Furthermore, a small number of gender differences—such as play patterns—emerge during childhood (Maccoby, 1990b; Serbin et al., 1993). Psychologists currently favor two leading theories about the development of gender: social learning theory and cognitive developmental theory.

Social Learning Theory   According to **social learning theory,** two major mechanisms explain how girls learn to act "feminine" and boys learn to act "masculine": (1) they receive rewards and punishments for their own behavior, and (2) they watch and imitate the behavior of other people (Mischel, 1966; Serbin et al., 1993). As you can see, this theory resembles the theory we examined in the previous section, stating that children acquire language by the principles of learning discussed in Chapter 6.

Social learning theory sounds plausible. Little Bobby wins smiles for playing with the fire truck, but his parents look horrified when he emerges from the bedroom wearing his sister's ballet costume. Furthermore, the models they see on television feature strong men, who solve problems and give orders, and submissive women, who are concerned primarily with family and romantic relationships (Gunter, 1986).

However, social learning explanations cannot be completely responsible for children's stereotypical behavior. For instance, parents treat their own sons and daughters fairly similarly (Jacklin, 1989; Lytton & Romney, 1991). Another problem for social learning theory is that children do not consistently prefer to imitate models who are the same gender as they are (Matlin, 1996a; Raskin & Israel, 1981). We need to look for additional explanations to supplement the social learning approach.

Cognitive Developmental Theories   According to several **cognitive developmental theories,** children's own thought processes are primarily responsible for the development of gender typing. Piaget emphasized that children actively engage in meaning-making, trying to make sense out of the objects and events in their world. Similarly, children actively work to make meaning out of the information they learn about gender.

Sandra Bem has developed cognitive developmental theory to emphasize gender schemas (Bem, 1985, 1993). As Chapter 7 (on memory) noted, a schema is a generalized idea that organizes our perceptions and thoughts. Sandra Bem's **gender schema theory** proposes that children use gender as an important schema to structure and guide their view of the world. In our culture, gender is extremely important, and children readily adopt gender schemas. They learn that the world should be divided into two important categories that are the polar opposites of each other—male and female.

Bem's gender schema theory acknowledges that we must incorporate social learning principles into cognitive developmental theory. Clearly, children develop some gender-related behaviors because they receive rewards and punishments for their behavior and because they imitate others—in addition to the influence of their own thought processes.

A study by Bigler (1995) highlights the importance of children's gender schemas. As part of her study, Bigler randomly assigned 6- to 9-year-old children either to control classrooms or to gender-emphasis classrooms during a 4-week summer school program. Teachers in the control classrooms were instructed not to emphasize gender in their remarks or in their treatment of the children. In contrast, teachers in the gender-emphasis classrooms used gender-segregated seating, with girls' and boys' desks on opposite sides of the classroom. The teachers also displayed boys' and girls' artwork on different bulletin boards, and they frequently instructed boys and girls to perform different activities. All children attended the program for four weeks.

The children who were already very aware of gender categories at the beginning of the study were not very influenced by the program. However, the nature of the program did influence those children who were initially unaware of gender categories. For example, the children who had been in the gender-emphasis classroom were more than twice as likely as children in the control condition to make stereotyped judgments about the kinds of jobs that males and females could hold. In short, children who are still forming their ideas about gender may learn to overemphasize gender if their teachers encourage these distinctions.

At present, gender schema theory seems to be the dominant explanation for how children acquire gender-related thoughts and behaviors. Gender schema theory has a major advantage over other theories: It acknowledges that we need complex explanations to account for the complexity of the way we think about gender and the way gender influences our actions.

Gender schema theory suggests that this boy learns how to act "masculine" and this girl learns how to act "feminine" because they have learned society's definitions of masculinity and femininity and because their own thoughts encourage the development of gender-stereotyped behavior.

Critical Thinking Exercise 10.3

Write down your answers to the following questions about gender.

a. Suppose that a group of researchers shows one photo of a man repeatedly, until an infant stops looking at it. Then the researchers show a photo of a woman, and the infant now looks at this photo for a long time. The same pattern of results is obtained when the photo of the woman is shown first. The researchers claim that their results demonstrate that infants can tell the difference between females and males. Why would you question these results?

b. Why was Bigler (1995) wise to analyze her data separately for the children who were initially aware of gender categories and those who were initially unaware?

SECTION SUMMARY: *GENDER-ROLE DEVELOPMENT*

1. Adults emphasize the importance of gender in the questions they ask parents of newborns and in their responses to infants—consistent with our culture's emphasis on gender.

2. Infants can distinguish between males and females.

3. Young children believe that males and females have different personalities; they also show gender segregation and ingroup favoritism.

4. The leading theories about gender typing include social learning theory and cognitive developmental theory (for example, Sandra Bem's gender schema theory).

PERSONALITY AND SOCIAL DEVELOPMENT

This textbook began with chapters on the biological aspects of behavior and then moved on to cognitive areas. The last part of the book will focus on individual differences and social relationships. Similarly, this chapter began by considering biological aspects of human development, such as prenatal and perceptual development. Then it moved on to three cognitive areas: memory, thinking, and language. The third topic, gender, combined cognitive development and social relationships. In this final section of the chapter, we consider personality and social development, foreshadowing the chapters in the last part of the book. An important concept in this section is **socialization,** the process by which children acquire the knowledge, values, skills, and behaviors that allow them to function effectively in adult society (Berns, 1997).

We must also emphasize that personality and social development depend closely on all the processes we have discussed in this chapter. When infants perfect their perceptual skills, they can recognize how the important people in their lives look, sound, and smell. These perceptual skills are necessary in forming social bonds with parents, siblings, and caretakers.

Children's memory development allows them to remember past social events and to recall rules about social interactions (Smetana, 1993). As children's thinking matures, their egocentrism declines. If they can take another person's point of view, they are less likely to act selfishly. As we emphasized earlier, language development enables children to talk about the social world and people's motivations—a necessary component of social development.

The development of gender roles also has important implications for personality and social behavior. For example, children acquire stereotypes, believing that men *should* be more aggressive, strong, and independent than women.

This section begins by considering early temperament—the origins of individual differences. We will also discuss self-concept, another important component of personality. When we examine children's social interactions, we'll look at their relationships with other people, the development of positive social interactions, the child care controversy, and children's ethnic backgrounds. The section ends with a discussion of the status of children in contemporary society.

Children's social interactions are facilitated by their abilities in perception, memory, thinking, and language.

Temperament

Temperament refers to individual differences in behavior that appear early in life; these differences show stability as the infant matures (Bates, 1994; Hartup & van Lieshout, 1995). For example, consider the two sisters in Figure 10.14. According to their mother, the sister on the right has always been relatively calm, whereas the sister on the left has consistently been more sensitive to stimuli.

Some studies suggest that children from different ethnic groups show early temperamental differences. For example, Kagan and his colleagues (1994) found that Chinese 4-month-olds in Beijing were significantly less active than White 4-month-olds in Boston and Dublin. The Chinese infants were also less irritable and less likely to produce speech sounds, in contrast to the American and Irish infants.

One major way in which children differ focuses on inhibition. **Inhibited children** are fearful of strangers and unfamiliar objects or events. In contrast, **uninhibited children** approach strangers and unfamiliar objects or events without hesitation (Robinson et al., 1992). In general, inhibited infants become inhibited children, and uninhibited infants remain uninhibited (Kagan et al., 1992; Kagan et al., 1993). Therefore, this research supports stability, rather than change.

FIGURE 10.14

Two siblings in the same family can differ tremendously in their temperament.

Self-Concept

The term **self-concept** refers to your thoughts and feelings about yourself as an individual. The self-concept begins to develop during infancy. As we will see in the next chapter, self-concepts become much more elaborate during adulthood, as people contemplate their abilities, priorities, and life goals.

As you might imagine, researchers cannot determine what young infants think about themselves, because research methods cannot assess such abstract information (Damon & Hart, 1992). However, older children can be tested with the mirror-and-rouge test. For example, Lewis and Brooks (1978) unobtrusively placed a spot of rouge on babies' faces, so that they were unaware they had been marked. Then the babies were allowed to look in the mirror. Infants between the ages of 9 and 12 months simply looked in the mirror but showed no evidence of self-recognition. However, the majority of children in the 21- to 24-month age range stared in the mirror and touched the rouge spot on their own face. As if to say "Hey, that's me!" they acknowledged that the children with the red spots were indeed themselves (Figure 10.15).

The psychodynamic theory of Erik Erikson (1950, 1968) provides one of the most comprehensive descriptions of the development of self-concept and identity (Hopkins, 1995). Erikson's theory proposes eight stages of development throughout the life cycle. We will consider the first four stages in this chapter; Chapter 11 (on adult development) considers the last four stages and also examines identity development in more detail.

Erikson suggested that an individual confronts a specific task or dilemma during each of the eight developmental stages. According to this theory, healthy development is more likely if the individual resolves the tasks successfully. As Table 10.3 shows, a child can presumably develop trust if caretakers provide food, warmth, and affection. During Stage 2, the toddler learns to walk and act independently; parents should encourage this independence, rather than making the toddler ashamed of these new efforts. In Stage 3, the child begins to plan activities without adults' help. Stage 4 applies to the school-age child, who can become competent in sports, academics, and social interactions.

Erikson's theory expanded on Sigmund Freud's psychoanalytic theory (which we'll examine in Chapter 13) by emphasizing normal development and social interactions. However, his theories cannot be adequately tested (Miller, 1993). For example, how could researchers objectively measure trust or mistrust in a 6-month-old? As a result, his theory may be widely discussed, but you should not assume that it is supported by empirical evidence.

FIGURE 10.15

This little girl shows self-recognition; she is touching the spot on her face that corresponds to the red spot she sees in the mirror.

TABLE 10.3   Erikson's Theory of Psychosocial Development (birth through childhood)

STAGE	AGE	PSYCHOSOCIAL TASK	DESCRIPTION OF TASK
1	0–1	Trust versus mistrust	The infant whose needs are met by caretakers develops a sense of trust in others.
2	1–3	Autonomy versus doubt	The toddler tries to learn independence and self-confidence.
3	3–6	Initiative versus guilt	The young child learns to initiate his or her own activities.
4	6–12	Competence versus inferiority	The child tries to develop skill in physical, cognitive, and social areas.

Source: Based on Erikson, 1950, 1968.

Note: A complete list of Erikson's eight psychosocial stages appears in Table 11.2 on Page 370.

Social Relationships

So far, we have looked at children's early personality characteristics and their growing sense of self. Of course, a child does not grow up in a vacuum, deprived of social interactions. Let's see how children interact with the other people in their life. We will begin with two aspects of relationships with parents: infants' attachments to their parents and the parents' styles of interacting with their children. We then explore children's interactions with siblings and peers.

Infants' Attachment to Their Parents   The term **attachment** refers to the close emotional bond of affection between an infant and his or her caregivers (Goldberg, 1993). As you might expect, some babies have a more positive attachment experience than others. According to the major classification system, a baby who shows **secure attachment** tends to use the caregiver as a secure base. A baby may wander away from this person for a while to explore the surroundings, returning frequently. After separation from the caregiver, the baby actively seeks interaction. Securely attached babies are especially likely to have sensitive, affectionate mothers (Isabella, 1993).

A baby who shows **anxious resistant attachment** displays a mixture of both seeking and resisting contact with the caregiver. Finally, a baby who shows **anxious avoidant attachment** easily moves away from the caregiver to explore the environment. After separation, the baby actively avoids interacting with this individual (Ainsworth, 1989; Sroufe et al., 1996).

In general, patterns of attachment show high stability during infancy and childhood (Ainsworth, 1990; Collins & Gunnar, 1990). Also, infant-mother and infant-father attachments are fairly similar. However, one difference is that positive interactions between mothers and babies are most likely to occur during caretaking, whereas fathers and babies are most likely to enjoy these interactions during play (Collins & Gunnar, 1990; Cox et al., 1992).

Bretherton (1992) points out that in a society where many families experience poverty and stress, children are less likely to have the advantage of secure attachment. Consistent with the sociocultural approach to psychology introduced in Chapter 1, contextual factors such as socioeconomic class can have an impact on development. Attachment patterns are also related to children's later adjustment. Securely attached infants are more likely to become competent, curious, and happy children with high self-esteem (Cummings & Davies, 1995; Sroufe et al., 1996).

Parenting Styles   We have seen that responsive, caring parents are more likely to have securely attached infants. Another important parenting factor is the kind of

Positive interactions between infants and fathers are especially likely to occur during play.

control that parents use with their children. Diana Baumrind (1971) proposed that the most effective parents are affectionate, but they also provide control when necessary. These **authoritative parents** respect each child's individuality, they are loving, and they allow children to express their own points of view. However, they have clear-out standards, which they uphold in a consistent fashion (Maccoby, 1992). Children with authoritative parents are more likely to be self-reliant, competent, contented, and socially responsible (Baumrind, 1971; Darling & Steinberg, 1993; Maccoby, 1994).

In contrast, **authoritarian parents** demand unquestioning obedience from their children. They punish children forcefully when children do not meet their standards, and they are less likely to be affectionate. Children from authoritarian families tend to be unhappy, distrustful, and ineffective in social interactions.

Finally, **permissive parents** make few demands on their children, allowing them to make their own decisions. In one extreme case, a 14-year-old son moved his parents out of their large bedroom suite and claimed it for himself, along with an expensive stereo system and television! You will not be surprised that he has never learned to live according to established rules, and he has few friends (Santrock & Yussen, 1989). In Baumrind's (1971) research, the children from permissive families were immature. They also had little self-control, and they explored less than children from authoritarian and authoritative families.

Most of the research on parenting styles has been conducted with European American samples. We do not know much about the influence of parenting styles in other cultural contexts. For example, Muret-Wagstaff & Moore (1989) reported on mother-infant pairs in a Minnesota sample of Hmong households, who had emigrated from Southeast Asia. About 80% of these infants lived in extended families, with grandmothers, aunts, and other adults. How do child rearing patterns operate in a family where many adults take responsibility for socializing young children? The recent emphasis on the sociocultural approach may inspire future research on a variety of ethnic backgrounds.

Interactions With Siblings So far, we have emphasized the importance of parents. However, 80% of children have siblings (Dunn, 1991). Sibling relationships differ tremendously. For some children, a sibling is an exciting affectionate playmate. Research in the United States, England, and Indonesia confirms that siblings often engage in pretend play about make-believe situations (Dunn, 1993; Farver & Wimbarti, 1995). For other children, a sibling may be a bossy, aggressive person who can make your life miserable (Dunn, 1993; Teti, 1992). In general, a child will adjust well to the birth of a younger sibling if he or she is skilled at taking the perspective of other people, rather than being egocentric, and if he or she is securely attached (Teti, 1992).

One of the most interesting recent findings about siblings is that two children growing up in the same household with the same parents are likely to be very different from each other. In fact, they often differ from one another almost as much as two unrelated children growing up in different families (Dunn, 1993; Dunn & Plomin, 1990). An important reason that siblings differ is called **nonshared environmental experiences;** parents treat each child differently, siblings create different environments for each other, and each child has different experiences outside the family. Furthermore, during late childhood, children often deliberately try *not* to be like their siblings, a process called **sibling deidentification** (Teti, 1992). Ironically, then, genetically similar siblings actively strive to be different from the people whom they have the greatest potential to resemble!

Interactions With Friends As children mature, they develop close relationships with people outside their family, and these relationships become increasingly important. The nature of friendship also changes as children mature. Young children base their friendships on rather superficial characteristics, such as living

Through interactions with their siblings, children learn how to play cooperatively.

near each other and liking to play the same games. However, by the time children reach the age of 9 or 10, they emphasize more abstract psychological qualities, such as loyalty, cooperation, commitment to the other person, and trustworthiness (Hartup, 1992; Rizzo, 1989). Two 10-year-old friends care about each other's feelings, not just about whether they like the same activities (Dunn, 1993; Erwin, 1993). In fact, these caring friendships may help encourage children to develop positive, prosocial behaviors toward other people—toward strangers, as well as family members and friends (Rizzo, 1989). We'll consider these prosocial interactions next.

Critical Thinking Exercise 10.4

Write down your answers to the following questions about social relationships.

a. Researchers have observed that fraternal twins (that is, twins who are not identical) are more similar than two siblings of different ages (Harris, 1995). Both kinds of siblings share, on the average, 50% of their genes. How would the information on sibling relationships help you interpret these findings?

b. Research on children's friendships tends to use either naturalistic observation or direct questioning of children (Newcomb & Bagwell, 1995). Which method would be most likely to be used with younger children, and which would be used with older children? Why would the methods tend to emphasize different components of friendship?

Prosocial Behavior

A student in my human development class described her 3-year-old nephew's concern for other family members. When his 6-month-old sister cries, he pats her back until she falls asleep. On several occasions when his mother was sleeping, he climbed into his sister's crib to play with her. As he explained, he did not want the baby's crying to wake their mother. This young boy's compassion for his sister and mother conflicts with Piaget's view that children are egocentric. Even young children can view the world from the perspective of another person and realize that a sister needs comforting and a mother needs sleep.

Prosocial behavior, or **altruism,** is voluntary action that benefits another person. Prosocial behavior can include comforting, helping, rescuing, sharing, and co-operating (Eisenberg, 1992; Zahn-Waxler & Smith, 1992). Even very young children can behave prosocially. Zahn-Waxler and her coauthors (1992) asked mothers to simulate various emotions during their normal interactions with their young children. For example, a mother might pretend to bump her head, say "ouch," and rub herself. More than half of all 13- to 15-month-olds responded with at least one prosocial behavior, usually hugging or patting. By 2 years of age, 26 of the 27 children studied showed prosocial behavior. Two-year-olds actively try to help someone who seems to be suffering. As children grow older, they are increasingly skilled at understanding other people's feelings (Eisenberg, 1992).

In general, prosocial children have parents who are nurturant and supportive, often providing a model of prosocial behavior (Eisenberg & Mussen, 1989; Zahn-Waxler & Smith, 1992). For instance, individuals who were active in the civil rights movement during the 1950s and 1960s were likely to have parents who had vigorously worked for social causes in previous decades (Mussen & Eisenberg-Berg, 1977). Children whose teachers are prosocially skilled are also more likely to comfort a crying classmate (Farver & Branstetter, 1994). Now that you are familiar

Even young children can be prosocial; in this photograph, a boy consoles his brother.

DEMONSTRATION 10.3   Observing Prosocial Behavior

Save this demonstration for the next time you are at a fast-food restaurant or other setting that has many children. Try to note any examples of prosocial behavior in these children, such as helping, comforting, complimenting, and sharing. Also note examples of antisocial behavior, such as aggression, negative comments, and selfishness. How do the two numbers compare? If you find a particularly prosocial or antisocial family group, can you identify any characteristics of the parents that might contribute to the children's behavior?

with some of the dimensions of prosocial behavior, try Demonstration 10.3. We will examine prosocial behavior again in Chapter 17, with a focus on explanations for altruism.

The Child Care Controversy

At present, about 60% of children younger than 6 years of age are cared for on a regular basis by people who are not their parents (Vandell et al., 1997). Statistics such as this raise a vitally important question: How do child care arrangements affect children?

Unfortunately, we cannot easily answer this question. In fact, the child care controversy highlights the theme that humans are extremely complex. The effects of child care on children seem to depend on a wide variety of such variables as the age, gender, and temperament of the child, the social and economic characteristics of the family, the quality of the day care center, and the number of hours spent each week in the day care center (Hofferth & Phillips, 1991; NICHD Early Child Care Research Network, 1998; Scarr & Eisenberg, 1993; Vandell et al., 1997).

Furthermore, we cannot draw firm conclusions about this issue because—for ethical reasons—the research cannot use the experimental method. Finally, our conclusions about child care are influenced by the dependent variable we choose. Let's look at three categories of dependent variables: cognitive development, attachment during infancy, and social relationships.

Cognitive Development   In general, the cognitive development of children who have been in a day care center is similar to children cared for at home—or in some cases is slightly more advanced. This conclusion holds true for tests of general intelligence, and also for tests of reading and mathematics ability (Scarr & Eisenberg, 1993; Vandell & Ramanan, 1992).

Attachment   For many years, psychologists had been concerned that infants who spend time in a day care center may not be securely attached to their mothers. However, a recent study conducted by 25 experts in infant development provides reassuring evidence (NICHD Early Child Care Research Network, 1998). These researchers studied more than 1,000 infant-mother pairs in 10 cities throughout the United States. This study confirms earlier findings that infants who experienced early day care were just as likely to be securely attached as infants who had no day care experience (Clarke-Stewart, 1989; McCartney & Phillips, 1988). The results also showed that children in poor-quality day care centers—who also had unresponsive mothers—were most likely to have attachment problems. However, a good mother could compensate for poor day care. Furthermore, good day care could also compensate for an unresponsive mother. Keep in mind the most important conclusion, though: Child care condition has no overall effect on attachment.

Social Development   The picture is mixed when we consider other components of social development. Children who have participated in day care tend to be more

The quality of care is a critical factor in the day care dilemma. Development is optimal when children can interact often with nurturant adults.

socially skilled in some areas. For example, they are more cooperative and confident in social interactions, and they are more skilled at taking another person's point of view (Phillips et al., 1987; Scarr & Eisenberg, 1993). However, some studies have reported that children in day care settings may be more aggressive (Haskins, 1985; Phillips et al., 1987). It's possible, though, that this behavior reflects independence, rather than aggression (Clarke-Stewart, 1992).

The Quality Issue Many psychologists are now approaching the child care controversy from a different perspective. They suggest that we should focus on the negative consequences of not providing high-quality child care. Research has repeatedly demonstrated that children are much more likely to thrive in high-quality day care centers (Howes et al., 1992; NICHD Early Child Care Research Network, 1998). Unfortunately, however, teachers and other staff members in day care centers are notoriously underpaid. Each year, about 40% of the staff leaves, in part because of low wages (Scarr & Eisenberg, 1993; Zigler & Gilman, 1993). During the coming years, people concerned about children need to work together to develop high-quality day care centers where the caregivers are warm and nurturing, and where children can develop cognitively, emotionally, and socially.

Children and Their Ethnic Backgrounds

The theme of individual differences has been prominent throughout this textbook. When we consider children from different ethnic backgrounds, we can appreciate even more clearly that children's life experiences may vary widely. We should note, incidentally, that definitions for ethnicity are controversial. However, we will use **ethnicity** to refer to groups that share the same nationality, culture, or language (Betancourt & López, 1993; Birman, 1994; Frable, 1997).

A related area of research, **cross-cultural psychology,** studies similarities and differences in psychological processes, as a function of membership in various cultural and ethnic groups (Berry et al., 1992). Cross-cultural research is likely to compare some behavior—perhaps a Piagetian conservation task—in two or more cultures (Matsumoto, 1996; Padilla, 1995).

In this discussion, we'll focus on ethnic diversity in North America. For example, Table 10.4 shows the number of U.S. residents in several major ethnic groups. By some estimates, the ethnic composition of the United States in the year 2050 will be

TABLE 10.4 Projected Estimate for the U.S. Population, by Major Ethnic Group, for the Year 2000

ETHNIC GROUP	ESTIMATED POPULATION
White	226,000,000
Black	35,000,000
Hispanic	31,000,000
Asian American	11,000,000
Native American	2,000,000

Source: Based on Day, 1996.

Note: Hispanic individuals may be of any race, so they may list themselves twice.

about half European American and about half members of other ethnic groups (Frable, 1997; U.S. Bureau of the Census, 1996).

Table 10.5 illustrates the ethnic diversity in Canada by showing the country of origin of its residents. In Canada, immigrants constitute 16% of the population (Badets, 1993; Dumas, 1990). Let's first consider each of four ethnic groups, and then we will look at the more general issue of ethnic bias.

Black Children   As Table 10.4 shows, about 11% of the U.S. population is Black. Incidentally, this textbook primarily uses the term *Black*—rather than *African American*—because *Black* includes Caribbean Americans and Black Canadians, as well as African Americans. Also, a Bureau of Labor Statistics survey of Black Americans reported that *Black* was the favored term ("Playing the Name Game," 1995).

We must be careful not to exaggerate the differences between Black and European American children. After all, most children in North America share cultural forces such as television programs, popular toys, and educational settings (Rowe et al., 1994). Also, we should not ignore the variation within each group. For example, about half of Black children live below the poverty line. However, the number of Black families with annual incomes greater than $50,000 has risen dramatically during recent years (Staples & Johnson, 1993). Like all other ethnic groups, Blacks represent a variety of social classes.

Despite this variation, Black families are usually more likely than European American families to focus on emotions and feelings. They also emphasize social connectedness, or responsibilities to a family or group, rather than the "rugged individualism" associated with European American families. Black families also value high levels of stimulation, preferring action that is lively and energetic (Berns, 1997; Boykin, 1986).

Many Black children grow up in extended families, where grandmothers, sisters, aunts, and cousins take care of each other's children (Collins, 1991). The

TABLE 10.5 The Country of Origin for Immigrants to Canada (based on Colombo, 1998)

COUNTRY OF ORIGIN (BY GEOGRAPHIC REGION)	NUMBER OF IMMIGRANTS
Europe	1,392,000
Asia	973,000
Caribbean	240,000
Latin America	210,000
Africa	98,000

extended family provides a stabilizing influence, especially among economically poor families.

By the time they reach the age of 3, children seem to be aware of such Black-White differences as skin color, hair texture, and facial features (Aboud, 1988). Also by the age of 3, the majority of children can identify their own race correctly (Katz & Kofkin, 1997).

We saw earlier in the chapter that children prefer to play with a child of their same gender. The results are more variable for ethnic-group preferences. In some research, preschoolers and kindergartners already prefer their own ethnic group (Finkelstein & Haskins, 1983; P. A. Katz, 1996). However, kindergartners in an extended naturalistic observation study showed no systematic preferences (Holmes, 1995). For example, one of the European American children in this study was asked whether friends must be the same color. He replied, "No, me and Henry gots different color hands and we're friends" (p. 79). Ethnic-group preferences probably depend on a variety of factors, such as teacher sensitivity, parental attitudes, and ethnic mix in the classroom.

Hispanic Children Hispanic or Latino individuals currently comprise 9% of the population, and this ethnic group is expected to outnumber Blacks within the next few years (Frable, 1997). *Hispanic* refers to all people of Latin American, Spanish, or Portuguese descent. They may share a language (either Spanish or Portuguese), values, and customs. However, a Mexican American child growing up in a farming region in central California may have very different experiences from a Puerto Rican child growing up in Manhattan or a Portuguese child growing up in Toronto.

Mexican Americans are the largest Hispanic subgroup in the United States. Many of the younger, college-educated Mexican Americans prefer to be called *Chicano* or *Chicana,* rather than *Hispanic* (Garbarino & Kostelny, 1992; Padilla, 1995). Mexican Americans often emphasize affiliation and the need for warm, supportive relationships (Berns, 1997). Some studies of children's social development conclude that Mexican American children show more cooperative behavior at a young age than do European American children (Martinez & Mendoza, 1984).

Once again, however, we must not exaggerate the differences between ethnic groups or assume that all members of the same ethnic group are similar. For example, Fry (1993) studied childrearing in two communities in Oaxaca, Mexico. Although the two communities were only 4 miles apart, they differed impressively. In one community, parents used verbal reasoning to discipline children, and these children were generally obedient and nonaggressive. In the other community, parents used physical punishment, and their children were often disobedient to parents and aggressive toward other children. In this case, the differences within a culture are extremely large.

Asian American Children Like Hispanics, Asian Americans come from many different countries. Asian Americans include—in order of population in the United States—Chinese, Filipinos, Japanese, Vietnamese, Koreans, Asian Indians, and more than 23 other ethnic-cultural groups (True, 1990). In Canada, the Chinese are among the fastest growing ethnic groups (Costa & Renaud, 1995). The majority of Chinese Canadians are immigrants, mostly from Hong Kong and the People's Republic of China, and most live in urban areas.

Asian Americans are often labeled the "model minority" because of their high education levels and relatively high incomes. Many cultural values of Asian Americans resemble those of middle-class European Americans. For example, both groups emphasize education and achievement for their children (Heath, 1995; Lin & Fu, 1990). However, Asian Americans typically emphasize family, duty, cooperation, and interpersonal harmony. In contrast, European Americans are more likely to value individuality and independence (Farver et al., 1995; Nagata, 1989). Also, Asian

Americans are often hesitant to reveal personal problems to people outside the family (Garbarino & Kostelny, 1992). We will consider the implications of this tendency when we discuss psychotherapy in Chapter 15.

Native American Children   According to estimates, more than 10 million North American Indians once resided on this continent (Trimble & Bagwell, 1995). As Table 10.4 showed, the current U.S. population of Native Americans is close to 2 million. Canadian data show about 1 million Native Canadians or aboriginals (Trimble & Bagwell, 1995).

Native Americans probably represent the most diverse ethnic group in the United States. In the 1990s, they included 200 different tribal languages and 517 separate native backgrounds. Native Americans may share a common geographic origin and a common history of being invaded and dispossessed by European Americans. However, their languages, values, and current lifestyles may have little in common (Garbarino & Kostelny, 1992; LaFromboise et al., 1993).

In general, Native Americans are likely to value independence in their children (Garbarino & Kostelny, 1992; LaFromboise & Lowe, 1989). For example, parents may encourage children to make their own decisions and develop independence at an early age. However, parents are also likely to emphasize cooperation, respect for elders, and helping people who need assistance (Berns, 1997).

Although we have mentioned some general characteristics of the parents and children of each ethnic group, we need to reemphasize the diversity within each group. Even if we focus on one specific subgroup—perhaps Chinese Americans—the differences *within* that subgroup are always greater than the differences *between* that subgroup and any other ethnic group (Bronstein & Quina, 1988).

Biases Against Children of Color   Patricia Romney, a college professor who is an African American, remembers her childhood experiences with a White girl (Romney et al., 1992). The two 8-year-olds were playing outside, and the White girl went inside briefly. She came out to announce that she could not play with Patricia any longer, because Patricia was colored. "What's that?" asked Patricia. "I don't know," replied the little girl. Of course that friendship never developed. Carlos Manjarréz, a Mexican American, remembers how a real estate agent tried to discourage his family from buying a home in the "White" suburbs (Manjarréz, 1991). It's easy to see how European American children learn prejudice from their parents. It's also easy to see how children of color can learn to be prejudiced against their own ethnic group (Aboud, 1988; Katz & Kofkin, 1997). Parents, educators, and therapists face a difficult task when they work to develop ethnic pride in children of color who live in a prejudiced society (Edelman, 1993; Hopson & Hopson, 1990).

In Chapter 16, we will examine in more detail the general nature of prejudice, discrimination, and stereotyping. When we consider how these biases develop in children, we need to examine how television provides children with a distorted view of ethnic diversity. Black children and adults are now fairly well represented on TV programs, although the characters often portray stereotypical roles. However, Hispanic children and adults are underrepresented (Greenberg & Brand, 1994). Furthermore, almost all Hispanic TV characters are men; Hispanic women scarcely exist on television. Also, Asians and Hispanics are typically portrayed either as villains or as victims of violence (Greenberg & Brand, 1994; Liebert & Sprafkin, 1988). A final problem is that people from different ethnic backgrounds rarely interact with one another on television (Greenberg & Brand, 1994; Liebert & Sprafkin, 1988).

When we think about children, we must consider their diversity. In North America, children represent a wide variety of ethnic groups whose cultural values and aspirations may differ substantially. Try to visualize a children's television show that could capture this diversity and portray these children playing with one another, as in Figure 10.16. This television program could provide children with models of prosocial behavior.

Another example of our theme of individual differences is represented in the diversity of ethnic groups in North America. These photos represent children from European American, Black, Hispanic, Asian, and Native American backgrounds.

FIGURE 10.16

Children in this New York neighborhood represent a variety of ethnic groups.

Critical Thinking Exercise 10.5

Write down your answers to the following questions about the child care controversy and about children's ethnicity.

a. Suppose that you read an article comparing high-quality and low-quality child care centers. The article reports that researchers had studied 300 children in the two kinds of centers (operationally defined in terms of the ratio of adult staff and the number of adult-child interactions per hour). The children in the high-quality center are found to be much more developed in their vocabulary and cognitive skills than the children in the low-quality center. Why would you be suspicious about whether the quality of the center actually *caused* the difference in children's cognitive development?

b. A group of U.S. researchers wants to compare 6- to 8-year-olds in both the United States and in rural Guatemala, with respect to their conservation of number (see Demonstration 10.1). What kinds of factors will they need to consider in order to make sure that the comparison is fair?

The Status of Children in North American Society

Most of us want to believe that children receive top priority in the United States. However, an international survey of children's health showed that 21 countries ranked better than the United States in infant mortality rate (Wegman, 1993). Countries such as Singapore, Spain, and Greece reported fewer infants dying before the age of 1 year. Canada fared much better, ranking seventh among the countries in this survey. Let's consider some other threats that North American children face as we approach the twenty-first century. These include health risks, poverty, violence, divorce, and the "hurried child" problem.

Health Risks Some of the threats that children currently face were unheard of just a few decades ago. Consider acquired immunodeficiency syndrome (AIDS), for example. By September 1997, U.S. pediatric AIDS cases numbered 7,902 (Centers for Disease Control, 1997). Other infants will die or face serious problems because their mothers used cocaine or other narcotics during pregnancy, as we discussed earlier in the chapter. Sadly, many children also die because they are physically abused by their caretakers. Between 1,200 and 5,000 U.S. children die each year from maltreatment (Finkelhor & Dziuba-Leatherman, 1994; Mattaini et al., 1996).

Poverty In the current era, the United States has a higher rate of child poverty than any other industrialized country (Huston, 1995). Currently, 24% of all children under the age of 6 live below the poverty line, which is operationally defined as an annual income of $15,569 for a family of four (Bronfenbrenner et al., 1996; Children's Defense Fund, 1997). As emphasized by the sociocultural approach to psychology, poverty has crucial consequences for children's welfare. Pregnant women with low incomes are not likely to receive prenatal care, and their infants and children also have more medical problems. Children living in poverty are also less likely to receive adequate nutrition, sensitive caregiving, and high-quality education (Children's Defense Fund, 1997; Huston, 1995).

Children and their parents now constitute more than one-third of all people in homeless shelters.

The poverty rate for Canada is lower than for the United States. In fact, Canadian children are about 40% less likely than U.S. children to live below the poverty line (Children's Defense Fund, 1997). However, some Canadian ethnic groups experience high poverty rates. For example, among aboriginal (Canadian Indian) groups, 44% of families live in poverty (Ryerse, 1990).

Consider, also, the lives of homeless children. According to one estimate, children and their parents now comprise 38% of all people in U.S. homeless shelters (Children's Defense Fund, 1997). Compared to other children, homeless children experience more health problems, hunger, poor nutrition, cognitive deficits, and psychological problems (Rafferty & Shinn, 1991).

Violence Children's sense of well-being can also be threatened by violence. In Chapter 6, we discussed the high incidence of violence on the television programs that students watch. Many children also encounter real-life violence. In fact, data reveal that a child is killed by gunshot every two hours in the United States (Children's Defense Fund, 1994). Damon (1995) points out some children actually become murderers. A typical issue of the daily newspaper reports an 11-year-old who slashed the throat of an 84-year-old woman, a 13-year-old who killed his 10-year-old longtime playmate, and a 5-year-old who shot his 3-year-old brother. Children can also kill themselves and others accidentally; more than 1.2 million latchkey children under the age of 12 have access to guns in their own homes (Melton, 1995; "Youths Learn Alternatives," 1992). As an editorial in one of the pediatric journals concludes, "The picture that emerges for some of our children is that they are awash in a sea of violence—at home, in the neighborhood, and in the media" (Fulginiti, 1992, p. 671).

Divorce Divorce is another potentially traumatic experience that can disrupt children's lives. Estimates show that between 40% and 50% of all children can expect to spend at least 5 years in a single-parent home. Many of these children will adjust successfully to their new life circumstances. However, a substantial number may suffer long-term negative effects (Furstenberg & Cherlin, 1991; Weitzman & Adair, 1988).

The "Hurried Child" Problem Others who are concerned about children's well-being point out that we are hurrying young people through childhood. For example, upper-class children are likely to feel academic pressure at an early age. One magazine article reported on a very expensive preschool program in Manhattan that routinely urges parents to arrange for tutoring for their 4-year-olds—at the cost of $75 an hour (Williams, 1996).

FIGURE 10.17

The "hurried child" is rushed through the stages of development, rather than being allowed to enjoy childhood.

David Elkind (1981, 1987) is a psychologist who is well known for his work in Piagetian research. Elkind points out Piaget's warning that children should not be pushed; instead, they should develop at their own pace. Many North American parents, however, want to rush their children through each stage of cognitive development as rapidly as possible. Parents buy designer jeans for their toddlers, equip them with miniature briefcases, and supply them with grown-up makeup and hairstyles (Figure 10.17). Elkind urges us not to hurry our children, but instead to allow them to enjoy their childhood.

In this chapter, we have seen that young children are miraculous human beings, capable of impressive perceptual, cognitive, and social skills. However, these miraculous beings face obstacles such as disease, deprivation, and life-threatening violence. Horowitz and O'Brien (1989) point out our responsibility to make life safer for children:

> Every child who does not function at a level commensurate with his or her possibilities, every child who is destined to make fewer contributions to society than society needs, and every child who does not take his or her place as a productive adult diminishes the power of that society's future. (p. 445)

SECTION SUMMARY: *PERSONALITY AND SOCIAL DEVELOPMENT*

1. Children's socialization is heavily influenced by their developing perceptual skills, cognitive abilities, and notions of gender roles.

2. Temperament (e.g., inhibited versus uninhibited style) shows some stability as children mature.

3. Erik Erikson's theory traces the developing self-concept through four childhood stages that emphasize trust, independence, planning, and competence.

4. Securely attached infants are more likely than anxious resistant or anxious avoidant infants to have sensitive, affectionate mothers.

5. Authoritative parents are more likely than authoritarian or permissive parents to have competent, contented, and socially responsible children.

6. Sibling relationships vary widely; furthermore, non-shared environmental experiences encourage siblings to differ impressively from one another.

7. As children mature, friends become increasingly important; also, friendships mature from being based on similar interests to an emphasis on loyalty and other abstract interpersonal qualities.

8. Prosocial behavior can be seen in children as young as 1 year of age; children are more likely to be prosocial if their parents and teachers have been prosocial.

9. The child care controversy is a complex issue; however, in general, children who have been in a day care situation are generally similar to children cared for at home in terms of cognitive development, attachment, and social interactions. The quality of the child care has a major impact on children's development.

10. Ethnic groups differ somewhat in their emphasis on social connectedness and cooperation, rather than individualism; however, within-group differences are substantial.

11. Television often provides children with a distorted view of ethnicity.

12. Children do not currently have top priority in North American society; some problems they face include AIDS, prenatal drug exposure, child abuse, poverty, homelessness, violence, divorce, and being pushed to grow up too fast.

REVIEW QUESTIONS

1. The introduction to this chapter presented three important issues in developmental psychology: the nature-nurture, continuity-stages, and stability-

change questions. Define each issue, and point out how one or more of them is important for the following topics: (a) early perceptual skills; (b) cognitive development; (c) infant temperament; and (d) Erikson's theory of self-concepts.

2. Briefly trace the course of prenatal development. Suppose you have a pregnant friend; what kinds of precautions would you suggest during her pregnancy?

3. Suppose that your friend has now delivered a healthy baby. What kinds of abilities could you tell her about that she might expect during the early weeks of the baby's life? Mention perceptual skills, memory, thinking (emphasizing the recent research here), and language.

4. Imagine that a family has a 4-year-old and a 12-year-old. Name some memory tasks on which these two children would be similar, and some on which they might differ; be sure to mention eyewitness testimony. How could memory strategies and metamemory help explain some of the differences?

5. How is Piaget's concept of egocentrism important in children's thinking? What does the research on language pragmatics and prosocial skills suggest about children's egocentrism?

6. Describe the major explanations of language acquisition and the major theories of gender-role development. How are some of the explanations similar?

7. What do infants and children know about gender? Also describe children's behavior and attitudes toward the other gender.

8. We discussed parents at several points throughout the chapter. How are parents relevant in language acquisition, gender roles, attachment, parenting style, ethnicity, and the current problems children face?

9. As this chapter emphasized, the differences within each ethnic group can be larger than the differences between two ethnic groups. Describe some of the *differences* within ethnic groups that were discussed in this chapter.

10. Imagine that you have been appointed as the director of a newly created national organization, which is designed to address the needs of children in the next decade. Imagine, also, that the funds are generous. What kinds of programs would you initiate to help children and provide support services for them?

Nᴇ𝗪 ᴛᴇʀᴍꜱ

development (p. 316)
nature-nurture question (p. 316)
continuity-stages question (p. 316)
stability-change question (p. 316)
longitudinal method (p. 317)
cross-sectional method (p. 317)
conception (p. 318)
fetal period (p. 318)
teratogens (p. 319)
fetal alcohol syndrome (FAS)
    (p. 319)
acuity (p. 320)
phonemes (p. 321)
operant conditioning (p. 323)
metamemory (p. 324)
meaning-making (p. 324)

assimilation (p. 325)
accommodation (p. 325)
sensorimotor period (p. 325)
object permanence (p. 325)
preoperational period (p. 325)
egocentrism (p. 325)
concrete operational period (p. 326)
conservation (p. 326)
formal operational period (p. 326)
habituation (p. 327)
syntax (p. 329)
telegraphic speech (p. 330)
pragmatics (p. 330)
child-directed speech (p. 331)
gender roles (p. 332)
gender segregation (p. 333)

ingroup favoritism (p. 334)
social learning theory (p. 334)
cognitive developmental theories
    (p. 334)
gender schema theory (p. 334)
socialization (p. 336)
temperament (p. 337)
inhibited children (p. 337)
uninhibited children (p. 337)
self-concept (p. 337)
attachment (p. 338)
secure attachment (p. 338)
anxious resistant attachment
    (p. 338)

anxious avoidant attachment (p. 338)
authoritative parents (p. 339)
authoritarian parents (p. 339)
permissive parents (p. 339)
nonshared environmental experiences
    (p. 339)
sibling deidentification (p. 339)
prosocial behavior (p. 340)
altruism (p. 340)
ethnicity (p. 342)
cross-cultural psychology (p. 342)

RECOMMENDED READINGS

Beal, C. R. (1994). *Boys and girls: The development of gender roles.* New York: McGraw-Hill. Beal's book is an interesting and wonderfully written examination of gender development. The topics include theories about gender-role development and how peers, teachers, and the media influence children's ideas about gender.

Children's Defense Fund. (1997) *The state of America's children.* Washington, DC: Author. CDF publishes a new volume of this series each year, typically focusing on family income, health issues, child care, and education. It includes excellent statistical information about the current status of children in the United States.

Eisenberg, N. (1992). *The caring child.* Cambridge, MA: Harvard University Press. Nancy Eisenberg's book on children's prosocial behavior covers children's motives for prosocial behavior, as well as how biology, socialization, and circumstances influence this activity.

Holmes, R. M. (1995). *How young children perceive race.* Thousand Oaks, CA: Sage. Robyn Holmes spent six years in preschool settings, observing how children view race; this is a fascinating and thought-provoking book.

Ninio, A., & Snow, C. E. (1996). *Pragmatic development: Essays in developmental science.* This is one of the most interesting books on children's language development, focusing on how children learn to become conversationalists.

Sroufe, L. A., Cooper, R. G., & DeHart, G. B. (1996). *Child development: Its nature and course* (3rd ed.). New York: McGraw-Hill. This mid-level textbook will be useful for students who want a clear and comprehensive overview of child development.

ANSWERS TO CRITICAL THINKING EXERCISES

Exercise 10.1

a. Although environmental (nurture) factors are certainly important, these children's musical talents are also influenced by genetics. Parents who are music teachers probably have some inborn musical talent, which they pass on through their genes to their children (nature).

b. The cross-sectional method can be used to complete a study in a much shorter time period, and it would be much less expensive to run. You would not need to worry about children dropping out of the study or moving away. You also would not need to worry that the children's abilities were measured in different years. A disadvantage would be that you would not be able to test whether children's knowledge showed stability versus change over time, because you measure them only once. One factor that is a potential disadvantage with the longitudinal method— changing patterns of education—would probably not be an issue for children whose ages differ by only four years.

Exercise 10.2

a. The dependent variable in Rovee-Collier's memory research was the kicking response. Piaget used manual search to examine infants' object permanence. Baillargeon used looking time.

b. Baillargeon and DeVos (1991) needed to establish that the infants looked equally at short and tall carrots in order to interpret the results for the test events (Figure 10.11, bottom two diagrams). Suppose that they simply compared the looking time for the two test events and the infants looked longer at the impossible event than at the possible event. A critic could argue that babies kept staring at this situation *not* because the tall carrot should have been visible through the opening, but because the tall carrot was somehow more interesting. In Baillargeon and DeVos's study, this explanation was ruled out because of similar looking time for the two carrots in the habituation phase.

Exercise 10.3

a. Perhaps the infant can indeed distinguish between the first and the second photo but is making the distinction on some characteristic other than gender (for example, hair color or presence versus absence of glasses). In order to conclude that infants can differentiate females versus males, the baby must first see a series of photos of *different people* of one gender and show habituation, and then show renewed interest in a photo of someone of the other gender.

b. If Bigler (1995) had simply lumped children from both classification-skills groups together, the overall difference between the control classroom and the gender-emphasis classroom might not have been significant. We wouldn't expect children who are knowledgeable about gender schemas to be influenced by just four weeks of classroom treatment, so their results should be analyzed separately from the children with low classification skills, for whom the treatment could have a major impact.

Exercise 10.4

a. Siblings who are not twins are likely to have different sets of friends. In contrast, fraternal twins are the same age, so they are more likely to have the same friends at school and in the neighborhood (Harris, 1995). As a result, nontwin siblings are likely to have more *nonshared environmental experiences,* which can encourage differences between the siblings.

b. Naturalistic observation would be more likely to be used with younger children, whose verbal skills are still somewhat limited. The researchers may therefore observe play patterns and actual behaviors between playmates. In contrast, researchers tend to ask older children questions about friendship. This technique is much more effective in assessing more abstract qualities such as loyalty and disclosing intimate thoughts. Although developmental differences are clearly important in the shift to emphasizing more abstract interpersonal qualities, the different kinds of methodologies may exaggerate the differences in the results for the two age groups.

Exercise 10.5

a. The basic problem is that families are not randomly assigned to a condition; instead, they can choose. As you might guess, well-educated parents are especially likely to look for high-quality child care centers, because they have been informed about the importance of quality care and they know what characteristics to look for (NICHD Early Child Care Research Network, 1998). So the children at high-quality centers are typically better at cognitive tasks, even before they begin attending the center. Carefully conducted research—like the NICHD study—takes this factor into account in analyzing the results.

b. One problem is that schooling will probably be a confounding variable, because many children in a developing country like Guatemala do not attend school. Another problem is that the interview questions would need to be carefully translated from English into the language the children speak (which may be an Indian language, rather than Spanish). Also, the researchers would need to be sure that the Guatemalan and U.S. children are equally familiar with the objects that are used in the conservation task.

DEVELOPMENT FROM ADOLESCENCE THROUGH OLD AGE

PHYSICAL AND PERCEPTUAL DEVELOPMENT

Physical Changes During Adolescence

Physical Changes During Adulthood

Changes in Perceptual Ability During Adulthood

COGNITIVE DEVELOPMENT

Memory in Adulthood

Thinking: Piaget's Approach

General Cognitive Performance

Moral Development

GENDER IN ADOLESCENCE AND ADULTHOOD

Work

Love Relationships

Parenthood

PERSONALITY AND SOCIAL DEVELOPMENT

Self-Concept and Identity

The Stability-Change Question

Interpersonal Relationships

Ethnicity Issues During Adolescence and Adulthood

Dealing With Death

In Depth: Attitudes Toward the Elderly and Their Consequences

Successful Aging

CHAPTER 11

Several years ago, I asked a 69-year-old friend to reflect about her life and about old age. At the age of 58, Anne Hardy and her husband Duane (shown in the photo above) left their comfortable community in Rochester, New York, to become full-time volunteers. They settled in the South, where they worked for several organizations that are concerned with civil rights and social justice. Anne wrote about this period in her life:

When our children were through college and on their own, our feeling was that it was time to close out the marketplace phase of our lives. We never had the empty-nest feeling. It was, instead, a kind of liberation, a time to move into a new phase. Just as marriage had been a new phase, followed by parenthood, this was another. The caring, the sharing of concerns, the readiness to be of help to each other when necessary, would continue with our children, unchanged by the fact that we were no longer living under one roof, but we were ready to move on, just as they were. We had both done a great deal of volunteer work in our free time for many years, and now we had the opportunity to do it full-time. Our needs are modest, so we were able to accept subsistence salaries until we were able to "retire" on Social Security, at which time we continued to work full-time but no longer drew salaries.

I am very conscious that my life hasn't been "typical," if there is such a thing. I've had many advantages denied to others. We have had fairly low income at times but were never really poor and certainly never hungry; my health has, for the most part, been good; we have loving, caring children; and best of all, I've had, in my husband, a superb companion and best friend. With today's economic stresses and disrupted families, I doubt it's a norm. . . .

At the age of 69, I still don't feel "old," although chronologically, I'm not "young." I think one ages—given reasonable health—as one has been gradually aging in all the years before, very much depending on the quality of life one has built. My interests haven't changed, except that we have the added joy of six grandchildren in our lives. Elderly people are as diverse as young people. Differences among them remain; previous likes and dislikes remain, for the most part. I am still me, "old" or not, though I feel that I have become more understanding, less judgmental, more open to new experiences, still trying to grow as a person. . . .

There are serious concerns and hopes about the future, naturally, both in regard to personal matters such as health and loss of close ones, and in regard to national and international events. What kind of world will our children and grandchildren inherit, if they inherit any world at all? I have lost much of my sense that we can influence the course of events; I have increasingly stronger conviction that we are in the hands of multinationals and conglomerates. . . . That feeling can be an immobilizing one. But to do nothing is to go along with what's happening. I know it's a cliché, but the future is now. *This is the only world any of us has, and if we don't like it, or if we are worried about the direction it's going, we have to work to change it.*

Anne Hardy's words illustrate a common thread that weaves throughout this chapter: the discrepancy between myth and reality. Her own life illustrates that elderly people typically remain optimistic and active. We'll also discuss the evidence against many other myths, pointing out that adolescents typically get along well with their parents, that lesbians and gay men are as well adjusted as heterosexual individuals, and that most people never experience a so-called midlife crisis. This chapter will also emphasize individual differences. For example, whereas most women do not experience an empty-nest feeling, some women do indeed have this reaction when their children leave home.

This is our second chapter on human development. As in the previous chapter, we will discuss physical and perceptual development, cognitive development, gender issues, and personality and social development. Our age range includes adolescence (the period between about 12 and the late teens), adulthood (from about 20 to 65), and later adulthood or old age (from about 65 onward).

PHYSICAL AND PERCEPTUAL DEVELOPMENT

Physical Changes During Adolescence

Puberty is the period of development in which a young person becomes physically capable of sexual reproduction (Nielsen, 1996). In the adolescent female, the production of estrogen rises rapidly during puberty. The elevated level of estrogen is responsible for breast development, broadening of the hips, and the beginning of menstruation. In the adolescent male, the production of androgen rises rapidly during puberty. The elevated androgen level is responsible for muscle development, increased body hair, and changes in the vocal cords. In summary, puberty has major consequences for both females and males (Dubas & Petersen, 1993).

Menarche and Menstruation   A girl's first menstrual period is termed **menarche** (pronounced "*men*-are-kee"). The average age of menarche in North America is currently about 13, but it can begin as early as 8 or as late as 16 (Golombok & Fivush, 1994; Golub, 1992). Thus, individual differences are obvious in the timing of menarche, and also in other milestones related to puberty.

Young women often have mixed emotions when their first menstrual period occurs. They are likely to describe their feelings as "excited but scared" or "happy and embarrassed" (Golub, 1992).

Menstruation is often accompanied by cramps, backache, and swelling (due to water retention). Menstrual pain is fairly common, though not every woman experiences it.

A more controversial topic is the so-called premenstrual syndrome. **Premenstrual syndrome (PMS)** is the name given to a variety of symptoms that may occur a few days before menstruation. These symptoms may include headache, painful breasts, and a variety of psychological reactions such as depression, anxiety, and irritability (Gallant et al., 1992; Golub, 1992). However, psychologists and medical researchers have no generally accepted definition of PMS. In fact, more than 200 different symptoms have been reported as part of PMS (Mitchell et al., 1992). In reality, some women may experience some of the symptoms associated with PMS—but not everyone does (Chrisler, 1996; Golub, 1992). Furthermore, in one study, women's moods depended more on the day of the week—whether it was Monday or Friday—than whether she was premenstrual or postmenstrual (Englander-Golden et al., 1986; McFarlane et al., 1988).

Let's also dispel another myth. In 1914, Leta Hollingworth demonstrated that women performed as well on cognitive tests when they were menstruating as at other times of the month. More recent researchers also agree that cognitive skills do not change throughout the menstrual cycle (Asso, 1983; Golub, 1992). In other words, a teenager should not panic if her period arrives the day before a major exam.

Children vary impressively in the age at which they reach puberty, as illustrated in this group of elementary school children.

Critical Thinking Exercise 11.1

Write down your answers to the following questions about menstruation.

a.   Given what you have just read about premenstrual syndrome, why would it be difficult to conduct research on this topic?

b.   Suppose that a young woman says, "I did much better on the SATs the second time I took them, because the first time, I had PMS." How would you critique this statement?

Puberty in Males   For males, the critical change during puberty is called spermarche. **Spermarche** (pronounced "*sperm*-are-kee") is the first experience with **ejaculation** (release of semen).

We know relatively little about young men's reactions to body changes during puberty. In general, they are somewhat positive about their first experience with ejaculation, though they seldom discuss it with others (Brooks-Gunn & Reiter, 1990). The following quotation captures one young man's impressions about puberty:

One reason that elderly drivers have a relatively high accident rate is that their reaction times are slower. Older drivers can compensate by taking precautions, such as not tailgating the driver ahead of them.

FIGURE 11.1

Scene at a store, as it would look to a young adult (top) and an older adult (bottom).

When I was 14 I went around for about two weeks with this dirty smudge on my upper lip. I kept trying to wash it off, but it wouldn't wash. Then I really looked at it and saw it was a mustache. So I shaved! For the first time. (Bell, 1980)

Physical Changes During Adulthood

Compared with the dramatic body changes during adolescence, the physical changes in adulthood are somewhat less dramatic. As adults grow older, their skin develops wrinkles, hair may grow thinner, and height may decrease. An older adult may still feel young. However, a glance in the mirror may reveal a person who looks older than expected (Whitbourne, 1996).

Female hormone levels begin to decrease around age 30, and the average woman experiences menopause between the ages of 45 and 55 (Alexander & LaRosa, 1994; Golub, 1992). **Menopause** occurs when menstrual periods have stopped for at least a year. Contrary to many myths, most menopausal women do not feel depressed or irritable (Alexander & La Rosa, 1994; Golub, 1992). Middle age may be a stressful time for many women. However, this stress can be traced to our culture's reaction to older women, rather than the experience of menopause.

Men may also experience physical changes during middle age. The **male climacteric** (pronounced "klie-*mack*-terr-ick") includes decreased fertility and decreased frequency of orgasm (Whitbourne, 1992). Male hormone levels do not seem to be correlated with mood. For men—as well as women—mood is related to stressful external factors, rather than to hormones.

A different physical change has more important consequences for older adults than either menopause or the male climacteric. Specifically, older adults have slower reaction times than younger adults (Cerella, 1995; Smith, 1996). Slower reaction time is one cause of the high rate of traffic accidents for older people, especially for those over the age of 75 (Carney, 1989).

How much longer can an elderly person expect to live? Data from the United States and Canada predict that the average 65-year-old man can currently expect to live to the age of 80; the average 65-year-old woman should reach the age of 84 ("Aging and the Canadian Population," 1996; Barinaga, 1991b). In Chapter 18, our discussion of health psychology will examine several factors related to longevity.

Changes in Perceptual Ability During Adulthood

Before examining perceptual changes during aging, let's discuss a potential methodological problem in studies comparing older and younger adults. Suppose that we test a group of college students, whose average age is 19, and a group of nursing home residents, whose average age is 78. Imagine that we find much higher scores for the college students on a test of speech perception. We cannot conclude that age is completely responsible for the difference in their scores, because the two groups also differ with respect to several confounding variables.

As discussed in Chapter 2, a **confounding variable** is a factor—other than the variable being studied—that is not equivalent in all conditions. For instance, the confounding variables in this example could include health, amount of education, and medications. In unbiased research, the elderly population being compared with college students should be healthy, well educated, and not taking medicines that could alter perceptual performance. Confounding variables like these three cannot account for all age-related differences, but they often explain a substantial portion (Birren & Schaie, 1996).

Vision The most significant change in the structure of the eye during aging is the thickening of the lens (shown in Figure 4.3). As a result, in an older person, the retina receives only one-third as much light as for a young adult. The lens also becomes less elastic, so that older adults have difficulty seeing nearby objects. Older people often need special glasses for reading and other close-up work. A final important consequence is that elderly people are more sensitive to glare (Weale, 1992: Whitbourne, 1996).

These visual changes, combined with decreased acuity in old age, produce distorted vision. Figure 11.1 shows how a grocery store might look to a young adult and an older adult (Pastalan, 1982). Fortunately, however, the most important contours and details are still retained. For most elderly people, vision is still adequate—especially with the help of corrective lenses.

Some visual problems arise in driving, however. For example, elderly people are more likely than young adults to report problems with reading signs, seeing through the windshield, and reading information on the instrument panel (Kline et al., 1992). Elderly adults also tend to have poor peripheral vision, compared to young adults. This aspect of visual attention is strongly related to traffic accidents (Ball & Rebok, 1994; Hoyer, 1995). For example, an elderly woman driver may look to the left as she prepares to turn left, and she may fail to see another car coming from her right.

Hearing Elderly people frequently have difficulty in hearing high-pitched tones. Somewhere between 10% and 35% of people over the age of 65 have trouble perceiving speech sounds. Elderly people usually hear even less when listening in a room that echoes (Schieber, 1992; Whitbourne, 1996). When speaking to an elderly person with hearing loss, try to lower the pitch of your voice and eliminate distracting background noises.

The Other Senses Researchers are not certain whether aging influences the skin senses. One problem is that elderly people vary even more than young adults in their sensitivities (Whitbourne, 1996). Consider the research on sensitivity to touch, temperature, and pain. In all three areas, some studies report that elderly adults are less sensitive than young adults. However, other studies report no age differences (Harkins, 1995; Whitbourne, 1996). Because of individual differences, some elderly people may be relatively insensitive to cold, which could cause a health problem in cold climates. However, other elderly people may be just as sensitive as younger adults to cold temperatures.

Elderly people are typically less sensitive to odors than younger adults, although some studies show no age changes (Stevens & Dadarwala, 1993; Whitbourne, 1996). As a consequence, some elderly people may be less likely than younger individuals to detect gas leaks or smoke from fires.

Although individual differences are large, taste sensitivity may decrease as we grow older (Schiffman, 1995; Whitbourne, 1996). Elderly people who are less sensitive to both smell and taste may complain that their food is less flavorful. As a consequence, they may oversalt their food or avoid nutritious food because it seems bland. Clearly, both these eating habits can create nutritional problems for elderly individuals.

Perceptual processes can change as we grow older. However, we need to reemphasize the theme of individual differences. You may know elderly people whose perceptual abilities have changed very little since they were teenagers.

Because sensitivity to odors and to taste tends to decrease with age, this dinner may not be as flavorful to this elderly man as it is to his younger relatives.

SECTION SUMMARY: *PHYSICAL AND PERCEPTUAL DEVELOPMENT*

1. The research on adolescence and old age reveals many discrepancies between myth and reality, as well as marked individual differences.

2. During puberty, girls develop breasts and begin to menstruate (menarche); boys develop muscles, body hair, and lower voices, and they experience their first ejaculation (spermarche).

3. During menopause, women's menstrual periods stop; male fertility also decreases during middle age. However, mood changes during middle age are not caused by hormonal changes.

4. Reaction times are slower for elderly people, contributing to an increased rate of driving accidents.

5. Visual changes during aging include difficulty seeing nearby objects, sensitivity to glare, reduced acuity, and decreased peripheral vision.

6. Although individual differences are large, some elderly people have difficulty perceiving speech sounds, skin senses (touch, temperature, and pain), odors, and tastes.

COGNITIVE DEVELOPMENT

Irene Hulicka (1982) shares an illustrative story about the way people judge cognitive errors by elderly people. A competent 78-year-old woman served a meal to her guests, and the meal was excellent except that she had used Clorox instead of vinegar in the salad dressing. Her concerned relatives attributed the error to an impaired memory and general intellectual decline, and they discussed placing her in a nursing home. As it turned out, someone else had placed the Clorox in the cupboard where the vinegar was kept. Understandably, she had reached for the wrong bottle, which was similar in size, shape, and color to the vinegar bottle.

Some time later, the same group of people were guests in another home. A young woman in search of hair spray reached into the bathroom cabinet and found a can of the right size and shape. She proceeded to drench her hair with Lysol. In this case, however, no one suggested that the younger woman should be institutionalized. Instead, they merely teased her about her absentmindedness. This example illustrates that a cognitive error can be interpreted differently, depending upon the age of the person who made the mistake.

In this section on cognitive development, we'll first consider memory in adulthood. Then we'll discuss thinking from both the Piagetian perspective and the perspective of intelligence measurement. Our final topic will be moral development.

Memory in Adulthood

As you grow older, your performance on some memory tasks may decline, but you will not notice any change on some other tasks. For instance, working memory is roughly equivalent for young and elderly adults when the task is straightforward (Craik, 1992; Smith, 1996). For example, a teenager and her grandmother should recall a phone number equally accurately several seconds after it was announced on the radio. However, age differences sometimes emerge on more complicated tasks. In a representative study by Craik, people were given short lists of unrelated words in random order, with the instructions to report the words in correct alphabetical order. On this task, the average young participant correctly reported 3.2 correct items, in contrast to only 1.7 correct items for the average elderly participant.

When we consider long-term memory, the age differences are small on tasks involving recognition. For example, a 70-year-old would be as likely as a 20-year-old to recognize a name as being familiar (Kausler, 1995; Lavigne & Finley, 1990). Age differences are also small on **implicit memory** tasks—those that require performing some activity. For instance, Light and her colleagues (1995) measured implicit memory in terms of the time required to pronounce unusual words. Implicit memory would be demonstrated when people pronounce a word they had seen on previous trials more quickly than a word they had not seen. On this task, participants between the ages of 64 and 78 received the same scores on implicit memory tasks as did the participants between the ages of 18 and 24. Other research confirms that implicit memory is similar for younger and older adults (La Voie & Light, 1994; Lovelace & Coon, 1991).

We've seen that age differences are small when the memory task involves fairly automatic processing, such as recognition or implicit memory. In contrast, the age differences are more substantial on long-term *recall* tasks. (Test your own long-term recall: Can you remember the name of the researcher who conducted the study on recalling words from working memory in alphabetical order?) In general, young adults perform significantly better than elderly adults on explicit recall tasks (G. Cohen et al., 1994; Zelinski & Gilewski, 1988). However, age differences are relatively small when participants have high verbal ability. For example, a study of university professors at the University of California at Berkeley showed that professors in their sixties remembered stories and scientific essays as well as professors in their thirties (Shimamura et al., 1995).

As you can see, the results of the research on memory are consistent with our theme of complexity. Do elderly people have memory difficulties? We cannot provide a simple response. Instead, the answer depends upon the characteristics of the memory task, as well as the individual's own intelligence.

Thinking: Piaget's Approach

In Chapter 10, we noted that Jean Piaget's theory of cognitive development proposed a final stage called formal operations. Teenagers and adults who are in the **formal operational period** can think scientifically and systematically (see Table 10.2).

Psychologists have conducted research to test whether adults typically reach the formal operational stage. Using a variety of tasks that measure the ability to reason abstractly and test hypotheses, they have concluded that Piaget may have been too optimistic. In fact, only 40% to 80% of adults in these studies have moved beyond concrete operations to formal operations (Kuhn, 1992; Ward & Overton, 1990). Naturally, people trained in abstract thinking usually perform better than untrained people, and some tests of formal operations are easier than others. However, we must conclude that people do not automatically progress from concrete operations to formal operations (Flavell, 1992). Although Piaget seems to have underestimated the cognitive abilities of infants, he apparently overestimated the logical skills of adults.

However, we need to emphasize our theme of individual differences once more. Some theorists now suggest that a small number of adults are capable of thinking at a level even more sophisticated than formal operations. During this more advanced **postformal-thought stage** of cognitive development, people can think creatively and ask intriguing new questions. They also solve complex problems that are not clear-cut, and they appreciate that a problem's solution may vary with the situation (Aiken, 1995; Labouvie-Vief, 1992). People typically show this highly sophisticated level of thinking in their domain of expertise, rather than in all areas—consistent with our conclusions about expertise in Chapter 8.

General Cognitive Performance

As we grow older, does our general cognitive ability tend to decline? Is your 80-year-old neighbor less intelligent than she was as a young adult? As you might imagine, the answer to this question depends on the specific cognitive skill that is being tested. For example, older adults are just as skilled as younger adults in solving problems about social relationships (Heidrich & Denney, 1994). The answer also depends on *how* the cognitive skill is being tested. For instance, Figure 11.2 shows how scores on a verbal test declined steadily when the data were gathered in a cross-sectional study, with different groups of individuals. In contrast, scores on the same test remained fairly steady when the data were gathered in a longitudinal study, following the same group of individuals across time (Schaie, 1994a).

Several theorists argue that some kinds of intelligence decline more than other kinds (Horn & Cattell, 1967). Specifically, they propose that **fluid intelligence**—or the ability to solve new problems—reaches a peak in the late teens and then declines slowly but steadily throughout adulthood. Fluid intelligence is related to neuronal breakdown during aging (Cockburn & Smith, 1991). Research using PET scans has shown that brain activity in the prefrontal cortex is reduced in elderly people, although brain activity remains relatively normal for other regions of the cortex (Grady et al., 1995; West, 1996). As Chapter 3 pointed out, the **prefrontal cortex** handles working

Will this elderly man remember what he has read as accurately as a younger person would? In some cases, his memory will be fine. However, the answer depends upon the nature of the task, how memory is tested, and his own verbal ability.

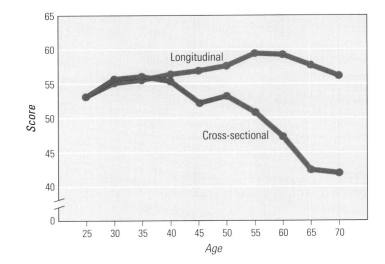

FIGURE 11.2

Age, Verbal Ability, and Method of Testing

Comparing cross-sectional and longitudinal studies on the relationship between age and scores on a verbal test.
Source: Based on Schaie, 1994a.

The Japanese film director Akira Kurosawa made the brilliant film Ran—*based on Shakespeare's* King Lear—*when he was 75 years old. Developmental theorists would argue that Kurosawa excelled at postformal thought and crystallized intelligence; these cognitive skills can continue to grow throughout adulthood.*

memory and other complex intellectual tasks. In summary, biological factors are at least partly responsible for the poorer scores on some complex problem-solving tests.

Theorists also propose that a second kind of intelligence continues to grow throughout adulthood (Horn & Cattell, 1967; Schaie, 1993a, 1994b; Sinnott, 1994). They call this kind of ability **crystallized intelligence,** and it involves specific acquired skills such as verbal ability. In general, research supports the distinction between these two kinds of intelligence and their different paths of development across the life course (Whitbourne, 1996).

Moral Development

Before you read further, try Demonstration 11.1. The moral dilemma in this story is one of 11 that Lawrence Kohlberg (1964, 1984) constructed to examine the development of moral thinking. Kohlberg analyzed the reasoning that people used for these moral dilemmas. He then created a stage theory of moral development, in the tradition of Piaget's theory of general cognitive development. In categorizing responses, Kohlberg emphasized people's moral reasoning rather than whether Heinz should commit the crime.

Kohlberg identified three broad periods of moral development, each divided into two stages. As you can see, the stages parallel those Piaget proposed. In both theories, thinking becomes less concrete and more focused on abstract principles as individuals mature. Let us examine each of the six stages, together with a representative answer to the moral dilemma about Heinz.

DEMONSTRATION 11.1 Moral Judgment

Read the following paragraph and then answer the question.

In Europe a woman was near death from a special kind of cancer. There was only one drug that the doctors thought might save her. It was a form of radium that a druggist in the same town had recently discovered. The drug was expensive to make, but the druggist was charging 10 times what the drug cost him to make. He paid $200 for the radium and charged $2,000 for a small dose of the drug. The sick woman's husband, Heinz, went to everyone he knew to borrow the money, but he could only get together $1,000, which is half of what it cost. He told the druggist that his wife was dying and asked him to sell it cheaper or let him pay later. But the druggist said, "No, I discovered the drug, and I am going to make money from it." So Heinz got desperate and broke into the man's store to steal the drug for his wife.

Question: Should Heinz have done this? Why or why not?

Source: Based on Kohlberg, 1969, p. 379.

Preconventional morality (in which decisions are based on rules that are made by other people):

Stage 1: Reasoning is based on avoiding punishment. For example, Heinz should not steal the drug because he might be sent to jail.

Stage 2: Reasoning is based on self-interest, with the hope that good deeds will be repaid. For example, Heinz should steal the drug because his wife will repay him after she recovers.

Conventional morality (in which decisions are based on internalized standards derived from interactions with others):

Stage 3: Reasoning is based on pleasing others and being a good person. For example, Heinz should steal the drug because his wife will admire him.

Stage 4: Reasoning is based on upholding the law. For example, Heinz should not steal because stealing breaks the law.

Postconventional morality (in which decisions are based on one's own abstract principles about right and wrong):

Stage 5: Reasoning is based on personal standards and the fact that it is best for society if people obey the law. For example, Heinz should not steal because it is bad for society if people steal whenever they become desperate.

Stage 6: Reasoning is based on personal standards, even if the standards conflict with the law. For example, Heinz should steal the drug because human life should be more important than upholding the law.

In general, the results of research on Kohlberg-type moral dilemmas show that Stage 1 responses are rare beyond adolescence. Stage 2 responses are the most common category for 10- and 12-year-olds, but they are rare in adults. Stage 3 and 4 reasonings are the most common categories throughout adolescence and young adulthood. In contrast, few people supply Stages 5 and 6 responses at any point during development (Colby et al., 1983; Rich & DeVitis, 1994).

Does the research support Kohlberg's theory of moral development? In general, people move forward from one stage to another, although some exceptions have been noted in the sequence (Helwig, 1997; Rich & DeVitis, 1994; Walker et al., 1995).

The earlier stages of Kohlberg's theory are generally supported by cross-cultural research. This research has examined such populations as rural Guatemalan Indians, Buddhist monks in Tibet, and Black Caribbean boys in Honduras (Boyes & Walker, 1988; Snarey, 1985). However, the later stages may be based too strongly on North American values. For example, Chinese culture holds that the highest level of moral development requires respect for one's elders, a belief that is not included in Kohlberg's theory (Helwig, 1997; Walker et al., 1995).

One of the major controversies about Kohlberg's theory focuses on gender comparisons. Carol Gilligan's (1982) book, *In a Different Voice,* argues that Kohlberg's theory is too narrow. Specifically, Gilligan points out that Kohlberg was only concerned about justice, which she asserts is a traditionally masculine value. Gilligan proposes that a comprehensive theory of moral development should also include traditionally feminine concerns such as caring, compassion, and social relationships.

However, we should emphasize that researchers find that men and women usually respond similarly on tests of moral reasoning (Clopton & Sorell, 1993; Darley & Schultz, 1990; Greeno & Maccoby, 1986). Males—as well as females—frequently emphasize the value of compassion. For example, Brabeck (1996) interviewed teenage boys in Guatemala. When asked about the characteristics they most valued, they emphasized helping other people and improving the community. In other words, women and men do *not* live in different moral worlds, with men emphasizing justice and women emphasizing social relations. The psychological similarities between men and women are typically more noteworthy than the differences (Matlin, 1996a).

Would this male social worker be less likely than a female to emphasize caring and compassion when working with clients? Although theorists such as Gilligan propose gender differences in moral reasoning, most research shows gender similarities.

These individuals are protesting against the School of the Americas, an organization run by the U.S. government that teaches Latin American soldiers how to torture prisoners and how to assassinate political leaders. Many such protesters argue that their moral convictions justify breaking the law (for example, by illegally entering the military facility) in order to publicize the immorality of the situation. This reasoning would represent Kohlberg's stage 6 level of morality.

Moral reasoning is related to other attitudes and behavior. For instance, people who have higher levels of moral development are more likely to be politically liberal. They are also more competent in dealing constructively with significant losses in their lives, such as the death of a family member (Emler et al., 1983; Lonky et al., 1984).

Critical Thinking Exercise 11.2

Write down your answers to the following questions about moral reasoning.

a. Suppose that a group of researchers wants to study gender comparisons in moral reasoning. They select 100 men, most of whom are professionals or executives, and 100 women of the same age, most of whom are not employed outside the home. They find that the men are more likely than the women to have reached Stages 5 or 6 in Kohlberg's theory. How would you critique this study?

b. Much of the research on morality has used moral dilemmas such as the one you saw in Demonstration 11.1. What would you say about the ecological validity of this study of moral development?

SECTION SUMMARY: *COGNITIVE DEVELOPMENT*

1. In general, elderly people show little decline on straightforward short-term memory tasks, recognition memory, and long-term implicit memory. They are likely to perform relatively poorly on complex short-term memory tasks and on long-term recall tasks (especially if the elderly person is low in verbal ability).

2. On Piagetian tasks, many adult participants do not reach the formal operational level. However, some reach a more advanced stage, called the postformal-thought stage.

3. On tests of general intelligence, the age trends depend upon the cognitive skill being tested and on whether the measurement is cross-sectional or longitudinal.

4. In general, fluid intelligence reaches a peak during the late teens and declines during later adulthood; crystalized intelligence continues to grow throughout adulthood.

5. Kohlberg proposed that moral reasoning develops through six stages; cross-cultural research partially supports his theory; men and women generally show similar patterns of moral reasoning.

GENDER IN ADOLESCENCE AND ADULTHOOD

In Chapter 10, we examined children's beliefs about gender as well as theories about gender-role development. Now let's discuss three important aspects of adolescence and adulthood: work, love relationships, and parenting. As you will see, gender is relevant in all three areas.

Work

In Canada, 80% of all clerical workers are female, in contrast to 2% of those in construction trades (Mackie, 1991). As Table 11.1 shows, certain occupations in the United States are almost exclusively female (e.g., nurses and kindergarten teachers) whereas others are almost exclusively male (e.g., carpenters and truck drivers). Gender clearly influences our work experiences. We'll look at three specific components of work: vocational choice, salary, and household work.

Vocational Choice   If you ask an adolescent boy what he wants to do for a living, he is likely to answer "be a carpenter or a mechanic" or else "be a lawyer or a doctor." He probably does not answer "be a nurse or a secretary," and most boys would never dream of responding, "I just want to be a husband and a father." As you might guess, males are more stereotyped in their career choices than females are (Betz & Fitzgerald, 1993; Phillips & Imhoff, 1997). Young men are socialized to avoid feminine areas. They are not likely to choose work that usually carries a lower salary and fewer opportunities for promotion (Mackie, 1991).

In contrast, young women are increasingly likely to pursue some of the stereotypically masculine professions. For example, in 1995, fully 42% of American medical students were female, in contrast to only 10% in 1967 (Barzansky et al., 1996; Jonas & Etzel, 1988). However, women are still seriously underrepresented in engineering and the sciences (Betz, 1992; Brush, 1991). Try Demonstration 11.2 to learn which factors tend to predict women's career choices.

Salary   Gender also influences salaries. If we consider full-time workers in the United States, the average female salary is only 75% of the average salary of men (Bureau of the Census, 1997). The comparable figure for Canada is 68% (Gee, 1995). Naturally, some of this pay discrepancy can be traced to the fact that males are more likely to enter high-paying fields. For example, mechanics are paid more than secretaries. However, pay discrepancies are typically found even within the same occupation. Consider a study by Olson & Frieze (1991), focusing on people who had graduated from the University of Pittsburgh master's program in business administration and were

TABLE 11.1   Percentage of U.S. Workers Who Are Female (selected occupations)

OCCUPATION	PERCENTAGE WHO ARE WOMEN
Carpenters	1%
Truck drivers	3%
Physicians	21%
Lawyers	24%
Nurses	95%
Kindergarten teachers	99%
Secretaries	99%

Sources: U.S. Department of Labor, 1989, 1990, 1994.

DEMONSTRATION 11.2 Women's Career Choices

Think about the most ambitious female student from your high school class—the one you thought was most likely to do well in a male-dominated career. Review the list of factors in the right-hand column, and place a check mark next to each item that describes this student in the column labeled "Most Ambitious Student." Then think of a female student from your high school class who planned a more traditional, stereotypically female career. Review the list of factors once more, placing a check mark in the second column next to each item that describes this second student. When you have finished, count whether there are more check marks for the first student than for the second one.

MOST AMBITIOUS STUDENT	MORE TRADITIONAL STUDENT	FACTORS THAT ARE GENERALLY ASSOCIATED WITH A WOMAN CHOOSING A NONTRADITIONAL CAREER
_____	_____	High ability
_____	_____	Liberated gender-role values
_____	_____	High self-esteem
_____	_____	Highly educated parents
_____	_____	Female role models
_____	_____	Employed mother or mother who was dissatisfied with her life
_____	_____	Supportive father
_____	_____	Strong academic self-concept
_____	_____	Work experience as adolescent

Source: Based on Betz and Fitzgerald, 1987; Betz, 1994b.

---

working in this field. Even after controlling for occupation and the university from which they received their degree, men earned an average of $5,300 a year more than women did. Similar discrepancies have been reported for librarians, engineers, and physicians (Baker, 1996; Frieze et al., 1994; Jagacinski et al., 1987).

Household Work Another, less visible kind of work is performed at home. Who makes the beds, prepares the meals, does the dishes, takes out the garbage, and picks up the socks? Most surveys show that U.S. and Canadian women perform between 60% and 75% of the home-related chores (Blumstein & Schwartz, 1991; Brayfield, 1992; Devereaux, 1993). Some studies have shown that men are doing slightly more housework than in earlier decades (Gilbert, 1994). Also, ethnicity can make a difference. For example, housework is more evenly divided among French Canadian couples than among English Canadian couples (Brayfield, 1992).

In one study, women did more housework than their husbands, even though both spouses had similar professional status. However, the women still felt guilty that they were not being "wifely" enough. As one woman said, "My sisters are very traditional, and my husband's family is super-traditional. They have wives who are not like me . . . subconsciously it bothers me" (Biernat & Wortman, 1991, p. 856).

In this section, we have seen that gender influences career choice, salaries, and the distribution of housework. Gender also has important implications for romantic relationships.

Love Relationships

On television, most adults are married—or else eagerly pursuing someone of the other gender (M. L. Moore, 1992). In this section, we'll consider some of the research on married couples. In addition, we will also examine other options that are portrayed much less often: lesbian and gay relationships, and remaining single.

Marriage In the United States and Canada, the typical age at first marriage is 24 to 26 years for women and 26 to 28 years for men (Saluter, 1994; Statistics Canada, 1990). A meta-analysis of research conducted in North America has shown that both women and men are happier if they are married than if they are not (Wood et al., 1989).

According to surveys, young married couples are the happiest of any age group (Hatfield & Rapson, 1993). Most research on newlyweds focuses primarily on White couples. In contrast, Jean Oggins and her colleagues (1993) studied 199 Black and 174 White newlywed couples. In general, the respondents were happiest if they felt that their partners valued them and showed this high regard through words and actions. Interestingly, White wives tended to reveal more about themselves than the White husbands did. However, no gender differences in self-disclosure were found for Black couples.

In a happy marriage, both wife and husband feel that their emotional needs are fulfilled, and each partner enriches the life of the other. Both people understand and respect each other, and both are concerned about one another's happiness and welfare (Stinnett et al., 1984; Turner & Helms, 1989). In general, happy couples are also likely to be skilled in interpreting each other's emotions. Both consider their spouses to be their best friend. Also, each partner is fairly high in stereotypically "feminine" traits such as being gentle, understanding, and affectionate (Antill, 1983; Bee, 1987; Whitbourne & Ebmeyer, 1990).

Reseachers have also examined a related issue in trying to predict whether a marriage will remain stable or whether it will end in a divorce (Birchler, 1992; Cate & Lloyd, 1992; Karney & Bradbury, 1995; Kurdek, 1991a, 1993; Levant, 1992; Mackey & O'Brien, 1995). The factors that are related to marriage stability include the following:

Research in North America has shown that both women and men are happier if they are married than if they are not.

1. Attaining high level of education

2. Lacking financial problems

3. Both being at least in their twenties at the time of marriage

4. Having no premarital births

5. Experiencing long acquaintance prior to marriage

6. Having parents who were happily married

7. Using appropriate conflict-resolution style

8. Trusting and respecting one another

Lesbian and Gay Relationships   When we use the terms **lesbians** and **gay males,** we are referring to individuals who are emotionally, psychologically, and sexually attracted to members of their own gender. In general, the terms *lesbians* and *gay male* are preferred to the term *homosexual,* which focuses too narrowly on the sexuality of the relationship. (Unfortunately, we have no appropriate substitutes for the word *heterosexual.* To me, the term *straight* sounds too rigid, and it implies moral correctness.)

Research suggests that between 40% and 80% lesbians and gay males are in a steady relationship (Kurdek, 1995; Peplau, 1988). Furthermore, surveys of lesbians,

Researchers have found that lesbians and gay men have relationships that are as satisfying as heterosexual relationships.

gay men, and heterosexuals have found no significant differences among the three groups on measures of satisfaction with the relationship (Kurdek, 1991b, 1995; Peplau, Veniegas, & Campbell, 1996). Contrary to many stereotypes, gays and lesbians typically report that their love relationships are stable, rather than temporary. For example, Peplau, Cochran, and Mays (1996) studied 398 Black lesbians and 325 Black gay men who were currently in love relationships. One question asked participants to rate the likelihood that they would still be in this relationship a year later. About two-thirds provided scores of 6 or 7 on a 7-point rating scale.

Research also shows that lesbians and gay males are similar to heterosexuals in their psychological adjustment and self-esteem (Gonsiorek, 1996; Gonsiorek & Weinrich, 1991; Herek, 1990; Savin-Williams, 1995). Furthermore, children raised in lesbian and gay households are similar to children raised in heterosexual households on characteristics such as intelligence, development, moral judgments, self-concepts, social competence, and gender identity (American Psychological Association, 1995; Cramer, 1986; Patterson, 1994, 1995; Tasker & Golombok, 1995).

So far, we have pointed out that gay males and lesbians tend to be in steady relationships, that they are generally well adjusted, and that their children are similar to children raised by heterosexuals. If you follow the media, however, you've probably seen much more coverage of a different issue: Is there a biological basis for being gay or lesbian? Some research suggests that sexual orientation may indeed be related to genetic, hormonal, or brain-structure factors (e.g., Bailey et al., 1993; Gladue, 1994; LeVay, 1993; Zhou et al., 1995).

However, the media typically do not explain the methodological flaws in these studies, and they typically oversimplify the results. For example, you may read in the newspaper about a study reporting lower testosterone levels in gay males. The report probably fails to mention that 20 studies found no difference based on sexual orientation, and two studies reported *higher* testosterone in gay males (Byne & Parsons, 1993). Furthermore, you may read about a study of identical twins; when one member of the pair is lesbian, her sister is also lesbian in 48% of the pairs (Bailey et al., 1993). But if genetic factors guarantee sexual orientation, we would expect that figure to be 100% (L. Ellis, 1996; Peplau et al., 1998). Thus, consistent with Theme 3, any explanation of sexual orientation must be complex in order to account for all the inconsistencies in the research. Biological factors probably play some role, but social factors must also be important (Bem, 1996; Byne & Parsons, 1993; Peplau et al., 1998).

Let's shift from a theoretic issue to a practical problem: Gay men and lesbians are often harmed by the homophobic remarks and actions of other people. **Homophobia** is an irrational fear, hatred, and intolerance of people who are lesbian or gay (Obear, 1991). People who have low levels of education and people who are very traditional in their ideas about gender are especially likely to be homophobic (Kite & Whitley, 1996). The abuse these people inflict upon gay men and lesbians may range from verbal harassment to armed assault (Pilkington & D'Augelli, 1995; Savin-Williams, 1994). For example, two gay men were holding hands while walking home. Two men in a car verbally harassed them, then drove up on the sidewalk to pin one man against the wall; the passenger then shot him in the chest (Freiberg, 1995). Homophobia is a significant problem. For instance, records gathered in nine cities reported 2,064 verbal or physical assaults against gays and lesbians in 1994 (Freiberg, 1995). As you might imagine, homophobia is low—and positive opinions are high—among individuals who have a friend or a relative who is gay or lesbian (Herek & Glunt, 1993).

Try to imagine how our culture's stereotypes about gays and lesbians would be reduced if we placed less emphasis on gender schemas (Bem, 1995). As we discussed in Chapter 10, gender is extremely important in our culture, and we encourage children to believe that males are very different from females. If we placed less emphasis on gender, then we would not be so concerned about the gender of people whom others choose to love.

Remaining Single Single people are often the objects of pity, if not outright scorn (Anderson & Stewart, 1994). In a study on attitudes toward single people, Etaugh and

Malstrom (1981) discovered that single people were perceived as being less sociable, less attractive, and less reliable in comparison with other people.

Single people believe that being single has both disadvantages and advantages. Some mention loneliness, though single people are not as lonely as the stereotypes suggest (Anderson & Stewart, 1994; Cargan & Melko, 1985).

One of the advantages most often mentioned is that single people enjoy independence and freedom (Dalton, 1992; Simon, 1987). For example, one woman who had never been married remarked, "I can pick up and go where I want, when I want, without having to ask anybody or thinking about taking care of anybody. My friends with husbands and families can't do that. I get to make decisions about myself for myself" (Dalton, 1992, p. 72).

In this section, we looked at three lifestyle options: marriage, gay relationships, and remaining single. Each of these may bring loneliness and frustration, yet each can also bring warm attachments and the opportunity for personal growth.

Critical Thinking Exercise 11.3

Write down your answers to the following questions about love relationships.

a. Suppose that a group of researchers wants to examine couples' satisfaction with marriage, as a function of the number of years of marriage. They conduct a longitudinal study on couples who have been married for 10 years, and then they resurvey those who are still together after 20 years of marriage. They find that the average marital satisfaction is greater on the 20-year data than on the 10-year data. What factor should you consider before you conclude that couples are more satisfied with marriage as the number of years of marriage increases?

b. LeVay (1993) wanted to determine whether brain structure is related to sexual orientation, and so he compared the size of the hypothalamus in the brains of 19 gay men who had died of AIDS and 16 heterosexual males, of whom 6 died of AIDS. He reported that the average hypothalamus size was much smaller in the gay men than in the heterosexual men. What confounding variable needs to be considered in this study? (Incidentally, this confounding variable was seldom mentioned in the media reports.)

Parenthood

The majority of North Americans become parents at some point in their lives. They often find that they become much more involved with parenthood than they had ever anticipated. For example, one father reported:

> It's been a lot of fun to watch her grow. . . . I just didn't have any idea of what being a father was all about. . . . And, I'm really attached. I find myself thinking about her at work, rushing to the day care center to pick her up, just because every day she learns something new and you just want to see it and kind of share it with her. (Grossman, 1987, p. 89)

A mother of twin daughters comments on some of the many ways her children have changed her life:

> In many ways the children have brought us together. They have given us a joint *aim* in life. . . . It's worth going on and getting things better and working hard because of the pleasure we can get from the children and what we can do for them. It gives you a reason for doing it all. (Boulton, 1983, p. 60)

For many women and men, parenthood represents a major life transition, because they realize that they are now responsible for the welfare of a new human being. For many years, psychologists concentrated their attention on mothers, ignoring men's reactions to fatherhood (Phares, 1992). Fortunately,

Fathers with nontraditional gender roles are more likely to spend time caring for their children and playing with them.

the recent research is beginning to examine fathers (e.g., Bornstein, 1995; Hewlett, 1992; Parke, 1995).

In general, the research shows that men and women are similar in their interest in becoming parents (Gerson, 1986). To some extent, fathers are increasing the amount of time they are spending with their children compared to similar studies conducted 25 years ago (Gilbert, 1994; P. Schwartz, 1994; Snarey, 1993). However, mothers spend between 65% and 80% more time than fathers interacting directly with their infants (Parke, 1995). As you might expect, fathers with nontraditional gender roles are more likely to help with child care.

SECTION SUMMARY: *GENDER IN ADOLESCENCE AND ADULTHOOD*

1. Men and women often pursue different kinds of careers; males' vocational choices are more stereotyped than females' choices; men and women earn significantly different salaries, even after controlling for confounding variables; women still do most of the housework.

2. According to one meta-analysis, married people are generally happier than unmarried people.

3. Researchers have identified a number of variables—such as education, conflict, resolution style, and trust—that are related to marriage stability, thus implying that successful marriages fit a pattern rather than being due to random factors.

4. Gay men and lesbians resemble heterosexuals in the quality of their relationships, their psychological adjustment, and their children's adjustment; the research on the biological basis of sexual orientation has serious flaws; many gay people experience the effects of homophobia.

5. Stereotypes often portray single people negatively; however, single people report that being single has both disadvantages and advantages.

6. Women and men have similar interests in becoming parents, though women typically spend more time performing child care activities.

PERSONALITY AND SOCIAL DEVELOPMENT

Think about the vastly different experiences that a group of 60-year-olds could have encountered during their six decades of life. We need to emphasize the theme of individual differences when we examine personality and social development, because these differences increase as people pass through adolescence and adulthood. This increased variability during aging is called **individual fanning out;** this concept emphasizes that 70-year-olds are more different from one another than 10-year-olds are (Whitbourne, 1997).

We'll begin this section by discussing self-concept. Our next topic is the stability-change question, one of the three developmental issues introduced in Chapter 10. Then we'll consider interpersonal relationships, ethnicity during adolescence and adulthood, dealing with death, and an "In Depth" feature on stereotypes about the elderly. Our final topic is successful aging.

Self-Concept and Identity

Chapter 10 introduced the term **self-concept,** or the schema of thoughts and feelings about oneself as an individual. We saw that toddlers can recognize themselves in a mirror and children develop feelings of competence. As you would expect, adolescents and adults have a much more differentiated sense of who they are and how they have changed. In discussing self-concepts beyond childhood, psychologists often prefer the term **identity,** which refers to an individual's self-rating of personal characteristics, considering biological, psychological, and social dimensions (Whitbourne, 1997). Let's focus on Erikson's theoretical approach to identity, as well as more recent research on adult identity.

Erikson's Psychosocial Approach   Chapter 10 introduced Erik Erikson's (1950, 1968) theory of identity development. Erickson argued that people confront a specific task during each of eight developmental stages. Table 11.2 reviews the first four stages, which describe childhood development, and adds the four stages that are important during adolescence and adulthood.

Chapter 10 discussed Piaget's theory of cognitive development, and an earlier part of this current chapter examined Kohlberg's theory of moral development. In Chapter 13, we will explore Freud's theory of personality development. However, none of these developmental theories matches Erikson's theory with respect to its attention to later adulthood. Erikson argues that individuals struggle with identity development throughout their life course.

As Table 11.2 shows, the major task for the adolescent in Stage 5 is to struggle with the question "Who am I, and where am I going?" If the previous stages have been successfully resolved, adolescents can explore social, personal, and occupational options. If these stages have not been adequately resolved, adolescents will be less socially mature (Nielsen, 1996). Erikson created the now-popular term *identity crisis* to refer to this stage. He argued that identity issues are particularly relevant for adolescents because of the major physical and cognitive changes young people experience, as well as their need to make decisions about occupations and education.

During Stage 6, the young adult develops an intimate relationship with another person. Erikson argues that an individual who does not develop intimacy will be overwhelmed by a sense of isolation. Young adults also struggle with career decisions.

In Stage 7, Erikson argues that generativity may be expressed in child rearing; by creative, productive work; and by volunteer activities that benefit other people. Social responsibility is also an important focus during this stage. Research by Peterson and his colleagues has confirmed that well-educated women in their forties frequently focus on generativity (Peterson & Klohnen, 1995; Peterson & Stewart, 1993, 1996). However, they found that many women began focusing on generativity at an even earlier age, during their twenties and thirties.

Erikson's Stage 8 requires looking back on your life accomplishments. At the beginning of the chapter, for example, you read about Anne Hardy's thoughts about conveying values to her children and her lifelong concern with working for racial equality and world peace. A person who can reminisce about a satisfying life achieves a sense of integrity, according to Erikson. In contrast, a person who has accomplished little may develop a sense of despair.

Recent Research on Adult Identity   Let's look at some of the more recent research on the question of adult identity. For example, Demonstration 11.3 is a modification of some questions Whitbourne (1986) explored during in-depth interviews of adults. She found that people considered their values to be a major part of their identity. One of the most frequently mentioned values was honesty—in other words, not stealing, cheating, or lying. Other frequently mentioned values were the Golden Rule (doing unto others as you would have them do unto you) and trying to get along well with others. In summary, then, Whitbourne's study demonstrated that adult identity emphasizes a concern for the well-being of other people.

Other research illustrates that culture has a major impact on identity and values. Specifically, North American and many Western European cultures emphasize that you must assert yourself and appreciate how you are different from others (Markus & Kitayama, 1991a; Raeff et al., 1995). In these **individualistic cultures,** a person's identity focuses on the idea that "I am a unique individual." In contrast, Asian, African, Hispanic, and many southern European cultures emphasize fitting in with others and living in interdependent relationships with them. In these **collectivist cultures,** a person's identity would focus on interconnectedness with others. Two popular sayings illustrate these two perspectives. In the United States, we say "The squeaky wheel gets the grease." In contrast, a popular Japanese saying is "The nail that stands out gets pounded down" (Markus & Kitayama, 1991a, p. 224).

According to the principle of individual fanning out, 70-year-olds differ more from one another than do 10-year-olds. These three elders include a competitive runner, an artist, and political activist Bella Abzug.

TABLE 11.2 Erickson's Theory of Psychosocial Development, From Birth Through Old Age

STAGE	AGE	PSYCHOSOCIAL TASK	DESCRIPTION OF TASK
1	0–1	Trust versus mistrust	The infant whose needs are met by a caretaker develops a sense of trust in others.
2	1–3	Autonomy versus doubt	The toddler tries to learn independence and self-confidence.
3	3–6	Initiative versus guilt	The young child learns to initiate his or her own activities.
4	6–12	Competence versus inferiority	The child tries to develop skill in physical, cognitive, and social areas.
5	12–19	Identity versus role confusion	The adolescent tries out several roles and forms an integrated, single identity.
6	20–40	Intimacy versus isolation	The young adult tries to form close, permanent relationships and to make career commitments.
7	40–65	Generativity versus stagnation	The middle-aged person tries to contribute to the world through family relationships, work productivity, and creativity.
8	65 on	Integrity versus despair	The elderly person thinks back on life, experiencing satisfaction or disappointment.

Source: Based on Erikson, 1950, 1968.

The Stability-Change Question

In Chapter 10 we considered the stability-change question when we asked whether infants maintain their personal characteristics as they mature into children. Now we need to consider the same issue in adulthood. The prominent American psychologist William James wrote a century ago, "For most of us, by the age of 30, the character

---

DEMONSTRATION 11.3 Important Values During Adulthood

Locate a friend or relative you would feel comfortable interviewing about personal issues. It would be ideal to locate someone at least 50 years old, but a younger person would be satisfactory. Tell this person that you will be conducting an informal interview about important values, and that he or she should feel free not to answer any questions that seem too personal. Each general question is followed by a probe, which you may find useful if your respondent requires clarification or hesitates about an answer.

1. Please describe for me your major values, the principles you try to live your life by.
   PROBE: What is important to you in the way you try to live your life?

2. How strongly do you feel about your values?
   PROBE: How important to you is it that you follow these values?

3. How do your values affect the way you feel about yourself as a person?
   PROBE: Do you judge yourself by your values? How do you come out with respect to these values?

4. Do you think your values are changing?
   PROBE: Do you have any questions or doubts about your values?

If yes: 5a. How are they changing?
   PROBE: What is it about your values that is changing?

If no: 5b. Do you think your values are likely to change in the future?
   PROBE: Do you think you will ever have questions about your values in the future?

Source: Based on Whitbourne, 1986, pp. 245–246.

Neurosurgeon Ben Carson visits Andrews University pre-med students.

has set like plaster, and will never soften again" (James, 1892, p. 124). In other words, James clearly cast his vote for "stability" in the great stability-change debate.

You might vote for "change," however, if you had known Benjamin Carson as an angry high school student and watched his transformation into a neurosurgeon. Ben Carson failed most of his math quizzes as a fifth-grader in inner-city Detroit. As a high school student, Ben was known for his violent temper. He would attack anyone who offended him, using a bottle, brick, knife, or any other handy weapon. One day, in a rage, he thrust a knife at a boy. The boy happened to be wearing a large metal belt buckle, which broke the blade on Ben's knife. Ben instantly realized that he could have killed another person. He ran home, closed himself into the bathroom, and sat on the edge of the tub. He thought and prayed, and then emerged three hours later with his anger gone. The anger never returned, and Ben focused his attention on his school work, achieving an A average in the remainder of high school. He was accepted to Yale University for his undergraduate work and the University of Michigan for medical school. Ben Carson became a neurosurgeon and later achieved fame for his surgery in separating conjoined twins (at one time referred to as Siamese twins) connected at the head (Woodford, 1989).

Personality Characteristics   Does the research evidence support the stability view of William James or the change view suggested by life transformations such as Ben Carson's? Do our personality characteristics remain consistent as we mature from teenagers into late adulthood? Naturally, people who experience traumatic events are less likely to show stability (Fiske & Chiriboga, 1990). Also, a study is less likely to demonstrate stability if researchers study long time spans—perhaps 30 years of personality development—rather than just one decade (Kogan, 1990).

In general, however, your personality characteristics at age 20 are correlated with those characteristics at age 50. For example, those who are more politically active as young people tend to remain more active than average in middle age; relatively unpolitical people tend to remain unpolitical (Franz & McClelland, 1994). In other words, we tend to keep our same standing—relative to other people—as we mature.

Several years ago, my mother attended the 50-year reunion of her high school class in Great Falls, Montana, and her report of the event meshed well with the research findings. For example, she noted moderate stability in the extent to which people were extraverted or outgoing. The high school senior who had been active in numerous school organizations was now, at age 68, the extraverted master of ceremonies for the reunion, whereas the quiet people were still quiet. Of course, the correlation between adolescent personality and adult personality was far from perfect, but it was impressively strong.

Midlife Crises   Another important issue related to the stability-change question is the so-called *midlife crisis*. You've probably read in popular magazines that adults are supposed to experience some kind of major change in their lives as they approach middle age. A typical article describes a happily married 39-year-old accountant who turns 40 and abruptly divorces his wife, abandons his children, and moves to southern California with a woman barely older than his offspring.

In reality, however, the research does not show widespread midlife crises (Chiriboga, 1989; Lieberman & Peskin, 1992). Furthermore, some people have a positive transition during midlife that allows them to lead a more creative and productive life (Gormly, 1997). We must conclude that individual differences are large with respect to midlife crises, and these crises are certainly *not* universal.

Interpersonal Relationships

We already considered a major interpersonal issue during adolescence and adulthood when we discussed love relationships. We'll now consider adolescent-parent interactions and patterns of friendship.

Adolescent-Parent Relationships   Perhaps you once read a teen novel containing a passage like this:

> All the scolding and criticism from her parents were simply too much for 15-year-old Meredith. Tears streaming down her pale cheeks, she ran into her bedroom, slamming the door behind her slender young legs. She hurled herself onto her bed, sobbing deeply into her lavender pillow. "I hate you, I hate you, I hate you!" she cried to her parents, in a voice choked with emotion.

Research shows that adolescents generally report feeling positive about their relationships with their parents.

Are the relationships between adolescents and their parents as stormy as the popular media suggest? In fact, we can reject the myth that adolescents constantly engage in fierce conflict with their parents. Instead, adolescents generally report feeling positive about their relationships with their parents (Galambos, 1992). Also, the arguments that adolescents have with their parents have been shown to be generally low in intensity (Smetana, 1996).

Naturally, parent-child relationships change during puberty (Holmbeck & Hill, 1991; Paikoff & Brooks-Gunn, 1991; Vangelisti, 1992). After all, adolescents are preparing to lead independent lives.

Judith Smetana (1996) explored adolescent-parent relationships in three different cultural groups: middle-class European American families, middle-class African American families, and Chinese families living in Hong Kong. From the discussion a little earlier of independence in White North Americans and interconnectedness in Asian and African cultures, you might expect the conflict to follow a similar pattern. Instead, Smetana found that the European American and the Chinese families had the most conflict, with lower conflict among the African American families. Most of the conflicts—for all three groups—were low in intensity and typically focused on activities, household chores, and personal appearance.

Friendship   Chapter 10 looked at friendship during childhood. We saw that these early friendships are based on concrete characteristics, such as similar interests.

However, adolescents base their friendships only partly on mutual interests. In addition, the friend must be dependable, trustworthy, and loyal. Adolescents know that a friend should be someone with whom you can have meaningful conversations about problems and experiences. Further, good friends must be able to resolve conflicts with each other (Collins & Repinski, 1994; Hartup, 1993). In choosing friends,

People who have good interactions with their friends are likely to be more satisfied with their lives.

adolescents tend to gravitate toward those who are typically similar in personality, attitudes, and values (Blieszner & Adams, 1992).

These deeper friendships during adolescence probably develop only after young people have lost most of their egocentrism—to use Piaget's term—and they can appreciate the perspective of another person. Also, Erikson's approach suggests that identity crises associated with Stage 5 must be resolved in order to develop truly intimate friendships.

The nature of friendships may change as people progress through adulthood. According to a study of friendships between the ages of 18 and 75, older men were more likely than younger men to emphasize concern and thoughtfulness. Older women were more likely than younger women to show more tolerance and less confrontation toward their friends (Fox et al., 1985). However, older adults tend to value the same characteristics in their friends as adolescents do: A friend should be a caring, dependable person with whom you can have good conversations (Rawlins, 1995).

Furthermore, life satisfaction during later adulthood seems to be correlated with positive interactions with friends (Rawlins, 1995; S. Rose, 1995). As an elderly man concluded in one interview, "Without friends, you're like a book that nobody bothers to pick up" (Fox et al., 1985, p. 500).

Critical Thinking Exercise 11.4

Write down your answers to the following questions about the stability-change question and interpersonal relationships.

a. Suppose you are describing to a friend how the research does not suggest that midlife crises are common. Your friend protests and then describes in great detail about a 43-year-old man who completely changed his life. How would you respond?

b. A study by Laursen (1995) on adolescent conflict examined a population of adolescents who lived at home with two parents and a sibling, and who had both a best friend and a romantic partner. The purpose of the study was to assess the number of daily conflicts the teenagers experienced. What are the advantages and disadvantages of using this kind of sample?

Ethnicity Issues During Adolescence and Adulthood

When we consider ethnicity and development, we must avoid stereotypes. We must also keep the theme of individual differences in mind; the members of an ethnic group vary widely from one another. Nevertheless, ethnic distinctions can be important in the lives of adolescents and adults. We now look at three important areas: adolescent academic achievement, biracial adolescents, and the experience of elderly people in different ethnic groups.

Academic Achievement During Adolescence   Table 11.3 shows the percentage of U.S. adults over the age of 24 who hold at least a bachelor's degree, as a function of ethnic group. As you can see, the percentages range from 9% for Native Americans and Hispanics to 37% for Asian Americans.

Black, Hispanic, and Native American adolescents are less likely than European American or Asian American students to attend college. One reason is that the academic environment is not perceived to be nurturing (Brown, 1994; Holden, 1991). Another issue is that Black, Hispanic, and Native American students are more likely than Asian American or European American students to withdraw from college before graduation (Aguirre & Martinez, 1993; Brown, 1994; Thompson, 1995; Tierney, 1993).

What are some of the factors that encourage academic success? Some successful students credit the high schools they attended. For example, Burciaga (1993) attended a school in El Paso, Texas, in which 70% of the students are Mexican, and 100% of the graduates go to college. He credits the faculty for their enthusiasm, values, and motivation that encourage every student to succeed.

Students of color who become successful in a challenging profession often attribute their success to a mentor who gave advice and encouragement. Many people of color who have achieved in the sciences point out that they lacked role models from their own ethnic background when they were in college. Eloy Rodriguez has a PhD in developmental biology. As he remarked, "I didn't see my first PhD role model Latino till the age of 28" (Holden, 1992).

Obviously, parents are also responsible for encouraging academic success (Holden, 1992). For example, Soto (1988) interviewed the parents of high- and low-achieving Puerto Rican children. The successful students were more likely to have parents who had high aspirations for their children. These parents were also more aware of their children's educational progress and more likely to praise their children for their achievements.

Interviews with successful Black students also show that parents' encouragement was an important factor (Lee, 1985). Another study concluded that Black students tended to receive higher grades if their parents encouraged them to develop racial pride and an appreciation of Black heritage (Bowman & Howard, 1985).

Another factor encouraging student success is called **bicultural efficacy,** which is a person's belief that he or she can live effectively within two different ethnic

TABLE 11.3	Percentage of Adults Over the Age of 24 With at Least a Bachelor's Degree, by Ethnic Group
ETHNIC GROUP	**PERCENTAGE WITH BACHELOR'S DEGREE**
Asian	37%
White	22%
Black	11%
Native American	9%
Hispanic	9%
Source: Based on Kominski, 1993.	

groups without compromising the sense of cultural identity (Birman, 1994; LaFromboise et al., 1993). For example, Native American college students who are high in bicultural efficacy have higher grades, better study habits, and a stronger commitment to academic success. The United States currently has 29 tribal-run colleges whose goal is to train Native Americans for careers, while learning more about their own heritage (Wright, 1996).

When psychologists examine ethnic differences in achievement, they also need to explain why Asian American students are generally so successful in school. In fact, Asian Americans are often stereotyped as the "ideal minority group." Many Asian students do excel in science and mathematics, both in North America and in Asia (e.g., Stevenson et al., 1993). For example, Asian American women are twice as likely as European American women to obtain a college degree (Root, 1995). However, we need to emphasize the large variability among the various Asian groups, as well as the variability within any single Asian group (Sue & Okazaki, 1990; Yatani, 1994).

Researchers do not believe that Asian Americans' academic success can be traced to a genetic explanation (Sue & Okazaki, 1990; Yatani, 1994). Instead, the differences can be traced to "nurture." Asian American parents encourage their children to feel a strong sense of obligation to their family (Lazur & Majors, 1995; Uba, 1994). Asian families traditionally set high standards for achievement (Lee, 1992). Another advantage for Asian American students is that their peers also value achievement, so they can win admiration from their friends for doing well in school (Steinberg et al., 1992).

However, many Asian American students complain that their families overemphasize success (Yatani, 1994). This focus on success is clearly stressful. Also, their families may discourage them from pursuing careers other than science and medicine. For example, a Chinese American student told me that she passionately wanted to become a psychologist. Unfortunately, her parents said that they would be ashamed of her, because their friends' daughters wanted to become doctors, physicists, and biologists.

Asian Americans also find that they may do well academically, but anti-Asian barriers keep them from participating in politics, sports, entertainment, and other influential or high-paying careers (Sue & Okazaki, 1990; Woo, 1989). In academic careers, Asian Americans are less likely to receive promotions. They are also less likely to be awarded leadership positions. Many have concluded that there is a "glass ceiling" for Asian Americans—a barrier that blocks their professional advancement (Miller, 1992).

In summary, ethnicity is related to academic achievement. Important factors that contribute to these differences include schools, parents, a student's own bicultural efficacy, the attitudes of peers, and racial discrimination.

Students who are high in bicultural efficacy tend to excel academically. At Little Big Horn Tribal College in Montana, students from the Crow tribe learn about their Native American heritage and also master the academic subjects taught at other colleges.

Biracial Adolescents   Melissa Steel's mother is a Black woman from Ghana, and her father is a European American man. She recalls her experience as an adolescent:

> Throughout middle school and high school, I got used to being unable to identify completely with my white friends, while feeling somehow guilty because I wasn't what my black classmates expected me to be. I gradually realized that my problems were more the result of divisions in American society than of deficiencies in my biracial upbringing. (Steel, 1995, p. 46)

The number of biracial families in the United States has increased by about 80% since 1980 (Steel, 1995). Many children in biracial families feel alienated from both groups, as Melissa Steel explained (Steel, 1995; Uba, 1994). This alienation may be encouraged by racist attitudes. In one well-publicized incident, a principal at a high school in Alabama tried to ban Black-White couples from attending the prom. One student, whose mother is Black and father is White, asked the principal, "Who should I go with to the prom?" He answered, "That's the problem. Your mom and dad made a mistake" (Gillem, 1996; Steel, 1995).

Many biracial adolescents ultimately decide to identify with both of their ethnic heritages, rather than choosing only one identity (Gillem, 1996; Rosenblatt et al., 1995). Those with biracial identity tend to have greater self-confidence and fewer

Melissa Steel, shown with her parents William and Adwoa and her brother Anim, eventually resolved her own questions about ethnic identity by realizing that she could simply be secure about herself, rather than needing to "choose sides."

psychological problems than those who "choose sides" and adopt a single racial identity. These individuals can view the world from an enriched perspective, rather than a single ethnic framework.

Ethnicity and Aging Elderly people of color experience some disadvantages and some advantages in comparison with elderly European American people. For example, the **double-jeopardy hypothesis** predicts that elderly members of ethnic minority groups will experience two kinds of prejudice, against both their age category and their ethnic category. The double-jeopardy hypothesis is indeed supported by the research on income. Elderly people of color are clearly more likely to live below the poverty line (American Psychiatric Association, 1994b; Padgett, 1995).

When we consider family support, however, Black elders seem to have the advantage over European American elders. For example, elderly Blacks are more likely than elderly European Americans to interact with and receive social support from their younger family members (Baker, 1994; Markides & Black, 1996).

Ethnic background also has an important influence on living arrangements. Specifically, elderly Asian Americans are more likely than members of other ethnic groups to live in the same home as their children—rather than with a spouse or alone (Lubben & Becerra, 1987; Tran, 1991).

We have seen that ethnicity may be related to financial status, family support, and living arrangements. However, ethnicity may have little impact on other aspects of growing old. For example, Native American, Hispanic, and European American elderly people report similar advantages and disadvantages to growing older (Harris et al., 1989). They value their freedom and their family relations, and they regret that their deteriorating health creates problems and limitations. Now let us turn our attention to a topic that is equally relevant for elderly people from all ethnic backgrounds: awareness of dying.

Studies generally show that elderly Black people are more likely than elderly European American people to receive social support from family members.

Dealing With Death

Erik Erikson and his coauthors (1986) interviewed elderly people in preparing their book *Vital Involvement in Old Age*. One respondent said, "You don't know whether you are going to be here tomorrow or not. Nobody does, of course, but when you are older your chances are more questionable." Many respondents did not hide their fear of death. As one person remarked, "On New Year's night, when they drop that ball, I am so glad I lived another year. I don't like to die at all! I am frightfully afraid of death!" (p. 65).

Life Review   We mentioned earlier that Erikson's Stage 8 emphasized looking back on one's life. This process is usually prompted by an awareness of death in the near future (Baltes, 1995). This **life review** is a special kind of reminiscing about the past in which an older person recalls previous experiences and tries to work through them to understand them more thoroughly (Sherman, 1991). Cognitive psychologists are now beginning to explore these life-review reports, because they are an important kind of autobiographical memory (Baltes, 1995).

New Developments in Death Education   Fortunately, the death-education movement has grown stronger in recent years. We now know, for example, that people do not pass through an orderly series of stages as they prepare for death (Aiken, 1995). Furthermore, ethnic group membership can have an important impact on a person's views of death (Brokenleg & Middleton, 1995; Chung, 1995). Many textbooks and other resources now offer both information and practical advice (e.g., Buckman, 1992; Kastenbaum, 1992; Wass & Neimeyer, 1995).

Also, health professionals and others who work with people who are dying now acknowledge that the traditional hospital setting is not a supportive, compassionate place. A relatively new development is called **hospice care,** in which death is viewed as normal, the family is involved in caring for the dying person, and medical care focuses on relieving pain, rather than keeping a person alive at all costs (Bee, 1992; Mor & Allen, 1995). Hospice programs can be based either in the hospital or in people's homes. However, their primary goal is to allow people with terminal illnesses to die with dignity.

IN DEPTH

Attitudes Toward the Elderly and Their Consequences

This chapter has probably encouraged you to think about your beliefs and opinions about elderly people. This "In Depth" feature explores how the media and the general public view the elderly. We'll also look at some cross-cultural comparisons and finish by seeing some practical consequences of these attitudes.

An important concept throughout this discussion is **ageism,** which is a bias against elderly people and the aging process. This ageist bias is encouraged by our North American culture, which emphasizes and values youthfulness. Ageism can include myths, negative attitudes, stereotypes, and outright discrimination (Schaie, 1993b; Whitbourne & Hulicka, 1990). According to ageist stereotypes, elderly people are more likely than young adults to be sickly, sexually inactive, ugly, mentally ill, inflexible, useless, depressed, and low in intelligence (Butler, 1995; Palmore, 1990). In each case, reality does not match the common stereotypes—a pattern we have noted repeatedly throughout this book.

How the Elderly Are Treated in the Media
The media advertisements make people feel guilty about aging skin and graying hair. Women are told to do something about their sagging jawline, and men are urged to buy expensive products to prevent baldness.

The elderly are clearly underrepresented in television programs (Fried et al., 1993). About 13% of U.S. residents are currently age 65 or older, yet less than 5% of the characters on television are in this age category (Bronfenbrenner et al., 1996; Passuth & Cook, 1985).

The next time you stop by a store that carries greeting cards, check out the birthday greetings for older adults. The example on the bottom in Figure 11.3 represents a large group of cards that show aging in a very negative light (Fried et al., 1993; Palmore, 1990). Even the fairly positive card on the top contains the ageist

FIGURE 11.3

Birthday cards for older adults sometimes use humor, or sometimes they portray aging in a negative light.

(IN DEPTH continued)
phrase "over the hill." Western artists also typically avoid painting elderly people. With a few exceptions—such as the Dutch painter Rembrandt—elderly people are either missing from paintings, or they are portrayed negatively (Hepworth, 1995). In short, elderly people are often underrepresented or misrepresented in media and art.

Attitudes Toward the Elderly

We need to emphasize that ageism, like many psychological concepts, is extremely complex. For example, Kite and Johnson (1988) performed a meta-analysis of previous research that showed a significant negative bias against the elderly. However, the judgments varied, depending on the characteristic that was being evaluated. For example, elderly people are judged to be fairly pleasant, but not very competent. Also, younger adults are more positive about specific elderly people than they are about elderly people in general. Other research has demonstrated—as you might expect—that people who have had frequent pleasant interactions with elderly people are more likely to report that elderly people are friendly, optimistic, and self-reliant (Knox et al., 1986).

Researchers have uncovered some evidence for the **double standard of aging,** which is the tendency to be more negative about elderly women than about elderly men. In general, though, college students tend to be more ageist than sexist (Kite et al., 1991). However, young people are likely to believe that elderly men are more intelligent than elderly women. In contrast, elderly women are seen as more passive and dependent than elderly men (Canetto et al., 1995; Kite et al., 1991).

We have discussed attitudes toward the elderly in some detail because they illustrate one of our themes: Psychological processes are complex. A simplistic view of ageism would suggest that everyone is guilty of stereotyping and discrimination toward all elderly people. However, reality is more complicated. To predict with any accuracy whether a person holds ageist views, we need to know what attributes of the elderly are being judged, whether the person is familiar with elderly individuals, and—in some cases—whether the elderly person is male or female.

Cross-Cultural Attitudes Toward the Elderly and Their Consequences

In Native American societies, the wisdom of the elderly is highly regarded (Reyos, 1997). Similarly, a young man living in the African country of Tanzania remarks that elderly women in his culture are considered to have special powers, old men are respected for their wisdom, and the elderly of both genders are valued for their knowledge of proverbs and traditions (Rich, 1994). In many cultures, attitudes toward the elderly are much more positive than in mainstream European American society.

These positive attitudes in other cultures certainly make the elderly feel more valued. However, recent evidence suggests that these attitudes also have important implications for cognitive functioning in the elderly. Becca Levy and Ellen Langer (1994) compared younger adults, whose average age was 22, with older adults, whose average age was 70, in three different populations: U.S. hearing adults, U.S. deaf adults, and Chinese hearing adults. Interestingly, previous researchers have found that young members of the deaf community consider older deaf adults to be wise leaders and role models (e.g., Padden & Humphries, 1988). Chinese elders are also highly respected and revered. Levy and Langer tested members of all six groups for their attitudes toward the elderly and for their long-term memory.

Levy and Langer found that both the young and the elderly adults in the deaf and the Chinese samples had significantly more positive attitudes about the ability and personal characteristics of elderly individuals, in contrast to the adults in the U.S. hearing sample. These findings replicated the earlier research.

Levy and Langer also administered a memory test to assess long-term, explicit memory. As you learned earlier in the chapter, in the section on cognitive development, this is precisely the kind of memory task that shows the greatest decline in standard research conducted in the United States. The memory task required participants to associate a photograph of an elderly person with an activity (e.g., "She

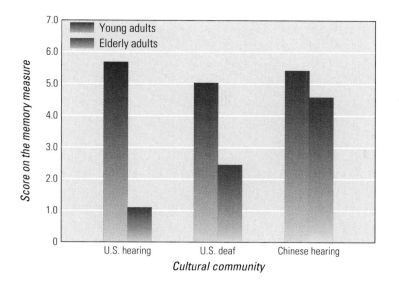

FIGURE 11.4

Memory Scores, as a Function of Age and Cultural Community
[Note: In this figure, the maximum score on the memory measure is 6.9]
Source: Based on Levy and Langer, 1994.

swims every day"). Everyone learned eight photo-activity pairs, and recall was tested after a 30-minute delay. A memory score was calculated for each participant, based on his or her score on four memory measures.

As you can see from Figure 11.4, the U.S. hearing sample replicates the previous research on long-term memory; the young adults perform much better than the elderly adults. The difference between the two age groups is much less for the deaf participants. Furthermore, the difference between the two age groups is not even statistically significant for the Chinese participants. Levy and Langer conclude that negative stereotypes can create a self-fulfilling prophecy when people believe that the elderly are supposed to show a decline in memory. These authors do not claim that stereotypes are the only factor associated with memory decline, and the study clearly merits replication. However, the study suggests that our attitudes can have important implications for memory in the elderly.

Critical Thinking Exercise 11.5

Write down your answers to the following questions about Levy and Langer's study.

a. How would you evaluate the ecological validity of the memory task, and what kind of precaution should the researchers consider in selecting the faces for the study?

b. What kind of precaution should the researchers take in selecting the sample of research participants?

Successful Aging

On the surface, elderly people might seem to have many reasons to be unhappy. We've noted that physical, perceptual, and cognitive changes can occur during normal aging. Poor health, limited income, the loss of friends, and fear of death could all contribute to pessimism in old age. Patronizing and ageist treatment—at least in the mainstream North American culture—might make elderly people feel even less competent.

Impressively, however, age seems to have little effect on people's sense of well-being, happiness, and self-esteem (Krause, 1991; Okun, 1995; Stacey & Gatz, 1991).

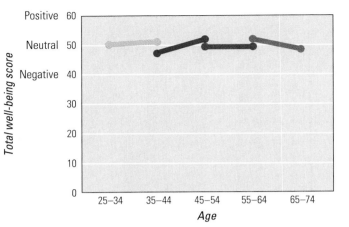

FIGURE 11.5

Life Satisfaction, as a Function of Age
Each respondent was interviewed on two occasions, nine years apart; the two dots at the ends of each line represent the same individuals. However, each of the four lines represents a different group.
Source: Based on Costa et al., 1987.

According to research by Krause and his coauthors, elderly people show an increased sense of control when they help other people.

Figure 11.5 shows data collected on nearly 5,000 people on two occasions, nine years apart (Costa et al., 1987). Each of the four lines therefore represents a longitudinal study across this nine-year time span. However, the study also used the cross-sectional method, because four different age groups are represented throughout the study. As you can see, people in all age categories are remarkably similar in their life satisfaction.

Consistent with our theme of individual differences, elderly people vary tremendously in their life satisfaction. Psychologists and other researchers have tried to identify the factors related to successful aging. For example, good physical health and social support are both crucial factors (Bass, 1995; Day, 1991; Schulz & Heckhausen, 1996).

Another important factor is a sense of control or self-determination (Landefeld et al., 1995; Rodin & Langer, 1977). For example, Landefeld and his colleagues (1995) studied 651 patients who were 70 years of age or older and who had been admitted to a hospital. Patients were randomly assigned to either a control group or an experimental group. The individuals in the experimental group stayed in a unit that promoted independence and featured an environment designed to promote competence (e.g., large clocks, uncluttered hallways). The results showed that the patients in the experimental group were better able to care for themselves and were less likely to require long-term care in an institution. In other words, a setting that encourages independence can have a major effect on successful aging.

Finally, research demonstrates that elderly people also benefit from the assistance they *give* to other people (Krause et al., 1992). By volunteering their services and offering support to others, elderly people develop greater feelings of personal control and higher levels of satisfaction with their lives.

SECTION SUMMARY: *PERSONALITY AND SOCIAL DEVELOPMENT*

1. Erikson's theory of identity development proposes that adolescents and adults struggle with identity, intimacy, generativity, and integrity.

2. More recent research on identity emphasizes that honesty and positive interpersonal interactions are critical components of identity and that different cultures have different perspectives on identity.

3. Adults show reasonable stability in their personality as they grow older; researchers do not find evidence for a universal midlife crisis.

4. In general, adolescents and their parents have reasonably positive interactions, although their conflict patterns may depend on culture.

5. Adolescent friendships are based on similar interests, dependability, and meaningful conversations; during later adulthood, people treat their friends with more concern and tolerance.

6. Factors that are relevant in ethnic comparisons in academic achievement include schools, parents, bicultural efficacy, the attitudes of peers, and racial discrimination.

7. Biracial adolescents often do not feel affiliated with either of their ethnic groups, or they may feel pressured to choose between their ethnic identities.

8. Elderly people of color experience greater disadvantages in terms of income, compared to European Americans; Black elders receive more social support from younger family members than do their European American counterparts; Asian Americans are more likely than older people of other ethnic groups to live with their children.

9. Elderly people are likely to conduct a life review; hospice care is an alternative to the traditional hospital setting for people with terminal illnesses.

10. Elderly people are often missing from the media or are represented negatively; people are often (but not always) negative about the elderly; a culture's attitudes about the elderly may be related to cognitive performance.

11. Age has little effect on people's sense of well-being; factors related to successful aging include physical health, social support, and a sense of independence.

Review Questions

1. The theme of individual differences appears many times in this chapter. Recall as many specific examples of this theme as possible, including the timing of puberty, changes in perception and memory during aging, moral development, and personality and social development.

2. Elderly people experience some deficits during the aging process, but in other respects, ability and performance do not decline. Discuss this statement with respect to reaction time, perception, memory, and performance on other cognitive tasks.

3. This chapter frequently discusses myths and stereotypes, in which the popular belief does not match reality. Discuss the popular misconceptions—as well as the research—about adolescent-parent relationships, midlife crises, gay men and lesbians, the elderly, and any other topics you can recall.

4. Imagine that you are going to be tutoring a 13-year-old student. Based on what you have read in this chapter, what might you expect about his or her physical development, moral development, career choices, identity development, and interpersonal relationships?

5. Gender is often relevant in the lives of adolescents and adults, although gender similarities are often found. Discuss gender comparisons in reactions to puberty, life expectancy, moral judgments, work, love relationships, and parenting.

6. Describe Erikson's last four stages of psychosocial development. Supply information from our discussions of work, love relationships, and death and dying to provide more details on the central tasks in each of these four stages.

7. How is ethnicity related to adolescent achievement? How is it related to the status of the elderly? Also discuss the situation of biracial individuals.

8. Try to imagine yourself and several friends—approximately your age—when you are 20 years older than now. What would the research on this group of people probably reveal about the stability-change issue? What would you predict from the principle of individual fanning out?

9. What is ageism, and how is it revealed in the media? Why is it difficult to predict when people will make ageist judgments? Finally, describe how ageism can potentially influence cognitive abilities.

10. We emphasized that researchers can reach the wrong conclusions if their study includes confounding variables. Explain how a study on life happiness across the life span might reach an incorrect conclusion if it failed to control several confounding variables. Begin by listing some potential confounding variables.

NEW TERMS

puberty (p. 354)
menarche (p. 355)
premenstrual syndrome (PMS)
   (p. 355)
spermarche (p. 355)
ejaculation (p. 355)
menopause (p. 356)
male climacteric (p. 356)
confounding variable (p. 356)
implicit memory (p. 358)
formal operational period (p. 359)
postformal-thought stage (p. 359)
fluid intelligence (p. 359)
prefrontal cortex (p. 359)
crystallized intelligence (p. 360)
preconventional morality (p. 361)

conventional morality (p. 361)
postconventional morality (p. 361)
lesbians (p. 365)
gay males (p. 365)
homophobia (p. 366)
individual fanning out (p. 368)
self-concept (p. 368)
identity (p. 368)
individualist cultures (p. 369)
collectivist cultures (p. 369)
bicultural efficacy (p. 374)
double-jeopardy hypothesis (p. 376)
life review (p. 377)
hospice care (p. 377)
ageism (p. 377)
double standard of aging (p. 378)

RECOMMENDED READINGS

Landrine, H. (Ed.). (1995). *Bringing cultural diversity to feminist psychology: Theory, research, and practice.* Washington, DC: American Psychological Association. This edited book examines how gender and ethnicity impact development. Four especially useful chapters focus on women in Native American, Latina, Asian American, and Black cultures.

Maddox, G. L. (Ed.). (1995). *The encyclopedia of aging* (2nd ed.). New York: Springer. Here's an ideal resource handbook for libraries, with short articles on hundreds of topics related to aging, which are written by well-known researchers in the discipline.

Nielsen, L. (1996). *Adolescence: A contemporary view* (3rd ed.). Fort Worth, TX: Harcourt Brace. Nielsen's comprehensive and readable textbook includes chapters on physical, cognitive, and social development; it also includes coverage of gender and ethnicity.

Whitbourne, S. K. (1996). *The aging individual: Physical and psychological perspectives.* New York: Springer. Whitbourne is a well-known researcher on adulthood; this book provides excellent coverage of such topics as aging of the cardiovascular, respiratory and nervous systems, as well as perception, cognition, and intelligence.

ANSWERS TO CRITICAL THINKING EXERCISES

Exercise 11.1

a. The problem is that we do not have a clear-cut *operational definition* for PMS, especially if 200 different symptoms have been listed for this syndrome. One researcher may examine anxiety, whereas another studies headaches. The controversy over PMS highlights our emphasis in Chapter 2 on the importance of precise operational definitions.

b. The data show that the phase of the menstrual cycle is not related to cognitive performance. By chance alone, some women will do worse when they are premenstrual—but some will do better. This young woman should consider other explanations, such as amount of sleep the previous night, anxiety, and previous experience with testing, in order to explain the difference in scores.

Exercise 11.2

a. One problem is that the men and women in these two samples differ in their daily experiences; the men are exposed to more legal and business interactions, whereas the women are more engaged in caretaking. This confounding variable could explain part of the gender difference. Also, the researchers should be certain that the men and women are equally well educated, because higher levels of moral reasoning are strongly correlated with education level (Speicher, 1994).

b. The brief description in Demonstration 11.1 is lacking in ecological validity, because it does not provide the kind of rich context we typically have when we make decisions in everyday life (such as Heinz's insurance status and how confident the doctors were about the effectiveness of the drug). Also, the dilemma offers only two alternatives—to steal or not to steal—whereas real-life dilemmas have numerous possible answers (Walker et al., 1995). In addition, in real life, we directly participate in moral dilemmas, often under time pressure, which is very different from leisurely reading a description of a dilemma.

Exercise 11.3

a. One problem with longitudinal studies is that people may drop out of the study for one reason or another. In this proposed study, an obvious group of people who will drop out are those who get divorced. The people who are divorced after 20 years are likely to be those who were least happily married after 10 years. One way to study this issue would be to omit those who were divorced after 20 years from the analysis of the 10-year data.

b. It's quite likely that people who have died of AIDS undergo some physical changes in brain structures such as the hypothalamus. As a result, the difference in hypothalamus size may be traceable to the disease, rather than to sexual orientation (Byne, 1995).

Exercise 11.4

a. Your friend has fallen victim to the situation in which a vivid example of just one individual is more persuasive than extensive objective data (a problem we discussed on Pages 22–23 of Chapter 1). You should acknowledge that some people indeed *do* experience midlife crises, but the phenomenon is far from universal.

b. Laursen (1995) wanted to obtain a sample of adolescents who all had a similar set of relationships with whom they could potentially experience a conflict. An adolescent who lived at home without a father or siblings—and who had no romantic relationship—would not have comparable opportunities for conflict. Laursen appropriately notes that he chose only individuals with these characteristics to ensure comparable data, although the negative side of this sample is that the data cannot be generalized to other adolescents.

Exercise 11.5

a. The nature of the task is relatively high in ecological validity; we often need to pair together a person's face and his or her interests and activities. However, other aspects of this task are lower in ecological validity—because we don't memorize names by looking at photos, and in the real world we see people in their natural settings, surrounded by real-life objects. The photos would need to be selected so that people in all groups are equally familiar with the stimuli. In this case, the U.S. samples saw European American faces, and the Chinese samples saw Chinese faces. (If the Chinese participants had seen European American faces, their memory scores would have been lower, and European Americans would have difficulty recalling Chinese faces.)

b. In selecting samples, researchers need to make sure that the young and the elderly samples are similar. In this case, Levy and Langer (1994) chose the U.S. samples from hearing and deaf community organizations. The Chinese samples were young workers at a pencil factory and elderly people who had retired from that factory.

MOTIVATION AND EMOTION

MOTIVATION

EMOTION

CHAPTER 12

If you've followed the career of ice skater Rudy Galindo, you know that his life story illustrates how motivation and emotion can influence a person's life. Rudy grew up in East San Jose, a neighborhood more known for its drugs and gangs than for its models of athletic achievement. Rudy's father was a Mexican American truck driver. His mother worked on an assembly line and has continually struggled with a severe psychological problem called bipolar disorder (sometimes called manic-depression).

Rudy began skating during elementary school, waking at 4:30 each morning for his daily lesson prior to school. As a second-grader, he developed a crush on an older boy—his first realization of his gay identity. From this nontraditional beginning, Rudy Galindo and his skating partner Kristi Yamaguchi went on to win first prize in the U.S. National Pairs Championship in 1989.

Soon afterward, Rudy's skating career spiraled downward. First, his partner Kristi left to skate on her own. Then, during a six-year period, his father died of a heart attack, and AIDS claimed the lives of his older brother and two coaches. After several disappointing skating seasons, he had basically given up hope of skating. However, he decided to try out for the 1996 national championships.

Rudy didn't have enough money to hire a professional coach, but his always-supportive sister Laura volunteered to coach him. Most ice skating fans had dismissed him, especially because his style was considered too ballet-like and feminine. Also, he had openly discussed his sexual orientation—a taboo subject in the world of ice skating.

On January 20, 1996, Rudy Galindo was the last participant to skate in the U.S. Men's Nationals. In a memorable performance—shown in the upper photo—he landed eight triple jumps perfectly. The audience of 10,869 rose to their feet, clapping wildly. Soon afterwards, the gay Mexican American man—who had been dismissed as a loser—was standing at the top of the awards podium to accept his prize. Tears streamed down his cheeks as he recalled the family members and other supporters who had died. And then they placed the gold medal around his neck (Galindo, 1997).

The first of two topics in this chapter, **motivation** focuses on *why* people behave in certain ways. Why did you eat a second slice of chocolate fudge cake, when you felt completely full before the first slice? Why is sexual motivation so strong that millions of people run the risk of both pregnancy and deadly diseases in order to satisfy that motivation? And why did Rudy Galindo—despite everyone's predictions—make a startling comeback to achieve his dreams of championship?

The second part of this chapter examines emotion. **Emotion** is a subjective experience or feeling that is accompanied by changes in physiological reactions and behavior. Notice, then, that emotion is a complex topic because it involves three components: subjective, physiological, and behavioral.

Consider how these three components of emotion might operate in a typical emotional situation. You have just received a phone call saying that a close friend has been in an automobile accident. He is in the intensive care unit at the hospital, in critical condition. Your subjective experiences include intense fear and concern, mingled with anxiety and surprise. Physiological reactions include an increase in heart rate and sweating. Behaviorally, your jaws drops, and your eyes widen.

The topics of motivation and emotion are intertwined in a complex fashion. Specifically, emotions are generally responsible for our motivated behavior. For example, your positive emotional reaction to a sexually attractive person motivates you to seek out this individual. Furthermore, while you are pursuing a motivated behavior, you have an emotional reaction. For example, people who are engaging in sexual behavior may experience a mixture of pleasure and guilt. Or consider achievement motivation. When the members of a basketball team are striving for the winning point in the final seconds of the last game of the tournament, they are likely to feel emotions such as anticipation, anger, fear, and joy.

Let us begin this chapter by considering the topic of motivation. In the second part of the chapter, we will explore emotion.

MOTIVATION

We humans frequently search for motives. The scandal newspaper at the supermarket asks why the well-known billionaire is leaving his second wife, or why the New Jersey mother sold her infant twins to buy a sports car for her new boyfriend. On a more literary level, consider the questions your English professor might raise in examining Shakespearean plays. Why did Iago want Othello to believe that his wife, Desdemona, had been unfaithful? Why did Richard III murder the young princes, who were the rightful heirs to the throne?

Our behavior and mental processes are activated by a variety of motives. Some motives are largely biological, emphasizing bodily needs such as hunger, thirst, and excretion. Others are primarily social motives, such as the needs for achievement, affiliation, and nurturance. Some of these motives are covered in other chapters. For example, we discussed the sleep motive in Chapter 5, and nurturance was examined in the parenthood section of Chapter 11. Chapter 16 considers affiliation and love, and Chapter 17 discusses aggression.

This chapter explores three representative human motives: hunger, sexuality, and achievement motivation. We'll begin with the most biological of these topics—hunger—and progress to the most cognitive of the three—achievement motivation. However, we'll see that even hunger is influenced by social and cognitive factors. Clearly, this most basic need is influenced by more complex variables than the simple nutritive value of food.

Hunger and Eating

The Roman Emperor Vitellius, not known for his vegetarian habits, was particularly fond of a stew containing flamingo tongues and peacock brains. People in modern-day China savor delicacies such as snake soup, wafer-thin slices of bear paw, and rat kebabs (Liu, 1991). Humans have no simple, universal rules that separate the delightful from the disgusting (Rozin, 1996).

We'll begin by looking at the biological basis of hunger and eating, and then we'll consider some external influences from the environment. Our last two topics in this discussion are obesity and eating disorders.

Biological Factors Regulating Eating Several internal factors trigger hunger and eating. For example, contractions of the empty stomach are partly responsible for the subjective experience of hunger. The hypothalamus and several body chemicals also play an important role.

Figure 3.13 on Page 89 illustrates the **hypothalamus,** which regulates eating and other motivated behaviors. The hypothalamus is responsible for **homeostasis,** or maintaining a constant, ideal internal state (Winn, 1995). The hypothalamus regulates homeostasis for body temperature, liquid intake, and food consumption. The research on the hypothalamus shows that different parts of this structure help regulate different components of the eating cycle. The mechanisms are complex, rather than operating in a simple on-off pattern (Logue, 1991; Winn, 1995).

Body chemistry is another biological factor that regulates hunger and eating. For example, the level of glucose is important. **Glucose** is a simple sugar nutrient that provides energy. In general, when the level of glucose in your bloodstream is low, you feel hungry. When the glucose level is high, you feel full. The blood glucose level seems to be monitored by **glucostats,** neurons that are sensitive to glucose levels. Researchers are not certain where the glucostats are located, but the hypothalamus receives their messages about glucose levels (Reeve, 1997).

Another important body chemical is **insulin,** which is a hormone secreted by the pancreas. Insulin plays an important role in converting blood glucose into stored fat. As you may know, diabetics have inadequate secretion or utilization of insulin; they often must receive insulin injections so that they can use glucose as a source of energy. Insulin therefore influences hunger indirectly, by decreasing glucose levels.

External Factors Regulating Eating Although hunger and eating can be influenced by our physiology, our eating habits are also determined by other factors. Obviously, the taste of a food influences how much we eat. We also learn food preferences in our culture. In fact, immigrant groups retain their preferences for ethnic foods long after they have mastered the language and customs of their new country (Booth, 1991; Rozin, 1996; Zellner, 1991).

My parents had an experience when they were living in Mexico that illustrates the importance of cultural food preferences. A Mexican geologist had been trying to convince them to try a special delicacy of his region, a worm that lived exclusively in the maguey plant. They had repeatedly declined politely. One day they were eating some particularly tasty tacos at his home. As my mother took another bite of her taco, a plump deep-fried worm fell to her plate. A moment earlier, the taco had tasted delicious. Once she realized that it contained a food rejected in her culture, she could not contemplate taking another bite.

Another important external factor is the social situation in which we eat. For example, we typically eat more food in the company of others than when we are alone (Zajonc, 1965).

Cultural factors can have an important influence on our food preferences. People who live in countries such as Portugal, Spain, and Thailand would relish a main course of sautéed squid. Many of you looking at this picture will not find your mouth watering as you contemplate that dish.

Obesity   In the United States, about 25% of men and 30% of women are considered to be obese. **Obesity** is defined as a body weight that is at least 20% above the desirable weight (Brownell & Rodin, 1994; Kuczmarski, 1992). We saw that the factors influencing eating are complex, involving both internal and external forces. Similarly, the causes of obesity are complex; overeating accounts for only part of the problem (Brownell & Wadden, 1992; Lichtman et al., 1992; Wooley et al., 1979).

If food intake cannot fully explain obesity, what can? Several other important factors include: (a) genetic makeup and metabolism; (b) set point; and (c) an exaggerated insulin response to the sights and smells of food.

Genetic predisposition makes some people more likely than others to become obese (Brownell & Wadden, 1992; Grilo & Pogue-Geile, 1991). In fact, estimates suggest that between 25% and 70% of the variation in body weight can be explained by genetic factors (Brownell & Rodin, 1994). Researchers have already identified an obesity gene in mice. However, the genetic basis of human obesity is undoubtedly more complex (Barinaga, 1996b; Marx, 1994; Zhang et al., 1994). One inherited factor in humans seems to be **metabolism,** or the energy required to maintain the body; people with slow metabolism gain more weight (Brownell & Wadden, 1992).

A second major explanation for obesity involves the notion called **set point,** a mechanism that seems to keep people at roughly the same weight throughout their adult lives (Zerbe, 1993). You probably know some people who manage to lose 15 pounds—with heroic effort. However, they gain it back several months later, even though they have been eating sensibly ever since the initial weight loss. By some estimates, as many as 95% of people who lose weight on a diet will return to their pre-diet weight within five years (Brownell & Rodin, 1994; Martin et al., 1991).

Dieting   Should people go on diets? This issue is controversial. On the one hand, many diets are unsuccessful, and our culture's concern with dieting seems to encourage eating disorders. On the other hand, overweight people are more likely to develop diabetes, high blood pressure, heart disease, and some cancers (Brownell & Rodin, 1994; Manson et al., 1995). Furthermore, overweight people are likely to experience discrimination in social, educational, and work settings (Gortmaker et al., 1993; Sargent & Blanchflower, 1994; Wing & Greeno, 1994). As a result, many obese people feel psychologically better after they have lost weight. A study of extremely obese individuals who had managed to lose at least 100 pounds revealed that these people would rather be their current normal weight than be an extremely obese multimillionaire (Rand & Macgregor, 1991).

One clear conclusion is that people whose weight is normal should *not* consider dieting. In fact, people who are slightly overweight and have trouble dieting should adopt a more positive attitude about their bodies (Burgard & Lyons, 1994; Chrisler, 1994). We should admire the wide variety of human shapes and sizes, rather than insisting that everyone be uniformly thin!

Furthermore, those of you who decide you must diet should remember that obesity is not limited to a single cause, so we should not expect a single cure. Table 12.1 lists some hints that may encourage weight loss.

Critical Thinking Exercise 12.1

Write down your answers to the following questions about obesity.

a. Suppose you see an extremely overweight couple and their overweight children at a shopping mall. Your first reaction is to suspect that the cause of their weight problem is genetic; the children have inherited the predisposition to gain weight. How else might you explain the situation?

b. The chapter noted that up to 95% of diets may be unsuccessful in the long run. However, the most pessimistic data on weight gain are obtained on individuals who are being treated in medical obesity clinics. The data on weight loss in the general population may be more optimistic about permanent weight loss (Brownell & Rodin, 1994). Why could this be true?

TABLE 12.1   Strategies That May Encourage Weight Loss

---

1. Substitute low-calorie foods for high-calorie foods (e.g., melon for dessert rather than brownies); especially avoid foods that are high in fat.
2. Take moderately small portions, and avoid sitting near additional sources of the food.
3. Slow down your eating rate by putting down your eating utensil from time to time and engaging in conversation.
4. Become aware of situations that encourage you to overeat (e.g., eat-all-you-want buffet restaurants), and arrange to avoid them.
5. Prior to a problem situation that you cannot avoid, plan a coping strategy (e.g., mentally rehearse how you will select only one cookie from a tray, rather than a handful).
6. If you do slip from time to time, do not condemn yourself and abandon your willpower. Set a modest goal for yourself and reward yourself (but not with food!) if you meet that goal.
7. Exercise to use up more calories; exercise also tends to increase your metabolic rate, which will make it easier to keep the weight off.

Eating Disorders   A young woman remarked, "When I say I overeat, it may not be what you think. I feel I'm gorging myself when I eat more than one cracker with peanut butter" (Bruch, 1978, p. 3). To save calories, she even avoided licking postage stamps. This woman has an eating disorder called **anorexia nervosa,** which is characterized by a refusal to maintain an appropriate body weight and an irrational concern about gaining weight (American Psychiatric Association, 1994a; Crisp, 1996). Anorexics feel fat, even when they look emaciated. The American Psychiatric Association (1994a) specifies that a person can be classified as anorexic if her or his body weight is 15% less than the weight specified on standard weight charts and if no known physical illness can account for the low weight.

About 90% to 98% of people with anorexia nervosa are females, and the most common age for the onset of this disorder is 12 to 18 (American Psychiatric Association, 1994a; Killen et al., 1992). However, clinicians need to be aware that older women—and men of all ages—can also become anorexic, even though young women are the most common victims. Although the data are not consistent, some studies show a lower incidence of anorexia among people of color, in comparison to European Americans (Osvold & Sodowsky, 1993; Wardle et al., 1993).

Anorexics tend to be high achievers who are overly perfectionistic and low in self-esteem. They are also likely to be depressed and high in anxiety (Connors, 1996; Graber et al., 1994). How can we interpret these relationships? Like many correlations, we cannot clearly define which is the cause and which is the effect (Chapter 2). For instance, does a depressed person develop anorexia? Alternatively, do anorexics become depressed because of their physiological, starved condition?

Anorexia nervosa is a life-threatening disorder, and 2% to 10% of anorexics die from it (American Psychiatric Association, 1994a; Kreipe et al., 1989). In anorexia, a person is more concerned about thinness than about maintaining a healthy body. As one father told me several years ago about his hospitalized anorexic daughter, "She'd rather be dead than fat." However that young woman has now kept a normal weight for four years. Fortunately, about half of anorexics will eventually recover and maintain a normal weight ("Eating Disorders—Part II," 1997).

Bulimia nervosa (pronounced "boo-*lih*-mee-ah") is characterized by binge eating, or episodes in which people consume huge amounts of food. Bulimics may eat up to 50,000 calories at a time. They gobble the food quickly, often with little enjoyment of its taste. Bulimics may also engage in some form of purging, such as vomiting or using laxatives (American Psychiatric Association, 1994a; Fairburn & Wilson, 1993). Like anorexics, bulimics are obsessed about food, eating, and body weight (Arnow, 1996; Striegel-Moore, 1993). Some bulimics—but not all—began binge eating after they had placed themselves on restrictive diets. For some people,

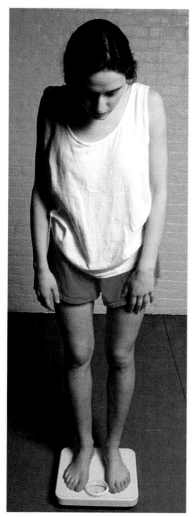

A person with anorexia nervosa has an irrational pursuit of thinness. For example, this young woman probably believes that she is overweight.

then, dieting can backfire and cause a harmful eating disorder (Lowe, 1993; S. S. Williams et al., 1996).

To some extent, eating disorders are encouraged by our culture's emphasis on slimness (Hesse-Biber, 1996). Slimness is important for men, but it is especially emphasized for women. Women are much more likely than men to be dissatisfied with their body size (Feingold & Mazzella, 1996; Tiggemann, 1992). Unfortunately, many women are trying to meet impossible standards. For example, only the thinnest 5% of women in the general North American population fall into the same weight category as fashion models (Kilbourne, 1994). In other words, the fashionable ideal excludes 95% of North American women! Average-weight women who admire these rail-thin women in the fashion magazines may develop eating disorders in order to achieve an inappropriate body weight. Our culture needs to set new standards that are not based on malnourished fashion models (Hsu, 1990).

Sexuality

Ideas and decisions about sexuality are an important component of many students' daily lives. For example, when students were asked to write about an important current conflict in their lives, one young woman wrote about a controversy that had dominated her relationship with her boyfriend for the last four years:

> The major issue which has always caused conflict in our relationship is sex. He wants to, I don't; but it's not that simple. . . . I just don't feel I am ready, there are things I want to do for myself first, before I get really deeply involved, and, never one to gamble, I don't want to chance anything. Besides, if something went wrong and if, for example, I got pregnant, I would be the one who was stuck. I have other reasons, though not so easily explained; it's a matter of self-esteem. I was raised in a very traditional environment, and I have my own dreams of how things will be. I want to wait until I am married. I know most people don't agree, they believe it is silly and prudish; but it is part of my moral code, something which I feel very strongly about, and something which is part of the many interwoven, inexplicable things which make up my identity.

To discuss the topic of sexuality, we need to consider topics as diverse as hormone levels and sexual passion—as well as personal moral codes. We'll begin by discussing biological factors that influence sexuality, as well as the external and cognitive factors. We'll then consider the sexual response cycle. Our final topic is sexual behavior, including some factors that must be considered whenever a person—such as the young woman quoted above—is making a decision about a sexual relationship.

Biological Factors   Hormone levels play a major role in the sexuality of most nonhuman primates. In human males and females, hormones are critically important. For instance, during puberty, the hypothalamus signals the pituitary gland to begin releasing special hormones. In the male, the pituitary produces a fairly constant level of hormones, whereas hormone production in females is cyclical. Hormones are clearly responsible for early sexual differentiation and for body changes during puberty. However, hormones are less important in regulating the pattern of human sexual behavior. For example, the level of testosterone in men is generally unrelated to their sexual activity (Udry & Campbell, 1994). For women, sexual desire and sexual behavior are not significantly higher at the time of ovulation than at other parts of the menstrual cycle (Kalat, 1995; Wade & Cirese, 1991). Sexual arousal in humans depends more on external and cognitive cues than on hormone levels.

External and Cognitive Factors   Touch is one of the most powerful sources of sexual arousal. A caress, a passionate kiss, or stroking the inside of the thigh—people vary in the kind of touch that they find most sexually stimulating.

Humans can also be effectively aroused by visual stimuli, either by the sight of a nude person or by erotic pictures. Research has demonstrated that men and women are similarly aroused when they see slides and movies showing foreplay and intercourse (Hyde, 1996a; Schmidt & Sigusch, 1970). However, we need to be concerned about some potential problems with viewing erotic material. For instance, Weaver and his colleagues (1984) found that men who had viewed a video of attractive nude females in provocative poses were likely to rate their girlfriends as less physically attractive. Furthermore, men who frequently read sexually explicit magazines are more likely than other men to believe that women enjoy forced sex—a rape myth that is clearly false (Malamuth & Check, 1985).

Touch and visual stimuli can be sexually arousing. However, human imagination and fantasy can create sexual excitement, even without the aid of external stimuli. An old saying captures the importance of these cognitive factors: "The brain is our most important erogenous zone."

Touch is an extremely powerful source of sexual arousal.

Sexual Arousal and Orgasm   Current models of the stages of sexual response emphasize cognitive factors. For example, a model proposed by Zilbergeld and Ellison (1980) emphasizes that sexual desire precedes several more physiological stages. Masters and Johnson (1966) proposed a classical model of a sexual response cycle in which both women and men initially experience excitement and a buildup to an orgasmic phase, followed by a resolution phase.

Additional research suggests that men and women are also fairly similar with respect to sexual fantasies during intercourse (Leitenberg & Hennig, 1995). Men and women also have similar psychological reactions to orgasm. Look at Demonstration 12.1 and try to determine whether a man or a woman wrote each description. In one study, people's guesses were no better than chance (Vance & Wagner, 1977).

Naturally, some gender differences are found in sexual reactions. For example, men are more likely than women to masturbate (Oliver & Hyde, 1993). Also, women are more likely than men to experience multiple orgasms (Hyde & De Lamater, 1997). However, women and men share more similarities than differences—even in the area of sexuality.

Sexual Behavior   Sexuality is more complex than our discussion of physiological processes might imply; let's shift our attention to sexual behavior.

DEMONSTRATION 12.1   Psychological Reactions to Orgasm

Each of these descriptions of an orgasm was written by a sexually experienced woman or man. Based on your ideas about gender, try to determine who wrote each passage. Place a *W* or an *M* in front of each description. The answers appear at the end of the chapter on Page 411.

_____ 1. A sudden feeling of lightheadedness followed by an intense feeling of relief and elation. A rush. Intense muscular spasms of the whole body. Sense of euphoria followed by deep peace and relaxation.

_____ 2. To me an orgasmic experience is the most satisfying *pleasure* that I have experienced in relation to any other type of satisfaction or pleasure that I've had which were nonsexually oriented.

_____ 3. It is like turning a water faucet on. You notice the oncoming flow but it can be turned on or off when desired. You feel the valves open and close and the fluid flow. An orgasm makes your head and body tingle.

_____ 4. A buildup of tension which starts to pulsate very fast, and there is a sudden release from the tension and desire to sleep.

_____ 5. It is a pleasant, tension-relieving muscular contraction. It relieves physical tension and mental anticipation.

_____ 6. A release of a very high level of tension, but ordinarily tension is unpleasant whereas the tension before orgasm is far from unpleasant.

_____ 7. An orgasm is a great release of tension with spasmodic reaction at the peak. This is exactly how it feels to me.

_____ 8. A building of tension, sometimes, and frustration until the climax. A *tightening* inside, palpitating rhythm, explosion, and warmth and peace.

Source: From Vance & Wagner, 1977, pp. 207–210.

A colleague recalled her graduate school professor saying that anything capable of a great deal of good can also create a great deal of harm (Smith, 1990). This statement clearly applies to sexuality. Under ideal circumstances, a sexual relationship can provide intense pleasure and feelings of intimacy. However—as described by the young woman at the beginning of this discussion—it can also lead to a loss of self-esteem and worry.

Sexual relationships can also create a great deal of harm with respect to sexually transmitted diseases such as AIDS. **AIDS (acquired immunodeficiency syndrome)** is a disease that destroys the body's natural immunity. AIDS will be discussed in more detail in Chapter 18.

Heterosexual individuals have an additional responsibility; they must make thoughtful and informed decisions about pregnancy and birth control. For example, by age 20, nearly 40% of all women in the United States have been pregnant at least once (U.S. Department of Health and Human Services, 1992). Each pregnant teenager faces a personal struggle, whether she chooses to have an abortion, to give up her child for adoption, or to spend the next 20 years raising the child.

Studies have demonstrated that teenagers are often uninformed—or *mis*informed about important aspects of sexuality (Hedgepeth & Helmich, 1996; Morrison, 1985). For instance, some believe that they cannot get pregnant the first time they have intercourse. Others believe that a person can get AIDS from masturbation. Moreover, even well-informed teenagers (and adults, too) may make an important cognitive error: They believe that the grim statistics about pregnancy rates without the use of contraceptives apply to *other* people, not to themselves (Morrison, 1985; Whitley & Hern, 1992).

We have noted some of the negative aspects of sexuality. An additional problem is that many people are harmed by sexual aggression. **Rape** is defined as vaginal, anal, or oral penetration—without the individual's consent. This penetration may be obtained by force, or by threat of physical harm, or when the victim is incapable of giving consent (Koss, 1993). Rape can be committed by a stranger, but data show that people who have been raped are likely to know those who raped them (Bridges, 1991; Koss et al., 1988; Ward, 1995; White, 1996). Unfortunately, most cases of rape go unreported (Gostin et al., 1994; Koss, 1993). However, estimates in the United States and Canada suggest that between 14% and 25% of women will be sexually assaulted in their lifetime (Calhoun & Atkeson, 1991; Michael et al., 1994; Statistics Canada, 1993).

Whereas rape typically involves physical violence or threatened violence, other kinds of sexual exploitation involve different threats, such as "Sleeping with me is the best way to get that promotion." This is an extreme example of **sexual harassment,** an activity that involves "deliberate or repeated comments, gestures, or physical contacts of a sexual nature that are unwanted by the recipient" (American Psychological Association, 1990, p. 393). Table 12.2 lists examples of both rape and sexual harassment.

In both rape and sexual harassment, one person has more power than another. In contrast, **consensual sexual interactions** are defined as participation in sexual relationships by people who freely choose to engage in that interaction (Allgeier, 1987). When two mature people respect each other (and when neither feels guilty about the relationship), sexual interactions can offer uniquely positive pleasures. Most of you reading this book will be making—and have made—decisions about sexuality. No book can make the decisions for you. The decisions must take into account the possibilities of both life-threatening disease and pregnancy. However, as Allgeier (1987, p. 11) writes, "Humans are blessed with a potential capacity for experiencing intense intimacy and connection, not to mention exquisite sensations, in the context of their sexual interactions with one another."

Sexual harassment is a problem in the workplace and in academic settings. This woman probably feels that the man is standing too close to her. However, if he is her boss, she may feel she should not complain.

TABLE 12.2 Examples of Rape and Sexual Harassment

RAPE

- A college sophomore attends a party, where she meets an attractive male who also seems to be a student. After dancing together for about 15 minutes, he suggests that they go outside to cool off. Once outside, he throws her down, knocks her out, and rapes her.
- A 67-year-old woman answers her door to find a man who says he is from a delivery company. He begins beating her head with a wrench, rapes her, and steals her TV and jewelry.
- A 25-year-old woman is attacked in a shopping mall parking lot by a stranger who uses a knife to force her into his car; he drives to a deserted area and rapes her.

SEXUAL HARASSMENT

- A woman takes a summer job in a restaurant. Her boss has been patting her and making suggestive comments for about a week, and then he suggests that they go to a motel after work that evening.
- A student at a community college is learning how to use a new machine. The instructor puts his hand on her inner thigh as he explains how to use the machine.
- A student at a university is taking a course required for her major. Last week she needed to talk to the course instructor about her paper, and he seemed too friendly, asking questions she thought were too personal. He asked her to come back today. This time, he says he would like to go to bed with her. She is repulsed by the idea, but she is afraid he may fail her in the course if she declines.

Sources: Examples based on Brownmiller, 1975; Burgess & Holmstrom, 1980; Dziech & Weiner, 1990; Koss & Harvey, 1991.

Critical Thinking Exercise 12.2

Write down your answers to the following questions about sexuality.

a. We discussed research in which men who frequently read sexually explicit magazines were more likely than other men to believe that women enjoy forced sex. Some might argue that these data demonstrate that pornography directly causes rape. Although this explanation may well be true, what other explanation can you suggest?

b. The U.S. government frequently assesses the incidence of rape through the National Crime Survey. The surveyor asks a question about rape *only* if someone responds "yes" to this earlier question: "Did someone try to attack you in some other way?" This survey estimates that less than 1% of women between the ages of 16 and 24 are raped each year (Koss, 1992). Why might 1% be an underestimate?

Achievement Motivation

Camara Barrett spent his childhood on the island of Jamaica, and he graduated first in his high school class in Brooklyn. He was also the class president and the editor of the school newspaper, while working 15 hours a week in a hospital. This story doesn't sound especially unusual, except that Camara lived in a homeless shelter. In fact, before his school helped to make arrangements for the shelter, he attended school during the day but had lived on the subway at night (Shanker, 1996).

Camara Barrett is clearly high in the **achievement motive;** he has the desire to do well on tasks, relative to a standard of achievement (Reeve, 1997). Researchers who study achievement motivation examine why some people persist on a task, when most would give up, and why others set unrealistically high goals for themselves (Graham, 1994). When we discussed the two other motives, hunger and sexuality, we examined underlying physiological components. In contrast, research on achievement motivation focuses almost exclusively on cognitive components.

Let's begin by examining individual differences in achievement motivation. Then we'll consider gender comparisons in this area, noting gender similarities in some aspects of achievement motivation—but also some gender differences. We'll then see how reward can sometimes—but not always—reduce a person's achievement-related behavior.

Individual Differences in Achievement Motivation   Achievement motivation is measured either with a questionnaire or with an assessment instrument called the Thematic Apperception Test (TAT), which Chapter 13 will consider in more detail. If you were to take the TAT, you would write a brief story about a series of ambiguous pictures. Your stories would be coded according to your emphasis on certain themes, such as your concern about achievement. Both questionnaires and the TAT are reasonably valid measures of achievement motivation (Spangler, 1992).

As you might expect, people who are high in achievement motivation tend to be superior students. They are also persistent on difficult tasks, and they seek out situations where they can receive feedback on their performance (Atkinson & Raynor, 1974; French & Thomas, 1958; McClelland, 1985; Reeve, 1992). High achievers also prefer working on tasks that depend on their personal efforts, rather than chance outcomes (McClelland, 1985).

High achievers also prefer working on more difficult tasks than low achievers (Locke & Latham, 1994). For example, Slade and Rush (1991) asked college students to work on a task that required responding to dials on a simulated aircraft instrument. Each person could select one of five difficulty levels. Based on achievement-motivation scores, the students had been previously classified as either high achievers or low achievers. As you can see from Figure 12.1, the two groups made similar choices for the first six blocks of trials. At this point, the low achievers then became less ambitious, whereas the high achievers continued to select the more difficult tasks.

Now that you have learned some of the important characteristics related to achievement motivation, you can informally assess your own achievement motivation by trying Demonstration 12.2.

Gender Comparisons in Achievement-Related Areas   In Chapter 11, we saw that women and men often pursue different careers. Relatively few women choose careers in professions such as medicine, law, and engineering. In the past, numerous psychologists have tried to explain women's absence in many careers in terms of personal "deficiencies" that inhibit their achievement.

In reality, however, men and women are similar in most characteristics related to achievement motivation. For example, men and women are similar in their

FIGURE 12.1

Task Choices and Achievement Motivation

Average difficulty of task choices, according to level of achievement motivation.

Source: Based on Slade & Rush, 1991.

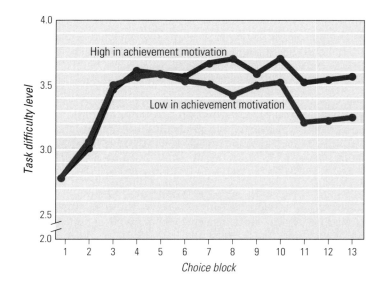

DEMONSTRATION 12.2 Informal Assessment of Achievement Motivation

Naturally, a quick test cannot accurately measure any quality as complex as achievement motivation. However, answer each of the following questions honestly with a "yes" or "no."

_____ 1. Do you enjoy doing tasks well, even when no one tells you to do a good job?

_____ 2. Do you feel great satisfaction in mastering a difficult task that you were not sure could be done?

_____ 3. Is success especially pleasurable when you have competed against other people?

_____ 4. Are you a good student (for instance, were you in the top 10% of your high school class)?

_____ 5. When you are working on a difficult task, do you persist even when you run into roadblocks?

_____ 6. Do you prefer a task for which you have personal responsibility, rather than one where chance plays an important role?

_____ 7. Do you like receiving feedback about how well you are doing when you are working on a project?

In general, people with a large number of "yes" answers tend to be high in achievement motivation, based on previous research (e.g., McClelland, 1985). Keep in mind, however, that you should not overgeneralize on the basis of a single, informal quiz.

overall achievement motive (Mednick & Thomas, 1993; Spence & Helmreich, 1983; Stewart & Chester, 1982). Men and women also do not differ in their **fear of success,** which is defined as worrying that success in competitive situations would lead to unpleasant consequences such as decreased popularity (Mednick & Thomas, 1993; Paludi, 1984).

However, gender differences sometimes appear in self-confidence. We know that women and men are similarly self-confident when they work on tasks considered "feminine," when the instructions do not encourage competition, and when clear feedback is provided (Hall, 1990; Lenney, 1977; Matlin, 1996a). However, in other cases, men are frequently more self-confident than women. Furthermore, women's self-confidence seems to be more influenced by the comments of others, whereas men's self-confidence remains relatively stable (Roberts, 1991; Roberts & Nolen-Hoeksema, 1989).

Men and women may differ on some components of achievement motivation, but the differences are not large enough to explain the striking differences in career choices. For example, only 1% of carpenters and 8% of engineers are women (U.S. Department of Labor, 1994). Instead, the gender differences are probably influenced by the kinds of gender stereotypes observed in young children (Chapter 10) and also in adults (Chapters 11 and 16).

The Paradoxical Effects of Reward on Achievement When he was a high school senior, Roger volunteered after school in a facility for profoundly retarded children. He enjoyed the work and felt gratified when, after hours of training, a child finally mastered a task. The following summer, one staff member left suddenly, and the facility was able to pay Roger for his work. However, when a permanent replacement was later hired, Roger was told that funds for his salary were no longer available, but he was welcome to work as a volunteer again. Roger politely declined; he was no longer interested in volunteering.

To explain the paradoxical effects of reward, we must consider **intrinsic motivation,** or the desire to perform an activity for its own sake. People are likely to do something when they find it inherently enjoyable (Deci & Ryan, 1990). In contrast, **extrinsic motivation** is the desire to perform an activity because of external rewards.

The problem is that extrinsic motivation can undermine intrinsic motivation. When people are intrinsically motivated to work on a task, and then they are offered a concrete, external reward—such as salary—intrinsic motivation often declines (Deci & Ryan, 1985; Tang & Hall, 1995). For instance, Roger's intrinsic motivation in working with retarded children probably decreased when he began

This man enjoys cooking and finds it intrinsically motivating. If he were to be paid for being a cook, his intrinsic motivation might decrease.

receiving a salary. Later, when the external reward is no longer available (e.g., no salary), people no longer spontaneously work on the task. The task is no longer appealing when extrinsic motivation has been taken away and when intrinsic motivation is low.

A simple operant-conditioning approach (Chapter 6) suggests that reward should increase the likelihood of performing a task. An appreciation of human complexity, however, suggests that reward can backfire.

A meta-analysis has shown that the research consistently supports the "backfiring" effect (Tang & Hall, 1995). That is, a concrete, external reward does reduce the likelihood of performing a task, once the reward is removed. Your intrinsic motivation also decreases when other people set deadlines, impose goals, and evaluate your performance (Deci & Ryan, 1990). We should emphasize, though, that the effect applies to concrete rewards. In contrast, praise and positive feedback are likely to increase a person's intrinsic motivation. In other words, parents can enhance their children's intrinsic motivation by congratulating them ("Maria, you are really doing well on that clarinet solo!"), rather than by offering material rewards.

Critical Thinking Exercise 12.3

Write down your answers to the following questions about achievement motivation.

a. Suppose you are reading a magazine intended for professional women, and it says that women are too low in self-confidence; professional women must raise their self-confidence up to the level found in men. From a critical-thinking perspective, how would you respond to this argument?

b. Suppose some researchers are interested in studying how reward influences intrinsic motivation, testing fifth-graders. During the first, baseline session, they observe that children really enjoy playing with watercolors. Next, during the second session, children are told that they will be given a toy for every good painting. Now their time spent with watercolors increases slightly. In the third session, they are told that they are free to play with the watercolors; however, no toys will be awarded. Their play time now drops significantly. Why would the data on this group of children *not* be sufficient to convince you that reward has backfired?

General Theories of Motivation

We have explored three different kinds of motivation: hunger, sexuality, and achievement. We've seen that biological factors explain some aspects of hunger and sexuality, but cognitive and social factors are crucial in all three areas. Now let's consider several theoretical approaches to all kinds of motivated behavior, not limiting ourself just to the three topics we have discussed. Why do we act? What energizes our behavior, sustains it, and directs it toward a certain goal? In this section, we will consider three current approaches to motivation. In Chapter 13, incidentally, we will examine a fourth important approach—Maslow's hierarchy of needs—in connection with Maslow's humanistic theory of personality.

Drive Theories   During the first half of the twentieth century, theorists argued that motivation could be explained by a concept called drive. **Drive** is the psychological energy from unmet needs that encourages an organism to do something (Weiner, 1991). For example, Clark Hull, who conducted laboratory research with rats, proposed that humans and other animals are motivated by four drives: hunger, thirst, sex, and the avoidance of pain. In Hull's theory, internal forces motivate us to do something to reduce these drives.

Drive theories may explain many aspects of thirst and hunger motivation, but they do not provide all the answers. For example, neither can explain why anorexics avoid eating (Reeve, 1997). Neither explains achievement motivation—let alone the paradoxical effects of reward. In short, drive theory lost popularity during the second half of the twentieth century as cognitive approaches became more prominent (Reeve, 1997). Currently, most psychologists acknowledge that humans think, plan ahead, and figure out how to reach their goals.

Intrinsic Motivation   In the discussion of achievement motivation, we explained how some kinds of rewards can decrease intrinsic motivation. However, we did not really examine the nature of intrinsic motivation, which is the second theoretical approach to motivation we'll discuss. This approach provides additional evidence for the connection between motivation and emotion.

The concept of intrinsic motivation was originally proposed by Robert White (1959). He argued that many behaviors—such as play and exploration—do not need to be reinforced in order to be performed. White argued that even young children have an internal force that encourages them to be competent. For example, I recall one of my daughters, at age 1, playing with a footstool that she had turned upside down. She would climb in and out, grinning each time about her sense of mastery. She did not look to her parents for praise. Instead, competent interaction with her environment was its own reward (Deci & Ryan, 1985).

Researchers have discovered that people who believe their work is intrinsically motivating are more satisfied with their lives (Graef et al., 1983). Try noticing how often your own activities are intrinsically motivating, rather than drive-reducing. For example, when pursuing a word in the dictionary, do you find yourself reading about other words—even though you cannot reduce any drive from learning about words such as *peplum* or *hendecagon?* When you see a couple together in a restaurant, do you try to gather clues so that you can determine whether they are well acquainted or on their first date? This curiosity cannot be explained by drive theory. However, at least for many people, curiosity is intrinsically motivating.

Incentive Theory   We have explored two approaches to motivation that emphasize internal forces within the organism. A person is motivated to act because of a driving tension or some internal force that encourages competence and inquiry.

In contrast, **incentive theory** emphasizes how external goals motivate us to respond. An attractive incentive energizes us to do something, and an unattractive incentive encourages us *not* to do something (Reeve, 1997). Incentive theory is consistent with the principles of operant conditioning discussed in Chapter 6. Incentive theory explains some aspects of achievement motivation. For example, a student is motivated by the incentive of good grades, and a college instructor is motivated by the incentive of a promotion.

We have reviewed three general theoretical explanations for motivated behavior. Drive theory can help explain some behaviors. However, the complexity of human behavior also requires more subtle and all-encompassing approaches, such as intrinsic motivation and incentive theory.

Robert White—and others who believe that many human activities are intrinsically motivating—argue that children feel pride in their accomplishments.

For these Olympic runners, drive theory probably explains very little. Instead, intrinsic motivation and incentive theory are better able to explain the complexity of human behavior.

SECTION SUMMARY: *MOTIVATION*

1.   Motivation and emotion are intertwined; emotion leads to motivation, and motivated behavior produces emotion.

2.   Hunger is partially regulated by biological factors such as stomach contractions, hypothalamic activity, and levels of glucose and insulin; however, exter-

nal factors such as culture and social setting are also influential.

3.   Explanations for obesity include food intake, genetic predisposition, metabolism, and set point.

4.   Overweight people often face health risks and discrimination.

5. Anorexia nervosa is a life-threatening pursuit of thinness; bulimia nervosa involves binge eating; both eating disorders are encouraged by our culture's emphasis on slimness, particularly for women.

6. In human sexuality, external and cognitive cues are more important determinants of arousal than hormones.

7. Women and men have somewhat similar sexual response cycles.

8. Important topics concerned with sexual behavior include sexually transmitted diseases, the risk of pregnancy, misinformation about sexuality, and the problems of rape and sexual harassment—as well as the sense of intimacy and connectedness that is part of consensual sexual interactions.

9. People who are high in achievement motivation are likely to be excellent students who are persistent; they prefer challenging tasks that provide feedback.

10. Men and women are similar in their achievement motive and their fear of success; however, men are often more self-confident than women.

11. Intrinsic motivation may decrease when people receive concrete rewards.

12. Three current theoretical explanations for motivation include drive, intrinsic motivation, and incentive theory.

EMOTION

Imagine the end of the opera *Rigoletto,* drained of its emotions. Rigoletto is determined to kill the Duke of Mantua, who has seduced Rigoletto's beloved daughter Gilda. In the dark, the hired assassin stabs someone in man's attire. Rigoletto discovers that it is Gilda, instead of the Duke. In the emotion-drained version, he calmly pronounces, "Gosh, we should have checked more carefully." Or consider the soap opera "The Young and the Restless." Chris is now married to Paul, who is increasingly eager to have children. But Chris still longs for Danny, her first husband and the one true love of her life. In the emotion-drained version, she performs a costs-benefits analysis and decides coolly, "Yes, I believe I'll stick with Paul." Without emotions, our lives would be dominated by cold cognitions, filmed in black and white instead of passionate purple and vibrant turquoise.

As we noted at the beginning of the chapter, the emotions in our daily lives are rich, complicated experiences that include subjective, behavioral, and physiological components. We'll begin this part of the chapter by exploring the subjective component of emotions, typically measured by the self-report method we discussed in Chapter 2. Next, the "In Depth" feature switches to the behavioral component of emotions, as we focus on facial expressions. Then we'll consider physiological reactions to these emotional states. Our last two topics are emotional intelligence and theories about emotion.

Many remaining chapters in this textbook also discuss some aspect of emotion. For instance, Chapters 14 and 15 examine mood disorders and therapy for these

---

DEMONSTRATION 12.3 Estimating Subjective Well-Being

Estimate the percentage of people in the United States who belong to each of the following categories:

1. What percentage become clinically depressed at some point in their lifetime? _____

2. What percentage report positive life satisfaction (that is, a rating above the neutral point on a scale)? _____

3. What percentage of nonhospitalized people who have chronic psychological disorders report more positive emotion than negative emotion? _____

4. What percentage of people who have complete quadriplegia (with both arms and both legs paralyzed) consider that their life is average or above average in happiness? _____

The answers to these questions, based by research by Diener and Diener (1996) and by Hellmich (1995), can be found at the end of the chapter.

disorders. Chapters 16 and 17 frequently explore our emotional reactions to other people. Finally, Chapter 18 considers how stress influences our physical health.

Subjective Emotional Reactions

Psychologists have not devised any perfectly objective measure that firmly establishes a person's subjective emotions along dimensions such as joy, sorrow, or embarrassment. However, most psychologists believe that people's self-reports are accurate reflections of their true feelings (Ortony et al., 1988; Scherer, 1986). In some studies, participants are instructed to rate their **subjective well-being,** which is their evaluation of their life satisfaction. Researchers in this area typically try to identify factors that may be correlated with subjective well-being. In other studies, participants evaluate their mood at that moment, a more specific assessment. One important example of this second kind of research focuses on how a person's mood influences cognitive processes.

Subjective Well-Being Before you read further, try Demonstration 12.3, which asks you to estimate the subjective well-being of various groups of people.

In general, subjective well-being is not correlated with demographic variables such as age, gender, ethnic group, and education (Diener, 1997; Diener & Larsen, 1994; Myers & Diener, 1995, 1996). Also, people who have physical disabilities are not substantially less happy than other people (Diener & Diener, 1993; Eysenck, 1990). Furthermore, subjective well-being is not strongly correlated with family income. As long as people have enough income to buy the essentials, extra money does not buy happiness (Myers & Diener, 1995, 1996).

So what factors *are* correlated with subjective well-being? These factors are primarily psychological variables, such as having a warm, intimate love relationship, supportive friends, a challenging, satisfying job, and good health (Myers, 1992; Myers & Diener, 1995). Each of these factors matches our commonsense impressions; the demographic factors that are *not* correlated with happiness are more surprising. Also, if you checked the correct answers to Demonstration 12.3, you learned that the majority of people are reasonably happy—even people who have every right to report unhappiness (Diener & Diener, 1996; Hellmich, 1995).

Cross-cultural researchers are beginning to explore another intriguing component of subjective well-being. Different cultures may have different interpretations of

Research demonstrates that people with physical disabilities are similar to other people in their subjective well-being.

what it means to be happy. In Chapter 11, we introduced the concept of individualistic versus collectivist cultures. In **individualistic cultures,** such as the United States and Canada, a person's identity focuses on his or her individual characteristics. Markus and Kitayama (1994) found that people in individualistic cultures tend to base their subjective well-being on their own personal achievements and feeling "like being at the top of the world." In contrast, in **collectivist cultures** such as Japan, a person's identity focuses on interconnectedness with others. Markus and Kitayama found that people in collectivist cultures tend to base their subjective well-being on feelings of interpersonal relationships with other people—the self in harmony with others.

In summary, a number of psychological variables are correlated with individual differences in subjective well-being. Furthermore, cultures differ in their interpretation of what it means to be happy.

The Influence of Mood on Cognitive Processes Have you ever noticed that you think more effectively when you are in a reasonably good mood? Alice M. Isen and her colleagues conducted a series of studies demonstrating that the independent variable of emotional state has an important influence on an impressive variety of dependent variables, measured by performance on cognitive tasks.

To manipulate the independent variable, Isen and her coauthors sometimes gave people small gifts like notepads, whereas people in the control group received no gift. In other studies, the experimental group might see a cartoon film (rather than a neutral film) or see a list of pleasant words (rather than neutral words).

The research showed that people in the experimental group (good mood) performed better than people in the control group (neutral mood) on a variety of cognitive tasks (Isen, 1994):

According to Isen's research, the positive mood of these students should encourage them to perform well on memory, problem-solving, and language tasks.

1. The number of words recalled on a memory task (Isen, Daubman, & Gorgoglione, 1987);

2. Scores on measures of creative problem solving (Isen, Daubman, & Nowicki, 1987);

3. The number of unusual words provided when people were asked to supply words related to a stimulus (Isen et al., 1985); and

4. The flexible use of word categories (Isen & Daubman, 1984; Isen et al., 1992).

Similarly, other researchers have found that people who are in a good mood are less likely to take unnecessary risks and to engage in other self-defeating behavior (Leith & Baumeister, 1996). We'll explore this issue again in Chapter 14, when we see that people with serious depression often experience cognitive problems.

Behavioral Emotional Reactions

A second component of emotions is our behavioral reactions: We react to an emotional experience by *doing* something. When a pleasant event occurs, we may jump up and down with excitement; when we are unhappy, we may complain (Kowalski, 1996) or tell a lie (DePaulo et al., 1996; Lewis & Saarni, 1993). However, the behavioral measure that psychologists typically examine is facial expression. These facial expressions are an important component of nonverbal communication, a topic we also discussed in Chapter 9. Here, however, we'll emphasize how facial expressions can convey emotions.

Before reading further, try Demonstration 12.4 to test your accuracy in interpreting facial expression. This "In Depth" feature examines the accuracy of decoding facial expressions and the possibility that facial expressions are somewhat universal.

DEMONSTRATION 12.4 Identifying Behavioral Emotional Reactions

Examine the photos below and match each one of the six emotions listed here. The answers appear on Page 411.

_____ 1. Fear   _____ 4. Disgust
_____ 2. Happiness   _____ 5. Surprise
_____ 3. Anger   _____ 6. Sadness

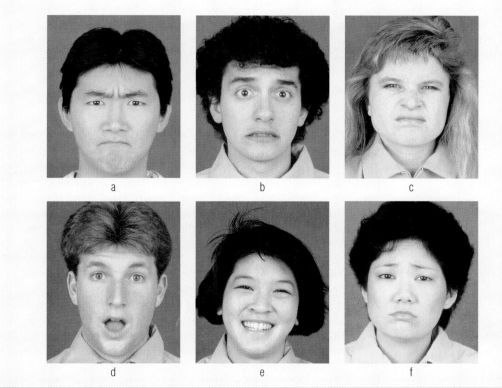

Accuracy in Decoding Emotions

As you might imagine, people vary tremendously in their ability to decode emotions. You may know someone who can sense your sadness, even when you are barely aware of it yourself. Another acquaintance may spend several hours with you, unaware that you are depressed. Research shows that the ability to decode nonverbal cues increases between childhood and adulthood, reaching a maximum between the ages of about 20 and 30 (Hall et al., 1978). Females tend to be somewhat better than males at decoding nonverbal expressions (Brody & Hall, 1993; Hall, 1984). Keep in mind, however, that you may know exceptions to these general tendencies. For example, can you think of a male friend who is better than most female friends at deciphering people's moods?

Check your accuracy on Demonstration 12.4. In general, people are fairly accurate in matching photos with their appropriate emotional labels (Ekman, 1994). For example, in a classic study, respondents were given photos like those in Demonstration 12.4 and were asked to select the appropriate emotional labels (Ekman, 1973). In general, people were fairly accurate. Happiness was correctly identified by 97%, surprise by 95%, and anger by 67%.

How accurate are we in decoding *false* facial expressions? We are not especially skilled at detecting which smiles are genuine and which are false, though we could be more accurate if we paid attention to the muscles surrounding the eyes (Ekman et al., 1990; Frank et al., 1993). Figure 12.2 shows both a genuine and a false smile.

Critical Thinking Exercise 12.4

Write down your answers to the following questions about subjective emotional reactions and accuracy in decoding emotions.

a. In the discussion of mood and cognitive performance, we described how Isen used the experimental method. She concluded, for example, that a good mood *caused* people to recall more items. Suppose, instead, that she gathers 100 participants, and they all rate their current mood. The 50 with the most positive mood remember significantly more times than the other 50 participants. Why couldn't she draw a causal conclusion from these results?

b. You saw that females are typically more accurate than males in decoding facial expressions. Suppose you are watching a TV show that says, "Nature has made it so that females have the genetically based ability to read people's emotions." How would you respond to this statement?

Genuine smile.

False smile.

FIGURE 12.2

Notice that in both a genuine and a false smile, the mouth expressions are similar. However, in the genuine smile, the skin is gathered slightly under the eye.

(IN DEPTH continued)

Are Interpretations of Facial Expressions Universal?

Do people from different cultures decode facial expressions in the same way? The answer seems to be that cultures are both similar and different in facial interpretations (Ekman, 1994; Mesquita & Frijda, 1992; Russell, 1994, 1995). In general, our immediate, involuntary facial expressions seem to be somewhat similar across cultures. Let's first examine these similarities, and then we'll see how people's delayed, more controlled facial expressions seem to depend more on one's culture.

In a typical study, Paul Ekman (1973) tested people in Brazil, Chile, Argentina, and Japan, using photographs similar to those in Demonstration 12.4. In each country, people were asked to name the emotion displayed in the photo. Across all four cultures, the average accuracy was 85% for all six emotions. Similar results were obtained in other cultures as diverse as New Guinea, Turkey, and Estonia (Ekman et al., 1987; Ekman & Friesen, 1971).

Reviewing all of the research, James Russell (1994, 1995) agrees that different cultures have similar interpretations of facial expressions. Figure 12.3 shows how people in various cultures responded to three facial expressions: happiness, surprise, and anger. The values on the vertical axis (median percentage agreement) shows the median percentage of participants who associated a smile with happiness, raised eyebrows with surprise, and a frown with anger.

As you can see, agreement depends both on the cultural group and on the emotion being tested. For instance, people who live in Western literate cultures (e.g., France) showed strong agreement, especially for the "happiness" interpretation. People who live in non-Western literate cultures (e.g., Japan) show somewhat lower agreement, though it's still far above chance. People who live in isolated illiterate cultures (e.g., a tribe in New Guinea that had no previous experience with Western culture) showed still less agreement on most facial expressions. Notice, however, that they did show high agreement on the happy facial expression.

Evolutionary psychologists are interested in these cross-cultural findings. After all, people in the isolated illiterate group had never before interacted with North Americans, and they had never seen facial expressions on our television programs. Still, they agree that a smile suggests happiness. Charles Darwin and others noted that monkeys show a similar smile when greeting or playing with other monkeys (Darwin, 1872/1965; van Hooff, 1976). This expression may have developed during evolution as a way of greeting an unfamiliar primate and communicating the message "I'm not planning to fight with you." Natural selection may therefore have favored those primates that could flash a smile at appropriate times. If so, then we humans may have an inborn, genetically based tendency to smile in

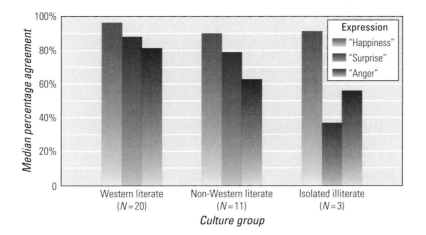

FIGURE 12.3

Interpretation of Facial Expressions
Agreement with the "standard" interpretation of facial expressions (e.g., that a smile means happiness), as a function of the cultural group and the facial expression.
Source: Based on Russell, 1995.

appropriate circumstances. However, other facial expressions—such as surprise—are not so universally understood. They cannot be easily explained from an evolutionary psychology perspective.

As we noted earlier, some immediate, involuntary facial expressions are similar across cultures. However, when we must control our facial expression, we tend to display the facial expression prescribed by our specific culture (Argyle, 1988; Ekman, 1984). These culture-specific prescriptions about who can show which emotion—and in what circumstance—are called **display rules** (Ekman, 1993). We often work on our emotions and facial expressions, trying to make them more consistent with cultural expectations (Hochschild, 1990). Consider the display rule in our culture that males should not cry. One man recalls an early experience in suppressing an emotional expression:

> I was in the sixth grade at the time my grandfather died. I remember being called to the office of the school where my mother was on the phone. . . . She told me what had happened and all I said was, "Oh." I went back to class and a friend asked me what happened and I said, "Nothing." I remember wanting very much just to cry and tell everyone what had happened. But a boy doesn't cry in the sixth grade for fear of being called a sissy. So I just went along as if nothing happened while deep down inside I was very sad and full of tears. (Hochschild, 1983, p. 67)

Let's consider a study that examined both immediate and delayed facial expressions. Ekman and Friesen (1969) studied both European Americans living in the United States and Japanese living in Japan. Each participant in the study watched an extremely unpleasant film about sinus surgery. Each person was seated alone in the room, and the facial expressions were secretly videotaped. The videotapes of the immediate facial expressions were highly similar for people in the two cultures; both groups showed disgust. Later, each person was interviewed about the film. In these delayed responses, the European Americans continued to show negative expressions, but the Japanese produced happy faces. An important Japanese display rule is that one should not display negative emotions when an authority is present (Ekman, 1984).

This study and related research suggest that we react to a situation with a facial expression that is reasonably uniform in many cultures. Moments later, however, we adopt the facial expression we have learned in our culture: An American boy conceals his sadness with a neutral countenance, and a Japanese man smiles to conceal his disgust.

Cross-cultural research suggests that people in different parts of the world should be reasonably accurate in identifying this emotional reaction as happiness.

In our culture, display rules demand that men conceal their sorrow. This man, holding a casket at a funeral, seems to be struggling to cover his sadness by trying to look brave.

If you were walking in a dark area and saw this shape, your amygdala would immediately respond, even before your cortex could analyze whether the shape is dangerous.

Physiological Emotional Reactions

In Chapter 3, we discussed the **autonomic division** of the nervous system, which helps control your glands, heart, blood vessels, and other internal organs. The autonomic nervous system has two components that respond in different ways to emotional experiences. In a frightening situation, the **sympathetic nervous system** prepares your body for action. Your heart beats faster, your pupils widen, and you sweat and blush. The sympathetic nervous system directs the release of the substances epinephrine and norepinephrine. When the danger has passed, the **parasympathetic nervous system** restores your body to its normal state. It slows your heartbeat, constricts your pupils, and inhibits the further release of epinephrine and norepinephrine.

In Chapter 3, we also noted that the limbic system plays a central role in emotional experiences. (See Figure 3.14.) The hypothalamus is important in motivated behavior such as eating, and it also plays an important role in emotion. Specifically, the hypothalamus reacts to stress by signaling the pituitary to release epinephrine, which is associated with the sympathetic nervous system (Kalin, 1993).

The amygdala is another key player within the limbic system (Kalin, 1993; LeDoux, 1995). The **amygdala** receives information from the cortex, but also from brain regions—such as the thalamus—that are involved in processing more primitive emotions (Derryberry & Tucker, 1992). This "early warning" from the thalamus allows you to respond to the first signs of danger, even before your cortex can analyze the information more completely. For example, suppose you are walking down a dark hallway at night, and suddenly a shape moves toward you. Your amygdala immediately responds to this early warning. At a more leisurely speed, the cortex can analyze whether the shape is dangerous or friendly.

Within the cortex, the two hemispheres seem to play somewhat different roles with respect to emotion. Specifically, the right hemisphere regulates our facial expression, and the left hemisphere deciphers emotional tone from the messages we hear (Gardner, 1994; Hauser, 1993). As we discussed in Chapter 3, each hemisphere is somewhat specialized in its activities.

We have seen that the autonomic nervous system and several structures in the brain are responsible for processing emotions. Let's now consider several physiological measures of emotion and then discuss a practical application: Are lie detector tests useful?

Physiological Measures People who study the biological components of emotion usually collect certain measures of activity in the autonomic nervous system. These measures may include heart rate, finger temperature, skin conductance (which measures skin perspiration), pulse, breathing rate, and muscular tension (Levenson et al., 1992). In general, heart rate is the most accurate measure for discriminating among emotions. However, even the best measures are far from consistent (Zajonc & McIntosh, 1992). Furthermore, two different emotions may produce similar physiological measures. For example, both fear and sadness are associated with faster heart rate and lower skin temperature (Levenson, 1992; Zajonc & McIntosh, 1992). Physiological measures therefore provide some indexes of emotional response. However, they cannot adequately discriminate among several emotions that are subjectively very different.

The Controversial "Lie Detector" Test Consider the case of Roger Coleman, a convicted murderer who vigorously proclaimed that he was innocent. In 1992, on the morning he was scheduled to be executed, he was given one final lie detector test. He failed that test, and so he was executed. He may have failed the lie detector test because he was indeed guilty. However, before his execution, four witnesses came forward to say that they had heard someone else confess to the crime. Thus, he may actually have been innocent but so anxious—in the face of death—that the polygraph was registering arousal, rather than guilt (Ford, 1996). Unfortunately, we have no way of determining what emotions Roger Coleman was experiencing that day.

A lie detector test, or—more properly—a **polygraph examination,** simultaneously measures several autonomic changes such as blood pressure, pulse, breathing patterns, and skin conductance. These measures are taken while a person is asked a structured series of questions. The examiner notes the pattern of arousal and decides on the basis of these measures whether the person being tested is telling the truth (Ford, 1996; Saxe et al., 1985). Note, however, that the polygraph does not *really* detect lies; instead, it detects emotional arousal.

Unfortunately, research on the polygraph exam shows that it is not a valid test. For example, people who can control their physiological reactions—or who take appropriate drugs—can lie successfully and "beat" the test. Other people with overly reactive autonomic nervous systems (perhaps including Roger Coleman) may tell the truth, yet the examiner would conclude otherwise (Bashore & Rapp, 1993; Ford, 1996).

Chapter 1 noted that applied psychologists emphasize the practical application of psychological knowledge. The investigation of polygraph testing is one example of how applied psychologists can influence public policy. The research demonstrates that autonomic measures typically show an unacceptably low correspondence with the truthfulness of the person being examined (Ford, 1996). As a result, most state and federal courts currently exclude or restrict the use of polygraph results. Also, most private employers are prohibited from using polygraphs to test their employees (Steinbrook, 1992). Neuroscientists are currently developing measures of brain electrical activity that may turn out to be more valid than the polygraph test (Bashore & Rapp, 1993). However, the usefulness of these new testing procedures has not yet been demonstrated.

The polygraph examination, commonly known as the lie detector test, is not a very valid measure, but you may nevertheless read about its use in legal and employment situations.

If this child is high in emotional intelligence, she will be able to understand why she is feeling so sad, and she will begin to change her mood.

Emotional Intelligence

In Chapter 8, we briefly mentioned emotional intelligence in connection with the new, broader views of intelligence. Let's now inspect this topic more thoroughly. **Emotional intelligence** includes the ability to perceive emotion accurately, to understand it, and to express it (Mayer & Salovey, 1997). People who are high in emotional intelligence understand that they cannot focus only on their own happiness. They also understand their own moods, as well as how to change these moods (Goleman, 1995; Greenspan, 1996; Mayer & Salovey, 1995, 1997).

Mayer and Salovey (1997) suggest that parents can help their children develop emotional intelligence by encouraging them to identify their emotions and understand how these feelings are connected to their actions. In school settings, children can learn about their emotions through the stories they read. As the reading lessons become more complex, the emotions of the story characters also become more complex. For instance, a child in a story may experience some mixture of joy, relief, and guilt. These ideas sound intriguing, though we do not yet have convincing evidence that emotional education can be effective.

Critical Thinking Exercise 12.5

Write down your answers to the following questions about physiological emotional reactions and emotional intelligence.

a. Chapter 2 discussed the psychological concepts of reliability and validity. How could you measure these two test attributes on the polygraph test?

b. Suppose a group of second grade teachers want to try teaching their students about emotional intelligence. The teachers spend about an hour each week discussing feelings with their students, reading stories about emotions, and role-playing emotional encounters. At the end of the school year, the teachers report that the training has made their students more emotionally mature. How would you critique this conclusion?

General Theories of Emotion

So far, we have explored the subjective, behavioral, and physiological aspects of emotion, as well as the concept of emotional intelligence. With this background, we can now consider an important question: How are emotional reactions produced? Suppose that you are watching a science fiction movie. Suddenly, when you least expect it, the shapeless blob leaps out of a tree to attack the hero. You experience terror. But exactly what forces produced that subjective experience of terror?

Like many questions, it's not clear that there *is* a problem until you start to think about it. One of the major issues in explaining emotions is the relative importance of physiological and cognitive forces. Is your terror produced by (1) your pounding heart, the knot in your digestive tract, and the physiological side effects from your terrified facial expression, or (2) your cognitive processes that assess the situation and choose the label "terror." We'll first consider some approaches that emphasize physiological explanations, and then we'll discuss two approaches that include cognitive factors.

The James-Lange Theory   William James, the first major American psychologist, explained emotional experience using a theory that seems to contradict common sense. Common sense suggests that, when you see the shapeless blob in the movie, you experience the emotion "terror," which sets off physiological reactions (such as a cramp in your digestive tract or increased blood pressure).

James (1890) argued, however, that the commonsense explanation placed the events in the wrong order. If he were watching the science fiction movie with you, he would claim that your perception of an emotion-arousing event immediately produces physiological reactions. These physiological reactions send a message to the brain, which produces the emotional experience of terror. Each emotion, James argued, is signaled by a specific physiological pattern. James emphasized physiological changes in the abdominal organs. At about the same time, another psychologist named Carl Lange suggested a similar theory, which emphasized physiological changes in the circulatory system. The **James-Lange theory** therefore proposes that physiological changes are the source of emotional feelings (Figure 12.4).

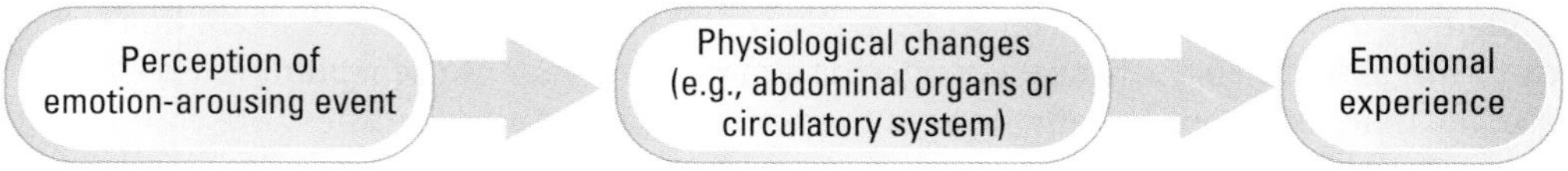

FIGURE 12.4

The James-Lange theory of emotion.

Some recent research provides support for the James-Lange theory (Ellsworth, 1994; Lang, 1994; Reisenzein et al., 1995). However, the new approach emphasizes feedback from facial expression, rather than from the abdominal organs or the circulatory system. According to the **facial feedback hypothesis,** changes in your facial expression can actually *cause* changes in your emotional state (Ekman & Davidson, 1993; Levenson et al., 1990; Zajonc, 1994). In other words, your terrified expression—when the shapeless blob leaps out of the tree—encourages you to feel terrified.

In a representative study, Strack and his coauthors (1988) asked participants to hold a pen either in their teeth or their mouth, as in Figure 12.5. If you try holding a pen in your teeth (without touching your lips), you'll find that your facial expression resembles a smile. However, if you hold a pen in your lips (without touching your teeth), your facial expression is reasonably grumpy. Notice, then, that people adopted either smiling or nonsmiling facial expressions without ever hearing any emotional labels like "smile." With the pen still in position,

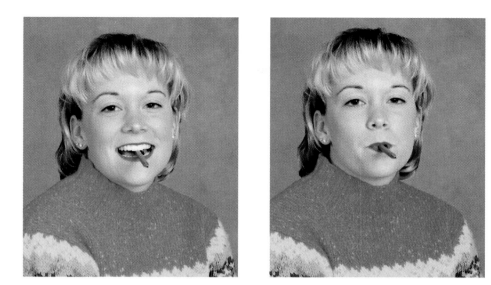

FIGURE 12.5

Strack and his colleagues (1988) would predict that this young woman should rate the comic pages as being funnier when she puts her lips in the configuration on the left, rather than the one on the right.

the participants rated a series of cartoons on a scale that ranged from "not at all funny" to "very funny." Impressively, the people wearing smiles judged the cartoons to be significantly funnier than did the unsmiling people! In general, then, the research on facial feedback shows that facial expression does have a modest effect on emotional experiences (Cornelius, 1996; Matsumoto, 1987; Omdahl, 1995).

The Schachter-Singer Theory   So far, you have heard about thumping hearts and knotted stomachs—a variety of ways in which physiological reactions might mediate emotional experiences. In the early 1960s, however, theorists began to emphasize that our cognitive interpretations might be relevant in forming our emotional experiences. Stanley Schachter and Jerome Singer (1962) proposed that these higher mental processes help us label whether we are experiencing joy or terror.

According to the **Schachter-Singer theory,** an emotion-producing event causes physiological arousal, and you examine the external environment to help you interpret that event. For example, if your heart is pounding, you try to figure out *why.* If a shapeless blob has suddenly appeared on the movie screen, you interpret your arousal as terror. If a very attractive person has just sat down next to you and is gazing into your eyes, you interpret this arousal very differently! As Figure 12.6 shows, the combination of physiological arousal and a cognitive label produces an emotional experience.

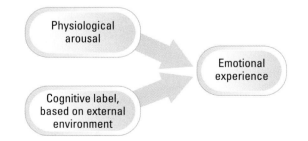

FIGURE 12.6

The Schachter-Singer theory of emotion.

Schachter and Singer (1962) designed a complex study to test their two-factor theory. They gave epinephrine injections to college men, which increased their arousal. Imagine that you are a participant in this study, and you have been told that the injection will cause no effects. Now you find yourself sitting in a room with a person who is either extremely happy (in one condition) or extremely hostile (in another condition). Your heart is pounding, and you are breathing rapidly. How can this be happening? You search around for a cognitive label, some emotional explanation for your reaction. If you are sitting with the happy person, it must be because you are happy. If you are sitting with the hostile person, it must be because you are angry.

In contrast, the participants in Schachter and Singer's other conditions were told about the effects of the epinephrine. Because these individuals could attribute their physiological experiences to the drug, the researchers hypothesized that their emotions would not be influenced by the other person in the room.

Schachter and Singer's experiment did not turn out exactly as their theory had predicted. Furthermore, the research has not been replicated (Plutchik, 1994; Reisenzein, 1983). A more contemporary theory, proposed by Carroll Izard, more fully explains the complexity of our emotional lives.

Izard's Theory Carroll Izard (pronounced "Ih-*zahrd*") has proposed the richest theory of emotions. **Izard's theory** suggests that two different kinds of emotion pathways are responsible for our feelings (Izard, 1989, 1991, 1993; Izard & Youngstrom, 1996). Cognition is not relevant for the first kind of emotional experience, but it is necessary for the second kind.

Imagine that it is late at night, your bedroom is dark, and you have emerged from bed for a drink of water. Suddenly you stub your toe on some object, and you are instantly angry. The sensation of pain leads *immediately* to anger. You do not need to evaluate the stimuli in the environment, and you do not need to speculate about who could have left the object in your path. In this example, cognition is not necessary to experience an emotional response.

One source of evidence that cognition is not essential in all emotions comes from studies with 2-month-old infants. When these infants received their immunizations, Izard and his colleagues (1983) observed that the pain from the shot produced an angry reaction. Other researchers have also observed a clearly angry facial expression in 4-month-olds when their arms are restrained (Stenberg & Campos, 1990).

This baby is illustrating the first kind of emotional reaction (noncognitive) in Izard's theory. The mother—holding the baby's arms while the nurse administers an injection—is illustrating the second kind, which requires cognitive processes.

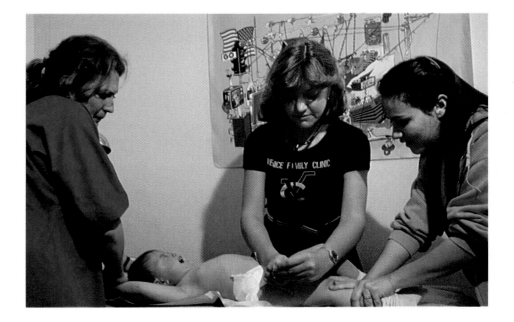

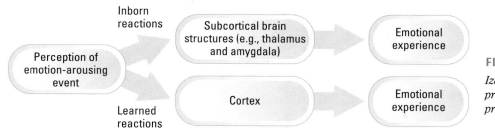

FIGURE 12.7

Izard's theory of emotion, which proposes two separate routes for the production of emotional experiences.

A cognitive explanation is not appropriate for these young infants, who cannot yet interpret or categorize the emotion-arousing events. Izard (1989) proposes that evolution has developed inborn nervous-system pathways for processing certain emotions very efficiently. The important brain structures in this pathway are the thalamus and the amygdala, as noted earlier, when we discussed physiological emotional reactions. The cortex plays no role in the inborn nervous-system pathway.

However, cognition is clearly required for other emotional reactions. Suppose that someone bumps into you on the sidewalk, and your immediate emotional response to the pain is anger. Then you notice that the person has a cast on his leg leg and is on crutches. Your anger is likely to be replaced by a second emotional response—perhaps pity. This more complex emotion cannot be generated by primitive brain structures such as the thalamus or the amygdala. The cortex is required to observe that the crutches and the cast identify this person as having a broken leg. The cortex is also required to decide that the accident was not intentional. This more leisurely kind of emotional reaction requires cognitive processes such as comparison, matching, appraisals, imagery, memory, and judgment (Izard, 1989, 1993). Figure 12.7 illustrates the two pathways for emotional reactions, as proposed in Izard's theory.

Let's briefly review the role of cognition in each theory of emotion. In the James-Lange theory, cognitions are not critical in determining our emotions. Instead, physiological changes are important. In the Schachter-Singer theory, however, cognitions are essential for interpreting physiological arousal ("Why is my heart pounding? It must be because I'm terrified by the sudden appearance of the shapeless blob.") Finally, in Izard's theory, cognitions are not involved in the basic emotional reaction demonstrated in infants and in some immediate reactions in adults. However, cognitions are essential for the more complex emotions that we adults experience. Some variant of Izard's theory will probably be most useful in explaining the variety and richness of human emotions.

SECTION SUMMARY: *EMOTION*

1. One kind of subjective emotional reaction, called subjective well-being, is not strongly correlated with age, gender, ethnic group, income, or disability; it is correlated with positive social relationships, a satisfying job, and good health; North Americans base their subjective well-being on more personal factors than do people in collectivist cultures.

2. Isen's work suggests that people in a happy mood perform better on memory, problem solving, and verbal tasks.

3. Behavioral emotional reactions are primarily assessed in terms of facial expression; adults tend to be more accurate than children in decoding facial expressions, and females tend to be more accurate than males; we are not especially accurate in decoding fake smiles.

4. People from different cultures tend to agree in decoding some immediate facial expressions (e.g., a smile) in the same way; the agreement is lower for other facial expressions. Also, the display rules that

influence our more delayed facial expressions tend to differ from one culture to the next.

5. Structures that produce our physiological emotional reactions include the sympathetic and the parasympathetic nervous system, the hypothalamus, the amygdala, and parts of the cortex.

6. Physiological measures cannot discriminate among different emotions; similarly, the polygraph examination is not very reliable in separating liars from people telling the truth.

7. Emotional intelligence refers to our ability to perceive, understand, and express emotion.

8. Some approaches to emotion include the James-Lange theory, the Schachter-Singer theory, and Izard's theory.

REVIEW QUESTIONS

1. Define the terms *motivation* and *emotion,* and point out how these two concepts are intertwined. Then think of an episode in your life that involved both motivation and emotion. What kind of motivation was relevant? Describe the three components of your emotional reaction (subjective, behavioral, and physiological).

2. Describe the internal factors related to hunger, eating, and obesity. Then describe the external factors related to our eating habits.

3. Many parts of the motivation section contrasted external and internal factors and their roles in determining motivation. Discuss the importance of both external and internal factors in determining sexual interactions and achievement motivation.

4. Throughout this chapter, we discussed gender comparisons. Note the areas within motivation and emotion in which these variables are important, as well as the areas in which they are usually irrelevant.

5. A major portion of the section on emotion emphasized the subjective, behavioral, and physiological components of emotions. What are the advantages and disadvantages of each index of emotion?

6. Suppose that a friend is puzzled about why polygraph examinations are no longer legal in many situations. Describe these tests, their results, and the reasons they are no longer widely used. Based on this chapter, do you think that jurors should decide a person's guilt on the basis of his or her facial expression?

7. This chapter discussed ethnic and cross-cultural issues at several points. Note the areas within motivation and emotion in which these variables are important, as well as areas in which they are usually irrelevant.

8. Cognitive performance depends on both motivational and emotional factors. Discuss several issues that would be important for teachers to know to enhance students' performance on academic tasks.

9. The discussion of cross-cultural aspects of facial expression covered both immediate and delayed facial responses. How would Izard's theory of emotions best explain these two kinds of responses?

10. This chapter examined three explanations for motivation and three explanations for emotion. Describe each theoretical approach, indicating which theory or theories best explain a wide variety of motivations and emotions.

NEW TERMS

motivation (p. 386)
emotion (p. 386)
hypothalamus (p. 387)
homeostasis (p. 387)
glucose (p. 387)
glucostats (p. 387)
insulin (p. 387)
obesity (p. 388)
metabolism (p. 388)
set point (p. 388)
anorexia nervosa (p. 389)
bulimia nervosa (p. 389)
acquired immunodeficiency
   syndrome (AIDS) (p. 392)
rape (p. 392)
sexual harassment (p. 392)
consensual sexual interactions
   (p. 392)
achievement motive (p. 393)
fear of success (p. 395)

intrinsic motivation (p. 395)
extrinsic motivation (p. 395)
drive (p. 396)
incentive theory (p. 397)
subjective well-being (p. 399)
individualistic cultures (p. 400)
collectivist cultures (p. 400)
display rules (p. 403)
autonomic division (p. 404)
sympathetic nervous system (p. 404)
parasympathetic nervous system
   (p. 404)
amygdala (p. 404)
polygraph examination (p. 405)
emotional intelligence (p. 405)
James-Lange theory (p. 406)
facial feedback hypothesis (p. 406)
Schachter-Singer theory (p. 407)
Izard's theory (p. 408)

RECOMMENDED READINGS

Fallon, P., Katzman, M. A., & Wooley, S. C. (Eds.). (1994). *Feminist perspectives on eating disorders.* New York: Guilford Press. This interesting book presents a variety of feminist perspectives on topics such as fashion, hunger, health issues for overweight women, and advertising.

Hyde, J. S., & De Lamater, J. D. (1997). *Understanding human sexuality* (6th ed.). New York: McGraw-Hill. Janet Hyde is well known for her work in the psychology of women; her husband, John De Lamater, enriches the book with a sociological perspective. Their comprehensive textbook includes material on physiological, behavioral, and cultural aspects of sexuality.

Lewis, M., & Haviland, J. M. (Eds.). (1994). *Handbook of emotions.* New York: Guilford Press. The 44 chapters in this handbook focus on such topics as the biological, subjective, and social aspects of emotion; it also includes chapters on nine selected emotions (e.g., disgust and anger).

Reeve, J. (1997). *Understanding motivation and emotion* (2nd ed.). Fort Worth, TX: Harcourt Brace. Reeve's mid-level textbook covers all the topics we discussed in Chapter 12, as well as personality and social aspects of motivation.

ANSWERS TO DEMONSTRATIONS

Demonstration 12.1
   1. W;   2. M;   3. W;   4. W;   5. M;   6. M;   7. M;   8. W

Demonstration 12.3
   1. 8–18%;   2. 82–84%;   3. 57%;   4. 84%

Demonstration 12.4

1. b; 2. e; 3. a; 4. c; 5. d; 6. f

ANSWERS TO CRITICAL THINKING EXERCISES

Exercise 12.1

a. First of all, remember that an estimated 25% to 70% of the variation in body weight appears to be genetic, which leaves 30% to 75% due to some other factor(s). Second, these family members probably live in the same house and eat basically the same food, so it's possible that their similar body size can be traced to similar eating habits.

b. The research on the weight-loss question has been done with selected samples. Some characteristics of these samples may make it more difficult for them to lose weight. For example, maybe only the people who are not successful losing weight on their own are likely to seek treatment in a medical clinic. Also, people with other medical or psychological problems may be overrepresented. As it happens, an estimated 25% to 50% of people in these samples are binge eaters, in contrast to only about 5% of overweight people in the general population (Brownell & Rodin, 1994). You will read about binge eating in the discussion of eating disorders, a little later in the chapter. Binge eaters would probably be less likely to achieve permanent weight loss.

Exercise 12.2

a. An alternative partial explanation may be that men who believe women enjoy forced sex may be more likely than other men to spend time reading sexually explicit magazines. In other words, we have a correlation here, and the direction of causality isn't clear.

b. The phrase "attack in some other way" may be too vague, so that a person who has been raped might not interpret this question to include rape. Furthermore, a person who has been held down forcibly by an acquaintance prior to sexual aggression might not realize that this assault involved an "attack," especially if no weapon was involved. Finally, rape is such an unpleasant experience and it is such a taboo subject to be discussed with a stranger that respondents would typically be reluctant to mention rape on a survey.

Exercise 12.3

a. From this discussion of gender comparisons, you know that men are often higher than women in their self-confidence, so the magazine is at least partly correct. However, a gender difference does not necessarily mean that women are somehow *deficient*. In fact, the gender difference may imply that men are too *high* in self-confidence, so perhaps men should lower their confidence to a more realistic level. In fact, we cannot know how to interpret this gender difference unless we have data informing us where the level of self-confidence should be. For example, suppose that males estimate that they will get 90% of items correct, and females estimate 70%. If both genders actually do get 70% correct, then the males are too high in self-confidence.

b. This proposed study needs a control group of children that never receive toys for good painting. Otherwise, we don't know why the experimental group has lower play time in the third session—it just may be that children grow bored with watercolors after two sessions, even if toys have never been awarded.

Exercise 12.4

a. Here's an example of the principle "Correlation does not necessarily imply causality." For example, it's possible that poor memory causes bad moods, especially if the participants were students (because those with poor memories would be less pleased with their grades). It's also possible that some third variable (e.g., stress level) could be related to both mood and memory. Isen used random assignment, as part of the experimental method, so she *can* draw causal conclusions.

b. Nothing about the data on gender suggests that females' ability to decode expressions is biologically based. A more likely possibility is that females are encouraged from a young age to try to decipher emotions, and they have had greater practice (Hall, 1984; Matlin, 1996a).

Exercise 12.5

a. You could do a study in which participants are asked a series of innocent questions (e.g., their birthdate, the city in which they were born, etc.). One researcher specifies that they must lie on certain items. A different researcher, who doesn't know which responses are lies, administers the polygraph test on two occasions. Reliability would be measured in terms of the consistency of the response (e.g., lying about the birthday produces an increase in heart rate). Validity could be established by seeing whether a change in these physiological measures is more likely for the "lie" answers than for the "truth" answers.

b. One problem with this informal study is that there is no control group; children without any such training might simply become more emotionally mature as they grow older during the school year. Also, we'd want to know whether the teachers had an objective operational definition for measuring emotional maturity. Finally, we would want to know whether the teachers' expectations could be at least partly responsible for the improvement.

THEORIES OF PERSONALITY

THE PSYCHODYNAMIC APPROACH

Structure of Personality

Freud's Methods

Stages of Psychosexual Development

Defense Mechanisms

Freudian Theory and Women

Other Psychodynamic Theories

Psychodynamic Theory and Projective Tests

Evaluation of the Psychodynamic Approach

THE HUMANISTIC APPROACH

Rogers's Person-Centered Approach

Maslow's Hierarchy of Needs

Evaluation of the Humanistic Approach

THE TRAIT APPROACH

Allport's Trait Theory

The Five-Factor Model

The Person-Situation Debate

The Biological Basis of Individual Differences

The Minnesota Multiphasic Personality Inventory

Evaluation of the Trait Approach

THE SOCIAL COGNITIVE APPROACH

Origins of the Social Cognitive Approach

Observational Learning

Reciprocal Influences

Self-Efficacy

In Depth: Cross-Cultural Views of the Self

Evaluation of the Social Cognitive Approach

CHAPTER 13

Abigail and Brittany Hensel are conjoined twins, produced by a single fertilized egg that somehow failed to divide completely into a pair of separate but identical twins. Together, they have a single pair of legs and a single pair of arms, but two separate heads, as you can see in the photo above. The two girls have the same genetic makeup, and they have shared virtually the same environment. However, their parents have encouraged them to pursue different interests. Abigail enjoys playing with animals, and Brittany likes to draw. Abigail likes blue leggings, but Brittany prefers pink. Sometimes they work together on projects, but other times they work independently. For example, at school they never copy each other's answers on tests.

Their parents report that the daughters have had different temperaments since infancy. Abigail is somewhat more impulsive, and she is usually the leader. Brittany is more reflective, and she is more interested in academics. Brittany wants to be a pilot, but Abigail is planning to become a dentist. (As their dad muses, it will be busy in the cockpit, while one daughter is flying and the other is working on someone's teeth.) However, sometimes the sisters seem to share the same thoughts. While watching television one day, Abigail asked her sister, "Are you thinking what I'm thinking?" Brittany replied "Yup," and they immediately ran off to the bedroom to read the same book (Miller & Doman, 1996).

The situation of Abigail and Brittany makes us ponder some intriguing questions. How do we define a person? On the practical level, how should the twins' classmates interpret the school rule that only two children can play simultaneously at the Play-Doh table? If Abigail and Brittany are there, can a third child join them? On the theoretical level, how can two people with nearly identical nature and nurture develop such different personalities?

As the story of Abigail and Brittany illustrates, personality is an inherently complicated topic—one that a variety of theorists have attempted to explain. In this chapter, we'll define **personality** as consistent patterns of thought, feelings, and behavior that originate within the individual (Burger, 1993). Notice, then, that we will focus on stable internal characteristics that help to explain our individual differences.

In this chapter, we will consider how four different theories explain personality processes:

1. The **psychodynamic approach,** which originated with Sigmund Freud, emphasizes childhood experiences and unconscious motivations and conflicts.

2. The **humanistic approach** argues that humans have enormous potential for personal growth.

3. The **trait approach** proposes that human personality is a combination of specific stable, internal personality characteristics—such as shyness or aggressiveness.

4. The **social cognitive approach** emphasizes social factors such as observational learning, and cognitive factors such as the way we think about the events in our lives.

Students in my introductory psychology class often wonder why psychologists feel compelled to examine personality theories. A theory is important, however, because it provides a general framework for understanding how personality operates, for explaining why people behave in certain ways, and for predicting how they will act in the future. In addition, each of the four approaches that we will discuss identifies critical questions that psychologists must address. Research therefore advances in a more orderly and systematic fashion (Mendelsohn, 1993; Monte, 1995).

In addition, the personality approach we adopt can influence our view of human nature (Rychlak, 1981). Suppose that a person firmly supports the psychodynamic view, which argues that humans are irrational, and they are governed by unconscious wishes. This individual would approach the judicial system differently than would someone who prefers the social cognitive view, which suggests that people commit crimes because they have observed antisocial models. Also, psychodynamic theorists would probably conclude that wars and other forms of interpersonal violence are inevitable. Firm supporters of the humanistic and social cognitive theories would disagree.

Finally, we will see in Chapter 14 that the various theories of personality provide different explanations for the origin of psychological disorders. The theories also take different approaches in treating these disorders, as we will see in Chapter 15.

In this chapter, we'll compare the four central theoretical approaches on the following dimensions:

1. What is the source of the data? Are the data obtained from an expert therapist, from an objective test, or from self-reports? Are the observations gathered from people in therapy or from a more general population?

2. What is the cause of behavior? Is the cause internal or external to the person?

3. What is the explanation for people's motivation? Is it optimistic, pessimistic, or neutral?

4. How comprehensive is the approach? Does it attempt to explain almost all behavior, or does it focus on isolated characteristics?

Let's discuss two precautions before we begin. First, these four perspectives do not need to be mutually exclusive. To some extent, the approaches focus on different aspects of human personality, so they do not conflict. We should not assume that one approach must be correct, and all others must be wrong. Instead, most psychologists favor one approach but admire some aspects of at least one other approach (Mischel, 1993).

A second precaution is that human personality is inherently complex, and so it cannot be captured adequately even by four different perspectives. In fact, each approach provides just a partial view of individuals. Theorists from each of the four perspectives have gathered information about personality for several decades. Still, we need additional decades—and perhaps even new perspectives—to describe human personality adequately.

THE PSYCHODYNAMIC APPROACH

We'll begin by describing the psychodynamic approach, which was the first theory that attempted to explain personality. The psychodynamic approach emphasizes three central ideas: (1) childhood experiences determine adult personality; (2) unconscious mental processes influence everyday behavior; and (3) unconscious conflict underlies most human behavior. Sigmund Freud was the founder of an earlier version of this theory, called the psychoanalytic approach. This narrower term, the **psychoanalytic approach,** refers specifically to Freud's original theory, developed about a century ago. Whereas Freud emphasized sexual forces, more recent psychodynamic theorists have emphasized social roles (Hale, 1995). Let's begin with Freud's psychoanalytic approach before we consider several of the more recent psychodynamic theories.

Sigmund Freud was born in 1856 and grew up in a Jewish family in Vienna, Austria. He was trained in medicine, with specific interests in neurology and psychological problems. We should emphasize that Freud's theories were controversial during an era known for its straitlaced attitudes toward sexuality. Another source of controversy was that Freud focused on the unconscious. In contrast, most theorists favored the views of Wilhelm Wundt. As we mentioned in Chapter 1, Wundt emphasized conscious experiences.

Freud's (1900/1953) groundbreaking book, *The Interpretation of Dreams,* was not well received. It sold only 351 copies in the first six years after publication (Gay, 1988). However, Freud's approach became more influential several decades later. In fact, his theory has been called "the single most sweeping contribution to the field of personality" (Phares, 1988, p. 75).

Many current psychologists have abandoned Freud; we will examine some of their criticisms later. However, his ideas still influence many areas of popular culture (Eisenman, 1994). Phrases such as "Freudian slip" and "unconscious" are part of our daily vocabulary. High school health textbooks present terms such as "reaction formation" and "repression" as if they were documented facts, rather than theoretical speculations.

In fact, at the college level, you'll typically hear more references to psychoanalytic concepts from humanities professors than from psychology professors (Kihlstrom, 1994; Lippmann, 1996; Welsh, 1994). Scholars in the humanities believe that a Freudian perspective can provide insights about a character's emotions and inner conflicts. However, some scholars may overinterpret the material. For example, Acocella

Sigmund Freud strolling in the mountains with his daughter Anna Freud (who also became a psychoanalyst).

Freudian theory would say that this child's superego prevents her from taking a forbidden cookie, which her id is urging her to consume.

(1995) describes an essay written by a humanities professor who wanted to demonstrate that the American novelist Willa Cather had been a lesbian. Cather describes a boat named *Berengaria,* and the essayist—in the Freudian tradition—tried to decode the symbol by rearranging the letters into phrases that presumably reveal "lesbian energies," such as *raring engine,* and *barrage* of *anger.* Willa Cather may indeed have been a lesbian, but the essayist should have known that Cather had just sailed back from Europe on an ocean liner called *Berengaria.* Critical thinkers in the humanities— as well as psychology—must consider alternative explanations. In this case, the correct explanation for *Berengaria* did not rely on any symbolism.

Let's begin our overview of the psychodynamic approach by considering Freud's basic theories on the structure of personality. We'll then discuss his methods, the stages of psychosexual development, Freud's views on defense mechanisms, and his representation of women. We'll end by considering some other psychodynamic theories, some personality tests designed to reveal hidden motives, and an evaluation of the psychodynamic approach.

Structure of Personality

Freud envisioned three basic components to personality: the id, the ego, and the superego (Freud, 1933/1964). He proposed that humans are born with an **id,** which is immature and illogical. The id consists of the basic drives—such as eating and sexual activities—and it provides the energy (or **libido**) for all human behavior. Freud also maintained that the id lacks moral judgment; it cannot distinguish between good and evil. The id is unconscious, a "hidden self" that can influence our everyday actions (Elliott, 1994).

The **ego,** in contrast, supposedly develops because the individual needs some factor that will mediate between the id and reality. For example, Freud argues that the ego helps young children delay their impulses until the situation is appropriate.

So far, we have an irrational id, governed by pleasure, and a cooler, calmer ego. Freud's third personality component is the **superego,** which includes a person's conscience, ideals, and values. Parents and society convey these principles. Because the society in Freud's era often discouraged sexual expression, Freud argued that the superego suppresses the sexual impulses.

In Freud's theory, then, the ego acts as a supervisor. The ego must negotiate a compromise between the id's drives and the superego's rules about moral behavior. In Freudian theory, personality is created through the constant conflict and interaction among the id, the ego, and the superego (Domjan, 1993).

Let's see how the id, ego, and superego are related to a person's awareness. Freud compared the human mind to an iceberg. As in Figure 13.1, only a small part of the iceberg rises above the surface of the water. This portion represents the **conscious,** which includes everything you are aware of at a particular moment. As Chapter 5 described, our conscious experiences include our awareness of the outside world and of our perceptions, thoughts, and feelings. As Figure 13.1 shows, only the ego and the superego are included in the conscious. (Note, however, that parts of both the ego and the superego lie below the conscious.) The id is entirely unconscious.

Freud was especially interested in the **unconscious,** which holds thoughts, feelings, and desires that are far below the level of a person's awareness, hidden from the outside world. Freud argued that your unconscious may hold denied wishes or a particularly traumatic childhood memory, for example (Cloninger, 1996). Freud proposed that traumatic memories can influence your behavior, even though you may not be consciously aware of them.

FIGURE 13.1

Freud's model of the conscious and the unconscious, similar to an iceberg. As you can see, the ego and the superego can be in the conscious or the unconscious, but the id is entirely unconscious.

Freud's Methods

In traditional psychoanalysis, the individual is seen several times a week, and analysis may continue for many years. Freud used three major psychoanalytic techniques. One technique, **free association,** requires patients to report anything that occurs to them; normal critical analysis should be suspended (Macmillan, 1992). The thoughts may be silly, irrational, and unrelated to the present time. For example, a woman in therapy may suddenly recall an image of a perfume bottle. Perhaps this image brings forth a childhood recollection, such as a fight with a brother near her mother's bureau. Freud argued that free association was one tool that allowed access to the unconscious.

A second Freudian method was dream analysis. As we noted in Chapter 5, Freud believed that the unconscious reveals itself though symbols in our dreams. Freud argued that the ego censors our thoughts when we are awake. However, the ego relaxes its control when we sleep, so that the unconscious is more obvious in our dreams (McGrath, 1992). People supposedly try to disguise their own wishes from themselves by constructing symbols. For example, an individual may report a dream about riding on a bull in an amusement-park carousel. This conscious, remembered story line of a dream is called its **manifest content.** The analyst may interpret the bull as a symbol of the person's father. These underlying, unconscious aspects of the dream (as interpreted by the analyst) are called the **latent content.** Try Demonstration 13.1 to see whether you can decode the latent content of a fairy tale.

In the third Freudian technique, the therapist interprets the patient's reactions. For instance, a modern-day analyst was helping a 2-year-old girl who was concerned about broken crayons (Chehrazi, 1986). This analyst interpreted the broken crayons as a symbol of the girl's wish for a penis.

Critical Thinking Exercise 13.1

Write down your answers to the following questions about Freud's psychoanalytic methods.

a. In Chapter 1, we noted that one requirement of critical thinking is to determine whether conclusions are supported by the evidence that has been presented. What evidence is presented that the dream about the carousel bull really does represent the dreamer's father?

b. One of the guidelines for critical thinking, mentioned in Chapter 1, is to consider other possible interpretations of an explanation. What other interpretations can you supply for the little girl's preoccupation with broken crayons?

DEMONSTRATION 13.1   Decoding a Fairy Tale

Psychoanalyst Bruno Bettelheim argues that children's fairy tales are filled with hidden messages, and children can translate the manifest content into the appropriate latent content at an unconscious level. Read the following summary of part of the fairy tale "Sleeping Beauty" and search for the latent-content items; place the corresponding number next to the relevant passage in the summary. To make the task more challenging, I listed four items irrelevant to the story.

Sleeping Beauty

A 15-year-old princess climbs a circular staircase, unlocks the door, and enters the forbidden little room. Inside, an old woman sits spinning cloth. Seeing the cylinder-shaped spindle, the young princess asks the old woman about the object that jumps in such an unusual fashion. She touches the spindle, her finger bleeds, and she falls into a deep sleep. After sleeping for 100 years, she is awakened by a kiss from the handsome prince. They are later married.

Possible Latent-Content Items

1. a brutal father figure
2. a penis
3. bowel movements
4. female genitals
5. sucking (oral needs)
6. menstruation
7. attachment to mother
8. sexual intercourse

Also, what is the implied message of this fairy tale? Check the end of the chapter (Page 448) for the answers to this demonstration.

Sources: Based on Bettelheim, 1977; McAdams, 1990.

Stages of Psychosexual Development

Freud's analysis of his patients persuaded him that psychological disorders have their origin in childhood. As a result, he argued that many aspects of adult personality can be explained by examining important early events. Freud argues that the libido is centered at different body parts—or **erogenous zones**—as the individual matures. The first erogenous zone is the mouth, followed at later ages by the anus, and finally the genitals. Pleasant stimulation presumably reduces the tension that the person experiences.

Freud also proposed that children experience conflicts between urges in these erogenous zones and the rules of society. For example, society demands that toddlers be toilet trained. Suppose that a conflict in a particular erogenous zone is not successfully resolved, because the individual is either overindulged or underindulged. Freud argued that this individual may experience a **fixation,** in which he or she is rigidly locked in conflict about that erogenous zone. Table 13.1 lists the five stages of psychosexual development. Let's explore them further.

During the **oral stage,** the mouth presumably experiences the most tension. The id tries to reduce this tension by encouraging the child to suck on nipples, thumbs, and pacifiers. Freud argued that a fixation during the later part of the oral period—after the child has teeth—produces an adult who is "bitingly" aggressive (Burger, 1993).

In the **anal stage,** the erogenous zone shifts to the anal region. Freud proposed that toddlers experience satisfaction when their anal region is stimulated, for instance by retaining or eliminating feces. Parents begin toilet training at this stage, insisting that the child must eliminate feces in the toilet. Conflict arises between the child's id and the new restrictions imposed by society. According to Freud's theory, a child may become fixated at the anal stage if this conflict is not successfully resolved. An individual may become "anal retentive," too orderly and overly concerned about being punctual. On the other hand, a person can become "anal expulsive," or messy and perpetually late.

During the **phallic stage,** the erogenous zone shifts to the sex organs, and the child presumably finds pleasure in masturbation. Freud proposed that boys in the phallic stage experience an Oedipus complex (pronounced "*Ed*-ih-pus). In the ancient Greek tragedy *Oedipus Rex,* King Oedipus unknowingly kills his father and marries his mother. Similarly, in psychoanalytic theory, an **Oedipus complex** is a

Freud argued that humans first experience tension in the mouth area, during the oral stage.

TABLE 13.1 **Freud's Five Stages of Psychosexual Development**

AGE	STAGE	DESCRIPTION
0–18 months	Oral stage	Stimulation of the mouth produces pleasure; the baby enjoys sucking, chewing, biting.
18–36 months	Anal stage	Stimulation of the anal region produces pleasure; the toddler experiences conflict over toilet training.
3–6 years	Phallic stage	Self-stimulation of the genitals produces pleasure; the child struggles with negative feelings about the same-gender parent.
6–puberty	Latency	Sexual feelings are repressed; the child avoids members of the other gender.
Puberty onward	Genital stage	Adolescent or adult has mature sexual feelings and experiences pleasure from sexual relationships with others.

conflict in which a boy's sexual impulses are directed toward his mother, and he views his father as a rival. The young boy is afraid that his father may punish him for these desires by castrating him, or cutting off his penis. A boy who develops normally will reduce this castration anxiety by identifying with his father, internalizing his father's values, and developing a strong superego.

Freud maintained that a girl in the phallic stage notices that she lacks a penis, so she experiences penis envy. She decides that her mother was responsible for castrating her and therefore develops hostile feelings for her mother. Meanwhile, her love for her father grows.

During the **latency stage,** children's sexual feelings are not obvious. Children are presumably ashamed and disgusted about sexual issues, and so they tend to avoid members of the other gender. As you may recall, Chapter 10 discussed that children are likely to show gender segregation. However, we have no evidence that any of these childhood behaviors are sexually motivated (Macmillan, 1992).

Freud's final stage of psychosexual development is the **genital stage;** during puberty, sexual urges reappear. Genital pleasure during the genital stage now arises from sexual relationships with others.

Defense Mechanisms

So far, we have examined Freud's ideas about the structure of personality, his methods for exploring personality, and his proposed stages of psychosexual development. Another central concept in Freud's psychoanalytical approach is called defense mechanisms. We emphasized earlier that the conflict among the id, the ego, and the superego is central in Freudian theory. Freud proposed that the id may express a particular desire; the superego responds that this desire is socially inappropriate. Then the ego tries to resolve this conflict. Often, it resolves the conflict by using **defense mechanisms,** which are mental activities designed to reduce the anxiety resulting from this conflict (Bond, 1995). Defense mechanisms are often harmless or even helpful, but rigid and severe defense mechanisms can cause psychological problems. Table 13.2 lists five selected defense mechanisms, which Sigmund Freud developed in collaboration with his daughter, Anna.

Notice that Freud's pessimism about people's motivations is often revealed in the defense mechanisms. For example, why are you helpful toward your neighbors? According to Freud, you really feel aggressive toward them (Wallach & Wallach, 1983). You shovel snow from their sidewalk every winter morning because of a reaction formation, designed to reduce the anxiety about your hatred.

Repression, the first defense mechanism listed in Table 13.2, is currently very controversial. As you may recall from the discussion in Chapter 7 (Pages 237–239), some therapists and theorists believe that people can temporarily forget about an especially traumatic event. More specifically, they argue that traumatized individuals may *repress* these memories (Horowitz, 1994). In contrast, cognitive psychology researchers are more likely to argue that the memories are not really repressed, and some people may even create false memories for events that did not really occur (Bower, 1990; Holmes, 1994). As we concluded in Chapter 7, each position in this controversy is probably at least partially correct (Schacter, 1996; Schooler, 1994).

Freudian Theory and Women

Before we consider other psychodynamic theorists, let's evaluate Freud's theory with respect to gender. During the last three decades, people who support the equality of women and men have argued that Freudian theory reveals gender biases (e.g., Greenspan, 1993; Lerman, 1986; Slipp, 1993). Freud's writing often refers to female inferiority, which he traces primarily to women's lack of a penis. Freud argued that when young girls notice that they are missing a penis, they "feel themselves heavily handicapped . . . and envy the boy's possession of it" (Freud, 1925/1976, p. 327).

TABLE 13.2 **Some Representative Defense Mechanisms Proposed by Freud**

DEFENSE MECHANISM*	DEFINITION	EXAMPLE
Repression	Pushing back unacceptable thoughts and feelings into the unconscious.	A rape victim cannot recall the details of the attack.
Regression	Acting in ways characteristic of earlier life stages.	A young adult, anxious on a trip to his parents' home, sits in the corner reading comic books, as he often did in grade school.
Reaction formation	Replacing an anxiety-producing feeling with its exact opposite, typically going overboard.	A man who is anxious about his attraction to gay men begins dating women several times a week.
Displacement	Redirecting an emotion (e.g., anger) toward someone who is less dangerous than the "real" object of that emotion.	A husband, angry at the way his boss treats him, screams at his wife.
Projection	Attributing your own unacceptable thoughts and feelings to another person.	An employee at a store, tempted to steal some merchandise, suspects that another employee is stealing.

Sources: Holmes, 1984b; Monte, 1995; Plutchik, 1995.
*These five defense mechanisms are listed with the New Terms at the end of this chapter.

Freud also argued that boys strongly identify with their fathers after resolving their Oedipal conflicts; girls cannot identify as strongly with their mothers because their struggle is milder. As a consequence, girls' superegos never develop fully (Freud, 1925/1976).

We should note that psychological research has not produced evidence for penis envy in females (Fisher & Greenberg, 1977; Lerman, 1986; Slipp, 1993). In fact, most young girls are unconcerned about genital differences. Some are even relieved that they lack this anatomical structure. Consider, for instance, the little girl who took a bath with a young male cousin and observed the genital differences in silence. Later, she said softly to her mother, "Isn't it a blessing he doesn't have it on his face?" (Tavris & Offir, 1977, p. 155). Most important, as we discussed in Chapter 11, men and women do not differ significantly in their moral development. In judging Freud, though, many psychodynamic theorists urge us to remember that he was writing in an era when women were considered inferior, so his ideas may partially reflect his own culture and historical context (Kurzweil, 1995).

Other Psychodynamic Theories

Sigmund Freud has influenced our thinking about personality both directly through his own writing and indirectly through the ideas of his followers. We will discuss two of these theorists—Carl Jung and Karen Horney— as well as the more recent object relations theory. You are already familiar with the best known of the theorists influenced by Freud—Erik Erikson; we discussed his eight stages of psychosocial development in Chapters 10 and 11. In general, you can see that these psychodynamic theorists emphasize social roles, whereas Freud emphasized sexual factors.

Jung's Theory   The Swiss analyst Carl Jung (pronounced "Yoong") supported Freud's notion of the unconscious (Jung, 1917/1953). In addition, he proposed an even deeper layer. Jung's **collective unconscious** presumably stores fragments from our ancestral past. Jung's theory proposes, then, that all humans share the same collective unconscious. The concept of a collective unconscious has been greeted more enthusiastically by artists and anthropologists than by psychologists (Robertson, 1995).

Horney's Theory   Karen Horney (pronounced "*Horn*-eye") challenged Freud's theory of penis envy and proposed that women are more likely to envy men's status in society than their genitals (Horney, 1926/1967; Mitchell & Black, 1995). Horney proposed that young children feel relatively helpless and threatened. Children develop several strategies to cope with the anxiety generated by this helplessness (Enns, 1989; Horney, 1945). Specifically, they can show affection or hostility toward others, or they can withdraw from relationships. Horney proposed that normal people balance the three strategies. However, psychological disorders develop when one strategy dominates personality.

Object-Relations Approach   We have summarized the ideas of two theorists who were strongly influenced by Freud. A more recent development is the **object-relations approach,** which focuses on the development of ideas about the self in relation to other people—especially during the first two years of life. This approach minimizes Freud's notion of drives and emphasizes the developing relationship between the self and objects—that is, significant people in the child's life (Klein, 1948; Monte, 1995; "Psychodynamic Therapy: Part II," 1991).

A prominent object-relations theorist is Nancy Chodorow (1978, 1989, 1994), who argues that Freud did not pay enough attention to mothers in his theory. Chodorow argues that boys and girls both identify with their mother initially. Infant girls grow up with a feeling of similarity to their mother, which develops into interdependence, or a connection with others in general. Infant boys, in contrast, must learn that they are different from their mothers in order to develop a male identity. As a consequence, the two genders face different potential problems in their relationships. Specifically, females may not develop sufficient independence, and males may not develop close attachments (Gilligan, 1982).

Psychodynamic Theory and Projective Tests

Another outgrowth of psychodynamic theory is the development of personality tests. In Chapter 2, we introduced the topic of psychological tests, and in Chapter 8 we examined intelligence testing. Theorists have also devised a variety of personality tests. In this section, we'll consider **projective tests,** in which responses to ambiguous stimuli presumably reflect a person's needs, emotions, and other personality characteristics (Hood & Johnson, 1991). In other words, people supposedly *project* their personality onto the test stimuli. Let's consider two projective tests: the Rorschach Inkblot Test and the Thematic Apperception Test. Be sure that you try Demonstration 13.2 before you read further.

DEMONSTRATION 13.2 Responding to an Inkblot

Look at the inkblot to the right, which is similar to those on the Rorschach Inkblot Test. Try to describe what the picture looks like and what it could be. Write down your answer. (You do not need to use complete sentences.)

When you have finished your description, go back over it and explain how you arrived at each part of that description. It is important to keep in mind, however, that this is not a true Rorschach Test, and that these tests cannot be interpreted adequately without expert training. Furthermore, as the text that follows will explain, many critics question its value.

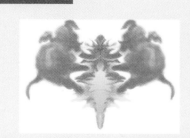

The Rorschach Inkblot Test Hermann Rorschach (1884–1922) developed an interest in inkblots as an adolescent. The test named after him remains extremely popular, despite its many critics (Butcher & Rouse, 1996; Dawes, 1994). In the **Rorschach Inkblot Test,** people respond to a series of ambiguous inkblots, and the responses are analyzed according to characteristics such as recurring themes, number of responses, the region of the inkblot that attracts attention, and whether the nature of the response is common or unusual (Groth-Marnat, 1990). The Rorschach is designed to be administered by rigorously trained professionals (Exner, 1993).

Consider how one woman responded to a card from the Rorschach Test, a black-and-white design similar to the colored inkblot you saw in Demonstration 13.2. Ms. T. reported that she saw "two elephants, two itty-bitty elephants . . . fighting over a roach—cockroach—in the middle . . . [The elephants] both got their—their snoz-zoolas—[half laughs] or their trunks or whatever you call them wrapped around the cockroach" (Allison et al., 1988, p. 203).

The therapist's interpretation of this response proposed that Ms. T.'s defense mechanisms had attempted to shrink a huge attacking creature into something small and playful. The interpretation also noted that she focused on the elephants' penislike trunks, yet she blocked momentarily on the specific name. As you can see, the Rorschach provides psychodynamically inclined professionals with a test rich with symbolic possibilities.

Some researchers argue that the Rorschach has moderate reliability (consistency) and validity—the ability to accurately measure psychological disturbances (Exner, 1993, 1996; Parker et al., 1988). However, others complain that the scoring is arbitrary and that people's scores are not correlated with their psychiatric diagnoses. These critics also point out that these negative findings have not been sufficiently publicized (Dawes, 1994; Wood et al., 1996a, 1996b). An additional problem is that the Rorschach has not been adequately tested with people of color (Velásquez & Callahan, 1992).

The Thematic Apperception Test The second most popular projective test is the TAT (Butcher & Rouse, 1996). The **TAT (Thematic Apperception Test)** consists of a series of ambiguous scenes; the test taker describes what is happening now, what happened in the past, and what will occur in the future. The TAT was first published by Christina Morgan and Henry Murray in 1935. In Chapter 12, we saw how the TAT is used to test achievement motivation. It has also been used to assess power motivation, and the test has been used to assess personality in psychiatric and in business settings (Butcher & Rouse, 1996; McClelland, 1993).

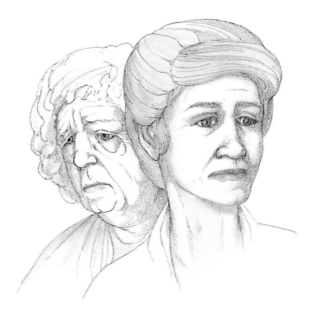

FIGURE 13.2

An item similar to those that appear on the Thematic Apperception Test.

Figure 13.2 shows a picture similar to those on the TAT. In responding to a picture like this, one woman wrote the following:

> This is a woman who has been quite troubled by memories of a mother she was resentful toward. She has feelings of sorrow for the way she treated her mother; her memories of her mother plague her. These feelings seem to be increasing as she grows older and sees her children treating her in the same way she treated her mother. (Aiken, 1989, p. 364)

The TAT was designed to bring forth unconscious tendencies that a person may be unwilling or unable to reveal, such as difficulties with one's parents. The test takers presumably project their personality traits onto one or more of the characters in the scene. The people administering and scoring the test must be professionally trained, as you can imagine. Furthermore, the results are often interpreted within a psychodynamic framework. For instance, when a person omits reference to a gun shown in a TAT picture, the examiner may conclude that he or she tends to repress aggressive impulses (Phares, 1988).

Research on the TAT shows that the reliability and validity measures are rather low when personality traits are assessed (Groth-Marnat, 1990; Kaplan & Saccuzo, 1993; Spangler, 1992). Furthermore, like the Rorschach, the TAT has primarily been tested with European American populations (Velásquez & Callahan, 1992).

Evaluation of Projective Tests   One major advantage of projective tests is that their purpose is disguised: Test takers are seldom aware how their responses will be interpreted (Anastasi, 1988). In contrast, people taking an objective self-report test often choose the most socially acceptable answer, even if another option is more truthful. For instance, a suicidal person may answer "No" to the question "Sometimes I think I may kill myself." However, he or she may spontaneously mention death on a projective test.

A second, related advantage proposed by psychodynamic psychologists is that test takers can presumably relax their defense mechanisms (such as repression) when taking a projective test. This relaxation supposedly allows the release of unconscious material (Groth-Marnat, 1990).

A significant disadvantage of projective tests is that they are not as standardized as objective tests. Several alternative scoring systems may be used, and the accuracy also depends on the examiner's professional training.

Most important, the reliability and the validity of projective tests may not be high, even when the examiners are well trained (Wolfe, 1998). A test is not useful when people receive inconsistent scores and when the test does not measure the characteristic it is supposed to measure!

Critical Thinking Exercise 13.2

Write down your answers to the following questions about projective tests.

a. A group of psychologists wants to test the validity of the Rorschach Inkblot Test. They give the test to 100 people who have requested treatment for a variety of psychological disorders. The psychologists score the Rorschach responses according to the established methods for detecting depression on the Rorschach. Next, these same psychologists diagnose these people on the basis of self-reported psychological symptoms. The psychologists discover that, of the 50 people diagnosed with depression, 40 also have high depression scores on the Rorschach. Of the 50 people diagnosed with other disorders, only 5 have high depression scores on the Rorschach. Why would you mistrust this validity study?

b. A student is taking the TAT in the hopes of being admitted to a special college program. The first card shows a violin, and he thinks he will receive a high score on this test if he finds a common thread interwoven through all the scenes. He painstakingly forces every story to revolve around violins and music. Why would this student's attempt to second-guess the purpose of this test lower the validity of the measure?

TABLE 13.3 A Summary of the Psychodynamic Approach	
	PSYCHODYNAMIC APPROACH
Source of Data	Obtained from expert analyst from people in therapy.
Cause of Behavior	Internal conflict, unconscious forces, childhood experiences.
Explanation for Motivation	Pessimistic explanation.
Comprehensiveness of Theory	Very comprehensive.

Evaluation of the Psychodynamic Approach

We have outlined Freud's theory and also briefly noted the contributions of three more recent theories. Let's now evaluate the psychodynamic approach, as represented by the prototype theorist, Sigmund Freud. Table 13.3 summarizes four important characteristics of psychodynamic theory.

What can we conclude about Freud's psychodynamic approach, roughly a century after it was formulated? By current standards, this theory has several major problems:

1. *It is difficult to test.* Psychodynamic theory emphasizes the unconscious. However, the unconscious rarely expresses itself directly, so this concept is difficult to measure. Also, consider the following problem: Suppose that an analyst suspects that a man is pessimistic. Any pessimistic feelings expressed during therapy will be taken as evidence of pessimism. However, any *optimistic* feelings will also be considered evidence of pessimism, because these feelings could be a reaction formation against the original pessimism. We cannot test a theory if it predicts both a particular characteristic and its opposite.

2. *When the theory is tested, the studies are often inadequate.* The psychodynamic approach has often been criticized for improper methodology (e.g., Dawes, 1994; Ewen, 1993). For instance, the observers may be biased, interpreting ambiguous observations so that they are consistent with a particular part of the theory. Critical Thinking Exercise 13.1 noted that the little girl's concern about broken crayons may have a more obvious explanation than penis envy. Also, Freud's theory was based on a nonrepresentative sample from a different era. We cannot generalize from a small sample of troubled, wealthy Viennese people—studied about a century ago—to a variety of cultures in the current era. Some psychodynamic theorists have conducted more rigorous research (e.g., Shulman, 1990; Silverman & Weinberger, 1985). However, other theorists argue that we still have no clear-cut evidence of basic Freudian concepts such as repression (e.g., Holmes, 1994).

3. *Freud's theory is biased against women.* As we noted earlier, Freud maintained that women have inferior moral judgment, a gender bias that is not supported by the research. He also proposed that women are **masochistic** (pronounced "mass-uh-*kiss*-tick"), which means that they would derive pleasure from being mistreated. This view does a disservice to women, and it encourages people to think—incorrectly—that women enjoy being battered or raped (Caplan & Caplan, 1994).

4. *It is too pessimistic about human nature.* Freudian theory proposes that our helpfulness can be traced to a reaction formation against our aggressive feelings.

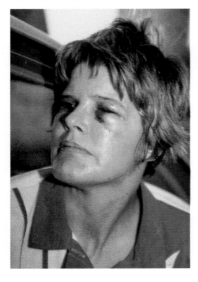

This woman is the victim of domestic violence. If she saw a therapist who argues that women are basically masochistic, she might have serious doubts about the potential for improving her life. For example, she might believe that if she leaves her husband, her "unconscious" will simply drive her into another masochistic relationship (Caplan & Caplan, 1994).

We do not help simply because we want to be moral or good (Wallach & Wallach, 1983). Also, the theory proposes that we act ethically because we fear punishment from our superegos. However, we saw in Chapter 10 that even very young children are helpful toward others—before their superegos could be well developed. As Wallach and Wallach point out, humans *are* basically concerned about others. Freud's explanation is unnecessarily indirect and negative.

We have described several problems with Freud's psychodynamic theory. Still, we need to remember that we cannot blame Freud for being unable to predict how our society would behave a century after he developed his theories. Here are some of the theory's strengths:

1. *It examines motivation and emotion.* We need to praise Freud for encouraging psychology to explore human motivations and emotions, rather than focusing only on thoughts and intellectual reactions. Freud's concept of the unconscious is clearly valuable to many current cognitive psychologists (e.g., Jacoby et al., 1992; Loftus & Klinger, 1992).

2. *Freud's theory is impressively comprehensive.* Sigmund Freud's approach is the most fully developed and comprehensive approach we'll consider in this chapter. He tried to explain an impressive range of human behaviors, addressing developmental patterns as well as psychological disorders. We have to admire Freud's brilliance and persistence in developing such an all-encompassing theory that was so strikingly different from the trends of his own culture.

SECTION SUMMARY: *THE PSYCHODYNAMIC APPROACH*

1. The psychodynamic approach emphasizes childhood experiences and unconscious motivations and conflicts; one kind of psychodynamic approach, Freud's psychoanalytic theory, was radically controversial when it was first proposed, but it eventually had a strong impact on psychology, popular culture, and the humanities.

2. Freud proposed three components of personality: the id, ego, and superego; the ego and the superego are partly represented in the conscious, whereas the id is completely unconscious.

3. Freud's methods include free association, dream analysis, and action interpretation.

4. Freud argued that the erogenous zone shifts throughout development, during the oral, anal, phallic, latency, and genital stages.

5. The psychoanalytic defense mechanisms include repression, regression, reaction formation, displacement, and projection.

6. Freud's theory emphasizes penis envy and less complete ethical development in women; these claims are not supported by the research.

7. Other psychodynamic theories have been proposed by Erikson (discussed in Chapters 10 and 11), Jung (collective unconscious), Horney (challenging penis envy; strategies of interacting with other people), and the object-relations approach (the self in relation to other people).

8. Two projective tests that are compatible with the psychodynamic approach are the Rorschach Inkblot Test and the Thematic Apperception Test (TAT), but these tests are not high in reliability or validity.

9. Criticisms of psychodynamic theory include the difficulty of testing it, inadequate research, its bias against women, and its extreme pessimism. Positive features include its emphasis on emotions and some useful theoretical concepts, as well as its comprehensive scope.

THE HUMANISTIC APPROACH

In contrast to the pessimism of the psychodynamic perspective, the humanistic approach optimistically argues that people have enormous potential for personal growth. The humanistic approach gained prominence in the early 1960s when Carl Rogers (1961) and Abraham Maslow (1962) published important books. Many psychologists were dissatisfied with the two dominant theories of that era. On the one hand, the psychodynamic approach proposed that human kindness and caring often arise from evil impulses. On the other hand, the behaviorist approach—which we discussed in Chapter 6—focused on animal research. How could experiments with rats and pigeons inform us about higher human goals, such as the search for truth and beauty? (We should note that the social cognitive approach had not yet been proposed, and the humanistic theorists did not consider the trait approach to be a full-fledged personality theory.)

Rogers, Maslow, and others developed the humanistic approach as an alternative to the psychodynamic and behaviorist approaches. Let's examine the ideas of these two most prominent humanistic theorists, and then we'll evaluate the humanistic approach.

Rogers's Person-Centered Approach

Carl Rogers (1902–1987) was born in Illinois and began his professional career working with troubled children, though he later extended his therapy to adults. Rogers's approach requires the therapist to try to see the world from each client's personal perspective, rather than from the therapist's own framework. Rogers emphasized that each of us interprets the same set of stimuli differently, so there are as many different "real worlds" as there are people on this planet (Rogers, 1980).

Self-Actualization   Carl Rogers used the term **self-actualization** to capture the natural, underlying tendency of humans to move forward and fulfill their true potential (Rogers, 1963, 1980; Thorne, 1992). He marveled that this actualizing tendency could persist, even in the most hostile environments. For example, Rogers often interacted with people in the back wards of large psychiatric hospitals. The lives of these clients had been terribly warped, yet Rogers believed that these people were still striving toward growth. Rogers emphasized that this active self-development tendency provided the underlying basis of the person-centered approach.

Personality Development   Carl Rogers proposed that even young children need to be highly regarded by other people. Children also need positive *self-regard*—to be esteemed by oneself as well as others. From his work with clients who had psychological disorders, Rogers found that self-actualizing tendencies were frequently stifled by restricting self-concepts. Specifically, these clients had often acted in ways that distorted their "true selves" in order to win positive regard from others.

Rogers proposed that most children experience **conditional positive regard;** parents withhold their love and approval if children fail to conform to their elders' standards. For instance, parents might award positive regard to their son only in certain conditions—for example, only if he makes the football team. However, they may withhold positive regard if he fails to achieve in athletics or if he succeeds in other areas, such as music or the debate club.

In contrast, Rogers believed that everyone should be given **unconditional positive regard,** which is a nonjudgmental and genuine love, without any strings attached (Ewen, 1993; Rogers, 1959). The research partly supports Rogers's ideas. As you may recall from Chapter 10, authoritarian parents, who demand unquestioning obedience, do tend to produce unhappy, ineffective offspring. However, permissive parents, who allow children to make all their own decisions, often produce immature offspring with little self-control. Unconditional positive regard does not necessarily encourage self-actualization. The most successful parenting style is authoritative, with both love and clear-cut standards.

Rogers argued that people strive toward growth, even in less-than-favorable surroundings.

Maslow's Hierarchy of Needs

Abraham Maslow (1908–1970) was born in Brooklyn, New York. As a young psychologist, he was initially attracted to behaviorism. However, when his first child was born, Maslow realized that behaviorism could not account for the miracle and mystery of human infancy (Cloninger, 1996).

Maslow is probably best known for his theoretical exploration of self-actualization, the important tendency to realize our own potential. Maslow proposed that our human motives are arranged in a hierarchy, with the most basic needs at the bottom. At the top are the more highly developed needs (esteem needs and—finally—self-actualization).

Figure 13.3 shows **Maslow's hierarchy of needs,** in which each lower need must be satisfied before the next level of need can be addressed. For instance, people whose homes have just been destroyed by a flood will primarily be concerned with physiological and safety needs, rather than the more lofty goal of self-actualization. Let's examine the five levels in Maslow's hierarchy, beginning with the most basic level.

1. *Physiological needs:* We need food, water, sleep, and sex. Notice that these needs are also those that motivate lower animals.

2. *Safety needs:* These needs include security, protection, and the avoidance of pain.

3. *Belongingness and love needs:* These needs focus on affiliation with other people, affection, and feeling loved; sexual relationships as an expression of affection can also be included in this category.

4. *Esteem needs:* We also need to respect ourselves and to win the esteem of other people. Otherwise we feel discouraged and inferior, according to Maslow, so we will not strive for the highest level of hierarchy.

5. *Self-actualization needs:* A person who has satisfied all the lower needs can seek self-actualization, attempting to reach her or his full potential.

Maslow became particularly intrigued with this highest level, self-actualization, and he devised a list of characteristics of self-actualized people. Demonstration 13.3 encourages you to think about some attributes of self-actualizers, based on Maslow's theory.

Later, Maslow began to identify other prominent people as self-actualizers. These were healthy, well-adjusted people who had used their full potential. The list included social worker Jane Addams, presidents Thomas Jefferson and Abraham Lincoln, first lady and social activist Eleanor Roosevelt, and physicist Albert Einstein.

Pioneer social worker Jane Addams was one of the people Maslow identified as a self-actualizer.

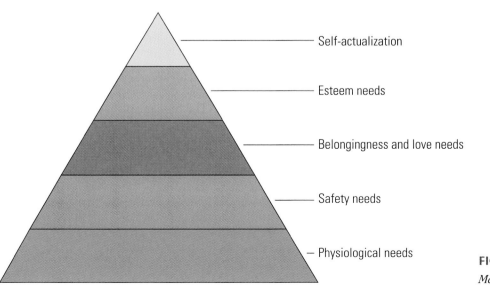

───── Self-actualization

───── Esteem needs

───── Belongingness and love needs

───── Safety needs

───── Physiological needs

FIGURE 13.3

Maslow's hierarchy of needs.

DEMONSTRATION 13.3 Qualities of a Self-Actualized Person

Think about someone you know who seems to be a self-actualized person, who has lived up to his or her potential. (Ideally, this is someone you know personally, so you are familiar with this person's qualities.) Now read each of the characteristics listed below and decide whether they apply to the person you know. Place an X in front of each one that does describe this person.

_____ An acceptance of himself or herself

_____ An acceptance of other people

_____ Involvement in some cause outside of himself or herself

_____ Very spontaneous in both actions and emotions

_____ Great need for privacy

_____ Focused on problems and solutions rather than himself or herself

_____ Resists pressures to conform

_____ Superior creativity

_____ Fresh appreciation of other people, rather than stereotyped reactions

_____ Strongly developed set of values

How many of these characteristics apply to your target person? If any did *not* apply, do you think that this person would be even more self-actualized if she or he possessed these qualities?

In addition, you might try evaluating several famous people on these dimensions. How would you rate Mother Theresa, various politicians, and some major entertainers?

Source: Based on Maslow, 1968, 1971.

Critical Thinking Exercise 13.3

Write down your answers to the following questions about the theories of Rogers and Maslow.

a. Several humanistic theorists want to test Rogers's notions about self-actualization and other theoretical concepts. How would research be more complicated because of Rogers's notion that we all interpret the world differently?

b. Maslow himself created a list of qualities of self-actualized people, many of which you saw in Demonstration 13.3. As a critical thinker, how would you evaluate this process for generating criteria?

Evaluation of the Humanistic Approach

Table 13.4 summarizes four important characteristics of the humanistic approach, contrasting it with the psychodynamic approach. As presented in the table, you can see that the data in the humanistic approach are gathered from people in therapy, in the case of Rogers; Maslow provided self-reports from nonclinical populations, and he also analyzed the writing of important historical figures (DeCarvalho, 1991). Behavior is motivated by self-concepts and the tendency to self-actualize. Compared with the psychodynamic approach, humanistic psychology proposes a blissfully optimistic view of human nature. Finally, the theory is reasonably comprehensive, though not as far-reaching as the psychodynamic approach.

The humanistic approach can be criticized for several reasons:

1. *It relies on subjective experience.* The humanistic approach emphasizes that reality lies in a person's own interpretation of the world. Some people have only a limited ability to express themselves, so their self-reports probably do not reflect their experiences (Phares, 1988). We are therefore left with somewhat limited data.

2. *The studies are often inadequate.* Both Rogers and Maslow examined a selected sample of people, who were more intelligent and verbal than average. Humanistic principles may not apply to other groups. Also, as Maslow (1971) admits and Critical Thinking Exercise 13.3 pointed out, the work on self-actualizing people isn't really *research*. His list is arbitrary, and the people he selected did not completely meet his criteria. For instance, Abraham Lincoln had periods of severe depression,

TABLE 13.4   A Comparison of the Humanistic Approach With the Psychodynamic Approach

	PSYCHODYNAMIC APPROACH	HUMANISTIC APPROACH
Source of Data	Obtained from expert analysis from people in therapy.	Obtained from self-reports from the general population and people in therapy.
Cause of Behavior	Internal conflict, unconscious forces, childhood experiences.	Self-concepts, self-actualizing tendencies.
Explanation for Motivation	Pessimistic explanation.	Optimistic explanation.
Comprehensiveness of Theory	Very comprehensive.	Fairly comprehensive.

and Eleanor Roosevelt's family relationships were not ideal. Much of the so-called support is too subjective, and little empirical research has been conducted on humanistic personality theory (Ewen, 1993).

3. *Humanistic theory is too selfish.* Altruism is not included in Maslow's hierarchy, and it is not central in many discussions of self-actualization. The theories emphasize personal goals, often ignoring our responsibilities toward others (Wallach & Wallach, 1983, 1990). Our globe is plagued with hundreds of problems. Should issues such as homelessness, social justice, and world peace be placed on the back burner while we all concentrate on self-actualization?

4. *It is too optimistic.* If you glance at today's newspaper, you will probably find little evidence that people are inherently good, striving toward self-actualization. Reported incidents of suicide, murder, battering, child abuse, and rape have all increased in recent decades, suggesting that the humanistic theory of personality is not realistic.

Despite these criticisms, humanistic psychology must be praised for its substantial strengths:

1. *Humanistic theory emphasizes the present and future.* The psychodynamic perspective makes us "captives of the past" (Phares, 1988, p. 217). In contrast, the humanistic perspective focuses on the present and the future. As we'll see in Chapter 15, these differing outlooks have implications for therapy. Psychodynamic therapists encourage clients to develop insight about earlier life events. In contrast, humanistic therapists encourage clients to change the way they live their lives in the future.

2. *It describes individual differences in perspective.* The humanistic approach deserves credit for pointing out that we each have different interpretations of reality. This point emphasizes human uniqueness and helps us understand how two individuals may have completely different viewpoints about the same issue.

3. *Humanistic theory provides an integrated view of humans.* As you'll soon see, trait theory and the social cognitive approach each offer glimpses of some component parts of personality. In contrast, humanistic theory emphasizes that each of us is a whole person, rather than a collection of isolated characteristics.

SECTION SUMMARY: *THE HUMANISTIC APPROACH*

1. The humanistic approach emphasizes the potential for personal growth.

2. Carl Rogers's person-centered approach points out that each of us perceives a different reality and that we strive toward self-actualization; everyone should receive unconditional positive regard.

3. Abraham Maslow's hierarchy proposes that our needs must be fulfilled in a specified order, from physiological, safety, and love to the higher needs of esteem and self-actualization; Maslow also specified a list of characteristics descriptive of self-actualized people.

4. The humanistic approach can be criticized for relying on subjective experience, as well as the inadequacy of the research, its emphasis on selfishness, and its excessive optimism. Its strengths include its focus on the present and future—rather than the past, its emphasis on different realities, and its integrated view of humans.

THE TRAIT APPROACH

Of the four personality approaches described in this chapter, the trait approach most strongly emphasizes our theme of individual differences. As we discussed in the introduction to this chapter, the trait approach proposes that personality is a combination of specific stable, internal personality characteristics called traits. Thus, a **trait** is a consistent tendency to have certain kinds of beliefs, desires, and behaviors (Wakefield, 1989).

Trait theorists often examine whether a trait remains stable across time. For example, if a person is outgoing at age 5, will he or she also be outgoing at age 55? You may recognize this issue as the stability-change question, which we examined in Chapters 10 and 11. Trait theorists also examine whether a trait remains stable across situations. For example, if a person is outgoing at work, will he or she also be outgoing in social situations?

In this section, we'll first examine the theory of Gordon Allport, a psychologist who was prominent in developing the trait approach. Then we'll discuss the influential five-factor model of personality, followed by the controversial person-situation debate. We'll also consider some of the biological research on personality, as well as the MMPI, the major current test of personality. We'll conclude this section by evaluating the trait approach.

Allport's Trait Theory

Gordon Allport (1897–1967) began his undergraduate years at Harvard University with C's and D's in his courses. It's hard to imagine how someone who began so unpromisingly and ended so prominently could have formulated a theory that focused on stability, rather than change. A lucky meeting with Sigmund Freud helps to explain the transformation. After arriving at Freud's office, Allport began the conversation by mentioning a 4-year-old boy he had met on the train who seemed to have been extremely concerned about getting dirty. At the end of the story, Freud gently asked Allport, "And was that little boy you?" (Allport, 1967, p. 8). At that point, Allport realized that the psychodynamic approach overemphasized hidden symbols and motivations. He resolved to focus, instead, on conscious motives and on personal traits.

Eventually, Allport (1937, 1961) decided to bring order to the study of personality by proposing three levels of traits:

1. A **cardinal trait** is one that dominates and shapes a person's behavior. For my daughter Beth, for example, a focused interest in infants and children shaped her life. At the age of 21 months, she showered affection and tiny gifts on her newborn sister. She studied early childhood education in college and started a Head-Start type program for preschoolers in Nicaragua. She's now teaching kindergarten in the Boston public schools. Perhaps you know someone who is

For this young woman, an intense interest in infants and children constitutes a cardinal trait.

obsessed with becoming wealthy, or another person whose life focus is religion. Allport proposed, however, that these cardinal traits are rare. Most of us lack a single overarching theme in our lives.

2. A **central trait** is a general characteristic, found to some degree in every person, that shapes much of our behavior. Some central traits could be honesty, cheerfulness, and shyness.

3. A **secondary trait** is a characteristic seen only in certain situations. These must be included to provide a complete picture of human complexity. Some typical secondary traits might be "uncomfortable in large crowds" and "likes to drive sports cars."

Allport argued that a person's unique pattern of traits determined his or her behavior. No two people are completely identical; as a result, no two people respond completely identically to the same environmental situation. As Allport said: "The same fire that melts the butter hardens the egg" (Allport, 1937, p. 102).

The Five-Factor Model

How many basic trait dimensions do we need to capture all the rich complexity of our personalities? Some researchers suggest as few as 2, whereas others propose as many as 16 basic traits (Mischel, 1993). The most widely accepted solution to the search for trait clusters is called the five-factor model (McCrae & Costa, 1997; L. R. Goldberg, 1993; Halverson et al., 1994). The **five-factor model,** also called the **Big Five traits,** proposes that the most important clusters of traits include extraversion, agreeableness, conscientiousness, emotional stability, and openness to experience.

Numerous studies have tested the five-factor model. For example, Havill and her coauthors (1994) discovered that U.S. mothers described their children using terms from the five clusters. In other words, the model seems appropriate for laypeople, as well as professional psychologists. Researchers have also found evidence of this five-factor model in cross-cultural studies with people in Canada, Finland, Poland, and Germany (Paunonen et al., 1992), and in Portugal, Israel, China, Korea, and Japan (Costa & McCrae, 1992a; McCrae & Costa, 1997). Therefore, the model is not limited to North American populations or to languages resembling English.

Costa and McCrae (1992b, 1995) have also developed a self-report test, called the NEO Personality Inventory, which is based on the five-factor model. Demonstration 13.4 is an informal version of this test. The reliability and validity measures on the NEO Personality Inventory are reasonably high (Goldsmith et al., 1994; McCrae & John, 1992).

As you can imagine, not all psychologists agree with the five-factor model (e.g., Block, 1995). In fairness, however, the model never claimed that these five dimensions capture all aspects of personality.

The Person-Situation Debate

A major ongoing controversy in studies examining the trait approach is called the person-situation debate. Like many other controversies in psychology, the **person-situation debate** features two extreme positions:

1. *Person:* Each person possesses stable, internal traits that cause him or her to act consistently in a variety of situations.

2. *Situation:* Each person does not possess stable internal traits. Instead, his or her behavior depends on the specific characteristics of each situation.

Psychologists who support trait theory typically favor the "person" position. In contrast, behaviorists in the tradition of B. F. Skinner believe that environmental

DEMONSTRATION 13.4 The Five-Factor Model

This demonstration allows you to assess yourself informally on each of the Big Five traits. Use the basic 7-point rating scale shown below, each time supplying a number in the blank space to indicate where you belong on a given scale (e.g., sociable-retiring). After you have rated yourself on the three scales that comprise each dimension, calculate an average (e.g., for extraversion). Which end of each dimension seems most characteristic of your personality? Please keep in mind, however, that any informal demonstration such as this is not intended to provide an accurate assessment.

1	2	3	4	5	6	7

1. Extraversion   (Average rating =   )

_____ Sociable   Retiring
_____ Enthusiastic   Unenthusiastic
_____ Affectionate   Reserved

2. Agreeableness   (Average rating =   )

_____ Sympathetic   Unsympathetic
_____ Trusting   Suspicious
_____ Helpful   Uncooperative

3. Conscientiousness   (Average rating =   )

_____ Well organized   Disorganized
_____ Careful   Careless
_____ Responsible   Irresponsible

4. Emotional Stability   (Average rating =   )

_____ Calm   Worrying
_____ Secure   Insecure
_____ Self-satisfied   Self-pitying

5. Openness to Experience   (Average rating =   )

_____ Imaginative   Down-to-earth
_____ Preference for variety   Preference for routine
_____ Independent   Conformity

Note: The "emotional stability" scale is sometimes called the "neuroticism" (instability) scale.
Source: Based on McCrae & Costa, 1986; McCrae & John, 1992.

---

stimuli are far more important, and thus they tend to agree with the "situation" position. To predict someone's response, they say, all we need to do is specify the external stimuli in a situation; we don't need to discuss any internal characteristics. Psychologists who favor the situation position might even suggest that we eliminate the personality chapter of introductory textbooks: Personality doesn't exist, and only situations count. Let's examine this controversy.

Mischel's Position   For many decades, personality psychologists had supported the person position, especially because it matches our common sense. Of course people are consistent! Julie is consistently unconcerned about other people, whereas Pete is always compassionate. A strong challenge to this position was presented by Walter Mischel (pronounced "Mih-*shell*"), who came from a behaviorist tradition.

Mischel (1968) examined dozens of earlier studies. He discovered that various behaviors that supposedly reflect the same internal trait are only weakly correlated with each other. For example, students' tendency to arrive on time for one event is correlated only +.19 with their tendency to arrive on time for another event (Dudycha, 1936). This very weak correlation does not support the person position.

But why do we persist in believing that personality characteristics are consistent across situations? Mischel (1968) argued that our perception is biased. For example, we usually see a person in only a limited set of situations. Think of someone

Cross-situational consistency is higher in an unconstrained situation like a picnic, where the situation has less formal structure and individual differences can reveal themselves.

from your high school whom you believe had a consistently friendly personality. You never saw this person on a college interview—where he or she may have acted timid and withdrawn. Mischel (1979) argued that each of us does show some slight personality consistency from one situation to another, but the people who know us tend to exaggerate that consistency.

Factors Related to Consistency   One intriguing finding is that people show more consistency if we measure their average behavior across several events, rather than just one single event (Epstein, 1983; Epstein & O'Brien, 1985; Rogers, 1995). This makes sense. You might be late to class one day, but early four other days. Your *average* punctuality for classes is probably correlated with your *average* punctuality for other events.

Furthermore, traits are more easily expressed in some situations than others (Buss, 1989; Kenrick & Funder, 1988; Wiggins & Pincus, 1992). For instance, some situations constrain our behavior, so the traits cannot be easily expressed. At a funeral, the friendly people will not act much different from the unfriendly people. However, at a picnic, individual differences will be strong. Cross-situational consistency will be higher if the situation is familiar, if people receive no instructions about how they should act, and if they are observed for a long time, rather than a brief period.

Conclusions About the Person-Situation Debate   Behavior is probably not as consistent across situations as our intuitions suggest; systematic biases encourage us to believe in traits too strongly. However, some consistency really does exist (Funder, 1993; 1995). Furthermore, the consistency can be reasonably high—in some situations, for some people, some traits, and some methods of measuring those traits. Obviously, our theme of complexity fits the data on the person-situation debate!

Walter Mischel began the debate in 1968, and about 30 years later, he suggested a new way to view the debate. Specifically, Mischel and his coauthor Yuichi Shoda (1995) reexamined some data from several studies and noticed that people really are fairly consistent in their personality if we carefully examine the external features of the situations they encounter.

For example, Mischel and Shoda examined the personality trait of "verbal aggression" in children. One child seemed to be fairly low in verbal aggression on some occasions, for example, but very high on this same trait on other occasions. On the surface, the child's personality appears to be inconsistent. When Mischel and Shoda reexamined the data, however, they found that this child was consistently low in aggression when a peer approached, but consistently very high in aggression when an

According to Mischel and Shoda (1995), we need to know the specific details of the situation before we can find personality consistency. For example, this child shows little verbal aggression when another child approaches, but he might be consistently aggressive when an adult issues a warning to him.

adult gave a warning. Other children showed different profiles. Most important, if we can specify the external features of the situation (e.g., "peer approaching" or "adult warning"), then people *can* show remarkable consistency in their personalities.

In Chapter 10, we saw that we could not answer which factor is more important in several debates. For example, both nature and nurture are important—not just one of them. Similarly, we cannot answer which factor is a better predictor of behavior—person or situation. Again, both are important. To predict how a person will behave, we need some measure of his or her internal traits, but we must also understand the specific characteristics of the external situation.

Critical Thinking Exercise 13.4

Write down your answers to the following questions about the five-factor model and about the person-situation debate.

a. Compare the kind of self-report test you took in Demonstration 13.4 (based on the five-factor model) with the Rorschach Test (the projective test on which Demonstration 13.2 is based). What are the advantages of each kind of test?

b. In Chapter 16, we will discuss the primacy effect, which proposes that we tend to maintain our first impression of someone even if he or she acts very differently on later occasions. Why would the primacy effect encourage us to believe that personality characteristics are more consistent than they really are?

The Biological Basis of Individual Differences

The trait theory argues that we can understand personality by examining the characteristics that people bring to the situation. For many psychologists, the next logical step is to examine the biological bases of those characteristics (Zuckerman, 1994a). The most active biological research focuses on the genetic basis of personality. You may recall that Chapter 3 discussed how genetic researchers have conducted twin studies on personality, as well as in other areas such as cognitive abilities and psychological disorders.

The popular press has widely publicized the research on identical twins who have been reared apart (e.g., Begley, 1996; C. Bouchard et al., 1990; Lykken et al., 1992). After all, it's fascinating to read about a pair of twins reared in separate homes who behave identically at the beach; both enter the water backwards and avoid water levels above their knees. Some critics suggest that the high degree of similarities between the twin pairs is partly due to a nonrandom sample (T. Adler, 1991b). Furthermore, we must remember from the discussion of decision making in Chapter 8 that many unusual-looking outcomes can occur by chance alone.

The research on twins reared together and apart typically reports a measure called **heritability,** which is an estimate of how much of the variation in a characteristic can be traced to differences in heredity, as opposed to differences in environment. For example, research on each of the personality characteristics in the five-factor model shows that the heritability is typically in the range of 25% to 55% (Hartup & van Lieshout, 1995; Viken et al., 1994; Zuckerman, 1995).

Psychologists have begun to examine the biological basis of some characteristics we have discussed in earlier chapters. For example, Chapter 12 examined **subjective well-being,** which is a person's evaluation of his or her life satisfaction. Research on the genetic basis of subjective well-being suggests that heritability is about 50% (Lykken & Tellegen, 1996). Keep in mind, however, that environmental factors are still responsible for about half of the variation in these characteristics. In other words, people whose parents are dissatisfied with their lives are not doomed to become miserable themselves. Instead, they can seek a more positive environment.

Consider a trait called sensation seeking. People who are high in **sensation seeking** actively look for adventure, new experiences, and risky situations (Zuckerman, 1993, 1994b). In general, the heritability for sensation seeking is estimated to be 58%, which is relatively high for personality traits. The research comparing high sensation seekers with low sensation seekers shows that the two groups differ in a variety of brain chemicals, including neurotransmitters, endorphins, and hormones (Zuckerman, 1994b, 1995). Recent studies have also focused on DNA analysis, identifying a genetic basis for the novelty-seeking component of sensation seeking (Benjamin et al., 1996; Ebstein et al., 1996). This is the first step toward understanding the specific genetic maps of personality.

In summary, then, biological factors seem to account for a substantial portion of individual differences in personality traits. Keep in mind, however, that other variables—primarily environmental factors—account for at least half of these individual differences.

The Minnesota Multiphasic Personality Inventory

The most widely used personality test in psychology is the **Minnesota Multiphasic Personality Inventory (MMPI),** an objective personality test that asks a large number of true-false questions in order to assess personality traits. The MMPI has also been extremely popular in research, with more than 4,000 reports on this instrument published between 1974 and 1994 (Butcher & Rouse, 1996).

To design the MMPI, Starke Hathaway and J. C. McKinley administered a wide range of questions to more than 800 psychiatric patients, who represented the major clinical subgroups such as depression and schizophrenia. They also administered the questions to more than 1,500 unhospitalized people, such as students and hospital visitors.

An item was selected for a particular scale of the MMPI only if the two groups—the group with psychological disorders and the normal group—showed significantly different response patterns. For example, people with a particular psychological disorder were much more likely than people in the control group to say "true" to the item "Someone has been trying to poison me." In each case, the *content* of the item is irrelevant; the critical point is whether the item discriminates between the normal group and the group with a psychological disorder.

In 1989, a revised form of the MMPI was published (Butcher et al., 1989). This new MMPI-2 is based on a larger, more ethnically diverse sample of test takers. The revised version also eliminated gender-biased language, outdated items, and items that assumed the test taker was Christian (Graham, 1990; Hood & Johnson, 1991).

The items on the new MMPI-2 are grouped into 15 clinical scales and 5 validity scales, making a total of 567 questions. Table 13.5 shows some examples of the scales, the characteristics they are designed to assess, and some hypothetical test items. Notice, for example, that the "lie scale" helps assess one aspect of validity. Anyone who says "yes" to the item "I smile at everyone I meet" cannot be telling the truth!

The reliability of the MMPI-2 is considered to be reasonably high for a personality test. The test-retest reliability measures generally range between .75 and .85 (Graham, 1990; Kaplan & Saccuzzo, 1993). Numerous studies have been conducted to establish the validity of the MMPI-2. For example, when married couples took the MMPI-2, each person's answers were highly correlated with his or her spouse's evaluation of the person on these same items (Butcher et al., 1990).

A reasonable amount of research on the MMPI has been conducted with Hispanic and Black individuals, but Asians and Native Americans have not been extensively studied (Greene, 1987; Valásquez & Callahan, 1992). Psychologists are encouraging researchers to conduct additional studies, keeping in mind the variety of different cultures within each ethnic group (Dana, 1988; LaFromboise et al., 1997; Puente, 1990).

Recent research on the biological approach to personality suggests that about half of the variation in personality characteristics, such as subjective well-being, can be traced to differences in heredity. In this case, heredity and environment are equally responsible for explaining why these family members would be similar in their reported life satisfaction.

TABLE 13.5 Some Examples of Scales From the Minnesota Multiphasic Personality Inventory

NAME OF SCALE	KIND OF SCALE	DESCRIPTION	HYPOTHETICAL TEST ITEM (answer indicating the disorder is in parentheses)
Depression Scale	Clinical	Derived from patients who show extreme pessimism and feelings of hopelessness.	"I usually feel that life is interesting and worthwhile." *(False)*
Psychopathic Deviate Scale	Clinical	Derived from patients who show extreme disregard for social customs and who show aggressiveness.	"My activities and interests are often criticized by others." *(True)*
Paranoia Scale	Clinical	Derived from patients who show abnormal suspiciousness or delusions.	"There are evil people trying to influence my mind." *(True)*
Lie Scale	Validity	Measures overly good self-image.	"I smile at everyone I meet." *(True)*

Source: Minnesota Multiphasic Personality Inventory-2. Copyright © by the Regents of the University of Minnesota 1942, 1943, (renewed 1970), 1989. Reproduced by permission of the publisher.

A major advantage of the MMPI-2 and other self-report tests is that they can be easily administered, even in large groups. The test can be computer scored; it does not require a trained examiner (Hood & Johnson, 1991). A disadvantage is the length of the test. After answering the first 500 questions on the MMPI, would you really answer the remaining 67 questions honestly and carefully? As you will see in the next chapter, the MMPI is considered to be a valuable tool when clinical psychologists need to diagnose a psychological disorder.

Evaluation of the Trait Approach

Table 13.6 summarizes four important characteristics of the trait approach, contrasting it with the other two approaches discussed so far. As you can see, the trait approach is very different from the psychodynamic approach. Although it is similar to the humanistic approach in the way the data are gathered, the two approaches differ considerably on the other three characteristics. The trait approach can be criticized for several reasons:

TABLE 13.6 A Comparison of the Trait Approach With the Psychodynamic and Humanistic Approaches

	PSYCHODYNAMIC APPROACH	HUMANISTIC APPROACH	TRAIT APPROACH
Source of Data	Obtained from expert analyst from people in therapy.	Obtained from self-reports from the general population and people in therapy.	Obtained from observation of behavior and questionnaire responses from the general population as well as people in therapy.
Cause of Behavior	Internal conflict, unconscious forces, childhood experiences.	Self-concepts, self-actualizing tendencies.	Stable, internal characteristics; some emphasize genetic basis
Explanation for Motivation	Pessimistic explanation.	Optimistic explanation.	Neutral explanation.
Comprehensiveness of Theory	Very comprehensive.	Fairly comprehensive.	Not very comprehensive.

1. *It is not an integrated theory.* In fact, the trait approach is really a research technique, rather than a theory. The approach produces a wealth of information about people's characteristics, but no comprehensive view of humanity. It does not examine unconscious forces, and it generally does not attempt to explain *why* people have certain traits to varying degrees. (The prominent exception here is the new biologically based research, which does attempt to uncover causality.)

2. *The trait approach underestimates the role of situations.* Taken to its extreme, trait theory predicts that people act consistently, even in different situations. As we saw in the research, however, people are not very predictable. A person may be aggressive in one circumstance and unaggressive in another. People are predictable only in certain circumstances and only when we know the details about the situation.

We cannot be too critical, however, because the trait approach never aspired to be comprehensive and integrated. It has been a valuable tool, with strengths including the following:

1. *The theory has generated information about traits.* A major emphasis of this approach is to look for trait consistency, independent of the situation. To its credit, the trait approach provides abundant information about internal characteristics, such as the stability of traits.

2. *The trait approach has helped develop personality measurement.* Trait theorists have clearly contributed to the measurement of personality. In this section, we emphasized the NEO Personality Inventory and the MMPI. In addition, personality researchers have developed hundreds of other tests to assess more specific personality traits.

SECTION SUMMARY: *THE TRAIT APPROACH*

1. Allport proposed three levels of personality traits: cardinal, central, and secondary; he suggested that the combination of these traits determines a person's behavior.

2. The five-factor model is the most widely accepted categorization of trait dimensions; these traits are extraversion, agreeableness, conscientiousness, emotional stability, and openness to experience.

3. The resolution to the person-situation debate seems to be that people have traits that are somewhat consistent across situations, though our cognitive biases enhance this apparent consistency.

4. Cross-situational consistency is higher in unconstrained situations, when instructions have not been given, and when the observation period is long; consistency is also higher for some people, some traits,

and some methods. Finally, Mischel and Shoda (1995) have suggested that personality is likely to be consistent once we know the specific psychological features of the situation.

5. Research suggests that heritability is reasonably high for personality characteristics in the five-factor model, for subjective well-being, and for sensation seeking; research on brain chemicals and genetics has been especially active for the personality trait of sensation seeking.

6. The trait approach is not an integrated theory—though it never aspired to be one—and the extreme form of the trait approach underestimates the importance of situations; however, it has inspired much research about traits and many useful personality tests, such as the NEO Personality Inventory and the MMPI.

THE SOCIAL COGNITIVE APPROACH

We began this chapter by exploring the psychodynamic approach, which argues that people are ruled by their sexual organs and by forces of unconscious conflict. Then we considered the humanistic approach, which proposes that people are ruled by more noble motives, such as the striving for self-actualization. Our third topic was the trait approach, which maintains that people are ruled by stable, internal characteristics that may have a genetic basis.

In contrast especially to the psychodynamic approach, the social cognitive approach makes humans seem much less passionate and much more levelheaded. In fact, some personality theorists have pointed out that you can read dozens of books about the social cognitive approach without ever learning that humans have genitals! The social cognitive approach focuses on the way people observe, evaluate, regulate, and think. This approach is consistent with the view of cognitive psychology we explored in the chapters on memory, thinking, and language. In Chapters 7, 8, and 9, we saw that humans actively process information—for example, when you read this paragraph in your textbook. The social cognitive approach to personality also emphasizes that humans actively process information about their own behavior, their social world, and their personal characteristics (Hattie, 1992; Magnusson & Törestad, 1993).

We'll begin by investigating the origins of this social cognitive approach, and then we'll review the basic concepts of observational learning. Our next topic is reciprocal influences—the concept that environmental factors, personal factors, and behaviors all interact to form an individual's personality. Next we'll consider self-efficacy, or people's sense that they are competent and effective. Then the "In Depth" feature focuses on cross-cultural views on the self. We'll conclude with an evaluation of the social cognitive approach.

Origins of the Social Cognitive Approach

The social cognitive approach traces its origins to behaviorism. As we discussed in Chapter 1, behaviorism emphasizes observable behavior, instead of unobservable mental processes. As we saw in Chapter 6, operant conditioning explains how reinforcement and punishment influence behavior. For example, you do your physics homework, and you are reinforced by good grades on exams, so you continue to do homework in the future.

In B. F. Skinner's behaviorist theory, we do not need to talk about internal characteristics when we discuss people's personal traits. For instance, we can explain the behavior of a friendly person in terms of past and present reinforcement and punishment—that is, external factors—and genetic factors. Skinner (1974) argued that we achieve nothing by discussing personality characteristics such as an "extraversion trait."

Albert Bandura is one of the major theorists who found Skinner's approach inadequate (Grusec, 1992). Bandura (1986) argues that people learn much more by observational learning than by operant conditioning. Bandura also emphasizes that people think about and interpret events. Unlike Skinner, Bandura argues that the human mind makes an important contribution to personality. Bandura (1986) called his approach social cognitive theory, because it emphasizes the contribution of social factors (e.g., observational learning) and thought (e.g., beliefs about competence) in explaining personality and behavior.

Observational Learning

Observational learning, a major component in the social cognitive approach, was discussed in Chapter 6, together with classical conditioning and operant conditioning. In **observational learning,** we learn new behaviors by watching and imitating the behavior of others (Bandura, 1986, 1989). However, other complex cognitive factors also play crucial rules in the development of personality.

Reciprocal Influences

My daughter Sally is outgoing and adventurous. At age 16, she went by herself to Mexico to perfect her Spanish, and she lived with a Mexican family. Sally made

Skinner's behaviorist approach argues that we can understand this politician's outgoing behavior by identifying genetic and environmental factors, without discussing internal characteristics.

dozens of friends, including members of a local band. On her last evening there, her Mexican family and friends arranged a surprise farewell party, and the band played backup while she sang solo on her favorite Latin American song, "Doce Rosas." I pictured myself at 16 and marvel at the difference in our personalities. I was not so outgoing, and I could never have gone alone to a foreign country. Also, the option of singing solo in Spanish would have been only slightly less horrifying than walking barefoot on hot coals.

Bandura (1986) has proposed an explanation for the way initial individual differences become even stronger through reciprocal influences. According to the principle of **reciprocal influences,** three factors—personal/cognitive, behavior, and environmental—all influence one another (Figure 13.4). As a consequence, initial tendencies can become even stronger.

As an example of reciprocal influences, consider a young woman who is outgoing and friendly and expects that she will be successful in interpersonal interactions (personal/cognitive). She will therefore be likely to introduce herself to strangers and react positively to them (behavior). Furthermore, someone who is outgoing and friendly is likely to seek out social situations, rather than sitting in her room (environment). The environment, in turn, promotes even more friendly behavior, more self-confidence, and an even greater expectation for success in interpersonal interactions. In contrast, a shy, withdrawn person will dread interpersonal interactions, avoid strangers, and stay away from social situations. This behavior and lack of exposure to new environments will encourage the person to become even more withdrawn and to expect future interactions to be unsuccessful.

Skinner's theory proposes that the environment shapes human behavior. In contrast, Bandura argues that the process is more complex; behavior can be a *cause,* as well as an *effect* (Cloninger, 1996). In fact, personality, behavior, and environment shape one another in a reciprocal fashion. This more complex approach is necessary to explain the impressive complexity of humans.

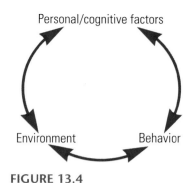

FIGURE 13.4

The principle of reciprocal influences.

Self-Efficacy

Let's examine the personal/cognitive part of Bandura's theory, because this component is most central to personality. Bandura (1986, 1997) believes that the most important personal/cognitive factor is self-efficacy. **Self-efficacy** is a person's belief in his or her ability to organize and perform the actions required to reach desired goals (Bandura, 1997). According to Bandura (1992b), your thoughts and expectations about success are more important than your actual behavior. For example, if you are trying to decide whether to try a new dance step in public, the relevant factor is whether you *think* you are a good dancer, not whether you *are* a good dancer!

Research confirms that people with a strong sense of self-efficacy do indeed manage their lives more successfully. In general, these people tend to be more persistent in school, intensifying their efforts when a task is difficult. They also have higher aspirations, as well as more flexible problem-solving strategies. They also have better metacognitive skills; they think about their thinking processes and regulate how they approach tasks (Bandura, 1997; Zimmerman, 1995). People who are confident about their abilities typically approach new challenges with optimism, and they set high goals for themselves (Bandura & Jourden, 1991). In contrast, people with low self-efficacy may set inappropriate goals, often leading to depression (Bandura, 1997).

When people with high self-efficacy are initially unsuccessful, they try a new approach and work harder. Bandura (1997) points out that the American poet and novelist Gertrude Stein submitted poems to a variety of editors for about 20 years before one was eventually accepted. How could reinforcement theory explain that persistence? Also, Vincent van Gogh sold only one painting during his lifetime. Still, both of these individuals persisted. In contrast, a person with low self-efficacy would give up when faced with such overwhelming rejection.

Bandura (1986, 1997) points out that self-efficacy is possible because humans can analyze their varied experiences and think about their own thought processes. In

Vincent van Gogh, the nineteenth century Dutch painter, is now well known for his colorful landscapes. However, he sold only one painting during his lifetime—an example of persistence arising from a sense of self-efficacy.

earlier chapters, we discussed metacognition (thinking about thinking). You can also think about your many other psychological attributes. Consider how often you have evaluated attributes such as your helpfulness, athletic ability, and friendliness. In fact, when you were reading the description of self-efficacy, you probably evaluated your own self-efficacy. We humans evaluate our skills and then use that information to regulate our future behavior (Bandura, 1991). The thoughts we have about ourselves are the focus of the "In Depth" feature that follows—an examination of our views of the self.

Cross-Cultural Views of the Self

In the past, virtually all of the theories and data in psychology have come from Western, northern-hemisphere populations, such as the United States, Canada, and Europe. However, about 70% of the people in the world live in other regions—Asia, Latin America, and Africa (Kitayama & Markus, 1995; Triandis, 1996). For many years, psychologists assumed that the basic principles of psychology—gathered on European American samples—could be accurately applied to other cultural groups. Now researchers have begun to study people living in other cultures. They sometimes conclude that these "basic principles" cannot be very basic if they do not apply to other cultures.

In Chapters 11 and 12, we introduced the concepts of individualistic and collectivist cultures. Let's review these terms, examining them in more depth, and then we'll see how people from these two kinds of cultural approaches have different views of personality and the self. First, however, try Demonstration 13.5, which assesses individualistic and collectivist values. See whether your pattern of answers is consistent with the culture to which you belong, keeping in mind that individual differences can be substantial for people from either of these two cultural backgrounds (Markus et al., 1996).

Individualistic Versus Collectivist Cultures

North American cultures and many Western European cultures emphasize an individualistic viewpoint. These **individualistic cultures** (also called **independent cultures**) maintain that you must assert yourself and appreciate how you are different from other people. In contrast, people in Asia, Africa, Latin America, and many southern European cultures—such as Italy and Greece—have a different perspective. These **collectivist cultures** (also called **interdependent cultures**) maintain that you must fit in with other people and live in interdependent relationships with them.

DEMONSTRATION 13.5 Assessing Values Related to Individualism and Collectivism

For each of the following items, write *true* if you think the statement is correct and *false* if not. Check Page 448 at the end of the chapter to see how to score your answers.

_____ 1. Without competition, it is not possible to have a good society.

_____ 2. I enjoy being unique and different from others.

_____ 3. I would do what would please my family, even if I detested that activity.

_____ 4. When another person does better than I do, I get tense and aroused.

_____ 5. It is important to me to maintain harmony within my group.

_____ 6. I rely on myself most of the time; I rarely rely on others.

_____ 7. I like sharing little things with my neighbors.

_____ 8. It is important to me that I respect the decisions made by my groups.

_____ 9. It is important that I do my job better than others.

_____ 10. I often do "my own thing."

_____ 11. I usually sacrifice my self-interest for the benefit of my group.

_____ 12. It is important to consult close friends and get their ideas before making a decision.

Source: Based on Singelis et al., 1995.

In Chapter 11, we saw that people in individualistic cultures base their identity on the characteristics that make them unique. In contrast, people in collectivist cultures base their identity on their interconnectedness with others. Later, in Chapter 12, we saw that people in individualistic cultures base their subjective well-being on their own personal happiness. In contrast, people in collectivist cultures base their subjective well-being on their sense of harmony with other people.

People in the two kinds of cultures also seem to view the self differently. For example, Hazel Markus and her colleagues (1996) discuss a study in which interviewers asked Japanese respondents, "How would you describe yourself to yourself?" The respondents struggled with this question, and their answers seemed vague and indirect. In contrast, U.S. respondents answered the same question easily and directly. For example, one American responded, "How long an answer would you like? I could talk all day about myself, you know, it's my favorite topic" (p. 885). Markus and her coauthors comment that this individualistic response would be considered extremely rude and inappropriate in Japanese culture. Let's look more closely at two components of cross-cultural views of personality: self-actualization and self-evaluation.

People in collectivist cultures are more likely than people in individualistic cultures to believe that a person should live in interdependent relationships with other people.

Self-Actualization in Individualistic and Collectivist Cultures

In the personality theories we have explored so far, the isolated individual is most important. Consider humanistic psychology, for example. Self-actualization is a central concept in Carl Rogers's theory, and it is the highest motivational level in Abraham Maslow's approach. Through self-actualization, a person achieves his or her individual potential; no larger group needs to be considered.

Is self-actualization equally important in other cultures? Harry Triandis and his colleagues (1990) showed that this characteristic may not always be desirable. These researchers conducted their research in both the United States and Hong Kong. In each location, they studied 40 **triads,** or groups of three individuals. Each triad was given one word at a time, and the three individuals were instructed to discuss this word and decide whether this characteristic was either important or unimportant in their culture. If 85% of the triads in one culture agreed—within one minute—that the characteristic was indeed important, then this characteristic was considered to be valuable in that culture. For example, all 40 of the Hong Kong triads decided within an average of three seconds that persistence is indeed important in their culture. According to the operational definition, therefore, persistence qualifies as a valuable characteristic. However, in the United States, persistence did not meet the criterion. How did self-actualization fare? In the United States, 39 of the 40 triads decided with an average of four seconds that self-actualization is important in the culture. In contrast, self-actualization did not meet the criterion in Hong Kong. These data suggest that the notion of self-actualization may be a highly valued personality characteristic in U.S. culture, but this humanistic concept would not rate at the top of a hierarchy in Hong Kong. Perhaps future personality theorists can determine whether this difference is maintained in other individualistic and collectivist societies. However, this "basic" principle of Maslow's hierarchy may not be equally useful in all cultures.

The Self-Serving Bias in Individualistic and Collectivist Cultures

We have pointed out that people in individualistic cultures focus on the self and on being superior to others in one's group. In contrast, people in collectivist cultures are encouraged to fit in, *not* to stand out. The research has consistently shown that people in North America tend to be self-serving when they evaluate themselves. That is, they give themselves high ratings on a variety of scales (e.g., Markus & Kitayama, 1991b; Matlin & Stang, 1978). Will people in collectivist cultures do the same, or will they avoid this tendency in order to fit in and maintain a sense of harmony with their group?

Hazel Markus and Shinobu Kitayama (1991b) compared U.S. college students studying in the United States and Japanese college students studying in Japan. They asked a series of questions based on a standard format: "What proportion of students have higher intellectual ability than yourself?" The questionnaire asked questions about abilities (intellectual ability, memory, and athletic ability), independence

TABLE 13.7   Judgments About the Percentage of People Who Are Superior to the Self in Each Specified Domain (averaged across all participants in each group)[*]

Domain	UNITED STATES		JAPAN	
	Men	Women	Men	Women
Abilities	36%	47%	49%	58%
Independence	33%	34%	46%	54%
Interdependence	30%	26%	40%	49%

Source: Markus & Kitayama (1991b).
[*]High numbers indicate modesty, and low numbers indicate a self-serving bias.

(IN DEPTH continued)
(independent; hold more strongly to their own view), and interdependence (more sympathetic; more warmhearted).

Table 13.7 shows the results for the men and women in the two cultures. The table lists the percentage of people whom the participant judged to be superior to himself or herself in each of the three domains. (A student who believes that he or she is just average on an attribute would therefore supply a rating of 50%.) Notice that the U.S. men are self-serving on all three characteristics. For example, they estimate that only 36% of the students on their campus have greater abilities than themselves. They have a self-serving bias because they believe relatively few students are better than themselves on this attribute. Notice that the U.S. women are self-serving with respect to both independence and interdependence—but not abilities. The Japanese men are relatively modest about their attributes, with just a hint of a self-serving bias for interdependence. Finally, the Japanese women show no evidence of a self-serving bias; in fact, they may even be *too* modest. They do not claim to have unique skills that make them stand out from their peer group.

Earlier in the chapter, we saw that the five-factor model applies reasonably well when people in other cultures rate their personality traits. However, we have seen in this "In Depth" feature that individualistic and collectivist cultures have different perspectives on the self. People in collectivist societies are reluctant to talk about themselves, they do not value self-actualization, and they do not tend to overrate their personal characteristics.

Critical Thinking Exercise 13.5

Write down your answers to the following questions about cross-cultural research on personality.

a. Analyze the questions in Demonstration 13.5 with respect to social desirability. Which responses would a person from an individualistic society provide in order to look good? How about a person from a collectivist society? Would the social desirability factor tend to increase or decrease the size of the difference between the two cultural groups?

b. In the study by Triandis and his colleagues (1990), the U.S. triads agreed, within the one-minute time limit, that self-actualization is a valuable characteristic; the Hong Kong students did not meet this criterion. Why would that finding be difficult to interpret if we didn't also learn that the Hong Kong students agreed, within the same time limit, that persistence is a valuable characteristic, but the U.S. students did not meet this criterion?

TABLE 13.8 **Contrasting the Four Approaches to Personality**

	PSYCHODYNAMIC APPROACH	HUMANISTIC APPROACH	TRAIT APPROACH	SOCIAL COGNITIVE APPROACH
Source of Data	Obtained from expert analyst from people in therapy.	Obtained from self-reports from the general population and people in therapy.	Obtained from observation of behavior and questionnaire responses from the general population as well as people in therapy.	Obtained from experiments, observation of behavior, and questionnaire responses from the general population.
Cause of Behavior	Internal conflict, unconscious forces, childhood experiences.	Self-concepts, self-actualizing tendencies.	Stable, internal characteristics; some emphasize genetic basis.	Reciprocal influence of personal/cognitive, behavior, and environment.
Explanation for Motivation	Pessimistic explanation.	Optimistic explanation.	Neutral explanation.	Neutral explanation.
Comprehensiveness of Theory	Very comprehensive.	Fairly comprehensive.	Not very comprehensive.	Not very comprehensive.

Evaluation of the Social Cognitive Approach

Table 13.8 summarizes four important characteristics of the social cognitive approach, contrasting it with the other three approaches discussed in this chapter. As you can see, it differs most from the psychodynamic approach. The social cognitive approach can be criticized for two major reasons:

1. *It is not comprehensive.* At present, the social cognitive approach is relatively narrow in scope. It does emphasize the importance of our thoughts about our own competence and how these thoughts organize our behavior. Still, the social cognitive approach underemphasizes emotions and sexual urges. Also, it has not examined in detail how personality develops from childhood to adulthood.

2. *It is not an integrated theory.* At present, the social cognitive approach consists of a collection of isolated ideas. We have observational learning, reciprocal influences, and self-efficacy from Bandura. Markus and others have examined notions of the self, and additional researchers are actively pursuing other components. However, a loose collection of ideas does not constitute a satisfying, cohesive theory.

The problems with the social cognitive approach certainly will not doom it to failure. Researchers are likely to tackle these two problems in the near future, and they may find some satisfying solutions. Furthermore, here are some of the strengths of the social cognitive approach:

1. *The theory is testable.* A major advantage of the social cognitive approach is that its proposals can be studied empirically, partly because the theories are specific, rather than general. In contrast, you'll recall that the psychodynamic approach is frequently too general to be tested.

2. *The social cognitive approach is compatible with other disciplines in psychology.* For example, this approach fits in successfully with the wealth of knowledge that psychologists have gathered on human cognitive processes. We have summarized this information in earlier chapters, when we discussed sensation and perception, learning, memory, cognition, language, and child and adult development; we'll also consider cognitive aspects of social psychology in Chapter 16. The same brain that collects information to make a decision or produce a sentence also manages to form a judgment about self-efficacy. Of the four approaches to personality considered in this chapter, the social cognitive approach is most compatible with other ongoing research on humans.

SECTION SUMMARY: *THE SOCIAL COGNITIVE APPROACH*

1. The origins of the social cognitive approach can be traced to behaviorism.

2. Observational learning explains how we acquire some personality characteristics.

3. The concept of reciprocal influences points out that personal/cognitive factors, behavior, and environment all influence one another.

4. People high in self-efficacy are persistent and have high aspirations; people low in self-efficacy may be at risk for depression.

5. The research on cross-cultural views of the self shows that people in collectivist societies—in comparison to people in individualistic societies—are reluctant to talk about themselves, they do not value self-actualization, and they do not tend to overrate their personal characteristics.

6. The social cognitive approach is neither comprehensive nor integrated; however, its strengths are that it is testable and that it is compatible with research in other psychological disciplines.

Review Questions

1. Imagine that a high school student you know has asked you to describe the chapter you have most recently read in your psychology textbook. Define the word *personality* and summarize each of the four approaches.

2. Try to reproduce the information in Table 13.8 from memory. Label the columns with the names of the four approaches (psychodynamic, humanistic, trait, and social cognitive). Label the rows with the four dimensions we considered (source of the data, cause of behavior, explanation for motivation, and outlook on humans). Then compare your table with Table 13.8.

3. Describe Freud's stages of normal human development. Now compare the following theorists with respect to their explanations about the origins of abnormal behavior: Freud, Horney, Rogers, a trait theorist who favors the biological approach, Skinner, and Bandura.

4. Imagine that you are a talk show host. The two invited guests today—miraculously—are Sigmund Freud and Carl Rogers. How might each respond to your questions: (a) Are wars inevitable? (b) Why do people sometimes perform heroic, altruistic acts? (c) What should people strive for in life?

5. What is self-actualization, in the views of Carl Rogers and Abraham Maslow? How does the research from the social cognitive perspective raise questions about this characteristic?

6. What is the person-situation debate? Think about a particularly noticeable trait of a close friend. Does this trait seem to persist across situations? Why might you tend to believe that this trait is more stable than it might really be? How would

Walter Mischel's most recent theory explain how the trait may depend upon the specific situation?

7. This chapter discussed several personality tests: the Rorschach, the TAT, the NEO Personality Inventory, and the MMPI. Which situations would be most appropriate for using each test? Where relevant, what are the advantages and disadvantages of each test?

8. Why does the cross-cultural research suggest that theorists must be careful about overgeneralizing their ideas to other cultures? We noted that part of the humanistic approach does not seem congruent with the values of collectivist cultures. How would psychodynamic theory, other aspects of humanistic theory, and social cognitive theory be likely to fare if they were tested cross-culturally?

9. How do the four approaches compare with respect to the emphasis on internal forces versus external stimuli? Also compare behaviorism on this dimension.

10. Which of the four approaches to personality do you find most appealing? If you had to design your own comprehensive theory, what features of the other three approaches would you incorporate? Can you list any aspects of personality that have not been addressed by any of these approaches?

New Terms

personality (p. 416)
psychodynamic approach (p. 416)
humanistic approach (p. 416)
trait approach (p. 416)
social cognitive approach (p. 416)
psychoanalytic approach (p. 417)
id (p. 418)
libido (p. 418)
ego (p. 418)
superego (p. 418)
conscious (p. 418)
unconscious (p. 418)
free association (p. 419)
manifest content (p. 419)
latent content (p. 419)
erogenous zones (p. 420)
fixation (p. 420)
oral stage (p. 420)
anal stage (p. 420)
phallic stage (p. 420)
Oedipus complex (p. 420)
latency stage (p. 421)
genital stage (p. 421)
defense mechanisms (p. 421)
repression (p. 422)
regression (p. 422)
reaction formation (p. 422)
displacement (p. 422)
projection (p. 422)
collective unconscious (p. 422)

object-relations approach (p. 423)
projective tests (p. 423)
Rorschach Inkblot Test (p. 424)
Thematic Apperception Test (TAT) (p. 424)
masochistic (p. 426)
self-actualization (p. 428)
conditional positive regard (p. 428)
unconditional positive regard (p. 428)
Maslow's hierarchy of needs (p. 429)
trait (p. 432)
cardinal trait (p. 432)
central trait (p. 433)
secondary trait (p. 433)
five-factor model (p. 433)
Big Five traits (p. 433)
person-situation debate (p. 433)
heritability (p. 436)
subjective well-being (p. 436)
sensation seeking (p. 437)
Minnesota Multiphasic Personality Inventory (MMPI) (p. 437)
observational learning (p. 440)
reciprocal influences (p. 441)
self-efficacy (p. 441)
individualistic cultures (p. 442)
independent cultures (p. 442)
collectivist cultures (p. 442)
interdependent cultures (p. 442)
triad (p. 443)

RECOMMENDED READINGS

Bandura, A. (1997). *Self-efficacy: The exercise of control.* New York: Freeman. Bandura's book explores self-efficacy from the social cognitive perspective and relates it to cognitive functioning, psychological and physical health, and efficacy in the political setting.

Cloninger, S. C. (1996). *Theories of personality: Understanding persons* (2nd ed.). Upper Saddle River, NJ: Prentice Hall. This mid-level textbook examines each of the major personality theories, using a clear and well-organized writing style. An interesting additional feature is that every chapter considers how that particular approach might explain the personality of two current or historical individuals (e.g., Mahatma Gandhi and Maya Angelou).

Markus, H. R., Kitayama, S., & Heiman, R. J. (1996). Culture and "basic" psychological principles. In E. T. Higgins & A. W. Kruglanski (Eds.), *Social psychology: Handbook of basic principles* (pp. 857–913). New York: Guilford Press. In addition to discussing cross-cultural views of the self, Hazel Markus and her colleagues examine the nature of culture and cross-cultural research on cognitive processes, motivation, and social psychology.

Zuckerman, M. (1994). *Behavioral expressions and biosocial bases of sensation seeking.* New York: Cambridge University Press. Here's an appropriate book for readers who are intrigued by the research on the biological basis of psychological traits, especially sensation seeking; after exploring this trait, Zuckerman discusses genetic and biochemical research in this area.

ANSWERS TO DEMONSTRATIONS

Demonstration 13.1

Climbing the staircase and unlocking the door symbolizes sexual intercourse (No. 8); the small forbidden room represents the female genitals (No. 4); the spindle is a symbol for a penis (No. 2); and pricking the finger indicates menstruation (No. 6). As far as I know, the other four items on the list are not symbolized in this fairy tale! Incidentally, Bettelheim tells us about the implied message for anxious little girls hearing this story: "Don't worry and don't try to hurry things—when the time is ripe, the impossible problem will be solved, as if all by itself" (p. 233). (We can only speculate whether females who wait for a kiss from a handsome prince are likely to thrive in the current era.)

Demonstration 13.5

Count the number of times you answered *true* to the following items: 1, 2, 4, 6, 9, and 10; these are the responses favored in individualistic cultures. Then count the number of times you answered *true* to the remaining items: 3, 5, 7, 8, 11, and 12; these are the responses favored in collectivist cultures. As an informal assessment of your own tendency, notice whether you supplied many more individualistic responses—characteristic of North Americans—or more collectivist responses—characteristic of people who emphasize interdependent relationships.

ANSWERS TO CRITICAL THINKING EXERCISES

Exercise 13.1

a. In the case of dream analysis, no convincing evidence could possibly be presented to demonstrate that a bull represents the dreamer's father. The dreamer may instead have seen a photo of a carousel (just as Willa Cather really had sailed on a ship called *Berengaria*). Basically, we cannot suggest any hypothesis about dream interpretation that could be objectively tested (Crews, 1996).

b. Another more likely possibility is that the little girl simply preferred unbroken crayons!

Exercise 13.2

a. To measure validity appropriately, you need to make certain that the comparison criterion (in this case, self-reported symptoms) will be truly independent. In this description, the people who gave the Rorschach Test may remember the depression scores from that test when they listen to the self-reported symptoms. That second judgment, which is based on the self-report, is likely to be biased (Wood et al., 1996a). The appropriate test would require that the psychologists who hear the self-report don't know about the individuals' Rorschach scores.

b. A test is valid if it measures what it is supposed to measure. In this case, the test might measure creativity or persistence. However, it probably would not measure the test taker's normal projected characteristics (perhaps achievement motivation, in this case).

Exercise 13.3

a. If we each have our own interpretations of the world, then it would be very difficult to find an operational definition for any concept. For example, what operational definition can we give for self-actualization? One person may feel self-actualized by quitting school and taking a job that most people would consider unchallenging; if it feels self-actualizing to that individual—but not to researchers—does it meet the criterion?

b. This list is based on Maslow's own personal criteria (Ewen, 1993). It is basically a test with no established validity or reliability. For instance, the criteria do not all seem essential for self-actualization; why does a person need to have a great need for privacy in order to be self-actualized, for example? Also, how could Maslow judge individuals along dimensions such as "an acceptance of himself or herself"—especially for the historical figure like Thomas Jefferson?

Exercise 13.4

a. One clear advantage of the Rorschach is that its purpose is disguised; the test taker doesn't know which responses will reflect psychological adjustment and which indicate psychological problems. In contrast, when you tried Demonstration 13.4, you probably noticed immediately that the responses *helpful* and *well organized* would be more socially acceptable than *uncooperative* and *disorganized*. People may be tempted to provide the socially acceptable answer, rather than the honest one. A psychodynamic theorist would also argue that people cannot relax their defense mechanisms with a self-report test. However, the self-report test uses a more standardized scoring system, and the self-report tests typically have higher validity.

b. If your first impressions tend to persist, then you will tend to have a biased perception of an acquaintance on future occasions. For example, if Linda seems to be friendly the first time you meet her, you will view her as being friendly when you see her in the future—even if she acts somewhat shy. To some extent, then, traits are partly in the minds of the beholder (Mischel, 1968).

Exercise 13.5

a. In general, people in individualistic societies would want to "look good" by supplying answers that portray themselves as being unique. As a result, they may sometimes give these responses, even if they do not truly apply to themselves. The same would hold true for people in collectivist societies, with respect to "fitting in." (However, you might find exceptions; my own impression is that most North Americans would also endorse Number 5, for social desirability reasons.) If people do respond according to the social desirability of these attributes in their society, then the difference between the two cultural groups would be increased.

b. If we knew only about the decisions regarding self-actualization, the results would be ambiguous. In particular, it might be possible that the Hong Kong students simply have a different way of making decisions, perhaps an etiquette about carefully reaching consensus that the U.S. students do not have. However, we also know that the Hong Kong students *could* reach consensus quickly about the value of persistence (and, incidentally, a number of other characteristics). We are therefore somewhat confident that the Hong Kong students do not really value self-actualization.

PSYCHOLOGICAL DISORDERS

CHAPTER 14

There is a particular kind of pain, elation, loneliness, and terror involved in this kind of madness. When you're high it's tremendous. The ideas and feelings are fast and frequent like shooting stars, and you follow them until you find better and brighter ones. . . . Feelings of ease, intensity, power, well-being, financial omnipotence, and euphoria pervade one's marrow. But, somewhere, this changes. The fast ideas are too fast, and there are far too many; overwhelming confusion replaces clarity. Memory goes. Humor and absorption on friends' faces are replaced by fear and concern. Everything previously moving with the grain is now against—you are irritable, angry, frightened, uncontrollable, and enmeshed totally in the blackest caves of the mind. You never knew those caves were there. (Jamison, 1996, p. 67)

This description of a psychological problem called bipolar disorder was written by Kay Jamison, who is shown in the photo above. Jamison has unusual expertise in this area: Not only has she written extensively on bipolar disorder, but she herself has lived with it since her senior year in high school. Her life had previously been normal, but suddenly she found herself transfixed by the beauty of the universe. After several days of feeling exhilarated, with little sleep, she crashed into depression. However, she recovered and then felt normal.

Several years later, as a new faculty member in clinical psychology, she experienced another bout of mania. This time she went on an unrestrained buying spree, a common characteristic of people with bipolar disorder. She bought expensive Rolex watches, elegant furniture, and a stuffed fox that she desperately thought she needed. Finally, she decided to get professional help. Jamison describes the strange sensation of being on the receiving end—answering the same questions that she had often asked the clients in her own practice.

Jamison still practices clinical psychology, and her bipolar disorder is reasonably well controlled with medication. She writes:

My high moods and hopes, having ridden briefly in the top car of the Ferris wheel, will, as suddenly as they came, plummet into a black and gray and tired heap. Time will pass, these moods will pass; and I will, eventually, be myself again. (p. 313)

Everyone reading this textbook has occasionally bought something that wasn't useful. Everyone has also felt depressed, at least occasionally. However, Kay Jamison has psychological problems that have frequently interfered with her normal functioning. Let's begin by discussing some general problems in defining, diagnosing, and explaining mental disorders, and then we will consider several specific categories of psychological problems.

BACKGROUND ON PSYCHOLOGICAL DISORDERS

Defining Psychological Disorders

No clear-cut boundary divides psychologically well-adjusted individuals from those with disorders. In fact, every criterion we propose is somewhat arbitrary and likely to produce some exceptions (Neale et al., 1996). However, psychologists often specify that **psychological disorders** include emotions, thoughts, and behaviors that are (1) maladaptive, (2) distressing, and (3) different from the social norms. Let us look more closely at these three components.

1. *Maladaptive:* Maladaptive means that the disorder interferes with normal functioning (Carson & Butcher, 1992). For example, we should be able to cope with everyday stress, but a person with an anxiety disorder feels tense, even under low-stress conditions. However, this criterion does not always hold true. Consider a person who is a transvestite, a person who wears clothing normally associated with the other gender. This characteristic is listed in the professional literature as a disorder, yet most transvestites are married and lead conventional lives (Neale et al., 1996).

2. *Distressing:* Psychological disorders generally cause personal distress and suffering (American Psychiatric Association, 1994a). If you have an anxiety disorder or if you experience severe depression, you will feel distressed. However, an important exception is a problem called antisocial personality disorder; people with this disorder are typically aggressive and they exploit other people, but they typically feel no guilt or personal distress.

3. *Different from the social norm:* Most people are depressed for some time after a love relationship has ended. However, a college student who remains depressed for two years would violate the social norm. But once again, the criterion is not absolute. People who rob banks do differ from the social norm, yet they would not be considered to have a psychological disorder. We should emphasize, too, that a behavior considered to be normal in one culture may be considered abnormal in another, as Figure 14.1 illustrates.

FIGURE 14.1

In Rajasthan, India, this woman's jewelry would look normal—though it would be considered abnormal in most communities in North America, because it would violate the social norm.

In short, the task of trying to define a psychological disorder points out the complexity we have emphasized in Theme 3. The criteria for psychological disorders (such as the three just listed here: maladaptive, distressing, and different from the social norm) are generally helpful in separating abnormal from normal. However, psychologists cannot construct firm criteria that are both necessary and sufficient for defining a psychological disorder.

Diagnosing Psychological Disorders

We have noted the difficulty of defining a psychological disorder; diagnosing a psychological disorder is equally challenging. The most frequently used resource for classifying psychological disorders is the ***Diagnostic and Statistical Manual of Mental Disorders (DSM).*** The first edition was published in 1952. The most recent edition, called the *DSM-IV* (or fourth edition), was published in 1994 (American Psychiatric Association, 1994a).

The *DSM-IV* describes the specific criteria that must be met in order to assign a particular diagnosis. However, the list of disorders and the criteria change over time to reflect recent research and current beliefs. For example, earlier editions of the *DSM* considered homosexuality to be a disorder. In contrast, homosexuality does not appear in the more recent editions of the *DSM* because mental health professionals now acknowledge that being gay or lesbian does not imply that someone has a psychological problem (American Psychiatric Association, 1994a; Widiger & Trull, 1991).

Some professionals object to any diagnostic instrument that tries to specify who is normal and who is not. Consider a classic study that added to the controversy. Dr. David Rosenhan, a psychologist, asked several other professionals to help test the validity of psychiatric diagnoses. Each person was instructed to arrive at a psychiatric hospital, complaining of just one symptom. In particular, they were to report that they heard voices during the last three weeks that said "empty," "hollow," and "thud." Otherwise they provided accurate information and acted normal. Rosenhan (1973) found that all the pseudopatients were admitted to the hospital with a diagnosis of schizophrenia—a very serious disorder. They were kept in the hospital an average of 19 days. Furthermore, the hospital staff interpreted the pseudopatients' *normal* behavior as being abnormal. For instance, when Rosenhan took notes, his note taking was considered a symptom of schizophrenia.

Rosenhan's study illustrated that psychiatric personnel have difficulty judging who is really disturbed and who is really normal. The study also demonstrated the effects of psychiatric labeling. Once an individual receives a label indicating a psychological disorder, all subsequent behavior is interpreted in terms of that label. To see how this can happen, try Demonstration 14.1. In Chapter 16, we will see additional examples of how stereotypes can influence people's interpretations of behavior.

DEMONSTRATION 14.1 How Labels Can Influence Our Perceptions

Look at the photograph of the person to the right. Imagine that she is a college student trying to think about job opportunities in her major. Describe how her facial expression is reflecting her thought processes. Now, shift gears. Imagine instead that she is a person who has been hearing voices during recent weeks that said "empty," "hollow," and "thud." Now describe how her facial expression is reflecting her thought processes. (Incidentally, she really is a college student.)

Chapter 13 considered the issue of validity in personality assessment. If people who are really normal are frequently diagnosed as being abnormal, then the instrument has a validity problem. Critics have noted that the *DSM-IV* is more valid than earlier versions, but problems still remain (Tavris, 1995; Wakefield, 1996). Furthermore, the *DSM-IV* may not be valid if it is strictly applied to ethnic groups other than European Americans (Cervantes & Arroyo, 1995; Morrison, 1995). For example, certain Native American groups believe in witches, which *DSM-IV* would consider a serious symptom of disordered thought. In general, the reliability of the *DSM-IV* is more impressive than its validity, though not close to the ideal reliability of 1.00 (Andreasen & Black, 1995).

Explaining Psychological Disorders

In this chapter, we'll examine the general categories of psychological disorders listed in Table 14.1. We'll also look at some of the explanations for these disorders. The explanations fall into four general categories, though clinicians often point out that any given disorder may have more than one explanation.

1. The *biological approach* explains disorders in terms of genetic factors, brain structure, neurotransmitters, hormones, and other biological factors. We have seen in previous chapters that psychological characteristics such as intelligence and risk-taking have a significant genetic component, and this chapter investigates the genetic basis for many psychological disorders. Some disorders are also associated with abnormal brain structures or inappropriate levels of neurotransmitters.

2. The *psychodynamic approach* argues that psychological disorders arise from two sources: unconscious conflict and the repression of traumatic childhood events (Chin, 1994). For example, suppose that a man feels unresolved anger toward his mother because he believes she rejected him during childhood. If the man's wife dies, this event may trigger emotions associated with his childhood experiences. In general, these theorists believe that psychological disorders may arise from unconscious processes such as (1) difficulty in repressing sexual and aggressive impulses and (2) the exaggerated use of defense mechanisms.

3. The *cognitive-behavioral approach* combines two perspectives that you'll recognize. Beginning early in the twentieth century, behaviorists emphasized the stimuli and reinforcers in the environment. Thus, psychological disorders can be explained by a person's learning history. For instance, behaviorists propose that depression is caused by a general decrease in reinforcement (Salinger, 1988). However,

---

TABLE 14.1 Psychological Disorders Discussed in Chapter 14

A. DISORDERS BASED ON ANXIETY
  1. Anxiety disorders
    a. Generalized anxiety disorder
    b. Panic disorder and agoraphobia
    c. Phobic disorders
    d. Obsessive-compulsive disorder
    e. Posttraumatic stress disorder
  2. Dissociative disorders
    a. Dissociative amnesia
    b. Dissociative identity disorder
      (multiple personality disorder)

B. MOOD DISORDERS
  1. Major depression
  2. Bipolar disorder
C. SCHIZOPHRENIA
D. PERSONALITY DISORDERS
  1. Obsessive-compulsive personality disorder
  2. Borderline personality disorder
  3. Antisocial personality disorder

current therapists are likely to integrate cognitive perspectives into their approach. Therefore, the **cognitive-behavioral approach** acknowledges behavioral principles and also emphasizes observational learning and cognitive interpretations of the world. For example, a child can acquire a fear of spiders by observing a parent's fearful behavior. An example of an inappropriate interpretation is a student who concludes that one low score on an exam indicates general incompetence in all academic areas.

The sociocultural approach emphasizes that people living in poverty experience more stress, which leads to psychological disorders.

    4. The *sociocultural approach* emphasizes how social and cultural factors influence mental health. For instance, we will note that schizophrenia is more common in lower social classes. People living in poverty—with inadequate food, poor housing, and the constant threat of crime—experience discrimination and low status. Similarly, women experience more of these stresses than men. In our "In Depth" feature, we'll explore some of the sociocultural explanations for the significantly higher rate of depression in women than in men. In short, the sociocultural perspective encourages us to look outside the individual to find the sources of psychological disorders. This perspective suggests that the real causes are poverty and biased treatment of certain groups of people (Mirowsky & Ross, 1989).

Prevalence of Psychological Disorders

A variety of research studies have attempted to estimate the prevalence of psychological disorders. As you can imagine, survey research on such a sensitive topic is extremely challenging. However, Kessler and his colleagues (1994) designed a survey to be administered by 158 trained interviewers. They interviewed more than 8,000 respondents between the ages of 15 and 54, throughout the United States. The sample was carefully selected to include people who varied on eight demographic variables, including age, gender, ethnicity, and education.

    The results of this survey allowed the researchers to make estimates of the lifetime prevalence of many psychological disorders, for the U. S. population. **Lifetime prevalence** is the likelihood that someone will experience a problem at some time within his or her lifetime. Overall, the lifetime prevalence for some kind of psychological disorder was 48%. The largest single problem was the abuse of alcohol and other substances; 27% are estimated to have these problems, which we discussed in Chapter 5. In addition, the lifetime prevalence for some kind of anxiety disorder is 25%, 19% for some kind of mood disorder, 3% for antisocial personality disorder, and 1% for schizophrenia. (The numbers add to more than 48% because many individuals had more than one disorder.)

Critical Thinking Exercise 14.1

Write down your answers to the following questions about the diagnosis and prevalence of psychological disorders.

a. A disorder called selective mutism means that a child consistently fails to speak in specific social situations, although he or she speaks in other social situations. Earlier versions of the *DSM* did not specify that the child must be familiar with the language used in that setting in order to "qualify" for the diagnosis of selective mutism. Would the diagnosis have been valid for a kindergartner from Haiti in a Boston classroom, who knew no English? Would the diagnosis have been reliable?

b. Suppose that a group of researchers decide to compare the prevalence of psychological disorders among European Americans and Asian Americans in the United States. They find that European Americans are twice as likely to report having a psychological disorder. They conclude that their study provides additional evidence that Asian Americans are the "model minority" because they are so mentally healthy. What's wrong with this conclusion?

SECTION SUMMARY: *BACKGROUND ON PSYCHOLOGICAL DISORDERS*

1. Psychological disorders involve behavior that is maladaptive, distressing, and different from social norms.

2. The *DSM-IV* is typically used to classify disorders, although critics object to clinicians' tendency to diagnose prematurely. Critics also question the validity of some criteria, though the reliability is fairly strong.

3. Theories about psychological disorders include the biological approach, the psychodynamic approach, the cognitive-behavioral approach, and the sociocultural approach.

4. Research on the lifetime prevalence of psychological disorders is 48%, with the most common problems being substance abuse, anxiety disorders, and mood disorders.

DISORDERS BASED ON ANXIETY

In this section, we'll consider many different disorders that are based on anxiety. People who experience these disorders usually report being unhappy, and their behavior is maladaptive. However, these people typically live in the community, rather than in a hospital setting. According to the data we just discussed, about one-quarter of U. S. residents will experience some kind of anxiety disorder within their lifetime (Kessler et al., 1994). In other words, millions of people are anxious, afraid, and functioning at a level substantially below their potential.

Let's begin by discussing the most common group of these disorders, known simply as anxiety disorders. Then we'll look briefly at a less common group, known as the dissociative disorders. First, turn back to Table 14.1 on Page 454 to see the general category structure of the 7 disorders we will discuss in this section on anxiety problems.

Anxiety Disorders

Most of us feel anxious from time to time. You may feel anxious when facing a test for which you are unprepared or when you are worried about the outcome of a friend's surgery. However, when anxiety persists—without any clear explanation—and when that anxiety causes intense suffering, these problems are called **anxiety disorders.** Let's consider five of these disorders: generalized anxiety disorder, panic disorder and agoraphobia, phobic disorders, obsessive-compulsive disorder, and posttraumatic stress disorder.

Generalized Anxiety Disorder   The everyday experience of people with **generalized anxiety disorder** is characterized by continuous long-lasting tension and worry. People with this disorder cannot identify a specific cause of their anxiety (hence the word *generalized*). They also have physical symptoms such as nausea, dizziness, and insomnia (American Psychiatric Association, 1994a; Michels & Marzuk, 1993a). Generalized anxiety disorder clearly disrupts normal thought process. For instance, 86% of people with this problem report difficulty concentrating (Beck et al., 1985). As you can imagine, a person with generalized anxiety disorder would have trouble taking an exam, performing competently at work, or enjoying a conversation with friends.

Agoraphobics become extremely anxious in places from which it is difficult to escape, such as this crowded subway car.

Panic Disorder and Agoraphobia   People with **panic disorder** experience recurrent panic attacks of overwhelming anxiety that occur suddenly and unexpectedly. Whereas generalized anxiety disorders are continuous, panic disorder involves specific panic attacks that are short-lasting and occur without warning. Someone in the midst of a panic attack may feel smothering sensations, severe chest pains, and a fear of dying (Sherbourne et al., 1996).

After several severe panic attacks, people often become very concerned about when their next panic attack will occur. If they are worried that they will not be able to escape to a safe place when the next attack occurs, the condition may lead to agoraphobia (Antony et al., 1992; Katon, 1991).

Agoraphobia is a disabling fear of being in situations where escape would be difficult. People with agoraphobia are afraid of situations such as traveling on a bus, being in a crowded restaurant, and leaving their home. About 70% of identified agoraphobics are female (Andreasen & Black, 1995; Kessler et al., 1994). Clearly, agoraphobia is disabling because it limits academic, social, and employment options.

Phobic Disorders   A **phobic disorder** is an excessive fear of a specific object, activity, or situation. The fear is irrational and out of proportion to the true danger. People with phobias avoid the feared object or situation, even if it means restricting their daily activities and missing pleasurable events (Öhman & Soares, 1993; Silverman & Kurtines, 1996).

Many phobias involve a specific fear about one kind of object or animal, such as snakes, spiders, and mice. Other phobic disorders include a fear of heights or a fear of flying in an airplane. Between 70% and 95% of people with specific phobias are female (American Psychiatric Association, 1994a; Kessler et al., 1994).

People who have a **social phobia** are excessively afraid of social situations, where they are afraid that they will do something embarrassing. More than half the U. S. population admits to being "shy" at least occasionally. However, people with social phobia are preoccupied with the possibility that someone will be evaluating them (Leary & Kowalski, 1995; "Social Phobia," 1994). Social phobia is slightly more common among women than among men (Hazen & Stein, 1995; Kessler et al., 1994). Notice that the phobic disorders are not as disabling as agoraphobia, but they certainly have an impact on a person's life.

A common phobia is a fear of heights. Someone with this kind of phobia might have trouble even looking out the window in a high building, or perhaps even looking at this photo of a construction worker.

Obsessive-Compulsive Disorder   Mild obsessive thoughts and compulsive actions are part of everyday experience for many of us. For example, we check a third time to make certain that an airplane ticket is safe in a pocket. In contrast, **obsessive-compulsive disorder** is a disabling condition that includes recurrent, time-consuming obsessions and/or compulsions (American Psychiatric Association, 1994a). **Obsessions** are unwanted, persistent thoughts that are unreasonable. A typical obsession would be inappropriate worry about becoming infected by shaking someone's hand or excessive concern that an accident might occur to a relative (Steketee, 1993).

Whereas obsessions focus on persistent *thoughts,* compulsions focus on persistent *actions.* That is, **compulsions** are repetitive behaviors performed absolutely systematically. For example, one man with obsessive-compulsive disorder felt a drop in his eye while passing a building. He had obsessive thoughts that someone with AIDS had spit out of a window. Those thoughts were turned into a compulsion. To reassure himself, he proceeded to knock on the door of every office in the 10-story building ("Obsessive-Compulsive Disorder—Part I," 1995). Common compulsions include hand washing, counting, and checking the location of an object.

Many veterans of the Vietnam War have experienced posttraumatic stress disorder. Reminders of the war, such as the Vietnam Veterans Memorial, may trigger flashback memories.

Posttraumatic Stress Disorder   Consider the case of a Vietnam veteran who sought help for his problems 10 years after his combat duty. During his year in Vietnam, his best friend was killed while he stood a few feet away. He himself had killed a young Vietcong boy by hitting him with a rifle butt. He reported that he still has nightmares about Vietnam and that he still jumps at the sound of a backfiring automobile. In moments of anger, he strikes his wife, and he often carries a gun. He also reported that he is constantly bored, depressed, and alienated ("Post-Traumatic Stress," 1991).

As the name implies, **posttraumatic stress disorder (PTSD)** is a pattern of disordered reactions following a traumatic event that the person has experienced or witnessed. These reactions may include extreme anxiety, irritability, emotional numbness, and flashbacks (Andreasen & Black, 1995; Freedy & Donkervoet, 1995; Stewart, 1996).

Researchers in the United States have focused on several major kinds of traumas that can lead to PTSD. The Vietnam War underscored the fact that people in combat may experience traumas, even if they are not physically wounded.

TABLE 14.2 The Anxiety Disorders

NAME	DESCRIPTION
a. Generalized anxiety disorder	Continuous long-lasting tension and worry
b. Panic disorder and agoraphobia	Recurrent attacks of overwhelming anxiety (panic disorder), which often lead to a fear of being in situations where escape would be difficult (agoraphobia)
c. Phobic disorders	Excessive fear of a specific object, activity, or situation (e. g., a social phobia)
d. Obsessive-compulsive disorder	Unwanted, persistent, unreasonable thoughts (obsessions) and repetitive behaviors performed systematically (obsessions)
e. Posttraumatic stress disorder (PTSD)	Disorders following a traumatic event; may include anxiety, irritability, numbness, and flashbacks

According to estimates, between 26% and 31% of Vietnam veterans who experienced combat developed posttraumatic stress disorder at some point in their lives (Weiss et al., 1992).

Individuals who have been raped or battered may also experience posttraumatic stress disorder (Waites, 1993). Furthermore, children and adults who have experienced natural and human-made disasters—including events such as nuclear accidents, earthquakes, and floods—can develop PTSD (Green & Solomon, 1995).

Table 14.2 summarizes the five major kinds of anxiety disorders we have discussed so far. After you try Critical Thinking Exercise 14.2, we'll consider an additional kind of problem related to anxiety, called dissociative disorders.

Critical Thinking Exercise 14.2

Write down your answers to the following questions about anxiety disorders.

a. We noted that women are more likely than men to be diagnosed with agoraphobia or a phobic disorder. Why would you be suspicious that the data may underestimate the number of males with these disorders?

b. Data on Vietnam War veterans suggest that Hispanic veterans had the highest incidence of PTSD, whereas European American veterans had the lowest incidence (Stewart, 1996). What further information would you want before concluding that different ethnic groups react differently to the stress of combat?

Dissociative Disorders

The dissociative disorders resemble the five anxiety disorders we just discussed because both are reactions to stress. However, the **dissociative disorders** are associated with much more severe psychological symptoms, and they are relatively rare. Ordinary people have an integrated sense of who they are. For example, they remember their life events, and they are aware of their stable personality characteristics. In contrast, the dissociative disorders are characterized by a splitting apart (or dissociation) of a person's identity, memory, and consciousness. These people suddenly lose their identity or their memory in dramatic ways (Andreasen & Black, 1995).

Dissociative Amnesia   In 1980, a Florida park ranger discovered a woman who was close to death. In fact, she was incoherent and covered with animal and insect bites. This woman, who was dubbed "Jane Doe," could remember neither her name nor her past (Carson & Butcher, 1992). A person who has **dissociative amnesia** forgets past experiences following a stressful event. We all have less than perfect memories, as Chapter 7 emphasized. However, a person with amnesia may forget an entire time period surrounding a traumatic event, or even his or her entire life history.

Dissociative Identity Disorder   The critical feature of amnesia is forgetting. In contrast, **dissociative identity disorder** is the diagnosis when a person has two or more distinct, well-developed personalities (American Psychiatric Association, 1994a). Incidentally, you may be familiar with the name used in previous editions of the *DSM:* **multiple personality disorder.** An individual with this disorder reports shifting from one personality to another dramatically different one, perhaps as often as every few minutes (Steinberg, 1995).

This woman, who came to be known as "Jane Doe," suffered from severe dissociative amnesia.

A person with dissociative identity disorder will often show one quiet, unassuming personality and one more assertive personality. For example, a 26-year-old woman named Effie was shy, somewhat depressed, and preferred to be alone (Morrison, 1995). When she first came to the mental health clinic, she reported that she had noticed "holes in her memory," lasting several days, about which she could remember nothing. During the next visit to the clinic, Effie seemed transformed. She announced that her name was Liz and immediately launched into a dramatic account of her adventures in the previous three days. She had met a man in the grocery store, and they had gone out for dinner and dancing. Afterwards, they had gone bar-hopping. When asked whether she knew Effie, she responded "I'm not saying that she isn't a decent human being, but you've met her—don't you think she's just a tad mousie?" Liz also reported that her father, a preacher, had sexually molested Effie when she was 13.

Dissociative identity disorder is a controversial topic. Some therapists argue that most of the people who claim to have multiple personalities are really telling the truth; they propose that this disorder arises from an intensely stressful event such as sexual abuse. Others argue that they are intentionally trying to deceive the therapist. Still others argue that the basic concept of dissociative identity disorder is flawed (L. M. Cohen et al., 1995; Kihlstrom et al., 1993; Spanos, 1994, 1996). These critics argue that the multiple personality is a social phenomenon in which a person plays several roles; it is not a genuine psychological disorder. Because this is a fairly recent controversy, we do not yet have a satisfying resolution.

Explaining Disorders Based on Anxiety

We have considered a variety of psychological disorders, each connected with anxiety. Some disorders, such as a specific phobia, may have little impact on an individual's day-to-day activities. Others, such as agoraphobia and dissociative identity disorder, cause major disruptions in a person's social relationships, work performance, and ability to enjoy life. How does anxiety arise, and why does it produce the particular symptoms we have outlined? Let's discuss how several explanations introduced at the beginning of the chapter account for some of these anxiety-based disorders.

The Biological Approach   Some of the disorders based on anxiety have a genetic component. For example, people with simple phobias, panic disorder, agoraphobia, obsessive-compulsive disorder, and posttraumatic stress disorder are more likely than people in a control group to have a close relative with an anxiety disorder (Papp et al.,

1994; True et al., 1993). However, we need to be cautious about accepting the research uncritically. A young woman may have inherited the disposition toward agoraphobia from her mother. However, she also had an opportunity to watch her mother's fearful behavior; observational learning could account for the daughter's modeling of her mother's agoraphobia.

Neuroscience research also suggests a biological component. For example, brain imaging studies have found heightened frontal lobe activity when a person who has a germ obsession is asked to hold a dirty towel ("Obsessive-Compulsive Disorder, Part II," 1995). Also, combat veterans with posttraumatic stress disorder show much more limbic system activity than control participants when they are shown combat-related scenes (Shin et al., 1996). A number of neurotransmitter abnormalities have also been identified for several of the anxiety disorders (Papp et al., 1994).

The Psychodynamic Approach Sigmund Freud suggested that anxiety can be caused by a variety of events, such as separation from mother or fear of castration (Freud, 1909; Andreasen & Black, 1995). Anxiety may therefore be a signal of unconscious fantasies about dangerous situations. This anxiety stimulates a variety of defense mechanisms (Cloitre & Shear, 1995). As we discussed in Chapter 13, psychodynamic theorists believe that these defense mechanisms may be helpful. However, psychological disorders result when the person overuses them. Although the psychodynamic theories are well developed, the research evidence is not persuasive (Cloitre & Shear, 1995).

The Cognitive-Behavioral Approach Behaviorists explain phobias in terms of classical conditioning, and this kind of learning may account for the acquisition of some phobias (e.g., Mattick et al., 1995; Öhman & Soares, 1993). However, most people with phobias cannot recall a traumatic conditioning event to account for their fears (Barlow, 1988; Mineka, 1986). Instead, most theorists who favor a learning approach now favor observational learning, rather than classical conditioning. For example, children learn to be afraid of dentists by modeling their parents' anxious behavior in the dentist's office (Bandura, 1986). Disorders are therefore produced by observing inappropriate models.

Cognitive theorists suggest that anxiety-related disorders come from specific biases in our cognitive processes. For example, people with social phobias are worried that people are evaluating them. For example, they have an **attentional bias;** they focus their attention on the feared object or situation (Mineka & Sutton, 1992). Compared to a normal person, people with phobias perceive stimuli related to their phobia more quickly, and they remember those stimuli more accurately (Brown et al., 1994; McNally, 1994). One women with a cat phobia, for example, noticed cats whenever she walked outside. As her phobia decreased during therapy, she commented, "This neighborhood doesn't seem to have as many cats as it did before" (Kent, 1991). This kind of attentional bias helps explain why a weak phobia can grow even stronger.

This man is experiencing a panic attack. Theorists have explained this disorder in terms of the biological, psychodynamic, cognitive-behavioral, and sociocultural approaches.

One of the most interesting demonstrations of attentional bias comes from the "emotional Stroop effect." You tried the standard Stroop task in Demonstration 5.1. The word *red* was printed in yellow ink; when asked to name the ink color, the word *red* kept interfering, delaying your response. Similarly, the emotional Stroop effect is demonstrated when people with anxiety disorders are asked to name the ink color of words related to their feared objects. For example, someone with a fear of spiders is instructed to name the ink colors of printed words such as *hairy* and *crawl*. They are significantly slower on these anxiety-related words than on control words; control participants show no difference. In other words, they are hyper-alert to concepts related to their phobia, and they show attentional bias to these stimuli (J. M. G. Williams et al., 1996).

The Sociocultural Approach We noted earlier that the majority of people with simple phobias and agoraphobia are female. The reasons for this finding are not clear, but gender stereotypes seem to encourage women to be dependent and unassertive.

Women are socialized to be dependent on other people, and agoraphobics seem to receive a stronger "dose" of this message. The fact that many urban settings really are *not* safe for women may contribute further to the problem (McHugh, 1996; Yonkers & Gurguis, 1995).

Combining the Approaches Researchers have not produced compelling evidence for the psychodynamic explanations of anxiety-based disorders. However, the other approaches can help us construct a general explanation. A genetic component has been identified for these disorders; other research has shown brain activity related to several of the disorders. Cognitive-behavioral research has demonstrated that anxiety-based disorders may be acquired by classical conditioning, observational learning, and cognitive biases. Finally, gender roles and some realistic dangers help to account for the gender differences in the prevalence of these disorders.

SECTION SUMMARY: *DISORDERS BASED ON ANXIETY*

1. People with generalized anxiety disorder have continuous long-lasting tension and worry, typically accompanied by disrupted thought processes.

2. Panic disorder is characterized by recurrent panic attacks of overwhelming anxiety, which may lead to agoraphobia—a fear of being unable to escape to a safe place when in an unpleasant situation.

3. Phobic disorders involve an excessive fear of a specific object, activity, or situation; people with a social phobia have an excessive fear of social situations.

4. People with obsessive-compulsive disorder have persistent, unwanted thoughts (obsessions) and repetitive behaviors that are based on those obsessions (compulsions).

5. Posttraumatic stress disorder may follow a traumatic event; symptoms may include extreme anxiety and irritability.

6. Two dissociative disorders are dissociative amnesia (forgetting one's past) and dissociative identity disorder (developing two or more distinct personalities).

7. The most useful explanations of these disorders related to anxiety combine the biological, cognitive-behavioral, and sociocultural approaches.

MOOD DISORDERS

The primary characteristic of **mood disorders** is persistent, extreme disturbances of mood or emotional state. The more common kind of mood disorder is called **major depression,** involving frequent episodes of intense hopelessness and lowered self-esteem. You are already familiar with the less common mood disorder called bipolar disorder—a mixture of depression and mania—from the story about Dr. Kay Jamison at the beginning of this chapter.

Let's begin by discussing the general characteristics of major depression. Then we'll examine in depth some explanations for the gender differences in depression. After an overview of bipolar disorder, we'll discuss several theoretical approaches to the explanation of mood disorders.

General Characteristics of Major Depression

Depression is a common psychological disorder. In fact, an estimated 17% of the general U. S. population will experience a major depressive episode at least once in their lives (Gotlib, 1992; Kessler et al., 1994). Table 14.3 shows nine criteria for a major depressive episode. A diagnosis of major depression requires evidence of at least five of these criteria.

People who are depressed often report physical problems, such as indigestion, headaches, backaches, and general pain. Depressed people are also more susceptible

TABLE 14.3 Criteria for Major Depressive Episode, as Listed in the *DSM-IV*

At least five of these nine symptoms must be present during a two-week period:

1. depressed mood

2. reduced interest in almost all activities

3. significant weight gain or weight loss, without dieting

4. insomnia or too much sleep

5. too much or too little motor activity

6. fatigue or loss of energy

7. feelings of worthlessness or guilt

8. reduced ability to concentrate or think

9. recurrent thoughts of death

Source: Reprinted with permission from the *Diagnostic and Statistical Manual of Mental Disorders,* Fourth Edition. Copyright 1994 American Psychiatric Association.

to infectious diseases, probably because of a weakened immune system. The average health care costs for depressed people is nearly double the costs for people who do not experience depression (Simon et al., 1995; Weisse, 1992). As you can imagine, these physical problems often make a person even more depressed. Let's focus, however, on the psychological components of depression—its emotional, behavioral, and cognitive aspects.

Emotions Depressed people describe themselves as feeling apathetic, discouraged, and hopeless. They expect few happy events in their future, and they describe themselves in very negative terms (Andersen et al., 1992; Gara et al., 1993). Depression is typically measured with a psychological test called the Beck Depression Inventory-II, which assesses emotional characteristics such as sadness, sense of failure, and guilt (Beck et al., 1996). This sense of despair is so prominent that it may spread to other people. For example, Joiner (1994) found that students whose roommates were depressed during the first weeks of college tended to become depressed themselves.

Behavior In addition to physical and emotional changes, severely depressed people also show behavioral changes. They are less able to do daily chores, let alone more challenging tasks at work (Andreasen & Black, 1995; Williams et al., 1988). Social behavior is also different for severely depressed people, in comparison to nondepressed people. Depressed people make fewer contacts with other people, and they avoid social interactions that might be somewhat risky (Gotlib, 1992; Pietromonaco & Rook, 1987). These tendencies can lead to further isolation.

Suicide is the most alarming behavioral problem associated with serious depression. About 15% of individuals with a major mood disorder commit suicide (Kral & Sakinofsky, 1994). Before you read further, try to answer the questions in Demonstration 14.2.

According to official figures, about 32,000 people in the United States killed themselves in 1994 ("Suicide—Part I," 1996). The suicide rate in Canada is even higher (Leenaars & Domino, 1993). Even these chilling statistics underestimate the incidence of suicide, because many people disguise their suicides to look like accidents.

Because depressed people avoid social interactions that might be risky, they become more isolated from other people.

DEMONSTRATION 14.2 Myths and Realities About Suicide

Decide whether each of the following questions about suicide is true or false. Then turn the page to see the correct answers in Table 14.4.

_____ 1. Most people who attempt suicide have never told anyone about their suicidal thoughts.
_____ 2. Men are more likely than women to attempt suicide.
_____ 3. Men are more likely than women to actually kill themselves by suicide.
_____ 4. A suicidal person truly wants to die.
_____ 5. A person who has attempted suicide is not likely to attempt suicide again.
_____ 6. Asking a person "Are you thinking about committing suicide?" will increase the risk of suicide.
_____ 7. When someone has been severely depressed and then suddenly seems quite relieved, the danger is over.
_____ 8. Suicide is equally common among the rich and the poor.

Ethnic-group differences have also been reported. Specifically, the suicide rate is especially high among Native Americans and Native Canadians, though the statistics vary widely among the different Native tribes (Gartrell et al., 1993; Howard-Pitney et al., 1992; Kirmayer, 1994). The reported suicide rate for Blacks is somewhat lower than the national average (Howard-Pitney et al., 1992; "Suicide—Part I," 1996). As Canetto and Lester (1995) emphasize, the cultural climate helps determine whether suicide is considered to be reasonably "acceptable" in a particular ethnic group.

This year, some of you reading this book will have a friend or family member who begins to talk about suicide. What should you do? Unfortunately, no simple formula can prevent suicide, but here is some general advice (Berman & Jobes, 1991; Burstow, 1992; Rickgarn, 1994; Slaby & Garfinkel, 1994):

1. *Take the suicide threat seriously.* People usually do give warnings about suicidal thoughts.

2. *Convey the message that you care and want to help.* Show genuine support and empathy for a suicidal person. Even if you don't know the person well, try to provide empathy and understanding.

3. *Try to clarify the central problem.* As we will discuss shortly, depressed people have cognitive difficulties. If you can help isolate the critical problem, the situation may not seem so overwhelming.

4. *If you think someone is suicidal, ask direct questions.* If this person does say that suicide is a possibility, ask if he or she has made any specific plans. This sounds like a gruesome question, but someone who has a specific plan is more likely to attempt suicide.

5. *Suggest alternative actions.* Offer other solutions to the central problem. However, do not adopt a falsely cheerful "everything will just work out" attitude, and do not suggest "just try to snap out of it." The object should be to help the person gain steadiness by seeing other possibilities.

6. *Encourage consulting a professional.* Even if you have talked someone out of a suicide attempt, the problem still needs further attention. Help the person locate a counselor or other professional, and offer to go along if it would be useful.

7. *The worst thing you can do is nothing.* Take action, and show concern. Ignoring the problem will not reduce the danger.

Cognitive Processes The list of criteria for major depression (Table 14.3 on Page 462) included "reduced ability to concentrate or think." Depressed people not only have trouble on a variety of memory and cognitive tasks; they also have somewhat

---

TABLE 14.4 Myths and Realities About Suicide: The Answers to Demonstration 14.2

1. *False.* At least 70% of people who attempt suicide have told someone about their intentions.

2. *False.* Women are at least twice as likely as men to attempt suicide.

3. *True.* Men are about 3 times as likely as women to die from suicide.

4. *False.* Ambivalence is common among suicidal people; they don't necessarily want to die, but they can't figure out how to live with the pain.

5. *False.* Somewhat less than half will attempt suicide again; however, those who can find professional help and can manage their lives afterwards are less likely to attempt suicide again.

6. *False.* Asking a direct, caring question may actually minimize the suicide risk because the person may have been looking for some sign that friends care.

7. *False.* On the contrary, you should *watch out* if someone who has been depressed suddenly seems happy, because this person is no longer ambivalent.

8. *True.* Suicide is found equally among all socioeconomic groups; unemployed people have high suicide rates, but so do physicians and dentists.

Sources: Berman & Jobes, 1991; Canetto, 1994; Rickgarn, 1994.

---

different thinking patterns, in comparison with nondepressed individuals. Let's look at several ways in which depression influences cognitive processes.

1. Depressed people have more difficulty on memory tasks, especially if they are severely depressed and especially on challenging tasks that require effortful processing (Burt et al., 1995; Hartlage et al., 1993; Hertel, 1994).

2. Depressed people remember more negative material than positive material, whereas nondepressed people usually remember more positive material than negative material (Gara et al., 1993; Gotlib, 1992). This biased recall has important implications for depressed people. Chapter 8 described the **availability heuristic,** in which we make estimates in terms of how easily we think of examples of something. If depressed people think of more examples of unhappy life events than happy life events, then the availability heuristic will encourage the conclusion, "Yes, my life is pretty miserable" (Mineka & Sutton, 1992).

3. Depressed people have negative views of themselves, and they have a pessimistic explanatory style (Gara et al., 1993; Gotlib & Hammen, 1992; Metalsky et al., 1993). If you have a **pessimistic explanatory style,** you believe that the causes of the sorrows in your life are permanent, widespread, and traceable to yourself. For example, a person with this style will explain a low grade on a test by saying, "My poor performance will last forever, it happens in most areas of my life, and it's all my fault" (Seligman, 1993). In contrast, nondepressed people have "positive illusions." In fact, they are often unrealistically optimistic about their skills and personal attributes (Taylor & Brown, 1994; Taylor & Gollwitzer, 1995).

Review the foregoing list of cognitive characteristics. Depressed people have cognitive difficulties, they remember more negative material, and they explain their lives in a negative way. Obviously, these cognitive biases can intensify the depression of individuals who are already discouraged and depressed. Before you read further, please try Demonstration 14.3.

Depressed people tend to explain unpleasant events as being permanent, widespread, and their own fault. For example, this unemployed man may believe he cannot get a job because he has never been competent—in any line of work—and it's his own fault.

DEMONSTRATION 14.3   Factors in a Male-Female Romantic Relationship

If you are a female in a romantic relationship with a male, answer the following questions from your own point of view. If you are a male in a romantic relationship with a female, try to answer the way your female partner would respond. Other students may wish to apply this demonstration to a particular male-female relationship with which they are familiar.

Answer each question *yes* or *no*. The scoring key appears at the end of the chapter on Page 479.

_____ 1. He is always trying to change me.
_____ 2. He respects my opinion.
_____ 3. He acts as though I am in the way.
_____ 4. He won't take no for an answer when he wants something.
_____ 5. He is always thinking of things that would please me.
_____ 6. He argues back, no matter what I say.
_____ 7. He lets me make up my own mind.
_____ 8. He wants to control everything I do.
_____ 9. He is happy to go along with my decisions.
_____ 10. He encourages me to follow my own interests.

IN DEPTH

Gender and Depression

Throughout this book, we will note that most gender differences are small. However, the gender differences in the prevalence of depression is an exception: This gender difference is large. In fact, in North America, women are 1.7 to 3.0 times more likely than men to experience depression during their lifetime (Kessler et al., 1994; Nolen-Hoeksema, 1990; Statistics Canada, 1992). The gender difference holds true for European American, Black, and Hispanic women in the United States (Russo & Green, 1993). Also, cross-cultural studies show that women are more likely than men to experience depression in countries as varied as Sweden, France, Taiwan, Korea, and Lebanon (Frodi & Ahnlund, 1995; Weissman et al., 1996).

Factors Related to Depression in Women

What kinds of factors are likely to be associated with depression in women? In Chapter 12, we saw that well-being is more closely related to personal factors than to demographic factors. The same pattern is true for depression. For example, women are somewhat more likely to become depressed if they work at low-paying jobs, rather than high-paying jobs (Russo, 1990). However, the following personal factors are even more important: (1) low self-esteem; (2) low sense of personal accomplishment; (3) traditional, feminine gender-typing; and (4) little sense of control over one's own life (Russo et al., 1993; Thornton & Leo, 1992).

Another important factor is the nature of the love relationship for married women. Schaefer and Burnett (1987) asked a group of married women a series of questions like the one in Demonstration 14.3. The study showed that women were significantly more likely to be depressed if their husbands were hostile, detached, or overly controlling. In contrast, those with supportive, encouraging husbands were unlikely to be depressed.

Why Are Women More Depressed?

It's easy to document the higher rates of depression among women. In contrast, it's challenging to explain these gender differences. Biologically based explanations do not offer satisfactory accounts for the prevalence of depression among women

Women are more likely than men to work at low-paying jobs and are therefore more likely to develop depression, according to one explanation for women's relatively high depression rate.

Part of the gender differences in depression can be accounted for by the way people respond to a depressed mood; women are often more likely than men to respond by ruminating or worrying about their problems.

(IN DEPTH continued)

(Nolen-Hoeksema, 1990; Schwartz & Schwartz, 1993). Let's consider several other explanations that *have* received support.

First, *women are more likely to have certain negative experiences in their lives.* For instance, many women are depressed because of unpleasant realities such as child-hood sexual abuse, rape, and battering (Strickland, 1992; Vasquez, 1994). They are also depressed because low-paying jobs provide little reward, in contrast to men's jobs. As we saw in Chapter 11, women also do much more housework than men, and this work is rarely rewarding. They also have less spare time for relaxing activities (Barnett et al., 1992; Nolen-Hoeksema & Jackson, 1996).

Second, *women's close relationships may tend to encourage depression.* Women are more likely to derive their sense of self from being "the wife of John Garcia" or "the mother of Pat and Chris." In contrast, John Garcia is likely to base his identity on his own accomplishments, perhaps, "the vice president of First National Bank." Re-search has shown that women tend to be depressed if they derive their identity from other people, rather than having their own independent sense of self (Jack, 1991; Warren & McEachren, 1985). In addition, women are less likely than men to say that their spouse understands them and brings out their best qualities (Fincham et al., 1997; McGrath et al., 1990).

Third, *women are more likely than men to worry (ruminate) about their depression.* Let's consider this possibility in detail. In a series of studies, Susan Nolen-Hoeksema (1987, 1990) observed that women are more likely than men to respond to a de-pressed mood by worrying. These **ruminative responses** are thoughts and behav-iors that encourage depressed people to focus their attention on their symptoms, as well as the possible causes and consequences of those depressed symptoms (Nolen-Hoeksema et al., 1993). Nolen-Hoeksema's (1987, 1990) research has shown that women are more likely than men to adopt a ruminative response style.

People can also react to depression by distracting themselves. These **distract-ing responses** are thoughts and behaviors that encourage depressed people to shift their attention away from their symptoms, concentrating instead on pleasant or neu-tral activities (Nolen-Hoeksema et al., 1993). Some of these distracting responses are maladaptive because they are dangerous (for example, using drugs or driving too fast). However, other distracting responses can lure depressed people away from de-pression (for example, working on a hobby or doing something enjoyable with friends). Nolen-Hoeksema's (1987, 1990) research has often shown that men are more likely than women to adopt a distracting response style. (However, we'll soon consider a study with no gender differences in the number of distracting responses.) Naturally, neither gender uses one response style exclusively. You probably know men with a ruminative style and women with a distracting style.

Let's consider why a ruminative response style might prolong depression. Focusing on your depression will bring unpleasant memories to mind. The availability of these negative thoughts will encourage people to decide that their lives are unhappy. Also, as you learned in Chapter 12, people solve problems better when they are in a good mood. Depressed people who keep ruminating cannot lift themselves into this positive state, so they are less likely to solve the problems that produced their depression. Notice, then, how well the principles of cognitive psychology help to explain aspects of depression.

Susan Nolen-Hoeksema, Jannay Morrow, and Barbara Fredrickson (1993) wanted to examine whether people with a ruminative response style tend to remain depressed for longer periods of time. To test this hypothesis, they asked female and male college students to keep track of their mood each day for 30 days. If the students had been de-pressed, they were instructed to rate how depressed they had been and how long the depressed mood had lasted. They also completed a form that asked how they had re-sponded to any depression; the questions asked them to indicate which of a variety of ruminative and distracting responses they had tried in reaction to their depression.

Nolen-Hoeksema and her colleagues found that people with a ruminative re-sponse style had a greater number of relatively severe and long-lasting depressive

TABLE 14.5 **Gender Comparisons of Ruminative and Distracting Responses to Depressed Moods (reported for a 30-day period)**

	WOMEN	MEN
Average number of severe depressed moods	6.28	4.00
Average number of ruminative responses	3.49	2.38
Average number of distracting responses	3.02	2.63

Source: Based on Nolen-Hoeksema et al., 1993.
Note: The first two comparisons are statistically significant; the third comparison is not.

episodes. That is, the number of ruminative responses they used was positively correlated with several measures of the intensity of depression. In this particular study, the number of distracting responses was not correlated with the intensity of depression. (Based on their theories, they had expected a *negative* correlation.)

These researchers found some significant gender differences. As Table 14.5 shows, women reported a significantly greater number of days in which they were severely depressed, in comparison to men. They also reported making a significantly greater number of ruminative responses to their depression. However, in this study—unlike in earlier research—women and men did not differ in their number of distracting responses.

Whether you are a man or a woman, what practical advice do these results suggest if you are feeling depressed? Basically, you can think briefly about the problem, but then do something that is enjoyable—something that keeps you from brooding. When your depressed mood has lifted somewhat, then you can begin to analyze the situation that made you depressed. Obviously, however, you should seek help from a mental health professional if your depression persists.

Critical Thinking Exercise 14.3

Write down your answers to the following questions about the research by Nolen-Hoeksema and her coauthors on gender, response style and depression.

a. In the study on college students, Nolen-Hoeksema and her coworkers (1993) found that the number of distracting responses was not significantly related to depression, and no gender differences were discovered. In Chapter 2, we noted that the operational definition of each variable can have an important impact on the results. If you were designing a replication study, what operational definition for distracting response style would you use that might be more strongly related to both depression and to gender?

b. We've seen that people who have a ruminative style are more likely to be depressed. Explain why we cannot conclude: "Using a ruminative response style tends to *make* people more depressed."

Bipolar Disorder

This chapter began with Dr. Kay Jamison's recollections about her own experiences with bipolar disorder. Take a moment to glance back at her description, and then we'll consider this disorder in more detail.

People with **bipolar disorder** experience some depressive episodes and some manic episodes. The same criteria you saw for the diagnosis of major depression are also used to diagnose the depressive phase of bipolar disorder (Jamison, 1993). In addition, people with bipolar disorder also experience occasional manic episodes. **Mania** is an abnormally positive, enthusiastic, overexcited state, accompanied by extremely high self-esteem (Andreasen & Black, 1995). The name *bipolar* suggests two polar opposites. Like the two poles of the earth, depression and mania represent opposite ends of the human emotional spectrum. As Kay Jamison (1996) described, she experienced weeks of bitter depression—intertwined with days of feeling intensely exhilarated.

About 1% to 2% of the U. S. population experiences bipolar disorder during their lifetime (American Psychiatric Association, 1995; Kessler et al., 1994; Weissman et al., 1996). Notice, then, that bipolar disorder is much less common than major depression. Also, unlike major depression, about the same number of women and men experience bipolar disorder (Kessler et al., 1994; Weissman et al., 1996). Some of the important characteristics of the manic phase of bipolar disorder include inflated self-esteem and increased talkativeness, moving quickly from topic to topic. During a manic episode, people may become deeply involved in pleasurable activities that will produce painful consequences at a later time (American Psychiatric Association, 1994a; Jamison, 1993). You'll recall Kay Jamison's description of her bizarre, expensive purchases, revealing the poor judgment often found during a manic episode.

People with bipolar disorder report exhilarating bursts of creativity during their manic phases. However, mania cannot last forever. The bubble bursts, and mood returns to normal—or it may crash into a depression. The painful consequences of some of the wild behavior often intensify the depression.

What causes mood disorders—both major depression and bipolar disorder? Why do people develop these life-altering conditions that influence so many psychological processes, in addition to emotions?

Explaining Mood Disorders

Researchers have been extremely active in pursuing explanations for mood disorders. The research on the biological approach examines both depression and bipolar disorder. In contrast, those who prefer psychological explanations have focused primarily on depression (Halgin & Whitbourne, 1997).

The Biological Approach   Genetic factors clearly influence a person's chances of developing a mood disorder; both depression and bipolar disorder have a significant inherited component (Gotlib & Hammen, 1992). For example, Kendler and his colleagues (1994) studied 15,000 pairs of twins and their families to determine the genetic component of depression. They derived a measure of **heritability,** an estimate of how much of the variation in depression could be traced to differences in heredity, as opposed to environment. According to this research, heritability was estimated to be between 52% and 56%. Other genetic research on bipolar disorder suggests that several genes are associated with this disorder (Morell, 1996; Papolos et al., 1996).

You may wonder exactly what factors are inherited. Researchers are reasonably convinced that the relevant factor is the balance in the neurotransmitter system. As Chapter 3 described, **neurotransmitters** are the chemical substances stored in the ends of axons, which allow electrical messages to be transmitted to nearby neurons. It's clear that mood disorders cannot be traced to just one neurotransmitter; the complexity we've noted throughout this book also applies to the biological explanation of mood disorders (Michels & Marzuk, 1993a). At present, researchers believe that norepinephrine and serotonin are among the relevant neurotransmitters.

The Psychodynamic Approach   As you'll recall, psychodynamic theorists emphasize that psychological disorders can be traced to childhood problems and unconscious conflict. Freud argued that depression is related to feelings of loss. For example, if a man's wife dies, this emotional experience may trigger emotions—such as anger—connected with his childhood (Halgin & Whitbourne, 1997; Mendelson, 1990). Other psychodynamic theorists argue that shame is a critical factor in depression (Tangney et al., 1992).

The Cognitive-Behavioral Approach   Contemporary cognitive-behavioral theorists emphasize that depression can be traced to maladaptive cognitive reactions to life events. In other words, depressed people interpret reality differently from nondepressed people, and this cognitive style is related to depression.

For instance, Aaron Beck's cognitive behavioral theory suggests that some people develop negative views of themselves and their life events (Beck, 1976, 1995; Segal, 1988). For example, Taylor (1989) describes a woman who had told her therapist she felt very depressed after seeing a movie. The movie had been extremely sad, and she could relate it to her own life. The therapist suggested selecting a happier movie, and so she did choose an upbeat one. On the following visit, she reported to the therapist that the movie had left her very depressed. After all, the happy movie showed her what she was missing, and the contrast with her own miserable life had made her more depressed than ever!

In general, cognitive-behavioral theorists point out that our cognitive processes can lead us to exaggerate our problems, ignore positive events, and misinterpret innocent statements. We can also develop a pessimistic explanatory style, as we noted earlier; our sorrows are permanent, widespread, and our own fault (Metalsky et al., 1993; Seligman, 1993). For people with this cognitive style, a relatively minor stress will leave them helpless and depressed.

The Sociocultural Approach   The sociocultural perspective suggests that we look to social pressures—rather than the individual—for explanations of depression. For example, we saw that women are 1.7 to 3.0 times more likely than men to develop depression. The sociocultural approach emphasizes that women's low status, more limited rewards, and social-emotional relationships will encourage depression.

Life is also more stressful for certain other groups in North America. For example, people who are economically poor do indeed have higher rates of depression (Mollica, 1989). Refugees and immigrants are also more likely to be depressed (Jenkins et al., 1991; Uba, 1994). Basically, people who lack a sense of control over important factors in their lives are at greater risk for depression (Albee, 1992).

Our culture's values may also encourage depression. Seligman (1989) reported that depression is about 20 times more likely for those born after 1950 than for those born before 1910. This increasing rate of depression has been confirmed in research examining depression rates in the United States, Canada, New Zealand, Sweden, Italy, and Korea (Cross-National Collaborative Group, 1992; Klerman & Weissman, 1989). Seligman (1989) argues that the rate of depression is increasing because current values emphasize material possessions and self-advancement, rather than concern for other people. People who emphasize selfish interests may feel that their lives are not especially meaningful, a situation that may encourage depression. Seligman offers a clear prescription for depression: We should be less concerned with ourselves and more concerned about the welfare of other people and the common good.

Combining the Approaches   How do all the pieces fit together in explaining depression? Let's consider a general explanation that combines the approaches. Keep in mind, however, that some factors in the model may not be relevant for everyone. For example, some individuals may not have any biological disposition toward depression; instead, their depression may be induced by overwhelming life stress.

Psychodynamic theorists believe that depression can be traced to some kind of shame or loss, such as the death of a close relative.

Seligman argues that people concerned about the welfare of others are less likely to develop depression. In this photo, volunteers are painting a home to help low-income residents.

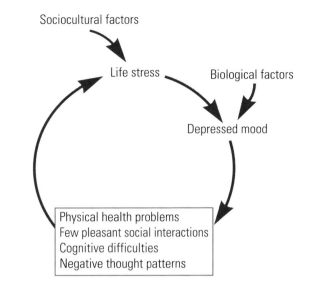

FIGURE 14.2

In the vicious cycle of depression, the symptoms generate even more depression. For example, sociocultural factors may contribute to life stress. Then, as the diathesis-stress model argues, the biological factors combine with life stress to produce a depressed mood. The symptoms of this depressed mood, in turn, create additional life stress.

An explanation that many theorists favor is called the diathesis-stress model. According to the **diathesis-stress model,** some people are born with a predisposition (that is, a *diathesis*) that makes them more likely to respond to a stressful situation by developing a psychological disorder. For example, a person with a biologically based tendency toward depression might respond to chronic pain by becoming depressed (Banks & Kerns, 1996). In contrast, a person with no such tendency might be able to live with the pain for several decades without developing depression. A diathesis-stress explanation has been supported for both depression and bipolar disorder (Johnson & Roberts, 1995; Metalsky & Joiner, 1992).

Figure 14.2 diagrams how the diathesis-stress model may work. Notice how life stress—often increased by sociocultural factors—combines with biological factors to produce a depressed mood. This depressed mood produces the four consequences we have discussed: (1) physical health problems; (2) few pleasant social interactions; (3) cognitive difficulties; and (4) negative thought patterns. These factors make life even more stressful, which increases depression still further. A vicious cycle begins, in which depression grows steadily worse. As we'll see in the next chapter, however, this vicious cycle can be interrupted, and depression can usually be treated successfully.

SECTION SUMMARY: *MOOD DISORDERS*

1. The characteristics of major depression include physical problems; apathy and negative emotions; fewer pleasant social interactions; contemplation of suicide; less effective cognitive skills; and negative views of themselves.

2. Women are much more likely than men to become depressed; risk factors for depression include a low-paying job, personal characteristics, and the nature of their love relationships.

3. Some potential explanations for the higher rate of depression among women include low gratification, the nature of their close relationships, and their response to depression.

4. People with bipolar disorders experience both depressive and manic episodes; during manic episodes, they exhibit inflated self-esteem, talkativeness, and overinvolvement in potentially harmful activities.

5. The complex explanation for mood disorders involves stressful events (often sociocultural in origin) frequently combined with biological factors. The depressed mood produces physical health problems, few positive social interactions, cognitive difficulties, and negative thought patterns. These four factors, in turn, create additional stress.

SCHIZOPHRENIA

Doug Hughes had led a fairly normal life until, at age 23, he began to hear strange voices. He was soon convinced that aliens had infiltrated the earth. Soon the voices that he heard began arguing with each other. A female voice might wonder, "Who would care if he died?" and a male voice might answer, "That's a joke! No one, of course!" (Keefe & Harvey, 1994, p. 16). Sometimes, faces appear out of nowhere to torment him, and sometimes he feels a woman stabbing him with a butter knife.

In the previous section, we examined depression and bipolar disorder, where disturbed mood is most prominent. In contrast, the most prominent feature of **schizophrenia** is severely disordered thoughts—although perceptions, emotions, social interactions, and behavior may also be disturbed. The name *schizophrenia* implies a splitting off from reality. In some cases, this disorganization is so extensive that individuals lose their contact with reality.

Roughly 1% of the U. S. and Canadian populations develop schizophrenia at some point during their lifetime (Gottesman, 1991; Kessler et al., 1994). Men and women are equally likely to develop schizophrenia.

What are some of the symptoms that make schizophrenia so disabling? What is its pattern of development? Finally, how can we explain this disorder that so profoundly alters virtually every aspect of a person's life?

This painting was created by a person with schizophrenia, who painted it while gazing at his own face in a mirror. The painting suggests the splitting off from reality that is characteristic of this disorder.

Characteristics of Schizophrenia

As you review the following characteristics, you should remember that individuals with schizophrenia differ dramatically, just as psychologically healthy people show wide individual differences (Theme 2).

Hallucinations   People with schizophrenia often experience **hallucinations,** which are strong mental images that seem like they truly occurred. The most common hallucinations are auditory, such as voices coming from outside one's head (McGuffin & Morrison, 1994).

Delusions   A **delusion** is a false belief that a person firmly holds, without any objective evidence. For example, a woman may believe that she has behaved immorally, even though she has not (Maher & Spitzer, 1993). The term **paranoid schizophrenia** is applied to individuals with one or more long-lasting delusions. For example, one man was extremely concerned that he would be bombarded by plums. He often raced through the halls of the psychiatric hospital, with wads of cotton protruding from his ears to prevent plums from entering his ears and growing there (Baur, 1991).

Disorganized Speech   People with schizophrenia have trouble focusing their speech. People with schizophrenia do not seem to show concern that a listener might be confused by the disorganization.

Some speech shows more interest in the sound of language than its meaning. Consider how one individual with schizophrenia responded when a psychologist asked about the color of a test item: "Looks like clay. Sounds like gray. Take you for a roll in the hay. Hay day. Mayday" (Chaika, 1985, p. 21).

Individuals with schizophrenia are also less skilled in other areas. For example, they may have difficulty on tests of memory and concept formation (Goldberg et al., 1990; May et al., 1995). Also, they seem to make less use of background knowledge and top-down processing (Hemsley, 1994). As you learned in Chapter 8, normal cognitive processes rely heavily on what we know from previous experience. Without the cohesiveness of top-down processing, thought and speech are disorganized and illogical.

An individual with schizophrenia may make unusual body movements or adopt abnormal body postures.

Attention Problems   As you learned in Chapter 5, normal people typically pay selective attention to one message, screening out the stream of other distracting stimuli and thoughts. For instance, as you are now reading, you can ignore the noise and the visual clutter that could divert you from your goal of completing this sentence. However, people with schizophrenia are easily distracted (McGuffin & Morrison, 1994).

Let's look at some of the research evidence on attention in schizophrenia. You'll recall that the Stroop task (Demonstration 5.1 on Page 157) is fairly difficult for normal individuals. People with schizophrenia are even more distracted than people with normal attention abilities (Cohen & Servan-Schreiber, 1992). Benioff (1995) describes the difficulty of working with schizophrenic individuals who become distracted by a cough, the slight squeak of a chair, or other noises we normally ignore.

Emotional Disturbances   People with schizophrenia often show **flat affect,** or little sign of either positive or negative emotion. In flat affect, the voice is a monotone, and the face has no expression. Other people with schizophrenia may show inappropriate emotions. For example, when I was a college student, I accompanied some people from a local psychiatric hospital to a performance of *The Sound of Music.* One man, with a diagnosis of schizophrenia, began to laugh out loud at one of the saddest parts of the play, when Maria decides she must leave the family to return to the abbey. The inappropriate emotions may be partly traceable to disorganized thought processes.

Social Problems   People with schizophrenia usually have trouble with interpersonal relationships (American Psychiatric Association, 1994a). Often they are socially withdrawn, as if in their own isolated world. In general, people with schizophrenia lack many of the everyday social skills that normal people take for granted.

Behavioral Disturbances   People with schizophrenia typically show motor disturbances (Crider, 1991). One individual may make facial grimaces, and another may adopt an abnormal body posture. Still others may stand rigidly immobile and unresponsive for hours, a situation called a **catatonic stupor.**

The Courses of Schizophrenia

Schizophrenia typically develops between the ages of 17 and 40, though an onset during childhood or old age is also possible (American Psychiatric Association, 1994a; Carpenter & Buchanan, 1994). Signs of the disorder seem to appear earlier. For example, researchers have examined home movies of children who developed schizophrenia during adulthood (Walker, 1994; Walker & Lewine, 1990). Trained viewers spotted characteristic attributes—such as lack of eye contact and physical clumsiness—during the first few years of life. However, a casual observer seldom notices anything unusual.

The disorder becomes obvious when the individual begins to withdraw socially or behave unusually. Major symptoms that develop later include hallucinations, delusions, and incoherent speech.

This section is titled "The *Courses* of Schizophrenia" because of the individual differences in outcome. In general, about one-quarter of people diagnosed with schizophrenia will recover substantially. About half will remain about the same, and about one-quarter will become more disturbed (Bradshaw & Mattingley, 1995; Wieselgren & Lindström, 1996). The outcome is typically better for people who were relatively well adjusted during the most severe period of the disorder and for people who begin drug therapy early (Carpenter & Strauss, 1991; "Schizophrenia Update," 1995).

Critical Thinking Exercise 14.4

Write down your answers to the following questions about research on early signs of schizophrenia.

a. We mentioned Walker's research on the early signs of schizophrenia in home movies of children who later developed the disorder. Why would you suspect that the sample is not representative of the U. S. population of people with schizophrenia?

b. Suppose that a group of researchers wants to determine whether adults with schizophrenia showed early signs of the disorder. They prepare a checklist of various symptoms, such as anxiety, thought disturbances, and unusual language patterns. Parents of these schizophrenic individuals are asked to recall their child's early years and note the relevant behaviors. Parents are asked to do the same for a sibling of this child, who did not have schizophrenia. They check more abnormal symptoms for the child with schizophrenia. Why would you be reluctant to conclude that adults with schizophrenia showed early "warning signs"?

Explaining Schizophrenia

How can we find an explanation for such a wide variety of disorders as hallucinations, delusions and disorganized thinking, as well as disturbances in attention, emotion, social interactions, and behavior? Let's look at several biological explanations before turning to the cognitive-behavioral and sociocultural approaches. (Because researchers rarely mention psychoanalytic explanations for schizophrenia, we won't discuss that approach here.)

Biological Approaches   Three major areas in which biological factors could operate are in the genetic transmission of schizophrenia, neurotransmitter abnormalities, and brain abnormalities.

The evidence strongly supports a genetic contribution to schizophrenia, probably involving more than one gene (Keefe & Harvey, 1994; Torrey, 1994). For example, suppose that Sheila has schizophrenia. If she has an identical twin, that twin stands about a 50% chance of having schizophrenia (Andreasen & Black, 1995; Gottesman, 1991). Remember that the incidence of schizophrenia in the general population is only 1%. However, a genetic explanation is only part of the story. If genetic factors were the only determinant, then we'd expect to find that an individual would have a 100% chance of developing schizophrenia if his or her identical twin has this disorder—rather than the 50% chance that researchers report.

Researchers have pursued a second biological mechanism for schizophrenia—the neurotransmitters. The most widely researched topic in this area is called the dopamine hypothesis. The **dopamine hypothesis** argues that schizophrenia is caused by too much dopamine at critical synapses in the brain. Some of the evidence is persuasive. For example, some of the drugs used to treat schizophrenia happen to block the dopamine receptors (Gottesman, 1991; Keefe & Harvey, 1994). As you might expect, however, the neurotransmitter mechanism is not that simple. For instance, if the drugs used to treat schizophrenia operate simply by blocking the receptors, then why does it take weeks—rather than minutes—for the improvements to occur (Pinel, 1997)? Furthermore, other neurotransmitters such as norepinephrine also seem to play a role in schizophrenia (Lieberman et al., 1994).

Now let's turn our attention to a third biological mechanism for schizophrenia—the structure of the brain. In the last decade, researchers have used brain-imaging techniques to explore the function and the structure of the brain in people with schizophrenia. For example, PET scans can trace chemical activity in various parts of the brain,

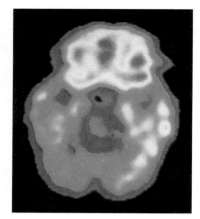

a. Normal individual

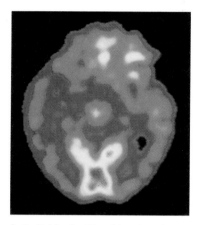

b. Individual with schizophrenia
FIGURE 14.3

PET scans made while participants were performing an attention task. (Red and yellow regions indicate high activity; blue and purple areas indicate low activity. Frontal lobe is at the top of each image.)

telling us which areas are most metabolically active. Figure 14.3a shows a PET scan of a normal volunteer, performing a task requiring attention, perhaps watching for a faint light to appear. Red and yellow indicate high activity levels. You can see that the frontal lobe (at the top of the image) is highly active. On contrast, the PET scan of a person with schizophrenia (Figure 14.3b) shows minimal activity in the frontal cortex (Gershon & Rieder, 1992).

The evidence is now persuasive that the frontal lobe of the cortex (more precisely, the prefrontal cortex) is underactive in people with schizophrenia (Cohen et al., 1997; Cohen & Servan-Schreiber, 1992). This finding makes sense. As we saw in Chapter 3, the prefrontal cortex handles working memory and other complex cognitive tasks like making plans—tasks that are often difficult for people with schizophrenia (Michels & Marzuk, 1993b).

Research on brain structure has also revealed that many people with schizophrenia have smaller-than-normal structures in their limbic system (Benes, 1996; Carpenter & Buchanan, 1994). This abnormality is probably related to some of the emotional problems of individuals with schizophrenia.

In short, biological explanations provide some enticing hints. The factors of genetics, neurotransmitters, and brain structure are undoubtedly important. However, we do not yet have a satisfying, complete explanation for the biology of schizophrenia.

The Cognitive-Behavioral Approach Unfortunately, researchers have been less active in developing psychological explanations to schizophrenia—in contrast to their eager pursuit of biological explanations. The most prominent explanations focus on family interactions. In particular, people who are trying to recover from a schizophrenic episode are more likely to have problems if (1) the family's communication patterns are fragmented and unclear; (2) family members are monitoring the individual too closely; and (3) family members frequently make critical comments. The research—conducted with both European American and Mexican American populations—tends to confirm that these family-interaction patterns are indeed important (Doane et al., 1989; Keefe & Harvey, 1994; McGlashan, 1994).

The Sociocultural Approach Our earlier discussion of the sociocultural approach to depression focused on gender. In contrast, the sociocultural approach to schizophrenia focuses on social class. Specifically, schizophrenia is reported more often in lower social classes, especially in urban areas (McGlashan, 1994; McGuffin & Morrison, 1994). Poverty creates long-term stress. Also, people who are economically disadvantaged often find that their lives are controlled by other people, such as an unreasonable boss or unsympathetic people in a welfare office. As a result, they may not have the opportunity to take charge of their lives and cope effectively with stress (McGlashan, 1994).

Combining the Approaches Any explanation of schizophrenia must somehow combine biological, cognitive-behavioral, and sociocultural explanations. After all, many people with a genetic predisposition toward schizophrenia will turn out to be well adjusted. Furthermore, many other people grow up in dysfunctional or impoverished families, yet they also will turn out to be well adjusted.

At present, the most likely explanation seems to be some variation of the diathesis-stress model. We applied this model to depression in the section on mood disorders. When we apply this model to schizophrenia, the diathesis is biological factors such as genetic predispositions, as well as factors such as prenatal disease (McGlashan, 1994). When individuals with these biological predispositions are faced with extreme stresses, such as family problems or sociocultural issues, they are likely to develop schizophrenia (Gottesman, 1991; Halgin & Whitbourne, 1997).

SECTION SUMMARY: *SCHIZOPHRENIA*

1. Schizophrenia is marked by a wide variety of symptoms that vary from person to person; these disorders include hallucinations, delusions, and disorganized thinking, as well as problems with attention, emotions, social interactions, and behavior.

2. Schizophrenia typically develops during adolescence and early adulthood; about one-quarter will recover substantially, half will remain the same, and one-quarter will become more disturbed.

3. Biological explanations for schizophrenia include the genetic transmission of schizophrenia, neuro-transmitter abnormalities, and brain-structure abnormalities.

4. Relevant cognitive-behavioral explanations for schizophrenia focus on the family's communication patterns, excessive monitoring, and critical comments; the sociocultural approach emphasizes that factors such as poverty can contribute to schizophrenia.

5. The diathesis-stress model argues that a biological predisposition toward schizophrenia combines with psychological and sociocultural stresses to produce the disorder.

PERSONALITY DISORDERS

In Chapter 13, we saw that personality traits are relatively stable ways in which individuals differ from one another. When personality traits become inflexible and maladaptive, they are called **personality disorders.** People with personality disorders typically share the following three problems (Links et al., 1996; Oldham, 1994; Perry & Vaillant, 1989):

1. An inflexible, maladaptive response to stress;

2. Problems at work and in social relationships; and

3. Frequent interpersonal conflicts.

Let's begin by considering two personality disorders briefly, and then we'll look at antisocial personality disorder in more detail.

The Variety of Personality Disorders

The *Diagnostic and Statistical Manual of Mental Disorders* lists numerous personality disorders. However, the diagnostic categories come from a variety of different schools of thought. As a result, the end product looks like a patchwork quilt with overlapping categories and no strong underlying theme (Trull, 1992).

An individual with **obsessive-compulsive personality disorder** tends to overemphasize details, conscientiousness, and rigid compliance with rules (Pfohl & Blum, 1995). Each of these characteristics is admirable—up to a certain point. However, this perfectionism can become such a major part of an individual's personality that he or she cannot complete a project or make a decision. For example, I know a young man who spent close to 10 minutes standing in front of an array of desserts, trying to decide which one to purchase. His friends were not amused.

In recent years, one of the most extensively researched personality disorders has been **borderline personality disorder,** which involves unstable interpersonal relationships, inappropriate anger, and impulsiveness (American Psychiatric Association, 1994a). Individuals with borderline personalities are likely to attempt suicide, and they are extremely resistant to psychotherapy (Horwitz et al., 1996).

Antisocial Personality Disorder

Of all the personality problems, antisocial personality disorder has attracted the most attention. As the name suggests, **antisocial personality disorder** is marked by a variety of antisocial behaviors, including lying, violence, and other actions

People with obsessive-compulsive personality disorder overemphasize details so much that they have great difficulty trying to make decisions about relatively minor issues, such as which sweater to wear.

that show little concern for the welfare of others (American Psychiatric Association, 1994a).

Consider the case of Milo Tark. When he was in seventh grade, he extorted money from younger schoolchildren. He joined the army at 19 but was discharged for using cocaine in the barracks. At 23, he was arrested for conning money from the elderly patrons at an automatic teller machine. He knew that the ATM machine was connected with the bank where his mother worked, but he hadn't considered how his criminal behavior could affect his mother. When he was asked about this potential problem, he yawned and said, "She can always get another job" (Morrison, 1995, p. 477).

According to estimates, between 3% and 6% of American males have this disorder, in contrast to about 1% of American females (Kessler et al., 1994; Perry & Vaillant, 1989). Notice, then, that the gender ratio is the reverse of the gender ratio for depression. (We should also note that males are currently more likely to develop substance abuse problems; these disorders were considered in Chapter 5.)

Let's consider some of the more common characteristics of antisocial personality disorder:

1. *Aggressiveness:* People with antisocial personality often become involved in physical fights. Spouse abuse and child beating are also common.

2. *Lack of guilt:* Antisocial personalities typically do not feel guilty about their immoral behavior or the harm it does to other people (Lykken, 1995). As a result, they seldom seek therapy. In fact, they fail to acknowledge any problem.

3. *Exploitation of others:* People with antisocial personality disorder typically exploit other people. They are often likable, outgoing, and charming. In fact, they may appear sincere when they apologize for wrongdoing. However, they typically continue to exploit the person to whom they have just apologized.

People in prison comprise the best publicized examples of antisocial personality disorder. However, clinicians who work with this disorder argue that it is underdiagnosed in more everyday settings (Widiger & Corbitt, 1995). Our competitive society tends to admire aggressive, clever, charming people who may bend the law, although they do not actually break it (Millon, 1981). The typical antisocial personality is probably more likely to be a successful businessperson than a mass murderer.

Some biological explanations have been proposed for antisocial personality disorder. For instance, this disorder seems to have a hereditary component (Lykken, 1995; Nigg & Goldsmith, 1994). Some argue that the disorder is related to frontal lobe problems (e. g., Lykken, 1995). This link makes sense, because the frontal lobe is responsible for inhibiting inappropriate actions. An individual with antisocial personality disorder actually performs these forbidden activities.

Psychological explanations typically emphasize that antisocial behavior develops when an aggressive, difficult child has not had the appropriate guidelines from parents (Lykken, 1995). Parents should also serve as appropriate models who encourage moral development in their children.

This disorder is difficult to treat. Individuals with disorders related to anxiety and those with mood disorders or schizophrenia seem tormented by their psychological problems, and thus welcome assistance. In contrast, people with antisocial personality disorder are unlikely to seek or accept help because they do not believe they have a problem. (We have discussed explanations for this complicated disorder only superficially; space does not permit a thorough presentation. For further possibilities, see David Lykken's 1995 book, *The Antisocial Personalities.*)

Ted Bundy was attractive and charming, yet he murdered many women, apparently without experiencing guilt. His characteristics are consistent with those of the antisocial personality.

Critical Thinking Exercise 14.5

Write down your answers to the following questions about antisocial personality disorder.

a. Suppose that a researcher wants to examine the biological basis of antisocial personality disorder, using people who meet the *DSM-IV* criteria. Suppose also that 27 of the participants meet the criteria because they break the law and are deceitful and impulsive; 33 meet the criteria because they are aggressive and irresponsible, never feeling guilty about their actions. If the researcher counted all 60 people in the same category, why would this present a problem for the study?

b. Suppose that this same researcher obtains the sample of participants from a nearby prison and concludes that people with antisocial personality disorder are likely to come from an economically poor background. Why would you question these results?

Throughout this chapter, we have examined psychological disorders in which humans become anxious, depressed, disorganized, and inflexible. The origins of these disorders are often mysterious. However, Higgins (1994) points out that we know even less about people who have resilience, or the ability to negotiate challenges and overcome stress, emerging more mature and emotionally competent. In fact, the real mystery of psychological disorders is that so many people continue to remain competent and caring in a world where natural disasters and our fellow humans present so many obstacles to a fulfilling life.

SECTION SUMMARY: *PERSONALITY DISORDERS*

1. Personality disorders are personality traits that have become inflexible and maladaptive; the various personality disorders are not especially similar to one another.

2. Obsessive-compulsive personality disorder overemphasizes details, conscientiousness, and compliance with rules; borderline personality disorder is characterized by unstable interpersonal relationships, inappropriate anger, and impulsiveness.

3. People with antisocial personality disorder frequently become violent and show little concern for others; this disorder has a genetic component, as well as a psychological explanation.

REVIEW QUESTIONS

1. We emphasized that no clear-cut boundary separates people with psychological disorders from those considered normal. Select an example of one anxiety disorder and one mood disorder. Provide an illustration of normal behavior that might resemble each disorder.

2. Suppose that a neighbor believes her adolescent child has a psychological disorder. Explain to her how a clinician is likely to make a diagnosis. What are some of the problems with the diagnosis process?

3. Make a diagram to indicate the classifications within the anxiety disorders and dissociative disorders. (This textbook lists 7 of them.) Describe each disorder and try to explain how each of these would affect a person's daily life.

4. Suppose that a college student named Susan has a strong family history of major depression. Create a scenario in which all the factors that encourage

depression (e. g., social interactions, cognitive factors, gender issues) do indeed operate in her case, leading to serious depression. Then repeat the process, this time examining life events and psychological characteristics that could make her resilient.

5. We noted that women and men differ in the prevalence of phobias, major depression, and antisocial personality disorder. Review the explanations for the greater prevalence of the first two disorders in women, and then speculate why antisocial problems are more prevalent among men.

6. We noted that people with schizophrenia experience intense disorganization. Describe how the thought processes, emotional experiences, and social interactions of schizophrenic individuals reflect this disorganization.

7. We examined a number of cognitive problems found among people who have disorders based on anxiety, mood disorders, and schizophrenia. (For example, each group exhibits some kind of problem with attention—though the nature of the problems differs.) Discuss as many of these as you can recall, using the terminology from earlier chapters in the book whenever possible.

8. What is the biological approach to psychological disorders? How does it account for disorders based on anxiety, mood disorders, and schizophrenia?

9. Describe the sociocultural approach to psychological disorders; then answer the following question, which anticipates an issue in Chapter 15: If you support a sociocultural explanation for these disorders, would you suggest only therapy for a person who had a disorder, or would you favor another solution?

10. List several important characteristics of a person with antisocial personality disorder; why does this disorder present a problem when we try to define psychological disorders? Contrast this disorder with major depression, using as many characteristics as possible.

N EW TERMS

psychological disorders (p. 452)
Diagnostic and Statistical Manual of Mental Disorders (DSM) (p. 453)
cognitive-behavioral approach (p. 455)
lifetime prevalence (p. 455)
anxiety disorders (p. 456)
generalized anxiety disorder (p. 456)
panic disorder (p. 456)
agoraphobia (p. 457)
phobic disorder (p. 457)
social phobia (p. 457)
obsessive-compulsive disorder (p. 457)
obsessions (p. 457)
compulsions (p. 457)
posttraumatic stress disorder (PTSD) (p. 457)

dissociative disorders (p. 458)
dissociative amnesia (p. 459)
dissociative identity disorder (p. 459)
multiple personality disorder (p. 459)
attentional bias (p. 460)
mood disorders (p. 461)
major depression (p. 461)
availability heuristic (p. 464)
pessimistic explanatory style (p. 464)
ruminative responses (p. 466)
distracting responses (p. 466)
bipolar disorder (p. 468)
mania (p. 468)
heritability (p. 468)
neurotransmitters (p. 468)
diathesis-stress model (p. 470)
schizophrenia (p. 471)
hallucinations (p. 471)
delusion (p. 471)
paranoid schizophrenia (p. 471)

flat affect (p. 472)
catatonic stupor (p. 472)
dopamine hypothesis (p. 473)
personality disorders (p. 475)
obsessive-compulsive personality
  disorder (p. 475)

borderline personality disorder
  (p. 475)
antisocial personality disorder (p. 475)

Recommended Readings

Al-Issa, I. (Ed.). (1995). *Handbook of culture and mental illness: An international perspective.* Madison, CT: International Universities Press. If you're curious about various psychological disorders in other countries, this resource is ideal. Among the countries described in this book are Egypt, Nigeria, India, Israel, Hungary, and Korea.

American Psychiatric Association. (1994). *Diagnostic and statistical manual of mental disorders* (4th ed.). Washington, DC: American Psychiatric Association. Although parts of the *DSM-IV* are controversial, this major reference book is clear and well organized, providing descriptions and criteria for each disorder, as well as information on its incidence and course of development.

Halgin, R. P., & Whitbourne, S. K. (1997). *Abnormal psychology: The human experience of psychological disorders* (2nd ed.). Madison, WI: Brown & Benchmark. Here's a wonderful undergraduate textbook that explains both the research side and the human side of psychological disorders.

Keefe, R. S. E., & Harvey, P. D. (1994). *Understanding schizophrenia: A guide to the new research on causes and treatment.* New York: Free Press. This book is intended for intelligent nonprofessionals; I especially admired the clear explanations of the biological research.

Lykken, D. T. (1995). *The antisocial personalities.* Hillsdale, NJ: Erlbaum. David Lykken is well known for his research on the genetic basis of personality, which we discussed in Chapter 13. Here, he examines antisocial personality disorders, with attention to both biological and psychological approaches.

Answers to Demonstrations

Demonstration 14.3

Count the number of times you said *yes* to the following questions: 1, 3, 4, 6, and 8; these items suggest that your relationship is likely to encourage depression in women. Now count the number of times you said *no* to the following questions: 2, 5, 7, 9, and 10; these items suggest that your relationship is less likely to encourage depression. Notice the relative number of items in each category.

Answers to Critical Thinking Exercises

Exercise 14.1

a. The diagnosis would not have been a valid indication of a psychological disorder; the child may be psychologically healthy and simply be struggling (presumably temporarily) with the language problem (Wakefield, 1996). However, the diagnosis would probably be reliable; for example, test-retest reliability would probably show that the child did not speak during either observation period. (Incidentally, the current *DSM-IV* emphasizes that the mutism must not be traceable to unfamiliarity with the language.)

b. As we'll see in Chapter 15, many Asian Americans are hesitant to discuss psychological disorders, especially with a stranger (Uba, 1994). We'd also need to know whether the Asian Americans were being interviewed using a language in which they were fluent. In this example, we'd be very hesitant about accepting the conclusions based on a dubious self-report technique with a potential confounding variable of language familiarity.

Exercise 14.2

a. These data are based on self-report. As you may recall from Chapter 2, we often find gender differences in self-report. Males may be hesitant about admitting that they are afraid of spiders, for instance. If we were to take physiological measures, however, we might find that the gender differences are smaller; men may show more phobias when assessed by physiological measures.

b. We would need to know whether Hispanic soldiers and European American soldiers were assigned to equally dangerous situations. The news reports at the time often mentioned that people of color were more likely to be killed in action than European American soldiers, who were typically given safer assignments. That factor might explain the relationship between ethnicity and PTSD (Stewart, 1996).

Exercise 14.3

a. The problem is that someone may use just one distracting response when trying to cope with depression. However, that one response may be extremely effective in reducing depression. In other words, the *number* of distracting responses is less important than the *quality* of those responses. As Nolen-Hoeksema and her colleagues (1993) point out, future research should ask people to rate how effective each response is in taking their minds off their troubles. This measure may be a more sensitive measure of the effectiveness of people's distracting response style. As a result, this measure might be significantly correlated with depression; also, gender differences might be found.

b. This research does not use an experimental design; people cannot be randomly assigned to a response style. It might be that the people who are more depressed at the beginning of the study would be more likely to use a ruminative style because they were more deeply depressed. In contrast, people who aren't very distressed might not brood or ruminate. In other words, a depressed mood may cause a ruminative response style, rather than the ruminative response style causing a depressed mood.

Exercise 14.4

a. As Walker and her colleagues (1994) note, the samples in this kind of research overrepresents people with high incomes—those who could afford the equipment necessary to take movies of their young children. Also, some ethnic groups may be less likely than European Americans to take movies of young children. Also, in order to obtain the movies, the individual with schizophrenia must still have contact with his or her parents; this sample may differ from those individuals who have lost contact.

b. As you know from Chapter 7, we can't always trust people's memories. It seems likely that parents might unintentionally reconstruct the early childhood experiences of their children to be more congruent with the current schema of "psychological disorders." In hindsight, a parent may report that this child was always different from the other siblings (Keefe & Harvey, 1994).

Exercise 14.5

a. The problem is that the general category of "antisocial personality disorder" really includes some very different characteristics. Therefore, the sample of individuals described here is rather like mixing apples and oranges. If the researcher groups all 60 people together, the results might be difficult to interpret. For example, let's suppose that the researcher does find partial evidence of reduced frontal lobe activity in this mixed group. The researcher wouldn't be able to explain why some people don't show this pattern. Perhaps the crucial characteristic connected with this reduced activity is impulsiveness. The study would be more useful if the researcher studied people who all met identical criteria, or if the researcher compared frontal lobe activity on one criterion at a time (e. g., first, breaking the law; second, exploiting others; and so on).

b. Here we have a sample that is not representative. It's possible that if the researcher also examined samples of people with antisocial personality disorder from the business world, these individuals would have come from middle-class and upper-middle-class backgrounds.

TREATING PSYCHOLOGICAL DISORDERS

PSYCHOTHERAPY APPROACHES

Psychodynamic Approaches

Humanistic Approaches

Cognitive-Behavioral Approaches

Other Psychotherapies

BIOLOGICAL TREATMENTS

Treating Anxiety Disorders

Treating Mood Disorders

Treating Schizophrenia

Conclusions About Biological Treatments

ISSUES IN TREATING PSYCHOLOGICAL DISORDERS

In Depth: Evaluating Therapeutic Approaches

Therapy and Gender

Therapy and Ethnic Group

Therapy and the Deaf

The Community Psychology Approach

CHAPTER 15

Consider the case of Mr. W., a 28-year-old Cambodian refugee who had visited the hospital emergency room in Seattle on several occasions. Each time, he experienced symptoms that suggested a heart attack. The medical tests were all negative, which led the physicians to suspect panic disorder.

The consulting psychiatrist encouraged Mr. W. to describe his earlier experiences during the political upheavals in Cambodia. At one point, Mr. W.'s father and a sister had died from starvation. Later, Mr. W. and his brother had managed to escape by walking more than 200 miles to Thailand. (The photo above illustrates families fleeing Cambodia during that era.) The two brothers spent three impoverished years in Thailand before immigrating to the United States. He had not been able to contact his family members—his mother and two surviving sisters—who had remained in Southeast Asia. Understandably, he still had frequent nightmares about the years of starvation.

Mr. W. was diagnosed as having both panic disorder and posttraumatic stress disorder. He received medication for his anxiety disorder, and he also went to therapy once a week. During this psychotherapy, he described in depth his family's sufferings during the three years. He also wrote a 50-page account of this period of his life, an experience that he felt was useful in reducing the trauma he had endured. He was able to taper the dose of the medication after six months in treatment, and he has been symptom free for several years (Katon, 1991).

M r. W.'s past experiences were unusually horrifying. However, the nature of his treatment was fairly standard. As you'll see, many psychological disorders are treated with a combination of drug treatment and one or more psychotherapy approaches. We'll begin by examining the major approaches to psychotherapy and then consider different kinds of biological treatments for three major classes of psychological disorders. The last part of the chapter raises important issues such as the evaluation of therapy, conducting therapy with diverse groups of clients, and the community mental health movement.

PSYCHOTHERAPY APPROACHES

Psychotherapy is a process in which a therapist aims to treat psychological problems. At present, professionals offer about 400 different kinds of psychotherapy (Garfield, 1995).

Professionals from many different academic backgrounds can provide therapy, as Table 15.1 shows. Furthermore, each type of professional can represent a variety of different theoretical orientations. We'll focus on the following three approaches:

1. *Psychodynamic therapy,* which attempts to provide insight into earlier experiences and current interpersonal relationships.

2. *Humanistic therapy,* which tries to remove the blocks to personal growth.

TABLE 15.1 Major Professionals Involved in Psychotherapy

TYPE	DESCRIPTION
Clinical and counseling psychologists	Psychologists with PhD degrees (with more emphasis on research) or PsyD degrees (with more emphasis on applied work). All have been trained to treat psychological disorders.
Psychiatrists	Physicians with MD degrees who specialize in treating psychological disorders.
Psychoanalysts	Usually psychiatrists (though sometimes psychologists) who have received training in the psychoanalytic techniques emphasized by Sigmund Freud and his followers.
Clinical social workers	People who have earned an MSW (Master of Social Work), which usually requires two years of study after a bachelor's degree.
Other therapists	People from a wide variety of backgrounds, including pastoral counselors (typically with a religious connection) and psychiatric nurses (with either an RN or a master's degree).

3. *Cognitive-behavioral therapy,* which focuses on correcting maladaptive thinking and inappropriate learning.

We need to emphasize, however, that few current therapists would confine themselves to the techniques associated with just one approach (Goldfried, 1995). The term **eclectic approach** applies to therapists who believe that they can be more effective if they use concepts and methods from more than one theoretical perspective (Neale et al., 1996).

Despite some flexibility, however, therapists usually prefer a treatment that is consistent with their theory of personality and their beliefs about the origins of psychological problems. For instance, a professional who traces problems to inappropriate thinking and learning would practice cognitive-behavioral therapy. In contrast, a professional who believes that disorders are caused by neurotransmitter imbalances will favor using the kind of drug therapy we discuss in the second section of this chapter. Finally, those who support a sociocultural explanation—that poverty and discrimination cause psychological problems—will favor a more global, community psychology approach, as discussed at the end of this chapter.

Let's now consider the major psychotherapy approaches. Later, after discussing biological treatments, we'll evaluate the effectiveness of various methods of treating psychological disorders.

Psychodynamic Approaches

Psychoanalysis, a therapy based on the psychoanalytic approach of Sigmund Freud, attempts to resolve problems by examining childhood experiences and making people aware of the conflicts buried in their unconscious. Let's first examine the classic psychoanalytic concepts. Then we'll consider some more recent developments in the psychodynamic approach; this broader perspective places more emphasis on social relationships.

Psychoanalytic Concepts Classical psychoanalysis requires many years of therapy, with perhaps three or four sessions each week, to allow in-depth probing of the unconscious (Wolitzky, 1995). An individual undergoing psychoanalysis would relax on a couch, such as the one shown in Figure 15.1. One important method Freud developed was **free association,** in which clients relax and express their thoughts freely and without censorship (Nye, 1992).

A second method Freud developed is **dream analysis,** in which the therapist interprets the hidden meaning of the patient's dream. After all, the patient is not really aware of the dream's meaning (Weiss, 1993). Freud proposed that both free association and dream analysis could be used to circumvent defense mechanisms such as repression.

Two other psychoanalytic concepts describe important processes that usually occur during psychoanalysis. These are transference and insight.

In **transference,** the client transfers a variety of positive and negative reactions associated with parents and other childhood authority figures, directing these emotions toward the therapist. These feelings may include anger, ambivalence, and jealousy of other patients. The therapist encourages transference, so that the client can reexperience the intense childhood emotions previously directed toward important adults (Eagle & Wolitzky, 1994; Wallerstein, 1995).

A second process, insight, describes the goal of classical psychoanalysis. The term **insight** refers to the client's awareness of the unconscious conflicts that cause his or her psychological problems. Insight grows gradually during the course of psychoanalysis as the therapist pieces together evidence from free associations, dream analysis, and transference. Conscious insight presumably releases the energy previously wasted on the conflict, allowing the individual to have a more satisfying life.

In recent years, however, therapists have questioned the value of classical psychoanalysis. The method is time-consuming and costly. It relies heavily on the recall of

FIGURE 15.1

In Freud's consulting room in Vienna, clients were encouraged to relax on this couch and supply free associations. Freud reasoned that repressions would be likely to weaken under these conditions.

In brief psychodynamic therapy, the therapist and the client agree upon a central issue that can be resolved relatively quickly; ideal candidates are bright and intelligent, interacting in a friendly fashion with the therapist.

early experiences. As you know from Chapters 7 and 10, our recall for these early experiences may be flawed (Brewin et al., 1993). Also, many clients cannot manage the level of abstract thinking required for psychoanalysis (Gabbard, 1995). These factors encouraged therapists who admired Freud to develop a variety of psychodynamic therapies.

Current Psychodynamic Approaches   In the current era, few therapists follow Freud's principles completely. One common adaptation of the classical approach is called brief psychodynamic therapy. This approach still incorporates some of the familiar terms, such as transference and defense mechanisms. However, **brief psychodynamic therapy** generally features these guidelines (DeAngelis, 1996; Hobbs, 1996; Messer & Warren, 1995):

1. Therapy can be accomplished within about 10 to 30 weekly sessions, rather than several years of daily meetings.

2. The therapist and the client work together to select one central issue that requires resolution, instead of Freud's intentionally broad scope.

3. Therapy emphasizes the individual's current social relationships, rather than early childhood experiences.

4. Self-motivated, intelligent people are ideal clients for brief psychodynamic therapy. In contrast, this approach is not suitable for individuals with schizophrenia, severe depression, or severe personality disorders.

Let's summarize one of the most popular brief psychodynamic therapies inspired by an American named Harry Stack Sullivan (1892–1949) and developed more recently by Myrna Weissman and Gerald Klerman (1990). **Interpersonal psychotherapy** (often abbreviated **IPT**) focuses on improving the quality of a person's current interactions with other people. The client and the therapist work together to identify specific problems that may be currently interfering with interpersonal relationships. These often include issues of grief, interpersonal arguments, role transitions, and lack of skill in social interactions (Andreasen & Black, 1995). When ITP is used to treat depression, the assumption is that mood disorders will improve once the interpersonal dilemma is resolved (Swartz & Markowitz, 1995).

Psychodynamic approaches no longer dominate psychotherapy as they did several decades ago, although interpersonal psychotherapy is popular. In the topics that follow, we'll consider some alternative therapies.

Critical Thinking Exercise 15.1

Write down your answers to the following questions about psychodynamic approaches to therapy.

a. From what you know about human memory, why would you be more likely to trust the clients' reports in ITP than in classical psychoanalytic therapy?

b. Suppose that a young woman is being treated for depression with classical psychoanalytic therapy. The woman repeatedly emphasizes that she had a fairly happy childhood; the therapist believes that this emphasis suggests she really experienced major conflicts in her early life. How would you approach this issue from a critical thinking perspective?

Humanistic Approaches

As we discussed in Chapter 13 when we explored personality theories, the humanistic approach emphasizes that humans have tremendous potential for personal growth and self-actualization. However, people can run into roadblocks. For example, parents may withhold their love and approval until a young person conforms to their standards; that is, parents often show conditional positive regard. The goals of **humanistic therapy** are to remove the blocks to personal growth and to help people appreciate their true selves. In general, this approach is used with less serious psychological disorders; it is rarely appropriate for disorders such as schizophrenia (Vitkus, 1996).

Carl Rogers's **person-centered therapy** attempts to focus on the individual's own point of view, instead of the therapist's interpretations. A central principle is that clients possess the tools and knowledge to solve their own personal difficulties (Lakin, 1996). Therapists must not lead their clients. Instead, they should act as companions, to help them surmount feelings of hopelessness and emerge with greater understanding on the other side (Rice & Greenberg, 1991; Rogers, 1986).

Rogers (1986) proposes that three characteristics are particularly likely to encourage growth in person-centered therapy:

1. **Congruence,** also known as genuineness, whereby the therapist expresses his or her genuine feelings, rather than maintaining a formal "I'm the expert" attitude;

2. **Unconditional positive regard,** or a positive, nonjudgmental attitude toward the client; and

3. **Empathic understanding,** or the therapist's accurate feelings about the client's emotions.

In Rogers's person-centered therapy, the client is central in discovering the answers; the therapist acts as a companion.

These characteristics allow the therapist to enter the client's world, creating a trusting relationship in which the client can move in useful directions (Gelso & Fretz, 1992; C. H. Patterson, 1996). In fact, an important goal of therapy is not merely to solve current problems, but also to promote psychological growth.

An important tool in person-centered therapy is **active listening,** in which the therapist attempts to understand both the content and the emotion of a client's statement. The therapist then communicates this understanding back to the client. The therapist should not simply echo the client's statements. Instead, the therapist is trying to determine whether his or her understanding of the situation is correct (Thorne, 1992). Although active listening originated in person-centered therapy, it is now standard in most other therapeutic approaches. Now try Demonstration 15.1, which features an example of person-centered therapy.

DEMONSTRATION 15.1 Person-Centered Therapy

In the following excerpted interview, Carl Rogers interacts with a 30-year-old divorced woman named Gloria, who has been having difficulty adjusting to her single life. As you read, try to understand Rogers's general method. Then read it again, paying particular attention to (1) the active-listening technique; (2) Rogers's congruence—that is, his genuineness, rather than pompous formality; (3) unconditional positive regard; and (4) empathic understanding.

Gloria is discussing how she enjoys "utopian moments" in her life, when she feels right about herself:

Rogers: I sense that in those utopian moments you feel kind of whole. You feel all in one piece . . .

Gloria: Yes, it gives me a choked-up feeling when you say that because I don't get that as often as I'd like. I like that whole feeling. That's real precious to me.

Rogers: I expect none of us get it as often as we'd like, but I really do understand it. [*Pause. Tears come to Gloria's eyes.*] That really does touch you, doesn't it?

Gloria: Yes, and you know what else I was just thinking? I—a dumb thing—that all of a sudden when I was talking to you I thought, "Gee, how nice I can talk to you and I want you to approve of me and I respect you, but I miss that my father couldn't talk to me like you are." I mean, I'd like to say, "Gee, I'd like you for my father." I don't even know why that came to me.

Rogers: You look to me like a pretty nice daughter. But you really do miss the fact that you couldn't be open with your own dad.

Source: Based on a film transcript, reported in Thorne (1992).

Cognitive-Behavioral Approaches

As the name suggests, **cognitive-behavioral therapy (CBT)** traces psychological disorders to inappropriate learning (behavioral factors) and to maladaptive thinking (cognitive factors). For many years, the two components of CBT existed separately. Behavioral therapists used their techniques, based on the principles of learning theory, to target specific learned behaviors. In contrast, cognitive therapists used their techniques—based on social learning theory, social cognitive principles, and cognitive psychology—to treat more generalized problems such as depression (Brewin, 1996).

In recent years, however, the two components are usually combined. Those who had previously been devoted to behavioral techniques admitted that they really needed to use imagery in treating disorders; early behaviorists had firmly rejected the concept of imagery. Also, those who had favored cognitive techniques saw the usefulness of some highly effective behavioral methods (Brewin, 1996). As a result, most people from these two traditions now call themselves cognitive-behavioral therapists. Let's begin by looking at some of the behavioral techniques inspired by classical and operant conditioning (Chapter 6), and then we'll examine some of the cognitive techniques based on the principles of cognitive psychology (Chapters 7 and 8).

Systemic desensitization is used to help people overcome a phobia about flying in an airplane. Training is especially effective when it involves contact with the feared object. This program includes a step in which clients experience a plane flight.

Systematic Desensitization   The goal of **systematic desensitization** is to reduce fear or anxiety by gradually exposing the client to increasingly anxiety-arousing versions of the feared stimulus, while he or she is relaxed. The purpose of systematic desensitization is to extinguish learned fearful reactions. During the first phase, the therapist and the client work together to construct a fear hierarchy, with the least anxiety-arousing items at the beginning and the most terrifying items at the end. Imagine a college student who is extremely nervous in dating, academic, and other social situations (Larkin & Edens, 1994). The easiest item on his list might be "playing video games alone in the dorm room, and my roommate walks in." His most difficult item might be "going to a large party alone."

The client is then trained in systematic relaxation, learning to relax all muscles while imagining being in a serene, beautiful setting. After the client has learned to relax, the therapist presents the easiest item in the fear hierarchy. If the client feels anxious, the therapist immediately encourages the relaxing imagery. Gradually, they work their way up through the hierarchy. The therapist often encourages the client to imagine the feared stimulus. Other times, therapy uses **in vivo treatment** (pronounced "in *vee*-voe"), in which the client actually interacts with the feared situation. For example, the final goal for treating a snake phobia using the in vivo approach might be for the client to handle a live snake. In general, in vivo treatment is more effective than therapy in which clients simply imagine the feared stimulus (Emmelkamp et al., 1992; Harris et al., 1991).

As you might imagine, systematic desensitization is especially useful in treating anxiety-based disorders. The technique has been used successfully with both adults and children, in treating problems such as simple phobia, social phobia, agoraphobia, obsessive-compulsive disorder, and posttraumatic stress disorder (Bowers, 1991; Williams & Gross, 1994; Zinbarg et al., 1992).

Exposure With Response Prevention   Another related method is used to treat individuals who have obsessive-compulsive disorder. Using the technique called **exposure with response prevention,** clients touch something that may be dirty, and then they are instructed to avoid the typical response of repetitive handwashing (Goisman, 1997). Schwartz and his colleagues (1996) found that people who had been treated with this technique were less likely to show compulsive behaviors. Before and after treatment, the researchers also conducted PET scans of each client's limbic system. Activity in this region was abnormally high—prior to treatment—when clients touched the dirty object, but it was substantially reduced after treatment.

Behavior Modification   As you may recall from Chapter 6, **behavior modification** systematically uses techniques from learning theory to change human behavior. Most often, appropriate behavior is shaped through the use of rewards and punishment, using operant conditioning techniques. For example, many psychiatric hospitals and group homes use a **token economy,** in which tokens such as poker chips are awarded for good behavior. The clients can later exchange these tokens for special privileges, objects, or activities (Williams & Gross, 1994).

If you are intrigued by behavior modification, you may wish to turn back to Demonstration 6.3 on Page 210. Keep in mind, however, that therapists who use behavior modification have undergone extensive training. Don't plan a major transformation on your own, or you may be disappointed.

Before we examine the cognitive side of the cognitive-behavioral approach, let's compare the behaviorist approaches we've just discussed with the extremely different psychodynamic approaches. Psychodynamic therapists believe that people are driven by hidden conflicts of which they are unaware. Psychodynamic therapy therefore addresses the underlying, unconscious dynamics, not the symptom. In contrast, behaviorists argue that the symptom *is* the problem. If we can effectively change the behavior, then we have eliminated the problem (Eysenck, 1991). Also, psychodynamic therapists often explore the past history that could have produced the problem. In contrast, behaviorists concentrate on the present, observable behavior.

Several different cognitive approaches within the cognitive-behavioral tradition emphasize that people are plagued by psychological disorders because their thinking is inappropriate or maladaptive. Recovery therefore requires a restructuring of the client's thoughts. Cognitive approaches have been standard therapy for depression for some time (Beck, 1995). However, cognitive approaches are now used in treating panic disorder (Adler, 1991c), schizophrenia (Kingdon & Turkington, 1994), and various disorders in children (Craighead et al., 1994; Larkin & Edens, 1994).

A variety of cognitive therapies have been developed in recent years. We'll feature Beck's cognitive therapy and then consider Ellis's rational emotive behavior therapy and Meichenbaum's stress management training in less detail. Although the specific components of these techniques differ, all three emphasize **cognitive restructuring,** an approach that focuses on changing the individual's maladaptive thought patterns.

Suppose that a student is reluctant to attempt college registration because he or she believes that others will interpret questions as a sign of stupidity. Cognitive therapy would suggest that the student should test the validity of these beliefs in an actual registration situation.

Beck's Cognitive Therapy   In Chapter 14, our discussion of the cognitive components of depression mentioned that depressed people have negative views about themselves and life events. **Beck's cognitive therapy** attempts to correct these systematic errors in reasoning, known as cognitive distortions, in order to treat depression. Some of the reasoning errors that this therapy addresses includes the following (Beck, 1991; Robins & Hayes, 1995):

1. Overgeneralization, or drawing a general rule from just a few isolated incidents and applying the conclusion to unrelated situations;

2. Mental filtering, or dwelling on one negative detail while ignoring the positive side;

3. "All-or-nothing" thinking, so that experiences must be either completely good or completely bad, rather than somewhere between the two extremes; and

4. Automatic thoughts, or negative ideas that emerge quickly and spontaneously.

Consider how Beck's cognitive therapy helped one young man who was planning to postpone his dream of going to college. He argued that people at the college would consider him stupid if he did not appear completely confident and sure of himself (Weishaar & Beck, 1987). The therapist urged him to design an "experiment" to

DEMONSTRATION 15.2 Testing the Accuracy of Your Beliefs

Identify a particular activity that you have always been reluctant to try. This activity—of course—should not be a dangerous one. However, it should be something that is slightly intimidating. Some examples include (1) introducing yourself to one of your college professors after class and asking a question; (2) going into the Career Planning Office to investigate some possible professions; (3) attending a lecture or an activity on campus by yourself; or (4) sitting next to strangers at lunchtime. For this demonstration, you will test your belief that the activity would not be successful.

Identify what you expect to happen during this test. Also identify how you will measure the expected results. (For example, if you sit near strangers, you might measure the number of people who talk to you during lunch.) Then actually test your hypothesis, keeping a positive attitude about the outcome. Of course, not every outcome will be as positive as in the case of the young man at registration who is described in the text. Still, you will probably find that the results were more positive than you had anticipated.

test his beliefs. At college registration, he asked several students for directions and for help with a complicated computerized list. Following the "experiment," he reported that every one of the students had been friendly, and they were often as confused as he. In fact, by gathering information through his questions, he was able to help other lost students. The "experiment" helped him develop a positive attitude toward college and toward his own abilities. Some time during the next week, try Demonstration 15.2 to see whether this method works for you, as well.

Many studies have demonstrated that cognitive therapy techniques such as Beck's are successful in helping people with severe depression, as well as less serious mood disorders treated in college counseling centers (Beck, 1991; Hollon & Beck, 1994; Robins & Hayes, 1995). For example, a meta-analysis combined the results of 69 studies testing the effectiveness of self-statement modification. The technique of **self-statement modification** encourages people to replace negative statements about themselves with more positive statements. The average person who used this technique was better adjusted after therapy than 77% of people in a control group (Dush et al., 1983). In other words, self-statement modification does not help everyone, but it is reasonably effective.

Critical Thinking Exercise 15.2

Write down your answers to the following questions about behavioral techniques and about Beck's cognitive therapy.

a. Suppose that you locate 20 studies on systematic desensitization. Averaging across all studies, you discover that 85% of the participants reported their symptoms improved after therapy. You also locate 20 studies on Beck's cognitive therapy. Averaging across all studies, you discover that 70% of all participants reported their symptoms improved after therapy. Assume that the studies were conducted appropriately and that the self-reports are accurate. Still, why couldn't you conclude that systematic desensitization is the more effective therapy technique?

b. In the story about the college student and registration, your textbook places quotation marks around the word *experiment*. This is the word that therapists often use to describe the method in which clients test their own beliefs. Why isn't this kind of test a true experiment?

Ellis's Rational Emotive Behavior Therapy This cognitive approach was founded in the 1950s by Albert Ellis. Ellis had originally tried a psychodynamic approach, but he felt that the technique was not particularly effective or efficient (Ellis, 1996). He became increasingly convinced that people's psychological disorders can be traced to irrational beliefs. Here are several of the unreasonable beliefs he frequently noticed among his clients (Ellis, 1996; Ellis & Harper, 1975).

1. "I must have love and approval from the people I care about—at *all* times."

2. "I must be completely successful, or else I am worthless."

3. "My living conditions must be absolutely pleasurable, or else I can't stand it."

Basically, **rational emotive behavior therapy (REBT)** encourages people to examine their beliefs carefully and rationally, to make positive statements about themselves, and to solve problems effectively. Ellis first works with his clients to detect irrational beliefs. These beliefs often contain words such as "should," "must," and "always." Ellis then urges clients to debate their irrational beliefs. Ellis (1996) focuses on his clients' present situation, not their past experiences, because he acknowledges that memory is often an inaccurate reconstruction of what really happened.

Consider how Ellis (1986) used the technique of debating irrational beliefs to help a woman named Jane, who was extremely anxious about social interactions, especially in talking with men. Ellis encouraged Jane to debate several unreasonable beliefs such as, "When I don't speak well and impress people, how does that make me a stupid, inadequate person?" (p. 281).

Jane was also encouraged to construct some positive statements to repeat to herself several times a day, such as, "I *can* speak up to others, even when I feel uncomfortable doing so." Finally, Ellis worked with her on strategies for solving practical problems, such as how to meet appropriate men. Notice, then, that REBT emphasizes behaviors, as well as cognitions. It encourages people to develop practical changes in behavior, not simply a new way of thinking about the world (Ellis, 1996).

In many respects, Aaron Beck's and Albert Ellis's approaches have similar goals, so it is easy to confuse them. However, Beck identifies a general tendency to develop a negative self-image, so that the client's entire attitude is generally pessimistic. In contrast, Ellis targets a small number of specific irrational beliefs. Still, cognitive-behavioral therapies can easily combine both techniques, together with the techniques of the next approach we'll consider.

Meichenbaum's Stress Management Training   Donald Meichenbaum (1985, 1993, 1995) agrees with Beck and Ellis that clients should use cognitive restructuring. However, his technique is more focused on reducing future stress, rather than reinterpreting past failures. Specifically, **stress management training** helps people to prepare for difficult or unpleasant situations by anticipating problems and practicing methods of controlling stress. Clients are taught relaxation techniques and problem-solving methods. They are also instructed to notice when their thinking becomes negative. Then they develop some helpful statements that can guide them through a crisis. For example, a young man might devise a series of statements he can say to himself when he gives a presentation in front of his speech communications class: "It's natural to feel tense" and "Worrying is only going to make me more nervous" and so on. Notice, then, that these cognitive statements can be used to guide and shape future behavior.

To summarize, the cognitive-behavioral therapies propose that psychological disorders are caused by inappropriate learning and by maladaptive thinking, not by unconscious conflicts (psychodynamic therapies) or by blocking of full development (humanistic therapies). Cognitive-behavioral therapies focus on current or future problems and use a variety of techniques to encourage clients to act and to think more appropriately. Table 15.2 summarizes the three major therapies we have discussed, so it can help you clarify the similarities and differences. We'll examine the effectiveness of these methods in a later section.

This student could reduce his nervousness during this class presentation by using Meichenbaum's techniques, including relaxation techniques and positive self-statements.

Other Psychotherapies

Even when we consider the numerous variations of the three major approaches to psychotherapy, the total is only a fraction of the hundreds of different kinds of therapy currently available. The diversity of these other approaches is fascinating. In

TABLE 15.2 The Three Major Approaches to Treating Psychological Disorders

	THERAPY APPROACH		
	Psychodynamic	**Humanistic**	**Cognitive-Behavioral**
1. Psychological component emphasized	Emotions	Emotions	Behaviors and thoughts
2. Source of the problem	Childhood problems and unconscious conflicts	Blocking of full development	Inappropriate learning and thinking
3. Focus of therapy	Bring the conflict to consciousness	Discover true emotions and goals	Correct undesirable behaviors and restructure inappropriate thinking
4. Techniques of therapy	Psychoanalysis, using free association and dream analysis	Conversations, largely guided by client	Systematic desensitization, behavior modification, self-statement modification, and stress management

Note: For simplicity's sake, the psychodynamic approach is represented by Freud's classic psychoanalytic treatment.

some, clients are encouraged to smash furniture and hurl insults; in others, they are trained to move their eyes in a specified pattern (Singer & Lalich, 1996). Also, dozens of books are available to help people address their problems without the aid of a therapist (Santrock et al., 1994). Let's limit our exploration to two general approaches that can be used with a variety of different therapies, including the three we have discussed. These general approaches are group therapy and family therapy.

Group Therapy In **group therapy,** the therapist works with a group of seven or eight people who have something in common. The therapist usually does not actively direct the conversation, but lets it unfold naturally. The group is encouraged to use its own resources and to develop a sense of belonging and common purpose (Schoenholtz-Read, 1994; Woody et al., 1989). A meta-analysis has confirmed the usefulness of group therapy (Burlingame et al., 1995).

One major advantage of group therapy is that it encourages people to realize that others have similar problems—they are not alone. Consider how group therapy can help gay men struggling in a society that is biased against gay people (Dworkin & Gutiérrez, 1992). In group therapy, the men do not need to hide their sexual orientation. They can rapidly identify with the group, while appreciating the diversity of gay relationships. Together, they can share strategies about dealing with mutual problems, such as relationships with family members or the experience of coming out (telling others that they are gay).

Family Therapy As the name implies, family therapy considers the entire family to be the client, rather than focusing on just one family member. According to the **family therapy** approach, families show recurring patterns of interactions, and many problems reflect disturbed relationships among several family members, rather than just a single person (Goldenberg & Goldenberg, 1991). Generally, therapy includes all members of the nuclear family—even younger children. The approach resembles group therapy, except that the family comprises a group with established patterns of interacting.

Like group therapy, family therapy has been adapted creatively to address a variety of current issues. For example, psychologists now use family therapy to work with troubled Hispanic adolescents and their families (Szapocznik & Kurtines, 1993). In many of these families, the parents are strongly loyal to their Latin American background, whereas the adolescents identify more strongly with U.S. culture.

The goal of the therapy is to encourage bicultural efficacy in both the parents and the adolescents. As Chapter 11 outlined, **bicultural efficacy** is a person's belief that he or she can live effectively within two different ethnic groups (Birman, 1994; LaFromboise et al., 1993). Therapists therefore try to reduce family conflict by encouraging all family members to appreciate the strengths of both cultures.

Critical Thinking Exercise 15.3

Write down your answers to the following questions about other psychotherapies.

a. Suppose that you have a neighbor who praises the new "Scream Psychotherapy" she has tried. She went to the therapist's office and shouted a series of phrases she had learned, such as "I'm angry" and "I feel stronger." After just a single session, she believes she is able to express her feelings more clearly. How would you analyze her conclusion from a critical-thinking perspective?

b. Imagine that you are designing a study to test the effectiveness of family therapy. You examine 100 families, randomly assigning the families to either the therapy group or the waiting-list control group. (These families will receive therapy at a later date.) What kinds of dependent variables could you measure to assess the effectiveness of the therapy?

SECTION SUMMARY: *PSYCHOTHERAPY APPROACHES*

1. Sigmund Freud's psychoanalytic technique uses free association and dream analysis to probe the unconscious; therapy emphasizes transference and insight.

2. Brief psychodynamic therapy approaches—such as interpersonal psychotherapy—focus more on current interactions with other people.

3. Humanistic approaches emphasize techniques such as congruence, unconditional positive regard, empathic understanding, and active listening.

4. Cognitive-behavioral approaches use behavioral techniques such as systematic desensitization, exposure with response prevention, and behavior modification; cognitive approaches emphasize cognitive restructuring and include Beck's cognitive therapy, Ellis's Rational Emotive Behavior Therapy, and Meichenbaum's stress management training.

5. Other approaches to therapy, which can also be combined with the previous methods, include group therapy and family therapy.

BIOLOGICAL TREATMENTS

We have discussed several psychotherapy approaches to treating disorders. People recall their dreams, figure out how to eliminate roadblocks, and devise alternative ways of viewing their lives. In all these approaches, therapists emphasize emotions, behaviors, and thoughts. In contrast, biological treatments focus on the physiology of the central nervous system—on neurotransmitters, rather than theories of personality.

As the name suggests, **drug therapies** treat psychological disorders with medication. In this chapter, we'll examine how drugs can be used to treat three important categories of disorders that were discussed in Chapter 14: anxiety disorders, mood disorders, and schizophrenia.

Treating Anxiety Disorders

More people receive medication for anxiety than for any other psychological disorder (Schatzberg & Cole, 1991). **Antianxiety drugs** reduce tension and create drowsiness by depressing activity in the central nervous system. These antianxiety drugs include

Antianxiety drugs may be useful for treating anxiety disorders, especially when combined with psychotherapy. However, side effects can be a problem.

Joan Nobiling, an advocate for people who have psychological disorders, believes that medication is an essential part of her treatment.

Valium and Librium. Unfortunately, physicians sometimes prescribe these drugs too freely, when therapy might be more helpful in examining the source of the anxiety (Hughes & Pierattini, 1992). In addition, these antianxiety drugs frequently produce side effects such as fatigue, memory disturbances, and poor balance. Furthermore, people who stop taking these drugs often report withdrawal symptoms such as irritability, depression, and insomnia (Gitlin, 1996). However, antianxiety drugs may be useful for the short-term treatment of anxiety disorders, especially in combination with psychotherapy (C. B. Taylor, 1995). For example, Mr. W., the Cambodian man described at the beginning of the chapter, seemed to be helped by six months of appropriate medication.

Treating Mood Disorders

As Chapter 14 described, about 17% of the U.S. population will experience a major depressive episode at least once in their lives (Kessler et al., 1994). Many of these individuals will seek drug treatment, and a much smaller number will be treated with electroconvulsive shock. Between 1% and 2% will experience bipolar disorder, which is typically treated with a substance called lithium.

Treating Major Depression With Drug Therapy   A variety of **antidepressant drugs** are used to treat the symptoms of depression. For many years, the two major classes of antidepressants were the MAO inhibitors and the tricyclics. These two kinds of medications work by different mechanisms, but both ultimately increase the effective levels of two relevant neurotransmitters—serotonin and norepinephrine. Each of these classes of antidepressants is reasonably helpful in relieving the symptoms of depression. However, each also needs to be prescribed with caution (Erickson & Goodwin, 1994; Potter et al., 1991).

In 1988, a new drug was introduced called Prozac, or fluoxetine; about 10 million people now take this antidepressant (Alloy et al., 1996). Prozac is a selective serotonin reuptake inhibitor (or SSRI); it works by selectively blocking the reabsorption of serotonin at the nerve endings. As a result, the activity of serotonin is enhanced. Many people greeted Prozac as the new "miracle drug," especially because it seemed to have less troublesome side effects. However, several studies have shown that Prozac and other new SSRIs are no more effective than the more established antidepressants (Greenberg et al., 1994). In addition, overdoses can be lethal.

Antidepressants cannot help everyone who suffers from depression. They are most effective for people who are severely depressed, who have had previous depressive episodes, and whose family history suggests a genetic component. However, many individuals do not respond to antidepressants. A further problem is that the drugs work slowly, often requiring up to six weeks for a person to respond (Erickson & Goodwin, 1994). In addition, overdoses can be lethal.

Despite their drawbacks, many people can function more normally with a combination of antidepressants and psychotherapy. For example, Joan Nobiling is an advocate for people with psychological disorders; she herself suffers from depression. In a presentation at my college, she pointed out how antidepressants allowed her to take full advantage of psychotherapy and other community support programs. As she said, "It's like someone who's drowning. They have to be able to get their head up from under the water to breathe. Then they can resume swimming" (Nobiling, 1991).

Treating Major Depression With Electroconvulsive Therapy   Let's now consider a kind of biological treatment that is sometimes used for severely depressed individuals who do not respond to antidepressants or who cannot take these antidepressants for medical reasons. In **electroconvulsive therapy (ECT),** a person receives an electric shock that produces a seizure, which often relieves the symptoms of severe depression when other treatments have failed. ECT should not be considered for mild or moderate depression, but it is helpful when a person is overwhelmingly preocuppied with suicide or has delusions as well as severe depression (Gitlin, 1996; Potter & Rudorfer, 1993).

A person scheduled for ECT is typically anesthetized and given a muscle relaxant to reduce body movement. Then an electric current of approximately 70 to 130 volts is passed through the brain. (See Figure 15.2.) The procedure is repeated periodically for several weeks. The procedure sounds frightening, so we need to dispel some common misunderstandings: (1) The modern ECT method is *not* painful, though it may be somewhat uncomfortable. (2) The seizure, rather than the shock itself, produces the helpful effects. (3) The success rate in treating major depression is high, especially when the electrical "dosage" and the electrode placement have been adjusted for individual differences (Alloy et al., 1996; Gitlin, 1996; Sackeim et al., 1993).

Obviously, electroconvulsive therapy should not be treated casually, especially because it is associated with some temporary memory loss. However, many people who are severely depressed—and who do not respond to antidepressant medication—consider ECT to be quite literally a lifesaver (DeBattista & Schatzberg, 1995; Gitlin, 1996; Potter & Rudorfer, 1993).

FIGURE 15.2

This woman is about to receive electroconvulsive therapy (ECT).

Critical Thinking Exercise 15.4

Write down your answers to the following questions about drug and ECT treatment for depression.

a. Suppose that a group of psychiatrists is testing a new kind of antidepressant. They randomly assign their depressed clients to two groups; half receive the medication, and half receive a **placebo,** a capsule that looks like a drug but actually is an inactive substance. They record which client is in which condition, and then two months later they interview the clients to determine their current level of depression. What's wrong with this study?

b. How would you design a relatively unbiased study to test the effectiveness of electroconvulsive therapy?

Treating Bipolar Disorder With Drug Therapy   The most effective treatment for bipolar disorder is **lithium.** As you may recall from a chemistry course, one of the elements in the periodic table is lithium—hardly a substance you'd expect to find in a chapter on treating psychological disorders. Nevertheless, about 70% to 80% of people with bipolar disorder will improve after taking lithium—significantly more than the percentage who respond to a placebo (American Psychiatric Association, 1995; Price & Heninger, 1994).

Lithium is especially effective in treating the mania phase of bipolar disorder. Therapeutic doses of lithium seem to affect all major neurotransmitters, but researchers cannot explain exactly *how* lithium works (Bowden, 1995; Price & Heninger, 1994). The level of lithium in the blood stream must be carefully monitored; an overdose can be toxic, and too little medication is ineffective (Gitlin, 1996). With the appropriate dose, most people begin responding to lithium within one or two weeks (Bowden, 1995). Unfortunately, however, people who are experiencing a manic episode may resist taking any medication because they do not wish to diminish their energy and productivity.

Treating Schizophrenia

Antipsychotic drugs reduce the symptoms of schizophrenia, such as hallucinations, delusions, and agitated motor movement. These drugs typically have little effect on symptoms such as flat affect and apathy (Buckley & Meltzer, 1995; Neale, 1997). Most antipsychotics operate by binding onto the receptors associated with the neurotransmitter dopamine. As a result, dopamine cannot reach the receptors; a reduction in dopamine diminishes many schizophrenic symptoms.

The major challenge in drug therapy for schizophrenia is to find a medication for which the **target effects** (or improvements of the major symptoms of a disorder) outweigh the **side effects** (undesirable medical or psychological problems). For example, antipsychotics often make people drowsy and less alert (Whitaker, 1992). A substantial proportion of people who take the standard antipsychotics also develop a condition called tardive dyskinesia (Buckley & Meltzer, 1995; Gitlin, 1996). **Tardive dyskinesia** is characterized by involuntary body movements and abnormal gait in walking.

One of the hopeful alternatives is an antipsychotic called clozapine. Clozapine seems to reduce many of the symptoms of schizophrenia, with minimal side effects (Buckley & Meltzer, 1995; Green & Patel, 1996). Clozapine apparently alters the levels of neurotransmitters in the prefrontal cortex, improving a person's ability to plan and pay attention (Green & Patel, 1996).

Conclusions About Biological Treatments

Without a doubt, drug therapies and electroconvulsive therapy are important components of treating many psychological disorders in the current era. In many cases, they can allow seriously disturbed clients to be more receptive to therapy. However, every biological treatment has some side effects. Also, consistent with the theme of individual differences, these treatments seem to help some people without improving others. Table 15.3 summarizes the major biological treatments.

Obviously, any drug or electroconvulsive treatment must be carefully monitored, noting any side effects as well as target effects. Furthermore, psychologists would strongly argue that any disorder serious enough to be treated medically should also require psychotherapy.

TABLE 15.3   Summary of Biological Treatments

PSYCHOLOGICAL DISORDER	KIND OF TREATMENT	BRAND NAMES	SIDE EFFECTS
Anxiety disorders	Antianxiety drugs	Valium, Librium	Fatigue, memory problems, poor balance, potential addiction
Mood disorder: major depression	Antidepressant drugs	MAO inhibitors: Nardil, Parnate	Weight gain, blood pressure problems when some foods are eaten
		Tricyclics: Tofranil, Elavil	Weight gain, nervousness
		SSRIs: Prozac, Zoloft	Anxiety, insomnia
	Electroconvulsive therapy (ECT)	—	Temporary disorientation, some memory loss
Mood disorder: bipolar disorder	Lithium	Eskalith, Lithobid, Lithonate	Weight gain, fatigue
Schizophrenia	Antipsychotic drugs	Thorazine (chlorpromazine), Mellaril, Stelazine	Potential tardive dyskinesia, drowsiness
		Clozapine	Weight gain, potential blood problem

Source: Based on Gitlin, 1996.

ISSUES IN TREATING PSYCHOLOGICAL DISORDERS

So far, we have emphasized a variety of psychological and biological approaches in treating psychological disorders. Now we'll consider several more general issues, beginning with an evaluation of various therapeutic approaches. Then we'll discuss therapy and gender, therapy with members of various ethnic groups, and therapy with deaf individuals. The chapter concludes with a discussion of community mental health.

Evaluating Therapeutic Approaches

Suppose that a friend seems deeply depressed. Should you recommend therapy? So far, you have read about a variety of approaches in which people explore hidden conflicts, remove roadblocks to personal growth, and adjust their maladaptive behaviors and thoughts. Let's begin by seeing whether people tend to believe that psychotherapy is helpful. Then we'll consider some meta-analyses that compare various therapeutic approaches. We'll conclude this "In Depth" feature with a discussion of the similarities among the therapies.

Self-Reports on the Effectiveness of Therapy

You are probably familiar with *Consumer Reports,* a magazine that asks consumers to rate everything from automobiles to shampoo. In its 1994 annual survey, however, it asked its readers whether they had any experience with therapy and how satisfied they had been with the experience ("Mental Health: Does Therapy Help?" 1995). The consultant on this project was Martin Seligman (1995), a clinical psychologist well known for his work with depression.

The survey was answered by about 7,000 individuals, and more than 2,800 said that they had consulted a mental health professional—most often a psychologist or a psychiatrist. Let's look at their responses on a scale derived by adding together their responses on three 100-point subscales: (1) how much the treatment had helped with the problems that led to therapy; (2) how satisfied they were with the therapist; and (3) how they felt at the time of the survey, compared with when they had begun therapy. Figure 15.3 shows the results, in relation to the amount of time the respondents had continued their therapy (Seligman, 1995). As you can see, satisfaction is related to the number of months or years spent in therapy.

About 90% of those who had felt either "very poor" or "fairly poor" at the time they began therapy reported feeling "very good," "good," or "so-so" at the time they completed the survey. Also, the respondents who had psychotherapy alone reported being as satisfied as those who had received psychotherapy plus medication (Seligman, 1995). According to this self-report survey, then, the respondents believed that therapy had served them well.

Critical Thinking Exercise 15.5

Write down your answers to the following questions about the Consumer Reports survey.

a. Would this sample of about 2,800 people have been representative of all the individuals who had experienced psychological problems? How could biases in the sample have distorted the results?

b. Seligman (1995) concluded: "Long-term therapy produced more improvement than short-term therapy" (p. 968). What other interpretation could you provide for the data in Figure 15.3?

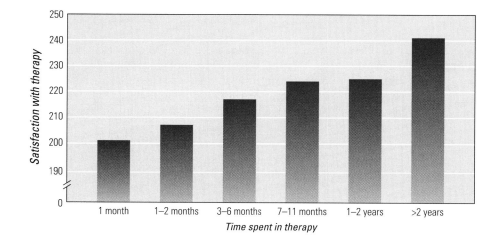

FIGURE 15.3

Overall Satisfaction With the Therapy Experience as a Function of the Time Spent in Therapy
(*Maximum score = 300*)
Source: Based on Seligman, 1995.

(IN DEPTH continued)

The *Consumer Reports* survey does demonstrate that a large number of people say they are satisfied with psychotherapy. However, be sure to check the answers to Critical Thinking Exercise 15.5 on Page 507 to see several reasons why we must be skeptical of these results. Another problem is that the self-reports were retrospective; people's memories may not have been accurate (Hollon, 1996). In addition, some of the respondents could have shown **spontaneous remission;** that is, they might have recovered without any therapy (Hall, 1996).

Meta-Analyses on the Effectiveness of Therapy

Hundreds of well-controlled studies have examined the effectiveness of psychotherapy. Researchers have gathered together a large number of these studies and conducted meta-analyses. The clear majority of these meta-analyses demonstrate that those who had therapy were better adjusted than those in control groups (Lipsey & Wilson, 1993).

A representative meta-analysis by John Weisz and his colleagues (1995) examined the effectiveness of psychotherapy with children and adolescents. This meta-analysis of 150 studies showed that individuals who had some form of cognitive-behavioral therapy were significantly better adjusted than those in the control groups. Psychodynamic and person-centered therapy were less effective. Also, the therapy was more effective for adolescent females than for adolescent males, young girls, or young boys.

All the research on the effectiveness of therapy has inspired two other questions: (1) Are some people especially responsive to certain therapies? and (2) Do the therapies share some underlying similarities?

Client-Treatment Interaction

For many years, educators have acknowledged that some children learn better with one teaching approach, whereas others learn better with an alternative method (Snow, 1977). In recent years, psychotherapists have proposed a similar pattern called **client-treatment interaction;** some kinds of clients may respond best to Therapy A, whereas other clients may respond best to Therapy B (Neale et al., 1996; Shoham-Salomon & Hannah, 1991). As Smith and Sechrest (1991) argue, the research on therapy has shown that the various therapy methods produce reasonably similar success rates. However, all therapies might be more successful if therapists and clients would work together more closely to match each client with an appropriate therapy. Perhaps Chris, who likes to examine his thoughts about relationships, would do best with interpersonal psychotherapy. In contrast, Pat might respond better to a cognitive-behavioral approach. Clearly, the idea of client-treatment interactions matches our two themes about individual differences and the complexity of human psychological processes.

Underlying Similarities in Therapies

Parts of this "In Depth" feature have focused on differences among the therapies. However, we must also emphasize the similarities. All therapies offer support, trust, reassurance, suggestions, and attention from the therapist. In all therapies, self-fulfilling prophecies may operate because clients anticipate that they *should* recover. Furthermore, all therapies share a common goal of reducing anxiety and improving the client's behavior, functioning, and self-efficacy—even though their specific routes to competent functioning may differ (Lambert et al., 1986; Strupp, 1986, 1996). Ideally, the therapist and client can form a **working alliance** in which the therapist's skills join together with the client's observational insights to enhance the counseling process (Gelso & Fretz, 1992).

In addition, an active ingredient in all therapies is the personality of the therapist. Effective therapists of all persuasions are people who are warm, genuine, and caring. Therapists who encourage trust and develop empathy with their clients are more likely to provide successful therapy, no matter which approach they favor (Kokotovic & Tracey, 1990).

Therapy and Gender

Before you read further, try Demonstration 15.3, which focuses on gender. Gender issues are often relevant in therapy because therapists may encourage traditional gender roles in both women and men. For example, a woman who is depressed because of her low status at work and in her family will become even more depressed if her therapist conveys the attitude that "I'm the one who knows everything, and you are relatively powerless." In contrast, therapy will be helpful if her therapist can treat her as a competent person who has definite strengths (Brabeck et al., 1997; Nadelson & Notman, 1995).

Some potential biases against women in therapy include encouraging women to maintain traditionally feminine gender roles and having low expectations for women clients (Espín, 1994; Hansen & Reekie, 1990). Another problem occurs when therapists have sexual relationships with their clients—obviously unethical conduct that can be especially harmful to clients who are feeling vulnerable (Canter et al., 1994; National Association of Social Workers, 1993). Clearly, therapists should not harm the very people they are hired to help. In addition, both men and women deserve to be treated in an unbiased fashion.

DEMONSTRATION 15.3 Beliefs About Gender

Read the following statements and place a checkmark in front of each statement with which you agree. This demonstration is discussed later in the chapter.

_____ 1. If a man and a woman are doing equally well at the same job, they should receive equal pay.

_____ 2. If a man and a woman are doing equally well at the same job and they have been employed an equal number of years, they should have the same chance of being promoted.

_____ 3. If a man and a woman perform equally well on an exam in a college course, they should receive the same grade.

_____ 4. If a man and a woman perform equally well throughout college and are equivalent on all important measures, they should have the same chance of receiving admission to graduate school.

_____ 5. If a man and a woman perform equally well throughout college and are equivalent on all important measures, they should have the same chance of being offered a prestigious job.

_____ 6. A man and a woman who are equally well qualified for political office should have an equal chance of being elected.

_____ 7. If a husband and a wife each spend the same number of hours on the job, they should spend the same number of hours on chores around the home.

_____ 8. A man has no right to physically abuse his wife, because she is not his "property."

In recent years, an increasing number of therapists have adopted a feminist approach to therapy. A **feminist** is a woman or man whose beliefs, values, attitudes, and actions reflect a high regard for women as human beings (Hunter College Women's Studies Collective, 1995). Check over your own answers to Demonstration 15.3. If you have checked a large number of these items, you are a feminist. Notice that the definition emphasizes that men can be feminists, if they respect women and men equally.

A **feminist approach to therapy** argues that men and women should be valued equally, that women's inferior status in society often causes psychological problems, and that gender-stereotyped behavior harms both women and men (Betz & Fitzgerald, 1993; Matlin, 1996a). Feminist therapists emphasize that the therapist and the client should be reasonably equal in power and that sociocultural factors must be addressed (Brown, 1995; Espín, 1994). Feminist therapy is often combined with other approaches, such as cognitive-behavioral therapy.

Leston Havens (1993), a psychiatrist at Harvard Medical School, remarks that the women's movement has altered the practice of therapy. He has often noticed that a woman's anxiety and depression may improve remarkably, once the therapist has acknowledged that the woman's home situation is indeed difficult.

Therapists have also begun to focus on the male gender role. They point out how the socialization of young men creates later difficulties in love relationships, as well as exaggerated attitudes about gender (Betz & Fitzgerald, 1993; Osherson, 1992). Feminist therapists encourage us to create new therapy techniques to help both men and women become more fully human.

Therapy and Ethnic Group

The U.S. Bureau of the Census (1996) has estimated that by the year 2000, 13% of the U.S. population will be Black, 11% Hispanic, 4% Asian, and 1% Native American. In Canada, one in six residents was born outside that country (Badets, 1993; Dumas, 1990). As a consequence, North American therapists need to be sensitive to different values and beliefs when they provide mental health services (Brown, 1995).

In general, European Americans are more likely than other ethnic groups to use mental health services and college counseling centers (Atkinson et al., 1993; Barney, 1994; Uba, 1994). Some of the reasons that people of color underuse these services include (1) shame in talking about personal problems to strangers; (2) suspiciousness of therapists, especially European American therapists; (3) language and economic barriers; (4) reluctance to recognize that help is necessary; and (5) culturally based preference for other interventions such as prayer.

In most cases, a person of color will not be able to see a therapist from his or her own ethnic background. For example, only about 4% of PhD-level psychologists belong to ethnic minority groups (Bernal & Castro, 1994; Hall, 1997)—but nearly 30% of the U.S. population belongs to these minority groups. Most people of color who need psychological help will therefore see someone from a different ethnic background.

As we noted, language can be another barrier. For example, most U.S. professionals are not fluent in Spanish, yet many Hispanic individuals speak little English. Vasquez (1994) describes a Spanish-speaking woman who came to a hospital emergency room, talking about pills. The E.R. physician spoke little Spanish, but he thought he had made her promise that she would not attempt suicide—and so he sent her home. Someone later discovered that she had tried to tell him she had already swallowed a lethal dose of pills and was trying to obtain help. If your first language is English, ask yourself whether you could understand the woman's message in your second language. Could you precisely capture the subtleties of anxiety, let alone the terrors of schizophrenia?

Bias Against Members of Some Ethnic Groups Although some research suggests that therapists are not racially biased, several other studies indicate that we need to be concerned (Atkinson et al., 1993; Gong-Guy et al., 1991; Sue & Sue, 1990). Consider, for example, an experiment in which European American psychiatrists were asked to make judgments about a 25-year-old male client, based on a three-page summary about this man. Each psychiatrist also received one of three additional descriptions (assigned at random). Specifically, the man was described variously as White with a high IQ, Black with a high IQ, or White with a low IQ. The psychiatrists judged the low-IQ White man to be more verbal, competent, and knowledgeable about psychology than the high-IQ Black man. The psychiatrists were also more likely to recommend drug treatment for the Black man than for either of the White men (Geller, 1988).

Therapy With People of Color We have noted many reasons why people of color may avoid seeking help. Therapists need to be flexible and eagerly committed to learning about the culture of those ethnic minority clients who do seek therapy. Here are some important general strategies that mental health professionals should keep in mind (Allodi, 1990; Bernal & Castro, 1994; Davis & Gelsomino, 1994; Fabrega, 1995; Hall, 1997; LaFromboise et al., 1994):

This photo illustrates the cuento *of Rosita who, feeling unloved by her mother and stepfather, decides to run away from home. As a runaway, she is exploited by unscrupulous circus owners. During one of her circus performances, she is happily reunited with her mother, who had been looking for her.*

1. Search the client's history for strengths that can promote the counseling process.

2. Show empathy, caring, and an appreciation of human potential.

3. Be aware of any biased beliefs or feelings that could interfere with the counseling relationship.

4. Learn about the general history, experiences, and cultural values of the client's ethnic group, but be aware of the diversity within any particular group; let the client teach you about his or her background, and take courses about ethnic diversity.

5. Be aware that refugees from some countries may have experienced torture, which is associated with high levels of anxiety and depression.

6. Be sensitive to issues of social class, which may have important effects on a client's life opportunities.

Researchers are also developing culture-sensitive techniques designed to *prevent* psychological disorders, not just to treat them. For example, a project with Puerto Rican children in New York City has successfully utilized *cuentos,* or Puerto Rican folktales (Costantino et al., 1986; Costantino et al., 1994; Malgady et al., 1990).

Therapy and the Deaf

As Chapter 4 noted, more than 28 million Americans have hearing disabilities (Soli, 1994); many have such limited hearing that they cannot communicate verbally. According to some estimates, about 40,000 deaf Americans experience serious psychological disorders, but only about 2% of these individuals receive the services they need (Pollard, 1996).

We discussed in the previous section how people who do not speak English can have difficulty communicating with therapists. The same is true for the Deaf. At present, few therapists are fluent in sign language, so deaf individuals seldom receive diagnosis and treatment. For example, Pollard (1996) describes a deaf man named Darryl, who had been admitted to a psychiatric hospital. However, because of communication difficulties, his problem could not be diagnosed until much later, when a psychologist who specialized in services to the Deaf noticed that Darryl's sign language was distorted in ways similar to the spoken-language patterns of hearing individuals with schizophrenia.

With the increased enrollment of deaf students in graduate psychology programs—as well as new programs for deaf clients—a larger proportion of deaf individuals will be able to participate in psychotherapy.

Fortunately, the picture is changing. Partly because of the Americans With Disabilities Act, deaf and hard-of-hearing students are beginning to enroll in graduate psychology programs (Pollard, 1996). In addition, therapists are starting to design specialized programs (Corker, 1994; Seppa, 1997). For example, group therapy is an especially effective way to reduce the isolation and potential embarrassment that many deaf individuals experience when they seek help for psychological problems.

The second theme of our textbook addresses the individual differences among individuals. An important component of this theme is that people differ with respect to the kind of therapy or drug treatment that is most helpful to them. Another important part of that theme is that therapists can best serve their clients by considering each individual's gender, ethnic group, and hearing ability.

The Community Psychology Approach

George Albee, a psychologist affiliated with the University of Vermont, describes his impressions when a cab driver took him to a psychiatric hospital in Brooklyn, New York, where Albee was scheduled to give a lecture:

> We drove through long stretches of Bedford-Stuyvesant, which looked a lot like a post–World War II bombed-out city. Buildings were boarded up, or scorched from fires; able-bodied men were passing around bottles in brown paper bags, teenagers who should have been in school were rapping on our cab windows and asking for quarters, teenage prostitutes shared the littered sidewalks with teenage mothers and teenage muggers. In short, we saw the pathology that characterizes this urban monument to an economic system which encourages discrimination, prejudice, involuntary unemployment, and that results in every form of social pathology. (Albee, 1987, p. 37)

Albee had arrived early, so he waited outside for an hour and was astonished to see a series of chauffeur-driven limousines pull up to the hospital entrance. A well-dressed woman emerged from each limousine. Obviously puzzled, Albee questioned one of the chauffeurs. The fellow responded, "Psychoanalysis . . . every day we bring our employers here for their hour-long psychoanalytic session." Albee suddenly realized that he was witnessing a prototype of the problems of the mental health system in the United States.

The irony is that millions of people with psychological problems will never speak with a therapist. In Chapter 14, we noted that 48% of the U.S. population will struggle with one of the psychological disorders we have discussed or with substance abuse (Kessler et al., 1994). One-on-one psychotherapy is beyond the reach of most troubled individuals.

In contrast to the individual approach, the **community psychology approach** focuses on social issues and institutions that influence groups and individuals; the goal is to optimize the well-being of community members by using innovative interventions (Duffy & Wong, 1996). This approach argues that (1) a top priority should be to prevent psychological disorders; (2) the current program of deinstitutionalization is not working; and (3) communities must offer a variety of services to help individuals with psychological problems.

Preventing Disorders As we saw in Chapter 14, the **sociocultural approach** emphasizes that psychological disorders are largely caused by social and cultural factors. As Albee argues, if we want to reduce the incidence of psychological problems, we must attack the crucial social problems, such as poverty, prejudice, unemployment, and so forth (cited in Freiberg, 1991). In other words, we should change society to eliminate discrimination on the basis of gender, ethnic group, disabilities, and other social categories—hardly an easy task! Notice that this approach—holding society accountable for problems—is very different from tracing psychological disorders to an individual person's biological makeup or past experiences. This approach is also much more radical.

Some of the prevention techniques recommended by community psychologists include the following (Alloy et al., 1996; Duffy & Wong, 1996; Reiss & Price, 1996):

1. Education, to help people alter their behavior and learn problem-solving skills;

2. Health care, especially good prenatal care and nutrition, to reduce the danger of brain damage in newborns;

3. Programs to promote feelings of competence and self-esteem among community members; and

4. Community intervention programs aimed at all age groups.

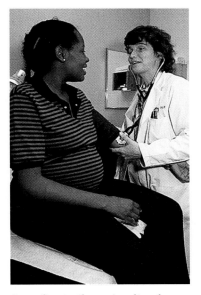

According to the sociocultural approach, the way to address psychological disorders is through health care, education, community organization, and promotion of self-esteem.

Only a small portion of the money that North Americans spend on mental health is funneled into prevention. As a consequence, most projects are small-scale, though the results are often encouraging. A typical project is the *cuento* approach with high-risk Puerto Rican children, described earlier. Another program assists elderly caregivers of disabled spouses, a population at risk for stress-related psychological problems (Mrazek & Haggerty, 1994). Because of limited finances, these are typically short-term programs that cannot provide the necessary long-term continuity. Ironically, more people die each year in the United States from suicide than from homicide (Muñoz et al., 1996), yet we have few comprehensive programs designed to prevent suicide and related psychological problems.

Deinstitutionalization Beginning in the late 1950s, the mental health system in the United States adopted a policy of **deinstitutionalization,** or discharging people from psychiatric hospitals into the community. In theory, this policy could be helpful because it would return people to the supportive environment of family and community. Deinstitutionalization could also encourage independence and coping abilities —certainly an admirable goal.

In practice, however, deinstitutionalization has not worked (Duffy & Wong, 1996). For instance, many people who would have been cared for in a psychiatric hospital now receive temporary care in general hospitals that aren't designed to treat psychological problems (Grob, 1994; Szasz, 1994). Instead of being treated in appropriate institutions, people with serious disorders such as schizophrenia and bipolar disorder are more likely to live in homeless shelters, in jails, and on the street (Baum & Burnes, 1993; Torrey, 1991).

The sad reality is that many people with serious psychological disorders are homeless (Baum & Burnes, 1993; Levine & Rog, 1990). Because they do not have an established residence, they are usually excluded from programs that offer long-term services to people with psychological disorders. Several researchers estimate that between 65% and 85% of the homeless population experience significant mental illness, alcoholism, drug problems—or some combination of the three (Baum & Burnes, 1993). Furthermore, the stress and instability of homelessness ensure that even mentally healthy people would develop psychological disorders. The problem is clearly a serious one that our institutions have not adequately addressed. The homelessness issue also illustrates how deinstitutionalization has failed. People with psychological problems are *not* being integrated into the community. Instead, they are being isolated, without appropriate supports and treatments.

According to studies, a large number of homeless people have psychological disorders.

Other Programs in the Community The community psychology approach argues that the problem of mental illness is too complex to be remedied by any single program (Duffy, 1998). Consistent with our complexity theme, a complicated problem requires complex, sophisticated solutions. A systematic approach would include community mental health centers, intermediate care facilities, hotlines, assistance for family members, and organizations for people with long-term mental illnesses.

Ideally, community mental health centers should offer education about preventing psychological disorders. They should also offer well-planned outpatient services, so that people could live at home and receive therapy at the center (Muñoz et al., 1996). These centers could provide systematic aftercare for people who have been released from a hospital.

Intermediate care facilities should also be available. For example, in a **halfway house,** people who have recently been discharged from a hospital live together with trained staff in a home and learn the skills necessary to live independently (Carling, 1995). Many communities sponsor a **crisis hotline,** a phone number to call for immediate counseling and comfort. Hotlines are designed to help people who are suicidal or have other psychological problems, as well as others experiencing a crisis—such as victims of rape and domestic violence. Hotline volunteers provide immediate counseling and information about services available in the community (Ackerman, 1997; Duffy, 1998).

The families of the mentally ill are another community resource. For example, the National Alliance for the Mentally Ill (NAMI) is a grassroots organization focused on improving the lives of people with severe psychological disorders. It educates the public, lobbies for better mental health care, and encourages families to support and share strategies with others in similar situations (Duffy, 1998).

Members of a community psychosocial group called Operation Friendship work together to do outreach with their membership.

An additional community resource is the people themselves—individuals who live with psychological disorders. One representative community organization is Operation Friendship, in Rochester, New York. Operation Friendship is a psychosocial club run by community members who have psychological disorders. People help themselves and each other with a variety of services and programs that include meals, trips, courses, and assistance in applying for jobs. Groups like Operation Friendship acknowledge that an important part of therapy is **empowerment,** or developing people's ability to actively control their own lives (Duffy, 1998).

Professionals acknowledge that the North American community mental health situation is far from ideal. Some of these professionals are beginning to examine the even graver problems in developing countries (e.g., Aponte, 1994; Desjarlais et al., 1995). As Aponte (1994) laments, economically disadvantaged people in North America would be considered relatively wealthy in most of Asia, Latin America, and other developing countries. Sadly, the kinds of community organizations and empowerment programs available in some parts of North America are extremely rare when we examine the global perspective.

SECTION SUMMARY: *ISSUES IN TREATING PSYCHOLOGICAL DISORDERS*

1. Research on psychotherapy shows in general that clients report they are satisfied with therapy; meta-analyses suggest that psychotherapy is typically effective.

2. According to the concept of client-treatment interaction, some clients respond well to one kind of therapy, whereas others may respond better to a different kind; however, successful therapists from all approaches are likely to be those who are warm and who encourage trust.

3. The feminist approach to therapy argues that men and women should be valued equally and that the therapist and the client should have more nearly equal power; therapists are now beginning to address potentially harmful aspects of the male gender role.

4. European Americans are more likely than other ethnic groups to use mental health services, and some research (but not all) shows bias against people of color; therapists need to be alert to potential biases and become informed about cultural diversity.

5. At present, few therapists are skilled in sign language, but specialized programs are now being developed for working with the deaf.

6. The community mental health approach emphasizes the prevention of disorders; appropriate follow-up for people discharged from hospitals; a network of community mental health centers, halfway houses, and crisis hotlines; and community organizations for the mentally ill that encourage empowerment.

Review Questions

1. In one sentence each, describe how the following approaches explain the origin of psychological disorders: psychodynamic, humanistic, cognitive-behavioral, biological, and sociocultural.

2. Briefly describe the therapeutic approach that corresponds to each of the theoretical approaches in the previous question.

3. Focusing on the classical psychoanalytic approach, describe two techniques that encourage the expression of the unconscious, as well as some important processes that may occur during analysis. Also, describe how interpersonal psychotherapy (IPT) differs from classical psychoanalysis.

4. Imagine that you are working at a summer camp for children with a variety of psychological problems. How might a therapist use the behavioral techniques of systematic desensitization, exposure with response prevention, and behavior modification to address these children's problems?

5. Suppose that a therapist finds the cognitive components of the cognitive-behavioral approaches—as well as humanistic approaches—particularly appealing. Describe how the approaches of Aaron Beck, Albert Ellis, and Carl Rogers could be integrated in treating someone who suffers from depression.

6. Your textbook described three behavioral techniques, as well as three cognitive approaches that cognitive-behavioral therapists might adopt. Describe each of these, and discuss how you could use several of these components to help address a personal problem you wish could be corrected.

7. Considering the biological treatments for psychological disorders, list the treatments that can be used for each of the following problems: (a) schizophrenia, (b) bipolar disorder, (c) anxiety, and (d) severe depression.

8. Suppose that a relative of yours is considering psychotherapy but wonders whether it would be worth the time and money. Based on the information presented in the "In Depth" feature, how would the research give you information for answering that question?

9. The community psychology approach emphasizes the concept of empowerment. How is that concept relevant to the sections of this chapter on gender and therapy and on ethnicity and therapy?

10. The chapter ends by considering the community approach to mental health. If finances were available, how could your own community provide services to help prevent psychological disorders and to help meet the needs of people with psychological problems?

New Terms

psychotherapy (p. 484)
eclectic approach (p. 485)
psychoanalysis (p. 485)
free association (p. 485)
dream analysis (p. 485)
transference (p. 485)
insight (p. 485)
brief psychodynamic therapy (p. 486)
interpersonal psychotherapy (IPT) (p. 486)

humanistic therapy (p. 487)
person-centered therapy (p. 487)
congruence (p. 487)
unconditional positive regard (p. 487)
empathic understanding (p. 487)
active listening (p. 487)
cognitive-behavioral therapy (CBT) (p. 488)
systematic desensitization (p. 488)
in vivo treatment (p. 488)

exposure with response prevention (p. 488)
behavior modification (p. 489)
token economy (p. 489)
cognitive restructuring (p. 489)
Beck's cognitive therapy (p. 489)
self-statement modification (p. 490)
rational emotive behavior therapy (REBT) (p. 491)
stress management training (p. 491)
group therapy (p. 492)
family therapy (p. 492)
bicultural efficacy (p. 493)
drug therapies (p. 493)
antianxiety drugs (p. 493)
antidepressant drugs (p. 494)
electroconvulsive therapy (ECT) (p. 494)

placebo (p. 495)
lithium (p. 495)
antipsychotic drugs (p. 495)
target effects (p. 496)
side effects (p. 496)
tardive dyskinesia (p. 496)
spontaneous remission (p. 498)
client-treatment interaction (p. 498)
working alliance (p. 499)
feminist (p. 500)
feminist approach to therapy (p. 500)
community psychology approach (p. 502)
sociocultural approach (p. 502)
deinstitutionalization (p. 503)
halfway house (p. 504)
crisis hotline (p. 504)
empowerment (p. 504)

Recommended readings

Comas-Díaz, L., & Greene, B. (Eds.). (1994). *Women of color: Integrating ethnic and gender identities in psychotherapy.* New York: Guilford Press. This book contains six chapters on a variety of ethnic groups, six chapters on therapeutic approaches, and five chapters on specific problems (e.g., women of color in battering relationships); it provides an excellent overview of both ethnicity and therapy.

Duffy, K. G., & Wong, F. Y. (1996). *Community psychology.* Boston: Allyn & Bacon. If you want to know more about the community mental health approach outlined in the last part of this chapter, this book provides details, as well as applications of community psychology in schools, the legal system, and health care.

Gitlin, M. J. (1996). *The psychotherapist's guide to psychopharmacology* (2nd ed.). New York: Free Press. Psychiatrist Michael Gitlin has written a clear guide to drug therapy and electroconvulsive therapy. I have often recommended this book to friends who want to know about medications prescribed for psychological disorders.

Van Hasselt, V. B., & Hersen, M. (Eds.). (1994). *Advanced abnormal psychology.* New York: Plenum. This book begins with chapters on research methods and on therapeutic approaches, then discusses major categories of disorders, and concludes with treatments of these disorders.

Answers to critical thinking exercises

Exercise 15.1

a. Chapter 7 emphasized that human memory is less than perfect; memory errors are especially likely for events that happened long ago. Chapter 10 also emphasized that children's memories can be biased by suggestions. Therefore, memory for early childhood events—as emphasized by the classical psychoanalytic approach—could be highly inaccurate. In contrast, ITP emphasizes current relationships; memory for these recent events will be much more accurate.

b. The problem is that the classical psychoanalytic therapy assumes that, when a client doesn't discuss or acknowledge a particular issue, then this behavior is a sign that the issue (e.g., unhappy childhood) really did occur. The truth may be that the woman did have a genuinely happy childhood, so that's why she "fails to remember" the unhappiness. From a critical-thinking perspective, this kind of explanation is not logical.

Exercise 15.2

a. The problem is that the two kinds of therapy are used to treat two different kinds of psychological problems. Systematic desensitization is used to treat phobias, a fairly specific problem that might therefore be relatively easy to correct. In contrast, Beck's cognitive therapy is used to treat depression, a much more generalized problem. Directly comparing the "success rate" for the two kinds of disorders is not a fair comparison.

b. This test is not a true experiment, because there is no comparison group. The young man is testing the statement "If I go to registration, people there will consider me stupid." To be a true experiment, we'd have to ask, "compared to what?" The test certainly did yield some useful information, but it was not an experiment because we did not have students randomly assigned to groups, with a manipulated independent variable.

Exercise 15.3

a. One question would be "more clearly than *what?*" She needs to have a comparison condition. Presumably, she means, "more clearly than before Scream Psychotherapy." If so, you might wonder how she would assess the ability to express her feelings (i.e., what dependent variables). You might also wonder if she would have shown similar improvement if she had no therapy, just the passage of time. Also, you might be suspicious that her "cure" was a result of her expectations, rather than the therapy itself.

b. You could ask the family members in both groups to rate their family interactions, for example on a 5-point rating scale. You could also ask family members to record the number of arguments they had, the number of conversations, and the number of positive remarks they had made to each other, during a specified time period.

Exercise 15.4

a. First of all, you would need to be certain that the clients were not aware whether they were in the medication condition or in the placebo-control study. However, the ideal study would use the double-blind technique, in which neither the researchers nor the clients knew which individuals received the drug and which received the placebo. (Another individual, for example, might mark the pill bottles either *A* or *B*.) Then, the psychiatrists' expectations could not influence the clients' reactions. In addition to methodological problems, this study raises serious ethical concerns: People in the placebo group believe they are receiving a drug, but they are not; the deception is a problem.

b. The effectiveness of ECT can be tested by comparing a group who receives real ECT with a group who receives "sham ECT," which would be all the ECT procedures such as anesthesia and electrode placement—but no electric current. (Obviously sham ECT is not an ideal control group, though.) Incidentally, the research clearly demonstrates that real ECT is more effective than sham treatment in reducing depression (Gitlin, 1996).

Exercise 15.5

a. First of all, people who read *Consumer Reports* are not representative of the U.S. population. They are more likely to be White, middle class, and fairly well educated. They are probably more likely than average to want to solve problems—like which shampoo to buy or how to get rid of their depression. People with severe psychological problems are probably *not* likely to subscribe. Then those who had the motivation to return the questionnaire would be even more likely than the average *Consumer Reports* subscriber to constitute an "elite," nonrepresentative sample, especially because people who had unpleasant psychotherapy experiences would be less likely to enjoy filling out the questionnaire. All these factors would bias the results so that respondents would be more pro-therapy than would have been obtained with a random sample.

b. Another possible interpretation is that those who were dissatisfied with therapy dropped out; only those who are still satisfied remain. Furthermore, those who have been spending the time and money on more than 2 years of therapy may need to convince themselves that therapy is worthwhile, in order to spend all the time and money on it.

SOCIAL COGNITION

ATTITUDES

How Attitudes Influence Behavior

Cognitive Dissonance

Attitude Change

PERSON PERCEPTION

Impression Formation

Attribution

STEREOTYPES, PREJUDICE, AND DISCRIMINATION

Racism

Sexism

In Depth: The Cognitive Basis of Stereotypes

Stereotypes and Self-Fulfilling Prophecies

Reducing Biases

CLOSE RELATIONSHIPS

Friendship

Love Relationships

CHAPTER 16

Consider the case of Colorado Governor Roy Romer—shown here at a press conference. Like most of us, Romer has held some stereotypes. Unlike most of us, however, Romer decided to learn more about one group of people whom he had stereotyped. His journey began when friends from his local Presbyterian church talked lovingly about their gay son. At that point, Romer told himself, "I need to understand this better." So he attended some meetings of a support group called Parents, Families, and Friends of Lesbians and Gays. He also studied the group's literature.

Some time later, his assistant told him she was a lesbian, and he knew how to be warmly supportive. As she recalls, he instantly replied, "Well, you're the same person to me now that you were 10 minutes ago." Shortly afterwards, he began setting up meetings with gay Colorado state government employees. Each person described his or her experiences, often mentioning the discrimination they had faced. A turning point came when one state employee refused to divulge his last name or his government position. As this man explained, he was certain he would be fired if his supervisor learned he was gay. Romer quickly realized that gay workers needed protection, so he issued an executive order forbidding any anti-gay job discrimination in the Colorado state government.

Romer didn't stop there. In 1992, he championed the efforts to defeat anti-gay legislation in his state. He is also creating a state Commission on the Rights and Responsibilities of Same Sex Relationships. As Romer told columnist Deb Price, "I believe that any gay person is equal in the sight of God to me." Romer also emphasized that people—heterosexual and gay alike—are more likely to thrive in long-term, committed relationships, rather than facing loneliness (Price, 1997).

An attitude is a psychological tendency that is expressed by an evaluation of something. For example, what is your attitude toward the needle-exchange program, in which drug addicts can exchange their used needles for clean ones, thereby reducing the spread of AIDS?

Our topic for the next two chapters is **social psychology,** which focuses on the way other people influence our thoughts, feelings, and behaviors. This first chapter examines **social cognition,** or how we think about other people and ourselves. Social cognition includes several topics that are illustrated in the story about Governor Romer. Specifically, we form *attitudes* about topics such as gay rights. Through *person perception,* we form impressions of other people; for example, Romer formed an impression of his assistant that did not change after she told him that she was a lesbian. We reveal our *stereotypes, prejudice,* and *discrimination* when we judge groups of individuals, such as gays and lesbians. Finally, we humans are eager to form *close relationships,* such as the friendships Romer formed with his staff members and the love relationships that these individuals described.

Chapter 17 will examine social influence—or how other people have an impact on group interactions, social pressure, conflict, and altruism. As you might expect, the topics in these two chapters are closely intertwined. For instance, if we have stereotypes about members of a group (Chapter 16), we are more likely to develop conflicts with them and less likely to show altruism (Chapter 17).

While you are reading about social cognition in the present chapter, remember that the human mind struggling to understand social relationships is the same human mind we examined in the earlier chapters on cognition. You learned in Chapter 8 that **cognition** involves the acquisition, storage, transformation, and use of knowledge. In this chapter, we focus specifically on acquiring, storing, transforming, and using social information.

In the earlier cognition chapters, we emphasized that humans are typically efficient and accurate; most errors are actually "smart," sensible errors. The same rules generally hold true for social cognition. We are surrounded by a complex social world, so rich with human interactions that we cannot achieve perfect accuracy. In fact, we approach the social world with the same kinds of heuristics we use for nonsocial stimuli (Hamilton et al., 1994). These **heuristics**—or general strategies that are usually accurate—are similar to the cognitive shortcuts discussed in earlier chapters. We are especially likely to use these heuristics when our cognitive capacity is overloaded (Fiske, 1993a). Still, we are admirably accurate and efficient, especially when we have appropriate information (Ajzen, 1996).

ATTITUDES

An **attitude** is a psychological tendency we express when we evaluate something or someone (Eagly & Chaiken, 1993). Your attitude toward something can be positive, neutral, or negative. Furthermore, these attitudes are represented in terms of

DEMONSTRATION 16.1   The Relationship Between Attitudes and Behavior

1. Think of an issue on which your attitudes are either strongly positive or strongly negative. Issue 1 can concern politics, the environment, an international issue, or something concerned with public policy.
2. Think of a second issue on which your attitudes are as close to neutral as possible. Issue 2 should also concern one of the topics listed above.
3. Now answer each of the following questions about your behavior regarding both Issue 1 and Issue 2 during the past three years:

	Issue 1	Issue 2
a. How many letters to the editor (e.g., of a newspaper) have you written?	_____	_____
b. How many local or national organizations do you belong to that are concerned with this issue?	_____	_____
c. How many letters to Congress have you written?	_____	_____
d. How many petitions have you signed on this issue?	_____	_____

4. Add up the numbers you listed for Issue 1 and then for Issue 2. If your total for Issue 1 is much higher than the total for Issue 2, then your attitudes do strongly influence your behavior. Otherwise, the two factors are not really related.

Source: Item 3 questions are based on Fiske et al., 1983.

structures in memory (Judd et al., 1991; Olson & Zanna, 1993). As a result, the principles of memory you learned in Chapter 7—such as the importance of schemas and the likelihood of forgetting—also apply to your attitudes.

Social psychologists typically examine three long-standing issues concerning attitudes: (1) What is the relationship between attitudes and behavior? (2) What happens when a person holds two inconsistent attitudes, as in the case of cognitive dissonance? and (3) What persuasion techniques produce the greatest attitude change?

How Attitudes Influence Behavior

Before you read further, try Demonstration 16.1. This demonstration is based on a study by Fiske and her colleagues (1983). These researchers wanted to examine the relationship between people's attitudes about nuclear war and their actual behavior. We would expect that people who have passionate attitudes about nuclear weapons issues (either pro or con) would *do* something significant, like writing letters. However, Fiske and her colleagues found that the correlation between intensity of attitudes and nuclear-issues behavior was only +.18, a relationship that is statistically significant, but very weak.

Research on environmental issues confirms that attitudes are not strongly correlated with behavior (Stern, 1992; D. D. Winter, 1996). Check your own responses to Demonstration 16.1 to see whether your behaviors are consistent with your attitudes.

Why isn't the correlation stronger between attitudes and behavior? One factor that reduces the strength of this correlation is that the stimulus situation may be less than ideal (Stern, 1992). For instance, maybe you would be happy to sign a petition concerning an issue you strongly support, but you have never been in the same room with a relevant petition. A second important factor is **subjective norms,** or your beliefs about what other people think you ought to do (Ajzen, 1991). If you feel your friends won't approve, you won't sign a petition. Finally, if you don't feel knowledgeable about a topic, you won't show behavior that is consistent with your attitudes (A. R. Davidson, 1995; Davidson et al., 1985). Perhaps you would like to write a letter to a newspaper, but you do not feel sufficiently well informed.

In short, attitudes and behavior are typically not strongly correlated with each other. However, under ideal circumstances, the correlation *is* strong (Bargh et al.,

If the stimulus situation is ideal, a person with a strong attitude about an issue often shows behavior that is consistent with that attitude. For example, this man can express his attitudes about environmental issues because a petition is available.

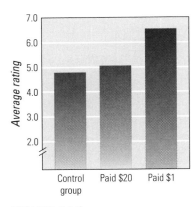

FIGURE 16.1

Attitudes toward a boring task, as a function of condition. High numbers indicate more positive attitudes.
Source: Based on Festinger and Carlsmith, 1959.

This young woman smoking a cigarette holds two dissonant cognitions: "I am smoking a cigarette" and "Cigarettes cause cancer and other harmful diseases." How would you guess she resolves this cognitive dissonance?

1996; Greenwald & Banaji, 1995). If the stimulus situation is perfect, if you think others approve, and if you are knowledgeable, then you will translate your attitudes into behavior.

Cognitive Dissonance

We have examined inconsistencies between attitudes and behaviors. But what happens when someone holds two inconsistent attitudes? For example, I know a young woman who had decided during high school that she would not apply to any colleges outside of her native state of New York. However, the college that offered the best program in her major turned out to be located in Boston—a city obviously outside New York's boundaries. In September, she found herself driving in the family car to attend school in Boston. Her behavior and current attitude clearly did not match her original attitude.

According to Leon Festinger's classic theory of **cognitive dissonance,** a discrepancy between two inconsistent cognitions produces psychological distress; people will be motivated to reduce this dissonance (discrepancy) by changing one of the cognitions (Festinger, 1964). The Boston-bound college student, for example, began to praise Boston's restaurants, sights, and shopping—feeling sorry for her high school classmates who had remained in New York.

To test the theory of cognitive dissonance, Festinger and Carlsmith (1959) instructed college students to perform an extremely boring task—turning pegs one-quarter of a rotation and then turning them back again. They continued for a full hour, undoubtedly producing the attitude "That was a boring study." Then students in one condition were offered $20 to persuade another person that the study had been exciting and interesting. Students in the second condition were offered only $1 for the same persuasion efforts. Students in the control group simply waited for a short period. At the end of the experiment, all the students were asked about their attitudes toward the dull task.

Surprisingly, the participants in the $1 group liked the task more than those in the other two groups. (See Figure 16.1.) Cognitive dissonance theory points out that participants are faced with a mismatch between one cognition ("That was a boring study.") and another cognition ("I have just told someone that the study was exciting."). Now the $20 participants could resolve the dissonance quite well; they justified the deceit because they had been paid $20 for a few minutes' work. The $1 participants could not use this justification. To reduce the dissonance, they modified their attitude toward the study, so that this attitude was more positive, consistent with the message they had conveyed when persuading the other individual.

Cognitive dissonance theory can be applied to a fairly wide range of situations (Gerard, 1994). For example, people who agree to undergo a challenging course of therapy for snake phobia show more improvement than those who choose a low-effort therapy (Olson & Zanna, 1993).

Critical Thinking Exercise 16.1

Write down your answers to the following questions about attitude-behavior consistency and cognitive dissonance.

a. Suppose a group of researchers wants to demonstrate that attitudes are consistent with behavior. They measure students' attitudes toward a controversial issue on campus. Three weeks later, they arrange a situation in which the three influential factors (stimulus situation, approval of others, and knowledge level) are all ideal. Then they see whether people sign petitions consistent with their attitudes. They find that attitudes do *not* predict behavior. Can you explain why?

b. Suppose that you are a learning theorist who supports reinforcement theory. What attitudes would you have expected for the $1 group and for the $20 group in Festinger and Carlsmith's study, relative to the control group?

Attitude Change

We have seen how people respond to an inconsistency in their attitudes. Now let's see how people's attitudes can be changed, as the result of persuasion. At the beginning of this chapter, we mentioned that the principles governing normal cognitions about nonsocial stimuli will also operate in social contexts. This generalization is especially clear in the area of persuasion, where we often employ the kind of heuristics discussed in earlier chapters.

In the current era, our world is overloaded with information. If you carefully weighed the pros and cons of every decision, you might find yourself, for example, at election time—long after the polls had closed—still trying to decide which candidate to select for mayor. As we saw in Chapter 8, we typically do not identify and analyze every relevant piece of information whenever we make a decision. Instead, we usually select just a few reliable features on which to base our decisions.

Several cognitive theories have been developed to explain how we make decisions about our attitudes (e.g., Petty & Cacioppo, 1986; Petty et al., 1995). Let's look at an approach that blends especially well with your background from Chapter 8, Shelly Chaiken's heuristic-systematic model (Chaiken et al., 1989; Chaiken et al., 1996). According to the **heuristic-systematic model,** persuasion can create attitude change by two separate routes: (1) when you are not involved in the issue or when you are not able to analyze a message, you rely on heuristics —the simple decision-making rules you have learned in the past; (2) when you are involved in the issue and when you have the ability to analyze it, you use systematic processing.

Think about whether your own responses to persuasion match the heuristic-systematic model. It seems to match my own experiences. I know that when I hear something regarding an issue I care about deeply, that message captures my attention completely. For instance, I've traveled several times to Central America, I have friends there, and dozens of other friends and relatives have also visited several Central American countries. When I see an article on Central America in a magazine, I read every word carefully and relate it to my previous knowledge (systematic processing). However, I am less informed and involved with Eastern Europe. If I read an article about an Eastern European country, I am less likely to process it analytically and more likely to judge its merits by certain commonsense guidelines (heuristic processing). For instance, I'll ask whether the author seems to have the appropriate expertise. In the interest of "cognitive economy," I take some shortcuts to help my decision making (Chaiken et al., 1996).

What are the heuristics that people use when someone is trying to persuade them, and they decide not to analyze the argument carefully? Researchers have discovered dozens of characteristics that affect persuasiveness (Chaiken et al., 1996; Lord, 1997). Let's consider three that are especially relevant to the heuristics of the heuristic-systematic model.

Expertise of the Persuader   When an authority speaks, we listen, and we are likely to change our attitude. Words from an expert make us stop searching for additional information, so this represents a heuristic, or shortcut for decision making. Characteristics such as education, occupation, experience, and credibility can establish a person's expertise (O'Keefe, 1990; Petty et al., 1997). For example, a classic study on expertise demonstrated that people were more persuaded by an article about a cure for the common cold when they thought it had appeared in the prestigious *New England Journal of Medicine,* rather than in the popular family magazine *Life* (Hovland & Weiss, 1951).

Attractiveness of the Persuader   The "In Depth" feature of Chapter 2 emphasized that attractive people have many advantages over less attractive people. It's certainly not fair, but attractive people are also more effective persuaders

Advertisers use physically attractive models to make their message more convincing. We seldom see ordinary-looking people in fashion ads.

CANALI

DEMONSTRATION 16.2 Preferences and Mirror Images

For this demonstration, find a location where you can arrange two mirrors, one of which can be moved. (An ideal setup is a medicine cabinet with a mirror on two of its doors.) Arrange the cabinet doors so that your image is directly reflected in one mirror, and the second captures a mirror image from the first mirror. Look at your own face and compare the two images of yourself. Which version of yourself do you think is more attractive?

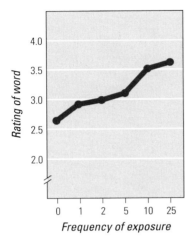

FIGURE 16.2

People rate nonsense words more positively if they have seen them frequently. In this figure, higher numbers indicate greater liking.
Source: Based on Zajonc, 1968.

(Garramone et al., 1990; O'Keefe, 1990; Petty et al., 1997). The next time you see a persuasive advertisement, ask yourself whether you would respond differently if the models were less physically appealing.

Frequency A third persuasion heuristic is the simplest of all: To convince people, simply repeat the message over and over (Petty et al., 1997). The classic research in this area was conducted by Robert Zajonc (pronounced "*Zye*-unce"). Zajonc (1968) showed participants some nonsense words—such as *CIVADRA* and *KADIRGA*—one at a time, at frequencies ranging from 0 to 25 exposures. Later, the participants rated how much they liked the various nonsense words. Figure 16.2 shows the clear-cut results. According to Zajonc's **mere exposure effect,** we often prefer items (objects, ideas, and people) with which we have had repeated contact. Now try Demonstration 16.2 at this point, before you read further.

The mere exposure effect holds true for a wide variety of stimuli presented in many different circumstances. A meta-analysis of the research showed that the effect is reasonably strong (Bornstein, 1989, 1993).

Incidentally, some researchers have been concerned that the mere exposure effect might be partially explained by demand characteristics. As we mentioned in Chapter 2, **demand characteristics** are clues that participants discover about the experiment, which suggest how they are supposed to respond. A clever study by Mita and his coauthors (1977) minimized demand characteristics, so that the participants were not aware that frequency had been manipulated. Specifically, some people in this experiment saw a photo of themselves printed the way people see themselves in a mirror. Other people saw the photo of themselves reversed, the way other people see them. The participants were much more positive about the mirror-image version, the one with which they were most familiar. However, their close friends preferred the reversed version—the image they had seen most often. Did your own response on Demonstration 16.2 confirm the mere exposure effect?

A study by Mita and his coauthors (1977) predicts that you'd prefer the left photo of Jim Lehrer, because it's oriented the way you usually see him. However, Jim Lehrer should prefer the photo on the right, the version he sees in the mirror each morning.

Critical Thinking Exercise 16.2

Write down your answers to the following questions about the mere exposure effect.

a. Suppose that you repeat Zajonc's classic mere-exposure study in simplified form. People see the nonsense words *IKTITAF* and *AFWORBU* zero times; they see *CIVADRA* and *ENANWAL* 5 times; they see *ZABULON* and *LOKANTA* 25 times. You discover that they rate the 25-exposure items much more positively than the 5-exposure items, which in turn they rate much more positively than the zero-exposure items. What confounding variable might explain your findings?

b. After identifying a general phenomenon, such as the mere exposure effect, psychologists often try to identify whether there are people or conditions for which the phenomenon does *not* apply. Would you expect the mere exposure effect to operate for people who are easily bored? When the stimuli are simple, would repeated exposure backfire, so that people dislike stimuli that are repeated too often?

Summary of Persuasion Factors   We have looked at three factors that can influence whether you will be persuaded to change your attitudes. Keep in mind, however, that these factors will not have much impact if you care strongly about an issue or if you choose to examine the issue carefully. For example, suppose that you strongly oppose nuclear power. You probably won't change your attitude, no matter how expert or attractive the people seem to be in the pronuclear advertisements, and no matter how often you see the ads. Instead, you will use systematic processing.

SECTION SUMMARY: *ATTITUDES*

1. Our thoughts about other people are governed by the same principles that govern our thoughts about nonsocial items.

2. Our attitudes often do not predict our behavior; the correlation is likely to be weak if the situation is not ideal, if subjective norms oppose the behavior, and if we are not well informed about the issue.

3. When we hold two contradictory attitudes, cognitive dissonance theory predicts that we will change one of those attitudes.

4. According to the heuristic-systematic model of persuasion, we use systematic processing when we care deeply about an issue and when we have the ability to analyze the message. In other situations, we rely on heuristics such as the expertise and attractiveness of the persuader, as well as the frequency of exposure.

PERSON PERCEPTION

Recently, I ate dinner with some friends in a Chicago restaurant. The waitress was incredibly extraverted and friendly, urging us *not* to order one of the dinner specials and to share the enormous salads, rather than requesting separate orders. As she proclaimed, "My family always raised me to be nice, so I don't want to cheat you." As she handed the bill to us, she declared with a smile, "Now the standard tip in this restaurant is 60% of the bill, and I won't let you out of the restaurant without it."

This restaurant interaction reminded me once more about the importance of person perception in our daily lives. **Person perception** is the area within social cognition that examines both impression formation and attribution. In **impression formation,** we integrate various pieces of information about a person. In the case of the waitress, for example, I quickly integrated characteristics such as extraverted, friendly, and witty. In **attribution,** we draw inferences about the reasons for a person's behavior (E. R. Smith, 1994). For example, I concluded that this waitress was friendly because of stable personality traits such as extraversion, friendliness, and wittiness. As I write these words, however, I realize that her behavior might be explained—instead—by the nature of the situation. In a different situation—where friendliness is less appropriate—she might even become an introvert. In this section, let's first discuss impression formation and then consider the related topic of attribution.

Impression Formation

We form an impression of someone by combining the available visual and auditory information about that person. If this impression is not accurate, however, we often face serious consequences. You might think that a friend would make an excellent roommate, but this person turns out to be extremely inconsiderate. You might ask a professor to write a letter of recommendation for you, but this professor's letter is much less enthusiastic than you expected.

We saw in the section on attitudes that psychologists interested in social cognition emphasize that we react to people much the same way that we react to nonsocial objects. Similarly, bottom-up and top-down processing work together in impression formation, in the same kind of coordinated fashion we use when we perceive nonsocial objects (Fiske, 1992). Also, we typically take mental shortcuts when we form impressions—just as we take mental shortcuts when we are deciding whether to change our attitudes. Let's consider how impression formation is influenced by two kinds of mental shortcuts: schemas and the primacy effect. Both of these shortcuts encourage us to form impressions quickly and effortlessly (Bargh, 1994). We'll also see how the self-fulfilling prophecy encourages people to live up to our expectations.

Schemas and Impression Formation In Chapter 7 (on memory), we introduced a useful concept called schemas. A **schema** is a simple, well-structured set of ideas. Chapter 7 emphasized our schemas about objects and events. Here, we'll focus on our schemas about other people.

A **person schema** consists of selected bits of information about a person, which we organize into a coherent, unified picture (Hamilton & Sherman, 1996; McConnell et al., 1994). For instance, you might form a schema for a student you met

What is your first impression of each of these students? If you are like most people, you quickly formed an impression. However, think about how you formed this impression, given that you possess so little information about these individuals.

DEMONSTRATION 16.3   The Primacy Effect

Read the following paragraphs about Jim:

1. Jim left the house to get some stationery. He walked out into the sun-filled street with two of his friends. Jim entered the stationery store and talked with an acquaintance while he waited for the clerk to catch his eye. On his way out, he stopped to chat with a school friend. While walking toward school, he met the young woman to whom he had been introduced the night before, and they talked for a short while.

2. After school, Jim left the classroom alone and started on his long walk home. Coming down the street toward him, he saw the young woman he had met on the previous evening. Jim crossed the street and entered a coffee shop, where he noticed a few familiar faces. Jim waited quietly until the counterman took his order. He sat down at a side table to finish his drink, and then went home.

Now describe Jim, noting especially whether he seemed to be friendly or shy.

Then, try to clear your head of your current impression of Jim, and read the two paragraphs about Jim in the reverse order, beginning with Paragraph 2 and ending with Paragraph 1. Does your impression of Jim seem different now?

yesterday: "She's the cheerleader type, with blond fluffy hair, a phony smile, expensive clothes, guys hanging around her . . . a definite airhead." You may have formed this schema after a 30-second conversation. Furthermore, you knit all the diverse pieces of information into a well-organized framework that oversimplifies what you really saw and heard during that conversation (Hamilton & Sherman, 1996; Zebrowitz, 1990). Once again, we find that social cognition emphasizes mental shortcuts. However, our schemas are not always accurate. For example, the blond student may be a physics major planning on graduate school—rather than an airhead.

The Primacy Effect   Before you read further, try Demonstration 16.3, which illustrates the primacy effect. Did Jim strike you differently when you read the paragraphs in the reverse order? The **primacy effect** is the tendency for early information to be considered more important than later information. Basically, we begin to create a schema on the basis of this early information, and this initial schema guides us as we "fill in the blanks" (Bierhoff, 1989).

The section on decision making in Chapter 8 introduced a similar effect, the anchoring and adjustment heuristic. That is, we make an initial guess that serves as an anchor, and then we make additional adjustments, based on other available information. This heuristic is less than ideal, however, because we often rely too strongly on our first guess, and we don't make large enough adjustments when we acquire additional information. Similarly, when you first read the paragraphs in Demonstration 16.3, you formed an impression based on Jim's many friendly interactions in Paragraph 1. You probably did not substantially adjust that first impression when the additional information in Paragraph 2 actually suggested that he was shy and introverted.

Demonstration 16.3 is based on a classic study by Luchins (1957). People who read Paragraph 1 before Paragraph 2 judged Jim to be friendly and outgoing. In contrast, those who read the paragraphs in the reverse order judged him to be shy and withdrawn. Additional research has confirmed that the primacy effect usually operates when we form impressions of other people (Lord, 1997; McKelvie, 1990).

Notice that the primacy effect is further evidence that we tend to simplify our social world. By relying too heavily on first impressions, we do not pay close attention to later information, and we tend to oversimplify. The problem is that oversimplification can lead to errors in impression formation.

How often do we make these impression-formation errors in everyday life? Social psychologists conclude that people are in fact reasonably accurate (Ambady & Rosenthal, 1992; Fiske, 1993a; Kenny, 1994). For example, Ambady and Rosenthal (1993) asked female college students to watch very brief videotapes of graduate teaching assistants, shown teaching a class; the students rated these individuals, based on just three 2-second clips of each teacher. Ambady and Rosenthal then obtained a second measure, which was the rating of each person's teaching skill. This rating was provided by a different group of students, who were actually enrolled in each teacher's classes that semester. Amazingly, the researchers found that the ratings based on *6 seconds* of videotape were correlated +.71 with the teachers' course ratings, supplied by a completely different sample of students!

However, even if we are reasonably accurate in our initial impressions, we should try to improve our accuracy. Specifically, when we try to judge people, we should ask whether we are placing too much emphasis on those first impressions. We can minimize the primacy effect by paying equal attention to more recent information.

Critical Thinking Exercise 16.3

Write down your answers to the following questions about Ambady and Rosenthal's (1993) study on the accuracy of first impressions.

a. This study obtained first-impression ratings from female undergraduates (presumably 18–22 years old), and the ratings emphasized nonverbal behavior. Based on what you know from Chapter 12 about factors that influence people's ability to decode facial expressions, do you think you could generalize these results to other groups of people?

b. A research assistant selected each 2-second clip from somewhat longer (10-second) clips made of each teacher. This research assistant did not know the hypotheses being tested or the ratings these teachers received from their classes. Why were these precautions necessary?

The Self-Fulfilling Prophecy So far, we have looked at two factors that can influence impression formation: schemas and the primacy effect. Now let's examine how your impressions of someone can actually influence that person's behavior. In a **self-fulfilling prophecy,** your expectations about someone lead him or her to act in ways that confirm your original expectations.

Consider this example, which I vividly recall from my seventh grade experience at summer camp. On the first day of camp, a girl named Jan immediately impressed us all with her sense of humor, her friendliness, and her athletic ability. We all tried to sit at Jan's table at mealtime, and we elected her to represent us at the camp council during the second week of camp. In fact, she remained our leader for the entire session. In September, I met another girl from Jan's school and eagerly asked how Jan was doing. She looked puzzled at my enthusiasm and asked, "Oh, you mean Jan, the fat girl?" At camp, our first impression of Jan had been extremely positive, and we continued to have high expectations for her; she then lived up to those high expectations. Students at her school apparently had different expectations, so she "became" a different person.

Notice that the self-fulfilling prophecy resembles a research-methods problem we discussed in Chapter 2. Specifically, participants in an experiment tend to fulfill the experimenter's expectations (Rosenthal, 1973). Researchers therefore need to be cautious about conveying these expectations to the participants.

The research on the self-fulfilling prophecy shows that our expectations can indeed influence another person's behavior (Blanck, 1993; Rosenthal, 1994, 1995). The effects are statistically significant, though they are not very strong. In a representative study, children in elementary school were told that they would be working with a child with a behavior problem (hyperactivity). The children interacted in a less friendly fashion with the supposedly hyperactive children than with control-group children (Harris et al., 1992). These supposedly hyperactive children, in turn, did not enjoy the social interaction, and they believed they had done poorly on the task. In short, one person's expectations can have an impact on another person's responses.

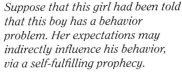

Suppose that this girl had been told that this boy has a behavior problem. Her expectations may indirectly influence his behavior, via a self-fulfilling prophecy.

The research suggests that teacher expectancy is especially powerful for girls, for students from lower socioeconomic status, and for African Americans (Jussim et al., 1996). Keep in mind, though, that self-fulfilling prophecies are relatively weak. Children of limited ability may indeed perform better when their teacher expects them to do well, but they probably will not rise to the top of the class (Darley & Oleson, 1993).

Attribution

Suppose that an acquaintance of yours is supposed to meet you at the library at 2:00. It's now 2:17, and there's no sign of him. We humans typically begin to look for attributions, which we defined earlier as reasons for a person's behavior. In this discussion, we'll focus primarily on our attributions for the behavior of other people. However, remember that we also make attributions for our own behavior. For example, we saw in Chapter 14 that people who are depressed have different attributional patterns (or explanatory styles) from those who are not depressed. For instance, if you are depressed, you might respond to a low test score by saying, "I'm just not meant to be in college." If you are not depressed, your attribution might be very different: "Well, that's not my best subject."

In general, we tend to choose one of two major kinds of attributions for another person's behavior (Brehm & Kassin, 1996). A **personal attribution** means that we emphasize how an internal trait—located within the person—is responsible for the behavior. These personal attributions may focus on that individual's ability, personality, or motivation. In contrast, a **situational attribution** means that we emphasize how a specific situation—some force located outside the person—is responsible for the behavior. These situational attributions may focus on the physical, social, or societal circumstances of an event.

For example, suppose that you see a television program about a woman on welfare. What attribution would you make for her poverty? If you favor a personal attribution, you might suggest that she lacks the motivation to get a proper job. If you favor a situational attribution, you'd prefer to blame the economic situation, lack of appropriate jobs, and other external circumstances. Interestingly, Wagstaff (1983) found that politically conservative people usually supply personal attributions for poverty, whereas politically liberal people favor situational attributions.

The research on attributions has been an especially active part of social cognition (e.g., Brehm & Kassin, 1996; Shaver & Kirk, 1996). We'll consider two

How would you explain why this woman is on welfare? Would you trace her situation to an internal problem, or to external factors such as temporary bad luck and a society based on inequalities?

consistent biases in the way people make attributions: the fundamental attribution error and the actor-observer bias.

The Fundamental Attribution Error According to the **fundamental attribution error,** we tend to overestimate the role of internal, personal causes and underestimate the role of external, situational causes. This error was named the *fundamental* attribution error because it originally seemed to be a fundamental or basic characteristic of social cognition. More recent cross-cultural research suggests that the fundamental attribution error may indeed be fundamental in **individualistic cultures** like those in the United States, Canada, and Northern Europe; in these cultures, a person's identity focuses on his or her individualistic characteristics. We tend to believe that people are motivated by internal forces, so they are responsible for their own behavior. In contrast, people in collectivist cultures are not as likely to commit the fundamental attribution error. In **collectivist cultures** such as India or China, people emphasize a person's social roles (Krull & Erickson, 1995; Triandis, 1995). For example, a man in India might explain a friend's lateness by believing that his responsibilities as a son or as a worker might have kept him from arriving promptly. This cross-cultural information emphasizes that the fundamental attribution error is learned within a culture, rather than being a fundamental characteristic of social cognition.

Let's see how the fundamental attribution error is illustrated by a representative study in the United States. Gilbert and Jones (1986) set up an intentionally artificial situation that demonstrated how people are reluctant to attribute a person's behavior to external forces. Imagine that you are participating in this study, and you report to the psychology lab. You are told to read a series of 14 questions to John, who is in another room. Furthermore, you will instruct John precisely about how he must respond to your questions. For instance, when you ask John, "What do you think of the legalization of marijuana?" the experimenter has told you that you must say to John, "Press the green button to indicate a liberal response." The experimenter has also made it clear to you that John has absolutely no opportunity to express his own personal opinion on the issue; John must supply only liberal responses.

John answers a total of 14 questions—always supplying the answer you have specifically given him. Then the experimenter tells you to rate John on a 15-point scale, with a rating of 1 being most liberal and a rating of 15 being most conservative. Wouldn't you want to say something like, "I can't possibly rate John, because I don't have a clue what he *really* thinks?" Actually, Gilbert and Jones found no such hesitation. Using this 15-point scale, participants gave a rating of 7.2 to the partners who had been instructed to supply liberal responses. Other participants, working with partners who had been instructed to supply conservative responses, gave these partners a rating of 9.7. This difference was clearly statistically significant. Even though the partners were obviously constrained by the situation, the participants thought that these partners really believed the statements they had been forced to make.

The fundamental attribution error is actually another variation of the familiar anchoring and adjustment heuristic. Basically, when we North Americans want to explain someone's behavior, we first establish an anchor by saying that the explanation is totally personal, a part of the person's internal character. Then we make some adjustments, pointing out how the situation is somewhat responsible. However, as we saw in Chapter 8, those adjustments are rarely large enough (Jones, 1990; Krull & Erickson, 1995). We are strongly governed by our top-down processes, which insist that people's personalities are responsible for their actions. As a result, we don't pay enough attention to the bottom-up information about the stimulus situation.

The Actor-Observer Bias Before you read further, try Demonstration 16.4, which asks you to make judgments about yourself and a friend.

If you are accustomed to seeing actor George Clooney in his role in the television show ER, *you are likely to believe that he is very macho and self-confident in his life outside of the television studio. However, the situation is really like the study by Gilbert and Jones (1986), because he is really just reciting the lines specified by the script (a situational factor). In other words, you will probably commit the fundamental attribution error.*

DEMONSTRATION 16.4 The Actor-Observer Bias

For each of the following characteristics, rate yourself by checking the item in Column A, the item in Column B, or the final option, "Depends on the situation." Put the letter *M* (for *Myself*) in the appropriate column. For example, are you serious, easygoing, or inconsistent?

COLUMN A	COLUMN B	DEPENDS ON THE SITUATION
1. _____ Serious	_____ Easygoing	_____
2. _____ Energetic	_____ Relaxed	_____
3. _____ Realistic	_____ Idealistic	_____
4. _____ Quiet	_____ Talkative	_____
5. _____ Cautious	_____ Bold	_____
6. _____ Uninhibited	_____ Self-controlled	_____
7. _____ Happy-go-lucky	_____ Conscientious	_____
8. _____ Future-oriented	_____ Present-oriented	_____
9. _____ Tough-minded	_____ Sensitive	_____
10. _____ Calm	_____ Intense	_____
11. _____ Lenient	_____ Firm	_____
12. _____ Reserved	_____ Emotionally expressive	_____

Now think about a friend—someone you know reasonably well, but not your best friend. With this person in mind, go through those 12 items once more, this time placing the letter *F* (for *Friend*) in Column A, Column B, or "Depends on the situation."

We saw that the fundamental attribution error leads us to attribute the behavior of other people to internal causes. However, we do not show this same attribution pattern for our own behavior. The **actor-observer bias** is the tendency to attribute our own behavior to external, situational causes, whereas we attribute the behavior of others to internal, personal causes. That is, we interpret behavior differently if we are explaining the behavior of the actor (ourselves) than if we are explaining the behavior of someone we are observing. Notice, then, that the actor-observer bias emphasizes that we make the fundamental attribution error when we judge others, but not when we judge ourselves.

Now check over your responses to Demonstration 16.4. Count up the number of "depends on the situation" responses you supplied for yourself, compared to the number for your friend. The actor-observer effect predicts that you will select many "depends on the situation" responses for yourself, because you believe that your behavior can be attributed to situational causes. In contrast, you envision your friend to be much more consistent; he or she is governed by stable, internal traits. Research similar to this demonstration has supported the actor-observer bias (Nisbett et al., 1973; Ross & Nisbett, 1991).

One likely explanation for the actor-observer bias is that people know so much about themselves. From past experience, you know that you are serious in some situations, but easygoing in others (Hewstone & Fincham, 1996). You have no similar wealth of experience with situational variability in the case of your friend.

The actor-observer bias is especially noticeable when something bad happens. We tend to manufacture excuses for our own behavior. We typically blame this unfortunate event on external factors beyond our control, instead of admitting we are personally responsible.

An unpleasant consequence of the actor-observer effect is that we often blame the victim when making judgments about a criminal incident. This blame-the-victim approach is especially likely in the case of rape (White & Sorenson, 1992). For example, Mrs. W. was a married, middle-aged woman who was raped by a stranger. She resisted to the best of her ability and received a knife wound and a concussion. Despite convincing evidence that she had been forcibly raped, everyone blamed her, including the police, the hospital staff, and even her own husband. For instance, a psychiatrist saw her for the first time—bleeding and battered—when she was admitted to the hospital. One of his first questions was, "Haven't you really been rushing toward this very thing all your life?" (Russell, 1975).

The actor-observer bias suggests that we should be more forgiving of other people. When a friend does something you consider wrong, ask yourself how you might explain this action if you were in your friend's shoes. Could external forces account for the behavior? When something tragic happens to other people, do not automatically begin searching for internal personality flaws that can allow you to conclude, "They got what they deserved."

Throughout this section on person perception, we have emphasized that people oversimplify their social worlds and make judgments that reflect certain systematic biases. As we discussed in earlier chapters, people are often governed by top-down processing. Our concepts, expectations, and prior knowledge help us achieve reasonably accurate person perception—though they can lead us astray. Of course, we also use bottom-up processing, attending to information we actually see and hear about other people. As a consequence, we are reasonably accurate in judging others. However, we can increase our accuracy by becoming aware of potential biases and correcting for these tendencies.

SECTION SUMMARY: *PERSON PERCEPTION*

1. In impression formation—one component of person perception—we often use a person schema, organizing information about a person into a coherent picture.

2. One bias that often operates in impression formation is the primacy effect, in which early information is more important than later information.

3. In self-fulfilling prophecy, our expectations about a person lead him or her to act in ways that confirm our original expectation.

4. According to the fundamental attribution error, we tend to attribute a person's behavior to internal, personal causes, rather than external, situational causes. However, the fundamental attribution error may be relatively rare in collectivist cultures.

5. According to the actor-observer bias, we commit the fundamental attribution error when judging other people; in contrast, we attribute our own behavior to external, situational causes.

STEREOTYPES, PREJUDICE, AND DISCRIMINATION

Uri Clinton, a law school student at Gonzaga University, received threatening letters during his campaign to become Gonzaga's representative to the American Bar Association. Incidentally, he was elected.

A student in a wheelchair confides that several elementary school classmates had been instructed by their parents not to play with her because she was different. A Black law school student, Uri Clinton, receives letters and telephone calls with racist messages. One letter warns him that there would be "hell to pay" if he is elected as the university's representative to the American Bar Association. An outstanding woman accountant is denied partnership in her firm, on the grounds that she is not "feminine" enough; she is told that she needs a course at charm school and should wear makeup and jewelry. A lesbian woman discovers that someone has thrown a brick—attached to a dead rat— through the window of her home.

In this section, we'll consider three interconnected concepts related to the foregoing examples. A **stereotype** is an organized set of beliefs about the characteristics of a group of people (Golombok & Fivush, 1994). Stereotypes are similar to the person schemas we discussed in the previous section. However, person schemas apply to individual people, whereas stereotypes apply to groups. Both person schemas and stereotypes encourage top-down processing, guiding the way we process social information (Hamilton & Sherman, 1994). As a result, we do not pay enough attention to the social information in the stimulus.

Whereas stereotypes emphasize beliefs and cognitive reactions, prejudice emphasizes attitudes and evaluations. **Prejudice** is an unreasonable negative attitude toward others because they belong to a particular group (Fishbein, 1996).

A third related term, **discrimination,** involves harmful actions against others because they belong to a particular group (Fishbein, 1996). We often see that stereotyped beliefs and prejudiced attitudes will reveal themselves in discriminatory behavior. For example, you may know someone who believes that Black people are lazy (a stereotype), has a negative attitude toward them (prejudice), and would refuse to hire Black people for a job (discrimination).

We have already noted some of these biases in earlier chapters. For instance, Chapter 2 addressed biases based on a person's appearance, and Chapter 11 examined biases against both gay people and the elderly. We've discussed biases about gender and ethnicity in many previous chapters. Stereotypes, prejudice, and discrimination also focus on religion, social class, and people with disabilities. (Can you think of other categories?)

We'll begin by looking at two of the most common biases, which have also been the most extensively researched: racism and sexism. Next is the "In Depth" feature, which discusses the cognitive basis of stereotypes, followed by some information about stereotypes and self-fulfilling prophecies. We'll end this section with some suggestions for reducing stereotypes and other biases.

Racism

Racism is bias against certain racial or ethnic groups; this bias can be revealed in stereotypes, prejudice, and discrimination. The United States has experienced a long history of racial bias. (See Figures 16.3 and 16.4.)

In recent years, the obvious forms of bigotry may be less prevalent. For example, Blacks and Whites no longer use separate drinking fountains. Still, we find abundant evidence of racism in many facets of everyday life. For example, a top CBS executive remarked at a staff meeting that African Americans are likely to watch late-night television because they don't need to go to work in the morning and because they don't have the attention span to watch hour-long dramas (Payne, 1996). Race-related violence is also reasonably common. For example, in Toronto, someone hurled a bomb into a club that was popular with South Asian teens (Hayes, 1992).

Racism is also obvious at the national level. For instance, the federal government is much harsher when companies violate the pollution laws in predominantly White areas. The average fine was $334,000 in communities where most residents are White, but only $44,000 in communities where most residents are people of color ("Coming Clean," 1992).

What kind of stereotypes do you have about these football players? Your top-down processing may prevent you from noticing specific information unique to each individual.

FIGURE 16.3

As recently as the 1960s, Black people faced discrimination in public places. These segregated drinking fountains were located in the county courthouse in Albany, Georgia.

FIGURE 16.4

During World War II, the U.S. government forced 120,000 Japanese Americans into internment camps, without any legal trial (Nagata & Crosby, 1991). This discrimination can be partly traced to racism. In this photo, a man bids farewell to his brother.

FIGURE 16.5

When they feel that a request for help is justified, White students help Black students almost as much as they help other White students. When a request for help is not justified, White students help Black students much less.
Source: Based on Frey and Gaertner, 1986.

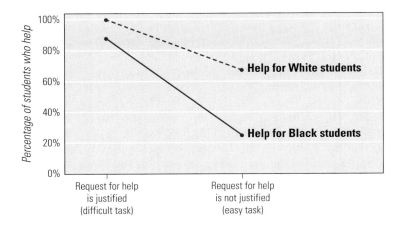

Nationwide surveys on Black-White relationships reveal some interesting data. For example, in one large-scale survey, 100% of Black individuals with college degrees agreed with the statement "Discrimination against Blacks is still very common today." In contrast, only 80% of the sample from the predominately White general population, with college degrees, agreed with that statement (Roach, 1997).

Contemporary racism is likely to be subtle, rather than obvious. For example, Frey and Gaertner (1986) randomly assigned White college women to one of two conditions, in which they were told that they would be working with a female partner in another room, who was either Black or White. This partner was working on a task that was described as either easy or difficult. During the work session, she sent a message requesting help on the task. Did the White students' responses depend on the perceived ethnicity of the partner?

Consistent with Theme 3, the results were complex. When the task was difficult—so the request for help appeared justified—the White students helped Black and White partners almost equally. However, when the task was easy—so the partner did not seem to be trying hard enough—the White students helped White partners more than twice as often as they helped Black partners. (See Figure 16.5.) In other words, they did not go out of their way to help Black partners unless the need seemed truly legitimate. When it was more acceptable to say no, these White students showed clear discrimination against Black partners.

Sexism

Sexism is bias toward people on the basis of their gender. A person is sexist who believes that women cannot be competent lawyers. An advertisement is also sexist if it portrays a man as a bumbling fool, trying to figure out how to change a baby's diaper (Cook, 1994). Institutions—as well as individuals—can be sexist, as well. Like racism, this bias can be revealed in stereotypes, prejudice, and discrimination.

Consider the case of sex discrimination that accountant Ann Hopkins (1996) brought to court. Hopkins was working at a prestigious accounting firm, Price Waterhouse. She was being considered for promotion to partnership, the only woman out of 88 candidates that year. (In the entire firm, only 7 of the 662 partners were women.) Hopkins had brought in business worth $25 million, at the top of the 88 candidates. However, the company did not promote her. The firm claimed that she lacked interpersonal skills, and they branded her "macho."

Ann Hopkins's lawsuit became the first Supreme Court case to use psychological research to document sex discrimination. Psychologist Susan Fiske and her colleagues provided documentation from the extensive research on gender stereotypes (Fiske, 1993b; Fiske et al., 1991). The Court eventually ruled that Price Waterhouse had indeed been guilty of sex discrimination. In 1991, Ann Hopkins was promoted to partner and was also awarded a financial settlement for back pay. As legal expert Theodore St. Antoine remarked, "The Court set down a pretty significant general principle that you can't treat a woman different from a man simply because you have this old-fashioned notion of what kind of lady-like decorum ought to be exhibited by a woman. . . . I think it will lead to some healthy soul-searching" (Walsh, 1996, p. xv).

Ann Hopkins is a highly competent accountant who was turned down for partner status because of sex discrimination. She won her lawsuit, which was ultimately decided by the Supreme Court.

Naturally, Ann Hopkins's court case did not eliminate the problem of the **glass ceiling,** the presumably invisible barriers in many professions that seem to block the advancement of women and people of color (Kaufman, 1995). For example, in 1996, less than 5% of the top business executives in the United States are women (Walsh, 1996).

In the current era, subtle sexism seems more common than obvious sexism in our daily lives. Glick and Fiske (1996) have attempted to capture this more complex kind of sexism with a scale they call the Ambivalent Sexism Inventory. They argue that modern sexism is based on ambivalence, rather than clear-cut dislike of women. As you can see in Demonstration 16.5, some questions assess "hostile sexism," the idea that women should be subordinate to men. However, other items emphasize that women are somewhat helpless. This is a more charitable kind of sexism, but it still emphasizes that women are *different* from men. The research demonstrated that men scored much higher than women on the hostile items. On the more charitable, "benevolent sexism" items, men also scored higher, but the gender differences weren't as large.

When we think about the topics of stereotypes, prejudice, and discrimination, we typically consider the damage done to women. However, men can also be victims of sexism. For example, Glick and his colleagues (1988) found that business professionals were more likely to interview a male—rather than a female—for a sales management job. For a dental receptionist job, however, they were much more likely to interview a female—rather than a male.

Gender stereotypes for both women and men still thrive in the media. Although some progress has been made, a glance at current magazines and television will convince you that women are relatively invisible in positions of importance. Also,

---

DEMONSTRATION 16.5 The Ambivalent Sexism Inventory

This demonstration includes selected items from the Ambivalent Sexism Inventory. For each item, indicate the degree to which you agree or disagree with the statement, using the following scale:

0	1	2	3	4	5
Disagree strongly	Disagree somewhat	Disagree slightly	Agree slightly	Agree somewhat	Agree strongly

_____ 1. Many women are actually seeking special favors, such as hiring policies that favor them over men, under the guise of asking for "equality."

_____ 2. Women should be cherished and protected by men.

_____ 3. Most women fail to appreciate fully all that men do for them.

_____ 4. Many women have a quality of purity that few men possess.

_____ 5. A good woman should be set on a pedestal by her man.

_____ 6. Most women interpret innocent remarks or acts as being sexist.

_____ 7. Once a woman gets a man to commit to her, she usually tries to put him on a tight leash.

_____ 8. In a disaster, women should be rescued before men.

_____ 9. Women seek to gain power by getting control over men.

_____ 10. No matter how accomplished he is, a man is not truly complete as a person unless he has the love of a woman.

When you have finished this test, check the scoring instructions at the end of the chapter on Page 539. Incidentally, the complete test includes 22 items, some of which are worded so that a highly sexist person would disagree with them.

Note: Readers should be aware that this shortened version of the Ambivalent Sexism Inventory has not been validated. The complete scale, appropriate for research or assessment purposes, can be found in Glick and Fiske (1996).

stereotypes dictate that men should look serious, businesslike, and macho, whereas women should look home-loving, sexy, and submissive (Matlin, 1996a; Wheeler, 1994).

The research on gender stereotypes often shows that the stereotypes about female and male characteristics are much more extreme than the actual gender differences (Martin, 1987). In fact, we often seem to carry an "illusion of gender differences," even on characteristics where men and women are fairly similar (Matlin, 1996a; Unger, 1979).

As in the case of schemas, our stereotypes reveal that we rely too heavily on top-down processing—specifically, our beliefs that women and men are different from each other. As a result, we don't pay enough attention to bottom-up processing—the actual behavior of women and men. If we looked more closely at the actual behavior, we could appreciate our similarities. The following "In Depth" feature examines how our cognitive processes encourage us to form and maintain stereotypes. After this feature, we'll see how stereotypes can play a role in self-fulfilling prophecies. Our discussion concludes with a section on reducing biases.

IN DEPTH

The Cognitive Basis of Stereotypes

Psychologists typically favor the **cognitive approach to stereotypes,** which argues that most stereotypes are produced by normal human thought processes (Hamilton et al., 1993; Hamilton, Stroessner, & Driscoll, 1994). One cognitive process that is characteristic of most humans is the tendency to divide the people we meet into categories, with the most common categories being gender, ethnicity, and age (Fiske, 1993a). We also categorize people on the basis of sexual orientation, religion, socioeconomic class, and other social attributes. This basic categorization process is a necessary part of stereotyping. We could not have stereotypes of women and men, for example, unless we first made a distinction between them.

Stereotypes help us simplify and organize the world by creating categories (Macrae et al., 1994; Snyder & Miene, 1994). For example, one important way we categorize people is on the basis of gender (Bem, 1993). We accomplish this gender categorization with very little thought. In fact, after you finish reading today, try *not* to pay attention to the gender of the first person you meet. It's very difficult to suppress this tendency to split the world in half, using gender as the great divide.

Once we have a stereotype in place, the stereotype often guides the way we cognitively process information. Consistent with Theme 1, we are typically quite accurate (Ottati & Lee, 1995). However, stereotypes can influence the way we perceive groups, remember group members, and evaluate those members. In general, stereotypes have the same kind of impact on our cognitive processes, whether these stereotypes focus on gender, ethnicity, age, sexual orientation, or any of the dozens of other categorizations we make. Let's now consider how stereotypes influence perception, memory, and evaluation.

Stereotypes and Perceptions of the Group

Cognitive psychologists propose that humans are so bombarded with stimuli that we simplify the world by creating categories. Two of the consequences of these categories are that we exaggerate the contrast between the categories and that we perceive our own group to have much more variation than any other groups.

Once we see people as members of a category or social group, we start perceiving them in a different way than we might otherwise. Specifically, we exaggerate the similarities *within* a group, and we exaggerate the differences *between* groups; this tendency is called **polarization.** For example, when we divide the world into the two groups "male" and "female," we tend to see all males as being fairly similar and

According to the cognitive approach to stereotypes, you would tend to categorize the people in this picture according to characteristics such as gender and ethnicity.

all females as being fairly similar. We also perceive the two categories—male and female—as being very different from each other. Sandra Bem (1993) points out that this gender polarization defines separate, mutually exclusive roles for men and women. This gender polarization also forces us to condemn individuals who deviate from this rigid role definition—as in the case of accountant Ann Hopkins, mentioned earlier.

When we exaggerate the contrast between women and men, we often lose sight of the diversity of people within each gender category (Tavris, 1992). As we have emphasized throughout this textbook, the characteristics of women and men tend to overlap. Unfortunately, however, gender polarization often creates an artificial gap between women and men. We also see other social categories—such as ethnicity and age—in the same polarized fashion.

A second perceptual consequence of stereotypes is that we are especially likely to perceive all members of another group as being similar to one another, a phenomenon known as **outgroup homogeneity** (Hilton & von Hippel, 1996). We perceive members of our own group to be reasonably diverse and heterogeneous, but people in that other group? "They are all the same!"

Notice what happens when we combine these two principles—polarization and outgroup homogeneity. We see our own group as being somewhat more homogeneous than it really is. However, people in those other groups are *especially* homogeneous.

Psychologists have uncovered evidence of outgroup homogeneity for many different groups of people in everyday situations (Ostrom et al., 1993; Ostrom & Sedikides, 1992). For example, White people tend to think that Black people are homogeneous (Linville & Jones, 1980). Young people think that old people are all the same, whereas old people think that young people are all the same (Brewer & Lui, 1984; Linville, 1982). And you will not be surprised to learn that engineering students think business students are highly similar, whereas business students think that engineering students are highly similar (Judd et al., 1991). Apparently, we are willing to believe that members of our own group display some amount of the individual differences that represent Theme 2 of this textbook. However, we deny this same diversity to people in other groups (Judd & Park, 1988).

Stereotypes and Memory

We have seen that stereotypes can influence perception. They can also influence memory, so that we remember attributes consistent with those stereotypes (Hamilton & Sherman, 1994; Hilton & von Hippel, 1996). Throughout this chapter, we have emphasized that our cognitive processes operate the same way, whether we think about

Suppose that you are watching a videotape of this woman, talking about her interests. Would you remember different things about her if you thought she was a doctor, rather than a hairdresser?

(IN DEPTH continued)

people or about objects and events. We saw in Chapter 7 that people sometimes—but not always—remember material consistent with a schema. Let's consider two studies in which people remember material consistent with a stereotype.

In one relevant study, Cann (1993) found that students recalled sentences like "Jane is a good nurse" better than "Jane is a bad nurse." When people work in a gender-*consistent* occupation, we expect successful performance, and so we recall their *competence*. In contrast, Cann's participants recalled sentences like "John is a bad nurse" better than "John is a good nurse." When people work in a gender-*inconsistent* occupation, we expect unsuccessful performance, and so we recall their *incompetence*. Notice how this memory bias could encourage a supervisor to remember a greater number of negative characteristics than positive characteristics for individuals who work in nontraditional occupations.

Let's consider a study by C. Neil Macrae and his colleagues (1993) in more detail. These researchers examined people's stereotypes about occupations—another social category where we have organized sets of beliefs concerning groups of people. These researchers decided to study undergraduate students' stereotypes about a female doctor and a female hairdresser. They therefore made a videotape of a woman discussing her entertainment interests. In the video, she mentioned 20 items considered typical of doctors, but not typical of hairdressers, such as an interest in politics and attending the opera. In the same video, the woman mentioned 20 items considered typical of hairdressers, but not typical of doctors, such as wearing short miniskirts and enjoying discos. Before viewing the video, students were told either that this woman was a doctor or a hairdresser.

Macrae and his colleagues also manipulated a second variable: the amount of additional information to be remembered while watching the video. Specifically, half of the students were instructed to remember an 8-digit number; the other half had no memory assignment. Notice why this variable is relevant: People might be especially likely to remember stereotype-consistent information when they must rehearse a number, because stereotypes are an energy-saving device. Stereotypes help us organize information, so they may be especially useful when people have the additional assignment of remembering a number.

Figure 16.6 shows the results of this study. As you can see, people with the additional memory load recalled more stereotype-consistent material than stereotype-inconsistent material. For example, if they believed they had watched a doctor, they might remember that she liked the opera but forget that she liked discos. In contrast, people with no additional memory load showed the reverse pattern; they recalled more stereotype-inconsistent material than stereotype-consistent material.

The research on stereotypes and memory is complex; as Macrae and his colleagues demonstrated, we don't always recall more of the stereotype-consistent material. However, biased recall is likely when we have other tasks to do at the same time and when our stereotypes are well developed (Fiske & Taylor, 1991; Hamilton & Sherman, 1994; Hilton & von Hippel, 1996.

Critical Thinking Exercise 16.4

Write down your answers to the following questions about the study by Macrae and his colleagues.

a. This study used 20 items considered stereotypical of female doctors and 20 considered stereotypical of female hairdressers. What would be a good method for obtaining these items?

b. The research suggests that people remember more stereotype-consistent information when they have other things to do at the same time. In everyday life, why is this principle relevant?

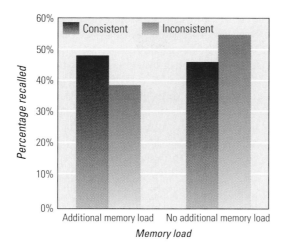

FIGURE 16.6

Recall of stereotype-consistent and stereotype-inconsistent information, as a function of memory load.
Source: Based on Macrae et al., 1993.

Stereotype and Evaluation

Two general factors operate when people evaluate individuals from different social groups. First, people generally downgrade individuals who belong to a group that is considered to have low status in a culture. For example, people tend to associate positive words with Whites and negative words with Blacks (Dovidio et al., 1986; Dovidio & Gaertner, 1993). Also, when students work together, they make more negative statements about female partners than male partners (Lott, 1987). People also judge a child's academic performance to be weaker if they think he or she is from a low socioeconomic background, rather than a high one (Darley & Gross, 1983).

However, people are not consistently biased against all members of a low-status group. For example, they may downgrade only women who are aggressive, but not less aggressive women (Eagly et al., 1992; Fiske & Stevens, 1993; Swim et al., 1989).

A second factor also operates during evaluation, especially when both groups are equal in status. Specifically, we tend to show **ingroup favoritism,** evaluating members of our own group more favorably than members of another group. In a representative study, Jennifer Crocker and her colleagues (1987) randomly assigned participants to either Group A or Group B by asking them to select a letter (A or B) from a box. The participants then sat at either Table A or Table B, and they were instructed not to talk to one another during the study. After several other tasks, all participants rated the members of both groups. The results showed that they rated members of their own group much more favorably. Other research has confirmed this ingroup favoritism (Brehm & Kassin, 1996; Schaller, 1992).

Notice, then, that we humans are accustomed to categorizing other humans. Even when we cannot categorize on the basis of obvious characteristics such as gender, ethnicity, social class, or occupation, we still seek ways to subdivide people. We may even use categories as clearly arbitrary as letters of the alphabet, randomly drawn from a box. Once we establish these categories, we often use stereotypes to simplify and bias our perceptions, memories, and evaluations of other members of our species. These biased cognitive processes, in turn, serve to maintain and strengthen our stereotypes.

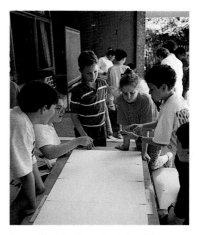

According to the principle of ingroup favoritism, the children interacting at the front of the photo should like their own group members better than they like the children in the group at the back of the photo. They will show ingroup favoritism, even if they were assigned to the groups entirely at random.

Stereotypes and Self-Fulfilling Prophecies

The earlier discussion of impression formation showed that self-fulfilling prophecies can influence behavior. Individuals often live up to the expectations that other

According to the research on self-fulfilling prophecies, this woman may begin acting in a more stereotypically feminine way if her boss has traditional views about women.

people have created. Self-fulfilling prophecies also operate in the case of stereotypes; people often live up to the expectations that other people have created for their social group. The effects of stereotypes are not confined to the cerebral cortex of the onlooker. Instead, they can guide the behavior of a person who has been stereotyped (Fiske & Taylor, 1991).

For example, self-fulfilling prophecies operate for gender. Specifically, women tend to act in a stereotypically feminine fashion when they interact with someone who seems to have traditional views about women (Deaux & Major, 1987; von Baeyer et al., 1981). Black job applicants may also perform more poorly when they are interviewed by someone who interacts with them in a racist fashion, rather than a friendly fashion (Taylor, 1993; Word et al., 1974). Stereotypes are especially likely to operate when we don't have much information about an individual, so we must rely on top-down processing (Fiske, 1993a; Matlin, 1996a).

Claude Steele and his colleagues recently identified a more subtle way in which stereotypes can influence performance. In brief, this research focuses on the academic performance of groups of people facing negative stereotypes. For example, the stereotype about women is that they are incompetent at math. The stereotype about Blacks is that they are incompetent at schoolwork. Picture, for example, an African American student named Henry. Henry received high grades in high school, he enjoys learning, and he is now in his first year of college. Midway through his first semester, Henry takes a challenging biology exam. He may encounter **stereotype threat,** a situational threat that may influence members of a group that is hampered by a negative stereotype, such as "low academic ability" (Steele, 1997; Steele & Aronson, 1995). Suppose that Henry is aware of this negative stereotype, and he believes that the biology exam is a test of his academic ability. He may "freeze," and perform worse on this exam than if he hadn't thought about this stereotype.

The research on stereotype threat suggests that special remedial programs for "Blacks only" or "women only" may backfire. The students in these programs may become especially aware of society's stereotypes about them because they have been selected for the program. They may begin to doubt their own ability. Instead, teachers who work with students from undervalued groups should give their students challenging work and convey the message that the students will perform well (Steele, 1997).

Reducing Biases

We have examined how stereotypes, prejudice, and discrimination can harm people, and we briefly considered Claude Steele's suggestions for improving students' performance. Let's consider some other ways of overcoming these biases.

Any serious attempt to overcome unequal treatment will require major changes in the structure of society and our institutions. For example, suppose that a corporation sincerely wants to promote more people of color into managerial positions. The plan will not be effective if only a single Hispanic person is advanced. This employee's "solo status" may encourage even more discrimination and racial tension. Also, suppose that just one Hispanic person is hired, and this person performs better than the stereotype. Others may say, "Well, Guillermo's not like all the rest of the Hispanics." In fact, researchers have found that a minority group must constitute roughly 20% of the larger group for discrimination to drop substantially (Pettigrew & Martin, 1987; Smith & Mackie, 1995). Let's look at some other approaches for reducing biases.

Contact Under Positive Circumstances We saw in the section on attitudes that mere familiarity with a stimulus often encourages more positive attitudes. However, simple contact between people from different social groups usually doesn't reduce prejudice unless the groups somehow have equal status (Lord, 1997; Stephan & Stephan, 1996). If you went to a school where the students belonged to several different ethnic groups, you may have noticed that voluntary segregation is common in public areas such as the cafeteria (Schofield, 1995).

Elliot Aronson and his colleagues devised a creative method for encouraging contact under positive circumstances. Specifically, they set up a situation in an ethnically diverse fifth grade classroom, ensuring that children could be similar in status (Aronson, 1995; Aronson et al., 1978). Aronson and his coworkers designed a **jigsaw classroom,** in which all the children must work together to ensure good grades— just as all the pieces must fit together in a jigsaw puzzle in order to complete the picture. For example, each member of a five-student learning group might receive one paragraph from a biography of Eleanor Roosevelt. Each child would learn just one piece of the puzzle, and then the children had to learn from one another in order to master the complete biography.

Consider the situation of Carlos, a Mexican American boy whose first language was Spanish. Initially, the other four children in the group were impatient with Carlos's halting English. However, a classroom assistant announced that the other students would need to know about Carlos's segment to succeed on the exam. The children quickly realized that they could learn more from Carlos by helping him communicate effectively. Soon they concluded that Carlos was much smarter than they had originally thought. The European American students began to like him, and he began to enjoy school more (Aronson, 1995). Research in the United States, Canada, Japan, and Israel has documented that college students as well as children can develop more positive attitudes toward individuals from other social groups when equal status is encouraged via a jigsaw classroom or some other cooperative learning setup (Aronson, 1991; Desforges et al., 1991).

Overcoming Mindlessness   Another technique for reducing biases requires us to overcome mindlessness. In the "In Depth" feature, we saw that humans have a strong tendency to categorize people into social groups. When we are trapped by these categories, we show mindlessness and fail to pay attention to the true qualities of individuals (Langer, 1989a). Some categorization is probably inevitable, but we should try to question these automatic categories.

Patricia Devine and her colleagues have shown that we can learn to inhibit our mindless, spontaneous stereotypes. At the same time, we can learn to activate newer, more thoughtful beliefs (Devine, 1995; Devine & Monteith, 1993).

In many cases, people who see themselves as being nonprejudiced will feel guilty and self-critical when they realize that they are responding in a stereotypical way (Monteith, 1996; Monteith et al., 1993). For example, suppose you see yourself as an individual who is not racist. You notice three Black adults on a street corner in the early afternoon, and you respond with the mindless stereotype, "Why don't they get a job?" However, the moment this stereotype comes to mind, you scold yourself, "I can't believe I actually thought that! I'm sounding like a racist." The guilt and the self-criticism you experience may play an important role in keeping you from automatically producing such stereotypes in the future.

Sometimes, other people can encourage us to be less biased. For example, students demonstrate less racism when they hear other students condemning racism (Blanchard, et al., 1991).

We have seen that we can inhibit stereotypes by criticizing our own automatic biases and by considering the opinions of other individuals. A third method of overcoming our mindless stereotypes is to express disapproval at racial slurs, sexist jokes, and other hurtful remarks. I once asked students in my

Students can reduce their own stereotypes by focusing on interests they have in common, rather than the categories that separate them.

psychology of women class to write anonymous descriptions about how their behavior had changed since taking the course. One student wrote that the previous week, one of his fraternity brothers had made a joke about rape. He said that it had been difficult, but he had responded that rape was not a joking matter. In other words, we can combat racism, sexism, ageism, homophobia—and other hate-filled biases—through the way we interact with our friends and family members (Smith, 1990).

If you are concerned about reducing some of your own stereotypes, try talking with someone from another social group. Focus on the characteristics you have in common, rather than the categories that separate you. Denise Burden-Patmon (1989), a professor of English, provides a useful example. She found herself standing in a downtown Boston train car, next to a young Black male whose dress and mannerisms suggested "problem youth." Most well-educated people would focus on the boundary that separated themselves from this young man.

However, Burden-Patmon took another approach that allowed her to overcome mindlessness. She turned to him and asked how he was feeling that day. He was initially shocked, but a wonderful conversation soon developed. She learned that he had abused drugs and had been in jail, but he responded warmly when he learned that she taught English. He then revealed that he had written some poetry while in jail. Soon he began to recite some of his poems on the train! A mutual appreciation of poetry allowed both of them to conquer an artificial category boundary.

SECTION SUMMARY: *STEREOTYPES, PREJUDICE, AND DISCRIMINATION*

1. A stereotype is an organized set of beliefs, prejudice is an unreasonable negative attitude, and discrimination involves harmful actions; these biases can focus on ethnicity, gender, appearance, sexual orientation, religion, social class, disabilities, and so on.

2. Racism is present at both the interpersonal level and the national level; an example of contemporary racism is the refusal to help Black people unless their need is obvious.

3. Sexism can be either blatant (as in the case of accountant Ann Hopkins) or subtle (as assessed by the "benevolent sexism" items on the Ambivalent Sexism Inventory); men—as well as women—can be harmed by sexism; gender differences are often smaller than stereotypes suggest.

4. According to the cognitive approach to stereotypes, the tendency to divide people into social groups serves as the basis for stereotypes, which then guide the way we perceive groups of people, remember them, and evaluate them.

5. Stereotypes encourage self-fulfilling prophecies; as Steele demonstrated, stereotype threat may hinder the academic performance of people belonging to stereotyped groups.

6. Ideas for reducing biases include increasing the number of members from other social groups in an organization, encouraging equal status for members of different groups, and various methods of overcoming mindlessness.

CLOSE RELATIONSHIPS

This chapter on social cognition has examined our thoughts about other people and ourselves. For example, the first section investigated how our attitudes can be influenced by other people. The section on person perception focused on the impressions we form of other people, as well as our attributions for their behavior. In the third section, we emphasized the negative aspects of social cognition when we examined systematic biases against certain social groups.

We'll end this chapter by considering close relationships, one positive aspect of social cognition. Chapters 10 and 11 examined friendship during childhood and adulthood, and Chapter 11 discussed the importance of love relationships in adults' lives. Now we'll focus on the social-psychological aspects of these close relationships.

As you read about close relationships, think about the way they may be influenced by the social processes we have discussed in the earlier sections of this chapter. For instance, cognitive dissonance may encourage you, over time, to like someone more (or less) than you did originally. Impression formation is a crucial factor during the initial phases of both friendship and love (Wood, 1993). Attributions are also relevant. For example, unhappily married people devise negative explanations for their spouse's misdeeds—"He brought me flowers because he feels guilty about something." In contrast, happily married people devise positive explanations for these behaviors—"He brought me flowers because he knows how happy they make me" (Bradbury et al., 1996; Fincham & Bradbury, 1993). Finally, stereotypes, prejudice, and discrimination may keep us from forming close relationships with individuals who belong to different social categories. Let's now focus on the important determinants of both friendship and love, and then we'll consider some theoretical approaches to love relationships.

Friendship

In recent years, psychologists have increased their research on close personal relationships (Baumeister & Leary, 1995; Vanzetti & Duck, 1996). One important question in this research focuses on the factors that influence our friendship choices. Among the most important are similarity, proximity, and attractiveness.

Similarity   Think about your closest friends: Why did those friendships develop? One of the strongest predictors of friendship is similarity (Brehm & Kassin, 1996; Simpson & Harris, 1994). For example, friends are likely to resemble each other on demographic characteristics such as ethnicity, age, education, religion, and socioeconomic status. Notice that this tendency fits well with the research on stereotyping; we categorize people according to these characteristics, and we show ingroup favoritism.

In general, people are likely to be friends with people who share similar attitudes on issues they consider important.

Friends are also likely to be similar in personality, mood, and attitudes (Brehm & Kassin, 1996; Simpson & Harris, 1994). For example, a woman who is a strong feminist is more likely to have a friend with similar views, rather than one who favors traditional gender roles. When it comes to choosing friends, opposites typically do *not* attract.

Proximity   Did your closest friend in high school live near you? Are your best friends from college the ones who sat next to you in class? In contrast, do you have trouble maintaining a friendship with someone you rarely see anymore? As you learned in the discussion of the mere exposure effect, we like something (or someone) better when exposure is frequent.

The classic study on proximity showed that people in an apartment complex were more likely to be friendly with their next-door neighbors—rather than someone from another building (Festinger et al., 1950). This research has been replicated with college students, soldiers, and senior citizens (Fehr, 1996; Simpson & Harris, 1994).

Attractiveness   We have seen the powerful effects of attractiveness throughout this book, most recently in the section on persuasion. As you might expect, we also tend to like attractive people (Fehr, 1996; Simpson & Harris, 1994).

Attractiveness also plays a role in friendship patterns. According to the **matching hypothesis,** we prefer friends who are similar to ourselves in attractiveness. For example, a meta-analysis of studies on same-gender friends showed that men tend to be similar to their friends in physical attractiveness (Feingold, 1988b). In contrast, however, women showed no matching tendencies. The explanation for these findings is not clear. Can you think of one?

We have seen that similarity, proximity, and attractiveness have an impact on friendship patterns. Now let's turn our attention to that more intense form of interpersonal attraction: love relationships.

Love Relationships

The son of a friend of mine fell in love for the first time when he was in college. This young man reported to his father that he couldn't concentrate on his courses or his part-time job. He simply couldn't stop thinking about his girlfriend! Or consider the middle-aged lesbian woman in the film *Out in Suburbia*. Speaking about the woman she loves, she remarked, "I really realized that I had fallen in love, and that all the loving feelings I had ever felt . . . I was feeling, and they were *so* intensified, and it was wonderful . . . it still is!"

This exploration of love relationships addresses two important issues: What variables predict love relationships? What theories have been proposed to explain love relationships?

Factors Related to Love Relationships   Many of the factors that are important in friendship are also important in love relationships. Consider similarity, for instance. Dating and married couples tend to be similar in age, ethnicity, social class, religion, education, and intelligence. Couples are also similar in their personalities, attitudes, and their tendency to reveal personal information about themselves (Brehm, 1992; Brehm & Kassin, 1996; Hatfield & Rapson, 1996; Hendrick et al., 1988).

Interestingly, people prefer those whose opinion of them matches their own self-image (Swann et al., 1992). Specifically, people with positive self-concepts are more committed to spouses who also think highly of them, compared with those whose spouses think poorly of them. This finding isn't surprising. However, people with negative self-concepts are more committed to spouses who think poorly of them, compared with those whose spouses think highly of them! As you can imagine, this second tendency can be destructive for a person with low self-esteem.

Proximity is also an important factor: We tend to fall in love with people who live nearby or whom we see often (Brehm, 1992). Although this doesn't sound very romantic, we typically fall in love with someone who is within driving distance (Buss, 1985).

Naturally, attractiveness is also important (Brehm, 1992; Hatfield & Rapson, 1996). In general, we prefer romantic partners who are reasonably attractive rather than unattractive. However, this preference is modified by a second familiar tendency. We tend to fall in love with people whose attractiveness matches our own (Feingold, 1988b).

Also, attractiveness matters more for a sexual relationship than for more permanent partnerships. Nevid (1984) asked students at a large eastern university to rate on a 5-point scale the degree to which they judged various personal characteristics to be important. The students provided ratings for both a "purely sexual relationship" and a "meaningful, long-term relationship." Table 16.1 shows the five most important characteristics for males judging females and for females judging males. As you can see, men and women differ somewhat in what they consider ideal traits in a partner for a purely sexual relationship: Specifically, men are likely to emphasize physical characteristics and attractiveness, whereas women also value personality characteristics (Feingold, 1992a; Hatfield & Rapson, 1993).

We tend to fall in love with people whose attractiveness matches our own.

TABLE 16.1   Characteristics That Males and Females Rate as Important for Sexual Relationships and for Meaningful Relationships

	MALES JUDGING FEMALES	FEMALES JUDGING MALES
SEXUAL RELATIONSHIP	Build/figure	Attractiveness
	Sexuality	Sexuality
	Attractiveness	Warmth
	Facial features	Personality
	Buttocks	Tenderness
MEANINGFUL RELATIONSHIP	Honesty	Honesty
	Personality	Fidelity
	Fidelity	Personality
	Sensitivity	Warmth
	Warmth	Kindness

Source: Based on Nevid, 1984.

Notice, however, that men and women are nearly identical in their judgments for meaningful relationships. Both want honesty, personality, fidelity, warmth, and sensitivity or kindness from a partner. These characteristics resemble qualities identified in an earlier study on couples in a noncollege population, where participants said the ideal partner would be a good companion, as well as considerate, honest, affectionate, dependable, intelligent, kind, understanding, interesting to talk to, and loyal (Buss & Barnes, 1986). Other researchers confirm that men and women emphasize similar characteristics when making judgments about meaningful relationships (Goodwin, 1990; Laner, 1989).

Theories About Love Relationships   Be sure to try Demonstration 16.6 before you read further in this section. This demonstration is based on research by Beverley

---

DEMONSTRATION 16.6   The Importance of Various Features of Love

Think about your ideas regarding love. Then read each characteristic listed here and rate how *central* each one is to the nature of love. If a term is an irrelevant feature of love, rate it 1. If a term is an important feature of love, rate it 8. Assign intermediate numbers to features that are somewhere in between. When you are done, check the end of the chapter on Page 539 to see how Fehr's students rated these items.

_____ 1. Respect
_____ 2. Sacrifice
_____ 3. Dependency
_____ 4. Trust
_____ 5. Energy

_____ 6. Patience
_____ 7. Caring
_____ 8. Security
_____ 9. Protectiveness
_____ 10. Uncertainty
_____ 11. Friendship
_____ 12. Contentment
_____ 13. Honesty
_____ 14. Scary
_____ 15. Laughing

Source: Based on Fehr, 1988.

Fehr (1988), who asked students in western Canada to rate whether various characteristics were central to their concept of love. Compare your own answers with those of Fehr's sample. Do you agree about which ones are important and which are largely irrelevant?

Fehr found that the items with the highest ratings were trust, caring, honesty, friendship, and respect. Similar findings were reported by students and patrons at a shopping mall in eastern Canada (Button & Collier, 1991; Fehr, 1993). In addition, a study in California found that men and women were similar in their ratings of the central attributes. This study also reported that the ratings provided by gays and lesbians were similar to those provided by heterosexuals (Rousar & Aron, 1990).

Other research by Fehr and her colleagues shows that people seem to have a prototype of love (Fehr, 1993; Fehr & Russell, 1991). As you may recall from Chapter 9, a **prototype** is the best example of a concept. For example, a prototypical vehicle is a car, rather than a wheelbarrow. Our prototype of love is an ideal characterized by friendship, caring, and trust. Qualities such as uncertainty, lust, or dependency do not match our general concept of love.

Whereas theorists such as Fehr focus on the nature of love, other theorists try to explain why people value certain characteristics in a romantic partner. One controversial explanation takes an evolutionary psychology approach. For example, Buss (1994, 1995b) argues that an evolutionary approach can explain why men and women have somewhat different ideas about ideal mates. Specifically, males are driven to have sex with as many females as they can, because their only contribution to reproduction is fertilization. The theory also argues that men should prefer healthy looking, attractive women, because they are most likely to be fertile. These healthy women can therefore produce numerous children.

Evolutionary psychologists also propose that women try to select a man who will be committed to a long-term relationship. After all, women not only give birth to children, but they must make sure that these children have enough resources. Evolutionary psychologists therefore argue that women look for men who are reliable and have good incomes (Buss, 1994).

In a large-scale study, Sprecher and her colleagues (1994) conducted a nationwide survey of more than 13,000 U.S. residents. In general, men tended to emphasize physical attractiveness more than women did, consistent with the research we discussed earlier. In contrast, women were more likely to emphasize earning potential in a mate. The results of this study are consistent with evolutionary approaches, but many alternative explanations could also be given.

Critical Thinking Exercise 16.5

Answer the following questions about preferences for romantic partners and the evolutionary psychology approach to love relationships.

a. The research illustrated in Table 16.1 relies on self-report. Why might this method be less than ideal? Can you think of a specific area in which the participants' responses might not be accurate?

b. Social psychologist Ellen Berscheid (1993) wrote this comment about the evolutionary psychology approach: "Unfortunately . . . , however, Mother Nature did not videotape the evolution of the human species for our analysis." As a result, she says, much of the theory about the origin of gender differences in behavior is "on a par with science fiction" (p. xii). What did she mean by these statements, with respect to research methods?

As you might imagine, many critics object to this evolutionary approach. For example, researchers interested in the growing area of men's studies object to the way this approach portrays males. For instance, Brooks (1997) points out that this approach exaggerates the gender differences and it tends to maintain the traditional gender-biased roles. (As you'll notice, the theory doesn't explain why men and women tend to prefer similar characteristics for a long-term romantic partner.)

As other critics point out, most research indicates that married men tend to be fairly monogamous, rather than having the numerous sexual relationships claimed by evolutionary theory (Mendoza & Shaver, 1995). Perhaps one of the most important criticisms, however, is that evolutionary approaches argue that these gender differences are inevitable. As a result, this argument can be used to justify why women should have lower status than men (Hatfield & Rapson, 1996).

We've looked at one theory that explains prototypes about love, as well as a theory that explains mate selection. A third theory examines how the nature of love relationships can be explained in terms of different relationship styles. Shaver and his colleagues proposed three categories of adult love-relationship styles. The names of these styles should remind you of similar terms from Chapter 10 (on child development) (Feeney & Noller, 1996; Hazan & Shaver, 1987; Shaver & Brennan, 1992; Shaver et al., 1988):

1. **Secure attachment style** means that you feel comfortable getting close to others and depending upon them.

2. **Avoidant attachment style** means that you feel somewhat uncomfortable getting close to others and trusting them completely.

3. **Anxious/ambivalent attachment style** means that you want to get closer to others than they would like; your intensity may scare away potential romantic partners.

Consistent with this theory's predictions, adult attachment style is fairly consistent with the attachment style an individual showed during childhood (Kirkpatrick & Davis, 1994).

As Hendrick and Hendrick (1992) point out in their book *Romantic Love,* the research on love relationships is too new to be confined to a single theory. With the current interest in research on close personal relationships, we can anticipate that many new theories will soon be developed.

SECTION SUMMARY: *CLOSE RELATIONSHIPS*

1. The most important determinants of friendship include similarity, proximity, and attractiveness.

2. Love relationships are also influenced by similarity, proximity, and attractiveness; however, attractiveness may be more important for purely sexual relationships than for permanent partnerships, and men may value an attractive partner more than women do.

3. Fehr suggests that we have a prototype for love relationships; this prototype emphasizes characteristics such as trust, caring, honesty, friendship, and respect.

4. The controversial evolutionary psychology approach to love relationships argues that men seek mates who are healthy looking and attractive, whereas women seek mates who are reliable and wealthy; critics argue that the theory portrays both women and men in an unfavorable light and that the data do not support the theory.

5. Shaver and his colleagues argue that people differ in their styles of romantic attachment, which may be secure, avoidant, or anxious/ambivalent.

Review Questions

1. Discuss the relationship between attitudes and behavior. Are they as closely related as you would have thought, prior to reading the chapter? Think of three issues from your own life where you have a strong attitude, and see whether the correspondence between your attitudes and your behavior depends on the three factors discussed on Pages 511–512.

2. Many parts of this chapter emphasize that we humans are overwhelmed by information, so we use shortcuts, schemas, and heuristics to simplify our social worlds. How is this theme relevant in persuasion, person perception, and stereotypes?

3. What factors influence (a) the likelihood that someone will persuade you, (b) your choice of a friend, and (c) your choice of a romantic partner? Point out the similarities among these three lists.

4. Explain the two routes described by the heuristic-systematic model. Then think about two occasions where you were persuaded by an advertisement or a presentation—one occasion for each of the two routes.

5. Why is the primacy effect important in connection with the concepts of the person schema and the self-fulfilling prophecy? Describe similar effects in connection with stereotypes.

6. Think of an occasion where you might have committed the fundamental attribution error when explaining someone's bad behavior, and point out how the actor-observer bias could have been relevant in this case. Do these two tendencies tend to make your self-image more positive or more negative than your image of other people?

7. Think of an occasion where you stereotyped someone on the basis of ethnicity, gender, or some other social characteristic. Discuss how that stereotyping was promoted by our tendency to categorize. Next, describe how your stereotype influenced your perceptions of that person's social group, as well as your memory and evaluations. Finally, note how these biases could be systematically reduced.

8. Our discussion of the nature of love relationships examined the prototype view, the evolutionary psychology approach, and the attachment approach. Briefly describe each of these three approaches. Then think of recent movies, TV shows, or books with which you are familiar. Which love relationship portrayed in these media is the closest to the prototypical ideal of love? Name one media couple who illustrate the pattern suggested by the evolutionary approach—and one who do not. Finally, name a person who represents each of the three attachment styles proposed by Shaver and his colleagues.

9. This chapter emphasized the importance of top-down processing in social cognition. Discuss how bottom-up processing also can be important in (a) the elaboration likelihood model, (b) the accuracy of person perception, (c) our ability to overcome stereotypes, and (d) the factors that influence our close relationships.

10. Many students take a psychology course to help them get along with other people. What practical advice have you learned in this chapter about (a) attitudes, (b) person perception, (c) stereotypes, prejudice, and discrimination, and (d) interpersonal attraction?

New Terms

social psychology (p. 510)   cognition (p. 510)
social cognition (p. 510)   heuristics (p. 510)

attitude (p. 510)
subjective norms (p. 511)
cognitive dissonance (p. 512)
heuristic-systematic model (p. 513)
mere exposure effect (p. 514)
demand characteristics (p. 514)
person perception (p. 515)
impression formation (p. 515)
attribution (p. 515)
schema (p. 516)
person schema (p. 516)
primacy effect (p. 517)
self-fulfilling prophecy (p. 518)
personal attribution (p. 519)
situational attribution (p. 519)
fundamental attribution error
   (p. 520)
individualistic cultures (p. 520)
collectivist cultures (p. 520)
actor-observer bias (p. 521)

stereotype (p. 522)
prejudice (p. 522)
discrimination (p. 523)
racism (p. 523)
sexism (p. 524)
glass ceiling (p. 525)
cognitive approach to stereotypes
   (p. 526)
polarization (p. 526)
outgroup homogeneity (p. 527)
ingroup favoritism (p. 529)
stereotype threat (p. 530)
jigsaw classroom (p. 531)
matching hypothesis (p. 533)
prototype (p. 536)
secure attachment style (p. 537)
avoidant attachment style (p. 537)
anxious/ambivalent attachment style
   (p. 537)

Recommended Readings

Brehm, S. S., & Kassin, S. M. (1996). *Social psychology* (3rd ed.). Boston: Houghton Mifflin. This superb textbook offers a clearly written overview of the field, with strong coverage of the recent research. In addition to covering the topics we presented in this chapter and on group processes, the book also includes chapters applying social psychology to law, business, and health.

Hatfield, E., & Rapson, R. L. (1993). *Love, sex, and intimacy: Cross-cultural perspectives.* New York: HarperCollins. Here's a well-written book about the research on topics such as romantic ideals, falling in love, passion, and breaking up.

Lord, C. G. (1997). *Social psychology.* Fort Worth, TX: Harcourt Brace. This mid-level textbook is especially strong on the research and theory about social cognition; applications of social psychology are integrated throughout the book.

Matlin, M. W. (1996). *The psychology of women* (3rd ed.). Fort Worth, TX: Harcourt Brace. My textbook takes a lifespan approach to women's lives, from infancy through old age. Gender stereotypes and discrimination are discussed throughout the book.

Petty, R. E., & Krosnick, J. A. (Eds.). (1995). *Attitude strength: Antecedents and consequences.* Mahwah, NJ: Erlbaum. Many of the major researchers in the social psychology of attitudes wrote chapters for this book; in addition to the topics you've already read about, you'll find information about attitude extremity, attitude importance, and ambivalence.

Answers to Demonstrations

Demonstration 16.5

Add together the total number of points from the following items: 1, 3, 6, 7, and 9. These represent the hostile sexism subscale. Then add together the total number of points from the following items: 2, 4, 5, 8, and 10. These represent the benevolent sexism subscale. Add these two subscale scores together to obtain an index of overall sexism.

Demonstration 16.6

Research by Fehr (1988) shows that students supplied the following average ratings: 1. Respect, 7.0; 2. Sacrifice, 5.4; 3. Dependency, 2.8; 4. Trust, 7.5; 5. Energy, 4.3; 6. Patience, 6.0;

7. Caring, 7.3; 8. Security, 5.0; 9. Protectiveness, 5.1; 10. Uncertainty, 2.9; 11. Friendship, 7.1; 12. Contentment, 5.8; 13. Honesty, 7.2; 14. Scary, 2.3; 15. Laughing, 5.5.

Answers to Critical Thinking Exercises

Exercise 16.1

a. The problem is that, under ideal circumstances, present attitudes should be correlated with present behavior. In this study, however, the delay is too long between the measure of attitudes and the measure of behavior; people's attitudes could have changed, especially if they learned new information.

b. Learning theory suggests a straightforward relationship; you like something better if you get a large reward, rather than a small reward. A learning theorist would expect to find the attitudes of the $1 group to be fairly similar to the attitudes of the control group. In contrast, you would expect the attitudes of the $20 group to be much more positive.

Exercise 16.2

a. The confounding variable is the initial pleasantness of the items: *ZABULON* and *LOKANTA* simply sound pleasant, whereas *IKTITAF* and *AFWORBU* are fairly unpleasant. To conduct the study properly, you must eliminate this confounding variable by presenting each nonsense word 25 times to some people, 10 times to others, and zero times to still others. With initial pleasantness controlled, you can draw firmer conclusions about the effect of the independent variable (frequency of exposure) on the dependent variable (liking).

b. People who are prone to boredom may show little or none of the mere exposure effect (Bornstein et al., 1990). Our theme of individual differences operates once more. Also, most people become bored when a simple stimulus is repeated very frequently (Bornstein et al., 1990).

Exercise 16.3

a. Females seem to be somewhat more skilled than males at "reading" nonverbal communication. Also, the most skilled age group is people between about 20 and 30, close to the ages of these students. As a result, this sample may be somewhat more talented than average at decoding nonverbal communication skills that might be related to teaching ratings.

b. If the research assistant had known the hypotheses being tested—as well as the class ratings these teachers had received—this individual might have clipped biased samples out of the 10-second videos. For example, the assistant could have clipped socially skilled segments from the videos of teachers who received high ratings, but grumpy, boring segments from the videos of teachers who received low ratings.

Exercise 16.4

a. You wouldn't want the list to be simply generated by the researchers, because they are older than the college students who will be tested, and they constitute a small sample. Instead, Macrae and his coworkers (1993) asked 10 students to make a list of characteristics typical of female doctors and another list of characteristics typical of female hairdressers. Then 10 different students rated these items in terms of whether they were characteristic of female doctors and, on a separate task, characteristic of female hairdressers. The researchers chose 20 items typical of doctors but not hairdressers and 20 items typical of hairdressers but not doctors. The method seems careful and appropriate.

b. In the laboratory, people typically do not have many distractions. In everyday life, however, we usually have many simultaneous stimuli and many things to think about. Therefore, in daily life, we may be more likely to remember stereotype-consistent information, rather than stereotype-inconsistent information.

Exercise 16.5

a. To some extent, people might report what they believe they *should* report. Also, their reports may not match what they actually would *do*, especially when choosing a partner for a meaningful relationship. Specifically, the responses in Table 16.1 don't mention any aspects of physical attractiveness. People probably *do* consider attractiveness when making real-life decisions regarding a long-term partner. Many people would probably never have the opportunity to find out about a potential partner's honesty or personality, because they considered this person unattractive.

b. Berscheid was suggesting that we can't really know whether the evolutionary psychology explanation is correct. If a videotape recording had been started in prehistory (obviously an impossibility), we would have some naturalistic observations to consult—but we don't have this option. In fact, none of the research methods can be used to test hypotheses about evolutionary psychology, so we cannot obtain clear-cut answers.

SOCIAL INFLUENCE

GROUP PROCESSES

    Social Roles

    Social Facilitation

    Social Loafing

    Group Polarization

    Groupthink

    Cross-Cultural Perspectives on Group Processes

YIELDING TO SOCIAL PRESSURE

    Conformity

    Compliance

    Obedience

AGGRESSION, CONFLICT, AND CONFLICT RESOLUTION

    Explaining Aggression

    Aggression and Gender

    Three Approaches to Conflict

    Conflict Escalation

    Interpersonal Conflict Resolution

    International Peacemaking and Peacebuilding

ALTRUISM

    Factors Affecting Altruism

    Altruism and Gender

    When People Do Not Help: The Bystander Effect

    In Depth: Explaining Altruism

CHAPTER 17

Suzie Valadez, 66 years old, works about 14 hours every day. Early in the morning, she prepares hundreds of sandwiches from food donated by a local supermarket chain in El Paso, Texas. Then she drives across the border in her beat-up van, to deliver the food to people in Ciudad Juarez, Mexico. Valadez began this work 28 years ago, as a single mother of four young children. She was also a high school dropout with only a limited Spanish vocabulary.

The people she helps in Mexico live next to a huge garbage dump, which used to be their major source of food before Valadez began her project. (The photo above shows Suzie Valadez, in the middle of the photo with dark glasses and a red skirt, together with the residents of this community.) The residents used to sort through the garbage to find discarded tortillas and vegetables. As a result, many people suffered from dysentery and other diseases transmitted by the insects and rodents living in the dump.

Suzie Valadez has made numerous personal sacrifices in order to help other people. For instance, her four children typically had little beyond the basic necessities. In fact, she sometimes gave away her own child's shoes if she saw a particularly needy Mexican child with bare feet.

Valadez has experienced great sorrow in her work. For instance, one year she made 12 coffins to bury the children who had died from poverty-related illness. However, her organization—Christ for Mexico Missions—has expanded its work to raise funds for a new medical building and a school in the community. This kind of progress helps her continue her mission with a sense of joy (Colby & Damon, 1992). Like many moral heroes, Suzie Valadez maintains her altruistic work without expecting any material rewards.

I n Chapter 16, we examined social cognition—our thoughts about other people. Now we'll shift our focus to behavior when we interact with other people. Specifically, we'll consider four topics: (1) group processes; (2) yielding to social pressure; (3) aggression; and (4) altruism—such as the altruism that defines the life of Suzie Valadez. Notice, then, that the first two sections examine the nature of group interactions, whereas the last two explore how our interactions can be either negative or positive.

GROUP PROCESSES

According to social psychologists, a **group** is defined as two or more people who influence one another through social interactions (Baron et al., 1993; Levine & Moreland, 1995). Think about a group to which you belong—maybe a social organization, an athletic team, or a group of students who often study together. In these interactions, the group members depend on one another, and they also influence one another. In this section, we'll discuss several processes that have probably occurred in your group. For example, people typically adopt social roles. Also, the presence of another person may influence performance, through either social facilitation or social loafing. In addition, the group may become more polarized and extreme when it makes a decision, and the group can make unwise decisions in an effort to preserve group harmony. We'll end this section by considering cross-cultural perspectives on the nature of groups.

Social Roles

As we will emphasize throughout this chapter, a group can influence its members in many different ways. One of the most powerful functions of a group is to create roles for its members. A **role** is the shared expectation about how someone in a group ought to behave (Hare, 1996; Wheelan, 1994). Some roles are defined by organizations and by families. For example, think about the different roles that a parent and a child play in your own family.

A prison system imposes one of the most clearly defined sets of roles. According to established policies and unwritten traditions, guards have all the power, and the prisoners must obey. Philip Zimbardo and his colleagues demonstrated the power of these roles when college men volunteered to play the parts of guards and prisoners in a simulated prison study (Haney et al., 1973; Zimbardo et al., 1973). By a flip of a coin, each student was assigned to either the guard or the prisoner role. The guards were given uniforms and were told to enforce certain prison rules. In contrast, the prisoners were "arrested" at their homes, and driven to "jail"—a prisonlike setup in the basement of the Stanford University psychology department.

Within a short time, the guards assumed the role of "guard." Some tried to be tough but fair, holding strictly to the prison rules. But about a third of them became cruel and abusive. They shouted commands, enjoyed imposing arbitrary rules, and treated the prisoners like animals.

In contrast, most in the prisoner role became depressed, apathetic, and helpless, but a few became rebellious and angry. In fact, the situation grew so intolerable that the study had to be abandoned after only six days. The line between roles and reality had become so blurry that it would have been unethical to continue the research.

The prisoners and guards readily assumed their roles in Zimbardo's simulated prison experiment.

We have seen that a group can encourage its members to act out specified roles. As we will see in the next two topics, a group can also influence its members' productivity through the processes known as social facilitation and social loafing.

Social Facilitation

Suppose that you need to accomplish a truly mindless task, such as washing dishes or raking leaves. Would you finish faster if someone else is nearby, rather than if you are alone? Now suppose that you are working on a difficult assignment, such as writing an essay about an incomprehensible poem or solving a set of challenging math problems. Would you rather be alone in a room or have someone else there with you?

Consistent with the complexity theme of this textbook, the presence of others sometimes helps performance—and sometimes hurts it. Specifically, on simple, well-learned tasks, we perform better when someone else is present. In contrast, on difficult, unfamiliar tasks, we perform worse when someone else is present (Guerin, 1993; Harkins, 1994; Zajonc, 1965). **Social facilitation** is the name of this tendency to do better on easy tasks and worse on difficult tasks when another person is nearby. Incidentally, you'll notice that this name is only half correct, because *facilitation* occurs only on easy tasks. More than 300 studies on social facilitation have been conducted, generally demonstrating that the presence of another person does indeed have an important influence on performance (Geen, 1991; Harkins, 1994; Mullen et al., 1997).

Why do you act differently when you are with another person, rather than alone? Guerin (1993) proposes that when another person is present, you become more alert, because you try to figure out whether this person will be interacting with you in some way. You also worry about how this person will evaluate you. These social concerns may encourage you to perform better on an easy task. However, this same alertness may make you nervous, so that you make errors on a challenging test.

Think how you can apply this information about social facilitation. For routine tasks, you may work better when others are around. However, for challenging assignments, try to find a location where you won't need to worry about social interactions.

Critical Thinking Exercise 17.1

Write down your answers to the following questions about social roles and social facilitation.

a. Analyze the Zimbardo prison study from the viewpoint of ethics. What precautions would you take to minimize potential harm?

b. Suppose that a research group designs the following study. They instruct a research participant to sit alone in a room, solving easy arithmetic problems. After 10 minutes, another student comes in and sits down in a chair in the corner of the room. The researchers test 50 students on this arithmetic task, and they find that the students receive significantly higher scores when solving problems with another student present. What's wrong with this conclusion?

Members of a group are likely to show social loafing; each will work less hard than if he or she were working independently.

Social Loafing

In social facilitation research, one person works on a task with another person nearby. In social loafing research, everyone works together on the same task. According to the principle of **social loafing,** each individual is less productive in a group than if he or she worked individually, because of reduced motivation and effort (Karau & Williams, 1993, 1995). The social loafing effect has been observed in sports teams, committees, and symphony orchestras. A meta-analysis has shown that the effect is moderately strong.

You can probably think of examples of social loafing from your own experience. However, the effect disappears and people work diligently when the task is interesting or relevant to their lives. It also disappears when people feel that their contributions are really necessary (Baron et al., 1993; Geen, 1991; Shepperd, 1995). After all, it's worth working hard if you feel that you are appreciated and can make a difference.

Group Polarization

Several years ago, the members of Students for Peace, a group at my college, decided to support a nationwide "Fast for El Salvador," and 32 of them signed a pledge to go without eating for one to three days. This was a position that was more extreme than most of them would have taken individually. At about the same time, the College Republicans passed a resolution to petition the student council to stop funding the Students for Peace organization. This, too, was a position that was more extreme than most of them would have taken individually.

In **group polarization,** group members take a more extreme position on a particular issue after discussing it among themselves than they would have taken without discussion (Clark, 1994). Thus, the average position of the Students for Peace became more liberal, whereas the average position of the College Republicans became more conservative. Notice, then, that the term *group polarization* means the whole group adopts a more extreme position after discussion. It does not mean that the attitudes *within* the group become more polarized; group members are not more likely to disagree with each other following discussion.

Notice, then, that a group is more than the sum of its parts. Something about the group process drives a group away from a safe, neutral position (Lord, 1997; Myers & Bishop, 1970). The group-polarization effect has been reported for a wide variety of groups. Football teams, courtroom juries, and gamblers all tend to make riskier decisions than individuals making decisions on their own (Clark, 1994; Lord, 1997; Whyte, 1993).

Groupthink

We have seen that a group can cause its members to make more extreme decisions through group polarization. In addition, a group can cause its members to make unwise decisions through groupthink. In **groupthink,** the group members try to achieve group harmony and consensus, and they place less emphasis on wise decision making. By focusing on the goal of consensus, they stop thinking critically. In Chapter 8, we examined how our decision making is guided by a small number of **heuristics**—a set of general strategies or problem-solving techniques that are usually accurate. When a group is tightly knit, the members often adopt an unspoken heuristic: "Preserve group harmony by going along uncritically with whatever consensus seems to be emerging" (Janis, 1989, p. 57).

Psychologists have examined several historic fiascos in which a government leader and his advisers were more concerned about group harmony than wise decisions. Some of these unwise decisions include President Kennedy's decision to invade Cuba in 1961, and President Johnson's decision to intensify the Vietnam War (Janis, 1982, 1989).

High-ranking officials (including Howard Baker, George Bush, and Frank Carlucci) who advised President Reagan seem to have shown symptoms of groupthink when they made the decision to pursue the Iran-Contra plan (Ettin, 1995).

Psychologist Mark Ettin (1995) has analyzed a more recent example of groupthink, the Iran-Contra scandal. During the 1980s, Congress had passed legislation saying that the United States government could not supply aid to the Nicaraguan Contras, a right-leaning rebel group that the United States had previously supported in its effort to undermine the duly elected, Nicaraguan government. Another government policy stated that the United States could not supply military weapons to countries that used terrorism (which included Iran). Nevertheless, President Reagan's advisers secretly arranged to sell military weapons to Iran, and to use the profits from those sales to support the Nicaraguan Contras. A small, cohesive group made a clearly unwise decision, one that violated the law, as well as the spirit of the U.S. Constitution (Ettin, 1995; Pratkanis & Aronson, 1992).

Some of the symptoms of groupthink include the following (Baron et al., 1993; Janis, 1989; Lord, 1997):

1. The illusion of invulnerability, in which group members believe that everything will work out because this group is special and morally superior;

2. The illusion of unanimity, in which people believe that group opinion is unanimous and unified; and

3. Direct pressure on dissenters, often suggesting that they are upsetting the group's harmony.

It's difficult to tell how often groupthink operates in real life, and it is often challenging to demonstrate in a laboratory setting (Aldag & Fuller, 1993; Fuller & Aldag, 1998; Tetlock et al., 1992). Groupthink has been shown to be more likely when a group is highly cohesive and when the group is isolated from the public view (Aronson et al., 1994; Turner et al., 1992).

How can we prevent groupthink? Janis (1982, 1989) made several proposals that would encourage critical thinking:

1. Arrange to spend a block of time surveying any troublesome warning signs;

2. Recommend that group members discuss the issue with people outside the group who seem to support other positions;

3. Hold a second-chance meeting after reaching the initial decision, to discuss any remaining doubts.

Cross-Cultural Perspectives on Group Processes

So far, we've seen a fairly pessimistic view of group processes. A group may cause its members to act like barbaric prison guards (social roles), to perform more poorly (social facilitation), to be less productive (social loafing), to adopt risky positions (group polarization), and to make unwise decisions (groupthink).

Hazel Markus and her colleagues (1996)—whose cross-cultural research we examined in earlier chapters—comment on this general view of social behavior. In particular, they point out that U.S. and Canadian psychologists approach social interactions with a very *asocial* model of the self. Specifically, the individual is competent and wise. But as soon as we join with other individuals, our wisdom flies out the window! Social situations somehow seem to compromise our behavior. From the individualistic perspective, the *individual* comes first.

Markus and her coauthors (1996) emphasize that people in collectivist societies see the world differently: The social group comes first, not last. These cultures focus on connectedness and interdependence. From this perspective, people's roles come first, and these roles help define an individual's identity. Furthermore, people in these cultures work more effectively in a group, rather than alone. For example, social loafing is much less common in collectivist societies.

In summary, a cross-cultural perspective forces us to reexamine our assumptions. In Chapter 16, we saw that the fundamental attribution error isn't really so fundamental. Instead, people in collectivist cultures believe that external factors are often responsible for the behavior of others. In this chapter, we see that individualistic societies place the individual first, and the group second. However, we can also adopt a collectivist perspective, by seeing the group as the primary human unit.

SECTION SUMMARY: *GROUP PROCESSES*

1. People adopt specified roles in a group situation; for example, in Zimbardo's simulated prison study, college men quickly assumed their roles as "guards" and "prisoners."

2. According to the research on social facilitation, the presence of others encourages people to perform better on easy tasks but worse on difficult tasks.

3. In social loafing, each person works less hard in a group than if he or she worked independently.

4. In group polarization, group members move toward a more extreme position following group discussion.

5. When group members emphasize harmony, rather than wise decision making, they may show

In collectivist societies such as this one in Ecuador, the group is the primary unit, and the individual is secondary.

groupthink; several precautions can encourage a more critical approach, thereby avoiding groupthink.

6. From the perspective of U.S. and Canadian researchers and an individualistic framework, the individual comes first and the group compromises the individual. From the perspective of collectivist cultures, the group comes first and helps to define the individual.

YIELDING TO SOCIAL PRESSURE

A student named Jim recalls a time he yielded to social pressure during the autumn before his 10th birthday. A new boy, Wally, had moved to the neighborhood, and several boys had decided to play a trick on the newcomer. To join their club, they said, Wally had to be buried under a pile of leaves. Reluctantly, Jim joined the other boys in heaping leaves upon Wally. The boys announced that they would return after 10 minutes to welcome Wally to the club. Of course, they planned never to return, but instead watched from a living room window as Wally emerged from the leaves half an hour later—damp, dirty, and disappointed. Jim wishes he could rewind the video and—resisting the lure of conformity—could say, "Don't do it, Wally!"

Social pressure certainly operates in some of the situations we discussed in the first section of this chapter. For example, social pressure may encourage some moderate group members toward group polarization. Now we need to focus more specifically on the nature of social pressure as we examine conformity, compliance, and obedience. We can view these three kinds of social influence along a continuum, with minimum social pressure for conformity, moderate pressure for compliance, and maximum pressure for obedience. Keep in mind, however, that social pressure can be used to encourage positive behavior, as well as harmful behavior. For example, the children in Jim's neighborhood could have pressured him to go door-to-door, collecting donations for UNICEF.

Conformity

Conformity refers to a change in beliefs or behaviors in response to group pressure when the group does not directly request this change (Zimbardo & Leippe, 1991). Let's begin by considering the classic study by Asch on conformity, and then we'll examine several factors that influence conformity. Finally, we'll see how conformity can be applied to environmental psychology.

The Asch Conformity Experiments Solomon Asch (1952, 1955) demonstrated that college students often conform with a group, even when this group adopts a position that is clearly incorrect. Imagine that you are participating in one of Asch's studies. You arrive in the laboratory and learn that you will be looking at a vertical line and deciding which of three other lines matches its length. (See Figure 17.1.) The experimenter asks you and several other students to

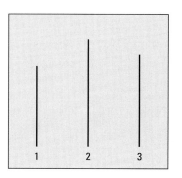

FIGURE 17.1

Conforming to Group Opinion
In Asch's classic study, participants were asked which of the three lines on the right matched the line on the left. Many conformed to the group opinion, even when it was clearly incorrect.
Source: Based on Asch, 1955.

The students in this group show a high degree of conformity in the clothes they wear. Do students at your college tend to conform with respect to their clothing?

announce your judgments aloud, according to your seating position. At first, the five people to your right and the one person to your left all supply the same judgments you give.

However, on the third trial, the first five people all give the wrong answer, supplying a comparison line that is clearly shorter than the line on the left. What should you do? As you may have guessed, all the other participants in Asch's study are confederates who have been hired by the experimenter to supply the wrong answer. In fact, you are the only genuine subject in this study, and the experimenter is measuring whether you conform with the rest of the group. We should note, incidentally, that the dependent measure is the subject's outward response; he or she may privately maintain a different opinion. When Asch originally performed the study, he found that the subjects conformed on 37% of the trials.

Factors Influencing Conformity   Asch's conformity setup is easily one of the most famous in social psychology. However, we need to point out that some researchers have found virtually no evidence of conformity (Lalancette & Standing, 1990; Perrin & Spencer, 1981). In general, the research in the United States and Canada shows that conformity has declined since Asch's era (Bond & Smith, 1996).

Researchers have discovered that a variety of factors influence the likelihood of conformity:

1. Conformity is more likely when a large number of people provide the wrong answer, rather than only two or three (Asch, 1955; Bond & Smith, 1996). Try Demonstration 17.1 to see whether you can discover the same effect.

DEMONSTRATION 17.1   The Influence of Group Size on Conformity

Persuade four other people to join you for a brief demonstration. Assemble your group near a classroom building or dormitory at least two stories high. One of you should stare persistently at a window on the top floor while the others stand some distance away. Note what percentage of the passersby look upward. Several minutes later, repeat the study with two people staring at the same window, and then—after appropriate intervals—repeat it with three and then four. (You remain behind to record the data.) Milgram and his coauthors (1969) found that conformity among passersby increased from 40% when one person looked up, to nearly 80% with five people looking up at the same window.

2. Women are somewhat more likely than men to conform, perhaps because they wish to preserve the social harmony of the group (Eagly & Wood, 1985; Rhodes & Wood, 1992).

3. People in collectivist countries tend to show higher levels of conformity than those in individualist countries (Bond & Smith, 1996; Triandis, 1994). Those in collectivist countries emphasize preserving the social harmony and "fitting in," whereas those in individualistic societies emphasize their own individual uniqueness.

4. People are less likely to conform if someone else in the group expresses a different viewpoint (Crano, 1994; Nemeth, 1994). When someone disagrees with the majority viewpoint—and this person makes a strong argument—group members may think more carefully about the issues. Some influential nonconformers from history include Galileo, Darwin, Christ, Freud, Marx, Einstein, and Gandhi (Crano, 1994).

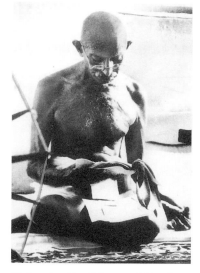

Mohandas Gandhi exemplifies the power of disagreeing with the majority viewpoint. His opposition to British rule in India caused other Indians to question the status quo and ultimately achieve Indian independence.

Conformity and Environmental Psychology We mentioned in Chapter 4 that **environmental psychology** studies interactions between people and the environment (Bell et al., 1996). We considered some social aspects of environmental psychology in Chapter 16; for example, we saw that violations of pollution laws receive larger fines in communities with mostly European American residents, rather than people of color.

Conformity plays an important role on college campuses that have prominent recycling containers for paper, glass, aluminum, and plastic. The social pressures encourage students to conform by recycling their garbage appropriately. As we mentioned earlier, social forces can promote positive social behavior, as well as harmful actions.

Environmental psychologists can also use the principles of conformity to encourage people to conserve water (Aronson et al., 1994). For example, one study showed that water conservation in college showers zoomed from 6% to 67% when several students were instructed to act as ideal models and turn off the shower while soaping up (Aronson, 1988).

We have been discussing conformity, the most subtle of the group-influence forces. Notice that conformity operates because group pressure encourages uniformity. No one *told* the participants in Asch's study, for instance, to choose Line 1. In this discussion we have seen that conformity is not always demonstrated, and that conformity is influenced by the number of people in the majority, as well as by gender, culture, and the presence of a different viewpoint.

Critical Thinking Exercise 17.2

Write down your answers to the following questions about conformity.

a. Asch's line-length study was conducted just as psychologists were beginning to express concerns about ethics (Korn, 1997). Why would this study raise ethical concerns today?

b. Suppose that some researchers want to do cross-cultural studies on conformity. They locate a number of universities in collectivist countries such as China, India, and Japan, as well as in several Latin American countries; they test conformity with students in these universities as well as students in the United States, Canada, and various European individualistic countries. Why might these samples of participants underestimate the difference between the two kinds of cultures?

If this resident allows the fundraiser to "put her foot in the door" she may find that a small request may later become a major commitment.

Compliance

Compliance means going along with a stated request from someone who does not have the specific authority to make you obey. Compliance can be contrasted with two other related concepts. *Persuasion,* considered in Chapter 16, usually refers to attitudes, whereas *compliance* refers to behavior. *Conformity,* which we just finished discussing, relies on more subtle group pressures, rather than a stated request. Two of the most effective compliance techniques are called the foot-in-the-door technique and the door-in-the-face technique.

The Foot-in-the-Door Technique   Has a friend ever asked you for a small favor—perhaps to borrow a cardboard box—and then you later found yourself performing a much larger favor, such as moving this friend into a new apartment? If so, your friend has mastered the foot-in-the-door technique. The **foot-in-the-door technique** is a two-step compliance method in which a person achieves compliance by first making a small request, and then later making a larger, related request (Cialdini, 1995).

Consider a study by Freedman and Fraser (1966). These researchers called 36 people at random from a telephone directory. The people who answered the phone were asked whether they would complete a short survey, and then the researchers asked eight simple questions such as "What brand of soap do you use in your kitchen sink?" The control group of 36 people was not contacted at this point, so these individuals had no opportunity to perform a small favor. Three days after the experimental group had been called, people in both groups were contacted about performing a large favor. They were asked to allow five or six men from the survey project to spend two hours going through their homes, classifying all household products. Of those who had first complied with the small favor, 53% agreed to the large favor. In contrast, of those who were asked just about the large favor, only 22% agreed.

Notice why the name *foot-in-the-door* is appropriate. Once the foot is inside the door, you soon find yourself inviting the entire salesperson in, and you are vulnerable to larger requests.

The Door-in-the-Face Technique   In the comic strip "Calvin and Hobbs," little Calvin asks, "Mom, can I set fire to my mattress?" She replies, "No, Calvin." He then asks, "Can I ride my tricycle on the roof?" "No, Calvin," she again replies. And then Calvin asks the real question: "Then can I have a cookie?" At his tender age, Calvin has already mastered the **door-in-the-face technique,** a two-step compliance technique in which a person achieves compliance by first making such a large request that it is certain to be denied, and then making a smaller, more reasonable request.

To test the door-in-the-face technique, Cialdini and his colleagues (1975) asked one sample of college students for a very large favor—to spend two hours each week as a counselor to juvenile delinquents, for a minimum of two years. As you can imagine, everybody refused. So then they asked the students if they would be willing to chaperone a group of juvenile delinquents on a day-long trip to the zoo. An impressive 50% said that they would. In contrast, when the researchers asked a similar sample of students for this relatively small favor—without first asking for the large favor—only 17% said yes. Replications of this research have demonstrated the effectiveness of the door-in-the-face technique (Cialdini, 1995).

Notice, incidentally, that the door-in-the-face technique relies on the anchoring-and-adjustment heuristic discussed in Chapter 8. After an outrageous initial anchor—for instance, hundreds of hours with juvenile delinquents—a single day sounds quite reasonable.

Obedience

So far, we have considered only relatively mild social pressure. A student selects a matching line that is clearly too short, consistent with the majority judgment (conformity), or someone agrees to let a research team into her home (compliance). The third kind of social pressure is stronger. In **obedience,** an authority specifically commands us to change our behavior. Let's first consider the Milgram obedience studies. Then we will look at some historical examples of obedience. This discussion ends with some conclusions about obedience.

Milgram's Obedience Studies   Stanley Milgram's research on obedience is clearly among the most famous studies in psychology (Blass, 1996). The introduction to Chapter 2 (on Pages 31–32) described this classic research; take a moment to review this procedure. Basically, an experimenter instructed individual participants to play the role of "teacher," delivering shock to the "learner" for every incorrect response. In reality, no one actually received shock; Milgram was measuring whether people would obey a command that would clearly harm another person (Milgram, 1963, 1974).

When Milgram described this study to psychologists and psychiatrists, most predicted that people would refuse to deliver more than a mere 150-volt shock. Contrast these predictions with the actual results. (See Figure 17.2.) In the proximity condition, the participant in the role of teacher sat in the same room as the learner, who cried out in response to the more painful shocks. In the voice-feedback condition, the teacher could hear the learner crying out in the same fashion from an adjacent room. As you can see in Figure 17.2, obedience was highest in the remote condition, where the learner was presumably sitting in an adjacent room and did not cry out. Only 35% of the participants refused to deliver the full amount of electric shock.

We should emphasize that many psychologists protested that these obedience studies were unethical (Baumrind, 1964; Brock & Brannon, 1994). As a result, no research using this obedience technique has been conducted since 1976. The ethical concerns are certainly appropriate. However, the research did provide valuable insights into the way we humans obey authority (Brock & Brannon, 1994; Milgram, 1964).

Historical Examples of Obedience   Milgram's experiments are powerful because they show us that ordinary people can perform actions that seriously violate their conscience. This behavior reminded everyone of the German citizens who had systematically slaughtered millions of innocent people between 1933 and 1945. These

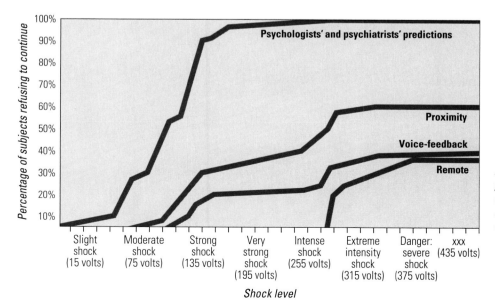

FIGURE 17.2

Results of Milgram's Research on Obedience
Figure shows the percentage of participants who refused to deliver a shock, as a function of shock level and task condition.
Source: Based on Milgram, 1974.

good citizens obeyed the commands of Nazi authorities. They built gas chambers and guarded death camps, producing the daily quotas of corpses with impressive efficiency (Milgram, 1974).

We can find many more recent examples of obedience in other countries. For example, Ignacio Martín-Baró was a social psychologist, teaching in El Salvador. During the 1980s, he conducted research on obedience, focusing on the repressive government in El Salvador and the blind obedience shown by El Salvadoran soldiers. For instance, Martín-Baró (1994) wrote that military soldiers may experience cognitive dissonance when a person in authority commands them to kill another human:

> This dissonance is generally taken into account in the training of those who, like soldiers, will be obligated by trade to kill other human beings. . . . The most common way the dissonance is prevented is through denial of one of the concepts: the humanity of the victim. So, although the soldier subscribes to the idea that "thou shalt not kill," he is taught to believe that "this person I'm killing isn't really a human being." (pp. 155–156)

Ironically, Martín-Baró was murdered by soldiers who were demonstrating blind obedience. In the middle of the night on November 16, 1989, the U.S.-trained soldiers of El Salvador's Atlacatl Battalion rounded up Martín-Baró, several Jesuit priests, their housekeeper, and her young daughter. The soldiers aimed their weapons at their captives' heads and murdered all eight individuals (Aron & Corne, 1994).

A quick glance at history reveals numerous other examples of blind obedience. For example, American soldiers slaughtered Vietnamese civilians—including women, elderly men, and babies—on many occasions during the Vietnam War (Bilton & Sim, 1992). More recently, troops in Iraq and in the former Yugoslavia have practiced "ethnic cleansing" (Brock & Brannon, 1994). You probably also remember learning in early 1997 that the Heaven's Gate cult guru, Marshall Herff Applewhite, urged his 38 followers to commit suicide (Miller, 1997).

In many cases, the power of the authority can be terrifying. In Nazi Europe, people were killed for defying authority. In Vietnam, soldiers who ignored an order in battle were sometimes executed on the spot (Bilton & Sim, 1992). However, people often obey an authority, even when the threat is minimal. The situation somehow leads us to believe we have no options.

Social psychologist Martín-Baró often lectured and wrote about the dangers of blind obedience. Sadly, he was assassinated for expressing these beliefs. This photo was taken the morning after he, his colleagues, a housekeeper, and her daughter were murdered by soldiers who had been blindly obedient. (Only four of the victims are shown here; Martín-Baró is the one in the blue shirt.)

Conclusions About Obedience   The Milgram research and the historical examples of obedience carry clear implications for our everyday lives. These examples also contribute to psychological theory. In Chapter 13, we pointed out that many psychologists emphasize the importance of the situation, rather than people's internal traits. In the case of the Milgram studies, people are more likely to obey if they are high in a trait involving a submissive attitude toward authority (Blass, 1991). However, the power of the situation is even stronger than personal traits. In a compelling situation, ordinary citizens seem to obey an authority unquestioningly.

Why do people obey experimenters in the Milgram studies and powerful leaders in real-life situations? One reason we obey is simple embarrassment. We would feel awkward saying, "No, I refuse." Another reason is related to an earlier discussion: Our role as subordinates encourages us to obey both military leaders and psychology researchers, even when we are wrongfully hurting other people.

A final reason we obey is that we sometimes display mindlessness, or failure to think through all the consequences of obedience (Langer, 1989a). We continue on, delivering the shock without critical analysis. These findings suggest some important advice. Whenever we find ourselves confronted by an illegal or inhumane command, we need to evaluate the situation critically and determine whether we can resist an immoral authority.

Dr. Martin Luther King, Jr., often urged people to consult their conscience, rather than obeying an immoral command. In this photo, King and other organizers lead the 1966 civil rights march in Selma, Alabama.

SECTION SUMMARY: *YIELDING TO SOCIAL PRESSURE*

1. In the Asch conformity studies, people often adopted the majority position, even when it was clearly incorrect; conformity depends on characteristics such as group size, gender, culture, and the presence of a dissenting viewpoint.

2. Two effective compliance methods are the foot-in-the-door technique (small request followed by large) and the door-in-the-face technique (large request followed by small).

3. In Milgram's obedience studies, participants usually obeyed the experimenter's commands, but obedience depended on the task conditions; numerous historical examples confirm that people frequently show obedience to immoral authorities; obedience is encouraged by embarrassment, social roles, and mindlessness.

AGGRESSION, CONFLICT, AND CONFLICT RESOLUTION

Several years ago, two boys murdered another boy. This homicide was especially grim because the murderers were 11 and 12 years old. They threw their 5-year-old victim from the 14th floor of a Chicago high-rise apartment because he had refused to steal candy for them. Virtually every day, we read some new horror, as sixth-graders plot to murder their teacher, teenagers slash the throat of a homeless man, and a troubled adult opens fire on a group of schoolchildren (Anderson & Bushman, 1997; Hayes, 1993). Meanwhile, the international news proclaims aggression on a larger scale. For example, during Rwanda's civil war of 1994, the Hutu majority in that African country systematically murdered at least 800,000 members of the Tutsi minority (Gourevitch, 1997)—within a period of just 100 days.

In addition to the startling, newsworthy acts of aggression we hear about in the media, we also confront more ordinary aggression in our daily lives. A fight breaks out during a hockey game. A friend reveals that her boyfriend beat her last night. Your roommate turns the radio up—rather than down—when you announce that you want to study. We can easily compile a long list of everyday aggressions.

This section begins with several theoretical explanations for aggression, and then we'll discuss gender comparisons in aggression. Next we'll consider

---

DEMONSTRATION 17.2 Beliefs About Aggression

Answer the following questions by writing *true* or *false* in front of each one. Some questions are discussed in the text; all answers appear at the end of the chapter on Page 571.

_____ 1. Humans are the only animals that often kill members of their own species.
_____ 2. Humans are instinctively aggressive.
_____ 3. Research demonstrates that men are consistently more aggressive than women.
_____ 4. Aggression can be controlled by participating in substitute activities, such as watching football games and violent movies.
_____ 5. If children are allowed to play aggressively, they will get it out of their system and be better adjusted in the long run.
_____ 6. Extremely violent behavior, such as child abuse and spouse abuse, is typically committed by people with psychological disorders.
_____ 7. Given the nature of human aggression, wars are inevitable.

Sources: Based on Aronson, 1988; Goldstein, 1989; Matlin, 1996a; Tedeschi & Felson, 1994.

---

approaches to conflict and conflict escalation. We'll complete this section by discussing conflict resolution.

Explaining Aggression

Before you read further, clarify your own beliefs about aggression by trying Demonstration 17.2. The term *aggression* has numerous different meanings (Coie & Dodge, 1998; Loeber & Hay, 1997). According to the definition we will use, **aggression** is behavior intended to hurt a person or other living organism (Baron & Richardson, 1994). Let's consider several current theoretical approaches to explaining aggression.

Biological Explanations The biological approach argues that biological factors can explain aggression and that individual differences in aggressiveness are inherited. In Chapters 3 and 12, you learned that structures in the limbic system seem to be associated with our emotions. Specifically, researchers have concluded that the amygdala (see Figure 3.14) is especially important in regulating aggression (Potegal, 1994). Also, Chapter 5 examined another potential biological factor connected with aggression: People who are under the influence of alcohol develop alcohol myopia, so that they process cues less accurately. As a result, they often become violent in social situations, because they don't consider the negative consequences of their violence (e.g., Ito et al., 1996).

We also have some evidence that aggressive tendencies are inherited, especially when these tendencies are measured in terms of criminal behavior (Baron & Richardson, 1994; Tedeschi & Felson, 1994). For example, one research team studied children who had been adopted at birth. Those who had an aggressive biological parent were more likely to be aggressive as adolescents, in contrast to adopted children who had no biological history of family aggression (Cadoret et al., 1995).

As we've said, brain structures regulate aggression, alcohol's physiological effects can increase aggression, and aggression tends to be inherited. However, these conclusions are *not* the same as saying that we humans have an "aggressive instinct" or that aggression is inevitable in our social interactions (Tedeschi & Felson, 1994). Instead, we can modify our behaviors so that we are more likely to act with empathy, rather than violence. Let's look at two theories that emphasize the importance of observational learning and cognitive processes.

Observational Learning Explanations In Chapter 6, we discussed experimental, quasi-experimental, and correlational research about television violence. These studies show that many children become more aggressive after they observe violent TV programs. Other research suggests that teenage suicide rates rise after a suicide case has been widely publicized by the media (Lore & Schultz, 1993). Observational learning therefore helps explain some aggression directed toward other people and toward oneself (Pepler & Slaby, 1994).

Let's consider a related question. Are people who view violent pornography likely to become more aggressive? Psychologists who have examined pornographic material emphasize that pornography often portrays sexual aggressors in a positive fashion, and these aggressors are seldom punished for their actions (Check & Malamuth, 1986; Linz et al., 1992). We should not be surprised to learn, then, that both college men and noncollege men who have been exposed to pornography are more likely than other men to believe the myth that women enjoy rape (Check, 1984; Malamuth & Check, 1985). Also, men who have seen a sexually violent movie are less likely than men in a control group to sympathize with a rape victim when they serve as jury members in a reenacted rape trial. That is, they are more likely to believe that a victim's injuries are not very severe, and they are more likely to consider the victim to be a worthless person (Donnerstein & Linz, 1984).

Other research shows that violent pornography also increases rape fantasies and tolerance for rapists. It also decreases support for women's rights (Donnerstein et al., 1987; Intons-Peterson & Roskos-Ewoldsen, 1989; Zillmann, 1992).

Men who have seen sexually violent movies are more likely to believe the myth that women enjoy rape and that rape victims are not seriously hurt by the rape incident.

Critical Thinking Exercise 17.3

Write down your answers to the following questions about the definition of aggression and about the ethics of aggression research.

a. In this chapter, aggression is defined as behavior intended to hurt a person or other living organism. What would have been *gained* by defining aggression as "behavior that hurts a person or other living organism"? What would have been *lost?*

b. What ethical concerns are raised by the study about men who are less sympathetic to rape victims after watching a sexually violent movie? How could a researcher address these concerns?

Social Cognitive Explanations According to social cognitive explanations, children develop aggressive tendencies because of maladaptive thinking about social situations (Coie & Dodge, 1998; Dodge, 1993). Consider, for example, a child who has not been invited to a classmate's birthday party. Some children will respond to this ambiguous social situation by saying, "Well, maybe Chris just had a small party." Other children who have developed aggressive **schemas** (well-structured sets of ideas) may respond by saying, "I hate Chris! Wait until he sees how I can get him back!" A child with this kind of maladaptive thinking will also misinterpret other people's behavior; a friendly comment will be misperceived as hostile (Loeber & Hay, 1997). Children with this maladaptive thinking may respond with hostile comments and aggressive behavior. If these maladaptive schemas persist, these aggressive children will become aggressive adults.

Many social interactions are ambiguous. For example, this girl may be offering a toy to this boy as a friendly gesture. Psychologists who favor a social cognitive explanation argue that some children may think about social situations maladaptively. For example, if this boy has developed aggressive schemas, he may interpret the gesture as a hostile joke.

Aggression and Gender

According to the stereotype, men are eager to fight and insult, whereas women are much less aggressive. However, research on gender comparisons in aggression shows that men and women are more similar than most people believe. For example, one review of the research showed that males were significantly more aggressive than females in only about one-third of the studies (Eagly, 1987).

Gender differences tend to be larger in studies of children than they are in studies of adults (Hyde, 1986b). Gender differences are also larger when aggression is measured in terms of physical injury or pain, rather than psychological harm (Eagly & Steffen, 1986). For example, typical research shows that men are more likely than women to deliver electric shock to somebody. However, men and women are equally likely to deliver insults. In some cases, women may even be more aggressive than men. For example, research in Argentina found that women were more likely than men to show aggression by gossip and social manipulation of other people (Hines & Fry, 1994). We need to readjust the cultural "lenses" we have acquired from the common stereotypes of our culture (White & Kowalski, 1994). Men are not consistently more aggressive than women.

The data show an additional important pattern. Gender differences are relatively small when we examine interactions with strangers. However, research throughout North America documents a high incidence of domestic violence; men are much more likely than women to injure their spouses severely (Browne, 1993; Morval, 1992). In fact, an estimated 2 to 4 million women in the United States are assaulted by their male partners each year (Browne, 1993; Stahly, 1996). A Canadian study reported that 45% of women over the age of 18 had experienced violence from husbands, boyfriends, or other men they knew ("Violence Against Women Survey," 1993). Victims of domestic violence often report that the experience was traumatic. For example, in one of my classes, a young woman vividly described how her ex-husband tracked her down in a new apartment and threw her through the bedroom wall. She told the class that the psychological terror of the experience was just as painful as the physical trauma.

Remember, though, that women and men are equally aggressive in many situations. Biological forces do *not* guarantee that men must be aggressive. People who accept the myth that men are inevitably more violent may erroneously believe that men are biologically incapable of controlling their tempers.

Three Approaches to Conflict

Conflict, which is closely related to aggression, is a perceived incompatibility of goals that occurs when the desires of one party interfere with the desires of another party (Rubin & Levinger, 1995; Smith & Mackie, 1995). Conflict can occur between two people—perhaps you and a classmate—or between two groups, such as the management and the workers in a factory. Conflict can also arise between two nations, as a glance at any newspaper demonstrates. Obviously, the dynamics change somewhat when we consider nations, rather than individuals. However, many of the same elements can be found in all conflicts.

Conflict analysts point out that the participants in a conflict can adopt three different approaches to a conflict. In a **lose-lose approach,** both parties will suffer a net loss. War is typically a lose-lose solution. For example, there were 127 wars and about 22 million deaths related to war between World War II and 1989 (Nelson, 1991; Sivard, 1989). Even the victor in a war usually loses more in terms of human suffering than any positive outcome that the war was supposed to accomplish.

Most competitive situations in business adopt a **win-lose approach,** in which one party's win is balanced by the other party's loss. A win-lose approach is also typical in competitive sports. If your favorite baseball team wins a game, the other team must lose.

In contrast, in a **win-win approach,** both parties benefit by cooperating. For example, people can decide to resolve the conflict by "expanding the pie" and increasing the available resources so that both sides can get what they want (Pruitt & Olczak, 1995).

Consider how two groups in southern California used the win-win approach to resolve a conflict. Two neighborhoods located next to each other had experienced increasing violence at their shared boundary. The conflict was heightened because one neighborhood had mostly Mexican American residents, whereas the other neighborhood had mostly gay male residents. Fortunately, some of the residents decided to address the violence and planned a street fair for everyone. The fair became an annual

Most wars represent a lose-lose approach to conflict, because both sides lose in terms of human suffering. For example, the conflict in the former Yugoslavia produced losses for both the Serbs (top photo) and the Bosnian Croats (bottom photo).

event. Also, the project—known as Sunset Junction Neighborhood Alliance—provided many opportunities for members of the two groups to plan and work cooperatively, rather than in conflict (Rebecca, 1983). Clearly, a win-win approach favors successful conflict resolution. In contrast, a lose-lose approach and a win-lose approach both encourage conflict escalation (Heitler, 1990; Smith & Mackie, 1995).

Many people think that conflict is inevitably wrong and unproductive. However, some nonaggressive conflict can be helpful when people enter the conflict with a win-win approach. In contrast, groupthink—an undesirable outcome—occurs because the group members want to avoid conflict at all costs. Also, conflict often nourishes social change (Levine & Thompson, 1996; Worchel et al., 1993). What would happen if civil rights reformers never expressed their disagreements with the status quo? Would we have wheelchair access to public places if people with disabilities had systematically kept quiet about their needs?

Some conflict can be productive. For example, people with disabilities probably would never have won wheelchair access to public transportation in some areas if they had kept quiet about their needs. Here, in Austin, Texas, a man boards a bus that is equipped with a hydraulic lift.

Conflict Escalation

Let's consider several factors that tend to fuel a conflict and encourage the parties to adopt either a lose-lose or a win-lose approach. These factors include issues proliferation, stereotypes, and enemy images.

Issues Proliferation   Often, a conflict starts small, but then each party points out additional grievances, which were not part of the original problem. The tendency for parties in a conflict to increase the number of controversial topics is called **issues proliferation** (Rubin et al., 1994). For instance, two roommates in conflict over an insulting remark may suddenly start dragging in each other's annoying habits and other long-forgotten injustices. Whenever you hear yourself saying, "And another thing . . ." in the midst of a conflict, you know that you are engaging in issues proliferation. You will be more likely to resolve a conflict when it remains more narrowly focused.

Stereotypes   In Chapter 16, we saw how stereotypes can distort reality. A similar stereotypical distortion occurs in conflict; we simplify an extremely complex situation into categories such as "the good guys" versus "the bad guys" (Rothbart, 1993; Smith, 1992).

Stereotypes also lead us to make attributional errors (Wessells, 1993). Consider two countries in conflict. The leaders in Country A make a concession, in an attempt to resolve the conflict. The leaders in Country B may conclude that Country A has evil, hidden motives for this concession. The truth is that the actions of other people are often ambiguous. If someone who has been quarreling with you for months does you a favor, don't automatically ask yourself, "I wonder what she wants from me?" Instead, consider several more charitable attributions.

Enemy Images   According to a concept called **enemy images,** we often see ourselves as good and peace-loving, whereas our enemies are evil, aggressive, and warlike. These enemies, however, also have an image of us. They see *themselves* as good and peace-loving, but they see *us* as evil, aggressive, and warlike (Bronfenbrenner, 1961; Moyer, 1985; Smith & Mackie, 1995). This biased perception by both sides in a conflict is called **mirror-image thinking.** Reality is usually more ambiguous; we all have our peace-loving and aggressive sides.

For example, many North Americans had negative images of Iraqis during the Gulf War of the early 1990s, especially because the U.S. government kept us from identifying with the Iraqi war victims (Craige, 1994). Iraq residents also had negative images of Americans (White, 1991). Furthermore, the same mirror-image thinking occurred during the conflict in the former Yugoslavia ("Enemy Images," 1992; Smith & Mackie, 1995). Enemy images help escalate conflict because they encourage us to think of our adversaries as evil, rather than as humans who share the same kinds of strengths and weaknesses we ourselves have.

Here are two enemy images from previous eras in U.S. history: the Germans in World War I (left), and the Japanese in World War II (right) (Keen, 1986). Note the exaggerated features and the dehumanized images in both illustrations.

Critical Thinking Exercise 17.4

Write down your answers to the following questions about enemy images.

a. The initial reports about the 1995 Oklahoma City bombing suggested that "Arab-looking individuals" had been the culprits. However, court trials concluded that the culprits were really homegrown European Americans. How do enemy images and the availability heuristic contribute to the original mistake?

b. Suppose that you want to study mirror-image thinking in two warring countries, and you plan to examine political cartoons in the newspapers of both countries for evidence of enemy images. (Imagine that you are fluent in the relevant languages.) Name some factors that could introduce biases into your study.

We are more likely to resolve conflicts successfully if we avoid issues proliferation, stereotyping, and enemy images. Let's consider some additional guidelines to conflict resolution at both the interpersonal and the international level.

Interpersonal Conflict Resolution

Try Demonstration 17.3 to prepare for this discussion about resolving interpersonal conflicts. Successful problem solving in a conflict situation depends on finding **perceived common ground,** or an alternative that satisfies the wishes of both parties. Perceived common ground is more likely if both parties perceive that the other is ready to solve the problem, if they trust each other, and if they have ongoing contact (Girard & Koch, 1996; Rubin et al., 1994).

Before you begin to resolve a conflict, consider whether any conflict actually exists! As you might guess from our discussion of social psychology, many conflicts are illusory; the two participants in the conflict may actually want the same goals (Carnevale & Pruitt, 1992; Girard & Koch, 1996). Also, keep in mind some advice from previous chapters in this textbook. In Chapter 8, you learned about creative problem solving. Conflicts can often be resolved by breaking a mental set or by figuring out innovative methods of expanding the number of options and the quantity of

DEMONSTRATION 17.3 Interpersonal Conflict

Take a moment to think about a recent conflict you have had with a friend or a romantic partner. This conflict can either be resolved, or it can be ongoing. How concerned are you about your own welfare in this conflict? To what extent are you concerned about the other person's welfare? Now examine the figure below. This diagram is called a *dual-concern model,* because it points out that our choices depend upon the relative concern we have about our own welfare and the welfare of another person (Carnevale & Pruitt, 1992; Rubin et al., 1994). Where would you place your own conflict on this diagram? If you selected "inaction"—that is, low concern about both your own and the other person's outcome—are you satisfied with the decision to do nothing? If you categorized the conflict as "yielding," decide whether you are content not to have your own preferences satisfied. (In fact, that solution may be ideal.) If the conflict falls in the "contending region," ask yourself whether you have considered the position of the other individual. Finally, if you categorized the conflict as "problem solving," this section provides the perfect opportunity to begin to resolve this conflict!

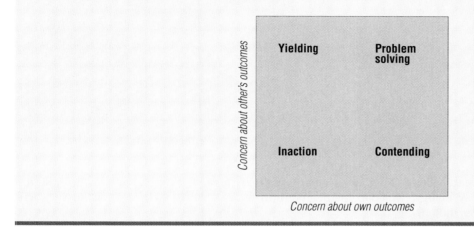

resources (Rubin, 1991). Chapter 16 also highlighted a variety of methods for reducing biases against people in other groups.

One of the most useful skills in creative problem solving is effective listening (Heitler, 1990; Raider, 1995). Try discovering what is *right* in the speaker's statements, not what is wrong. Also, focus on what the other person is saying, rather than on the response you plan to make. Try to imagine how the situation appears from his or her perspective.

Your goal in conflict resolution should be to identify a win-win solution that meets both parties' wishes. If that approach is not successful, work to identify the issues that have the highest priority, discarding the less important ones.

A promising new development focuses on conflict management programs for young students, beginning in elementary school (Girard & Koch, 1996; Raider, 1995). Through the Community Board Program, for example, selected children receive training. These conflict managers resolve conflicts that arise on the playground or at lunch (Amsler, 1991). These programs seem to be successful in reducing the incidence of school violence (Deutsch, 1993; Raider, 1995). In the long run, this kind of strategy may be more useful than current school practices that simply focus on avoiding violence (McCarthy, 1993).

International Peacemaking and Peacebuilding

Researchers argue that conflicts between individuals, groups, communities, and nations all share certain basic similarities, such as a perceived incompatibility of goals and a mixture of motives. Also, the same conflict-resolution principles can be used in many disputes that seem superficially different (Bunker & Rubin, 1995; Rubin & Levinger, 1995).

The topic of international peacemaking has a surprisingly long history. In fact, William James encouraged the American Psychological Association to pursue peace research in 1910 (Kimmel & VandenBos, 1992). Currently, international

In the Community Board Program, these two conflict managers try to resolve a conflict that has arisen on the playground.

peacemaking is part of an interdisciplinary area within psychology called **political psychology,** which combines political science with psychology (primarily social psychology).

As I write this chapter in late 1997, the United States is not currently participating in an armed conflict. However, we spend about $635 billion each year on military expenses, and the stockpile of nuclear weapons is frightening. (Also, we may be involved in another conflict by the time you read this book.) A major problem with these large-scale international conflicts is that high levels of tension can produce cognitive rigidity, so that the political leaders may have trouble devising new alternatives and options (Carnevale & Pruitt, 1992; Deutsch, 1983).

Reactive Devaluation One barrier that has important implications for international conflict resolution is called reactive devaluation (Ross, 1992; Ross & Stillinger, 1991). According to the concept of **reactive devaluation,** the mere act of offering a particular concession makes that offer less attractive to the recipient. Our enemy images force us to devalue anything proposed by "the enemy"—even an idea that would benefit both sides. For example, in 1986, California residents were asked to evaluate a proposal for nuclear disarmament. When they were told that a U.S. leader had made the proposal, 90% approved; when they were told it had been made by a Soviet leader, only 44% approved. (Incidentally, beware of reactive devaluation in your own interpersonal conflicts, as well!)

At the end of the twentieth century, the United States had so many nuclear weapons that they represented roughly 200,000 times the force of the nuclear bomb that destroyed Hiroshima in World War II.

GRIT One technique of conflict resolution that is especially useful in international peacemaking is called GRIT. **GRIT (Graduated and Reciprocated Initiatives in Tension Reduction)** consists of a series of steps in which one party announces a modest step it will take to reduce tension, and this party actually takes the step. For example, one country might provide humanitarian aid to its rival. Then this party invites the second party to reciprocate in some way. If the second party does reciprocate, the first party then starts another round of these initiatives (Blumberg, 1996; Fisher, 1990; Osgood, 1962). Once the process begins, each side becomes increasingly committed to conflict resolution (Rubin, 1991).

One important application of GRIT occurred in 1963, when President Kennedy decided to try to de-escalate conflict with the Soviet Union, and Soviet Premier Nikita Krushchev reciprocated. In fact, the two countries even signed a treaty limiting nuclear testing (Christie, 1997; Smith & Mackie, 1995). Unfortunately, this period of reduced conflict ended when the United States became involved in Vietnam, introducing a new source of tension. However, this successful de-escalation is one example of the value of GRIT in international conflict.

Peacebuilding   In recent years, psychologists have become interested in peacebuilding, which is more than simply the absence of war (Christie, 1997; Wagner, 1993). Specifically, **peacebuilding** is an active process that attempts to improve relationships between parties in a post-conflict situation and also tries to prevent conflict before it arises (Christie, 1997). Recently, the American Psychological Association formed the Division on Peace Psychology, which sponsors a journal called *Peace and Conflict*. William James's request for psychologists to focus on peace research was therefore fulfilled, although the delay was nearly a century.

SECTION SUMMARY: *AGGRESSION, CONFLICT, AND CONFLICT RESOLUTION*

1. Aggressive tendencies seem to be inherited and to have biological correlates, but humans do not have an "aggressive instinct"; observational learning and social cognitive explanations are important.

2. About one-third of studies on aggression and gender show males to be more aggressive than females; gender differences are largest in studies of children and in research on physical violence; in addition, men are much more likely than women to assault their domestic partners.

3. Conflict escalates with a lose-lose or a win-lose approach—rather than with a win-win approach; it

also escalates when the situation includes issues proliferation, stereotypes, and enemy images.

4. Interpersonal conflict resolution is encouraged by factors such as finding perceived common ground, eliminating illusory conflict, creative problem solving, and effective listening.

5. International peacemaking is often hampered by factors such as reactive devaluation; in contrast, strategies such as GRIT (Graduated and Reciprocated Initiatives in Tension Reduction) and peacebuilding are essential in avoiding devastating wars.

ALTRUISM

In 1944, a young Swedish diplomat named Raoul Wallenberg was sent into Budapest, Hungary, with instructions from the Swedish Foreign Ministry to save as many Jews as possible from the Nazis. Wallenberg was an imaginative young man whose heroes were Charlie Chaplin and the Marx brothers. Wallenberg decided to collect an assortment of official-looking Hungarian documents, such as driver's licenses and tax receipts, and to try to pass them off to the Germans as "Swedish protective passports." In a typical act of creative heroism, he climbed on top of a moving train carrying hundreds of Jews to the death camps. He then ran along the roof, dropping the "passports" through the air vents. Finally, he ordered the train to stop and release all the "Swedish citizens." Raoul Wallenberg eventually saved more than 100,000 women, men, and children through creative but exceptionally risky actions (Fogelman, 1994; "Wallenberg," 1990).

Raoul Wallenberg resembles Suzie Valadez, the woman described at the beginning of the chapter, who brings food and supplies to people living near the Mexican garbage dump. Both demonstrate **altruism,** a voluntary helpfulness that is motivated by concern about the welfare of other people, rather than by the possibility of personal reward (Midlarsky & Kahana, 1994).

Let's begin our discussion of altruism by examining several factors that influence altruism, and then we'll consider gender comparisons in altruism. Our third topic in this section is the bystander effect, a situation in which people *avoid* altruism. Finally, the "In Depth" feature examines a question that makes altruism especially mysterious: How can we explain altruism, especially because people often act so admirably when they have no prospect of reward?

Raoul Wallenberg, the young Swedish diplomat who saved more than 100,000 Jews from the Nazis during World War II.

Factors Affecting Altruism

Throughout the two chapters on social psychology, we have emphasized how the situation influences our social interactions. Situational factors are also important when we consider altruism. Let's consider several of these situational factors.

1. You are more likely to be altruistic when you have seen another person serving as a model for altruistic behavior (Schroeder et al., 1995). Research by Ervin Staub (1974) showed that people are more altruistic when a nearby person remarks that someone really needs help. Incidentally, Ervin Staub's personal decision to study altruism was probably influenced by observing another individual's altruism. As a 6-year-old child living in Hungary, Staub was one of the many people rescued from the Nazis by Raoul Wallenberg (Fogelman, 1994).

2. Altruism is more likely when people are not in a rush, hurrying off to other pressing duties (Darley & Batson, 1973; Schroeder et al., 1995).

3. Altruism is more common in rural areas and small towns than it is in large cities (Kohn, 1990; Levine et al., 1994). This same pattern holds true in cross-cultural research (Triandis, 1994).

These three determinants of altruism depend on the situation and changeable circumstances. However, researchers have also discovered systematic individual differences in altruism that seem to be genetically based (e.g., Carlo et al., 1991; Eisenberg, 1993; Schroeder et al., 1995). These altruistic tendencies persist as children mature into adulthood, emphasizing once again our theme of individual differences. Try Demonstration 17.4 to test your own altruistic tendencies.

An interesting study on individual differences in altruism was conducted by Samuel and Pearl Oliner (1988). They interviewed more than 700 people who had rescued Jews in Nazi Europe during World War II. These individuals risked their own lives to help others—even total strangers. The Oliners found that these people were much more likely than those who had not been rescuers to report a strong sense of empathy and feeling of attachment to other people, including people they did not know.

DEMONSTRATION 17.4 Testing Altruism

This test is a shortened version of the self-report altruism scale, devised by Rushton and his colleagues (1981). In each case, indicate how often you have performed each action.

	Never 0	Once 1	More than once 2	Often 3	Very often 4
1. I have given directions to a stranger.	___	___	___	___	___
2. I have given money to a stranger who needed it (or asked me for it.)	___	___	___	___	___
3. I have done volunteer work for charity.	___	___	___	___	___
4. I have given money to a charity.	___	___	___	___	___
5. I have helped carry a stranger's belongings (books, parcels, etc.).	___	___	___	___	___
6. I have delayed an elevator and held the door open for a stranger.	___	___	___	___	___
7. I have pointed out a clerk's error (in a bank, at the supermarket) in undercharging me for an item.	___	___	___	___	___
8. I have helped a classmate whom I did not know that well with a homework assignment when my knowledge was greater than his or hers.	___	___	___	___	___

When you have completed the items, calculate your score by adding together the numbers at the top that correspond to your answers. The maximum score on this version of the altruism scale is 32 points.

The Oliners found that altruistic people were likely to come from families who encouraged their children to think how their own actions would have consequences for other people. This focus seems likely to encourage compassion. The parents themselves also served as models of altruistic behavior. Children were encouraged to ignore social class, race, and religion in choosing their friends. As a result, these same children grew into adults who could appreciate the similarities that bind all humans to one another. They were less likely to emphasize the kinds of boundaries that separate "us" from "them." In Chapter 16, we saw that discrimination can be reduced when we try to overcome boundaries. The Oliners' study emphasizes how the ability to overcome boundaries can also produce empathy and altruism toward all humanity.

Altruism and Gender

In general, men and women are similar in their altruism. In a representative study, for example, visitors to a Toronto science museum read three stories. In each story, they could choose either an altruistic or a selfish response (Mills et al., 1989). The results showed that both women and men chose the altruistic option 75% of the time.

A meta-analysis of the research on gender comparisons in altruism showed that males were slightly more helpful than females in their interactions with strangers (Eagly & Crowley, 1986). However, the gender differences were very inconsistent across studies. In general, men were more helpful when an audience was present, but gender similarities were found when no one else was present.

Social psychologists typically study altruism toward strangers, a kind of altruism normally associated with males (Eagly, 1987). In contrast, they rarely study how people help family members and friends, a kind of altruism normally associated with females. In one of these studies, students read scenarios in which a friend asks for help with a personal problem; the female students reported greater willingness to help than did the male students (Belansky & Boggiano, 1994).

In summary, men and women are more similar than different when we consider overall altruism, though gender differences may arise in some situations (Eagly, 1996). This gender similarity theme has been repeated throughout the textbook, with respect to both cognitive and social characteristics.

Critical Thinking Exercise 17.5

Write down your answers to the following questions about gender and altruism.

a. Research on helping strangers shows that men are more helpful than women in tasks such as picking up a hitchhiker. In contrast, men and women are similar on tasks such as answering a stranger who asks "Excuse me, could you tell me what time it is?" (Eagly & Crowley, 1986). Can you think of an explanation that may help account for these inconsistencies?

b. We discussed the study by Belansky and Boggiano (1994), showing that women reported greater willingness to help a friend in difficulty. Can you think of an explanation that may help to account for this gender difference?

When People Do Not Help: The Bystander Effect

So far, we have considered a number of factors related to altruism. Now let's consider situations where people often *fail* to help, even when they know someone is in danger. This apparent apathy is called the **bystander effect,** a phenomenon in which the presence of other people inhibits helpfulness.

This bystander puzzle was first brought to public attention in 1964. Kitty Genovese was walking toward her apartment building in the early morning when a man

According to the bystander effect, a person is less likely to help someone in need if other people are around.

stabbed her. She screamed, "Oh, my God, he stabbed me! Please help me! Please help me!" The man left briefly, but then returned to attack her a second time. She shouted, "I'm dying! I'm dying." He drove away this time, but was soon back. This last time, he stabbed her again and then raped her before she died (Dowd, 1984; Shear, 1989).

The puzzling part of this murder was that 38 neighbors heard or saw at least part of the crime. In fact, 18 witnessed all three attacks. However, not one of them summoned the police until more than half an hour after the initial attack, when it was too late.

The remarkable apathy of these bystanders inspired Bibb Latané and John Darley (1968) to study the effect in the laboratory. Each participant in their study was led into a small room. Then he or she was instructed to discuss personal problems through an intercom system, presumably with one, two, or five other people in nearby rooms. After an uneventful beginning, one of the other people mentioned that he had a seizure disorder. Soon afterwards, he began to stutter badly and then cry out that he was having a seizure. Latané and Darley observed whether the participant rushed out to help the young man.

They discovered that 100% of the participants rushed to get help when they thought they were in a two-person group (i.e., each person thought he or she was the only one who could find help for the person having the seizure). However, only 62% of the participants sought help when they thought they were part of a six-person group. When people think they are part of a larger group, no individual feels responsible for helping, an effect called **diffusion of responsibility.** You can see that diffusion of responsibility is related to the social loafing we discussed earlier. Numerous studies in a variety of laboratory and real-life settings have confirmed that people are significantly less likely to help when other people are nearby (Batson, 1995; Latané & Nida, 1981). We can therefore add group size to the list of variables that influence altruism.

IN DEPTH

Explaining Altruism

One of the classic puzzles about social behavior is why humans perform actions that help society. *Why* does Suzie Valadez spend the majority of her waking hours passing out sandwiches at a garbage dump? *Why* did Raoul Wallenberg repeatedly risk his life to save thousands of Jews during World War II?

This "In Depth" feature focuses primarily on the research of one psychologist, C. Daniel Batson. His research provides an excellent example of a systematic series of studies designed to test a specific hypothesis: Will people help others, even when there is no possibility of personal benefit? Batson (1995) agrees that altruism is often selfishly motivated. However, people are sometimes purely altruistic and not the least bit selfish.

Batson (1995) proposes that we often help other people because we experience **empathy,** which means that we feel the same pain, suffering, or other emotion that someone else feels (Aronson et al., 1994). For example, you may feel empathy for a friend who didn't get the job he hoped for. According to Batson's **empathy-altruism hypothesis,** empathy has the power to motivate us to be altruistic. From previous research, we know that people are more likely to perform altruistic actions when they experience empathy (e.g., Davis, 1996; Eisenberg & Miller, 1987). This makes sense; we are more eager to help people if we experience some of the same emotions that they feel.

We mentioned that altruism is often selfishly motivated. Specifically, we may help other people for two major selfish reasons: (1) we want to *avoid* the personal pain of seeing someone suffer or else the guilt of not helping someone in distress; and (2) we want to share vicariously the joy that someone feels when his or her life improves. Notice, then, that these reasons represent two different kinds of selfishness; the first avoids personal pain and the second seeks out personal pleasure.

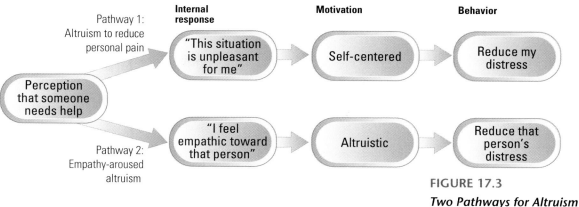

Pathway 1:
Altruism to reduce
personal pain

**Internal
response**

Motivation

Behavior

"This situation
is unpleasant
for me"

Self-centered

Reduce my
distress

Perception
that someone
needs help

"I feel
empathic toward
that person"

Altruistic

Reduce that
person's
distress

Pathway 2:
Empathy-aroused
altruism

FIGURE 17.3

Two Pathways for Altruism
Source: Based on Batson, 1987, 1995.

Batson's primary contribution to the research on altruism is that he has demonstrated how people can be altruistic when their empathy is aroused, even when neither the "avoiding personal pain" nor the "seeking vicarious joy" hypothesis can operate. Let's consider the research comparing the empathy-altruism hypothesis with each of these two more selfish hypotheses, and then we'll consider more evidence for the empathy-altruism hypothesis.

The Empathy-Altruism Hypothesis Versus Avoiding Personal Pain

As we noted, Batson agrees that we sometimes help other people because we want to avoid personal pain and guilt. He emphasizes, however, that even when selfish motives are missing, we often help other people—as long as we experience empathy. Figure 17.3 diagrams these two pathways.

Let's consider a representative study that demonstrates altruism, even when that altruism does not involve avoiding personal pain. College students were told that they would be working with another student named Elaine, who would be receiving electric shocks while she performs a task. One at a time, these students watched Elaine describe on closed-circuit TV how she was thrown from a horse onto an electric fence as a child. These shocks remind her of that trauma. The experimenter then asks participants whether they would be willing to trade places with Elaine and receive the shocks (Batson et al., 1981).

Batson and his colleagues (1981) led half of the participants to believe that their own interests and values were very similar to Elaine's; the other half were led to believe that they were very different from Elaine. Thus, the first group should have higher empathy for Elaine than would the second group. A second variable in this study was difficulty of escape. In the easy-escape condition, people were told that they could leave after viewing two trials in which Elaine suffered. In the difficult-escape condition, people could either watch Elaine suffer for 10 trials, or they could switch places with her.

Let's consider the results for the two low-empathy conditions. (See Figure 17.4.) When empathy was low and participants could easily escape, most participants left the experiment; few were altruistic. However when empathy was low but escape was difficult, people often volunteered to trade places with Elaine. Apparently, those people wanted to reduce the pain of watching someone else suffer, consistent with Pathway 1 in Figure 17.3.

Now let's consider the results for the two high-empathy conditions, in which people were encouraged to feel genuine compassion for Elaine. Consistent with Batson's empathy-altruism hypothesis, when empathy is aroused, people are highly likely to be altruistic. The participants in both high-empathy conditions were highly likely to help, whether escape was easy or difficult. If the avoidance of personal pain is the only reason for altruism, then participants in the easy-escape, high-empathy condition would have rushed to leave the experiment. Instead, about 90% of them

FIGURE 17.4

Altruism and Empathy

Percentage of people who help a needy person, as a function of the level of empathy and how difficult it would be for them to escape watching the victim's pain.
Source: Based on Batson et al., 1981.

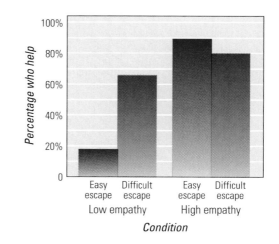

(IN DEPTH continued)
volunteered to trade places with Elaine. As Batson (1995) argues, we humans can have a genuine desire to improve others' welfare for altruistic reasons, and not simply because of our own selfishness.

The Empathy-Altruism Hypothesis Versus Vicarious Joy

Another possible explanation for human altruism focuses on a different form of selfishness. Maybe when we feel empathy with other people, we help them because we hope to share their joy vicariously when the situation improves (Smith et al., 1989). This motivation sounds somewhat more noble than the "avoiding personal pain" rationale. However, this explanation still emphasizes that our own emotional goals motivate our helpfulness.

Indeed, we often do help others because we imagine ourselves feeling joyous when their lives improve. However, Batson and his colleagues (1991) tested whether people can be altruistic, even when they know they'll never learn whether the victim's situation will improve. In a representative study, 83% of participants volunteered to help a fellow student, even when it was clear that they would never hear about the outcome of their altruism. The explanation for their helpfulness seems to have been empathy-inspired altruism, rather than vicarious joy.

More Evidence for the Empathy-Altruism Hypothesis

Let's consider one final study about the empathy-altruism hypothesis. The research we've looked at so far used helping responses as the dependent variable. In a more recent study, Batson and Weeks (1996) examined mood change as the dependent variable.

In this research, participants believed that they were helping another student. Half of the participants received instructions that encouraged low empathy; the other half received high-empathy instructions. When they later learned that their efforts had not actually helped the other student, those in the high-empathy condition were much sadder. In short, empathy is a powerful motivating force that encourages our altruism.

Conclusions About Altruism

In summary, the research has shown that we can be altruistic for a variety of reasons. We can be altruistic because we want to avoid personal pain and guilt. We are sometimes altruistic because we want to experience vicarious joy. However, we can also be altruistic when neither of those more selfish rationales is relevant. Instead, we help other people because we feel a bond with them. Our empathy is aroused; we want to reduce their distress and improve their lives.

When's the last time your investment yielded a 100 percent return?

Probably never. So here's an investment tip that will produce spectacular results year after year.

The *American Friends Service Committee* (AFSC) built a transformer, two pumping stations and water canals for the villages of Ngoc and Cung in Viet Nam. *Investment*: $30,000. *Yield*: Two annual crops instead of one, doubling the rice harvest and making a third crop of vegetables possible.

Venturing in Viet Nam continuously since 1966, *ASFC* knows that irrigation projects can end hunger and achieve food security. We share these goals with the ethnic minorities we serve in the poorest provinces.

Water works also have spin-off benefits. Clean water improves public health, relieves the long portages by women and girls and frees the girls for school. Electricity also means labor-saving rice mills and potential for light industry.

AFSC underwrites its food goals with better seed, livestock care, rice banks, contour farming in the eroded highlands, small revolving loans ($20 usually) and medical assistance.

Cast some bread upon the waters. Even though *AFSC* isn't listed on the *NYSE*, join our limited partnership and invest in Viet Nam with us. Please mail or phone in your gift today.

American Friends Service Committee Development Office, 1501 Cherry St., Philadelphia, PA 19102

My gift to help Quaker Service underwrite irrigation projects in Thanh Hoa Province:

❑$35 ❑$50 ❑$100 ❑$250 ❑$500
❑Other_____

Name

Address

City/State/Zip   HM197
VISA/Mastercard 1-888-588-AFSC
Photo by Lady Borton, AFSC Field Director, Hanoi.

According to Batson's empathy-arousal hypothesis, people will want to donate to the organization described in this ad because their empathy has been aroused. Batson and his colleagues argue that people will be altruistic, even when their generosity will not help them avoid personal pain and even when they cannot experience vicarious joy.

SECTION SUMMARY: *ALTRUISM*

1. Factors that encourage altruism include watching an altruistic model, lack of time pressure, and a rural or small-town setting; altruistic people usually come from families who encouraged compassion and emphasized overcoming boundaries between people.

2. Men are somewhat more helpful than females in their interactions with strangers, especially when an audience is present; women may be somewhat more helpful with family members and friends; overall, gender differences in helpfulness are not large.

3. Research on the bystander effect shows that we are less likely to help when other people are present, largely through the diffusion of responsibility.

4. We sometimes help others because we want to avoid pain and guilt or because we want to experience vicarious joy. However, Batson's empathy-altruism hypothesis argues that we can be altruistic because we feel an empathic bond with others, which encourages us to help them.

REVIEW QUESTIONS

1. This chapter examined many ways in which being in a group can influence a person's performance. Discuss this issue, being sure to mention social roles, social facilitation, social loafing, group polarization, groupthink, conformity, and the bystander effect. Also mention how a cross-cultural perspective helps us reinterpret our views about groups.

2. Some of the material in this chapter is related to the discussion of social cognition in the previous chapter. Discuss how social cognition factors—such as the self-fulfilling prophecy and the cognitive basis of stereotyping—are related to

social roles, stereotyping in conflict situations, enemy images, and any other topics you believe to be relevant.

3. From your own experience in group settings, try to recall examples of group polarization, groupthink, and conformity. Can you think of an occasion when a single person with an opposing opinion kept others from complying with a majority viewpoint?

4. We noted that conformity, compliance, and obedience can be placed along a continuum in terms of increasing social pressure. Discuss the nature of the social pressure in each case, and then describe how each of these three kinds of social pressure could be used to encourage a group to behave altruistically.

5. Discuss the possible explanations for both aggression and altruism, trying to point out parallels when possible.

6. We discussed gender issues as they relate to four topics in this chapter: conformity, aggression, pornography, and altruism. Summarize the conclusions in these four areas.

7. Using an example of a conflict you are currently facing, outline how you could help increase the perceived common ground. What other steps could you take to resolve this conflict? Finally, how would knowledge about reactive devaluation and GRIT help you begin to resolve the conflict?

8. The discussion of international peacemaking emphasized the GRIT model. However, much of the material on interpersonal conflict resolution is also relevant for international peacemaking. Imagine that you are advising the leaders of two countries that are currently in conflict. What specific guidelines would be relevant for them? Why would the empathy-altruism hypothesis be relevant, as well?

9. Based on what you know about altruism, describe all the factors that increase the likelihood of altruism. In other words, if you were in a situation where you needed help, describe the characteristics of the setting, the helper, and the relationship between yourself and the helper that would increase altruistic behavior.

10. Many of the principles in this chapter have implications for working with children and adolescents. Imagine that you are teaching elementary or high school. Choose one grade level, and turn back to the chapter outline. Point out how almost every topic could help you understand your students' current behavior or encourage them to be better human beings.

New Terms

group (p. 544)
role (p. 544)
social facilitation (p. 545)
social loafing (p. 546)
group polarization (p. 546)
groupthink (p. 546)
heuristics (p. 546)
conformity (p. 549)
environmental psychology (p. 551)
compliance (p. 552)
foot-in-the-door technique (p. 552)

door-in-the-face technique (p. 552)
obedience (p. 553)
aggression (p. 556)
schemas (p. 557)
conflict (p. 558)
lose-lose approach (p. 558)
win-lose approach (p. 558)
win-win approach (p. 558)
issues proliferation (p. 559)
enemy images (p. 559)
mirror-image thinking (p. 559)

perceived common ground (p. 560) peacebuilding (p. 563)
political psychology (p. 562)   altruism (p. 563)
reactive devaluation (p. 562)   bystander effect (p. 565)
GRIT (Graduated and Reciprocated diffusion of responsibility (p. 566)
    Initiatives in Tension Reduction) empathy (p. 566)
    (p. 562)   empathy-altruis hypothesis (p. 566)

Recommended Readings

Chrisler, J. C., Golden, C., & Rozee, P. D. (Eds.). (1996). *Lectures on the psychology of women.* New York: McGraw-Hill. This book features 24 very readable chapters on the psychology of women and gender; especially relevant to issues regarding social influence are the chapters on altruism, battered women, and fear of rape.

Cialdini, R. B. (1993). *Influence: Science and practice* (3rd ed.). New York: HarperCollins. Cialdini has written a fascinating book, filled with numerous examples and good reviews of the research on group influence.

Colby, A., & Damon, W. (1992). *Some do care: Contemporary lives of moral commitment.* New York: Free Press. Colby and Damon's book remains one of my favorites in social psychology. The portraits of altruistic individuals are superb, and the book includes thoughtful analyses of the moral basis of behavior.

Schroeder, D. A., Penner, L. A., Dovidio, J. F., & Piliavin, J. A. (1995). *The psychology of helping and altruism: Problems and puzzles.* New York: McGraw-Hill. Some of the topics explored in this excellent book include situational determinants of altruism, explanations of altruism, and the development of altruism.

Tesser, A. (Ed.). (1995). *Advanced social psychology.* New York: McGraw-Hill. The 12 chapters in this textbook focus on topics such as social influence, altruism (in a chapter written by Batson), aggression, and group processes.

Answers to Demonstrations

Demonstration 17.2
    1. True; 2. False; 3. False; 4. False; 5. False; 6. False; 7. False.

Answers to Critical Thinking Exercises

Exercise 17.1
    a. The researchers would need to be concerned about the ethical principle that experimenters should avoid potential harm. Presumably, they would not have allowed the "guards" to physically harm the "prisoners." However, some mental harm might occur from the prisoners' mental torment and from the guards' realizations that they could so easily torment other people. Ethical principles demand that the researchers extensively debrief the participants, and the researchers did do this. They also administered questionnaires later on, and the participants' responses indicated that their recovery had been satisfactory (Zimbardo et al., 1972). The research provided valuable information that even encouraged prison reform. Still, we need to be concerned that some participants may have experienced psychological harm.
    b. The problem is that the study has an important confounding variable. Specifically, the better performance in the second half of the study may be due to a practice effect. The other student was always present in the second half, when the participants had already had the opportunity to "warm up." One way to conduct the study would be to have the other student present at

the beginning (but not at the end) for half of the participants, and present at the end (but not at the beginning) for the other half of the participants. The researchers could then determine whether performance is better in the person-present condition, because they have equated for amount of practice.

Exercise 17.2

a. As Asch (1956) himself noted, the situation is embarrassing for the participant. In a typical study, a young man is placed in a situation, without his consent, in which he usually reveals something personal—that he is a conformist. None of the others in the group face this danger. Asch expressed his great concern about this problem. In debriefing the participants, he tried to treat them with great respect and encourage their collaboration in trying to discover how conformity might work (Korn, 1997).

b. A major problem would be that by studying college students in the collectivist culture, the researchers would obtain a biased sample that overrepresented wealthy, well-educated individuals who would also be more likely to be influenced by Western, individualistic values (Bond & Smith, 1996). Research with uneducated people in rural communities might reveal even greater differences between the collectivist cultures and the individualistic cultures.

Exercise 17.3

a. By dropping the part of the definition that emphasizes *intention,* the operational definition of aggression would be more straightforward and easy to measure. After all, we can measure amount of damage fairly easily; if we emphasize that a person intended to hurt someone else, we must request self-reports (which would be unreliable) or some behavioral index that the aggressor meant harm. On the other hand, if we dropped the requirement about intentions, then we would have to include cases where harm occurred accidentally (e.g., you stumbled in a dark movie theater and stepped on someone's foot). This alternate definition doesn't capture the hurtful spirit that most of us mean by the word *aggression.*

b. We would need to be concerned that people who view this material might become less sympathetic to victims of rape in the real world, outside the laboratory. Researchers must therefore include appropriate debriefing about the harmful physical and psychological effects of rape. Participants with this kind of careful debriefing have been found to be *less* accepting (rather than more accepting) of rape myths than participants in the control group (Intons-Peterson et al., 1989; Malamuth & Check, 1984). Obviously, the debriefing statement must be carefully prepared and persuasively delivered.

Exercise 17.4

a. The enemy images research suggests that people from Middle Eastern backgrounds were negatively portrayed during the Gulf War; we heard little positive information about this "outgroup" (Rothbart, 1993). Also, the villains portrayed on television usually have dark hair and complexions, rather than light features. As a result, during the aftermath of the traumatic bombing, images of dark "villains" would come readily to mind (i.e., be highly available).

b. One problem would be experimenter bias, because you have the expectation that you will see these distortions. Another problem would be that it's difficult to measure enemy images in an unbiased way. For example, the photos on Page 560 both show distortions, but the nature of the distortion is different in these two examples. It would be difficult to assign objective numbers, based on operational definitions. Also, the newspapers may have biases about what they are willing to publish; you could not generalize your findings to the entire culture.

Exercise 17.5

a. Picking up a stranger is more likely to be dangerous for a woman than for a man; women may therefore be less likely than men to help in this situation (Eagly, 1996). In contrast, telling someone the time of day is nonthreatening for both women and men, so neither gender should hesitate to help on the basis of safety. In fact, Eagly and Crowley (1986) demonstrated that research results were much more likely to show gender differences if the task was potentially dangerous for women.

b. Notice that the Belansky and Boggiano (1994) study assessed people's *reported* willingness to help friends. As we noted in Chapter 2, gender differences often emerge when the dependent variable is operationally defined in terms of self-report. If we could observe behavior, rather than using self-report, the gender differences might be smaller.

HEALTH PSYCHOLOGY, STRESS, AND COPING

CHAPTER 18

Every year, natural disasters affect the lives of thousands of North Americans. Life is proceeding forward with its normal quota of joys and hassles, and then this routine is upset by a hurricane, an earthquake, a tornado, or a flood.

Ellen Gerrity and Peter Steinglass (1994) interviewed families in Tucker County, West Virginia, whose homes had been completely destroyed during a flood similar to the one shown in the photo above. These families had evacuated their homes in the middle of the night and then returned to find that their homes had washed away, with most of the contents waterlogged and unsalvageable. In the months that followed, these families experienced intense stress as they faced the loss of their house, their favorite possessions, and the meaning of "home."

Some people, understandably, saw the flood as a turning point in their lives, when everything became grim. Sixteen months after the flood, a young man reported as follows:

Before the flood I hardly got into trouble. I used to have a job working at the drug store. As soon as the flood hit, that messed me up. Then we moved out of town and I got to hanging around with the wrong people. I broke into a store and I just got sent off. That's what happened after the flood . . . and I see it as caused by the flood. If it hadn't happened, I wouldn't have been in this institution [prison] and I wouldn't have broken into the store. (Gerrity & Steinglass, 1994, p. 235)

Other individuals coped with this tragedy by reordering their priorities. The experience had indeed been traumatic, but living through the disaster had forced them to realize the aspects of life they most cherished. An older married woman responded, three months after the flood:

Losing the things I lost, I don't put the value on material things now that I did before, and I don't intend to in the future. There were things I thought I had to have that I

*didn't need. In the future I think I'll be more careful in buying and not just have
a lot of things cluttering up the house. All those things were just gone in a matter of hours. It took you 20 years to put in that house. I've talked to different
people that really, losing their material things had really affected them bad. To
me, none of us lost our lives or got injured, and that's really more important.
(Gerrity & Steinglass, 1994, p. 232)*

Stress and coping can have important implications for one's physical health—as
well as one's mental health—as we will see in this chapter. **Health psychology**
attempts to understand how people stay healthy, why they engage in risky behavior, why they develop illnesses, and how they react to illnesses (S. E. Taylor, 1995).
Health psychology is therefore an example of **applied psychology,** because it emphasizes practical applications of psychological research.

Health psychology is especially important in the current era, as we realize that
many fatal diseases have a psychological component. When people died a century ago in
North America, the most common causes were infectious diseases, such as pneumonia
and tuberculosis. In contrast, the current leading causes of death are heart disease, cancer, lung diseases, and other problems that can be partly traced to emotional and behavioral factors such as stress, cigarette smoking, and improper diet (Brannon & Feist, 1992).

A discussion of health psychology provides a useful conclusion to an introductory psychology textbook, because so many diverse research areas can be applied to
this topic. In particular, this chapter emphasizes the application of research on
biopsychology, emotions, personality, and social psychology.

We'll begin with a section on stress and coping, noting that stressful emotional experiences are often linked with serious illness. The second section of this
chapter emphasizes individual differences in health. It also examines how ethnicity,
social class, and gender are related to health. The last two sections explore two health
issues that are especially crucial in the current decade: AIDS and cigarette smoking.
These two topics may initially seem to have little in common. However, in both cases,
risky behavior can be life-threatening. In both cases, social psychologists work together with health psychologists, medical professionals, and educators to develop
persuasive techniques to help people change their attitudes and their behavior.

STRESS AND COPING

Stress is the negative emotional experience that occurs when demands on a person are
greater than his or her response capabilities (Kaplan, 1996a; S. E. Taylor, 1995). Let's
begin our discussion of stress by considering a general overview of stress. Then we'll
look at several sources of stress, the effects of stress, and methods of coping with stress.

An Overview of Stress

In 1956, Hans Selye developed a classic model of stress. According to the model—
called **general adaptation syndrome**—a **stressor** (or unpleasant situation) produces
three stages of response. During the **alarm phase,** the individual prepares for action,

activating the sympathetic division of the nervous system. The goal is to regain **homeostasis,** or a state of internal balance. During the **resistance** phase, the body tries to cope with the stressor by releasing stress hormones; blood pressure, heart rate, and respiration all increase. Toward the end of resistance, the activity decreases in the sympathetic system and increases in the parasympathetic system. If the stressor persists, then the **exhaustion phase** follows: the parasympathetic system is now dominant, and the individual may develop physical illnesses (Selye, 1956).

However, theorists have argued that Selye's model is limited because it does not assign a large enough role to psychological factors (Stroebe & Stroebe, 1995; S. E. Taylor, 1995). According to Lazarus's **cognitive appraisal approach,** our cognitive processes help us decide whether we interpret an event as being stressful (Lazarus, 1991; Lazarus & Folkman, 1984). Consistent with the theme of this book, we differ from one another in the way we interpret the same event. Some people believe that they can overcome obstacles and cope effectively; others are overwhelmed by the situation (Park & Folkman, 1997).

Sources of Stress

If you compiled a list of all the sources of stress that you, your family, and your friends have faced, that list could be partitioned into three major categories: catastrophes, important life events, and daily hassles.

Catastrophes   A catastrophe is a large-scale disaster that affects numerous people and causes extensive damage. The West Virginia flood mentioned in the introduction to this chapter was certainly a catastrophe. Catastrophes also include major earthquakes, hurricanes, widespread war, toxic-waste contamination, and nuclear accidents (Adams & Adams, 1984; Baum & Fleming, 1993; Ursano et al., 1994). Hovanitz (1993) reviewed the research on the relationship between catastrophes and health, reporting that health problems increased in 14 of the 15 catastrophes that had been studied.

Important Life Events   A second category of stressors is major life events. Try Demonstration 18.1 before you read further. This demonstration is based on a scale developed by Yeaworth and her colleagues (1980) for use with students. Notice that all the items listed are not necessarily "bad"; even a happy, positive event can be stressful. This scale is similar to a variety of other questionnaires designed for older adults, such as the Social Readjustment Rating Scale (S. Cohen et al., 1995; Holmes & Rahe, 1967). On most of these scales, the minimum score for any event is 0 and the maximum score is 100.

People differ in their reactions to the same event. This couple is enjoying their wedding, but other couples might perceive their wedding to be a stressful occasion.

DEMONSTRATION 18.1   The Life Change Event Scale

The following items are part of a scale developed by Yeaworth and her coauthors (1980) for use with students; this scale assesses stress from major life changes. If you add up the total number of points for all these stressful events that have occurred within the last year, individuals with higher total scores would be more likely to develop physical illnesses. However, please note that this list does not include all items on the scale, so your informal assessment of life-change events may not be strongly correlated with health.

EVENT	VALUE
Parents getting divorced or separated	86
Family member (other than yourself) having trouble with alcohol	79
Parent or relative in your family (other than yourself) getting very sick	74
Breaking up with a close girlfriend or boyfriend	74
Parent losing a job	69
Starting a new school	57
Moving to a new home	51
Starting a job	34
Brother or sister getting married	26

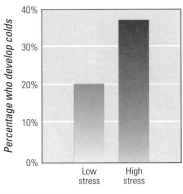

FIGURE 18.1

Percentage of colds diagnosed for students with low perceived stress versus high perceived stress.
Source: Based on S. Cohen et al., 1993.

Daily hassles—such as romantic problems—may be even more important than major life events in predicting the likelihood of illness.

Many studies have shown that people with high total scores on these life event scales are likely to develop physical illnesses such as tuberculosis, diabetes, arthritis, heart disease, and multiple sclerosis (S. Cohen et al., 1995; Holmes & Masuda, 1974; Hovanitz, 1993). In general, the correlation between life events and illness is lower than +.30. In other words, these stressful life events are moderately related to illness (S. Cohen et al., 1995). However, we would not expect the correlation between life events and illness to be extremely high. After all, individuals respond in different ways to the same presumably stressful event.

Sometimes, the relationship is stronger when we assess *perceived* stress, a measure that emphasizes cognitive appraisal. For example, Cohen and his colleagues (1993) recruited volunteers and exposed them to a low dose of an infectious respiratory virus. Medical professionals examined them repeatedly to determine whether they developed colds. The participants also filled out several questionnaires about the stress factors in their lives. One of the most useful measures was perceived stress. As Figure 18.1 shows, those who reported higher perceived stress were much more likely to develop colds.

One specific category of life stressors has inspired extensive research. Specifically, people who are responsible for taking care of family members with serious illnesses are likely to develop illnesses themselves (Lepore, 1995; Taylor et al., 1997). For example, you may know someone who is taking care of a spouse who has Alzheimer's disease or is recovering from heart disease, a stroke, or cancer. This caregiver is especially likely to develop a stress-related disease. Many communities offer services to caregivers who need temporary breaks from the experience of chronic stress. These programs probably benefit the caregivers' mental and physical health.

Daily Hassles Think for a moment about your most stress-filled days. A student I know described a miserable day that included an unreasonable biology test, a car with a dead battery, getting stuck in a friend's snowy driveway, and rushing from school to rehearse for a play. Kohn and his colleagues (1990) developed a Hassles Scale, which showed that college students' hassles tended to cluster into five categories: academic difficulties, time pressure, alienation from academics, romantic problems, and assorted social problems. Scales measuring daily hassles are correlated with health problems in both college students and older adults (Herbert & Cohen, 1996; Kohn et al., 1991; Kohn & MacDonald, 1992).

Interestingly, research often shows that the accumulation of daily hassles is a better predictor of future illness than is a scale that only counts the major life events (Eckenrode, 1984; Lazarus, 1984). For example, Robert Williams and his colleagues (1992) studied Navajo Indians in Arizona and discovered that the number of daily hassles was more helpful than major life events in predicting which individuals would require hospitalization.

We have seen that catastrophes, major life events, and minor daily hassles create stress, which in turn encourages physical illness. However, consider these two cautions: (1) Individual differences in people's interpretation and management of stress may be even more important than these environmental events; we'll address these individual differences in the second section of this chapter. (2) The relationship between stress and illness is moderately strong, but the correlation is far from perfect. Do not assume that every cold or heart attack has been created by stress!

Stress and the Immune System

Chapter 6 introduced the new field of **psychoneuroimmunology,** an interdisciplinary area that examines the relationship between the central nervous system and the immune system (Cohen & Herbert, 1996). We also noted in that discussion that the **immune system** protects our bodies from damage by invading bacteria, viruses, and parasites. **Lymphocytes** are the central players in the immune system; they are the white blood cells that defend the body against infection and other harmful agents. These lymphocytes divide rapidly when the body is threatened by these harmful agents (Cohen & Herbert, 1996). Research in both the laboratory and in naturalistic settings has shown that stress can reduce the number of lymphocytes. For example, studies have shown that lymphocyte production is decreased after the death of a spouse (Adler & Matthews, 1994; Schleifer et al., 1983). The brain registers stress, and it indirectly regulates lymphocyte production through both the peripheral nervous system and the endocrine glands (Maier et al., 1994).

Lymphocytes are key factors in the immune system. (In this photo, the lymphocytes are magnified about 1,000 times.)

Coping With Stress

Coping refers to the thoughts and behaviors we use to handle stress or anticipated stress. As you might imagine, individual differences in coping styles are impressively large (Aldwin et al., 1996). This theme about variability was emphasized for me when two of my friends became widows after their husbands had died of cancer. One woman asked her husband's friends to conduct the memorial service, because she knew it would be too stressful for her to speak. Another friend organized the service herself, greeting all who attended with warmth and strength. As she buried the urn with his ashes in her backyard, she smiled and said, "Well, I'm burying Sam here for now. But if I move, I'll just dig him up and bury him again." Both women had been equally close to their husbands, but they responded in very different ways to the stressful event.

Let's begin our discussion of coping with stress by contrasting problem-focused coping and emotion-focused coping. Then we'll consider social support as a form of coping.

Problem-Focused Coping Versus Emotion-Focused Coping Researchers often divide coping strategies into two major categories: problem-focused coping and emotion-focused coping (Lazarus, 1993; Lazarus & Folkman, 1984; Taylor & Aspinwall, 1996). **Problem-focused coping** includes taking direct action to solve problems as well as changing your thoughts. These two problem-focused strategies attempt to alter the problem that is creating the stress. In contrast, **emotion-focused coping** attempts to regulate emotional responses to the problem. Let's consider these two basic approaches.

1. *Problem-focused coping:* One problem-focused coping response is direct action. In a stressful situation, you try to define the problem, generate several possible solutions, and determine the costs and benefits of each alternative. You then select among these alternatives and move forward. We discussed this kind of approach in the problem-solving section of Chapter 8, as well as in the conflict-resolution section of Chapter 17. Research shows that people who tend to use this strategy are likely to experience lower levels of stress. Also, no consistent gender differences have been observed in the tendency to use direct action as a coping strategy (D'Zurilla & Sheedy, 1991; Lazarus, 1993).

A second kind of problem-focused coping can be directed inward. You can reduce stress by cognitive adjustments such as shifting your level of aspiration. For example, a student whose grades seem too low for medical school may decide to pursue a less challenging health-related career. This kind of internal coping strategy is called **cognitive reappraisal** (Lazarus & Folkman, 1984).

Most researchers examine how we respond to a situation that is already stressful. However, Aspinwall & Taylor (1997) emphasize that we also need to consider proactive coping. In **proactive coping,** we make efforts in advance to prevent a potentially stressful event or to reduce its impact before the event actually occurs. For example, a California resident may use proactive coping to prepare for a possible earthquake, by purchasing earthquake insurance and earthquake-related supplies. Proactive coping is especially effective because individuals can deal with the stressor before it becomes overwhelming (Aspinwall & Taylor, 1997).

Short-term denial can sometimes be adaptive. These victims of the January 1994 earthquake in Los Angeles could have developed psychological disorders if they did not show some denial in the hours following this disaster.

We are more likely to use problem-focused coping—either direct action or cognitive reappraisal—when we believe that the situation can actually be changed. When we believe that nothing can be done about a stressful situation, we typically try emotion-focused forms of coping (Taylor & Aspinwall, 1996).

2. *Emotion-focused coping:* The second major category of coping strategies consists of denial, seeking social support, and miscellaneous stress-reduction approaches; these are examples of emotion-focused coping.

Denial is the refusal to recognize the reality of a stressful life situation (Schafer, 1996). Some denial may be adaptive immediately after an event because it prevents us from being overwhelmed with panic. Denial allows us to process new information in tolerable doses. For instance, the survivors of Hiroshima's atomic bombing would probably have developed severe psychological disorders if they had not used denial to avoid thinking about widespread death and destruction (Lifton, 1967). However, high levels of denial long after the trauma can be harmful, because the individual may resist using helpful problem-focused coping (S. E. Taylor, 1995).

We'll examine a second kind of emotion-focused coping in the next section when we note the advantages of seeking social support. Other emotion-focused strategies for coping include exercise, relaxation, and laughter (Dubbert, 1992; Schafer, 1992). Some people also manage to find some positive benefits from their stressful situation. Like the woman at the beginning of the chapter who had lived through the West Virginia floods, they report that the experience forced them to reexamine their emotions and reorder their life priorities (Aldwin et al., 1996).

Social Support and Coping Many people cope with stress by seeking support from other people. Our family and friends can provide emotional reassurance, boost our self-esteem, and express their caring concern. Companions and confidants can enhance both our emotional and physical well-being (Connidis & Davies, 1990, 1992).

Social support helps people cope with stress-related illnesses.

Several large-scale studies confirm that social support is related to health status (Brannon & Feist, 1992; "Hearts and Minds," 1997; S. E. Taylor, 1995). For example, a study of more than 700 men—all 50 years of age at the beginning of the study—contrasted individuals who engaged in many social activities and individuals who had few social activities (Orth-Gomér, 1994). The study controlled for risk factors such as blood pressure and amount of exercise, as well as age. The results showed that the men with few social contacts were more than 3 times as likely as the highly social men to have a heart attack by age 56. Another analysis of the same men used a different operational definition for social support—degree of attachment to the closest family member. The men with low attachment were more than twice as likely to experience a heart attack by age 56, in comparison to the men with high attachment (Orth-Gomér, 1994).

Social support also seems to help people cope with a variety of stress-related illnesses (Burleson, 1994; Hobfoll, 1988; S. E. Taylor, 1995). However, we need to be cautious in interpreting these data because most of the research is correlational, or else it includes potential confounding variables. Suppose, for example, that a study reports higher cancer recovery rates for individuals with high social support, rather than low social support. Unless the study is carefully conducted, an alternative explanation might be that a person with severe symptoms tends to drive away the people who might provide social support.

In general, however, the research suggests that social support actually *causes* modest improvements in health (Cohen, 1991; Orth-Gomér, 1994). Social support serves as a buffer that allows people to interpret threatening events as being less stressful. Also, social support enhances general self-esteem and well-being.

Some research suggests that people who discuss their traumatic experiences with others may actually improve the functioning of their immune system (Pennebaker, 1995, 1997; Schwartz & Kline, 1995). For example, Pennebaker and his coauthors (1988) asked healthy undergraduates to write about either superficial topics (control group) or traumatic experiences (experimental group) during brief daily sessions. Measures on the immune system showed that lymphocytes were more responsive in those students who had discussed their traumatic experiences. The experimental group also showed a drop in the number of visits to the health center, relative to the control group.

Critical Thinking Exercise 18.1

Write down your answers to the following questions about emotion-focused coping and the effects of social support.

a. Suppose that a friend tells you, "You know, laughing really can improve your health. I had a cold last week, and I decided to just stay in bed and pamper myself by watching a lot of situation comedies. And by the next day, I was better!" List at least three problems with this conclusion.

b. The research on social support is challenging for a number of reasons. One important reason is that we can construct many alternative operational definitions for social support. Suggest at least three useful operational definitions for the concept of social support.

SECTION SUMMARY: *STRESS AND COPING*

1. Selye's model of stress, called general adaptation syndrome, includes three stages of response: alarm, resistance, and exhaustion; Lazarus's approach emphasizes that we use cognitive appraisal to help us decide whether we interpret an event to be stressful.

2. Stress-related illnesses are somewhat correlated with measures of three kinds of stress: catastrophes, important life events, and minor daily hassles.

3. According to research in psychoneuroimmunology, stressful life events are associated with a decrease in lymphocyte production; the brain registers stress and

communicates to the immune system through the peripheral nervous system and the endocrine glands.

4. Problem-focused coping includes direct problem solving and cognitive adjustment; emotion-focused coping includes denial, seeking social support, and other tactics designed to reduce stress.

5. Social support appears to help reduce the incidence of heart attacks, and it helps people recover from a variety of other stress-related illnesses; discussing one's previous traumatic events may also provide health benefits.

DEMONSTRATION 18.2 Assessing Hostility

The following items are similar to those items from the MMPI, which Barefoot and his colleagues (1983) used to assess hostility. In front of each item, write *true* if the statement is true about you and *false* if the statement is false. Check your responses against the key at the end of the chapter.

_____ 1. When someone does something wrong, I feel obligated to do something wrong in return.

_____ 2. Many times I've been in the position of taking orders from someone less competent than myself.

_____ 3. Most people are so incompetent that they need a lot of argument to help them see the truth.

_____ 4. My relatives tend to think highly of me.

_____ 5. People usually understand my way of doing things.

_____ 6. It seems perfectly fair to take advantage of people if the opportunity is just sitting there.

_____ 7. I make friends with people because they are likely to be useful to me.

_____ 8. I often find that people let me down.

_____ 9. Even when people are rude to me, I try to be gentle in return.

_____ 10. I usually try to cover up my poor opinion of a person so that he or she never knows how I feel.

PSYCHOSOCIAL FACTORS RELATED TO HEALTH AND ILLNESS

When we considered sources of stress in the previous section, we discussed forces in the environment that are related to stress and illness. A devastating flood, the death of a family member, and countless daily hassles all predict health problems. However, we also need to consider individual differences in the way people respond to those external forces. These internal factors may be just as important as the forces in the environment. We'll first consider two personality characteristics and then discuss three social categories: gender, ethnicity, and social class.

Type A Behavior Pattern and Hostility

Researchers initially proposed that a general personality pattern designated as "Type A" was a risk factor for heart disease. However, more careful research demonstrated that only the hostility component of this personality pattern was the "deadly" factor. Try Demonstration 18.2 now, and then we'll look more closely at the research.

In an influential book, Friedman and Rosenman (1974) proposed that people can be divided into two basic categories. People with the **Type A behavior pattern** are aggressive, competitive, hostile, and impatient. These people speak rapidly and work quickly. They also respond to hassles with irritation and hostility (Lyness, 1993; Rosenman, 1990).

In contrast, people with the **Type B behavior pattern** are more relaxed and easygoing; they are seldom impatient or hostile. For example, I know a woman with Type B characteristics who did not discover until three weeks after the switch to daylight savings time that her watch had been an hour off. She is simply unconcerned about time.

More detailed research has shown, however, that the two original categories were too broad; they included many personality characteristics that are not closely related to heart disease (Adler & Matthews, 1994; Friedman et al., 1994). For example, people who work hard and move fast will be categorized as Type A, but most of them tend to be well-adjusted and healthy.

One particular component of Type A behavior, however, *does* predict heart disease: hostility. Specifically, people who are at high risk for heart problems tend to be hostile, bitter, suspicious, controlling, and frustrated (Adler & Matthews, 1994; Friedman et al., 1994). These individuals tend to view the world as a hostile place, and they are equally suspicious about the human race. Apparently, hostile people do not cope well with stress. They are also less likely to follow their physicians' recommendations about issues such as diet and medication (Friedman et al., 1994).

Hostility and Type A behavior pattern are the personality attributes that have received the most attention. However, let's consider another relevant characteristic: psychological control.

The most dangerous component of the Type A behavior pattern may actually be hostility.

Psychological Control

A student described a disturbing experience she had while working in a nursing home. She had befriended a woman living in that home who had been a psychiatrist. The student was interested in the psychiatrist's remarks about Freudian theory, as well as her comments about how the nurses' treatment of other residents was likely to make those people feel helpless. The student then went off to college for two months; on returning, she sought out the psychiatrist. Astonishingly, the psychiatrist no longer recognized the student, and she no longer talked. In fact, the elderly woman looked transformed. She was no longer neatly dressed and carefully groomed. Now her blouse was improperly buttoned, and her hair was disheveled. The nursing home records showed no evidence of a stroke or other organic reason for her decline. Naturally, some purely medical condition could still be responsible, but psychological control may be the relevant factor.

In Chapter 11, we discussed how nursing homes can take away people's sense of psychological control. Elderly people who have lost this sense of control may show a decline in physical health. In contrast, nursing homes can encourage residents to make their own decisions about daily activities in order to establish a sense of control. These individuals who exercise psychological control tend to be happier and live longer than those with standard nursing home care (Rodin & Langer, 1977).

Psychological control is important when we consider illness at any age, not just for elderly residents of nursing homes. When people develop serious illnesses, they often feel powerless and vulnerable. If they believe they can do something to influence their future health, they feel more powerful (Helgeson, 1992, 1994; S. E. Taylor, 1995). In general, research shows that people high in psychological control take better care of themselves, for example, by reading articles about healthful habits and by asking questions when they visit their physicians.

Research indicates that people who are high in psychological control are more likely to follow the advice of a physician—for example, getting regular exercise after a stroke.

Gender

As Table 18.1 shows, women in three major ethnic groups have a longer life expectancy than men (Giachello, 1996). One factor that may contribute to gender differences in longevity is employment patterns. Men are more likely to have hazardous jobs, such as construction work or police work. Men are also more likely to consume alcohol and other harmful drugs, and they are more likely to die in motor vehicle accidents (S. E. Taylor, 1995).

One factor that may benefit women's health is that they are more likely to visit their health care provider (S. E. Taylor, 1995; Travis, 1993). They may also be more sensitive to problems concerning their own health. In contrast, the male gender role encourages men to be physically "tough," rarely complaining about symptoms of illness. Perhaps women are more likely to consult physicians during the early stages of a disease, before it becomes fatal. As we have emphasized throughout this book, gender roles and gender stereotypes may be harmful for males, as well as females.

Consistent with Theme 3, the causes are complex. No single factor accounts for gender differences in life expectancy. The explanation must focus on a variety of factors, such as employment patterns, risky behavior, and health habits.

In every ethnic group, men have a shorter life expectancy than women. The explanation for this gender difference is complex, including factors such as employment in dangerous occupations, risky behavior, and health habits.

Ethnicity

Ethnicity is relevant to health psychology because members of some ethnic groups are more likely to experience certain health problems and illnesses. For example, both Native Americans and Native Canadians are more likely than Whites to experience drug and alcohol problems (Center for Substance Abuse Treatment, 1994; Gfellner, 1994). In the United States, Blacks are more likely than Whites to die of cancer and AIDS.

TABLE 18.1 Gender Differences in Life Expectancy (in years) for Three Major Ethnic Groups

	ETHNIC GROUP		
	European American	Black	Hispanic
Women	79	73	77
Men	73	65	70

Source: Based on Giachello, 1996.

Health care for immigrants may be more effective when people seek traditional healing customs in addition to standard U.S. medical care. In this photo, a man purchases items from a botanica, *an herbal stall in Mexican culture, which sells herbs, potions, and roots intended to help the users improve their health.*

Also, Black infants are more than twice as likely as White infants to die in the first year of life (Bayne-Smith, 1996a; Meyerowitz et al., 1998; Phillip, 1993). Table 18.1 emphasized *gender* differences in life expectancy, but look at that table once more to see the large *ethnic* differences in life expectancy.

Ethnicity can combine with social class, gender, and area of residence, leading to extremely dangerous health risks. For example, Black men in the Harlem region of New York City are less likely to reach the age of 65 than men living in Bangladesh (McCord & Freeman, 1990).

Ethnic background has an additional influence on health care: We must also consider the interactions between immigrants and European American doctors. For example, many Hispanic patients have difficulty describing their symptoms to physicians who do not speak Spanish (Seijo et al., 1995).

Physicians trained in U.S. and Canadian medical schools need to be sensitive as well to the health care practices of other cultures. For example, 10,000 members of the Hmong tribe in Laos have settled in Minnesota. The Hmong often prefer to seek care from shamans, ritual healers from the Southeast Asian tradition. Physicians can learn to coordinate their medical care with other healing methods. For example, a child with an ear infection might take an antimicrobial medicine prescribed by a U.S.-trained doctor, as well as an herbal mixture recommended by the shaman. Similarly, Mexican Americans may combine medicine from a U.S.-trained doctor with herbs purchased at a *botanica* (Mayers, 1989; Risser & Mazur, 1995). Herbal medicines may indeed have healing properties. In addition, cultural beliefs should be respected (unless the practice is known to be harmful). As we have seen, psychological factors can influence the immune system and other health processes.

IN DEPTH

Socioeconomic Status

We've just seen that ethnicity can have an important effect on life expectancy and other measures of health. As you might imagine, social class is at least partly responsible for some of those ethnic differences. That is, European Americans may tend to be healthier than members of other ethnic groups because of factors related to personal income and education. Let's now focus our attention on socioeconomic status.

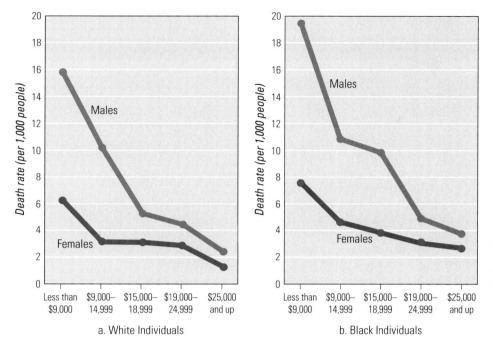

FIGURE 18.2

Annual Death Rate for Male and Female Blacks and Whites (as a function of family income)
Source: Based on Pappas et al., 1993.

Socioeconomic status (SES) is a social-class ranking that is based on factors such as educational attainment, income, occupation, and family prestige (Kornblum, 1994). Socioeconomic status is often called **social class.**

Socioeconomic status is among the most powerful predictors of life expectancy, health, and illness (Adler et al., 1994). For example, an adult with an income of less than $9,000 per year is roughly 5 times as likely to die in any given year as someone with an income greater than $25,000 per year (Pappas et al., 1993). Figure 18.2 shows the details of a study by Gregory Pappas and his colleagues. As you can see, income is strongly related to death rate for both Whites and Blacks and for both men and women. The results are similar when socioeconomic status is operationally defined in terms of education, rather than income. For example, a Black woman with less than 12 years of school is roughly 3 times as likely to die in any given year as a Black woman with a college degree (Pappas et al., 1993).

Other researchers have also found that social class has a major impact on death rate and on the likelihood of a variety of serious diseases (e.g., Adler et al., 1994; Adler & Coriell, 1997; Kitagawa & Hauser, 1973). The major challenge, however, is explaining *why* social class is so strongly correlated with various health measures. Consistent with Theme 3 of this book, the explanation is extremely complex because numerous factors help account for the social class differences. Let's look at three general categories of factors: physical environment, health behavior, and psychological characteristics.

Physical Environment

One important factor in the relationship between social class and health is that people who live in impoverished neighborhoods are more likely to be exposed to chemical dangers such as air pollution, water pollution, hazardous wastes, and pesticides (Coriell & Adler, 1997). Economically poor people are also more likely than wealthy people to be victims of crime.

You may have figured out another environmental factor related to social class. Economically poor people are more likely to live in crowded housing situations. Crowded living conditions promote the spread of infectious diseases (Coriell & Adler,

One factor that helps explain the relationship between social class and health is that individuals from lower social classes are more likely to receive treatment in clinics, with lower quality care and lack of treatment continuity.

(IN DEPTH continued)

1997). In short, environmental factors can explain part of the relationship between social class and health.

Health Behavior

Nancy Adler and her colleagues at University of California, San Francisco, have also identified a variety of health behaviors that help explain the connection between social class and health. For example, social class is strongly linked to cigarette smoking; lower social class individuals smoke more, whether we define social class in terms of income or education (Adler et al., 1994). Lower social class individuals are also more likely to be obese (Adler et al., 1994). As we saw in Chapter 12, obese people are more likely to experience health problems.

Economically disadvantaged people also do not have the same access to high-quality health care that the upper classes enjoy (Brislin, 1993; Rodin & Salovey, 1989). People from lower social classes are less likely to have a personal physician, and they are more likely to receive treatment in clinics. The quality of health care suffers when a different physician is seen on each visit.

Psychological Characteristics

In addition to physical environment and health behavior, psychological characteristics may also explain the relationship between social class and health. For example, social class is related to depression. A Canadian study showed a depression rate of 2% in a high SES group, 4% in an average SES group, and 12% in a low SES group (Murphy et al., 1991). As you may recall from Chapter 14, depressed people are more likely than nondepressed people to experience a variety of health problems.

Social class is also related to psychological stress. For example, lower SES people are more likely to live in a stressful neighborhood. Economic pressures and unemployment produce additional stress (Adler et al., 1994). As you know from the first section of this chapter, major life events and daily hassles are both associated with health problems.

You may be surprised to learn that social class is also related to several psychological factors discussed earlier in this second section of the chapter. For example, social class is related to hostility (Coriell & Adler, 1997; Adler et al., 1994). That is, lower SES individuals are more likely to be hostile and angry—whether you measure SES in terms of education or personal income. Social class is also related to psychological control; lower SES individuals are less likely to feel in control of their lives.

Conclusions about SES and Health

We have seen that a wide variety of factors could contribute to the social class differences in health. Once we appreciate the complexity of the issues, we can understand why the differences won't be erased by a single, one-shot "cure" for the problem—such as improving the health clinics in lower social class areas. (Though, of course, we must start somewhere!) Also, it is significant that the social class differences in health are *increasing*—rather than decreasing—as the differences between the rich and the poor grow larger in the United States (Adler et al., 1994).

Addressing the problem of social class differences in health requires an interdisciplinary approach. In Chapter 3, we saw that research in biopsychology requires the interdisciplinary approach provided by psychologists, biologists, and medical researchers. In Chapter 17, we saw that the research on international conflict resolution requires psychologists and political scientists to work together. Tackling the problem of social class and health is also interdisciplinary. For example, Nancy Adler—one of the leaders in the field—is currently working with other psychologists—as well as sociologists, anthropologists, biologists, and medical researchers—to define the problems and to begin determining how they can be corrected (Kent, 1997).

Critical Thinking Exercise 18.2

Write down your answers to the following questions about social class and health.

a. We defined socioeconomic status as a social-class ranking based on factors such as educational attainment, income, occupation, and family prestige. Most of the studies on social class and health examine very large samples of people. Why do you suppose that the operational definition of social class focuses on either educational attainment or income?

b. In the data we discussed, lower SES individuals are more likely to have health problems. However, a few diseases show a different pattern. For example, breast cancer is more common among *higher* SES women. One risk factor for breast cancer is delayed childbearing—specifically, not giving birth before the age of 30 (Adler & Coriell, 1997). How could this risk factor help explain the positive correlation between breast cancer and SES?

SECTION SUMMARY: *PSYCHOSOCIAL FACTORS RELATED TO HEALTH AND ILLNESS*

1. Hostility appears to be the component of Type A behavior pattern that best predicts heart disease.

2. Psychological control is also related to health; people high in control typically want to influence their future health.

3. Women live longer than men, in part because of employment, less risky behavior, and better health habits.

4. Ethnic group differences are found in illness and life expectancy; health care providers must be sensitive to the health-related practices of their immigrant patients.

5. Socioeconomic status is a powerful predictor of health status, for reasons that include physical environment, health behavior, and psychological characteristics.

ACQUIRED IMMUNODEFICIENCY SYNDROME (AIDS)

We began this chapter by discussing stress, a factor that contributes to many health problems. We then considered how health is associated with two personality characteristics, as well as gender, ethnicity, and social class. In the last two sections of this chapter, we'll discuss two health hazards that are critically important in the current era: AIDS and smoking.

We often have no control over the way we die. The evening news describes the horrifying wreck of a car hit head-on by a drunk driver; the innocent victim had no way of avoiding death. But the irony of AIDS and smoking is that we can control whether we have unsafe sex or share needles with someone who might have AIDS. We also have the potential to avoid smoking. Still, thousands of people court suicide every day by engaging in risky behavior. Health psychologists are challenged to find methods to help people change their high-risk activities. Let's begin by discussing AIDS and then consider smoking in the final section.

Acquired immunodeficiency syndrome (AIDS) is a viral disease that weakens the immune system and is spread by infected blood, semen, and vaginal secretions. As of June 1997, more than 379,000 U.S. residents have died of AIDS. By the year 2000, an estimated 40 million people throughout the world will be HIV-positive (Centers for Disease Control, 1997; Freiberg, 1998). (For current data and other information related to AIDS, you can call the Centers for Disease Control's National AIDS Hotline at 1-800-342-2437.)

AIDS is an important topic in health psychology because the disease is spread primarily by high-risk behavior. At present, no medicine can prevent or cure AIDS. Therefore, the primary method of halting AIDS is through education and changes in behavior. Our overview of AIDS begins with some background information and then discusses psychological aspects of AIDS and AIDS prevention.

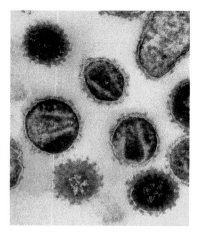

Several human immunodeficiency viruses (HIV), magnified 240,000 times.

Medical Aspects of AIDS

AIDS is caused by a virus called **human immunodeficiency virus (HIV),** which has the potential to destroy part of the immune system. In particular, HIV invades certain white blood cells called T-helper lymphocyte cells. These particular cells resemble the conductor of a symphony, because they direct the other branches of the immune system to fight disease (Kalichman, 1996). Inside these lymphocytes, the HIV replicates itself. As it replicates, it destroys the lymphocytes. Ironically, then, HIV destroys the specific lymphocytes that are most important in fighting disease.

When HIV destroys a lymphocyte, the virus is released and infects other lymphocytes. As a consequence, the immune system is substantially weakened (Kelly, 1995).

Some people infected with HIV may develop symptoms such as swollen lymph glands, fatigue, unexplained fevers, and diarrhea (Kalichman, 1996). However, many HIV-positive individuals may have no symptoms, and so they do not realize that they are infected. Still, a person with HIV is very contagious during the first few weeks after the infection begins (Coffin, 1995; Hoffman, 1996). The average incubation period between the initial HIV infection and the diagnosis is estimated to be 10 years or more (Coffin, 1995; Schneiderman et al., 1994).

AIDS is actually the end stage of the HIV infection. AIDS is the illness that occurs when the individual becomes seriously ill because other infections have taken advantage of the severely weakened immune system (Kalichman, 1996; Kelly, 1995). A formal diagnosis of AIDS is typically made after an HIV-positive individual develops a severe illness. One of the most common of these illnesses is *Pneumocystis carinii* pneumonia, a disease that is particularly deadly for people whose immune system no longer works properly. Another severe illness is Kaposi's sarcoma, a cancer that harms the cells inside certain small blood vessels (Kalichman, 1996; Kelly, 1995). Tragically, once the AIDS diagnosis is established, the life expectancy may be only two years (Kalichman, 1996). However, this life expectancy information is frequently changing for those individuals who can afford the new "drug cocktails." Once again, social class has an important impact on an individual's health.

Transmission of AIDS

FIGURE 18.3

This poster emphasizes that no population is immune to AIDS.

As the poster in Figure 18.3 illustrates, anyone can get AIDS who engages in risky behavior with an infected person. Unfortunately, it is usually impossible to tell whether a person is infected, even though college students think they can make that

Anyone can get AIDS from sexual contact or sharing needles with an infected person. **Call 1-800-541-AIDS**
But we know how to prevent AIDS. Learn how to protect yourself.

New York State Health Department

distinction by talking with someone (Swann et al., 1995). Keep in mind that any contact with blood, semen, or vaginal secretions is potentially dangerous.

At present, transmission through sexual contact is responsible for between 75% and 85% of HIV infections (Royce et al., 1997). Gay and bisexual males who have had anal intercourse without condom protection are at high risk for AIDS (Kalichman, 1996). In contrast, lesbian women are at relatively low risk for AIDS if they have never had unsafe sex with men and if they have never used IV drugs—although no one is perfectly risk-free (Clay, 1997).

Heterosexuals are also at risk for AIDS. For instance, the number of individuals who contracted AIDS through heterosexual intercourse quadrupled between 1989 and 1995 (Kalichman, 1996). A woman who has intercourse with an HIV-positive man runs a risk 12 times greater than that of a man who has intercourse with an HIV-positive woman (Morokoff et al., 1995; Padian et al., 1990). Unfortunately, heterosexual women and men often resist taking appropriate precautions, because they believe that they are not at risk for AIDS.

Intravenous drug users are at high risk for developing AIDS (Kalichman, 1996; Murphy & Kelly, 1994). HIV is transmitted by needles previously used by individuals who are HIV-positive. HIV can also be transmitted via contaminated blood. In addition, babies who are born to infected mothers can develop AIDS. In the United States, 7,902 cases of pediatric AIDS had been reported by June 1997 (Centers for Disease Control, 1997).

In the first part of this chapter, we saw how people could acquire a disease through years of accumulated stressful experiences. In the case of AIDS, a single act—lasting only minutes—can lead to a fatal illness.

Living With AIDS

HIV can have several direct effects on the central nervous system. When lymphocytes have been infected with HIV, they secrete substances that change the levels of certain neurotransmitters, such as dopamine. Brain-imaging techniques also show tissue damage among people with AIDS, in both the cortex and in other brain structures (Parsons, 1996b). Not surprisingly, then, people with AIDS often experience cognitive problems. They have trouble paying attention, remembering, and using language. Problems with motor coordination are also common (Hoffman, 1996; Parsons, 1996b).

As you might imagine, HIV-positive individuals are likely to experience depression (Kalichman & Sikkema, 1994; Lyketsos et al., 1993). Anxiety, anger, and guilt are also common (Kalichman & Sikkema, 1994).

Some people respond to a diagnosis of AIDS with denial (Hoffman, 1996). In fact, Taylor and her colleagues (1992) reported the astonishing finding that men who knew they tested positive for HIV were significantly *more* optimistic about not developing AIDS than men who knew they had tested negative. Those who deny that they have AIDS are not likely to take precautions against infecting other people. As a consequence, the disease spreads even further.

Many people living with AIDS report feeling rejected and patronized by other people. As one woman with AIDS wrote:

> My family couldn't accept it at all. My brothers . . . they wouldn't let the kids come to the party, they thought they could catch it from the food. I tried to talk, particularly to my brother, and he said it's not the fact he doesn't care, it's that he's scared, particularly of catching the virus but also about "Are you going to live, are you going to die?" (Henderson, 1992, p. 26)

What is the most effective way to cope with the terror of having AIDS? In general, people who use active coping strategies are likely to have the highest self-esteem and the least depression (Hoffman, 1996; Namir et al., 1987). Some of these active strategies include talking to people, increasing physical exercise, and

According to research, people with AIDS who take an active approach to life are likely to be relatively well adjusted. Volunteering at an AIDS office such as this one might promote psychological adjustment.

becoming involved in AIDS-related political activities. We discussed the importance of social support earlier in this chapter. This feeling of connectedness and concern is also vitally important when people are trying to cope with AIDS (Celentano & Sonnega, 1991; Hoffman, 1996).

AIDS-Prevention Programs

At present, we have no vaccine against AIDS and no cure for the disease. Health psychologists who focus on AIDS often design programs to educate people about AIDS and to help prevent AIDS. An underlying problem in designing these programs is one we raised in Chapter 16: Attitudes are often unrelated to behavior. That is, people know that the consequences of high-risk behavior can be deadly, and they certainly have negative *attitudes* about acquiring AIDS—but their *behavior* may still be risky. Education has persuaded an impressive number of people to avoid AIDS risk. Still, the success rate is far from satisfactory. AIDS prevention requires further reduction in two areas: high-risk sexual behavior and IV drug abuse.

High-Risk Sexual Behavior   Many people simply fail to realize that they are engaging in risky sexual behavior. For example, in one survey of university students, 75% said that they faced a lower-than-average risk of contracting AIDS, compared to their peers. Just 20% said that they had an average risk, and only 5% said they had an above-average risk (Moore & Rosenthal, 1991). Unless this sample was biased, we would expect 50% to rate themselves as average or above-average. A good number of students are apparently trying to fool themselves about the risks of AIDs.

According to the research, only a small percentage of sexually active people regularly use a condom (Campbell et al., 1992; Kalichman, 1995). Alarmingly, women with the largest number of sexual partners are *less* likely to use condoms regularly than women who had just one partner (Campbell et al., 1992; MacDonald et al., 1990).

The data on estimated AIDS risk and on condom use illustrate that cognitive biases can sometimes lead people to act irrationally, a tendency we examined in Chapter 8. Try Demonstration 18.3 to illustrate another cognitive bias. As Chapter 8 discussed, the **framing effect** shows that people are influenced by the background context and the wording of a question when they make a decision. See whether the people you question are more likely to say "yes" when the condoms are described in terms of a 90% success rate, rather than a 10% failure rate (Linville et al., 1993). As Chapter 8 pointed out, people make different decisions when they hear "success rate," rather than "failure rate."

At present, gay men in North America face greater risks of contracting AIDS than do heterosexuals. Research shows that older gay men have reduced the incidence of risky sexual behavior. However, gay men under the age of 25 often take unwise risks (Gelman, 1993; Rosenberg, 1995).

DEMONSTRATION 18.3   The Framing Effect and Judgments About Condom Effectiveness

When you have a convenient opportunity, ask a number of friends about condom effectiveness. The two questions below present alternative versions of the same information. Ask Question 1 to half of your sample, and ask Question 2 to the other half. Keep track of the number of "yes" responses from each group. Does the way the question is framed affect your friends' responses?

1. A particular brand of condoms has been found to have a 90% success rate. Should the manufacturers of this condom be allowed to advertise that it is an effective way to reduce the risk of AIDS?

2. A particular brand of condoms has been found to have a 10% failure rate. Should the manufacturers of this condom be allowed to advertise that it is an effective way to reduce the risk of AIDS?

Source: Based on Linville et al., 1993.

How can people be persuaded to take AIDS more seriously? As you might expect, no single approach can be effective when the issue is so complex. Most high schools now include information about AIDS. Most also emphasize that abstinence is the best way to prevent AIDS. However, researchers have concluded that the "Just Say No" approach is an unrealistic way to address the issue of AIDS prevention (Ruder et al., 1990; Stryker et al., 1995). The most effective programs take a more comprehensive approach (Kelly et al., 1993; Maddux, 1994). For example, social cognitive programs examine students' belief systems and discuss emotional concerns. They also work on self-efficacy issues. As we saw in Chapter 13, Bandura's concept of **self-efficacy** is the feeling people have that they are competent and effective (Bandura, 1992a).

People also need to be reached through community groups and the media, as well as school programs (Choi & Coates, 1994; Levine et al., 1993). We need to be more creative in persuading sexually active men and women to convert their *attitudes* about the danger of AIDS into less risky *behavior*.

High-Risk IV Drug Abuse   We have known for decades that IV drug abuse is highly risky. However, those risks increased drastically when AIDS began to spread. Now, an injection of a mind-altering drug can also include an injection of the HIV virus.

Programs focusing on IV drug users emphasize the dangers of shared needles, and they may make clean syringes available to decrease the spread of infection. These programs are generally effective (Coates et al., 1996; Choi & Coates, 1994).

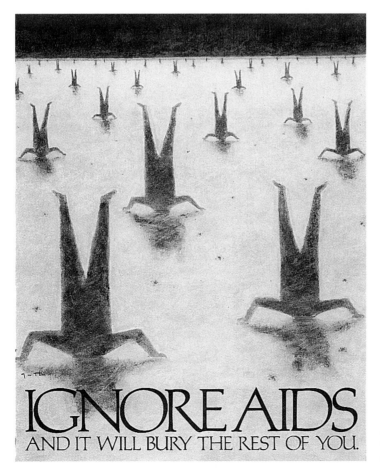

Media campaigns have produced effective ads like this one, encouraging AIDS prevention.

Unfortunately, however, drug users are often sexually promiscuous as well, and they seldom use condoms. As a consequence, HIV-infected drug abusers are likely to spread the disease to their sexual partners.

Most drug abusers are not likely to think extensively about future plans, including the risks of developing AIDS. Unfortunately, people who do not think about the future are not likely to worry about health issues. They are also not likely to change their high-risk behaviors. In summary, this population is likely to remain at high risk for this deadly disease.

??? Critical Thinking Exercise 18.3

Write down your answers to the following questions about AIDS.

a. Several studies have shown that community programs, designed to teach gay men about AIDS risks, have been effective in increasing the use of condoms. Why should we be reluctant to generalize these results beyond the sample of individuals who are studied?

b. Why would it be virtually impossible to conduct a true *experiment* to test the effectiveness of a program in which IV-drug users receive clean needles and syringes in exchange for used ones?

SECTION SUMMARY: *ACQUIRED IMMUNODEFICIENCY SYNDROME (AIDS)*

1. AIDS is caused by HIV, a virus that destroys a vitally important part of the immune system; early symptoms in an HIV-positive individual include swollen lymph glands, fatigue, fevers, and diarrhea.

2. The formal diagnosis of AIDS is given when an HIV-positive person develops a severe illness such as pneumonia or cancer.

3. People with the highest risk of AIDS include people who engage in unprotected intercourse with an infected person—whether they are gay, bisexual, or heterosexual—as well as IV drug users.

4. AIDS can directly affect neurotransmitters and brain tissue; depression, anxiety, anger, and guilt are common psychological reactions.

5. AIDS-prevention programs must attempt to change people's negative attitudes about acquiring AIDS into a reduction of high-risk behavior, with respect to both sexual behavior and IV-drug use.

SMOKING

Cigarette smoking is the major preventable cause of death in North America (Napier et al., 1996; Villeneuve & Morrison, 1995). Health psychologists are interested in the smoking issue, especially because they need to understand why a habit so clearly dangerous as smoking should be so difficult to overcome.

Let's begin by examining the demographics of smoking, as well as the health consequences. Then we'll explore two interrelated topics: trying to stop smoking and preventing people from beginning to smoke.

The Demographics of Smoking

At present, about 24% of women and 28% of men in the United States smoke cigarettes (Gold, 1995; Shumaker & Smith, 1995). However, the gender gap is narrowing. For example, a survey in Canada showed that males and females between the ages of 15 and 24 are equally likely to smoke (Eliany, 1992).

It is difficult to draw conclusions about ethnic differences in smoking rates, because the results vary according to gender and age. Overall, however, Native Americans seem to have the highest smoking rate, Blacks, Hispanics, and Whites have intermediate rates, and Asians have the lowest rate (Maisto et al., 1995; Mermelstein & Borrelli, 1995). Once again, however, we find that we cannot draw simple conclusions about ethnicity. For example, one of the highest smoking rates can be found among male immigrants from Southeast Asia. Between 57% and 72% report that they smoke cigarettes (Chen, 1992). In other words, the ethnic group with the lowest overall smoking rate (Asian) includes a subgroup with an astonishingly high smoking rate.

In the "In Depth" feature, we focused on the relationship between social class and health. One index of social class—educational status—is probably the factor that best predicts smoking. As you might imagine, college-educated individuals are much less likely to smoke than those who have not completed college or high school (Maisto et al., 1995; Mermelstein & Borrelli, 1995).

Health Consequences of Smoking

According to recent estimates, between 400,000 and 550,000 deaths each year can be traced to tobacco (Gold, 1995; Napier et al., 1996). As some have pointed out with irony, the tobacco industry is the only business that regularly kills its best customers. One researcher estimates that a smoker loses seven minutes of life for each cigarette that is smoked (Gold, 1995). Here are some of the health hazards that produce illness and early death in smokers:

1. *Lung cancer:* Every year, more than 130,000 U.S. residents and more than 11,000 Canadian residents die from lung cancer caused by smoking (Napier et al., 1996; Villeneuve & Morrison, 1995). If you smoke, you increase your risk of developing lung cancer by as much as 3,000% (Taubes, 1995).

2. *Other lung diseases:* Cigarette smokers are also much more likely than nonsmokers to develop asthma, respiratory infections, and emphysema, a serious disease that harms the lung tissue and makes breathing more difficult (Napier et al., 1996).

3. *Other cancers:* Smokers also develop cancer in regions of the body other than the lung. Smokers are more likely to develop cancer of the mouth, the larynx, the esophagus, the digestive system, the bladder, the kidney, the pancreas, the colon, and—in women—the cervix (Gold, 1995; Napier et al., 1996).

4. *Heart disease:* Cigarette smoking causes about 200,000 deaths from heart disease each year in the United States (Napier et al., 1996). However, if you *stop* smoking, within three years your risk for heart disease will be the same as for nonsmokers (Gold, 1995).

5. *Strokes:* Smoking decreases the blood supply to the brain, by constricting the blood vessels. As a result, smokers are 250% more likely than nonsmokers to experience a stroke (Napier et al., 1996).

Every year, we learn about some new danger that smokers face. For example, did you know that smokers are more likely than nonsmokers to be involved in automobile accidents, or that smokers run an increased risk of blindness ("Cigarettes May Promote Blindness," 1996; Spilich et al., 1992)? Fires started by cigarettes also claim many lives each year. In addition, Chapter 10 noted that pregnant women who smoke are likely to harm their unborn children. Furthermore, about 3,000 lung cancer deaths each year—as well as other health problems—can be traced to secondhand smoke (Committee on Substance Abuse, 1994; Cowley, 1992). Because cigarettes cause so much harm to both smokers and their families, many smokers want to stop. Let's now consider efforts to quit smoking.

An increasing number of businesses and public places have no-smoking policies.

Trying to Stop Smoking

About half of all smokers eventually quit, yet only 5% succeed on the first attempt (Goldstein, 1994; "Nicotine Dependence—Part I," 1997). Why is quitting so difficult? Let's first consider the barriers to quitting, and then we'll discuss some smoking-cessation techniques.

Barriers to Quitting   Researchers have concluded that the nicotine in tobacco is actually addicting (Heishman et al., 1997; Piasecki et al., 1997). Nicotine causes a physical dependence—similar to drugs such as heroin and cocaine, which were discussed in Chapter 5. In fact, smokers who have used heroin and cocaine heavily often report that these illegal drugs were easier to give up than cigarettes ("Nicotine Dependence—Part I," 1997). Some nicotine withdrawal symptoms include anxiety, hunger, irritability, and restlessness.

External forces also make it difficult to stop smoking. Breaking the habit is more difficult if your peers smoke. However, an increasing number of colleges, work sites, and public places have adopted no-smoking policies. As a result, the environment may help encourage those who want to stop smoking.

Another external barrier to giving up cigarettes is the tobacco industry, which spends billions of dollars each year to advertise and promote cigarettes (Gold, 1995). Advertisements show slender, glamorous people, surrounded by friends and enjoying life to the fullest. The advertisers are clearly aware of the factors we discussed in Chapter 16 that persuade potential buyers.

Smoking-Cessation Programs   About 1.5 million Americans stop smoking each year (Lichtenstein & Glasgow, 1992). One group of people who are particularly likely to quit smoking are those who have recently suffered a heart attack (Jeffery, 1989; Weinstein, 1989). Perhaps the decision-making heuristic of availability works for these people (Chapter 8). A vivid example of a recent life-threatening trauma comes readily to mind when they are tempted to light up a cigarette.

Health psychologists point out that physicians should take the opportunity during routine physical exams to advise smokers about the health risks of smoking. Physicians should also give their patients appropriate literature and help them develop a concrete plan for giving up cigarettes (Werner, 1995). Chapter 17 discussed how the expertise of the persuader is an important factor in persuasion, so physicians should have the potential to be convincing. They could be especially influential if they increase their patients' cognitive dissonance. Patients need to appreciate the discrepancy between their beliefs about the dangers of smoking and their actions of continuing to smoke.

About 90% of smokers who quit manage to do so on their own ("Nicotine Dependence—Part II," 1997). However, a variety of smoking-cessation programs are available (Maisto et al., 1995; Stroebe & Stroebe, 1995). They often use cognitive-behavioral techniques. One approach, for example, requires individuals to deposit money, to be returned only if the smoker successfully gives up cigarettes. Other approaches emphasize developing a feeling of self-efficacy in order to develop appropriate resistance ("Nicotine Dependence—Part II," 1997). When a group of people who know one another enroll in one of these programs, the peer pressure to stop smoking can be another useful incentive.

The most effective smoking-cessation programs use more than one approach (Lichtenstein & Glasgow, 1992; Stroebe & Stroebe, 1995) and might include using transdermal patches—small "nicotine patches" worn directly on the skin. Psychological components of a comprehensive antismoking campaign should include specific recommendations from physicians, enrollment in a smoking-cessation program, and antismoking messages from the media.

The American Cancer Society has developed effective no-smoking ads aimed at teenagers.

Smoking-Prevention Programs

The nicotine habit is so hard to break, however, that even the most successful approaches are not particularly effective in getting people to stop smoking. Instead, most health psychologists argue that it's more effective to keep people from starting an addiction to cigarettes in the first place. Most users acquire their habit before they are 18, so these smoking-prevention programs must target young people (Kessler et al., 1997).

Smoking-prevention programs need to emphasize that the majority of young people do not smoke; nonsmoking is therefore the norm. Ideal programs should begin with children in elementary school and should focus on the socially undesirable aspects of smoking—for example, "Cigarettes smell bad"—as well as the health problems (Epps et al., 1995; Stroebe & Stroebe, 1995). The most effective programs also train students how to resist peer pressures to try cigarettes. Some feature presentations by attractive, socially skilled older teenagers—an idea that takes advantage of several of the persuasion principles we discussed in Chapter 17.

Perhaps even more important than these isolated efforts would be a more broad-based approach in which smoking advertisements are more strictly regulated and the price of cigarettes is drastically raised. In addition, the smoking-prevention programs need to train young people to take their lives and their health more seriously. A primary advantage of such an approach would be to encourage adolescents to become more aware of their future plans. People who think about the future are more concerned about staying healthy and avoiding activities that would jeopardize their longevity.

Critical Thinking Exercise 18.4

Write down your answers to the following questions about smoking.

a. Suppose that a large-scale study finds that the rate of automobile accidents is twice as high for teenager smokers as for teenage nonsmokers. What other factors would you need to consider before determining that smoking causes automobile accidents?

b. Suppose that a friend argues, "Well, it's clear that education leads people to think better, and so they know they shouldn't smoke." What other kinds of explanations could you suggest for the fact that educated people smoke less, and what confounding variables would you include in your argument?

SECTION SUMMARY: *SMOKING*

1. Gender differences in smoking rates are small, and ethnic differences are complex; education is strongly correlated with smoking.

2. Health consequences of smoking include lung cancer, other lung diseases, other cancers, heart disease, and strokes.

3. Smoking is difficult to stop, especially because nicotine is addicting; helpful strategies include physicians' advice, programs that include cognitive-behavioral techniques, and groups that create peer pressure to not smoke.

4. Smoking-prevention programs should begin early, emphasize social advantages of not smoking, teach resistance strategies, and include messages from appropriate older teens; in addition, these programs should encourage a future orientation.

REVIEW QUESTIONS

1. This question will help you review parts of the entire textbook. Make a list of the 17 previous chapter titles. Then skim this chapter on health psychology, stress, and coping. As you skim, make notes next to each of the other chapter titles whenever you see a relevant application.

2. Try to recall a recent time when you experienced stress. Relate that experience to Selye's general adaptation syndrome model, using relevant terminology, as well as Lazarus's cognitive appraisal approach. Which of the three major categories of stress sources seems most relevant to that situation, and what coping strategies did you use?

3. The section on stress and coping describes how stress influences the immune system. What does AIDS do to the immune system, and how might the coping responses of people living with AIDS have some influence on the course of their disease?

4. Suppose that a middle-aged relative tells you that he has read that people who are time conscious and always "on the go" are more likely than relaxed people to die of a heart attack. How would you explain the current findings on this topic?

5. The section on psychological control emphasized that control may actually increase longevity. Think about an elderly person you know, and list some of the ways in which this individual could achieve greater personal control over life events. Briefly describe several methods in which psychological control could influence longevity.

6. How are gender and ethnicity relevant in (a) general health and illness, (b) likelihood of getting AIDS, and (c) smoking?

7. The "In Depth" feature in this chapter focused on socioeconomic status and health. Prepare an outline of the three major categories of factors that help explain the effect—physical environment, health behavior, and psychological characteristics—filling in as many of the explanations within each category as you can recall. Then double-check Pages 585–586 to make certain that your list is complete.

8. Imagine that you have been appointed to coordinate a state education committee on teaching health issues to junior high students. What techniques would you use to encourage health-conscious lifestyles? What kind of media approaches would you use to supplement the school program?

9. In both the section on AIDS and the section on smoking, we discussed how people persist in risky behaviors, even though they know that these activities are dangerous. How are the topics of AIDS and smoking related, and how are they different?

10. How are an individual's thoughts about the future relevant to both AIDS and smoking? How could this concept also be applied to helping people make long-range plans for dealing with stress?

NEW TERMS

health psychology (p. 576)
applied psychology (p. 576)
stress (p. 576)
general adaptation syndrome (p. 576)
stressor (p. 576)
alarm phase (p. 576)
homeostasis (p. 577)
resistance (p. 577)
exhaustion phase (p. 577)
cognitive appraisal approach (p. 577)
psychoneuroimmunology (p. 578)
immune system (p. 578)
lymphocytes (p. 578)
coping (p. 579)

problem-focused coping (p. 579)
emotion-focused coping (p. 579)
cognitive reappraisal (p. 579)
proactive coping (p. 579)
denial (p. 580)
Type A behavior pattern (p. 582)
Type B behavior pattern (p. 582)
socioeconomic status (SES) (p. 585)
social class (p. 585)
acquired immunodeficiency syndrome (AIDS) (p. 587)
human immunodeficiency virus (HIV) (p. 588)
framing effect (p. 590)
self-efficacy (p. 591)

RECOMMENDED READINGS

Adler, N. E., et al. (1994). Socioeconomic status and health: The challenge of the gradient. *American Psychologist, 49,* 15–24. This article by Nancy Adler and her colleagues presents a comprehensive and clear overview of this complex topic.

Bayne-Smith, M. (Ed.). (1996). *Race, gender, and health.* Thousand Oaks, CA: Sage. Here's a book that examines ethnicity and gender in a variety of ethnic groups, with respect to health issues.

Gold, M. S. (1995). *Tobacco.* New York: Plenum. Mark Gold's book examines the history of tobacco use, the nature of its addictive properties, its health effects, and treatment and prevention programs.

Kalichman, S. C. (1996). *Answering your questions about AIDS.* Washington, DC: American Psychological Association. I'd recommend this book for a clear overview of the topic, in question-and-answer format; its level is appropriate for college students.

Kaplan, H. B. (Ed.). (1996). *Psychosocial stress: Perspectives on structure, theory, life-course, and methods.* San Diego: Academic Press. This book contains 10 chapters on a variety of topics related to stress, such as the nature of stress, coping with stress, and methodological issues.

ANSWERS TO DEMONSTRATIONS

Demonstration 18.2

Give yourself 1 point for every *true* response you provided for these items: 1, 2, 3, 6, 7, and 8. Give yourself an additional point for every *false* response you provided for these items:

4, 5, 9, and 10. In general, those with higher scores tend to be higher in hostility than those with low scores.

ANSWERS TO CRITICAL THINKING EXERCISES

Exercise 18.1

a. Like so many informal observations, this observation is plagued by many confounding variables. First of all, your friend might have been almost well already and would have recovered just as rapidly without any special treatment. Second, maybe it was the pampering and rest—rather than the sitcoms—that hastened the recovery. Third, maybe your friend behaved differently in some other way on the "sitcom day," and this other behavior might have been helpful. Fourth, your friend may have expected to recover, and this optimistic expectation was helpful. Fifth, your friend's reporting may have been biased, so that persisting symptoms of a cold were ignored.

b. We could measure social support in terms of the number of close friends and/or relatives, the average rated closeness of those individuals, the rated closeness of the best friend, the number of social interactions in a given period of time, the number of social events attended in a given period of time, the number of social communications (e.g., telephone, e-mail) in a given period of time, and so forth. We could also measure the attitudes of the people who were listed as close friends and relatives, with respect to the individual we are studying. We have literally dozens of possible operational definitions!

Exercise 18.2

a. These two variables (educational attainment and income) are much easier to measure and report objectively. Also, some studies are based on census data, and these variables are coded in the census. In contrast, people might disagree on the relative prestige of different occupations, and family prestige would be even more controversial.

b. Women who are highly educated (and therefore higher SES) are likely to postpone child-bearing or decide not to have children. In contrast, less educated women have children at an earlier age. We need to emphasize, however, that of women who actually *develop* breast cancer, higher SES women are more likely to survive (Adler & Coriell, 1997).

Exercise 18.3

a. The sample of people would not have been representative of the population at risk for AIDS. The sample doesn't specifically contain IV-drug users or women. It is probably more likely to include men who are "out," rather than "in the closet"—so it's possible they are physically healthier and experience less stress (Cole et al., 1996). The men are probably likely to be older, better educated, and more likely to have social support. In addition, they are eager to learn about health issues. In other words, this is a group that might be more conscientious about their health than most other people, and therefore more likely to accept the precautions.

b. Conducting a controlled experiment would be almost impossible, because you could not randomly assign people to the exchange-program versus control group. A quasi-experiment would be more reasonable, with pairs of neighborhoods matched for appropriate variables. Half of the neighborhoods have the program; half do not. Even so, the problem of measuring the dependent variable would be extremely challenging.

Exercise 18.4

a. The problem is that smokers and nonsmokers differ in numerous ways from each other—in addition to the variable of smoking. Smokers are likely to differ in education, health attitudes, alcohol consumption, use of seat belts, risk-taking, and so forth (Stroebe & Stroebe, 1995). In addition, even if all these variables were controlled, we would not know from these data whether the important factor was some chemical ingredient in the cigarettes or the distraction caused by the activity of smoking.

b. It is possible that highly educated people are more oriented toward future plans, so that they are less likely to engage in an activity that harms their future health. (However, it may be that this future orientation causes an increased likelihood of attending college.) Other confounding variables would include parents' income, parents' education, the individual's own intelligence, whether peers smoked, and ethnicity.

APPENDIX
STATISTICAL PROCEDURES AND CALCULATIONS

In Chapter 2 (on research methods), you saw how statistics can be used in psychology. You learned about descriptive statistics—specifically, central tendency and variability—as well as inferential statistics. That information provided an essential background for the research discussed throughout the textbook.

For many of you, this course in introductory psychology will be your only exposure to statistical methods. Therefore, you may want to know some more details about statistical procedures and calculations. Consider several examples of situations where statistics might be useful for you:

1. You may pursue a career in business, and your boss has asked you to construct a frequency distribution to show the number of sick days reported by the 73 company employees during the previous year.

2. You may teach grade school, and you want to know how to interpret the percentile scores that are listed for your students on their last standardized mathematics test.

3. You may become a physician. Perhaps you are concerned about a woman with bulimia nervosa. Her weight is about average for her height, but you notice that her weight during the daily weigh-ins is too variable. You want to calculate the standard deviation for these weights.

Let's consider how each of these issues can be addressed by considering three topics: (1) frequency distributions and graphs, (2) percentiles, and (3) standard deviations. This information also provides a brief preview of these topics for those of you who will take a statistics course in the future. Most psychology majors are required to take a statistics course. It is also frequently required for students majoring in sociology, political science, mathematics, economics, education, and biology.

FREQUENCY DISTRIBUTIONS AND GRAPHS

A **frequency distribution** is a summary of data that shows how often each score occurs. To construct a frequency distribution, divide the entire range of scores into equal intervals. Then tally the number of scores that fall in each interval.

TABLE A.1 Frequency Distribution of the Number of Sick Days Reported by 73 Employees for the Previous Year

INTERVAL	NUMBER OF EMPLOYEES IN EACH INTERVAL
0–1	22
2–3	9
4–5	6
6–7	8
8–9	7
10–11	8
12–13	6
14–15	4
16–17	2
18+	1

Suppose, for example, that you have been instructed to construct a frequency distribution and a histogram illustrating the number of employee sick days. Your first step is to construct a table like Table A.1.

A frequency distribution allows you to summarize a large amount of data into one well-organized table. However, you may want to convert these data into a figure that provides a more visual representation. You might, therefore, decide to construct a **histogram,** which is a graphic representation of a frequency distribution. Figure A.1 is a histogram of the data in Table A.1. As you

FIGURE A.1

A Histogram of the Frequency Distribution in Table A.1 (illustrating the number of sick days reported by 73 employees for the previous year)

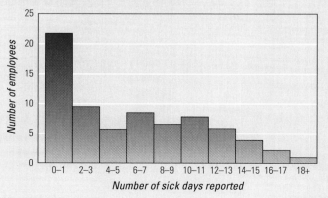

can see, the height of each bar represents how often each score occurs. Many people feel that they can appreciate the general trend in data more quickly by looking at a histogram than by consulting a less visual frequency distribution, presented in table form.

Psychologists often summarize their data in histograms and other figures. Advertisers also use graphs, especially when they want to illustrate how their product outperforms the competing brands. Unfortunately, however, the graphs can be constructed so that they distort reality. Critical thinkers need to know how to read figures accurately, as well as reading verbal material accurately.

For example, suppose that the Gonif Educational Corporation runs a program for high school seniors, helping them to prepare for the Scholastic Achievement Test (SAT). A student from your high school shows you Gonif's brochure, which includes a graph. The graph illustrates the average number of points that students improve on the test, after taking the Gonif review course. The graph also includes comparison data for two competing courses. Based on the data in Figure A.2, this student is prepared to send off a check to the Gonif Corporation.

However, you should caution the student to pay close attention to the numbers on the *y*-axis of the graph. Note that they start with 30, rather than 0, and each unit on the graph is just 1 point on the test. This kind of graph distorts the results, exaggerating the size of the differences among the three preparation courses. Notice that a more appropriate graph, such as the one in Figure A.3, shows that the three courses produce nearly identical improvements in test scores.

FIGURE A.2

This graph compares three review courses, using an inappropriate y-axis that distorts the differences.

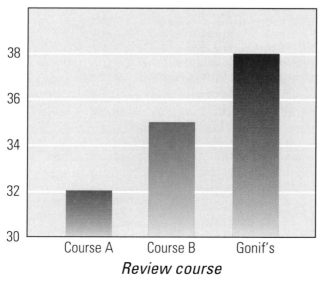

Review course

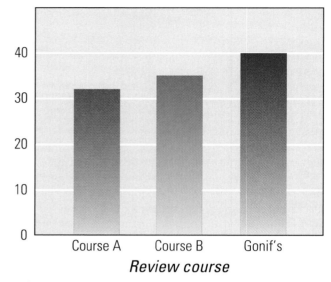

Review course

FIGURE A.3

This graph compares three review courses, using a more appropriate y-axis that emphasizes the similarities.

PERCENTILES

You probably noticed the terms *percentile score* or *percentile rank* if you took a standardized test such as the Scholastic Achievement Test (SAT) when you were applying for college. For example, if you took the SAT in November of 1997, a score of 550 on the verbal portion was listed as the 64th percentile. A **percentile score** indicates the percentage of people who received scores below your own score. In this case, if you received a percentile score of 75, this would mean that 75% of the people who took the test received a score lower than you did. A percentile score is useful because it allows you to understand where your score falls relative to other scores.

Percentile scores are especially important in education. Suppose that you are a fourth grade teacher who is trying to figure out why one of your students, Gordon, is doing poorly in mathematics. You consult Gordon's records and discover that his raw score on the mathematics portion of a standardized test from last year is 27. A raw score, by itself, is meaningless. You have no hint about whether a 27 is low, medium, or high.

Most standardized tests therefore list a percentile score next to the raw score. Suppose that Gordon's percentile score is 73. You would then know that Gordon scored higher than 73% of students; his performance on that test was clearly above average. You would conclude that Gordon seems to have the skill to perform the work. You might suspect a motivational problem or a specific learning disability associated with a particular kind of mathematical skill.

Note, incidentally, that a student cannot obtain a percentile score of 100. That score would mean the student scored higher than 100% of students, including himself or herself—a logical impossibility! Instead, an extremely high raw score is often assigned a percentile score of 99+. For example, in November 1997, a verbal SAT score of 800 was assigned a percentile score of 99+. Also, note that a percentile score of 50 means the student has received a score that is at the median of the distribution. As discussed in Chapter 2, the **median** is the score that falls precisely in the middle of a distribution of scores. Figure A.4 illustrates several percentile scores.

STANDARD DEVIATIONS

As we discussed in Chapter 2, a **standard deviation** is a measure of **variability**, or the extent to which scores differ from one another. Variability can easily be measured in terms of **range**, or the difference between the highest and lowest scores in a distribution. However, the range takes into account only *two* scores. Psychologists are much more likely to measure variability in terms of the standard deviation, which uses *all* scores in calculating the "spread-outedness" of these scores. The standard deviation is based on the distance of each score from the mean. Turn back to Figure 2.12 to contrast one distribution, whose standard deviation is 5.7, with a second distribution, whose standard deviation is only 2.2.

Imagine that you are a physician who is monitoring a woman with bulimia nervosa. You are particularly concerned about the fact that her weight seems to vary too much from one day to the next—which suggests that she may be bingeing on some days and restricting her intake on other days. Suppose that she reports to your office on six consecutive days and you record her weight each time:

FIGURE A.4

Examples of Percentile Scores
Note: *30th percentile means that 30% of test takers received scores lower than this particular score.*

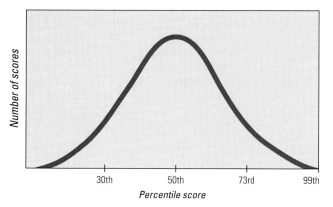

| 123 | 125 | 122 | 125 | 130 | 125 |

To calculate the standard deviation, you will use this formula, expressed in words instead of symbols:

$$\text{Standard deviation} = \sqrt{\frac{\text{Sum of (deviations)}^2}{\text{Number of scores}}}$$

Let's go through the procedure, step by step.

1. Calculate the mean of the scores.

$$
\begin{array}{r}
123 \\
125 \\
122 \\
125 \\
130 \\
\underline{125} \\
750
\end{array}
$$

$$6\overline{)750} \quad \text{Mean (symbolized } \overline{X}) = 125$$

2. Subtract the mean from each of your scores. Check your accuracy; the sum of these new deviation scores should equal zero.

Score		Mean		Deviation score
123	–	125	=	–2
125	–	125	=	0
122	–	125	=	–3
125	–	125	=	0
130	–	125	=	+5
125	–	125	=	0
				0 √

3. Take each of these deviation scores, square it, and add together these squared deviation scores.

Deviation score	Squared deviation score
–2	$(-2)^2 = 4$
0	$(0)^2 = 0$
–3	$(-3)^2 = 9$
0	$(0)^2 = 0$
+5	$(+5)^2 = 25$
0	$(0)^2 = \underline{0}$

Sum of the squared deviation
scores   38

4. Divide the sum of the deviation scores by the number of observations you made.

$$6\overline{)38} \quad \frac{6.3}{}$$

5. Take the square root of the number you calculated in step 4.

$$\sqrt{6.3} = 2.5$$

Notice that large standard deviations indicate greater variability in the scores. Suppose, for example, that you were to calculate a standard deviation of 2.5 for a bulimic woman's weight measurements, prior to the beginning of therapy. Suppose that the standard deviation of her weight measurements, after several months of therapy, was 1.1. You might note that the newer set of weight measurements was less variable. (However, you would actually need to conduct a statistical test on your data to determine whether that decrease had been statistically significant.)

Chapter 2 discussed the terms *mean* and *range*, which are relatively straightforward concepts. You can easily see how both these terms are related to the actual scores in the distribution. In contrast, when we look at the weight scores from our example—123, 125, 122, 125, 130, and 125—a standard deviation of 2.5 does not seem closely related to these scores.

One helpful point that makes the standard deviation seem more concrete is this: When you have a large number of scores in a typical distribution, 68% of the scores lie within one standard deviation of each side of the mean. That is, roughly one-third of all scores lie between the mean and a point one standard deviation *above* the mean. Furthermore, roughly one-third of all scores lie between the mean and a point one standard deviation *below* the mean. The remaining one-third of all scores lie outside these boundaries (specifically, one-sixth above the boundary and one-sixth below the boundary). Figure A.5 illustrates this general principle. (Note, incidentally, that in the case of the hypothetical bulimic woman, one-third of her weight scores lie outside of the interval 125 ± 2.5.)

As a further example, let's also relate standard deviations to IQ scores, because you are probably familiar with the scores that are typical on intelligence tests (Chapter 8). On many IQ tests, the size of the standard deviation is 15. As you now know, about 68% of IQ scores should lie within one standard deviation of each side of the mean. This means that if the mean is 100, then 68% of individuals should receive scores between 85 and 115.

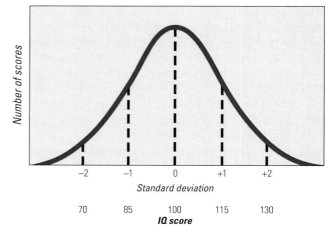

FIGURE A.6

The distribution of scores on an IQ test, showing scores one and two standard deviations away from the mean. (Note: Roughly two-thirds—68%—of IQ scores lie within one standard deviation of the mean; 95% of IQ scores lie within two standard deviations of the mean.)

Figure A.6 notes, also, that 95% of all scores lie within two standard deviations of each side of the mean—that is, between IQ scores of 70 and 130.

Finally, we must emphasize that most psychologists use computers to calculate the majority of statistical measures. When you need to calculate the standard deviation for six scores, as we did earlier, you can easily figure out a standard deviation using a calculator. However, the process quickly becomes cumbersome as the number of scores increases. With the aid of a statistical package for the computer, psychologists simply enter all the scores in a distribution. The printout supplies a variety of useful information, such as the mean, median, frequency distribution, histogram, and standard deviation.

New terms

frequency distribution (p. 601)	median (p. 603)
histogram (p. 601)	standard deviation (p. 603)
percentile score (p. 602)	variability (p. 603)
	range (p. 603)

FIGURE A.5

A distribution of scores, showing the mean and points one standard deviation above and below the mean.

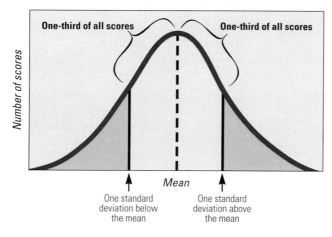

GLOSSARY

A guide has been provided for words whose pronunciation may be ambiguous; the accented syllable is indicated by italics.

Accommodation Piaget's concept proposing that humans change their thought structures to fit the stimuli they encounter.

Acetylcholine (ACh) In the nervous system, a neurotransmitter found in synapses in the brain, where it is important in such functions as arousal, attention, memory, aggression, sexuality, and thirst. ACh can also be found at the junction between neurons and muscle fibers, where it acts as an excitatory neurotransmitter, causing muscle fibers to contract.

Achievement motive Desire to do well relative to a standard of excellence.

Acquired immunodeficiency syndrome (AIDS) Sexually transmitted viral disease—spread by infected blood, semen, or vaginal secretions—that destroys the body's natural immunity to diseases. Once the immune system has been destroyed, diseases such as pneumonia and cancer can take over, leading eventually to death.

Acquisition In general, the process of learning a new response. In classical conditioning, acquisition involves producing a conditioned response to a conditioned stimulus. Pertaining to memory, acquisition is the first stage of remembering in which we perceive the item and record its important features.

Action potential Rapid change in the electrical charge of an axon.

Activation-synthesis hypothesis In the neurocognitive model of the function of dreams, a core concept which proposes that the hindbrain sends a haphazard pattern of signals to the cerebral cortex (activation), and then the cerebral cortex tries to make sense out of these random signals (synthesis).

Active listening In person-centered therapy, technique by which the therapist attempts to understand both the content and the emotion of a client's statement.

Active touch Touch perception in which we actively explore and touch objects.

Actor-observer bias Tendency to attribute our own behavior to external, situational causes, whereas we attribute others' behavior to internal, personal causes.

Acuity Ability to see precise details.

Adaptation Phenomenon in which the perceived intensity of a repeated stimulus decreases over time. For example, touch adaptation guarantees that we stop noticing touch after a few minutes of mild constant pressure.

Addiction A pattern of behavior in which people repetitively and compulsively take a psychoactive drug.

Adoption studies Studies to determine whether adopted children are more like their biological parents (who contribute genes) or their adoptive parents (who contribute a home environment).

Adrenal glands Two structures on top of the kidneys that produce several dozen kinds of hormones, including sex hormones, epinephrine, and hormones that regulate the concentration of minerals in the body and the concentration of sugar in the blood.

Age regression During hypnosis, a hypnotized person is given suggestions to re-experience an event that occurred at an earlier age and to act like and feel like a person of that particular age.

Ageism Bias against elderly people and the aging process. This bias can include myths, negative attitudes, stereotypes, and outright discrimination.

Aggression A deliberate attempt to injure or hurt a person or other living organism.

Agoraphobia Type of anxiety disorder involving fear of being in situations or public places where escape would be difficult.

AIDS *See* Acquired immunodeficiency syndrome.

Alarm phase First phase of the general adaptation syndrome (response to stress), during which the individual prepares for action.

Alcohol myopia A state in which the effect of alcohol causes a person to process fewer cues and to process them less accurately.

Altruism Action that benefits another person, including comforting, helping, sharing, rescuing, and cooperating. Acts of concern for other people, without any hope of reward. Also known as prosocial behavior.

Alzheimer's disease Disorder that involves a severe decline in memory, language, and thinking skills, gradually worsening over time.

Amnesia Loss of memory.

Amplitude In vision, the height of the light wave; amplitude is related to the brightness of a visual stimulus. In audition, the size of the change in pressure created by the sound wave; amplitude is related to the loudness of the auditory stimulus.

Amygdala Part of the limbic system that receives information from the cortex and other regions of the brain that are responsible for processing more primitive emotions.

Anal stage One of the stages of psychosexual development during which the erogenous zone presumably shifts to the anal region. Freud proposed that toddlers experience satisfaction when their anal region is stimulated by retaining or eliminating feces.

Analogy approach In problem solving, a strategy in which persons use a solution to an earlier problem to help solve a new one.

Anchoring and adjustment heuristic Strategy for making an estimate in which people begin by guessing a first approximation (an anchor) and then make adjustments to that number on the basis of additional information. Typically, people rely too heavily on the anchor, and their adjustments are too small.

Androgen hormones Hormones that produce changes in males during early prenatal development, guiding the development of the male reproductive system.

Anorexia nervosa Eating disorder that is characterized by an irrational pursuit of thinness and concern about gaining weight. Anorexics feel fat, even when they look emaciated. The American Psychiatric Association specifies that a person can be classified as anorexic if body weight is 15% less than specified on standard weight charts and if no known illness accounts for the low weight.

Anterograde amnesia An impaired ability to form long-term memory for new information after a brain injury.

Antianxiety drugs Drugs designed to reduce tension and create drowsiness by depressing activity in the central nervous system. Examples include Valium and Librium.

Antidepressant drugs Drugs designed to help make a person's mood more positive. Examples include the MAO inhibitors, the tricyclics, and Prozac.

Antipsychotic drugs Drugs that reduce the symptoms of schizophrenia such as agitation, confusion, delusions, and hallucinations.

Antisocial personality disorder Type of personality disorder characterized by a variety of antisocial behaviors, including lying, violence, and other actions that show little concern for the welfare of others.

Anxiety disorders Anxiety that persists without any clear explanation and that causes intense suffering. Five types of anxiety disorders are generalized anxiety disorders, panic disorders and agoraphobia, phobic disorders, obsessive-compulsive disorders, and posttraumatic stress disorders.

Anxious/ambivalent attachment style Adult love-relationship style in which the individual wants to get closer to others than they would like; the individual's intensity sometimes scares people away.

Anxious avoidant attachment Type of attachment in which a baby enjoys exploration; after separation, the baby actively avoids the caretaker.

Anxious resistant attachment Type of attachment in which a baby displays a mixture of seeking and resisting contact with the caregiver.

Aphasia Language difficulty caused by damage to the speech area of the brain.

Applied psychologists Psychologists whose focus is on changing both behaviors and mental processes.

Applied psychology Area of psychology emphasizing practical applications of psychological research.

Aptitude test Test designed to predict future success on the basis of current performance. Aptitude tests draw their material from a broad range of human experience, including information gained outside the classroom.

Assimilation Piaget's concept proposing that humans use and modify stimuli they encounter in terms of their current thought structure.

Associative visual agnosia (ag-*know*-zhia) A disorder in which a person with no general disorder (such as Alzheimer's disease) cannot recognize objects by sight.

Attachment Close emotional bond of affection between an infant and his or her caregivers.

Attention Concentration of mental activity.

Attentional bias A social-cognitive explanation for phobias which proposes that people with phobias focus their attention on feared aspects of the environment.

Attitude Psychological tendency that is expressed by an evaluation of something.

Attribution In person perception, the explanation we create about the reasons for our own behavior and the behavior of other people. Attributions often focus on causal explanations for success or failure.

Auditory canal Tube running inward from the outer ear, through which sound enters.

Auditory cortex Portion of the cortex primarily located in a deep groove on each side of the surface of the brain. The auditory cortex codes both simple and complex auditory stimuli.

Auditory nerve Bundle of axons that carries information from the inner ear toward higher levels of auditory processing.

Authoritarian parents Parenting style in which parents demand unquestioning obedience from their children, punish children forcefully when children do not meet their standards, and are less likely to be affectionate with their children.

Authoritative parents Effective parenting style in which parents are affectionate but provide control when necessary. Parents respect each child's individuality, they are loving, and they allow children to express their own points of view. However, they have clear-cut standards, which they uphold in a consistent fashion.

Autism A disorder in which a person's social interactions and language skills are extremely limited.

Autobiographical memory Memory for events from a person's own life.

Autonomic division In the nervous system, the division that helps control the glands, blood vessels, intestines, heart, and other internal organs. The autonomic nervous system usually works automatically, unlike the somatic division.

Availability heuristic General strategy used when people estimate frequency or probability in terms of how easy it is to think of examples of something.

Avoidant attachment style Adult love-relationship style in which the individual feels somewhat uncomfortable getting close to others and trusting them completely.

Axon In the nervous system, the long fiber that carries information away from the cell body toward other neurons.

Balanced-placebo design Research design consisting of four groups of participants, half of whom expect that they will be doing something (e.g. drinking alcohol) and half of whom do not. Half of the participants actually do receive something (e.g. alcohol) and half receive a placebo. This research design is used to sort out the effects of the variable itself (e.g. alcohol), as opposed to the effects of people's expectations about how they should behave.

Base rate How often the item occurs in the population.

Baseline measure In behavior modification, the response rate before beginning the behavior modification program.

Basilar membrane Specialized membrane in the cochlea of the inner ear that contains hair cells (the receptors for hearing).

Beck's cognitive therapy Therapy that attempts to correct systematic errors in reasoning known as cognitive distortions.

Behavior modification The systematic use of techniques from learning theory to change human behavior.

Behavioral measures In a research study, measurement that objectively records people's observable behavior.

Behaviorism Approach to psychology that emphasizes the study of observable behavior instead of hidden mental processes.

Biased sample In a research study, a sample in which some members of the population are more likely to be chosen than others.

Bicultural efficacy A person's belief that he or she can live effectively within two different ethnic groups without compromising the sense of cultural identity.

Big Five traits In personality research, the five most important clusters of personality traits, including extraversion, agreeableness, conscientiousness, emotional stability, and openness to experience.

Bilingual A person who uses two languages that differ in speech sounds, vocabulary, and syntax.

Binge drinking Alcohol consumption of four or more drinks in a row for a woman and five or more drinks in a row for a man at least once in a two-week period.

Binocular In depth perception, factors requiring two eyes to provide information about distance.

Binocular disparity In vision, source of distance information provided by two eyes that present slightly different views of the world. The difference between the two retinal images of an object is known as binocular disparity.

Binocular vision Characteristic of the human visual system based on both eyes working together and having partially overlapping fields of view.

Biological approach Approach to psychology, also called neuroscience approach, that proposes that each behavior, emotion, and thought is caused by a physical event in the brain or other part of the nervous system.

Biological motion In motion perception, the pattern of movement exhibited by people and other living things.

Biological preparedness Built-in bias ensuring that some relationships between stimuli and responses will be learned more readily than others.

Biology Scientific discipline that examines the structure and function of living things.

Biopsychology Scientific study of the biology of behavior and mental processes.

Bipolar cells In the eye, cells that receive the electrical message converted from light by the rods and cones. The bipolar cells then pass this electrical message on to the ganglion cells.

Bipolar disorder Mood disorder in which the individual experiences both depressive episodes and manic episodes.

Blind spot In the eye, the location where the optic nerve leaves the retina. Neither rods nor cones inhabit the blind spot, so a person cannot see anything that reaches this part of the retina.

Borderline personality disorder Type of personality disorder characterized by unstable interpersonal relationships, inappropriate anger, unstable mood, and impulsiveness.

Bottom-up processing In perception, processing that depends on the information from the senses at the bottom (or most basic) level of perception, with sensory information flowing from this low level upward to the higher, more cognitive levels.

Brief psychodynamic therapy Psychodynamic therapy with the following general attributes: (1) therapy is likely to consist of 10 to 30 weekly sessions; (2) the therapist and client select a specific, central issue that requires resolution; and (3) the individual's current social problems are emphasized.

Brightness The quality of a visual stimulus, which is determined by the height or amplitude of a light wave; psychological reaction corresponding to the intensity of light wave.

Broca's aphasia A condition in which a person's speech is slow, effortful, and grammatically simple.

Bulimia nervosa (boo-*lih*-mee-ah) Eating disorder characterized by binge eating, or episodes in which people consume huge amounts of food. Bulimics also engage in some form of purging, such as vomiting or using laxatives.

Bystander effect Apparent apathy and inaction in the face of crisis, where the presence of other people inhibits helpfulness.

Cardinal trait In Allport's theory, personality trait that dominates and shapes behavior.

Case study Research method that is an in-depth description and analysis of a single person or group. The data typically include an interview, observation, and test scores. Most often, the individual selected for a case study is highly unusual.

Catatonic stupor Symptom of schizophrenia in which a person stands rigidly immobile and unresponsive for hours.

Cell body In the nervous system, the area of the neuron that contains the cell nucleus, as well as other structures that help the cell function properly.

Central executive In Alan Baddeley's model of working memory, the component that integrates information from the phonological loop and the visuospatial working memory, as well as material retrieved from long-term memory. The central executive also plays a major role in planning and controlling behavior.

Central nervous system Portion of the nervous system that includes the spinal cord and brain.

Central tendency Statistical measure of the most typical, characteristic score (mean, median, or mode).

Central trait In Allport's theory, a general characteristic, found to some degree in every person, such as honesty, extraversion, or cheerfulness.

Cerebellum A structure located at the lower rear of the brain that plays an important role in learning, in maintaining posture, and in controlling motor movements.

Cerebral cortex Outer surface of the two cerebral hemispheres of the brain; it processes all perceptions and complex thoughts.

Child-directed speech Language spoken by adults to children using simple vocabulary with emphasis on important words, well-formed sentences, long pauses, slow rate of speech, and a high-pitch voice.

Chromosomes Rod-shaped structures carrying genetic information in virtually every cell of the body. In humans, the genes are located on 23 pairs of chromosomes.

Circadian rhythm Daily cycle lasting approximately 24 hours, with each cycle including both a sleeping and waking period.

Classical conditioning Conditioning in which people learn that certain environmental stimuli can predict certain responses.

Client-treatment interaction Model proposing that some clients respond well to Therapy A, whereas other clients respond well to Therapy B. Theorists suggest that therapy is more successful if each client could be matched with an appropriate therapy.

Clinical psychologists Psychologists who assess and treat people with psychological disorders. On the basis of an interview and psychological tests, clinical psychologists provide a diagnosis of the problem followed by either individual or group psychotherapy.

Cochlea Bony, fluid-filled coil in the ear that contains the auditory receptors.

Cognition Mental activities involving the acquisition, storage, transformation, and use of knowledge.

Cognitive appraisal approach Lazarus's idea that our cognitive processes help us decide whether we interpret an event as stressful.

Cognitive approach Approach that focuses on unobservable mental processes such as perceiving, remembering, thinking, and understanding.

Cognitive approach to stereotypes Approach stating that most stereotypes are products of normal human thought processes, such as categorization.

Cognitive-behavioral approach Therapy that acknowledges behav-ioral principles and also emphasizes observational learning and cognitive interpretations of the world.

Cognitive-behavioral therapy (CBT) Therapy in which psychological disorders are traced to inappropriate learning and maladaptive thinking.

Cognitive-developmental theory Theory of gender development stating that children's own thought processes are primarily responsible for the development of gender-related behavior.

Cognitive dissonance A discrepancy between two inconsistent cognitions produces psychological distress. People will be motivated to reduce this dissonance by changing one of the cognitions.

Cognitive modeling In educational psychology, the technique in which a teacher performs actions while verbalizing reasons for those actions. The teacher models not only correct procedures, but also how to cope with errors.

Cognitive psychologists Psychologists who conduct research on topics such as memory, thinking, and language.

Cognitive reappraisal Problem-focused coping strategies that attempt to reduce stress by internal cognitive adjustments, such as shifting one's level of aspiration.

Cognitive restructuring Therapeutic approach that emphasizes changing one's maladaptive thought patterns.

Collective unconscious According to Jung, the second, deeper layer of the unconscious that stores memory fragments from our ancestral past. All humans presumably share the same collective unconscious.

Collectivist cultures Cultures in which a person's identity focuses on interconnectedness with others (e.g. Latin American countries). Also called interdependent cultures.

Color constancy Phenomenon by which an object's perceived hue tends to stay the same, despite changes in illumination.

Color deficiency Difficulty in discriminating between different colors. Although relatively rare in females, about 8% of males have color deficiency.

Community psychology approach Approach to psychotherapy that em-phasizes social issues and institutions that influence groups and individuals. The goal is to optimize the well-being of community members.

Compliance Going along with a stated request from someone who does not have the specific authority to make you obey.

Compulsions Repetitive behaviors performed according to certain rules, often linked with obsessive thoughts. People with compulsions usually realize that their compulsive behavior is unreasonable. Common compulsions include hand washing, counting, and checking the location of an object.

Computed tomography (CT scan) Imaging technique that passes X-ray beams through the head from a variety of angles, plotting a two-dimensional picture that resembles a horizontal "slice" through the brain. Then the patient's head is moved either up or down; eventually, an entire series of computer-generated pictures is assembled.

Conception Point at which a sperm cell from the father fertilizes an egg cell (ovum) from the mother.

Concrete operational period One of Piaget's four periods of human development, during which children acquire important mental operations, that is, methods of manipulating information mentally.

Concussion A disruption of neurological function produced by trauma, such as a direct blow to the head.

Conditional positive regard According to Carl Rogers, the situation in which positive regard is given only in certain conditions; moreover, parents and other important people withhold their love and approval if the child fails to conform to their own standards.

Conditioned response In classical conditioning, the response that is elicited by the conditioned stimulus.

Conditioned stimulus In classical conditioning, the stimulus that is predictive of the unconditioned stimulus.

Conduction deafness Type of deafness involving problems in either the outer or the middle ear. These disabilities always involve a problem with the mechanical aspects of the auditory system, so that sound cannot be conducted appropriately from the eardrum to the receptors.

Cones Photoreceptors used for color vision under well-lit conditions.

Confabulation A major problem with "hypnotically refreshed" memory, in which hypnotized people may simply make up an item in memory to replace one that they cannot retrieve.

Conflict Interpersonal process that occurs when the goals of one party interfere with the actions of another party.

Conformity Change in beliefs or behaviors in response to group pressure when the group does not directly request this change.

Confounding variable or factors In an experiment, any variable—other than the independent variable—that is not equivalent in all conditions.

Congruence In person-centered therapy, the therapist expresses what he or she genuinely feels, rather than maintaining a formal "I'm the expert" attitude; also known as genuineness.

Conjunction fallacy Mistake in decision making in which people judge the probability of the conjunction (two events occurring together) to be greater than the probability of one single event.

Connectionist approach An influential model in cognitive psychology that proposes that the activation of one cue leads to the activation of other related concepts. Also known as parallel distributed processing approach or PDP approach.

Conscious In psychoanalytic theory, the conscious includes everything you are aware of at a particular moment. Our conscious experiences include our awareness of the outside world and of our perceptions, thoughts, and feelings.

Consciousness Awareness of the environment and of our perceptions, thoughts, and feelings.

Consensual sexual interactions Participation in sexual relationship by fully informed adults who freely choose to engage in mutual sexual stimulation.

Conservation According to Piaget, the mental operation by which children realize that a given quantity stays the same, no matter how its shape or physical arrangement may change.

Constancy Tendency to perceive objects as having constant characteristics (such as size and shape), despite changes in the information about them that reaches the eyes.

Constructionist view With respect to inferences, the view that readers usually draw inferences about the causes of events and the relationships between events.

Constructivist approach In memory, the approach that we continually revise our past in order to reflect our current knowledge.

Content validity In testing, a test's ability to cover the complete range of material that it is supposed to cover.

Continuity-stages question Is development a gradual process, with adults simply having a greater *quantity* of some particular skill? Alternatively, do children and adults differ in the *quality* of their psychological processes? Although many skills show continuity throughout development, there is evidence for stages in several areas of development.

Continuous reinforcement schedule In operant conditioning, situations in which the subject is reinforced on every correct trial.

Contralateral arrangement Crossover arrangement of the two hemispheres of the brain in which the right side of the cortex is more strongly connected with the left side of the body and the left side of the cortex is more strongly connected with the right side of the body.

Control condition In an experiment, the group that is left unchanged; in contrast to the experimental condition, they receive no special treatment.

Conventional morality Morality in which decisions are based on internalized standards derived from interactions with others.

Coping Thoughts and behaviors we use to handle stress or anticipated stress.

Cornea In the eye, the clear membrane just in front of the iris, with a curved surface that helps to bend light rays when they enter the eye.

Corpus callosum Bridge between the two hemispheres of the brain; a thick bundle of about 200 million nerve fibers that permits communication between the two hemispheres.

Correlation coefficient In correlational research, a number (symbolized as *r*) that indicates the direction and the strength of a relationship between two variables. The correlation coefficient can range between −1.00 and +1.00.

Correlational research Research in which psychologists try to determine whether two variables or measures are related. In correlational research, behavior can be observed in real-life settings, with neither random assignment to groups nor the manipulation of independent variables.

Counseling psychologists Psychologists who assess and treat people with less severe psychological problems than those treated by clinical psychologists. Some provide marriage or career counseling; others work in college mental health clinics.

Creativity Ability to produce unusual, high-quality solutions when solving problems.

Crisis hotline Community service that provides a phone number to call for immediate counseling and comfort. Hotline volunteers provide counseling and information about services available in the community. These services are used not only by people who have already been hospitalized for a psychological disorder, but also by others who are experiencing a crisis—such as rape victims, drug abusers, victims of domestic violence, and people considering suicide.

Criterion Willingness to say, "I detect the stimulus," when it is not clear whether the stimulus has been presented.

Criterion validity In testing, a test's ability to predict a person's performance on a second measure—that is, an independent criterion.

Critical thinking Thinking that involves deciding what to believe and how to act after carefully evaluating the evidence and the reasoning in a situation. Critical thinking requires that you ask good questions, determine whether conclusions are supported by the evidence presented, and suggest alternative interpretations of the evidence.

Cross-cultural psychology Study of similarities and differences in psychological processes of members of various cultures and ethnic groups.

Cross-sectional method Research method used by developmental psychologists in which researchers test individuals of different ages at the same time.

Crystallized intelligence Mental ability that involves specific acquired skills such as a verbal ability. Crystallized intelligence continues to grow throughout adulthood.

Cultural-familial retardation Mental retardation with no clear organic cause. Individuals may be retarded because they received fewer genes for high intelligence from their parents, because they grew up in an economically impoverished situation, or a combination of these two factors.

Dark adaptation Increase in sensitivity that occurs as the eyes remain in the dark.

Debriefing In a research study, telling the participants afterward about the purpose of the study, the nature of the anticipated results, and any deceptions used.

Decay theory Theory that each item in memory decays spontaneously as time passes.

Decision making Cognitive task that requires making a choice about the likelihood of uncertain events, for example, when people make estimates about frequency when only scanty evidence is available.

Deep structure Pertaining to sentence structure, the underlying, more abstract representation of the sentence.

Default assignment In the connectionist approach to memory, the process by which a person fills in missing information about an item, based on information about similar items.

Defense mechanisms In Freudian theory, mental activities designed to reduce the tension resulting from a desire of the id that the superego finds socially inappropriate.

Deinstitutionalization Program adopted by the mental health system to discharge people from mental hospitals into the community. In theory, this policy could be useful because it could return people to the supportive environment of family and friends and encourage independence and coping abilities. In practice, the policy has created problems.

Delusion False belief that a person firmly holds, despite any objective evidence.

Demand characteristics In a research study, the clues discovered by the participants about the purpose of the study, including rumors they hear about the study, which suggest how they are supposed to respond.

Demographic information Characteristics often used to classify people, such as gender, age, marital status, race, education, income, and so forth.

Dendrites In the nervous system, slender, branched fibers that carry neural impulses in the direction of the cell body in a neuron.

Denial Refusal to recognize the reality of stressful external events.

Dependent variable In an experiment, the variable that concerns the responses the participants make; it is a measure of their behavior.

Depressants Psychoactive drugs that depress central nervous system functioning. These substances reduce pain and tension, and slow down thinking and actions. Depressants include tranquilizers, barbiturates, opiates, and alcohol.

Depth of processing The method used to mentally process stimuli; deep processing makes material more memorable than shallow processing.

Descriptive statistics Statistics that provide some measure of central tendency ("What is the typical score?") and variability ("Are the other scores clustered closely around the typical score, or are they more spread out?")

Detection In detection studies, psychologists provide low-intensity stimuli and record whether people report them. Two major approaches to detection are the classical psychophysics approach and the signal detection theory approach.

Detection threshold In the classical psychophysics approach, the smallest amount of energy required for the observer to report the stimulus on half (50%) of the trials.

Development Changes in physical, cognitive, and social abilities that occur throughout the life span.

Developmental psychologists Psychologists who examine how humans mature and change throughout the life span.

Diagnostic and Statistical Manual of Mental Disorders (DSM) Manual for classifying psychological disorders, containing descriptions of the major categories of disorders, as well as a description of specific criteria that must be met before a diagnosis can be assigned.

Diathesis-stress model Model stating that people are born with a predisposition (diathesis) to respond to a stressful situation by developing a psychological disorder.

Dichotic listening task (die-*kot*-ick) Task in which people wear earphones that present two different simultaneous messages, one to each ear. Listeners are instructed to repeat a message presented to one ear while ignoring a different message presented to the other ear.

Diffusion of responsibility Situation in which, when people think they are part of a larger group, no individual feels responsible for helping.

Discourse Language units that are larger than a sentence.

Discrimination In psychophysics, discrimination is the determination of whether two stimuli are distinguishably different.

Discrimination In social psychology, discrimination involves action against a person or a group of people.

Discriminative stimulus In operant conditioning, a stimulus signaling that a response will be reinforced.

Displacement Defense mechanism that involves redirecting emotional feelings (e.g. anger) to a substitute target.

Display rules Culture-specific prescriptions about who can show which emotion, and in what circumstance. For instance, a display rule in our culture says that males should not cry.

Dissociative amnesia Psychological disorder involving the forgetting of past experiences following a stressful event. Dissociative amnesia is characterized by extensive memory loss.

Dissociative disorders Psychological disorder involving the splitting off (or dissociating) of a person's identity, memory, or consciousness.

Dissociative identity disorder Psychological disorder that occurs when a person has two or more distinct, well-developed personalities. Typically the personalities are dramatically different from each other, and there is a distinct unawareness of the other personalities. Previously known as multiple personality disorder.

Distinctive features In visual perception, characteristics of letters and other stimuli such as straight versus curved lines.

Distracting responses Thoughts and behaviors that cause depressed people to shift their attention away from their symptoms.

Divided attention Situation in which people try to distribute their attention among two or more competing tasks.

Door-in-the-face technique Two-step compliance technique in which an influencer achieves compliance by first making a request that is so large it is certain to be denied, and then making a smaller, more reasonable request.

Dopamine In the nervous system, an inhibitory neurotransmitter for muscle fibers.

Dopamine hypothesis Hypothesis that schizophrenia is caused by too much dopamine at critical synapses in the brain.

Double-jeopardy hypothesis Prediction that elderly members of ethnic minority groups will experience two kinds of prejudice, against both their age category and their ethnic category.

Double standard of aging The tendency to be more negative about elderly women than about elderly men.

Down syndrome Genetic abnormality involving an extra chromosome added to the 21st pair of chromosomes. Individuals with Down syndrome are typically retarded and have smaller brain size. When interacting with other people, they are often friendly and cheerful.

Dream analysis Psychoanalytic technique in which the therapist interprets the hidden meaning of the client's dream. Freud argued that dream analysis could circumvent repression.

Drive In motivation, the psychological energy from unmet needs that propels the organism to action.

Drug therapies Treatment of psychological disorders with medication.

Dual-route hypothesis Influential model of reading which states that we can reach a word's meaning through either of two routes: (1) direct recognition of the printed word or (2) by sounding the word out and then locating the word's meaning.

Eardrum Thin membrane that vibrates in sequence with the sound waves.

Echoic memory Auditory sensory memory, which is so fragile that it usually fades within 2 seconds.

Eclectic approach Approach to psychotherapy that selects what seems best from a variety of theoretical perspectives.

Ecological validity A principle stating that results obtained in research should be generalizable to real-life settings.

Ego In psychoanalytic theory, the component of the personality that deals with the outside world. The ego serves as a mediator between the id and reality.

Egocentrism According to Piaget, the phenomenon of a child seeing the world from only one point of view—his or her own.

Ejaculation Release of semen.

Electroconvulsive therapy (ECT) During this treatment, a person receives a series of electric shocks that produce convulsions, which often relieve the symptoms of severe depression where other treatments have failed.

Electroencephalography (EEG) Technique in which electrodes are placed on the scalp, and the electrical message from the thousands of neurons beneath the electrodes are then recorded on graph paper. The EEG is helpful in diagnosing brain disease and also provides useful information about brain activity when people are sleeping.

Emblem A gesture that is clearly understood by most members of a culture. Each emblem can be translated into a verbal phrase.

Emotion Subjective experience or feeling that is accompanied by changes in physiological reactions and behavior.

Emotion-focused coping Method of coping with stress that is directed at regulating emotional responses to the problem.

Emotional intelligence Ability to perceive emotion accurately, to understand it, and to express it.

Empathic understanding In person-centered therapy, the therapist's accurate feelings about the client's emotions.

Empathy Emotional reaction that involves a subjective grasp of another person's feelings or experiences.

Empathy-altruism hypothesis Hypothesis stating that empathy has the power to motivate altruism.

Empirical evidence Scientific evidence obtained by careful observation and experimentation.

Empowerment Development of a sense of self-worth and control over one's own life.

Encoding Pertaining to memory, the first stage of remembering, in which we transform sensory stimuli into a form that can be placed in memory.

Encoding specificity principle Principle stating that recall is better if the retrieval context is like the encoding context.

Endocrine system Collection of glands that release their chemicals (hormones) into the bloodstream.

Endorphins In the nervous system, chemicals that occur naturally in the brain and that, when released, decrease a person's sensitivity to pain.

Enemy images Tendency for us to see ourselves as good and peace-loving, whereas our enemies are evil, aggressive, and warlike.

Environmental psychology The applied area of psychology that studies interactions between people and their environment.

Epinephrine Hormone manufactured by the adrenal glands; epinephrine makes the heart pound vigorously due to fright.

Erogenous zones In psychoanalytic theory, parts of the body in which the libido is centered.

Estrogen hormones Hormones that influence changes in females at puberty.

Ethnicity   Concept referring to groups that share the same nationality, culture, or language.

Evolutionary psychology   A branch of psychology which proposes that psychological mechanisms have evolved in humans to solve specific adaptive problems.

Evolutionary theory   The theory that various species gradually change over the course of many generations in order to adapt better to their environments.

Excitatory potential   In the nervous system, the vesicles release a neurotransmitter that excites the postsynaptic neuron, which—as a consequence—is more likely to produce an action potential.

Exhaustion phase   Third phase of the general adaptation syndrome (response to stress) that occurs if the stressor persists. When the individual uses up the available resources, he or she is likely to develop physical problems and illnesses.

Experiment   Research design in which researchers systematically manipulate a variable under controlled conditions and observe how the participants respond. If the behavior changes when only the manipulated behavior is changed, then the researchers can conclude that they have discovered a cause-and-effect relationship.

Experimental condition   In an experiment, the group that is changed in some way. A particular variable is present in the experimental condition that is absent in the control condition.

Experimental method   Research method in which researchers manipulate the independent variable to determine its effects on the dependent variable, that is, the behavior of the participants in the experiment.

Experimenter expectancy effect   A term meaning that a researcher's biases and expectations can influence the outcome of an experiment.

Expertise   Demonstration of consistently exceptional performance on representative tasks for a particular area.

Explicit memory   The conscious recollection of a person's previous experiences.

Exposure with response prevention   Treatment of individuals with obsessive-compulsive disorder in which they are instructed to touch something that may be dirty and then avoid the typical response of repetitive handwashing.

Extinction   In classical conditioning, the gradual disappearance of a conditioned response that happens when a conditioned stimulus is repeatedly presented without the unconditioned stimulus.

Extrinsic motivation   Desire to perform an activity because of external rewards.

Facial feedback hypothesis   Theory of emotion stating that changes in facial expression can cause changes in a person's emotional state.

Family therapy   Psychotherapy that considers the entire family—not just one family member—to be the client. According to the family therapy approach, families show recurring patterns of interactions, and many problems involve disturbed relationships among several family members rather than just a single person.

Fear of success   Worry that success in competitive achievement situations will lead to unpleasant consequences such as unpopularity.

Feminist   A woman or man whose beliefs, values, and attitudes reflect a high regard for women as human beings.

Feminist approach to therapy   Approach to psychotherapy emphasizing that men and women should be valued equally, that women's inferior status in society often causes psychological problems, and that gender-stereotyped behavior harms both women and men. Feminist therapists argue that the therapist and client should be reasonably equal in power.

Fetal alcohol syndrome   Condition of children born to women who drank alcohol heavily during pregnancy. These children have characteristic facial features, including widely spaced eyes and flattened noses, and experience retarded physical growth and mental retardation.

Fetal period   The developing human from 2 months after conception until the baby is born about 7 months later.

Figure-ground relationship   In shape perception, when two areas share a common boundary, the figure is the distinct shape with clearly defined edges. The ground is the part that forms the background in the scene.

First language   The bilingual speaker's native language.

Five-factor model   In personality research, the five most important clusters of personality traits, including extraversion, agreeableness, conscientiousness, emotional stability, and openness to experience. Also known as the Big Five traits.

Fixation   In psychoanalytic theory, becoming rigidly locked in conflict about a particular erogenous zone.

Fixed-interval schedule   In operant learning, situations in which reinforcement is given for the first correct response made after the specified period of time has passed.

Fixed-ratio schedule   In operant learning, situations in which reinforcement is given after a fixed number of responses have been made.

Flashbulb memory   Phenomenon whereby people often have very vivid memories of a situation in which they first learned of a surprising and emotionally arousing event.

Flat affect   Little sign of either positive or negative emotion, often characteristic of schizophrenics. In flat affect, the voice is a monotone, and the face has no expression.

Flavor   Experience of taste, smell, touch, temperature, and pain associated with substances in the mouth.

Fluid intelligence   Ability to solve new problems. Fluid intelligence reaches a peak in the late teens and then declines slowly but steadily throughout adulthood.

Focused attention   Complicated kind of search that requires processing objects one at a time and focusing attention to identify each object.

Foot-in-the-door technique   Two-step compliance technique in which an influencer achieves compliance with a small request before making a larger request. People who have said "yes" to a small favor are more likely to say "yes" to a larger favor, in contrast to those who were only asked about the larger favor.

Forebrain   The largest part of the brain in humans, consisting of the following structures: cerebral cortex, thalamus, hypothalamus, pituitary gland, and limbic system.

Formal operational period   One of Piaget's four stages of human development, in which teenagers and adults can think scientifically and systematically, solve problems without the help of concrete representation, contemplate complex ideas, and think flexibly about a variety of problems.

Fovea   (*foe*-vee-uh) In the eye, the tiny region of the retina in which vision is the most precise.

Framing effect   In decision making, the situation in which people are influenced by the following factors that should be ignored: (1) the background context of the decision, and (2) the way in which a question is worded.

Fraternal twins   Twins who came from two separate eggs and are thus no more genetically similar than two siblings.

Free association   A psychoanalytic technique which requires a patient to report anything that occurs to them; normal critical analysis should be suspended.

Free running   Natural tendency for humans to adopt a 25-hour cycle when deprived of zeitgebers.

Frequency   Number of cycles a sound wave completes in one second.

Frequency distribution   In statistics, a summary of data that shows how often each score occurs.

Frequency theory   Theory of auditory processing proposing that the entire basilar membrane vibrates at a frequency that matches the frequency of a tone.

Frontal lobe   Part of the cerebral cortex that includes the motor cortex, which controls voluntary movement for different parts of the body. The frontal lobe also includes the prefrontal cortex, which is responsible for complex cognitive tasks.

Functional fixedness   Barrier to problem solving in which the function assigned to an object tends to remain fixed or stable.

Functional magnetic resonance imaging (fMRI)   Imaging technique which is a modification of the MRI and produces images of the increase in blood flow to the brain.

Functionalism   Approach to psychology proposing that psychological processes are adaptive; they allow humans to survive and to adapt successfully to their surroundings.

Fundamental attribution error   Tendency to overestimate the role of internal, personal causes and underestimate the role of external, situational causes in explaining the behavior of other people.

***g* factor**   According to Spearman, a single, general mental ability, underlying all the varying kinds of intelligence.

Ganglion cells   In the eye, cells that collect synaptic messages from the bipolar cells and send this information (in the form of action potentials) out of the eye, in the direction of the brain.

Gardner's theory of multiple intelligences   Theory that proposes seven different components of intelligence: (1) language ability, (2) logical-mathematical thinking, (3) spatial thinking, (4) musical thinking, (5) bodily kinesthetic thinking, (6) interpersonal thinking, (7) intrapersonal thinking.

Gate-control theory   Theory proposing that people experience pain only if pain messages pass through a gate in the spinal cord on their route to the brain. When the gate is open, people experience pain. However, the brain can send messages to the spinal cord, indicating that the gate should be closed, thereby blocking pain messages from reaching the brain. As a consequence, people feel no pain.

Gay males   Men who are emotionally, psychologically, and sexually attracted to other men.

Gender roles   Set of expectations about appropriate activities for females and males.

Gender schema theory   Theory proposing that children use gender as an important schema to structure and guide their view of the world.

Gender segregation   Tendency to associate with persons of the same gender.

General adaptation syndrome (GAS)   Model of stress, developed by Hans Selye, consisting of three stages of response to stressful situations: (1) the alarm phase, (2) the resistance phase, and (3) the exhaustion phase.

Generalized anxiety disorders   Disorders characterized by continuous, long-lasting worry and tension. People with this disorder cannot identify a specific cause of their anxiety. They also have physical symptoms such as nausea, dizziness, and muscle tension.

Genes   Basic units of genetics. In humans, the genes are located on 23 pairs of chromosomes in virtually every cell of the body.

Genital stage   Final stage of psychosexual development in which, during puberty, sexual urges presumably reappear and the genitals once again become an erogenous zone. Freud argued that genital pleasure during the genital stage arises from sexual relationships with others.

Genome   A full set of genes for any given organism.

Gestalt approach   (geh-*shtahlt*) Approach to perception that emphasizes that humans perceive objects as well-organized, whole structures rather than as separated, isolated parts.

Gestalt laws of grouping   (geh-*shtahlt*) In vision and shape perception, the four laws of Gestalt grouping are (1) the law of proximity; (2) the law of similarity; (3) the law of good continuation; (4) the law of closure.

Gestures   Movements that accompany speech.

Gifted   Based on the definition of most school districts, individuals with IQs over 130, roughly the top 2%. Some argue that giftedness includes exceptional creativity, leadership skills, or artistic abilities. Others propose that people are gifted only if they meet all of the three criteria: (1) above-average ability, (2) creativity, and (3) focused motivation for completing a project.

Glass ceiling   The presumably invisible barrier in many professions that seems to block the advancement of women and people of color.

Glucose   Simple sugar nutrient that provides energy.

Glucostats   Neurons that are sensitive to glucose levels.

Gonads   Sex glands, including the testes in males and the ovaries in females. The gonads produce a variety of hormones that are crucial in sexual development and reproduction.

Gonorrhea Bacterial sexually transmitted disease that infects the genital membranes.

Graceful degradation In the connectionist approach to memory, the brain's ability to provide partial memory.

Graded structure In the prototype approach to meaning, the assumption that all members of a category are *not* created equal. Instead, a category has a graded structure in which the most representative or prototypical members have priority, and the category's nonprototypical members have lower status.

GRIT (Graduated and Reciprocated Initiatives in Tension Reduction) Conflict resolution technique, especially useful in international peacemaking, that consists of a series of steps in which one party announces a step it will take to reduce tension, the party actually takes the step, then the party states its expectations for some kind of reciprocation. If the other party reciprocates, the first party then starts another round of these initiatives.

Group Two or more people who influence one another through social interaction.

Group polarization Phenomenon in which group members take a more extreme position on a particular issue after discussing it than they would have taken without discussion.

Group therapy Psychotherapy conducted with an interacting group of 7 or 8 people who have something in common. The therapist usually does not actively direct the conversation, but lets it unfold naturally. The group is encouraged to use its own resources and to develop a sense of belonging and common goals.

Groupthink Situation in which the harmony of a group becomes more important than wise decision making. The group members work hard to maintain a positive view of the group's functioning, and they stop thinking critically.

Habituation Situation whereby a stimulus is presented many times until the individual stops responding to it.

Hair cells In the ear, the receptors for hearing, which are embedded in a part of the cochlea called the basilar membrane.

Halfway house Intermediate care facility in which people who have recently been discharged from a hospital live together with trained staff in a home and learn the skills necessary to live independently.

Hallucinations Strong mental images that seem as if they truly occurred in the absence of physical stimuli. The most common hallucinations are auditory, such as voices coming from outside one's head, but they may also include visions, smells, tastes, and skin-sense hallucinations.

Hallucinogens Chemical substances that alter people's perceptions of reality and may cause vivid hallucinations. Hallucinogens include several synthetic drugs such as LSD, as well as substances extracted from plants such as marijuana.

Health psychology Study of how people stay healthy, why they engage in risky behavior, why they develop illnesses and how they react to illnesses.

Heritability In the nature-nurture question, the extent to which the variation in some characteristic can be traced to differences in heredity as opposed to differences in environment. The heritability index can vary between 0% (little of the variation can be traced to heredity) to 100% (almost all of the variation can be traced to heredity).

Heuristic-systematic model Approach that persuasion can create attitude change by two separate routes: (1) when you are not involved in the issue or when you are not able to analyze a message, you rely on heuristics (simple decision-making rules) that you may have learned in the past; (2) when you are involved in the issue and when you have the ability to analyze it, you use systematic processing.

Heuristics General problem-solving techniques that are typically accurate.

Hierarchy System in which items are arranged in a series of classes, from the most general to the most specific.

Hindbrain Structure located in the bottom portion of the brain and consisting of the medulla, pons, cerebellum, reticular formation.

Histogram Graph in which the data are arranged so that they show the frequency of each score.

Homeostasis The maintenance of constant, ideal internal environment; state of internal balance or stability. The hypothalamus regulates homeostatis for body temperature, liquid intake, and food intake.

Homophobia Irrational, persistent fear and contempt for gay people.

Hormones Chemicals released by the endocrine system. Hormones circulate through all parts of the bloodstream, yet they influence only specific target organs.

Hospice care The goal of hospice care is to allow people with terminal illnesses to die with dignity. In hospices, death is viewed as normal, the family is involved in caring for the dying person, and medical care focuses on relieving pain rather than keeping a person alive at all costs.

Hue Color of a visual stimulus, determined in part by the wavelength of the light.

Human immunodeficiency virus (HIV) Virus with the potential to destroy part of the immune system through invasion of white bloods cells called T-helper lymphocytes.

Humanistic approach Approach emphasizing that humans have enormous potential for personal growth. They have the ability to care deeply for other people and to establish meaningful, productive lives for themselves.

Humanistic therapy Psychotherapy designed to remove the blocks to personal growth and to help people appreciate their true selves. An example is Carl Rogers's person-centered therapy.

Hypnosis Social interaction in which one person (the subject) responds to suggestions offered by another person (the hypnotist); the subject will experience changes in thoughts, feelings, or behavior based on these suggestions.

Hypothalamus That part of the brain lying just below the thalamus and controlling the autonomic nervous system. Several distinct clusters of neurons regulate different kinds of motivated behavior such as eating, drinking, sexual behavior, aggression, and activity level.

Hypothesis Tentative set of beliefs about the nature of the world, a statement about what is expected to happen if certain conditions are true. A hypothesis tells what relationship a researcher expects to find between an independent variable and a dependent variable.

Iconic memory (eye-*conn*-ick) Visual sensory memory, which is so fragile that it usually fades before we can recall all of it.

Id In psychoanalytic theory, the component of personality that consists of the basic drives, such as eating and sexual activity, providing the energy (or libido) for all human behavior. The id lacks moral judgment and it is unconscious.

Identical twins Twins who came from a single fertilized egg and are genetically identical.

Identity An individual's self-rating of personal characteristics.

Illusion Discrepancy between perception and reality that occurs as a result of normal sensory processes. Illusions lead us to make errors in the orientation of lines, in the lengths of lines, and in the perception of contours.

Illusory contour A figure in which we see edges even though they are not physically present.

Illustrator Nonverbal action that accompanies speech and quite literally provides an illustration.

Immune system System that protects the body against infection, allergies, bacteria, viruses, and other dangers.

Implicit memory Memory that involves performing a task and assessing whether that action is influenced by past experience.

Impression formation Integration of various pieces of information about a person.

In vivo treatment (in *vee*-voe) In systematic desensitization, a technique in which clients interact with the actual feared object.

Incentive theory Motivation theory that emphasizes how external goals motivate people to respond and to act. An incentive occurs before people actually do something, and it energizes them to do something—if the incentive is attractive—or *not* do something—if the incentive is unattractive.

Independent cultures Cultures in which a person's identity focuses on themselves as an individual (e.g., United States and Canada). Also called individualistic cultures.

Independent variable In an experiment, the variable that the experimenters manipulate.

In-depth interview Research method that requires the interviewer to gather answers to open-ended questions, often over a period of many hours or days.

Individual fanning out Increased variability during aging; the fact that individual differences increase as people grow older. For example, 60-year-olds are more different from one another than 10-year-olds are.

Individualistic cultures Cultures in which a person's identity focuses on themselves as an individual (e.g., United States and Canada). Also called independent cultures.

Industrial/organizational psychologists Psychologists who focus on human behavior in business and industry. Some help organizations hire and train employees, others study the work setting, and others measure consumer attitudes.

Inferential statistics Statistics used when researchers want to draw conclusions about their data based on evidence. Inferential statistics provide a formal procedure for using data to test for statistical significance.

Ingroup favoritism Tendency, influenced by stereotypes, to evaluate members of our own group more favorably than members of another group.

Inhibited children Children who are fearful of strangers and unfamiliar objects or events.

Inhibitory potential In the nervous system, the vesicles release a neurotransmitter that inhibits the postsynaptic neuron which, as a consequence, is less likely to produce an action potential.

Insight In psychoanalysis, the client's awareness of the unconscious conflicts causing his or her psychological problems. Insight grows gradually during the course of psychoanalysis as the therapist pieces together evidence from free association, dream analysis, and transference.

Insomnia Difficulty in falling asleep and/or remaining asleep.

Instinctive drift Principle indicating that when an animal is engaged in operant conditioning, its behavior will drift in the direction of instinctive behaviors related to the task it is learning.

Instrumental conditioning Type of conditioning that involves learning to make a response because it produces a reinforcing effect and learning not to make a response because it produces a punishing effect. Also known as operant conditioning.

Insulin Hormone secreted by the pancreas that plays an important role in converting blood glucose into stored fat.

Intelligence Ability to master the information and skills needed to succeed within a particular culture. Intelligence therefore includes a wide range of cognitive skills, such as perception, learning, memory, problem solving, and reasoning.

Intelligence quotient (IQ) Performance on intelligence tests can be scored and transformed into an intelligence quotient, which is currently computed by assigning a score of 100 to a person whose performance is average for a particular age group. Higher and lower IQ scores are then based on where a person's score fall in comparison to the average.

Interdependent cultures Cultures in which a person's identity focuses on interconnectedness with others (e.g., Latin American countries). Also called collectivist cultures.

Interference theory Belief that forgetting occurs because other items get in the way of the information a person wants to remember.

Interpersonal psychotherapy (ITP) Psychodynamic therapy that focuses on improving the quality of a person's current interaction with other people. The client and therapist work to identify specific problems that may be currently interfering with interpersonal relationships.

Intrinsic motivation Desire to perform an activity for its own sake. People are likely to do something—and to do it well—when they find it inherently enjoyable.

Intrinsic punishment Internalized sense of dissatisfaction for poor performance.

Intrinsic reinforcement Internalized sense of satisfaction at performing well.

Introspection Observation of one's own conscious psychological reactions.

Iris In the eye, a ring of muscles just behind the cornea that contract and dilate to change the amount of light that enters the eye. The color of the iris can range from pale blue to dark brown.

Issues proliferation Tendency for parties in a conflict to increase the number of controversial topics, thus increasing the areas of conflict.

Izard's theory (Ih-*zahrd*) Theory of emotion suggesting that two different kinds of emotion pathways are responsible for our feelings. Cognition is not necessary for the first kind of emotional experience, but it is for the second kind.

James-Lange theory Theory of emotion proposing that physiological changes are the source of emotional feelings.

Jet lag Disturbances in body rhythm caused by airplane journeys involving time zone changes.

Jigsaw classroom Method of encouraging equal status in an interracial classroom in which all children must work together to ensure good grades.

Just-noticeable difference (jnd) Smallest change needed in physical stimulus in order for the observer to notice the change.

Keyword method In memory improvement, method using visual imagery to link a key word with another word.

Latency stage One of the stages of psychosexual development during which children's sexual feelings presumably remain in the repressed state in which they were left at the end of the phallic stage. According to Freud, children are presumably ashamed and disgusted about sexual issues, and so they tend to avoid members of the other gender.

Latent content Underlying, unconscious aspects of a dream.

Lateralization Brain hemispheric specialization (with the left hemisphere being more competent on language tasks and the right hemisphere being more competent on spatial tasks). Although the two brain hemispheres have somewhat different functions, these differences should not be exaggerated.

Law of closure In shape perception, the law stating that a figure with a gap will be perceived as a closed, intact figure.

Law of effect In operant conditioning, responses resulting in rewarding consequences are learned, whereas responses with punishing consequences are weakened and not learned.

Law of good continuation In shape perception, the law stating that people tend to perceive smooth, continuous lines, rather than discontinuous fragments.

Law of proximity In shape perception, the law stating that objects near each other tend to be perceived as a unit.

Law of similarity In shape perception, the law stating that objects similar to each other tend to be perceived as a unit.

Learning Relatively permanent change in behavior or knowledge due to experience.

Lens In the eye, the structure directly behind the iris and the pupil that changes shape to focus on objects that are nearby or far away. The lens helps bend the light rays so that they gather in focus at the back of the eye, at a point on or near the retina.

Lesbians Women who are emotionally, psychologically, and sexually attracted to other women.

Lesion A wound or disruption of the brain. Lesions can be produced in laboratory animals to confirm some hypotheses about the functions of brain structure.

Libido Energy for all human behavior provided by the id.

Life review Special kind of reminiscing about the past in which an older person recalls past experiences and tries to work through them to understand them more thoroughly.

Lifetime prevalence The likelihood that someone will experience a psychological disorder at some point in life.

Limbic system A portion of the forebrain that helps regulate emotions and plays a critical role in motivation, learning, and memory. The system has several components such as the hippocampus and amygdala.

Linearization problem Dilemma involving speech productions, in which people may have a general thought they want to express, or a mental image that needs to be conveyed verbally. These ideas need to be translated into a statement that is linear, with one word following after another in a line.

Lithium Chemical that is useful in treating bipolar disorder.

Localization The ability to determine the direction from which a sound is coming.

Long-term memory (LTM) A relatively permanent kind of memory, which has an enormous capacity. LTM stores memories that are decades old, as well as memories that arrived a few minutes ago.

Long-term potentiation In memory research, the phenomenon in which brief electrical stimulation leaves the neuron highly responsive to the same kind of stimulation in the future.

Longitudinal method Research method used by developmental psychologists in which researchers select one group of individuals who are the same age and then retest them periodically as they grow older.

Lose-lose approach Approach to conflict in which both parties will suffer a net loss. War is an example of the lose-lose approach.

Loudness Psychological reaction that corresponds to the physical characteristic of amplitude; loudness is measured in decibels (dB).

Lymphocytes White blood cells, part of the immune system, that defend the body against viruses and other harmful agents.

Magnetic resonance imaging (MRI) Imaging technique used to provide a picture of the living human brain by passing a strong (but harmless) magnetic field through a patient's head. The MRI scanner picks up radiation from hydrogen molecules, providing a picture of a "slice" of the human brain.

Major depression Mood disorder characterized by frequent episodes of intense hopelessness and lowered self-esteem.

Male climacteric (klie-*mack*-terr-ick) Physical change experienced by men during middle age that includes decreased fertility and decreased frequency of orgasm.

Mania Mood disorder characterized by an abnormally positive, over-excited state, accompanied by high self-esteem.

Manifest content The conscious, remembered story line of a dream.

Masculine generic The use of masculine nouns and pronouns to refer to all human beings, instead of males alone.

Maslow's hierarchy of needs Theory stating that human motives are arranged in a hierarchy, with the most basic needs (physiological, safety, belongingness, and love) at the bottom and the more highly developed needs (esteem and self-actualization) at the top. Each lower need must presumably be satisfied before the next level of need can be addressed.

Masochistic (mass-uh-*kiss*-tick) Deriving pleasure from being mistreated.

Matching hypothesis In friendship, we prefer friends who are similar to ourselves in attractiveness.

Matrix Chart that represents all possible combinations. In problem solving, a matrix is an excellent way to keep track of items, particularly when the problem is complex.

Mean In statistics, a measure of central tendency that is the simple average of all scores, obtained by adding all the scores together and dividing by the number of scores.

Meaning-making Children's active attempts to make sense out of their world and their experiences. They try to construct general principles based on these experiences.

Means-end analysis In problem solving, the problem solver divides the problem into a number of subproblems, or smaller problems. Each of these subproblems is solved by removing the barriers between the original situation and the goal.

Median In statistics, a measure of central tendency that is the score which falls precisely in the middle of a distribution of scores. To calculate a median, arrange the scores in order from lowest to highest and identify the score in the middle, with half the scores above and half the scores below.

Meditation Technique for focusing attention and avoiding worried thoughts.

Medulla That part of the brain found just above the spinal cord and important in several basic functions, such as controlling breathing and heart rate.

Memory Storing of information over time, involving encoding, storage, and retrieval.

Menarche (*men*-are-kee) The first menstrual period.

Menopause Time when menstrual periods have stopped for at least a year.

Mental control The influence we exercise over our consciousness.

Mental imagery Mental representations of things that are not physically present.

Mental retardation Features include (1) intellectual functioning that is significantly below average, (2) difficulty functioning in two or more skill areas, and (3) onset prior to age 18.

Mental set Barrier to problem solving in which problem solvers keep using the same solution they have used in previous problems, even though there may be easier ways of approaching the problem.

Mere exposure effect Tendency to prefer items (objects, ideas, and people) with which we have had repeated contact.

Meta-analysis Systematic, statistical method for synthesizing the results from numerous studies on a given topic, yielding a single number that indicates whether a particular factor has an overall effect on behavior.

Metabolism Energy required to maintain the body; people with slow metabolism gain more weight.

Metacognition Knowledge and awareness about a person's own thought processes.

Metacomprehension Thoughts about a person's own reading comprehension.

Metalinguistics Knowledge about the form and structure of language.

Metamemory Knowledge and awareness of a person's own memory.

Midbrain The part of the brain that continues upward from the pons portion of the hindbrain. All the signals that pass between the spinal cord and the forebrain—as well as visual information—must pass through this structure.

Mindlessness Barrier to problem solving in which a person uses information too rigidly, without becoming aware of the potentially novel characteristics of the current situation.

Minnesota Multiphasic Personality Inventory (MMPI) Objective personality test that asks a large number of true-false questions in order to assess personality traits.

Mirror-image thinking In a conflict, biased perception by both sides in which each side sees itself as good and peace-loving and the other side as evil, aggressive, and warlike.

Mnemonics Use of a strategy to help memory.

Mode In statistics, a measure of central tendency that is the score which occurs most often in a group of scores. The mode can be established by inspecting the data and noting which number appears most frequently.

Modeling Learning new behaviors by watching and imitating the behavior of others (models). Also known as observational learning and social learning.

Monocular In depth perception, factors seen with one eye that can provide information about distance.

Mood disorders Psychological disorders characterized by persistent, extreme disturbances of mood or emotional state. Examples include major depression, bipolar disorder, and mania.

Motivation The reason people behave the way they do. Some motives are biological (e.g., hunger) and other are social (e.g., need for nurturance).

Multiple personality disorder Psychological disorder that occurs when a person has two or more distinct, well-developed personalities. Typically the personalities are dramatically different from each other, and there is a distinct unawareness of the other personalities. Currently known as dissociative identity disorder.

Multiple sclerosis (MS) Disease that destroys the myelin sheath, causing numbness, weakness, visual disturbances, and motor problems.

Myelin sheath Insulating material (part fat and part protein) that coats the larger axons in the nervous system.

Natural selection A central concept in evolutionary theory in which the better adapted members of a species are more likely to stay alive until they produce offspring.

Naturalistic observation Research method in which individuals are examined in their natural environment, performing their natural behaviors in response to natural stimuli in order to gather information about typical behavior.

Nature In the nature-nurture question, nature refers to differences between people determined by the genes they inherited from their biological parents.

Nature-nurture question Can development be primarily explained by nature or by genetics? Alternatively, is development primarily determined by nurture, that is, by learning and experience? The appropriate answer is that development is determined by both nature and nurture.

Negative correlation In correlational research, the situation in which people who receive a high score on Variable 1 usually receive a *low* score on Variable 2; people with a low score on Variable 1 usually receive a *high* score on Variable 2. A strong negative correlation coefficient will be close to −1.00.

Negative hallucinations Hypnotic phenomenon in which subjects can be encouraged *not* to see objects that are present.

Negative reinforcement In operant conditioning, something negative that is taken away or avoided after the correct response has been made.

Neodissociation theory Theory of hypnosis, proposed by Ernest Hilgard, which emphasizes that hypnosis produces a dissociation or division in consciousness. As a result, behaviors, thoughts, and feelings operate independently, as if there are two separate channels.

Nerve deafness Type of deafness involving problems in the inner ear, specifically in the cochlea or auditory nerve.

Nerves Bundles of axons from neurons in the peripheral nervous system. Nerves carry communication between the peripheral nervous system and the central nervous system.

Network model Theory of meaning proposing that concepts are organized in memory in a netlike pattern, with many interconnections. The meaning of a particular concept, such as *apple*, depends on the concepts to which it is connected.

Neurocognitive model Model of the function of dreams, developed by J. Allan Hobson and John Antrobus and based on neurophysiology and cognitive psychology. A core concept is the activation-synthesis hypothesis, which proposes that the hindbrain sends a haphazard pattern of signals to the cerebral cortex (activation), and then the cerebral cortex tries to make sense out of all these random signals (synthesis).

Neurolinguistics The discipline that examines the relationship between the brain and language.

Neuromodulators In the nervous system, chemical substances acting at the synapse to modify the effects of neurotransmitters, either increasing or decreasing neuronal activity. Neuromodulators are also likely to spread beyond the synapse and influence more distant neurons.

Neuron In the nervous system, a specialized cell that processes, stores, and transmits information throughout the body.

Neuroscience approach Approach to psychology, also called biological approach, which proposes that each behavior, emotion, and thought is caused by a physical event in the brain or other part of the nervous system.

Neurotransmitters In the nervous system, chemical substances stored in the neurons that alter the electrical activity of the postsynaptic neuron.

Nictitating-membrane reflex In rabbits, the response of an unusual inner eyelid that slides over a rabbit's eye to protect it when a puff of air is presented.

Nightmare Dream that occurs during REM sleep which produces anxiety or fear.

Noise Sound that is unwanted.

Nonshared environmental experiences Differences between siblings due to the fact that parents treat each child differently, siblings create different environments for each other, and each child has different experiences outside the family.

Nonverbal communication All human communications that do not involve words, including tone of voice, hand movements, posture, rate of speaking, and facial expression.

Norms In testing, established standards of performance on the test. An individual's score on the test can be interpreted by comparing the score with those standards.

Novices Those individuals who have not acquired expertise in a specific area.

Nurture In the nature-nurture question, nurture refers to differences between people determined by the way they were reared—that is, by their environment.

Obedience Social pressure in which an authority specifically commands us to change our behavior.

Obesity Condition in which a person is 20% or more above the desirable weight.

Object permanence The knowledge that an object exists even if it is temporarily out of sight.

Object-relations approach Psychodynamic approach that focuses on the nature and development of ideas about the self in relation to other people. This approach minimizes Freud's notion of drives and emphasizes the developing relationship between the self and objects—that is, significant persons.

Observational learning Learning of new behaviors by watching and imitating the behavior of others. Also known as modeling and social learning.

Obsessions Persistent, unwanted thoughts that are unreasonable. Typical obsessions include inappropriate worry over germs or illness and excessive concerns about other people.

Obsessive-compulsive disorder Disabling conditions that involve recurrent, time-consuming obsessions and/or compulsions.

Obsessive-compulsive personality disorder Type of personality disorder characterized by a personality that overemphasizes details, conscientiousness, and rigid compliance with rules.

Occipital lobe (ox-*sip*-ih-tul) The part of the cerebral cortex at the back of the head. An important part of this region of the brain is the visual cortex.

Oedipus complex (*ed*-ih-pus) In psychoanalysis, a conflict in which a boy's sexual impulses are directed toward his mother and he views his father as a rival. The young boy is afraid that his father may punish him for his desires by castrating him. A boy who develops normally will reduce this fear by identifying with his father, internalizing his father's values, and developing a strong superego.

Operant conditioning Type of conditioning that involves learning to make a response because it produces a reinforcing effect and learning not to make a response because it produces a punishing effect. Also known as instrumental conditioning.

Operational definition In a research study, a precise definition that specifies exactly what operations will be performed and how the concept is to be measured.

Opiates Class of depressants that includes drugs such as morphine and heroin. These psychoactive drugs suppress pain and encourage sleep. They imitate the action of endorphins.

Opponent-process theory In color perception, a theory describing the mechanisms of ganglion cells and other cells closer to the cortex; specifically, these cells respond by increasing their activity when one color is present and decreasing their activity when another color is present.

Optic nerve In the eye, the collection of ganglion-cell axons that travel out of the eye and onward to higher levels of visual processing.

Oral stage One of the stages of psychosexual development during which the mouth presumably experiences the most tension. According to Freud, the id tries to reduce this tension by encouraging the child to suck on nipples, thumbs, and pacifiers.

Organic retardation Mental retardation caused by a genetic disorder (such as Down syndrome) or by physical damage to the brain caused by an infectious disease, Fetal Alcohol Syndrome, or medical complications from a premature delivery.

Outcome research Controlled experiments on the effectiveness of psychotherapy.

Outgroup homogeneity Perception influenced by stereotypes that all members of another group are similar, whereas members of one's own group are perceived as diverse and heterogeneous.

Pain A complex perceptual experience involving sensory, emotional, and evaluative components. Pain can produce stress, depression, and lowered immunity.

Panic disorder Type of anxiety disorder marked by recurrent panic attacks of overwhelming anxiety that occur suddenly and unexpectedly. Someone in the midst of a panic attack may feel smothering sensations, severe chest pains, and a fear of dying.

Paralanguage The use of vocal cues other than the words themselves, such as voice tone, pitch, pauses, and inflection of the voice.

Parallel distributed processing approach (PDP approach) Pertaining to cognitive psychology, the model that proposes that the activation of one cue leads to the activation of other, related concepts. Also known as the connectionist approach.

Parallel search Searching long-term memory by handling all the characteristics at the same time.

Paranoid schizophrenic Person with one or more persistent, bizarre delusions.

Parasympathetic nervous system Part of the autonomic nervous system that tends to slow down body functions and conserve energy.

Parietal lobe (puh-*rye*-ih-tull) Part of the cerebral cortex, upward and forward from the occipital lobe. The parietal lobe registers information about body movement, the location of body parts, and touch. At the front of the parietal lobe is the somatosensory cortex, the part of the brain that handles the skin senses.

Parkinson's disease Disease traced to a deficit in dopamine production, with symptoms such as tremors of the hands, altered body posture, and difficulty walking, caused by deterioration in the neurons in the part of the brain that releases dopamine.

Partial reinforcement schedule In operant conditioning, situations in which the subject is reinforced only part of the time. Also known as intermittent reinforcement.

Passive touch Touch perception in which an object touches the skin.

Past-life regression During hypnosis, a person is supposedly age-regressed beyond birth until a "past life personality" is reinstated; this proposed phenomenon has not been empirically demonstrated.

Peacebuilding An active process that attempts to improve relationships between parties in a post-conflict situation and tries to prevent conflict before it arises.

Perceived common ground In a conflict situation, the likelihood of finding an alternative that satisfies both parties' wishes.

Percentile score Standardized test score that indicates the percentage of people who received scores below your own score.

Perception Interpretation of basic sensations; perception involves organization and meaning.

Peripheral nervous system Everything in the nervous system except the brain and spinal cord. The peripheral nervous system transmits messages from the sensory receptors to the central nervous system and back out from the central nervous system to the muscles and glands.

Permissive parenting Parenting style in which parents make few demands on their children, allowing them to make their own decisions. Children from permissive families tend to be immature; they have little self-control, and they explore less than children from authoritarian and authoritative families.

Person attribution Type of attribution indicating that we believe that an internal trait, located within the person, was responsible for the behavior—in contrast to situation attribution.

Person-centered therapy Psychotherapy developed by Carl Rogers that attempts to focus on the person's own point of view, instead of the therapist's interpretations. Rogers proposed three conditions that are likely to encourage growth in person-centered therapy: congruence, unconditional positive regard, and empathic understanding.

Person perception Area within social cognition that examines both impression formation (integrating various pieces of information about a person) and attribution (the explanations we create about the reasons for our own behavior and the behavior of others).

Person schema Generalized idea about a person that consists of selected bits of information about the person, organized into a coherent picture.

Person-situation debate Controversy with the following positions: The *person* position states that each person possesses stable, internal traits that cause him or her to act consistently in a variety of situations. The *situation* position states that each person does not possess stable, internal traits; instead, his or her behavior depends upon the specific characteristics of each situation.

Personal attribution Emphasis on an internal trait as responsible for a person's behavior.

Personality Pattern of consistent feelings, thoughts, and behaviors that originate within the individual.

Personality disorders Psychological disorders in which personality traits become inflexible and maladaptive. People with personality disorders typically share these problems: (1) a disability at work and in social relationships, (2) frequent interpersonal conflicts, (3) an ability to cause distress to other people, and (4) a maladaptive response to stress.

Personality psychologists Psychologists who investigate how people are influenced by relatively stable inner factors.

Pessimistic explanatory style Depressed person's belief that their sorrows are permanent, widespread, and traceable to themselves.

PET scan *See* Positron emission tomography.

Phallic stage One of the stages of psychosexual development during which the erogenous zone presumably shifts to the sex organs, and the child presumably finds pleasure in masturbation. Freud proposed that boys in the phallic stage experience an Oedipus complex.

Phantom limb pain Phenomenon reported by about 70% of people who have had an arm or leg amputated;

they continue to report pain in the missing limb even though there are no longer any pain receptors.

Phobias Intense, irrational fears of particular objects or situations.

Phobic disorder Type of anxiety disorder involving excessive fear of a specific object, activity, or situation. This fear is out of proportion to the true danger, and it cannot be eliminated by rational thought.

Phoneme Basic unit of speech, such as the sounds *th*, *a*, and *t* in the word *that*.

Phonemic restoration Situation in which people think that they hear a phoneme, even though the correct sound vibrations never reach their ears.

Phonological loop In Alan Baddeley's model of working memory, the component that stores a limited number of sounds. Memories in the phonological loop decay within 2 seconds unless the material is rehearsed.

Physiological measures In a research study, measurements that are objective recordings of physiological states such as heart rate, breathing rate, perspiration, and brain activity.

Pitch Psychological reaction that corresponds to the frequency of a tone.

Pituitary gland Hormone-producing gland attached by a stalk to the bottom part of the hypothalamus and regulated by the hypothalamus. The pituitary gland manufactures its own hormones (such as growth hormone) and also regulates the other hormonal glands in the body.

Place theory Theory of auditory processing proposing that each frequency of vibration causes a particular place on the basilar membrane to vibrate.

Placebo (pluh-*see*-bow) Inactive substance given to a control group instead of a medication.

Placebo effect (pluh-*see*-bow) Phenomenon that occurs when a person is given a substance that contains no active ingredient and yet experiences some relief from specific symptoms.

Polarization Exaggeration of the similarities within the group, as well as exaggerating the differences between groups.

Political psychology Interdisciplinary area within psychology that combines political science with psychology. Includes international peacemaking.

Polygraph examination Lie detector test that simultaneously measures several autonomic changes such as blood pressure, pulse, breathing patterns, and skin conductance. These measures are taken while a person is asked a structured series of questions. The examiner notes the pattern of arousal and decides on the basis of these data whether the person being tested is innocent or guilty.

Pons Structure in the brain, located above the medulla. Functions as a bridge, connecting the lower brain regions with the higher brain regions. The pons is important in muscle control, such as facial expression and skillful use of fingers.

Positive correlation In correlational research, the situation in which people who receive a high score on Variable 1 are likely to receive a high score on Variable 2; people who receive a low score on Variable 1 are likely to receive a low score on Variable 2. A strong positive correlation coefficient will be close to +1.00.

Positive hallucinations Hypnotic phenomenon in which subjects can be encouraged to perceive objects that are not present.

Positive reinforcement In operant conditioning, something positive that is added to the situation after the correct response has been made.

Positron emission tomography (PET scan) Imaging technique that provides a picture of the living brain by tracing the chemical activity of various parts of the living brain. A radioactive chemical is injected into blood vessels that carry the chemical to the brain, and the active cells in the brain temporarily accumulate the chemical. A machine then passes X-ray beams through the head.

Postconventional morality Morality in which decisions are based on one's own abstract principles about right and wrong.

Postformal-thought stage In Piaget's approach, the stage at which people can think creatively and ask intriguing questions. People generally show this highly sophisticated level of thinking in their domain of expertise rather than in all areas.

Posttraumatic stress disorder (PTSD) Pattern of disordered reactions following a traumatic event. These reactions may include anxiety, irritability, inability to concentrate, and emotional numbness, as well as flashbacks to the traumatic event.

Practical significance In a research study, results having some important, practical implications for the real world.

Pragmatics Social aspects of language involving how people use language to communicate and to accomplish their social goals. Pragmatics includes listeners' background knowledge, conversational interactions, and politeness.

Preattentive processing In attention, the automatic registration of the features in a display of objects.

Preconventional morality Morality in which decisions are based on rules made by other people.

Prefrontal cortex Part of the cerebral cortex responsible for complex cognitive tasks, such as making plans, forming concepts, and inhibiting inappropriate actions.

Prejudice Negative attitude toward others because they belong to a particular group.

Premenstrual syndrome (PMS) Variety of symptoms that may occur during the week preceding menstruation, including headache, painful breasts, and a variety of psychological reactions such as depression, anxiety, and irritability.

Preoperational period One of Piaget's four major periods of human development, during which language develops. The child can now represent thought by using symbols and words, rather than simple physical actions.

Prepared childbirth Technique using relaxation and distraction to reduce perception of pain during childbirth.

Primacy effect Tendency for early information to be considered more important than later information.

Primary reinforcer Reinforcer that can satisfy a basic biological need, most likely food or water.

Proactive coping Taking steps in advance to prevent a potentially stressful event or to reduce its impact.

Proactive interference Phenomenon by which old memories work in a forward direction to interfere with new memories.

Problem-focused coping Method of coping with stress that includes taking direct action to solve problems as well as changing one's thoughts.

Problem solving Mental activity used when persons want to achieve a certain goal and the path to this goal is not immediately obvious.

Projection Defense mechanism that involves attributing your own unacceptable feelings to another person.

Projective tests Psychological tests that ask people to respond to a standard set of stimuli that are vague and ambiguous. These stimuli presumably evoke a person's feelings, needs, and personality characteristics. The two most common projective tests are the Rorschach Inkblot Test and the Thematic Apperception Test (TAT).

Prosocial behavior Action that benefits another person, including comforting, helping, sharing, rescuing, and cooperating. Also known as altruism.

Prosopagnosia (pro-soap-ag-*know*-zhia) A very specific kind of associative visual agnosia in which a person has difficulty recognizing human faces following brain damage.

Prototype Pertaining to concepts, the best example of a concept. People establish meaning by placing items in categories.

Prototype approach Pertaining to meaning, theory proposing that people decide whether an item belongs to a category by comparing that item with a prototype.

Psychiatrists Professionals who receive training in medicine, rather than psychology, with an orientation toward treating certain disorders with medication.

Psychoactive drugs Chemical substances that influence the brain, altering consciousness and producing psychological changes. Psychoactive drugs usually work via the neurotransmitters.

Psychoanalysis Therapy technique based on the psychoanalytic theory of Sigmund Freud; it attempts to resolve problems by examining childhood experiences and making

people aware of the conflicts buried in their unconscious.

Psychoanalytic approach Psychodynamic approach that refers specifically to Sigmund Freud's original theory.

Psychodynamic approach Approach that emphasizes childhood experience as determinant of adult personality and unconscious mental processes and conflict as influences on most human behavior.

Psychological disorders Disorders involving behavior that is (1) distressing, (2) maladaptive, and (3) different from the social norms.

Psychological test Objective, standardized measure of a sample of behavior.

Psychology Scientific study of behavior and mental processes.

Psychoneuroimmunology An interdisciplinary area that examines the relationship between the central nervous system and the immune system.

Psychophysics Area of psychology that examines the relationship between physical stimuli (such as sights or sounds) and our psychological reactions to those stimuli.

Psychotherapy Treatment of psychological disorders by a psychotherapist.

Puberty Period of development in which a young person becomes physically capable of sexual reproduction.

Punishment In operant conditioning, something negative that is added or something positive that is taken away following an inappropriate response. Punishment tends to decrease the probability of the response that it follows; however, it does not automatically increase the frequency of the appropriate behavior.

Pupil In the eye, the opening in the center of the iris.

Pursuit movement Eye movement used for tracking a moving object.

Quasi-experiment Research study resembling an experiment but lacking random assignment of participants to groups. Instead, researchers locate a situation in which groups already exist that differ substantially from each other.

Racism Bias against certain racial or ethnic groups; this bias can be revealed in stereotypes, prejudice, or discrimination.

Random assignment In an experiment, the process by which people are assigned to experimental groups using a system—such as a coin toss—ensuring that everybody has an equal chance of being assigned to any one group. If the number of participants is sufficiently large, then random assignment usually guarantees that the various groups will be reasonably similar with respect to important characteristics.

Random sample In a research study, a sample in which every member of the population has an equal chance of being selected. When a sample is random, it is more likely to be a representative sample, in which the characteristics of the sample are similar to the characteristics of the population.

Range In statistics, a measure of variability that is the difference between the highest and the lowest scores.

Rape Vaginal, oral, or anal penetration without the individual's consent.

Rational Emotive Behavior Therapy (REBT) Cognitive therapy developed by Albert Ellis that encourages people to examine their beliefs carefully and rationally, to make positive statements about themselves, and to solve problems effectively.

Reaction formation Defense mechanism that involves replacing an anxiety-producing feeling with its exact opposite, typically going overboard.

Reactive devaluation Barrier to international conflict resolution in which the mere act of offering a particular concession makes that offer less attractive to the recipient.

Recall Measure of explicit memory that asks a person to reproduce items that had been learned earlier.

Receptor cells In the eye, retinal cells that respond to light; the two kinds are cones and rods.

Reciprocal influences Principle stating that initial individual differences become even stronger because of three factors—personal/cognitive, behavior, and environment—all influencing each other.

Recognition Measure of explicit memory that asks a person to identify which items on a list had been learned earlier.

Recognition-by-components theory Theory stating that more complex patterns are recognized in terms of their parts, or components. The underlying assumption is that an object can be represented as an arrangement of simple three-dimensional shapes (geons).

Regression Defense mechanism that involves acting in ways characteristic of earlier life stages.

Rehearse In memory, the repetition of items to be remembered.

Reliability In testing, the consistency of a person's scores. This consistency is established by reexamining the test takers with the same test on two different occasions, or by some other method of measuring the stability of the scores.

REM sleep Rapid eye movement during sleep, associated with dreaming, in which delta waves disappear and neurons in the cerebral cortex become much more active.

Replications Studies in which a phenomenon is tested several times, often under different conditions.

Representative sample In a research study, a sample in which the characteristics of the sample are similar to the characteristics of the population.

Representativeness heuristic General strategy used when people decide whether the sample they are judging matches the appropriate prototype. For example, tossing a coin five times and getting five heads would violate the representativeness heuristic.

Repression Defense mechanism that involves pushing back unpleasant feelings and unacceptable thoughts into the unconscious.

Resistance phase Second phase of the general adaptation syndrome (response to stress) during which the body tries to cope with the stressor by releasing stress hormones. In addition, measures such as blood pressure, heart rate, respiration, and body temperature all increase.

Reticular formation That part of the brain running up from the hindbrain through to the midbrain with axons reaching upward into the cerebral cortex at the top of the brain. Important in attention and in sleep, as well as simple learning tasks.

Retina In the eye, the structure that absorbs light rays and converts them into patterns of action potentials that can be transmitted to the brain by the neurons.

Retinotopic arrangement Correspondence between the pattern of information on the retina (the sensory receptors inside the eye) and the pattern of information on part of the visual cortex.

Retrieval Pertaining to memory, the third stage of remembering in which we successfully locate the item and use it.

Retrieval failure Theory specifying that memory failures occur when the proper retrieval cues are not available.

Retroactive interference Phenomenon by which new memories work in a backward direction to interfere with old memories.

Rods Photoreceptors used for the perception of blacks, grays, and whites. When the lighting is poor, rods function better than cones.

Role Shared expectation about how someone in a group ought to behave.

Rorschach Inkblot Test Projective test in which people respond to a series of ambiguous inkblots, and the responses are analyzed according to characteristics such as recurring themes, number of responses, the region of the inkblot that attracts attention, and whether the nature of the response is common or unusual.

Ruminative responses Thoughts and behaviors that cause depressed people to focus their attention on their symptoms.

Saccadic movement (suh-*kaad*-dick) Rapid, jumpy movement of the eye from one location to the next, necessary to bring the fovea into position over the object we want to see clearly. Saccadic movements are used in reading.

Sample Individuals selected because they are representative of the population to be studied, with the intention of discovering something about the population from which the sample was drawn.

Schachter-Singer theory Theory of emotion stating that an emotion-arousing event causes physiological arousal; people examine the external environment to help interpret that event.

Schema (*skee*-muh) In observational learning, a generalized idea that captures the important components, but not every exact detail. Pertaining to memory and person perception, a generalized idea about objects, people, and events that are encountered frequently.

Schizophrenia Psychological disorder that involves severely disordered thoughts, although perceptual, emotional, social, and behavioral processes may also be disturbed. People with schizophrenia experience disorganized thought processes. In some cases, this disorganization is so extensive that individuals lose contact with reality.

Scholastic Assessment Test (SAT) A test designed specifically to measure aptitude for college work.

Scientific method Basis for psychology research, consisting of four basic steps: (1) identification of the research problem; (2) design and conducting of a study including gathering appropriate data; (3) examination of the data; (4) communication of the results.

Second language The bilingual speaker's non-native language.

Secondary reinforcer Reinforcer that does not satisfy a basic biological need but acquires its rewarding power by association with another established reinforcer.

Secondary trait In Allport's theory, a characteristic seen only in certain situations, such as "uncomfortable in large crowds" and "likes to drive sports cars."

Secure attachment Positive attachment experience in which an infant tends to use the caretaker as a secure base for exploration. A baby may wander away from the caregiver for a while to explore the surroundings, returning frequently; after separation from a caregiver, the baby actively seeks interaction.

Secure attachment style Adult love-relationship style in which the individual feels comfortable getting close to others and depending on them.

Selective attention Focusing attention on one of several simultaneous messages, ignoring everything else.

Self-actualization In Carl Rogers's person-centered approach, the nat-

ural, inborn tendency for humans to fulfill their true potential.

Self-concept Schema of thoughts and feelings about oneself as an individual.

Self-efficacy Person's belief in his or her ability to organize and perform actions required to reach desired goals.

Self-fulfilling prophecy Situation in which your expectations about someone leads him or her to act in ways that confirm your original expectation.

Self-reference effect In memory, the deepest, most effective way of processing stimuli which is in terms of our own experience.

Self-report Research method for assessing psychological processes in which participants report their own thoughts, emotions, behaviors, or intentions. Self-reports are commonly measured with a rating scale.

Self-statement modification Therapeutic technique in which people are encouraged to replace negative statements about themselves with more positive statements.

Sensation Immediate, basic experiences generated by simple stimuli.

Sensation seeking A trait in people who actively look for adventure, new experiences, and risky situations.

Sensitivity In psychophysics, the ability to detect a weak stimulus.

Sensorimotor period One of Piaget's four major periods of human development, in which the infant's major cognitive tasks include sensory activities (such as seeing and hearing) and motor activities (such as kicking, sucking, and reaching).

Sensory memory Storage system that records information from the senses with reasonable accuracy as the information first enters the memory. The capacity of sensory memory is relatively large, but each item fades extremely quickly—in less than two seconds.

Serial search Searching long-term memory by handling the characteristics one at a time.

Set point Mechanism that seems to keep people at roughly the same weight throughout their adult lives.

Sex chromosomes One of 23 pairs of chromosomes that determines whether someone is male or female. Females have a pair of sex chromo-

somes called X chromosomes (XX); males have one sex chromosome called X and one called Y (XY).

Sexism Bias toward people on the basis of their gender, which can be revealed in stereotypes, prejudice, and discrimination.

Sexual harassment Unwelcome sexual advance, request for sexual favors, or other verbal or physical conduct of a sexual nature.

Shape constancy Phenomenon in which an object's perceived shape stays the same, despite changes in its orientation toward the viewer.

Shaping In operant conditioning, the systematic reinforcement of gradual improvements toward the desired behavior.

Shift schedules Work schedules in which people work during the normal sleeping hours. As a consequence, these workers sleep fewer hours, and they wake up more often during sleep.

Short-term memory (STM) Memory that contains only the small amount of material we are currently using. Memories in STM are reasonably fragile; they can be lost from memory within about 30 seconds unless they are somehow repeated or rehearsed. Also known as working memory.

Sibling deidentification Process during late childhood whereby children often deliberately try *not* to be like their siblings.

Side effects Undesirable medical or psychological problems due to the use of medication.

Signal detection theory In contrast to the classical psychophysics approach, signal detection theory assesses both the observer's sensitivity (or ability to detect a weak stimulus) and the observer's criterion (or willingness to say, "I detect the stimulus," when it is not clear whether the stimulus has been presented). Expectations and prior knowledge influence the probability of the observer's recognition.

Single-cell recording technique Method for obtaining precise recordings of brain activity by inserting a microelectrode next to (or even into) a single neuron.

Situational attribution Type of attribution indicating that we believe that the specific situation—a force located outside the person—was responsible for the behavior. Situation attributions may involve the physical, social, or societal explanations for why an event occurred.

Size constancy Phenomenon in which an object's perceived size stays the same, even though the distance changes between the viewer and the object.

Sleep State during which the body is less active and people are less responsive to the environment; however, the neurons in the brain are active.

Sleep apnea Disorder involving frequent lapses of breathing during sleep. A person with sleep apnea may experience interrupted breathing more than 300 times each night. Each time, the individual wakes up briefly and then begins to breathe normally again.

Slip of the tongue Error in which sounds are rearranged between two or more different words.

Social class Socioeconomic status.

Social cognition How we think about other people and ourselves.

Social cognitive approach Approach to personality that emphasizes observational learning and the central importance of cognitive factors.

Social constructionist viewpoint With respect to gender, the argument that we actively organize and construct our view of the world and what is means to be female or male in our society. Our culture provides us with a body of knowledge, which operates like a set of lenses through which we try to make sense of the events the occur in the world.

Social facilitation Tendency to do better on easy tasks and worse on difficult tasks when another person is present.

Social learning Learning new behaviors by watching and imitating the behavior of others in a social situation. Also known as observational learning and modeling.

Social learning theory With respect to gender development, the theory explaining that girls learn to act "feminine" and boys learn to act "masculine" through two major mechanisms: (1) they receive rewards and punishments for their own behavior; and (2) they watch and imitate the behavior of others.

Social loafing Phenomenon in which each individual works less hard in a group than if he or she worked independently.

Social phobia Type of phobic disorder in which people are excessively afraid of social situations, because they are afraid they will do something embarrassing.

Social psychologists Psychologists who examine how our thoughts, feelings, and behaviors are influenced by other people.

Social psychology Approach to psychology focusing on the way that other people influence our thoughts, feelings, and behaviors.

Social role theory Theory of hypnosis, first proposed by William James and later developed by Theodore Barber, stressing that the hypnotized person simply acts out a social role consistent with the social situation.

Socialization The process by which children acquire the knowledge, values, skills, and behaviors that allow them to function effectively in adult society.

Sociocognitive perspective The perspective that the behavior of hypnotized individuals can be traced to their attempts to understand the social situation.

Sociocultural approach Approach that proposes that human behavior and mental processes are strongly influenced by social context, which includes factors such as culture, ethnic group, and gender. Pertaining to psychological disorders, an approach emphasizing that social and cultural factors (poverty, prejudice, unemployment, and so forth) are largely responsible for these disorders.

Socioeconomic status Social-class ranking based on factors such as educational attainment, income, occupation, and family prestige.

Sociology Scientific discipline that examines how groups and institutions function in society.

Somatic division In the nervous system, sensory neurons that transmit sensory information into the central nervous system, as well as motor neurons that carry motor commands out of the central nervous system to the muscles.

Somatosensory cortex The part of the brain that handles skin senses.

Sound Perception of successive air pressure changes.

Sound waves Tiny disturbances in air pressure that cause sound.

Spacing effect A rule about practice in which persons will recall more material if they distribute their practice throughout several study sessions. In contrast, persons will remember less material if they mass their learning into a single, uninterrupted session.

Spermarche (*sperm*-are-kee) During puberty, males' first experience with ejaculation (release of semen).

Spinal cord Column of neurons that runs from the base of the brain, down the center of the back, and is protected by a series of bones; one of the components of the central nervous system.

Spontaneous recovery In classical conditioning, the reappearance of the conditioned response after previous extinction.

Spontaneous remission Recovery from a psychological disorder, without any therapy.

Spreading activation According to network models, once the name of a concept is perceived, that particular location becomes activated and the activation spreads from that location to other concepts with which it is connected.

Stability-change question Do people maintain their personal characteristics as they mature from infants into adults (stability)? Alternatively, do these characteristics shift (change)? The stability-change question asks whether the individuals in a group maintain the same relative ranks on a particular characteristic as they grow older. There is some stability as infants mature into children.

Standard deviation Measure of variability; the extent to which scores differ from each other and deviate from the mean.

Standardization In testing, the process of determining norms on a group of people who have taken a test under uniform conditions.

Statistical significance In inferential statistics, the situation in which the findings are likely to be due to a real difference between two groups, rather than due to chance alone.

Stereotype Organized set of beliefs about the characteristics of a group of people. Similar to personal schemas, except that a schema applies to an individual person and a stereotype applies to a group.

Stereotype threat   A situational threat that may influence members of a group that is hampered by a negative stereotype such as "low academic ability."

Stimulants   Chemicals that increase central nervous system functioning by increasing the release of neurotransmitters such as dopamine in the cortex and the reticular activating system. Stimulants include caffeine, nicotine, the amphetamines, and cocaine.

Stimulus discrimination   Process whereby organisms learn to differentiate between similar stimuli.

Stimulus generalization   In classical conditioning, the tendency for similar stimuli other than the original conditioned stimulus to produce the conditioned response.

Storage   Pertaining to memory, the second stage of remembering in which we hold the information in memory for later use.

Stress   Negative emotional experience that occurs when demands on a person are greater than his or her response capabilities.

Stress-induced analgesia   Phenomenon in which psychological stress triggers the release of endorphins, making painful stimuli seem less intense.

Stress management training   Therapeutic technique that helps people prepare for difficult or unpleasant situations by anticipating problems and practicing methods of controlling stress (relaxation techniques, problem-solving methods, and developing helpful statements that can guide them through a crisis).

Stressor   Unpleasant situation that produces stress.

Stroke   Disorder in which a blood clot or some other obstruction reduces blood flow to a region of the brain.

Stroop effect   Phenomenon in which people take much longer to say the color of a stimulus when it is used to print an inappropriate color name, rather than appearing as a simple solid color.

Structural features   In problem solving, these are the underlying features that must be understood in order to solve the problem correctly.

Structuralism   Approach to psychology that examines the structure of the mind and the organization of the basic elements of sensations, feelings, and images.

Subjective norms   Our beliefs about what other people think we ought to do.

Subjective well-being   Person's evaluation of his or her life satisfaction.

Superego   In psychoanalytic theory, the component of the personality that includes individual personal conscience, ideals, and values. The superego acquires its principles from society, via the parents.

Surface features   In problem solving, these are the specific objects and terms used in the question.

Surface structure   Pertaining to sentence structure, the structure that is represented by the words which are actually spoken or written.

Survey method   Research method in which researchers select a large group of people and ask them questions about their behaviors or thoughts. Typically, the researchers also collect demographic information about the characteristics often used to classify people, such as gender, age, marital status, race, education, and income.

Sympathetic nervous system   Part of the autonomic nervous system that prepares the body for action through the secretion of epinephrine.

Synapse   In the nervous system, the location at which the axon of one neuron connects with the dendrite of a neighboring neuron.

Syntax   In grammar, the organizational rules for determining word order, sentencing organization, and relationships among words.

Systematic desensitization   Behaviorist approach to reducing fear or anxiety by exposing clients to increasingly anxiety-arousing stimuli while they are relaxed.

Tardive dyskinesia   Condition caused by side effects from using antipsychotic drugs, characterized by involuntary body movements and abnormal gait in walking.

Target effects   Improvement of the major symptoms of a disorder through the use of medication.

Taste   Perceptions created when a substance makes contact with the special receptors in the mouth.

Taste aversion   Development of an intense dislike for a food through classical conditioning.

Telegraphic speech   Characteristic of children's early sentences, that include nouns and verbs but leave out the extra words such as prepositions and articles that only serve grammatical functions.

Temperament   Individual differences in behavior that are present early in life and show stability as the individual matures.

Temporal lobes   Part of the cerebral cortex that is located on the sides of the head. The temporal lobes contain the auditory cortex, which processes information about sounds, speech, and music. Parts of the temporal lobes are also important in processing complex visual stimuli.

Teratogens   (*terr*-uh-tuh-jens) Substances in prenatal environment that may cause abnormalities.

Terminal buttons   In the nervous system, the knobs located at the far end of the axon.

Test-retest reliability   Method of measuring the reliability of a test in which the identical test is administered on two occasions, usually one day to several weeks apart. The test-retest reliability is high if each person's score is similar on the two tests.

Thalamus   Plays an important role in perception. Nearly all sensory information is processed by the thalamus on its route from the sensory receptors to the cerebral cortex and is organized and transformed there.

Thematic Apperception Test (TAT)   Projective test that consists of a series of ambiguous scenes, which the test taker is invited to describe, telling what is happening now, what happened in the past, and what will occur in the future.

Theory of misapplied constancy   Theory of illusions proposing that observers interpret certain cues for maintaining size constancy.

Thinking   Manipulation of mental representations to reach a conclusion.

Thought suppression   Intentional, conscious removal of a thought from consciousness.

Thyroid gland   Gland that regulates the body's metabolism through the production of a hormone.

Timbre (*tam*-burr) Sound quality of a tone.

Tip-of-the-nose phenomenon Ability to recognize that an odor is familiar, combined with the inability to identify its name.

Tip-of-the-tongue experience People's sensation of being confident that they know the word for which they are searching, yet cannot recall it.

Token economy Tool in behavior modification in which good behavior is quickly reinforced by a symbol or token; the tokens can then be accumulated and exchanged for a reinforcer.

Tolerance Condition in which the same amount of a psychoactive drug has a reduced effect.

Top-down processing In perception, processing that emphasizes the importance of the observers' concepts, expectations, and prior knowledge—the kinds of information stored at the top (or highest level) of perception.

Total time hypothesis Principle stating that the amount a person learns depends on the total amount of time he or she devotes to learning.

Trait Consistent tendency to have certain kinds of beliefs, desires, behaviors, and so forth.

Trait approach Approach to personality proposing that human personality is a combination of specific stable, internal personality characteristics, such as shyness or aggressiveness.

Transference In psychoanalysis, the process by which the client transfers a variety of positive and negative reactions associated with parents and other childhood authority figures, directing these feelings toward the therapist.

Triads Groups of three individuals.

Trichromatic theory Theory of color vision stating that the retina contains three kinds of cones, each sensitive to light from a different portion of the spectrum.

Twin studies Research that compares identical and fraternal twins.

Type A behavior pattern Personality type with such characteristics as ambitiousness, aggressiveness, competitiveness, and impatience. People with Type A behaviors speak rapidly and work quickly; they are also likely to respond to hassles with irritation and hostility.

Type B behavior pattern Personality type of people who are relaxed and easygoing and are seldom impatient or hostile.

Unconditional positive regard According to Carl Rogers, total, genuine love without special conditions or strings attached.

Unconditioned response In classical conditioning, an unlearned response to a stimulus.

Unconditioned stimulus In classical conditioning, the stimulus that elicits an unlearned response.

Unconscious In psychoanalytic theory, psychic processes—thoughts and desires—that are far below the level of conscious awareness.

Uninhibited children Children who approach strangers and unfamiliar objects or events without hesitation.

Validity In testing, a test's accuracy in measuring what it is supposed to measure.

Variability In statistics, the measures that indicate the extent to which the scores are spread out, that is, how much the scores differ from one another. The standard deviation and range are measures of variability.

Variable-interval schedule In operant learning, situations in which reinforcement is given for the first response made after a varying period of time has passed.

Variable-ratio schedule In operant learning, situations in which reinforcement is given after a varying number of responses have been made.

Vicarious punishment In observational learning, punishment of the learner that occurs when the model receives punishment.

Vicarious reinforcement In observational learning, reinforcement of the learner that occurs when the model receives reinforcement.

Vigilance tasks Tasks that require detecting and responding to a stimulus.

Visual acuity Ability to see precise details in a scene.

Visual cortex Outer part of the brain that is concerned with vision, located at the back of the brain just above the neck.

Visuo-spatial working memory In Alan Baddeley's model of working memory, the component that stores visual and spatial information.

Wavelength Distance between two peaks of light, which travel in waves. This distance is measured in nanometers (nm). Wavelength is a characteristic of light that helps to determine the hue or color of a visual stimulus.

Weber's law (*Vay*-bur) According to Weber's law, a weak or small stimulus does not require much change before a person notices that the stimulus has changed; a strong or large stimulus requires a proportionately greater change before a person notices that it has changed.

Wechsler scales (*Wex*-ler) A series of verbal and nonverbal (performance) questions used to measure intelligence.

Well-controlled study Experiment in which researchers use precautions, such as random assignment, to reduce confounding variables. With a well-controlled study, researchers can feel more confident about drawing cause-and-effect conclusions.

Wernicke's aphasia (*Ver*-nih-keez) A condition that produces speech that is too abundant, often lacking content, and in which there are serious difficulties understanding speech.

Whorfian hypothesis Hypothesis stating that the structure of language influences the structure of thought.

Win-lose approach Approach to conflict in which one party's win is balanced by the other party's loss. Most business competitive situations and competitive sports involve win-lose situations.

Win-win approach Approach to conflict in which both parties gain by cooperating. A win-win approach favors successful conflict resolution.

Withdrawal symptoms Undesirable effects of discontinued use of a psychoactive drug. These symptoms vary, depending upon the psychoactive drug, but may include nausea, intense depression, agitation, abdominal cramps, and muscle spasms.

Word-superiority effect In shape and pattern recognition, letters are perceived more accurately when they appear in words rather than in strings of unrelated letters or by themselves.

Working alliance   In psychotherapy, the therapist and the client form a working alliance in which the therapist's skills join together with the client's observational insights

to facilitate the counseling process.

Working memory   Short-term memory is sometimes called working memory because it handles the material we are currently working with, rather than items not attended to in sensory memory or items stored in long-term memory.

Zeitgebers   (*tsite*-gay-burs) Clues that help people adopt a 24-hour cycle, such as clocks and watches, the position of the sun, outdoor temperature, and mealtimes.

Zero correlation   In correlational research, a correlation that indicates no substantial relationship between the two variables.

REFERENCES

Aboud, F. (1988). *Children and prejudice.* Oxford, England: Blackwell.

Abraham, W. C., Corballis, M., & White, K. G. (1991). Introduction. In W. C. Abraham, M. Corballis, & K. G. White (Eds.), *Memory mechanisms: A tribute to G. V. Goddard* (pp. xv–xxii). Hillsdale, NJ: Erlbaum.

Abrams, R. A. (1994). The forces that move the eyes. *Current Directions in Psychological Science, 3,* 65–67.

Ackerman, D. (1990). *A natural history of the senses.* New York: Random House.

Ackerman, D. (1997, April). A slender thread: Crisis hotline counseling. *Harvard Mental Health Letter,* pp. 4–5.

Acocella, J. (1995, November 27). Cather and the academy. *New Yorker,* pp. 56–71.

Adams, P. R., & Adams, G. R. (1984). Mount Saint Helens's ashfall: Evidence for a disaster stress reaction. *American Psychologist, 39,* 252–260.

Adams, R. L., Parsons, O. A., Culbertson, J. L., & Nixon, S. J. (Eds.). (1996). *Neuropsychology for clinical practice: Etiology, assessment, and treatment of common neurological disorders.* Washington, DC: American Psychological Association.

Ader, R. (1995). The role of conditioning in pharmacotherapy. In A. Harrington (Ed.), *Placebo.* Cambridge, MA: Harvard University Press.

Ader, R., & Cohen, N. (1985). CNS-immune system interactions: Conditioning phenomena. *Behavioral and Brain Sciences, 8,* 379–394.

Ader, R., & Cohen, N. (1993). Psychoneuroimmunology: Conditioning and stress. *Annual Review of Psychology, 44,* 53–85.

Adler, J., & Hall, C. (1995, June 5). Surgery at 33,000 feet. *Newsweek,* p. 36.

Adler, N. E., & Coriell, M. (1997). Socioeconomic status and women's health. In S. J. Gallant, G. P. Keita, & R. Royak-Schaler (Eds.), *Health care for women: Psychological, social, and behavioral influences* (pp. 11–23). Washington, DC: American Psychological Association.

Adler, N. E., & Matthews, K. (1994). Health psychology: Why do some people get sick and some stay well? *Annual Review of Psychology, 45,* 229–259.

Adler, N. E., et al. (1994). Socioeconomic status and health. *American Psychologist, 49,* 15–24.

Adler, T. (1991a, July). Memory researcher wins Troland Award. *APA Monitor, 22* (7), p. 12.

Adler, T. (1991b, January). Seeing double? Controversial twins study is widely reported, debated. *APA Monitor,* pp. 1, 8.

Adler, T. (1991c, November). Therapy may best treat panic disorder. *APA Monitor,* p. 10.

Adler, T. (1993, September). Scientists have a clearer view of body's descent into sleep. *APA Monitor,* p. 21.

Aggleton, J. P. (Ed.). (1992). *The amygdala: Neurobiological aspects of emotion, memory, and mental dysfunction.* New York: Wiley.

Aging and the Canadian population. (1996). *About Canada.* [Brochure]. Sackville, New Brunswick: Center for Canadian Studies, Mount Allison University.

Agnati, L. F., Bjelke, B., & Fuxe, K. (1992, July–August). Volume transmission in the brain. *American Scientist, 80,* 362–373.

Aguirre, A., Jr., & Martinez, R. O. (1993). *Chicanos in higher education: Issues and dilemmas for the 21st century.* Washington, DC: George Washington University, School of Education and Human Development.

Aiken, L. R. (1989). *Assessment of personality.* Boston: Allyn & Bacon.

Aiken, L. R. (1995). *Aging: An introduction to gerontology.* Thousand Oaks, CA: Sage.

Ainsworth, M. D. S. (1989). Attachments beyond infancy. *American Psychologist, 44,* 709–716.

Ainsworth, M. D. S. (1990). Epilogue. In M. T. Greenberg, D. Cicchetti, & E. M. Cummings (Eds.), *Attachment in the preschool years: Theory, research, and intervention* (pp. 463–487). Chicago: University of Chicago Press.

Aitken, R. J. (1995). The complexities of conception. *Science, 269,* 39–40.

Ajzen, I. (1991). The theory of planned behavior. *Organizational Behavior and Human Decision Processes, 50,* 179–211.

Ajzen, I. (1996). The social psychology of decision making. In E. T. Higgins & A. W. Kruglanski (Eds.), *Social psychology: Handbook of basic principles* (pp. 279–325). New York: Guilford Press.

Albee, G. W. (1987). Powerlessness, politics, and prevention. The community mental health approach. In F. Hurrelmann, F. X. Kaufmann, & F. Lösel (Eds.), *Social intervention: Potential and constraints* (pp. 37–52). Berlin: de Gruyter.

Albee, G. W. (1992). Genes don't hurt people: People hurt people [Review of the book *Social causes of psychological distress*]. *Contemporary Psychology, 37,* 16–17.

Albert, M. S. (1992). Alzheimer's disease: Cognitive aspects. In L. R. Squire (Ed.), *Encyclopedia of learning and memory* (pp. 20–22). New York: Macmillan.

Aldag, R. J., & Fuller, S. R. (1993). Beyond fiasco: A reappraisal of the groupthink phenomenon and a new model of group decision processes. *Psychological Bulletin, 113,* 533–552.

Aldhous, P. (1992). Twin studies go back to the womb. *Science, 257,* 165.

Aldwin, C. M., Sutton, K. J., & Lachman, M. (1996). The development of coping resources in adulthood. *Journal of Personality, 64,* 837–871.

Alexander, L. L., & LaRosa, J. H. (1994). *New dimensions in women's health.* Boston: Jones & Bartlett.

Alexander, M. P. (1997). Aphasia: Clinical and anatomic aspects. In T. E. Feinberg & M. J. Farah (Eds.), *Behavioral neurology and neuropsychology* (pp. 133–149). New York: McGraw-Hill.

Al-Issa, A. (Ed.). (1995). *Handbook of culture and mental illness: An international perspective.* Madison, CT: International Universities Press.

Allgeier, E. R. (1987). Coercive versus consensual sexual interactions. In V. P. Makosky (Ed.), *The G. Stanley Hall lecture series* (Vol. 7, pp. 7–63). Washington, DC: American Psychological Association.

Allison, J., Blatt, S. J., & Zimet, C. N. (1988). *The Interpretation of psychological tests.* Washington, DC: Hemisphere.

Allodi, F. (1990). Refugees as victims of torture and trauma. In W. H. Holtzman & T. H. Bornemann (Eds.), *Mental health of immigrants and refugees* (pp. 245–252). Austin, TX: University of Texas Press.

Alloy, L. B., Acocella, J., & Bootzin, R. R. (1996). *Abnormal psychology* (7th ed.). New York: McGraw-Hill.

Allport, G. W. (1937). *Personality: A psychological interpretation.* New York: Holt.

Allport, G. W. (1961). *Pattern and growth in personality.* New York: Holt.

Allport, G. W. (1967). Gordon W. Allport. In E. G. Boring & G. Lindzey (Eds.), *A history of psychology in autobiography* (Vol. 5). New York: Appleton-Century-Crofts.

Almagor, U. (1990). Some thoughts on common scents. *Journal for the Theory of Social Behaviour, 20,* 181–195.

Alper, J. (1993). EEG + MRI: A sum greater than the parts. *Science, 261,* 559.

Alpert, J. L. (1996). Professional practice, psychological science, and the recovered memory debate. In K. Pezdek & W. P. Banks (Eds.), *The recovered memory/false memory debate* (pp. 325–340). San Diego, CA: Academic Press.

Alvarez, C. (1987). El hilo que nos une: Becoming a Puerto Rican woman. In R. Benmayor, A. Juarbe, C. Alvarez, & B. Vázquez (Eds.), *Stories to live by: Continuity and change in three generations of Puerto Rican women* (pp. 24–42). New York: Centro de Estudios Puertoriqueños (Hunter College).

Amabile, T. M. (1983). *The social psychology of creativity.* New York: Springer-Verlag.

Amabile, T. M. (1990). Within you, without you: The social psychology of creativity, and beyond. In M. A. Runco & R. S. Albert (Eds.), *Theories of creativity* (pp. 61–91). Newbury Park, CA: Sage.

Amabile, T. M. (1994). The atmosphere of pure work: Creativity in research and development. In W. R. Shadish & S. Fuller (Eds.), *The social psychology of science* (pp. 316–328). New York: Guilford Press.

Amabile, T. M. (1996). *Creativity in context.* Boulder, CO: Westview Press.

Ambady, N., & Rosenthal, R. (1992). Thin slices of expressive behavior as predictors of interpersonal consequences: A meta-analysis. *Psychological Bulletin, 111,* 256–274.

Ambady, N., & Rosenthal, R. (1993). Half a minute: Predicting teacher evaluations from thin slices of nonverbal behavior and physical attractiveness. *Journal of Personality and Social Psychology, 64,* 431–441.

American Academy of Pediatrics. (1991). Marijuana: A continuing concern for pediatricians. *Pediatrics, 88,* 1070–1072.

American Psychiatric Association. (1994a). *Diagnostic and statistical manual of mental disorders* (4th ed.). Washington, DC: Author.

American Psychiatric Association. (1994b). *Ethnic minority elderly.* Washington, DC: Author.

American Psychiatric Association. (1995). *Practice guideline for treatment of patients with bipolar disorder.* Washington, DC: Author.

American Psychological Association. (1973). *Ethical principles in the conduct of research with human participants.* Washington, DC: Author.

American Psychological Association. (1990). Ethical principles of psychologists. *American Psychologist, 45,* 390–395.

American Psychological Association. (1992). Ethical principles of psychologists and code of conduct. *American Psychologist, 47,* 1597–1611.

American Psychological Association. (1994). *Publication manual of the American Psychological Association* (4th ed.). Washington, DC: American Psychological Association.

American Psychological Association. (1996). Interim report of the working group on investigation of memories of childhood abuse. In K. Pezdek & W. P. Banks (Eds.), *The recovered memory/false memory debate* (pp. 371–372). San Diego, CA: Academic Press.

Amsler, T. (1991, Fall–Winter). The fourth "R": School conflict resolution comes of age. *Peace Reporter,* p. 7.

Anastasi, A. (1988). *Psychological testing* (6th ed.). New York: Macmillan.

Anch, A. M., Browman, C. P., Mitler, M. M., & Walsh, J. K. (1988). *Sleep: A scientific perspective.* Englewood Cliffs, NJ: Prentice Hall.

Andersen, S. M., Spielman, L. A., & Bargh, J. A. (1992). Future-event schemas and certainty about the future: Automaticity in depressives' future-event predictions. *Journal of Personality and Social Psychology, 63,* 711–723.

Anderson, C. A., & Bushman, B. J. (1997). External validity of "trivial" experiments: The case of laboratory aggression. *Review of General Psychology, 1,* 19–41.

Anderson, C. A., Krull, D. S., & Weiner, B. (1996). Explanations: Processes and consequences. In E. T. Higgins & A. W. Kruglanski (Eds.), *Social psychology: Handbook of basic principles* (pp. 271–296). New York: Guilford Press.

Anderson, C. M., & Stewart, S. (1994). *Flying solo: Single women in midlife.* New York: Norton.

Anderson, J. R. (1990). *The adaptive character of thought.* Hillsdale, NJ: Erlbaum.

Anderson, J. R. (1993). Problem solving and learning. *American Psychologist, 48,* 35–44.

Anderson, R. (1992). *The aftermath of stroke: The experience of patients and their families.* Cambridge: Cambridge University Press.

Anderson, S. J., & Conway, M. A. (1993). Investigating the structure of autobiographical memories. *Journal of Experimental Psychology: Learning, Memory, and Cognition, 19,* 1178–1196.

Andreasen, N. C., et al. (1994). Thalamic abnormalities in schizophrenia visualized through magnetic resonance image averaging. *Science, 266,* 294–297.

Andreasen, N. C., & Black, D. W. (1995). *Introductory textbook of psychiatry* (2nd ed.). Washington, DC: American Psychiatric Press.

Angoff, W. H., & Johnson, E. G. (1988). *A study of the differential impact of curriculum on aptitude test scores.* Princeton, NJ: Educational Testing Service.

Antill, J. K. (1983). Sex role complementarity versus similarity in married couples. *Journal of Personality and Social Psychology, 45,* 145–155.

Antony, M. M., Brown, T. A., & Barlow, D. H. (1992). Current perspectives on panic and panic disorder. *Current Directions in Psychological Science, 1,* 79–82.

Antrobus, J. (1990). The neurocognition of sleep mentation: Rapid eye movements, visual imagery, and dreaming. In R. R. Bootzin, J. F. Kihlstrom, & D. L. Schacter (Eds.), *Sleep and cognition* (pp. 1–24). Washington, DC: American Psychological Association.

Antrobus, J. (1991). Dreaming: Cognitive processes during cortical activation and high afferent thresholds. *Psychological Review, 98,* 96–121.

Antrobus, J., & Bertini, M. (1992). Introduction. In J. S. Antrobus & M. Bertini (Eds.), *The neuropsychology of sleep and dreaming* (pp. 1–14). Hillsdale, NJ: Erlbaum.

Aponte, H. J. (1994). *Bread and spirit: Therapy with the new poor.* New York: Norton.

Argyle, M. (1988). *Bodily communication* (2nd ed.). London: Methuen.

Aries, E. (1996). *Men and women in interaction: Reconsidering the differences.* New York: Oxford University Press.

Arnow, B. (1996). Cognitive-behavioral therapy for bulimia nervosa. In J. Werne (Ed.), *Treating eating disorders* (pp. 101–141). San Francisco: Jossey-Bass.

Aron, A., & Corne, S. (1994). Introduction. In A. Aron & S. Corne (Eds.), *Writings for a liberation psychology* (pp. 1–11). Cambridge, MA: Harvard University Press.

Aronson, E. (1988). *The social animal* (5th ed.). New York: Freeman.

Aronson, E. (1991). How to change behavior. In R. C. Curtis & G. Stricker (Eds.), *How people change: Inside and outside therapy* (pp. 101–112). New York: Plenum.

Aronson, E. (1995). *The social animal* (7th ed.). New York: Freeman.

Aronson, E., et al. (1978). *The jigsaw classroom.* Beverly Hills, CA: Sage.

Aronson, E., Wilson, T. D., & Akert, R. M. (1994). *Social psychology: The heart and the mind.* New York: HarperCollins.

Asch, S. E. (1952). *Social psychology.* Englewood Cliffs, NJ: Prentice Hall.

Asch, S. E. (1955). Opinions and social pressures. *Scientific American, 193* (5), 31–35.

Asch, S. E. (1956). Studies of independence and conformity: I. A minority of one against a unanimous majority. *Psychological Monographs, 70* (Whole No. 416).

Aslin, R. N., & Smith, L. B. (1988). Perceptual development. *Annual Review of Psychology, 39,* 435–473.

Aspinwall, L. G., & Taylor, S. E. (1997). A stitch in time: Self-regulation and proactive coping. *Psychological Bulletin, 121,* 417–436.

Asso, D. (1983). *The real menstrual cycle.* Chichester, England: Wiley.

Atkinson, D. R., Morten, G., & Sue, D. W. (1993). *Counseling American minorities* (4th ed.). Madison, WI: Brown & Benchmark.

Atkinson, J. W., & Raynor, J. O. (Eds.). (1974). *Motivation and achievement.* Washington, DC: Winston.

Atkinson, R. C., & Shiffrin, R. M. (1968). Human memory: A proposed system and its control processes. In K. W. Spence & J. T. Spence (Eds.), *The psychology of learning and motivation: Advances in research and theory* (Vol. 2). New York: Academic Press.

Azar, B. (1995a, December). Mental disabilities and the brain-gene link. *APA Monitor,* p. 18.

Azar, B. (1996, September). Students need a broader outlook on careers. *APA Monitor,* p. 35.

Azuma, S. D., & Chasnoff, I. J. (1993). Outcome of children prenatally exposed to cocaine and other drugs: A path analysis of three-year data. *Pediatrics, 92,* 396–402.

Babkoff, H., Caspy, T., Mikulincer, M., & Sing, H. C. (1991). Monotonic and rhythmic influences: A challenge for sleep deprivation research. *Psychological Bulletin, 109,* 411–428.

Baddeley, A. D. (1982). *Your memory: A user's guide.* New York: Macmillan.

Baddeley, A. D. (1986). *Working memory.* Oxford: Oxford University Press.

Baddeley, A. D. (1990). *Human memory: Theory and practice.* Boston: Allyn & Bacon.

Baddeley, A. D. (1992). Working memory. *Science, 255,* 556–559.

Baddeley, A. D. (1993). *Your memory: A user's guide.* London: Prion.

Baddeley, A. D., & Hitch, G. J. (1974). Working memory. In G. Bower (Ed.), *Recent advances in learning and memory* (Vol. 8, pp. 47–90). New York: Academic Press.

Baddeley, A. D., Thomson, N., & Buchanan, M. (1975). Word length and the structure of short-term memory. *Journal of Verbal Learning and Verbal Behavior, 14,* 575–589.

Bader, E. J. (1996, Spring). Manage my moods. *On the Issues,* pp. 51–53.

Badets, J. (1993, Summer). Canada's immigrants: Recent trends. *Canadian Social Trends,* pp. 8–11.

Bahrick, H. P., Bahrick, L. E., Bahrick, A. S., & Bahrick, P. E. (1993). Maintenance of foreign language vocabulary and the spacing effect. *Psychological Science, 4,* 316–321.

Bahrick, H. P., et al. (1994). Fifty years of language maintenance and language dominance in bilingual Hispanic immigrants. *Journal of Experimental Psychology: General, 123,* 264–283.

Bailey, J. M., Pillard, R. C., Neale, M. C., & Agyei, Y. (1993). Heritable factors influence sexual orientation in women. *Archives of General Psychiatry, 50,* 217–223.

Baillargeon, R. (1986). Representing the existence and the location of hidden objects: Object permanence in 6- and 8-month-old infants. *Cognition, 23,* 21–41.

Baillargeon, R. (1992). The object concept revisited. In C. E. Cranrud (Ed.), *Visual perception and cognition in infancy.* Carnegie-Mellon Symposia on Cognition (Vol. 23). Hillsdale, NJ: Erlbaum.

Baillargeon, R. (1994). How do infants learn about the physical world? *Current Directions in Psychological Science, 3,* 133–140.

Baillargeon, R., & DeVos, J. (1991). Object permanence in young infants: Further evidence. *Child Development, 62,* 1227–1246.

Baillargeon, R., Spelke, E. S., & Wasserman, S. (1985). Object permanence in five-month-olds. *Cognition, 20,* 191–208.

Bair, F. E. (1993). *Alzheimer's, stroke, and 29 other neurological disorders sourcebook.* Detroit: Omnigraphics.

Baker, F. M. (1994). Issues in the psychiatric care of African American elders. In American Psychiatric Association (Ed.), *Ethnic minority elderly* (pp. 21–62). Washington, DC: American Psychiatric Association.

Baker, L. C. (1996). Differences in earnings between male and female physicians. *New England Journal of Medicine, 334,* 960–964.

Bales, J. (1988, December). Vincennes: Findings could have helped avert tragedy, scientists tell Hill panel. *APA Monitor,* pp. 10–11.

Ball, K., & Rebok, G. (1994). Evaluating the driving ability of older adults. *The Journal of Applied Gerontology, 13,* 20–38.

Balota, D. A., Pollatsek, A., & Rayner, K. (1985). The interaction of contextual constraints and parafoveal visual information in reading. *Cognitive Psychology, 17,* 364–390.

Baltes, P. B. (1995). Life review: Reminiscence. In G. L. Maddox (Ed.), *The encyclopedia of aging* (2nd ed., pp. 563–564). New York: Springer.

Baltes, P. B., & Kliegl, R. (1989). On the dynamics between growth and decline in the aging of intelligence and memory. In K. Poeck (Ed.), *Proceedings of the 13th World Congress of Neurology.* Heidelberg: Springer.

Banaji, M. R., & Crowder, R. G. (1989). The bankruptcy of everyday memory. *American Psychologist, 44,* 1185–1193.

Bandura, A. (1963, October 22). What TV violence can do to your child. *Look,* pp. 46–52.

Bandura, A. (1986). *Social foundations of thought and action: A social cognitive theory.* Englewood Cliffs, NJ: Prentice Hall.

Bandura, A. (1989). Social cognitive theory. *Annals of Child Development, 6,* 1–60.

Bandura, A. (1991). Social cognitive theory of self-regulation. *Organizational Behavior and Human Decision Processes, 50,* 248–287.

Bandura, A. (1992a). Observational learning. In L. R. Squire (Ed.), *Encyclopedia of learning and memory* (pp. 492–495). New York: Macmillan.

Bandura, A. (1992b). Self-efficacy: Thought control of action. In R. Schwarzer (Ed.), *Self-efficacy: Thought control of action* (pp. 3–38). Washington, DC: Hemisphere.

Bandura, A. (1994). Social cognitive theory of mass communication. In J. Bryant & D. Zillmann (Eds.), *Media effects: Advances in theory and research* (pp. 61–90). Hillsdale, NJ: Erlbaum.

Bandura, A. (1997). *Self-efficacy: The exercise of control.* New York: Freeman.

Bandura, A., & Jourden, F. J. (1991). Self-regulatory mechanisms governing the impact of social comparison on complex decision making. *Journal of Personality and Social Psychology, 60,* 941–951.

Bandura, A., Ross, D., & Ross, S. A. (1961). Transmission of aggression through imitation of aggressive models. *Journal of Abnormal and Social Psychology, 63,* 575–582.

Bandura, A., Ross, D., & Ross, S. A. (1963). Imitation of film-mediated aggressive models. *Journal of Abnormal and Social Psychology, 66,* 311–318.

Banks, S. M., & Kerns, R. D. (1996). Explaining high rates of depression in chronic pain: A diathesis-stress framework. *Psychological Bulletin, 119,* 95–110.

Banks, W. P., & Krajicek, D. (1991). Perception. *Annual Review of Psychology, 42,* 305–331.

Barber, T. X. (1979). Suggested ("hypnotic") behavior: The trance paradigm versus an alternative paradigm. In E. Fromm & R. E. Shor (Eds.), *Hypnosis: Developments in research and new perspectives* (pp. 217–274). Chicago: Aldine.

Barber, T. X. (1986). Realities of stage hypnosis. In B. Zilbergeld, M. G. Edelstien, & D. L. Araoz (Eds.), *Hypnosis: Questions and answers* (pp. 22–27). New York: Norton.

Barclay, C. R. (1986). Schematization of autobiographical memory. In D. C. Rubin (Ed.), *Autobiographical memory* (pp. 82–99). New York: Cambridge University Press.

Barclay, C. R. (1993). Remembering ourselves. In G. M. Davies & R. H. Logie (Eds.), *Memory in everyday life* (pp. 285–323). Amsterdam: North-Holland.

Barefoot, J. C., Dahlstrom, W. G., & Williams, R. B., Jr. (1983). Hostility, CHD incidence, and total mortality. A 25-year follow-up study of 255 physicians. *Psychosomatic Medicine, 45,* 59–63.

Bargh, J. A. (1994). The four horsemen of automaticity: Awareness, intention, efficiency, and control in social cognition. In R. S. Wyer, Jr., & T. K. Srull (Eds.), *Handbook of social cognition* (2nd ed., Vol. 1, pp. 1–40). Hillsdale, NJ: Erlbaum.

Bargh, J. A., Chaiken, S., Raymond, P., & Hymes, C. (1996). The automatic evaluation effect: Unconditional automatic attitude activation with a pronunciation task. *Journal of Experimental Social Psychology, 32,* 104–128.

Barinaga, M. (1991a). How the nose knows: Olfactory receptor cloned. *Science, 252,* 209–210.

Barinaga, M. (1991b). How long is the human life-span? *Science, 254,* 936–938.

Barinaga, M. (1994a). Watching the brain remake itself. *Science, 266,* 1475–1476.

Barinaga, M. (1994b). Old protein provides new clue to nerve regeneration puzzle. *Science, 265,* 1800–1801.

Barinaga, M. (1995a). Dendrites shed their dull image. *Science, 268,* 200–201.

Barinaga, M. (1995b). Remapping the motor cortex. *Science, 268,* 1696–1698.

Barinaga, M. (1995c). New Alzheimer's gene found. *Science, 268,* 1845–1846.

Barinaga, M. (1996a). The cerebellum: Movement coordinator or much more? *Science, 272,* 482–483.

Barinaga, M. (1996b). Obesity: Leptin receptor weighs in. *Science, 271,* 29.

Barker, L. M. (1994). *Learning and behavior: A psychobiological perspective.* New York: Macmillan.

Barkow, J. H., Cosmides, L., & Tooby, J. (Eds.). (1992). *The adapted mind: Evolutionary psychology and the generation of culture.* New York: Oxford University Press.

Barlow, D. H. (1988). *Anxiety and its disorders.* New York: Guilford Press.

Barnett, R. C., Marshall, N. L., & Singer, J. D. (1992). Job experiences over time, multiple roles, and women's mental health: A longitudinal study. *Journal of Personality and Social Psychology, 62,* 634–644.

Barney, D. D. (1994). Use of mental health services by American Indian and Alaska Native elders. *American Indian and Alaska Native Mental Health Research, 5,* 1014.

Baron, J. (1991). Some thinking is irrational. *Behavioral and Brain Sciences, 14,* 486–487.

Baron, R. A., & Richardson, D. R. (1994). *Human aggression* (2nd ed.). New York: Plenum.

Baron, R. S., Kerr, N. L., & Miller, N. (1993). *Group process, group decision, group action.* Pacific Grove, CA: Brooks/Cole.

Barrett, G. V., & Depinet, R. L. (1991). A reconsideration of testing for competence rather than for intelligence. *American Psychologist, 46,* 1012–1024.

Barsalou, L. W. (1989). Intra-concept similarity and its implications for inter-concept similarity. In S. Vosniadou & A. Ortony (Eds.), *Similarity and analogical reasoning* (pp. 76–121). New York: Cambridge University Press.

Barsalou, L. W. (1993). Flexibility, structure, and linguistic vagary in concepts: Manifestations of a compositional system of perceptual symbols. In A. F. Collins, S. E. Gathercole, M. A. Conway, & P. E. Morris (Eds.), *Theories of memory* (pp. 29–101). Hove, England: Erlbaum.

Bartoshuk, L. M. (1991a). Taste, smell, and pleasure. In R. C. Bolles (Ed.), *The hedonics of taste* (pp. 15–28). Hillsdale, NJ: Erlbaum.

Bartoshuk, L. M. (1991b). Sensory factors in eating behavior. *Bulletin of the Psychonomic Society, 29,* 250–255.

Bartoshuk, L. M., & Beauchamp, G. K. (1994). Chemical senses. *Annual Review of Psychology, 45,* 419–449.

Barzansky, B., Jonas, H. S., & Etzel, S. I. (1996). Educational programs in US medical schools, 1995–1996. *JAMA, 276,* 714–719.

Basher, S. K. (1991). Personal communication.

Bashore, T. R., & Rapp, P. E. (1993). Are there alternatives to traditional polygraph procedures? *Psychological Bulletin, 113,* 3–22.

Bass, S. A. (Ed.). (1995). *Older and active: How Americans over 55 are contributing to society.* New Haven, CT: Yale University Press.

Bates, E., Dale, P. S., & Thal, D. (1995). Individual differences and their implications for theories of language development. In P. Fletcher & B. MacWhinney (Eds.), *The handbook of child language* (pp. 96–151). Cambridge, MA: Blackwell.

Bates, E., Thal, D., & Janowsky, J. S. (1992). Early language development and its neural correlates. In I. Rapin & S. Segalowitz (Eds.), *Handbook of neuropsychology* (Vol. 6). Amsterdam: Elsevier.

Bates, J. E. (1994). Introduction. In J. E. Bates &T. D. Wachs (Eds.), *Temperament: Individual differences at the interface of biology and behavior* (pp. 1–14). Washington, DC: American Psychological Association.

Batson, C. D. (1987). Prosocial motivation: Is it ever truly altruistic? *Advances in Experimental Social Psychology, 20,* 65–122.

Batson, C. D. (1995). Prosocial motivation: Why do we help others? In A. Tesser (Ed.), *Advanced social psychology* (pp. 332–381). New York: McGraw-Hill.

Batson, C. D., et al. (1981). Is empathic emotion a source of altruistic motivation? *Journal of Personality and Social Psychology, 40,* 290–302.

Batson, C. D., et al. (1991). Empathic joy and the empathy-altruism hypothesis. *Journal of Personality and Social Psychology, 61,* 413–426.

Batson, C. D., & Weeks, J. L. (1996). Mood effects of unsuccessful helping: Another test of the empathy-altruism hypothesis. *Personality and Social Psychology Bulletin, 22,* 148–157.

Baum, A., & Fleming, I. (1993). Implications of psychological research on stress and technological accidents. *American Psychologist, 48,* 665–672.

Baum, A. S., & Burnes, D. W. (1993). *A nation in denial: The truth of homelessness.* Boulder, CO: Westview Press.

Baumeister, R. F., & Leary, M. R. (1995). The need to belong: Desire for interpersonal attachments as a fundamental human motivation. *Psychological Bulletin, 117,* 497–529.

Baumrind, D. (1964). Some thoughts on ethics of research: After reading Milgram's "Behavioral Study of Obedience." *American Psychologist, 19,* 421–423.

Baumrind, D. (1971). Current patterns of parental authority. *Developmental Psychology Monographs, 4* (1, Pt. 2).

Baur, S. (1991). *The dinosaur man: Tales of madness and enchantment from the back ward.* New York: HarperCollins.

Bayne-Smith, M. (1996a). Health and women of color: A contextual overview. In M. Bayne-Smith (Ed.), *Race, gender, and health* (pp. 1–42). Thousand Oaks, CA: Sage.

Bayne-Smith, M. (Ed.). (1996b). *Race, gender, and health.* Thousand Oaks, CA: Sage.

Beal, C. R. (1994). *Boys and girls: The development of gender roles.* New York: McGraw-Hill.

Beall, A. E. (1993). A social constructionist view of gender. In A. E. Beall & R. J. Sternberg (Eds.), *The psychology of gender* (pp. 127–147). New York: Guilford Press.

Beatty, W. W. (1996). Multiple sclerosis. In R. L. Adams, O. A. Parsons, J. L. Culbertson, & S. J. Nixon (Eds.), *Neuropsychology for clinical practice: Etiology, assessment, and treatment of common neurological disorders* (pp. 225–242). Washington, DC: American Psychological Association.

Bechara, A., et al. (1995). Double dissociation of conditioning and declarative knowledge relative to the amygdala and hippocampus in humans. *Science, 269,* 1115–1118.

Beck, A. T. (1976). *Cognitive therapy and the emotional disorders.* New York: International Universities Press.

Beck, A. T. (1991). Cognitive therapy: A 30-year retrospective. *American Psychologist, 46,* 368–375.

Beck, A. T. (1995). Cognitive therapy: Past, present, and future. In M. J. Mahoney (Ed.), *Cognitive and constructive psychotherapies* (pp. 29–40). New York: Springer.

Beck, A. T., Emery, G., & Greenberg, R. L. (1985). *Anxiety disorders and phobias: A cognitive perspective.* New York: Basic Books.

Beck, A. T., Steer, R. A., & Brown, G. K. (1996). *Beck Depression Inventory-II.* San Antonio, TX: Psychological Corporation.

Bédard, J., & Chi, M. T. H. (1992). Expertise. *Current Directions in Psychological Science, 1,* 135–139.

Bee, H. L. (1987). *The journey of adulthood.* New York: Macmillan.

Bee, H. L. (1992). *The journey of adulthood* (2nd ed.). New York: Macmillan.

Beers, S. R. (1992). Cognitive effects of mild head injury in children and adolescents. *Neuropsychology Review, 3,* 281–320.

Beers, S. R., Goldstein, G., & Katz, L. J. (1994). Neuropsychological differences between college students with learning disabilities and those with mild head injury. *Journal of Learning Disabilities, 27,* 315–324.

Begley, S. (1996, October 14). Born happy? *Newsweek,* pp. 78–80.

Beilin, H. (1992). Piaget's enduring contribution to developmental psychology. *Development Psychology, 28,* 191–204.

Belansky, E. S., & Boggiano, A. K. (1994). Predicting helping behaviors: The role of gender and instrumental/expressive self-schemata. *Sex Roles, 30,* 647–661.

Bell, P. A., Greene, T. C., Fisher, J. D., & Baum, A. (1996). *Environmental psychology* (4th ed.). Fort Worth, TX: Harcourt Brace.

Bell, R. (1980). *Changing bodies, changing lives.* New York: Random House.

Bellack, A. S., Hersen, M., & Kazdin, A. E. (Eds.). (1990). *International handbook of behavior modification and therapy* (2nd ed.). New York: Plenum.

Bellezza, F. S. (1996). Mnemonic method to enhance storage and retrieval. In E. Bjork & R. Bjork (Eds.), *Handbook of perception and cognition* (Vol. 10). San Diego, CA: Academic Press.

Bem, D. J. (1996). Exotic becomes erotic: A developmental theory of sexual orientation. *Psychological Review, 103,* 320–335.

Bem, S. L. (1985). Androgyny and gender schema theory: A conceptual and empirical integration. In T. B. Sonderegger (Ed.), *Nebraska Symposium on Motivation, 1984: Psychology and gender* (pp. 179–226). Lincoln: University of Nebraska Press.

Bem, S. L. (1993). *The lenses of gender: Transforming the debate on sexual inequality.* New Haven, CT: Yale University Press.

Bem, S. L. (1995). Dismantling gender polarization and compulsory heterosexuality: Should we turn the volume down or up? *Journal of Sex Research, 32,* 329–334.

Benes, F. M. (1996, November). Altered neural circuits in schizophrenia. *Harvard Mental Health Letter,* pp. 5–7.

Benioff, L. (1995). What is it like to have schizophrenia? In S. Vinogradov (Ed.), *Treating schizophrenia* (pp. 81–107). San Francisco: Jossey-Bass.

Benjamin, J., et al. (1996). Population and familial association between the D4 domanine receptor gene and measures of novelty seeking. *Nature Genetics, 12,* 81–84.

Benjamin, L. T., Jr., et al. (1992). Wundt's American doctoral students. *American Psychologist, 47,* 123–131.

Benmayor, R. (1987). "For every story there is another story which stands before it." In R. Benmayor, A. Juarbe, C. Alvarez, & B. Vázquez (Eds.), *Stories to live by: Continuity and change in three generations of Puerto Rican women* (pp. 1–13). New York: Centro de Estudios Puertorriqueños (Hunter College).

Benson, D. F. (1994). *The neurology of thinking.* New York: Oxford University Press.

Berglund, B., & Engen, T. (1993). A comparison of self-adaptation and cross-adaptation to odorants presented singly and in mixtures. *Perception, 22,* 103–111.

Berman, A. L., & Jobes, D. A. (1991). *Adolescent suicide assessment and intervention.* Washington, DC: American Psychological Association.

Bernal, M. E., & Castro, F. G. (1994). Are clinical psychologists prepared for service and research with ethnic minorities? *American Psychologist, 49,* 797–805.

Berns, R. M. (1997). *Child, family, school, community: Socialization and support* (4th ed.). Fort Worth, TX: Harcourt Brace.

Bernstein, I. L. (1978). Learned taste aversions in children receiving chemotherapy. *Science, 200,* 1302–1303.

Bernstein, I. L. (1991). Development of taste preferences. In R. C. Bolles (Ed.), *Development of taste preferences* (pp. 143–157). Hillsdale, NJ: Erlbaum.

Bernstein, I. L., & Meachum, C. L. (1990). Food aversion learning: Its impact on appetite. In E. D. Capaldi & T. L. Powley (Eds.), *Taste, experience, and feeding* (pp. 170–178). Washington, DC: American Psychological Association.

Berntson, G. G., Cacioppo, J. T., Quigley, K. S., & Fabro, V. T. (1994). Autonomic space and psychophysiological response. *Psychophysiology, 31,* 44–61.

Berry, J. W., Poortinga, Y. H., Segall, M. H., & Dasen, P. R. (1992). *Cross-cultural psychology: Research and applications.* New York: Cambridge University Press.

Berscheid, E. (1993). Foreword. In A. E. Beall & R. J. Sternberg (Eds.), *The psychology of gender* (pp. vii–xvii). New York: Guilford Press.

Bertenthal, B. I. (1996). Origins and early development of perception, action, and representation. *Annual Review of Psychology, 47,* 431–459.

Bertenthal, B. I., & Pinto, J. (1994). Global processing of biological motions. *Psychological Science, 5,* 221–225.

Betancourt, H., & López, S. R. (1993). The study of culture, ethnicity, and race in American psychology. *American Psychologist, 48,* 629–637.

Bettelheim, B. (1977). *The uses of enchantment: The meaning and importance of fairy tales.* New York: Vintage Books.

Betz, N. E. (1992). Career counseling for women in the sciences and engineering. In W. B. Walsh & S. H. Osipow (Eds.), *Career counseling for women.* Hillsdale, NJ: Erlbaum.

Betz, N. E. (1994a). Career counseling for women in the sciences and engineering. In W. B. Walsh & S. H. Osipow (Eds.), *Career counseling for women* (pp. 237–261). Hillsdale, NJ: Erlbaum.

Betz, N. E. (1994b). Basic issues and concepts in career counseling for women. In W. B. Walsh & S. H. Osipow (Eds.), *Career counseling for women* (pp. 1–41). Hillsdale, NJ: Erlbaum.

Betz, N. E., & Fitzgerald, L. F. (1987). *The career psychology of women.* New York: Academic Press.

Betz, N. E., & Fitzgerald, L. F. (1993). Individuality and diversity: Theory and research in counseling psychology. *Annual Review of Psychology, 44,* 343–381.

Bialystok, E. (1988). Levels of bilingualism and levels of linguistic awareness. *Developmental Psychology, 24,* 560–567.

Bialystok, E. (1991). Metalinguistic dimensions of bilingual language proficiency. In E. Bialystok (Ed.), *Language processing in bilingual children* (pp. 113–140). Cambridge: Cambridge University Press.

Bialystok, E. (1992). Selective attention in cognitive processing: The bilingual edge. In R. J. Harris (Ed.), *Cognitive processing in bilinguals* (pp. 501–513). Amsterdam: Elsevier.

Bialystok, E., & Hakuta, K. (1994). *In other words: The science and psychology of second-language acquisition.* New York: Basic Books.

Bickerton, D. (1995). *Language and human behavior.* Seattle: University of Washington Press.

Biederman, I. (1987). Recognition-by-components: A theory of human image understanding. *Psychological Review, 94,* 115–147.

Biederman, I. (1990). Higher-level vision. In E. N. Osherson, S. M. Kosslyn, & J. M. Hollerbach (Eds.), *An invitation to cognitive science* (Vol. 2, pp. 41–72). Cambridge, MA: MIT Press.

Biederman, I., Hilton, H. J., & Hummel, J. E. (1991). Pattern goodness and pattern recognition. InG. R. Lockhead & J. R. Pomerantz (Eds.), *The perception of structure* (pp. 73–95). Washington, DC: American Psychological Association.

Bierhoff, H. (1989). *Person perception and attribution.* Marburg, Germany: Springer-Verlag.

Biernat, M., & Wortman, C. B. (1991). Sharing of home responsibilities between professionally employed women and their husbands. *Journal of Personality and Social Psychology, 60,* 844–860.

Bigler, R. S. (1995). The role of classification skill in moderating environmental influences on children's gender stereotyping: A study of the functional use of gender in the classroom. *Child Development, 66,* 1072–1087.

Bilton, M., & Sim, K. (1992). *Four hours in My Lai.* New York: Penguin.

Bilyk, S. (1992). Personal communication.

Birch, J. (1993). *Diagnosis of defective colour vision.* Oxford: Oxford University Press.

Birman, D. (1994). Acculturation and human diversity in a multicultural society. In E. J. Trickett, R. J. Watts, & D. Birman (Eds.), *Human diversity: Perspectives on people in context* (pp. 261–284). San Francisco: Jossey-Bass.

Birnbaum, M. H., Anderson, C. J., & Hynan, L. G. (1990). Theories of bias in probability judgment. In J. P. Caverni, J. M. Fabre, & M. Gonzalez (Eds.), *Cognitive biases* (pp. 477–498). Amsterdam: Elsevier.

Birren, J. E., & Schaie, K. W. (Eds.). (1996). *Handbook of the psychology of aging* (4th ed.). San Diego, CA: Academic Press.

Bischoping, K. (1993). Gender differences in conversational topics, 1922–1990. *Sex Roles, 28,* 1–18.

Bishop, E. G., Dickson, A. L., & Allen, M. T. (1990). Psychometric intelligence and performance on selective reminding. *Clinical Neuropsychologist, 4,* 141–150.

Bjork, D. W. (1993). *B. F. Skinner: A life.* New York: Basic Books.

Bjork, R. A., & Richardson-Klavehn, A. (1987). On the puzzling relationship between environmental context and human memory. In C. Izawa (Ed.), *Current issues in cognitive processes* (pp. 313–344). Hillsdale, NJ: Erlbaum.

Blackburn, C. (1988, April). Matters of taste. *Piedmont Airlines,* pp. 24–27.

Blanchard, F. A., Lilly, T., & Vaughn, L. A. (1991). Reducing the expression of racial prejudice. *Psychological Science, 2,* 101–105.

Blanck, P. D. (Ed.). (1993). *Interpersonal expectations: Theory, research, and applications.* New York: Cambridge University Press.

Blass, T. (1991). Understanding behavior in the Milgram obedience experiment: The role of personality, situations, and their interactions. *Journal of Personality and Social Psychology, 60,* 398–413.

Blass, T. (1996). Experimental invention and controversy: The life and work of Stanley Milgram. *General Psychologist, 32,* 47–55.

Blieszner, R., & Adams, R. G. (1992). *Adult friendship.* Newbury Park, CA: Sage.

Bliss, T. V. P., & Lømo, T. (1973). Long-lasting potentiation of synaptic transmission in the dentate area of the anaesthetized rabbit following stimulation of the perforant path. *Journal of Physiology, 232,* 331–356.

Block, J. (1995). A contrarian view of the five-factor approach to personality description. *Psychological Bulletin, 117,* 187–215.

Blum, D. (1994). *The monkey wars.* New York: Oxford University Press.

Blum, J. S., Chow, K. L., & Pribram, K. H. (1950). A behavioral analysis of the organization of the parieto-temporo-preoccipital cortex. *Journal of Comparative Neurology, 93,* 53–100.

Blumberg, H. H. (1996). Cooperation, competition, and conflict resolution. In A. P. Hare, H. H. Blumberg, M. F. Davies, & M. V. Kent (Eds.), *Small groups: An introduction* (pp. 149–159). Westport, CT: Praeger.

Blumenthal, A. L. (1975). A reappraisal of Wilhelm Wundt. *American Psychologist, 30,* 1081–1088.

Blumstein, P. W., & Schwartz, P. (1991). Money and ideology: Their impact on power and the division of household labor. In R. L. Blumberg (Ed.), *Gender, family, and economy: The triple overlap* (pp. 261–268). Newbury Park, CA: Sage.

Blumstein, S. E. (1995). The neurobiology of language. In J. L. Miller & P. D. Eimas (Eds.), *Speech, language, and communication* (pp. 339–370). San Diego, CA: Academic Press.

Bock, J. K. (1987). Co-ordinating words and syntax in speech plans. In A. W. Ellis (Ed.), *Progress in the psychology of language* (Vol. 3, pp. 337–390). London: Erlbaum.

Bock, K. (1995). Sentence production: From mind to mouth. In J. L. Miller & P. D. Eimas (Eds.), *Speech, language, and communication* (pp. 181–216). San Diego, CA: Academic Press.

Boesch-Achermann, H., & Boesch, C. (1993). Tool use in wild chimpanzees: New light from dark forests. *Current Directions in Psychological Science, 2,* 18–21.

Bohannon, J. N., III. (1993). Theoretical approaches to language acquisition. In J. B. Gleason (Ed.), *The development of language* (pp. 239–297). New York: Macmillan.

Bond, M. P. (1995). The development and properties of the Defense Style Questionnaire. In H. P. Conte & R. Plutchik (Eds.), *Ego defenses: Theory and measurement* (pp. 202–220). New York: Wiley.

Bond, R., & Smith, P. B. (1996). Culture and conformity: A meta-analysis of studies using Asch's (1952b, 1956) line judgment task. *Psychological Bulletin, 119,* 111–137.

Boneau, C. A. (1992). Observations on psychology's past and future. *American Psychologist, 47,* 1586–1596.

Bonnet, M. H., & Arand, D. A. (1994). Impact of the level of physiological arousal on estimates of sleep latency. In R. D. Ogilvie & J. R. Harsh (Eds.), *Sleep onset: Normal and abnormal processes* (pp. 127–139). Washington, DC: American Psychological Association.

Booth, D. A. (1991). Learned ingestive motivation and the pleasures of the palate. In R. C. Bolles (Ed.), *The hedonics of taste)* (pp. 29–58). Hillsdale, NJ: Erlbaum.

Bornstein, M. H. (1992). Perception across the life span. In M. H. Bornstein & M. E. Lamb (Eds.), *Development psychology: An advanced textbook* (3rd ed.). Hillsdale, NJ: Erlbaum.

Bornstein, M. H. (Ed.). (1995). *Handbook of parenting.* Mahwah, NJ: Erlbaum.

Bornstein, M. H., et al. (1992). Functional analysis of the contents of maternal speech to infants of 5 and 13 months in four cultures: Argentina, France, Japan, and the United States. *Developmental Psychology, 28,* 593–603.

Bornstein, R. F. (1989). Exposure and affect: Overview and meta-analysis of research, 1968–1987. *Psychological Bulletin, 106,* 265–289.

Bornstein, R. F., Kale, A. R., & Cornell, K. R. (1990). Boredom as a limiting condition on the mere exposure effect. *Journal of Personality and Social Psychology, 58,* 791–800.

Botman, H. I., & Crovitz, H. F. (1989–1990). Dream reports and autobiographical memory. *Imagination, Cognition and Personality, 9,* 213–224.

Bouchard, C., et al. (1990). The response to long-term overfeeding in identical twins. *New England Journal of Medicine, 322,* 1477–1487.

Boulton, M. G. (1983). *On being a mother.* London: Tavistock.

Bouton, M. E. (1994a). Conditioning, remembering, and forgetting. *Journal of Experimental Psychology: Animal Behavior Processes, 20,* 219–231.

Bouton, M. E. (1994b). Context, ambiguity, and classical conditioning. *Current Directions in Psychological Science, 3,* 49–53.

Bowden, C. L. (1995). Treatment of bipolar disorders. In A. F. Schatzberg & C. B. Nemeroff (Eds.), *The American Psychiatric Press textbook of psychopharmacology* (pp. 603–614). Washington, DC: American Psychiatric Association.

Bower, G. H. (1990). Awareness, the unconscious, and repression: An experimental psychologist's perspective. In J. L. Singer (Ed.), *Repression and dissociation* (pp. 209–230). Chicago: University of Chicago.

Bower, G. H., Clark, M. C., Lesgold, A. M., & Winzenz, D. (1969). Hierarchical retrieval schemes in recall of categorized word lists. *Journal of Verbal Learning and Verbal Behavior, 8,* 323–343.

Bower, G. H., & Winzenz, G. (1970). Comparison of associative learning strategies. *Psychonomic Science, 20,* 119–120.

Bowers, W. A. (1991). Psychosocial treatment for simple phobia, obsessive-compulsive disorder, post-traumatic stress disorder, and social phobia. In W. Coryell & G. Winokur (Eds.), *The clinical management of anxiety disorders* (pp. 28–40). New York: Oxford University Press.

Bowman, P. J., & Howard, C. (1985). Race-related socialization, motivation, and academic achievement: A study of black youths in three-generation families. *Journal of the American Academy of Child Psychiatry, 24,* 134–141.

Boyes, M. C., & Walker, L. J. (1988). Implications of cultural diversity for the universality claims of Kohlberg's theory of moral reasoning. *Human Development, 31,* 44–59.

Boykin, A. W. (1986). The triple quandary and the schooling of Afro-American children. In U. Neisser (Ed.), *The school achievement of minority children* (pp. 57–92). Hillsdale, NJ: Erlbaum.

Brabeck, M. M. (1996). The moral self, values, and circles of belonging. In K. F. Wyche & F. J. Crosby (Eds.), *Women's ethnicities: Journeys through psychology* (pp. 145–165). Boulder, CO: Westview Press.

Brabeck, M. M., et al. (1997). Feminist theory and psychological practice. In N. Johnson & J. Worell (Eds.), *Feminist visions: New directions for education and practice.* Washington, DC: American Psychological Association.

Bradbury, T. N., Beach, S. R. H., Fincham, F. D., & Nelson, G. M. (1996). Attributions and behavior in functional and dysfunctional marriages. *Journal of Consulting and Clinical Psychology, 64,* 569–576.

Bradshaw, J. L., & Mattingley, J. B. (1995). *Clinical neuropsychology: Behavioral and brain science.* San Diego, CA: Academic Press.

Brainard, D. H., Wandell, B. A., & Chichilnisky, E. J. (1993). Color constancy: From physics to appearance. *Current Directions in Psychological Science, 2,* 165–170.

Brainerd, C. J. (1996). Piaget: A centennial celebration. *Psychological Science, 7,* 191–195

Brain Imaging and Psychiatry—Part I. (1997, January). *Harvard Mental Health Letter, 13,* 1–4.

Brake, M. (1994, March 14). Needed: A license to drink. *Newsweek,* 11.

Brannon, L., & Feist, J. (1992). *Health psychology: An introduction to behavior and health* (2nd ed.). Belmont, CA: Wadsworth.

Bransford, J. D., & Franks, J. J. (1971). Abstraction of linguistic ideas. *Cognitive Psychology, 2,* 331–350.

Brayfield, A. A. (1992). Employment resources and housework in Canada. *Journal of Marriage and the Family, 54,* 19–30.

Brehm, S. S. (1992). *Intimate relationships* (2nd ed.). New York: McGraw-Hill.

Brehm, S. S., & Kassin, S. M. (1996). *Social psychology* (3rd ed.). Boston: Houghton Mifflin.

Breland, K., & Breland, M. (1961). The misbehavior of organisms. *American Psychologist, 16,* 681–684.

Bretherton, I. (1992). Attachment and bonding. In V. B. Van Hasselt & M. Hersen (Eds.), *Handbook of social development: A lifespan perspective* (pp. 133–155). New York: Plenum.

Brewer, M. B., & Lui, L. (1984). Categorization of the elderly by the elderly: Effects of perceiver's category membership. *Personality and Social Psychology Bulletin, 10,* 585–595.

Brewer, R. D., et al. (1994). The risk of dying in alcohol-related automobile crashes among habitual drunk drivers. *New England Journal of Medicine, 331,* 513–539.

Brewer, W. F. (1992). The theoretical and empirical status of the flashbulb memory hypothesis. In E. Winograd & U. Neisser (Eds.), *Affect and accuracy in recall: Studies of "flashbulb" memories* (pp. 274–305). New York: Cambridge University Press.

Brewer, W. F., & Treyens, J. C. (1981). Role of schemata in memory for places. *Cognitive Psychology, 13,* 207–230.

Brewin, C. R. (1996). Theoretical foundations of cognitive-behavior therapy for anxiety and depression. *Annual Review of Psychology, 47,* 33–57.

Brewin, C. R., Andrews, B., & Gotlib, I. A. (1993). Psychopathology and early experience: A reappraisal of retrospective reports. *Psychological Bulletin, 113,* 82–98.

Bridgeman, B., & Wendler, C. (1991). Gender differences in predictors of college mathematics performance and in college mathematics course grades. *Journal of Educational Psychology, 83,* 275–289.

Bridges, J. S. (1991). Perceptions of date and stranger rape: A difference in sex role expectations and rape-supportive beliefs. *Sex Roles, 24,* 291–307.

Briere, J., & Conte, J. (1993). Self-reported amnesia for abuse in adults molested as children. *Journal of Traumatic Stress, 6,* 21–31.

Brinkman, S. D. (1995). Psychological theory about Alzheimer's disease [Review of the book *Neuropsychology of Alzheimer's disease and other dementias*]. *Contemporary Psychology, 40,* 681–682.

Brislin, R. (1993). *Understanding culture's influence on behavior.* Fort Worth: Harcourt Brace Jovanovich.

Broberg, D. J., & Bernstein, I. L. (1987). Candy as a scapegoat in the prevention of food aversions in children receiving chemotherapy. *Cancer, 60,* 2344–2347.

Broca, P. (1861). Remarques sur la siège de la faculté du langage articulé, suivees d'une observation d'aphémie (perte de la parole). *Bulletin de la Societe Anatomique (Paris), 36,* 330–357.

Brock, T. C., & Brannon, L. A. (1994). Milgram's last call [Review of the book *The individual in a social world*]. *Contemporary Psychology, 39,* 258–259.

Brody, L. R., & Hall, J. A. (1993). Gender and emotion. In M. Lewis & J. M. Haviland (Eds.), *Handbook of emotions* (pp. 447–460). New York: Guilford Press.

Brody, N. (1992). *Intelligence* (2nd ed.). San Diego, CA: Academic Press.

Brokenleg, M., & Middleton, D. (1995). Native Americans: Adapting, yet retaining. In K. P. Monteiro (Ed.), *Ethnicity and psychology: African-, Asian-, Latino- and Native-American psychologies.* Dubuque, IA: Kendall/Hunt.

Bronfenbrenner, U. (1961). The mirror image in Soviet-American relations: A social psychologist's report. *Journal of Social Issues, 17,* 45–46.

Bronfenbrenner, U., & Ceci, S. J. (1994). Nature-nurture reconceptualized in developmental perspective: A bioecological model. *Psychological Review, 101,* 568–586.

Bronfenbrenner, U., et al. (1996). *The state of Americans.* New York: Free Press.

Bronstein, P. A., & Quina, K. (1988). Perspectives on gender balance and cultural diversity in the teaching of psychology. In P. A. Bronstein & K. Quina (Eds.), *Teaching a psychology of people: Resources for gender and sociocultural awareness* (pp. 3–11). Washington, DC: American Psychological Association.

Brooke, O. G., et al. (1989). Effects on birth weight of smoking, alcohol, caffeine, socioeconomic factors, and psychosocial stress. *British Medical Journal, 298,* 795–801.

Brooks, C. I. (1987). Superiority of women in statistics achievement. *Teaching of Psychology, 14,* 45.

Brooks, G. R. (1997, Spring). Our voice can make a difference. *Society for the Psychological Study of Men and Masculinity Bulletin,* pp. 1–3.

Brooks-Gunn, J., & Reiter, E. O. (1990). The role of pubertal processes. In S. Shirley Feldman & G. R. Elliott (Eds.), *At the threshold: The developing adolescent* (pp. 16–53). Cambridge, MA: Harvard University Press.

Brown, A. S. (1991). A review of the tip-of-the-tongue experience. *Psychological Bulletin, 109,* 204–223.

Brown, D. (1996, December 9–15). The marijuana riddle. *Washington Post National Weekly Edition,* p. 35.

Brown, D. E. (1991). *Human universals.* Philadelphia: Temple University Press.

Brown, G. G., & Bornstein, R. A. (1991). Anatomic imaging methods for neurobehavioral studies. In R. A. Bornstein & G. G. Brown (Eds.), *Neurobehavioral aspects of cerebrovascular diseases* (pp. 83–108). New York: Oxford University Press.

Brown, H. D., et al. (1994). Can patients with obsessive-compulsive disorder discriminate between percepts and mental images? A signal detection analysis. *Journal of Abnormal Psychology, 103,* 445–454.

Brown, L. S. (1995). Cultural diversity in feminist therapy: Theory and practice. In H. Landrine (Ed.), *Bringing cultural diversity to feminist psychology* (pp. 143–161). Washington, DC: American Psychological Association.

Brown, L. S. (1996). On the construction of truth and falsity: Whose memory, whose history. In K. Pezdek & W. P. Banks (Eds.), *The recovered memory/false memory debate* (pp. 341–353). San Diego, CA: Academic Press.

Brown, O. G. (1994). *Debunking the myth: Stories of African-American University Students.* Bloomington, IN: Phi Delta Kappa Educational Foundation.

Brown, P. (1991). *The hypnotic brain: Hypnotherapy and social communication.* New Haven: Yale University Press.

Brown, P., & Levinson, S. C. (1987). *Politeness: Some universals of language usage.* Cambridge: Cambridge University Press.

Brown, R., & Kulik, J. (1977). Flashbulb memories. *Cognition, 5,* 73–99.

Brown, R., & McNeill, D. (1966). The "tip of the tongue" phenomenon. *Journal of Verbal Learning and Verbal Behavior, 5,* 325–377.

Browne, A. (1993). Violence against women by male partners: Prevalence, outcomes, and policy implications. *American Psychologist, 48,* 1077–1087.

Brownell, K. D., & Rodin, J. (1994). The dieting maelstrom: Is it possible and advisable to lose weight? *American Psychologist, 49,* 781–791.

Brownell, K. D., & Wadden, T. A. (1992). Etiology and treatment of obesity: Understanding a serious, prevalent, and refractory disorder. *Journal of Consulting and Clinical Psychology, 60,* 505–517.

Brownmiller, S. (1975). *Against our will: Men, women, and rape.* New York: Bantam.

Bruce, V., & Green, P. (1990). *Visual perception: Physiology, psychology, and ecology* (2nd ed.). Hove, England: Erlbaum.

Bruch, H. (1978). *The golden cage: The enigma of anorexia nervosa.* Cambridge, MA: Harvard University Press.

Brush, S. G. (1991). Women in science and engineering. *American Scientist, 79,* 404–419.

Bryant, J., & Zillmann, D. (Eds.). (1994). *Media effects: Advances in theory and research.* Hillsdale, NJ: Erlbaum.

Buck, L., & Axel, R. (1991). A novel multigene family may encode odorant receptors: A molecular basis for odor recognition. *Cell, 65,* 175–187.

Buckley, K. W. (1989). *Mechanical man: John Broadus Watson and the beginnings of behaviorism.* New York: Guilford Press.

Buckley, P. F., & Meltzer, H. Y. (1995). Treatment of schizophrenia. In A. F. Schatzberg & C. B. Nemeroff (Eds.), *The*

American Psychiatric Press textbook of psychopharmacology (pp. 615–639). Washington, DC: American Psychiatric Association.

Buckman, R. (1992). *"I don't know what to say" . . . How to help and support someone who is dying.* New York: Vintage Books.

Buehler, R., Griffin, D., & Ross, M. (1994). Exploring the "planning fallacy." Why people underestimate their task completion times. *Journal of Personality and Social Psychology, 67,* 366–381.

Bunker, B. B., & Rubin, J. Z. (1995). Introduction: Conflict, cooperation and justice. In B. B. Bunker et al. (Eds.), *Conflict, cooperation and justice* (pp. 1–9). San Francisco: Jossey-Bass.

Burciaga, J. A. (1993). *Drink culture: Chicanismo.* Santa Barbara, CA: Capra Press.

Burden-Patmon, D. (1989, December). Stand and deliver: Achieving against the odds. *Wheelock Bulletin,* pp. 2, 15.

Bureau of the Census. (1997). *Statistical abstract of the United States 1997* (117th ed.). Austin, TX: Hoover's Business Press.

Burgard, D., & Lyons, P. (1994). Alternatives in obesity treatment: Focusing on health for fat women. In P. Fallon, M. A. Katzman, & S. C. Wooley (Eds.), *Feminist perspectives on eating disorders* (pp. 212–230). New York: Guilford Press.

Burger, J. M. (1993). *Personality* (3rd ed.). Pacific Grove, CA: Brooks/Cole.

Burgess, A. W., & Holmstrom, L. L. (1980). Rape typology and the coping behavior of rape victims. In S. L. McCombie (Ed.), *The rape crisis intervention handbook* (pp. 27–40). New York: Plenum.

Burgoon, M. (1990). Language and social influence. In H. Giles & W. P. Robinson (Eds.), *Handbook of language and social psychology* (pp. 51–72). Chichester, England: Wiley.

Burleson, B. R. (1994). Comforting messages: Significance, approaches, and effects. In B. Burleson, T. Albrecht, & I. Sarason (Eds.), *Communication of social support: Messages, interactions, relationships, and community* (pp. 3–28). Thousand Oaks, CA: Sage.

Burstow, B. (1992). *Radical feminist therapy: Working in the context of violence.* Newbury Park, CA: Sage.

Burt, D. B., Zembar, M. J., & Niederehe, G. (1995). Depression and memory impairment: A meta-analysis of the association, its pattern, and specificity. *Psychological Bulletin, 117,* 285–305.

Bushman, B. J., & Cooper, H. M. (1990). Effects of alcohol on human aggression: An integrative research review. *Psychological Bulletin, 107,* 341–354.

Buss, A. H. (1989). Personality as traits. *American Psychologist, 44,* 1378–1388.

Buss, D. M. (1985, January–February). Human mate selection. *American Scientist,* pp. 47–51.

Buss, D. M. (1994). *The evolution of desire: Strategies of human mating.* New York: Basic Books.

Buss, D. M. (1995a). Evolutionary psychology: A new paradigm for psychological science. *Psychological Inquiry, 6,* 1–30.

Buss, D. M. (1995b). Psychological sex differences: Origins through sexual selection. *American Psychologist, 50,* 164–168.

Buss, D. M., & Barnes, M. (1986). Preferences in human mate selection. *Journal of Personality and Social Psychology, 50,* 559–570.

Butcher, J. N., et al. (1989). *Minnesota Multiphasic Personality Inventory (MMPI-2). Manual for administration and scoring.* Minneapolis: University of Minnesota Press.

Butcher, J. N., et al. (1990). *Development and use of the MMPI-2 content scales.* Minneapolis: University of Minnesota Press.

Butcher, J. N., & Rouse, S. V. (1996). Personality: Individual differences and clinical assessment. *Annual Review of Psychology, 47,* 87–111.

Butler, D. (1992). *The musician's guide to perception and cognition.* New York: Macmillan.

Butler, R. N. (1995). Ageism. In G. L. Maddox (Ed.), *The encyclopedia of aging* (2nd ed., pp. 35–36). New York: Springer.

Button, C. M., & Collier, D. R. (1991, June). *A comparison of people's concepts of love and romantic love.* Paper presented at the Canadian Psychological Association Conference, Calgary, Alberta.

Buysse, D. J., & Nofzinger, E. A. (1994). Sleep in depression: Longitudinal perspectives. *Review of Psychiatry, 13,* 651–675.

Byne, W. (1995). Science and belief: Psychobiological research on sexual orientation. *Journal of Homosexuality, 28,* 303–344.

Byne, W., & Parsons, B. (1993). Human sexual orientation. *Archives of General Psychiatry, 50,* 228–239.

Cabanac, M. (1996). In search of the science of consciousness [Review of the book *Consciousness in philosophy and cognitive neuroscience*]. *Contemporary Psychology, 41,* 166–167.

Cadoret, R. J., et al. (1995). Genetic-environmental interaction in the genesis of aggressivity and conduct disorders. *Archives of General Psychiatry, 52,* 916–924.

Cage, M. C. (1994, October 12). Spanish, sí! *The Chronicle of Higher Education,* pp. A15, A17.

Cain, W. S. (1988). Olfaction. In R. C. Atkinson, R. J. Herrnstein, G. Lindzey, & R. D. Luce (Eds.), *Stevens' handbook of experimental psychology* (2nd ed., Vol. 1, pp. 409–459). New York: Wiley.

Calhoun, K. S., & Atkeson, B. M. (1991). *Treatment of rape victims: Facilitating psychosocial adjustment.* Elmsford, NY: Pergamon.

Calvin, W. H. (1994, October). The emergence of intelligence. *Scientific American,* pp. 101–107.

Cameron, D., McAlinden, F., & O'Leary, K. (1993). Lakoff in context: The social and linguistic functions of tag questions. In S. Jackson (Ed.), *Women's studies: Essential readings* (pp. 421–426). New York: New York University Press.

Campbell, S. M., Peplau, L. A., & DeBro, S. C. (1992). Women, men, and condoms: Attitudes and experiences of heterosexual college students. *Psychology of Women Quarterly, 16,* 273–288.

Canadian Psychological Association. (1991). *Canadian code of ethics for psychologists.* Old Chelsea, Québec: Author.

Candland, D. K. (1993). *Feral children and clever animals.* New York: Oxford University Press.

Canetto, S. S. (1994). Gender issues in the treatment of suicidal individuals. In A. A. Leenaars, J. T. Maltsberger, &

R. A. Neimeyer (Eds.), *Treatment of suicidal people* (pp. 115–126). Washington, DC: Taylor & Francis.

Canetto, S. S., Kaminski, P. L., & Felicio, D. M. (1995). Typical and optimal aging in women and men: Is there a double standard? *International Journal of Aging and Human Development, 40,* 187–207.

Canetto, S. S., & Lester, D. (1995). *Women and suicidal behavior.* New York: Springer.

Cann, A. (1993). Evaluation expectations and the gender schema: Is failed inconsistency better? *Sex Roles, 28,* 677–678.

Cannon, J. T. (1996). *The psychology of pain.* Paper presented at the Northeastern Conference for Teachers of Psychology, Ithaca, NY.

Canter, M. B., Bennett, B. E., Jones, S. E., & Nagy, T. F. (1994). *Ethics for psychologists: A commentary on the APA Ethics Code.* Washington, DC: American Psychological Association.

Caplan, P. J., & Caplan, J. B. (1994). *Thinking critically about research on sex and gender.* New York: HarperCollins.

Caramazza, A., Yenni-Komshian, G., Zurif, E., & Carbone, E. (1973). The acquisition of a new phonological contrast: The case of stop consonants in French-English bilinguals. *Journal of the Acoustical Society of America, 54,* 421–428.

Cardon, L., et al. (1994). Quantitative trait locus for reading disability on Chromosome 6. *Science, 266,* 276–279.

Cargan, L., & Melko, M. (1985). Being single on Noah's ark. In L. Cargan (Ed.), *Marriage and family: Coping with change.* Belmont, CA: Wadsworth.

Carling, P. J. (1995). *Return to community.* New York: Guilford Press.

Carlo, G., et al. (1991). The altruistic personality: In what contexts is it apparent? *Journal of Personality and Social Psychology, 61,* 450–458.

Carlson, E. R. (1995). Evaluating the credibility of sources: A missing link in the teaching of critical thinking. *Teaching of Psychology, 22,* 39–41.

Carlson, N. R. (1994). *Physiology of behavior* (5th ed.). Boston: Allyn & Bacon.

Carnevale, P. J., & Pruitt, D. G. (1992). Negotiation and mediation. *Annual Review of Psychology, 43,* 531–582.

Carney, J. (1989, January 16). Can a driver be too old? *Time,* p. 28.

Carpenter, W. T., Jr., & Buchanan, R. W. (1994). Schizophrenia. *New England Journal of Medicine, 330,* 681–690.

Carpenter, W. T., Jr., & Strauss, J. S. (1991). The prediction of outcome in schizophrenia IV: Eleven-year follow-up of the Washington IPSS cohort. *Journal of Nervous and Mental Disease, 179,* 517–525.

Carroll, D. W. (1994). *Psychology of language* (2nd ed.). Pacific Grove, CA: Brooks/Cole.

Carroll, J. B. (1992). Cognitive abilities: The state of the art. *Psychological Science, 3,* 266–270.

Carroll, J. B. (1993). *Human cognitive abilities: A survey of factor-analytic studies.* New York: Cambridge University Press.

Carson, R. C., & Butcher, J. N. (1992). *Abnormal psychology and modern life* (9th ed.). New York: HarperCollins.

Carver, R. P. (1990). *Reading rate: A review of research and theory.* San Diego, CA: Academic Press.

Case, R. (1987). The structure and process of intellectual development. *International Journal of Psychology, 22,* 571–607.

Cassell, E. J. (1990). Introduction: The nature of suffering and the goals of medicine. In T. W. Miller (Ed.), *Chronic pain* (Vol. 1, pp. xix–xxxv). Madison, CT: International Universities Press.

Cate, R. M., & Lloyd, S. A. (1992). *Courtship.* Newbury Park, CA: Sage.

Ceci, S. J. (1994). Education, achievement, and general intelligence: What ever happened to the *psycho* in *psychometrics? Psychological Inquiry, 5,* 197–201.

Ceci, S. J. (1996). *On intelligence: A bioecological treatise on intellectual development* (Expanded Ed.). Cambridge, MA: Harvard University Press.

Ceci, S. J., & Bruck, M. (1993). Suggestibility of the child witness: A historical review and synthesis. *Psychological Bulletin, 113,* 403–439.

Ceci, S. J., & Bruck, M. (1995). *Jeopardy in the courtroom: A scientific analysis of children's testimony.* Washington, DC: American Psychological Association.

Celentano, D. D., & Sonnega, A. B. (1991). Coping processes and strategies and personal resources among persons with HIV-spectrum disease. In P. I. Ahmed (Ed.), *Living and dying with AIDS* (pp. 105–121). New York: Plenum.

Center for Substance Abuse Treatment. (1994). *Practical approaches in the treatment of women who abuse alcohol and other drugs.* Rockville, MD: Department of Health and Human Services, Public Health Service.

Centers for Disease Control. (1997, June). *HIV/AIDS Surveillance Report, 9(1).* Atlanta, GA: Author.

Centerwall, B. S. (1992). Television and violence: The scale of the problem and where to go from here. *JAMA, 267,* 3059–3063.

Cerella, J. (1995). Reaction time. In G. L. Maddox (Ed.), *The encyclopedia of aging* (2nd ed., pp. 792–795). New York: Springer.

Cernoch, J. M., & Porter, R. H. (1985). Recognition of maternal axillary odors by infants. *Child Development, 56,* 1593–1598.

Cervantes, R. C., & Arroyo, W. (1995). Cultural considerations in the use of DSM-IV with Hispanic children and adolescents. In A. M. Padilla (Ed.), *Hispanic psychology: Critical issues in theory and research.* Thousand Oaks, CA: Sage.

Chaika, E. (1985, August). Crazy talk. *Psychology Today, 19,* 30–35.

Chaiken, S., Liberman, A., & Eagly, A. H. (1989). Heuristic and systematic processing within and beyond the persuasion context. In J. S. Uleman & J. A. Bargh (Eds.), *Unintended thought: Limits of awareness, attention, and control* (pp. 212–252). New York: Guilford Press.

Chaiken, S., Wood, W., & Eagly, A. H. (1996). Principles of persuasion. In E. T. Higgins & A. W. Kruglanski (Eds.), *Social psychology: Handbook of basic principles* (pp. 702–742). New York: Guilford Press.

Chalmers, D. J. (1995, December). The puzzle of conscious experience. *Scientific American,* pp. 80–86.

Changeux, J. (1993, November). Chemical signaling in the brain. *Scientific American,* pp. 58–62.

Chaves, J. F. (1993). Hypnosis in pain management. In J. W. Rhue, S. J. Lynn, & I. Kirsch (Eds.), *Handbook of clinical hypnosis* (pp. 511–532). Washington, DC: American Psychological Association.

Check, J. V. P. (1984). *The effects of violent and nonviolent pornography.* Ottawa: Canadian Department of Justice.

Check, J. V. P., & Malamuth, N. M. (1986). Pornography and social aggression: A social learning theory analysis. In M. L. McLaughlin (Ed.), *Communication yearbook* (Vol. 9, pp. 181–213). Beverly Hills, CA: Sage.

Chehrazi, S. (1986). Female psychology. *Journal of the American Psychoanalytic Association, 34,* 111–162.

Chen, M. S. (1992). *Healthy Asian Americans–Pacific Islanders: Model or myth?* Paper presented at the annual convention of the American Psychological Association, Washington, DC.

Cherry, E. C. (1953). Some experiments on the recognition of speech with one and with two ears. *Journal of Acoustical Society of America, 25,* 975–979.

Chialant, D., & Caramazza, A. (1995). Where is morphology and how is it processed? The case of written word recognition. In L. B. Feldman (Ed.), *Morphological aspects of language processing* (pp. 55–76). Hillsdale, NJ: Erlbaum.

Children's Defense Fund. (1994). *Special report: Violence.* Washington, DC: Author.

Children's Defense Fund. (1997). *The state of America's children: Yearbook 1997.* Washington, DC: Author.

Chin, J. L. (1994). Psychodynamic approaches. In L. Comas Díaz & Beverly Greene (Eds.), *Women of color: Integrating ethnic and gender identities in psychotherapy* (pp. 194–222). New York: Guilford Press.

Chipman, S. F. (1994). Gender and school learning: Mathematics. In T. Husen & T. H. Postelthwaite (Eds.), *International encyclopedia of education.* London: Pergamon.

Chiriboga, D. A. (1989). Mental health at the midpoint: Crisis, challenge, or relief? In S. Hunter & M. Sundel (Eds.), *Midlife myths: Issues, findings, and practice implications* (pp. 116–144). Newbury Park, CA: Sage.

Chodorow, N. J. (1978). *The reproduction of mothering.* Berkeley: University of California Press.

Chodorow, N. J. (1989). *Feminism and psychoanalytic theory.* New Haven, CT: Yale University Press.

Chodorow, N. J. (1994). *Femininities, masculinities, sexualities: Freud and beyond.* Lexington: University Press of Kentucky.

Choi, K. H., & Coates, T. J. (1994). Prevention of HIV infection. *AIDS, 8,* 1371–1389.

Chomsky, N. (1957). *Syntactic structures.* The Hague: Mouton.

Chomsky, N. (1965). *Aspects of the theory of syntax.* Cambridge, MA: MIT Press.

Chomsky, N. (1988). *Language and problems of knowledge: The Managua Lectures.* Cambridge, MA: MIT Press.

Chrisler, J. C. (1996). PMS as a culture-bound syndrome. In J. C. Chrisler, C. Golden, & P. D. Rozee (Eds.), *Lectures on the psychology of women* (pp. 106–121). New York: McGraw-Hill.

Chrisler, J. C., Golden, C., & Rozee, P. D. (Eds.). (1996). *Lectures on the psychology of women.* New York: McGraw-Hill.

Christie, D. J. (1997). Peacebuilding: The human needs approach locally and globally. *Peace and Conflict: Journal of Peace Psychology,* in press.

Chung, C. (1995). Death and dying: A Vietnamese cultural perspective. In K. P. Monteiro (Ed.), *Ethnicity and psychology: African-, Asian-, Latino- and Native-American psychologies* (pp. 138–171). Dubuque, IA: Kendall/Hunt.

Churchland, P. S., & Sejnowski, T. J. (1992). *The computational brain.* Cambridge, MA: MIT Press.

Cialdini, R. B. (1993). *Influence: Science and practice* (3rd ed.). New York: HarperCollins.

Cialdini, R. B. (1995). Principles and techniques of social influence. In A. Tesser (Ed.), *Advanced social psychology* (pp. 257–281). New York: McGraw-Hill.

Cialdini, R. B., et al. (1975). Reciprocal concessions procedure for inducing compliance: The door-in-the-face technique. *Journal of Personality and Social Psychology, 31,* 206–215.

Cigarettes may promote blindness. (1996, October 21). *Newsweek,* p. 73.

Clark, E. V. (1991). Acquisitional principles in lexical development. In S. A. Gelman & J. P. Byrnes (Eds.), *Perspectives on language and thought: Interrelations in development* (pp. 31–71). New York: Cambridge University Press.

Clark, H. H. (1991). Words, the world, and their possibilities. In G. R. Lockhead & J. R. Pomerantz (Eds.), *The perception of structure* (pp. 263–277). Washington, DC: American Psychological Association.

Clark, H. H. (1992). *Arenas of language use.* Chicago: University of Chicago Press.

Clark, H. H. (1996). *Using language.* New York: Cambridge University Press.

Clark, H. H., & Brennan, S. E. (1991). Grounding in communication. In L. R. Resnick, J. M. Levine, & S. D. Teasley (Eds.), *Perspectives on socially shared cognition* (pp. 127–149). Washington, DC: American Psychological Association.

Clark, H. H., & Clark, E. V. (1977). *Psychology and language: An introduction to psycholinguistics.* New York: Harcourt Brace Jovanovich.

Clark, H. H., & Wilkes-Gibbs, D. (1986). Referring as a collaborative process. *Cognition, 22,* 1–39.

Clark, R. D., III. (1994). A few parallels between polarization and minority influence. In N. L. Kerr & M. E. Winters (Eds.), *Minority influence* (pp. 47–66). Chicago: Nelson-Hall.

Clarke-Stewart, A. (1989). Infant day care: Maligned or malignant. *American Psychologist, 44,* 266–273.

Clarke-Stewart, A. (1992). Consequences of child care—One more time: A rejoinder. In A. Booth (Ed.), *Child care in the 1990s: Trends and consequences* (pp. 116–124). Hillsdale, NJ: Erlbaum.

Clay, R. A. (1997, February). HIV risk among lesbians is higher than most realize. *APA Monitor,* p. 40.

Clement, J. (1991). Nonformal reasoning in experts and in science students: The use of analogies, extreme cases, and physical intuition. In J. Voss, D. Perkins, & J. Siegel (Eds.), *Informal reasoning and education.* Hillsdale, NJ: Erlbaum.

Cloitre, M., & Shear, M. K. (1995). Psychodynamic perspectives. In M. B. Stein (Ed.), *Social phobia: Clinical and research perspectives* (pp. 163–187). Washington, DC: American Psychiatric Association.

Cloninger, S. C. (1996). *Theories of personality: Understanding persons* (2nd ed.). Upper Saddle River, NJ: Prentice Hall.

Clopton, N. A., & Sorell, G. T. (1993). Gender differences in moral reasoning: Stable or situational? *Psychology of Women Quarterly, 17,* 85–101.

Coates, T. J., et al. (1996). HIV prevention in the developed countries. *Lancet,* in press.

Cockburn, J., & Smith, P. T. (1991). The relative influence of intelligence and age on everyday memory. *Journal of Gerontology: Psychological Sciences, 46,* P31–P36.

Coffin, J. M. (1995). HIV population dynamics in vivo: Implications for genetic variation, pathogenesis, and therapy. *Science, 267,* 483–489.

Cohen, G., Conway, M. A., & Maylor, E. A. (1994). Flashbulb memories in older adults. *Psychology and Aging, 9,* 454–463.

Cohen, J. (1994). The earth is round (*p* < .05). *American Psychologist, 49,* 997–1003.

Cohen, J. D., Braver, T. S., & O. Reilly, R. C. (1997). A computational approach to prefrontal cortex, cognitive control, and schizophrenia: Recent developments and current challenges. *Philosophical Transactions of the Royal Society, Biological Sciences,* in press.

Cohen, J. D., et al. (1994). Activation of the prefrontal cortex in a nonspatial working memory task with functional MRI. *Human Brain Mapping, 1,* 293–304.

Cohen, J. D., & Servan-Schreiber, D. (1992). Context, cortex, and dopamine: A connectionist approach to behavior and biology in schizophrenia. *Psychological Review, 99,* 45–77.

Cohen, L. M., Berzoff, J. N., & Elin, M. R. (Eds.). (1995). *Dissociative identity disorder: Theoretical and treatment controversies.* Northvale, NJ: Jason Aronson.

Cohen, M. W. (1993). Three paradigms for view-ing decision biases. In G. A. Klein, J. Orasanu, R. Calderwood, & C. E. Zsambok (Eds.), *Decision making in action: Models and methods* (pp. 36–50). Norwood, NJ: Ablex.

Cohen, N. J., & Eichenbaum, H. (1993). *Memory, amnesia, and the hippocampal system.* Cambridge, MA: MIT Press.

Cohen, R. J., Swerdlik, M. E., & Smith, D. K. (1992). *Psychological testing and assessment: An introduction to tests and measurement* (2nd ed.). Mountain View, CA: Mayfield.

Cohen, S. (1991). Social supports and physical health: symptoms, health behaviors, and infectious disease. In E. Mark Cummings, A. L. Greene, & K. H. Karraker (Eds.), *Life-span developmental psychology: Perspectives on stress and coping* (pp. 213–234). Hillsdale, NJ: Erlbaum.

Cohen, S., & Herbert, T. B. (1996). Health psychology: Psychological factors and physical disease from the perspective of human psychoneuroimmunology. *Annual Review of Psychology, 47,* 113–142.

Cohen, S., Kessler, R. C., & Gordon, L. U. (1995). Strategies for measuring stress in studies of psychiatric and physical disorders. In S. Cohen, R. C. Kessler, & L. U. Gordon (Eds.), *Measuring stress: A guide for health and social scientists* (pp. 3–26). New York: Oxford University Press.

Cohen, S., Tyrrell, D. A. J., & Smith, A. P. (1993). Negative life events, perceived stress, negative affect, and susceptibility to the common cold. *Journal of Personality and Social Psychology, 64,* 131–140.

Coie, J. D., & Dodge, K. A. (1998). Aggression and antisocial behavior. In W. Damon & N. Eisenberg (Eds.), *Handbook of child psychology* (5th ed., Vol. 3). New York: Wiley.

Coile, D. C., & Miller, N. E. (1984). How radical animal activists try to mislead humane people. *American Psychologist, 39,* 700–701.

Colby, A., & Damon, W. (1992). *Some do care: Contemporary lives of moral commitment.* New York: Free Press.

Colby, A., Kohlberg, L., Gibbs, J., & Lieberman, M. (1983). A longitudinal study of moral judgment. *Monographs of the Society for Child Development* (Serial No. 201).

Cole, S. W., et al. (1996). Elevated physical health risk among gay men who conceal their homosexual identity. *Health Psychology, 15,* 243–251.

Coleman, R. M. (1986). *Wide awake at 3:00 A.M.* New York: Freeman.

Collaer, M. L., & Hines, M. (1995). Human behavioral sex differences: A role for gonadal hormones during early development? *Psychological Bulletin, 118,* 55–107.

Collins, A. M., & Loftus, E. F. (1975). A spreading-activation theory of semantic memory. *Psychological Review, 82,* 407–428.

Collins, M. A., & Zebrowitz, L. A. (1995). The contributions of appearance to occupational outcomes in civilian and military settings. *Journal of Applied Social Psychology, 25,* 129–163.

Collins, P. H. (1991). The meaning of motherhood in Black culture and Black mother/daughter relationships. In P. Bell-Scott, B. Guy-Sheftall, J. J. Royster, J. Sims-Wood, M. DeCosta-Willis, &L. Fultz (Eds.), *Double stitch: Black women write about mothers and daughters* (pp. 42–60). Boston: Beacon.

Collins, W. A., & Gunnar, M. R. (1990). Social and personality development. *Annual Review of Psychology, 41,* 387–416.

Collins, W. A., & Repinski, D. J. (1994). Relationships during adolescence: Continuity and change in interpersonal perspective. In R. Montemayor, G. R. Adams, & T. P. Gullotta (Eds.), *Personal relationships during adolescence* (pp. 7–36). Thousand Oaks, CA: Sage.

Colombo, J. R. (1998). *The 1998 Canadian global almanac.* Toronto: Macmillan Canada.

Coltheart, M., & Rastle, K. (1994). Serial processing in reading aloud: Evidence for dual-route models of reading. *Journal of Experimental Psychology: Human Perception and Performance, 20,* 1197–1211.

Colwill, R. M., & Rescorla, R. A. (1990). Evidence for the hierarchical structure of instrumental learning. *Animal Learning and Behavior, 18,* 71–82.

Comas-Díaz, L., & Greene, B. (Eds.). (1994). *Women of color: Integrating ethnic and gender identities in psychotherapies.* New York: Guilford Press.

Coming clean. (1992, September 21). *Newsweek,* p. 6.

Committee on Communications, American Academy of Pediatrics. (1995). Children, adolescents, and television. *Pediatrics, 96,* 786–787.

Committee on Substance Abuse. (1994). Tobacco-free environment: An imperative for the health of children and adolescents. *Pediatrics, 93,* 866–868.

Committee on the Use of Animals in Research. (1991). *Science, medicine, and animals.* Washington, DC: National Academy Press.

Comstock, G., & Strasburger, V. C. (1993). Media violence: Q & A. *Adolescent Medicine, 4,* 495–509.

Condry, J. C. (1989). *The psychology of television.* Hillsdale, NJ: Erlbaum.

Condry, J. C., & Condry, S. (1976). Sex differences: A study of the eye of the beholder. *Child Development, 47,* 812–819.

Connidis, I. A., & Davies, L. (1990). Confidants and companions in later life: The place of family and friends. *Journal of Gerontology: Social Sciences, 45,* S141–S149.

Connidis, I. A., & Davies, L. (1992). Confidants and companions: Choices in later life. *Journal of Gerontology: Social Sciences, 47,* S115–S122.

Connors, M. E. (1996). Developmental vulnerabilities for eating disorders. In L. Smolak, M. P. Levine, & R. Striegel-Moore (Eds.), *The developmental psychopathology of eating disorders* (pp. 285–310). Mahwah, NJ: Erlbaum.

Conway, M. A. (1995). *Flashbulb memories.* Hove, England: Erlbaum.

Conway, M. A., et al. (1994). The formation of flashbulb memories. *Memory & Cognition, 22,* 326–343.

Cook, M., Mineka, S., Wolkenstein, B., & Laitsch, K. (1985). Observational conditioning of snake fears in unrelated rhesus monkeys. *Journal of Abnormal Psychology, 95,* 195–207.

Cook, S. W. (1994). Men: Powerful or powerless? [Review of the book *The myth of male power: Why men are the disposable sex*]. *Contemporary Psychology, 39,* 972–973.

Cooke, P. (1992, November 2). Noises out: What it's doing to you. *New York,* pp. 29–39.

Coon, D. J. (1994). "Not a creature of reason": The alleged impact of Watsonian behaviorism on advertising in the 1920s. In J. T. Todd & E. K. Morris (Eds.), *Modern perspectives on John B. Watson and classical behaviorism* (pp. 37–63). Westport, CT: Greenwood.

Cooper, H., & Hedges, L. V. (1994). Research synthesis as a scientific enterprise. In H. Cooper & L. V. Hedges (Eds.), *The handbook of research synthesis* (pp. 3–28). New York: Russell Sage Foundation.

Cooper, W. E., Tye-Murray, N., & Eady, S. J. (1985). Acoustical cues to the reconstruction of missing words in speech perception. *Perception & Psychophysics, 38,* 30–40.

Coren, S. (1981). The interaction between eye movements and visual illusions. In D. F. Fisher, R. A. Monty, & J. W. Senders (Eds.), *Eye movements: Cognition and visual perception.* Hillsdale, NJ: Erlbaum.

Coren, S. (1996). *Sleep thieves: An eye-opening exploration into the science and mysteries of sleep.* New York: Free Press.

Coren, S., & Girgus, J. S. (1978). *Seeing is deceiving: The psychology of visual illusions.* Hillsdale, NJ: Erlbaum.

Coren, S., & Porac, C. (1983). Subjective contours and apparent depth: A direct test. *Perception & Psychophysics, 33,* 197–200.

Coren, S., Ward, L. M., & Enns, J. T. (1994). *Sensation and perception* (4th ed.). Fort Worth, TX: Harcourt Brace.

Coriell, M., & Adler, N. E. (1997). Social ordering and health. In B. S. McEwen (Ed.), *Handbook of endocrinology,* in press.

Corker, M. (1994). *Counselling—The deaf challenge.* London: Kingsley.

Corkin, S. (1984). Lasting consequences of medial temporal lobectomy: Clinical cause and experimental findings in H. M. *Seminars in Neurology, 4,* 249, 259.

Cornelius, R. R. (1996). *The science of emotion: Research and tradition in the psychology of emotions.* Upper Saddle River, NJ: Prentice Hall.

Costa, P. T., Jr., & McCrae, R. R. (1992a). Four ways five factors are basic. *Personality and Individual Differences, 13,* 653–665.

Costa, P. T., Jr., & McCrae, R. R. (1992b). Normal personality assessment in clinical practice: The NEO Personality Inventory. *Psychological Assessment, 4,* 5–13.

Costa, P. T., Jr., & McCrae, R. R. (1995). Solid ground in the wetlands of personality: A reply to Block. *Psychological Bulletin, 117,* 216–220.

Costa, P. T., Jr., et al. (1987). Longitudinal analyses of psychological well-being in a national sample: Stability of mean levels. *Journal of Gerontology, 42,* 50–55.

Costa, R., & Renaud, V. (1995, Winter). The Chinese in Canada. *Canadian Social Trends,* pp. 22–26.

Costantino, G. (1992). Overcoming bias in educational assessment of Hispanic students. In K. F. Geisinger (Ed.), *Psychological testing of Hispanics* (pp. 89–97). Washington, DC: American Psychological Association.

Costantino, G., Malgady, R. G., & Rogler, L. H. (1986). Cuento therapy: A culturally sensitive modality for Puerto Rican children. *Journal of Consulting and Clinical Psychology, 54,* 639–645.

Costantino, G., Malgady, R. G., & Rogler, L. H. (1994). Storytelling through pictures: Culturally sensitive psychotherapy for Hispanic children and adolescents. *Journal of Clinical Child Psychology, 23,* 13–20.

Cotman, C. W., & Lynch, G. S. (1990). The neurobiology of learning and memory. In P. D. Eimas & A. M. Galaburda (Eds.), *Neurobiology of cognition* (pp. 201–241). Cambridge, MA: MIT Press.

Cotton, R. (1990). Is there still too much extrapolation from data on middle-aged white men? *JAMA, 263,* 1049–1055.

Courtois, C. A. (1996). Informed clinical practice and the delayed memory controversy. In K. Pezdek & W. P. Banks (Eds.), *The recovered memory/false memory debate* (pp. 355–370). San Diego, CA: Academic Press.

Cowan, G., & Hoffman, C. D. (1986). Gender stereotyping in young children: Evidence to support a concept-learning approach. *Sex Roles, 14,* 11–22.

Cowan, N. (1994). Mechanisms of verbal short-term memory. *Current Directions in Psychological Science, 3,* 185–189.

Cowey, A. (1994). Cortical visual areas and the neurobiology of higher visual processes. In M. J. Farah & G. Ratcliff (Eds.), *The neuropsychology of high-level vision: Collected tutorial essays* (pp. 3–31). Hillsdale, NJ: Erlbaum.

Cowley, G. (1991, August 19). Sweet dreams or nightmare? *Newsweek,* pp. 44–51.

Cowley, G. (1992, June 29). Poison at home and at work. *Newsweek,* p. 55.

Cowley, G., & Church, V. (1992, May 18). Live longer with vitamin C. *Newsweek,* p. 60.

Cox, D. R., et al. (1994). Assessing mapping progress in the human genome project. *Science, 265,* 2031–2032.

Cox, M. J., Owen, M. T., Henderson, V. K., & Margand, N. A. (1992). Prediction of infant-father and infant-mother attachment. *Developmental Psychology, 28,* 474–483.

Craig, K. D., & Grunau, R. V. E. (1993). Neonatal pain perception and behavioral measures. In K. J. S. Anand & P. J. McGrath (Eds.), *Pain in neonates* (pp. 67–105). Amsterdam: Elsevier.

Craige, B. J. (1994, January 12). Multiculturalism and the Vietnam syndrome. *Chronicle of Higher Education,* p. B3.

Craighead, L. W., Craighead, W. E., Kazdin, A. E., & Mahoney, M. J. (Eds.). (1994). *Cognitive and behavioral interventions.* Boston: Allyn & Bacon.

Craik, F. I. M. (1977). Depth of processing in recall and recognition. In S. Dornic (Ed.), *Attention and performance* (Vol. 6). Hillsdale, NJ: Erlbaum.

Craik, F. I. M. (1990). Changes in memory with normal aging: A functional view. In R. J. Wurtman (Ed.), *Advances in*

Neurology, Vol. 51: Alzheimer's Disease (pp. 201–205). New York: Raven.

Craik, F. I. M. (1992). Memory changes in normal aging. In R. Kostavic, S. Knezevic, H. Wisniewski, & G. Spilich (Eds.), *Neurodevelopment, aging and cognition*. Boston: Birkhauser.

Craik, F. I. M., & Lockhart, R. S. (1972). Levels of processing: A framework for memory research. *Journal of Verbal Learning and Verbal Behavior, 11,* 671–684.

Cramer, D. (1986). Gay parents and their children: A review of research and practical implications. *Journal of Counseling and Development, 64,* 504–507.

Crano, W. D. (1994). Context, comparison, and change. In S. Moscovici, A. Mucchi-Faina, & A. Maass (Eds.), *Minority influence* (pp. 17–46). Chicago: Nelson-Hall.

Cravatt, B. F., et al. (1995). Chemical characterization of a family of brain lipids that induce sleep. *Science, 268,* 1506–1509.

Craven, B. J., & Foster, D. H. (1992). An operational approach to colour constancy. *Vision Research, 32,* 1359–1366.

Crawford, H. J., Kitner-Triolo, M., Clarke, S. W., & Olesko, B. (1992). Transient positive and negative experiences accompanying stage hypnosis. *Journal of Abnormal Psychology, 101,* 663–667.

Crawford, M. (1995). *Talking difference: On gender and language.* Thousand Oaks, CA: Sage.

Crawford, M., Chaffin, R., & Fitton, L. (1995). Cognition in social context. *Learning and Individual Differences, 7,* 341–362.

Crews, F. (1996). The verdict on Freud [Review of the book *Freud evaluated: The completed arc*]. *Psychological Science, 7,* 63–68.

Crick, F. (1994). *The astonishing hypothesis: The scientific search for the soul.* New York: Scribner's.

Crider, A. (1991). Motor disturbances in schizophrenia. *Behavioral and Brain Sciences, 14,* 22–23.

Crisp, A. H. (1996). Anorexia nervosa in a young male. In J. Werne (Ed.), *Treating eating disorders* (pp. 1–30). San Francisco: Jossey-Bass.

Crocker, J., Thompson, L. L., McGraw, K. M., & Ingerman, C. (1987). Downward comparison, prejudice, and evaluation of others: Effects of self-esteem and threat. *Journal of Personality and Social Psychology, 52,* 907–916.

Crossen, C. (1994). *Tainted truth: The manipulation of fact in America.* New York: Simon & Schuster.

Cross-National Collaborative Group. (1992). The changing rate of major depression: Cross-national comparisons. *JAMA, 268,* 3098–3105.

Crowder, R. G. (1982). Decay of auditory memory in vowel discrimination. *Journal of Experimental Psychology: Learning, Memory, and Cognition, 8,* 153–162.

Crowder, R. G. (1992). Sensory memory. In L. S. Squire (Ed.), *Encyclopedia of learning and memory* (pp. 588–590). New York: Macmillan.

Crowder, R. G., & Wagner, R. K. (1992). *The psychology of reading: An introduction* (2nd ed.). New York: Oxford University Press.

Cummings, E. M., & Davies, P. T. (1995). The impact of parents on their children: An emotional security perspective. *Annals of Child Development, 10,* 167–208.

Cummins, D. D. (1992). Role of analogical reasoning in the induction of problem categories. *Journal of Experi-mental Psychology: Learning, Memory, and Cognition, 18,* 1103–1124.

Cummins, D. D. (1994). Analogical reasoning. In V. S. Ramachandran (Ed.), *Encyclopedia of human behavior* (Vol. 1, pp. 125–130). San Diego, CA: Academic Press.

Cutler, A. (1987). Speaking for the listening. In A. Allport, D. MacKay, W. Prinz, & E. Scheerer (Eds.), *Language perception and production* (pp. 24–40). London: Academic Press.

Cutler, B. L., & Penrod, S. D. (1995). *Mistaken identification: The eyewitness, psychology, and the law.* New York: Cambridge University Press.

Cutting, J. E. (1983). Perceiving and recovering structure from events. In SIGGRAPH/SIGART Interdisciplinary Workshop (Ed.), *Motion: Representation and perception.* New York: Association for Computing Machinery.

Cutting, J. E., & Vishton, P. M. (1995). Perceiving layout and knowing distances: The integration, relative potency, and contextual use of different information about depth. In W. Epstein & S. J. Rogers (Eds.), *Perception of space and motion* (pp. 69–118). Orlando: Academic Press.

Cutting, J. E., Vishton, P. M., & Braren, P. A. (1995). How we avoid collisions with stationary and moving obstacles. *Psychological Review, 102,* 627–651.

Dahl, R. E., Scher, M. S., Williamson, D. E., Robles, N., & Day, N. (1995). A longitudinal study of prenatal marijuana use. *Archives of Pediatric and Adolescent Medicine, 149,* 145–150.

Dalton, S. T. (1992). Lived experience of never-married women. *Issues in Mental Health Nursing, 13,* 69–80.

D'Amico, D. J. (1994). Diseases of the retina. *New England Journal of Medicine, 331,* 95–106.

Damon, W. (1995). *Greater expectations: Overcoming the culture of indulgence in America's homes and schools.* New York: Free Press.

Damon, W., & Hart, D. (1992). Self-understanding and its role in social and moral development. In M. H. Bornstein & M. E. Lamb (Eds.), *Developmental psychology: An advanced textbook* (3rd ed., pp. 421–464). Hillsdale, NJ: Erlbaum.

Dana, R. H. (1988). Culturally diverse groups and MMPI interpretation. *Professional Psychology: Research and Practice, 19,* 490–495.

Danziger, K. (1990). *Constructing the subject: Historical origins of psychological research.* Cambridge, England: Cambridge University Press.

Darley, J. M., & Batson, C. D. (1973). From Jerusalem to Jericho: A study of situational and dispositional variables in helping behavior. *Journal of Personality and Social Psychology, 27,* 269–275.

Darley, J. M., & Gross, P. H. (1983). A hypothesis-confirming bias in labeling effects. *Journal of Personality and Social Psychology, 44,* 20–33.

Darley, J. M., & Oleson, K. C. (1993). Introduction to research on interpersonal expectations. In P. D. Blanck (Ed.), *Interpersonal expectations: Theory, research, and applications* (pp. 45–63). New York: Cambridge University Press.

Darley, J. M., & Schultz, T. R. (1990). Moral judgments: Their content and acquisition. *Annual Review of Psychology, 41,* 525–556.

Dartnall, H. J. A., Bowmaker, J. J., & Mollon, J. D. (1983). Microspectrophotometry of human photoreceptors. In

J. D. Mollon & L. T. Sharpe (Eds.), *Color vision* (pp. 69–80). London: Academic Press.

Darwin, C. (1859). *The origin of species.* London: John Murray.

Darwin, C. (1872/reprinted 1965). *The expression of the emotions in man and animals.* Chicago: University of Chicago Press.

Darwin, C. J., Turvey, M. T., & Crowder, R. G. (1972). An auditory analogue of the Sperling partial report procedure: Evidence for brief auditory storage. *Cognitive Psychology, 3,* 255–267.

Das, N. (1992). Personal communication.

Daum, I., & Schugens, M. M. (1996). On the cerebellum and classical conditioning. *Current Directions in Psychological Science, 5,* 58–61.

Davidson, A. R. (1995). From attitudes to actions to attitude change: The effects of amount and accuracy of information. In R. E. Petty & J. A. Krosnick (Eds.), *Attitude strength: Antecedents and consequences* (pp. 315–336). Mahwah, NJ: Erlbaum.

Davidson, A. R., Yantis, S., Norwood, M., & Montano, D. E. (1985). Amount of information about the attitude object and attitude-behavior consistency. *Journal of Personality and Social Psychology, 49,* 1184–1198.

Davidson, D. (1995). The representativeness heuristic and the conjunction fallacy effect in children's decision making. *Merrill-Palmer Quarterly, 41,* 328–346.

Davies, G. M., & Logie, R. H. (Eds.). (1993). *Memory in everyday life.* Amsterdam: North-Holland.

Davis, G. A., & Rimm, S. B. (1989). *Education of the gifted and talented* (2nd ed.). Englewood Cliffs, NJ: Prentice Hall.

Davis, L. E., & Gelsomino, J. (1994). An assessment of practitioner cross-racial treatment experiences. *Social Work, 39,* 116–123.

Davis, M. H. (1996). *Empathy: A social psychological approach.* Boulder, CO: Westview Press.

Dawes, R. M. (1988). *Rational choice in an uncertain world.* San Diego: Harcourt Brace Jovanovich.

Dawes, R. M. (1994). *House of cards: Psychology and psychotherapy built on myth.* New York: Free Press.

Day, J. C. (1996). *Population projections of the United States by age, sex, race, and Hispanic origin: 1995–2050.* Washington, DC: U.S. Bureau of the Census.

DeAngelis, T. (1996, September). Psychoanalysis adapts to the 1990s. *APA Monitor,* pp. 1, 43.

Deaux, K., & Major, B. (1987). Putting gender into context: An interactive model of gender-related behavior. *Psychological Review, 94,* 369–389.

Deaux, K., & Wrightsman, L. S. (1988). *Social psychology* (5th ed.). Pacific Grove, CA: Brooks/Cole.

DeBattista, C., & Schatzberg, A. F. (1995). Somatic therapy. In I. D. Glick (Ed.), *Treating depression* (pp. 153–181). San Francisco: Jossey-Bass.

DeCarvalho, R. J. (1991). *The founders of humanistic psychology.* New York: Praeger.

Deci, E. L., & Ryan, R. M. (1985). *Intrinsic motivation and self-determination in human behavior.* New York: Plenum.

Deci, E. L., & Ryan, R. M. (1990). A motivational approach to self: Integration in personality. *Nebraska Symposium on Motivation, 38,* 237–288.

DeFries, J. C., Plomin, R., & LaBuda, M. C. (1987). Genetic stability of cognitive development from childhood to adulthood. *Developmental Psychology, 23,* 4–12.

De Graef, P. (1992). Scene-context effects and models of real-world perception. In K. Rayner (Ed.), *Eye movements and visual cognition: Scene perception and reading* (pp. 243–259). New York: Springer-Verlag.

DeHart, G. (1990). Personal communication.

DelGiudice, G. T. (1986). The relationship between sibling jealousy and presence at a sibling's birth. *Birth, 13,* 250–254.

Dell, G. S. (1986). A spreading-activation theory of retrieval in sentence production. *Psychological Review, 93,* 283–321.

Dell, G. S. (1990). Effects of frequency and vocabulary type on phonological speech errors. *Language and Cognitive Processes, 5,* 313–349.

Dell, G. S., & Brown, P. M. (1991). Mechanisms for listener-adaptation in language production: Limiting the role of the "model of the listener." In D. J. Napoli & J. A. Kegl (Eds.), *Bridges between psychology and linquistics: A Swarthmore Festschrift for Lila Gleitman* (pp. 105–129). Hillsdale, NJ: Erlbaum.

Dember, W. N. (1990). William James on sensation and perception. *Psychological Science, 1,* 163–166.

Dempster, F. N. (1981). Memory span: Sources of individual and developmental differences. *Psychological Bulletin, 89,* 63–100.

Dempster, F. N. (1988). The spacing effect: A case study in the failure to apply the results of psychological research. *American Psychologist, 43,* 627–634.

Denmark, F., Russo, N. F., Frieze, I. H., & Sechzer, J. A. (1988). Guidelines for avoiding sexism in psychological research: A report of the Ad Hoc Committee on Nonsexist Research. *American Psychologist, 43,* 582–585.

DePaulo, B. M. (1992). Nonverbal behavior and self-presentation. *Psychological Bulletin, 111,* 203–243.

DePaulo, B. M., et al. (1996). Lying in everyday life. *Journal of Personality and Social Psychology, 70,* 979–995.

Derryberry, D., & Tucker, D. M. (1992). Neural mechanisms of emotion. *Journal of Consulting and Clinical Psychology, 60,* 329–338.

Desforges, D. M., et al. (1991). Effects of structured cooperative contact on changing negative attitudes toward stigmatized social groups. *Journal of Personality and Social Psychology, 60,* 531–544.

Desimone, R. (1991). Face selective cells in the temporal cortex of monkeys. *Journal of Cognitive Neuroscience, 3,* 1–8.

Desimone, R., Albright, T. D., Gross, C. G., & Bruce, C. (1984). Stimulus selective properties of inferior temporal neurons in the macaque. *Journal of Neuroscience, 4,* 2051–2062.

Desjarlais, R., Eisenberg, L., Good, B., & Kleinman, A. (1995). *World mental health: Problems and priorities in low-income countries.* New York: Oxford University Press.

Desor, J. A., & Beauchamp, G. K. (1974). The human capacity to transmit olfactory information. *Perception & Psychophysics, 16,* 551–556.

Deutsch, M. (1983). The prevention of World War III: A psychological perspective. *Political Psychology, 4,* 3–31.

Deutsch, M. (1993). Educating for a peaceful world. *American Psychologist, 48,* 510–517.

Devereaux, M. S. (1993, Autumn). Time use of Canadians in 1992. *Canadian Social Trends,* pp. 13–35.

de Villiers, P. A., & de Villiers, J. G. (1992). Language development. In M. H. Bornstein & M. E. Lamb (Eds.), *Develop-*

mental psychology: An advanced textbook (3rd ed., pp. 337–420). Hillsdale, NJ: Erlbaum.

Devine, P. G. (1995). *Breaking the prejudice habit: Pro-gress and prospects.* Paper presented at the annual meeting of the American Psychological Association, New York City.

Devine, P. G., & Monteith, M. J. (1993). The role of discrepancy associated affect in prejudice reduction. In D. M. Mackie & D. L. Hamilton (Eds.), *Affect, cognition, and stereotyping: Interactive processes in intergroup perception.* Orlando: Academic Press.

de Wijk, R. A., Schab, F. R., & Cain, W. S. (1995). Odor identification. In F. R. Schab & R. G. Crowder (Eds.), *Memory for odors* (pp. 21–37). Mahwah, NJ: Erlbaum.

Dewji, N., & Singer, S. J. (1996). Genetic clues to Alzheimer's disease. *Science, 271,* 159–160.

Diaz, R. M. (1985). Bilingual cognitive development: Addressing three gaps in current research. *Child Development, 56,* 1376–1388.

Diener, E. (1997). Subjective well-being and personality. In D. Barone, M. Hersen, & V. Van Hasselt (Eds.), *Advanced personality.* New York: Plenum.

Diener, E., & Diener, C. (1993). *Most people in the United States are happy and satisfied.* Unpublished manuscript.

Diener, E., & Diener, C. (1996). Most people are happy. *Psychological Science, 7,* 181–185.

Diener, E., & Larsen, R. J. (1994). The experience of emotional well-being. In M. Lewis & J. M. Haviland (Eds.), *Handbook of emotions* (pp. 405–415). New York: Guilford Press.

Diener, E., Wolsic, B., & Fujita, F. (1995). Physical attractiveness and subjective well-being. *Journal of Personality and Social Psychology, 69,* 120–129.

DiLollo, V., & Bischof, W. F. (1995). Inverse-intensity effect in duration of visible persistence. *Psychological Bulletin, 118,* 223–237.

Dinges, D. F., & Kribbs, N. B. (1991). Performing while sleepy: Effects of experimentally-induced sleepiness. In T. H. Monk (Ed.), *Sleep, sleepiness and performance* (pp. 97–128). Chichester, England: Wiley.

Dion, K. K. (1986). Stereotyping based on physical attractiveness: Issues and conceptual perspectives. In C. P. Herman, M. P. Zanna, & E. T. Higgins (Eds.), *Physical appearance, stigma, and social behavior: The Ontario Symposium* (Vol. 3, pp. 7–21). Hillsdale, NJ: Erlbaum.

Doane, J. A., et al. (1989). Parental communication deviance and schizophrenia: A cross-cultural comparison of Mexican- and Anglo-Americans. *Journal of Abnormal Psychology, 98,* 487–490.

Dodes, J. E. (1997, January–February). The mysterious placebo. *Skeptical Inquirer,* pp. 44–45.

Dodge, K. A. (1993). Social-cognitive mechanisms in the development of conduct disorder and depression. *Annual Review of Psychology, 44,* 559–584.

Dodge, S. (1992, April 15). Colleges are trying ways to enhance academic advising. *Chronicle of Higher Education,* pp. A41–A42.

Dodwell, P. C. (1993). From the top down. *Canadian Psychology/ Psychologie Canadienne, 34,* 137–151.

Domjan, M. (1993). *The principles of learning and behavior* (3rd ed.). Pacific Grove, CA: Brooks/Cole.

Domjan, M., & Purdy, J. E. (1995). Animal research in psychology: More than meets the eye of the general psychology student. *American Psychologist, 50,* 496–503.

Donnerstein, E., & Linz, D. (1984, January). Sexual violence in the media: A warning. *Psychology Today,* pp. 14–15.

Donnerstein, E., Linz, D., & Penrod, S. (1987). *The question of pornography.* New York: Free Press.

Dorfman, D. D. (1995). Soft science with a neoconservative agenda [Review of the book *The Bell Curve*]. *Contemporary Psychology, 40,* 419–421.

Dovidio, J. F., Evans, N., & Tyler, R. B. (1986). Racial stereotypes: The contents of their cognitive representations. *Journal of Experimental Social Psychology, 22,* 22–37.

Dovidio, J. F., & Gaertner, S. L. (1993). Stereotypes and evaluative intergroup bias. In D. M. Mackie & D. L. Hamilton (Eds.), *Affect, cognition, and stereotyping: Interactive processes in group perception* (pp. 167–193). San Diego, CA: Academic Press.

Dowd, M. (1984, March 12). Twenty years after the murder of Kitty Genovese, the question remains: Why? *New York Times,* pp. B1, B4.

Druckman, D., & Bjork, R. A. (1991). *The mind's eye: Enhancing human performance.* Washington, DC: National Academy Press.

Dubas, J. S., & Petersen, A. C. (1993). Female pubertal development. In M. Sugar (Ed.), *Female adolescent development* (2nd ed., pp. 3–26). New York: Brunner/Mazel.

Dubbert, P. M. (1992). Exercise in behavioral medicine. *Journal of Consulting and Clinical Psychology, 60,* 613–618.

Dubow, E. F., & Miller, L. S. (1996). Television violence viewing and aggressive behavior. In T. M. MacBeth (Ed.), *Tuning in to young viewers: Social science perspectives on television* (pp. 117–147). Thousand Oaks, CA: Sage.

Dudycha, G. J. (1936). An objective study of punctuality in relation to personality and achievement. *Archives of Psychology, 204,* 1–319.

Duffy, K. G. (1998). Community psychology. In S. Cullari (Ed.), *Foundations of clinical psychology.* Boston: Allyn & Bacon.

Duffy, K. G., & Wong, F. Y. (1996). *Community psychology.* Boston: Allyn & Bacon.

Dumas, J. (1990). *Report on the demographic situation in Canada 1990.* Ottawa: Statistics Canada.

Duncker, K. (1945). On problem solving. *Psychological Monographs, 58* (Whole No. 270).

Dunn, J. F. (1991). Sibling influences. In M. Lewis & S. Feinman (Eds.), *Social influences and socialization in infancy* (pp. 97–109). New York: Plenum.

Dunn, J. F. (1993). *Young children's close relationships: Beyond attachment.* Newbury Park, CA: Sage.

Dunn, J. F., & Plomin, R. (1990). *Separate lives: Why siblings are so different.* New York: Basic Books.

Dunn, L. M. (1987). *Bilingual Hispanic children on the U.S. mainland: A review of research on their cognitive, linguistic, and scholastic development.* Circle Pines, MN: American Guidance Service.

Dusek, D. E., & Girdano, D. A. (1987). *Drugs: A factual account* (4th ed.). New York: Random House.

Dush, D. M., Hirt, M. L., & Schroeder, H. (1983). Self-statement modification with adults: A meta-analysis. *Psychological Bulletin, 94,* 408–422.

Dworkin, S. H., & Gutiérrez, F. J. (Eds.). (1992). *Counseling gay men and lesbians: Journey to the end of the rainbow.* Alexandria, VA: American Association for Counseling and Development.

Dwyan, J., & Bowers, K. (1983). The use of hypnosis to enhance recall. *Science, 222,* 184–185.

Dziech, B. W., & Weiner, L. (1990). *The lecherous professor: Sexual harassment on campus* (2nd ed.). Urbana: University of Illinois Press.

D'Zurilla, T. J., & Sheedy, C. F. (1991). Relation between social problem-solving ability and subsequent level of psychological stress in college students. *Journal of Personality and Social Psychology, 61,* 841–846.

Eagle, M., & Wolitzky, D. (1994). Dynamic psychotherapy. In V. B. Van Hasselt & M. Hersen (Eds.), *Advanced abnormal psychology* (pp. 475–495). New York: Plenum.

Eagly, A. H. (1987). *Sex differences in social behavior: A social-role interpretation.* Hillsdale, NJ: Erlbaum.

Eagly, A. H. (1996). Gender and altruism. In J. C. Chrisler, C. Golden, & P. D. Rozee (Eds.), *Lectures on the psychology of women* (pp. 42–73). New York: McGraw-Hill.

Eagly, A. H., Ashmore, R. D., Makhijani, M. G., & Longo, L. C. (1991). What is beautiful is good, but . . . : A meta-analytic review of research on the physical attractiveness stereotype. *Psychological Bulletin, 110,* 109–128.

Eagly, A. H., & Chaiken, S. (1993). *The psychology of attitudes.* Fort Worth, TX: Harcourt Brace Jovanovich.

Eagly, A. H., & Crowley, M. (1986). Gender and helping behavior: A meta-analytic review of the social psychological literature. *Psychological Bulletin, 100,* 283–308.

Eagly, A. H., Makhijani, M. G., & Klonsky, B. G. (1992). Gender and the evaluation of leaders: A meta-analysis. *Psychological Bulletin, 111,* 3–22.

Eagly, A. H., & Steffen, V. J. (1986). Gender and aggressive behavior: A meta-analytic review of the social psychological literature. *Psychological Bulletin, 100,* 309–330.

Eagly, A. H., & Wood, W. (1985). Gender and influenceability: Stereotype versus behavior. In V. E. O'Leary, R. K. Unger, & B. S. Wallston (Eds.), *Women, gender and social psychology* (pp. 225–256). Hillsdale, NJ: Erlbaum.

Eating disorders—Part II. (1997, November). *Harvard Mental Health Letter,* pp. 1–5.

Ebbinghaus, H. (1885). *Über das Gedachtnis.* Leipzig: Duncker & Humblot.

Ebstein, R. P., et al. (1996). Dopamine D4 receptor (D4DR) exon III polymorphism associated with the human personality trait of novelty seeking. *Nature Genetics, 12,* 78–80.

Eccles, J. S. (1989). Bringing young women to math and science. In M. Crawford & M. Gentry (Eds.), *Gender and thought* (pp. 36–58). New York: Springer-Verlag.

Eckenrode, J. (1984). Impact of chronic and acute stressors on daily reports of mood. *Journal of Personality and Social Psychology, 46,* 907–918.

Edelman, M. W. (1993). *The measure of our success: A letter to my children and yours.* New York: HarperCollins.

Edwards, A. J. (1993). *Dementia.* New York: Plenum.

Eich, E. (1995). Searching for mood dependent memory. *Psychological Science, 6,* 67–75.

Eimas, P. D., Siqueland, E. R., Jusczyk, R., & Vigorito, J. (1971). Speech perception in infants. *Science, 171,* 303–306.

Eisenberg, N. (1992). *The caring child.* Cambridge, MA: Harvard University Press.

Eisenberg, N. (1993). Does true altruism exist? [Review of the book *The altruism question: Toward a social-psychological answer*]. *Contemporary Psychology, 38,* 350–351.

Eisenberg, N., & Lennon, R. (1983). Sex differences in empathy and related capacities. *Psychological Bulletin, 94,* 100–131.

Eisenberg, N., & Miller, P. A. (1987). The relation of empathy in prosocial and related behaviors. *Psychological Bulletin, 101,* 91–119.

Eisenberger, R., & Cameron, J. (1996). Detrimental effects of reward: Reality or myth? *American Psychologist, 51,* 1153–1166.

Eisenberger, R., & Selbst, M. (1994). Does reward increase or decrease creativity? *Journal of Personality and Social Psychology, 66,* 1116–1127.

Eisenman, R. (1994). *Studies in personality, social, and clinical psychology: Nonobvious findings.* Lanham, MD: University Press.

Ekman, P. (1973). Cross-cultural studies of facial expression. In P. Ekman (Ed.), *Darwin and facial expression* (pp. 169–222). New York: Academic Press.

Ekman, P. (1976, Summer). Nonverbal communication/Movements with precise meaning. *Journal of Communication, 26,* 13–26.

Ekman, P. (1984). Expression and the nature of emotion. In K. R. Scherer & P. Ekman (Eds.), *Approaches to emotion* (pp. 319–343). Hillsdale, NJ: Erlbaum.

Ekman, P. (1993). Facial expression and emotion. *American Psychologist, 48,* 384–392.

Ekman, P. (1994). Antecedent events and emotion metaphors. In P. Ekman & R. J. Davidson (Eds.), *The nature of emotion: Fundamental questions* (pp. 146–171). New York: Oxford University Press.

Ekman, P., & Davidson, R. J. (1993). Voluntary smiling changes regional brain activity. *Psychological Science, 4,* 342–345.

Ekman, P., Davidson, R. J., & Friesen, W. V. (1990). The Duchenne smile: Emotional expression and brain physiology, II. *Journal of Personality and Social Psychology, 58,* 342–353.

Ekman, P., & Friesen, W. V. (1969). The repertoire of nonverbal behavior: Categories, origins, usage, and coding. *Semiotica, 1,* 49–98.

Ekman, P., & Friesen, W. V. (1971). Constants across cultures in the face and emotion. *Journal of Personality and Social Psychology, 17,* 124–129.

Ekman, P., et al. (1987). Universals and cultural differences in the judgments of facial expressions of emotion. *Journal of Personality and Social Psychology, 53,* 712–717.

Eliany, M. (1992, Autumn). Alcohol and drug consumption among Canadian youth. *Canadian Social Trends,* pp. 10–13.

Eliany, M., Wortley, S., & Adlaf, E. (1992). *Alcohol and other drug use by Canadian youth.* Toronto: Minister of Supply and Services Canada.

Elkind, D. (1981). *The hurried child: Growing up too fast too soon.* Reading, MA: Addison-Wesley.

Elkind, D. (1987). *Miseducation: Preschoolers at risk.* New York: Knopf.

Elliott, A. (1994). *Psychoanalytic theory: An introduction.* Oxford, England: Blackwell.

Ellis, A. (1986). Rational-emotive therapy. In I. L. Kutash & A. Wolf (Eds.), *Psychotherapist's casebook* (pp. 277–287). San Francisco: Jossey-Bass.

Ellis, A. (1996). *Better, deeper, and more enduring brief therapy: The rational emotive behavior therapy approach.* New York: Brunner/Mazel.

Ellis, A., & Harper, R. A. (1975). *A new guide to rational living.* North Hollywood, CA: Wilshire.

Ellis, L. (1996). The role of perinatal factors in determining sexual orientation. In R. C. Savin-Williams & K. Cohen (Eds.), *The lives of lesbians, gays, and bisexuals: Children to adults* (pp. 35–70). Fort Worth: TX: Harcourt Brace.

Ellsworth, P. C. (1994). William James and emotion: Is a century of fame worth a century of misunderstanding? *Psychological Review, 101,* 222–229.

Elms, A. C. (1995). Obedience in retrospect. *Journal of Social Issues, 51,* 21–31.

Emler, N., Renwick, S., & Malone, B. (1983). The relationship between moral reasoning and political orientation. *Journal of Personality and Social Psychology, 45,* 1073–1080.

Emmelkamp, P. M. G., Bouman, T. K., & Scholing, A. (1992). *Anxiety disorders: A practitioner's guide.* Chichester, England: Wiley.

Enemy images in Croatia and Serbia documented. (1992, Fall). *Psychologists for Social Responsibility Newsletter, 11* (3), p. 4.

Engen, T. (1987). Remembering odors and their names. *American Scientist, 75,* 497–503.

Engen, T. (1991). *Odor sensation and memory.* Westport, CT: Praeger.

Englander-Golden, P., Sonleitner, F. J., Whitmore, M. R., & Corbley, G. J. M. (1986). Social and menstrual cycles: Methodological and substantive findings. In V. L. Olesen & N. F. Woods (Eds.), *Culture, society and menstruation* (pp. 77–96). Washington, DC: Hemisphere.

Engle, R. W., Fidler, D. S., & Reynolds, L. H. (1981). Does echoic memory develop? *Journal of Experimental Child Psychology, 32,* 459–473.

Enns, C. Z. (1989). Toward teaching inclusive personality theories. *Teaching of Psychology, 16,* 111–117.

Epps, R. P., Manley, M. W., & Glynn, T. J. (1995). Tobacco use among adolescents: Strategies for prevention. *Pediatric Clinics of North America, 42,* 389–402.

Epstein, R. (1991). Skinner, creativity, and the problem of spontaneous behavior. *Psychological Science, 2,* 362–370.

Epstein, S. (1983). Aggregation and beyond: Some basic issues on the prediction of behavior. *Journal of Personality, 51,* 360–392.

Epstein, S., & O'Brien, E. J. (1985). The person-situation debate in historical and current perspective. *Psychological Bulletin, 98,* 513–537.

Epstein, W. (1995). The metatheoretical context. In W. Epstein & S. J. Rogers (Eds.), *Perception of space and motion* (pp. 1–22). Orlando: Academic Press.

Erickson, H. M., Jr., & Goodwin, D. W. (1994). Pharmacologic interventions. In V. B. Van Hasselt & M. Hersen (Eds.), *Advanced abnormal psychology* (pp. 513–523). New York: Plenum.

Erickson, M. H. (1980). Hypnosis: A general review. In E. L. Rossi (Ed.), *The collected papers of Milton H. Erickson on hypnosis* (Vol. 3, pp. 13–20). New York: Irvington. (Original work published in 1941.)

Ericsson, K. A., & Charness, N. (1994). Expert performance: Its structure and acquisition. *American Psychologist, 49,* 725–747.

Ericsson, K. A., & Kintsch, W. (1995). Long-term working memory. *Psychological Review, 102,* 211–245.

Ericsson, K. A., & Lehmann, A. C. (1996). Expert and exceptional performance: Evidence of maximal adaptation to task constraints. *Annual Review of Psychology, 47,* 273–305.

Erikson, E. H. (1950). *Childhood and society.* New York: Norton.

Erikson, E. H. (1968). *Identity: Youth and crisis.* New York: Norton.

Erikson, E. H., Erikson, J. M., & Kivnick, H. Q. (1986). *Vital involvement in old age.* New York: Norton.

Eron, L. D. (1993). *The problem of media violence and children's behavior.* New York: Guggenheim Foundation.

Eron, L. D. (1995a, August). *Media violence: How it affects kids and what can be done about it.* Paper presented at the annual meeting of the American Psychological Association, New York City.

Eron, L. D. (1995b). Media violence. *Pediatric Annals, 24,* 84–87.

Eron, L. D., & Huesmann, L. R. (1987). Television as a source of maltreatment of children. *School Psychology Review, 16,* 195–202.

Erwin, P. (1993). *Friendship and peer relations in children.* Chichester, England: Wiley.

Espín, O. M. (1994). Feminist approaches. in L. Comas-Díaz & B. Greene (Eds.), *Women of color: Integrating ethnic and gender identities in psychotherapy* (pp. 265–286). New York: Guilford Press.

Estes, W. K. (1991). Cognitive architectures from the standpoint of an experimental psychologist. *Annual Review of Psychology, 42,* 1–28.

Etaugh, C., & Malstrom, J. (1981). The effect of marital status on person perception. *Journal of Marriage and the Family, 43,* 801–805.

Ettin, M. P. (1995). The group process in President Reagan's National Security Council during the Iran-Contra affair—Revisited. In M. F. Ettin, J. W. Fidler, & B. D. Cohen (Eds.), *Group process and political dynamics* (pp. 75–108). Madison, CT: International Universities Press.

Evans, E. F. (1982a). Functional anatomy of the auditory system. In H. B. Barlow & J. D. Mollon (Eds.), *The senses* (pp. 251–306). Cambridge: Cambridge University Press.

Evans, E. F. (1982b). Basic physics and psychophysics of sound. In H. B. Barlow & J. D. Mollon (Eds.), *The senses* (pp. 239–250). Cambridge: Cambridge University Press.

Evans, G. W., Hygge, S., & Bullinger, M. (1995). Chronic noise and psychological stress. *Psychological Science, 6,* 333–338.

Evans, J. St. B. T., Newstead, S. E., & Byrne, R. M. J. (1993). *Human reasoning: The psychology of deduction.* Hove, England: Erlbaum.

Evans, R. B. (1990). William James and his *Principles.* In M. G. Johnson & T. B. Henley (Eds.), *Reflections on The Principles of Psychology: William James after a century* (pp. 11–31). Hillsdale, NJ: Erlbaum.

Ewen, R. B. (1993). *An introduction to theories of personality* (4th ed.). Hillsdale, NJ: Erlbaum.

Exner, J. E., Jr. (1993). *The Rorschach: A comprehensive system: Vol. 1. Basic foundations* (3rd ed.). New York: Wiley.

Exner, J. E., Jr. (1996). A comment on "The comprehensive system for the Rorschach": A critical examination. *Psychological Science, 7,* 11–13.

Eysenck, H. J. (1991). Behavioral psychotherapy. In C. E. Walker (Ed.), *Clinical psychology: Historical and research foundations* (pp. 417–442). New York: Plenum.

Eysenck, M. W. (1990). *Happiness: Facts and myths.* Hillsdale, NJ: Erlbaum.

Eysenck, M. W. (1991). Creativity. In M. W. Eysenck (Ed.), *The Blackwell dictionary of cognitive psychology* (pp. 86–87). Oxford, England: Blackwell.

Fabrega, H., Jr. (1995). Hispanic mental health research. In A. M. Padilla (Ed.), *Hispanic psychology* (pp. 107–132). Thousand Oaks, CA: Sage.

Faden, R. R., Beauchamp, T. L., & King, N. M. P. (1986). *A history and theory of informed consent.* New York: Oxford University Press.

Fagot, B. I., & Leinbach, M. D. (1993). Gender-role development in young children: From discrimination to labeling. *Developmental Review, 13,* 205–224.

Fairbairn, W. R. D. (1952). *Psychoanalytic studies of the personality.* London: Routledge & Kegan Paul.

Fairburn, C. G., & Wilson, G. T. (1993). Binge eating: Definition and classification. In C. G. Fairburn & G. T. Wilson (Eds.), *Binge eating: Nature, assessment, and treatment* (pp. 3–14). Washington, DC: American Psychiatric Press.

Fallon, P., Katzman, M. A., & Wooley, S. C. (Eds.). (1994). *Feminist perspectives on eating disorders.* New York: Guilford Press.

Fancher, R. E. (1985). *The intelligence men: Makers of the IQ controversy.* New York: Norton.

Fantz, R. E. (1961). The origin of form perception. *Scientific American, 204* (5), 66–72.

Farah, M. J. (1990). *Visual agnosia: Disorders of object recognition and what they tell us about normal vision.* Cambridge, MA: MIT Press.

Farah, M. J. (1994). Specialization within visual object recognition: Clues from prosopagnosia and alexia. In M. J. Farah & G. Ratcliff (Eds.), *The neuropsychology of high-level vision: Collected tutorial essays* (pp. 133–146). Hillsdale, NJ: Erlbaum.

Farah, M. J. (1996). Is face recognition "special"? Evidence from neuropsychology. *Behavioural Brain Research, 76,* 181–189.

Farah, M. J., Levinson, K. L., & Klein, K. L. (1995). Face perception and within-category discrimination in prosopagnosia. *Neuropsychologia, 33,* 661–674.

Farah, M. J., McMullen, P. A., & Meyer, M. M. (1991). Can recognition of living things be selectively impaired? *Neuropsychologia, 29,* 185–193.

Farah, M. J., & Ratcliff, G. (Eds.). (1994). The neuropsychology of high-level vision: Collected tutorial essays. Hillsdale, NJ: Erlbaum.

Farah, M. J., Wilson, K. D., Drain, H. M., & Tanaka, J. R. (1995). The inverted face inversion effect in prosopagnosia: Evidence for mandatory, face-specific perceptual mechanisms. *Vision Research, 35,* 2089–2093.

Farthing, G. W. (1992). *The psychology of consciousness.* Englewood Cliffs, NJ: Prentice Hall.

Farver, J. A. M., Kim, Y. K., & Lee, Y. (1995). Cultural differences in Korean- and Anglo-American preschoolers' social interaction and play behaviors. *Child Development, 66,* 1088–1099.

Farver, J. A. M., & Wimbarti, S. (1995). Indonesian children's play with their mothers and older siblings. *Child Development, 66,* 1493–1503.

Favreau, O. E. (1993). Do the Ns justify the means? Null hypothesis testing applied to sex and other differences. *Canadian Psychology/Psychologie Canadienne, 34,* 64–78.

Feeney, J., & Noller, P. (1996). *Adult attachment.* Thousand Oaks, CA: Sage.

Fehr, B. (1988). Prototype analysis of the concepts of love and commitment. *Journal of Personality and Social Psychology, 55,* 557–579.

Fehr, B. (1993). How do I love thee . . .? Let me consult my prototype. In S. Duck (Ed.), *Individuals in relationships.* Newbury Park, CA: Sage.

Fehr, B. (1996). *Friendship processes.* Thousand Oaks, CA: Sage.

Fehr, B., & Russell, J. A. (1991). The concept of love viewed from a prototype perspective. *Journal of Personality and Social Psychology, 60,* 425–438.

Feingold, A. (1988a). Cognitive gender differences are disappearing. *American Psychologist, 43,* 95–103.

Feingold, A. (1988b). Matching for attractiveness in romantic partners and same-sex friends: A meta-analysis and theoretical critique. *Psychological Bulletin, 104,* 226–235.

Feingold, A. (1992a). Good-looking people are not what we think. *Psychological Bulletin, 111,* 304–341.

Feingold, A. (1992b). Gender differences in mate selection preferences: A test of the parental investment model. *Psychological Bulletin, 112,* 125–139.

Feingold, A. (1993). Cognitive gender differences: A developmental perspective. *Sex Roles, 29,* 91–112.

Feingold, A., & Mazzella, R. (1996, Fall). Gender differences in body image are increasing. *General Psychologist, 32,* 90–98.

Fenson, L., et al. (1991). *The MacArthur Communicative Development Inventories: Technical manual.* San Diego: San Diego State University.

Fernald, A. (1991). Prosody in speech to children: Prelinguistic and linguistic functions. *Annals of Child Development, 8,* 43–80.

Fernald, A., & Mazzie, C. (1991). Prosody and focus in speech to infants and adults. *Developmental Psychology, 27,* 209–221.

Fernandez, E., & Turk, D. C. (1989). The utility of cognitive coping strategies for altering pain perception: A meta-analysis. *Pain, 38,* 123–135.

Fernandez, E., & Turk, D. C. (1992). Sensory and affective components of pain: Separation and synthesis. *Psychological Bulletin, 112,* 205–217.

Feroce, A. (1992). *Class assignment on confounding variables.* Geneseo, NY: SUNY Geneseo.

Ferreira, F. (1994). Eye movements and the study of cognitive processing [Review of the book *Eye movements and visual cognition: Scene perception and reading*]. *Contemporary Psychology, 39,* 1087–1090.

Ferster, D., & Spruston, N. (1995). Cracking the neuronal code. *Science, 270,* 756–757.

Festinger, L. (1964). *Conflict, decision, and dissonance.* Stanford, CA: Stanford University Press.

Festinger, L., & Carlsmith, J. M. (1959). Cognitive consequences of forced compliance. *Journal of Abnormal and Social Psychology, 58,* 203–210.

Field, T. M. (1993). The therapeutic effects of touch. In G. G. Brannigan & M. R. Merrens (Eds.), *The undaunted psychologist:*

Adventures in research (pp. 2–11). Philadelphia: Temple University Press.

Field, T. M. (Ed.). (1995). *Touch in early development.* Hillsdale, NJ: Erlbaum.

Fincham, F. D., Beach, S. R. H., Harold, G. T., & Osborn, L. N. (1997). Marital satisfaction and depression: Different causal relationships for men and women? *Psychological Science, 8,* 351–357.

Fincham, F. D., & Bradbury, T. N. (1993). Marital satisfaction, depression, and attributions: A longitudinal analysis. *Journal of Personality and Social Psychology, 64,* 442–452.

Finkelhor, D., & Dziuba-Leatherman, J. (1994). Victimization of children. *American Psychologist, 49,* 173–183.

Finkelstein, N. W., & Haskins, R. (1983). Kindergarten children prefer same-color peers. *Child Development, 54,* 502–508.

Finn, K. L. (1991, Fall). Uncovering a hidden problem. *University of Michigan Medical Center Advance,* pp. 2–12.

Finn, K. L. (1996, Spring). From toe tags to body bags. *Advance,* 14–19.

Fiorito, G. (1993). Social learning in invertebrates: Response. *Science, 259,* 1629.

Fiorito, G., & Scotto, P. (1992). Observational learning in *Octopus vulgaris. Science, 256,* 545.

Fischhoff, B. (1992). Giving advice: Decision theory perspectives on sexual assault. *American Psychologist, 47,* 577–588.

Fischhoff, B. (1996). The real world: What good is it? *Organizational Behavior and Human Decision Processes, 65,* 232–248.

Fischman, M. W., & Foltin, R. W. (1991). Cocaine and the amphetamines. In I. B. Glass (Ed.), *The international handbook of addiction behaviour* (pp. 85–89). London: Routledge.

Fishbein, H. D. (1996). *Peer prejudice and discrimination.* Boulder, CO: Westview Press.

Fisher, C. B., & Fyrberg, D. (1994). Participant partners: College students weigh the costs and benefits of deceptive research. *American Psychologist, 49,* 417–427.

Fisher, R. J. (1990). *The social psychology of intergroup and international conflict resolution.* New York: Springer-Verlag.

Fisher, S., & Greenberg, R. P. (1977). *The scientific credibility of Freud's theories and therapy.* New York: Basic Books.

Fiske, M., & Chiriboga, D. A. (1990). *Change and continuity in adult life.* San Francisco: Jossey-Bass.

Fiske, S. T. (1992). Thinking is for doing: Portraits of social cognition from Daguerreotype to laserphoto. *Journal of Personality and Social Psychology, 63,* 877–889.

Fiske, S. T. (1993a). Social cognition and social perception. *Annual Review of Psychology, 44,* 155–194.

Fiske, S. T. (1993b). Controlling other people: The impact of power on stereotyping. *American Psychologist, 48,* 621–628.

Fiske, S. T., et al. (1991). Social science research on trial: Use of sex stereotyping research in *Price Waterhouse v. Hopkins. American Psychologist, 46,* 1049–1060.

Fiske, S. T., Pratto, F., & Pavelchak, M. A. (1983). Citizens' images of nuclear war: Content and consequences. *Journal of Social Issues, 39,* 41–65.

Fiske, S. T., & Stevens, L. E. (1993). What's so special about sex? Gender stereotyping and discrimination. In S. Oskamp & M. Costanzo (Eds.), *Gender issues in contemporary society* (pp. 173–196). Newbury Park, CA: Sage.

Fiske, S. T., & Taylor, S. E. (1991). *Social cognition* (2nd ed.). New York: McGraw-Hill.

Flavell, J. H. (1992). Cognitive development: Past, present, and future. *Developmental Psychology, 28,* 998–1005.

Flavell, J. H. (1996). Piaget's legacy. *Psychological Science, 7,* 200–203.

Flores d'Arcais, G. B. (1988). Language perception in F. J. Newmeyer (Ed.), *Linguistics: The Cambridge survey* (Vol. 3, pp. 97–123). Cambridge: Cambridge University Press.

Foddy, W. (1993). *Constructing questions for interviews and questionnaires: Theory and practice in social research.* New York: Cambridge University Press.

Foertsch, J., & Gernsbacher, M. A. (1997). In search of gender neutrality: Is singular *they* a cognitively efficient substitute for generic *he? Psychological Science, 8,* 106–111.

Fogelman, E. (1994). *Conscience and courage: Rescuers of Jews during the Holocaust.* New York: Anchor.

Foley, J. M. (1980). Binocular distance perception. *Psychological Review, 87,* 411–434.

Foley, J. M. (1985). Binocular distance perception: Egocentric distance tasks. *Journal of Experimental Psychology: Human Perception and Performance, 11,* 132–149.

Foley, M. A., Foley, H. J., Durso, F. T., & Smith, N. K. (1997). Investigations of closure processes: What source-monitoring judgments suggest about what is "closing." *Memory & Cognition, 25,* 140–155.

Ford, C. V. (1996). *Lies! Lies!! Lies!!!: The psychology of deceit.* Washington, DC: American Psychological Association.

Forth-Finnegan, J. L. (1991). Sugar and spice and everything nice: Gender socialization and women's addiction—A literature review. In C. Bepko (Ed.), *Feminism and addiction* (pp. 19–48). New York: Haworth.

Foti, R. J., & Lord, R. G. (1987). Prototypes and scripts: The effects of alternative methods of processing information on rating accuracy. *Organizational Behavior and Human Decision Processes, 39,* 318–340.

Fox, L. H., Tobin, D., & Brody, L. (1979). Sex-role socialization and achievement in mathematics. In M. A. Wittig & A. C. Petersen (Eds.), *Sex-related differences in cognitive functioning* (pp. 303–332). New York: Academic Press.

Fox, M., Gibbs, M., & Auerback, D. (1985). Age and gender dimensions of friendship. *Psychology of Women Quarterly, 9,* 489–501.

Frable, D. E. S. (1997). Gender, racial, ethnic, sexual, and class identities. *Annual Review of Psychology, 48,* 139–162.

Frank, M. G., Ekman, P., & Friesen, W. V. (1993). Behavioral markers and recognizability of the smile of enjoyment. *Journal of Personality and Social Psychology, 64,* 83–93.

Franz, C. E., & McClelland, D. C. (1994). Lives of women and men active in the social protests of the 1960s: A longitudinal study. *Journal of Personality and Social Psychology, 66,* 196–205.

Freedman, J. L. (1986). Television violence and aggression: A rejoinder. *Psychological Bulletin, 100,* 372–378.

Freedman, J. L. (1992). Television violence and aggression: What psychologists should tell the public. In P. Suedfeld & P. E. Tetlock (Eds.), *Psychology and social policy* (pp. 179–189). New York: Hemisphere.

Freedman, J. L., & Fraser, S. C. (1966). Compliance without pressure: The foot-in-the-door technique. *Journal of Personality and Social Psychology, 4,* 195–203.

Freedy, J. R., & Donkervoet, J. C. (1995). Traumatic stress: An overview of the field. In J. R. Freedy & S. E. Hobfoll (Eds.), *Traumatic stress: From theory to practice* (pp. 3–28). New York: Plenum.

Freiberg, P. (1991, January). The guru of prevention calls for social change. *APA Monitor,* pp. 28–29.

Freiberg, P. (1995, June). Psychologists examine attacks on homosexuals. *APA Monitor,* pp. 30–31.

Freiberg, P. (1998, February). We know how to stop the spread of AIDS: So why can't we? *APA Monitor,* p. 32.

French, E. G., & Thomas, F. H. (1958). The relationship of achievement motivation to problem-solving effectiveness. *Journal of Abnormal and Social Psychology, 56,* 45–48.

Freud, S. (1900/1953). *The interpretation of dreams.* London: Hogarth.

Freud, S. (1909). Analysis of a phobia in a five-year-old boy. In *The standard edition of the complete psychological works of Sigmund Freud.* London: Hogarth.

Freud, S. (1925/1976). Some physical consequences of the anatomical distinction between the sexes. In J. Strachey (Ed., Trans.), *The complete psychological works: Standard edition* (Vol. 19). New York: Norton.

Freud, S. (1933/1964). New introductory lectures on psychoanalysis. In J. Strachey (Ed.), *The standard edition of the complete psychological works of Sigmund Freud* (Vol. 23). London: Hogarth.

Frey, D. L., & Gaertner, S. L. (1986). Helping and the avoidance of inappropriate interracial behavior: A strategy that perpetuates a nonprejudiced self image. *Journal of Personality and Social Psychology, 50,* 1083–1090.

Frick, R. W. (1988). Issues of representation and limited capacity in the auditory short-term store. *British Journal of Psychology, 79,* 213–240.

Frick, R. W. (1990). The visual suffix effect in tests of the visual short-term store. *Bulletin of the Psychonomic Society, 28,* 101–104.

Fried, S., Van Booven, D., & MacQuarrie, C. (1993). *Older adulthood: Learning activities for understanding aging.* Baltimore: Health Professions Press.

Friedman, H. S., Hawley, P. H., & Tucker, J. S. (1994). Personality, health, and longevity. *Current Directions in Psychological Science, 3,* 37–41.

Friedman, L., Bliwise, D. L., Yesavage, J. A., & Salom, S. R. (1991). A preliminary study comparing sleep restriction and relaxation treatments for insomnia in older adults. *Journal of Gerontology, 46,* P1–P8.

Friedman, M., & Rosenman, R. (1974). *Type A behavior pattern and your heart.* New York: Knopf.

Frieze, I. H., Olson, J. E., & Katz, J. M. (1994). Understanding the characteristics and experiences of women in male- and female-dominated fields. In M. R. Stevenson (Ed.), *Gender roles through the life span* (pp. 151–202). Muncie, IN: Ball State University Press.

Frisch, D. (1993). Reasons for framing effects. *Organizational Behavior and Human Decision Processes, 54,* 399–429.

Frodi, A., & Ahnlund, K. (1995). *Gender differences in the vulnerability to depression.* Paper presented at the convention of the Eastern Psychological Association, Boston.

Fromkin, V. A. (1998). Speech production. In J. B. Berko-Gleason & N. B. Ratner (Eds.), *Psycholinguistics* (2nd ed., pp. 309–346). Fort Worth, TX: Harcourt Brace Jovanovich.

Frumkes, T. E. (1990). Classic and modern psychophysical studies of dark and light adaptation and their relationship to underlying retinal function. In K. N. Leibovic (Ed.), *Science of vision* (pp. 172–210). New York: Springer-Verlag.

Fruzzetti, A. E., Toland, K., Teller, S. A., & Loftus, E. F. (1992). Memory and eyewitness testimony. In M. Gruneberg & P. Morris (Eds.), *Aspects of memory* (2nd ed., Vol. 1, pp. 18–50). New York: Routledge.

Fry, D. P. (1993). The intergenerational transmission of disciplinary practices and approaches to conflict. *Human Organization, 52,* 176–185.

Fucci, D., Petrosino, L., Schuster, S. B., & Wagner, S. (1990). Comparison of lingual vibrotactile suprathreshold numerical responses in men and women: Effects of threshold shift during magnitude-estimation scaling. *Perceptual and Motor Skills, 70,* 483–492.

Fulginiti, V. A. (1992). Editorial: Violence and children in the United States. *American Journal of Diseases of Children, 146,* 671–672.

Fuller, S. R., & Aldag, R. J. (1996). Organizational Tonypandy: Lessons from the groupthink fiasco. *Organizational Behavior and Human Decision Processes,* in press.

Funder, D. C. (1993). Judgments as data for personality and developmental psychology: Error versus accuracy. In D. C. Funder, R. D. Parke, C. Tomlinson-Keasey, & K. Widaman (Eds.), *Studying lives through time: Personality and development* (pp. 121–146). Washington, DC: American Psychological Association.

Funder, D. C. (1995). On the accuracy of personality judgment: A realistic approach. *Psychological Review, 102,* 652–670.

Furstenberg, F. F., & Cherlin, A. J. (1991). *Divided families: What happens to children when parents part.* Cambridge, MA: Harvard University Press.

Fussell, S. R., & Kraus, R. M. (1992). Coordination of speakers' assumptions about what others know. *Journal of Personality and Social Psychology, 62,* 378–391.

Gabbard, G. O. (1995). Psychodynamic psychotherapies. In G. O. Gabbard (Ed.), *Treatment of psychiatric disorders* (2nd ed., Vol. 1, pp. 1205–1220). Washington, DC: American Psychiatric Press.

Gabrieli, J. D. E., Cohen, N. L., & Corkin, S. (1988). The impaired learning of semantic knowledge following bilateral medial temporal-lobe resection. *Brain and Cognition, 7,* 157–177.

Gaffan, D., & Harrison, S. (1987). Amygdalectomy and disconnection in visual learning for auditory secondary reinforcement by monkeys. *Journal of Neuroscience, 7,* 2285–2292.

Galambos, N. L. (1992). Parent-child relations. *Current Directions in Psychological Science, 1,* 146–149.

Galambos, S. J., & Goldin-Meadow, S. (1990). The effects of learning two languages on levels of metalinguistic awareness. *Cognition, 34,* 1–56.

Galambos, S. J., & Hakuta, K. (1988). Subject-specific and task-specific characteristics of metalinguistic awareness in bilingual children. *Applied Psycholinguistics, 9,* 141–162.

Galanter, E. (1962). Contemporary psychophysics. In R. Brown, E. Galanter, E. H. Hess, & G. Mandler (Eds.), *New directions in psychology.* New York: Holt, Rinehart and Winston.

Galindo, R. (1997). *Icebreaker: The autobiography of Rudy Galindo.* New York: Pocket Books.

Gallant, S. J., et al. (1992). Using daily ratings to confirm pre-menstrual syndrome/late luteal phase dysphoric disorder: Part I. Effects of demand characteristics and expectations. *Psychosomatic Medicine, 54,* 149–166.

Gallistel, C. R. (1990). *The organization of learning.* Cambridge, MA: MIT Press.

Gannon, L., et al. (1992). Sex bias in psychological research: Progress or complacency. *American Psychologist, 47,* 389–396.

Gao, J., et al. (1996). Cerebellum implicated in sensory acquisition and discrimination rather than motor control. *Science, 272,* 545–547.

Gara, M. A., et al. (1993). Perception of self and other in major depression. *Journal of Abnormal Psychology, 102,* 93–100.

Garbarino, J., & Kostelny, K. (1992). Cultural diversity and identity formation. In J. Garbarino (Ed.), *Children and families in the social environment* (pp. 179–199). New York: de Gruyter.

Garcia, J. (1984). Evolution of learning mechanisms. in B. L. Hammond (Ed.), *Psychology and learning.* Washington, DC: American Psychological Association.

Garcia, J., & Koelling, R. (1966). Relation of cue to consequence in avoidance learning. *Psychonomic Science, 4,* 123–124.

Garcia, J., McGowan, G. K., & Green, K. F. (1972). Biological constraints on conditioning. In A. H. Black & W. F. Prokasy (Eds.), *Classical conditioning II: Current research and theory.* New York: Appleton-Century-Crofts.

Gardner, H. (1983). *Frames of mind: The theory of multiple intelligences.* New York: Basic Books.

Gardner, H. (1985). *The mind's new science: A history of the cognitive revolution.* New York: Basic Books.

Gardner, H. (1988, Summer). Multiple intelligences in today's schools. *Human Intelligence Newsletter, 9* (2), 1–2.

Gardner, H. (1993). *Multiple intelligences: The theory in practice.* New York: Basic Books.

Gardner, H. (1994). The stories of the right hemisphere. *Nebraska Symposium on Motivation, 41,* 57–69.

Gardner, R. C., & Lambert, W. E. (1959). Motivational variables in second-language acquisition. *Canadian Journal of Psychology, 13,* 266–272.

Garfield, S. L. (1995). *Psychotherapy: An eclectic-integrative approach* (2nd ed.). New York: Wiley.

Garramone, G. M., Steele, M. E., & Pinkelton, B. (1990). The role of cognitive schemata in determining candidate characteristic effects. In F. Biocca (Ed.), *Television and political advertising* (Vol. 1, pp. 311–328). Hillsdale, NJ: Erlbaum.

Garry, M., & Loftus, E. F. (1994). Pseudomemories without hypnosis. *International Journal of Clinical and Experimental Hypnosis, 42,* 363–378.

Gartrell, J. W., Jarvis, G. K., & Derksen, L. (1993). Suicidality among adolescent Alberta Indians. *Suicide and Life-Threatening Behavior, 23,* 366–373.

Gastil, J. (1990). Generic pronouns and sexist language: The oxymoronic character of masculine generics. *Sex Roles, 23,* 629–643.

Gathercole, S. E. (1992). The nature and uses of working memory. In P. Morris & M. Gruneberg (Eds.), *Theoretical aspects of memory* (2nd ed., pp. 50–78). New York: Routledge.

Gathercole, S. E., & Baddeley, A. D. (1993). *Working memory and language.* Hove, England: Erlbaum.

Gazzaniga, M. S. (1983). Right hemisphere language following brain bisection. *American Psychologist, 38,* 525–537.

Gazzaniga, M. S. (1992). *Nature's mind: The biological roots of thinking, emotions, sexuality, language, and intelligence.* New York: Basic Books.

Gazzaniga, M. S., & LeDoux, J. E. (1978). *The integrated mind.* New York: Plenum.

Geary, D. C. (1995). Sexual selection and sex differences in spatial cognition. *Learning and Individual Differences, 7,* 289–301.

Gee, E. M. (1995). Contemporary diversities. InN. Mandell & A. Duffy (Eds.), *Canadian families: Diversity, conflict and change* (pp. 79–109). Toronto: Butterworths.

Geen, R. G. (1991). Social motivation. *Annual Review of Psychology, 42,* 377–399.

Geen, R. G. (1994). Television and aggression: Recent developments in research and theory. In D. Zillman, J. Bryant, & A. C. Huston (Eds.), *Media, children, and the family: Social scientific, psychodynamic, and clinical perspectives* (pp. 151–162). Hillsdale, NJ: Erlbaum.

Geiselman, R. E. (1992). Hypnosis and memory. InL. R. Squire (Ed.), *Encyclopedia of learning and memory* (pp. 255–259). New York: Macmillan.

Geisinger, K. F. (Ed.). (1992). *Psychological testing of Hispanics.* Washington, DC: American Psychological Association.

Geller, J. D. (1988). Racial bias in the evaluation of patients for psychotherapy. In L. Comas-Díaz & E. Griffith (Eds.), *Clinical guidelines in cross-cultural mental health* (pp. 112–134). New York: Wiley.

Gelman, D. (1993, January 11). The young and the reckless. *Newsweek,* pp. 60–61.

Gelso, C. J., & Fretz, B. R. (1992). *Counseling psychology.* Fort Worth, TX: Harcourt Brace Jovanovich.

Gender-specific pain relief. (1993, July 11). *Los Angeles Daily News,* p. C1.

Genesee, F., Tucker, R., & Lambert, W. E. (1975). Communication skills of bilingual children. *Child Development, 46,* 1010–1014.

Geraghty, M. (1996, July 19). More students quitting college before sophomore year, data show. *Chronicle of Higher Education,* pp. A35–A36.

Gerard, H. B. (1994). A retrospective review of Festinger's *A Theory of Cognitive Dissonance. Contemporary Psychology, 39,* 1013–1017.

Gernsbacher, M. A. (Ed.). (1994). *Handbook of psycholinguistics.* San Diego, CA: Academic Press.

Gerrity, E. T., & Steinglass, P. (1994). Relocation stress following natural disaster. In R. J. Ursano, B. G. McCaughey, & C. S. Fullerton (Eds.), *Individual and community responses to trauma and disaster* (pp. 220–247). New York: Cambridge University Press.

Gershon, E. S., & Rieder, R. O. (1992, September). Major disorders of mind and brain. *Scientific American,* pp. 127–133.

Gerson, M. J. (1986). The prospect of parenthood for women and men. *Psychology of Women Quarterly, 10,* 49–62.

Gettys, C. F., Mehle, T., & Fisher, S. (1986). Plausibility assessments in hypothesis generation. *Organizational Behavior and Human Decision Processes, 37,* 14–33.

Gfellner, B. M. (1994). A matched-group comparison of drug use and problem behavior among Canadian Indian and White adolescents. *Journal of Early Adolescence, 14,* 24–48.

Giachello, A. L. (1996). Latino women. In M. Bayne-Smith (Ed.), *Race, gender, and health* (pp. 121–171). Thousand Oaks, CA: Sage.

Gibbons, B. (1992, February). Alcohol, the legal drug. *National Geographic,* pp. 2–35.

Gibbs, L., et al. (1995). A measure of critical thinking about practice. *Research on Social Work Practice, 5,* 193–204.

Gibson, E. J. (1969). *Principles of perceptual learning and development.* Englewood Cliffs, NJ: Prentice Hall.

Gibson, E. J., & Walk, R. D. (1960). The "visual cliff." *Scientific American, 202* (4), 64–71.

Gibson, J. J. (1959). Perception as a function of stimulation. In S. Koch (Ed.), *Psychology: A study of a science* (Vol. 1, pp. 456–501). New York: McGraw-Hill.

Gibson, J. J. (1979). *The ecological approach to visual perception.* Boston: Houghton Mifflin.

Giedd, J. N., et al. (1994). Quantitative morphology of the corpus callosum in attention deficit hyperactivity disorder. *American Journal of Psychiatry, 151,* 665–669.

Gigerenzer, G., & Hoffrage, U. (1995). How to improve Bayesian reasoning without instruction: Frequency formats. *Psychological Review, 102,* 684–704.

Gilbert, D. T., & Jones, E. E. (1986). Perceiver-induced constraint: Interpretations of self-generated reality. *Journal of Personality and Social Psychology, 50,* 269–280.

Gilbert, L. A. (1994). Current perspectives on dual-career families. *Current Directions in Psychological Science, 3,* 101–105.

Gilbert, M. J. (1989). Alcohol use among Latino adolescents: What we know and what we need to know. In B. Segal (Ed.), *Perspectives on adolescent drug use* (pp. 35–53). New York: Haworth.

Gillam, B. (1980). Geometric illusions. *Scientific American, 242,* 102–111.

Gillem, A. (1996). Beyond double jeopardy: Female, biracial, and perceived to be Black. In J. C. Chrisler, C. Golden, & P. D. Rozee (Eds.), *Lectures on the psychology of women* (pp. 198–209). New York: McGraw-Hill.

Gilley, D. W. (1993). Behavioral and affective disturbances in Alzheimer's disease. In R. W. Parks, R. F. Zec, & R. S. Wilson (Eds.), *Neuropsychology of Alzheimer's disease and other dementias* (pp. 112–137). New York: Oxford University Press.

Gilligan, C. (1982). *In a different voice.* Cambridge, MA: Harvard University Press.

Gilovich, T. (1991). *How we know what isn't so: The fallibility of human reason in everyday life.* New York: Free Press.

Ginsburg, H. P., & Opper, S. (1988). *Piaget's theory of intellectual development* (3rd ed.). Englewood Cliffs, NJ: Prentice Hall.

Girard, K., & Koch, S. J. (1996). *Conflict resolution in the schools: A manual for educators.* San Francisco: Jossey-Bass.

Gitlin, M. J. (1996). *The psychotherapist's guide to psychopharmacology* (2nd ed.). New York: Free Press.

Gladue, B. A. (1994). The biopsychology of sexual orientation. *Current Directions in Psychological Science, 3,* 150–154.

Glaser, R., & Chi, M. T. H. (1988). Overview. In M. T. H. Chi, R. Glaser, & M. J. Farr (Eds.), *The nature of expertise* (pp. xv–xxxvi). Hillsdale, NJ: Erlbaum.

Glees, P. (1988). *The human brain.* Cambridge: Cambridge University Press.

Glick, P., & Fiske, S. T. (1996). The Ambivalent Sexism Inventory: Differentiating hostile and benevolent sexism. *Journal of Personality and Social Psychology, 70,* 491–512.

Glick, P., Zion, C., & Nelson, C. (1988). What mediates sex discrimination in hiring decisions? *Journal of Personality and Social Psychology, 55,* 178–186.

Gogel, W. C. (1977). The metric of visual space. In W. Epstein (Ed.), *Stability and constancy in visual perception: Mechanisms and processes.* New York: Wiley.

Goisman, R. M. (1997, May). Cognitive-behavioral therapy today. *Harvard Mental Health Letter,* pp. 4–7.

Gold, M. S. (1993). *Cocaine.* New York: Plenum.

Gold, M. S. (1995). *Tobacco.* New York: Plenum.

Goldberg, L. R. (1993). The structure of phenotypic personality traits. *American Psychologist, 48,* 26–34.

Goldberg, M. E., & Bruce, C. J. (1986). The role of the arcuate frontal eye fields in the generation of saccadic eye movements. In H. J. Freund, U. Buttner, B. Cohen, & J. Noth (Eds.), *Progress in brain research* (Vol. 64, pp. 143–174). Amsterdam: Elsevier.

Goldberg, S. (1993). Early attachment: A passing fancy or a long term affair? *Canadian Psychology/Psychologie Canadienne, 34,* 307–314.

Goldberg, T. E., et al. (1990). Neuropsychological assessment of monzygotic twins discordant for schizophrenia. *Archives of General Psychiatry, 47,* 1066–1072.

Goldenberg, I., & Goldenberg, H. (1991). *Family therapy: An overview* (3rd ed.). Pacific Grove, CA: Brooks/Cole.

Goldfried, M. R. (1995). *From cognitive-behavior therapy to psychotherapy integration.* New York: Springer.

Goldman, M. S., Brown, S. A., Christiansen, B. A., & Smith, G. T. (1991). Alcoholism and memory: Broadening the scope of alcohol-expectancy research. *Psychological Bulletin, 110,* 137–146.

Goldman-Rakic, P. S. (1988). Topography of cognition: Parallel distributed networks in primate association cortex. *Annual Review of Neuroscience, 11,* 137–156.

Goldsmith, H. H. (1993). Nature-nurture issues in behavior-genetic context: Overcoming barriers to communication. In R. Plomin & G. E. McClearn (Eds.), *Nature, nurture, and psychology.* Washington, DC: American Psychological Association.

Goldsmith, H. H., Losoya, S. H., & Bradshaw, S. H. (1994). Genetics of personality: A twin study of the five-factor model and parent-offspring analyses. In C. H. Halverson, Jr., G. A. Kohnstamm, & R. P. Martin (Eds.), *The developing structure of temperament and personality from infancy to adulthood* (pp. 241–265). Hillsdale, NJ: Erlbaum.

Goldstein, A. (1976). Opioid peptides endorphins in pituitary and brain. *Science, 193,* 1081–1086.

Goldstein, A. (1994). *Addiction: From biology to drug policy.* New York: Freeman.

Goldstein, E. B. (1989). *Sensation and perception* (3rd ed.). Belmont, CA: Wadsworth.

Goldstein, E. B. (1996). *Sensation and perception* (4th ed.). Pacific Grove, CA: Brooks/Cole.

Goleman, D. (1995). *Emotional intelligence.* New York: Bantam.

Golombok, S., & Fivush, R. (1994). *Gender development.* New York: Cambridge University Press.

Golub, S. (1992). *Periods: From menarche to menopause.* Newbury Park, CA: Sage.

Gong-Guy, E., Cravens, R. B., & Patterson, T. E. (1991). Clinical issues in mental health service delivery to refugees. *American Psychologist, 46,* 642–648.

Gonsiorek, J. C. (1996). Mental health and sexual orientation. In R. C. Savin-Williams & K. Cohen (Eds.), *The lives of lesbians, gays, and bisexuals: Children to adults* (pp. 462–478). Fort Worth, TX: Harcourt Brace.

Gonsiorek, J. C., & Weinrich, J. D. (Eds.). (1991). *Homosexuality: Research implications for public policy.* Newbury Park, CA: Sage.

Goodglass, H. (1993). *Understanding aphasia.* San Diego, CA: Academic Press.

Goodman, G. S., & Bottoms, B. L. (Eds.). (1993). *Child victims, child witnesses: Understanding and improving testimony.* New York: Guilford Press.

Goodman, G. S., et al. (1996). Predictors of accurate and inaccurate memories of traumatic events experienced in childhood. In K. Pezdek & W. P. Banks (Eds.), *The recovered memory/false memory debate* (pp. 3–28). San Diego, CA: Academic Press.

Goodwin, C. J. (1991). Misportraying Pavlov's apparatus. *American Journal of Psychology, 104,* 135–141.

Goodwin, R. (1990). Sex differences among partner preferences: Are the sexes really very similar? *Sex Roles, 23,* 501–513.

Gordon, I. E., & Earle, D. C. (1992). Visual illusions: A short review. *Australian Journal of Psychology, 44,* 153–156.

Gormly, A. V. (1997). *Lifespan human development* (6th ed.). Fort Worth, TX: Harcourt Brace.

Gortmaker, S. L., et al. (1993). Social and economic consequences of overweight in adolescence and young adulthood. *New England Journal of Medicine, 329,* 1008–1012.

Gostin, L. O., et al. (1994). HIV testing, counseling, and prophylaxis after sexual assault. *JAMA, 271,* 1436–1444.

Gotlib, I. H. (1992). Interpersonal and cognitive aspects of depression. *Current Directions in Psychological Science, 1,* 149–154.

Gotlib, I. H., & Hammen, C. L. (1992). *Psychological aspects of depression: Toward a cognitive-interpersonal integration.* Chichester, England: Wiley.

Gottesman, I. I. (1991). *Schizophrenia genesis: The origins of madness.* New York: Freeman.

Gottfried, A. W., Gottfried, A. E., Bathurst, K., & Guerin, D. W. (1994). *Gifted IQ: Early developmental aspects.* New York: Plenum.

Gould, J. L., & Marler, P. (1987). Learning by instinct. *Scientific American, 256* (1), 74–85.

Gourevitch, P. (1997, January 20). The return. *New Yorker,* pp. 44–54.

Graber, J. A., Brooks-Gunn, J., Paikoff, R. L., & Warren, M. P. (1994). Prediction of eating problems: An 8-year study of adolescent girls. *Developmental Psychology, 30,* 823–834.

Grady, C. L., et al. (1995). Age-related reductions in human recognition memory due to impaired encoding. *Science, 269,* 218–221.

Graef, R., Csikszentmihalyi, M., & Gianinno, S. M. (1983). Measuring intrinsic motivation in everyday life. *Leisure Studies, 2,* 155–168.

Graesser, A. C., & Kreuz, R. J. (1993). A theory of inference generation during text comprehension. *Discourse Processes, 16,* 145–160.

Graesser, A. C., Millis, K. K., & Zwaan, R. A. (1997). Discourse comprehension. *Annual Review of Psychology, 48,* 163–189.

Grafman, J. (1989). Plans, actions, and mental sets: Managerial knowledge units in the frontal lobes. In E. Perecman (Ed.), *Integrating theory and practice in clinical neuropsychology* (pp. 93–138). Hillsdale, NJ: Erlbaum.

Graham, J. R. (1990). *MMPI-2: Assessing personality and psychopathology.* New York: Oxford University Press.

Graham, S. (1994). Classroom motivation from an attributional perspective. In H. F. O'Neil, Jr., & M. Drillings (Eds.), *Motivation: Theory and research* (pp. 31–48). Hillsdale, NJ: Erlbaum.

Graige, B. J. (1994, January 12). Multiculturalism and the Vietnam syndrome. *Chronicle of Higher Education,* p. B3.

Grantham, D. W. (1995). Spatial hearing and related phenomena. In B. C. J. Moore (Ed.), *Hearing* (pp. 297–345). San Diego, CA: Academic Press.

Gray, J. (1992). *Men are from Mars, women are from Venus.* New York: HarperCollins.

Gray, P. (1996). Incorporating evolutionary theory into the teaching of psychology. *Teaching of Psychology, 23,* 207–214.

Green, A. I., & Patel, J. K. (1996, December). The new pharacology of schizophrenia. *Harvard Mental Health Letter,* pp. 6–7.

Green, B. L., & Solomon, S. D. (1995). *The mental health impact of natural and technological disasters.* In J. R. Freedy & S. E. Hobfoll (Eds.), (pp. 163–180). New York: Plenum.

Green, D. G., & Powers, M. K. (1982). Mechanisms of light adaptation in rat retina. *Vision Research, 22,* 209–216.

Green, D. P., Kahneman, D., & Kunreuther, H. (1994). How the scope and method of public funding affect willingness to pay for public goods. *Public Opinion Quarterly, 58,* 49–67.

Green, G. M. (1996). *Pragmatics and natural language understanding* (2nd ed.). Mahwah, NJ: Erlbaum.

Greenberg, B. S. (1975). British children and television violence. *Public Opinion Quarterly, 39,* 521–547.

Greenberg, B. S., & Brand, J. E. (1994). Minorities and the mass media: 1970s to 1990s. In J. Bryant & D. Zillman (Eds.), *Media effects: Advances in theory and research* (pp. 273–314). Hillsdale, NJ: Erlbaum.

Greenberg, J. (1990). Employee theft as a reaction to underpayment inequity: The hidden cost of pay cuts. *Journal of Applied Psychology, 75,* 561–568.

Greenberg, R. P., et al. (1994). A meta-analysis of fluoxetine outcome in the treatment of depression. *Journal of Nervous and Mental Disease, 182,* 547–551.

Greene, R. L. (1987). Ethnicity and MMPI performance: A review. *Journal of Consulting and Clinical Psychology, 55,* 497–512.

Greene, R. L. (1992). *Human memory: Paradigms and paradoxes.* Hillsdale, NJ: Erlbaum.

Greenfield, P. M., & Savage-Rumbaugh, S. (1991). Imitation, grammatical development, and the invention of protogrammar by an ape. In N. A. Krasnegor, D. M. Rumbaugh, R. L. Schiefelbusch, & M. Studdert-Kennedy (Eds.), *Biological and behavioral determinants of language development* (pp. 235–258). Hillsdale, NJ: Erlbaum.

Greengard, P., Valtorta, F., Czernik, A. J., & Benfenati, F. (1993). Synaptic vesicle phosphoproteins and regulation of synaptic function. *Science, 259,* 780–785.

Greeno, C. G., & Maccoby, E. E. (1986). How different is the "different voice"? *Signs, 11,* 310–316.

Greeno, J. G. (1977). Process of understanding in problem solving. In J. J. Castellan, Jr., D. B. Pisoni, & G. R. Potts (Eds.), *Cognitive theory* (Vol. 2, pp. 43–84). Hillsdale, NJ: Erlbaum.

Greeno, J. G. (1991). A view of mathematical problem solving in school. In M. U. Smith (Ed.), *Toward a unified theory of problem solving* (pp. 69–98). Hillsdale, NJ: Erlbaum.

Greenough, W. T. (1991). The animal rights assertions: A researcher's perspective. *Psychological Science Agenda, 4* (3), 10–12.

Greenough, W. T. (1992). Animal rights replies distort(ed) and misinform(ed). *Psychological Science, 3,* 142.

Greenspan, M. (1993). *A new approach to women and therapy* (2nd ed.). Bradenton, FL: Human Services Institute.

Greenspan, S. (1996). Am I jealous, or is it my stupid amygdala? [Review of the book *Emotional intelligence*]. *Contemporary Psychology, 41,* 1206.

Greenwald, A. G., & Banaji, M. R. (1995). Implicit social cognition: Attitudes, self-esteem, and stereotypes. *Psychological Review, 102,* 4–27.

Greenwald, A. G., Spangenberg, E. R., Pratkanis, A. R., & Eskenazi, J. (1991). Double-blind tests of subliminal self-help audiotapes. *Psychological Science, 2,* 119–122.

Griffin, D. R. (1991, November). Essay: Animal thinking. *Scientific American, 265* (5), p. 144.

Griffin, D. W., & Varey, C. A. (1996). Towards a consensus on overconfidence. *Organizational Behavior and Human Decision Processes, 65,* 227–231.

Griffith, P. L., & Olson, M. W. (1992). Phonemic awareness helps beginning readers break the code. *The Reading Teacher, 45,* 516–523.

Grilo, C. M., & Pogue-Geile, M. F. (1991). The nature of environmental influences on weight and obesity: A behavioral genetic analysis. *Psychological Bulletin, 110,* 520–537.

Grinspoon, L., & Bakalar, J. B. (1994). The war on drugs—A peace proposal. *New England Journal of Medicine, 330,* 357–360.

Grob, G. N. (1994). *The mad among us: A history of the care of America's mentally ill.* New York: Free Press.

Grossman, F. K. (1987). Separate and together: Men's autonomy and affiliation in the transition to parenthood. In P. W. Berman & F. A. Pedersen (Eds.), *Men's transitions to parenthood: Longitudinal studies of early family experience* (pp. 89–112). Hillsdale, NJ: Erlbaum.

Groth-Marnat, G. (1990). *Handbook of psychological assessment* (2nd ed.). New York: Wiley.

Grusec, J. E. (1992). Social learning theory and developmental psychology: The legacies of Robert Sears and Albert Bandura. *Developmental Psychology, 28,* 776–786.

Guerin, B. (1993). *Social facilitation.* Cambridge: Cambridge University Press.

Gulick, W. L., Gescheider, G. A., & Frisina, R. D. (1989). *Hearing: Physiological acoustics, neural coding, and psychoacoustics.* New York: Oxford University Press.

Gunter, B. (1986). *Television and sex role stereotyping.* London: Libbey.

Gunter, B. (1994). The question of media violence. In J. Bryant & D. Zillmann (Eds.), *Media effects: Advances in theory and research* (pp. 163–211). Hillsdale, NJ: Erlbaum.

Guthrie, R. V. (1998). *Even the rat was white: A historical view of psychology* (2nd ed.). Boston: Allyn & Bacon.

Haaland, K. Y. (1992). Introduction to the special section on the emotional concomitants of brain damage. *Journal of Consulting and Clinical Psychology, 60,* 327–328.

Haensly, P. A., & Reynolds, C. R. (1989). Creativity and intelligence. In J. A. Glover, R. R. Ronning, & C. R. Reynolds (Eds.), *Handbook of creativity* (pp. 135–145). New York: Plenum.

Hagen, M. A. (1985). James J. Gibson's ecological approach to visual perception. In S. Koch & D. E. Leary (Eds.), *A century of psychology as science* (pp. 231–249). New York: McGraw-Hill.

Hale, N. G., Jr. (1995). *The rise and crisis of psychoanalysis in the United States: Freud and the Americans, 1917–1985.* New York: Oxford University Press.

Halgin, R. P., & Whitbourne, S. K. (1997). *Abnormal psychology: The human experience of psychological disorders.* Dubuque, IA: Brown & Benchmark.

Hall, C. C. I. (1997). Cultural malpractice. The growing obsolescence of psychology with the changing U.S. population. *American Psychologist, 52,* 642–651.

Hall, E. G. (1990). The effect of performer gender, performer skill level, and opponent gender on self-confidence in a competitive situation. *Sex Roles, 23,* 33–41.

Hall, J. A. (1984). *Nonverbal sex differences: Communication accuracy and expressive style.* Baltimore: Johns Hopkins University Press.

Hall, J. A. (1987). On explaining gender differences: The case of nonverbal communication. In P. Shaver & C. Hendrick (Eds.), *Sex and gender* (pp. 177–200). Newbury Park, CA: Sage.

Hall, J. A. (1996). *Using reader surveys as scientific data.* Paper presented at the annual convention of the American Psychological Association, Toronto.

Hall, J. A., et al. (1978, May). Decoding wordless messages. *Human Nature,* pp. 68–75.

Hall, J. A., & Veccia, E. M. (1990). More "touching" observations: New insights on men, women, and interpersonal touch. *Journal of Personality and Social Psychology, 59,* 1155–1162.

Halpern, D. F. (1992). *Sex differences in cognitive abilities* (2nd ed.). Hillsdale, NJ: Erlbaum.

Halpern, D. F. (1996a). *Thought and knowledge: Introduction to critical thinking* (3rd ed.). Mahwah, NJ: Erlbaum.

Halpern, D. F. (1996b). Changing data, changing minds: What the data on cognitive sex differences tell us and what we hear. *Learning and Individual Differences, 8,* 73–82.

Halpern, D. F., Hansen, C., & Riefer, D. (1990). Analogies as an aid to understanding and memory. *Journal of Educational Psychology, 82,* 298–305.

Halpern, D. F., Salzman, B., Harrison, W., & Widaman, K. (1983). The multiple determination of illusory contours: 2. An empirical investigation. *Perception, 12,* 293–303.

Halpern, D. F., & Wright, T. M. (1996). A process-oriented model of cognitive sex differences. *Learning and Individual Differences, 8,* 3–24.

Halpin, J. A., Puff, C. R., Mason, H. F., & Marston, S. P. (1984). Self-reference and incidental recall by children. *Bulletin of the Psychonomic Society, 22,* 87–89.

Halverson, C. F., Jr., Kohnstamm, G. A., & Martin, R. P. (Eds.). (1994). *The developing structure of temperament and personality from infancy to adulthood.* Hillsdale, NJ: Erlbaum.

Hamel, J. (1993). *Case study methods.* Newbury Park, CA: Sage.

Hamers, J. F., & Blanc, M. H. A. (1989). *Bilinguality and bilingualism.* Cambridge: Cambridge University Press.

Hamid, M. S., Garner, R., & Parenté, R. (1996). Improving reading rate and reading comprehension with iconic memory training. *Cognitive Technology, 1,* 19–24.

Hamilton, D. L., Devine, P. G., & Ostrom, T. M. (1994). Social cognition and classic issues in social psychology. In P. G. Devine, D. L. Hamilton, & T. M. Ostrom (Eds.), *Social cognition: Impact on social psychology* (pp. 1–13). San Diego, CA: Academic Press.

Hamilton, D. L., & Sherman, J. W. (1994). Stereotypes. In R. S. Wyer, Jr., & T. K. Srull (Eds.), *Handbook of social cognition* (2nd ed., Vol. 2, pp. 1–68). Hillsdale, NJ: Erlbaum.

Hamilton, D. L., & Sherman, S. J. (1996). Perceiving persons and groups. *Psychological Review, 103,* 336–355.

Hamilton, D. L., Stroessner, S. J., & Driscoll, D. M. (1994). *Social cognition and the study of stereotyping* (pp. 291–321). San Diego, CA: Academic Press.

Hamilton, D. L., Stroessner, S. J., & Mackie, D. M. (1993). The influence of affect on stereotyping: The case of illusory correlations. In D. M. Mackie & D. L. Hamilton (Eds.), *Affect, cognition, and stereotyping: Interactive processes in group perception* (pp. 39–61). San Diego, CA: Academic Press.

Handel, S. (1995). Timbre perception and auditory object identification. In B. C. J. Moore (Ed.), *Hearing* (pp. 425–461). San Diego, CA: Academic Press.

Haney, C., Banks, C., & Zimbardo, P. (1973). Interpersonal dynamics in a simulated prison. *International Journal of Criminology and Penology, 1,* 69–97.

Hansen, F. J., & Reekie, L. J. (1990). Sex differences in clinical judgments of male and female therapists. *Sex Roles, 23,* 51–64.

Hardin, C., & Banaji, M. R. (1993). The influence of language on thought. *Social Cognition, 11,* 277–308.

Hardy, J. A., & Higgins, G. A. (1992). Alzheimer's disease: The amyloid cascade hypothesis. *Science, 256,* 184–185.

Hare, A. P. (1996). Roles and relationships. In A. P. Hare, H. H. Blumberg, M. F. Davies, & M. V. Kent (Eds.), *Small groups: An introduction* (pp. 81–95). Westport, CT: Praeger.

Hargadon, R., Bowers, K. S., & Woody, E. Z. (1995). Does counterpain imagery mediate hypnotic analgesia? *Journal of Abnormal Psychology, 104,* 508–516.

Harkins, S. G. (1994). Theory in social psychology: A matter of taste? [Review of the book *Social facilitation*]. *Contemporary Psychology, 39,* 1025–1026.

Harkins, S. W. (1995). Pain. In G. L. Maddox (Ed.), *The encyclopedia of aging* (2nd ed., pp. 725–726). New York: Springer.

Härnqvist, K. (1968). Relative changes in intelligence from 13 to 18. *Scandinavian Journal of Psychology, 9,* 50–82.

Harris, B. (1979). Whatever happened to little Albert? *American Psychologist, 34,* 151–160.

Harris, J. R. (1995). Where is the child's environment? A group socialization theory of development. *Psychological Review, 102,* 458–489.

Harris, M. B., Begay, C., & Page, P. (1989). Activities, family relationships and feelings about aging in a multicultural elderly sample. *International Journal of Aging and Human Development, 29,* 103–117.

Harris, M. J., et al. (1992). Self-fulfilling effects of stigmatizing information on children's social interactions. *Journal of Personality and Social Psychology, 63,* 41–50.

Harris, S. L., Alessandri, M., & Nathan, A. M. (1991). Behavior therapy with children. In M. Hersen, A. E. Kazdin, & A. Bellack (Eds.), *The clinical psychology handbook* (2nd ed., pp. 567–579). New York: Pergamon.

Hartlage, S., Alloy, L. B., Vázquez, C., & Dykman, B. (1993). Automatic and effortful processing in depression. *Psychological Bulletin, 113,* 247–278.

Hartman, B. J. (1982). An exploratory study of the effects of disco music on the auditory and vestibular systems. *Journal of Auditory Research, 22,* 271–274.

Hartmann, E. (1993). Nightmares. In M. Carskadon (Ed.), *Encyclopedia of sleep and dreaming* (pp. 406–408). New York: Macmillan.

Hartshorne, M. F. (1995). Positron emission tomography. In W. W. Orrison, J. D. Lewine, J. A. Sanders, & M. F. Hartshorne (Eds.), *Functional brain imaging* (pp. 187–212). St. Louis: Mosby.

Hartup, W. W. (1992). Friendships and their developmental significance. In H. McGurk (Ed.), *Childhood social development: Contemporary perspectives* (pp. 175–205). Hillsdale, NJ: Erlbaum.

Hartup, W. W. (1993). Adolescents and their friends. In B. Laursen (Ed.), *Close friendships in adolescence.* San Francisco: Jossey-Bass.

Hartup, W. W., & van Lieshout, C. F. M. (1995). Personality development in social context. *Annual Review of Psychology, 46,* 655–687.

Haskins, R. (1985). Public aggression among children with varying day care experience. *Child Development, 56,* 689–703.

Hatfield, E., & Rapson, R. L. (1993). *Love, sex, and intimacy: Their psychology, biology, and history.* New York: HarperCollins.

Hatfield, E., & Rapson, R. L. (1996). *Love and sex: Cross-cultural perspectives.* Boston: Allyn & Bacon.

Hatfield, E., & Sprecher, S. (1986). *Mirror, mirror . . . The importance of looks in everyday life.* Albany: State University of New York Press.

Hattie, J. (1992). *Self-concept.* Hillsdale, NJ: Erlbaum.

Hauser, M. D. (1993). Right hemisphere dominance for the production of facial expression in monkeys. *Science, 261,* 475–477.

Havens, L. (1993). *Coming to life: Reflections on the art of psychotherapy.* Cambridge, MA: Harvard University Press.

Havill, V. L., Allen, K., Halverson, C. F., & Kohnstamm, G. A. (1994). Parents' use of Big Five categories in their natural language descriptions of children. In C. F. Halverson, Jr., G. A. Kohnstamm, & R. P. Martin (Eds.), *The developing structure of temperament and personality from infancy to adulthood* (pp. 371–386). Hillsdale, NJ: Erlbaum.

Hayes, D. (1992, October). The dances, the firebomb, and the clash of cultures. *Toronto Life,* pp. 39–43, 119–124.

Hayes, D. W. (1993, July 29). An education in violence. *Black Issues in Higher Education,* pp. 18–22.

Hayes, J. R. (1989a). Cognitive processes in creativity. In J. A. Glover, R. R. Ronning, & C. R. Reynolds (Eds.), *Handbook of creativity* (pp. 135–145). New York: Plenum.

Hayes, J. R. (1989b). *The complete problem solver* (2nd ed.). Hillsdale, NJ: Erlbaum.

Hayes, N. (1994). *Principles of comparative psychology.* Hillsdale, NJ: Erlbaum.

Hazan, C., & Shaver, P. (1987). Romantic love conceptualized as an attachment process. *Journal of Personality and Social Psychology, 52,* 511–524.

Hazen, A. L., & Stein, M. B. (1995). Clinical phenomenology and comorbidity (1995). In M. B. Stein (Ed.), *Social phobia: Clinical and research perspectives* (pp. 3–41). Washington, DC: American Psychiatric Press.

Healy, A. F., & McNamara, D. S. (1996). Verbal learning and memory: Does the modal model still work? *Annual Review of Psychology, 47,* 143–172.

Hearts and minds—Part II (1997, August). *Harvard Mental Health Letter,* pp. 1–4.

Heath, D. T. (1995). Parents' socialization of children. In B. B. Ingoldsby & S. Smith (Eds.), *Families in multicultural perspective* (pp. 161–186). New York: Guilford Press.

Heath, L., Kruttschnitt, C., & Ward, D. (1986). Television and violent criminal behavior: Beyond the Bobo doll. *Victims and Violence, 1,* 177–190.

Hedgepeth, E., & Helmich, J. (1996). *Teaching about sexuality and HIV.* New York: New York University Press.

Heeger, D. J. (1994). The representation of visual stimuli in primary visual cortex. *Current Directions in Psychological Science, 3,* 159–163.

Heidrich, S. M., & Denney, N. W. (1994). Does social problem solving differ from other types of problem solving during the adult years? *Experimental Aging Research, 20,* 105–126.

Heishman, S. J., Kozlowski, L. T., & Henningfield, J. E. (1997). Nicotine addiction: Implications for public health policy. *Journal of Social Issues, 53,* 13–33.

Heitler, S. M. (1990). *From conflict to resolution.* New York: Norton.

Helgeson, V. S. (1992). Moderators of the relation between perceived control and adjustment to chronic illness. *Journal of Personality and Social Psychology, 63,* 656–666.

Helgeson, V. S. (1994). Relation of agency and communion to well-being: Evidence and potential explanations. *Psychological Bulletin, 116,* 412–428.

Heller, M. A. (1991). Introduction. In M. A. Heller & W. Schiff (Eds.), *The psychology of touch* (pp. 1–19). Hillsdale, NJ: Erlbaum.

Heller, M. A., & Schiff, W. (1991). Conclusions: The future of touch. In M. A. Heller & W. Schiff (Eds.), *The psychology of touch* (pp. 327–337). Hillsdale, NJ: Erlbaum.

Hellige, J. B. (1991). Cerebral laterality and metacontrol. In F. L. Kitterle (Ed.), *Cerebral laterality: Theory and research* (pp. 117–132). Hillsdale, NJ: Erlbaum.

Hellige, J. B. (1993a). *Hemispheric asymmetry: What's right and what's left.* Cambridge, MA: Harvard University Press.

Hellige, J. B. (1993b). Unity of thought and action: Varieties of interaction between the left and right cerebral hemispheres. *Current Directions in Psychological Science, 2,* 21–25.

Hellige, J. B., et al. (1994). Individual variation in hemispheric asymmetry: Multitask study of effects related to handedness and sex. *Journal of Experimental Psychology: General, 123,* 235–256.

Hellmich, N. (1995, June 9). Optimism often survives spinal cord injuries. *USA Today,* p. 4D.

Helwig, C. C. (1997). Making moral cognition respectable (again): A retrospective review of Lawrence Kohlberg. *Contemporary Psychology, 42,* 191–195.

Hemsley, D. R. (1994). Perceptual and cognitive abnormalities as the bases for schizophrenic symptoms. In A. S. David & J. C. Cutting (Eds.), *The neuropsychology of schizophrenia* (pp. 97–116). Hove, England: Erlbaum.

Henderson, S. (1992). Living with the virus: Perspectives from HIV-positive women in London. In N. Dorn, S. Henderson, & N. South (Eds.), *AIDS: Women, drugs, and social care* (pp. 8–29). London: Falmer.

Hendrick, S. S., & Hendrick, C. (1992). *Romantic love.* Newbury Park, CA: Sage.

Hendrick, S. S., Hendrick, C., & Adler, N. L. (1988). Romantic relationships: Love, satisfaction, and staying together. *Journal of Personality and Social Psychology, 54,* 980–988.

Hepworth, M. (1995). Images of old age. In J. F. Nussbaum & J. Coupland (Eds.), *Handbook of communication and aging research* (pp. 5–37). Mahwah, NJ: Erlbaum.

Herbert, T. B., & Cohen, S. (1996). Measurement issues in research on psychosocial stress. In H. B. Kaplan (Ed.), *Psychosocial stress: Perspectives on structure, theory, life-course, and methods* (pp. 295–332). San Diego, CA: Academic Press.

Herek, G. M. (1990). Gay people and government security clearances: A social science perspective. *American Psychologist, 45,* 1035–1042.

Herek, G. M., & Glunt, E. K. (1993). Interpersonal contact and heterosexuals' attitudes toward gay men: Results from a national survey. *Journal of Sex Research, 30,* 239–244.

Hergenhahn, B. R. (1988). *An introduction to theories of learning* (3rd ed.). Englewood Cliffs, NJ: Prentice Hall.

Herrmann, D. J. (1991). *Super memory.* Emmaus, PA: Rodale.

Herrnstein, R. J. (1984). Objects, categories, and discriminative stimuli. In H. L. Roitblat, T. G. Bever, & H. S. Terrace (Eds.), *Animal cognition* (pp. 233–261). Hillsdale, NJ: Erlbaum.

Herrnstein, R. J., Loveland, D. H., & Cable, D. (1976). Natural concepts in pigeons. *Journal of Experimental Psychology: Animal Behavior Processes, 2,* 285–302.

Herrnstein, R. J., & Murray, C. (1994). *The bell curve: Intelligence and class structure in American life.* New York: Free Press.

Hertel, P. T. (1994). Depression and memory: Are impairments remediable through attentional control? *Current Directions in Psychological Science, 3,* 190–193.

Hesse-Biber, S. (1996). *Am I thin enough yet?* New York: Oxford University Press.

Hewlett, B. S. (Ed.). (1992). *Father-child relations: Cultural and biosocial contexts.* New York: Aldine de Gruyter.

Hewstone, M., & Fincham, F. (1996). Attribution theory and research: Basic issues and applications. In M. Hewstone, W. Stroebe, & G. M. Stephenson (Eds.), *Introduction to social psychology* (2nd ed., pp. 167–204). Oxford: Blackwell.

Heyes, C. M., & Galef, B. G., Jr. (Eds.). (1996). *Social learning in animals: The roots of culture.* San Diego, CA: Academic Press.

Hicks, R. A., et al. (1990). Self-reported sleep durations of college students: Normative data for 1978–79 and 1988–89. *Perceptual and Motor Skills, 70,* 370.

Higgins, G. O. (1994). *Resilient adults: Overcoming a cruel past.* San Francisco: Jossey-Bass.

Hilgard, E. R. (1987). *Psychology in America: A historical survey.* San Diego, CA: Harcourt Brace Jovanovich.

Hilgard, E. R. (1991). Suggestibility and suggestions as related to hypnosis. In J. F. Schumaker (Ed.), *Human suggestibility: Advances in theory, research, and application* (pp. 37–58). New York: Routledge, Chapman and Hall.

Hilgard, E. R., Leary, D. E., & McGuire, G. R. (1991). History of psychology: A survey and critical assessment. *Annual Review of Psychology, 42,* 79–107.

Hill, R. D., Evankovich, K. D., Sheikh, J. I., & Yesavage, J. A. (1987). Imagery mnemonic training in a patient with primary degenerative dementia. *Psychology and Aging, 2,* 204–205.

Hilton, J. L., & von Hippel, W. (1996). Stereotypes. *Annual Review of Psychology, 47,* 237–271.

Hines, N. J., & Fry, D. P. (1994). Indirect modes of aggression among women of Buenos Aires, Argentina. *Sex Roles, 30,* 213–236.

Hinsz, V. B., & Tindale, R. S. (1992). Ambiguity and human versus technological sources of information in judgments involving base rate and individuating information. *Journal of Applied Social Psychology, 22,* 973–997.

Hirst, W. (1988). Improving memory. In M. S. Gazzaniga (Ed.), *Perspectives in memory research* (pp. 219–244). Cambridge, MA: Bradford.

Hirst, W. (1995). Cognitive aspects of consciousness. In M. S. Gazzaniga (Ed.), *The cognitive neurosciences* (pp. 1307–1319). Cambridge, MA: MIT Press.

Hobbs, M. (1996). Short-term dynamic psychotherapy. In S. Bloch (Ed.), *An introduction to the psychotherapies* (3rd ed., pp. 52–83). New York: Oxford University Press.

Hobfoll, S. E. (1988). *The ecology of stress.* New York: Hemisphere.

Hobson, J. A. (1988). *The dreaming brain.* New York: Basic Books.

Hobson, J. A. (1990). Activation, input source, and modulation: A neurocognitive model of the state of the brain-mind. In R. R. Bootzin, J. F. Kihlstrom, & D. L. Schacter (Eds.), *Sleep and cognition* (pp. 25–40). Washington, DC: American Psychological Association.

Hobson, J. A., & Stickgold, R. (1995). The conscious state paradigm: A neurocognitive approach to waking, sleeping, and dreaming. In M. S. Gazzaniga (Ed.), *The cognitive neurosciences*(pp. 1373–1389). Cambridge, MA: MIT Press.

Hochschild, A. R. (1983). *The managed heart.* Berkeley: University of California Press.

Hochschild, A. R. (1990). Ideology and emotion management: A perspective and path for future research. In T. D. Kemper (Ed.), *Research agendas in the sociology of emotions* (pp. 117–142). Albany: State University of New York Press.

Hofferth, S. L., & Phillips, D. A. (Eds.). (1991). Child care policy research [Special issue]. *Journal of Social Issues, 47* (2).

Hoffman, M. A. (1996). *Counseling clients with HIV disease: Assessment, intervention, and prevention.* New York: Guilford Press.

Hogarth, R. (1987). *Judgement and choice* (2nd ed.). Chichester, England: Wiley.

Holden, C. (1991). Minorities need more nurture. *Science, 254,* 796.

Holden, C. (1992). Minority survivors tell their tales. *Science, 258,* 1204–1206.

Hollon, S. D. (1996). The efficacy and effectiveness of psychotherapy relative to medications. *American Psychologist, 51,* 1025–1030.

Hollon, S. D., & Beck, A. T. (1994). Cognitive and cognitive-behavioral therapies. In A. E. Bergin & S. L. Garfield (Eds.), *Handbook of psychotherapy and behavior change* (4th ed.). New York: Wiley.

Holloway, M. (1991, March). Trends in pharmacology: R_x for addiction. *Scientific American, 264* (3), 95–103.

Holmbeck, G. N., & Hill, J. P. (1991). Conflictive engagement, positive affect, and menarche in families with seventh-grade girls. *Child Development, 62,* 1030–1048.

Holmes, D. S. (1984a). Meditation and somatic arousal reduction: A review of the experimental evidence. *American Psychologist, 39,* 1–10.

Holmes, D. S. (1984b). Defense mechanisms. InR. Corsini (Ed.), *Encyclopedia of psychology* (Vol. 1, pp. 347–350). New York: Wiley.

Holmes, D. S. (1987). The influence of meditation versus rest on physiological arousal: A second examination. In M. A. West (Ed.), *The psychology of meditation* (pp. 81–103). New York: Oxford University Press.

Holmes, D. S. (1994, June). Is there evidence for repression? Doubtful. *Harvard Mental Health Letter,* pp. 4–6.

Holmes, R. M. (1995). *How young children perceive race.* Thousand Oaks, CA: Sage.

Holmes, T. H., & Masuda, M. (1974). Life change and illness susceptibility. In B. S. Dohrenwend &B. P. Dohrenwend (Eds.), *Stressful life events: Their nature and effects* (pp. 45–72). New York: Wiley.

Holmes, T. H., & Rahe, R. H. (1967). The social readjustment rating scale. *Journal of Psychosomatic Research, 11,* 213–218.

Holyoak, K. J., & Thagard, P. (1997). The analogical mind. *American Psychologist, 52,* 35–44.

Honer, W. G., Geiwirtz, G., & Turey, M. (1987, August 22). Psychosis and violence in cocaine smokers. *Lancet, 8556,* 451.

Hood, A. B., & Johnson, R. W. (1991). *Assessment in counseling: A guide to the use of psychological assessment procedures.*

Alexandria, VA: American Association for Counseling and Development.

Hood, D. C., & Finkelstein, M. A. (1986). Sensitivity to light. In K. R. Boff, L. Kaufman, & M. P. Thomas (Eds.), *Handbook of perception and human performance* (pp. 5-1–5-66). New York: Wiley.

Hoosain, R. (1991). *Psycholinguistic implications for linguistic relativity: A case study of Chinese.* Hillsdale, NJ: Erlbaum.

Hopkins, A. B. (1996). *So ordered: Making partner the hard way.* Amherst: University of Massachusetts Press.

Hopkins, J. R. (1995). Erik Homburger Erikson (1902–1994). *American Psychologist, 50,* 796–797.

Hopson, D. P., & Hopson, D. S. (1990). *Different and wonderful: Raising Black children in a race-conscious society.* New York: Prentice Hall.

Hoptman, M. J., & Davidson, R. J. (1994). How and why do the two cerebral hemispheres interact? *Psychological Bulletin, 116,* 195–219.

Horgan, J. (1993, June). Trends in behavioral genetics: Eugenics revisited. *Scientific American,* pp. 123–131.

Horn, J. L. (1989). Cognitive diversity: A framework of learning. In P. L. Ackerman, R. J. Sternberg, & R. Glaser (Eds.), *Learning and individual differences: Advances in theory and research* (pp. 61–116). New York: Freeman.

Horn, J. L., & Cattell, R. B. (1967). Age differences in fluid and crystallized intelligence. *Acta psychologica, 26,* 107–129.

Horney, K. (1926/1967). The flight from womanhood. In H. Kelman (Ed.), *Feminine psychology* (pp. 54–70). New York: Norton.

Horney, K. (1945). *Our inner conflicts.* New York: Norton.

Horowitz, F. D., & O'Brien, M. (1989). In the interest of the nation: A reflective essay on the state of our knowledge and the challenges before us. *American Psychologist, 44,* 441–445.

Horowitz, M. J. (1994, July). Does repression exist? Yes. *Harvard Mental Health Letter,* pp. 4–6.

Horwitz, L., et al. (1996). *Borderline personality disorder.* Washington, DC: American Psychiatric Press.

Houston, J. P. (1991). *Fundamentals of learning and memory* (4th ed.). Fort Worth, TX: Harcourt Brace Jovanovich.

Hovanitz, C. A. (1993). Physical health risks associated with aftermath of disaster: Basic paths of influence and their implications for preventative intervention. *Journal of Social Behavior and Personality, 8,* 213–254.

Hovland, C. I., & Weiss, W. (1951). The influence of source credibility on communication effectiveness. *Public Opinion Quarterly, 15,* 635–650.

How often do abused children become child abusers? (1991, July). *Harvard Mental Health Letter,* p. 8.

Howard, R. W. (1995). *Learning and memory: Major ideas, principles, issues and applications.* Westport, CT: Praeger.

Howard-Pitney, B., et al. (1992). Psychological and social indicators of suicide ideation and suicide attempts in Zuni adolescents. *Journal of Consulting and Clinical Psychology, 60,* 473–476.

Howe, M. L., Kelland, A., Bryant-Brown, L., & Clark, S. L. (1992a). Measuring the development of children's amnesia and hypermnesia. In M. L. Howe, C. J. Brainerd, & V. F. Reyna (Eds.), *Development of long-term retention* (pp. 56–102). New York: Springer-Verlag.

Howe, M. L., O'Sullivan, J. T., & Marche, T. A. (1992b). Toward a theory of the development of long-term retention. In M. L. Howe, C. J. Brainerd, & V. F. Reyna (Eds.), *Development of long-term retention* (pp. 245–255). New York: Springer-Verlag.

Howes, C., Phillips, D. A., & Whitebook, M. (1992). Thresholds of quality: Implications for the social development of children in center-based child care. *Child Development, 63,* 449–460.

Hoyer, W. J. (1995). Vision and visual perception. In G. L. Maddox (Ed.), *The encyclopedia of aging* (2nd ed., pp. 956–957). New York: Springer.

Hser, Y., Anglin, M. D., & Powers, K. (1993). A 24-year follow-up of California narcotics addicts. *Archives of General Psychiatry, 50,* 577–584.

Hsu, L. K. G. (1990). *Eating disorders.* New York: Guilford Press.

Hubel, D. H. (1982). Explorations of the primary visual cortex, 1955–1978. *Nature, 299,* 515–524.

Hubel, D. H., & Wiesel, T. N. (1965). Receptive fields of single neurons in two nonstriate visual areas (18 and 19) of the cat. *Journal of Neurophysiology, 28,* 229–289.

Hubel, D. H., & Wiesel, T. N. (1979). Brain mechanisms and vision. *Scientific American, 241* (3), 150–162.

Hudson, R. A. (1996). *Sociolinguistics* (2nd ed.). Cambridge: Cambridge University Press.

Hudson, T. J., et al. (1995). An STS-based map of the human genome. *Science, 270,* 1945–1954.

Hudspeth, A. J. (1989). How the ear's works work. *Nature, 341,* 397–404.

Huesmann, L. R. (1986). Psychological processes promoting the relation between exposure to media violence and aggressive behavior by the viewer. *Journal of Social Issues, 42,* 125–139.

Huesmann, L. R., & Eron, L. D. (Eds.). (1986). *Television and the aggressive child: A cross-national comparison.* Hillsdale, NJ: Erlbaum.

Huesmann, L. R., Eron, L. D., Berkowitz, L., & Chaffee, S. (1992). The effects of television violence on aggression: A reply to a skeptic. In P. Suedfeld & P. E. Tetlock (Eds.), *Psychology and social policy* (pp. 191–200). New York: Hemisphere.

Hugdahl, K., et al. (1995). Brain mechanisms in human classical conditioning: A PET blood flow study. *NeuroReport, 6,* 1723–1728.

Hughes, J. N., & Hasbrouck, J. E. (1996). Television violence: Implications for violence prevention. *School Psychology Review, 25,* 134–151.

Hughes, J. R., & Pierattini, R. A. (1992). An introduction to pharmacotherapy for mental disorders. In J. Grabowski & G. R. VandenBos (Eds.), *Psychopharmacology: Basic mechanisms and applied interventions* (pp. 97–125). Washington, DC: American Psychological Association.

Huitema, J. S., Dopkins, S., Klin, C. M., & Myers, J. L. (1993). Connecting goals and actions during reading. *Journal of Experimental Psychology: Learning, Memory, and Cognition, 19,* 1053–1060.

Hulicka, I. M. (1982). Memory functioning in late adulthood. In F. I. M. Craik & S. Trehub (Eds.), *Aging and cognitive processes* (pp. 331–351). New York: Plenum.

Hull, J. G., & Bond, C. F. (1986). Social and behavioral consequences of alcohol consumption and expectancy: A meta-analysis. *Psychological Bulletin, 99,* 347–360.

Hunt, E., Streissguth, A. P., Kerr, B., & Olson, H. C. (1995). Mothers' alcohol consumption during pregnancy: Effects on spatial-visual reasoning in 14-year-old children. *Psychological Science, 6,* 339–342.

Hunter College Women's Studies Collective (1995). *Women's realities, women's choices* (2nd ed.). New York: Oxford University Press.

Hurtado, A., & Gurin, P. (1995). Ethnic identity and bilingualism attitudes. In A. M. Padillo (Ed.), *Hispanic psychology: Critical issues in theory and research* (pp. 89–103). Thousand Oaks, CA: Sage.

Huston, A. C. (1995, August). *Children in poverty and public policy.* Paper presented at the Annual Meeting of the American Psychological Association, New York City.

Huttenlocher, J., & Goodman, J. (1987). The time to identify spoken words. In A. Allport, D. MacKay, W. Prinz, & E. Scheerer (Eds.), *Language perception and production* (pp. 431–444). London: Academic Press.

Hyde, J. S. (1986a). Introduction: Meta-analysis and the psychology of gender. In J. S. Hyde & M. C. Linn (Eds.), *The psychology of gender: Advances through meta-analysis* (pp. 1–13). Baltimore: Johns Hopkins University Press.

Hyde, J. S. (1986b). Gender differences in aggression. In J. S. Hyde & M. C. Linn (Eds.), *The psychology of gender: Advances through meta-analysis* (pp. 51–66). Baltimore: Johns Hopkins University Press.

Hyde, J. S. (1996a). *Half the human experience: The psychology of women* (5th ed.). Lexington, MA: Heath.

Hyde, J. S. (1996b). A process-oriented model of cognitive sex differences. *Learning and Individual Differences, 8,* 33–38.

Hyde, J. S., & DeLamater, J. D. (1997). *Understanding human sexuality* (6th ed.). New York: McGraw-Hill.

Hyde, J. S., Fennema, E., & Lamon, S. J. (1990). Gender differences in mathematics performance: A meta-analysis. *Psychological Bulletin, 107,* 139–155.

Hyde, J. S., & Linn, M. C. (1988). Gender differences in verbal ability: A meta-analysis. *Psychological Bulletin, 104,* 53–69.

Hypnosis. (1991, April). *Harvard Mental Health Letter,* pp. 1–4.

Iaccino, J. F. (1993). *Left brain-right brain differences: Inquiries, evidence, and new approaches.* Hillsdale, NJ: Erlbaum.

Ianazzi, C. (1992). Personal communication.

Innis, N. K. (1992). Animal psychology in America as revealed in APA presidential addresses. *Journal of Experimental Psychology: Animal Behavior Processes, 18,* 3–11.

Intons-Peterson, M. J., & Reddel, M. (1984). What do people ask about a neonate? *Developmental Psychology, 20,* 358–359.

Intons-Peterson, M. J., & Roskos-Ewoldsen, B. (1989). Mitigating the effects of violent pornography. In S. Gubar & J. Hoff (Eds.), *For adult users only: The dilemma of violent pornography* (pp. 218–239). Bloomington: Indiana University Press.

Intons-Peterson, M. J., et al. (1989). Will educational materials reduce negative effects of exposure to sexual violence? *Journal of Social and Clinical Psychology, 8,* 256–275.

Irving, G. A. (1997). Psychology of chronic pain. In G. A. Irving & M. Wallace (Eds.), *Pain management for the practicing physician.* New York: Churchill Livingstone.

Irwin, D. E. (1992). Visual memory within and across fixations. In K. Rayner (Ed.), *Eye movements and visual cognition* (pp. 146–165). New York: Springer-Verlag.

Irwin, D. E. (1996). Integrating information across saccadic eye movements. *Current Directions in Psychological Science, 5,* 94–100.

Isaacson, R. L. (1993). Toward an understanding of the limbic system. In G. G. Brannigan & M. R. Merrens (Eds.), *The undaunted psychologist: Adventures in research* (pp. 31–42). Philadelphia: Temple University Press.

Isabella, R. A. (1993). Origins of attachment: Maternal interactive behavior across the first year. *Child Development, 64,* 605–621.

Isen, A. M. (1994). Positive affect and decision making. In M. Lewis & J. M. Haviland (Eds.), *Handbook of emotions* (pp. 261–277). New York: Guilford Press.

Isen, A. M., & Daubman, K. A. (1984). The influence of affect on categorization. *Journal of Personality and Social Psychology, 47,* 1206–1217.

Isen, A. M., Daubman, K. A., & Gorgoglione, J. M. (1987). The influence of positive affect on cognitive organization: Implications for education. In R. E. Snow & M. J. Farr (Eds.), *Aptitude, learning, and instruction* (Vol. 3, pp. 143–164). Hillsdale, NJ: Erlbaum.

Isen, A. M., Daubman, K. A., & Nowicki, G. P. (1987). *Journal of Personality and Social Psychology, 52,* 1122–1131.

Isen, A. M., Johnson, M. M. S., Mertz, E., & Robinson, G. F. (1985). The influence of positive affect on the unusualness of word associations. *Journal of Personality and Social Psychology, 48,* 1413–1426.

Isen, A. M., Niedenthal, P. M., & Cantor, N. (1992). An influence of positive affect on social categorization. *Motivation and Emotion, 16,* 65–78.

Ito, T. A., Miller, N., & Pollock, V. E. (1996). Alcohol and aggression: A meta-analysis on the moderating effects of inhibitory cues, triggering events, and self-focused attention. *Psychological Bulletin, 120,* 60–82.

Ivry, R. B. (1992). An alternative to associative learning theories. [Review of the book *The organization of learning*]. *Contemporary Psychology, 37,* 209–210.

Ivry, R. B., & Lebby, P. C. (1993). Hemispheric differences in auditory perception are similar to those found in visual perception. *Psychological Science, 4,* 41–45.

Iwata, B. A., Vollmer, T. R., Zarcone, J. R., & Rodgers, T. A. (1993). Treatment classification and selection based on behavioral function. In R. Van Houten & S. Axelrod (Eds.), *Behavior analysis and treatment* (pp. 101–125). New York: Plenum.

Izard, C. E. (1989). The structure and functions of emotions: Implications for cognition, motivation, and personality. In I. S. Cohen (Ed.), *The G. Stanley Hall Lecture Series* (Vol. 9, pp. 37–73). Washington, DC: American Psychological Association.

Izard, C. E. (1991). *The psychology of emotions.* New York: Plenum.

Izard, C. E. (1993). Four systems for emotion activation: Cognitive and noncognitive processes. *Psychological Review, 100,* 68–90.

Izard, C. E., Hembree, E. A., Dougherty, L. M., & Spizzirri, C. C. (1983). Changes in facial expressions of 2- and 19-month-old infants following acute pain. *Developmental Psychology, 19,* 418–426.

Izard, C. E., & Youngstrom, E. A. (1996). The activation and regulation of fear and anxiety. *Nebraska Symposium on Motivation, 43,* 1–59.

Jack, D. C. (1991). *Silencing the self: Women and depression.* Cambridge, MA: Harvard University Press.

Jackendoff, R. (1994). *Patterns in the mind.* New York: Basic Books.

Jacklin, C. N. (1989). Female and male: Issues of gender. *American Psychologist, 44,* 127–133.

Jackson, N. E., & Butterfield, E. C. (1986). A conception of giftedness designed to promote research. In R. J. Sternberg & J. E. Davidson (Eds.), *Conceptions of giftedness* (pp. 151–181). New York: Cambridge University Press.

Jacobs, J. E. (1991). Influence of gender stereotypes on parent and child mathematics attitudes. *Journal of Educational Psychology, 83,* 518–527.

Jacoby, L. L., Lindsay, D. S., & Toth, J. P. (1992). Unconscious influences revealed: Attention, awareness, and control. *American Psychologist, 47,* 802–809.

Jaffe, J. H. (1991). Opiates. In I. B. Glass (Ed.), *The international handbook of addiction behaviour* (pp. 64–68). London: Tavistock/Routledge.

Jagacinski, C. M., LeBold, W. K., & Linden, K. W. (1987). The relative career advancement of men and women engineers in the United States. *Work and Stress, 1,* 235–247.

James, W. (1890). *The principles of psychology.* New York: Holt.

James, W. (1892). *Psychology: The briefer course.* New York: Holt.

Jameson, D., & Hurvich, L. M. (1989). Essay concerning color constancy. *Annual Review of Psychology, 40,* 1–22.

Jamison, K. R. (1993). *Touched with fire: Manic-depressive illness and the artistic temperament.* New York: Free Press.

Jamison, K. R. (1996). *An unquiet mind: A memoir of moods and madness.* New York: Vintage Books.

Janis, I. L. (1982). *Groupthink: Psychological studies of policy decisions and fiascoes.* Boston: Houghton Mifflin.

Janis, I. L. (1989). *Crucial decisions: Leadership in policymaking and crisis management.* New York: Free Press.

Jarboe, J. (1990, May). The way out. *Texas Monthly,* pp. 102–104, 146–154.

Jay, T. (1992). *Cursing in America.* Philadelphia: Benjamins.

Jeffery, R. W. (1989). Risk behaviors and health: Contrasting individual and population perspectives. *American Psychologist, 44,* 1194–1202.

Jenkins, J. H., Kleinman, A., & Good, B. J. (1991). Cross-cultural studies of depression. In J. Becker & A. Kleinman (Eds.), *Psychosocial aspects of depression* (pp. 67–99). Hillsdale, NJ: Erlbaum.

Jenkins, J. J. (1974). Remember that old theory of memory? Well, forget it. *American Psychologist, 29,* 785–795.

Jenkins, M. R., & Culbertson, J. L. (1996). Prenatal exposure to alcohol. In R. L. Adams, O. A. Parsons, J. L. Culbertson, & S. J. Noxon (Eds.), *Neuropsychology for clinical practice: Etiology, assessment, and treatment of common neurological disorders.* Washington, DC: American Psychological Association.

Jensen, A. R. (1969). How much can we boost IQ and scholastic achievement? *Harvard Educational Review, 39,* 1–123.

Jespersen, O. (1922). *Language.* London: Allen and Unwin.

Joanette, Y., & Brownell, H. H. (1990). Introduction. In Y. Joanette & H. H. Brownell (Eds.), *Discourse ability and brain damage: Theoretical and empirical perspectives* (pp. xiii–xvi). New York: Springer-Verlag.

Johansson, G. (1975). Visual motion perception. *Scientific American, 232,* 76–88.

Johansson, G. (1985). About visual event perception. In W. H. Warren, Jr., & R. W. Shaw (Eds.), *Persistence and change: Proceedings of the First International Conference on Event Perception* (pp. 29–54). Hillsdale, NJ: Erlbaum.

Johansson, G. (1994). Gunnar Johansson: A practical theorist. In G. Jansson, S. S. Bergström, & W. Epstein (Eds.), *Perceiving events and objects* (pp. 3–25). Hillsdale, NJ: Erlbaum.

Johansson, G., von Hofsten, C., & Jansson, G. (1980). Event perception. *Annual Review of Psychology, 31,* 27–63.

Johnson, B. A. (1991). Cannabis. In I. B. Glass (Ed.), *The international handbook of addiction behaviour* (pp. 69–76). London: Tavistock/Routledge.

Johnson, M. K., & Hermann, A. M. (1995). Semantic relations and Alzheimer's disease: An early and disproportionate deficit in functional knowledge. *Journal of the International Neuropsychological Society, 1,* 568–574.

Johnson, R. D. (1987). Making judgments when information is missing: Inferences, biases, and framing effects. *Acta Psychologica, 66,* 69–72.

Johnson, S. L., & Roberts, J. E. (1995). Life events and bipolar disorder: Implications from biological theories. *Psychological Bulletin, 117,* 434–449.

Johnson, T. P., Hougland, J. G., Jr., & Moore, R. W. (1991). Sex differences in reporting sensitive behavior: A comparison of interview methods. *Sex Roles, 24,* 669–680.

Johnson-Laird, P. N. (1988). *The computer and the mind: An introduction to cognitive science.* Cambridge, MA: Harvard University Press.

Johnston, L. D., O'Malley, P. M., & Bachman, J. G. (1991). *Drug use among American high school seniors, college students and young adults, 1975–1990.* Rockville, MD: National Institute on Drug Abuse.

Joiner, T. E., Jr. (1994). Contagious depression: Existence, specificity to depressed symptoms, and the role of reassurance seeking. *Journal of Personality and Social Psychology, 67,* 287–296.

Jonas, H. S., & Etzel, S. I. (1988). Graduate medical education. *Journal of the American Medical Association, 260,* 1063–1071.

Jones, E. E. (1990). *Interpersonal perception.* New York: Freeman.

Jordan, N. (1989, June). Spare the rod, spare the child. *Psychology Today,* p. 16.

Jordan, T. R., & Bevan, K. M. (1994). Word superiority over isolated letters: The neglected case of forward masking. *Memory & Cognition, 22,* 133–144.

Josephs, R. A., & Steele, C. M. (1990). The two faces of alcohol myopia: Attentional mediation of psychological stress. *Journal of Abnormal Psychology, 99,* 115–126.

Josephson, W. L. (1987). Television violence and children's aggression: Testing the priming, social script, and disinhibition predictions. *Journal of Personality and Social Psychology, 53,* 882–890.

Jou, J., & Harris, R. J. (1992). The effect of divided attention on speech production. *Bulletin of the Psychonomic Society, 30,* 301–304.

Joy, L. A., Kimball, M. M., & Zabrack, M. L. (1986). Television and children's aggressive behavior. In T. M. Williams (Ed.), *The impact of television: A natural experiment in three communities*(pp. 303 –360). Orlando: Academic Press.

Judd, C. M., & Park, B. (1988). Out-group homogeneity: Judgments of variability at the individual and group levels. *Journal of Personality and Social Psychology, 54,* 778–788.

Judd, C. M., Ryan, C. S., & Park, B. (1991). Accuracy in the judgment of in-group and out-group variability. *Journal of Personality and Social Psychology, 61,* 366–379.

Julien, R. M. (1995). *A primer of drug action* (7th ed.). New York: Freeman.

Jung, C. G. (1917/1953). On the psychology of the unconscious. In H. Read, M. Fordham, & G. Adler (Eds.), *Collected works of C. G. Jung* (Vol. 7). Princeton, NJ: Princeton University Press.

Jusczyk, P. W. (1986). Speech perception. In K. R. Boff, L. Kaufman, & J. P. Thomas (Eds.), *Handbook of perception and human performance*(pp. 27.1–27.5). Hillsdale, NJ: Erlbaum.

Jussim, L., Eccles, J., & Madon, S. (1996). Social perception, social stereotypes, and teacher expectations: Accuracy and the quest for the powerful self-fulfilling prophecy. *Advances in Experimental Social Psychology, 28,* 281–388.

Kadlec, H., & Townsend, J. T. (1992). Signal detection analyses of dimensional interactions. InF. G. Ashby (Ed.), *Multidimensional models of perception and cognition* (pp. 181–231). Hillsdale, NJ: Erlbaum.

Kagan, J., et al. (1994). Reactivity in infants: A cross-national comparison. *Developmental Psychology, 30,* 342–345.

Kahn, D., & Hobson, J. A. (1994, May). Self-organization and the dreaming brain. *Harvard Mental Health Letter,* 3–5.

Kahneman, D., & Tversky, A. (1972). Subjective probability: A judgment of representativeness. *Cognitive Psychology, 3,* 430–454.

Kahneman, D., & Tversky, A. (1973). On the psychology of prediction. *Psychological Review, 80,* 237–251.

Kahneman, D., & Tversky, A. (1984). Choices, values, and frames. *American Psychologist, 39,* 341–350.

Kail, R. V., Jr. (1984). *The development of memory in children* (2nd ed.). New York: Freeman.

Kail, R. V., Jr. (1992). Processing speed, speech rate, and memory. *Developmental Psychology, 28,* 899–904.

Kaiser, P. K., & Boynton, R. M. (1996). *Human color vision* (2nd ed.). Washington, DC: Optical Society of America.

Kaitz, M. (1992). Recognition of familiar individuals by touch. *Physiology and Behavior, 52,* 565–567.

Kalat, J. W. (1988). *Biological psychology* (3rd ed.). Belmont, CA: Wadsworth.

Kalat, J. W. (1995). *Biological psychology* (5th ed.). Pacific Grove, CA: Brooks/Cole.

Kalichman, S. C. (1995). *Understanding AIDS: A guide for mental health professionals.* Washington, DC: American Psychological Association.

Kalichman, S. C. (1996). *Answering your questions about AIDS.* Washington, DC: American Psychological Association.

Kalichman, S. C., & Sikkema, K. J. (1994). Psychological sequelae of HIV infection and AIDS: Review of empirical findings. *Clinical Psychology Review, 14,* 611–632.

Kalin, N. H. (1993, May). The neurobiology of fear. *Scientific American,* pp. 94–101.

Kanizsa, G. (1976). Subjective contours. *Scientific American, 234* (4), 48–52.

Kantrowitz, B. (1993, June 28). He's the next best thing: A student of genius. *Newsweek,* pp. 47–48.

Kaplan, H. B. (1996a). Perspectives on psychosocial stress. In H. B. Kaplan (Ed.), *Psychosocial stress: Perspectives on structure, theory, life-course, and methods* (pp. 3–24). San Diego, CA: Academic Press.

Kaplan, H. B. (Ed.). (1996b). *Psychosocial stress: Perspectives on structure, theory, life-course, and methods.* San Diego, CA: Academic Press.

Kaplan, R. M., & Saccuzzo, D. P. (1993). *Psychological testing: Principles, applications, and issues* (3rd ed.). Pacific Grove, CA: Brooks/Cole.

Karau, S. J., & Williams, K. D. (1993). Social loafing: A meta-analytic review and theoretical integration. *Journal of Personality and Social Psychology, 65,* 681–706.

Karau, S. J., & Williams, K. D. (1995). Social loafing: Research findings, implications, and future directions. *Current Directions in Psychological Science, 4,* 134–140.

Karney, B. R., & Bradbury, T. N. (1995). The longitudinal course of marital quality and stability: A review of theory, method, and research. *Psychological Bulletin, 118,* 3–34.

Kassin, S. M., & Sommers, S. R. (1997). Inadmissible testimony, instructions to disregard, and the jury: Substantive versus procedural considerations. *Personality and Social Psychology Bulletin, 23,* 1046–1054.

Kastenbaum, R. (1992). *The psychology of death* (2nd ed.). New York: Springer.

Katon, W. (1991). *Panic disorder in the medical setting.* Washington, DC: American Psychiatric Press.

Katz, P. A. (1996). Raising feminists. *Psychology of Women Quarterly, 20,* 323–340.

Katz, P. A., & Kofkin, J. A. (1997). Race, gender and young children. In S. S. Luther, J. A. Burack,D. Cicchetti, & J. Weisz (Eds.), *Developmental psychopathology: Perspectives on risk and disorder.* New York: Cambridge University Press.

Katz, P. A., & Ksansnak, K. R. (1994). Developmental aspects of gender role flexibility and traditionality in middle childhood and adolescence. *Developmental Psychology, 30,* 272–282.

Katz, S. (1996). Personal communication.

Katz, S., & Lautenschlager, G. J. (1994). Answering reading comprehension items without passages on the SAT-I, the ACT, and the GRE. *Educational Assessment, 2,* 295–308.

Katz, S., Lautenschlager, G. J., Blackburn, A. B., & Harris, F. H. (1990). Answering reading comprehension items without passages on the SAT. *Psychological Science, 1,* 122–127.

Kaufman, D. R. (1995). Professional women: How real are the recent gains? In J. Freeman (Ed.), *Women: A feminist perspective* (5th ed., pp. 287–305). Mountain View, CA: Mayfield.

Kausler, D. H. (1995). Memory and memory theory. In G. L. Maddox (Ed.), *The encyclopedia of aging* (2nd ed., pp. 612–615). New York: Springer.

Kazdin, A. E. (1994). *Behavior modification in applied settings* (5th ed.). Pacific Grove, CA: Brooks/Cole.

Keefe, R. S. E., & Harvey, P. D. (1994). *Understanding schizophrenia: A guide to the new research on causes and treatment.* New York: Free Press.

Keen, S. (1986). *Faces of the enemy: Reflections of the hostile imagination.* San Francisco: Harper & Row.

Keith, T. Z., et al. (1986). Parental involvement, homework, and TV time: Direct and indirect effects on high school achievement. *Journal of Educational Psychology, 78,* 373–380.

Keith-Spiegel, P. (1990). Personal communication.

Keith-Spiegel, P., & Koocher, G. P. (1985). *Ethics in psychology.* Hillsdale, NJ: Erlbaum.

Kellerman, A. L., et al. (1993). Gun ownership as a risk factor for homicide in the home. *New England Journal of Medicine, 329,* 1084–1119.

Kellogg, R. T. (1988). Attentional overload and writing performance: Effects of rough draft and outline strategies. *Journal of Experimental Psychology: Learning, Memory, and Cognition, 14,* 355–365.

Kellogg, R. T. (1994). *The psychology of writing.* New York: Oxford University Press.

Kelly, J. A. (1995). *Changing HIV risk behavior: Practical strategies.* New York: Guilford Press.

Kelly, J. A., Murphy, D. A., Sikkema, K. J., & Kalichman, S. C. (1993). Psychological interventions to prevent HIV infection are urgently needed. *American Psychologist, 48,* 1023–1034.

Kelly, M. H., Bock, J. K., & Keil, F. C. (1986). Prototypicality in a linguistic context: Effects on sentence structure. *Journal of Memory and Language, 25,* 59–74.

Kemper, S. (1984). When to speak like a lady. *Sex Roles, 10,* 435–444.

Kendler, K. S., et al. (1994). Sources of individual differences in depressive symptoms: Analysis of two samples of twins and their families. *American Journal of Psychiatry, 51,* 1605–1614.

Kenny, D. A. (1994). *Interpersonal perception: A social relations analysis.* New York: Guilford Press.

Kent, D. (1990, May). A conversation with Claude Steele. *APS Observer,* pp. 11–17.

Kent, D. (1997, May–June). Healthcare's redefinition drives research on relation between health and wealth. *APS Observer,* pp. 12–13, 38.

Kent, G. (1991). Anxiety. In W. Dryden & R. Rentoul (Eds.), *Adult clinical problems: A cognitive-behavioural approach* (pp. 27–55). London: Routledge.

Keren, G. (1987). Facing uncertainty in the game of bridge: A calibration study. *Organizational Behavior and Human Decision Processes, 39,* 98–114.

Kessen, W. (1996). American psychology just before Piaget. *Psychological Science, 7,* 196–199.

Kessler, D. A., et al. (1997). Nicotine addiction: A pediatric disease. *Journal of Pediatrics, 130,* 518–524.

Kessler, R. C., et al. (1994). Lifetime and 12-month prevalence of DSM-III-R psychiatric disorders in the United States. *Archives of General Psychiatry, 51,* 8–19.

Khatena, J. (1992). *Gifted: Challenge and response for education.* Itasca, IL: Peacock.

Kiang, N. Y., & Peake, W. T. (1988). Physics and physiology of hearing. In R. C. Atkinson, R. J. Hernstein, G. Lindzey, & R. D. Luce (Eds.), *Stevens' handbook of experimental psychology* (2nd ed., Vol. I, pp. 277–326). New York: Wiley.

Kihlstrom, J. F. (1985). Hypnosis. *Annual Review of Psychology, 36,* 385–418.

Kihlstrom, J. F. (1994). Persons transcendent, persons embedded [Review of the book *Fifty years of personality psychology*]. *Contemporary Psychology, 39,* 705–706.

Kihlstrom, J. F. (1995, September). On the validity of psychology experiments. *APS Observer,* pp. 10–11.

Kihlstrom, J. F., & Barnhardt, T. M. (1993). The self-regulation of memory: For better and for worse, with and without hypnosis. In D. M. Wegner & J. W. Pennebaker (Eds.), *Handbook of mental control* (pp. 88–125). Englewood Cliffs, NJ: Prentice Hall.

Kihlstrom, J. F., Barnhardt, T. M., & Tataryn, D. J. (1992). Implicit perception. In R. F. Bernstein & T. S. Pittman (Eds.), *Perception without awareness: Cognitive, clinical, and social perspectives* (pp. 17–54). New York: Guilford Press.

Kihlstrom, J. F., Tataryn, D. J., & Hoyt, I. P. (1993). Dissociative disorders. In P. B. Sutker & H. E. Adams (Eds.), *Comprehensive handbook of psychopathology* (2nd ed., pp. 203–234). New York: Plenum.

Kilbourne, J. (1994). Still killing us softly: Advertising and the obsession with thinness. In P. Fallon, M. A. Katzman, & S. C. Wooley (Eds.), *Feminist perspectives on eating disorders* (pp. 395–418). New York: Guilford Press.

Killackey, H. P. (1990). The neocortex and memory storage. In J. L. McGaugh, N. M. Weinberger, & G. Lynch (Eds.), *Brain organization and memory: Cells, systems, and circuits* (pp. 265–270). New York: Oxford University Press.

Killen, J. D., et al. (1992). Is puberty a risk factor for eating disorders? *American Journal of Diseases of Children, 146,* 323–325.

Kimball, M. M. (1989). A new perspective on women's math achievement. *Psychological Bulletin, 105,* 198–214.

Kimble, G. A. (1992). *A modest proposal for a minor revolution in the language of psychology.* Paper presented at the convention of the American Psychological Society.

Kimble, G. A. (1994). Evolution of the nature-nurture issue in the history of psychology. In R. Plomin & G. E. McClearn (Eds.), *Nature, nurture, and psychology* (pp. 3–25). Washington, DC: American Psychological Association.

Kimble, G. A. (1996). *Psychology: The hope of a science.* Cambridge, MA: MIT Press.

Kimmel, P. R., & VandenBos, G. R. (1992). *Peace: Abstracts of the psychological and behavioral literature, 1967–1990.* Washington, DC: American Psychological Association.

Kimura, D. (1992, September). Sex differences in the brain. *Scientific American, 267,* 118–125.

Kimura, D. (1993). *Neuromotor mechanisms in human communication.* New York: Oxford University Press.

King, A. (1992). Facilitating elaborative learning through guided student-generated questioning. *Educational Psychologist, 27,* 111–126.

Kingdon, D. G., & Turkington, D. (1994). *Cognitive-behavioral therapy of schizophrenia.* New York: Guilford Press.

Kinomura, S., Larsson, J., Gulyás, B., & Roland, P. E. (1996). Activation by attention of the human reticular formation and thalamic intralaminar nuclei. *Science, 271,* 513–515.

Kirkpatrick, L. A., & Davis, K. E. (1994). Attachment style, gender, and relationship stability: A longitudinal analysis. *Journal of Personality and Social Psychology, 66,* 502–512.

Kirmayer, L. J. (1994). Suicide among Canadian aboriginal peoples. *Transcultural Psychiatric Research Review, 31*, 3–58.

Kirsch, I., & Lynn, S. J. (1995). The altered state of hypnosis: Changes in the theoretical landscape. *American Psychologist, 50*, 846–858.

Kirsch, I., Lynn, S. J., & Rhue, J. W. (1993). Introduction to clinical hypnosis. In J. W. Rhue, S. J. Lynn, & I. Kirsch (Eds.), *Handbook of clinical hypnosis* (pp. 3–22). Washington, DC: American Psychological Association.

Kitagawa, E. M., & Hauser, P. M. (Eds.). (1973). *Differential mortality in the United States: A study in socioeconomic epidemiology.* Cambridge, MA: Harvard University Press.

Kitayama, S., & Markus, H. R. (1995). Culture and self: Implications for internationalizing psychology. In N. R. Goldberge & J. B. Veroff (Eds.), *The culture and psychology reader* (pp. 366–383). New York: New York University Press.

Kite, M. E., Deaux, K., & Miele, M. (1991). Stereotypes of young and old: Does age outweigh gender? *Psychology and Aging, 6*, 19–27.

Kite, M. E., & Johnson, B. T. (1988). Attitudes toward older and younger adults: A meta-analysis. *Psychology and Aging, 3*, 233–244.

Kite, M. E., & Whitley, B. E., Jr. (1996). Sex differences in attitudes toward homosexual persons, behaviors, and civil rights: A meta-analysis. *Personality and Social Psychology Bulletin, 22*, 336–353.

Klein, B. E. K., & Klein, R. (1995). Protecting vision. *New England Journal of Medicine, 332*, 1228–1229.

Klein, J. D., et al. (1993). Adolescents' risky behavior and mass media use. *Pediatrics, 92*, 24–31.

Klein, M. (1948). *Contributions to psychoanalysis, 1921–1945.* London: Hogarth.

Klein, S. B., & Kihlstrom, J. F. (1986). Elaboration, organization, and the self-reference effect in memory. *Journal of Experimental Psychology: General, 115*, 26–38.

Klerman, G. L., & Weissman, M. M. (1989). Increasing rates of depression. *JAMA, 261*, 2229–2235.

Kline, D. W., et al. (1992). Vision, aging, and driving: The problems of older drivers. *Journal of Gerontology: Psychological Sciences, 47*, P27–P34.

Kline, P. (1993). *The handbook of psychological testing.* New York: Routledge.

Knox, V. J., Gekoski, W. L., Johnson, E. A. (1986). Contact with and perceptions of the elderly. *Gerontologist, 26*, 309–313.

Koelega, H. S. (1995). Alcohol and vigilance performance: A review. *Psychopharmacology, 118*, 233–249.

Koelega, H. S. (1996). Sustained attention. InO. Newmann & A. F. Sanders (Eds.), *Handbook of perception and action* (Vol. 3, pp. 277–331). San Diego, CA: Academic Press.

Kogan, N. (1990). Personality and aging. In J. E. Birren & K. W. Schaie (Eds.), *Handbook of the psychology of aging* (3rd ed., pp. 330–346). San Diego, CA: Academic Press.

Kohlberg, L. (1964). The development of moral character and moral ideology. In M. Hoffman &L. Hoffman (Eds.), *Review of child development research* (Vol. 1). New York: Russell Sage Foundation.

Kohlberg, L. (1969). Stage and sequence: The cognitive-developmental approach to socialization. In D. A. Goslin (Ed.), *Handbook of socialization theory and research.* Chicago: Rand McNally.

Kohlberg, L. (1984). *Essays on moral development: Vol. 2. The psychology of moral development.* San Francisco: Freeman.

Kohn, A. (1988, April). You know what they say . . . *Psychology Today,* pp. 36–41.

Kohn, A. (1990). *The brighter side of human nature.* New York: Basic Books.

Kohn, P. M., Lafreniere, K., & Gurevich, M. (1990). The inventory of college students' recent life experiences: A decontaminated hassles scale for a special population. *Journal of Behavioral Medicine, 13*, 619–630.

Kohn, P. M., Lafreniere, K., & Gurevich, M. (1991). Hassles, health, and personality. *Journal of Personality and Social Psychology, 61*, 478–482.

Kohn, P. M., & MacDonald, J. E. (1992). Hassles, anxiety, and negative well-being. *Anxiety, Stress, and Coping, 5*, 151–163.

Kokotovic, A., & Tracey, T. (1990). Working alliance in the early phase of counseling. *Journal of Counseling Psychology, 37*, 16–21.

Kominski, R. (1993, September). *We the Americans: Our education.* Washington, DC: U.S. Bureau of the Census.

Korn, J. H. (1997). *Illusions of reality: A history of deception in social psychology.* Albany: State University of New York Press.

Kornblum, W. (1994). *Sociology in a changing world* (3rd ed.). Fort Worth, TX: Harcourt Brace.

Koss, M. P. (1992). The underdetection of rape: Methodological choices influence incidence estimates. *Journal of Social Issues, 48*, 61–75.

Koss, M. P. (1993). Rape: Scope, impact, interventions, and public policy responses. *American Psychologist, 48*, 1062–1069.

Koss, M. P., Dinero, T. E., Siebel, C. A., & Cox, S. L. (1988). Stranger and acquaintance rape: Are there differences in the victim's experience? *Psychology of Women Quarterly, 12*, 1–24.

Koss, M. P., & Harvey, M. R. (1991). *The rape victim: Clinical and community interventions* (2nd ed.). Newbury Park, CA: Sage.

Kosslyn, S. M., Anderson, A. K., Hillger, L. A., & Hamilton, S. E. (1994). Hemispheric differences in sizes of receptive fields or attentional biases? *Neuropsychology, 8*, 139–147.

Kosslyn, S. M., & Koenig, O. (1992). *Wet mind: The new cognitive neuroscience.* New York: Free Press.

Kowalski, R. M. (1996). Complaints and complaining: Functions, antecedents, and consequences. *Psychological Bulletin, 119*, 179–196.

Kral, M. J., & Sakinofsky, I. (1994). A clinical model for suicide risk assessment. In A. A. Leenars, J. T. Maltsberger, & R. A. Neimeyer (Eds.), *Treatment of suicidal people* (pp. 19–31). Washington, DC: Taylor & Francis.

Krause, N. (1991). Stressful events and life satisfaction among elderly men and women. *Journal of Gerontology: Social Sciences, 46*, S84–S92.

Krause, N., Herzog, A. R., & Baker, E. (1992). Providing support to others and well-being in later life. *Journal of Gerontology: Psychological Sciences, 47*, P300–P311.

Kreipe, R. E., Churchill, B. H., & Strauss, J. (1989). Long-term outcome of adolescents with anorexia nervosa. *American Journal of Diseases of Children, 143*, 1322–1327.

Kronauer, R. E. (1994). Circadian rhythms. In R. Cooper (Ed.), *Sleep* (pp. 96–134). London: Chapman & Hall.

Krueger, L. E. (1992). The word-superiority effect and phonological recoding. *Memory & Cognition, 20,* 685–694.

Krull, D. S., & Erickson, D. J. (1995). Inferential hopscotch: How people draw social inferences from behavior. *Current Directions in Psychological Science, 4,* 35–38.

Kryter, K. D. (1994). *The handbook of hearing and the effects of noise: Physiology, psychology, and public health.* San Diego, CA: Academic Press.

Kuczmarski, R. J. (1992). Prevalence of overweight and weight gain in the United States. *American Journal of Clinical Nutrition, 55* (Supplement), 495S–502S.

Kuhl, P. K. (1994). Speech perception. In F. D. Minifie (Ed.), *Introduction to communication sciences and disorders* (pp. 77–148). San Diego, CA: Singular Publishing Group.

Kuhn, D. (1992). Cognitive development. In M. H. Bornstein & M. E. Lamb (Eds.), *Developmental psychology: An advanced textbook* (3rd ed.). Hillsdale, NJ: Erlbaum.

Kurdek, L. A. (1991a). Predictors of increases in marital distress in newlywed couples: A 3-year prospective longitudinal study. *Developmental Psychology, 27,* 627–636.

Kurdek, L. A. (1991b). Correlates of relationship satisfaction of cohabiting gay and lesbian couples: Integration of contextual, investment, and problem-solving models. *Journal of Personality and Social Psychology, 61,* 910–922.

Kurdek, L. A. (1993). Predicting marital dissolution: A 5-year prospective longitudinal study of newlywed couples. *Journal of Personality and Social Psychology, 64,* 221–242.

Kurdek, L. A. (1995). Assessing multiple determinants of relationship commitment in cohabiting gay, cohabiting lesbian, dating heterosexual, and married heterosexual couples. *Family Relations, 44,* 261–266.

Kurzweil, E. (1995). *Freudians and feminists.* Boulder, CO: Westview Press.

Kymissis, E., & Poulson, C. L. (1990). The history of imitation in learning theory: The language acquisition process. *Journal of the Experimental Analysis of Behavior, 54,* 113–127.

LaBerge, S. (1990). Lucid dreaming: Psychophysiological studies of consciousness during REM sleep. In R. R. Bootzin, J. F. Kihlstrom, & D. L. Schacter (Eds.), *Sleep and cognition* (pp. 109–126). Washington, DC: American Psychological Association.

Labouvie-Vief, G. (1992). A neo-Piagetian perspective on adult cognitive development. In R. J. Sternberg & C. A. Berg (Eds.), *Intellectual development* (pp. 197–228). Cambridge: Cambridge University Press.

LaFrance, M. (1992). Gender and interruptions: Individual infraction or violation of the social order? *Psychology of Women Quarterly, 16,* 497–512.

LaFromboise, T. D., Berman, J. S., & Sohi, B. K. (1994). American Indian women. In L. Comas-Díaz & B. Greene (Eds.), *Women of color: Integrating ethnic and gender identities in psychotherapy* (pp. 30–71). New York: Guilford Press.

LaFromboise, T. D., Choney, S. B., James, A., & Running Wolf, P. R. (1997). American Indian women and psychology. In H. Landrine (Ed.), *Bringing cultural diversity to feminist psychology: Theory, research, and practice* (pp. 197–239). Washington, DC: American Psychological Association.

LaFromboise, T. D., Coleman, H. L. K., & Gerton, J. (1993). Psychological impact of biculturalism: Evidence and theory. *Psychological Bulletin, 114,* 395–412.

LaFromboise, T. D., & Lowe, K. (1989). American Indian children and adolescents. In J. Gibbs &L. Huang (Eds.), *Children of color: Psychological interventions with minority youth.* San Francisco: Jossey-Bass.

Lakin, M. (1996, Summer). Carl Rogers and the culture of psychotherapy. *General Psychologist, 32,* 62–68.

Lalancette, M., & Standing, L. (1990). Asch fails again. *Social Behavior and Personality, 18,* 7–12.

Lambert, M. J., Shapiro, D. A., & Bergin, A. E. (1986). The effectiveness of psychotherapy. In S. L. Garfield & A. E. Bergin (Eds.), *Handbook of psychotherapy and behavior change* (pp. 157–211). New York: Wiley.

Lambert, W. E. (1990). Persistent issues in bilingualism. In B. Harley, P. Allen, J. Cummins, & M. Swain (Eds.), *The development of second language proficiency* (pp. 201–218). Cambridge: Cambridge University Press.

Lambert, W. E. (1992). Challenging established views on social issues. *American Psychologist, 47,* 533–542.

Lambert, W. E., Genesee, F., Holobow, N., & Chartrand, L. (1991). *Bilingual education for majority English-speaking children.* Montreal: McGill University, Psychology Department.

Laming, D. (1985). Some principles of sensory analysis. *Psychological Review, 92,* 462–485.

Landefeld, C. S., et al. (1995). A randomized trial of care in a hospital medical unit especially designed to improve the functional outcomes of acutely ill older patients. *New England Journal of Medicine, 332,* 1338–1344.

Landrine, H. (Ed.). (1995). *Bringing cultural diversity to feminist psychology: Theory, research, and practice.* Washington, DC: American Psychological Association.

Landry, M. J. (1994). *Understanding drugs of abuse: The processes of addiction, treatment, and recovery.* Washington, DC: American Psychiatric Press.

Laner, M. R. (1989). Competitive vs. noncompetitive styles: Which is most valued in courtship? *Sex Roles, 20,* 165–172.

Lang, P. J. (1994). The varieties of emotional experience: A meditation on James-Lange theory. *Psychological Review, 101,* 211–221.

Langer, E. J. (1989a). *Mindfulness.* Reading, MA: Addison-Wesley.

Langer, E. J. (1989b). Minding matters: The consequences of mindlessness-mindfulness. *Advances in Experimental Social Psychology, 22,* 137–173.

Langer, E. J., & Piper, A. I. (1987). The prevention of mindlessness. *Journal of Personality and Social Psychology, 53,* 280–287.

Langlois, J. H., & Musselman, L. (1995). Myths and mysteries of beauty. In D. R. Calhoun (Ed.), *1996 Yearbook of science and the future* (pp. 40–61). Chicago: Encyclopaedia Britannica.

Langlois, J. H., Ritter, J. M., Roggman, L. A., & Vaughn, L. S. (1991). Facial diversity and infant preferences for attractive faces. *Developmental Psychology, 27,* 79–84.

Larkin, J. H., & Simon, H. A. (1987). Why a diagram is (sometimes) worth ten thousand words. *Cognitive Science, 11,* 65–99.

Larkin, K. T., & Edens, J. L. (1994). Behavior therapy. In V. B. Van Hasselt & M. Hersen (Eds.), *Advanced abnormal psychology* (pp. 497–512). New York: Plenum.

Latané, B., & Darley, J. M. (1968). Group inhibition of bystander intervention. *Journal of Personality and Social Psychology, 10,* 215–221.

Latané, B., & Nida, S. (1981). Ten years of research on group size and helping. *Psychological Bulletin, 89,* 308–324.

Lattal, K. A. (Ed.). (1992). Reflections on B. F. Skinner and psychology [Special issue]. *American Psychologist, 47* (11).

Laursen, B. (1995). Conflict and social interaction in adolescent relationships. *Journal of Research on Adolescence, 5,* 55–70.

Lavigne, V. D., & Finley, G. E. (1990). Memory in middle-aged adults. *Educational Gerontology, 16,* 447–461.

La Voie, D., & Light, L. L. (1994). Adult age differences in repetition priming: A meta-analysis. *Psychology and Aging, 9,* 539–553.

Lavond, D. G., Lincoln, J. S., McCormick, D. A., & Thompson, R. F. (1984). Effect of bilateral lesions of the dentate and interpositus nuclei on conditioning of heart-rate and nictitating membrane/eyelid response in the rabbit. *Brain Research, 305,* 323–330.

Law, D. J., Pellegrino, J. W., & Hunt, E. B. (1993). Comparing the tortoise and the hare: Gender differences and experience in dynamic spatial reasoning tasks. *Psychological Science, 4,* 35–40.

Lawless, H. T., & Engen, T. (1977). Associations to odors: Interference, memories, and verbal labeling. *Journal of Experimental Psychology: Human Learning and Memory, 3,* 52–59.

Lazarus, R. S. (1984). Puzzles in the study of daily hassles. *Journal of Behavioral Medicine, 7,* 375–389.

Lazarus, R. S. (1991). *Emotion and adaptation.* New York: Oxford University Press.

Lazarus, R. S. (1993). From psychological stress to the emotions: A history of changing outlooks. *Annual Review of Psychology, 44,* 1–21.

Lazarus, R. S., & Folkman, S. (1984). *Stress, appraisal, and coping.* New York: Springer.

Lazur, R. F., & Majors, R. (1995). Men of color: ethnocultural variations of male gender role strain. In R. F. Levant & W. S. Pollack (Eds.), *A new psychology of men* (pp. 337–358). New York: Basic Books.

Leary, M. R., & Kowalski, R. M. (1995). *Social anxiety.* New York: Guilford Press.

Leather, J., & James, A. (1996). Second language speech. In W. C. Ritchie & T. K. Bhatia (Eds.), *Handbook of second language acquisition* (pp. 269–316). San Diego, CA: Academic Press.

LeDoux, J. E. (1995). Emotion: Clues from the brain. *Annual Review of Psychology, 46,* 209–235.

Lee, C. (1985). Successful rural black adolescents. A psychosocial profile. *Adolescence, 77,* 131–141.

Lee, L. C. (1992). *The search for universals: Whatever happened to race and culture?* Paper presented at the convention of the American Psychological Association, Washington, DC.

Leenaars, A. A., & Domino, G. (1993). A comparison of community attitudes towards suicide in Windsor and Los Angeles. *Canadian Journal of Behaioural Science, 25,* 253–266.

Leichtman, M. D., & Ceci, S. J. (1995). The effects of stereotypes and suggestions on preschoolers' reports. *Developmental Psychology, 31,* 568–578.

Leigh, B. C. (1989). In search of the seven dwarves: Issues of measurement and meaning in alcohol expectancy research. *Psychologial Bulletin, 105,* 362–373.

Leinbach, M. D., & Fagot, B. I. (1991). Attractiveness in young children: Sex-differentiated reactions of adults. *Sex Roles, 25,* 269–284.

Leitenberg, H., & Hennig, K. (1995). Sexual fantasy. *Psychological Bulletin, 117,* 469–496.

Leith, K. P., & Baumeister, R. F. (1996). Why do bad moods increase self-defeating behavior?: Emotion, risk-taking, and self-regulation. *Journal of Personality and Social Psychology, 71,* 1250–1267.

Lenney, E. (1977). Women's self-confidence in achievement settings. *Psychological Bulletin, 84,* 1–13.

Lennie, P. (1980). Parallel visual pathways: A review. *Vision Review, 20,* 561–594.

Lepore, S. J. (1995). Measurement of chronic stressors. In S. Cohen, R. C. Kessler, & L. U. Gordon (Eds.), *Measuring stress: A guide for health and social scientists* (pp. 102–120). New York: Oxford University Press.

Lerman, H. (1986). From Freud to feminist personality theory: Getting here from there. *Psychology of Women Quarterly, 10,* 1–18.

Levant, R. F. (1992). Toward the reconstruction of masculinity. *Journal of Family Psychology, 5,* 379–402.

LeVay, S. (1993). *The sexual brain.* Cambridge, MA: MIT Press.

Levelt, W. J. M. (1989). *Speaking: From intention to articulation.* Cambridge, MA: MIT Press.

Levelt, W. J. M. (1994). The skill of speaking. In P. Bertelson, P. Eelen, & G. d'Ydewalle (Eds.), *International perspectives on psychological science* (Vol. 1, pp. 89–103). Hove, England: Erlbaum.

Levenson, R. W. (1992). Autonomic nervous system differences among emotions. *Psychology Science, 3,* 23–27.

Levenson, R. W., Ekman, P., & Friesen. W. V. (1990). Voluntary facial action generates emotion-specific autonomic nervous system activity. *Psychophysiology, 27,* 363–384.

Levenson, R. W., Ekman, P., Heider, K., & Friesen, W. V. (1992). Emotion and autonomic nervous system activity in the Minangkabau of West Sumatra. *Journal of Personality and Social Psychology, 62,* 972–988.

Leventhal, E. A. (1994). Gender and aging: Women and their aging. In V. J. Adesso, D. M. Reddy, & R. Fleming (Eds.), *Psychological perspectives on women's health* (pp. 11–35). Washington, DC: Taylor & Francis.

Levine, G., & Parkinson, S. (1994). *Experimental methods in psychology.* Hillsdale, NJ: Erlbaum.

Levine, I. S., & Rog, D. J. (1990). Mental health services for homeless mentally ill persons: Federal initiatives and current service trends. *American Psychologist, 45,* 963–968.

Levine, J. M., & Moreland, R. L. (1990). Progress in small group research. *Annual Review of Psychology, 41,* 585–634.

Levine, J. M., & Moreland, R. L. (1995). Group processes. In A. Tesser (Ed.), *Advanced social psychology* (pp. 418–465). New York: McGraw-Hill.

Levine, J. M., & Thompson, L. (1996). Conflict in groups. In E. T. Higgins & A. W. Kruglanski (Eds.), *Social psychology:*

Handbook of basic principles (pp. 745–776). New York: Guilford Press.

Levine, M., Toro, P. A., & Perkins, D. V. (1993). Social and community interventions. *Annual Review of Psychology, 44,* 525–558.

Levine, R. V. (1990, September–October). The pace of life. *American Scientist,* pp. 451–459.

Levine, R. V. (1993, October). Cities with heart. *American Demographics,* pp. 46–54.

Levine, R. V., Martinez, T. S., Brase, G., & Sorenson, K. (1994). Helping in 36 U.S. cities. *Journal of Personality and Social Psychology, 67,* 69–82.

Levy, B., & Langer, E. (1994). Aging free from negative stereotypes: Successful memory in China and among the American Deaf. *Journal of Personality and Social Psychology, 66,* 989–997.

Lewandowsky, S., & Li, S. C. (1995). Catastrophic interference in neural networks: Causes, solutions, and data. In F. N. Dempster & C. J. Brainerd (Eds.), *Interference and inhibition in cognition* (pp. 329–361). San Diego, CA: Academic Press.

Lewis, E. R., Everhart, T. E., & Zeevi, Y. Y. (1969). Study of neural organization in Aplysia with the scanning electron microscope. *Science, 165,* 1140–1143.

Lewis, J. W., et al. (1984). Neural, neurochemical, and hormonal bases of stress-induced analgesia. In L. Kruger & J. C. Liebeskind (Eds.), *Neural mechanisms of pain* (pp. 227–288). New York: Raven.

Lewis, M., & Brooks, J. (1978). Self-knowledge in emotional development. In M. Lewis & L. Rosenblum (Eds.), *The development of affect* (pp. 205–226). New York: Plenum.

Lewis, M., & Haviland, J. M. (Eds.). (1994). *Handbook of emotions.* New York: Guilford Press.

Lewis, M., & Saarni, C. (Eds.). (1993). *Lying and deception in everyday life.* New York: HarperCollins.

Lichtenstein, E., & Glasgow, R. E. (1992). Smoking cessation: What have we learned over the past decade? *Journal of Consulting nad Clinical Psychology, 60,* 518–527.

Lichtman, S. W., et al. (1992). Discrepancy between self-reported and actual caloric intake and exercise in obese subjects. *New England Journal of Medicine, 327,* 1893–1898.

Lieberman, D. A. (1990). *Learning: Behavior and cognition.* Belmont, CA: Wadsworth.

Lieberman, J. A., Brown, A. S., & Gorman, J. M. (1994). Schizophrenia. *Review of Psychiatry, 13,* 133–170.

Lieberman, M. A., & Peskin, H. (1992). Adult life crises. In J. E. Birren, R. B. Sloane, & G. D. Cohen (Eds.), *Handbook of mental health and aging* (2nd ed., pp. 119–143). San Diego, CA: Academic Press.

Liebert, R. M., & Sprafkin, J. (1988). *The early window* (3rd ed.). Elmsford, NY: Pergamon.

Lifton, R. J. (1967). *Death in life: Survivors of Hiroshima.* New York: Simon & Schuster.

Light, L. L., La Voie, D., & Kennison, R. (1995). Repetition priming of nonwords in young and older adults. *Journal of Experimental Psychology: Learning, Memory, and Cognition, 21,* 327–346.

Lin, C. C., & Fu, V. R. (1990). A comparison of child-rearing practices among Chinese, immigrant Chinese, and Caucasian-American parents. *Child Development, 61,* 429–433.

Lindsay, D. S., & Read, J. D. (1994). Psychotherapy and memories of childhood sexual abuse: A cognitive perspective. *Applied Cognitive Psychology, 8,* 281–338.

Links, P. S., Boiago, I., & Allnut, S. (1996). Understanding and recognizing personality disorders. In P. S. Links (Ed.), *Clinical assessment and management of severe personality disorders*(pp. 1–19). Washington, DC: American Psychological Association.

Linn, M. C. (1992). Gender differences in educational achievement. In Educational Testing Service (Ed.), *Sex equity in educational opportunity, achievement, and testing. Proceedings of the 1991 Invitational Conference of the Educational Testing Service.* Princeton, NJ: Educational Testing Service.

Linn, M. C., & Peterson, A. C. (1986). A meta-analysis of gender differences in spatial ability: Implications for mathematics and science achievement. In J. S. Hyde & M. C. Linn (Eds.), *The psychology of gender: Advances through meta-analysis* (pp. 67–101). Baltimore: Johns Hopkins University Press.

Linville, P. W. (1982). The complexity-extremity effect and age-based stereotyping. *Journal of Personality and Social Psychology, 42,* 193–211.

Linville, P. W., Fischer, G. W., & Fischhoff, B. (1993). AIDS risk perceptions and decision biases. InJ. B. Pryor & G. D. Reeder (Eds.), *The social psychology of HIV infection* (pp. 5–38). Hillsdale, NJ: Erlbaum.

Linville, P. W., & Jones, E. E. (1980). Polarized appraisals of out-group members. *Journal of Personality and Social Psychology, 38,* 689–703.

Linz, D., Wilson, B. J., & Donnerstein, E. (1992). Sexual violence in the mass media: Legal solutions, warnings, and mitigation through education. *Journal of Social Issues, 48,* 145–172.

Lippmann, P. (1996). Freud, the ambitious writer of fiction: A view from the English department [Review of the book *Freud's wishful dream book*]. *Contemporary Psychology, 41,* 555–556.

Lipsitt, L. P., & VandenBos, G. R. (1992). Foreward. In M. Glantz & R. Pickens (Eds.), *Vulnerability to drug abuse* (pp. xv–xvi). Washington, DC: American Psychological Association.

Liu, M. (1991, July 29). Pass a snake, hold the rat. *Newsweek,* p. 35.

Liu, S. S. (1971). Differential conditioning and stimulus generalization of the rabbit's nictitating membrane response. *Journal of Comparative and Physiological Psychology, 77,* 136–142.

Livingston, M. (1993). Psychoprophylactic method (Lamaze). In B. L. Rothman (Ed.), *Encyclopedia of childbearing: Critical perspectives* (pp. 343–345). Phoenix: Oryx.

Livingstone, M. S. (1987). Art, illusion and the visual system. *Scientific American, 258* (1), 78–85.

Locke, E. A., & Latham, G. P. (1994). Goal setting theory. In H. F. O'Neil, Jr., & M. Drillings (Eds.), *Motivation: Theory and research* (pp. 13–29). Hillsdale, NJ: Erlbaum.

Locke, J. L. (1994). Phases in the child's development of language. *American Scientist, 82,* 436–445.

Locurto, C. (1989). The dark side of hegemony. *Behavioral and Brain Sciences, 12,* 153–154.

Locurto, C. (1991). *Sense and nonsense about IQ: The case for uniqueness.* New York: Praeger.

Loeber, R., & Hay, D. (1997). Key issues in the development of aggression and violence from childhood to early adulthood. *Annual Review of Psychology, 48*, 371–410.

Loehlin, J. C. (1992). *Genes and environment in personality development*. Newbury Park, CA: Sage.

Loehlin, J. C., Willerman, L., & Horn, J. M. (1988). Human behavior genetics. *Annual Review of Psychology, 39*, 101–133.

Loftus, E. F. (1991). The glitter of everyday memory . . . and the gold. *American Psychologist, 46*, 16–18.

Loftus, E. F. (1992). When a lie becomes memory's truth: Memory distortion after exposure to misinformation. *Current Directions in Psychological Science, 1*, 121–123.

Loftus, E. F. (1993). The reality of repressed memory. *American Psychologist, 48*, 518–537.

Loftus, E. F., & Ketcham, K. (1991). *Witness for the defense*. New York: St. Martin's Press.

Loftus, E. F., & Ketcham, K. (1994). *The myth of repressed memory*. New York: St. Martin's Press.

Loftus, E. F., & Klinger, M. R. (1992). Is the unconscious smart or dumb? *American Psychologist, 47*, 761–765.

Loftus, E. F., Miller, D. G., & Burns, H. J. (1978). Semantic integration of verbal information into a visual memory. *Journal of Experimental Psychology, 4*, 19–31.

Logie, R. H. (1993). Working memory in everyday cognition. In G. M. Davies & R. H. Logie (Eds.), *Memory in everyday life* (pp. 173–239). Amsterdam: North-Holland.

Logie, R. H. (1995). *Visuo-spatial working memory*. Hove, England: Erlbaum.

Logue, A. W. (1991). *The psychology of eating and drinking: An introduction*. New York: Freeman.

Lonky, E., Kaus, C. R., & Roodin, P. A. (1984). Life experience and mode of coping: Relation to moral judgment in adulthood. *Developmental Psychology, 20*, 1159–1167.

Lord, C. G. (1997). *Social psychology*. Fort Worth, TX: Harcourt Brace.

Lore, R. K., & Schultz, L. A. (1993). Control of human aggression: A comparative perspective. *American Psychologist, 48*, 16–25.

Lott, B. (1987). Sexist discrimination as distancing behavior: I. A laboratory demonstration. *Psychology of Women Quarterly, 13*, 341–355.

Lourenço, O., & Machado, A. (1996). In defense of Piaget's theory: A reply to 10 common criticisms. *Psychological Review, 103*, 143–164.

Lovelace, E. A., & Coon, V. E. (1991). Aging and word finding: Reverse vocabulary and Cloze tests. *Bulletin of the Psychonomic Society, 29*, 33–35.

Lowe, M. R. (1993). The effects of dieting on eating behavior: A three-factor model. *Psychological Bulletin, 114*, 100–121.

Lu, Z.-L., Williamson, S. J., & Kaufman, L. (1992). Behavioral lifetime of human auditory sensory memory predicted by physiological measures. *Science, 258*, 1668–1670.

Lubben, J. E., & Becerra, R. M. (1987). Social support among Black, Mexican, and Chinese elderly. In D. E. Gelfand & C. M. Barresi (Eds.), *Ethnic dimensions of aging* (pp. 130–144). New York: Springer.

Luce, R. D., & Krumhansl, C. L. (1988). Measurement, scaling, and psychophysics. In R. C. Atkinson, R. J. Herrnstein, G. Lindzey, & R. D. Luce (Eds.), *Stevens' handbook of experimental psychology* (2nd ed., pp. 3–74). New York: Wiley.

Luchins, A. S. (1957). Primacy-recency in impression formation. In C. I. Hovland (Ed.), *The order of presentation in persuasion* (pp. 33–61). New Haven, CT: Yale University Press.

Lutz, J. (1994). *Introduction to learning and memory*. Pacific Grove, CA: Brooks/Cole.

Lyketsos, C. G., et al. (1993). Depressive symptoms as predictors of medical outcomes in HIV infection. *JAMA, 270*, 2563–2577.

Lykken, D. T. (1995). *The antisocial personalities*. Hillsdale, NJ: Erlbaum.

Lykken, D. T., McGue, M., Tellegan, A., & Bouchard, T. J., Jr. (1992). Emergenesis: Genetic traits that may not run in families. *American Psychologist, 47*, 1565–1577.

Lykken, D. T., & Tellegan, A. (1996). Happiness is a stochastic phenomenon. *Psychological Science, 7*, 186–189.

Lyness, S. A. (1993). Predictors of differences between Type A and B individuals in heart rate and blood pressure reactivity. *Psychological Bulletin, 14*, 266–295.

Lynn, S. J., Kirsch, I., Neufield, J., & Rhue, J. W. (1996). Clinical hypnosis: Assessment, applications, and treatment considerations. In S. J. Lynn, I. Kirsch, & J. W. Rhue (Eds.), *Casebook of clinical hypnosis* (pp. 3–30). Washington, DC: American Psychological Association.

Lyons, W. (1986). *The disappearance of introspection*. Cambridge, MA: MIT Press.

Lytton, H., & Romney, D. M. (1991). Parents' differential socialization of boys and girls: A meta-analysis. *Psychological Bulletin, 109*, 267–296.

MacBeth, T. M. (Ed.). (1996). *Tuning in to young viewers: Social science perspectives on television*. Thousand Oaks, CA: Sage.

Maccoby, E. E. (1990a). *Gender differentiation: Explanatory viewpoints*. Paper presented at the convention of the American Psychological Society, Dallas.

Maccoby, E. E. (1990b). Gender and relationships: A developmental account. *American Psychologist, 45*, 513–520.

Maccoby, E. E. (1992). The role of parents in the socialization of children: An historical overview. *Developmental Psychology, 28*, 1006–1017.

Maccoby, E. E., & Jacklin, C. N. (1974). *The psychology of sex differences*. Stanford, CA: Stanford University Press.

Maccoby, E. E., & Jacklin, C. N. (1987). Gender segregation in childhood. In H. Reese (Ed.), *Advances in child development and behavior* (Vol. 20, pp. 239–288). New York: Academic Press.

MacDonald, N. E., et al. (1990). High-risk STD/HIV behavior among college students. *JAMA, 263*, 3155–3159.

MacDonald, T. K., Zanna, M. P., & Fong, G. T. (1995). Decision making in altered states: Effects of alcohol on attitudes toward drinking and driving. *Journal of Personality and Social Psychology, 68*, 973–985.

Mace, F. C., Lalli, J. S., Lalli, E. P., & Shea, M. C. (1993). Functional analysis and treatment of aberrant behavior. In R. Van Houten & S. Axelrod (Eds.), *Behavior analysis and treatment* (pp. 75–99). New York: Plenum.

Mackenzie, B. (1984). Explaining race differences in IQ: The logic, the methodology, and the evidence. *American Psychologist, 39*, 1214–1233.

Mackey, R. A., & O'Brien, B. A. (1995). *Lasting marriages: Men and women growing together*. Westport, CT: Praeger.

Mackie, M. (1991). *Gender relations in Canada: Further explorations.* Toronto: Butterworths.

MacLeod, C. M. (1991). Half a century of research on the Stroop effect: An integrative review. *Psychological Bulletin, 109,* 163–203.

MacLeod, C. M., & Campbell, L. (1992). Memory accessibility and probability judgments: An experimental evaluation of the availability heuristic. *Journal of Personality and Social Psychology, 63,* 890–902.

Macmillan, M. (1992). The sources of Freud's methods for gathering and evaluating clincial data. In T. Gelfand & J. Kerr (Eds.), *Freud and the history of psychoanalysis* (pp. 99–151). Hillsdale, NJ: Analytic Press.

Macrae, C. N., Hewstone, M., & Griffiths, R. J. (1993). Processing load and memory for stereotype-based information. *European Journal of Social Psychology, 23,* 77–87.

Macrae, C. N., Milne, A. B., & Bodenhausen, G. V. (1994). Stereotypes as energy-saving devices: A peek inside the cognitive toolbox. *Journal of Personality and Social Psychology, 66,* 37–47.

Maddox, G. L. (Ed.). (1995). *The encyclopedia of aging* (2nd ed.). New York: Springer.

Maddux, J. E. (1994, Fall). Social cognitive theories of behavior change: Basic principles and issues in the prevention of AIDS. *General Psychologist, 30,* 90–95.

Magnusson, D., & Törestad, B. (1993). A holistic view of personality: A model revisited. *Annual Review of Psychology, 44,* 427–452.

Maher, B. A., & Spitzer, M. (1993). Delusions. In C. G. Costello (Ed.), *Symptoms of schizophrenia* (pp. 92–120). New York: Wiley.

Maier, S. F., Watkins, L. R., & Fleshner, M. (1994). Psychoneuroimmunology: The interface between behavior, brain, and immunity. *American Psychologist, 49,* 1004–1017.

Maisto, S. A., Galizio, M., & Connors, G. J. (1995). *Drug use and abuse* (2nd ed.). Fort Worth, TX: Harcourt Brace.

Maki, R. H., & Berry, S. L. (1984). Metacomprehension of text material. *Journal of Experimental Psychology: Learning, Memory, and Cognition, 10,* 663–679.

Maki, R. H., & Serra, M. (1992). The basis of test prediction for text material. *Journal of Experimental Psychology: Learning, Memory, and Cognition, 18,* 116–126.

Malamuth, N. M., & Check, J. V. P. (1984). Debriefing effectiveness following exposure to pornographic rape depictions. *Journal of Sex Research, 20,* 1–13.

Malamuth, N. M., & Check, J. V. P. (1985). The effects of aggressive pornography on beliefs in rape myths: Individual differences. *Journal of Research in Personality, 19,* 299–320.

Males, M. (1996, November–December). Another anti-teen fix. *Extra!,* 15–17.

Malgady, R. G., Rogler, L. H., & Costantino, G. (1990). Culturally sensitive psychotherapy for Puerto Rican children and adolescents: A program of treatment outcome research. *Journal of Consulting and Clinical Psychology, 58,* 704–712.

Malinosky-Rummell, R., & Hansen, D. J. (1993). Long-term consequences of childhood physical abuse. *Psychological Bulletin, 114,* 68–79.

Mandler, J. M. (1992). The foundations of conceptual thought in infancy. *Cognitive Development, 7,* 273–285.

Mandler, J. M., & McDonough, L. (1993). Concept formation in infancy. *Cognitive Development, 8,* 291–318.

Manjarréz, C. A. (1991). *Mis palabras.* In D. Schoem (Ed.), *Inside separate worlds: Life stories of young Blacks, Jews, and Latinos* (pp. 50–63). Ann Arbor: University of Michigan Press.

Manson, J. E., et al. (1995). Body weight and mortality among women. *New England Journal of Medicine, 333,* 677–692.

Marcus, R. F. (1986). Naturalistic observation ofcooperation, helping, and sharing and their associations with empathy and affect. InC. Zahn-Waxler, E. M. Cummings, & R. Iannotti (Eds.), *Altruism and aggression* (pp. 256–279). Cambridge: Cambridge University Press.

Markides, K. S., & Black, S. A. (1996). Race, ethnicity, and aging: The impact of inequality. In R. H. Binstock & L. K. George (Eds.), *Handbook of aging and the social sciences* (4th ed., pp. 153–170). San Diego, CA: Academic Press.

Markus, H. R., & Kitayama, S. (1991a). Culture and self: Implications for cognition, emotion, and motivation. *Psychological Review, 98,* 224–253.

Markus, H. R., & Kitayama, S. (1991b). Cultural variation in the self-concept. In J. Strauss & G. R. Goethals (Eds.), *The self: Interdisciplinary approaches* (pp. 18–48). New York: Springer-Verlag.

Markus, H. R., & Kitayama, S. (1994). The cultural construction of self and emotion: Implications for social behavior. In S. Kitayama & H. R. Marcus (Eds.), *Emotion and culture: Empirical studies of mutual influence* (pp. 89–130). Washington, DC: American Psychological Association.

Markus, H. R., Kitayama, S., & Heiman, R. J. (1996). Culture and "basic" psychological principles. In E. T. Higgins & A. W. Kruglanski (Eds.), *Social psychology: Handbook of basic principles* (pp. 857–913). New York: Guilford Press.

Marín, G., & Marín, B. V. (1991). *Research with Hispanic populations.* Newbury Park, CA: Sage.

Martin, C. L. (1987). A ratio measure of sex stereotyping. *Journal of Personality and Social Psychology, 52,* 489–499.

Martin, D. W. (1990). *Doing psychology experiments* (3rd ed.). Monterey, CA: Brooks/Cole.

Martin, G., & Pear, J. (1992). *Behavior modification: What it is and how to do it* (4th ed.). Englewood Cliffs, NJ: Prentice Hall.

Martin, M. (1994). The philosophical importance of the Rosenthal effect. In M. Martin & L. C. McIntyre (Eds.), *Readings in the philosophy of social science* (pp. 585–596). Cambridge, MA: MIT Press.

Martin, R. J., White, B. D., & Hulsey, M. G. (1991). The regulation of body weight. *American Scientist, 79,* 528–541.

Martín-Baró, I. (1994). The psychological value of violent political repression. In A. Aron & S. Corne (Eds.), *Writings for a liberation psychology* (pp. 151–167). Cambridge, MA: Harvard University Press.

Martinez, J. L., Jr., & Mendoza, R. H. (Eds.). (1984). *Chicano psychology* (2nd ed.). New York: Aca-demic Press.

Martyna, W. (1980). Beyond the "He/Man" approach: The case for nonsexist language. *Signs, 5,* 482–493.

Marx, J. (1994). Obesity gene discovery may help solve weighty problem. *Science, 266,* 1477–1478.

Marx, J. (1995). A new guide to the human genome. *Science, 270,* 1919–1920.

Masland, R. H. (1996). Unscrambling color vision. *Science, 271,* 616–617.

Maslow, A. H. (1962). *Toward a psychology of being.* Princeton, NJ: Van Nostrand.

Maslow, A. H. (1968). *Toward a psychology of being* (2nd ed.). Princeton, NJ: Van Nostrand.

Maslow, A. H. (1971). *The farther reaches of human nature.* New York: Viking.

Massaro, D. W. (1987). *Speech perception by ear and eye.* Hillsdale, NJ: Erlbaum.

Masters, W. H., & Johnson, V. E. (1966). *Human sexual response.* Boston: Little, Brown.

Mastropieri, M. A., & Scruggs, T. E. (1991). *Teaching students ways to remember: Strategies for learning mnemonically.* Cambridge, MA: Brookline.

Mathie, V. A. (1993). Promoting active learning in psychology classes. In T. V. McGovern (Ed.), *Handbook for enhancing undergraduate education in psychology* (pp. 183–214). Washington, DC: American Psychological Association.

Matlin, M. W. (1996a). *The psychology of women* (3rd ed.). Fort Worth, TX: Harcourt Brace.

Matlin, M. W. (1996b). *"But I thought I was going to ace that test!": Metacognition and the college student.* Paper presented at the Middle Tennessee Psychology Conference, Nashville.

Matlin, M. W. (1998). *Cognition* (4th ed.). Fort Worth, TX: Harcourt Brace.

Matlin, M. W., & Foley, H. J. (1997). *Sensation and perception* (4th ed.). Boston: Allyn & Bacon.

Matlin, M. W., & Stang, D. J. (1978). *The Pollyanna Principle: Selectivity in language, memory, and thought.* Cambridge, MA: Schenkman.

Matson, J. L. (1990). *Handbook of behavior modification with the mentally retarded* (2nd ed.). New York: Plenum.

Matsumoto, D. (1987). The role of facial response in the experience of emotion: More methodological problems and a meta-analysis. *Journal of Personality and Social Psychology, 52,* 769–774.

Matsumoto, D. (1996). *Culture and psychology.* Pacific Grove, CA: Brooks/Cole.

Mattaini, M. A., McGowan, B. G., & Williams, G. (1996). Child maltreatment. In M. A. Mattaini & B. A. Thyer (Eds.), *Finding solutions to social problems: Behavioral strategies for change* (pp. 223–266). Washington, DC: American Psychological Association.

Maunsell, J. H. R. (1995). The brain's visual world: Representation of visual targets in cerebral cortex. *Science, 270,* 764–769.

May, C. P., Kane, M. J., & Hasher, L. (1995). Determinants of negative priming. *Psychological Bulletin, 118,* 35–54.

Mayer, J. D., & Salovey, P. (1995). Emotional intelligence and the construction and regulation of feelings. *Applied and Preventative Psychology, 4,* 197–208.

Mayer, J. D., & Salovey, P. (1997). What is emotional intelligence? In P. Salovey & D. Sluyter (Eds.), *Emotional development, emotional literacy, and emotional intelligence.* New York: Basic Books.

Mayer, R. E. (1988). *Teaching for thinking: Research on the teachability of thinking skills.* Paper presented at the Convention of the American Psychological Association, Atlanta.

Mayer, R. E. (1991). Problem solving. In M. W. Eysenck (Ed.), *The Blackwell dictionary of cognitive psychology* (pp. 284–288). Oxford, England: Blackwell.

Mayers, R. S. (1989). Use of folk medicine by elderly Mexican-American women. *Journal of Drug Issues, 19,* 283–295.

Mayes, L. C., Bornstein, M. H., Chawarska, K., & Granger, R. H. (1995). Information processing and developmental assessments in 3-month-old infants exposed prenatally to cocaine. *Pediatrics, 95,* 539–545.

Mazur, J. E. (1993). Predicting the strength of a conditioned reinforcer: Effects of delay and uncertainty. *Current Directions in Psychological Science, 2,* 70–74.

McAdams, D. P. (1990). *The person: An introduction to personality psychology.* San Diego: Harcourt Brace Jovanovich.

McCann, C. D., & Higgins, E. T. (1990). Social cognition and communication. In H. Giles & W. P. Robinson (Eds.), *Handbook of Language and Social Psychology* (pp. 13–32). Chichester, England: Wiley.

McCarthy, C. (1993, August 9). Arm students with non-violent conflict resolutions. *Liberal Opinion,* p. 1.

McCartney, K., & Phillips, D. (1988). Motherhood and child care. In B. Birns & D. H. Hay (Eds.), *The different faces of motherhood* (pp. 157–183). New York: Plenum.

McClelland, A. G. R., & Bolger, F. (1994). The calibration of subjective probabilities: Theories and models 1980–1984. In G. Wright & P. Ayton (Eds.), *Subjective probability* (pp. 453–482). Chichester, England: Wiley.

McClelland, D. C. (1985). *Human motivation.* Glenview, IL: Scott, Foresman.

McClelland, D. C. (1993). Motives and health. In G. G. Brannigan & M. R. Merrens (Eds.), *The undaunted psychologist: Adventures in research* (pp. 128–141). Philadelphia: Temple University Press.

McClelland, J. L. (1981). Retrieving general and specific knowledge from stored knowledge of specifics. *Proceedings of the Third Annual Conference of the Cognitive Science Society,* 170–172.

McClelland, J. L., McNaughton, B. L., & O'Reilly, R. C. (1995). Why there are complementary learning systems in the hippocampus and neocortex: Insights from the successes and failures of connectionist models of learning and memory. *Psychological Review, 102,* 419–457.

McClelland, J. L., Rumelhart, D. E., & the PDP Research Group. (1986). *Parallel distributed processing* (Vol. 2). Cambridge, MA: MIT Press.

McCloskey, M. (1992). Special versus ordinary memory mechanisms in the genesis of flashbulb memories. In E. Winograd & U. Neisser (Eds.), *Affect and accuracy in recall: Studies of "flashbulb" memories* (pp. 227–235). New York: Cambridge University Press.

McConnell, A. R., Sherman, S. J., & Hamilton, D. L. (1994). Online and memory-based aspects of individual and group target judgments. *Journal of Personality and Social Psychology, 67,* 173–185.

McCord, C., & Freeman, H. P. (1990). Excess mortality in Harlem. *New England Journal of Medicine, 322,* 173–177.

McCormick, D. A., Clark, G. A., Lavond, D. G., & Thompson, R. F. (1982). Initial localization of the memory trace for a basic form of learning. *Proceedings of the National Academy of Science, 79,* 2731–2742.

McCrae, R. R., & Costa, P. T., Jr. (1986). Clinical assessment can benefit from recent advances in personality psychology. *American Psychologist, 41,* 1001–1003.

McCrae, R. R., & Costa, P. T., Jr. (1997). Personality trait structure as a human universal. *American Psychologist, 52,* 509–516.

McCrae, R. R., & John, O. P. (1992). An introduction to the five-factor model and its applications. *Journal of Personality, 60,* 175–215.

McDonald, J. L. (1997). Language acquisition: The acquisition of linguistic structure in normal and special populations. *Annual Review of Psychology, 48,* 215–241.

McFarlane, J., Martin, C. L., & Williams, T. M. (1988). Mood fluctuations: Women versus men and menstrual versus other cycles. *Psychology of Women Quarterly, 12,* 201–223.

McGaugh, J. L. (1989). Involvement of hormonal and neuromodulatory systems in the regulation of memory storage. *Annual Review of Neuroscience, 12,* 255–287.

McGaugh, J. L., & Gold, P. E. (1988). Hormonal modulation of memory. In R. B. Brush & S. Levine (Eds.), *Psychoendocrinology.* New York: Aca-demic Press.

McGlashan, T. H. (1994). Psychosocial treatments of schizophrenia. In N. C. Andreasen (Ed.), *Schizophrenia: From mind to molecule* (pp. 189–215). Washington, DC: American Psychiatric Association.

McGovern, T. V., & Reich, J. N. (1996). A comment on the *Quality Principles. American Psychologist, 51,* 252–255.

McGrath, E., Keita, G. P., Strickland, B. R., & Russo, N. F. (Eds.). (1990). *Women and depression.* Washington, DC: American Psychological Association.

McGrath, W. J. (1992). Freud and the force of history. In T. Gelfand & J. Kerr (Eds.), *Freud and the history of psychoanalysis* (pp. 79–97). Hillsdale, NJ: Analytic Press.

McGuffin, P. W., & Morrison, R. L. (1994). Schizophrenia. In V. B. Van Hasselt & M. Hersen (Eds.), *Advanced abnormal psychology* (pp. 315–334). New York: Plenum.

McGuinness, D. M. (1985). Sensorimotor biases in cognitive development. In R. L. Hall (Ed.), *Male-female differences: A biocultural perspective* (pp. 57–126). New York: Praeger.

McGuire, P. K., Shah, G. M. S., & Murray, R. M. (1993). Increased blood flow in Broca's area during auditory hallucinations in schizophrenia. *Lancet, 342,* 703–706.

McHugh, M. C. (1996). A feminist approach to agoraphobia. In J. C. Chrisler, C. Golden, & P. D. Rozee (Eds.), *Lectures on the psychology of women* (pp. 339–357). New York: McGraw-Hill.

McHugh, M. C., Koeske, R. D., & Frieze, I. H. (1986). Issues to consider in conducting nonsexist psychological research: A guide for researchers. *American Psychologist, 41,* 879–890.

McKee, S. P., & Welch, L. (1992). The precision of size constancy. *Vision Research, 32,* 1447–1460.

McKelvie, S. J. (1990). The Asch primacy effect: Robust but not infallible. *Journal of Social Behavior and Personality, 5,* 135–150.

McKelvie, S. J. (1992). *Grappling with confusion: Experiences with the methods course.* Paper presented at Canadian Psychological Association, Québec City.

McKim, W. A. (1991). *Drugs and behavior: An introduction to behavioral pharmacology* (2nd ed.). Englewood Cliffs, NJ: Prentice Hall.

McLaughlin, B., & Heredia, R. (1996). Information-processing approaches to research on second language acquisition and use. In W. C. Ritchie & T. K. Bhatia (Eds.), *Handbook of second language acquisition* (pp. 213–228). San Diego, CA: Academic Press.

McMullen, L. (1992). *Sex differences in spoken language: Empirical truth or mythic truth?* Presented at the annual convention of the Canadian Psychological Association. Québec City.

McNally, J. L. (1998). *Geneseo freshman class profiles 1975–1997: Based on American Council of Education student information form.* Unpublished report.

McNally, R. J. (1994). Cognitive bias in panic disorder. *Current Directions in Psychological Science, 3,* 129–132.

McNeill, D. (1985). So you think gestures are nonverbal? *Psychological Review, 92,* 350–371.

Mead, J. (1996, Winter). The other third of life. *Buffalo Physician,* 12–17.

Mednick, M. T., & Thomas, V. (1993). Women and the psychology of achievement: A view from the eighties. In F. L. Denmark & M. A. Paludi (Eds.), *Psychology of women: A handbook of issues and theories* (pp. 585–626). Westport, CT: Greenwood.

Meichenbaum, D. (1985). *Stress inoculation training.* New York: Pergamon.

Meichenbaum, D. (1993). The personal journey of a psychotherapist and his mother. In G. G. Brannigan & M. R. Merrens (Eds.), *The undaunted psychologist* (pp. 189–201). Philadelphia: Temple University Press.

Meichenbaum, D. (1995). Changing conceptions of cognitive behavior modification: Retrospect and prospect. In M. J. Mahoney (Ed.), *Cognitive and constructive psychotherapies* (pp. 20–26). New York: Springer.

Meier, S. T. (1994). *The chronic crisis in psychological measurement and assessment: A historical survey.* San Diego, CA: Academic Press.

Meier, S. T., & Davis, S. R. (1990). Trends in reporting psychometric properties of scales used in counseling psychology research. *Journal of Counseling Psychology, 37,* 113–115.

Melton, G. B. (1995). Bringing psychology to Capitol Hill: Briefings on child and family policy. *American Psychologist, 50,* 766–770.

Melzack, R. (1986). Neurophysiological foundations of pain. In R. A. Sternbach (Ed.), *The psychology of pain* (pp. 1–24). New York: Raven.

Melzack, R. (1990). The tragedy of needless pain. *Scientific American, 262,* 27–33.

Melzack, R. (1992, April). Phantom limbs. *Scientific American, 266,* 120–126.

Melzack, R., & Wall, P. D. (1965). Pain mechanisms: A new theory. *Science, 150,* 971–979.

Mendelsohn, G. A. (1993). It's time to put theories of personality in their place, or, Allport and Stagner got it right, why can't we? In K. H. Craik, R. Hogan, & R. N. Wolfe (Eds.), *Fifty years of personality psychology* (pp. 103–115). New York: Plenum.

Mendelson, M. (1990). Psychoanalytic views on depression. In B. B. Wolman & G. Stricker (Eds.), *Depressive disorders: Facts, theories, and treatment methods* (pp. 22–37). New York: Wiley.

Mennella, J. A., & Beauchamp, G. K. (1996). The early development of human flavor preferences. In E. D. Capaldi (Ed.), *Why we eat what we eat: The psychology of eating* (pp. 83–112). Washington, DC: American Psychological Association.

Mensink, G., & Raaijmakers, J. G. W. (1988). A model for interference nad forgetting. *Psychological Review, 95,* 434–455.

Mental health: Does therapy help? (1995, November). *Consumer Reports,* 734–739.

Menyuk, P., Liebergot, J. W., & Schultz, M. C. (1995). *Early language development in full-term and premature infants.* Hillsdale, NJ: Erlbaum.

Mercer, J. R. (1988). Ethnic differences in IQ scores: What do they mean? (A response to Lloyd Dunn). *Hispanic Journal of Behavioral Sciences, 10,* 199–218.

Mermelstein, R. J., & Borrelli, B. (1995). Women and smoking. In A. L. Stanton & S. L. Gallant (Eds.), *The psychology of women's health* (pp. 309–348). Washington, DC: American Psychological Association.

Mervis, C. B., Catlin, J., & Rosch, E. (1976). Relationships among goodness-of-example, category norms, and word frequency. *Bulletin of the Psychonomic Society, 7,* 283–284.

Mesquita, B., & Frijda, N. (1992). Cultural variations in emotions: A review. *Psychological Bulletin, 112,* 179–204.

Messer, S. B., & Warren, C. S. (1995). *Models of brief psychodynamic therapy: A comparative approach.* New York: Guilford Press.

Metalsky, G. I., & Joiner, T. E., Jr. (1992). Vulnerability to depressive symptomatology: A prospective test of the diathesis-stress and causal mediation components of the hopelessness theory of depression. *Journal of Personality and Social Psychology, 63,* 667–675.

Metalsky, G. I., Joiner, T. E., Jr., Hardin, T. S., & Abramson, L. Y. (1993). Depressive reactions to failure in a naturalistic setting: A test of the hopelessness and self-esteem theories of depression. *Journal of Abnormal Psychology, 102,* 101–109.

Metcalfe, J., Funnell, M., & Gazzanica, M. S. (1995). Right-hemisphere memory superiority: Studies of a split-brain patient. *Psychological Science, 6,* 157–164.

Metcalfe, J., & Shimamura, A. P. (Eds.). (1994). *Metacognition: Knowing about knowing.* Cambridge, MA: MIT Press.

Meyer, G. E., & Petry, S. (1987). Top-down and bottom-up: The illusory contour as a microcosm of issues in perception. In S. Petry & G. E. Meyer (Eds.), *The perception of illusory contours* (pp. 3–26). New York: Springer-Verlag.

Meyerowitz, B. E., Richardson, J., Hudson, S., & Leedham, B. (1998). Ethnicity and cancer outcomes: Behavioral and psychosocial considerations. *Psychological Bulletin, 123,* 47–70.

Michael, J. (1985). Fundamental research and behaviour modification. In C. F. Lowe, M. Richelle, D. E. Blackman, & C. M. Bradshaw (Eds.), *Behaviour analysis and contemporary psychology* (pp. 159–170). London: Erlbaum.

Michael, R. T., Gagnon, J. H., Laumann, E. O., & Kolata, G. (1994). *Sex in America: A definitive survey.* Boston: Little, Brown.

Michel, A. (1980). *The story of Nim the chimp who learned language.* New York: Knopf.

Michels, R., & Marzuk, P. M. (1993a). Progress in psychiatry (second of two parts). *New England Journal of Medicine, 329,* 628–638.

Michels, R., & Marzuk, P. M. (1993b). Progress in psychiatry (first of two parts). *New England Journal of Medicine, 329,* 552–560.

Midanik, L. T., & Clark, W. B. (1995). Drinking-related problems in the United States: Description and trends, 1984–1990. *Journal of Studies on Alcohol, 56,* 395–402.

Middlebrooks, J. C., & Green, D. M. (1991). Sound localization by human listeners. *Annual Review of Psychology, 42,* 135–159.

Middleton, F. A., & Strick, P. L. (1994). Anatomical evidence for cerebellar and basal ganglia involvement in higher cognitive function. *Science, 266,* 458–461

Midkiff, E. E., & Bernstein, I. L. (1985). Targets of learned food aversions in humans. *Physiology and Behavior, 34,* 839–841.

Midlarsky, E., & Kahana, E. (1994). *Altruism in later life.* Thousand Oaks, CA: Sage.

Milgram, S. (1963). Behavioral studies of obedience. *Journal of Abnormal and Social Psychology, 67,* 371–378.

Milgram, S. (1964). Issues in the study of obedience: A reply to Baumrind. *American Psychologist, 19,* 848–852.

Milgram, S. (1974). *Obedience to authority.* New York: Harper & Row.

Milgram, S., Bickman, L., & Berkowitz, L. (1969). Note on the drawing power of crowds of different size. *Journal of Personality and Social Psychology, 13,* 79–82.

Miller, A. G., Collins, B. E., & Brief, D. E. (1995a). Perspectives on obedience to authority: The legacy of the Milgram experiments. *Journal of Social Issues, 51,* 1–19.

Miller, A. G., Collins, B. E., & Brief, D. E. (Eds.). (1995b). Perspectives on obedience to authority: The legacy of the Milgram experiments [Special issue]. *Journal of Social Issues, 51,* (3).

Miller, G. A. (1956). The magical number seven, plus or minus two: Some limits on our capacity for processing information. *Psychological Review, 63,* 81–97.

Miller, G. A. (1962). *Psychology: The science of mental life.* New York: Harper & Row.

Miller, G. A. (1967). The psycholinguists. In G. A. Miller (Ed.), *The psychology of communication* (pp. 70–92). London: Penguin.

Miller, G. A. (1991). *The science of words.* New York: Freeman.

Miller, J. L., & Eimas, P. D. (1995). Speech perception: From signal to word. *Annual Review of Psychology, 46,* 467–492.

Miller, K., & Doman, J. M. R. (1996, April). Together forever. *Life,* pp. 44–56.

Miller, M. (1997, April 14). Secrets of the cult. *Newsweek,* pp. 29–37.

Miller, N. E. (1985). The value of behavioral research on animals. *American Psychologist, 40,* 423–440.

Miller, N. E. (1991). Commentary on Ulrich: Need to check truthfulness of statements by opponents of animal research. *Psychological Science, 2,* 422–423.

Miller, P. H. (1993). *Theories of developmental psychology* (3rd ed.). New York: Freeman.

Miller, R. J., Hennessy, R. T., & Leibowitz, H. W. (1973). The effect of hypnotic ablation of the background on the magnitude of the Ponzo perspective illusion. *International Journal of Clincial and Experimental Hypnosis, 21,* 180–191.

Miller, R. R., Barnet, R. C., & Grahame, N. J. (1995). Assessment of the Rescorla-Wagner model. *Psychological Bulletin, 117,* 363–386.

Miller, S. K. (1992). Asian-Americans bump against glass ceilings. *Science, 258,* 1224–1228.

Millon, T. (1981). *Disorders of personality.* New York: Wiley.

Mills, J. (1984). Self-posed behavior of females and males in photographs. *Sex Roles, 10,* 633–637.

Mills, R. S. L., Pedersen, J., & Grusec, J. E. (1989). Sex differences in reasoning and emotion about altruism. *Sex Roles, 20,* 603–621.

Milner, B. R. (1966). Amnesia following operation on the temporal lobes. In C. W. M. Whitty & O. L. Zangwill (Eds.), *Amnesia following operation on the temporal lobes* (pp. 109–133). London: Butterworths.

Milner, B. R. (1970). Memory and medial temporal regions of the brain. In K. H. Pribram & D. E. Broadbent (Eds.), *Biology of memory* (pp. 29–50). Orlando, FL: Academic Press.

Mindell, J. A. (1993). Infancy, normal sleep patterns in. In M. A. Carskadon (Ed.), *Encyclopedia of sleeping and dreaming* (pp. 304–306). New York: Macmillan.

Mineka, S. (1986). The frightful complexity of the origins of fears. In J. B. Overmier & F. R. Brush (Eds.), *Affect, conditioning, and cognition: Essays on the determinants of behavior.* Hillsdale, NJ: Erlbaum.

Mineka, S., Davidson, M., Cook, M., Keir, R. (1984). Observational conditioning of snake fear in rhesus monkeys. *Journal of Abnormal Psychology, 93,* 355–372.

Mineka, S., & Sutton, S. K. (1992). Cognitive biases and the emotional disorders. *Psychological Science, 3,* 65–69.

Mingay, D., Bickart, B., Sudman, S., & Blair, J. (1994). Self and proxy reports of everyday events. In N. Schwartz & S. Sudman (Eds.), *Autobiographical memory and the validity of retrospective reports* (pp. 235–250). New York: Springer-Verlag.

Mirowsky, J., & Ross, C. E. (1989). *Social causes of psychological distress.* New York: Aldine de Gruyter.

Mischel, W. (1966). A social-learning view of sex differences in behavior. In E. Maccoby (Ed.), *The development of sex differences* (pp. 56–81). Stanford, CA: Stanford University Press.

Mischel, W. (1968). *Personality and assessment.* New York: Wiley.

Mischel, W. (1979). On the interface of cognition and personality: Beyond the person-situation debate. *American Psychologist, 34,* 740–754.

Mischel, W. (1993). *Introduction to personality* (5th ed.). Fort Worth, TX: Harcourt Brace Jovanovich.

Mischel, W., & Shoda, Y. (1995). A cognitive-affective system theory of personality: Reconceptualizing situations, dispositions, dynamics, and invariance in personality structure. *Psychological Review, 102,* 246–268.

Miserandino, M. (1991). Memory and the seven dwarfs. *Teaching of Psychology, 18,* 169–171.

Mishkin, M. (1966). Visual mechanisms beyond the striate cortex. In R. Russel (Ed.), *Frontiers in physiological psychology* (pp. 93–119). New York: Academic Press.

Mishkin, M., & Appenzeller, T. (1987). The anatomy of memory. *Scientific American, 256,* (6), 80–89.

Mita, T. H., Dermer, M., & Knight, J. (1977). Reversed facial images and the mere-exposure hypothesis. *Journal of Personality and Social Psychology, 35,* 597–601.

Mitchell, D. B. (1991). Implicit memory, explicit theories [Review of the book *Implicit memory: Theoretical issues*]. *Contemporary Psychology, 36,* 1060–1061.

Mitchell, E. S., et al. (1992). Methodological issues in the definition of premenstrual syndrome. In A. J. Dan & L. L. Lewis (Eds.), *Menstrual health in women's lives* (pp. 7–14). Urbana: University of Illinois Press.

Mitchell, S. A., & Black, M. J. (1995). *Freud and beyond: A history of modern psychoanalytic thought.* New York: Basic Books.

Moffitt, T. E., et al. (1993). The natural history of change in intellectual performance: Who changes? How much? Is it meaningful? *Journal of Child Psychology and Psychiatry, 34,* 455–506.

Mogil, J. S., et al. (1993). Sex differences in the antagonism of swim stress-induced analgesia: Effects of gonadectomy and estrogen replacement. *Pain, 53,* 17–25.

Moliterno, D. J., et al. (1994). Coronary-artery vasoconstriction induced by cocaine, cigarette smoking, or both. *New England Journal of Medicine, 330,* 454–459.

Mollica, R. F. (1989). Mood disorders: Epidemiology. In H. I. Kaplan & B. J. Sadock (Eds.), *Comprehensive textbook of psychiatry/V* (5th ed., Vol. 1, pp. 859–867). Baltimore: Williams & Wilkins.

Monk, T. H., et al. (1991). Circadian characteristics of healthy 80-year-olds and their relationship to objectively recorded sleep. *Journal of Gerontology, 46,* M171–M175.

Monte, C. F. (1995). *Beneath the mask: An introduction to theories of personality.* Fort Worth, TX: Harcourt Brace.

Monteith, M. J. (1996). Affective reactions to prejudice-related discrepant responses: The impact of standard salience. *Personality and Social Psychology Bulletin, 22,* 48–59.

Monteith, M. J., Devine, P. G., & Zuwerink, J. R. (1993). Self-directed versus other-directed affect as a consequence of prejudice-related discrepancies. *Journal of Personality and Social Psychology, 64,* 198–210.

Moorcroft, W. H. (1993). *Sleep, dreaming, and sleep disorders: An introduction* (2nd ed.). Lanham, MD: University Press.

Moore, M. L. (1992). The family as portrayed on prime-time television, 1947–1990: Structure and characteristics. *Sex Roles, 26,* 41–61.

Moore, S., & Rosenthal, D. (1991). Adolescent invulnerability and perceptions of AIDS risk. *Journal of Adolescent Research, 6,* 164–180.

Moore, T. E. (1991). *Subliminal auditory self-help tapes.* Paper presented at the annual convention of the American Psychological Association, San Francisco.

Moore, T. E. (1992a). Subliminal perception: Facts and fallacies. *Skeptical Inquirer, 16,* 273–281.

Moore, T. E. (1992b). *Subliminal self-help: Fact or artifact?* Paper presented at the annual convention of the American Psychological Association, Washington, DC.

Mor, V., & Allen, S. (1995). Hospice. In G. L. Maddox (Ed.), *The encyclopedia of aging* (2nd ed., pp. 475–477). New York: Springer.

Morell, V. (1996). Manic-depression findings spark polarized debate. *Science, 272,* 31–32.

Morin, C. M. (1993). *Insomnia: Psychological assessment and management.* New York: Guilford Press.

Morin, C. M., Culbert, J. P., Schwartz, S. M. (1994). Nonpharmacological interventions for insomina: A meta-analysis of treatment efficacy. *American Journal of Psychiatry, 151,* 1172–1180.

Morokoff, P. J., Harlow, L. L., & Quina, K. (1995). Women and AIDS. In A. L. Stanton & S. J. Gallant (Eds.), *The psychology of women's health* (pp. 117–169). Washington, DC: American Psychological Association.

Morrison, D. M. (1985). Adolescent contraceptive behavior: A review. *Psychological Bulletin, 98,* 538–568.

Morrison, J. (1995). *DSM-IV made easy: The clinician's guide to diagnosis.* New York: Guilford Press.

Morton, J., & Johnson, M. (1991). The perception of facial structure in infancy. In G. R. Lockhead & J. R. Pomerantz (Eds.), *The perception of structure* (pp. 317–325). Washington, DC: American Psychological Association.

Morval, M. V. G. (1992). Á propos de la violence familiale. *Canadian Psychology/Psychogie Canadienne, 33,* 144–150.

Moyer, R. S. (1985). *Teaching psychology courses about the nuclear arms race.* Paper presented at meeting of the Massachusetts Psychological Association.

Mrazek, P. J., & Haggerty, R. J. (Eds.). (1994). *Reducing risks for mental disorders.* Washington, DC: National Academy Press.

Mullen, B., Bryant, B., & Driskell, J. E. (1997). The presence of others and arousal: An integration. *Group Dynamics, 1,* 52–64.

Munglani, R., & Jones, J. G. (1992). Sleep and general anaesthesia as altered states of consciousness. *Journal of Psychopharmacology, 6,* 399–409.

Muñoz, R. F., Mrazek, P. J., & Haggerty, R. J. (1996). Institute of Medicine report on prevention of mental disorders. *American Psychologist, 51,* 1116–1122.

Mura, R. (1987). Sex-related differences in expectations of success in undergraduate mathematics. *Journal for Research in Mathematics Education, 18,* 15–24.

Muret-Wagstaff, S., & Moore, S. G. (1989). The Hmong in America: Infant behavior and rearing practices. In J. K. Nugent, B. M. Lester, & T. B. Brazelton (Eds.), *The cultural context of infancy* (Vol. 1, pp. 319–339). Norwood, NJ: Ablex.

Murphy, D. A., & Kelly, J. A. (1994). Women's health: The impact of the expanding AIDS epidemic. In V. J. Adesso, D. M. Reddy, & R. Fleming (Eds.), *Psychological perspectives on women's health* (pp. 285–312). Washington, DC: Taylor & Francis.

Murphy, J. M., et al. (1991). Depression and anxiety in relation to social status. *Archives of General Psychiatry, 48,* 223–229.

Murray, B. (1995, November). Gender gap in math scores is closing. *APA Monitor,* p. 43.

Myers, D. G. (1992). *The pursuit of happiness.* New York: Morrow.

Myers, D. G., & Bishop, G. D. (1970). Discussion effects on racial attitudes. *Science, 169,* 778–779.

Myers, D. G., & Diener, E. (1995). Who is happy? *Psychological Science, 6,* 10–19.

Myers, D. G., & Diener, E. (1996, May). The pursuit of happiness. *Scientific American,* pp. 70–72.

Myers, N. A., & Perlmutter, M. (1978). Memory in the years from two to five. In P. A. Ornstein (Ed.), *Memory development in children* (pp. 191–218). Hillsdale, NJ: Erlbaum.

Nadelson, C. C., & Notman, M. T. (1995). Gender issues in psychiatric treatment. In G. O. Gabbard (Ed.), *Treatments of psychiatric disorders* (2nd ed., Vol. 1, pp. 35–53). Washington, DC: American Psychiatric Press.

Nagata, D. K. (1989). Japanese American children and aolescents. In J. T. Gibbs & L. N. Huang (Eds.), *Children of color.* San Francisco: Jossey-Bass.

Nagata, D. K., & Crosby, F. (1991). Comparisons, justice, and the internment of Japanese-Americans. In J. Suls & T. A. Wills (Eds.), *Social comparison: Contemporary theory and research* (pp. 347–368). Hillsdale, NJ: Erlbaum.

Nakatani, C. H., & Hirschberg, J. (1994). A corpus-based study of repair cues in spontaneous speech. *Journal of the Acoustical Society of America, 95,* 1603–1616.

Nakayama, K., & Shimojo, S. (1992). Experiencing and perceiving visual surfaces. *Science, 257,* 1357–1363.

Namir, S., Wolcott, D. L., Fawzy, F. I., & Alumbaugh, M. J. (1987). Coping with AIDS: Psychological and health implications. *Journal of Applied Social Psychology, 1987, 17,* 309–328.

Napier, K., London, W. M., Whelan, E. M., & Case, A. G. (1996). *Cigarettes: What the warning label doesn't tell you.* New York: American Council on Science and Health.

Nash, M. (1987). What, if anything, is regressed about hypnotic age regression? A review of the empirical literature. *Psychological Bulletin, 102,* 42–52.

National Association of Social Workers. (1993). *Code of ethics of the National Association of Social Workers.* Washington, DC: Author.

National Institute on Drug Abuse. (1989). *National household survey on drug abuse: 1988 population estimates.* Washington, DC: U.S. Government Printing Office.

Neale, J. M. (1997). Some (fairly) new drugs for treating schizophrenia [Review of the book *The new pharmacotherapy of schizophrenia*]. *Contemporary Psychology, 42,* 315–316.

Neale, J. N., Davison, G. C., & Haaga, D. A. F. (1996). *Exploring abnormal psychology.* New York: Wiley.

Nebes, R. D. (1992). Cognitive dysfunction in Alzheimer's disease. In F. I. M. Craik & T. A. Salthouse (Eds.), *The handbook of aging and cognition* (pp. 373–445). Hillsdale, NJ: Erlbaum.

Nebes, R. D., & Brady, C. B. (1992). Generalized cognitive slowing and severity of dementia in Alzheimer's disease: Implications for the interpretation of response-time data. *Journal of Clinical and Experimental Neuropsychology, 14,* 317–326.

Neisser, U. (1987). From direct perception to conceptual structure. In U. Neisser (Ed.), *Concepts and conceptual development* (pp. 11–24). New York: Cambridge University Press.

Neisser, U., et al. (1996). Intelligence: Knowns and unknowns. *American Psychologist, 51,* 77–101.

Neisser, U., & Harsch, N. (1992). Phantom flashbulbs: False recollections of hearing the news about *Challenger.* In E. Winograd & U. Neisser (Eds.), *Affect and accuracy in recall* (pp. 9–31). New York: Cambridge University Press.

Nelson, D. L. (1993). Implicit memory. In P. E. Morris & M. Gruneberg (Eds.), *Aspects of memory* (Vol. 2). London: Routledge.

Nelson, L. (1991). Psychological factors in war and peacemaking. *Contemporary Social Psychology, 15,* 172–178.

Nelson, T. O. (1992). *Consciousness and metacognition.* Paper presented at the convention of the American Psychological Association, Washington, DC.

Nelson, T. O. (1996). Consciousness and metacognition. *American Psychologist, 51,* 102–116.

Nelson, T. O., Dunlosky, J., Graf, A., & Narens, L. (1994). Utilization of metacognitive judgments in the allocation of study during multitrial learning. *Psychological Science, 5,* 207–213.

Nelson, T. O., & Leonesio, R. J. (1988). Allocation of self-paced study time and the "labor-in-vain effect." *Journal of*

Experimental Psychology: Learning, Memory, and Cognition, 14, 676–686.

Nemeth, C. J. (1994). The value of minority dissent. In S. Moscovici, A. Mucchi-Faina, & A. Maass (Eds.), *Minority influence* (pp. 3–15). Chicago: Nelson-Hall.

Nevid, J. S. (1984). Sex differences in factors of romantic attraction. *Sex Roles, 11,* 401–411.

Newcomb, A. F., & Bagwell, C. L. (1995). Children's friendship relations: A meta-analytic review. *Psychological Bulletin, 117,* 306–347.

Newman, B., O'Grady, M. A., Ryan, C. S., & Hemmes, N. S. (1993). Pavlovian conditioning of the tickle response of human subjects: Temporal and delay conditioning. *Perceptual and Motor Skills, 77,* 779–785.

NICHD Early Child Care Research Network. (1997). The effects of infant child care on infant-mother attachment security: Results of the NICHD Study of Early Child Care. *Child Development, 68,* 860–879.

Nicholls, J. G., Martin, A. R., & Wallace, B. G. (1992). *From neuron to brain: A cellular and molecular approach to the function of the nervous system* (3rd ed.). Sunderland, MA: Sinauer.

Nickerson, R. S. (1990). William James on reasoning. *Psychological Science, 1,* 167–171.

Nickerson, R. S., & Adams, M. J. (1979). Long-term memory for a common object. *Cognitive Psychology, 11,* 287–307.

Nicotine dependence—Part I. (1997, May). *Harvard Mental Health Letter, 13,* pp. 1–4.

Nicotine dependence—Part II. (1997, June). *Harvard Mental Health Letter, 13,* pp. 1–4.

Nieburg, P., Marks, J. S., McLaren, N. M., & Remington, P. L. (1985). The fetal tobacco syndrome. *JAMA, 253,* 2998–2999.

Nielsen, L. (1996). *Adolescence: A contemporary view* (3rd ed.). Fort Worth, TX: Harcourt Brace.

Nigg, J. T., & Goldsmith, H. H. (1994). Genetics of personality disorders: Perspectives from personality and psychopathology research. *Psychological Bulletin, 115,* 346–380.

NIH/CEPH Collaborative Mapping Group. (1992). A comprehensive genetic linkage map of the human genome. *Science, 258,* 67–86.

Ninio, A., & Snow, C. E. (1996). *Pragmatic development: Essays in developmental science.* Boulder, CO: Westview Press.

Nisbett, R. E. (1995). Race, IQ, and scientism. In S. Fraser (Ed.), *The bell curve wars: Race, intelligence, and the future of America* (pp. 36–57). New York: Basic Books.

Nisbett, R. E., Caputo, C., Legant, P., & Maracek, J. (1973). Behavior as seen by the actor and as seen by the observer. *Journal of Personality and Social Psychology, 27,* 154–164.

Nisbett, R. E., & Ross, L. (1980). *Human inference: Strategies and shortcomings of social judgment.* Englewood Cliffs, NJ: Prentice Hall.

Nisbett, R. E., & Wilson, T. D. (1977). Telling more than we can know. Verbal reports on mental processes. *Psychological Review, 84,* 231–259.

Nissani, M. (1994). Conceptual conservation: An understated variable in human affairs? *Social Science Journal, 31,* 307–318.

Nixon, S. J. (1996). Alzheimer's disease and vascular dementia. In R. L. Adams, O. A. Parsons, J. L. Culbertson, & S. J. Nixon (Eds.), *Neuropsychology for clinical practice: Etiology, as-*

sessment, and treatment of common neurological disorders (pp. 65–105). Washington, DC: American Psychological Association.

Nobiling, J. (1991). Personal communication.

Nodine, B. F. (1994, August). *G. Stanley Hall Lecture: Students write to learn in psychology classes: Joining the discourse community.* Paper presented at the annual convention of the American Psychological Association, Los Angeles.

Nofsinger, R. E. (1991). *Everyday conversation.* Newbury Park, CA: Sage.

Nolen-Hoeksema, S. (1987). Sex differences in unipolar depression: Evidence and theory. *Psychological Bulletin, 101,* 259–282.

Nolen-Hoeksema, S. (1990). *Sex differences in depression.* Stanford, CA: Stanford University Press.

Nolen-Hoeksema, S., & Jackson, B. (1996). *Ruminative coping and the gender differences in depression.* Paper presented at the annual convention of the American Psychological Association, Toronto.

Nolen-Hoeksema, S., Morrow, J., & Fredrickson, B. L. (1993). Response styles and the duration of episodes of depressed mood. *Journal of Abnormal Psychology, 102,* 20–28.

Nolen-Hoeksema, S., Parker, L. E., & Larson, J. (1994). Ruminative coping with depressed mood following loss. *Journal of Personality and Social Psychology, 67,* 92–104.

Norrick, N. R. (1993). *Conversational joking: Humor in everyday talk.* Bloomington: Indiana University Press.

Northcraft, G. B., & Neale, M. A. (1987). Experts, amateurs, and real estate: An anchoring-and-adjustment perspective on property pricing decisions. *Organizational Behavior and Human Decision Processes, 39,* 84–97.

Novick, L. R. (1988). Analogical transfer, problem similarity, and expertise. *Journal of Experimental Psychology: Learning, Memory, and Cognition, 14,* 510–520.

Novick, L. R., & Coté, N. (1992). *The nature of expertise in anagram solution.* Proceedings of the Fourteenth Annual Conference of the Cognitive Science Society (pp. 450–455). Hillsdale, NJ: Erlbaum.

Novy, D. M., Nelson, D. V., Francis, D. J., & Turk, D. C. (1995). Perspectives of chronic pain: An evaluative comparison of restrictive and comprehensive models. *Psychological Bulletin, 118,* 238–247.

Nowak, R. (1994). Breast cancer gene offers surprises. *Science, 265,* 1796–1799.

Nye, R. D. (1992). *Three psychologies: Perspectives from Freud, Skinner, and Rogers* (4th ed.). Pacific Grove, CA: Brooks/Cole.

Obear, K. (1991). Homophobia. In N. J. Evans & V. A. Wall (Eds.), *Beyond tolerance: Gays, lesbians and bisexuals on campus* (pp. 39–66). Lanham, MD: American College Personnel Association.

Obsessive-compulsive disorder—Part I. (1995, November). *Harvard Mental Health Letter,* pp. 1–3.

Obsessive-compulsive disorder—Part II. (1995, December). *Harvard Mental Health Letter,* pp. 1–3.

O'Donnell, J. M. (1985). *The origins of behaviorism: American psychology, 1870–1920.* New York: New York University Press.

Office for Protection From Research Risks. (1986). *Public Health Service policy on humane care and use of laboratory animals.* Bethesda, MD: National Institutes of Health.

Oggins, J., Veroff, J., & Leber, D. (1993). Perceptions of marital interaction among Black and White newlyweds. *Journal of Personality and Social Psychology, 65,* 494–511.

Öhman, A., & Soares, J. J. E. (1993). On the automatic nature of phobic fear: Conditioned electrodermal responses to masked fear-relevant stimuli. *Journal of Abnormal Psychology, 102,* 121–132.

Ohzawa, I., DeAngelis, G. C., & Freeman, R. D. (1990). Stereoscopic depth discrimination in the visual cortex: Neurons ideally suited as disparity detectors. *Science, 249,* 1037–1041.

O'Keefe, D. J. (1990). *Persuasion: Theory and research.* Newbury Park, CA: Sage.

Okun, M. A. (1995). Subjective well-being. In G. Maddox (Ed.), *The encyclopedia of aging* (pp. 909–912). New York: Springer.

Oldfield, S. R., & Parker, S. P. A. (1986). Acuity of sound localisation: A topography of auditory space: III. Monaural hearing conditions. *Perception, 15,* 67–81.

Oldham, J. M. (1994). Personality disorders: Current perspectives. *JAMA, 272,* 1770–1776.

Olds, D. L., Henderson, C. R., & Tatelbaum, R. (1994). Intellectual impairment in chidren of women who smoke cigarettes during pregnancy. *Pediatrics, 93,* 221–233.

Oliner, S. P., & Oliner, P. M. (1988). *The altruistic personality.* New York: Free Press.

Oliver, M. B., & Hyde, J. S. (1993). Gender differences in sexuality: A meta-analysis. *Psychological Bulletin, 114,* 29–51.

Olson, J. E., & Frieze, I. H. (1991). A decade of change for U.S. managers. *Equal Opportunities International, 10,* 19–23.

Olson, J. M., & Zanna, M. P. (1993). Attitudes and attitude change. *Annual Review of Psychology, 44,* 117–154.

Omdahl, B. L. (1995). *Cognitive appraisal, emotion, and empathy.* Mahwah, NJ: Erlbaum.

O'Neill, P., Miller, R. (Producers), & Chaplin, D. (Director). (1995). *Not in our town* [Film]. (Available from California Working Group, P.O. Box 10326, Oakland, CA 94610)

Orne, M. T. (1951). The mechanisms of hypnotic age regression: An experimental study. *Journal of Abnormal Psychology, 46,* 213–225.

Orne, M. T. (1962). On the social psychology of the psychological experiment: With particular reference to demand characteristics and their implications. *American Psychologist, 17,* 776–783.

Orne, M. T. (1986). The validity of memories retrieved in hypnosis. In B. Zilbergeld, M. G. Edelstien, & D. L. Araoz (Eds.), *Hypnosis: Questions and answers* (pp. 45–46). New York: Norton.

Orth-Gomér, K. (1994). International epidemiological evidence for a relationship between social support and cardiovascular disease. In S. A. Shumaker & S. M. Czajkowski (Eds.), *Social support and cardiovascular disease* (pp. 97–117). New York: Plenum.

Ortony, A., Clore, G. L., & Collins, A. (1988). *The cognitive structure of emotions.* Cambridge: Cambridge University Press.

Osgood, C. E. (1962). *An alternative to war or surrender.* Urbana: University of Illinois Press.

O'Shea, R. P., Blackburn, S. G., & Ono, H. (1994). Contrast as a depth cue. *Vision Research, 34,* 1595–1604.

Osherson, S. (1992). *Wrestling with love: How men struggle with intimacy with women, children, parents, and each other.* New York: Fawcett.

Ostrom, T. M., Carpenter, S. L., Sedikides, C., & Li, F. (1993). Differential processing of in-group and out-group information. *Journal of Personality and Social Psychology, 64,* 21–34.

Ostrom, T. M., & Sedikides, C. (1992). Out-group homogeneity effects in natural and minimal groups. *Psychological Bulletin, 112,* 536–552.

Osvold, L. L., & Sodowsky, G. R. (1993). Eating disorders of White American, racial and ethnic minority American, and international women. *Journal of Multicultural Counseling and Development, 21,* 143–154.

Oswald, I. (1987a). Sleep. In R. L. Gregory (Ed.), *The Oxford companion to the mind* (pp. 718–719). New York: Oxford University Press.

Oswald, I. (1987b). Dreaming. In R. L. Gregory (Ed.), *The Oxford companion to the mind* (pp. 201–203). New York: Oxford University Press.

Ottati, V., & Lee, Y. T. (1995). Accuracy: A neglected component of stereotype research. In Y. T. Lee, L. J. Jussim, & C. R. McCauley (Eds.), *Stereotype accuracy: Toward appreciating group differences* (pp. 29–59). Washington, DC: American Psychological Association.

Owens, R. E., Jr. (1996). *Language development: An introduction* (4th ed.). Boston: Allyn & Bacon.

Padden, C., & Humphries, T. (1988). *Deaf in America: Voices from a culture.* Cambridge, MA: Harvard University Press.

Padgett, D. K. (Ed.). (1995). *Handbook on ethnicity, aging, and mental health.* Westport, CT: Greenwood.

Padian, N. S., Shiboski, S. S., & Jewell, N. (1990, June). The relative efficiency of female-to-male HIV sexual transmission. *Proceedings of the Sixth International Conference on AIDS.* Abstract No. Th.C. 101, p. 159.

Padilla, A. M. (1988). Early psychological assessments of Mexican-American children. *Journal of the History of the Behavioral Sciences, 24,* 111–117.

Padilla, A. M. (1995). Introduction to Hispanic psychology. In A. M. Padilla (Ed.), *Hispanic psychology: Critical issues in theory and research* (pp. xi–xxi). Thousand Oaks, CA: Sage.

Pagliaro, L. A. (1996, Winter). Everything goes better with coke? *Psynopsis,* p. 20.

Paik, H., & Comstock, G. (1994). The effects of television violence on antisocial behavior: A meta-analysis. *Communication Research, 21,* 516–546.

Paikoff, R. L., & Brooks-Gunn, J. (1991). Do parent-child relationships change during puberty? *Psychological Bulletin, 110,* 47–66.

Paivio, A. (1995). Imagery and memory. In M. S. Gazzaniga (Ed.), *The cognitive neurosciences* (pp. 977–986). Cambridge, MA: MIT Press.

Pallis, C. A. (1955). Impaired identification of faces and places with agnosia for colors. *Journal of Neurology, Neurosurgery and Psychiatry, 18,* 218–224.

Palmer, S. E. (1992). Common region: A new principle of perceptual grouping. *Cognitive Psychology, 24,* 436–447.

Palmer, S. E., Neff, J., & Beck, D. (1996). Late influences on perceptual grouping: Amodal completion. *Psychonomic Bulletin and Review, 3,* 75–80.

Palmer, S. E., & Rock, I. (1994). Rethinking perceptual organization: The role of uniform connectedness. *Psychonomic Bulletin and Review, 1,* 29–55.

Palmore, E. B. (1990). *Ageism negative and positive.* New York: Springer.

Paludi, M. A. (1984). Psychometric properties and underlying assumptions of four objective measures of fear of success. *Sex Roles, 10,* 765–781.

Panksepp, J. (1986). The neurochemistry of behavior. *Annual Review of Psychology, 37,* 77–107.

Papolos, D. F., et al. (1996). Bipolar spectrum disorders in patients diagnosed with velo-cardio-facial syndrome. *American Journal of Psychiatry, 153,* 1541–1547.

Papp, L. A., Coplan, J., & Gorman, J. M. (1994). *Review of Psychiatry, 13,* 187–205.

Pappas, G., Queen, S., Hadden, W., & Fisher, G. (1993). The increasing disparity in mortality between socioeconomic groups in the United States, 1960 and 1986. *New England Journal of Medicine, 329,* 103–109.

Park, C. L., & Folkman, S. (1997). Meaning in the context of stress and coping. *Review of General Psychology, 1,* 115–144.

Parke, R. D. (1995). Fathers and families. In M. H. Bornstein (Ed.), *Handbook of parenting* (Vol. 3, pp. 27–63). Mahwah, NJ: Erlbaum.

Parker, K. C. H., Hanson, R. K., & Hunsley, J. (1988). MMPI, Rorschach, and WAIS: A meta-analytic comparison of reliability, stability, and validity. *Psychological Bulletin, 103,* 367–373.

Parks, T. E. (1986). Illusory figures: A (mostly) atheoretical review. *Psychological Bulletin, 95,* 282–300.

Parsons, O. A. (1996a). Alcohol abuse and alcoholism. In R. L. Adams, O. A. Parsons, J. L. Culbertson, & S. J. Nixon (Eds.), *Neuropsychology for clinical practice: Etiology, assessment, and treatment of common neurological disorders* (pp. 175–201). Washington, DC: American Psychological Association.

Parsons, O. A. (1996b). Human immunodeficiency virus (HIV-1). In R. L. Adams, O. A. Parsons, J. L. Culbertson, & S. J. Nixon (Eds.), *Neuropsychology for clinical practice: Etiology, assessment, and treatment of common neurological disorders* (pp. 203–224). Washington, DC: American Psychological Association.

Partridge, L. D., & Partridge, L. D. (1993). *The nervous system: Its function and its interaction with the world.* Cambridge, MA: MIT Press.

Pascalis, O., et al. (1995). Mother's face recognition by neonates: A replication and an extension. *Infant Behavior and Development, 18,* 79–85.

Passingham, R. E. (1993). *The frontal lobes and voluntary action.* New York: Oxford University Press.

Passuth, P. M., & Cook, F. L. (1985). Effects of television viewing on knowledge and attitudes about older adults: A critical re-examination. *Gerontologist, 25,* 69–77.

Pastalan, L. A. (1982). Environmental design and adaptation to the visual environment of the elderly. In R. Sekuler, D. Kline, & K. Dismukes (Eds.), *Handbook of perception* (Vol. 4). New York: Academic Press.

Patterson, C. H. (1996). Still relevant—Still revolutionary. *Contemporary Psychology, 41,* 759–762.

Patterson, C. J. (1994). Children of the lesbian baby boom: Behavioral adjustment, self-concepts, and sex role identity. In B. Greene & G. M. Herek (Eds.), *Lesbian and gay psychology: Theory, research and clinical applications* (pp. 156–175). Thousand Oaks, CA: Sage.

Patterson, C. J. (1995). Adoption of minor children by lesbian and gay adults: A social science perspective. *Duke Journal of Gender Law and Policy, 2,* 191–205.

Patterson, C. J. (1996). Lesbian and gay parents and their children. In R. C. Savin-Williams & K. M. Cohen (Eds.), *The lives of lesbians, gays, and bisexuals: Children to adults* (pp. 274–304). Fort Worth, TX: Harcourt Brace.

Patterson, D. R., Everett, J. J., Burns, G. L., & Marvin, J. A. (1992). Hypnosis for the treatment of burn pain. *Journal of Consulting and Clinical Psychology, 60,* 713–717.

Patterson, M. L. (1983). *Nonverbal behavior: A functional perspective.* New York: Springer-Verlag.

Paul, R. (1992). *Critical thinking* (2nd ed.). Santa Rosa, CA: Foundation for Critical Thinking.

Paunonen, S. V., Jackson, D. N., Trzebinski, J., & Forsterling, F. (1992). Personality structure across cultures: A multimethod evaluation. *Journal of Personality and Social Psychology, 62,* 447–456.

Pavlov, I. P. (1927). *Conditioned reflexes.* London: Oxford University Press.

Payne, D. G., & Wenger, M. J. (1992). Improving memory through practice. In D. J. Herrmann, H. Weingartner, A. Searleman, & C. McEvoy (Eds.), *Memory improvement: Implications for memory theory* (pp. 187–209). New York: Springer-Verlag.

Payne, J. W., Bettman, J. R., & Johnson, E. J. (1992). Behavioral decision research: A constructive processing perspective. *Annual Review of Psychology, 43,* 87–131.

Payne, L. (1996, February 5). CBS exec slanders Black viewers. *Liberal Opinion,* p. 28.

Peal, E., & Lambert, W. E. (1962). The relation of bilingualism to intelligence. *Psychological Monographs,* 546.

Pendergrast, M. (1995). *Victims of memory: Incest accusations and shattered lives.* Hinesburg, VT: Upper Access.

Pennebaker, J. W. (1995). Emotion, disclosure, and health: An overview. In J. W. Pennebaker (Ed.), *Emotion, disclosure, and health* (pp. 3–10). Washington, DC: American Psychological Association.

Pennebaker, J. W. (1997). Writing about emotional experiences as a therapeutic process. *Psychological Science, 8,* 162–173.

Pennebaker, J. W., Kiecolt-Glaser, J. K., & Glaser, R. (1988). Disclosure of traumas and immune function: Health implications for psychotherapy. *Journal of Consulting and Clinical Psychology, 56,* 239–245.

Peplau, L. A. (1988, July). *Research on lesbian and gay relationships: A decade review.* Paper presented at the International Conference on Personal Relationships, University of British Columbia, Vancouver.

Peplau, L. A., Cochran, S. D., & Mays, V. M. (1996). A national survey of the intimate relationships of African American lesbians and gay men: A look at commitment, satisfaction, sexual behavior and HIV disease. In B. Greene & G. Herek (Eds.), *Psychological perspectives on lesbian and gay issues:*

Ethnic and cultural diversity among lesbians and gay men. Newbury Park, CA: Sage.

Peplau, L. A., et al. (1997). A critique of Bem's "exotic becomes erotic" theory of sexual orientation, *Psychological Review,* in press.

Peplau, L. A., Veniegas, R. C., & Campbell, S. M. (1996). Gay and lesbian relationships. In R. C. Savin-Williams & K. Cohen (Eds.), *The lives of lesbians, gays, and bisexuals: Children to adults* (pp. 250–273). Fort Worth, TX: Harcourt Brace.

Pepler, D. J., & Slaby, R. G. (1994). Theoretical and developmental perspectives on youth and violence. In L. D. Eron, J. H. Gentry, & P. Schlegel (Eds.), *Reasons to hope* (pp. 27–58). Washington, DC: American Psychological Association.

Perfetti, C. A. (1993). Why inferences might be restricted. *Discourse Processes, 16,* 181–192.

Perkins, D. N. (1981). *The mind's best work.* Cambridge, MA: Harvard University Press.

Perkins, D. N. (1995). *Outsmarting IQ: The emerging science of learnable intelligence.* New York: Free Press.

Pernanen, K. (1991). *Alcohol in human violence.* New York: Guilford Press.

Perrin, S., & Spencer, C. (1981). Independence or conformity in the Asch experiment as a reflection of cultural and situational factors. *British Journal of Social Psychology, 20,* 205–209.

Perry, J. C., & Vaillant, G. E. (1989). Personality disorders. In H. I. Kaplan & B. J. Sadock (Eds.), *Comprehensive textbook of psychiatry/V*(5th ed., Vol. 2., pp. 1352–1387). Baltimore: Williams & Wilkins.

Perry, N. W., & Wrightsman, L. S. (1991). *The child witness: Legal issues and dilemmas.* Newbury Park, CA: Sage.

Pert, C. B., & Snyder, S. H. (1973). Opiate receptor: Demonstration in nervous tissue. *Science, 179,* 1011–1014.

Peterson, B. E., & Klohnen, E. C. (1995). Realization of generativity in two samples of women at midlife. *Psychology and Aging, 10,* 20–29.

Peterson, B. E., & Stewart, A. J. (1993). Generativity and social motives in young adults. *Journal of Personality and Social Psychology, 65,* 186–198.

Peterson, B. E., & Stewart, A. J. (1996). Antecedents and contexts of generativity motivation at midlife. *Psychology and Aging, 11,* 21–33.

Peterson, M. A. (1994). Object recognition processes can and do operate before figure-ground organization. *Current Directions in Psychological Science, 3,* 105–111.

Peterson, M. A., & Gibson, B. S. (1994). Object recognition contributions to figure-ground organization: Operations on outlines and subjective contours. *Perception and Psychophysics, 56,* 551–564.

Peterson, S. E., et al. (1989). Positron emission tomographic studies of the processing of single words. *Journal of Cognitive Neuroscience, 1,* 153–170.

Petitto, L. A., & Marentette, P. F. (1991). Babbling in the manual mode: Evidence for the ontogeny of language. *Science, 251,* 1493–1496.

Petraitis, J., Flay, B. R., & Miller, T. Q. (1995). Reviewing theories of adolescent substance use: Organizing pieces in the puzzle. *Psychological Bulletin, 117,* 67–86.

Petrosino, M. A., Fucci, D., Harris, D., & Randolph-Tyler, E. (1988). Lingual vibrotactile/auditory magnitude estimation and cross-modal matching: Comparison of suprathreshold responses in men and women. *Perceptual and Motor Skills, 67,* 291–300.

Pettigrew, T. F., & Martin, J. (1987). Shaping the organizational context for Black American inclusion. *Journal of Social Issues, 43,* 41–78.

Petty, R. E., & Cacioppo, J. T. (1986). *Communication and persuasion.* New York: Springer-Verlag.

Petty, R. E., Haugtvedt, C. P., & Smith, S. M. (1995). Elaboration as a determinant of attitude strength: Creating attitudes that are persistent, resistant, and predictive of behavior. In R. E. Petty & J. A. Krosnick (Eds.), *Attitude strength: Antecedents and consequences* (pp. 93–130). Mahwah, NJ: Erlbaum.

Petty, R. E., & Krosnick, J. A. (Eds.). (1995). *Attitude strength: Antecedents and consequences.* Mahwah, NJ: Erlbaum.

Petty, R. E., Wegener, D. T., & Fabrigar, L. R. (1997). Attitudes and attitude change. *Annual Review of Psychology, 48,* 609–647.

Pezdek, K., & Banks, W. P. (Eds.). (1996). *The recovered memory/false memory debate.* San Diego, CA: Academic Press.

Pfohl, B., & Blum, N. (1995). Obsessive-compulsive personality disorder. In W. J. Livesley (Ed.), *The DSM-IV personality disorders* (pp. 261–276). New York: Guilford Press.

Phares, E. J. (1988). *Introduction to personality*(2nd ed.). Glenview, IL: Scott, Foresman.

Phares, V. (1992). Where's Poppa? The relative lack of attention to the role of fathers in child and adolescent psychopathology. *American Psychologist, 47,* 656–664.

Phillip, M. (1993, April 8). AIDS: Fighting a killer through education. *Black Issues in Higher Education,* pp. 22–23.

Phillips, D., McCartney, K., & Scarr, S. (1987). Child-care quality and children's social development. *Developmental Psychology, 23,* 537–543.

Phillips, D. P., & Brugge, J. F. (1985). Progress in neurophysiology of sound localization. *Annual Review of Psychology, 36,* 245–274.

Phillips, S. D., & Imhoff, A. R. (1997). Women and career development: A decade of research. *Annual Review of Psychology, 48,* 31–59.

Piaget, J. (1983). Piaget's theory. In P. H. Mussen (Ed.), *Handbook of child psychology* (4th ed., Vol. 1, pp. 103–128). New York: Wiley.

Piasecki, T. M., et al. (1997). Listening to nicotine: Negative affect and the smoking withdrawal conundrum. *Psychological Science, 8,* 184–189.

Pich, E. M., et al. (1997). Common neural substrates for the addictive properties of nicotine and cocaine. *Science, 275,* 83–86.

Pickles, J. O. (1988). *An introduction to the physiology of hearing* (2nd ed.). London: Academic Press.

Pierce, W. D., & Epling, W. F. (1995). *Behavior analysis and learning.* Englewood Cliffs, NJ: Prentice Hall.

Pietromonaco, P. R., & Rook, K. S. (1987). Decision style in depression: The contribution of perceived risks versus benefits. *Journal of Personality and Social Psychology, 52,* 399–408.

Pilkington, N. W., & D'Augelli, A. R. (1995). Victimization of lesbian, gay, and bisexual youth in community settings. *Journal of Community Psychology, 23,* 34–56.

Pinel, J. P. J. (1997). *Biopsychology* (3rd ed.). Boston: Allyn & Bacon.

Pinker, S. (1993). The central problem for the psycholinguist. In G. Harman (Ed.), *Conceptions of the human mind* (pp. 59–84). Hillsdale, NJ: Erlbaum.

Pinker, S., & Birdsong, D. (1979). Speakers' sensitivity to rules of frozen word order. *Journal of Verbal Learning and Verbal Behavior, 18,* 497–508.

Pion, G. M., et al. (1996). The shifting gender composition of psychology: Trends and implications for the discipline. *American Psychologist, 51,* 509–528.

Plaut, D. C., & Farah, M. J. (1990). Visual object representation: Interpreting neurophysiological data within a computational framework. *Journal of Cognitive Neuroscience, 2,* 320–343.

Playing the name game. (1995, November 20). *Newsweek,* p. 81.

Plomin, R. (1990). The role of inheritance in behavior. *Science, 248,* 183–188.

Plomin, R., DeFries, J. C., & McClearn, G. E. (1990). *Behavioral genetics: A primer* (2nd ed.). New York: Freeman.

Plomin, R., & Neiderhiser, J. M. (1992). Genetics and experience. *Current Directions in Psychological Science, 1,* 160–163.

Plomin, R., & Rende, R. (1991). Human behavioral genetics. *Annual Review of Psychology, 42,* 161–190.

Plous, S. (1991). An attitude survey of animal rights activists. *Psychological Science, 2,* 194–196.

Plous, S. (1993). *The psychology of judgment and decision making.* New York: McGraw-Hill.

Plous, S. (1994, Fall). William James' *other* concern: Racial injustice in America. *General Psychologist, 30,* 80–88.

Plutchik, R. (1994). *The psychology and biology of emotion.* New York: HarperCollins.

Plutchik, R. (1995). A theory of ego defenses. In H. R. Conte & R. Plutchik (Eds.), *Ego defenses: Theory and measurement* (pp. 13–37). New York: Wiley.

Poggio, G. F. (1995). Stereoscopic processing in monkey visual cortex: A review. In T. V. Papathomas, C. Chubb, A. Gorea, & E. Kowler (Eds.), *Early vision and beyond* (pp. 43–53). Cambridge, MA: MIT Press.

Pollard, R. Q., Jr. (1996). Professional psychology and deaf people: The emergence of a discipline. *American Psychologist, 51,* 389–396.

Pool, R. (1994). *The dynamic brain.* Washington, DC: National Academy Press.

Popplestone, J. A., & McPherson, M. W. (1994). *An illustrated history of American psychology.* Madison, WI: Brown & Benchmark.

Posner, M. I. (1994). Attention: The mechanisms of consciousness. *Proceedings of the National Academy of Science, 91,* 7398–7403.

Posner, M. I. (1996, September). Attention and psychopathology. *Harvard Mental Health Letter,* pp. 5–6.

Posner, M. I., & Raichle, M. E. (1994). *Images of mind.* New York: Freeman.

Postman, N., & Powers, S. (1992). *How to watch TV news.* New York: Penguin.

Post-traumatic stress: Part I. (1991, February). *Harvard Mental Health Letter,* pp. 1–4.

Potegal, M. (1994). Aggressive arousal: The amygdala connection. In M. Potegal & J. F. Knutson (Eds.), *The dynamics of aggression* (pp. 73–111). Hillsdale, NJ: Erlbaum.

Potter, W. Z., & Rudorfer, M. V. (1993). Electroconvulsive therapy—A modern medical procedure. *New England Journal of Medicine, 328,* 882–883.

Potter, W. Z., Rudorfer, M. V., & Manji, H. (1991). The pharmacologic treatment of depression. *New England Journal of Medicine, 325,* 633–641.

Potts, R., Huston, A. C., & Wright, J. C. (1986). The effects of television form and violent content on boys' attention and social behavior. *Journal of Experimental Child Psychology, 41,* 1–17.

Poulton, E. C. (1989). *Bias in quantifying judgments.* Hillsdale, NJ: Erlbaum.

Powers, S., & López, R. L. (1985). Perceptual, motor and verbal skills of monolingual and bilingual Hispanic children: A discriminant analysis. *Perceptual and Motor Skills, 60,* 999–1002.

Powlishta, K. K. (1995a). Intergroup processes in childhood: Social categorization and sex role development. *Developmental Psychology, 31,* 781–788.

Powlishta, K. K. (1995b). Gender bias in children's perceptions of personality traits. *Sex Roles, 32,* 17–28.

Powlishta, K. K. (1995c, May). Gender segregation among children: Understanding the "cootie phenomenon." *Young Children,* pp. 61–69.

Powlishta, K. K., Serbin, L. A., Doyle, A., & White, D. R. (1994). Gender, ethnic, and body type biases: The generality of prejudice in childhood. *Developmental Psychology, 30,* 526–536.

Pratkanis, A., & Aronson, E. (1992). *Age of propaganda: The everyday use and abuse of persuasion.* New York: Freeman.

Premack, D. (1996). Piggyback with Darwin [Review of the book *The adapted mind: Evolutionary psychology and the generation of culture*]. *Contemporary Psychology, 41,* 207–212.

Pressley, M., & El-Dinary, P. B. (1992). Memory strategy instruction that promotes good information processing. In D. J. Herrmann, H. Weingartner, A. Searleman, & C. McEvoy (Eds.), *Memory improvement: Implications for memory theory* (pp. 79–100). New York: Springer-Verlag.

Pressley, M., & Ghatala, E. S. (1988). Delusions about performance on multiple-choice comprehension tests. *Reading Research Quarterly, 23,* 454–464.

Pribram, K. H. (1954). Toward a science of neuropsychology: Method and data. In R. A. Patton (Ed.), *Current trends in psychology and the behavioral science* (pp. 115–152). Pittsburgh: University of Pittsburgh Press.

Price, D. (1997, July 28). Colorado's governor champions legal rights of gay people. *Liberal Opinion,* p. 29.

Price, D. L., & Sisodia, S. S. (1992). Alzheimer's disease: Neural and molecular basis. In L. S. Squire (Ed.), *Encyclopedia of learning and memory* (pp. 22–25). New York: Macmillan.

Price, L. H., & Heninger, G. R. (1994). Lithium in the treatment of mood disorders. *New England Journal of Medicine, 331,* 591–598.

Prigatano, G. P. (1992). Personality disturbances associated with traumatic brain injury. *Journal of Consulting and Clinical Psychology, 60,* 360–368.

Prince, D. A. (1995). Thirty years among cortical neurons. In M. J. Gutnick & I. Mody (Eds.), *The cortical neuron* (pp. 3–23). New York: Oxford University Press.

Pruitt, D. G., & Olczak, P. V. (1995). Beyond hope: Approaches to resolving seemingly intractable conflict. In B. B. Bunker et al. (Eds.), *Conflict, cooperation, and justice* (pp. 59–92). San Francisco: Jossey-Bass.

Psychodynamic Therapy—Part II (1991, December). *Harvard Mental Health Letter,* pp. 1–4.

Puente, A. E. (1990). Psychological assessment of minority group members. In G. Goldstein & M. Hersen (Eds.), *Handbook of psychological assessment* (2nd ed., pp. 505–520). New York: Pergamon.

Pugh, E. N., Jr. (1988). Vision: Physics and retinal physiology. In R. C. Atkinson, R. J. Herrnstein, G. Lindzey, & R. D. Luce (Eds.), *Stevens' handbook of experimental psychology* (2nd ed., Vol. 1, pp. 75–163). New York: Wiley.

Pyke, S. W. (1995, Winter). "Shaping our future": The National Conference on Graduate Education. *Psynopsis,* p. 8.

Pyke, S. W., & Greenglass, E. R. (1997, January). Women and organizational structures: An avenue to influence. *Newsletter of the CAP/SCP,* pp. 5–8.

Rachlin, H. (1994). *Behavior and mind: The roots of modern psychology.* New York: Oxford University Press.

Rados, R., & Cartwright, R. D. (1982). Where do dreams come from? *Journal of Abnormal Psychology, 91,* 433–436.

Raeff, C., Greenfield, P. M., & Quiroz, B. (1995, March). *Developing interpersonal relationships in the cultural contexts of individualism and collectivism.* Paper presented at the Society for Research in Child Development, Indianapolis.

Rafferty, Y., & Shinn, M. (1991). The impact of homelessness on children. *American Psychologist, 46,* 1170–1179.

Raichle, M. E. (1994, April). Visualizing the mind. *Scientific American,* pp. 58–64.

Raider, E. (1995). Conflict resolution training in schools: Translating theory into applied skills. In B. B. Bunker et al. (Eds.), *Conflict, cooperation, and justice* (pp. 93–121). San Francisco: Jossey-Bass.

Rajagopal, I. (1990). The glass ceiling in the vertical mosaic: Indian immigrants in Canada. *Canadian Ethnic Studies, 22,* 96–101.

Ramachandran, V. S. (1987). Visual perception of surfaces: A biological theory. In S. Petry & G. E. Meyer (Eds.), *The perception of illusory contours* (pp. 93–108). New York: Springer-Verlag.

Ramachandran, V. S. (1992a). Filling in gaps in perception: Part 1. *Current Directions in Psychological Science, 1,* 199–205.

Ramachandran, V. S. (1992b, May). Blind spots. *Scientific American, 266,* 86–91.

Ramachandran, V. S. (1993). Filling in gaps in perception: Part 2. Scotomas and phantom limbs. *Current Directions in Psychological Science, 2,* 56–65.

Ramachandran, V. S., & Gregory, R. L. (1991). Perceptual filling in of artificially induced scotomas in human vision. *Nature, 350,* 699–702.

Rand, C. S. W., & Macgregor, A. M. C. (1991). Successful weight loss following obesity surgery and the perceived liability of morbid obesity. *International Journal of Obesity, 15,* 577–579.

Raskin, P. A., & Israel, A. C. (1981). Sex-role imitation in children: Effects of sex of child, sex of model, and sex-role appropriateness of modeled behavior. *Sex Roles, 7,* 1067–1076.

Ratner, H. H., & Foley, M. A. (1994). A unifying framework for the development of children's memory for activity. In H. W.

Reese (Ed.), *Advances in child development and behavior* (Vol. 25, pp. 33–105). New York: Academic Press.

Rattan, A. I., & Rattan, G. (1987). A historical perspective on the nature of intelligence. In R. S. Dean (Ed.), *Introduction to assessing human intelligence* (pp. 5–28). Springfield, IL: Thomas.

Rauscher, F. H., Krauss, R. M., & Chen, Y. (1996). Gesture, speech, and lexical access: The role of lexical movements in speech production. *Psychological Science, 7,* 226–231.

Rawlins, W. K. (1995). Friendships in later life. In J. F. Nussbaum & J. Coupland (Eds.), *Handbook of communication and aging research* (pp. 227–257). Mahwah, NJ: Erlbaum.

Raymond, J. L., Lisberger, S. G., & Mauk, M. D. (1996). The cerebellum: A neuronal learning machine? *Science, 272,* 1126–1131.

Rayner, K. (Ed.). (1992). *Eye movements and visual cognition: Scene perception and reading.* New York: Springer-Verlag.

Rayner, K. (1993). Eye movements in reading: Recent developments. *Current Directions in Psychological Science, 2,* 81–85.

Rayner, K., & Pollatsek, A. (1987). Eye movements in reading: A tutorial review. In M. Coltheart (Ed.), *Attention and performance XII: The psychology of reading.* Hillsdale, NJ: Erlbaum.

Read, J. D., Yuille, J. C., & Tollestrup, P. (1992). Recollections of a robbery: Effects of arousal and alcohol upon recall and person identification. *Law and Human Behavior, 16,* 425–446.

Read, S. J., & Cesa, I. L. (1991). This reminds me of the time when . . . : Expectation failures in reminding and explanation. *Journal of Experimental Social Psychology, 27,* 1–25.

Rebecca, M. (1983). Personal communication.

Rebok, G. W., Brandt, J., & Folstein, M. (1990, April–June). Longitudinal cognitive decline in patients with Alzheimer's disease. *Journal of Geriatric Psychiatry and Neurology, 3,* 91–97.

Rebok, G. W., & Folstein, M. F. (1993). Dementia. *Journal of Neuropsychiatry, 5,* 265–276.

Rebok, G. W., & Folstein, M. F. (1994, February). Challenges in diagnosing and treating Alzheimer's disease. *Psychiatric Times,* pp. 22–24.

Ree, M. J., & Earles, J. A. (1992). Intelligence is the best predictor of job performance. *Current Directions in Psychological Science, 1,* 86–89.

Reeve, J. (1992). *Understanding motivation and emotion.* Fort Worth, TX: Harcourt Brace Jovanovich.

Reeve, J. (1997). *Understanding motivation and emotion* (2nd ed.). Fort Worth, TX: Harcourt Brace.

Reeves, L. M., & Weisberg, R. W. (1993). On the concrete nature of human thinking: Content and context in analogical transfer. *Educational Psychology, 13,* 245–258.

Reeves, L. M., & Weisberg, R. W. (1994). The role of content and abstract information in analogical transfer. *Educational Psychology, 13,* 245–258.

Register, P. A., & Kihlstrom, J. F. (1987). Hypnotic effects on hypermnesia. *International Journal of Clinical and Experimental Hypnosis, 35,* 155–169.

Reicher, G. M. (1969). Perceptual recognition as a function of meaningfulness of stimulus materials. *Journal of Experimental Psychology, 81,* 275–280.

Reinitz, M. T., Morrissey, J., & Demb, J. (1994). Role of attention in face encoding. *Journal of Experimental Psychology: Learning, Memory, and Cognition, 20,* 161–168.

Reisenzein, R. (1983). The Schachter theory of emotion: Two decades later. *Psychological Bulletin, 94,* 239–264.

Reisenzein, R., Meyer, W. U., & Schützwohl, A. (1995). James and the physical basis of emotion: A comment on Ellsworth. *Psychological Review, 102,* 757–761.

Reiss, D., & Price, R. H. (1996). National research agenda for prevention research. *American Psychologist, 51,* 1109–1115.

Rempel-Clower, N. L., Zola, S. M., Squire, L. R., & Amaral, D. G. (1996). Three cases of enduring memory impairment after bilateral damage limited to the hippocampal formation. *Journal of Neuroscience, 16,* 5233–5255.

Renzulli, J. S. (1986). The three-ring conception of giftedness: A developmental model for creative productivity. In R. J. Sternberg & J. E. Davidson (Eds.), *Conceptions of giftedness* (pp. 53–92). New York: Cambridge University Press.

Rescorla, R. A. (1968). Probability of shock in the presence and absence of CS in fear conditioning. *Journal of Comparative and Physiological Psychology, 66,* 1–5.

Rescorla, R. A. (1988). Pavlovian conditioning: It's not what you think it is. *American Psychologist, 43,* 151–160.

Rescorla, R. A. (1991). Associative relations in instrumental learning: The Eighteenth Bartlett Memorial Lecture. *Quarterly Journal of Experimental Psychology, 43B,* 1–23.

Rescorla, R. A., & Wagner, A. R. (1972). A theory of Pavlovian conditioning: Variations in the effectiveness of reinforcement and nonreinforcement. In A. H. Black & W. F. Prokasy (Eds.), *Classical conditioning II: Current research and theory* (pp. 64–99). New York: Appleton-Century-Crofts.

Resnick, S. M. (1992). Positron emission tomography in psychiatric illness. *Current Directions in Psychological Science, 1,* 92–98.

Restak, R. M. (1994). *The modular brain.* New York: Macmillan.

Revusky, S. H. (1971). The role of interference in association over a delay. In W. K. Honig & P. H. R. James (Eds.), *Animal memory* (pp. 155–213). New York: Academic Press.

Reynolds, A. G. (1991). The cognitive consequences of bilingualism. In A. G. Reynolds (Ed.), *Bilingualism, multiculturalism, and second language learning: The McGill conference in honour of Wallace E. Lambert* (pp. 145–182). Hillsdale, NJ: Erlbaum.

Reyos, N. (1997, Spring). Native American/American Indian culture and its influence on male identity development. *Society for the Psychological Study of Men and Masculinity Bulletin, 2,* 17–18.

Ricciardelli, L. A. (1992). Creativity and bilingualism. *Journal of Creative Behavior, 26,* 242–259.

Rice, L. N., & Greenberg, L. S. (1991). Two affective change events in client-centered therapy. In J. D. Safran & L. S. Greenberg (Eds.), *Emotion, psychotherapy, and change* (pp. 197–226). New York: Guilford Press.

Rice, M. L. (1989). Children's language acquisition. *American Psychologist, 44,* 149–156.

Rich, J. (1994, March). Growing old gracefully. *Maryknoll, 88,* 7–11.

Rich, J. M., & DeVitis, J. L. (1994). *Theories of moral development* (2nd ed.). Springfield, IL: Thomas.

Richards, A., et al. (1992). Effects of mood manipulation and anxiety on performance if an emotional Stroop task. *British Journal of Psychology, 83,* 479–491.

Richardson, J. T. E., & Zucco, G. M. (1989). Cognition and olfaction: A review. *Psychological Bulletin, 105,* 352–360.

Richardson, K. (1991). *Understanding intelligence.* Buckingham, England: Open University Press.

Rickgarn, R. L. V. (1994). *Perspectives on college student suicide.* Amityville, NJ: Baywood.

Rieser, P. A., & Underwood, L. E. (1990). Disorders of growth and short stature: Medical overview. In C. S. Holmes (Ed.), *Psychoneuroendocrinology: Brain, behavior, and hormonal interaactions* (pp. 10–16). New York: Springer-Verlag.

Risser, A. L., & Mazur, L. J. (1995). Use of folk remedies in a Hispanic population. *Archives of Pediatric and Adolescent Medicine, 149,* 978–988.

Ritts, V., Patterson, M. L., & Tubbs, M. E. (1992). Expectations, impressions, and judgments of physically attractive students: A review. *Review of Educational Research, 62,* 413–426.

Rivers, P. C. (1994). *Alcohol and human behavior: Theory, research, and practice.* Englewood Cliffs, NJ: Prentice Hall.

Rizzo, T. A. (1989). *Friendship development among children in school.* Norwood, NJ: Ablex.

Roach, R. (1997, July 10). Racial attitudes: Gaps narrow for young people. *Black Issues in Higher Education,* pp. 12–13.

Roberts, L. (1992). Two chromosomes down, 22 to go. *Science, 258,* 28–30.

Roberts, T. (1991). Gender and the influence of evaluations on self-assessments in achievement settings. *Psychological Bulletin, 109,* 297–308.

Roberts, T., & Nolen-Hoeksema, S. (1989). Sex differences in reactions to evaluative feedback. *Sex Roles, 21,* 725–747.

Robertson, R. (1995). *Jungian archetypes: Jung, Gödel, and the history of archetypes.* York Beach, ME: Nicholas-Hays.

Robins, C. J., & Hayes, A. M. (1995). An appraisal of cognitive therapy. In M. J. Mahoney (Ed.), *Cognitive and constructive therapies* (pp. 41–63). New York: Springer.

Robinson, J. L., Kagan, J., Reznick, J. S., & Corley, R. (1992). The heritability of inhibited and uninhibited behavior: A twin study. *Developmental Psychology, 28,* 1030–1037.

Rock, I. (1983). *The logic of perception.* Cambridge, MA: MIT Press.

Rock, I. (1987). A problem-solving approach to illusory contours. In S. Petry & G. E. Meyer (Eds.), *The perception of illusory contours* (pp. 62–70). New York: Springer-Verlag.

Rock, R., & Mitchener, K. (1992). Further evidence of failure of reversal of ambiguous figures by uninformed subjects. *Perception, 21,* 39–45.

Rodgers, J. E. (1982). The malleable memory of eyewitnesses. *Science Digest, 3,* 32–35.

Rodin, J., & Langer, E. J. (1977). Long-term effects of a control-relevant intervention with the institutionalized aged. *Journal of Personality and Social Psychology, 35,* 897–902.

Rodin, J., & Salovey, P. (1989). Health psychology. *Annual Review of Psychology, 40,* 533–579.

Rodin, J., Schooler, C., & Schaie, K. W. (Eds.). (1990). *Self-directedness: Causes and effects throughout the life course.* Hillsdale, NJ: Erlbaum.

Roediger, H. L., III, & McDermott, K. B. (1995). Creating false memories: Remembering words not presented in lists. *Journal of Experimental Psychology: Learning, Memory, and Cognition, 21,* 803–814.

Rogers, C. R. (1959). A theory of therapy, personality, and interpersonal relationships, as developed in the client-centered framework. In S. Koch (Ed.), *Psychology: A study of a science* (Vol. 3). New York: McGraw-Hill.

Rogers, C. R. (1961). *On becoming a person: A therapist's view of psychotherapy.* Boston: Houghton Mifflin.

Rogers, C. R. (1963). Actualizing tendency in relation to "motives" and to consciousness. In M. R. Jones (Ed.), *Nebraska symposium on motivation* (pp. 1–24). Lincoln: University of Nebraska Press.

Rogers, C. R. (1980). *A way of being.* Boston: Houghton Mifflin.

Rogers, C. R. (1986). Client-centered therapy. In I. L. Kutash & A. Wolf (Eds.), *Psychotherapist's casebook* (pp. 197–208). San Francisco: Jossey-Bass.

Rogers, S. (1995). Perceiving pictorial space. In W. Epstein & S. J. Rogers (Eds.), *Perception of space and motion* (pp. 119–163). Orlando, FL: Academic Press.

Rogers, T. B. (1983). Emotion, imagery, and verbal codes: A closer look at an increasingly complex interaction. In J. Yuille (Ed.), *Imagery, memory, and cognition* (pp. 285–305). Hillsdale, NJ: Erlbaum.

Rogers, T. B. (1995). *The psychological testing enterprises: An introduction.* Pacific Grove, CA: Brooks/Cole.

Rogers, T. B., Kuiper, N. A., & Kirker, W. S. (1977). Self-reference and the encoding of personal information. *Journal of Personality and Social Psychology, 35,* 677–688.

Roitblat, H. L. (1987). *Introduction to comparative cognition.* New York: Freeman.

Roitblat, H. L., & von Fersen, L. (1992). Comparative cognition: Representations and processes in learning and memory. *Annual Review of Psychology, 43,* 671–710.

Romaine, S. (1996). Bilingualism. In W. C. Ritchie & T. K. Bhatia (Eds.), *Handbook of second language acquisition* (pp. 571–604). San Diego, CA: Academic Press.

Romney, P., Tatum, B., & Jones, J. (1992). Feminist strategies for teaching about oppression: The importance of process. *Women's Studies Quarterly, 20,* 95–110.

Root, M. P. P. (1995). The psychology of Asian American women. In H. Landrine (Ed.), *Bringing cultural diversity to feminist psychology: Theory, research, and practice* (pp. 265–301). Washington, DC: American Psychological Association.

Rosch, E. H. (1973). Natural categories. *Cognitive Psychology, 4,* 328–350.

Rosch, E. H., & Mervis, C. B. (1975). Family resemblances: Studies in the internal structure of categories. *Cognitive Psychology, 7,* 573–605.

Rose, R. J. (1995). Genes and human behavior. *Annual Review of Psychology, 46,* 625–654.

Rose, S. (1995). Women's friendships. In J. C. Chrisler & A. H. Henstreet (Eds.), *Variations on a theme: Diversity and the psychology of women* (pp. 79–105). Albany: State University of New York Press.

Rosekrans, M., & Hartup, W. (1967). Imitative influences of consistent and inconsistent response consequences to a model on aggressive behavior in children. *Journal of Personality and Social Psychology, 7,* 429–434.

Rosen, C. M. (1987, September). The eerie world of reunited twins. *Discover,* 36–46.

Rosenberg, P. S. (1995). Scope of the AIDS epidemic in the United States. *Science, 270,* 1372–1375.

Rosenberg, S. (1993). Chomsky's theory of language: Some recent observations. *Psychological Science, 4,* 15–19.

Rosenblatt, P. C., Karis, T. A., & Powell, R. D. (1995). *Multiracial couples: Black and White voices.* Thousand Oaks, CA: Sage.

Rosenhan, D. L. (1973). On being sane in insane places. *Science, 179,* 250–258.

Rosenman, R. H. (1990). Type A behaviour pattern: A personal overview. *Journal of Social Behavior and Personality, 5,* 1–24.

Rosenthal, R. (1968, September). Self-fulfilling prophecy. *Psychology Today, 2* (4), pp. 44–51.

Rosenthal, R. (1973, September). The Pygmalion effect lives. *Psychology Today, 7* (4), pp. 56–63.

Rosenthal, R. (1993). Interpersonal expectations: some antecedents and some consequences. In P. D. Blanck (Ed.), *Interpersonal expectations: Theory, research, and applications* (pp. 3–24). New York: Cambridge University Press.

Rosenthal, R. (1994). Interpersonal expectancy effects: A 30-year perspective. *Current Directions in Psychological Science, 3,* 176–179.

Rosenthal, R. (1995). Critiquing *Pygmalion:* A 25-year perspective. *Current Directions in Psychological Science, 4,* 171–172.

Ross, L. (1992, August). *Reactive devaluation and other barriers to dispute resolution.* Paper presented at the Annual Convention of the American Psychological Association, Washington, DC.

Ross, L., & Nisbett, R. E. (1991). *The person and the situation: Perspectives of social psychology.* New York: McGraw-Hill.

Ross, L., & Stillinger, C. (1991). Barriers to conflict resolution. *Negotiation Journal, 7,* 389–404.

Ross, M., & Buehler, R. (1994). Creative remembering. In U. Neisser & R. Fivush (Eds.), *The remembering self: Construction and accuracy in the self-narrative* (pp. 205–235). New York: Cambridge University Press.

Rosser, R. (1994). *Cognitive development: Psychological and biological perspectives.* Boston: Allyn & Bacon.

Rotberg, I. C. (1995). Myths about test score comparisons. *Science, 270,* 1446–1448.

Rothbart, M. K. (1993). Intergroup perception and social conflict. In S. Worchel & J. A. Simpson (Eds.), *Conflict between people and groups* (pp. 93–109). Chicago: Nelson-Hall.

Rotton, J., & Kelly, I. W. (1985). Much ado about the full moon: A meta-analysis of lunar-lunacy research. *Psychological Bulletin, 97,* 286–306.

Rousar, E. E., III, & Aron, A. (1990, July). *Valuing, altruism, and the concept of love.* Paper presented at the Fifth International Conference on Personal Relationships, Oxford, England.

Rovee-Collier, C. K., Borza, M. A., Adler, S. A., & Boller, K. (1993). Infants' eyewitness testimony: Effects of postevent information on a prior memory representation. *Memory & Cognition, 21,* 267–279.

Rovee-Collier, C. K., & Boller, K. (1995). Current theory and research on infant learning and memory: Application to early intervention. *Infants and Young Children, 7,* 1–12.

Rovee-Collier, C. K., & Hayne, H. (1987). Reactivation of infant memory: Implications for cognitive development. *Advances in Child Development and Behavior, 20,* 185–238.

Rowe, D. C., Vazsonyi, A. T., & Flannery, D. J. (1994). No more than skin deep: Ethnic and racial similarity in developmental process. *Psychological Review, 101,* 396–413.

Royce, J. E., & Scratchley, D. (1996). *Alcoholism and other drug problems.* New York: Free Press.

Royce, R. A., Sena, A., Cates, W., & Cohen, M. S. (1997). Sexual transmission of HIV. *New England Journal of Medicine, 336,* 1072–1078.

Rozée, P. D., & Van Boemel, G. (1989). The psychological effects of war trauma and abuse on older Cambodian refugee women. *Women & Therapy, 8,* 23–50.

Rozin, P. (1996). Towards a psychology of food and eating: From motivation to module to model to marker, morality, meaning, and metaphor. *Current Directions in Psychological Science, 5,* 18–24.

Rubin, D. C., & Kontis, T. C. (1983). A schema for common cents. *Memory & Cognition, 11,* 335–341.

Rubin, D. H., et al. (1986, August 23). Effect of passive smoking on birth-weight. *Lancet, 8504,* pp. 415–417.

Rubin, D. L., & Greene, K. (1992). Gender-typical style in written language. *Research in the Teaching of English, 26,* 7–40.

Rubin, D. L., & Greene, K. (1994). The suppressed voice hypothesis in women's writing: Effects of revision on gender-typical style. In D. L. Rubin (Ed.), *Composing social identity in written language* (pp. 133–149). Hillsdale, NJ: Erlbaum.

Rubin, E. (1915/1958). Synoplevede Figurer. Copenhagen: Cyldendalske. Abridged translation by M. Wertheimer: Figure and ground. In D. C. Beardsley & M. Wertheimer (Eds.), *Readings in perception.* Princeton, NJ: Van Nostrand.

Rubin, J. Z. (1991). The timing of ripeness and the ripeness of timing. In L. Kriesberg & S. J. Thorson (Eds.), *Timing and the deescalation of international conflicts.* Syracuse: Syracuse University Press.

Rubin, J. Z., & Levinger, G. (1995). Levels of analysis: In search of generalizable knowledge. In B. B. Bunker et al. (Eds.), *Conflict, cooperation, and justice* (pp. 13–38). San Francisco: Jossey-Bass.

Rubin, J. Z., Pruitt, D. G., & Kim, S. H. (1994). *Social conflict: Escalation, stalemate, and settlement* (2nd ed.). New York: McGraw-Hill.

Ruder, A. M, Flam, R., Flatto, D., & Curran, A. S. (1990). AIDS education: Evaluation of school and worksite based presentations. *New York State Journal of Medicine, 90,* 129–133.

Rueckl, J. G. (1993). Making new connections [Review of the book *Connectionism and the mind: An introduction to parallel processing in networks*]. *Contemporary Psychology, 38,* 58–59.

Ruff, R. M. (1993). Understanding behavioral problems following brain trauma. [Review of the book, *Traumatic brain injury and neuropsychological impairment: Sensorimotor, cognitive, emotional, and adaptive problems of children and adults*]. *Contemporary Psychology, 38,* 155.

Rumbaugh, D. M. (1993). Learning about primates' learning, language, and cognition. In G. G. Brannigan & M. R. Merrens (Eds.), *The undaunted psychologist: Adventures in research* (pp. 90–109). Philadelphia: Temple University Press.

Rumelhart, D. E., McClelland, J. L., & the PDP Research Group. (1986). *Parallel distributed processing* (Vol. 1). Cambridge, MA: MIT Press.

Rushton, J. P., Chrisjohn, R. D., & Fekken, G. C. (1981). The altruistic personality and the self-report altruism scale. *Personality and Individual Differences, 2,* 293–302.

Rushton, W. A. H. (1958). Kinetics of cone pigments measured objectively in the living human fovea. *Annals of the New York Academy of Science, 74,* 291–304.

Russell, D. (1975). *The politics of rape.* New York: Stein and Day.

Russell, J. A. (1994). Is there universal recognition of emotion from facial expression? A review of the cross-cultural studies. *Psychological Bulletin, 115,* 102–141.

Russell, J. A. (1995). Facial expressions of emotion: What lies beyond minimal universality? *Psychological Bulletin, 118,* 379–391.

Russo, N. F. (1983). Psychology's foremothers: Their achievements in context. In A. N. O'Connell & N. F. Russo (Eds.), *Models of achievement* (pp. 9–24). New York: Columbia University Press.

Russo, N. F. (1990). Overview: Forging research priorities for women's mental health. *American Psychologist, 45,* 368–373.

Russo, N. F., & Green, B. L. (1993). Women and mental health. In F. L. Denmark & M. A. Paludi (Eds.), *Psychology of women: A handbook of issues and theories* (pp. 379–436). Westport, CT: Greenwood.

Russo, N. F., Green, B. L., & Knight, G. (1993). The relationship of gender, self-esteem, and instrumentality to depressive symptomotology. *Journal of Social and Clinical Psychology, 12,* 218–236.

Rychlak, J. F. (1981). *Instructor's manual to Introduction to Personality and Psychotherapy* (2nd ed.). Boston: Houghton Mifflin.

Ryerse, C. (1990). *Thursday's child: Child poverty in Canada.* Ottawa, Ontario: National Youth in Care Network.

Sackeim, H. A., et al. (1993). Effects of stimulus intensity and electrode placement on the efficacy and cognitive effects of electroconvulsive therapy. *New England Journal of Medicine, 328,* 839–846.

Sacks, O. (1995a, January 9). Prodigies. *New Yorker,* pp. 44–65.

Sacks, O. (1995b). *An anthropologist on Mars.* New York: Vintage Books.

Saffran, J. R., Aslin, R. N., & Newport, E. L. (1996). Statistical learning by 8-month-old infants. *Science, 274,* 1926–1928.

Safire, W. (1979, May 27). "I led the pigeons to the flag." *New York Times Magazine,* pp. 9–10.

Salinger, K. (1988). The future of behavior analysis in psychopathology. *Behavior Analysis, 23,* 53–60.

Saluter, A. F. (1994). *Marital status and living arrangements: March 1993.* Washington, DC: U.S. Government Printing Office.

Samuel, A. G. (1996). Does lexical information influence the perceptual restoration of phonemes? *Journal of Experimental Psychology: General, 125,* 28–51.

Samuel, A. G. (1997). Lexical activation produces potent phonemic percepts. *Cognitive Psychology, 32,* 97–127.

Sanders, B., Soares, M. O., & D'Aquila, J. M. (1982). The sex difference on one test of spatial visualization: A nontrivial difference. *Child Development, 53,* 1106–1110.

Sanes, J. N., et al. (1995). Shared neural substrates controlling hand movements in human motor cortex. *Science, 268,* 1775–1777.

Sanna, L. J. (1992). Self-efficacy theory: Implications for social facilitation and social loafing. *Journal of Personality and Social Psychology, 62,* 774–786.

Santrock, J. W., Minnet, A. M., & Campbell, B. D. (1994). *The authoritative guide to self-help books.* New York: Guilford Press.

Santrock, J. W., & Yussen, S. R. (1989). *Child development* (4th ed.). Dubuque, IA: Brown.

Sargent, J. D., & Blanchflower, D. G. (1994). Obesity and stature in adolescence and earnings in young adulthood. *Archives of Pediatric and Adolescent Medicine, 148,* 681–687.

Sarno, M. T. (1991). Management of aphasia. In R. A. Bornstein & G. G. Brown (Eds.), *Neurobehavioral aspects of cerebrovascular disease*(pp. 314–336). New York: Oxford University Press.

Savage-Rumbaugh, S., & Lewin, R. (1994). *Kanzi: The ape at the brink of the human mind.* New York: Wiley.

Savin-Williams, R. C. (1994). Verbal and physical abuse as stressors in the lives of lesbian, gay male, and bisexual youths: Associations with school problems, running away, substance abuse, prostitution, and suicide. *Journal of Consulting and Clinical Psychology, 62,* 261–269.

Savin-Williams, R. C. (1995). An exploratory study of pubertal maturation timing and self-esteem among gay and bisexual male youths. *Developmental Psychology, 31,* 56–64.

Sax, L. J., Astin, A. W., Korn, W. S., & Mahoney, K. M. (1997). *The American freshman: National norms for Fall 1997.* Los Angeles: Higher Education Research Institute.

Saxe, L., Dougherty, D., & Cross, T. (1985). The validity of polygraph testing: Scientific analysis and public controversy. *American Psychologist, 40,* 355–366.

Scarborough, E. (1994). Recognition for women: The problem of linkage. In H. E. Adler & R. W. Rieber (Eds.), *Aspects of the history of psychology in America: 1892–1992* (pp. 101–112). Washington, DC: American Psychological Association.

Scarborough, E., & Furumoto, L. (1987). *Untold lives: The first generation of American women psychologists.* New York: Columbia University Press.

Scarr, S. (1984). Intelligence: What an introductory psychology student might want to know. In A. M. Rogers & C. J. Scheirer (Eds.), *The G. Stanley Hall Lecture Series* (Vol. 4, pp. 61–99). Washington, DC: American Psychological Association.

Scarr, S. (1996). Best of human behavior genetics [Review of the book *Twins as a tool of behavioral genetics*]. *Contemporary Psychology, 41,* 149–150.

Scarr, S., & Eisenberg, M. (1993). Child care research: Issues, perspectives, and results. *Annual Review of Psychology, 44,* 613–644.

Scarr, S., & Weinberg, R. A. (1976). IQ test performance of black children adopted by white families. *American Psychologist, 31,* 726–739.

Schachter, S., & Singer, J. E. (1962). Cognitive, social, and physiological determinants of emotional state. *Psychological Review, 69,* 379–399.

Schacter, D. L. (1992). Understanding implicit memory: A cognitive neuroscience approach. *American Psychologist, 47,* 559–569.

Schacter, D. L. (1995). Memory distortion: History and current status. In D. L. Schacter, J. T. Coyle, G. D. Fishbach, M. M. Mesulam, & L. E. Sullivan (Eds.), *Memory distortion: How minds, brains and societies reconstruct the past.* Cambridge, MA: Harvard University Press.

Schacter, D. L. (1996). *Searching for memory: The brain, the mind, and the past.* New York: Basic Books.

Schacter, D. L., Church, B., & Treadwell, J. (1994). Implicit memory in amnesic patients: Evidence for spared auditory priming. *Psychological Science, 5,* 20–25.

Schacter, D. L., et al. (1996). Neuroanatomical correlates of veridical and illusory recognition memory: Evidence from positron emission tomography. *Neuron, 17,* 267–274.

Schaefer, E. S., & Burnett, C. K. (1987). Stability and predictability of quality of women's marital relationships and demoralization. *Journal of Personality and Social Psychology, 53,* 1129–1136.

Schafe, G. E., & Bernstein, I. L. (1996). Taste aversion learning. In E. D. Capaldi (Ed.), Why we eat what we eat: The psychology of eating (pp. 31–51). Washington, DC: American Psychological Association.

Schafer, W. (1992). *Stress management for wellness* (2nd ed.). Fort Worth, TX: Harcourt Brace Jovanovich.

Schafer, W. (1996). *Stress management for wellness* (3rd ed.). Fort Worth, TX: Harcourt Brace.

Schaie, K. W. (1993a). The Seattle longitudinal studies of adult intelligence. *Current Directions in Psychological Science, 2,* 171–175.

Schaie, K. W. (1993b). Ageist language in psychological research. *American Psychologist, 48,* 49–51.

Schaie, K. W. (1994a). Developmental designs revisited. In S. H. Cohen & H. W. Reese (Eds.), *Life-span developmental psychology: Methodological contributions* (pp. 45–64). Hillsdale, NJ: Erlbaum.

Schaie, K. W. (1994b). The course of adult intellectual development. *American Psychologist, 49,* 304–313.

Schaller, M. (1992). In-group favoritism and statistical reasoning in social inference: Implications for formation and maintenance of group stereotypes. *Journal of Personality and Social Psychology, 63,* 61–74.

Schank, R. C., & Abelson, R. P. (1995). So all knowledge isn't stories? In R. S. Wyer, Jr. (Ed.), *Knowledge and memory: The real story* (pp. 1–85). Hillsdale, NJ: Erlbaum.

Schatzberg, A. F., & Cole, J. O. (1991). *Manual of clinical psychopharmacology* (2nd ed.). Washington, DC: American Psychiatric Press.

Schatzman, M., & Fenwick, P. (1994). Dreams and dreaming. In R. Cooper (Ed.), *Sleep* (pp. 212–242). London: Chapman & Hall Medical.

Schellenberg, G. D., et al. (1992). Genetic linkage evidence for a familial Alzheimer's disease locus on Chromosome 13. *Science, 258,* 668–671.

Scherer, K. R. (1986). Studying emotion empirically: Issues and a paradigm for research. In K. R. Scherer, H. G. Wallbott, & A. B. Summerfield (Eds.), *Experiencing emotion.* Cambridge: Cambridge University Press.

Schieber, F. (1992). Aging and the senses. In J. E. Birren, R. B. Sloane, & G. D. Cohen (Eds.), *Handbook of mental health and aging* (2nd ed.,pp. 251–306). San Diego, CA: Academic Press.

Schiffman, S. S. (1995). Taste. In G. L. Maddox (Ed.), *The encyclopedia of aging* (2nd ed., pp. 920–922). New York: Springer.

Schiller, P. H. (1994). Area V4 of the primate visual cortex. *Current Directions in Psychological Science,* 89–96.

Schizophrenia update—Part II. (1995, July). *Harvard Mental Health Letter,* pp. 1–5.

Schleifer, S. J., et al. (1983). Suppression of lymphocyte stimulation following bereavement. *Journal of the American Medical Association, 250,* 374–377.

Schlesinger, K. (1985). A brief introduction to ahistory of psychology. In G. A. Kimble &K. Schlesinger (Eds.), *Topics in the history of psychology* (Vol. 1, pp. 1–20). Hillsdale, NJ: Erlbaum.

Schmajuk, N. A., & Blair, H. T. (1993). Stimulus configuration, spatial learning, and hippocampal function. *Behavioural Brain Research, 59,* 103–117.

Schmajuk, N. A., & DiCarlo, J. J. (1991). A neural network approach to hippocampal function in classical conditioning. *Behavioral Neuroscience, 105,* 82–110.

Schmajuk, N. A., & DiCarlo, J. J. (1992). Stimulus configuration, classical conditioning, and hippocampal function. *Psychological Review, 99,* 268–305.

Schmidt, G., & Sigusch, V. (1970). Sex differences in response to psychosexual stimulation by films and slides. *Journal of Sex Research, 6,* 268–283.

Schnaitter, R. (1987). American practicality and America's psychology [Review of the book *The origins of behaviorism: American psychology, 1870–1920*]. *Contemporary Psychology, 32,* 736–737.

Schnapf, J. L., & Baylor, D. A. (1987). How photoreceptor cells respond to light. *Scientific American, 256* (4), 40–47.

Schneider, W. (1993). Variety of working memory as seen in biology and in connectionist/control architectures. *Memory and Cognition, 21,* 184–192.

Schneiderman, N., et al. (1994). HIV-1, immunity, and behavior. In R. Glaser & J. K. Kiecolt-Glaser (Eds.), *Handbook of human stress and immunity* (pp. 267–300). San Diego, CA: Academic Press.

Schoenholtz-Read, J. (1994). Selection of group intervention. In H. S. Bernard & K. R. MacKenzie (Eds.), *Basics of group psychotherapy* (pp. 157–188). New York: Guilford Press.

Schofield, J. W. (1995). Promoting positive intergroup relations in school settings. In W. D. Hawley & A. W. Jackson (Eds.), *Toward a common destiny* (pp. 257–289). San Francisco: Jossey-Bass.

Schooler, J. W. (1994). Seeking the core: The issues and evidence surrounding recovered accounts of sexual trauma. *Consciousness and Cognition, 3,* 452–469.

Schreiber, T. A., & Sergent, S. D. (1996, November). *Eyewitness memory and misleading suggestions: Toward a resolution of the memory impairment/nonimpairment debate.* Paper presented at the annual convention of the Psychonomic Society.

Schroeder, D. A., Penner, L. A., Dovidio, J. F., & Piliavin, J. A. (1995). *The psychology of helping and altruism: Problems and puzzles.* New York: McGraw-Hill.

Schultz, D. P., & Schultz, S. E. (1996). *A history of modern psychology* (6th ed.). Fort Worth, TX: Harcourt Brace.

Schunk, D. H. (1991). *Learning theories: An educational perspective.* New York: Macmillan.

Schwartz, A., & Schwartz, R. M. (1993). *Depression: Theories and treatments.* New York: Columbia University Press.

Schwartz, B. (1989). *Psychology of learning and behavior* (3rd ed.). New York: Norton.

Schwartz, G. E., & Kline, J. P. (1995). Repression, emotional disclosure, and health: Theoretical, empirical, and clinical considerations. In J. W. Pennebaker (Ed.), *Emotion, disclosure, and health* (pp. 177–193). Washington, DC: American Psychological Association.

Schwartz, J. M., et al. (1996). Systematic changes in cerebral glucose metabolic rate after successful behavior modification treatment of obsessive-compulsive disorder. *Archives of General Psychiatry, 53,* 109–113.

Schwartz, P. (1994). *Peer marriage: How love between equals really works.* New York: Free Press.

Schwartz, R. (1994). *Vision: Variations on some Berkeleian themes.* Cambridge, MA: Blackwell.

Schwartz, R. H. (1995). LSD: Its rise, fall, and renewed popularity among high school students. *Pediatric Clinics of North America, 42,* 403–413.

Schwartz, S. H. (1971). Modes of representation and problem solving: Well evolved is half solved. *Journal of Experimental Psychology, 91,* 347–350.

Schwartz-Bickenbach, D., et al. (1987). Smoking and passive smoking during pregnancy and early infancy: Effects on birth weight, lactation period, and nicotine concentrations in mother's milk and infant's urine. *Toxicology Letters, 35,* 73–81.

Schweickert, P., & Boruff, B. (1986). Short-term memory capacity: Magic number of magic spell? *Journal of Experimental Psychology: Learning, Memory, and Cognition, 12,* 419–425.

Scinto, L. F., et al. (1994). A potential noninvasive neurobiological test for Alzheimer's disease. *Science, 266,* 1051–1054.

Scott, S. (1973). *The relation of divergent thinking to bilingualism: Cause or effect?* Unpublished manuscript. McGill University, Psychology Department.

Scoville, W. B., & Milner, B. (1957). Loss of recent memory after bilateral hippocampal lesions. *Journal of Neurology, Neurosurgery, and Psychiatry, 20,* 11–21.

Scruggs, T. E., Mastropieri, M. A., Jorgensen, C., & Monson, J. (1986). Effective mnemonic strategies for gifted learners. *Journal of the Education of the Gifted, 9,* 105–121.

Seabrook, J. (1993, January 11). The flash of genius. *New Yorker,* pp. 38–52.

Segal, N. L. (1993). Twin, sibling, and adoption methods: Tests of evolutionary hypotheses. *American Psychologist, 48,* 943–956.

Segal, Z. V. (1988). Appraisal of the self-schema construct in cognitive models of depression. *Psychological Bulletin, 103,* 147–162.

Seijo, R., Gomez, H., & Freidenberg, J. (1995). Language as a communication barrier in medical care for Hispanic patients. In A. M. Padilla (Ed.), *Hispanic psychology* (pp. 169–181). Thousand Oaks, CA: Sage.

Seith, P. (1992). Personal communication.

Seligman, M. E. P. (1989). Research in clinical psychology: Why is there so much depression today? In I. S. Cohen (Ed.), *The G. Stanley Hall Lecture Series* (Vol. 9, pp. 75–96). Washington, DC: American Psychological Association.

Seligman, M. E. P. (1993). *What you can change . . . and what you can't.* New York: Fawcett Columbine.

Seligman, M. E. P. (1995). The effectiveness of psychotherapy: The *Consumer Reports* study. *American Psychologist, 50,* 965–974.

Selnow, G. W. (1985). Sex differences in uses and perceptions of profanity. *Sex Roles, 12,* 303–312.

Selye, H. (1956). *The stress of life.* New York: McGraw-Hill.

Seppa, N. (1997, July). Hard-of-hearing clients often hide their disability. *APA Monitor,* p. 28.

Serbin, L. A., & O'Leary, K. D. (1975, December). How nursery schools teach girls to shut up. *Psychology Today, 9,* 57–58, 102–103.

Serbin, L. A., Powlishta, K. K., & Gulko, J. (1993). The development of sex typing in middle childhood. *Monographs of the Society for Research in Child Development, 58,* 1–73.

Sereno, M. I., et al. (1995). Borders of multiple visual areas in humans revealed by functional magnetic resonance imaging. *Science, 268,* 889–893.

Sexton, M., & Hebel, R. (1984). A clinical trial of change in maternal smoking and its effect on birth weight. *Journal of the American Medical Association, 251,* 911–915.

Shafir, E. B. (1993). Choosing versus rejecting: Why some options are both better and worse than others. *Memory & Cognition, 21,* 546–556.

Shafir, E. B., Smith, E. E., & Osherson, D. N. (1990). Typicality and reasoning fallacies. *Memory & Cognition, 18,* 229–239.

Shanker, A. (1996, September). A real role model. *On Campus,* p. 5.

Shapiro, D. H. (1984). Overview: Clinical and physiological comparison of meditation with other self-control strategies. In D. H. Shapiro & R. N. Walsh (Eds.), *Meditation: Classic and contemporary perspectives* (pp. 5–11). New York: Aldine.

Sharpe, D., Adair, J. G., & Roese, N. J. (1992). Twenty years of deception research: A decline in subjects' trust? *Personality and Social Psychology Bulletin, 18,* 585–590.

Shatz, M. (1994). *A toddler's life: Becoming a person.* New York: Oxford University Press.

Shatz, M., & Gelman, R. (1973). The development of communication skills. Modifications in the speech of young children as a function of listener. *Monographs of the Society for Research in Child Development, 38* (2, Serial No. 152).

Shaver, K. G., & Kirk, D. L. (1996). The quest for meaning in social behavior. *Contemporary Psychology, 41,* 423–426.

Shaver, P. R., & Brennan, K. A. (1992). Attachment styles and the "big five" personality traits: Their connections with each other and with romantic relationship outcomes. *Personality and Social Psychology Bulletin, 18,* 536–545.

Shaver, P. R., Hazan, C., & Bradshaw, D. (1988). Love as attachment: The integration of three behavioral systems. In R. J. Sternberg & M. L. Barnes (Eds.), *The psychology of love* (pp. 68–99). New Haven, CT: Yale University Press.

Shaywitz, S. E., Shaywitz, B. A., Fletcher, J. M., & Escobar, M. D. (1990). Prevalence of reading disability in boys and girls. *Journal of the American Medical Association, 264,* 998–1002.

Shea, C. (1994, September 7). "Gender gap" on examinations shrank again this year. *Chronicle of Higher Education,* p. A54.

Shea, M. T., et al. (1992). Course of depressive symptoms over follow-up: Findings from the National Institute of Mental Health Treatment of Depression Collaborative Research Program. *Archives of General Psychiatry, 49,* 782–787.

Shear, M. (1989, March–April). Murder evokes rage. *New Directions for Women,* p. 6.

Sheehan, P. W. (1988). Memory distortion in hypnosis. *International Journal of Clinical and Experimental Hypnosis, 36,* 296–311.

Shepperd, J. A. (1995). Remedying motivation and productivity loss in collective settings. *Current Directions in Psychological Science, 4,* 131–134.

Sherbourne, C. D., Wells, K. B., & Judd, L. L. (1996). Functioning and well-being of patients with panic disorder. *American Journal of Psychiatry, 153,* 213–218.

Sherin, J. E., Shiromani, P. J., McCarley, R. W., & Saper, C. B. (1996). Activation of ventrolateral preoptic neurons during sleep. *Science, 271,* 216–219.

Sherman, E. (1991). *Reminiscence and the self in old age.* New York: Springer.

Sherrill, R., Jr. (1991). Natural wholes: Wolfgang Köhler and Gestalt theory. In G. A. Kimble, M. Wertheimer, & C. White (Eds.), *Portraits of pioneers in psychology* (pp. 256–273). Washington, DC: American Psychological Association.

Sheth, B. R., Sharma, J., Rao, S. C., & Sur, M. (1996). Orientation maps of subjective contours in visual cortex. *Science, 274,* 2110–2115.

Shiloh, S. (1994). Heuristics and biases in health decision making: Their expression in genetic counseling. In L. Heath, R. S. Tindale, J. Edwards, E. J. Posavac, F. B. Bryant, E. Henderson-King, Y. Suarez-Balcazar, & J. Myers (Eds.), *Applications of heuristics and biases to social issues* (pp. 13–30). New York: Plenum.

Shimamura, A. P., Berry, J. M., Mangels, J. A., Rusting, P. L., & Jurica, P. J. (1995). Memory and cognitive abilities in university professors: Evidence for successful aging. *Psychological Science, 6,* 271–277.

Shin, L. M., et al. (1997). Visual imagery and perception in postraumatic stress disorder: A positron emission tomographic investigation. *Archives of General Psychiatry, 54,* 233–241.

Shoham-Salomon, V., & Hannah, M. T. (1991). Client-treatment interaction in the study of differential change processes. *Journal of Consulting and Clinical Psychology, 59,* 217–225.

Shulman, D. G. (1990). The investigation of psychoanalytic theory by means of the experimental method. *International Journal of Psycho-Analysis, 71,* 487–498.

Shumaker, S. A., & Smith, T. R. (1995). Women and coronary heart disease: A psychological perspective. In A. L. Stanton & S. Gallant (Eds.), *The psychology of women's health* (pp. 25–49). Washington, DC: American Psychological Association.

Siegal, M. (1996). Conversation and cognition. In R. Gelman & T. K. Au (Eds.), *Perceptual and cognitive development* (pp. 243–282). San Diego, CA: Academic Press.

Siegler, R. S., & Ellis, S. (1996). Piaget on childhood. *Psychological Science, 7,* 211–215.

Silverman, L. H., & Weinberger, J. (1985). Mommy and I are one: Implications for psychotherapy. *American Psychologist, 12,* 1296–1308.

Silverman, W. K., & Kurtines, W. M. (1996). *Anxiety and phobic disorders: A pragmatic approach.* New York: Plenum.

Silverstein, B. (1989). Enemy images: The psychology of U.S. attitudes and cognitions regarding the Soviet Union. *American Psychologist, 44,* 903–913.

Simon, B. L. (1987). *Never married women.* Philadelphia: Temple University Press.

Simon, L. (1998). *Genuine reality: A life of William James.* New York: Harcourt Brace.

Simon, G. E., VonKorff, M., & Barlow, W. (1995). Health care costs of primary care patients with recognized depression. *Archives of General Psychiatry, 52,* 850–856.

Simon, H. A. (1992). What is an "explanation" of behavior. *Psychological Science, 3,* 150–161.

Simons, J. M., Finlay, B., & Yang, A. (1991). *The adolescent and young adult fact book.* Washington, DC: Children's Defense Fund.

Simpson, J. A., & Harris, B. A. (1994). Interpersonal attraction. In A. L. Weber & J. H. Harvey (Eds.), *Perspectives on close relationships* (pp. 45–66). Boston: Allyn & Bacon.

Singelis, T., Triandis, H. C., Bhawuk, D., & Gelfand, M. (1995). Horizontal and vertical individualism and collectivism: A theoretical and methodological refinement. *Cross-Cultural Psychology, 29,* 240–275.

Singer, J. L., & Singer, D. G. (1981). *Television, imagination, and aggression: A study of preschoolers.* Hillsdale, NJ: Erlbaum.

Singer, J. L., Singer, D. G., & Rapaczynski, W. (1984, Spring). Family patterns and television viewing as predictors of children's beliefs and aggression. *Journal of Communication, 34,* 73–89.

Singer, M. T., & Lalich, J. (1996). *"Crazy" therapies.* San Francisco: Jossey-Bass.

Singleton, C. H. (1987). Sex roles in cognition. In D. J. Hargreaves & A. M. Colley (Eds.), *The psychology of sex roles* (pp. 60–91). New York: Hemisphere.

Sinnott, J. D. (Ed.). (1994). *Interdisciplinary handbook of adult lifespan learning.* Westport, CT: Greenwood.

Sivard, R. L. (1989). *World military and social expenditures, 1989.* Washington, DC: World Priorities.

Skinner, B. F. (1953). *Science and human behavior.* New York: Macmillan.

Skinner, B. F. (1957). *Verbal behavior.* Englewood Cliffs, NJ: Prentice Hall.

Skinner, B. F. (1971). *Beyond freedom and dignity.* New York: Knopf.

Skinner, B. F. (1988a, June). Skinner joins aversives debate. *APA Monitor, 19,* 22–23

Skinner, B. F. (1988b, August). *The school of the future.* Paper presented at the meeting of the American Psychological Association, Atlanta.

Slade, L. A., & Rush, M. C. (1991). Achievement motivation and the dynamics of task difficulty choices. *Journal of Personality and Social Psychology, 60,* 165–172.

Sleep disorders. (1994, August). *Harvard Mental Health Letter,* pp. 1–4.

Slipp, S. (1993). *The Freudian mystique: Freud, women, and feminism.* New York: New York University Press.

Slobin, D. I. (1985). *The cross-linguistic study of language acquisition* (Vols. 1 & 2). Hillsdale, NJ: Erlbaum.

Slovic, P., Fischhoff, B., & Lichtenstein, S. (1982). Facts versus fears: Understanding perceived risk. In D. Kahneman, P. Slovic, & A. Tversky (Eds.), *Judgment under uncertainty: Heuristics and biases* (pp. 463–489). New York: Cambridge University Press.

Slovic, P., Fischhoff, B., & Lichtenstein, S. (1988). Response mode, framing, and information-processing effects in risk assessment. In D. E. Bell, H. Raiffa, & A. Tversky (Eds.), *Decision making: Descriptive, normative, and prescriptive interactions* (pp. 152–166). Cambridge: Cambridge University Press.

Slovic, P., Kunreuther, H., & White, G. F. (1974). Decision processes, rationality and adjustment to natural hazards. In G. F. White (Ed.), *Natural hazards, local, national and global.* New York: Oxford University Press.

Small, M. Y. (1990). *Cognitive development.* San Diego, CA: Harcourt Brace Jovanovich.

Smetana, J. G. (1993). Understanding of social rules. In M. Bennett (Ed.), *The development of social cognition: The child as psychologist* (pp. 111–141). New York: Guilford Press.

Smetana, J. G. (1996, August). *Autonomy and authority in adolescent-parent relationships.* Paper presented at the International Society for the Study of Behavioral Development Conference, Quebec City.

Smith, A. D. (1996). Memory. In J. E. Birren & K. W. Schaie (Eds.), *Handbook of the psychology of aging* (4th ed.). San Diego, CA: Academic Press.

Smith, A. P., & Jones, D. M. (1992). Noise and performance. In D. M. Jones & A. P. Smith (Eds.), *Handbook of human performance* (Vol. 1, pp. 1–28). San Diego, CA: Academic Press.

Smith, B., & Sechrest, L. (1991). Treatment of aptitude × treatment interactions. *Journal of Consulting and Clinical Psychology, 59,* 233–244.

Smith, E. R. (1994). Social cognition contributions to attribution theory and research: Theory and research. In P. G. Devine, D. L. Hamilton, & T. M. Ostrom (Eds.), *Social cognition: Impact on social psychology* (pp. 77–108). San Diego, CA: Academic Press.

Smith, E. R., & Mackie, D. M. (1995). *Social psychology.* New York: Worth.

Smith, G. J. (1985). Facial and full-length ratings of attractiveness related to the social interactions of young children. *Sex Roles, 12,* 287–293.

Smith, K. D., Keating, J. P., & Stotland, E. (1989). Altruism revisited: The effect of denying feedback on a victim's status to empathic witnesses. *Journal of Personality and Social Psychology, 57,* 641–650.

Smith, M. B. (1992). Nationalism, ethnocentrism, and the new world order. *Journal of Humanistic Psychology, 32,* 76–91.

Smith, M. S. (1990). Personal communication.

Smith, R. (1988). Does the history of psychology have a subject? *History of the Human Sciences, 1,* 147–177.

Smith, S. E., & Walker, W. J. (1988). Sex differences on New York state regents examinations: Support for the differential course-taking hypothesis. *Journal of Research in Mathematics Education, 19,* 81–85.

Smith, S. M. (1988). Environmental context-dependent memory. In G. M. Davies & D. M. Thomson (Eds.), *Memory in context: Context in memory* (pp. 13–34). Chichester, England: Wiley.

Smith, S. M., Glenberg, A., & Bjork, R. A. (1978). Environmental context and human memory. *Memory & Cognition, 6,* 342–353.

Smyth, M. M., Collins, A. F., Morris, P. E., & Levy, P. (1994). *Cognition in action* (2nd ed.). Hove, England: Erlbaum.

Snarey, J. R. (1985). Cross-cultural universality of social-moral development: A critical review of Kohlbergian research. *Psychological Bulletin, 97,* 202–232.

Snarey, J. R. (1993). *How fathers care for the next generation: A four-decade study.* Cambridge, MA: Harvard University Press.

Snodgrass, J. G., Levy-Berger, G., & Haydon, M. (1985). *Human experimental psychology.* New York: Oxford University Press.

Snow, C. E. (1998). Bilingualism and second language acquisition. In J. B. Berko-Gleason & N. B. Ratner (Eds.), *Psycholinguistics* (2nd ed., pp. 453–481). Fort Worth, TX: Harcourt Brace Jovanovich.

Snow, R. E. (1977). Individual differences and instructional theory. *Educational Researcher, 6,* 11–15.

Snyder, M., & Miene, P. (1994). On the functions of stereotypes and prejudice. In M. P. Zanna & J. M. Olson (Eds.), *The psychology of prejudice: The Ontario symposium* (Vol. 7, pp. 33–54). Hillsdale, NJ: Erlbaum.

Snyder, T. D., Hoffman, C. M., & Geddes, C. M. (1996). *Digest of educational statistics 1996.* Washington, DC: U.S. Department of Education.

Social phobia—Part I. (1994, October). *Harvard Mental Health Letter,* pp. 1–3.

Sokal, M. M. (1992). Origins and early years of the American Psychological Association: 1890 to 1906. In R. B. Evans, V. S. Sexton, & T. C. Cadwallader (Eds.), *The American Psychological Association: A historical perspective* (pp. 43–71). Washington, DC: American Psychological Association.

Soken, N. H., & Pick, A. D. (1992). Intermodal perception of happy and angry expressive behaviors by seven-month-old infants. *Child Development, 63,* 787–795.

Soli, S. D. (1994, Autumn). Hearing aids: Today and tomorrow. *Echoes: Newsletter of the Acoustical Society of America,* pp. 1–5.

Soll, J. B. (1996). Determinants of overconfidence and miscalibration: The roles of random error and ecological structure. *Organizational Behavior and Human Decision Processes, 65,* 117–137.

Solomon, P. R., et al. (1983). Hippocampus and trace conditioning of the rabbit's nictitating membrane response. *Neuroscience Abstracts, 9,* 645.

Solso, R. L. (1995). *Cognitive psychology* (4th ed.). Boston: Allyn & Bacon.

Soto, L. D. (1988). The home environment of higher and lower achieving Puerto Rican children. *Hispanic Journal of Behavioral Sciences, 10,* 161–167.

Soukup, V. M., & Adams, R. L. (1996). Parkinson's disease. In R. L. Adams, O. A. Parsons, J. L. Culbertson, & S. J. Nixon (Eds.), *Neuropsychology for clinical practice: Etiology, assessment, and treatment of common neurological disorders* (pp. 243–267). Washington, DC: American Psychological Association.

Spangler, W. D. (1992). Validity of questionnaire and TAT measures of need for achievement: Two meta-analyses. *Psychological Bulletin, 112,* 140–154.

Spanos, N. P. (1991). A sociocognitive approach to hypnosis. In S. J. Lynn & J. W. Rhue (Eds.), *Theories of hypnosis: Current models and perspectives* (pp. 324–361). New York: Guilford Press.

Spanos, N. P. (1994). Multiple identity enactments and multiple personality disorder: A sociocognitive perspective. *Psychological Bulletin, 116,* 143–165.

Spanos, N. P. (1996). *Multiple identities and false memories: A sociocognitive perspective.* Washington, DC: American Psychological Association.

Spanos, N. P., et al. (1991). Secondary identity enactments during hypnotic past-life regression: A sociocognitive perspective. *Journal of Personality and Social Psychology, 61,* 308–320.

Spanos, N. P., Flynn, D. M., & Gabora, N. J. (1989). Suggested negative visual hallucinations in hypnotic subjects: When no means yes. *British Journal of Clinical Hypnosis, 6,* 63–67.

Spearman, C. (1904). "General intelligence" objectively determined and measured. *American Journal of Psychology, 15,* 201–293.

Spearman, C. (1923). *The nature of "intelligence" and the principles of cognition.* London: Macmillan.

Speicher, B. (1994). Family patterns of moral judgment during adolescence and early adulthood. *Developmental Psychology, 30,* 624–632.

Spelke, E. S., et al. (1994). Early knowledge of object motion: Continuity and inertia. *Cognition, 51,* 131–176.

Spelke, H. W., Hirst, W., & Neisser, U. (1976). Skills of divided attention. *Cognition, 4,* 215–230.

Spence, J. T., & Helmreich, R. L. (1983). Achievement-related motives and behaviors. In J. T. Spence (Ed.), *Achievement and achievement motives* (pp. 7–68). San Francisco: Freeman.

Sperling, G. (1960). The information available in brief visual presentations. *Psychological Monographs, 74,* 1–29.

Sperling, S. (1988). *Animal liberators: Researchers and morality.* Berkeley: University of California Press.

Sperry, R. W. (1982). Some effects of disconnecting the cerebral hemispheres. *Science, 217,* 1223–1226.

Sperry, R. W. (1993). The impact and promise of the cognitive revolution. *American Psychologist, 48,* 878–885.

Spiegel, D., Bierre, P., & Rootenberg, J. (1989). Hypnotic alteration of somatosensory perception. *American Journal of Psychiatry, 146,* 749–754.

Spielberger, C. D., & Starr, L. M. (1994). Curiosity and exploratory behavior. In H. F. O'Neill, Jr., & Drillings, M. (Eds.), *Motivation: Theory and research* (pp. 221–243). Hillsdale, NJ: Erlbaum.

Spilich, G. J., June, L., & Renner, J. (1992). Cigarette smoking and cognitive performance. *British Journal of Addiction, 87,* 1313–1326.

Sprafkin, J., Gadow, K. D., & Grayson, P. (1987). Effects of viewing aggressive cartoons on the behavior of learning disabled children. *Journal of Child Psychology and Psychiatry and Allied Disciplines, 28,* 387–398.

Sprecher, S., Sullivan, Q., & Hatfield, E. (1994). Mate selection preferences: Gender differences examined in a national sample. *Journal of Personality and Social Psychology, 66,* 1074–1080.

Springer, S. P., & Deutsch, G. (1989). *Left brain, right brain* (3rd ed.). New York: Freeman.

Squier, L. H., & Domhoff, G. W. (1998). The presentation of dreaming and dreams in introductory psychology textbooks: A critical examination. *Dreaming,* in press.

Squire, L. R. (1987). *Memory and brain.* New York: Oxford University Press.

Squire, L. R. (1992a). Memory and the hippocampus: A synthesis from findings with rats, monkeys, and humans. *Psychological Review, 99,* 195–231.

Squire, L. R. (1992b). *Encyclopedia of learning and memory.* New York: Macmillan.

Squire, L. R., & Knowlton, B. J. (1994). Memory, hippocampus, and brain systems. In M. Gazzaniga (Ed.), *The cognitive neurosciences* (pp. 825–837). Cambridge, MA: MIT Press.

Squire, L. R., Knowlton, B., & Musen, G. (1993). The structure and organization of memory. *Annual Review of Psychology, 44,* 453–495.

Sroufe, L. A., Cooper, R. G., & DeHart, G. B. (1996). *Child development: Its nature and course.* New York: McGraw-Hill.

Stacey, C. A., & Gatz, M. (1991). Cross-sectional age differences and longitudinal change on the Bradburn Affect Balance Scale. *Journal of Gerontology: Psychological Sciences, 46,* P76–P78.

Stahly, G. B. (1996). Battered women: Why don't they just leave? In J. C. Chrisler, C. Golden, & P. D. Rozee (Eds.), *Lectures on the psychology of women* (pp. 288–306). New York: McGraw-Hill.

Stanley, J. C. (1995). What happens subsequently to persons identified as being "gifted" or talented? [Review of the book *Beyond Terman: Contemporary longitudinal studies of giftedness and talent*]. *Contemporary Psychology, 40,* 763–764.

Stanovich, K. E. (1998). *How to think straight about psychology* (5th ed.). New York: Longman.

Staples, R., & Johnson, L. B. (1993). *Black families at the crossroads: Challenges and prospects.* San Francisco: Jossey-Bass.

Staples, S. L. (1996). Human response to environmental noise: Psychological research and public policy. *American Psychologist, 51,* 143–150.

Statistics Canada. (1990). *Health reports, marriages, Supplement 16.* Ottawa: Author.

Statistics Canada. (1992). *Mental health statistics, 1989–90.* Ottawa: Author.

Statistics Canada. (1993, November 18). The violence against women survey. *Daily,* pp. 1–9.

Staub, E. (1974). Helping a distressed person: Social, personality, and stimulus determinants. InL. Berkowitz (Ed.), *Advances in experimental social psychology* (Vol. 7, pp. 293–341). New York: Academic Press.

Steel, M. (1995, Spring). New colors. *Teaching Tolerance,* pp. 44–49.

Steele, C. M. (1997). A threat in the air: How stereotypes shape intellectual identity and performance. *American Psychologist, 52,* 613–629.

Steele, C. M., & Aronson, J. (1995). Stereotype threat and intellectual test performance of African Americans. *Journal of Personality and Social Psychology, 69,* 797–811.

Steele, C. M., & Josephs, R. A. (1990). Alcohol myopia: Its prized and dangerous effects. *American Psychologist, 45,* 921–933.

Steinberg, L., Dornbusch, S. M., & Brown, B. B. (1992). Ethnic differences in adolescent achievement: An ecological perspective. *American Psychologist, 47,* 723–729.

Steinbrook, R. (1992). The polygraph test—A flawed diagnostic method. *New England Journal of Medicine, 327,* 122–123.

Steinmetz, G. (1992, February). The preventable tragedy: Fetal alcohol syndrome. *National Geographic,* pp. 36–39.

Steketee, G. S. (1993). *Treatment of obsessive-compulsive disorder.* New York: Guilford Press.

Stenberg, C. R., & Campos, J. J. (1990). The development of anger expressions in infancy. In N. L. Stein, B. Leventhal, & T. Trabasso (Eds.), *Psychological and biological approaches to emotion* (pp. 247–282). Hillsdale, NJ: Erlbaum.

Stepanski, E. J. (1993). Insomnia. In M. A. Carskadon (Ed.), *Encyclopedia of sleep and dreaming* (pp. 309–313). New York: Macmillan.

Stephan, C. W., & Langlois, J. H. (1984). Baby beautiful: Adult attributions of infant competence as a function of infant attractiveness. *Child Development, 55,* 576–585.

Stephan, W. G., & Stephan, C. W. (1996). *Intergroup relations.* Boulder, CO: Westview Press.

Stephens, R. S., & Roffman, R. A. (1993). Adult marijuana dependence. In J. S. Baer, G. A. Marlatt, & R. J. McMahon (Eds.), *Addictive behavior across the life span: Prevention, treatment, and policy issues* (pp. 202–218). Newbury Park, CA: Sage.

Stern, P. C. (1992). Psychological dimensions of global environmental change. *Annual Review of Psychology, 43,* 269–302.

Sternbach, R. A. (1968). *Pain: A psychophysiological analysis.* New York: Academic Press.

Sternbach, R. A. (1978). Psychological dimensions and perceptual analyses, including pathologies of pain. In E. C. Carterette & M. P. Friedman (Eds.), *Handbook of perception* (Vol. 6B). New York: Academic Press.

Sternberg, R. J. (1986). *Intelligence applied.* San Diego, CA: Harcourt Brace Jovanovich.

Sternberg, R. J. (1990a). *Metaphors of mind: Conceptions of the nature of intelligence.* Cambridge: Cambridge University Press.

Sternberg, R. J. (1990b). Wisdom and its relations to intelligence and creativity. In R. J. Sternberg (Ed.), *Wisdom: Its nature, origins, and development* (pp. 142–159). New York: Cambridge University Press.

Sternberg, R. J., Conway, B. E., Ketron, J. L., & Bernstein, M. (1981), People's conception of intelligence. *Journal of Personality and Social Psychology, 41,* 37–55.

Sternberg, R. J., & Lubart, T. I. (1995). *Defying the crowd: Cultivating creativity in a culture of conformity.* New York: Free Press.

Sternberg, R. J., & Lubart, T. I. (1996). Investing in creativity. *American Psychologist, 51,* 677–688.

Stevens, C. F. (1995). Cortical synaptic transmission: An overview. In M. J. Gutnick & I. Mody (Eds.), *The cortical neuron* (pp. 27–51). New York: Oxford University Press.

Stevens, J. C., & Dadarwala, A. D. (1993). Variability of olfactory threshold and its role in assessment of aging. *Perception & Psychophysics, 54,* 296–302.

Stevenson, H. W., Chen, C., & Lee, S. Y. (1993). Math-ematics achievement of Chinese, Japanese, and American children: Ten years later. *Science, 259,* 53–58.

Stewart, A. J., & Chester, N. L. (1982). Sex differences in human social motives: Achievement, affiliation, and power. In A. J. Stewart (Ed.), *Motivation and society* (pp. 172–218). San Francisco: Jossey-Bass.

Stewart, S. H. (1996). Alcohol abuse in individuals exposed to trauma: A critical review. *Psychological Bulletin, 120,* 83–112.

Stillings, N. A., et al. (1995). *Cognitive science: An introduction* (2nd ed.). Cambridge, MA: MIT Press.

Stinnett, N., Walters, J., & Kaye, E. (1984). *Relationships in marriage and the family* (2nd ed.). New York: Macmillan.

Stoppard, J. M., & Gruchy, C. D. G. (1993). Gender, context, and expression of positive emotion. *Personality and Social Psychology Bulletin, 19,* 143–150.

Strack, F., Martin, L. L., & Stepper, S. (1988). Inhibiting and facilitating conditions of facial expressions: A non-obtrusive test of the facial feedback hypothesis. *Journal of Personality and Social Psychology, 54,* 768–777.

Strange, J., & Shapiro, H. (1991). Tripping the light fantastic: The phenomenon of the hallucinogens. In I. B. Glass (Ed.), *The international handbook of addiction behaviour* (pp. 77–84). London: Tavistock/Routledge.

Strange, P. G. (1992). *Brain biochemistry and brain disorders.* New York: Oxford University Press.

Strasburger, V. C. (1991). Children, adolescents, and television. *Feelings and their medical significance, 33* (1), pp. 1–6.

Strauch, I., & Meier, B. (1996). *In search of dreams.* Albany: State University of New York Press.

Straus, M. A., & Gelles, R. J. (1980). *Behind closed doors: Violence in the American family.* New York: Anchor/Doubleday.

Streissguth, A. P., Bookstein, F. L., Sampson, P. D., & Barr, H. M. (1993). *The enduring effects of prenatal alcohol exposure on child development.* Ann Arbor: University of Michigan Press.

Strickland, B. R. (1992). Women and depression. *Current Directions in Psychological Science, 1,* 132–135.

Striegel-Moore, R. H. (1993). Etiology of binge eating: A developmental perspective. In C. G. Fairburn & G. T. Wilson (Eds.), *Binge eating: Nature, assessment, and treatment* (pp. 144–172). New York: Guilford Press.

Stroebe, W., & Stroebe, M. S. (1995). *Social psychology and health.* Pacific Grove, CA: Brooks/Cole.

Stroop, J. R. (1935). Studies of interference in serial verbal reactions. *Journal of Experimental Psychology, 18,* 643–662.

Strupp, H. H. (1986). Psychotherapy: Research, practice, and public policy (how to avoid dead ends). *American Psychologist, 41,* 120–130.

Strupp, H. H. (1996). The tripartite model and the *Consumer Reports* study. *American Psychologist, 51,* 1017–1024.

Stryker, J., et al. (1995). Prevention of HIV infection: Looking back, looking ahead. *JAMA, 1995,* 1143–1148.

Stumpf, H. (1995). Gender differences in performance on tests of cognitive abilities: Experimental design issues and empirical results. *Learning and Individual Differences, 7,* 275–287.

Stuss, D. T. (1991). Self, awareness, and the frontal lobes: A neuropsychological perspective. In J. Strauss & G. R. Goethals (Eds.), *The self: Interdisciplinary approaches* (pp. 255–278). New York: Springer-Verlag.

Stuss, D. T., & Benson, D. F. (1984). Neuropsychological studies of the frontal lobe. *Psychological Bulletin, 95,* 3–28.

Stuss, D. T., Gow, C. A., & Hetherington, C. R. (1992). "No longer Gage" Frontal lobe dysfunction and emotional changes. *Journal of Consulting and Clinical Psychology, 60,* 349–359.

Subrahmanyam, K., & Greenfield, P. M. (1994). Effect of video game practice on spatial skills in girls and boys. *Journal of Applied Developmental Psychology, 15,* 13–32.

Sudman, S., Bradburn, N. M., & Schwartz, N. (1996). *Thinking about answers: The application of cognitive processes to survey methodology.* San Francisco: Jossey-Bass.

Sue, D. W., & Sue, D. (1990). *Counseling the culturally different: Theory and practice* (2nd ed.). New York: Wiley.

Sue, S. (1992). *Asian American psychology: The untold story.* Paper presented at the convention of the American Psychological Association, Washington, DC.

Sue, S., & Okazaki, S. (1990). Asian-American educational achievements: A phenomenon in search of an explanation. *American Psychologist, 45,* 913–920.

Sugg, M. J., & McDonald, J. E. (1994). Time course of inhibition in color-response and word-response versions of the Stroop task. *Journal of Experimental Psychology: Human Perception and Performance, 20,* 647–675.

Suicide—Part I. (1996, November). *Harvard Mental Health Letter,* pp. 1–5.

Sulzer-Azaroff, B., & Mayer, G. R. (1991). *Behavior analysis for lasting change.* Fort Worth, TX: Harcourt Brace Jovanovich.

Sussman, N. M., & Rosenfeld, H. M. (1982). Influence of culture, language, and sex on conversational distance. *Journal of Personality and Social Psychology, 42,* 66–74.

Suzuki-Slakter, N. S. (1988). Elaboration and metamemory during adolescence. *Contemporary Educational Psychology, 13,* 206–220.

Swann, W. B., Jr., Hixon, J. G., & De La Ronde, C. (1992). Embracing the bitter "truth": Negative self-concepts and marital commitment. *Psychological Science, 3,* 118–121.

Swann, W. B., Jr., Silvera, D. H., & Proske, C. U. (1995). On "knowing your partner": Dangerous illusions in the age of AIDS? *Personal Relationships, 2,* 173–186.

Swanson, L. W. (1992). Hippocampus. In L. R. Squire (Ed.), *Encyclopedia of learning and memory* (pp. 217–219). New York: Macmillan.

Swartz, H. A., & Markowitz, J. C. (1995). Interpersonal psychotherapy. In I. D. Glick & I. D. Yalom (Eds.), *Treating depression* (pp. 71–94). San Francisco: Jossey-Bass.

Swets, J. A. (1996). *Signal detection theory and ROC analysis in psychology and diagnostics: Collected papers.* Mahwah, NJ: Erlbaum.

Swim, J., Borgida, E., Maruyama, G., & Myers, D. G. (1989). Joan McKay versus John McKay: Do gender stereotypes bias evaluations? *Psychological Bulletin, 105,* 409–429.

Szapocznik, J., & Kurtines, W. M. (1993). Family psychology and cultural diversity. *American Psychologist, 48,* 100–407.

Szasz, T. (1994). *Cruel compassion: Psychiatric control of society's unwanted.* New York: Wiley.

Szymczyk, J. (1995, August 14). Animals, vegetables and minerals. *Newsweek,* p. 10.

Talbot, J. D., et al. (1991). Multiple representations of pain in human cerebral cortex. *Science, 251,* 1355–1358.

Tang, S. H., & Hall, V. (1995). The overjustification effect: A meta-analysis. *Applied Cognitive Psychology, 9,* 365–404.

Tangney, J. P., Wagner, P., & Gramzow, R. (1992). Proneness to shame, proneness to guilt, and psychopathology. *Journal of Abnormal Psychology, 101,* 469–478.

Tannen, D. (1990). *You just don't understand: Women and men in conversation.* New York: Ballantine.

Tannen, D. (1994). *Talking from nine to five.* New York: Morrow.

Tasker, F., & Golombok, S. (1995). Adults raised as children in lesbian families. *American Journal of Orthopsychiatry, 65,* 203–215.

Tauber, R. T. (1988). Overcoming misunderstanding about the concept of negative reinforcement. *Teaching of Psychology, 15,* 152–153.

Taubes, G. (1994). Averaged brains pinpoint a site for schizophrenia. *Science, 266,* 221.

Taubes, G. (1995). Epidemiology faces its limits. *Science, 269,* 164–169.

Tavris, C. (1992). *The mismeasure of woman.* New York: Simon & Schuster.

Tavris, C. (1995, Fall). Diagnosis and the DSM: The illusion of science in psychiatry. *General Psychologist, 31,* 72–76.

Tavris, C., & Offir, C. (1977). *The longest war: Sex differences in perspective.* New York: Harcourt Brace Jovanovich.

Taylor, C. B. (1995). Treatment of anxiety disorders. In A. F. Schatzberg & C. B. Nemeroff (Eds.), *Textbook of psychopharmacology* (pp. 641–655). Washington, DC: American Psychiatric Press.

Taylor, I., & Taylor, M. M. (1990). *Psycholinguistics: Learning and using language.* Englewood Cliffs, NJ: Prentice Hall.

Taylor, M. C. (1993). Expectancies and the perpetuation of racial inequity. In P. D. Blanck (Ed.), *Interpersonal expectations: Theory, research, and applications* (pp. 88–124). New York: Cambridge University Press.

Taylor, S. E. (1989). *Positive illusions.* New York: Basic Books.

Taylor, S. E. (1995). *Health psychology* (3rd ed.). New York: McGraw-Hill.

Taylor, S. E., & Aspinwall, L. G. (1996). Mediating and moderating processes in psychosocial stress. In H. B. Kaplan (Ed.), *Psychosocial stress: Perspectives on structure, theory, life-course, and methods* (pp. 71–110). San Diego, CA: Academic Press.

Taylor, S. E., & Brown, J. D. (1988). Illusion and well-being: A social psychological perspective on mental health. *Psychological Bulletin, 103,* 193–210.

Taylor, S. E., & Brown, J. D. (1994). Positive illusions and well-being revisited: Separating fact from fiction. *Psychological Bulletin, 116,* 21–27.

Taylor, S. E., & Gollwitzer, P. M. (1995). Effects of mindset on positive illusions. *Journal of Personality and Social Psychology, 69,* 213–226.

Taylor, S. E., et al. (1992). Optimism, coping, psychological distress, and high-risk sexual behavior among men at risk for acquired immunodeficiency syndrome (AIDS). *Journal of Personality and Social Psychology, 63,* 460–473.

Taylor, S. E., Repetti, R. L., & Seeman, T. (1997). Health psychology: What is an unhealthy environment and how does it get under the skin? *Annual Review of Psychology, 48,* 411–447.

Tedeschi, J. T., & Felson, R. B. (1994). *Violence, aggression, and coercive actions.* Washington, DC: American Psychological Association.

Teghtsoonian, M. (1983). Olfaction: Perception's Cinderella. *Contemporary Psychology, 28,* 763–764.

Teri, L., & Wagner, A. (1992). Alzheimer's disease and depression. *Journal of Consulting and Clinical Psychology, 60,* 379–391.

Terrace, H. S. (1979). *Nim.* New York: Knopf.

Terry, P. (1995). Psychobiology. In C. R. Hollin (Ed.), *Contemporary psychology: An introduction* (pp. 145–164). London: Taylor & Francis.

Tesser, A. (1993). The importance of heritability in psychological research: The case of attitudes. *Pscyhological Review, 100,* 129–142.

Tesser, A. (Ed.). (1995). *Advanced social psychology.* New York: McGraw-Hill.

Teti, D. M. (1992). Sibling interaction. In V. B. Van Hasselt & M. Hersen (Eds.), *Handbook of social development: A lifespan perspective* (pp. 201–226). New York: Plenum.

Tetlock, P. E., et al. (1992). Assessing political group dynamics: A test of the groupthink model. *Journal of Personality and Social Psychology, 63,* 403–425.

Thomas, J. C. (1974). An analysis of behavior in the Hobbits-Orcs program. *Cognitive Psychology, 6,* 257–269.

Thomas, M. H., & Wang, A. Y. (1996). Learning by the keyword mnemonic: Looking for long-term benefits. *Journal of Experimental Psychology: Applied, 2,* 330–342.

Thompson, E., Palacios, A., & Varela, F. J. (1992). Ways of coloring: Comparative color vision as a case study for cognitive science. *Behavioral and Brain Sciences, 15,* 1–74.

Thompson, G. L. (1995, June 15). School dropouts: Despite progress, minority rates still exceed whites'. *Black Issues in Higher Education,* pp. 24–26.

Thompson, R. F. (1993). *The brain: A neuroscience primer* (2nd ed.). New York: Freeman.

Thompson, R. F. (1994). Behaviorism and neuroscience. *Psychological Review, 101,* 259–265.

Thompson, R. F., & Donegan, N. H. (1986). The search for the engram. In J. L. Martinez & R. P. Kesner (Eds.), *Learning and memory: A biological view* (pp. 3–52). San Diego, CA: Academic Press.

Thorndike, E. L. (1898). Animal intelligence: An experimental study of the associative processes in animals. *Psychological Monographs, 2* (Whole no. 8).

Thorndike, E. L. (1913). *Educational psychology.* New York: Teachers College Press.

Thorne, B. (1992). *Carl Rogers.* Thousand Oaks, CA: Sage.

Thornton, B., & Leo, R. (1992). Gender typing, importance of multiple roles, and mental health consequences for women. *Sex Roles, 27,* 307–317.

Tielsch, J. M., et al. (1995). The prevalence of blindness and visual impairment among nursing home residents in Baltimore. *New England Journal of Medicine, 332,* 1205–1209.

Tierney, W. G. (1993). The college experience of Native Americans: A critical analysis. In L. Weis & M. Fine (Eds.), *Beyond silenced voices: Class, race, and gender in United States schools* (pp. 309–323). Albany: State University of New York Press.

Tiggemann, M. (1992). Body-size dissatisfaction: Individual differences in age and gender, and relationship with self-esteem. *Personality and Individual Differences, 13,* 39–43.

Todd, J. T. (1994). What psychology has to say about John B. Watson: Classical behaviorism in psychology textbooks, 1920–1989. In J. R. Ross & E. K. Morris (Eds.), *Modern perspectives on John B. Watson and classical behaviorism* (pp. 75–107). Westport, CT: Greenwood.

Todd, J. T., & Morris, E. K. (Eds.). (1995). *Modern perspectives on B. F. Skinner and contemporary behaviorism.* Westport, CT: Greenwood.

Toms, M., Morris, N., & Foley, P. (1994). Characteristics of visual interference with visuospatial working memory. *British Journal of Psychology, 85,* 131–144.

Torrey, E. F. (1991, March). Care of the mentally ill. *Harvard Mental Health Letter,* p. 8.

Torrey, E. F. (1994). *Schizophrenia and manic-depressive disorder.* New York: Basic Books.

Tran, T. V. (1991). Family living arrangement and social adjustment among three ethnic groups of elderly Indochinese refugees. *International Journal of Aging and Human Development, 32,* 91–102.

Travis, C. B. (1993). Women and health. In F. L. Denmark & M. A. Paludi (Eds.), *Psychology of women: A handbook of issues and theories* (pp. 283–323). Westport, CT: Greenwood.

Treatment of drug abuse and addiction—Part III. (1995, October). *Harvard Mental Health Letter,* pp. 1–4.

Trehub, A. (1991). *The cognitive brain.* Cambridge, MA: MIT Press.

Treisman, A. M. (1986, November). Features and objects in visual processing. *Scientific American, 255,* (5), 114B–125.

Treisman, A. M. (1991). Search, similarity, and integration of features between and within dimensions. *Journal of Experimental Psychology: Human Perception and Performance, 17,* 652–676.

Treisman, A. M. (1993). The perception of features and objects. In A. Baddeley & L. Weiskrantz (Eds.), *Attention: Selection, awareness, and control* (pp. 5–35). Oxford, England: Clarendon.

Treisman, A. M., & Gelade, G. (1980). A feature-integration theory of attention. *Cognitive Psychology, 12,* 97–136.

Triandis, H. C. (1994). *Culture and social behavior.* New York: McGraw-Hill.

Triandis, H. C. (1995). *Individualism and collectivism.* Boulder, CO: Westview Press.

Triandis, H. C. (1996). The psychological measurement of cultural syndromes. *American Psychologist, 51,* 407–415.

Triandis, H. C., Bontempo, R., Leung, K., & Hui, C. K. (1990). A method for determining cultural, demographic, and personal constructs. *Journal of Cross-Cultural Psychology, 21,* 302–318.

Trimble, J. E., & Bagwell, W. M. (1995). *North American Indians and Alaska Natives: Abstracts of the psychological and behavioral literature, 1967–1994.* Washington, DC: American Psychological Association.

Trosman, H. (1993). Freud's dream theory. In M. Carskadon (Ed.), *Encyclopedia of sleep and dreaming* (pp. 251–254). New York: Macmillan.

True, R. H. (1990). Psychotherapeutic issues with Asian American women. *Sex Roles, 22,* 477–486.

True, W. R., et al. (1993). A twin study of genetic and environmental contributions to liability for posttraumatic stress symptoms. *Archives of General Psychiatry, 50,* 257–264.

Trull, T. J. (1992). Personality disorder diagnoses: How valid are they? [Review of the book *Personality disorders: New perspectives on diagnostic validity*]. *Contemporary Psychology, 37,* 231–232.

Tsai, M., & Uemura, A. (1988). Asian Americans: The struggles, the conflicts, and the successes. In P. A. Bronstein & K. Quina (Eds.), *Teaching a psychology of people* (pp. 125–133). Washington, DC: American Psychological Association.

Tulving, E. (1983). *Elements of episodic memory.* New York: Oxford University Press.

Turcotte, P. (1993, Summer). Mixed-language couples and their children. *Canadian Social Trends,* pp. 15–17.

Turk, D. C. (1994). Perspectives on chronic pain: The role of psychological factors. *Current Directions in Psychological Science, 3,* 45–48.

Turk, D. C., & Melzack, R. (1992). The measurement of pain and the assessment of people experiencing pain. In D. C. Turk & R. Melzack (Eds.), *Handbook of pain assessment* (pp. 3–12). New York: Guilford Press.

Turk, D. C., & Rudy, T. E. (1992). Classification logic and strategies in chronic pain. In D. C. Turk & R. Melzack (Eds.), *Handbook of pain assessment* (pp. 409–428). New York: Guilford Press.

Turkheimer, E. (1991). Individual and group differences in adoption studies of IQ. *Psychological Bulletin, 110,* 392–405.

Turkington, C. (1993, January). New definition of retardation includes the need for support. *APA Monitor,* pp. 26–27.

Turkkan, J. S. (1989a). Classical conditioning: The new hegemony. *Behavioral and Brain Sciences, 12,* 121–179.

Turkkan, J. S. (1989b). Classical conditioning beyond the reflex: An uneasy rebirth. *Behavioral and Brain Sciences, 12,* 161–179.

Turner, J. A., et al. (1994). The importance of placebo effects in pain treatment and research. *JAMA, 271,* 1609–1614.

Turner, J. S., & Helms, D. B. (1989). *Contemporary adulthood* (4th ed.). New York: Holt, Rinehart and Winston.

Turner, M. E., Pratkanis, A. R., Probasco, P., & Leve, C. (1992). Threat, cohesion, and group effectiveness: Testing a social identity maintenance perspective on groupthink. *Journal of Personality and Social Psychology, 63,* 781–796.

Turner, R. J., & Wheaton, B. (1995). Checklist measurement of stressful life events. In S. Cohen, R. C. Kessler, & L. U. Gordon (Eds.), *Measuring stress: A guide for health and social scientists* (pp. 29–58). New York: Oxford University Press.

Turvey, M. T. (1996). Dynamic touch. *American Psychologist, 51,* 1134–1152.

Tversky, A., & Kahneman, D. (1973). Availability: A heuristic for judging frequency and probability. *Cognitive Psychology, 5,* 207–232.

Tversky, A., & Kahneman, D. (1974). Judgment under uncertainty: Heuristics and biases. *Science, 185,* 1124–1131.

Tversky, A., & Kahneman, D. (1982). Judgment under uncertainty: Heuristics and biases. In D. Kahneman, P. Slovic, & A. Tversky (Eds.), *Judgment under uncertainty: Heuristics and biases* (pp. 3–20). New York: Cambridge University Press.

Tversky, A., & Kahneman, D. (1983). Extensional versus intuitive reasoning: The conjunction fallacy in probability judgment. *Psychological Review, 90,* 293–315.

Uba, L. (1994). *Asian Americans: Personality patterns, identity, and mental health.* New York: Guilford Press.

Udry, J. R., & Campbell, B. C. (1994). Getting started on sexual behavior. In A. S. Rossi (Ed.), *Sexuality across the life cycle* (pp. 187–207). Chicago: University of Chicago Press.

Ullman, S. (1983). The measurement of visual motion. *Trends in NeuroSciences, 6,* 177–179.

Unger, R. K. (1979). Toward a redefinition of sex and gender. *American Psychologist, 34,* 1085–1094.

Unger, R. K., & Crawford, C. (1996). *Women and gender: A feminist psychology* (2nd ed.). New York: McGraw-Hill.

Ungerleider, L. G. (1995). Functional brain imaging studies of cortical mechanisms for memory. *Science, 270,* 769–775.

Update on Alzheimer's disease. (1995, February). *Harvard Mental Health Letter,* pp. 1–5.

Ursano, R. J., McCaughey, B. G., & Fullerton, C. S. (Eds.). (1994). *Individual and community responses to trauma and disaster.* New York: Cambridge University Press.

U.S. Bureau of the Census. (1992). *Statistical abstract of the United States 1992.* Washington, DC: U.S. Government Printing Office.

U.S. Bureau of the Census. (1996). *Population projections of the United States by age, sex, race and Hispanic origin: 1995 to 2050.* (Population Characteristics Service, P-25, No. 1130). Washington, DC: U.S. Government Printing Office.

U.S. Department of Health and Human Services. (1992). *Healthy people 2000: National health promotion and disease prevention objectives.* Washington, DC: Public Health Service.

U.S. Department of Labor. (1989). *Handbook of labor statistics.* Washington, DC: U.S. Government Printing Office.

U.S. Department of Labor. (1990). *Supplementary Report Series: Detailed occupation and other characteristics from the EEO file for the United States.* Washington, DC: U.S. Government Printing Office.

U.S. Department of Labor. (1994). *1993 Handbook on women workers: Trends and issues.* Washington, DC: U.S. Government Printing Office.

Vance, E. B., & Wagner, N. N. (1977). Written descriptions of orgasm: A study of sex differences. In D. Byrne & L. A. Byrne (Eds.), *Exploring human sexuality* (pp. 201–212). New York: Crowell.

Van de Castle, R. L. (1993). Content of dreams. In M. Carskadon (Ed.), *Encyclopedia of sleep and dreaming* (pp. 136–139). New York: Macmillan.

Vandell, D. L., Pierce, K., & Stright, A. (1997). Child care and children's development. In G. Bear, K. Minke, & A. Thomas (Eds.), *Children's needs II: Psychological perspectives.* Bethesda, MD: National Association of School Psychologists.

Vandell, D. L., & Ramanan, J. (1992). Effects of early and recent maternal employment on children from low-income families. *Child Development, 63,* 938–949.

Van Den Bergh, N. (1991). Having bitten the apple: A feminist perspective on addictions. In N. Van Den Bergh (Ed.), *Feminist perspectives on addictions* (pp. 3–30). New York: Springer.

VanderStoep, S. W., & Seifert, C. M. (1994). Problem solving, transfer, and thinking. In P. R. Pintrich, D. R. Brown, & C. E. Weinstein (Eds.), *Student motivation, cognition, and learning: Essays in honor of Wilbert J. McKeachie* (pp. 27–49). Hillsdale, NJ: Erlbaum.

Van Essen, D. C., Anderson, C. H., & Felleman, D. J. (1992). Information processing in the primate visual system: An integrated systems perspective. *Science, 255,* 419–422.

Vangelisti, A. L. (1992). Older adolescents' perceptions of communication problems with their parents. *Journal of Adolescent Research, 7,* 382–402.

Van Hasselt, V. B., & Hersen, M. (Eds.). (1994). *Advanced abnorml psychology.* New York: Plenum.

van Hooff, J. A. (1976). The comparison of facial expression in man and higher primates. In M. von Cranach (Ed.), *Methods of inference from animal to human behaviour.* Chicago: Aldine.

Van Houten, R., & Doleys, D. M. (1983). Are social reprimands effective? In S. Axelrod & J. Apsche (Eds.), *The effects of punishment on human behavior* (pp. 45–70). New York: Academic Press.

Vanzetti, N., & Duck, S. (1996). Preface. In N. Vanzetti & S. Duck (Eds.), *A lifetime of relationships* (pp. xvii–xx). Pacific Grove, CA: Brooks/Cole.

Vasquez, M. J. T. (1994). Latinas. In L. Comas-Díaz & B. Greene (Eds.), *Women of color: Integrating ethnic and gender identities in psychotherapy* (pp. 114–138). New York: Guilford Press.

Vasta, R., Haith, M. M., & Miller, S. A. (1995). *Child psychology: The modern science* (2nd ed.). New York: Wiley.

Vasta, R., Knott, J. A., & Gaze, C. E. (1996). Can spatial training erase the gender differences on the water-level task? *Psychology of Women Quarterly, 20,* 549–567.

Vaughan, D., Asbury, T., & Riordan-Eva, P. (1995). *General ophthalmology* (14th ed.). East Norwalk, CT: Appleton & Lange.

Vega, W. A., Kolody, B., Hwang, J., & Noble, A. (1993). Prevalence and magnitude of perinatal substance exposures in California. *New England Journal of Medicine, 329,* 850–854.

Velásquez, R. J., & Callahan, W. J. (1992). Psychological testing of Hispanic Americans in clinical settings: Overview and issues. In K. F. Geisinger (Ed.), *Psychological testing of Hispanics* (pp. 253–265). Washington, DC: American Psychological Association.

Venn, J. (1986). Hypnosis and the Lamaze method: A reply to Wideman and Singer. *American Psychologist, 41,* 475–476.

Vihman, M. M., et al. (1994). External sources of individual differences? A cross-linguistic analysis of the phonetics of mothers' speech to 1-year-old children. *Developmental Psychology, 30,* 651–662.

Viken, R. J., Rose, R. J., Kaprio, J., & Koskenvuo, M. (1994). A developmental genetic analysis of adult personality: Extraversion and neuroticism from 18 to 59 years of age. *Journal of Personality and Social Psychology, 66,* 722–730.

Villeneuve, P. J., & Morrison, H. I. (1995, Winter). Trends in mortality from smoking-related cancers, 1950–1991. *Canadian Social Trends,* pp. 8–11.

Violence against women survey. (1993, November 18). *Daily Statistics Canada,* pp. 1–10.

Vitkus, J. (1996). *Casebook in abnormal psychology* (3rd ed.). New York: McGraw-Hill.

von Baeyer, C. L., Sherk, D. L., & Zanna, M. P. (1981). Impression management in the job interview: When the female applicant meets the male "chauvinist" interviewer. *Personality and Social Psychology Bulletin, 7,* 45–51.

Vorhees, C. V., & Mollnow, E. (1987). Behavioral teratogenesis: Long-term influences on behavior from early exposure to environmental agents. In J. D. Osofsky (Ed.), *Handbook of infant development* (2nd ed., pp. 913–971). New York: Wiley.

Voyer, D. (1996). On the magnitude of laterality effects and sex differences in functional lateralities. *Laterality, 1,* 51–83.

Voyer, D., Voyer, S., & Bryden, M. P. (1995). Magnitude of sex differences in spatial abilities: A meta-analysis and consideration of critical variables. *Psychological Bulletin, 117,* 250–270.

Wade, C. (1995). Using writing to develop and assess critical thinking. *Teaching of Psychology, 22,* 24–28.

Wade, C., & Cirese, S. (1991). *Human sexuality* (2nd ed.). San Diego, CA: Harcourt Brace Jovanovich.

Wade, N. J., & Swanston, M. (1991). *Visual perception: An introduction.* New York: Routledge, Chapman and Hall.

Wagner, R. V. (1993). The differential psychological effects of positive and negative approaches to peace. In V. K. Kool (Ed.), *Nonviolence: Social and psychological issues* (pp. 79–84). Lanham, MD: University Press.

Wagstaff, G. F. (1983). Attitudes to poverty, the Protestant ethic, and political affiliation: A preliminary investigation. *Social Behavior and Personality, 11*, 45–47.

Wainer, H., & Steinberg, L. S. (1992). Sex differences in performance on the mathematics section of the Scholastic Aptitude Test: A bidirectional validity study. *Harvard Educational Review, 62*, 323–336.

Waites, E. A. (1993). *Trauma and survival: Post-traumatic and dissociative disorders in women.* New York: Norton.

Wakefield, H., & Underwager, R. (1994). *Return of the furies: An investigation into recovered memory therapy.* Peru, IL: Open Court.

Wakefield, J. C. (1989). Level of explanation in personality theory. In D. M. Buss & N. Cantor (Eds.), *Personality psychology: Recent trends and emerging directions* (pp. 333–346). New York: Springer-Verlag.

Wakefield, J. C. (1996). DSM-IV: Are we making diagnostic progress? [Review of the book *Diagnostic and statistical manual of mental disorders (DSM-IV)*]. *Contemporary Psychology, 41*, 646–652.

Walker, E. F. (1994). Developmentally moderated expressions of the neuropathology underlying schizophrenia. *Schizophrenia Bulletin, 20*, 453–480.

Walker, E. F., & Lewine, R. R. J. (1990). Prediction of adult-onset schizophrenia from childhood home movies of the patients. *American Journal of Psychiatry, 147*, 1052–1056.

Walker, E. F., Savoie, T., & Davis, D. (1994). Neuromotor precursors of schizophrenia. *Schizophrenia Bulletin, 20*, 441–451.

Walker, G., Eric, K., Pivnick, A., & Drucker, E. (1991). A descriptive outline of a program for cocaine-using mothers and their babies. In C. Bepko (Ed.), *Feminism and addiction* (pp. 7–17). New York: Haworth.

Walker, L. J., Pitts, R. C., Hennig, K. H., & Matsuba, M. K. (1995). Reasoning about morality and real-life moral problems. In M. Killen & D. Hart (Eds.), *Morality in everyday life: Developmental perspectives* (pp. 371–407). New York: Cambridge University Press.

Walker-Andrews, A. S. (1986). Intermodal perception of expressive behaviors: Relation of eye and voice? *Developmental Psychology, 22*, 373–377.

Wallace, B. C. (1991). *Crack cocaine: A practical treatment approach for the chemically dependent.* New York: Brunner/Mazel.

Wallach, M. A., & Wallach, L. (1983). *Psychology's sanction for selfishness.* San Francisco: Freeman.

Wallach, M. A., & Wallach, L. (1990). *Rethinking goodness.* Albany: State University of New York Press.

Wallenberg. (1990, Autumn). *Giraffe Gazette*, p. 6.

Wallerstein, R. S. (1995). *The talking cures: The psychoanalyses and the psychotherapies.* New Haven, CT: Yale University Press.

Wallis, C. (1984, July 11). Unlocking pain's secrets. *Time*, pp. 58–66.

Wallman, J. (1992). *Aping language.* New York: Cambridge University Press.

Walsh, M. R. (1996). Foreward. In A. B. Hopkins, *So ordered: Making partner the hard way* (pp. ix–xv). Amherst: University of Massachusetts Press.

Walton, G. E., Bower, N. J., & Bower, T. G. R. (1992). Recognition of familiar faces by newborns. *Infant Behavior and Development, 15*, 265–269.

Ward, C. A. (1995). *Attitudes toward rape: Feminist and social psychological perspectives.* Thousand Oaks, CA: Sage.

Ward, S. L., & Overton, W. F. (1990). Semantic familiarity, relevance, and the development of deductive reasoning. *Developmental Psychology, 26*, 488–493.

Wardle, J., Bindra, R., Fairclough, B., & Westcome, A. (1993). Culture and body image: Body perception and weight concern in young Asian and Caucasian British women. *Journal of Community and Applied Social Psychology, 3*, 173–181.

Warr, P., & Parry, G. (1982). Paid employment and women's psychological well-being. *Psychological Bulletin, 91*, 498–516.

Warren, L. W., & McEachren, L. (1985). Derived identity and depressive symptomatology in women differing in marital and employment status. *Psychology of Women Quarterly, 9*, 133–144.

Warren, R. M. (1984). Perceptual restoration of obliterated sounds. *Psychological Bulletin, 96*, 371–383.

Warren, R. M., & Warren, R. P. (1970, December). Auditory illusions and confusions. *Scientific American, 223* (6), 30–36.

Warrington, E. K., & Weiskrantz, L. (1970). Amnesic syndrome: Consolidation or retrieval? *Nature, 228*, 629–630.

Wass, H., & Neimeyer, R. A. (Eds.). (1995). *Dying: Facing the facts* (3rd ed.). Philadelphia: Taylor & Francis.

Watson, D. L., & Tharp, R. G. (1993). *Self-directed behavior: Self-modification for personal adjustment* (6th ed.). Pacific Grove, CA: Brooks/Cole.

Watson, J. B. (1913). Psychology as the behaviorist views it. *Psychological Review, 20*, 158–177.

Watson, J. B., & Rayner, R. (1920). Conditioned emotional reactions. *Journal of Experimental Psychology, 3*, 1–14.

Weale, R. A. (1992). *The senescence of human vision.* New York: Oxford University Press.

Weaver, C. A., III. (1993). Do you need a "flash" to form a flashbulb memory? *Journal of Experimental Psychology, General, 122*, 39–46.

Weaver, J. B., Masland, J. L., & Zillman, D. (1984). Effect of erotica on young men's aesthetic perception of their female sexual partners. *Perceptual and Motor Skills, 58*, 929–930.

Webb, J. T., & Kleine, P. A. (1993). Assessing gifted and talented children. In J. L. Culbertson & D. J. Willis (Eds.), *Testing young children* (pp. 383–407). Austin, TX: Pro-Ed.

Webb, W. B. (1992). *Sleep: The gentle tyrant* (2nd ed.). Bolton, MA: Anker.

Weber, E. U., Böckenholt, U., Hilton, D. J., & Wallace, B. (1993). Determinants of diagnostic hypothesis generation: Effects of information, base rates, and experience. *Journal of Experimental Psychology: Learning, Memory, and Cognition, 19*, 1131–1164.

Wechsler, H., Deutsch, C., & Dowdall, G. (1995, April 14). Too many colleges are still in denial about alcohol abuse. *Chronicle of Higher Education*, B1–B2.

Wechsler, H., et al. (1994). Health and behavioral consequences of binge drinking in college: A national survey of students at 140 campuses. *JAMA, 272*, 1672–1677.

Wegman, M. E. (1993). Annual summary of vital statistics—1992. *Pediatrics, 92,* 743–754.

Wegner, D. M. (1992). You can't always think what you want: Problems in the suppression of unwanted thoughts. *Advances in Experimental Social Psychology, 25,* 193–225.

Wegner, D. M., & Gold, D. B. (1995). Fanning old flames: Emotional and cognitive effects of suppressing thoughts of a past relationship. *Journal of Personality and Social Psychology, 68,* 782–792.

Wegner, D. M., & Pennebaker, J. W. (Eds.). (1993). *Handbook of mental control.* Englewood Cliffs, NJ: Prentice Hall.

Wegner, D. M., Schneider, D. J., Carter, S., III, & White, L. (1987). Paradoxical effects of thought suppression. *Journal of Personality and Social Psychology, 53,* 5–13.

Wegner, D. M., & Wenzlaff, R. M. (1996). Mental control. In E. T. Higgins & A. W. Kruglanski (Eds.), *Social psychology: Handbook of basic principles* (pp. 466–492). New York: Guilford Press.

Weiner, B. (1991). Metaphors in motivation and attribution. *American Psychologist,* 921–930.

Weinstein, L. N., Schwartz, D. G., & Arkin, A. M. (1991). Qualitative aspects of sleep mentation. In S. J. Ellman & J. S. Antrobus (Eds.), *The mind in sleep: Psychology and psychophysiology* (2nd ed., pp. 172–213). New York: Wiley.

Weinstein, N. D. (1989). Effects of personal experience on self-protective behavior. *Psychological Bulletin, 105,* 31–50.

Weinstein, S. (1968). Intensive and extensive aspects of tactile sensitivity as a function of body part, sex, and laterality. In D. R. Kenshalo (Ed.), *The skin senses.* Springfield, IL: Thomas.

Weisberg, R. W., & Suls, J. M. (1973). An information-processing model of Duncker's candle problem. *Cognitive Psychology, 4,* 255–276.

Weishaar, M. E., & Beck, A. T. (1987). Cognitive therapy. In W. Dryden & W. L. Golden (Eds.), *Cognitive-behavioural approaches to psychotherapy* (pp. 61–91). Cambridge, England: Hemisphere.

Weiss, D. S., et al. (1992). The prevalence of lifetime and partial post-traumatic stress disorder in Vietnam theater veterans. *Journal of Traumatic Stress, 5,* 265–376.

Weiss, J. (1993). *How psychotherapy works: Process and technique.* New York: Guilford Press.

Weiss, R. S. (1994). *Learning from strangers: The art and method of qualitative interview studies.* New York: Free Press.

Weisse, C. S. (1992). Depression and immunocompetence: A review of the literature. *Psychological Bulletin, 111,* 475–489.

Weissman, M. M., et al. (1996). Cross-national epidemiology of major depression and bipolar disorder. *JAMA, 276,* 293–299.

Weissman, M. M., & Klerman, G. L. (1990). Interpersonal psychotherapy for depression. In B. B. Wolman & G. Stricker (Eds.), *Depressive disorders: Facts, theories and treatment methods* (pp. 379–395). New York: Wiley.

Weisz, J., et al. (1995). Effects of psychotherapy with children and adolescents revisited: A meta-analysis of treatment outcome studies. *Psychological Bulletin, 117,* 450–468.

Weitzman, M., & Adair, R. (1988). Divorce and children. *Pediatric Clinics of North America, 35,* 1313–1323.

Welsh, A. (1994). *Freud's wishful dream book.* Princeton, NJ: Princeton University Press.

Welsh, J. P., & Harvey, J. A. (1992). The role of the cerebellum in voluntary and reflexive movements: History and current status. In R. Llinás & C. Sotelo (Eds.), *The cerebellum revisited* (pp. 301–334). New York: Springer-Verlag.

Wenderoth, P. (1992). Perceptual illusions. *Australian Journal of Psychology, 44,* 147–151.

Werker, J. F. (1994). Cross-language speech perception: Development change does not involve loss. In J. G. Goodman & H. C. Nusbaum (Eds.), *The development of speech perception: The transition from speech sounds to spoken words* (pp. 93–120). Cambridge, MA: MIT Press.

Werker, J. F., & Tees, R. C. (1984). Cross-language speech perception: Evidence for perceptual reorganization during the first year of life. *Infant Behavior and Development, 7,* 49–63.

Werner, M. J. (1995). Principles of brief intervention for adolescent alcohol, tobacco, and other drug use. *Pediatric Clinics of North America, 42,* 335–349.

Wessells, M. G. (1993). Psychological obstacles to peace. In V. K. Kool (Ed.), *Nonviolence: Social and psychological issues* (pp. 25–35). Lanham, MD: University Press.

West, R. L. (1996). An application of prefrontal cortex function theory to cognitive aging. *Psychological Bulletin, 120,* 272–292.

Westbrook, P. R. (1993). Apnea. In M. A. Carskadon (Ed.), *Encyclopedia of sleep and dreaming* (pp. 45–50). New York: Macmillan.

Wheelan, S. A. (1994). *Group processes: A developmental perspective.* Boston: Allyn & Bacon.

Wheelan, S. A., & Verdi, A. F. (1992). Differences in male and female patterns of communication in groups: A methodological artifact? *Sex Roles, 27,* 1–15.

Wheeler, C. (1994, September–October). How much ink do women get? *Executive Female,* p. 51.

Whitaker, L. C. (1992). *Schizophrenic disorders: Sense and nonsense in conceptualization, assessment, and treatment.* New York: Plenum.

Whitbourne, S. K. (1986). *The me I know: A study of adult identity.* New York: Springer-Verlag.

Whitbourne, S. K. (1992). Sexuality in the aging male. In L. Glasse & J. Hendricks (Eds.), *Gender & aging* (pp. 45–57). Amityville, NY: Baywood.

Whitbourne, S. K. (1996). *The aging individual: Physical and psychological perspectives.* New York: Springer.

Whitbourne, S. K. (1997). Identity and adaptation to the aging process. In C. Ryff & V. Marshall (Eds.), *Self and society in aging processes,* in press.

Whitbourne, S. K., & Ebmeyer, J. B. (1990). *Identity and intimacy in marriage.* New York: Springer-Verlag.

Whitbourne, S. K., & Hulicka, I. M. (1990). Ageism in undergraduate psychology texts. *American Psychologist, 45,* 1127–1136.

White, J. W. (1996, August). *Sexual revictimization: Sexual scripts and dating rituals.* Paper presented at the convention of the American Psychological Association, Toronto.

White, J. W., & Kowalski, R. M. (1994). Reconstructing the myth of the non-aggressive woman: A feminist analysis. *Psychology of Women Quarterly, 18,* 487–508.

White, J. W., & Sorenson, S. B. (1992). A sociocultural view of sexual assault: From discrepancy to diversity. *Journal of Social Issues, 48,* 187–195.

White, N. M., & Milner, P. M. (1992). The psychobiology of reinforcers. *Annual Review of Psychology, 43,* 443–471.

White, R. K. (1991). Enemy images in the UnitedNations–Iraq and East-West conflicts. In R. W. Rieber (Ed.), *The psychology of war and peace: The image of the enemy* (pp. 59–70). New York: Plenum.

White, R. W. (1959). Motivation reconsidered: The concept of competence. *Psychological Review, 66,* 297–333.

Whitley, B. E., Jr. (1996). *Principles of research in behavioral science.* Mountain View, CA: Mayfield.

Whitley, B. E., Jr., & Hern, A. L. (1992). *Sexual experience, perceived invulnerability to pregnancy, and the use of effective contraception.* Paper presented at the meeting of the Eastern Psychological Association, Boston.

Whitman, T. L., Hantula, D. A., & Spence, B. H. (1990). Current issues in behavior modification with mentally retarded persons. In J. L. Matson (Ed.), *Handbook of behavior modification with the mentally retarded* (2nd ed., pp. 9–50). New York: Plenum.

Whorf, B. L. (1956). Science and linguistics. In J. B. Carroll (Ed.), *Language, thought, and reality: Selected writings of Benjamin Lee Whorf.* Cambridge, MA: MIT Press.

Whyte, G. (1993). Escalating commitment in individual and group decision making: A prospect theory approach. *Organizational Behavior and Human Decision Making, 54,* 430–455.

Whyte, G., & Sebenius, J. K. (1997). The effect of multiple anchors on anchoring in individual and group judgment. *Organizational Behavior and Human Decision Processes, 69,* 75–85.

Widiger, T. A., & Corbitt, E. M. (1995). Antisocial personality disorder. In W. J. Livesley (Ed.), *The DSM-IV personality disorders* (pp. 103–126). New York: Guilford Press.

Widiger, T. A., & Trull, T. J. (1991). Diagnosis and clinical assessment. *Annual Review of Psychology, 42,* 109–133.

Widom, C. S. (1989). Does violence beget violence? A critical examination of the literature. *Psychological Bulletin, 106,* 3–28.

Wiertelak, E. P., Maier, S. F., & Watkins, L. R. (1992). Cholecystokinin antianalgesia: Safety cues abolish morphine analgesia. *Science, 256,* 830–833.

Wieselgren, I. M., & Lindström, L. H. (1996). A prospective 1–5-year outcome study in first-admitted and readmitted schizophrenic patients. *Acta Psychiatrica Scandinavica, 93,* 9–19.

Wiggins, J. S., & Pincus, A. L. (1992). Personality: Structure and assessment. *Annual Review of Psychology, 43,* 473–504.

Williams, A. (1996, March 4). It pays to study. *New York Magazine,* p. 14.

Williams, D. A., Overmier, J. B., & LoLordo, V. M. (1992). A reevaluation of Rescorla's early dictums about Pavlovian conditioned inhibition. *Psychological Bulletin, 111,* 275–290.

Williams, J. M. G., Mathews, A., & MacLeod, C. (1996). The emotional Stroop task and psychopathology. *Psychological Bulletin, 120,* 3–24.

Williams, J. M. G., Watts, F. N., MacLeod, C., & Mathews, A. (1988). *Cognitive psychology and emotional disorders.* Chichester, England: Wiley.

Williams, M. A., & Gross, A. M. (1994). Behavior therapy. In V. B. Van Hasselt & M. Hersen (Ed.), *Advanced abnormal psychology* (pp. 419–441). New York: Plenum.

Williams, R., Zyzanski, S. J., & Wright, A. L. (1992). Life events and daily hassles and uplifts as predictors of hospitalization and outpatient visitation. *Social Science and Medicine, 34,* 763–768.

Williams, S. S., et al. (1996). Restrained eating among adolescents: Dieters are not always bingers and bingers are not always dieters. *Health Psychology, 15,* 176–184.

Williamson, D. J. G., Scott, J. G., & Adams, R. L. (1996). Traumatic brain injury. In R. L. Adams, O. A. Parsons, J. L. Culbertson, & S. J. Nixon (Eds.), *Neuropsychology for clinical practice: Etiology, assessment, and treatment of common neurological disorders* (pp. 9–64). Washington, DC: American Psychological Association.

Willig, A. C. (1988). A case of blaming the victim: The Dunn monograph on bilingual Hispanic children on the U.S. mainland. *Hispanic Journal of Behavioral Science, 10,* 219–236.

Willson, A., & Lloyd, B. (1990). Gender vs. power: Self-posed behavior revisited. *Sex Roles, 23,* 91–98.

Wilson, M. N. (1986). The black extended family: An analytical consideration. *Developmental Psychology, 22,* 246–258.

Winckelgren, I. (1992). How the brain "sees" borders where there are none. *Science, 256,* 1520–1521.

Wing, R. R., & Greeno, C. G. (1994). Behavioural and psychosocial aspects of obesity and its treatment. *Baillière's Clinical Endocrinology and Metabolism, 8,* 689–703.

Wingfield, A., & Titone, D. (1998). Sentence processing. In J. B. Gleason & N. B. Ratner (Eds.), *Psycholinguistics* (2nd ed., pp. 227–274). Fort Worth, TX: Harcourt Brace.

Winn, P. (1995). The lateral hypothalamus and motivated behavior: An old syndrome reassessed and a new perspective gained. *Current Directions in Psychological Science, 4,* 182–187.

Winter, D. D. (1996). *Ecological psychology: Healing the split between planet and self.* New York: HarperCollins.

Witelson, S. F. (1995). Neuroanatomical bases of hemispheric functional specialization in the human brain: Possible developmental factors. In F. L. Kitterle (Ed.), *Hemispheric communication: Mechanisms and models* (pp. 61–84). Hillsdale, NJ: Erlbaum.

Wolf, N. (1991). *The beauty myth: How images of beauty are used against women.* New York: Morrow.

Wolfe, R. N. (1998). *Personality research: Can it be a self-correcting discipline?* Paper presented at the annual meeting of the Eastern Psychological Association, Boston.

Wolford, G., Taylor, H. A., & Beck, J. R. (1990). The conjunction fallacy? *Memory & Cognition, 18,* 47–53.

Wolitzky, D. L. (1995). The theory and practice of traditional psychoanalytic psychotherapy. In A. S. Gurman & S. B. Messer (Eds.), *Essential psychotherapies: Theories and practice* (pp. 12–54). New York: Guilford Press.

Wolraich, M. L., Wilson, D. B., & White, J. W. (1995). The effect of sugar on behavior or cognition in children: A meta-analysis. *JAMA, 274,* 1617–1621.

Woo, D. (1989). The gap between striving and achieving: The case of Asian American women. In Asian Women United of California (Eds.), *Making waves: An anthology of writings by and about Asian American women* (pp. 185–194). Boston: Beacon.

Wood, J. M., Nezworski, M. T., & Stejskal, W. J. (1996a). The comprehensive system for the Rorschach: A critical examination. *Psychological Science, 7,* 3–10.

Wood, J. M., Nezworski, M. T., & Stejskal, W. J. (1996b). Thinking critically about the comprehensive system for the Rorschach: A reply to Exner. *Psychological Science, 7*, 14–17.

Wood, N., & Cowan, N. (1995). The cocktail party phenomenon revisited: How frequent are attention shifts to one's name in an irrelevant auditory channel? *Journal of Experimental Psychology: Learning, Memory, and Cognition, 21*, 255–260.

Wood, R. (1993). Deceptive schemata: Initial impressions of others. In P. J. Kalbfleisch (Ed.), *Interpersonal communication: Evolving interpersonal relationships* (pp. 69–86). Hillsdale, NJ: Erlbaum.

Wood, W., Rhodes, N., & Whelan, M. (1989). Sex differences in positive well-being: A consideration of emotional style and marital status. *Psychological Bulletin, 106*, 249–264.

Wood, W., Wong, F. Y., & Chachere, J. G. (1991). Effects of media violence on viewers' aggression in unconstrained social interaction. *Psychological Bulletin, 109*, 271–383.

Woodford, J. (1989, February). The transformation of Benjamin Carson. *Michigan Today*, pp. 6–7.

Woodward, A. L., & Markman, E. M. (1998). Early word learning. In W. Damon (Series Ed.) &D. Kuhn & R. Siegler (Eds.), *Handbook of child psychology* (Vol. 2: *Cognition, perception and language*, pp. 371–420). New York: Wiley.

Woody, R. H., Hansen, J. C., & Rossberg, R. H. (1989). *Counseling psychology: Strategies and services.* Pacific Grove, CA: Brooks/Cole.

Wooley, S., Wooly, O. W., & Dyrenforth, S. (1979). Theoretical, practical, and social issues in behavioral treatments of obesity. *Journal of Applied Behavior Analysis, 12*, 3–25.

Worchel, S., Coutant-Sassic, D, & Wong, F. (1993). Toward a more balanced view of conflict: There is a positive side. In S. Worchel & J. A. Simpson (Eds.), *Conflict between people and groups: Causes, processes, and resolutions* (pp. 76–89). Chicago: Nelson-Hall.

Word, C. H., Zanna, M. P., & Cooper, J. (1974). The nonverbal mediation of self-fulfilling prophecies in intersocial interaction. *Journal of Experimental Social Psychology, 10*, 109–120.

Wright, S. W. (1996, December 12). "Frontiers of opportunity" for tribal colleges. *Black Issues in Higher Education*, pp. 28–29.

Wundt, W. (1912/1973). *An introduction to psychology* (R. Pintner, Translator). London: Allen. Reproduced by Arno Press, New York.

Yatani, C. (1994). School performance of Asian-American and Asian children: Myth and fact. In E. Tobach & B. Rosoff (Eds.), *Challenging racism and sexism: Alternatives to genetic explanations* (pp. 295–308). New York: Feminist Press.

Yates, J. F. (1990). *Judgment and decision making.* Englewood Cliffs, NJ: Prentice Hall.

Yates, J. F., Lee, J.-W., & Shinotsuka, H. (1996). Beliefs about overconfidence, including its cross-national variation. *Organizational Behavior and Human Decision Processes, 65*, 138–147.

Yeast meets west. (1995, February 13). *People*, p. 192.

Yeaworth, R. C., et al. (1980). The development of an adolescent life change event scale. *Adolescence, 15*, 91–98.

Yellott, J. I. (1981). Binocular depth inversion. *Scientific American, 245*, (1), 148–159.

Yeni-Komshian, G. H. (1998). Speech perception. In J. B. Gleason & N. B. Ratner (Eds.), *Psycholinguistics* (2nd ed., pp. 107–156). Fort Worth, TX: Harcourt Brace Jovanovich.

Yerkes, R. M., & Morgulis, S. (1909). The method of Pawlow in animal psychology. *Psychological Bulletin, 6*, 257–273.

Yonas, A., & Owsley, C. (1987). Development of visual space perception. In P. Salapatek & L. Cohen (Eds.), *Handbook of infant perception* (pp. 79–122). Orlando, FL: Academic Press.

Yonkers, K. A., & Gurguis, G. (1995). Gender differences in the prevalence and expression of anxiety disorders. In M. V. Seeman (Ed.), *Gender and psychopathology* (pp. 113–130). Washington, DC: American Psychiatric Press.

Yost, W. A. (1992). Auditory perception and sound source determination. *Current Directions in Psychological Science, 1*, 179–184.

Youths learn alternatives to violence. (1992, September). *Children's Defense Fund Reports, 13*, 1, 4.

Zahn-Waxler, C., Radke-Yarrow, M., Wagner, E., & Chapman, M. (1992). Development of concern for others. *Development Psychology, 28*, 126–136.

Zahn-Waxler, C., & Smith, K. D. (1992). The development of prosocial behavior. In V. B. Van Hasselt & M. Hersen (Eds.), *Handbook of social development: A lifespan perspective* (pp. 229–256). New York: Plenum.

Zajonc, R. B. (1965). Social facilitation. *Science, 149*, 269–275.

Zajonc, R. B. (1968). Attitudinal effects of mere exposure. *Journal of Personality and Social Psychology Monograph, 9* (1–29, Pt. 2).

Zajonc, R. B. (1994). Emotional expression and temperature modulation. In S. H. M. van Goozen,N. E. Van de Poll, & J. A. Sergeant (Eds.), *Emotions: Essays on emotion theory* (pp. 3–27). Hillsdale, NJ: Erlbaum.

Zajonc, R. B., & McIntosh, D. N. (1992). Emotions research: Some promising questions and some questionable promises. *Psychological Sciences, 3*, 70–74.

Zebrowitz, L. A. (1990). *Social perception.* Pacific Grove: CA: Brooks/Cole.

Zec, R. F. (1993). Neuropsychological functioning in Alzheimer's disease. In R. W. Parks, R. F. Zec, & R. S. Wilson (Eds.), *Neuropsychology of Alzheimer's disease and other dementias* (pp 3–80). New York: Oxford University Press.

Zeki, S. (1992, September). The visual image in mind and brain. *Scientific American, 267*, 68–76.

Zelinski, E. M., & Gilewski, M. J. (1988). Memory for prose and aging: A meta-analysis. In M. L. Howe & C. J. Brainerd (Eds.), *Cognitive development in adulthood: Progress in cognitive development research* (pp. 133–158). New York: Springer-Verlag.

Zellner, D. A. (1991). How foods get to be liked: Some general mechanisms and some special cases. In R. C. Bolles (Ed.), *The hedonics of taste* (pp. 199–217). Hillsdale, NJ: Erlbaum.

Zerbe, K. J. (1993). *Eating disorders: A guide for the perplexed.* Washington, DC: American Psychiatric Press.

Zhang, Y., et al. (1994). Positional cloning of the mouse obese gene and its human homologue. *Nature, 372*, 425–432.

Zhou, J. H., Hofman, M. A., Gooren, L. J. G., & Swaab, D. F. (1995). A sex difference in the human brain and its relation to transsexuality. *Nature, 378*, 68–70.

Zigler, E. F., & Gilman, E. (1993). Day care in America: What is needed? *Pediatrics, 91*, 175–178.

Zigler, E. F., & Hodapp, R. M. (1991). Behavioral functioning in individuals with mental retardation. *Annual Review of Psychology, 42,* 29–50.

Zilbergeld, B., & Ellison, C. R. (1980). Desire discrepancies and arousal problems in sex therapy. InS. R. Leiblum & L. A. Pervin (Eds.), *Principles and practice of sex therapy.* New York: Guilford Press.

Zillmann, D. (1992). Pornography research, social advocacy, and public policy. In P. Suedfeld & P. E. Tetlock (Eds.), *Psychology and social policy* (pp. 165–178). New York: Hemisphere.

Zimbardo, P. G., Haney, C., & Banks, W. C. (1973, April 8). A Pirandellian prison. *New York Times Magazine,* pp. 38–60.

Zimbardo, P. G., Haney, C., Banks, W. C., & Jaffe, D. (1972). *The psychology of imprisonment: Privation, power, and pathology.* Unpublished paper, Stanford University.

Zimbardo, P. G., & Leippe, M. R. (1991). *The psychology of attitude change and social influence.* New York: McGraw-Hill.

Zimmerman, B. J. (1995). Self-efficacy and educational development. In A. Bandura (Ed.), *Self-efficacy in changing societies* (pp. 202–231). New York: Cambridge University Press.

Zinbarg, R. E., Barlow, D. H., Brown, T. A., & Hertz, R. M. (1992). Cognitive-behavioral approaches to the nature and treatment of anxiety disorders. *Annual Review of Psychology, 43,* 235–267.

Zivin, J. A., & Choi, D. W. (1991, July). Stroke therapy. *Scientific American, 265,* 56–63.

Zuckerman, B., & Frank, D. (1994). Prenatal cocaine exposure: Nine years later. *Journal of Pediatrics, 124,* 731–733.

Zuckerman, M. (1993). Out of sensory deprivation and into sensation seeking: A personal and scientific journey. In G. G. Brannigan & M. R. Merrens (Eds.), *The undaunted psychologist: Adventures in research* (pp. 44–57). Philadelphia: Temple University Press.

Zuckerman, M. (1994a). Impulsive unsocialized sensation seeking: The biological foundations of a basic dimension of personality. In J. E. Bates & T. D. Wachs (Eds.), *Temperament: Individual differences at the interface of biology and behavior* (pp. 219–255). Washington, DC: American Psychological Association.

Zuckerman, M. (1994b). *Behavioral expressions and biosocial bases of sensation seeking.* New York: Cambridge University Press.

Zuckerman, M. (1995). Good and bad humors: Biochemical bases of personality and its disorder. *Psychological Science, 6,* 325–332.

Zurif, E. (1992). Aphasia. In L. R. Squire (Ed.), *Encyclopedia of learning and memory* (pp. 41–43). New York: Macmillan.

PHOTO CREDITS

Chapter 1 p. 3, © Billings Gazette, Billings, MT; p. 5, © Christopher Morrow/Stock, Boston; p. 6 (top), Corbis-Bettmann; p. 6 (bottom), Archives of the History of American Psychology; p. 8 (top left), Corbis-Bettmann; p. 8 (top left middle), Archives of the History of American Psychology; p. 8 (top right middle), Courtesy of Wellesley College Archives; p. 8 (top right), © Department of Manuscripts and University Archives Cornell University Library; p. 8 (bottom left), Archives of the History of American Psychology; p. 8 (bottom left middle), Archives of the History of American Psychology; p. 8 (bottom right middle), Culver Pictures; p. 8 (bottom right), Archives of the History of American Psychology; p. 9, © Yves de Braine/Black Star; p. 10, © Chris J. Johnson/Stock, Boston; p. 11, Corbis-Bettmann; p. 12, Courtesy of The Carl Rogers Memorial Library; p. 13, © Hank Morgan/Rainbow; p. 14 (top right), © Drew Appleby; p. 14 (top left), © John P. Fox/Beaver College; p. 14 (bottom left), © Robert V. Guthrie Collection; p. 15 (top), © Robert V. Guthrie Collection; p. 15 (bottom), Courtesy of Dr. Stanley Sue; p. 17, © Robert E. Daemmrich/Tony Stone Images; p. 18, © Steve Sherman; p. 19, © Robin Sachs; p. 21, © Deborah Davis/PhotoEdit; p. 24, © Alejandro Balaguer/Sygma.

Chapter 2 p. 31, Photograph of Stanley Milgram with shock generator, permission granted by Alexandra Milgram; p. 35, © Comstock; p. 38 (top), © Drew Appleby; p. 38 (bottom), © Jeff Greenberg/PhotoEdit; p. 46, St. Mark's, Venice from Floating Cities , M. Joseph 1991 © Stephen Wiltshire; p. 47, © Rob Nelson/Black Star; p. 50, © 1998 R. Pretzer/LUXE; p. 52, © David Frazier; p. 54, © Ron Pretzer/LUXE; p. 57 (top), © Will & Deni McIntyre/Photo Researchers; p. 57 (bottom), © Myrleen Ferguson/PhotoEdit; p. 61, © Stephen Collins/Photo Researchers; p. 62, © 1998 Robin Sachs; p. 67, © David Frazier; p. 68, © Louise Wadsworth.

Chapter 3 p. 75, © Tony Freeman/PhotoEdit; p. 77, © Phototake; p. 78, © Omikron/Science Source/Photo Researchers; p. 82, © 1993 Hank Morgan/Rainbow; p. 83, Courtesy of Drs. Michael Phelps and John C. Mazziotta, UCLA School of Medicine; p. 84, © Dan McCoy/Rainbow; p. 88, © Steven Labuzetta; p. 91, © 1991 Custom Medical Stock Photography; p. 94, © David Madison/Tony Stone Images; p. 97, © Ron Pretzer/LUXE; p. 98, © Will McIntyre/Science Source/Photo Researchers; p. 99 (top), © 1991 Richard Falco/Black Star; p. 99 (middle), © Tony Latham/Tony Stone Images; p. 99 (bottom), Dr. Dennis Dickson, Albert Einstein College of Medicine/Peter Arnold, Inc.; p. 100, Dr. Dennis Dickson, Albert Einstein College of Medicine/Peter Arnold, Inc.; p. 102 (both), Reprinted from Neuropsychologia, 33, Farah, M. J., Levinson, K. L., & Klein, K. L., Face perception and within–category discrimination in prosopagnosia, 661–674, 1995, with permission from Elsevier Science; p. 104, © Biophoto Associates/Science Source/Photo Researchers; p. 105 (top), © James Schnepf/Gamma Liaison; p. 105 (bottom left), © Rhoda Sidney/PhotoEdit; p. 105 (bottom right), AP/Wide World Photos; p. 107 (both), © Breck P. Kent.

Chapter 4 p. 113, © Myrleen Ferguson/PhotoEdit; p. 114, © Kenneth A. Deitcher/The Wildlife Collection; p. 116, © Bill Gallery/Stock, Boston; p. 119, Courtesy of Dr. E. R. Lewis, University of California at Berkeley; p. 123, © Elinore Matlin; p. 127 (top), © Bill Aron/PhotoEdit; p. 127 (bottom), "The Forest Has Eyes" © Bev Doolittle, courtesy of The Greenwich Workshop, Inc. For more information on the limited edition fine art prints by Bev Doolittle, call 1-800-577-0666; p. 128 (top left), © Drew Appleby; p. 128 (top right), © Ron Pretzer/LUXE; p. 128 (bottom left), © Joel Gordon 1987; p. 128 (bottom right), © Ron Pretzer/LUXE; p. 130 (top), © Sverker Runeson/Uppsala Universitet; p. 130 (bottom), © Glen Allison/Tony Stone Images; p. 131 (top), © Ric Ergenbright; p. 131 (bottom), © Gary Randorf/Adirondack Council; p. 132 (both), from We Who Believe in Freedom (jacket cover) by Bernice Johnson Reagon. Copyright. Used by permission of Doubleday, a division of Bantam Doubleday Dell Publishing Group, Inc. Photo © 1998 R. Pretzer/LUXE; p. 138 (top), © Dr. G. Bredberg/Science Photo Library/Photo Researchers; p. 138 (bottom), © Jeff Greenberg/PhotoEdit; p. 139 (top), © Van Cliburn Foundation, Katia Skanavi, finalist of the 10th Van Cliburn International Piano Competition, Fort Worth, TX; p. 139 (bottom left), © David Young-Wolff/PhotoEdit; p. 139 (bottom right), © David Young-Wolff/PhotoEdit; p. 140, © 1996, Joan Marcus, Carol Rosegg; p. 141 (top), Courtesy of House Ear Institute; p. 141 (bottom), © Phil Borden/PhotoEdit; p. 142, © Louise Wadsworth; p. 143, © Bob Daemmrich/Stock, Boston; p. 144, © Stephen Dunn/Allsport; p. 145, © Louise Wadsworth; p. 147, © A. K. Das.

Chapter 5 p. 153, © Thomas Treuter, Photojournalist, all rights reserved; p. 155, © R. J. Erwin 1990/Photo Researchers; p. 156, © Drew Appleby; p. 159, © Owen Franken/Stock, Boston; p. 160, © Daudier/Jerrican/Photo Researchers; p. 165 (left), © Bildarchiv Foto Marburg/Art Resource; p. 165 (right), The Detroit Institute of Arts, gift of Mr. and Mrs. Bert L. Smokler and Mr. and Mrs. Lawrence Fleischman; p. 167, © 1982 Pier Angelo Simone; p. 169, © Joel Gordon 1993; p. 173, © Drew Appleby; p. 174, © Kal Muller/Woodfin Camp; p. 177, © David Parker/Photo Researchers.

Chapter 6 p. 187, © 1998 Robin Sachs; p. 189, © Lee Snider/The Image Works; p. 193 (top), © Gabe Palmer/The Stock Market; p. 193 (bottom), © Steven Lunetta; p. 194 (top), © Matthew McVay/Stock, Boston; p. 194 (bottom), © Burbank/The Image Works; p. 195, © Guy Connolly/US Department of Agriculture; p. 196, © David Frazier; p. 197, © Drew Appleby; p. 198, © C.C. Duncan/Medical Images Inc.; p. 201, © Dr. Robert Epstein; p. 202, © Louise Wadsworth; p. 203, Coulbourn Instruments, L. L. C.; p. 205, © J. Pickerell/The Image Works; p. 207 (all), courtesy Dr. R. J. Herrnstein, Harvard University; p. 208, © Breck P. Kent/Animals, Animals; p. 209, © 1998 Robin Sachs; p. 210, © Charles Gupton/Stock, Boston; p. 211, © J. Pickerell/The Image Works; p. 213, © Roy Morsch/The Stock Market; p. 214, ©

Jodi Buren; p. 217, © Robert Brenner/PhotoEdit; p. 219, © Louise Wadsworth.

Chapter 7 p. 225, © Drew Appleby; p. 227, © Doug Mazza-pica/Black Star; p. 228 (top), © Ron Pretzer/LUXE; p. 228 (bottom), © Ron Pretzer/LUXE; p. 229 (top), © Drew Appleby; p. 229 (bottom), © Drew Appleby; p. 235, © Drew Appleby; p. 236 (both), Corbis-Bettmann; p. 238, © Spencer Grant/PhotoEdit; p. 240, © Drew Appleby; p. 241, © Louise Wadsworth; p. 242, © David Frazier; p. 243, © B. Daemmrich/The Image Works; p. 246, © Breck P. Kent; p. 247, © Louise Wadsworth; p. 248, © David Frazier; p. 251, © Drew Appleby.

Chapter 8 p. 257 (both), © Rex USA Ltd.; p. 258, © Tony Free-man/PhotoEdit; p. 261, © Alan Odie/PhotoEdit; p. 262 (top), © Ron Pretzer/LUXE; p. 262 (both), AP/Wide World Photos; p. 265, © Joseph Nettis/Tony Stone Images; p. 267, © F. Hoffmann/The Image Works; p. 268, © Ron Pretzer/LUXE; p. 270, © Drew Appleby; p. 271, © Ron Pretzer/Luxe; p. 272, © Louise Wadsworth; p. 273, Reuters/Corbis-Bettmann; p. 276, © B. Daemmrich/The Image Works; p. 278, © B. Daemmrich/The Image Works; p. 279, © Louise Wadsworth; p. 280, © Patrick Harbron/Outline; p. 281 (top left), © Drew Appleby; p. 281 (top right), © R. Lord/The Image Works; p. 281 (bottom), © M. B. Gross/Cathedral High School; p. 283, © Joyce Lockwood; p. 284, © Tony Freeman/PhotoEdit; p. 288, © Ron Pretzer/LUXE.

Chapter 9 p. 291, Courtesy of H. Terrace; p. 294, © Elinore Matlin; p. 295 (top), © Calvin Larsen/Photo Researchers; p. 295 (bottom), © Jim Corwin/Photo Researchers; p. 297, © Drew Appleby; p. 298, courtesy of Marcus E. Raichle, M.D., Washington University School of Medicine; p. 299, © Louise Wadsworth; p. 302, © Dr. Arnold Matlin; p. 304, © Dr. Arnold Matlin; p. 305, © GSU/Language Research Center; p. 306, © Bruce Ayres/Tony Stone Images; p. 308, © Network Pro/The Image Works; p. 309, © Ron Pretzer/LUXE.

Chapter 10 p. 315 (top), courtesy of Children's Defense Fund; p. 315 (bottom), Marian Wright Edelman, used by permission of Johnson Publishing Co.; p. 317, © B. Daemmrich/The Image Works; p. 318, © Francis Leroy, Biocosmos/Science Photo Library/Photo Researchers; p. 319, © Petit Format/Nestle/Science Scource, Photo Researchers; p. 320 (top, left to right), © George Steinmetz; p. 320 (bottom), by permission of The American Cancer Society; p. 321, © Elizabeth Robbins/Courtesy of Dr. Richard D. Walk; p. 322, © Barbara Filet/Tony Stone Images; p. 323, Courtesy of Carolyn Rovee-Collier; p. 324, © Louise Wadsworth; p. 325, © W. Hille/Leo deWys; p. 326 (both), © Louise Wadsworth; p. 327 (all), © Louise Wadsworth; p. 329 (top), © Kenneth Garrett/FPG; p. 329 (bottom), © Lee Kuhn/FPG; p. 330 (top), © Myrleen Ferguson/PhotoEdit; p. 330 (bottom), © Julie Houck/Stock, Boston; p. 331, © Robert Frerck/Tony Stone Images; p. 333 (top), © Michael A. Keller/The Stock Market; p. 333 (bottom), © Joan Trasdale/The Stock Market; p. 335 (top), © Philip Jon Bailey/Stock, Boston; p. 335 (bottom), © Dale Durfee/Tony Stone Images; p. 336, © Crews/The Image Works; p. 337 (top), © Louise Wadsworth; p. 337 (bottom), © Dan McCoy/Rainbow; p. 338, © Labat/Jerrican/Photo Researchers; p. 339, © Robert Brenner/PhotoEdit; p. 340, © Don Smetzer/Tony Stone Images; p. 342, © Kenneth Murray/Photo Researchers; p. 345 (top), © Esbin-Anderson/The Image Works; p. 345 (top middle), © Bob Daemmrich/The Image Works; p. 345 (middle), © Robert Foothorap/Black Star; p. 345 (bottom middle), ©

Renee Lynn/Photo Researchers; p. 345 (bottom), © Lawrence Migdale/Photo Researchers; p. 346, © John Chaisson/Gamma-Liaison; p. 347, © Tony Freeman/PhotoEdit; p. 348, © Myrleen Ferguson/PhotoEdit.

Chapter 11 p. 353, courtesy of Duane Hardy; p. 355, © David Young-Wolff/PhotoEdit; p. 356 (all), © Gary A. Conner/PhotoEdit; p. 357, © M. Bernsau/The Image Works; p. 359, © Drew Appleby; p. 360, AP/Wide World Photos; p. 361, © Michael Newman/PhotoEdit; p. 362, SOA Watch; p. 365 (top), © Louise Wadsworth; p. 365 (bottom left), © Mark Richards/PhotoEdit; p. 365 (bottom right), © PhotoEdit; p. 367, © Amy C. Etra/PhotoEdit; p. 369 (top), © Okoniewski/The Image Works; p. 369 (middle), © David Young-Wolff/PhotoEdit; p. 369 (bottom), AP/Wide World Photos; p. 371, © Ernie Medina/Andrews University; p. 372, © Rhoda Sidney/Monkmeyer Press; p. 373, © Elinore Matlin; p. 375, © Dilip Mehta/Woodfin Camp; p. 376 (top), William Steel; p. 376 (bottom), © Michael Schwarz/The Image Works; p. 378 (both), © Ron Pretzer/LUXE; p. 380, © K. Preuss/The Image Works.

Chapter 12 p. 385 (both), © Otto Greule/Allsport; p. 387, © Felicia Martinez/PhotoEdit; p. 389, © Arlene Collins/Monkmeyer Press; p. 391, © Charles Gupton/Stock, Boston; p. 392, © Bruce Ayers/Tony Stone Images; p. 396, © Drew Appleby; p. 397 (top), © Tony Freeman/PhotoEdit; p. 397 (bottom), AP/Wide World Photos; p. 399, © Randy Matusow/Monkmeyer Press; p. 400, © Drew Appleby; p. 401 (all), Matsumoto and Ekman, Japanese and Caucasian Facial Expressions of Emotion, 1988; p. 402 (both), Dr. Paul Ekman, Human Interaction Laboratory; p. 403 (top), © Richard Lord; p. 403 (bottom), © Michael Grecco/Stock, Boston; p. 404, © David Young-Wolff/PhotoEdit; p. 405 (top), © Robert E. Daemmrich/Tony Stone Images; p. 405 (bottom), © Pascal Crapet/Tony Stone Images; p. 407 (both), © Drew Appleby; p. 408, © Alan Oddie/PhotoEdit.

Chapter 13 p. 415, © 1996 Steve Wewerka/Impact Visuals; p. 417, © Mary Evans Picture Library, London; p. 418, © Louise Wadsworth; p. 420, © Margaret Matlin; p. 426, © Michael Newman/PhotoEdit; p. 428, © Margot Granitsas/Photo Researchers; p. 429, Jane Addams Memorial Collection, University of Illinois at Chicago; p. 432, © Arnold H. Matlin; p. 435 (top), © Bachmann/PhotoEdit; p. 435 (bottom), © David Young-Wolff/PhotoEdit; p. 437, © Tony Freeman/PhotoEdit; p. 440, © David Young-Wolff/PhotoEdit; p. 441, © PhotoEdit; p. 443, © Myrleen Ferguson/PhotoEdit.

Chapter 14 p. 451, © Theo Westenberger/The Gamma Liaison Network; p. 452, © Robert Frerck/Tony Stone Images; p. 453, © Drew Appleby; p. 455, © Joe Sohm/The Image Works; p. 456, © Robert Brenner/PhotoEdit; p. 457 (top), © Pat Souders/Tony Stone Images; p. 457 (bottom), © Catherine Ursillo/Photo Researchers; p. 459, © Susan Greenwood/Gamma Liaison; p. 460, © Robert Rathe/Stock, Boston; p. 462, © Myrleen Ferguson/PhotoEdit; p. 464, © Andy Sacks/Tony Stone Images; p. 466 (top), © Billy Barnes/Stock, Boston; p. 466 (bottom), © David Young-Wolff/PhotoEdit; p. 469 (top), © Jeff Greenberg/PhotoEdit; p. 469 (bottom), © Robert E. Daemmrich/Tony Stone Images; p. 471, courtesy of Edward Adamson; p. 472, © Nelson/CMSP; p. 474 (both), data provided by Dr. Monte S. Buchsbaum; p. 475, © Drew Appleby; p. 476, AP/Wide World Photos.

Chapter 15 p. 483, © Gamma Liaison; p. 485, AP/Wide World Photos; p. 486, © Michael Newman/PhotoEdit; p. 487, © Michael

Newman/PhotoEdit; p. 488, © Rick Friedman/Black Star; p. 489, © Bob Daemmrich/The Image Works; p. 491, © Drew Appleby; p. 494 (top), © Stephen Freisch/Stock, Boston; p. 494 (bottom), courtesy of Dr. Joan Nobiling; p. 495, © Will McIntyre/Science Source/Photo Researchers; p. 501, Fordham University/Lutheran Medical Center; p. 502, © Michael Newman/PhotoEdit; p. 503 (top), © Steve Leonard/Tony Stone Images; p. 503 (bottom), © M. Dwyer/Stock, Boston; p. 504, courtesy of Operation Friendship.

Chapter 16 p. 509, © Diana Walker/Gamma Liaison; p. 510, © Gary Wagner; p. 511, © Seth Resnick/Stock, Boston; p. 512, © Richard Hutchings/PhotoEdit; p. 513, Canali; p. 514 (both), © Bob Daemmrich/Stock, Boston; p. 516, © Mark Richards/PhotoEdit; p. 518, © Tony Freeman/PhotoEdit; p. 519, © B. Daemmrich/The Image Works; p. 520, AP/Wide World Photos; p. 522, AP/Wide World Photos; p. 523 (top), © S. Skjold/PhotoEdit; p. 523 (middle), © Danny Lyon/Magnum; p. 523 (bottom), © Jack Iwata/National Japanese-American Historical Society; p. 525, © Terry Ashe/Time Magazine; p. 527, © Comstock; p. 528, © Michael Newman/PhotoEdit; p. 529, © David Young-Wolff/PhotoEdit; p. 530, © Blair Seitz/Photo Researchers; p. 532, © Ron Pretzer/Luxe; p. 533, © Ramey/Stock, Boston; p. 534 (top), © A. Carey/The Image Works; p. 534 (bottom), © Myrleen Ferguson/PhotoEdit.

Chapter 17 p. 543, courtesy of Irma Tovar, Christ for Mexico Missions; p. 545 (all), Philip Zimbardo/Stanford University; p. 546, © Peter Grumann/The Image Bank; p. 547 AP/Wide World Photos 548, © Steve Maines/Stock, Boston; p. 550, © David R. Frazier Photolibrary; p. 551, AP/Wide World Photos; p. 552, © C. Lord; p. 554, © P. Chauvel/Sygma; p. 555, © 1966 Steve Chapiro/Black Star; p. 557 (top), © Roswell Angier/Stock, Boston; p. 557 (bottom), © Mary Kate Denny/PhotoEdit; p. 558 (both), AP/Wide World Photos; p. 559, © Bob Daemmrich/The Image Works; p. 560 (both), The National Archive; p. 562 (top), courtesy of the Community Board, San Francisco; p. 562 (bottom), © The Stock Market; p. 563, courtesy of the Raoul Wallenberg Committee; p. 566, © Robert Brenner/PhotoEdit; p. 569, photo by Lady Borton, AFSC, Field Director.

Chapter 18 p. 575, © Okoniewski/The Image Works; p. 577, © Esbin Anders/The Image Works; p. 578, © Drew Appleby; p. 579, © CNRI/Science Photo Library/Photo Researchers; p. 580 (top), AP/Wide World Photos; p. 580 (bottom), © Jim W. Grace/Photo Researchers; p. 582, © Grant Le Duc/Monkmeyer Press; p. 583 (top), © David Frazier; p. 583 (bottom), © Gary Conner/PhotoEdit; p. 584, © Eric Lars Bakke; p. 586, © Mark Richards/PhotoEdit; p. 588 (top), © Oliver Meckes/Gelderblom/Photo Researchers; p. 588 (bottom), New York City Board of Health; p. 590, © Mary Kate Denny/PhotoEdit; p. 591, New York State Department of Health; p. 594, © Michael Grecco/Stock, Boston; p. 595, by permission of The American Cancer Society.

Copyright Acknowledgments

FIGURE 2.2 American Psychological Association, p. 565, by J. Greenberg from *Journal of Applied Psychology*, 75. Copyright © 1990 by the American Psychological Association. Reprinted with permission.

FIGURE 3.22 Elsevier Science, from *Neuropsychologia*, 29(2), Martha Farah, "Can Recognition of Living Things be Selectively Impaired?," pp. 185–193. Copyright © 1991, with permission of Elsevier Science.

TABLE 4.1 Eugene Galanter, 1962, *Contemporary Psychophysics*, in NEW DIRECTIONS IN PSYCHOLOGY, New York: Holt, Rinehart and Winston, p. 97. Reprinted with permission of the author.

FIGURE 4.25 Jerome Kuhl, "Subjective Contours" by G. Kanizsa from *Scientific American*, 75, 1976. Reprinted by permission of the artist.

FIGURE 5.10 Science, "The Use of Hypnosis to Enhance Recall" by J. Dwyan and K. Bowers from *Science*. Copyright © 1983 by American Association for the Advancement of Science. Reprinted with permission.

FIGURE 6.5 American Psychological Association, "Differential Conditioning & Stimulus Generalization" by S. Liu from *Journal of Comparative & Physiological Psychology*. Copyright © 1971 by the American Psychological Association. Reprinted with permission.

FIGURE 6.15 Academic Press, THE IMPACT OF TELEVISION by L. Joy. Copyright © 1986 by Academic Press. Reprinted with permission.

DEMONSTRATION 7.6 American Psychological Association, *Journal of Experimental Psychology*, 21, pp. 803–814, "Learning, Memory, and Cognition" by H. L. Roediger, III & K. B. McDermott. Copyright © 1995 by the American Psychological Association. Reprinted with permission.

DEMONSTRATION 7.7 American Psychological Association, "Schemata and Memory for Stories" by J. Jenkins from *American Psychologist*, 29, pp. 785–795. Copyright © 1974 by the American Psychological Association. Reprinted with permission.

DEMONSTRATION 8.9 Barron's Educational Series, HOW TO PREPARE FOR THE SCHOLASTIC APTITUDE TEST, 14/e, by S. Brownstein. Reprinted with permission.

DEMONSTRATION 8.9 Newsweek, "The Search for the Elusive 1600," p. 60, March 14, 1994. Copyright © 1994, Newsweek, Inc. All rights reserved. Reprinted by permission.

TABLE 8.2 Academic Press, ORGANIZATIONAL BEHAVIOR AND HUMAN DECISION PROCESSES by D. Frisch, pp. 399–429. Copyright © 1993 by Academic Press. Reprinted with permission.

FIGURE 8.1 Dr. Theresa Amabile, PhD., "The Influence of Evaluation Expectation and Working Condition on Creativity" from THE SOCIAL PSYCHOLOGY OF CREATIVITY. Copyright © 1983 by Theresa Amabile. Reprinted by permission of author.

FIGURE 9.2 Bell-Atlantic, "What You Should Know about Automatic Dialing Services." Courtesy of Bell-Atlantic.

CHAPTER 10 OPENER Beacon Press from THE MEASURE OF OUR SUCCESS by Marian Wright Edelman. Copyright © 1992 by Marian Wright Edelman. Reprinted by permission of Beacon Press, Boston.

FIGURE 10.14 American Psychological Association, "Intergroup Processes in Childhood" by K.K. Powlishta from *Developmental Psychology*, 31, p. 784. Copyright © 1995 by the American Psychological Association. Reprinted with permission.

FIGURE 11.2 K.W. Schaie, "Developmental Designs Revisited" from LIFE-SPAN DEVELOPMENTAL PSYCHOLOGY by S. H. Cohen & H. W. Reese, eds., pp. 45–64. Copyright © 1994. Reprinted by permission of the artist and Lawrence Erlbaum Associates, Inc.

FIGURE 11.5 Paul Costa, "The Stability of Mean Levels" from THE JOURNEY OF ADULTHOOD, 2/e, by H. Bee. Copyright © 1992. Reprinted by permission.

FIGURE 12.3 American Psychological Association, "Achievement Motivation and the Dynamics of Task Difficulty Choices" by L. Slade and M. Rush from *Journal of Personality & Social Psychology*, 60, pp. 165–172. Copyright © 1991 by the American Psychological Association. Reprinted with permission.

FIGURE 12.5 American Psychological Association, "Facial Expressions of Emotion" by J. Russell from *Psychological Bulletin*, 118, pp. 379–391. Copyright © 1991 by the American Psychological Association. Reprinted with permission.

DEMONSTRATION 13.4 American Psychological Association, "Clinical Assessment Can Benefit from Recent Advances" by R. McCrae & P. Costa, Jr. from *American Psychologist*, 41, p. 1002. Copyright © 1986 by the American Psychological Association. Reprinted with permission.

DEMONSTRATION 13.5 Sage Publications, "Horizontal and Vertical Individualism and Collectivism . . ." by T. Singelis, H.C. Triandis, D. Bhawuk & M. Gelfand from *Cross-Cultural Research*, 29, pp. 240–275. Copyright © 1995 by Sage Publications. Reprinted by permission of Sage Publications.

TABLE 13.5 University of Minnesota Press, MINNESOTA MULTI-PHASIC PERSONALITY INVENTORY-2. Copyright © by the Regents of the University of Minnesota, 1942, 1943,1951, 1967 (renewed 1970), 1989. Reproduced by permission of the publisher.

TABLE 13.7 Springer-Verlag, *The Self: Interdisciplinary Approaches* edited by Strauss & Goethals (1991), table 2.2. Reprinted by permission of Springer-Verlag New York. Any further reproduction is strictly prohibited.

TABLE 14.4 American Psychiatric Association, DIAGNOSTIC & STATISTICAL MANUAL OF MENTAL DISORDERS, 4/e. Copyright © 1994. Reprinted with permission of the American Psychiatric Association.

TABLE 14.6 American Psychological Association, "Response Styles and the Duration of Episodes of Depressed Mood" by S. Nolen-Hoeksema, J. Morrow & B. L. Fredrickson from *Journal of Abnormal Psychology*, 102, pp. 20–28. Copyright © 1993 by the American Psychological Association. Reprinted with permission.

FIGURE 15.4 American Psychological Association, "The Effectiveness of Psychotherapy" by P. Seligman from *American Psychologist*, 50, pp. 965–974. Copyright © 1995 by the American Psychological Association. Reprinted with permission.

DEMONSTRATION 16.6 Dr. Peter Glick, "The Ambivalent Sexism Inventory" from *Journal of Personality and Social Psychology*, 70(3), pp. 491–512. Reprinted by permission of the author.

TABLE 16.1 J. Nevid, "Sex Differences in Factors of Romantic Attraction" from SEX ROLES. Copyright © 1984. Reprinted by permission of Plenum Publishing Corp.

FIGURE 16.2 American Psychological Association, "The Attitudinal Effects of Mere Exposure" by R. Zajonc from *Journal of Personality & Social Psychology*, 9, p. 14. Copyright © 1968 by the American Psychological Association. Reprinted with permission.

FIGURE 16.5 American Psychological Association, "Helping and the Avoidance of Inappropriate Interracial Behavior" by D. Frey & S. Gaertner from *Journal of Personality & Social Psychology*, 50, p. 1086. Copyright © 1986 by the American Psychological Association. Reprinted with permission.

FIGURE 16.6 John Wiley & Sons, Ltd., *European Journal of Social Psychology*, 23, p. 83, "Processing Load and Memory for Stereotype-based Information" by C.M. Hewstone, R. J. Griffiths. Copyright © John Wiley & Sons Limited. Reproduced with permission.

FIGURE 17.6 American Psychological Association, "Is Empathic Emotion a Source of Altruistic Motivation?" by C. Batson from *Journal of Personality & Social Psychology*, p. 290–302. Copyright © 1981 by the American Psychological Association. Reprinted with permission.

FIGURE 18.1 American Psychological Association, "Negative Life Events, Perceived Stress, Negative Affect & Susceptibility to the Common Cold" by S. Cohen from *Journal of Personality & Social Psychology*, 64, p. 135. Copyright © 1993 by the American Psychological Association. Reprinted with permission.

Name Index

SUBJECT INDEX